ACTORS ON ACTING FOR THE SCREEN

GARLAND REFERENCE LIBRARY
OF THE HUMANITIES
(VOL. 899)

ACTORS ON ACTING FOR THE SCREEN

Roles and Collaborations

edited by

Doug Tomlinson

GARLAND PUBLISHING, INC.
New York & London / 1994

Library of Congress Cataloging-in-Publication Data

Tomlinson, Doug, 1949–1992.
Actors on acting for the screen : roles and collaborations / Doug Tomlinson.
p. cm. — (Garland reference library of the humanities ; vol. 899)
Includes bibliographical references.
ISBN 0–8240–5619–1 (alk. paper)
1. Motion picture acting. I. Title. II. Series.
PN1995.9.A26T66 1994
791.43'028—dc20 92–40094
CIP

Printed on acid-free, 250-year-life paper
Manufactured in the United States of America

DEDICATED TO JAY LEYDA

1910-1988

SCHOLAR

TEACHER

FRIEND

and

JIM CLINTON

1957-1989

FRIEND

CONTENTS

ACKNOWLEDGMENTS

The material in this volume was researched in a number of locales. I wish to thank the staffs of the following libraries who were gracious in their help: The Lincoln Center Library for the Performing Arts in New York, The Academy of Motion Picture Arts and Sciences Library in Los Angeles, The British Film Institute Libraries in London and Berkhamsted, The New York Public Library, The Toronto Public Library and The Harry A. Sprague Library at Montclair State College.

I wish also to acknowledge the inspiration of Jay Leyda, the support of Bill Simon of NYU while I was beginning this project, and Dean Phil Cohen of Montclair State College who supported me in the final difficult stages. Barry Jacobs generously provided translations from Swedish. Paula Ladenburg and Phyllis Korper of Garland Publishing Inc. have my respect for their patience and support. Sharon Maffetone and William Beech helped with the enormously tedious job of indexing this volume. William M. Drew provided a model of rigorous research. My college provided me necessary computer facilities; but the biggest debt is to Jim Myers, whose computer expertise and gentle patience helped me bring this project to its final stages.

I also wish to acknowledge certain publications which have been responsible for numerous entries in this volume and who have clearly made a commitment to in-depth investigative interviewing. Among the most important are: *American Film*, *Film Comment*, *Films & Filming*, *Focus on Film*, *Interview*, *The New York Times*, *The Saturday Evening Post*, and *Playboy*. Certain interviewers must also be acknowledged. Among the most consistently strong questioners have been: David Galligan of *Drama-Logue*, Gordon Gow of *Films & Filming*, Judy Klemesrud and Howard Thompson of *The New York Times*, Lawrence Linderman and Lawrence Grobel of *Playboy*, Roger Ebert of *The Chicago Sun-Times*, Leonard Maltin of *Film Fan Monthly* and Charles Higham and Rex Reed whose work appears in a variety of publications. The American Film Institute must be congratulated for their Oral History/Dialogue on Film seminars for their excellence. *The Saturday Evening Post* is to be praised for their excellent series, "The Role I Liked Best," which provided much excellent material. Among the many interview anthologies, those by Judith Crist (*Take 22*), William M. Drew (*Speaking of Silents*), John Kobal (*People Will Talk*) and Lillian and Helen Ross (*The Player*) were particularly rich in material. Among the publishing houses which have a clear commitment to books on the cinema and its artists are: The Putnam Berkley Group, Alfred A. Knopf, St. Martin's Press, Doubleday & Co.

All material—with very few exceptions—is copyright of the source listed; the search for copyright holders on out of print publications was extensive, complicated and difficult. A trip to The Library of Congress in Washington D.C. was particularly frustrating as addresses of copyright holders are not kept current.

Special note is made of the following at the request of the publishers: Interviews with Joan Bennett, Willem Dafoe, Lillian Gish, James Mason and Fay Wray reprinted with permission of the Publisher, Salem Press Inc. Copyright © 1982, 1983 and 1987 by Frank N. Magill; interviews with Barnard Hughes and Geraldine Page used by permission of Sterling Publishing Company, Inc., 387 Park Ave S. NY, NY 10016 from *Actors on Acting* by Joanmarie Kalter, © by Sterling Publishing Co, Inc.; excerpts from *Jerry Lewis in Person* by Jerry Lewis with Herb Gluck reprinted with the permission of Atheneum Publishers, an imprint of Macmillan Publishing Company, copyright © 1982, by Jerry Lewis and Herb Gluck; excerpts from *Jack Nicholson: Face to Face* by Christopher Fryer and Robert David Crane—copyright © 1975 by Christopher Fryer and Robert David Crane, reprinted with permission of the publisher, M. Evans & Co.; excerpts from *Veronica: The Autobiography of Veronica Lake* by Veronica Lake with Donald Bain, copyright © 1971 by The Citadel Press. Published by arrangement with Carol Publishing Group; excerpts from *Jack Lemmon: His Films and Career*, revised edition, by Joe Baltake. Copyright © 1986, 1977 by Joe Baltake. Published with arrangement with Carol Publishing Group. A Citadel Press Book; excerpts from *Conversations with Joan Crawford* by Roy Newquist. Published by arrangement with Carol Publishing Group. A Citadel Press Book; excerpts from *People Will Talk* by John Kobal, copyright © 1986 by the Kobal Collection, Ltd. Reprinted by permission of Alfred A. Knopf, Inc.; excerpts from *Myrna Loy: Being and Becoming* by Myrna Loy and James

Kotsilibas-Davis are copyright © 1987 by James Kotsilibas-Davis and Myrna Loy. Reprinted by permission of Alfred A. Knopf, Inc.; excerpts from *It's a Wonderful Life Book* by Jeanine Basinger, copyright © 1986 by Wesleyan University Film Archive. Reprinted by permission of Alfred A. Knopf, Inc.; excerpts from *Lauren Bacall by Myself* by Lauren Bacall, copyright © 1978 by Caprigo, Inc. Reprinted by permission of Alfred A. Knopf, Inc.; excerpts from *This Life* by Sidney Poitier copyright © 1980 by Sidney Poitier. Reprinted by permission of Alfred A. Knopf, Inc.; excerpts from *The Parade's Gone By* by Kevin Brownlow are copyright © 1968 by Kevin Brownlow and are reprinted by permission of Sterling Lord Literistic, Inc.; excerpts from *Norma: The Story of Norma Shearer* by Laurence J. Quirk, *On the Other Hand: A Life Story* by Fay Wray, *Actors: A Celebration* by Rita Gam, *Yvonne: An Autobiography* by Yvonne DeCarlo, *Ladies' Man* by Paul Henreid, *Three Phases of Eve* by Eve Arden, *Faye Dunaway* by Allan Hunter and *Walter Matthau* by Allan Hunter are copyright St. Martin's Press Inc., New York; excerpts from *Up in the Clouds, Gentlemen, Please* by John Mills are copyright © 1980 by John Mills. Reprinted by permission of Ticknor & Fields, a Houghton Mifflin Company. All rights reserved; the excerpt from *Nostalgia Isn't What It Used to Be* by Simone Signoret is copyright © 1978 by Harper & Row Publishers, Inc. Reprinted by permission of HarperCollins Publishers; the excerpts from *Kate: The Life of Katharine Hepburn* by Charles Higham are reprinted by permission of W.W. Norton & Company, Inc. Copyright © 1975 by Charles Higham; the excerpt from *Don't Fall off the Mountain* by Shirley MacLaine is reprinted by permission of W. W. Norton & Company, Inc. Copyright © 1970 by Shirley MacLaine; the excerpt from *The Griffith Actresses* is copyright © by Anthony Slide; the excerpt from *This 'n' That* by Bette Davis is reprinted by permission of The Putnam Publishing Group, copyright © 1987 by Bette Davis; the excerpts from *Lana: The Lady, The Legend, The Truth* by Lana Turner and Hollis Alpert. Copyright © 1982 by Eltee Productions and Hollis Alpert. Used by permission of the publisher, Dutton, an imprint of New American Library, a division of Penguin Books USA Inc.; excerpts from *Spencer Tracy: Tragic Idol* by Bill Davidson. Copyright © 1987 by Bill Davidson. Used by permission of the publisher, Dutton, an imprint of New American Library, a division of Penguin Books USA Inc; the excerpt from *Nostalgia Isn't What It Used To Be* by Simone Signoret. Copyright © 1978 by Harper & Row Publishers, Inc. Reprinted by permission of Harper Collins Publishers; the excerpts from *The Bennett Playbill* by Joan Bennett. Copyright © 1970 by Joan Bennett. Reprinted by permission of Henry Holt Company, Inc.; excerpt from *The Ragman's Son*, copyright © 1988 by Kirk Douglas. Reprinted by permission of Simon & Schuster; excerpts from *The Player* are copyright © 1962 by Lillian Ross and Helen Ross, renewed 1990 by Lillian Ross are reprinted by permission of Simon & Schuster; excerpts from *Marlene* by Marlene Dietrich are used by permission of Grove Weidenfeld. Copyright © 1989; the excerpts from *Take 22: Moviemakers on Moviemaking* by Judith Crist and co-edited by Shirley Sealey (New York: Crossroad/Continuum 1991); reprinted by permission; excerpts from Raymond Massey's *From a Hundred Different Lives* are Copyright © by Raymond Massey. By permission of Little, Brown and Company; the excerpt from *Diahan Carroll* with Ross Firestone is Copyright © 1986 by Diahan Carroll and Ross Firestone. By permission of Little, Brown and Company; the excerpt from *My Wonderful World of Comedy* by Buster Keaton and Charles Samuels are Copyright © 1960 by Buster Keaton and are reprinted by permission of Stealing Lord Literistic Inc.

Excerpts from *The New York Herald Tribune* © 1917, 1934, 1936, 1937, 1938, 1939, 1941, 1942, 1943, 1944, 1948, 1951, 1952, 1955, 1956, 1957, 1958, 1959, 1960, 1962, 1963, 1964, 1965 and 1967 New York Herald Tribune, Inc. All rights reserved. Reprinted by permission; all excerpts from *The New York Post* are reprinted by permission of *The New York Post*; all interviews from *The New York Times* are reprinted by permission © *The New York Times* 1927, 1937, 1938, 1940, 1941, 1942, 1943, 1947, 1949, 1950, 1952, 1953, 1954, 1955,1956, 1958, 1960, 1961, 1963, 1964, 1965, 1966, 1967, 1968, 1969, 1970, 1971, 1972, 1973, 1974, 1975, 1976, 1977, 1978, 1979, 1980, 1981, 1982, 1983, 1984, 1985, 1986, 1987, 1988, 1989, 1990, 1991; interview with Judy Davis, copyright of *The San Francisco Chronicle*; excerpts from interviews with Samantha Eggar, Jane Fonda, Cary Grant, Warren Beatty, Ernest Borgnine, Jeremy Irons, Sissy Spacek are reprinted with permission of The Toronto Star Syndicate.

The interview with Linda Hunt, originally published in *The New Yorker*, is from "A Part in the Play", reprinted by permission, © 1990 Cynthia Zarin; interview with Richard Widmark, originally published in *The New Yorker*, is from "The Player, Part III," © 1961, 1989 by Lillian and Helen Ross, reprinted by permission; interview with Talia Shire reprinted with the permission of United Press International; excerpts from the interview with Tom Cruise, "I Had to Grow Up Fast" © 1989 originally published in *Parade Magazine* by Ellen Hawkes are used by permission of The Wallace Literary Agency, Inc., and *Parade Magazine.*

Excerpts from the *Playboy* Interview: Al Pacino are copyright *Playboy Magazine* © 1979 by *Playboy*. Used with permission. All rights reserved; excerpts from the *Playboy* Interview: Susan Sarandon are copyright *Playboy Magazine* © 1989 by *Playboy*. Used with permission. All rights reserved; excerpts from the *Playboy* interview: Roy Scheider are copyright Playboy Magazine © 1980 by *Playboy*. Used with permission. All rights reserved; excerpts from the *Playboy* Interview: Donald Sutherland are copyright © 1981 by *Playboy*. Used with permission. All rights reserved; excerpts from the *Playboy* Interview: Kathleen Turner, are copyright *Playboy Magazine* © 1986. Used with permission. All rights reserved; other excerpts from Playboy Magazine — Julie Andrews, Robert Blake, Marlon Brando, Richard Burton, Michael Caine, John Cassavetes, Sean Connery, Tom Cruise, Clint Eastwood, Henry Fonda, Peter Fonda, Elliott Gould, Tom Hanks, Goldie Hawn, Barbara Hershey, Jack Lemmon, Groucho Marx, Paul Newman, Jack Nicholson, Peter O'Toole, Robert Redford, George C. Scott, Sylvester Stallone, Barbra Streisand, John Travolta, Mae West and Robin Williams are used by permission of *Playboy*, copyright © *Playboy Magazine*; excerpts from *Screen Actor* reprinted with permission from The Screen Actors Guild; excerpts from *Rolling Stone* are by permission of Straight Arrow Publishers and *Rolling Stone*; interviews from *Seventeen* are reprinted with the permission of SEVENTEEN Magazine, copyright by News America Publications, Inc. All rights reserved; the article by Alexander Knox from *Hollywood Quarterly* Vol 1 #1, Oct 1945 pp 110-111 © 1945, The Regents of the University of California; the interviews with Robert Redford, Oliver Reed and George C. Scott are reprinted with permission of Penthouse International Ltd. © 1973, 1976 and 1980; excerpts from *Film Comment* © 1969, 1972, 1973 by Film Comment Publishing Company. Reprinted by permission of The Film Society of Lincoln Center; excerpts from *Film Comment* © 1974, 1975, 1980, 1987, 1988, 1989 by The Film Society of Lincoln Center. All rights reserved; excerpts from interviews in *New York* or *Cue* magazines with Kathy Baker, Jeff Bridges, Tony Curtis, Morgan Freeman, Robert Redford, Mikhail Baryshnikov, Jill Clayburgh, Jane Fonda, Rosalind Russell, Gene Wilder and Joe Pesci are copyright © 1991 K-111 Magazine Corporation. All rights reserved. Reprinted with the permission of *New York* magazine; the interviews with Claire Dubrey in *The Silent Picture* is copyright © by Anthony Slide; the excerpt from Clint Eastwood's article on Don Siegel is reprinted by permission of the Mr. Eastwood © 1991; the excerpts from the interviews with William Holden and John Wayne for the Arizona Historical Society Oral History Project are granted by the Society. The Holden interview is AV-0086, the Wayne interview is AV-0084.

Several publishers and individuals proved impossible to locate due to the cessation of their publishing endeavors. I tried long and hard to find the following: Kaleidoscope Press and Don Shay; *American Classic Screen* and Traditions Press; Julia Cameron; Bernard Friedman; Bertha Klausner; Iron Eyes Cody and Everest House; Elm Tree Books/Hamish Hamilton Ltd.; Ben Fong-Torres; Robert Seidenberg; Louis Biancolli; Mike Bygrave and Joan Goodman; Guy Garcia; Hollis Alpert; Lori J. Smith; Bruce Cook; Mitch Tuchman; Joseph McBride; Bobbs-Merrill Publishing Co.; *After Dark*; *New Times*; *Focus on Film*; *The Sunday Worker*; *Screen Stars*; *Photon*; *Filmograph*; *Crawdaddy*; *Film Weekly*; *Hollywood Filmograph*; *Movie Digest*; *Silver Screen*; *The New York Telegraph*; *L.A. Weekly*; *The Brooklyn Daily Eagle*; Abelard Schuman Publishers.

I have used this material without permission and invite these individuals or companies to respond. My attempts to reach you were valiant. Certain variations in credit format are at the request of the publication quoted.

Note: Dr. Tomlinson was terminally ill when he was trying to finish this book. Apologies are due if any copyrights have been neglected.

INTRODUCTION

In assembling this volume of reminiscences by actors and actresses I have focussed on three central issues in the film performer's work: the genesis and development of a role, the working relationship of the performer and director, and the working relationship between fellow performers. These three areas of discussion provide the clearest insight into the work of the film performer and often provide the most interesting revelations about the success, failure or significance of any particular cinematic characterization or film.

Discussion of the genesis and development of a cinematic characterization can provide significant insight into both the process of the individual performer and the art of film performance. The range of approaches to characterization is enormously varied: while some individuals have a standard procedure which they follow with each role, others approach each project in a way which develops from the screenwriter's description of the character to be portrayed, while others depend on the director to indicate a process. As Simone Signoret wrote in her autobiography:

> There are those actors who explain to you that they know exactly how they're going to do the part; that they're experienced enough to avoid coming a cropper over this and that. And then there is the other method, which is to have no method at all. This is mine. I didn't choose it, nor did I decide that it was a method; it's just the only one that suits me. I feel a real need not to think, not to analyze.
>
> When I'm filming I need someone who's going to think and analyze for me—the director. He's the one who has to pull the whole thing together. This is the only way I can work, and what a luxury it is. One comes offering oneself, as it were, with all that one hopes one is capable of doing—and I'm emphasizing the lack of certainty—and above all, bringing something to a part one hasn't chosen oneself.[1]

The variety of starting points is equally fascinating: some performers like to dress the character or find the hairstyle in order to find the interior life while others like to analyze the interior life in order to find the exterior qualities; some search for animal images to find the physical characterization while others find historical or fictional characters upon which to base their interpretation; some find the voice first then use that as a key to the rest of the character, while others find the voice only after discovering the way a character moves. Ultimately, some performers claim they "live" a role, others that they "feel" a role, while yet others say they "think" a role.

While the individual performer may do a great deal of work on his or her own, the development of a characterization is generally done in collaboration with or under the supervision of the director of the film. Of interest both theoretically and practically is the director's overall aesthetic with regards to performance, whether he or she prefers to privilege performance as a central mode of cinematic expression or whether he or she prefers to make performance secondary to the aesthetic designs of cinematographic expression. Just as there is a wide variety of approaches to the work of the performer, so too, there is a wide variety of directorial styles which impact on the work of the performer: some directors are "cattle herders" who have no regard for the input of the performers who are generally seen as an impediment to the achievement of visual imagery; others are more theatrically oriented directors who prefer to indulge in extensive rehearsal before cameras turn; yet others are intuitive artists who simply prefer to turn on the camera and let a scene evolve by letting performers and technicians exercise the accumulated knowledge and experience of their craft. The actor must adapt. As Karl Malden indicated in a 1964 interview for *Cinema* about his work methods:

> With Kazan I can work one way, with Hitchcock I'll have to work another way, with Frankenheimer I'll work a third way. [2]

Beyond these matters of performance and directorial aesthetics, how do matters of casting and collaboration between performers affect the development of individual characters and character relationships? How, ultimately, do they affect the finished film? Can the issue of who is cast opposite whom have a significant effect on how a film is received and a performance is perceived?[3] What happens when styles of performance clash, or when a performer who is supposed to portray a character in harmony with his co-stars cannot rise above political or personality differences, or when performers are simply mismatched for the needs of the drama? How does one work with an animal co-star, with a child co-star, when the co-star is your spouse? We often read that a particular performer is "difficult"; what does that mean for other performers on the set?

While these issues were the main focus of my research, other experiences of performing for the screen came to the fore and I have included a number as illustrations of other considerations: the effect technology — styles of lighting, camera angle or sound recording, for example — can have on the performer's intended portrayal; the differences for the performer when the image is being filmed for standard ratio projection and when it is being filmed for Cinemascope; the effect of developing and playing scenes so as not to provoke the censor; the effect of post-production decisions such as the altering of a performance moment by music, the dubbing in of sound or voice effects, or the unanticipated juxtaposition of images.

In assembling this anthology, I have chosen an alphabetical organization by performer. One can, however, approach the text in a variety of ways. One alternate method would be to read a reminiscence by a particular performer then check the index to see who else reminisces about working with that individual on the same film, with the particular director or co-star who is the subject of the reminiscence, or with that individual on other projects. For example, one might read the section on Marlon Brando where he speaks of working with Elia Kazan on *On the Waterfront*, then find in the index that his co-star Rod Steiger also speaks of that same experience. One might then compare their experiences to those of others who reminisce about working with Kazan on other projects: Carroll Baker, James Dean, Robert De Niro, Andy Griffith, Deborah Kerr, Vivien Leigh, Karl Malden, Gregory Peck, Lee Remick, Ethel Waters, Richard Widmark, and Natalie Wood. One could then check to see who else reminisces about working with Marlon Brando on other projects and find that the list includes John Gielgud, Vivien Leigh, Sophia Loren, Karl Malden, James Mason, Martin Sheen, Maureen Stapleton, Joanne Woodward and Teresa Wright. In this way a composite picture of a performer covering a number of films over a period of time could effectively be drawn.

If one is more concerned with examining the performance aesthetic of a particular director, one need only turn to the index to begin constructing an overall appreciation. For example, if one is interested in the question of whether Alfred Hitchcock really treated his actors like cattle, as the myth goes, one can find that the index includes several entries which make reference to that director: Ingrid Bergman, Doris Day, Marlene Dietrich, Henry Fonda, Joan Fontaine, John Gielgud, Cary Grant, Tippi Hedren, Janet Leigh, Karl Malden, Vera Miles, Gregory Peck, Anthony Perkins, Claude Rains, Michael Redgrave, Eva Marie Saint, James Stewart and Teresa Wright.

By examining a number of directors in this fashion, one can begin to appreciate the aesthetic spectrum of the film director's use of and attitude toward the work of the film performer. One can read of the wide range of approaches, from a director like Robert Bresson who distrusts the techniques of acting and courts no collaboration with his performers ("models" as he calls them), to Elia Kazan, a former actor who cherishes the actor's technique and encourages active performer input. In selecting entries for this anthology, every attempt was made to ensure that all major directors were the subject of at least one reminiscence on their approach to directing performers so as to ensure that a wide variety of directorial aesthetics was available for examination.

Another way of using the text: if one is more interested in a particular film, one might check the index under the title and see which cast members from that film speak of the experience. If one is interested in *Gone With the Wind*, for example, one will find comments by three of the pictures' stars — Olivia De Havilland, Clark Gable and Vivien Leigh. Many other films are the subject of such multiple reminiscences. For example, both Jane Fonda and Donald Sutherland speak of working on *Klute*, both William Hurt and Kathleen Turner speak of *Body Heat* and Laurence Olivier, Marilyn Monroe and Dame Sybil Thorndike all speak of *The Prince and the Showgirl.*

This book is not meant as a pantheon. Certain performers who are included in almost every survey of film performance are not represented here. Similarly, this volume is not meant to be an examination of individual performers; it is meant to be a collage of film performance experiences. The amount of material included under any individual's name is in no way meant to signify their importance in the history of film performance, nor is the material included meant to signify that these reminiscences represent their greatest or only significant achievements. Often interesting information is provided when a performer discusses why a performance or collaboration *failed.*

The omission of certain celebrated performers or performances is not a reflection of personal taste; rather it is the result of my inability to locate *appropriate* material. How long did I search for a quote from Greta Garbo on her work in the 1930s? Why was I unable to find a suitable quote from Maximilian Schell speaking of his in *Judgment at Nuremberg*? And why is there no extensive record of Spencer Tracy speaking of his many cinematic collaborations with Katharine Hepburn?

The clipping files at the research libraries I worked in contain a great deal of material on most film personalities. The standard research bibliographies also provide many other sources for material. The reason for the lack of certain material resides in journalistic trends: unfortunately, far too many interviewers have been more obsessed with asking questions about the personal lives of their subjects than exploring the intricacies of artistic creativity.[4] When involved in research on performers one becomes exasperated reading of social lives, eating habits and leisure pursuits. One Hollywood columnist who interviewed a number of individuals I had hoped to include repeatedly asked such significant questions as: What is your favorite color?; What is your favorite flower?; What are your sleeping habits?; What is your wardrobe like? Unfortunately, many performers have become so disgusted with this line of questioning that they have refused to do interviews or if forced to, have been resistant and often commented openly on the inane nature of the situation. While in England in 1959, Cary Grant expressed his frustration thus:

> Why are we talking? Whom am I talking to? A *well* person is not likely to read about me. Why? Because it is all trivia. People are conditioned to read trivia about actors and acting. Lots of actors are philosophers but the newspapers don't want to print what we are. Our audiences expect to hear nothing about us except trivia, egotistical trivia.[5]

Thankfully, certain artists have been able to maintain a posture that insists "talk of my art, not of me." In fact, certain artists are represented with more material in this volume by virtue of the fact that they have been able to insist upon discussing their art and not their private lives.

Unfortunately, however, others have agreed to talk of themselves, but simply and often adamantly refused to talk about the art of performance. Montgomery Clift told interviewers that if they wanted to know anything about how he worked as an artist, they should ask his artistic collaborators;[6] when, in a 1986 interview, Sean Penn was asked how he developed a role like that of Brad Whitewood, Jr. in *At Close Range*, he replied:

> I have a standard answer to that question: Any discussion defeats the purpose of what is on the screen. [Talking about] preparation is all hogwash; it takes the mystery out of movies. I don't want to know how some guy wore the same socks for months to prepare for a role; then when I see the movie that's all I can think about — dirty socks.[7]

Sandy Dennis and Shirley Knight, two actresses known predominantly for their work in the theater, spoke noisily of nothing but the "idiocy of Hollywood"; these two self-professed "serious actresses" had nothing to say about their work on the screen. Actors with other occupations generally spoke of their other endeavors instead of their work in film, Frank Sinatra being a good case in point. And perhaps most unfortunately, some key players are not represented here either because they were never asked about their work or because I could not locate any material worth using. I regret the absence of the following voices: Judith Anderson, Dana Andrews, Fay Bainter, Theda Bara, Richard Barthelmess, William Bendix, Constance Bennett, Buelah Bondi, Louis Calhern, Lee J. Cobb, Jane Darwell, Dan Duryea, José Ferrer, Sir Cedric Hardwicke, Van Heflin, Oscar Homolka, Miriam Hopkins, Trevor Howard, John Ireland, Ben Johnson, Celia Johnson, Van Johnson, Jennifer Jones, Arthur Kennedy, Alan Ladd, Herbert Marshall, Burgess Meredith, Sal Mineo, Mabel Normand, Tyrone Power, Richard Pryor, Ralph Richardson, George Sanders, Margaret Sullavan, Robert Walker and Keenan Wynn. Other major figures for whom I have found far too little material include Jean Arthur, Ethel Barrymore, John Barrymore, Humphrey Bogart, Agnes Moorehead, Maximilian Schell, Spencer Tracy.... I also regret the lack of material from certain performers who stopped granting interviews: As Greta Garbo said in 1940:

> I don't like to talk to people because I can't express myself satisfactorily. I am misunderstood. I don't say things I mean to say. This barrier to self-expression makes me keep to myself.[8]

Researching some of the cinema's earliest performers proved to be most difficult for in the earliest days of cinema, little but the self was discussed. Art and the artistic process were seemingly of little consequence to the editors and journalists of the day. The state of recording technology also meant that most early interviews were reported in prose with only the odd phrase placed in quotes. Quite often such brief quotes were used out of context. In a 1961 interview, Gary Cooper expressed a common frustration with those early days:

> I learned very early in my career that nothing you ever say gets quoted verbatim by the press. So for many years I just clammed up and didn't say anything.[9]

In researching this volume, I relied on a variety of sources including autobiographies, biographies, newspapers, magazines (both general and film specific), interview anthologies, press releases, documentary films, radio and television broadcasts, and unpublished interviews.[10]

One does not use this source material without certain trepidation: when approaching a research project of this nature, one becomes immediately aware of a variety of forces that come into play when an individual writes or speaks of personal experiences. When reading an autobiography or feature article by a performer, one must do so with a skeptical eye and thus be able to divine a seemingly accurate account of artistic process from self-congratulation or aggressive self-criticism or malicious vindictiveness.

When reading an interview in a newspaper or magazine, one must be able to sense immediately whether an interview is working and the interviewee is giving honestly. One must recognize that when the ego of the interviewer gets in the way, for example, the words accredited to the interviewee might not be the most accurate or may be quoted out of context. As Robert Redford admitted when asked by a *Playboy* interviewer why he was reluctant to be interviewed:

> I haven't had very good luck with interviews. I guess the press is fallible, human like all of us, but too often I've found myself in a situation where I felt the interviewer didn't have an open mind. He came in with a prejudice, or maybe just an angle on what I was all about, or should be all about.[11]

One must similarly be suspect of interviews given while an interviewee is on a press junket publicizing a new film as the exigencies of this format often necessitate or engender a lack of critical distance from the work, the director, co-workers and the self. Quotations found in press releases from a star's agent or studio must also be approached advisedly.

The interviewee's motivations may also be suspect: one might have agreed to the interview solely for public attention — the boost to the box office or the star's image. As Shelley Winters admitted in her autobiography:

> When a columnist or writer has a deadline to meet, he calls me and says, "Shelley, give me an interview," and I say, "Listen, give me a break. You know everything I've done since I was born." And he answers, "You'll think of something." I say, "Okay," and then take Marlon's advice about imaginary histories, birthplaces, etc. and give them a story that's funny and absolutely contrary to the truth. They don't care. They've got a story, and I guess it adds to "The Winters Tale."[12]

Finally, the researcher must also be aware that attitudes toward a work or a director can change and that one must avoid quotations which are either imbued with sentimentality (tributes in obituaries or at career celebrations) or are extraordinarily bitter (resulting from strained personal relations); one must look beyond the tone to the substance of the experience detailed. Whenever I had severe reservations about the veracity of a discussion of process or collaboration, I sought substantiating material by the same performer in another source. Whenever substantiation was not found, the entry was dropped from consideration.[13]

To those who wish to question the veracity of all reminiscenses, I justify my laying forth of this material by insisting that even when a teller recounts a dubious truth, at the very least a valuable point about process will have been illustrated. The historian's task is to research and selectively re-present; the theorist's task is to analyze the historian's archaeological findings in a specific context.

My friend and mentor Jay Leyda always spoke of publishing material that not only illuminated our own research interests, but which also provided material from which others could work. In a letter regarding this volume he wrote: "Stick to our first motto: Nothing that can't be used by somebody." In this collection, my intention has been to sow the seeds of other projects which will explore the work of the film performer.

A

F. Murray ABRAHAM [1939-]

Born: Pittsburgh. Studies at The University of Texas—El Paso and with Uta Hagen at The Herbert Berghof Studios in New York, and work on the stage including Broadway (from 1968), preceded his film debut in Serpico (1973, Sidney Lumet). In 1984, he played Salieri opposite Tom Hulce's Mozart in Milos Forman's Amadeus:

What do you do when you're a mediocre composer confronted with a genius? Many people would simply quit. But Salieri didn't destroy his work or kill himself. He said no to fate. There are two lines which were unfortunately cut from the movie, where the priest hearing his confession says to him, "May God forgive you," and Salieri replies, "He may, but I shall never forgive Him." I like that spirit. I think he was a courageous, crazy man.

—Abraham, interviewed by Stephen Farber for *The New York Times*, 20 Sept 1984

Milos has a voracious appetite for life and he shakes a film like a bull. He can't abide an unreal moment. He'll cut you cold and make you start again. That was a godsend to me. Milos has an eye you can trust and that allows you to relax. If you don't trust your director, you direct yourself and your performance is self-conscious.

—Abraham, interviewed by Aljean Harmetz for *The New York Times*, 24 Mar 1985

Joss ACKLAND [1928-]

Born: London, England. Studies at The Central School of Speech and Drama and work on the London stage (from 1945) preceded his film debut in Seven Days to Noon (1950, John Boulting). In 1987, he played Sir Jock Delves Broughton in Michael Radford's White Mischief (1987):

Broughton was very satisfying. The major difficulty was to make a man without personality interesting, but cast and crew began to treat me like a decent old buffer and I felt at least that I had become the man. What was exciting was to play someone who betrayed no emotions and concealed everything behind a respectable façade. But as the movie progressed a turmoil was building inside the man like a volcano, until it erupted into madness. Shooting out of context meant each scene had to begin with the correct balance of unseen torment and I had to be sure to betray nothing to actors or the camera and at the same time arrange that future audiences would sense what was really going on. Another complication was that Michael had travelled a new road in film making. Normally there is someone in a movie with whom the audience can identify and travel with in the story.... But *White Mischief* was concerned with a group of selfish unsympathetic characters who could be observed, but never joined.

—Ackland, in his *I Must Be in There Somewhere: An Autobiography by Joss Ackland* (London: Hodder & Stoughton, 1989)

Brian AHERNE [1902-1986]

Born: King's Norton, Worcestershire, England. Despite a stage debut at age 8 in Birmingham, he studied to be an architect. After a year on the job (1921-22), he returned to the theatre, then moved into films. Although he had appeared in a number of silent films while still living in England — his debut was The Eleventh Command (1924, George A. Cooper) — it was in Hollywood that his career was established, beginning with Song of Songs (1933, Rouben Mamoulian). Early in his Hollywood career, he worked with director W.S. Van Dyke on I Live My Life (1935):

I Live My Life was gay and often amusing, rather better than the average comedy of its time. Miss [Joan] Crawford was friendly and extremely professional, and dear Frank Morgan gave one of his inimitable comic performances. I remember the picture chiefly for the pleasure I got from watching the director, W.S. Van Dyke. An ex-captain in the U.S. Marines, he was a tall, thin, wiry man with a twinkle in his eye and usually a full tumbler of neat gin in his hand. He addressed all men as "kid" and all women as "honey."

"All I ask, kid," he said to me before starting, "is that you know your lines and that you are on the set at ten to nine in the morning, ready to shoot at nine. I shall never keep you after six. You will enjoy the picture." I did.

Shooting a motion picture with Van was much like shooting a television show today. One take was enough for him. He liked experienced actors because they were more likely to give him the scene on the first take....

Most of the great directors of that day made many takes — indeed, it seemed the more important they were, the more they made, finally printing three or four and perhaps holding a couple of others so that they could make a choice in the projection room. Van never went in a projection room. I expressed my astonishment.

"Kid," he said, his blue eyes twinkling, "those big shots in the front office have to find something to do to justify their big salaries. They like to cut. I let 'em do it. I direct and then I go home. That's why they love me!"

"But suppose they chose the wrong takes or angles?" I asked.

He winked at me. "I know what I'm doin' kid," he said. "I don't give 'em any choice. All they gotta do is join my stuff together."

I knew [Maximilian in *Juarez* (1939)] would be a great part for me because, on my visit to Mexico some years before, I had seen all the Maximilian relics and photographs and I knew that with the aid of a good make-up I would look uncannily like the tragic Emperor....

It is always interesting to actors to watch directors at work and to see how differently they go about it. *Juarez* was directed by William Dieterle, a very tall, precise German with dark, burning eyes and strictly formal manners, who had a fixed belief in numerology. On the day of my test he asked my birth date and did some rapid calculation on a bit of paper.... His script was a Bible, of which not one syllable could be changed, and he always wore white cotton gloves on the set in case it should be necessary, in getting the exact angle he wanted, to touch the face of a player. Most directors say "Camera!" or "Action!" to start a scene, but I can still hear Dieterle's classic actor's voice saying, "Here we...go!"

By contrast, I worked for Hal Roach on *Captain Fury* [1939], immediately following *Juarez*, and on his set things were entirely different. Hal, who had come up from silent movies with his Laurel and Hardy series and the Our Gang comedy shorts, was used to more free and easy ways. He set out to make a picture from the famous Australian novel *For the Term of His Natural Life*, but shortly before starting, discovered that he didn't have the rights. Nothing daunted, he improvised from day to day a somewhat similar story which he called *Captain Fury*, giving the cast dialogue out of his head as he went along, line by line. He would point at us in turn, "Now you say this, you say that, and" — pause for thought — "what could you say then....?"

—Aherne, in his *A Proper Job* (Boston: Houghton Mifflin, 1969)

Danny AIELLO [1933-]

Born: New York City. Work as a master of ceremonies and straight man at The Improvisation in N.Y. and on tour preceded his film debut in Bang the Drum Slowly (1973, John Hancock). In 1989, he played Sal in Spike Lee's Do the Right Thing:

People say [Sal] is a bigot. I don't think he is a bigot. He is a man of deeds. He shows by deeds he is not prejudiced or bigoted. [The racial epithets he uses] are not the words of a bigot, but the words of a man who has a limited vocabulary and grew up in the streets.

—Aiello, interviewed by Lawrence Van Gelder for *The New York Times*, 7 July 1989

Q. Was the action of smashing the ghetto blaster hard to justify?

A. Yeah, the work happened to justify the act — I've always wanted to smash one. Very few people that I know in the city of New York have not at some time or other wanted to smash one of those fuckin' things. So it didn't take too much to raise my dander.

But right in the scene itself I had all that I needed. First of all, there were words used that were not scripted. Giancarlo Esposito called me a guinea bastard. When he called me that, I looked at him, I said, "What did you say, you nigger motherfucker?" That wasn't scripted either. What we did was we got into street shit. I called him a black motherfucker; he said, "You guinea fuck." And all of that was real. I'm saying *real*. We were shouting at the top of our lungs — and we didn't shout in control....

It's right for [Sal] to use that language. I thought he was a fair man. Even if he was unfair, he was unfair to *everybody*. He was unfair to his sons [John Turturro and Richard Edson], and he treated Mookie [Spike Lee] probably better than he treated his own sons....

When I first saw the script, I said to Spike, "Why is this guy in the fuckin' neighborhood? Why is he there? I mean, this is stupid. If you want to, you could go to Vietnam and make money too." I had to resolve in my own mind, he was there because he wanted to be there. Because he liked the people there....

[I say] "I've been here for 25 years. You see these people, you see the kids? These people grew up on my pizza — yeah, you laugh, but I'm proud of that." Now, I said this is too fuckin' corny, no one's going to believe it. But they did and it made him a full-bodied, complex fuckin' character.

—Aiello, interviewed by Gavin Smith for *Film Comment*, July/Aug 1991

What made it work with us [Aiello and Spike Lee] was that we were fully honest and open. I told him right away that I was 300-degrees to the right of Ronald Reagan and that I love Larry Bird and the Boston Celtics. I'll go to my death saying that Howard Beach was a turf thing, not a racial thing. Spike feels differently. He has great black pride. And I have great white pride. But we got along great.

—Aiello, interviewed by Patrick Goldstein for *The Los Angeles Times*, 24 Sept 1989

Q. What did you notice about [Woody] Allen as a director [on *The Purple Rose of Cairo* (1985) and *Radio Days* (1987)]?

A. I think when he casts you, he's directed you. He knows who he's got. And his directing is very minimal. He is an intellectual, but he speaks in the smallest, most understood verbal tones: Be a little less angry, be a little more angry; be a little less happy, be a little more happy; take the edge off the anger....

I don't think I did my best work with Woody. I think if there's self-intimidation, with me it probably happened with Woody more than anyone else.

Q. What do you mean?

A. I expected so much of myself working with Woody, I never felt totally free. I put too much on myself.... I always wanted to give Woody more.

—Aiello, interviewed by Gavin Smith for *Film Comment*, July\Aug 1991

Eddie ALBERT [1908-]

Born: Edward Albert Heimberger in Rock Island, Illinois; father of Edward Albert [1951-]. Studies at The University of Minnesota, work on radio (with Grace Bradt), and on Broadway (from 1935) preceded his film debut in Brother Rat (1938, William Keighley), a role he originated on the stage. In 1956, he played Cooney in Robert Aldrich's Attack!:

I had been in combat as a naval officer. I was commended for bravery in battle. Two or three days later I wondered, "Was I brave, or was I a coward just trying to get out of action?" Is there such a thing as a coward? During action, the coward rationalizes his actions. James Poe showed in the script that the coward does not exist at the moment. It's only the outsiders who say this later, who put this view on it.

Aldrich approved of my approach. He had sympathy for Cooney. He made Cooney *understandable*. He wasn't just a cheap villain. That was the moral base. Bob brought it out with a sense of compassion, of pity. But he's got to be killed; he's a danger. He rationalized himself out of responsibility....

Aldrich's greatest virtue [was] his love for conflict.... He would build an antagonism, even while the scene was rolling. During one scene with [Jack] Palance and [Lee] Marvin at the table, Aldrich had goaded Palance to such an extent that I felt he might take a punch at me. I even moved my foot under the table so that I could duck if he did....

I was the kind of actor [Aldrich] liked — professional, grown-up, responsible — just like he was. He was a terribly strong man, perhaps too inflexible, too hot-tempered. He might have saved himself some harm had he been more flexible. But he did not suffer fools gladly. He was an intelligent, compassionate man, with genuine sympathy for the underdog. He found much wrong in the world and he hated it. He was a hard worker.... On the set, he was a great general; the set was professionally run and you were expected to do your job. He would listen to me, but he wasn't one for talk. He was not one of those directors who talk through a scene; to him, that was a kind of artistic masturbation. He was too intense. He was a man of action. He wanted to get on with it. [Albert also worked on Aldrich's *The Longest Yard* (1974) and *Hustle* (1975).]

—Albert, interviewed by Edwin T. Arnold and Eugene L. Miller, Jr. for *The Films and Career of Robert Aldrich* (Knoxville: The University of Tennessee Press, 1986)

Jane ALEXANDER [1939-]

Born: Jane Quigley in Boston. Studies at Sarah Lawrence College (math) and The University of Edinburgh, success at The Edinburgh Drama Festival, and brief U.S. stage work preceded her film debut as Eleanor Blackman in The Great White Hope (1970, Martin Ritt), a role she had played on Broadway. In 1976, she played the bookkeeper in Alan J. Pakula's All the President's Men:

I like to find characters we can look up to, aspire to.... The character I play in *All the President's Men* has that element of courage that I love. She's a very, very scared person. Her job is at stake. Her sense of morality has been overturned. Possibly her life is in danger. And yet she makes a commitment during that scene — and that's why it's a good scene — to divulge what she knows, to help turn the tables. It's an act of courage on her part.

—Alexander, interviewed by Robert Berkvist for *The New York Times*, 2 May 1976

[In reading a script] you can pick out the scenes that are going to be cut; you can even pick out a whole character that can be cut.

Now I took a very small role in a film called *All the President's Men*, the part of the bookkeeper. I knew when I took that part there was no way they could cut either of her scenes because they were absolutely crucial to the plot. It's no fun ending up on the cutting room floor, as many people will tell you. I have had scenes of mine go but I knew beforehand these scenes would go and have even told the director, "I know you can drop this." So when people worry about structuring their part and stuff like that I try and cover certain aspects in those scenes that might be cut — character aspects.

It's not why I choose a role but it's one of the considerations. I just turned down a role in a film. One of the people connected with it said, "Oh, isn't she a wonderful character?" But nothing about this character was integral to the plot; if anything had to go in the script it would have been her, so I said, "I'm not interested."

—Alexander, interviewed by David Galligan for *Drama-Logue*, 19-25 Mar 1987

The role [of Lillian in *Brubaker* (1980)] is underwritten. I came in too late. Bob Rafelson was released as director several weeks after the shooting began. The part was first written for a man. Bob Redford thought it a good idea to have a woman. Then Stuart Rosenberg came in to direct and he only had a few days. The part was not carefully thought out.

Lillian's position is a good one. I would have liked to see her outside the office and with Redford. The problem with making the aide a woman is that they didn't want a physical relationship to blur the intention of the film.

—Alexander, interviewed by Ann Guarino for *The Daily News*, 18 June 1980

Q. Did [you] have any trouble getting into character on the set of *Testament* [1983, Lynne Littman]?

A. Not at all. If you've ever worried about what would happen to your family if the madness [of nuclear war] is allowed to destroy the world, you don't need much encouragement. All you need is that fear, and I think that fear is within all of us....

I've been on the board of a Women's Action for Nuclear Disarmament for three years. It was founded by Helen Caldicott who was head of Physicians for Social Responsibility. She was interested in establishing an organization that would become grass roots and would primarily focus attention on the women because she felt that women would provide the turning point, just simple women all across the country who would say, "Hey, wait a minute. We're talkin' about our kids...."

I spoke to Helen Caldicott, and she's a doctor, so I do have a good idea of what [the aftermath of a bomb drop] would be like.

—Alexander, interviewed by James Verniere for *The Aquarian Weekly*, 24 Nov 1983

William ALLAND [1916-]

Born: Delmar, Delaware. An actor with Orson Welles' Mercury Theater in New York, he made his film debut as Thompson in Welles' Citizen Kane (1941):

I played the reporter, and the voice of the *March of Time*, but I also walked through Orson's scenes for him. I wasn't the stand-in; there was a stand-in for lighting purposes. When the scene had been lighted and Orson rehearsed his part, I studied his choreography and repeated it as Orson watched from behind the camera.

Then I had the responsibility of watching Orson during the scene and approving or rejecting the take. I didn't pass artistic judgment; I merely checked to see if Orson was getting what he wanted. After each scene, he would glance at me. If I smiled, the take was okay. If I remained poker-faced, he'd shoot it again.

There was one scene which stands out above all others in my memory; that was the one in which Orson broke up the roomful of furniture in a rage. You must realize that Orson never liked himself as an actor. He had the idea that he should have been feeling more, that he intellectualized too much and never achieved the emotion of losing himself in a part.

When he came to the furniture-breaking scene, he set up four cameras, because he obviously couldn't do the scene many times. He did the scene just twice, and each time he threw himself into the action with a fervor I had never seen in him. It was absolutely electric; you felt as if you were in the presence of a man coming apart. Orson staggered out of the set with his hands bleeding and his face flushed. He almost swooned, yet he was exultant. "I really felt it," he exclaimed. "I really felt it."

Strangely, that scene didn't have the same power when it appeared on the screen. It might have been how it was cut, or because there hadn't been close-in shots to depict his rage. The scene in the picture was only a mild reflection of what I had witnessed on that movie stage.

—Alland, in *Action*, May/June 1969

Nancy ALLEN [1950-]

Born: New York City. Studies at The High School of Performing Arts in N.Y. and at The Lee Strasberg Theater Institute, work in commercials and as a model preceded her film debut in The Last Detail (1973, Hal Ashby). She worked with Brian De Palma (to whom she was married 1979 to 1984) on four films; in the third — Dressed to Kill (1980) she played Liz Blake:

I gave her a lot of things that I strive for in my own life. Independence and the ability to have confidence in yourself and your work and to not give a damn what anyone else thinks. You know, to stand behind your decisions. I think a lot of people got off on the wrong track...and said: "Oh, she's a hooker...isn't that terrible." In fact, I worked very hard to make her very content with what she was doing.... [She was] basically self-reliant and just a very together woman.

—Allen, interviewed by Dan Fieldstad for *Movie Guide*, July 1981

There has been a strange, violent reaction to Sally [in *Blow-Out* (1981, Brian De Palma)], and it's a total mystery to me. Brian and I felt so sure that people would fall in love with her. I think some people resent that I'm Mrs. Brian De Palma. Some writers are actually comparing us to Hearst and Marion Davies! Someone in *The Daily News* wrote a piece saying that I'm a good actress who's being manipulated by my husband. How dare anyone presume I was being manipulated by my husband. I created Sally! I am responsible for her.

People like to be able to pigeonhole a character, and typically you'd expect someone like Sally to be a bad person, or if she shows any goodness, she must be a hooker with the heart of gold. Well, Sally isn't like that. As the part was written, she was more stereotyped, but I worked with Brian and John [Travolta — with whom she had worked on *Carrie* (1976, Brian De Palma)] to play against that. I wanted to make Sally a little bit liberated. She is not an educated or articulate woman, but she has perfectly good instincts. Her problem is that she doesn't trust them....

Why does Sally agree to participate in the plot to embarrass the presidential candidate in the first place? I guess the answer is tossed off in a line in a scene that goes by very quickly, but it's when she says, "Those men who stick their hands in the cookie jar deserve to get them cut off." Sally is performing a service to women. Oh, partially she does it for money, but she's not a passive victim. She's a person who's very determined to make her mark. [Allen also worked on De Palma's *Home Movies* (1979).]

—Allen, interviewed by Seth Cagin for *The Soho Weekly News*, 26 Aug 1981

Sally [in *Blow Out*] wasn't very smart; she did have common sense. She fit into the modern world — always looking out for herself first, always after a quick buck. This was in contrast to John's character, the disillusioned idealist, dreaming of a world that disappeared 20 years ago.

The thing that made Sally work for me wasn't her past or present situation — it was her future. I felt she had to have a goal in life, and Brian was good enough to let me add that facet. I looked for the key which would give her character validity, and developed it from the fact that she worked behind a cosmetic counter. It was only natural that she wanted to make up Hollywood stars. Though the audience knows she'll never get to California, Sally does have a spark of hope in her life....

I don't see Sally as a hooker. Sally does not sleep with the men she sets up. She has convinced herself that she's *helping* the men's wives, exposing their cheating and hypocrisy. And, in the back of her mind, she feels she will meet someone who can give her the ticket to Hollywood.

Sally is very different from Liz Blake, who was very independent, and genuinely *liked* being a prostitute. Liz didn't depend on anyone, even though she needed help. They were extremes: Liz was very cool and emotionless, while Sally is all emotion and heart.

Brian writes a skeleton script then asks for thoughts and feelings about the individual parts. Sally's character wasn't very strong in the original draft, so we made changes to improve her during rehearsals. John Travolta and I worked together for about a week, *opening up* our scenes. We did a lot of improvising, which Brian utilized in rewriting the final screenplay. We also had the opportunity to perform the entire movie in sequence, like a play, during rehearsals. This helped us to get a fix on the personal interrelationships....

By the time Brian is ready to shoot, most dramatic problems are solved, leaving him free to concentrate on his storyboards. Because of the way he uses the camera, he finds it vital to pinpoint the trouble spots as early as possible.

It is also to an actor's advantage to know exactly what he or she is going to say before going to the set, because working on a Brian De Palma film is extremely difficult. You have to make speeches and hit marks precisely in order to meet his constantly moving camera. Two-shots and close-ups are usually easy, but when the camera is tracking, it may require ten takes to coordinate *all* the activities.

—Allen, interviewed by Lynn Parks for *Prevue*, Nov/Dec 1981

Q. So how was Paul Verhoeven to work with on *RoboCop* [1987]?

A. It was a very intense experience, but very exciting. Paul is a desperately inspired artist, a very creative man with a real high level of artistic excellence in his work which kind of gets your juices going...at the same time he's very playful and a lot of fun....

A film becomes a director's point of view, very much so in my opinion, although there's some directors whose movies lack personality. But a Paul Verhoeven film, a Spielberg film [she had worked on his *1941* (1979)], a Brian De Palma feature...any of those people are very much on the edge, directing a lot of things that are not in the script. When an actor is on the set, he's very vulnerable to the director, and I would say that with Paul I felt a lot more secure. [Allen reprised her role in *RoboCop 2* (1990, Irvin Kershner).]

—Allen, interviewed by Jeremy Clarke for *Films & Filming*, Feb 1988

Woody ALLEN [1935-]

Born: Alan Stewart Konigsberg in Brooklyn, N.Y. A gag writer turned stand-up comedian, he made his debut as an actor in What's New Pussycat? (1965, Clive Donner), which he also wrote. In 1969, he became a successful director/actor with Take the Money and Run:

Q. You've said you've gotten more aggressive in your performances....

A. I am more aggressive on the screen. I'm willing to step out more and give myself more verbal jokes and physical jokes and spend more time on myself and take responsibility. A good example of that was *Sleeper* [1973]. In *Bananas* [1971] and *Take the Money and Run* the scripts are hilariously funny to read. They're kind of actor-proof. The jokes are there. If the guy takes a serum in his arm and turns into a rabbi [in *Take the Money and Run*], you could have fifty actors do that and people are going to laugh if they like that joke — it's self-contained. But in *Sleeper* the script is not very funny and I relied on myself to make it funny. I went in with a lot more trepidation with the flying packs and the big vegetables and the robot suits. There were no jokes there. It was what I was going to do with it. I was willing to take that chance. I would never have done that two years ago.

—Allen, interviewed by Leonard Probst for *Off-Camera* (New York: Stein & Day, 1975)

I decided to take a chance [with *The Front* (1976, Martin Ritt)]. From the beginning, I had enormous reservations about doing a film which I had not written and over which I would have no directorial control. I wasn't sure how I would feel being a hired actor in a dramatic movie, and I said, "If you want a guy to make *conversation*, hire Jack Nicholson."

I felt uncomfortable throughout the whole process, not being able to improvise and change things. And I could never judge how things were going. My only yardstick is funniness. I can look at the dailies on one of my own movies, and maybe I don't look too attractive up on that screen or maybe I don't move so gracefully, but I just *know* when it's funny, and I know immediately when something is missing. But when I look at the dailies on a dramatic film, I'm all at sea....

The reason I did *The Front* was that the *subject* was worthwhile. Martin Ritt and [screenwriter] Walter Bernstein lived through the blacklist and survived it with dignity, so I didn't mind deferring to their judgment....

—Allen, interviewed by Lee Guthrie for *Woody Allen: A Biography* (New York: Drake Publishers, 1978)

People got it into their heads that *Annie Hall* [1977] was autobiographical, and I couldn't convince them that it wasn't. And they thought *Manhattan* [1979] was autobiography. Because I make the lead character a comic or a writer, I play it myself. I can't play an atomic scientist. I'm not going to make the lead a mechanic. I know the language of certain people.

—Allen, interviewed by William E. Geist for *Rolling Stone*, 9 Apr 1987

[Sandy Bates in *Stardust Memories* (1980) is] a very sick, neurotic almost nervous-break-down film director. I didn't want this guy to be necessarily likable. I wanted him to be surly and upset: not a saint or an angel, but a man with real problems who finds that art doesn't save you. So many people were outraged that I dared to suggest an ambivalent, love/hate relationship between an audience and a celebrity; and then shortly after *Stardust Memories* opened, John Lennon was shot by the very guy who had asked him for his autograph earlier in the day. I feel that obtains. The guy who asks Sandy for his autograph on the boardwalk and says, "You're my favorite comedian" in the middle of the picture, later, in Sandy's fantasy, comes up and shoots him. This is what happens with celebrities — one day people love you, the next day they want to kill you. And the celebrity also feels that way toward the audience; because in the movie Sandy hallucinates that the guy shoots him; but in fact Sandy is the one who has the gun. So the celebrity imagines that the fan will do to him what in fact he wants to do to the fan. But people don't want to hear this — this is an unpleasant truth to dramatize.

—Allen, interviewed by Diane Jacobs for *...but we need the eggs: The Magic of Woody Allen* (New York: St. Martin's Press, 1982)

June ALLYSON [1917-]

Born: Ella Greisman in Lucerne, N.Y. Trained as a dancer, she was invited to make her feature film debut in Best Foot Forward (1943, Edward Buzzell) in a role she had created on Broadway. While waiting for that film to go into production, she made Girl Crazy (1943, Norman Taurog):

I felt incredibly lucky, in my first movie role, to be singing a song to Mickey Rooney....

Thank God I did my first movie scene with him. He was surprisingly sensitive to my needs and helped me through a nerve-racking day.

After rehearsals we started shooting. I was terrified by the complexity of movie acting — trying to remember all the things you have to do — simultaneously or in sequence — flirt with Mickey, sing, hold the note, move to that mark, smile, look there, hold that note. I had a sexy song and I was supposed to show Mickey around a lot during the number. He was a rich smart-alek kid who comes to a nightclub. I was supposed to be a Betty Hutton type, a little tough....

Mickey was like a big brother. Never again would I act with anyone who was greater at helping me along and making me look good by playing to me. I'm sure that had he wanted to, he could have made me all but invisible by drawing attention to himself. It would have been easy for such a master craftsman, but Mickey was a generous human being.

—Allyson, in her (with Frances Spatz Leighton) *June Allyson* (New York: G.P. Putnam's Sons, 1982)

The wistful, dewey-eyed, tremulous-of-the-lower-lip June Allyson — the character known to movie-goers — was born when I made *Two Girls and a Sailor* [1944, Richard Thorpe] with Van Johnson and Gloria DeHaven. The script called for me, as one of two competing sisters, to take Van away from Gloria. This just didn't make sense. Gloria is an absolutely beautiful girl and it was ridiculous to believe that Van would choose me over Gloria.

The studio executives finally agreed to allow me to test for the shy, plain girl, and I appeared wearing short bangs and no make-up. Gloria was a walking dream. Of course the test showed me pathetic and wistful, while Gloria was glamorous and sexy. Our roles were switched and "June Allyson" became more than a name; she became the Girl Next Door.

—Allyson, as told to John Maynard for *The Saturday Evening Post*, 14 Dec 1957

When I read the script [of *The Stratton Story* (1949)], I saw there was very little in it for the girl, so I said I wouldn't do it. M-G-M told me I wouldn't be suspended for refusing to make the film but I was still wanted for it. Then I put up the argument that studio officials — not me — claimed I was one of their biggest stars and asked why they didn't protect their property.... Then I went to Sam Wood, who was to direct the film, and explained that doing the picture was no wish of mine and that I'd have to depend upon him.

My part in that film was strictly Sam Wood. He and Jimmy Stewart would come to my dressing room after working hours and cook up whole scenes for me. Jimmy would say, "June's my wife. She's the big star. Moviegoers won't want to look at me; they want to look at her." So we rebuilt the whole picture around that idea.

—Allyson, interviewed by Hedda Hopper for *Photoplay Magazine*, Oct 1952

Q. After their [M-G-M] rather shoddy treatment, you left and went straight into one of the biggest smash hits of your career, *The Glenn Miller Story* [1954, Anthony Mann]. How did that come about?

A. Jimmy Stewart called me. It was at the time of negotiation, and though I didn't want to stay at Metro they were offering me a deal and Richard [husband Dick Powell] said I might as well take it. Just a day or two before I was supposed to sign the contracts, Jimmy called me and said, "Hey, I've got two films that I want to do and I won't do them without you." I said, "Marvelous, what are they?" and he told me *The Glenn Miller Story* and *Strategic Air Command* [1955, Anthony Mann]. He said, "I'll send the scripts over," but I said, "Don't bother, I'll do them, I don't have to read the scripts".... So, I didn't re-sign with Metro, I did the two films with Jimmy instead. It was the best thing I could have done, but I didn't do it because I was wise. I did it because Jimmy asked me.

—Allyson, interviewed by Tom Vallance for *Films & Filming*, July 1982

Even Richard [Powell] opposed me violently when I decided to make *The Shrike* [1955, José Ferrer]. All my advisors said no. But it was a challenge I could not resist. For years I had been the Perfect Wife: to Jim Stewart, to Alan Ladd, to Van Johnson, to Bill Holden; even on the screen to Dick Powell.

And now, in *The Shrike*, in the adaptation of the Broadway play with José Ferrer, I would be far from the perfect wife. I would indeed be a monster of a wife, one of the least attractive in the history of the theater.

—Allyson, as told to John Maynard for *The Saturday Evening Post*, 21 Dec 1957

Don AMECHE [1908-]

Born: Dominic Amici in Kenosha, Wisconsin. While studying law at The University of Wisconsin, he acted with a stock company in Madison. A brief Broadway appearance and a tour with Texas Guinan's vaudeville show and work on radio then led to his film debut in Sins of Man (1936, Otto Brower and Gregory Ratoff). That same year he co-starred with Loretta Young in Henry King's Ramona:

Of all the actresses I worked with, I believe Loretta Young did as much for me as anyone else. When we were making *Ramona*, there were several times when technical problems of motion pictures would stump me. Loretta always went out of her way to help me. She was never too busy to explain puzzling aspects of acting in pictures. Her cooperation made my first days in Hollywood much easier and taught me a great deal of the ins and outs of motion picture technique. I still maintain that Loretta is one of the finest technicians in Hollywood. [They worked together on 4 other films: *Ladies in Love* (1936, Edward H. Griffith), *Love is News* (1937, Tay Garnett), *Love Under Fire* (1937, George Marshall) and *The Story of Alexander Graham Bell* (1939, Irving Cummings).]

—Ameche, interviewed by Jack Holland for *Movies*, 1940

Q. You worked three times with Henry King, one of the top directors on the 20th [Century-Fox] lot.

A. Yes. I made *Ramona*, *In Old Chicago* [1938] and *Alexander's Ragtime Band* [1938] with Henry. He was a severe man, a very stern man. He was a man who thought he could do anything. He could fix the nets that they'd use for above when the sun was overhead. He thought he could do it better than anyone else, and maybe he could, I don't know. But he was a kind of dictatorial person, very much wanted his own way, and got it....

Q. How about Allan Dwan [on *The Three Musketeers* (1939)]?

A. He was like King, a really severe man, and inclined to pick on people a little bit when he found someone he could do that to. It was a trait I didn't like particularly. He did have ability but I just didn't like the browbeating quality....

Q. You were loaned to Paramount for the classic comedy, *Midnight* (1939).... What was director Mitchell Leisen like on the set?

A. Very gentle, allowed a tremendous latitude to the performers, depended a great deal upon them, as a matter of fact. He was the opposite of somebody like Henry King.

Q. How was John Barrymore to work with? [*Midnight*] was in his later years, past his prime.

A. He was wonderful, and I don't think personally that he was past his prime at all. He was reading all his lines off of a cardboard, and he didn't have to do that at all. It was just that he was lazy and he knew he could get by with it. But he didn't have to. I got to know John quite well. I don't think John ever lost his ability. It's just that he got a little lackadaisical about the energy he wanted to expend.

—Ameche, interviewed by John A. Gallagher for *Quirk's Reviews*, Oct 1987

[Mrs. Gilbert Grosvenor, the eldest daughter of Alexander Graham Bell] was very much interested in the production [of *The Story of Alexander Graham Bell*] and she did a great deal to help us in our characterizations by recalling for us all the little mannerisms and gestures of the people we were playing. Bell, for example, in moments of emotional stress, used to run his right hand constantly through his hair, an action I adopted for my work in the part.

—Ameche, interviewed in an unsourced, undated article in the files of The New York Public Library for the Performing Arts

Q. In *Heaven Can Wait* [1943] you played Henry Van Cleve for Ernst Lubitsch. Is it true that he acted out the parts for his actors?

A. He would if it was necessary, but he didn't do a great deal of that on *Heaven Can Wait*. That's my favorite picture of all the pictures I've made, and it's primarily because it was directed by Ernst Lubitsch.... No one came near him in the field of satire. Ernst had an odd outlook on life, a satirical outlook on life. When he and Sam Raphaelson finished writing the picture, they spent eight months polishing the script before we started shooting. The first day, he assembled the whole cast and he told us, "These are the facts and I beg you don't change anything because this is the way I would like it." He was totally persistent in getting exactly what he wanted. He'd go at it and at it and at it. This won't hurt anyone at all, but Gene Tierney couldn't quite come to one scene, and he just kept at her and at her until he broke her completely down. When shortly after, she straightened herself around, he rolled the camera and got exactly what he wanted. He knew how to do it. He didn't do it unless he had to, but he was a totally dedicated man to his art.

—Ameche, interviewed by John A. Gallagher for *Quirk's Reviews*, Dec 1987

My role in *Trading Places* [1983, John Landis] was easy. Playing Ralph Bellamy's brother, well, they were so black and white, there was only one direction to take — the meaner they could be, the better it was. Very effective, I thought.

It was all there on paper in sustained scenes. Longer scenes *are* easier, though there really isn't a hell of a lot of difference in the way I work as a performer — it's just that when the scenes are short, one doesn't have that little satisfaction of saying, "This is quite a good scene...."

John Landis is magnificent — *damn*, he's a good director! And, he's also a nice man — considerate — oh, he was a joy!

By that, though, I'm not implying that Ron Howard [on *Cocoon* (1985)] is not! I could almost see what was happening with John — he's so specific, I knew exactly what he wanted. Ron knows what he wants, but in a different way, a way his actors aren't always aware of. I just had to go entirely on what Ron said — whatever he asked me for, I tried to give it.

When Ron shot the scene in *Cocoon* with Wilford [Brimley], Hume [Cronyn] and me walking through the woods, we did 12 takes, and he told us to vary the dialogue if we felt like it.

—Ameche, interviewed by Kim Howard Johnson for *Starlog*, June 1986

I have never played a character like Gino [in *Things Change* (1988, David Mamet)] before. But I knew I could do it because I understand the Italian mentality: I was around Italians during my childhood. My father was from Italy. The accent I used for Gino is totally my father's — he had that until he died. And like Gino, he was a man of integrity, according to his standards....

David went into great depth about every scene we did. My view of Gino had to agree with his. Back in my studio days at 20th Century-Fox, if a director was doing a property written by somebody else, I felt that I always had the latitude of questioning the character relationships. And I did many times. But in this case, David had co-written the script with Shel Silverstein. He knew the character, and all you had to do was ask him about whatever you didn't understand, which I did. I was totally trying to give him what he wanted.

You see, I had watched David's first film, *House of Games* [1987] before I took the part. I just thought it was wonderful. I would've done anything he asked me to do, truthfully, after seeing that.

—Ameche, interviewed by Myra Forsberg for *The New York Times*, 16 Oct 1988

Julie ANDREWS [1935-]

Born: Julia Wells in Walton-on-Thames, England. A childhood stage performer (at 13, she gave a royal command performance for the Queen), her career developed to major status with her portrayal (at age 21) of Eliza Doolittle in My Fair Lady on the London and Broadway stages. She made her film debut in Mary Poppins (1964, Robert Stevenson):

I chose *The Americanization of Emily* [1964, Arthur Hiller] for my next film after *Mary Poppins* because it proposed another challenge. It was a straight dramatic role with no singing or dancing to fall back on. I'd have to act. It would also give me the chance to prove to myself and the public that I could do something besides musical comedy. I absolutely adored playing Emily. I had never done a straight part before.... I was at a loss without songs at first — at least in *Mary Poppins* I would always take comfort in the knowledge that I would be doing a song and would feel secure eventually. But in *Emily* there were no songs to hang on to.

—Andrews, quoted by Robert Windeler in *Julie Andrews* (New York: G.P. Putnam's Sons, 1970)

It occurred to me that Maria [in *The Sound of Music* (1965, Robert Wise)] *couldn't* be sweetness and light with seven kids on her hands all the time. Seven kids would have to get on one's nerves, at some point or other, so I tried once in a while to show that I might be slightly exhausted by them.

—Andrews, interviewed by Roy Newquist for *Showcase* (New York: G.P. Putnam's Sons, 1966)

When Blake [Edwards] cast Dudley [Moore in *10* (1979) as the replacement for George Segal], I said, "Well, surely you don't want *me* now, because it's going to look so ridiculous — I do tower over him."

Edwards: By about eight inches.

Andrews: I was thinking, foolishly, that I would be terribly embarrassed and that Dudley would be terribly embarrassed. But Blake said, "No, no, no. I think it would be great — it would make the relationship more unusual." So I said, "Well, give me something to relate to. Why would she fall in love with this pipsqueak — who is adorable, admittedly — but why?" And he said, "Okay, if he were just a butcher down the street you probably wouldn't be interested in him; but if he were a very, very talented man...." First of all he cited Frank Sinatra and Ava Gardner; he was quite small and she was quite tall and, for a while, they connected very well. Also, a great friend of ours is André Previn, who is not very tall, but he's the most dynamic man to meet and talk to, and so bright and intelligent and *very* attractive. When Blake mentioned André and said to relate to *him*, I said, "Ah, now I see what you mean. If I think of Dudley in that light I can do it." And it worked.

—Andrews (and Blake Edwards), interviewed at Judith Crist's Tarrytown seminar, 27-29 Nov 1981; repr. in *Take 22*, co-ed by Judith Crist and Shirley Sealy (New York: Viking Press, 1984)

Victor/Victoria [1982, Blake Edwards] was a very difficult, multifaceted role. I mean, I'd sometimes be playing a woman trying to pretend to be a man, then sometimes play a man with a woman's feelings and sometimes just be straight on. There were so many things to work out. As someone who likes to be in control, I felt *wobbly*. There was something else, too: When you get older, you kind of get on to yourself. You know the tricks you play to get by, and you like them less and less if you care about your work. I was trying hard to get away from them and was sometimes falling back, and so I wasn't as pleased as I'd like to have been with my performance. Not that Blake didn't help me enormously and bring out something good; he did. But looking back on it now, I wish I'd had more time, done fewer tricks and said lines differently.

—Andrews, interviewed (with Blake Edwards) by Lawrence Linderman for *Playboy*, Dec 1982

As Robert Preston says in [*Victor/Victoria*], there are all sorts of men that act in all sorts of ways. But as a general rule, I find that men are more still than ladies. They're not as busy. I used that stillness as sort of a safety measure: when in doubt, stand still.

—Andrews, interviewed by Leslie Bennetts for *The New York Times*, 14 Mar 1982

At first [*That's Life* (1986, Blake Edwards)] was very intimidating. We all wondered if we could say the words well enough to do Blake justice. But it became very liberating after a while. Blake always works with instant tape-playback built into the camera, so we were able to see what we were doing as we went along, and refer to it. When we realized it was working, it really became exciting....

I had thought perhaps we [Andrews and her youngest daughter, Emma Walton] would be embarrassed with each other: that really playing mother and daughter wouldn't work, especially since we were playing with some real overtones of our own lives. But it didn't get in the way. In fact, it was such a contributive thing and so shared that we really do have a good feeling about what we captured. Like the scene in her bedroom when I consoled her. Those things really came from having done it with her before. [Andrews and Edwards married in 1969. In addition to the above, she has appeared in 4 other Edwards films: *Darling Lili* (1970), *The Tamarind Seed* (1974), *S.O.B.* (1981) and *The Man Who Loved Women* (1983).]

—Andrews, interviewed by Kevin McKelvey for *The Hollywood Reporter*, 24 Nov 1986

ANN-MARGRET [1941-]

Born: Ann-Margret Olson in Stockholm, Sweden. After World War II, her family settled 40 miles from Chicago. Music and dance lessons led her to night club work. Spotted in Las Vegas by George Burns, she was asked to join his Sahara Hotel act. Work in television preceded her film debut as Bette Davis' daughter in Pocketful of Miracles (1961, Frank Capra). A major turning point in her film career was her performance as Bobbie in Carnal Knowledge (1971, Mike Nichols):

Q. What caused the divorce between Bobbie and Jonathan [Jack Nicholson]?

A. I think it came to the point of no return, where she realized that this man kept getting older, but did not change. I think any woman will agree, that if after a few years a man like this hasn't changed, and she's done everything she possibly can, then there's no changing him. The fact is that he doesn't want to change, or he's unable to change. So, it's a question of Bobbie living in a world where she's giving everything she had, and he was giving nothing. She wasn't a dummy. She wanted love in return.

When they got married she thought he loved her. She didn't know to what extent he was mentally disturbed. That didn't come out until much later. It was very frightening to Bobbie to watch this person that she'd had so much fun with in the beginning just change into a maniac.

Q. Was your section of the film shot sequentially, building up until the end?

A. Yes, thank goodness. It made it so much easier.

Q. How did you prepare for the explosive argument scene with Jack?

A. Very carefully.... Mike and Jack both knew that I was terribly nervous about it. I would stay in my dressing room the whole time, when I wasn't in front of the camera, and think morose thoughts and just stay in the character. It was very nice, because the weather at the time in Canada was a kind of somber, cool climate, and it helped. I just sat there, going over my lines in my head, not talking to anybody, just so I could stay in that kind of mood....

I remember one scene where I was sitting on the bed, and I said I wanted to get married. Well, I don't know how Mike knew this, but I'm an only child and I'm very close to my father, and my father is a very quiet, gentle man, and he has a way of just putting his hand on my head that makes me just fall apart. It just makes me feel all loved and protected, and just everything. It just rips me apart. I don't know how Mike knew this, but before the scene he didn't say anything. He just came over to where I was sitting, and he put his hand on my head, five seconds before the camera started. And he stood there, and then said, "O.K., roll 'em." And the tears just started. He didn't know me. He didn't know that part of me. It shook me up.

—Ann-Margret, interviewed by Robert David Crane and Christopher Fryer for *Jack Nicholson: Face to Face* (New York: M. Evans & Co., 1975)

[Jack Nicholson] was so giving [on *Carnal Knowledge*]. For example, in one of the really emotional scenes that we had in the bedroom, there was a close-up of me reacting to what he was doing. And although he wasn't on camera himself, just to help me he really gave his off-screen acting its full strength. He was jumping on the bed and screaming, so violently and so loudly that he went home with laryngitis. All for the benefit of *my* close-up. He's so unselfish.

Ken [Russell] wanted me to have a nervous breakdown on screen, and by the seventh day [of shooting the champagne, chocolate sauce and baked beans scene in *Tommy* (1975)], that's exactly what I was having. I felt like a caged animal within those four walls. Mind you, at first it was a sensual feeling, because the soapsuds [champagne] were warm and the chocolate was warm. And that was very enjoyable. But at the end it was ice cold, and I was a mess.

There was no stand-in. I did everything.... When the first stream of beans came out I was just thrown back by the sheer force of it. That was quite a shock. We did it several times. I was covered in it. Then they'd put me under the shower and get rid of all the stuff. They washed my hair, and dried it, and curled it. They put on fresh make-up, and brought me a fresh cat suit.... We did it again. They put me in the shower again. And over and over.... I'd realized when I read the scene that it would really have to be *dealt* with. Obviously Ken thought so too, because he saved it until the very end of my shooting schedule.

—Ann-Margret, interviewed by Gordon Gow for *Films & Filming*, Jan 1976

Roscoe "Fatty" ARBUCKLE [1887-1933]

Born: Smith Center, Kansas. Work in vaudeville, the fairgrounds and musical comedy led him to work as an extra in 1909, first at Universal and then at Keystone. In 1916, he directed and starred in The Waiter's Ball:

Q. What pictures have you most enjoyed making?

A. None of them. There is too much worry in working them out. A comedy scenario isn't like a drama. We have nothing but the skeleton of a plot to work on, and we fill it out with our own gags.

Q. Just what is the significance of the word "gag"?

A. A gag is a piece of by-play which has no direct connection with the plot. For instance, take this picture we are working on [*The Waiter's Ball* (1916)]. Most of the scenes are laid in a restaurant. Al [St. John] is a waiter. I am a cook. A patron orders fish. Al calls the order to the kitchen. We thought it would be funny to have a live fish, with me chasing it. Then we decided to have the fish jump through the kitchen door into the restaurant, and have everybody join in the fun. We tried it out, and by adding each other's suggestions, made the "gag". Really, some of our best comedy scenes are developed this way.

Q. Do you prefer serious parts?

A. Well, of course we all like to do the "heavy" but no audience will stand for me in anything but light comedy. I started as the "Fat Boy," and I'll never get away from it. However, as far as the comedy itself is concerned, I prefer it to drama. To me it is a study of human nature. You put a character in a certain farcical situation, and then figure out what he will do. What he does must be typical. For the audience laughs not only at the screen comedy, but also, in some degree, because the same sort of incident has happened to them. It should be burlesque rather than slapstick, for burlesque is the highest type of dramatic art.

—Arbuckle, interviewed by Robert F. Moore for *Motion Picture Classic*, Nov 1916

Eve ARDEN [1912-1990]

Born: Eunice Quedens in Mill Valley, California. Work in stock at San Francisco's Alcazar Theater and on California's "citrus circuit" preceded her film debut in The Song of Love (1929, Erle C. Kenton). In 1936, she worked for director Gregory La Cava on Stage Door in a role which helped establish her typical character:

Mr. La Cava said, "I work differently from many directors, and my writer and I write most of our scenes as we go, so I can't offer you a specific part, but I like certain qualities I see in you and want very much to use you in the picture"....

A week or so later I turned up for a reading. All the girls in the group [Katharine Hepburn, Lucille Ball, Ginger Rogers, Gail Patrick, Andrea Leeds and Ann Miller] were assembled, and sheets containing lines were handed around. Lines one, two, three, et cetera, were tossed to us like bones to puppies. I had immediately spotted two lines I was drooling over....

When the reading started, however, the first of the juicy lines was greeted by complete silence. Finally, I could stand it no longer. "If no one wants this, I'll take it," I said bravely, read it, and was rewarded with a laugh. Katharine Hepburn hooted from her perch on a ladder overlooking us. "She's the one to watch out for, girls." She laughed. No more than a minute later, the second line came due. I couldn't believe it when again no one read it. This time I didn't wait so long. "Well, if you gals don't know a good line when you see it!" I read it.

The next day Mr. La Cava called me in. "I've been trying to think how we could give this character something different than the others. Got any ideas?"

I didn't have, but finally said, "I just got a couple of cats from the pound and have had a few funny experiences; maybe I could be the girl with a cat. Maybe I call it Henry, but it turns out to be a pregnant Henrietta." I looked none too hopefully at my director, but he grinned and said, "Not bad...."

When we shot the first day, I was to be cracking peanuts as I walked around talking to the girls. A little stymied with only two hands, I draped Henry around my neck and he hung there peacefully. Greg yelled, "Hey, that's great. Will he stay?"

In my first scene in the picture I appeared to be wearing a fur scarf over my blouse until the fur scarf's tail switched angrily into the air.

The director who made the biggest impression on me of any I ever worked with [was] Ernst Lubitsch. A swarthy, short man, lips constantly mouthing a large cigar, he was an inventive director with a great mind for comedy. He was wonderful to work with, and he made you feel free to offer a line or a bit of business, without offending you in the least if he turned it down.

The picture was *That Uncertain Feeling* [1941], with Melvyn Douglas and lovely Merle Oberon. I was amused and impressed watching Ernst, who, without removing his cigar, demonstrated to Merle how to be seductive — and he really was, stogie and all.

—Arden, in her *Three Phases of Eve* (New York: St. Martin's Press, 1985)

Alan ARKIN [1934-]

Born: New York City. Studies at Los Angeles City College, work as a member of a popular folk group, The Tarriers, with Second City in Chicago and on Broadway, preceded his feature film debut as Rozanov in The Russians are Coming, The Russians are Coming (1966, Norman Jewison):

I prepare for a role in a strange way. I don't read the script very many times. I don't consciously think of it. I just find that it stays in my mind all the time until I get locked onto an image of the person I'm supposed to be. If that doesn't happen, I consider myself in deep trouble, but usually it means that the character doesn't know who *he* is. Like when I was doing *The Russians are Coming*. I felt terribly strange and awkward and I thought it was because this was my first movie and a lot was riding on it. But then I caught myself and said, wait a minute! — this is exactly what Rozanov feels! The strangeness and the sense of not knowing the language were his feelings, not mine. I was giving myself the right signals, but in my insecurity I misinterpreted them.

—Arkin, interviewed by Barry Farrell for *Life*, 2 Oct 1970

It's easier to play a blind man than a deaf man. An actor's job is to listen and I can't listen in this role [as John Singer in *The Heart is a Lonely Hunter* (1967, Robert Ellis Miller)] because I'm not supposed to hear what anybody is saying. You can close your eyes and not see, but you can't put contact lenses in your ears. I visited a deaf-mute school in Montgomery.... I found an infinite variety in character, personality and intelligence. Some are very straight-laced, others talk a blue streak. So there is no one way to play a mute. This character remains a million miles away from me, so I have to look for details in the role to make it real. Like the script said, "He reaches in his pocket for loose change." I didn't feel he would have loose things in his pocket, so we got a little change purse. I carry a watch fob with a gold chain, and a Mark Cross pencil. I planned the way he arranges things meticulously in a little toilet kit in his room. I don't know if audiences will notice these details, but they've made this mute come true for me.

—Arkin, interviewed by Rex Reed for *The New York Times*, 10 Dec 1967

Q. You said you look for the keys in characters that you play: the signals that characters throw off for you. For instance, in Singer, you had to find what it was that was the essence that gave you the whole concept; a clue of what to do.

A. With Singer, it will surprise you, I think. With Singer, it was as much as anything the fact that he was a manipulator in that every relationship he had with everybody in that film was one where he could feel superior to them. He never put himself in a situation for a moment where he was vulnerable to anybody.

Q. And once you decided that, that's the way you played him all the way through?

A. I wouldn't have played it that way all the way through if it didn't work. I won't jam an idea into something that won't contain that idea. I found as I played through several scenes that it continued to work throughout the entire thing. Not only did it continue to work, but the appearance that man gives is of being exactly the opposite.

Q. Well, then the odd thing is that I'm thinking of Singer as being a vulnerable man who was on the verge of breaking down all the time.

A. Right. Also true. But the thing about him that kept him together was the idea that he was manipulating his environment. That he would associate with nobody who could get to him. This is what made him vulnerable. If I had played him as an open, giving person....

Q. It would have been sentimental.

A. He would have been healthy, and would not have committed suicide. There had to be something in the way I played him that led to his suicide.

Q. In other words, that was his fatal flaw.

A. Yes. It wasn't something in the script or something I talked about with anybody. What destroyed him was the fact that he really did not allow anybody to get to him. One of the great laws of acting is that if you have something to do that must be done, don't do it. Do the opposite.

—Arkin, interviewed by Lewis Funke for *Actors Talk About Theatre* (Chicago: The Dramatic Publishing Co., 1977)

I had an interesting talk with [novelist] Joe Heller about Yossarian. I said I had three or four ideas about how to play him [in *Catch-22* (1970, Mike Nichols)]. In parts of the book, he's a complete paranoid. He's totally caught up in the idea that people are out to destroy him. In other sections, he's a buoyant free spirit. In others, he's an active rebel. Heller said chances are they're all right. It seemed a little contradictory, but it's all the same thing. Yossarian reveres his own life, which is a good thing.

—Arkin, interviewed by Mel Gussow for *Holiday*, Oct 1966

Richard ARLEN [1899-1976]

Born: St. Paul, Minnesota. A member of Canada's Royal Flying Corps during World War I, he began work after the war as a sports writer in Duluth. Many jobs followed before he landed in Hollywood where he became a lab assistant at the D.W. Griffith Studio. While delivering film, he broke his leg in a motorcycle accident on the Paramount lot and ended up on crutches. As a gesture, they gave him work as an extra in crowd scenes. He went on to star in Wings *(1927, William Wellman):*

For Wellman, the picture was a labor of love. He'd been a pilot in the Lafayette Flying Corps, and he was going to tell the story of the outfit dramatically but honestly and authentically. *Wings* had a big budget, and the studio wanted the protection of established stars. The brass wondered about Wellman's sanity when he cast me and Buddy Rogers as the male leads. So far as audiences were concerned, we were nobodies. Clara Bow was the only star in it. Wellman also gave Gary Cooper, who was then an unknown, a bit in the picture.

We spent six and a half months shooting it in San Antonio, Texas, using the entire United

States Air Corps, which consisted of four pursuit planes. There was no trick photography. Buddy and I, who played young lieutenants, did our own flying, and we did all the aerial dogfights ourselves.

—Arlen, interviewed by Walter Wagner for *You Must Remember This* (New York: G.P. Putnam's Sons, 1975)

George ARLISS [1868-1946]

Born: Augustus George Andrews in London, England; father of director Leslie Arliss. Work on the London stage (from 1884) led Arliss to tour America; he stayed twenty years. Although he made his film debut in The Devil (1921, James Young) in a role he had created on the stage, it was his stage success, Disraeli, filmed in 1921 as a silent film (by Henry Kolker) and again in 1929 with sound for which he is best remembered:

With Al Green as director, the filming of *Disraeli* [1929] was almost too easy. I had appeared in the play for five consecutive years, so the only lines I had to memorize were those occasional scenes which were added in order to clarify the story. I played the part exactly as I had acted it in the theatre, with certain obvious concessions to the requirements of the screen. Flo [Mrs. George Arliss] of course, played her old part of Lady Beaconsfield. I don't think we lost any of the values that we had discovered in the theatre....

It took us until the end of July to finish the film.... Residents in Hollywood will tell you that the summers are just lovely, but I feel bound to record that at Busch's Gardens, where we did the Garden Party scene, I often had to change my linen three or four times in a morning in order to be faithful to Disraeli's reputation for punctilious dressing....

—Arliss, in his *My Ten Years in the Studios* (Boston: Little, Brown & Co., 1940)

Desi ARNAZ [1917-1986]

Born: Desiderio Alberto Arnaz y De Acha in Santiago, Cuba. A career as a singer, band leader and stage actor preceded his film debut in Too Many Girls (1940, George Abbott), a role he had previously played on Broadway. The following year, he played opposite Adolphe Menjou in Father Takes a Wife (1941, Jack Hively):

Menjou had a wonderful sense of humor and knew every trick of the trade. We were doing a scene in a taxicab and were supposed to get out of the cab to go into a hotel. As we got out of the taxicab, Menjou first and me second, I was supposed to be saying a line. We did it and the director yelled, "Cut!"

"Let's do it again," he said, "but, Desi, when you get out of the taxicab, clear yourself from behind Menjou so that the camera can see you."

"Okay," I said.

We did it again. Menjou came out of the taxicab with that great flair he had — and I was covered again as I spoke the line.

"Cut!"

I had a lot of respect for Mr. Menjou. I admired him very much in all his pictures. I knew he'd been in pictures for a long, long time and that he was one of the best character actors in the business so I didn't dare say anything.

The director told me, "Desi, you were covered again."

"Well, I'm having a little trouble clearing myself. Mr. Menjou takes up most of the room when we come out of there."

"Adolphe will take it all if he can get away with it. Just don't let him."

"Okay, I'll give it another try."

We did it again, and again I failed.

"Cut!"

Back in the taxicab.

I said, "Mr. Menjou, you've got to help me out a little bit because the director is giving me hell. He wants me to clear myself from behind when we come out of the taxicab so he can see my face when I say my line. I've tried to clear myself five times now and I haven't been very successful.

He answered, "Every actor for himself!"

"Every actor for himself?" I asked.

"That's right."

The next time we came out of the cab, I gave him a real shove and he almost went on his ass.

"Cut!"

Back inside the cab.

"That's going a little overboard to clear yourself, isn't it?" asked Adolphe.

"Well, every actor for himself, Mr. Menjou."

He laughed. "You'll do fine out here; you learn fast."

In the next take we didn't have any trouble and he was very helpful to me for the rest of the picture.

—Arnaz, in his *A Book* (New York: Wm. Morrow & Co., 1976)

Edward ARNOLD [1890-1956]

Born: Guenther Schneider in New York City. Work on the stage, both amateur and professional, notably with The Ben Greet Shakespearean Players preceded his film debut as a cowboy at the Essanay Studios in Chicago in 1915. His first major role was as Jack Brennan opposite Joan Crawford in Sadie McKee (1934, Clarence Brown):

Most masculine roles are played entirely in one key. But the part of Jack Brennan in *Sadie McKee* offered a fine opportunity for a nicely varied characterization. Brennan was a charming, wealthy man about town, who loved to entertain and did it very well. He also loved Sadie McKee...and he loved to drink. Because Brennan was a brainy man and a person of some refinement, he lost no week ends, but he did get frequently and thoroughly irrigated.

This last factor, combined with the charm and sentiment in his make-up made the role a very interesting one to play. It was a sympathetic role, too. The audience, I think, was always pulling for Brennan; they wanted to see him win back Sadie McKee, especially after he gave up drinking to try to make her happy. When he lost her, the audience's sympathy for him was increased.

—Arnold, in *The Saturday Evening Post*, 1 May 1948

A lot of people think that James Buchanan Brady [in *Diamond Jim* (1935, Edward Sutherland)] was a super-salesman. But I don't think he ever really sold a bill of goods. What he sold was himself. He capitalized on his personality — which was much easier than selling goods. Diamond Jim was an exploiter of himself, and the imposing "front" he put up was his ivory tower.

Q. How do you feel about playing him?

A. If I can do Diamond Jim as well as I did that millionaire "drunk" in *Sadie McKee* I'll be happy. That part is the best I've ever done. And Joan Crawford is one of the best troupers I've ever worked with. That girl just hands it all to you on a platter, and you can't go wrong.

I was scared stiff when George Arliss sent for me to play Louis XIII in *Cardinal Richelieu* [1935, Rowland V. Lee]. To make matters worse, an actor who had been in one of his pictures warned me, "Don't forget to go to the barber's every day and have the back of your neck shaved, because that's all they'll ever see of you." I went to Arliss shaking. He looked at me and remarked: "I must apologize. I don't remember ever having seen you on the screen." I told him, "I don't go to see all your pictures." With a dry smile, he replied, "I don't blame you." We got along beautifully. Arliss is a charming man, and very generous. He taught me what *not* to do.

—Arnold, interviewed by Charles Darnton for *Photoplay Magazine*, July 1935

Jean ARTHUR [1905-1991]

Born: Gladys Greene in New York City. Work as a model preceded her film debut in a bit role in John Ford's Cameo Kirby in 1923. After several films, she then worked on Broadway and toured in stock before becoming a major film star in the mid-30s. In 1936, she played Babe Bennett opposite Gary Cooper as Mr. Deeds in Frank Capra's Mr. Deeds Goes to Town. The following year, Cooper and Arthur co-starred again in Cecil B. DeMille's The Plainsman:

Cooper was the most exciting. He was always prompt on the set. Very quiet and never wasted time. He was a big, strong person, who always gave you good support. He had tremendous strength for holding a scene together.

—Arthur, interviewed by Kay Gardella for *The Sunday News*, 28 Aug 1966

[Calamity Jane in *The Plainsman*] is completely free and unhampered. She doesn't know what conventions are and she wouldn't care if she did. I had to learn to use a bullwhip, because Calamity was a two-fisted bullwhacking beauty. Practicing on DeMille, I cut him across the wrist with it. He's been so splendid. He wouldn't let me strike an extra he had hired to be struck until I had first practiced on *him*.

And another thing I like about Calamity, she doesn't dress like anybody else you've ever seen on the screen; she doesn't talk or think like the average heroine. She's in love with Wild Bill Hickok — our Mr. Cooper — and she has healthy, generous human instincts. And that's all she knows.

—Arthur, interviewed by Ted Towne for *Movie Classic*, Jan 1937

You've no idea how realistically [*History is Made at Night* (1937)] was staged. Frank Borzage, who directed the picture is a nut for mood and detail. He managed to create such tension and confusion on the set that most of us actually believed that we were drowning. There were only three lines in the original script to describe the terror of the passengers, but out of those three lines Borzage built a sea disaster which worked us all into such a pitch that we didn't have to be directed to shriek and cry. We really were scared stiff.

—Arthur, interviewed by Irene Thirer for *The New York Post*, 11 Mar 1937

Dame Peggy ASHCROFT [1907-1991]

Born: Edith Margaret Ashcroft in Croydon, England. Studies with Elsie Fogerty at The Central School of Dramatic Art and work on stage (from 1926) preceded her film debut in The Wandering Jew (1933, Maurice Elvey). In 1984, she played Mrs. Moore in David Lean's adaptation of E.M. Forster's A Passage to India:

Mrs. Moore tells Aziz [Victor Banerjee] in the mosque that "God is here" and [He] will see if she has taken off her shoes as she should in the mosque. That impresses Aziz. I think the fact that he can respond and feel at home with an English woman is simply extraordinary to him.... They somehow meet because they are both perhaps a little naive and spontaneous, and they both want to like each other.

Both [Mrs. Moore and Barbie Batchelor in *Jewel in the Crown* (1984, for TV) are] Christian women. And they both have a deep questioning of their faith brought about by their being in India.

—Ashcroft, interviewed by Andrew Robinson for *Sight & Sound*, Summer 1984

Fred ASTAIRE [1899-1987]

Born: Frederick Austerlitz in Omaha, Nebraska. Following dance lessons at Claude Alvienne's School in N.Y., he and his sister, Adele, became a popular vaudeville and musical comedy team. When Adele retired to marry in 1932, Fred continued as a solo act. Considered by one studio executive to be unsuitable for film work, Fred found support in David O. Selznick who gave him his first role (as himself) in Dancing Lady (1933, Robert Z. Leonard). Later that year Astaire was teamed with Ginger Rogers at RKO for Flying Down to Rio (Thornton Freeland), the first of ten films together; their sixth was Swing Time (1936, George Stevens):

Swing Time opened at the Music Hall in New York to smash business and a nifty press. Some critics referred to it as the best of all our films. We were listed as the number-one box-office attraction in several national polls. But as the weeks went on, there was a premature falling-off of attendance. The signs that the cycle was running its course were beginning to show.

The slightest decline in a situation like this shows up tremendously, of course, so what we'll call a "concernment" started. After completing *Shall We Dance?* [1937, Mark Sandrich] with Ginger, I asked for and all hands at the studio agreed to, a picture away from her, to keep us from getting in a rut.

Ginger was for it too, and she was immediately assigned to *Stage Door* [1937, Gregory La Cava], with Katharine Hepburn. [Unlike Fred, Ginger was making non-team pictures during the early years of their partnership.]

[Producer] Pan Berman had been planning my picture ahead and he told me that *Damsel in Distress* [1937, George Stevens] was already under way with a [George and Ira] Gershwin score. I prepared myself for another siege of attacks because my usual partner would not be with me this time. Ginger and I had not announced any permanent dissolution; in fact, we had our next meeting all planned to follow this slight intermission. We were to do *Carefree* [1938, Mark Sandrich], with a [Irving] Berlin score....

At first there was a discussion about Ruby Keeler's playing *Damsel*, but the part called for a more British type. It was finally settled that Joan Fontaine, the lovely young actress recently signed at RKO, would play the part. Joan and I did only one dance together, and though she was not a dancer, she handled it beautifully. George Burns and Gracie Allen also were in the cast, and that, of course, opened up many new avenues of *divertissement*. George brought along an idea for a dance in which we three would use whisk brooms for props....

Damsel wasn't a big success, but accomplished what we tried to do. The great divide had taken place....

Pan Berman had already scheduled *The Story of Vernon and Irene Castle* [1939, H.C. Potter] to follow *Carefree*. That was to be the last of the series. Announcements of the farewell film for

Astaire and Rogers were released about September of 1938....

The Castles was not an easy one to get on the screen, because of the personal obligations when doing a story about someone still living. But we had Irene Castle on hand in an advisory capacity. She naturally was very particular about every detail.

The present generation cannot possibly realize the rage created by Vernon and Irene Castle. They were easily the most potent factor in the development of ballroom dancing, and were received with such acclaim both professionally and socially that it is almost impossible to describe it.

They were a tremendous influence on Adele and me — not that we copied them, but we did appropriate some of their ballroom steps and style for our vaudeville act. Having been imbued with the idolatrous feeling for so long, I was doubly intent upon pleasing Irene as far as my portrayal of Vernon was concerned. She had told me sometime before that when and if their story was done, I was her choice for the role of Vernon. [Astaire and Rogers' other films together were: *The Gay Divorcée* (1934, Mark Sandrich), *Roberta* (1935, William D. Seiter), *Top Hat* (1935, Mark Sandrich), *Follow the Fleet* (1936, Mark Sandrich); they were reunited ten years later for *The Barkleys of Broadway* (1949, Charles Walters) after Judy Garland withdrew from the project as production began.]

—Astaire, in *McCalls*, Apr 1959

By the time [songwriters Irving Berlin, George and Ira Gershwin, and Cole Porter] came to me with a song, it was generally finished or at least had taken shape, although they'd tell me what they were doing while they were writing. They knew they were writing for me; they knew what I wanted and what I could do. They never pressed me to do any of the numbers I didn't think were right for me — not that there were many of these.

They liked the way I sang songs. I got their lyrics over, I stuck to the tune, and I phrased the way they liked. They all mentioned that, and it's something I've always been flattered by because I'm not a vocalist, by any means. But to have these men say they'd rather have me sing a song than some of these vocalists was very encouraging.

Holiday Inn [1942, Mark Sandrich] was conceived for Bing Crosby and me. I went over to Paramount to co-star in it. I wasn't at that studio. Irving [Berlin] had discussed the score with me. He was always asking, "How do you like *this*, kid? How do you like *that*?" And I'd have an idea or I wouldn't or I'd say, "There's a scene coming up here. How can we do *this*? Maybe we can do something like *that*?" But usually it would confuse Irving if you suggested too much, because things came to *him*; and if you told him, he'd start worrying and try to get something along the lines *you* wanted....

Easter Parade [1948, Charles Walters] was the last of [Berlin's] films that I made. It was originally intended for Gene Kelly; then he broke his ankle and I took his place. There had to be a certain amount of rewriting, but I inherited some things that suited me very well. Judy [Garland] and I had that tramp number, "A Couple of Swells." It was a good "business" number....

—Astaire, interviewed by Joseph Lederer for *After Dark*, Oct 1973

Dancing for the movies is an ordeal. You live in a sweatbox. By the time rehearsals are over and I'm ready to shoot the picture, I'm skin and bones, too gaunt to photograph. I used to average eight months of work on a musical, rehearsing dance numbers the first three. Filming might begin with a couple of dance numbers, followed by scenes with dialogue. At the end, when the movie was finished and the actors had checked out, I'd go to work on whatever solo numbers were left over....

Q. Can you plan a dance on paper?

A. No, that's not the way mine began. I used to suffer from insomnia, and I'd get ideas at four in the morning.... Dancing on the ceiling [in *Royal Wedding* (1951, Stanley Donen)] — I got that idea almost four years before I was able to put it on the screen.... I had no idea it would turn out to be so complicated.

Q. How did you work it? Did you spin the camera?

A. Nothing that simple. I was the only element that stayed vertical. The whole room — floor, walls, and ceiling — revolved, as did the camera and the cameraman, all lashed tight in one piece. All sorts of unexpected things happened. I wanted to get it, without cuts, in one take. First of all, some of the furniture came loose; I almost got hit by a table that came crashing down. We had that fixed and then we discovered that when the room was upside down I got disoriented. I couldn't tell where anything was. And a tailcoat was out — there was a gravity problem with the tails. I did it in a tightly fitting short jacket.

—Astaire, interviewed by Jon Whitcomb for *Cosmopolitan*, Sept 1961

[*Daddy Long Legs* (1955) is] my first go at CinemaScope, or is it the other way around. Even with all the added width, basically you do more or less the same things as before — except for one thing. You don't dance toward center so much, the way Leslie Caron and I did at rehearsals.... Jean Negulesco, our director, said, "You've gotta keep those sides filled."

—Astaire, interviewed by Howard Thompson for *The New York Times*, 15 May 1955

I enjoyed doing *Silk Stockings* [1957, Rouben Mamoulian] with Cyd Charisse. It had all those good songs that Cole [Porter] had already composed for the Broadway version. He wrote an added number called "The Ritz Roll and Rock." We were trying to kid rock 'n' roll. The dance was all right because there were a lot of other people involved in it, but I hated the way I sang the song. Nobody else seemed to mind; but when I heard it, I absolutely wanted to walk out of the theater. It wasn't a great song to begin with, but it didn't have to be *that* bad. The way I sang it is the way I don't like to see *anybody* sing a song — especially me. I overdid, overplayed it. I could have simplified it more. But you get keyed up on a certain day and maybe do something that doesn't please you.

—Astaire, interviewed by Joseph Lederer for *After Dark*, Oct 1973

Mary ASTOR [1906-1987]

Born: Lucille Langhanke in Quincy, Illinois. She made her film debut in Sentimental Tommy, (1921, John S. Robertson). Three years later she played opposite John Barrymore in Beau Brummel (1924, Harry Beaumont):

I was a little uncertain and worried about the scenes I was to play with him. Perhaps I was a little awed by the magnificence of the Barrymore tradition. Now I know why people like to play with him. He brings them out by relieving them of all self-consciousness. He sweeps them into the romantic mood of the scene by his manner, bearing and gesture. You forget yourself and become the girl in the story, because he makes a certain appeal to the imagination. And he always plays with the greatest sincerity. Mr. Barrymore has the faculty of putting everyone at ease. He engenders instant confidence.

—Astor, in *Photoplay Magazine*, June 1924

In [*Holiday* (1930, Edward H. Griffith)] it was impossible to "overlap," which is natural in conversation. In fact one couldn't pick up a cue very quickly; there had to be time for the sound man to switch off one mike and switch on another, and that required a beat more than is natural. And the sound man was king. If he couldn't hear it, we couldn't shoot it.... You couldn't talk and pace up and down. For example, if the action started with you standing beside a table and then included a move to a chair by the fireplace, you could speak into a mike at the table, but you couldn't talk on the way over; you'd have to wait until you sat down — where there was another mike in the fireplace!

—Astor, in her *A Life on Film* (New York: Delacorte Press, 1971)

I played the other woman [in *Red Dust* (1932, Victor Fleming)]. The vamp era was past, so I didn't have to be a slinky siren. I just wore clothes that were a little smarter, and made up my mouth more heavily.

—Astor, interviewed for *Modern Screen*, Jan 1941

Stage 18 — or was it 16? — where the interiors [of *Red Dust*] were filmed; hot, no air conditioning then, just big fans; damp from the constant use of rain machines. Vic being tough about our complaints, "So what! Everybody sweats in the tropics. Let it show, that's the way it is...."

Personally I thought [Paul] Muni was a very attractive man, and as an actor he was very scholarly and as dedicated and hardworking as the character he was playing [in *The World Changes* (1933, Mervyn LeRoy)].... I *didn't* approve of his method of working: his total attention was to externals, makeup, hair, clothing, manner of walking, gesturing. Every word of the script memorized and actually recorded and rerecorded before he ever went on the set. And the theory that if your eyes twinkled you convey humor, if you shook your fist and shouted and allowed spittle to form on your lips, presto! you were an angry man. Okay. So I didn't agree with him....

—Astor, in her *A Life on Film* (New York: Delacorte Press, 1971)

The Maltese Falcon [1941] was John Huston's first job of directing — he had done the adaptation — and my friend "Bogey," Humphrey Bogart, was to star. The picture was a completely new conception of the "gangster movie"; it was the story not of hoodlums, but of a group of evil though intelligent people playing for very high stakes. I played the part of a crook, an unscrupulous girl who changed her name as she would change her hat, and who at the end admitted she "had always been a liar." John proved to be a wonderful director, with his dynamic personality and his keen insight into people. You either loved him or hated him, but you worked hard for him; his enthusiasm affected everyone on the set like wine. He had the picture well organized, so that things got done in a miraculously short time. And we had fun — zany, lighthearted fun. We were an unusually "close" company; players usually like to get away from each other at lunch time, but we would all go together across to the Lakeside Golf Club, where a big table was set on the patio for us. The normally frowned-on preluncheon drink was a must. We often took an hour and a half, and still we stayed ahead of schedule. I remember one scene near the end of the picture, very complicated technically; it ran about six minutes — and six minutes of script is an average good day's work. We rehearsed the scene before going home one evening, and all the camera moves were carefully plotted. The next morning we shot it in one take and went swimming at Lakeside the rest of the day. [Astor worked with Huston again on *Across the Pacific* (1942).]

—Astor, in her *My Story: An Autobiography* (Garden City, N.Y.: Doubleday & Co., 1959)

I have heard people say [Humphrey Bogart] wasn't *really* a good actor. I don't go along with that. It is true his personality dominated the character he was playing — but the character gained by it. His technical skill was quite brilliant. His precision timing was no accident. He kept other actors on their toes because he *listened* to them, he watched, he *looked* at them. [She worked with Bogart a second time on *Across the Pacific*.]

—Astor, in her *A Life on Film* (New York: Delacorte Press, 1971)

The role of Sandra [in *The Great Lie* (1941)] wasn't sympathetic, but it was fascinating to me. She was a ruthless, cold-blooded woman, selfish and at times cruel....

As originally written, my part was not nearly so important as Bette [Davis]'s. But Bette decided the most interesting feature of the story was the conflict between the two women, and thought it should be built up.

"I don't care if people are not impressed with my performance," she said, "just as long as they are impressed by the conflict between us. I want your role to be at least as important as mine." Later, Bette rearranged scenes and dialogue to equalize the parts and, when *The Great Lie* premiered, she sent me the heart-warming wire, "Baby, we did it."

—Astor, in *The Saturday Evening Post*, 15 Nov 1947

I worked out the way this poor alley cat [Pat, in *Act of Violence* (1949)] should look, and insisted firmly (with director Fred Zinnemann's help) that the one dress in the picture would *not* be made at the MGM wardrobe, but be found on a rack at the cheapest department store. We made the hem uneven, put a few cigarette burns and some stains on the front. I wore bracelets that rattled and jangled and stiletto-heeled slippers. I had the heels sanded off at the edges to make walking uncomfortable. I wore a fall, a long unbecoming hairpiece that came to my shoulder. And I put on very dark nail polish and chipped it. I used no foundation makeup, just too much lipstick and too much mascara — both "bled," that is, smeared, just a little. Zinney said, "You look just right!" And the camera helped with "bad" lighting.

—Astor, in her *A Life on Film* (New York: Delacorte Press, 1971)

Lew AYRES [1908-]

Born: Minneapolis, Minnesota. Work as a musician preceded his film debut as an extra in Fairways and Foul. In 1930, he played Paul Baumer in Lewis Milestone's adaptation of Erich Maria Remarque's All Quiet on the Western Front:

It puzzled me when I was chosen to play "Paul" in the greatest story of the war, *All Quiet on the Western Front.* Until I began rehearsing my part on the Universal lot, I had never held a rifle in my hands. I was a youngster of four when the United States entered the war. As a boy, I can't remember ever having played "war" or "soldiers". I have read few war stories. Military glory has never intrigued me in the slightest. On first thought, it seemed that the leading role...should have been given to someone whom war fascinated.

As our picture is nearing completion, however, it has all come to me clearly. Erich Maria Remarque didn't write of soldiers as soldiers. He wrote of them as human beings. Paul wasn't essentially a soldier. He was simply a schoolboy, who had started to write a play and who lived with his books. War broke out. He was pressed into service.

Paul never wanted to be a soldier. He didn't want to go to war.

You will remember his words in Remarque's novel: "We are eighteen and had begun to love life and the world; and we had to shoot it to pieces. The first bomb, the first explosion, burst in our hearts."

Standing in the trenches during the terrific bombardment scenes of the picture, I realized what Remarque meant.

Understand that I do not wish to underrate patriotism. There is no finer quality. Remarque's patriotism is unquestionable. His characters fought loyally for their fatherland. But Remarque saw beneath the surface of nationalism.

He saw human beings instead of uniforms.

I felt Remarque's human sympathy most keenly in the scene in which I, as Paul, kill a French soldier, and realize for the first time that it is a man, a fellow human being. I have slain, not merely an enemy. I thrust a knife into him while we are alone in a shell-hole and then, as he is dying, try to save his life and pledge myself madly to provide and care for his dependents if I survive the war.

—Ayres, in *The Universal Weekly*, Vol 31 #3.

[In *All Quiet on the Western Front*] I feel I've been responsible for showing millions of men, women and children throughout the world the utter futility of war. I'll never cease being grateful for a role that enabled me to preach what I sincerely believe — that all of us, regardless of race or nationality, are destroyed spiritually by the horror of modern warfare.

—Ayres, interviewed for *The Brooklyn Daily Eagle*, 22 Oct 1939

B

Lauren BACALL [1924-]

Born: Betty Joan Perske in New York City. Dance studies and work as a model led to a Broadway debut in 1942. In March of 1943, she was the cover model of Harper's Bazaar and from that exposure came an invitation to Hollywood from Howard Hawks, who cast her opposite Humphrey Bogart in To Have and Have Not (1944); married in 1945, Bogart and Bacall made a second film for Hawks — The Big Sleep (1946). Their other films together were Dark Passage (1947, Delmer Daves) and Key Largo (1948, John Huston):

"You've been walking to the door like a model," [Bogart] said [on the set of *To Have and Have Not*]. "You must always realize in a scene that you have just come from someplace else. Ask yourself: What was I doing before? Was I filing my nails? Combing my hair? You should have an attitude when you walk to the door."

I never forgot his advice. Ever since then, whenever I've had to play a scene, I've always thought, "What was I doing before this?" It couldn't be simpler, but most people never think of it.

—Bacall, interviewed by Joe Hyams for *Bogart & Bacall* (New York: Warner Books, 1976)

Howard [Hawks] had a brilliantly creative work method. Each morning when we got to the set, he, Bogie, and I and whoever else might be in the scene, and the script girl would sit in a circle in canvas chairs with our names on them and read the scene. Almost unfailingly Howard would bring in additional dialogue for the scenes of sex and innuendo between Bogie and me. After we'd gone over the words several times and changed whatever Bogie or Howard thought should be changed, Howard would ask an electrician for a work light — one light on the set — and we'd go through the scene on the set to see how it felt. Howard said, "Move around — see where it feels most comfortable." Only after all that had been worked out did he call Sid Hickox and talk about camera set-ups. It is the perfect way for movie actors to work, but of course it takes time....

—Bacall, in her *By Myself* (New York: Alfred A. Knopf, 1978)

Jim BACKUS [1913-1989]

Born: Cleveland, Ohio. Studies at The American Academy of Dramatic Arts, work in stock, vaudeville and on radio (as both announcer and actor) preceded his film debut in Easy Living (1949, Jacques Tourneur). The voice of Mr. Magoo in the UPA cartoons of the 1950s, he played James Dean's father in Rebel Without a Cause (1955, Nicholas Ray):

Before we started the actual shooting of *Rebel Without a Cause* Nick Ray got Jimmy and me together and we spent a lot of time discussing the relationship between the father and son and analyzed the motivation of each scene, rather than simply going over the dialogue. We studied the entire script in continuity instead of the usual movie practice of learning isolated scenes as they come up in the shooting schedule. The picture was shot that way too...from the beginning to the end in sequence wherever it was economically possible.

James Dean worked very closely with Nick. May I say that this is the first time in the history of motion pictures that a twenty-four-year-old boy, with only one movie to his credit, was practically the co-director. Jimmy insisted on utter realism, and, looking back, I sometimes wonder how we finished so violent a picture without someone getting seriously injured.

A great many people, including members of our craft, seem to feel that Jimmy had some sort of secret weapon or magic formula. I do not go along with this. I know that if anyone was ever dedicated to the art of acting, it was Jimmy. He had the greatest power of concentration I have ever encountered. He prepared himself so well in advance for any scene he was playing, that the lines were not simply something he had memorized — they were actually a very real part of him. Before the take of any scene, he would go off by himself for five or ten minutes and think about what he had to do, to the exclusion of everything else. He returned when he felt he was enough in character to shoot the scene.

On the stage, an actor has a chance to build and sustain a character, and through his evening performance, to finally reach a climax. Unfortunately, this cannot be done in motion pictures, and many times you have to plunge "cold" into a highly emotional scene. When this was the case, Jimmy would key himself up by vigorously jumping up and down, shadow boxing, or climbing up and down a fifty-foot ladder that ran to the top of the sound stage. In one scene in *Rebel* he was brought into Juvenile Hall on a charge of drunk and disorderly conduct. The scene called for him to have an intensely dramatic argument with the officer in charge, and end up by hysterically banging on the desk in frustration and rage. Before the actual filming of the scene, he kept the cast and crew waiting for one whole hour....

Jimmy spent the hour preparing for his scene, sitting in his darkened dressing room with a record player blasting out the Ride of the Valkyrie, and drinking a quart of cheap red wine. When he felt ready, he stormed out, strode onto the set, did the scene, which was practically a seven-minute monologue, in one take, so brilliantly that even the hard-boiled crew cheered and applauded. He played that scene so intensely that he broke two small bones in his hand when he beat on the desk, which he practically demolished.

—Backus, in his *Rocks on the Roof* (New York: G.P. Putnam's Sons, 1958)

I patterned Magoo after my father — partly, that is. He is hard of hearing, but he hears much more than he lets on and he's nearsighted, but he sees plenty.

—Backus, interviewed by Louella O. Parsons for *Pictorial TView*, 6 Dec 1959

Olga BACLANOVA [1899-1974]

Born: Moscow. After performing on Broadway with The Moscow Art Theater, she was brought to Hollywood where she made her film debut as an extra in The Dove (1928, Roland West). Later that year she appeared in Josef von Sternberg's The Docks of New York:

I tried to learn my parts like a human being. And I tried to play them that way. [von Sternberg] wanted me to play a scene a certain way — I felt this was not right. "Why do you tell me to do that?" I asked him.

"Do what I told you," he said. "Just because you were at the Moscow Art Theatre, don't think that you understand everything. Follow me."

So I started to do what he wanted.

"It's terrible! It's awful!" he shouted. We argued, and he yelled at me, and I was so scared I cried like a baby. And that, of course, was what he wanted. The scene in the picture was very good.

When *The Docks of New York* came out, he said, "You see what I did for you?"

—Baclanova, interviewed by Kevin Brownlow for *The Parade's Gone By* (New York: Alfred A. Knopf, 1969)

Kevin BACON [1958-]

Born: Philadelphia. Studies at Circle in the Square and work with The Equity Library Theater, both in N.Y., preceded his film debut in National Lampoon's Animal House (1978, John Landis). In 1982, he played Fenwick in Barry Levinson's Diner:

Q. Was the camaraderie between the actors on screen in *Diner* real?

A. Yes, it was. There's a kind of connection that was made there that will always exist. While we were shooting, there was a tremendous sense of camaraderie. I think that the fact that nobody was a real movie star helped a lot. We were guys who were just happy to be working on a movie. We all came from different places, different backgrounds. We were thrown into this town [Baltimore] none of us knew anything about. We were on location, which was exciting and fun. So you hang out when you have time to kill.

—Bacon, interviewed by Roberta Smoodin for *Playgirl*, May 1987

Levinson hadn't developed any kind of approach to actors, didn't know how to talk to them. He said, "Just do a little more...a little...uh, do a *thing*." To me he would say: "Do less, do less, do less." It's a cliché about movies, but you still have to be told. He would listen to us banter, or start the movie rolling before a scene and keep it rolling after — some of the best stuff in the movie came that way.

—Bacon, interviewed by Don Shewey for *Caught in the Act: New York Actors Face to Face* (New York: New American Library, 1986)

Carroll BAKER [1931-]

Born: Johnstown, Pennsylvania. Work as a chorus girl preceded her film debut in Easy to Love (1953, Charles Walters). After enrolling in The Actors Studio in N.Y. and appearing on Broadway, she returned to Hollywood to play Luz Benedict II in Giant (1956, George Stevens):

It is traditional for film companies to issue each afternoon a call sheet which lists the scenes to be filmed the following day, and the equipment and actors required for those proposed scenes. It is also expedient, because the cost of moving a crane to location, for example, runs to thousands of dollars. George Stevens, however, refused to be bound by this tradition and insisted upon everything from props to horses to cranes being ready and waiting at all times, with each and every actor standing by in full makeup and costume — including the stars. Even though Elizabeth [Taylor] and Rock [Hudson] had by far the largest roles, not even their parts demanded that they be on the set continuously; but they too were made to follow this strenuous and inconsiderate schedule....

Elizabeth and Rock took this seemingly senseless routine in stride, but after three days of doing nothing, Jimmy [Dean] blew his stack and refused to report for the fourth. Stevens claimed that Jimmy's behavior cost the company a day of lost production. As no one knew what George intended to film, this claim could have been either genuine or simply meant to teach Jimmy a lesson. Nonetheless, as contracted actors, it was our duty to report to work as instructed....

George was a very intelligent man, and he must have realized that Jimmy's behavior was prompted by insecurity and jealousy. But he refused to cater to Jimmy and demanded of him that he act like a grown-up and a professional. There are many directors, even superb ones, who would have been phony with Jimmy in order to get a performance — appeasing him on the set and then complaining bitterly about him behind his back. But George was a straightforward, no-nonsense, ex-Army officer. He told Jimmy what he thought of his conduct to his face and never changed that story when relating it to others. But George was also generous in his appreciation of well-acted scenes, never withholding his praise. Any reprimand was directed only at the misdeed itself and never carried over into the artistic area....

Whether it was in Marfa or in Hollywood, it was a great experience to work with Jimmy Dean. He was at once fully committed to the scene, entirely responsive to the other actor or actors, and yet a fierce competitor for first place. He was so driven to be better than anyone else that when it looked like a tie, he wasn't above fighting dirty to regain an edge....

It was just three short weeks after having finished *Giant* that I was in Benoit, Mississippi, to begin preliminary work on...[*Baby Doll* (1956)]. Gadge [Elia Kazan] had presented us with all the tools of the craft to work with: He took us to the location nearly a month in advance of the filming so that we could get the feel of the South, learn about the local people, and, he hoped, perfect a Mississippi drawl.

I left New York with the idea that Baby Doll Meighan was a totally bizarre invention of Tennessee [Williams]. What I learned was that girls like her were far from fictitious. Every element and quality that I needed to justify her was there to be discovered in the women of Benoit. Even the name "Baby Doll" was commonly used! One man told me, "Yeah, we sure do use that name. Why, my sister's name is Baby Doll, and we used to have a pet cow called Baby Doll."

Although I was playing a girl of nineteen, I found the perfect model for her in Ellie May, an eighty-year-old Southern belle. Ellie May spoke in a combination of Mississippi dialect and baby talk. The moment I heard her, I knew that those speech patterns were deliciously right for the part. From then on I spent hours with Ellie May....

Before the rehearsals began, Gadge took each actor aside for a long, private conversation. He wanted to know us as individuals. He wanted to know every attitude, hang up, and quirk, what made us tick. He delved deeply into the analogy between the character's traits and our own. "What of yourself can you use?" was one of his main questions. "If you believe that aspect of the character is different from you, what can you bring from your own life which will be similar....?"

One day Gadge took us all through the house and asked each of us, "Which do you think would be your room? What would you have in your room? Milly [Dunnock], what would you have in the kitchen? Karl [Malden], where would you keep your tools and which tools would you have? Carroll, what would you have by your crib and in the bathroom? Eli [Wallach], what would Vicarro wear?" Little wonder that there wasn't one costume, one piece of furniture, or one prop that wasn't familiar and just right — every detail had been so well worked out....

In rehearsal Gadge turned me and Eli loose on the grounds of the house and told us, "Use everything, try everything, go wild, don't be afraid to do anything no matter how silly it might seem. Anything that comes into your heads, be courageous — try it. Let me see it. It will be weeks before we set anything, so now is the time to experiment....

I had a scene in which I was waiting in the open car for Archie Lee [Karl Malden]. The script indicated that all of the local men standing outside the store made fun of Archie Lee as he exited the store and walked to the car. Because the whole town knew that the marriage had not been consummated and that Baby Doll was still a virgin, the local men were always jeering. Gadge also wanted something visual to hinge the laughter on. He asked Karl and me, "Can either of you think of something that you might be doing? Something that might motivate the jeering?" I said, "My daddy was a traveling salesman, and whenever I used to wait for him in the car, he would always bring me an ice cream cone." Gadge threw his cap down in the dusty street, and stamped and hollered for joy. "That's perfect, perfect," he howled. "It will make Archie Lee feel silly and doubly humiliated having to cross in front of the guys with a dripping ice cream cone. It is a perfect childish prop for you. I'll shoot Archie Lee's reactions and those of the crowd as you lick the cone, and we'll have our sexual connotations there, too...."

No scene was rigidly plotted, so during a take the camera operator was trained to follow the actors whatever they might do, to be alert for any unexpected movement or gesture, and to guide the camera accordingly. If we began to edge out of frame and there was a split-second decision to be made, the operator knew that Gadge relied on him not to halt, but to make that decision. At one moment in the "swing scene," my head drifted sideways and hung over the swing nearly to the ground. It was lovely the way the operator caught that spontaneous dip.

—Baker, in her *Baby Doll* (New York: Arbor House, 1983)

Kathy BAKER [1951-]

Born: Midland, Texas. Acting studies at the California Institute of the Arts, a degree in French at USC Berkeley, studies at Cordon Bleu in Paris, and work on the stage (notably with The Magic Theater in San Francisco and off-Broadway) preceded her film debut in The Right Stuff (1983, Philip Kaufman). She played Punchy opposite Morgan Freeman in Street Smart (1987, Jerry Schatzberg):

[In the scissors attack scene] I trusted Morgan so much, I could give myself over to it completely. Kathy Baker wasn't afraid, so I was free to let the character be totally scared out of her mind. Another thing about Morgan: Originally, we were shooting that scene on his face, but after a couple of takes he said, "No, no, this isn't my scene, this is Kathy's scene," and he reached out and put his hand over my face — "*This* is where it's happening" — and that's the way it is in the film. How many actors would do that?

—Baker, interviewed by Ross Wetzsteon for *New York*, 14 Mar 1988

My character [Charlie in *Clean and Sober* (1988)] is more addicted to men and to her relationship with Lenny [Luca Bercovici, her abusive boyfriend] than to drugs. She's one of those women in a no-win relationship: she needs someone who doesn't treat her well. She can't get out of that relationship. She fools herself into thinking he needs her....

There was one woman there [at an Alcoholics Anonymous meeting she, director Glenn Gordon Caron and co-star Michael Keaton attended] who told an amazing story. She doesn't know how much she helped me. It was about how much pain she was in and how she didn't think she could make it one more day without a drink. But it was also about a relationship. She was dying to pick up the phone to call a guy she knew was bad for her. She had to try to keep herself from both. Like my character, she's had a double addiction.

—Baker, interviewed by Nina Darnton for *The New York Post*, 26 Aug 1988

[With Charlie] I was trying to be still. These kind of people — an addict, a depressed person, even someone who works all day in a steel mill — they don't show a lot on their faces. So I was trying very hard to be the kind of person who just *is*.

—Baker, interviewed by David Edelstein for *The Village Voice*, 30 Aug 1988

Stanley BAKER [1927-1976]

Born: Ferndale, Wales. After being noticed in a school play, he soon appeared on the London and Birmingham stages. He made his screen debut in Undercover (1943, Sergei Nolbandov). In 1967, he played Charly in Joseph Losey's Accident:

Q. What sort of role did Harold Pinter play on *Accident*?

A. As with most of Losey's pictures we had a period of preproduction when we sat down together — Harold Pinter as well — and thrashed out what everybody was about which is quite normal when you're dealing with someone like Losey. But at that stage, most scriptwriters drop out entirely and I think that's probably a good thing because it must be an anxious time for them, but Pinter was quite different. He was there most days and because he had been involved with the previous discussions with the actors he knew what we were all trying to achieve, and if, as an actor, you needed reaffirming about any particular point you could always get an intelligent and objective reply from him. It was marvelous that he was there but I wouldn't use it as a method for most writers. It could be dangerous: it depends on the attitude of the writer.

Q. How did you achieve the superb pace and throwaway dialogue at the dinner table and round the tennis court? You know, the "All of a heap" and Uriah Heep stuff?

A. A lot of that came out of the actors themselves and the playing of the scene. It wasn't written down specifically in black and white. We were only able to use that sort of Pinterish dialogue because we were working with him before and were involved in the situation.

—Baker, in *Films & Filming*, Aug 1970

Q. Can you tell us something of your relationship with Losey?

A. Well, I don't know what to say about my relationship with Losey except that I think that it was Losey who really made me first properly aware about being an actor — probably how involved an actor should be in what he is doing — up until that stage everything was full of excitement. [Baker also worked on Losey's *Blind Date* (1959), *The Criminal* (1960) and *Eve* (1962).]

—Baker, interviewed by Clive James at The National Film Theatre, 2 Nov 1972

Bob BALABAN [1945-]

Born: Chicago, to the youngest of seven brothers who owned the Balaban & Katz chain of theaters in Chicago. His uncle, Barney Balaban, was a long-time president of Paramount Pictures and his grandfather, Sam Katz, was once head of production at MGM. Studies with Second City in Chicago, at Colgate University and NYU, and work as Linus in the stage version of You're a Good Man, Charlie Brown preceded his film debut in Midnight Cowboy (1969, John Schlesinger). He is the author of CE3K Diary (1977), about the making of Close Encounters of the Third Kind (1977, Steven Spielberg), in which he played scientist David Laughlin:

Steven's wonderful to work with. He is organized, really efficient, and energetic. Steven's also a sort of sympathetic person who watches out for you. He works with actors very well. Steven is definitely very interested in all the technical things, but don't forget that if you're in a scene where 8000 spaceships are supposed to be floating above your head and all that you're doing is walking around looking at them, you wouldn't expect the director to spend a lot of time telling you things. In *Close Encounters*, we had a month where they photographed us from so far away that we were almost invisible. We just had to maintain different positions so that later on the film footage would match with where we had been in the previous camera coverage. They used that film for those shots of us running around on the mountain where you saw us waving in the distance. It was great for me because I got to stand around all that time with [François]

Truffaut! I got to talk with this most fascinating idol of mine for hours.

[William Hurt, Blair Brown and I] all knew of each other before [*Altered States* (1979, Ken Russell)] brought us together...and then we made it a point to start to know each other before we began working. It was especially important because we play friends.... We got together a bunch of times.... Bill had been doing a lot of research for his part so he gave me some books that he'd been reading that he had found very helpful in understanding the film's subject matter.... Bill had tried sensory deprivation....

I suppose I thought Ken might be a director who paid more attention to technical details before I worked with him, but not after. Ken's very concerned with the actors and not just whether the light is falling on the right spot on your nose. Ken's pretty casual in a good way. As a result, the atmosphere on the set was very relaxed, which I like. We rehearsed for three weeks prior to filming, which was good because there's a lot of dialogue in *Altered States*.... When we worked, Ken would talk to you and work *with* you.

—Balaban, interviewed by James H. Burns for *Starlog*, Mar 1981

Sidney Lumet, the director [of *Prince of the City* (1981)], told me to play the prosecutor as someone in total, demoniacal demand. He told me to think of someone who was tremendously alive and repressed, like a guy who plays chess with people for the sheer power over other people.

—Balaban, interviewed by Judy Klemesrud for *The New York Times*, 10 Jan 1982

Lucille BALL [1911-1989]

Born: Jamestown, N.Y. Work as a model preceded her film debut as a Goldwyn Girl in Roman Scandals (1933, Frank Tuttle). In 1940, she played Bubbles in Dorothy Arzner's Dance, Girl, Dance:

Do you know I never was so scared as when I went into [*Dance, Girl, Dance*]. Just thinking of my part as Bubbles, the "Tiger Lily" made me tremble. It was my break of breaks, this picture, and I didn't want to make people dislike me. I didn't see how they could do anything else, because I had to be mean to Maureen O'Hara, who had the sweet girl role in the picture.

I had to steal Louis Hayward from Maureen. I had to slap her face, pummel her on the stage of a burlesque theater...and be generally hateful. But the character was a real one. I had known girls like that. The part had meat on the bones....

—Ball, interviewed by John Castle for *Motion Picture*, Jan 1941

Charles Laughton once said to me, "If you ever play a witch, play the witchiest witch who ever breathed." Gloria [in *The Big Street* (1942, Irving Reis)] was a witch, a girl with a foolish, unhealthy obsession which made her more ruthless than Scarlett O'Hara. It was anything but a sympathetic part. But it was exciting because it was so meaty — so rich in humor, pathos and tragedy. All my previous roles had been much easier, therefore less interesting. The challenging difficulty of portraying Gloria adequately was what made the task so much fun. And the fun was enhanced by being cast with one of my favorite leading men; the convincing sincerity with which Henry Fonda plays a part inspires everyone around him.

—Ball, in *The Saturday Evening Post*, 23 Mar 1946

I was in pictures and I didn't dig it too much because I wasn't typecast. I like to be typed. I made my mind up to that a long time ago, and when television came along I said, "Gee, this is my chance to be typed," which is quite the opposite of what most people want to do. To me I thought that was marvelous because I'd been 15 years in pictures and I'd always be playing someone else even though I was maybe the same type of career girl, maybe the same type of model, or the same type of prostitute or whatever the hell it was. But still there was a similarity to everything, but it wasn't a type — a real recognizable type so if you'd see me you could recognize me from pictures past....

Q. I have a question about the role of Mame [in *Mame* (1974, Gene Saks)]. Did you keep that close to the Lucy character?

A. I got as far away from it as I could.... People have asked me to do Mame throughout the years...and I always turned it down — I never had time to do it.... Then when I finally got the part, I said, "Now look, fellas, let's be very careful in these parts that are supposed to be Lucy-isms. I don't want to mug too much, I don't want to walk on the side of my boots like Auntie Mame did when everything would get her. I didn't want to do any of that." So I didn't. I was very careful. I didn't want to be plain little Lucy.

—Ball, interviewed for *Dialogue on Film*, May/June 1974

Anne BANCROFT [1931-]

Born: Anna Maria Italiano in The Bronx, N.Y. Studies at The American Academy of Dramatic Arts in N.Y. and work on the stage preceded her film debut in Don't Bother to Knock (1952, Roy Baker). Returning to New York in the late '50s, she studied at The Herbert Berghof Studio and made a triumphant return to the stage. She then returned to film in her second Broadway success, as Annie Sullivan in The Miracle Worker (1962, Arthur Penn).

[Working with Marilyn Monroe on *Don't Bother to Knock*] was a remarkable experience! Because it was one of those very rare times, in all my experiences in Hollywood, when I felt that give-and-take that can only happen when you are working with good actors. Marilyn played the part of a babysitter who has done some very destructive things to this child, and everyone in this hotel had become aware of it. It was the scene where they were bringing her down to the lobby to be held for the police. I was just somebody in the lobby; and I was to walk over to her and react, that's all; and there was to be a close-up of her and a close-up of me — you know, to show my reaction. Well, I moved toward her, and I saw that girl — of course, she wasn't the big sex symbol she later became, and she wasn't famous, so there was nothing I had to forget or shake off. There was just this scene of one woman seeing another woman who was helpless and in pain, and she *was* helpless and in pain. It was so real. I responded; I really reacted to her. She moved me so that tears came into my eyes. Believe me, such moments happened rarely, if ever again, in the early things I was doing out there.

—Bancroft, interviewed by James Robert Haspiel for *Films in Review* (NY), Jan 1980

Q. What did you do about learning about Annie Sullivan?

A. I read everything there was to read about her. Every book that was ever written about her, I read.

Q. And did you go where she came from, to her home?

A. We went up to Boston.... I saw her letters, her handwriting, you know, walked through the places she walked through. But, of course, it's not the same. And besides, I didn't find that very helpful anyway. I don't find those things helpful, you know those exterior things. The only thing I really find helpful, I found the books very helpful, and, of course, most of all I find the script the most helpful thing....

Q. Nevertheless, you seem to do a lot of this external research.

A. Well, I do all those things, you see, but I find that they give me the least amount of help. Most I discard. The most amount of help comes from, you know, my author's concept and then my director's image, and, you know, my own, which I get from the things that I read in the script, and these internal things that I do with myself, you know — where am I the same as Annie and where am I different from Annie?

Q. When you read *The Miracle Worker* for the first time, did the character assume proportions immediately, or is this something you think about for a long time?

A. Oh, no. Every once in a while it'll hit you and there it is, you know. It's like, you look at the script of *The Miracle Worker*. Now what is the script, you know, what is the whole thing about? It's about a woman who, if she does not teach this child, both she and the child will perish. Now, of course, I have nothing like that in my own life so I have to take something else in my life which I have to say, now if I don't do a certain thing, I will perish. So, well, it's kind of a parallel to her struggle.

—Bancroft, interviewed by Lewis Funke and John E. Booth for *Show*, Oct 1961

I felt deeply about [Jo Armitage in *The Pumpkin Eater* (1964, Jack Clayton)].... She was a universal character.... Don't get the idea this is a case history, but it's interesting to know that the expert view is that I'm basically a neurotic hysteric who cannot mesh her romantic fantasies with reality and is consequently suffering from reactive depression.

—Bancroft, interviewed by Stephen Watts for *The New York Times*, 6 Oct 1963

[John] Ford was the first really, really wonderful powerful director that I worked with. He was a funny fellow and very ornery. We'd all sit around, reading the script and if he didn't like the page he'd just rip it out. It was outrageous and how anybody was going to put that film together was beyond me. He wasn't really looney but he appeared to be because he took advantage of the power that he had.... I'm the Duke Wayne of that film [*Seven Women* (1966).]

—Bancroft, interviewed by Allan Hunter for *Films & Filming*, May 1987

I never dug deeper in my life [than for the part of Mrs. Robinson in *The Graduate* (1967, Mike Nichols)]. I had conceived her as a less calculating woman. But Mike's theory about it was clear: All grown-ups were bad and all kids were wonderful. I didn't see it, but we rehearsed for two weeks and gradually that side of her character emerged.

—Bancroft, interviewed by Paul Rosenfield for *The Los Angeles Times*, 14 Oct 1984

I identified with Emma [in *The Turning Point* (1978, Herbert Ross)] because I too made a choice in my life to have a career, and no matter what I would have that career — and pay the price.

—Bancroft, interviewed by James Robert Haspiel for *Films in Review* (NY), Jan 1980

Q. Did you do any research into the psychological side of being parent of a gay person [for *Torch Song Trilogy* (1988, Paul Bogart)]?

A. I'm well equipped with a good imagination. However, I never really thought of it as being a different problem than any mother might have with a child that disappoints her in her desires for that child. Mothers have dreams for their children and their children hardly ever reach those dreams. Very rarely do children actually become what their mothers want them to. Also, I think in this movie there is another aspect of the mother releasing the son [Harvey Fierstein as Arnold] and the son wanting to be released from the mother. You know, that good ol' breaking away. Here he is in his thirties, and he hasn't broken away from his mother yet — nor she from him.

—Bancroft, interviewed by James A. Baggett for *Christopher Street* #128, 1988

Tallulah BANKHEAD [1903-1968]

Born: Huntsville, Alabama. Against the wishes of her family (her father was Congressman William B. Bankhead), Tallulah took up a career as an actress after winning a Photoplay Magazine beauty contest (by mail); she appeared in only one film as a result: When Men Betray (1918, Ivan Abramson). In the 1920s, her fame was established in London where she was known for her extravagant behavior (off-stage and on) and the effect she had on her "gallery" fans. After eight years in London, she then made her Broadway debut. In 1931, she returned to American film, but after an initial six picture deal, worked rarely in that medium, preferring the stage:

Tarnished Lady [1931] was the work of Donald Ogden Stewart, a literate and amusing writer. I was fortunate, too, in that it was to be directed by George Cukor. Both Stewart and Cukor were stage veterans. All three of us were having our first fling on the talking screen, pioneers in a garrulous new medium. In the back of my skull stewed the notion that the fifty grand I would pick up in ten weeks would enable me to return to England, scotch the rumours that I had abdicated under pressure, wipe out my debts. A lot I cared if Paramount exercised its options. I was fated, or so I thought, for loftier adventures....

Was [*Tarnished Lady*] any good? In a word, NO! Though it had a fine director, a first-rate writer, and a luminous, er, star, it was a fizzle. Why? For the same reason that though the eggs, the cracker crumbs and the salt used for a soufflé may be topnotch the resultant dish may be rancid. The picture was made by trial and error. What appeared on the screen showed it.

Hitchcock offered me $75,000 to play the leading role in *Lifeboat* [1944], and off I dashed to Hollywood. It had been eleven years since I faced a camera....

Flouting the screen's bylaws, canons and taboos, Hitchcock confined the entire action of the picture to a forty-foot lifeboat adrift at sea. The plight of the passengers was the result of a U-boat torpedo. Although the derelict craft was supposed to wallow for days in the Atlantic, beset by hurricane, death and destruction, the picture was made in a studio with the drifters photographed against a bogus ocean. In the trade these are called process shots. In the picture the players were shivering from cold, but in its making I sweltered for fifteen weeks. I had to wear a mink coat. Blazing lights were focused on my every move. In a bow to authenticity, tons of water were sloshed over us at intervals.

I was black and blue from the downpours and the lurchings. Thanks to the heat, the singeing lights, the fake fog, submersions followed by rapid dryings-out, I came up with pneumonia early in November. Temperature 104 degrees, and rising.

A Dr. Fox dosed me with sulpha drugs. After three days I tottered back to the boat, rubber-legged and dizzy. Three more days amid the ice and brine and the bluster of the Nazi agent [Walter Slezak] who hoped to do us all in, and my temperature shot up to 104 again. Guess what this time? Another case of pneumonia!

—Bankhead, in her *Tallulah* (London: Victor Gollancz Ltd., 1952)

Screen roles...depend on skillful cutting, careful cameramen, retakes and — this above all — fine directing. Alfred Hitchcock directed *Lifeboat*.... Happily, he and I shared the same idea about acting — that it should be as natural as possible.

—Bankhead, in *The Saturday Evening Post*, 18 Dec 1948

Binnie BARNES [1906-]

Born: Gitelle Barnes in London, England. Brought to the British Film industry by Alexander Korda who saw her perform as a ballroom dancer, she made her screen debut in his production of Night in Montmarte (1931, Leslie Hiscott). One of her earliest successes was as Katherine Howard in The Private Life of Henry VIII (1933, Alexander Korda):

We were Korda's young ladies — Merle Oberon, Wendy Barrie, Elsa Lanchester and myself. He didn't have very much money at that time and he decided to make *Henry VIII*, and put us all in it. Charles Laughton was the only one who was an outside man with a big name, and he took a piece of the picture. He was very smart.... All I knew was that I wanted to eat tomorrow, so I was very happy to do anything. Halfway through the picture, Korda ran out of money, so he loaned me out to British International Pictures, to Lupino Lane, who was a director and comedian.... For this he got 200 pounds, Mr. Korda did, for eight weeks and when he raised enough money we went back and continued *Henry VIII*. I only got my contract money, which was 35 pounds a week....

Q. How was Korda as a director?

A. Fantastic. He was the most marvelous man, with a great deal of patience with us young girls, because we were like colts, always kicking up our heels. He had a lot of patience to hold us down. John Loder was in the picture, and Robert Donat played my lover. We were all very young, playing up like mad; we had a marvelous time, but Korda had a way of bringing us all back to earth. I learned a lot in that picture from Charles Laughton, who before every scene would take me back away from everybody and walk up and down. He was sort of a method actor, who had never been to a method school. He would walk up and down with me to calm me and say, "Shut up, be quiet, let's do the scene."

Q. Did he talk about his character a lot?

A. Oh yes. He was very keen on his character, and played that man always, at night, at home.

—Barnes, interviewed by Leonard Maltin for *Film Fan Monthly*, Jan 1974

Ethel BARRYMORE [1879-1959]

Born: Ethel Blythe in Philadelphia. A convent education and a distinguished career on the stage preceded her film debut in The Nightingale (1914, Augustus Thomas). She made only one film between 1919 and 1944, that being Rasputin and the Empress (1932, Richard Boleslavsky), in which she appeared with her brothers John and Lionel; she returned to the screen in None But the Lonely Heart (1944, Clifford Odets):

[*None But the Lonely Heart*] was hard work, but it was interesting and everything was so well organized that it was a pleasure to be involved in it. Last time I was out there [in Hollywood] making pictures, everything was done haphazardly. There was no such thing as a completed script. The night before we were to work, they would hand us something written on the back of an envelope. That would be our part, to learn for the next day.

But that's all changed. Clifford Odets wrote [this] script. It was completed, in perfect shape, before we went to work. Everything had been arranged in the same way. Everything was expertly done. In those circumstances it is easy to work hard.

—Barrymore, interviewed in an unsourced, undated article in the files of The New York Public Library for the Performing Arts

John BARRYMORE [1882-1942]

Born: John Blythe in Philadelphia. Work as a cartoonist for a New York newspaper and as an actor on Broadway (from 1901) preceded his film debut in An American Citizen (1914, J. Searle Dawley). Among his many silent screen successes was the dual role in Dr. Jekyll and Mr. Hyde (1920):

I have made up my mind to one thing. Hereafter I am going to watch the cutting and editing of my pictures. It may be painful to be obliged to look at myself day in and day out, but I am going to do it. The performance of the actor is made, not in the studio, but in the cutting room....

John Robertson, my director, and I worked out [the transformation scene] very carefully. We wanted to create a certain mood, to build up suspense. So we were careful to see that no one could insert an episode showing me as a school boy walking down a lane at Mamaroneck with a slate under my arm. They do put in things like that, you know, to prove that the hero isn't a bad fellow at heart....

You see, on the stage the actor has time to create a mood, to build up a character, to time a scene. In the movies, his performance is turned over to a cutter who can do what he likes with it.

—Barrymore, interviewed by Agnes Smith for *Photoplay Magazine*, Aug 1925

I had a good director on my last picture [*The Tempest* (1928)] — Sam Taylor, who used to direct Harold Lloyd. Because he has a comedy sense he knows a great deal about how people really act, which isn't emotionally.

I like *Tempest*.... Certainly Camilla Horn is delightful — a lusty German girl with a big appetite.... The reason she looked so fragile in *Faust* [1926] was merely because Murnau put her in corners and made her think of sad things like virtue.

—Barrymore, interviewed by Ruth Waterbury for *Photoplay Magazine*, Aug 1928

I didn't have to act to be Jaffe [in *Twentieth Century* (1934, Howard Hawks)]. I needed only to close my eyes and live over again the happiest days of my life. The character was so cleverly written that I could actually feel the peculiarities of such a man — a humbug, a faker, and a ham, but through it all, a man with a heart and soul.

—Barrymore, quoted by John Kobler in his *Damned in Paradise: The Life of John Barrymore* (New York: Atheneum, 1977)

I lived with Oscar Jaffe, under a dozen different names, for thirty years. I was raised, weaned and taught my faults by his peers. And is he real? He's as real as the grease-paint the old sinner would bleed if you cut his throat. I haven't a memory he doesn't live in, under one name or another. In him I see Jed Harris and Morris Gest and William Brady and [David] Belasco and a healthy portion of the house of Barrymore.

Just consider these clothes, this wide-brimmed hat, this turned-up coat collar, this big, black tie. Every item is the brand of one or another of those rare old showmen who were the heroes of my childhood, the mentors of my adolescence, and, I guess, the goats of my blunders. They were my teachers, my friends, my critics and my examples.

—Barrymore, interviewed in an unsourced, undated article in the files of The New York Public Library for the Performing Arts

Lionel BARRYMORE [1878-1954]

Born: Lionel Blythe in Philadelphia. Work in the theater preceded his film career. Between 1912 and 1928, he worked for D.W. Griffith on over 35 films:

Griffith drove his actors to get what he wanted. Hard-bitten players like me he largely let alone, but when he worked with his younger people, especially the Gish girls, he directed them minutely in every gestture they made, from the lifting of an eyelid to the correct way to scream.

—Barrymore, as told to Cameron Shipp in *The Saturday Evening Post*, 26 Aug 1950

Between Ethel and Jack and me, we always knew better as professionals than to blow the duke with competitive mugging. We had besides an experienced respect for each other, and for my part I was certain that reprisals would be lethal.

Exhibit A in the Hollywood indictment of my brother and me as scene-stealers is the sequence in *Rasputin and the Empress* [1932, Richard Boleslavsky] in which we fought. Jack is the Prince and I am the Mad Monk. In shooting the film, we created an unholy row for a week on the Metro lot as we rolled, tugged, hit, bit, gouged, and wrestled in what purported to be a bloody and dreadful encounter. Jack finally did me in with a poker. But before my demise the director took pains to show facial expressions as the Battle of the Barrymores grovelled into its final throes. First Jack's angry face, then mine. Then Jack's. Then mine. He downs me. I pop up, eyes to camera. I down him. He pops up. Profile to camera. It is commonly alleged that the fight took so long because each of us was battling for the limelight.

This wasn't, of course, the case. We could not have arranged these things. We were doing as we were told, and if the editor [Tom Held] put the film together in a certain way, it was not our fault.

Once, however, I did deliberately connive to theft a scene from my redoubtable relative. Money was involved.

When we were making *Night Flight* [1933], our fifth and last film together, Jack played the role of the superintendent of a South American airport. I was an old man who had to be sent for and bawled out by the boss. All the lines and all the action were Jack's.

Clarence Brown, who was directing, considered this a larceny-proof act for Jack and put up a wager.

"I will lay you ten dollars that this is one bit that Lionel cannot possibly steal from you," he said.

"Taken," said Jack. "He will snatch it if he has to hang from the chandelier."

As played, Jack completely dominated the scene. He was brilliant in his rhetoric and his action while I stood dumbly in front of his desk taking the dressing-down without a word to say or a movement to make.

I turned slowly, a bleak and defeated figure, droop-shouldered, and stumbled for the door. The big scene was still Jack's and I was through. I couldn't think of any way to make the act mine with my back to the camera and one second to go before Clarence was due to call "Cut!"

But just then it occurred to me to reach around and rub my bottom.

Jack wagged his head and turned to Clarence.

"Now there, sir, is a brother to be proud of," he said. "Pay me the ten dollars...." [Lionel and John's other films together were: *Arsene Lupin* (1932, Jack Conway), *Grand Hotel* (1932, Edmund Goulding) and *Dinner at Eight* (1933, George Cukor — although they did not share any scenes).]

Next to Miss Garbo [with whom I worked on *The Temptress* (1926, Maurice Stiller), *Mata Hari* (1932, George Fitzmaurice), *Grand Hotel* (1932, Edmund Goulding) and *Camille* (1936, George Cukor)] the most awesome actress I have encountered in Hollywood is Margaret O'Brien....

One day when I was working in *Dr. Gillespie's Criminal Case* [(1943), one of fourteen films in which he played the wheelchair bound Dr. Gillespie], the director [Willis Goldbeck] brought over a mite in pigtails. She was wearing a long hospital nightgown and I was told that she was to play the little sick girl in the story. She was shy and polite and small, only five years old.

I thought — out loud, after she made her curtsy and departed: "How bloody awful. She'll be bringing lollipops to the set and getting them tangled in everybody's hair...."

I soon realized that Margaret could perform like no youngster I or anybody else had ever seen. When she takes over, you might as well imagine yourself a design on the wallpaper. You could stand on your head and no audience would notice you. [Barrymore's Gillespie films included: *Young Dr. Kildare* (1938), *Calling Dr. Kildare* (1939), *The Secret of Dr. Kildare* (1939), *Dr. Kildare's Strange Case* (1940), *Dr. Kildare Goes Home* (1940), *Dr. Kildare's Crisis* (1940), *The People Vs. Dr. Kildare* (1941), *Dr. Kildare's Wedding Day* (1941), *Calling Dr. Gillespie* (1942, all Harold S. Bucquet); *Dr. Kildare's Victory* (1941, W.S. Van Dyke II); *Dr. Gillespie's New Assistant* (1942), *Dr. Gillespie's Criminal Case* (1943), *Three Men in White* (1944), *Between Two Women* (1944) and *Dark Delusion* (1947, all Willis Goldbeck).]

—Barrymore, in his, as told to Cameron Shipp, *We Barrymores* (New York: Appleton-Century-Crofts, Inc., 1951)

Mikhail BARYSHNIKOV [1948-]

Born: Riga, Latvia. Work with the Kirov Ballet in Leningrad, then the American Ballet Theater and The New York City Ballet preceded his film debut as Yuri in The Turning Point (1977, Herbert Ross):

[Yuri] was not a very complicated character, not a developed characterization that would need very extensive acting ability. The real problem is to have naturalness and freedom. The language problems for me were the biggest ones: speaking English clearly gave me difficulty in being free with my body. I worked hard on that....

Dancing for the camera is most difficult from a professional point of view.... Doing the sequences over and over is so unlike the performance situation, and things like the super-intensified lighting make the atmosphere very strenuous. It's challenging because film is forever; it has to be perfect, and you cannot depend on the impulse of a live audience to carry you to certain performance excitement. It means a need for very clean and pluperfect execution.

—Baryshnikov, interviewed by William Wolf for *Cue*, 29 Oct-11 Nov 1977

Alan BATES [1934-]

Born: Allestree, Derbyshire, England. Studies at The Royal Academy of Dramatic Art in London and work on the stage preceded his film debut in The Entertainer (1960, Tony Richardson). Throughout his film career he has maintained an active profile on the London stage, occasionally bringing a stage role to the screen, as in The Caretaker (1963, Clive Donner):

[*The Caretaker*] was essentially a piece of theatre. But I don't want to call it filmed theatre, because I think Clive Donner's direction got far beyond that. Nevertheless, the speeches and the conception of the characters are to a certain extent stylized, although the treatment was very simple and realistic. Since I'd done it in the theatre, there was some necessary adjustment for the film, particularly in my part — because the scenes with Donald Pleasence can be almost music hall, the word play between them. In the theatre you can play it straight out like a revue. In the cinema you just can't do that. So it took on a different emphasis. Those scenes became more sinister than funny, I think. The character is sinister anyway, of course, but I think the closer you are the more sinister he is — because you see much more of his interior mind, whereas in the theatre the emphasis was on his funny lines.

The part of Basil [in *Zorba the Greek* (1964, Michael Cacoyannis)] was a problem — he just didn't know himself. It's the author figure, and you can never get to the bottom of it when that's the case.... You can never explore those [author] characters fully, because the authors haven't been able to do so with themselves. They can write about their brothers and their sisters, and all the other characters, fantastically clearly. But not themselves. As for my role [in *Women in Love* (1970, Ken Russell)], the author figure again, [D.H.] Lawrence had written "himself" more objectively.... He's very complex and deep, of course, and there are many layers to him, but nevertheless it's easier to take a line on the Lawrence-figure of Birkin. I think I gave it a certain humour, a lightness. Perhaps I could have made him at times more bitter or dark — perhaps more unpleasant, just at times. Lawrence does often portray a side of him that is unpleasant. But I took my cue from reading about Lawrence, and learning that he did have a terrific sense of humor and liked playing practical jokes. And that sort of went into my mind, and I think the degree of lightness I gave it is quite valuable to the film. It could have been a heavy and ponderous performance if I'd thought about it in any other way....

The run and the wrestling were really what Lawrence was all about. Physical contact. Contact with the earth, contact with the ground, contact with each other — expressed physically, not only sexually. The point of discussion about that fight [with Oliver Reed] is — yes, it's got sexual undertones, but it's first and foremost a physical contact, as an expression of need or of friendship. A need to expend yourself. The reason they fight is because each of them is in a particular extreme state in his life. They both lived in a very constricted society. And to me that kind of explosion, although it's got an intellectual side to it too, is a natural thing. It's extreme, but it's not unnatural.

—Bates, interviewed by Gordon Gow for *Films & Filming*, June 1971

If I ever had a part that made me probe beneath the surface of a character, it is that of Yakov Bok in *The Fixer* [1968, John Frankenheimer]. Only slowly, through the awful pressure and humiliation he endures does it dawn on him who he is and what circumstances he is in. It is only at the end that he knows and he doesn't care whether he lives or dies, as long as it's truthful. As he says at one point in the drama, "Suffering I can gladly do without. I hate the taste of it. But if I must suffer, let it be for something."

—Bates, interviewed for the press packet for *The Fixer* (MGM, 1968)

I don't see Saul [in *An Unmarried Woman* (1978, Paul Mazursky)] particularly in that way [too good to be true]. He's not necessarily a Prince Charming. He's just someone who has found some kind of equilibrium and strength in life. But at the same time I think there is a streak of selfishness in him. His work comes first and he obviously had a disastrous first marriage. But he's found a way of laughing at it.

—Bates, interviewed by Judy Klemesrud for *The New York Times*, 16 Apr 1978

Kathy BATES [1948-]

Born: Memphis, Tennessee. Studies at Southern Methodist University preceded her film debut in Taking Off (1971, Milos Forman). In 1990, she played Annie Wilkes in Rob Reiner's adaptation of Stephen King's Misery:

Q. *Misery* was written and directed by men, but it's an equal battle between one man and one woman. And she doesn't really lose, does she?

A. I don't think she does, because I think she makes Paul [James Caan] fight to the very last ounce for what he wants and what he believes. On one level, it was like he met the devil. I prefer to think of it in terms of my response to the novel: that he was reborn. In the book, Paul Sheldon begins unconscious. And Stephen King refers to Annie Wilkes as this African goddess. He has two words on the frontispiece, "Africa" and "goddess," and there are all these references to bees and the queen bee. To my mind, he was getting into something very primitive — Mother Earth, Rebirth, Nature.

These are things I think about. Maybe this is going off the deep end, but as we readdress ourselves to Mother Earth in this day and age...and as women begin to take more power in society, and as men and women begin to balance the masculine and the feminine in themselves, I do think we are "Reinventing Eve," to steal the titles of Kim Chernin's books. And I think that's very exciting.

—Bates, interviewed by Michael Lassell for *Interview*, Aug 1991

Annie isn't a monster in a horror movie, she's a human being who is a psychopath. Her humanness comes from her inmost dreams and hopes, however crazy they may be.

—Bates, interviewed by David Sacks for *The New York Times*, 27 Jan 1991

Anne BAXTER [1923-1985]

Born: Michigan City, Indiana; granddaughter of Frank Lloyd Wright. Acting classes with Maria Ouspenskaya and work on Broadway (from age 12) and in summer stock, preceded her film debut in Twenty Mule Team (1940, Richard Thorpe). In 1942, she played Lucy Morgan in Orson Welles' The Magnificent Ambersons:

Orson works his players hard, but he's wonderful to work with. Remember the sleigh scene in the picture — where I was thrown out into the snow with Tim Holt? That scene was made in a downtown ice house at 2 in the morning. Orson realized by dinnertime that we weren't getting anywhere. I'd stiffen up every time I had to fall from the sleigh. So he took us all out to dinner and gave me three glasses of sparkling Moselle. After that it was easy falling out of the sleigh.

—Baxter, interviewed by Sheilah Graham for *The Newark Evening News*, 16 July 1943

So far, Orson Welles is my favorite director. He gives you the feeling when you go into a scene that you are doing something no one has ever done before. He takes the trouble to know every member of his cast so well that he understands exactly how to approach him and get his best work for each scene. You get very tired, physically and emotionally working for Orson, but it is worth it.

—Baxter, in *Photoplay/Movie-Mirror*, Sept 1943

Many movie parts for girls are what I call stooge roles, just a succession of reactions to things a man says and does. Mouche means "little fly" in French, and by her own choice and strength of character Mouche [in *Five Graves to Cairo* (1943)] flew in the face of destruction, fighting even Marshal Rommel himself to gain her personal goal in the war. Here was no stooge part; just the opposite — a girl who was indomitable and decisive, and yet delicately feminine....

There were wonderful people to work with. Meeting Von Stroheim — Rommel...was exhilarating: I found him so charming, humorous, unusual in his technique, and so shrewd about maintaining the legend of his terrible ferocity. Miles Mander and Akim Tamiroff were inspiring associates too. And holding all the satisfying elements together was Billy Wilder, an imaginative, exciting director with a quick sense of new things to do with the camera and with people. Finally there was the fact that while the picture was being made, things weren't going well for the Allies. As the French girl I was portraying struggled with the fearful Rommel, there was the feeling of being deep in the maelstrom of the great war myself — an unforgettably moving experience.

—Baxter, in *The Saturday Evening Post*, 2 Mar 1946

Sophie [in *The Razor's Edge* (1946, Edmund Goulding)] was *not* a sex symbol. She was an alcoholic.... She was a nice, poor girl from Chicago whose heart is broken in Paris.

—Baxter, interviewed by Judy Klemesrud for *The New York Times*, 22 Aug 1971

Warner BAXTER [1891-1951]

Born: Columbus, Ohio. Work on the stage in Louisville, Kentucky, in vaudeville, and in stock in Los Angeles preceded his film debut in Her Own Money (1914, Joseph Henabery). In 1934, he played the title role in Frank Capra's Broadway Bill:

For the first time in my life, I have played myself as I am in private life. The picture is *Broadway Bill.* Never before had I achieved the dream of every actor — complete naturalness. And strangely enough, I spent the first week of the picture fumbling around, wondering how to handle the part! Then Frank Capra gave me a clue when he presented me with a picture for the den of my new home, and inscribed it, "To Warner Baxter, who will succeed best when he is himself!"

Immediately, I applied this advice to the role, and found that I was handicapped neither by weighty dialogue nor by plot action. The man acted as I would act in similar situations, and the lines were in my own terms. His qualities, I think, are mine. You won't see a fictional character on the screen in this picture. The fellow *is* Warner Baxter!

—Baxter, interviewed by Mark Dowling for *Movie Classic*, Feb 1935

In the days of Murrieta [in *Robin Hood of El Dorado* (1936, William Wellman)], shortly after the discovery of gold in California, a man was an "outlaw" usually because he had a personal grievance, a vow to fulfill. Murrieta, for instance, became a bandit because he avenged the murders of his wife [Margo] and his brother [Carlos de Valdez] by killing the Americans who had wronged him. When he tried to return to the settlements he found a price on his head; he turned to banditry because it was the only course open to him.

Even as a bandit he was not a ruthless killer. He liked a fair fight. He was always seen at the head of his men, taking his chances with them. In matters of personal grievance it was a matter of which of the antagonists was quicker on the draw....

The years have given a new perspective to outlaws like Murrieta, Vasquez and others of their times.... It has been discovered that these men did almost as much good with their loot as they did harm in getting it.

Then too, there was no middle-class; a man was a respected citizen or he was an outlaw. Outlaws did not masquerade as respected citizens; they had a certain fierce pride in their station in life.

—Baxter, interviewed for *The Brooklyn Daily Eagle*, 15 Mar 1936

Ned BEATTY [1937-]

Born: Louisville, Kentucky. Seventeen years of stage work preceded his film debut in Deliverance (1972, John Boorman):

Q. Is there a key to understanding the character you play in *Deliverance*?

A. For that character, the strongest thing was to be liked. You very often have to have "through lines." Sometimes through lines don't just mean anything to the audience or anybody else. They're just that thing that you can always bring to the scene, that will always have life for you. And as an actor, you have to give it a name because you're within a formalized structure. The behavior in itself won't quite do. It's like a trick that you can go back to.

For that particular through line, even though *Deliverance* was about white water canoeing and woods, I decided to use a cocker spaniel. I very often use an animal image. And all the time under the kind of salesman outer shell, I wanted my character to be somebody who desperately wanted to be liked, and desperately wanted to be accepted.

Network [1976, Sidney Lumet] is the only film that I've ever been in that was said word for word the way it was written. And as far as I know, no one was ever asked to play it word for word. It was a consensus of opinion that that's what should be done. It was a literate movie, and the action took place in order to fill in the words. Most filmmaking doesn't follow that pattern. Most film scripts aren't that literate. That was very special. It just had to be done that way. [The script was by Paddy Chayefsky.]

—Beatty, interviewed for *Dialogue on Film*, *American Film*, Dec 1980

Warren BEATTY [1937-]

Born: Warren Beaty in Richmond, Virginia; brother of Shirley MacLaine. Studies at Northwestern University School of Speech and with Stella Adler, and work in radio, TV, and on Broadway preceded his film debut in Splendor in the Grass (1961, Elia Kazan). He made his first of two films with Arthur Penn — Mickey One — in 1965:

We had a lot of trouble on [*Mickey One*] because I didn't know what the hell Arthur was trying to do and I tried to find out. I had nothing to do with the real construction of that film. I didn't know what Penn wanted. I did the best I could. I'm not sure that he knew himself.

But let's say that he did know. Arthur felt that I never really trusted him on it, and he was absolutely right....

Q. In *Mickey One* where the character is a comedian, the comic technique seems a little strained....

A. I had the same feeling.... It could be that I just couldn't bring it off. But my feelings were that the words were not funny.... Maybe I should have made them funny. I don't know.

Q. Did you purposefully try to keep Mickey as a second-class comedian?

A. This was the way it was written. I didn't take any liberties with *Mickey One*. I didn't do any writing on it. None. So there was even a kind of speech pattern written into the script. I never got with it to my own satisfaction.

It's difficult to define what's going to be funny in that situation and that was always my complaint with Arthur, that the jokes were some attempt to attain some sort of universality, some appeal to intellect that I didn't find funny at all. I felt that they were pretentious jokes.

—Beatty, interviewed by Mike Wilmington and Gerald Peary for *The Daily Cardinal* and *The Velvet Light Trap*; publ. in *The Velvet Light Trap*, Winter 1972/73

[Bonnie Parker and Clyde Barrow] were great figures — I wouldn't say heroes — but they were great *figures* certainly in the imagination of the populace during the time of the depression. Because it was not only an economic depression; it was a depression of imagination as well. There was very little that lent itself to being admired; and it was not at all uncommon during the filming of *Bonnie and Clyde* [1967, Arthur Penn] for somebody to come up to us and show us an enormous scrapbook in which they had kept for over thirty years every single thing that had been written about Bonnie and Clyde. I remember a lady coming up to us and saying that she had made Bonnie's funeral dress, and she went into her house and brought out a piece of the material from which she had made it. Almost without exception, each time we moved to a new location, we'd find somebody — at least one person and usually more — who remembered them with considerable reverence.

—Beatty, interviewed in an unsourced, undated article in the files at The New York Public Library for the Performing Arts

I watched [the rushes] on *McCabe and Mrs. Miller* [1971] because Robert Altman wanted me to participate very heavily in the writing and construction of the film. I watched the rushes to see what the hell we should do next.

I like Bob very much. We kind of discarded the original script and I found myself writing most of the scenes. I wrote all my dialogue. The frog joke is mine.... Bob works in such a way that he wants a high level of participation from people.

Q. How did you like the part of McCabe?

A. I like to play schmucks. Cocky schmucks. Guys who think they know it all but don't. It's been the story of my life to think I knew what I was talking about and later find out that I didn't. I enjoy that. I think it's funny; I think it's ridiculous. I like to enjoy what I'm doing. McCabe made me laugh all during that movie....

I probably wouldn't have done so much work on that film had not Julie [Christie] been in it. Because of my relationship with her I wanted to work a little harder on it.

It's difficult. It makes the relationship at home a little difficult. It makes the relationship at work a little better because I know that girl loves me and she knows that I love her. So we always know when we work together that we'd go out of our way to assist the other person. [Beatty and Christie worked together again on *Shampoo* (1975, Hal Ashby) and *Heaven Can Wait* (1978, Warren Beatty and Buck Henry).]

—Beatty, interviewed by Mike Wilmington and Gerald Peary for *The Daily Cardinal* and *The Velvet Light Trap*; publ. in *The Velvet Light Trap*, Winter 1972/73

George [in *Shampoo*] is a composite of a whole bunch of male hairdressers I interviewed in Beverly Hills. Yes, I did my research thoroughly. I gave shampoos to some ladies. I soaked up the atmosphere of the beauty salons. I did my homework on how rich women talk under the hair dryer. But this is a hyper-sexual comedy with a difference — cruel, cold and tough. The people in it are all shallow and hypocritical, exploiting each other for economic reasons. Poor George is the equivalent of the dumb blonde, used and then discarded at the end, in this case by women. From the perpetual youthful Adonis, he winds up 40ish, realizing he hasn't grown up.

—Beatty, interviewed by Frank Rasky for *The Toronto Star*, 14 Mar 1975

Q. How do you interpret your switch from John Reed [in *Reds* (1981, Warren Beatty)] to Dick Tracy [in *Dick Tracy* (1990, Warren Beatty)]? You're obviously going for easy assimilation this time.

A. Well, there's something about Dick Tracy that gives me permission to be outlandishly heroic and clear-cut in dealing with good and evil, with love versus duty, with the wish for family. Tracy is completely good. What gives me the right to say this? The match of his yellow hat and yellow raincoat. The bright, twinkling stars you see behind his head. And the moon. The music tells me he's good. It affords me the chance to be naive in a way that somehow doesn't embarrass me.

Q. Where's Tracy's famous pointy nose and chin? How come you make the actors who play criminals wear doughy makeup and yet you've done nothing to alter your face?

A. See, it was the literal interpretation of the Tracy face that kept me from playing the part for a while. But when I began to realize that no one has that face, I felt I would be as good as anybody else. Even so, I tried prosthetics and makeup to approximate the nose and chin. I didn't look like Tracy. And you know what? Nobody does. I just looked silly.

—Beatty, interviewed by Bill Zehme for *Rolling Stone*, 31 May 1990

Wallace BEERY [1884-1949]

Born: Kansas City, Missouri. Work with the circus and on stage preceded his 1908 film debut as an extra in New Rochelle, N.Y.:

My first real film start came in 1910 in the old *Swedie* comedies with Ben Turpin.... I played a Swedish maid, dresses and all. The routine called for Turpin to knock me down. He did. Then I'd knock him down. Then came the chase — and everybody was knocked down.

Keystone offered me a job. I grabbed it, and the bopping business started all over again. Doug Fairbanks pulled me from under a boot and put me in the role of Richard Lion-Heart [in *Robin Hood* (1922, directed by Allan Dwan and produced by Fairbanks)]. A series of villain and humorous roles followed. Too easy. So, in 1927-28 I teamed up with Raymond Hatton for *Behind the Front* [1927, Edward Sutherland], *Fireman, Save My Child* [1927, Sutherland] and *Now We're in the Air* [1927, Frank Strayer]. The old swing-and-duck routine again.... Then sound. It looked like "Good Bye, Mr. Chips" for Mr. Beery.

Irving Thalberg came to the rescue. He reached the decision that characters should talk as they look. He cast me as Butch in *The Big House* [1930, George Hill]. It's been clear sailing ever since....

—Beery, interviewed by Ed Sullivan for *The New York Herald Tribune*, 20 July 1941

Don't let anybody tell you that Jackie [Cooper] is a genius, or any other kind of a freak.... If Jackie were a genius, he would have done that last great crying scene in *The Champ* [1931, King Vidor] from within — without quite knowing how or why he did it. But Jackie knew why he did that scene: we told him "Red" Golden, his idol and assistant director on the film had been fired! It was a dirty trick to play on the kid because we knew he'd take it hard. He took it just as any other normal kid would take the news of a lost pal — and that's what you saw on the screen. That alone should prove that Jackie isn't any spoiled child prodigy. He's just a healthy, normal little boy who happens to be a born actor.

—Beery, interviewed by Dorothy Manners for *Movie Classic*, Apr 1932

Most screen characters are either very good or very bad, a fact that often disturbs an actor as much as it does an intelligent observer. For no man is completely made from one piece of cloth, all good or all bad, all cruel or all tender. Instead, each person is a mixture of many things, and Pancho Villa was an especially interesting blend of evil and good.

He was an entirely human person, and that is one of the big reasons why I enjoyed playing the part in the picture *Viva Villa* [1934, Jack Conway]. Sometimes, when he was under the influence of the highly spiritual Francisco Madero [Henry B. Walthall], Villa was as nice as a boy just before Christmas. At other times, as when he faced the treacherous General Pascal, played by Joseph Schildkraut, he was ruthless. Villa was ignorant, yet shrewd; he was a great leader, yet he was bossed by his wife; he had moments of drunken rage, and periods of surprising softness....

I had read a lot about Villa before I took the role, and this reading made me respect him more. If he had had a good education, he might have made Mexico a great president; as it was, he gave history another colorful figure. His death scene was typical. He had been fatally shot by an old enemy [Donald Cook as Don Felipe] and was taken to a butcher shop to die. There a newspaperman [Stuart Erwin as Johnny Sykes], searching for some way to comfort him in his last moments, promised him a fine obituary. Villa, almost childlike and always an exhibitionist, was comforted; he gasped out his thanks and died.

—Beery, in *The Saturday Evening Post*, 21 Feb 1948

Villa had many faults. He was very far from a model of virtue. He knew little about the niceties of life, and nothing whatever about formal conventions. He lacked culture and polish. Sometimes he was brutal.

But I always had the feeling, and tried to put it into the picture, that Villa in his heart was somewhat bewildered by all the fuss he stirred up. He always reminded me of a little boy playing Robin Hood with muskets and swords and lives and human hearts, and wondering why everybody was so much interested in his games.

And he was true to his friendships. A man who has that trait can't be all bad.... He never betrayed a friendship, although he was merciless in his punishment of friends who tried to betray him....

He was a silent, reserved man. He had only five loves in his whole life — for his country, for the idealistic Francisco Madero, for women, for an American newspaperman who won his affection and for his soldiers. These loves he never betrayed.

If his love affairs were robust and unconventional, that was because he knew no other way to make love. If his hates were bitter, so were his friendships sincere.

—Beery, interviewed for the pressbook for *Viva Villa* (MGM, 1934)

Madge BELLAMY [1899-1990]

Born: Margaret Philpott in Hillsboro, Texas. Studies at Miss Wallack's dance school and work as a dancer and on Broadway (from 1918) preceded her film debut in The Riddle: Woman (1920, Edward Jose). In 1922, she played the title role in Maurice Tourneur's Lorna Doone:

Maurice Tourneur directed me in *Lorna Doone* and I don't think he gave a darn about acting. No matter what you did, it was all right with him. Once we did a scene in which I was supposed to go up, kiss the guy, and then some other business followed. Mr. Tourneur said, "Stop, that's all, okay."

I said, "But we haven't finished the scene."

"Yes," he said, "but that cloud was just right up there."

He was more interested in the pictorial style. It was an absolute for him. For instance, in the wedding scene which was at a distance, I was late to the set so he shot it without me although I was the bride. If you look close, you'll see there's no bride but it didn't matter because it was a long shot. I said, "Why couldn't you have waited just a minute?"

He said, "Well, the atmospheric conditions were just too perfect to wait."

I think personally that Jack Ford was one of the most lovable people I've ever known.... The strange thing about him was that he appeared uninterested when you were doing a scene. He'd usually let his brother Eddie rehearse it and then he'd come over and look at it. He might make some slight change or something, but he wasn't picayunish at all. He didn't seem to be terribly involved unless it was an action scene. If you were to fall off a horse, he'd have you do it over and over again, but if it was just a simple love scene, he didn't appear to be terribly interested. So he didn't pay too much attention to what you were doing unless it was something dangerous and exciting. Then he'd wake up and work hard at it. I don't think he was greatly interested in women's parts. I know it worried me because in *The Iron Horse* [1924] he hardly gave me any direction at all. In fact, I think that if I hadn't been in it, my absence would not have been noted.

I did *Sandy* [1926] and I danced the Charleston on a table. After that, I starred in a series of flapper comedies for Fox. I tried everything to be funny.... I didn't imitate other flappers like Clara Bow and Colleen Moore. In fact, you'll be surprised but I copied Harry Langdon. I used to think that at my worst I looked a little like him and, in some way, he just suited my style exactly. So I consciously imitated him more than anyone else and I do think I was a pretty good comedienne.... I loved Harry Beaumont who directed *Sandy*. Oh, he was a darling, very easy, patient and kind.

—Bellamy, interviewed (1983) by William M. Drew for *Speaking of Silents: First Ladies of the Screen* (Vestal, N.Y.: The Vestal Press, Inc., 1989)

A few years ago during a talk to the cinema students at UCLA, I described how different directors would direct a scene. [Allan] Dwan [on *Summer Bachelors* (1926)] used sarcasm. He would say, for instance, "To the left, you see your love approaching. You fear that he doesn't love you any more. He comes up and kisses you tenderly. You burst into tears of happiness and relief — if you can manage it....

[Frank] Borzage [on *The Dixie Merchant* (1921)] was just as emotional, but quieter. He would weep as he directed. He would sob, "You see him. He means everything to you. He may not love you anymore! He is your whole life! — Doesn't he care for you now?" By this time Borzage would be in tears. "He kisses you! Oh, what joy!" Frank would be too choked up to go on.

When Lewis Milestone was King Vidor's assistant on *Love Never Dies* [1921], he directed some of my scenes. I think that King Vidor was helping Milestone start his own directing career. Their method was my favorite. They would take me aside and explain exactly what they wanted, then keep on taking the scene until they got it. This is the method that Vidor used in the silent days.

—Bellamy, in her *A Darling of the Twenties* (Vestal, N.Y.: The Vestal Press, Inc., 1989)

Ralph BELLAMY [1904-1991]

Born: Chicago. Working as a bellboy at The Palisades Tavern in California, he was given the job of cleaning the shoes of Louise Lively, then on location for Wings of Morn (1919, J. Gordon Edwards). When he expressed a desire to be an actor, she found him a small part in the film. Back in Chicago, he formed his own troupe in 1922 — The North Shore Players — and toured the midwest; in 1927, he formed The Ralph Bellamy Players. In 1929, he made his Broadway debut; the following year he was offered a film contract and made his debut in The Secret Six (1931, George Hill). Here he speaks of the problems posed to performers by the restrictions of the Hays Office:

At one point in a picture at Fox with Sally Eilers called *Second Hand Wife* [1933], we were in an elaborate hotel bedroom on our honeymoon. We were about to retire when a phone call came with word of an accident to my little daughter by my first marriage. I quickly left to go to her and, quite late at night, returned to find Sally in an enticing nightgown, sound asleep on top of one of the twin beds. I was in pajamas.

The direction then was: you get into the other bed and turn out the light — fade out.

I told the director, Hamilton MacFadden, "If I do that it'll be the biggest laugh in the picture. It's our wedding night! I have to do something besides get into another bed and go to sleep, no matter how late it is or how tired I might be."

This was during the days of the Hays Office and rigid adherence to an industry-wide code of moral "don'ts." MacFadden agreed but he said he was helpless. He had orders to shoot the script the way it was written.

—Bellamy, in his *When the Smoke Hits the Fan* (Garden City, N.Y.: Doubleday & Co., 1979)

Dan Kelly called, and said, "Report to the studio Monday morning to do *The Awful Truth* [1937]." I said, "To play what? Where's the script?" He said, "I don't know, I guess they'll get it to you." I said, "Who else is in it?" He said, "Cary Grant and Irene Dunne." So I tried to get Harry [Cohn], and I got him the Friday before, and said, "I've got to talk to you about this. What am I playing?" He said, "Just leave it to Leo McCarey. Leo McCarey is a great director, and we're going to be all right. I'm not going to tell you anything." I said, "How am I going to play a part if I don't know anything about it?" He said it would be a Westerner, from Oklahoma. I said, "That's not much of a lead.... Would you mind if I go and see Leo?" He said, "Go ahead." So I called Leo at his house.... I went out to his house, and I said, "I want to talk to you about *The Awful Truth*." He said, "It's going to be great!" I said, "But what's the part?" He said, "Oh, don't worry, don't worry." It all seemed so indefinite and nebulous. So then this call came to show up Monday morning, and I said, "What kind of clothes?" They said, "Just bring a lot of clothes."

I was being nasty. I got made up, and I brought all the clothes I could carry onto the set. Leo came over, said hello. I said, "Leo, I don't know what the part is. I don't know how to dress it. I was told to bring a lot of clothes, so I've got a lot of clothes." He said, "What have you got on?" I said, "Odd jackets and trousers." He said, "Let me see it — just the thing!" It was just the way I came to the studio. He said, "Come over here," so I went over, and he had Irene sitting at a piano in front of the camera, and she was saying, "Leo, I can't, you can't ask me to do this." Irene and I said hello, and Leo said, "Can you sing?" I said, "I can't get from one note to the next." He laughed. "That's exactly what I want!" He said, "You're an Oklahoman." I said, "What kind of Oklahoman?" He said, "Just be an Oklahoman for the moment. I'll tell you about the rest of it later. Do you know *Home on the Range*?" I said, "I know the words, but I can't sing it." He said, "It's perfect! Irene, do you think you could do it?" She said, "You know I don't read music very well," and Leo thought this was funny. The camera was all set up, and Leo said, "Let's try one." The camera's running, she's playing *Home on the Range* and I'm singing it, and it's just *awful*. We finished, there's no place else to go, and nobody said, "Cut." We finally looked up, and McCarey was doubled up under the camera. He said, "That's it! Cut, print it." Irene and I didn't know what the hell we were doing. She was mad. I had no idea what the part was. Cary came in, did a scene, and he was put off. At the end of the day, Irene was in tears, Cary went to Harry Cohn.... Next morning, McCarey came in, and he had a piece of paper a few inches long; he said, "I've got something here I think would be very funny. You come in here, and you come in over there...and then we'll see what happens." So there we are coming through doors, and the dog is running through, and everything. And he's chuckling gleefully. Well, a couple of days later we saw what was happening. We shot that in less than six weeks, without a script. Leo knew all the time what he was going to do, but he was the only one who did. After a couple of days, we were willing to be putty in his hands.

—Bellamy, interviewed by Leonard Maltin for *Film Fan Monthly*, Sept 1970

Q. What were Howard Hawks' working methods like on *His Girl Friday* [1940]?

A. Very meticulous. He was great to work with. You had to do it his way. He had done his homework. This was a remake, as you know, of *The Front Page* [1931, Lewis Milestone]. They scattered the parts all around.... I played the leading lady!

Howard knew exactly what his day's work was going to be. He knew all his setups. We'd finish a shot, or a single coming through the door or whatever. It soon became evident that it was useless to discuss changing anything in the script with Howard. He'd say, "No, no, do it the way it is." I must say he was right.... They had it the way they wanted it, the script, and he was going to shoot it that way. But he was a quiet man. The set was always quiet. He had complete command of the entire company, and [was] a real gentleman.

—Bellamy, interviewed by John Gallagher for *Films in Review* (NY), Jan 1984

Joan BENNETT [1910-1990]

Born: Palisades, New Jersey. Daughter of actor Richard Bennett [1873-1944] and younger sister of actress Constance Bennett [1904-1965], she began her acting career as an extra in Power (1928, Howard Higgin). She made her Broadway debut the same year. Her first major film role was opposite Ronald Colman in Bulldog Drummond (1929):

In those days before the union controls of The Screen Actors' Guild, directors could work their companies around the clock if they chose, and the filming of *Bulldog Drummond* brought me the first brush with Hollywood temperament — not mine, but the director's, Richard Jones. At one point, the company worked until three in the morning, with a seven-o'clock makeup call the next day, ready to shoot on the set at nine. Ronald Colman put up with the schedule for a few days, then announced that he would not appear the following day until noon, no matter what the call might be, and if we had scenes with him we could take our choice of arriving before then or not. At that point I was so tired I jumped at the chance for a few extra hours of rest and the next day reported to the makeup department in plenty of time to be on the set when Colman arrived. The director greeted me with a blast. "What do you mean by not reporting at nine o'clock?" I explained that since all of my scenes were with Mr. Colman, I saw no reason to appear earlier just to watch the crew set up the scenes. "You do as you're told, young lady," he answered. "You're new at this business." Certainly he was right about that, but I felt his demands were unfair and unreasonable....

Robert Benchley once complained that a whole generation grew up thinking that every great man of history had looked like George Arliss, for in the late twenties and thirties he was cast as Disraeli, Voltaire, Alexander Hamilton, Cardinal Richelieu and other historical figures. When I worked with him [on *Disraeli* (1929, Alfred E. Green)], he was almost a legend and I was hopelessly in awe of him. He had a professional reputation for perfection and it was well deserved. Extraordinarily meticulous in his work, we rehearsed two weeks before the shooting began, a rarity in those days, and he demanded everything planned out ahead of time. Although he was a sweet and gentle man, he was absolutely inflexible about his working schedule. On the very stroke of five o'clock, he doffed his toupee, handed it to his valet, Jenner, and walked out. It was the signal that Mr. Arliss was through, and no amount of cajoling or pleas for "just one more take," had any effect whatever....

—Bennett, in her (with Lois Kibbee) *The Bennett Playbill* (New York: Holt, Rinehart & Winston, 1970)

Little Women [1933, George Cukor] with Kate Hepburn, Frances Dee, and Jean Parker was a joy to make. It was a very happy company. Director George Cukor was wonderful to work with and so was Kate. When George wanted us all on the set, he would yell, "Come, you four bitches." I was pregnant with Melinda at the time...and I had to go to George and tell him because there was a scene which called for me to take a fall. When I said I would not be able to do it, he simply said, "Okay, we'll give it to Kate." He was wonderful.

—Bennett, interviewed by Ronald Bowers for *Magill's Cinema Annual 1983*, ed. by Frank N. Magill (Englewood Cliffs, N.J.: Salem Press, 1983)

Early in 1941, I made my first film with the incomparable director, Fritz Lang, a circumstance that would be an important boost for me as an actress. The film was *Man Hunt*.... I played a Cockney, and for weeks before the shooting began I worked on the accent with Queenie Leonard, an English music hall performer. It was the only movie I ever made in which I knew the entire script, like a play, beforehand. Conquering the dialect was tricky enough, but the real challenge came in working with Fritz Lang....

Fritz was terribly exacting and demanding and working with him was sometimes abrasive, but he commanded great respect, and I performed better under his direction than at any other time in my career. Almost always I did what I was told, and we developed a great working rapport....

[The success of *Woman in the Window* (1944, Fritz Lang)] equaled that of *Man Hunt*, and ours seemed a fortuitous working relationship. I did a couple of films after that, neither of which pleased me very much, and it was then [husband, producer] Walter [Wanger], Fritz and I formed an independent producing company and arranged to distribute through Universal.... Our first film as an organization was *Scarlet Street* [1945], with a cast headed by Edward G. Robinson and me. It was another hit and a good omen for the newly formed company.

All the proceeds from the successful *Scarlet Street* went into the next Wanger-Bennett-Lang film, *Secret Beyond the Door* with Michael Redgrave, in 1948. But Fritz was a real Jekyll-and-Hyde character, calm and purposeful one moment, and off on a tirade the next. At script conferences he was rebellious, on the set he was outrageous and demanding. I remember he wouldn't use doubles for Michael Redgrave and me for a sequence in a burning house. We fled, terrified, through scorching flames, time and again....

Fritz and I had some thrilling arguments during the filming. When he was in a successful period, he was impossible and Darryl Zanuck told me, "Let him have one good resounding flop and he'll be adorable." He got it in *Secret Beyond the Door*. It flopped and Fritz was adorable at once....

—Bennett, in her (with Lois Kibbee) *The Bennett Playbill* (New York: Holt, Rinehart & Winston, 1970)

Jack BENNY [1894-1974]

Born: Benjamin Kubelsky in Chicago. Work in vaudeville preceded his film debut in The Hollywood Revue of 1929 (Charles Reisner). He is best remembered for his role as Josef Tura, in To Be or Not To Be (1942):

When Ernst Lubitsch asked me to play the Polish Shakespearean actor I was afraid. I told him that he needed a young, handsome leading man...a hero who would give the girls a thrill. Ernst said he had written it with me in mind.

—Benny, interviewed for *The Los Angeles Examiner*; quoted in *Jack Benny* by Irving A. Fein (New York: G.P. Putnam's Sons, 1976)

[Lubitsch's] method of direction was perfect for me. He would act out the whole scene — and then he'd say, "Now let's see how you'd do it." He'd give me the movements and then let me do them my own way.

—Benny, quoted in *The Wit and Wisdom of Hollywood* by Max Wilk (New York: Atheneum, 1971)

Tom BERENGER [1950-]

Born: Chicago. College theatrics at The University of Missouri, studies at the HB Studio in N.Y. and work on the off-Broadway stage and on TV preceded his film debut in Beyond the Door (1975, Oliver Hellman). In 1983, he played Sam in Lawrence Kasdan's The Big Chill:

[Sam] doesn't take what he's doing very seriously. He doesn't take acting very seriously. He doesn't take himself being an actor very seriously. And at this point in his life he doesn't take himself seriously anymore. I don't think he's doing what he wants to do and I think that probably other people are telling him what to do and so he doesn't enjoy it and he doesn't go home at night fulfilled.

He just goes home at night kind of empty. And I think that some of the other characters have this big fantasy about him. They see him on TV in their living rooms every Friday and they're very excited for him. They think it's great. He's making big money and he's doing this and that and they just assume that he must be a very happy person. And their lives aren't so happy. But his life is really no better than theirs.

—Berenger, interviewed by Lewis Archibald for *The Aquarian Weekly*, 5 Oct 1983

My first part was as a psychopath in *Looking for Mr. Goodbar* [1977, Richard Brooks], but I've done soft characters too — in *Eddie and the Cruisers* [1983, Martin Davidson] and *The Big Chill*. [Staff Sergeant Bob] Barnes [in *Platoon* (1986, Oliver Stone)] isn't really the same kind of psychopath as the guy in *Goodbar*. He's beginning to lose his morality, by the end he does lose it, but I had compassion for him. He's a victim, not just of his background but of what the war's done to him.

—Berenger, interviewed for *The New York Times*, 16 Jan 1987

Q. In *Betrayed* [1988, Costa-Gavras] you play [Gary] a racist, a less-than-likable character.

A. You can't think that you're playing a villain or you'll end up with a cartoon. You have to think about him as a person and he's also a hero. He won the Silver Star. He's incredibly nostalgic about the way things were when he was a kid. He feels the whole country has gone totally out of control. [Gary is] a seemingly very happy guy with a nice family.

—Berenger, interviewed by Dan Yakir for *Us*, 3 Oct 1988

Marisa BERENSON [1948-]

Born: New York City. A fashion model, she made her film debut in Cabaret (1972, Bob Fosse); her second major role was as Lady Lyndon in Barry Lyndon (1975, Stanley Kubrick):

In the original script, the character had a lot of dialogue, and it was only during rehearsals that Stanley started cutting down on the lines. He felt they weren't necessary in getting across the basic vulnerability and ultimate disillusionment of the woman. He thought it could be done better through expressions and attitudes.

—Berenson, interviewed by Gordon Stoneham for *The Ottawa Citizen*, 7 Feb 1976

Candice BERGEN [1946-]

Born: Los Angeles. Daughter of comedian/ventriloquist Edgar Bergen [1903-1978], she made her film debut as one of The Group (1966, Sidney Lumet). In 1971, she played Susan opposite Jack Nicholson and Art Garfunkel in Mike Nichols' Carnal Knowledge:

[Mike Nichols] was the first director to identify the concern with control that had always impeded me and to address the fear that lay behind it. He cracked my control when a scene required him to, and capitalized on it when it was consistent with the character. In an early scene in which I met Artie [Garfunkel] at a mixer, Mike told me to try taking my skirt off for the tight two-shot and playing the scene in my slip. It

produced just the right edge of discomfort, the precise note of nervousness the scene demanded.
—Bergen, in her *Knock Wood* (New York: Simon & Schuster, 1984)

I really wanted to make a film where I was pushed, where I knew from the start what kind of a film it was. I knew Lina [Wertmuller] would make demands and stretch me. She worked night and day [on *The End of the World in Our Usual Bed in a Night Full of Rain* (1977), Wertmuller's first English language film] forcing me to drop my defenses and wear through my protective armor. She did it with total force....

Some directors break through your armor by hugging you and loving you. She never stopped assaulting me. The content of the film was the most depressing, despairing, despondent stuff.

I spent four weeks crying every day, then two weeks in the rain with water pouring all over me, screaming all night. Every day was a psychodrama. But I can usually charm people and if it's important, I can win them over. I never felt I could win her over.

I was perversely opposite to what she wanted. She kept saying, "Be more Italian!" and I kept thinking, "Well, why didn't she hire Silvano Mangano?"
—Bergen, interviewed by Rex Reed for *The Toronto Star*, 19 Feb 1978

In the role of a woman [Jessica Potter in *Starting Over* (1979, Alan J. Pakula)] who abandons a happy marriage to pursue, with a singular lack of talent, a recording career, I was called on at two points in the script to sing. Very badly. This in itself was not a reach for me, as I sing very badly under any circumstances. But as I worked on the songs in the weeks before shooting, I realized with a sense of dread that in order for the songs to work and be funny I had to be willing to make a complete fool of myself. It only succeeded when done honestly, with no editorializing, no holding back. The second I worried about seeming stupid and pulled back in fear, it fizzled. *Pretending* to sing badly was not only redundant; it was hedging my bets.... I saw that as soon as I played it safe, I was sunk. I had to be committed and unself-conscious. Committed, in this case, to unmasking the fool in myself. Nothing less would do....

Once I had dreaded the first day's shooting because it was then that I was meant to sing my first song; but when the time came, I burst on the set like Ethel Merman, eager to strut my stuff. Worried earlier about the abject humiliation such a display before the crew would bring, I now shrieked happily while they grinned — holding pillows over their ears — and waited good-naturedly for me to stop....
—Bergen, in her *Knock Wood* (New York: Simon & Schuster, 1984)

Ingrid BERGMAN [1915-1982]

Born: Stockholm; mother of Isabella Rossellini. Studies at The Royal Dramatic Theater School in Stockholm preceded her film debut in Munkbrogreven (1934, Sigurd Wallen and Edvin Adolphson). She made her Hollywood debut in a remake of Intermezzo (1939, Gregory Ratoff) in which she had starred for Gustaf Molander in 1936:

[David O. Selznick] was impossible. He never could make up his mind, you know, that that was it — he always wanted something better. We went over and over my entrance because he wanted my arrival in the American film world to be like a shock that would just hit people between the eyes.... Now, *my* entrance was opening a door, hanging my coat up and stopping to watch a father looking at his little girl play the piano — there wasn't much I could do to make a tremendous impression. I can't tell you how many times I did it and redid it....

Q. It was more Selznick's movie than Gregory Ratoff's?

A. Yes. To be honest, it wasn't much Ratoff's movie. We had the Swedish version and a moviola on the set which we watched and did very much what the Swedish director had done. Leslie Howard rehearsed the dialogue with me and helped an awful lot. And what with Selznick and all his retakes. I have to say that Ratoff took a back seat there. I don't know how he felt about it. Sometimes he'd shout a lot on the set when he had to wait too long for some lighting or something. Yes, he was temperamental, but he was also a dear, sweet man. And very funny. His accent was very funny to listen to. He used to come up to me and say, "You don't read the line right. Listen to me...." And Ruth [Roberts] came up and said, "For God's sake, don't listen to him! Listen to *me*!" Because his accent was worse than mine.
—Bergman, interviewed by John Kobal (1972) for *People Will Talk* (New York: Alfred A. Knopf, 1985)

Robert Montgomery came into my dressing room the first day [of *Rage in Heaven* (1941)]. I knew that he had starred in Metro's *Night Must Fall* [1937, Richard Thorpe] as a psychopath some time before and had been a great success, and I suppose Metro was trying to repeat the success with him playing a similar role. But Bob had other ideas. He was very nice about it, but he was not going to act, he said. I didn't understand what he meant. He was an actor and he wasn't going to act?

"I'm very sorry to do this to you, but I'm forced to do this movie, so I intend to just say the lines but not act."

"But how does that work?"

"I don't know how it works, I don't care. I'm not going to do what they tell me to do. I'll listen but I shan't take any notice, I'll just say my lines blah-blah but I shan't act."

Then he explained. He was under contract to Metro-Goldwyn-Mayer, a seven-year contract that most actors had in those days, and he got paid every month, and they stipulated how many movies and what sort of movies they were. Now Robert was very popular, a superb comedian and much in demand, so as soon as he finished one movie he was pushed into another. It was a conveyor-belt system and he was exhausted. He had pleaded with them: "No more movies...I'm dead tired. I just can't go into another movie. I want to be with my family. I want to have a month off, go somewhere with the kids." But they had told him, "Nothing doing." So he was here in *Rage in Heaven.* "If I refuse they'll suspend me without pay. I've got a wife, children, a big house, a swimming pool. I need the money.... But I'm going to make my protest."

He said the same thing to George Sanders, who nodded his head and looked wise, but I don't think he understood anymore than I did. Until we started to film. Then we understood. The director would explain what he wanted to Bob, and Bob would look up at the sky as if he wasn't hearing a word and the director would say, "Now Bob, have you understood what I'm talking about?" and Bob would answer, "Now are we going to shoot this scene? Right, let's get going." And he'd go straight into this blah-blah-blah act of his, no inflections, nothing, same speed, same pace.

The first director lasted two weeks. Then the second one came in and Robert Montgomery went on the same way, his face just an impassive mask. So the second director quit and that's when they brought in Mr. W.S. Van Dyke II....

The picture was put together, released, and Bob Montgomery got the most glorious reviews because he gave such an original performance. You see, he was a light comedian, the rage of Hollywood, everybody adored him, and here was Bob being out of character, this absolutely flat performance as a psychopath, and people thought it was great. They didn't think he had it in him. So it turned out very well. For him.

In *Intermezzo* I played the nice piano teacher. In *Adam* [*Had Four Sons* (1941, Gregory Ratoff)] the nice housekeeper, in *Rage in Heaven* I was a nice refugee. Now they gave me the part of another sweet girl in *Dr. Jekyll and Mr. Hyde* [1941, Victor Fleming], and I really was fed up having to play it again. I went to Mr. Fleming and I said, "Couldn't we switch, and let Lana Turner play the fiancée, and I play the little tart in the bar, the naughty little Ivy?"

He laughed. "That's impossible. How can you with your looks? It's not to be believed."

"What do you know? You look at me and you look at the three pictures I've done and you know it's the same part I'm playing, but *I am an actress*!"

He grinned and said, "I don't believe you can play it; I mean a barmaid, a tart...it's Lana Turner's part."

"Will you let me do a test?"

"But David Selznick will *never* let you do a test. You've made three big pictures. A test means you're not sure that you can do it, which means you're not a *star*, and Mr. Selznick is not taking that sort of chance with one of *his* stars."

"Can we make a test without telling him?"

Fleming looked surprised: "You mean you'd really do that?"

"Of course I would. I'm dying to play *that* part. Come, let's run a test."

In great secrecy Victor got a cameraman and crew one night and I did the test. A lot of people afterwards asked me why. To begin with I loved this girl, this barmaid Ivy. I thought about her all the time. I thought how she would react, how she would behave. Besides, I simply had to get different parts; I could not remain typed as a Hollywood peaches-and-cream girl.

The test impressed Victor Fleming, and he rang up David Selznick and said, "David, I'm going to switch the parts. Ingrid is going to play Ivy."

David screamed, "But she just can't play that sort of role." You see David believed the Hollywood legend: the elevator boy always plays the elevator boy, the drunk's a drunk, the nurse always a nurse. In Hollywood you got yourself one role and played it forever. That's what the audience wants to see, they said, the same old performance, the familiar face....

Victor Fleming was marvelous. Although I'd known many fine directors in Sweden, this man added another dimension to what I'd known before. As soon as he came close to me I could tell by his eyes what he wanted me to do, and this happened with very few directors in my career; I could tell if he was satisfied, in doubt, or delighted. He got performances out of me which very often I didn't think I was capable of. The scene when he wanted a frightened distraught hysterical girl, faced by the terrifying Mr. Hyde — I just couldn't do it. So eventually he took me by the shoulder with one hand, spun me around, and struck me backwards and forwards across the face — hard — it hurt. I could feel the tears of what? surprise, shame — running down my cheeks. I was shattered by his action. I stood there weeping, while he strode back to the camera and shouted "Action!" Even the camera crew were struck dumb, as I wept my way through the scene. But he got the performance he wanted.... [She worked with Fleming again on *Joan of Arc* (1948).]

A close-up can...invent things that aren't there at all. In *Casablanca* [1942, Michael Curtiz] there was often nothing in my face, nothing at all. But the audiences put into my face what they thought I was giving. They were inventing my thoughts the way they wanted them: they were doing the acting for me.

I so loved that Maria [in *For Whom the Bell Tolls* (1943, Sam Wood)]. When I first thought I'd got the part I'd worked on it relentlessly. I studied everything that Hemingway had written about the girl. I shut myself up for days just studying being that girl. I thought: a woman in love forgets herself, her own interests. All she is thinking of is the man she loves. What she means to him. How she can make him happy. She simply lives to fit his needs.

—Bergman, in her (with Alan Burgess) *My Story* (New York: Delacorte Press, 1980)

I first met Gary Cooper in Nevada where *For Whom the Bell Tolls* was being shot. I was replacing another actress who had worked on the film for a short time, and I was very scared, very frightened. Gary Cooper was a famous actor. When I did begin to work, I found him to be an extremely kind, very simple person who kept to himself and didn't join in much with the others. One of the things I liked about him from the very start was his size. He is the tallest leading man I have worked with, and working with him was one of the few times when I did not have to slouch over for a leading man.

As an actor, I think he was extremely good. I remember one time I was standing next to him and he started talking very quietly. I couldn't make out what he was saying. I asked him to repeat what he had said, and he told me that he hadn't been speaking. He had been rehearsing his lines. It had sounded so natural that I couldn't tell then or in the film when he was acting. You never noticed that he was working. He spoke quietly, never tried to do an interpretation like an Alec Guinness. Instead he did little things with his face and his hands, little things you didn't even know were there until you saw the rushes and realized how tremendously effective he was....

He did get along extremely well with our director Sam Wood, and while we were making *For Whom the Bell Tolls*, we read a novel, *Saratoga Trunk*. I wanted very much to do it, to change my type, to put on a dark wig and makeup and play this emotional woman. The three of us agreed to make *Saratoga Trunk* as soon as we could [released 1945]. I also remember we discussed the possibility of Gary and I doing *The African Queen*, but, as you know, we did not.

—Bergman, interviewed by Stuart Kaminsky for *Coop* (New York: St. Martin's Press, 1980)

Leo McCarey was wonderful....

The boxing sequence, for instance, in *Bells of St. Mary's* [1945, Leo McCarey] — that was completely unrehearsed. We didn't know what would happen. So [McCarey] gave me the words and showed me what to do and then we just shot it several times and new things would keep coming in. Just little touches — doing things with your feet, looking worried about your clothes, a way of pushing your hair back, that sort of thing. Cukor explains everything in such detail that sometimes you feel like saying, "Please don't say any more because my mind is so full of explanations." I used to tease him by saying if it were a little line like "Have a cup of tea," he would say what kind of a cup it was and what kind of tea it was until you got so worried you couldn't say the line....

—Bergman, interviewed by John Kobal (1972) for *People Will Talk* (New York: Alfred A. Knopf, 1985)

Q. [Jean] Renoir [with whom she worked on *Elena et les hommes* (1956)] is on record as saying that Leo McCarey is one of the greatest American directors because he really understands people. Did you feel this?

A. Oh, yes. I think he understood people very well. He was a terribly funny man — the jokes that went on, and the gaiety! He always had a piano on the set [of *The Bells of St. Mary's*]; he used to play the piano while people were changing the lights or rehearsing. He was a very easy-going man. He also liked to improvise. I mean he had his story, but if he suddenly thought of something, he said, "Throw that away, let's do it this way." He would change everything.

—Bergman, interviewed by Robin Wood for *Film Comment*, July/Aug 1974

Hitch is a magnificently prepared director. There is nothing that he does not know about the picture he is going to do. Every angle and every set-up he had prepared at home with a small miniature set of what is being built in the studio. He does not even look into the camera — as he says "I know what it looks like." I don't know any other director that works this way. Of course he wants it primarily his way, but if an actor has some ideas he is, however, willing to let the actors try them. He will listen and sometimes I thought I had made myself clear and that Hitch was going to change his set-up. But, as a rule, he used to get his way by simply saying — "If you can't do it my way, fake it." It was a very good lesson for me, as many times when I can not win a battle with a director, I would remember Hitch saying, "Fake it." [She also worked Hitchcock's *Spellbound* (1945), *Notorious* (1946) and *Under Capricorn* (1949).]

—Bergman, in a letter to *Take One*, May 1976

When I was 15, I found out about Joan of Arc, and though I am not a Catholic, she became my favorite saint. I developed a tremendous love and admiration for her. She, too, was a timid child, but with great dignity and courage. She became the character I liked to play most. I learned everything I could about her. I found out that she wanted to get married and have children. I especially loved her sense of humor. I read and reread the record of her trial because I admired her for never being trapped by the questions of her inquisitors. [Bergman played Joan twice on film (*Joan of Arc*, 1948 and *Joan at the Stake*, 1954, Roberto Rossellini) and twice on stage (*Joan of Lorraine*, 1946 and *Joan of Arc at the Stake*, 1954).]

—Bergman, interviewed by Bill Davidson for *Look*, 2 Sept 1958

The script [of *Under Capricorn*] is interesting now, we've got a pretty good end, but Hitch's new technique I don't like. I have had no experience with it yet, for my first entrance was just a normal shot. But I have watched him with the others. It is so frightening for actors and crew.... I think Hitch and I will have some arguments. He wanted to shoot a whole roll of film, the camera following me everywhere and the sets and furniture being pulled away. It meant we had to rehearse a whole day without shooting and then shoot the scenes the following day. It made everybody nervous, but he insisted. We already had one little argument about my entrance and I got my way. I know I always can with him, but I dislike the argument....

Under Capricorn is half finished. The other day I burst. The camera was supposed to follow me around for eleven whole minutes, which meant we had to rehearse a whole day with the walls or furniture falling backwards as the camera went through, and of course that couldn't be done fast enough. So I told Hitch off. How I hate this new technique of his. How I suffer and loathe every minute on the set. My two leading men, Michael Wilding and Joe Cotten, just sat there and said nothing, but I know they agree with me, and I said enough for the whole cast. Little Hitch just left. Never said a word. Just went home.... oh dear....

—Bergman, in letters to Ruth Roberts, Aug 1948; repr. in her *My Story* (New York: Delacorte Press, 1980)

Q. One could perhaps make a basic distinction in film acting styles between acting a role and being a role. Would you accept a distinction of that kind between many of your Hollywood performances — such as your work in Hitchcock's films which are great acting performances — and the sense one has from the Rossellini films that you are not really acting, you are somehow so inside the part that you're are living it?

A. Yes, well that's what [Rossellini] always wanted and that's why he didn't like rehearsing too much. And he also didn't want to give the actors the dialogue in advance, because he said then they would repeat it and look in the mirror and see what effect they have. He disliked actors, because he always thought they were kind of phony people and very vain and that they wanted to look their best. So therefore he was trying to stop them by not giving the dialogue until the last minute, and take one or two takes and not any more, so that there would not be anything that was mechanical....

Now, for an actress like myself, and for George Sanders [in *Voyage to Italy* (1953)], it was difficult, because were not used to that. We were used to acting. But I tried as much as possible to come into the mood of these other amateurs. It was very, very hard, because I never knew when they had finished their dialogue and when my cue came up, so on my face there was always a worried expression and I was concerned about their performance and couldn't therefore always think of my own.

I remember one very funny scene in *Stromboli* [1949]. He had lots of amateurs from the island playing with me. First of all they didn't know English and I didn't know Italian and I spoke my lines in English. The whole thing was going to be dubbed as they always did in those days with films. He had put a thread around their toes in the shoes, as they never knew when to come in with their dialogue, and he had them on strings, so he pulled them when that one should speak; and he pulled the other one, so when he pulled them they spoke their dialogue....

—Bergman, interviewed by Robin Wood for *Film Comment*, July/Aug 1974

George Sanders had been told by Roberto that he liked his type, and that he was going to fit in absolutely with the husband and wife story of Colette's *Duo*. Unfortunately, by the time George arrived, Roberto had discovered that the rights were already sold. So now he had an actor and he didn't have a story. Of course that didn't bother Roberto. He would write another script.

George Sanders looked at me and said, "What is this? I'm coming here to do *Duo* and now it's going to be something else? He's changed his mind?"

I said, "Yes," because I knew Roberto was making up the story as he went along so as not to lose George Sanders. I was quite bewildered too, but I thought Roberto is Roberto; he might do another magnificent *Open City*. After all, we're going to Naples and he'll be inspired there....

Of course he couldn't get used to Roberto's habits. Like me, he'd been trained in Hollywood: shooting schedules, prepared dialogue, efficiency, speed....

It simply defeated him. I remember in Amalfi, in the hotel room we used as a dressing room, the tears were just pouring down his cheeks, and I said, "What's happened to you? What's the matter?"

"I am so unhappy in this movie, that's the matter. There's no dialogue. I don't know what's going to happen tomorrow. It's just impossible. I can't take it."

"Look, we'll write our own dialogue for the next scene. We'll write it now, and then we'll rehearse it."

"But what good does that do? It won't be any better tomorrow because we rehearse it." [Bergman's other films with Rossellini were: *Europa '51* (1951), *We, the Women* (1953), *Joan at the Stake* (1954) and *Fear* (1954).]

—Bergman, in her (with Alan Burgess) *My Story* (New York: Delacorte Press, 1980)

I've been told there are dozens of books about her [Anastasia], but I don't want to read them. Nor do I want to talk with the woman now living in Germany who claims to be Anastasia. It would just confuse me. You see, *I* am Anastasia [in *Anastasia* (1956, Anatole Litvak).]

—Bergman, interviewed by Mary Worthington Jones for *Photoplay Magazine*, Oct 1956

Jeannie BERLIN [1949-]

Born: Los Angeles; daughter of Elaine May [1932-]. Brief acting studies preceded her film debut in a bit part in Alice's Restaurant (1969, Arthur Penn). In 1972, she played Lila in her mother's The Heartbreak Kid:

When I got the part of Lila, I was a little bit afraid of the role. You see, I didn't want to make that girl stupid. It would have been so easy to do Lila stupid. I don't think Lila was stupid. I think every single thing she did was justified to her. I mean, she thought she was being nice. And she really was terrifically in love [with her husband, played by Charles Grodin]....

[Q. Did you like being directed by your mother?]

A. It was a dream. A pleasure. Terrific. No scenes, no traumas. Working on the film with her was incredible. *She's* incredible. In the film, it was a director-actress relationship. That's *all* it was. There was nothing about mother-daughter relationship. She directed me the way she directed everybody else, which was allowing you to "go" — to do what your impulses told you to do.

—Berlin, interviewed by John Gruen for *The New York Times*, 7 Jan 1973

Charles BICKFORD [1891-1967]

Born: Cambridge, Massachusetts. Studies at The Massachusetts Institute of Technology, and work in burlesque and stock preceded his Broadway debut in 1919. When sound terrorized Hollywood, Bickford was one of the many stage players offered a movie contract. He made his debut in Dynamite (1930), the first of five films for Cecil B. DeMille:

That first working morning, I watched in fascination as [De Mille] mapped out the mechanics of the first scene. Every move he made found the script clerk, chair bearer and megaphone bearer moving with him like shadows, always but an arm's length behind him. They were trained to anticipate his every wish. If he wanted his megaphone, he had merely to extend his hand and it would be immediately placed in his grasp. If he were about to sit, he didn't look to see if the chair was there. He just sat....

The first scene was one in which I, about to be executed for a murder which I did not commit, say "Goodbye" to my nine-year-old sister [Muriel McCormac]. Needless to say, Sis and I love each other very, very much and the scene as written was pretty mawkish stuff. What happened next I wouldn't believe except that it happened to me.

I was in my dressing room awaiting the call to rehearse when suddenly all activity on the set abruptly ceased. I heard the first assistant call for, and get, utter silence. From somewhere came the sound of music — soft music, and played with consummate feeling. A spinet player and a fiddler were pulling out all the stops as they played that tried-and-true old tear-jerker, *Hearts and Flowers*.

A minute later an assistant director rapped discreetly on my door and in hushed tones said, "We're ready for you, Mr. Bickford."

Responding immediately, I blithely walked onto the set where everyone, including the crew, stood with doleful expressions and bowed heads. Putting two and two together, I jumped to the conclusion that a gag was being pulled on me because of the sentimentality of the scene I was about to play....

Going along with the joke I struck a pose and began to declaim, "Friends, Romans, countrymen...."

[DeMille] was really concerned at my flippancy and explained in solemn tones that the music...was necessary in order to create in me the proper degree of emotional intensity demanded by the scene.

Coming from the top producer-director of his time and delivered to an actor of my experience and standing, his statement was hardly to be taken seriously. Once again I suspected a rib. "You have to be kidding," I said.

Once again I was wrong. He was painfully serious. "I never joke where my work is concerned, Mr. Bickford. And that's what we're here for, to work. I have found that music is of material help in creating a mood."

Since to some extent we all use individual methods to obtain results and as this musical gimmick appeared to have worked for him, I was bound to respect it. On the other hand it could not possibly work for me, inspiring in me as it did nothing but derisive mirth. As I did not wish to be rude, insulting, or even mildly disrespectful, it was up to me to come up with an intelligent refute....

"To put it bluntly: if the time ever comes when I need this type of stimulus to make me act, I'll go back to swinging a pick for a living." [Bickford also worked on DeMille's *The Squaw Man* (1931), *This Day and Age* (1933), *The Plainsman* (1937) and *Reap the Wild Wind* (1942).]

As for my associates during the *Anna Christie* engagement [1932], I couldn't have asked for a more compatible group. Garbo was consistently charming. Those two old pros, Marie Dressler and George Marion were a delight to work with. The director, Clarence Brown, was an amiable gent. Frances Marion, who adapted the play for the screen, was intelligent and a charming woman. Irving Thalberg, personally supervising the production, was at all times constructively critical and consistently agreeable.

Complete harmony is rare on a movie set and had it not been for my lack of enthusiasm for the play and for the role, it would have been a perfect assignment.

—Bickford, in his *Bulls, Balls, Bicycles and Actors* (New York: Paul S. Eriksson, 1965)

Too many characters in too many pictures are single-track persons instead of well-rounded individuals. The best roles are those with varied qualities; the others are apt to be monotonous.... Clancy, the butler [in *The Farmer's Daughter* (1947, H.C. Potter)]...was a good example of this.... He was a warm, human person with a good sense of humor. He demonstrated this warmth by encouraging a romance between a maid in the house [Loretta Young] and the son of the family [Joseph Cotten]. Yet he showed how hard-boiled he could be by throwing a crooked politician bodily out of the house.

—Bickford, in *The Saturday Evening Post*, 25 Sept 1948

[In *Whirlpool* (1949, Otto Preminger)] I play a detective who is different from the radio and movie variety. He's an intelligent human being with education, a psychological approach to the problem, and sentiment which doesn't degenerate into sentimentality.

—Bickford, interviewed by Hedda Hopper for *The Chicago Tribune*, 1949

Karen BLACK [1942-]

Born: Karen Ziegler in Park Ridge, Illinois. Studies at Northwestern University and with Lee Strasberg at The Actors Studio, and work both on and off Broadway preceded her film debut in You're a Big Boy Now (1966, Francis Ford Coppola). In 1970, she played Rayette opposite Jack Nicholson in Bob Rafelson's Five Easy Pieces:

I loved Rayette. From the first time I read for the part I thought she was great. She's alive. Alive! And she has a way of being happy. The way she's happy is that she doesn't think too much. She's not stupid, she just doesn't think too much. She doesn't bother herself with significances — analyses and interpretations of what happens around her. All she knows is there's the man I love, there's my cat, there's the plant I'm feeding. And she wants her man to be faithful.

But the main thing about her is that she survives and bounces back. She cries a lot and does all those numbers, but she's always back. I guess when finally he left her she would have gone home and had her baby — if she were pregnant. I chose to not choose whether she was or not. I mean, I didn't consider that she was, because if she had been it would have been communicated to the audience somehow, and I didn't want that.

—Black, interviewed by Tim Mulligan for *Show*, May 1971

In his films, [Robert Altman] radio mikes you and you're not aware of where the camera is, and then you invent things. Most of the things I said in *Nashville* [1975] were totally improvised. He enjoys all that; he admires the process. He has a feeling about it, that it can't be right or wrong. It's just some strange poetry that exists. He doesn't pounce on you and you don't feel crowded or feel that he is watching you critically. He never says you play the line wrong; he lets you make your choices. He believes in what is true for you and that's all he's interested in. [She worked with Altman again on both stage and screen versions of *Come Back to the Five and Dime, Jimmy Dean, Jimmy Dean* (1982).]

—Black, interviewed by Doug Tomlinson at the press conference for the Broadway production of *Come Back to the 5 and Dime, Jimmy Dean, Jimmy Dean*, 19 Feb 1982

Faye [in *The Day of the Locust* (1975, John Schlesinger)] is a very abrupt girl. She's very unpredictable. You can only be that unpredictable if you're terribly well off or if you're not plugged in....

Q. Did you like working with Schlesinger?

A. I did, yes. He has an adorable personality. He always seems to be letting you in on some secret or another. I think he may be, but I was never sure. It's like telling you something only for you. It's very private. He's a man who has a very high standard. He cares a terrific amount if the standard is reached.

—Black, interviewed by Peter Lester for *Interview*, May 1975

Robert BLAKE [1934-]

Born: Michael Gubitosi in Nutley, New Jersey. A part of the family act, "The Three Little Hillbillies" from age two, he entered the film industry in an Our Gang short before making his feature film debut in Andy Hardy's Double Life (1943, George Seitz). In 1947, he worked opposite John Garfield in Jean Negulesco's Humoresque:

Q. Of all the actors you worked with as a child, who made the biggest impression on you?

A. I only made one picture with John Garfield, but it would have to be him. It was *Humoresque*, and I played him as a boy. He taught me a lot about acting and about life. I remember I had a real tough scene in the movie. I was out on a fire escape, but of course, it was on a sound stage, and there was all this activity around. It was a tough scene, and I couldn't concentrate because of the crew moving around. Garfield just happened to be there, you know, sort of looking things over. He saw the trouble I was in, and he cleared the set. I mean, he cleared the entire sound stage. If you can imagine it, there was not a soul there but him and me. He just looked at me and said, "OK, kid, play the scene."

And so I went through it a couple of times, and it was fine. And he said to me, "Just remember, you're an actor. None of these people would be working without you. Respect yourself, and respect your art."

—Blake, interviewed by Bruce Cook for *American Film*, Dec 1978/Jan 1979

It's part of an actor's job to interpret the unconscious of the author. What I felt Truman [Capote] was really writing about in [*In*] *Cold Blood* [1967, Richard Brooks] was this: Everybody knows what a murderer is a millionth of a second after he pulls the trigger. But what is he a millionth of a second *before* he pulls the trigger? I don't think anybody has an answer to it. It's not as simple as asking what makes a person kill or what the neurotic elements are that lead a person to become a murderer.

—Blake, interviewed by Lawrence Linderman and Karen Colaianni Johnson for *Playboy*, June 1977

Joan BLONDELL [1909-1979]

Born: New York City. Touring with the family vaudeville act preceded a career on Broadway. Her role opposite James Cagney in Penny Arcade (1929) led to both being brought to Hollywood for the film version (Sinner's Holiday — 1930, John Adolfi); this successful teaming was repeated in six more films. She appeared in five films either directed or choreographed by Busby Berkeley, beginning with Golddiggers of 1933 (1933, Mervyn LeRoy):

[Berkeley] was marvelous. He was a ringmaster, there was no question of that, but everyone was young, and happy; it was kind of hard, really. The hours were long, but he knew exactly what he wanted and had everything coordinated in his mind. There was nothing rattled about it at all. It was just done — one, two, three — precisely.

—Blondell, interviewed by Leonard Maltin for *Film Fan Monthly*, Sept 1969

[Berkeley] was a wild man — he had to be. He had to do insane shots. Three story-high stages were built for him — you know, you could hardly see him up there. He'd begin on an "S" with two little birds and then pull back and go round that set with 500 girls and 200 pianos, etc., and then come right back up again and sit down on those birds. But he was fabulous. He was strict, but he had to be because he had a mass of things to organize. He rehearsed crazily, like a general with an army. But I always liked him very much and found him fun. [She also worked with Berkeley on *Footlight Parade* (1933, Lloyd Bacon), *Dames* (1934, Ray Enright), *Stagestruck* (1937, Busby Berkeley) and *Golddiggers of 1937* (1937, Lloyd Bacon).]

It was difficult, working and having children. I made six pictures carrying my son and eight with my daughter. They'd get me behind desks and tables and things to hide my tummy! I'd have off about two weeks to have the poor child and then get right back to work. The only other vacation I had was in the middle of a picture called *Back in Circulation* [1937, Ray Enright] with Pat O'Brien. My appendix blew up and they took me to the hospital. Well, the shooting was nearly over and they wanted me to start in on another one, but the doctor said I couldn't leave the hospital. They made a deal with the doctor to take me by stretcher to my house up on Lookout Mountain, and they had the set designer come and make what looked like the scene we were in when my appendix burst. There was a crew of sixty up there — sound and cameras and everything — and they changed the end of the story so I could be sick in bed! They didn't waste any time at all with me!

—Blondell, interviewed by John Kobal for *Focus on Film*, Spring 1976

Thank God censorship has improved since then. They cut the best scene in the picture [*A Tree Grows in Brooklyn* (1945, Elia Kazan)]....

Aunt Cissy, who is a very sweet, good woman, works in a rubber factory. Her profession is kept very quiet by everybody in the family. She takes the colorful tins the contraceptives are placed in — they have girls' faces on them and names like Agnes or Betsy — and gives them to the children to play with.

One day she accidently leaves a rubber in a tin. The little boy [Ted Donaldson] asks me about it, and in the most beautiful writing the author, Betty Smith, did, Cissy tries to explain to the children what the rubber is; not by talking about the actual thing, but about love and life itself. It was very simply done, and all of us players hugged each other spontaneously at the end of the scene. It was marvelous and the Legion of Decency made us take it out.

—Blondell, interviewed by Charles Higham for *The New York Times*, 20 Aug 1972

I'm from the one-two-kick school of acting, and this movie [*Opening Night* (1977, John Cassavetes)] threw me for a loop at first....

You never know where the camera is; Cassavetes follows you around the corner, into the phone booth, under the bed, everywhere. I couldn't tell when the actors were having a private conversation and when they were actually changing the lines of the script. They were always so *natural.* I must say, it's lovely not having to stick to all the author's ifs, ands and buts....

But don't ask me if *Opening Night* is supposed to be a comedy or a drama. I'll have to see it before I can tell.

—Blondell, interviewed by Guy Flatley for *The New York Times*, 11 Feb 1977

Claire BLOOM [1931-]

Born: North Finchley, London, England. Studies at The Guildhall School of Music and Drama and The Central School of Speech and Drama in London and work on radio and the stage preceded her film debut in The Blind Goddess *(1948, Harold French). Her second film was Charles Chaplin's* Limelight *(1952):*

The weather [in Los Angeles] was always fine and so we rehearsed in the garden of their house, Chaplin, Jerry Epstein, and I. Chaplin was the same director he'd been at the screen test: he told me what to do, I did it. He was never in repose for a moment, always moving, demonstrating a gesture, setting a scene, explaining a shot, always trying to make me aware of (so that in the end I would take for granted) the nearness of the camera. He asked for certain effects that to me seemed raw and naive and outdated. But they were his style, as much a part of the performer as his cane and his bowler, and now he expected these effects from me. Willing and eager — and adoring — I gave myself over to them and to him. I saw how clear to him was every nuance of the performance as it would register on the movie screen. Nothing was left to chance. There was no such thing as chance. There was only his genius....

The arrival of Buster Keaton was greatly anticipated by us all. He hadn't been in films for many years and was to appear with Chaplin in the final theatre sequence — Keaton as a nearsighted and cracked professor of the keyboard, Chaplin as an inspired and cracked violinist. Keaton was fifty-six when he made *Limelight*, but gave the impression of having suffered through a life twice that long. From his lined face and grave expression one would have thought that he had neither known a lighthearted moment nor was able to instigate one. His reserve was extreme, as was his isolation. He remained to himself on the set, until one day, to my astonishment, he took from his pocket a colour postcard of a large Hollywood mansion and showed it to me. It was the sort of postcard that tourists pick up in Hollywood drugstores. In the friendliest, most intimate way, he explained to me that it had once been his home. That was it. He retreated back into silence and never addressed a word to me again. In his scene with Chaplin, however, he was brilliantly alive with invention. Some of his gags may even have been a little too incandescent for Chaplin, because, laugh as he did at the rushes in the screening room, Chaplin didn't see fit to allow them all into the final version of the film.

—Bloom, in her *Limelight and After* (New York: Harper & Row, 1982)

Ann BLYTH [1928-]

Born: Mt. Kisco, N.Y. Work on radio (from age 5) and on Broadway (from age 13) preceded her screen debut in Chip Off the Old Block *(1944, Charles Lamont). She received her first major role the following year as Veda in Michael Curtiz'* Mildred Pierce:

After [*Mildred Pierce*] was released people constantly stopped me on the street to tell me how awful I was. Some of them added such stormy statements as "I could have slapped your face...."

All this criticism made me very happy. For as Veda I was supposed to be just as irritatingly obnoxious as the criticism suggests. Thus, the harsher the comments, the better I liked them.

The role itself was an actress' dream, full of wonderful variations. At one minute the audience might think Veda was to be pitied, but soon afterward they would be despising her for her greediness and plain brattishness. Even when Veda was outwardly charming, I had to play her so the audience would know she could never be anything but bad.

Although I still don't know how she managed it, Joan Crawford made me feel completely at ease.... She was wonderful to me.

—Blyth, in *The Saturday Evening Post*, 25 Mar 1950

I'll always be grateful to Mike [Curtiz]. From the time he first cast me against my type in *Mildred Pierce*, he's never lost faith in me as an actress.

I've discovered it's impossible to please all of the people all of the time. Some people feel I should cut down the 'sweetness and light,' while others feel I should never play a shady lady. Certainly, I don't want to make a career of playing 'scarlet women' on the screen, nor would I ever want to become identified with a series of unsavory characters. But Helen [in *The Helen Morgan Story* (1957, Michael Curtiz)], I feel, was neither.

She was a woman who yearned for affection in her early life and later, when great professional success came to her, it was as if she sought to buy her way into people's hearts. She was generous to the point that she would give blank checks to acquaintances in need, and she let her heart run away with her head in more important matters. She was constantly falling in love with the wrong man, but she was sincere in her love. That they weren't good for her couldn't change her feeling toward them. I don't think she had any great, driving ambition, but rather had a great loneliness which she tried to get rid of by surrounding herself with 'bought' friends. Although she had a magnificent talent, she felt insecure with it, and I think this insecurity led her finally down the alcoholic trail to where she literally drank herself to death.

There was no meanness in Helen Morgan, only sadness. She wasn't a bad woman, but a good woman who lost her way. I've met many people who've had part of Helen Morgan in them, particularly in Hollywood. People, who have that same loneliness, that same insecurity, people without an anchor, without a faith, who have plenty of money to buy whatever they need or want except the things that money can't buy — love and friends. I feel sorry for these people, just as I felt sorry for Helen Morgan — but I don't call them bad....

We don't dwell too long or too brutally on the rougher aspects of Helen's life. Mike Curtiz felt, and I believe rightly so, that if it were a choice between entertainment quality or just piling on stark reality, the former should be chosen. After all, no *one* motion picture can really do full justice to a person's life.

—Blyth, interviewed by Dick Sheppard for *Photoplay Magazine*, Dec 1957

Eleanor BOARDMAN [1898-1991]

Born: Philadelphia. Work as a model for Eastman Kodak and studies at The Academy of Fine Arts in Philadelphia preceded her film debut in The Stranger's Banquet (1922, Marshall Neilan). In 1923, she played Rena Fairchild/Sydney Fairchild in Three Wise Fools, the first of six films she made with King Vidor, to whom she was married from 1926-1933. In 1928, she played Mary in Vidor's The Crowd:

I worked more with Vidor than with any other director so perhaps I paid more attention to his direction.... As a director, he was very quiet and he talked more about the mood of the scene. He was very clever inasmuch as he didn't take a lot of footage that he wasn't going to use.... We wouldn't have a rehearsal. Very often, we'd end up using the first take instead of the second or third.

Vidor always studies reality to make everything believable about a scene and to make the audience feel it. Being from Galveston, Texas, he's a bit inarticulate. He's a man who doesn't speak very much but he feels.

When we made *The Crowd*, Vidor knew pretty much what he wanted. He wanted a boy and a girl going through life with difficulties, living without any money, trying to make a go of life in America without education or background. I played the feminine lead and James Murray was the leading man....

I didn't wear any make-up in *The Crowd*. I wasn't allowed to dress in anything but rags — no glamour at all. It helped to make it up to date. [Her third film with Vidor was *Bardelys the Magnificent* (1926).]

—Boardman, interviewed 1980 by William M. Drew for *Speaking of Silents: First Ladies of the Screen* (Vestal, N.Y.: The Vestal Press, 1989)

Dirk BOGARDE [1921-]

Born: Derek van den Bogaerde in Hampstead, England. After beginning a career as a scenic designer and commercial artist, he joined The Amersham Repertory Company in 1939. After Word War II service in Army intelligence, he made his film debut in a bit part in Dancing with Crime (1947, John P. Carstairs). In 1963, he played Barrett in The Servant, the first of four films with Joseph Losey:

Every film which I had made before this, with very few exceptions, was timed by a stop-watch. That is to say, every look, every move, every gesture even, every speech and even a run-along-a-busy-street was ruled by the vicious, staggering move of the stop-watch hand. Films cost money.

Time is money. Waste, even intelligent waste, was not tolerated....

With Losey there was none of this. No frantic cry from the Script Girl that a scene, a speech, a move even, had overrun its time; it was a sublime luxury. Not a form of self-indulgence (that is to be avoided at all costs, it is both false and ugly to watch) but an exhilarating form of developing someone else, of letting another person, so to speak, inhabit the empty vessels of one's body and mind. Under Losey's shrewd, watching eye, and with Bumble Dawson's simple, brilliant, designs for the clothes he would wear and live in, we started together to build the character of Barrett.

It is important to make it clear at this juncture that a brilliant designer, and Bumble was one of the very best, has a great deal to do with an actor's performance. I am an actor who works from the outside in, rather than the reverse. Once I can wear the clothes which my alter-ego has chosen to wear, then I begin the process of his development from inside the layers. Each item selected by her was carefully chosen by Losey, down to the tie-pin: a tight, shiny, blue serge suit, black shoes which squeaked a little, lending a disturbing sense of secret arrival, pork-pie hat with a jay's feather, a Fair Isle sweater, shrunken, darned at the elbows, a nylon scarf with horses' heads and stirrups. A mean, shabby outfit for a mean and shabby man.

For me the most important element of the wardrobe are always the shoes. From the shoes I can find the walk I must use; from the walk comes the stance, since naturally the spine is balanced on the feet. From the stance the shoulders may sag or become hunched, the neck might be thinly erect, or slip suggestively to one side or the other, the arms hang or are braced. In the chosen clothes one's body starts to form another's; another person walks and breathes in the shabby, serge suit. The whole is carried by the softly squeaking shoes. Thus the shape is arrived at; the physical frame.

Next the detail. Brylcreemed hair, flat to the head, a little scurfy round the back and in the parting, white puddingy face, damp hands (arms which hang loosely often have damp hands at their extremities, I don't know why). Glazed, aggrieved eyes, and then the walk to blend the assembly together. These details are always obtained from observing other people; an extension of my father's childhood game of "Pots and Pans." Always examine, question, the little things which go to make up human behavior....

Like all the greatest directors, Losey never tells one what to do, or how to do it. Ever. Only what not to do. Which is very different. You give him your character and he will watch it develop, encouraging or modifying, always taking what is offered and using it deftly. You only know that you have done it to his ultimate satisfaction when he says, "Print!" at the end of a take. There is no waste of chatter, no great in-depth discussions about motivation, no mumbo-jumbo about identification, soul, or truth....

—Bogarde, in his *Snakes and Ladders* (London: Chatto and Windus, 1978)

From my point of view, [*The Servant*] cost me very little emotionally, because I'm nothing to do with the man I played. So therefore it was much easier to expand my realms of fantasy and imagination and become a north country bastard called Barrett.

It was much harder to be in *Accident* [1967], because that *has* got something to do with me. I think it's the best film Losey and I have made together, although I don't know whether he'd agree with me. In *Accident* I had to sublimate my own personal feelings, because I don't believe in actors *being* — actors have got to act. So there I had to take the essence of my own feeling, and act it. *Accident* was close to me. Barrett in *The Servant* wasn't. I knew about that kind of man, and his compulsion to dominate. I'd seen it happen. I had a batman in the war. He was from a brass foundry in the north of England. He was like Barrett.... Later in life, I had a servant of my own and he was another Barrett.... He said to my parents, "Never mind — I'll make a proper little gentleman of him yet." That was when I was at least 30. He had shoes that squeaked. He had hair like Barrett. I modelled the whole performance on him.

The character in *Accident*, as distinct from a gentleman, is really a *gentle* man. A loser-out. A quiet man who is lost and settles for something. I'm a loser, but we all are, aren't we? I'm a loser in hundreds of ways....

—Bogarde, interviewed by Gordon Gow for *Films & Filming*, May 1971

Each one [of the four films which I made with Losey] was a bitter, exhausting, desperate battle. It never got any better; only Losey's obstinacy, determination, belief, optimism and unflagging courage managed to get us through; that coupled with a crew who also believed and a growing company, as he called it, of actors who were also prepared to put money second to career. In order to get any of these films made we all had to work for very modest salaries with the vague promises of percentages which we were seldom to see. No one got rich, in any possible degree from these enterprises. But we were enriched in our values; and that is what mattered most to us all.... [Bogarde's other films with Losey were *King and Country* (1964) and *Modesty Blaise* (1966).]

—Bogarde, in his *Snakes and Ladders* (London: Chatto and Windus, 1978)

[In *The Fixer* (1968, John Frankenheimer)] I defend the Jew [Alan Bates] accused of the ritual murder of a child. I switched it slightly; used that *King and Country* exasperated lawyer character again. It's a very small part, but lovely. We changed the attorney from a bourgeois to a more aristocratic man, just to point up that not only is the Jew of this story doomed, but also the aristocrat and his class.

—Bogarde, interviewed by Liz Smith for *The New York Times*, 11 Feb 1968

I put all the clothes and the shoes that I wore for the character [in *Accident*] into a trunk and locked them up. I wore them later in *Justine* [1969, George Cukor], the whole gear.... Pursewarden was a different man. Yet the same sort of man. I tried to do as much for Lawrence Durrell's original writing as the Americans tried to undo. I tried to stay faithful to Durrell. Pursewarden in *Justine* was very much a failure, a losing man. So the clothes that I had worn for *Accident* fitted him very well.

—Bogarde, interviewed by Gordon Gow for *Films & Filming*, May 1971

Providence [1977, Alain Resnais] was about one long night in the life of a dying novelist [John Gielgud] who, racked with pain, filled with drink and pills, is struggling to create a new work. Using the members of his family for his characters; muddled with the past, in terror of the future, filled with anger, spleen, and guilt, aware of swiftly approaching death.

"How am I going to play this cold rage-less barrister my father has invented?" I asked Resnais. "Obviously he is detested for some reason so I suppose that he must show detestable signs? Have I got that right?" I was never absolutely certain.

Resnais smiled his cool Breton smile, shrugged, spread his hands; inferring, in those eloquent movements, that it was up to me to work it out.

I was very perplexed; but suddenly I hit on an idea that I should play the role for him in three different ways, and whichever performance of the role he liked, and thought correct, we would stick with.

"You could play it three different ways?"

"I think so. Let's try. I'll play it absolutely straight — cold, attacking barrister; then in the style of, well...Congreve, the Restoration comedies; and then I'll give you my impersonation of Rex Harrison being bloody. Which shall we try first?"

I think that it was really the only time that I saw Resnais laugh with pleasure. But he also considered the suggestion with care. He was undecided how it should be played himself.

We did the scene three times, as suggested. He thought the Rex Harrison effort was possibly going a little too far, although it was funny, and finally settled for the high style of Restoration to begin with, mixed with the cold, attacking barrister, and here and there he suggested that I might add a pinch, just a pinch, of Rex Harrison. Which when I did always broke him up, to such an extent that he once fell off a chair.

I had started to shape my character, bearing in mind at all times that I must carry with it echoes and traces of Gielgud's *own* personality. Like father, then like son.

—Bogarde, in his *Snakes and Ladders* (London: Chatto and Windus, 1978)

Everyone came up to the house to have lunch and "iron out the bumps" in the script [of *Despair* (1979) Rainer Werner Fassbinder's first English language film]. We sat round the tin table, pencils posed, scripts before us, while Mr. [Tom] Stoppard feverishly re-wrote passages and then read them, eagerly aloud, while Fassbinder shrugged from time to time, showing a marked indifference to what was going on, and frequently yawned.

It was perfectly clear to me, after half an hour of this, that he would make *his* version of *Despair*, when the time came, and do exactly what he wanted. Which is precisely what he did....

If Rainer had a fault it was that he found it completely impossible to concentrate, think, or create, in anything which remotely approximated silence. He had to work in a vortex of sound: torrents of sound; it was something with which one quickly came to terms. Or perished.

From the moment that he roared up to the set (wherever it was) in his vastly expensive motorcar, until the moment that he left, usually far later than the rest of us for he stayed on writing, planning, and setting up, in detailed drawings, his shots for the next day, he worked in a shuddering blast of music. Maria Callas at full pitch in both

"Tosca" and "Norma"; sometimes, as a light relief, the entire score of "Evita", which made the very air vibrate, on other occasions "Der Rosenkavalier" over and over again.

A very different atmosphere to the saintly, cloistered, hush which had reigned at all times on *Providence*.

But then this was a film about madness; perhaps it all helped....

Rainer's work was extraordinarily similar to that of [Luchino] Visconti's; despite their age difference, they both behaved, on set, in much the same manner. Both had an incredible knowledge of the camera: the first essential. Both knew how it could be made to function; they had the same feeling for movement on the screen, of the all-important (and often-neglected) "pacing" of a film, from start to finish, of composition, of texture, and probably most of all they shared that strange ability to explore and probe into the very depths of character which one had offered them.

They took what one gave and built upon it, layer upon layer of physical and mental strata, so that eventually, together, we could produce a man, entire. Plus soul.

Exhausting, exhilarating, rewarding and draining, finally. But that was the way that I liked my cinema. It was the only way I could really work. [Bogarde worked with Visconti on *The Damned* (1969) and *Death in Venice* (1971).]

—Bogarde, in his *An Orderly Man* (London: Chatto & Windus, 1983)

Humphrey BOGART [1899-1957]

Born: New York City. A term in the U.S. Navy and work on Broadway preceded his film debut in the short film Broadway's Like That (1929, Murray Roth). He began a screen career as a hoodlum in The Petrified Forest (1936) as Duke Mantee, a role he had played on the Broadway stage:

Leslie Howard and I played our respective parts for a year and a half, but when Warners' bought the screen rights and signed up Leslie Howard they tested several actors for the Mantee part, and finally settled on Edward G. Robinson, who had won a reputation in tough-guy roles. Unhappy about this, I cabled Leslie, who was in Scotland, and he promptly informed the studio that if I didn't play Mantee, he would not play either. So I got the job.

Duke was my first heavy role, and I like heavies, having no desire to be sympathetic or romantic. Roles like those Van Johnson gets would give me the screaming meemies. Good people in pictures are often dull; besides, heavy roles do more for an actor....

A particularly pleasant feature about playing Mantee was that Director Archie Mayo let me do the part with stage technique. This is rare in translating stage parts to the screen, because many people think stage technique is all wrong for pictures. There was, too, the pleasure of working with people I had been with before — Howard and Bette Davis, with whom I had played in her first picture, *Bad Sister* [1931, Hobart Henley]. [He played opposite Davis again in *Marked Woman* (1937, Lloyd Bacon), *Kid Galahad* (1937, Michael Curtiz) and *Dark Victory* (1939, Edmund Goulding).]

—Bogart, in *The Saturday Evening Post*, 14 Dec 1946

Speaking of *The Roaring Twenties* [1939, Raoul Walsh], I did a scene in that which, I understand, makes strong men sicken. Scene where Jeffrey Lynn and I are in the trenches, remember, and Jeff takes a bead on a German soldier, a mere kid...and says to me, "I can't do it, he's not more than fifteen," and I say "Yeah, well, he'll never see sixteen" — and let him have it. Remember that? Why, even guys at the studio thought I'd better cut that scene. But not me. I never soften my roles.

I won't be a phony in my characterization and pat little kiddies on the head before I bop 'em off just to appeal to the Molls. Not me. I don't care if fans think I'm tough. I don't have to care.... I'm never placed in the position where I'm the "draw." I say an actor should do only what he's hired to do. He shouldn't "soften" his job. I don't care what people think about me, say about me or print about me. I'm the heavy and it won't hurt a bit. I can take it.

—Bogart, interviewed by Gladys Hall for *Motion Picture*, Apr 1940

[Audiences have] seen me with my face set hard for gangster roles and don't stop to think that maybe there's a trick to setting it hard, and that I can unset it, too. Anyway, even a sour-puss can have a sense of humor. That's what I liked about *It All Came True* [1940, Lewis Seiler]. It gave me a chance to prove it. Mind you, I'm no wit. I've got to have some very brilliant man write me devastating things to say. I'm no clown, but a lot of things strike me terribly funny.

—Bogart, interviewed by George Benjamin for *Modern Screen*, Dec 1940

I am not, by nature, an adventurous man. I do not seek danger and discomfort. But I believed so strongly in the story of *The African Queen* [1951] that I welcomed the chance to make the picture in Nairobi, Africa, with Katharine Hepburn, Director John Huston and a great crew. We all believed in the honesty and charm of the story. And I wanted to get out of that trench coat I wear in the movies whether I'm a heel or a saint and whether I go out to murder or to save humanity.

—Bogart, in *The American Weekly*, 31 Aug 1952

That Huston, there's the only real genius in Hollywood, a real poet. But he's murder to work with during the last three weeks of shooting. Always restless, wanting to quit for some new idea. [Bogart worked on five other Huston films: *The Maltese Falcon* (1941), *Across the Pacific* (1942), *The Treasure of the Sierra Madre* (1948), *Key Largo* (1949) and *Beat the Devil* (1953).]

—Bogart, interviewed by Howard Thompson for *The New York Times*, 2 Mar 1952

Ernest BORGNINE [1917-]

Born: Ermes Borgnino in Hamden, Connecticut. After serving in the navy, he studied acting at The Randall School of Dramatic Art in Hartford through the G.I. Bill of Rights. Work with The Barter Theater in Abingdon, Virginia, preceded his film debut in The Mob *(1951, Robert Parrish). A significant experience came while observing co-star Spencer Tracy in* Bad Day at Black Rock *(1954, John Sturges):*

I'll never forget that long scene he did with Robert Ryan outside the gas station.... I said to myself, "How can an actor hide himself from the audience, just bending over and looking up occasionally?" I could see that Ryan was trying to do everything but drop his pants. But there was Mr. Tracy, this man was talking to the *ground*, for Christ's sake, and only once in a while would he look up. I never saw anybody do that, just talking to the ground, and everyone's attention was riveted on *him*. It was just right for the character of Macreedy and Mr. Tracy thought up that way of doing it.

—Borgnine, interviewed by Bill Davidson for *Spencer Tracy: Tragic Idol* (New York: E.P. Dutton, 1987)

[Delbert] Mann knew me from live television plays he had directed in New York, and he thought I could play Marty [in *Marty* (1955)]. But [playwright Paddy] Chayefsky was skeptical and the role certainly was a far cry from the bad-guy parts I had just been doing in Hollywood.

I had to get the western twang out of my voice and start talking like a Bronx butcher before Chayefsky would listen. Then I auditioned by reading practically the whole script aloud, with Paddy himself reading all the other parts.

After a while we got to the point where my old Italian mother [Esther Minciotti] in the story is encouraging Marty to overcome his shyness and get out and meet some girls. She tells him, "Go on, put on your blue suit and go down there. You'll meet a lot of tomatoes." And Marty looks at her with his whole soul in his eyes and says, "All right, I'll put on my blue suit, but you know what I'll get from it? A broken heart. Maw, I'm just an ugly, ugly man!" Right at that point the role got under my skin so much that I turned around and started to bawl. And when I turned back and looked at Chayefsky a moment later, he was crying. And so was Delbert Mann. And at that instant I said to myself, "You've got it!"

—Borgnine, interviewed by Clyde Gilmour for *The Toronto Star*, 2 Dec 1972

Richard Brooks, the director [of *The Catered Affair* (1956)] had a reputation for eating actors alive. Bette [Davis] and I were working on our first scene together and there was something wrong with it. I realized it was the timing and suggested to Bette that we pace the scene differently. It worked. Brooks was astonished; in fact, he was furious. He called me a goddam thinking actor and Bette and I were pretty much on our own after that.

—Borgnine, interviewed by Arthur Bell for *The New York Times*, 17 June 1973

I had been working on a picture called *The Split* [1968, Gordon Flemyng] with Gene Hackman and Warren Oates just prior to doing *Wild Bunch* [1969, Sam Peckinpah]. I had signed to do *Wild Bunch* because I had never had the opportunity to work with Bill Holden before. So one day Warren, who had worked with Peckinpah [twice previously — *Ride the Wild Country* (1961) and *Major Dundee* (1964)], said to me only half-joking, "Wait till you meet that guy Peckinpah. He'll eat you alive!".... By total chance as we were finishing *The Split*...I broke a bone in my foot. So in order to fulfill my commitment to

Wild Bunch, I had them fit me with a walking cast on my left foot....

The way the picture was to open we were supposed to look like soldiers while in reality we were going to rob this railway office. And fortunately, the military leggings we had to wear fit right over the cast and special boot I had to have on. So except for a slight limp, you'd never know it was there.

Then we started shooting, and although we didn't shoot the picture in sequence, this particular thing with us dressed up as soldiers that opens the picture was scheduled first. Well, getting me inside the railway office was no trouble, but getting me out and across the street while there's this war going on with the bounty hunters who had ambushed us — that presented more of a problem. So Sam came up to me and said, "Borgnine, how in the Christ are we going to get you across that street?" And I said, "Will you leave it to me?" And he said, "What do you have in mind?" I said: "Just leave it to me. Crank your cameras and I'll be okay." So he said, "Okay, go ahead," and walked away.

Well, they started to roll the cameras, and I came out of that office and jumped behind that bloody watering trough. Then when I got the signal to move, I rolled across the street to where the horses were, firing at the same time. So when it was over, Sam came up to me with this big grin on his face and he says, "Ya lovable son of a bitch, that was great! Thank you!" That was all. But I had passed the test, and we never had a harsh word between us.

—Borgnine, interviewed by Garner Simmons for *Peckinpah: A Portrait in Montage* (Austin: The University of Texas Press, 1982)

What I do is so devilishly easy. No Stanislavsky. I don't chart out the life histories of the people I play. If I did, I'd be in trouble. I work with my heart and my head and naturally my emotions follow. Like for *Emperor* [*of the North* (1973, Robert Aldrich)], I said to myself, "You're an ugly sonofabitch" and really uglied myself up inside. Then, when we were ready to shoot, I prayed to the good Lord above and started to curse because it took cursing to put me in the mood.

—Borgnine, interviewed by Arthur Bell for *The New York Times*, 17 June 1973

Charles BOYER [1897-1978]

Born: Figeac, France. Philosophy studies at The Sorbonne, drama studies at The Paris Conservatory, and work on the stage (from 1920) preceded his film debut in L'Homme du Large (1920, Marcel L'Herbier). In Hollywood from 1929; in 1937, he played Napoleon opposite Greta Garbo as Marie Walewska in Clarence Brown's Conquest:

It was [Napoleon's great devotion to a cause] which made my job easier. You see, there were certain periods in my life when I could not escape from the set pattern which I had mapped out for myself. Many times there were temptations trying to tear me away, but always there was something inside me which forced me to live out the years of the particular devotion which engrossed me. So you see I had sympathy with Napoleon. My parallel is, of course, in no way comparable to his, but it did help me.

—Boyer, interviewed by Anita Kilore in an unsourced, undated article in files of The New York Public Library for the Performing Arts

I am a man of many loves in *Hold Back the Dawn* [1941, Mitchell Leisen] — a sort of international "heel" — a man who lives by his wits and his way with women....

Frankly, I was worried about playing a role which could be compared to my Pepe le Moko in *Algiers* [1938, John Cromwell]. But when Mitchell Leisen told me the entire story...how the rogue, Georges, who has many loves, is at last taught the meaning of true love by the sweet unsophisticated Emmy [Olivia De Havilland], then I knew that the role promised to be one of the best I have ever had.

—Boyer, in the pressbook for *Hold Back the Dawn* (Paramount Studios, 1941)

It is because men like Duc in *All This and Heaven, Too* [1940, Anatole Litvak], Michel in *Love Affair* [1939, Leo McCarey], Georges in *Hold Back the Dawn*...have light and shade to them, that I like to play them. They are men that are human. We all have light and shade to us. We all have weaknesses and strengths, capacities for good and for evil....

However, I say that most of the men I have played on the screen have been heels. Georges...is a simon-pure heel, until almost the end.

I would not like to play a character who was one hundred per cent cad and remained so because there is no such man. I believe there is so much good in the worst of us and so much bad in the best of us.... If Georges had not changed, I would not have attempted him because I am a believer that the movies should give us something to dream about and something to lift us. As we should give each other something to dream about, we should try to lift each other up when we can. I would always refuse to do something I felt would be definitely harmful, something that would set a bad example and an influence in the wrong way.

—Boyer, interviewed by Gladys Hall for *Motion Picture*; in an undated clipping in the files of The New York Public Library for the Performing Arts

I knew very little about [Ingrid Bergman] actually when we first met on the set of *Gaslight* [1944, George Cukor]. I had seen her pictures, and listened to people talk about her, and I was naturally very curious....

She was more like the European women with whom I had worked in Paris. Her first concern was her role, the woman she must portray. She was to play a wife who believed she was going crazy, and for preparation she had read a formidable number of books on psychiatry.

With the first scenes I discovered that she is the most daring performer I have ever known. Ingrid will stop at nothing to keep her performance from being even faintly phony....

—Boyer, as told to Howard Sharpe for *Modern Screen*, May 1947

Lorraine BRACCO [1955-]

Born: Brooklyn, N.Y. Work as a model in Europe and studies with Stella Adler and at The Actors Studio in N.Y. preceded her American film debut as Ellie in Ridley Scott's Someone to Watch Over Me (1987):

The importance of my character is coping with being alone. Women know what it is to be in that situation — left alone with a child to bring up in this world. It's life and it's tough and it's hard out there. I wanted to play it truthfully — without the music and hearts and flowers....

When I read the script, I thought: "I know her, I can do her." She was supposed to be the victim, but I said I would never stand for that — I'd kick and scream and fight and yell. I'm a real New Yorker that way. I think they chose me because of my temperament.

—Bracco, interviewed by Nina Darnton for *The New York Post*, 12 Oct 1987

I made a conscious choice not to meet [the real Karen Hill in preparation for *GoodFellas* (1990, Martin Scorsese)]. I thought it would be better if the creation came from me. I used her life with her parents as an emotional guideline for the role. Sh was really repressed as a child, coming from an Orthodox Jewish background, and marrying Henry Hill [Ray Liotta] when she was 19 was all about her breaking out and doing what she wanted to feel good. She married him and stayed with him for all the wrong reasons. She was a mentally abused woman who felt she had no place to go. She would have considered divorce more of a failure than a salvation.

—Bracco, interviewed by Alex Witchel for *The New York Times*, 27 Sept 1990

If I didn't make my work [in *GoodFellas*] important, it would probably end up on the cutting room floor. Marty said to me, "I know you think I only make men's movies, but I really like this character Karen." But I think if push came to shove, if the performance wasn't there, he would have geared the film more to Ray and the boys, so I felt a little bit of extra pressure on me.

— Bracco, interviewed by Susan Linfield for *The New York Times*, 16 Sept 1990

Eddie BRACKEN [1920-]

Born: Astoria, N.Y. A child star on the vaudeville and nightclub stages, he made his film debut in the comedy short series, Our Gang. Following work on Broadway, he made his feature film debut in Too Many Girls (1940, George Abbott). In 1944, he made two films for Preston Sturges:

Two roles conceived by Preston Sturges, whom I consider the best writer and director in the movies, were the most enjoyable I ever portrayed. One was Norval Jones in *The Miracle of Morgan's Creek*, but my top choice is Woodrow Truesmith, the young marine in *Hail the Conquering Hero*, who was ashamed of his medical discharge and allowed some of his military buddies to maneuver him into passing as a hero. Since this hilarious story had plenty of seriousness in it, I got a chance to play some straight dramatic interludes — something every comedian yearns to do.

Woodrow was an almost foolproof part, the interpreting of it really easy. When Sturges writes a script, he doesn't draw his characters with words on paper; he paints them. Beyond that, his skillful directing and the gay, informal atmosphere he maintains on the set make every scene a delightful task. In between shots, he sits around telling amusing or dramatic stories from his own experience or deftly leading the others on to do so. He blends the actors, the extras and the crew members into a kind of big, amiable family.

Another factor contributing to the pleasure of the role was the presence in the cast of Bill Demarest, in my judgment, the most talented character actor on the screen. He stimulates you to do your best work; anybody in a scene with Bill has to work darn hard to be noticed at all.

—Bracken, in *The Saturday Evening Post*, 23 Feb 1946

Kenneth BRANAGH [1960-]

Born: Belfast, Ireland. Amateur theatrics and studies at The Royal Academy of Dramatic Art preceded work on the London stage. In 1989, he made his film debut as an actor/director with Henry V:

I wanted to make [Henry] as human as possible, but as vulnerable as possible. Because it was part of a film that wanted to boost morale, Olivier's performance [in *Henry V* (1945)] presented a tremendously resolved, glamorous, handsome hero. But the text indicates a man of doubt who has to suppress his own innate violence, who is volatile and unpredictable. I wanted to close in with the camera, to see the unsettled inner man, the flickers of uncertainty in his eyes. The medium allowed me to release that bit of performance. Harry just ain't black and white.

—Branagh, interviewed by Graham Fuller for *Film Comment*, Nov/Dec 1989

Klaus-Maria BRANDAUER [1944-]

Born: Ault Ausee, Austria. Studies at The Academy of Music and Dramatic Art in Stuttgart, West Germany and much work on the stages of West Germany and Austria preceded his film debut in The Salzburg Connection (1972, Otto Preminger). Returning to the stage, he did not make a second film until 1979. American acclaim came with his role as Baron Bror Blixen in Out of Africa (1986, Sydney Pollack):

I thought, what can I do to make this "baddie" interesting and believable? Then by accident I met the nephew of Bror Blixen, who described him as a wonderful person, a great hunter who had a wonderful relationship with nature — and even with Karen Blixen's lover, Denys Finch-Hatton. His nephew said, "Please do everything to make him charming, because he was a charming man." His wish really "covered" my own wish, so I tried "to make publicity" for Bror.

[After seeing Sydney Pollack play the agent in *Tootsie* (1983)] I had the feeling he must be able to understand the problems of actors, and I was right. It's hard to create a sense of family with several hundred people on location, but he did that in Africa.

We [Brandauer, Meryl Streep as Karen Blixen and Robert Redford as Denys Finch-Hatton] had a very simple relationship — no complications at all. I don't think you can make a movie alone. You need others to create a tension, a rapport, and they were wonderful. You have to have a personality, some kind of charisma on the screen that has nothing to do with the part or even the creating of the part. It's a presence, and they both have that.

—Brandauer, interviewed by Kevin Thomas for *The Los Angeles Times*; repr. in *The New York Post*, 1 Mar 1986

Marlon BRANDO [1924-]

Born: Omaha, Nebraska, where his mother ran a local drama group. Expelled from Shattuck Military Academy, he moved to N.Y. and studied acting with Stella Adler and at The Actors Studio. His portrayal of Stanley Kowalski in the Broadway version of Tennessee Williams' A Streetcar Named Desire brought him offers from Hollywood; he made his debut in The Men (1950, Fred Zinnemann), followed by the film version of Streetcar (1951, Elia Kazan):

Kowalski typified a personality to me that I hated and despised and thought completely destructive and dangerously ignorant. He was nasty, brutal, insensitive and wretched.

—Brando, interviewed for *Movie Play*, Sept 1956

[Kowalski] is intolerant, and selfish, a man without sensitivity, without any kind of morality.

—Brando, interviewed by Hyman Goldberg for *The New York Mirror Magazine*, 28 Oct 1962

[In *The Wild One* (1953, Laslo Benedek)] I'm a motorcycle hipster who hates authority, cornball and two-beat. What I really want is to go whaling [wailing?] all the time. I'm a real down hipster, if you dig me, who's aware of what's shaking. We're a fly bunch of boys who will do anything to defy the law. D'ya dig me?

—Brando, interviewed by J.W. Richardson for *Silver Screen*, July 1953

The making of *The Wild One* was a disappointment to me. There are so many kids who are confused today. This problem has not been intelligently articulated in entertainment today. *The Wild One* script ambled and was not focused. At that time Stanley Kramer was having difficulties with Columbia Studios and was not able to oversee the production as he usually did. [Kramer was the producer of Brando's debut, *The Men*].

—Brando, in an unsourced, undated article in the files of The New York Public Library for the Performing Arts

Playboy: Was [the cab scene with Rod Steiger in *On the Waterfront* (1954, Elia Kazan)] a well-rehearsed scene or did Kazan just put the two of you there to act spontaneously?

Brando: We improvised a lot. Kazan is the best actor's director you could ever want, because he was an actor himself.... He understands things that other directors do not. He also inspired me. Most actors are expected to come with their parts in their pockets and their emotions spring-loaded; when the director says, "OK, hit it," they go into a time slip. But Kazan brought a lot of things to the actor and he invited you to argue with him. He's one of the few directors creative and understanding enough to know where the actor's trying to go. He'd let you play a scene almost any way you'd want.

As it was written, you had this guy pulling a gun on his brother. I said, "That's not believable; I don't believe one brother would shoot the other." The script never prepared you for it, it just wasn't believable; it was incredible. So I did it as if he *couldn't* believe it, and that was incorporated into the scene.

—Brando, interviewed by Lawrence Grobel for *Playboy*, Jan 1979

I had to learn Japanese by rote, copying the inflections [for *The Teahouse of the August Moon* (1956, Daniel Mann)]. I have no feeling for the words. I'm flying blind as far as that is concerned. I would play many times a tape recording of my lines as spoken by a native. My teacher and I would repeat over and over again the same line until I could imitate him.

To learn broken English was just as difficult. I learned by listening to Japanese speak English. I found that they cannot say, F, L or R. My broken English is not too authentic. If it were too accurate no one in the United States would understand it. So I edited the broken English I heard to keep just enough of its flavor.

—Brando, interviewed by Ray Falk for *The New York Times*, 10 June 1956

A lot of directors want to know everything. Some directors don't want to know anything. Some directors wait for you to bring everything to them....

[Charlie] Chaplin [for whom he worked on *A Countess From Hong Kong* (1966)] is a man whose talent is such that you have to gamble. First off, comedy is his backyard. He's a genius, a cinematic genius. A comedic talent without peer. You don't know that he's senile. Personally, he's a dreadful person. I didn't care much for him. Nasty and sadistic and mean....

[John Huston — with whom he worked on *Reflections in a Golden Eye* (1967)]...listens. Some guys listen, some guys are auditory; some guys are visual. Some guys are both. He's an auditory guy and he can tell by the tone of your voice whether you're cracking or not. But he leaves you alone pretty good.

—Brando, interviewed by Chris Hodenfield for *Rolling Stone*, 20 May 1976

I'm glad Bob Evans gave me the part [of Don Corleone in *The Godfather* (1972, Francis Ford Coppola)] because I felt the picture made a useful commentary on corporate thinking in this country.... Because the Mafia patterned itself so closely on the corporation, and dealt in a hard-nosed way with money, and with politics, it prospered.... To me, a key phrase is that whenever they wanted to kill somebody it was always a matter of policy. Before pulling the trigger, they told him, "Just business. Nothing personal."

—Brando, interviewed by Shana Alexander for *Life*, 10 Mar 1972

Don Corleone is just any ordinary American business magnate who is trying to do the best he can for the group he represents and for his family. I think the tactics the Don used aren't much different from those General Motors used against

Ralph Nader. Unlike some corporate heads, Corleone has an unwavering loyalty for the people that have given support to him and his causes and he takes care of his own. He is a man of deep principle and the natural question arises as to how such a man can countenance the killing of people. But the American Government does the same thing for reasons that are not much different from those of the Mafia. And big business kills us all the time — with cars and cigarettes and pollution — and they do it knowingly.

—Brando, interviewed by Steve Saler for *Newsweek*, 13 Mar 1972

Shakespeare said something that was remarkable. You don't hear it very often. He said, "There is no art that finds the mind's construction on the face." Meaning that there is the art of poetry, music or dancing, architecture or painting, whatever. But to find people's minds by their face, especially their face, is an art and it's not recognized as an art.

[Bernardo] Bertolucci has that and so does Gillo Pontecorvo. Gadge [Kazan] also knows when things are in and when they're out.... He works viscerally and on instinct. Bertolucci is extraordinary in his ability to perceive...he's a poet. Some directors are difficult to work for; Gillo is very difficult to work for, very highly disciplined. But Bertolucci is easy to work for. [Brando worked with Bertolucci on *Last Tango in Paris* (1973) and with Pontecorvo on *Burn!* (1970).]

Q. Different intuitions? Different manipulations?

A. Definitely. Gillo has a very stringent and disciplined technique. Kazan would say "Go out and rehearse this scene and bring me something back." He takes about eight points out of 12 or 11, and you argue with him. He'll give you points and there's no ego involved. He's a guy that works without ego. There might be a difference of interpretation. But he's got the last word on that. That's the director's privilege.

—Brando, interviewed by Chris Hodenfield for *Rolling Stone*, 20 May 1976

For the first 20 pages of script [of *The Missouri Breaks* (1976, Arthur Penn)], I'm the character everyone is talking about. "He's coming, he's coming." On page 21, I arrive.... Poor Jack Nicholson. He's right at the center, cranking the whole thing out, while I'm zipping around like a firefly. I wanted the character to be different, a serious study of the American Indian. But Arthur Penn said, "Gee, Marlon, not at these prices (1.5 million for Brando)." So I countered, "Arthur, at least let me have some fun."

—Brando, interviewed for *Time*, 24 May 1976

Walter BRENNAN [1894-1974]

Born: Swampscott, Massachusetts. Work in vaudeville and stock preceded his career in Hollywood, first as an extra and stuntman, then as a supporting character beginning with The Ridin' Rowdy (1927, Richard Thorpe). He worked opposite Gary Cooper in six films beginning with Wedding Night (1935, King Vidor); their fourth pairing was Meet John Doe (1941, Frank Capra):

Something he never discusses is his theories about acting. The ham in him never comes out, somehow. I used to think he didn't have any theories. I used to think he was just a great personality — who was relying on his personality to get him by. But I've changed my mind. I'm convinced that he's a great actor. There were scenes in *Meet John Doe* when he wasn't Cooper, but another guy; and he was still convincing. I think he has the whole business figured out. The secret is being natural. And he knows how to be natural — how to make a character part of himself. Take a look at that scene where he's supposed to be desperate from hunger. You never saw a hungrier-looking man. And you should have seen the lunch he tucked away before he did that scene! You'd be convinced, too, that he's a great actor....

I don't know anybody who treats others better than Coop does. He's pleasant to everybody. He doesn't have one set of manners with certain people, and a different set with others. He's the same with everybody. And when somebody wins his trust, nobody or nothing can swerve him from being loyal to that person. He's as generous as they come — but he doesn't go in for grandstand generosity. He's no show-off at the expense of others. He's too sensitive for that....

Do you suppose I would ever have won that Academy Award for *The Westerner* [1940, William Wyler] if Cooper hadn't been the guy he is? The answer is No. He could have made it plenty tough for me to do any standing out in that part. He was the star, and I was only a featured player. He could have demanded that my scenes be cut, or demanded all kinds of changes — which other stars, in the same spot, might have done. He never resents anybody else's part. Jealousy is out of his line....

I've worked with him under all kinds of conditions, good and bad, hot and cold, indoors and out, and I'm going right out on a limb and say I'd rather work with him than any other star I know. He relaxes me. [Brennan also worked with Cooper on *The Cowboy and the Lady* (1939, H.C. Potter), *Sergeant York* (1941, Howard Hawks) and *The Pride of the Yankees* (1942, Sam Wood).]

—Brennan, as told to James Reid for *Screen Life*, July 1941

Evelyn BRENT [1899-1975]

Born: Mary Elizabeth Riggs in Tampa, Florida; educated in New York City. While still in high school, she worked as a film extra. After a number of small parts, she then appeared on the London stage in 1920. In Hollywood from 1923, she worked with Josef von Sternberg on three films, beginning with Underworld (1927):

In the opening shot of *Underworld* I was to come down some stairs into the nightclub and [von Sternberg] had feathers down on the stairs before my feet came into the shot. This took a long time camera-wise to get, but when I saw it I realized why he wanted it. It stamped the whole character. The breeze took a couple of feathers and then my feet came in and the camera panned up.... He knew as much about cameras as any cameraman did. That was where a lot of the time was spent. And in those days we didn't have any stand-ins, we did the standing in ourselves. He would have it all mapped out. You'd stand under those hot lights while they'd move 'em all around. All this before you get to the scene, and you're exhausted. I never minded it, because Joe was a stickler for making you see rushes every day. It helped you to get an understanding of what he was taking the time to try to do. He got very angry if anybody missed seeing the rushes. We used to go in every day. He was tough to work with, but I like working. I could only wish they had more directors like him....

[He] had a great feeling for a picture. The actors were not as important as the sweep of the story, the actors moved against it.... The actors were incidental, they furthered the story, the action, instead of him concentrating on the actors only....

Q. Perhaps you could talk about *The Last Command* [1928, von Sternberg]. Did you consider it special to be in an Emil Jannings film?

A. Yeah.... I think Joe and Jannings got along well, Jannings had a great respect for Joe. And Joe had a way of involving you in a thing. If he was hot on a scene, he'd work with everybody. Jannings was wonderful to work with because he was one of the few big stars who, if an extra woman had one little scene, he would work with her behind the camera — you know, do his part. Most of them slough that and get away from it. But he was always very considerate of the other people. [Her third film for von Sternberg was *Drag Net* (1928).]

—Brent, interviewed by John Kobal (1972) for *People Will Talk* (New York: Alfred A. Knopf, 1985)

Beau BRIDGES [1941-]

Born: Lloyd Bridges III; brother of Jeff and son of Lloyd II [1913-]. Studies at UCLA and The University of Hawaii and bit roles in films and TV preceded his feature film debut in The Incident (1967, Larry Peerce). In 1989, he played Frank Baker in Steve Clovis' The Fabulous Baker Boys:

I thought the script was incredible. I said, "This is about me and my brother." Then after the movie came out people came up and said, "Boy, is that about you and your brother!" I think the key is that Steve Clovis...wrote about families, and it showed....

I like to be in charge, to plan, to know what the destination is. Loose ends can make me nervous. My brother in the movie is a jazz guy, an understated guy who doesn't talk alot. That's very much like Jeff. His work as an actor is very jazzy, he constantly fools you, surprises you. Yet the characters do get to switch around. Frank gets in touch with his emotions and Jack sees there's more to life than just pounding the keys in a bar.

We tried not to cut up the script but there are things that were unconscious. When I say goodbye to Jeff, all my life I've grabbed his crotch, and as he goes with both hands to protect himself, I hit him on top of his head! He's never been able to stop it so it's in the movie.

—Bridges, interviewed by Debbi K. Swanson for *Drama-Logue*, 4-10 Jan 1990

Jeff BRIDGES [1949-]

Born: Los Angeles; son of Lloyd and brother of Beau Bridges. A film debut at age 4 months as Jane Greer's baby in The Company She Keeps (1950, John Cromwell), brief study at The Herbert Berghof Studio in N.Y. and a few bit parts with his brother, Beau, in their father's TV series, Sea Hunt, preceded his first major film role in Halls of Anger (1969, Paul Bogart):

When I was 20, I did a movie called *Halls of Anger*, about busing white kids into a black school. I played a guy who tries to participate and adapt. He goes out for sports, tries to be friendly. And they keep beating the shit out of him. He keeps coming back and the black kids keep beating the shit out of him. And then there is this last scene that I have with Calvin Lockhart, who plays the boy's principal. He tells me to stick with it, to not leave the school. It was a big emotional scene for me. And I really happened to get off. I had a cathartic experience doing the scene. We filmed for half a day and I really got empty. And it taught me a lesson; a cathartic scene for the actor is not necessarily a cathartic scene for the filmgoer.

—Bridges, interviewed by Tim Cahill for *Rolling Stone*, 27 Jan 1977

What [*Bad Company* (1972)] is about is the kind of relationship the director, Bob Benton, has had with his writing partner, David Newman. At least that's what Bob used to tell us when we'd gather at his place on weekends to sip Wild Turkey and talk about the characters while we were on location in Emporia, Kansas. He told us he and Newman had a very tight relationship, where they would fight and break up, fight, and break up.

I was supposed to be Newman, who is a long-haired freaky kind of guy. Barry Brown was Benton, who is more prim and uptight, and the marvelous thing is that Bob *knows* that about himself, and talks about it. I remember him telling me once that he hated Newman incredibly after they had had a falling out — but then they got back together again.

—Bridges, interviewed by Judy Klemesrud for *The New York Times*, 22 Oct 1972

Q. Did you enjoy working with John Huston in *Winter Kills* [1979, William Richert]?

A. Very much. He had directed *Fat City* [1972] and it was very interesting how different it was working with him as an actor. In *Fat City*, he really didn't go out of his way...to make me feel especially comfortable. I think he liked that little edge he was getting, kind of keeping me on my toes. Working with him as an actor, he went out of his way to let everyone know he was just one of the boys, one of the players, and he was very respectful of the director — really terrific to work with.

—Bridges, interviewed by Tom Teicholz for *Interview*, Apr 1983

[*Jagged Edge* (1985, Richard Marquand)] was difficult because I had to get in touch with the evil side. I learned so much about evil in general. For me, the price of evil is the loss of love.

Q. How did you go about creating that character, or any character?

A. I usually get a physical image of the guy. I make a list of the different people this guy reminds me of. I patterned [Jack Forrester in *Jagged Edge*] on Werner Erhard (founder of est) a little bit. I'm a fan of his, but you never know what his motives are. What his motives are doesn't really matter. I liked his serenity, his stance, his posture. I used all that.

—Bridges, interviewed by Jay Scott for *The Globe & Mail*, 20 Dec 1986

[For *Starman* (1984, John Carpenter)] I watched the reactions [of my two daughters]. I remember one evening Susie and I had to get ready for some formal affair. Of course, we were late, and I was trying to get my bowtie straight. Belle came over to me, grabbed my leg, and started kissing it, "I love you, Daddy," she kept saying.

When she finished, I looked at her face and saw that she had makeup on. Well, the makeup smeared all over my pants. I screamed at her, and she looked so hurt and startled.

I used that look in the movie, particularly in one scene where I bring a deer back to life. A hunter punches me in the face, and I'm shocked because, like Belle, I was just showing love....

Doing the part of Starman, I really learned something. As an actor, you can pull off the corniest things if you do them with a certain freshness. Concepts like family and love have a lot of meaning. Even Starman seeing the rain for the first time can be exciting. You just can't be afraid of being sentimental or clichéd. For the most part, sophistication gets in our way.

—Bridges, interviewed by Patricia Morrisroe for *New York*, 17 Dec 1984

Matthew BRODERICK [1962-]

Born: New York City; son of James Broderick [1927-1982]. Acting at New York's Walden School led to work off-Broadway where he made his debut opposite his father in Horton Foote's On Valentine's Day. Further studies with Uta Hagen and Robert Leonard and work on Broadway preceded his film debut in Max Dugan Returns (1982, Herbert Ross). He played the title role in Ferris Bueller's Day Off (1986, John Hughes):

Ferris is not polite.... I think he's a little pushy and a little shady. He certainly cares a lot about his friends. He's someone I'd like to know but not be in the same restaurant with. I think of him as a great tour guide.

—Broderick, interviewed by Stephen M. Silverman for *The New York Post*, 10 June 1986

In the beginning [of *Torch Song Trilogy* (1988, Paul Bogart)] it's clear that [Alan] has no family, no place to hang his hat. So, his story is largely about trying to find some sort of security, which is what I think Arnold [Harvey Fierstein] represents to him — somebody who is stable and proud of being gay and who is not hiding....

Q. Did you feel like a victim while you were filming that scene [the bashing]?

A. The feeling — when I did it — was not really about being gay. It was about the violence that people do to other people. I'm half-Jewish, and my ancestors have had violent acts committed against them.... When you're getting hit with a bat, it's not about being gay. It's about violence that men do to other men.

—Broderick, interviewed by James A. Baggett for *Christopher Street* #128, 1988

The first step [in preparation for the role of Robert Gould Shaw in *Glory* (1989, Edward Zwick)] was to try to learn as much as I could about the real person. That was mostly from letters, photographs, descriptions of other people, a poem about him by Emerson. The thing I had to try to do was bring myself into that situation. I didn't want to be an imitation of my idea of what Shaw must have been like.

I thought of somebody who was suddenly given an enormous responsibility. I also tried to think of him coming from a strong background of abolitionists and literary people. I think the ideals of Thoreau and Emerson were all bred into him. I think that goes with him when he leads the regiment. It's not just him alone; it's his cause. His whole background comes with him.

—Broderick, interviewed by Lawrence Van Gelder for *The New York Times*, 22 Dec 1989

One thing that impressed me a lot [about working with Marlon Brando on *The Freshman* (1990, Andrew Bergman)] — he doesn't compromise. If he doesn't have a good take on a scene — he doesn't understand it, or he doesn't have something good to do — he'll change it or wait till someone can explain it to him so he can understand it. He'll change lines or the staging or how it's played. I think the director was, for the most part, thrilled. None of it was destructive. He doesn't monopolize a scene. He's very open to other people. He gets everybody in a mood of not settling.

—Broderick, interviewed by Martin Kasindorf for *Newsday*, 18 July 1990

Q. One of the great moments from *The Freshman* is when Brando gives you a big kiss on the lips. How did that scene evolve?

A. Simple. It was in the script. In the movie, my character is always trying to leave Brando's employ because he gets wind that it is not legal. Every time I try to quit, Brando tries to suck me in closer: "I never had a son," he says. He holds my hand. It keeps escalating. Finally, he grabs my face and kisses me.

—Broderick, interviewed by Rod Lurie for *The West Side Spirit*, 31 July 1990

Clive BROOK [1887-1974]

Born: Clifford Brook in London, England. Studies at London Polytechnic and work in provincial theater preceded his 1920 London stage debut and his first film (Trent's Last Case — 1920, Richard Garrick). In 1924, he was brought to Hollywood by Thomas Ince. In 1932, he played "Doc" Hardy opposite Marlene Dietrich in Josef von Sternberg's Shanghai Express:

[von Sternberg] was a great man to wear an actor down. Poor Lawrence Grant, on *Shanghai Express*, was kept hard at it from nine until six one day until the poor man burst into tears. "I don't think I can go on, Mr. von Sternberg."

"You have done it! The last take is good."

On the same picture, he asked me what I thought of some rushes. "But Jo," I protested, "everyone is talking in the same dreary monotone."

"Exactly," he replied, "I want that. This is The Shanghai Express. Everyone must talk like a train."

—Brook, interviewed by Kevin Brownlow (1965) for *The Parade's Gone By* (New York: Alfred A. Knopf, 1969)

Louise BROOKS [1906-1985]

Born: Cherryvale, Kansas. A student of Ruth St. Denis and a member of both George White's Scandals and The Ziegfeld Follies, she made her film debut in The Street of Forgotten Men (1925, Herbert Brenon). She then appeared as Lulu in G.W. Pabst's Pandora's Box (1929); upon her return to Hollywood, she received more mediocre parts. She retired from the screen in 1938 and in 1956 became an avoid chronicler of Hollywood history. Among her early roles was a small part in A Girl in Every Port (1928, Howard Hawks):

Howard Hawks was the perfect director. He didn't do anything at all. He would sit, look very, very beautiful, tall and graceful, leaning against anything he could lean against, and watch the scene; and the person who did all the directing was that big ham Victor McLaglen....

Mal St. Clair was just the opposite and I hated the pictures I did with him [*A Social Celebrity* (1926), *The Show Off* (1926) and *The Canary Murder Case* (1929)].... Mal came from the mugging school of [Mack] Sennett and he did everything by making faces, and he would mug out a scene for me and then send me into the scene, and I would be so embarrassed. I tried my best to please him and yet not to make all these mugging faces that date so terribly.... I felt Mal was a really terrible director, although I thought he was a charming man, a lovely man.

—Brooks, interviewed by John Kobal (1965 and 1982) for *People Will Talk* (New York: Alfred A.Knopf, 1985)

[William Wellman] directed the opening sequence of *Beggars of Life* [1928] with a sure, dramatic swiftness lacking in the rest of the film. It's pace did not accord with [Benjamin] Glazer's artistic conception of the tragedy and thereafter the action grew slower without increasing the film's content....

So intrigued was I by the quiet sadism practiced by Billy behind the camera, especially in his direction of women, that I began to investigate his past life. From him I learnt nothing because he was extremely shy in conversation with women. A slim handsome young man, more than a director he resembled an actor who was uncertain in his part.

—Brooks, in *Film Culture*, Spring 1972

Joe E. BROWN [1892-1973]

Born: Holgate, Ohio. Work in the circus, vaudeville and burlesque and on Broadway preceded his film debut in Crooks Can't Win (1928, Ralph Ince):

Ralph Ince was a good teacher, an inspired director, a successful producer, and one of the best friends I ever had in Hollywood. He belonged to that old-time school of director-producers who could shoot "off the cuff" with one cameraman, one electrician, and one prop-and-scenery man.... His scripts generally were only a few pages of notes but he had the story so thoroughly worked out in his mind that he never faltered or paused to think what came next when he was directing.

When he was making a picture he would take up his position just back of the cameraman, or to one side just out of range. On several occasions he became so carried away with the scene he was putting his actors through that his flailing arms knocked the camera over. Of course, this was in the days of the silent picture and all noise, voices, or music off stage were calculated to help the actors through their scenes. He liked to direct love scenes and sequences that exhibited strong human emotions. In a love scene he'd stand behind the camera and yell, "O.K., now, walk towards her. Now take her in your arms. Look at her for a moment as if you'd like to eat her. Ah, you love her, you adore her! Now, kiss her...hold it! O.K., cut!"

The command he had over his actors was nothing short of hypnotic. [Brown also worked on Ince's *Hit of the Show* (1928).]

—Brown, in his (as told to Ralph Hancock) *Laughter is a Wonderful Thing* (New York: A.S. Barnes, 1956)

Three things made the role [of Elmer in *Elmer the Great* (1933)] uniquely pleasant for me. One was the fact that Mervyn LeRoy...knew and loved baseball, and therefore understood the situations completely. Another was that Elmer was a touching, convincing character who could be brought clearly to life and be a natural, unforced source of laughs. Too often my roles had involved routines which had nothing to do with the characters, so that the laughs had to be artificially manufactured.

But the best thing about the part was that during the days when I played ball on small-town teams in Ohio, Indiana and Michigan I had come to know and admire many Elmers.

Some people misunderstood Elmer's character — thought he was just a braggart. He wasn't, really. When Elmer said of Alexander, the great pitcher, "He's good too," he was just being honest about the unswerving faith he had in himself.

—Brown, in *The Saturday Evening Post*, 9 Nov 1946

Mervyn LeRoy's particular idiosyncrasy was the habit of talking with an accent throughout the making of a picture and using a different accent for each picture. For instance, day after day while on the set he would speak and give directions in a Dutch accent. "Vell, vot's da matter? Come on, come on, let's get dis show rollink!" We'd answer in the same accent.

Perhaps during the shooting of the next picture he would switch to an Irish accent. And the accent was never determined by the subject or any characters in the story. The actor and the technicians all fell in with the gag and any stranger walking on to the set would have thought we were all a bunch of foreigners. Only when the cameras were rolling would the actors speak in their natural voices. [Brown worked with LeRoy three additional times: *Top Speed* (1930), *Broad-Minded* (1931) and *Local Boy Makes Good* (1931).]

[Flute, in *A Midsummer Night's Dream* (1935, Max Reinhardt and William Dieterle)] was the one and only role I ever signed to play without first understanding the part. Had I known more about Shakespeare I would not have attempted it. If you know your Shakespeare you know the role is that of an addlepated fellow who is forced to play a female role in the amateur show being strenuously put on to celebrate the marriage of the Duke of Athens. I was...scared, and obviously wrong as a female impersonator. But that's why Reinhardt put me in it. My look of shame and guilt was just what the role required. Reinhardt insisted that I play it straight.

—Brown, in his (as told to Ralph Hancock) *Laughter is a Wonderful Thing* (New York: A.S. Barnes, 1956)

Yul BRYNNER [1915-1985]

Born: Taidje Kahn on Sakhalen Island. Work with Michael Chekhov's Shakespeare Co. and on Broadway and as a TV director preceded his film debut in Port of New York (1949, Laslo Benedek). In 1956, he portrayed the King of Siam in Walter Lang's adaptation of The King and I, a role Brynner had played on Broadway:

[In *The King and I*] I played a man. You never act like a king when you are playing a king. The people around you act as if you are king.

—Brynner, interviewed by Cameron Shipp for *Redbook*, May 1957

The king I portrayed spent seventeen years in a monastery because that was the only way he could find time to study. In the monastery he adopted the haircut used by the priests and monks in Siam. He must have found it extremely comfortable and decided that never would he bother with hair again.

—Brynner, interviewed by Pete Martin for *The Saturday Evening Post*, 22 Nov 1958

The King of Siam is the story of a fierce, refined, violent, bestial kind of man, but [who] lives in the utmost refinement. His behavior is barbarian. But he himself lives in splendor, robed in sheer silks, ornamented with the finest jewels. He dabbles uncertainly in literature and the arts, not at all sure of anything, particularly his own authority.

—Brynner, interviewed by Robert Williams in an unsourced, undated article in the files of The New York Public Library for the Performing Arts

When I reached out to ask Deborah [Kerr] to dance [in *The King and I*], that gesture without any words or further action, should have explained the completeness of [my] desire.

—Brynner, interviewed for an unsourced, undated clipping in the files of The New York Public Library for the Performing Arts

[On *The Ten Commandments* (1956), Cecil B. DeMille and I] worked together in a sort of pantomime. After a scene was shot, if he liked it, he would nod at me with a little twinkle in his eye. If he didn't like it, he would merely turn to the crew and say, "Let's shoot it again." I'd look at him in a questioning way and he'd look back and say the particular word in the dialogue he wanted changed. Then he would go through it again, with the change he wanted. It was like going to school every day.

—Brynner, interviewed by Fern Marja for *The New York Post*, 30 Sept 1956

[Major Surov in *The Journey* (1959, Anatole Litvak)] is exactly the kind of guy who lives in a rigidly accepted formula.... What happens to guys like him who go out in the world and see what's happening around them is the story.

Any time a guy gives up the individual authority factor for the authority of the system, he is bound to have a tremendous upheaval when he finally sees life as it is.

The costume is Russian, but the man has the human problem. Regardless of what he is, I play him as a human being. This is the thing I always try to do with a part, regardless of how unknown and strange the character is.

When you play a character you try to be kind of an archtype which represents more than just one man. This man is like others I have played — a bastard with a heart of gold.

—Brynner, interviewed by Joe Hyams for *The New York Herald Tribune*, 12 June 1958

John BRYSON

A freelance photographer and former picture editor for Life, Bryson became a friend of Sam Peckinpah's who later cast him in The Getaway (1972):

I guess Sam saw something or other in me he figured he could put to use — my big shambling walk or something. One thing I'm certain of, though — he didn't cast me in the film out of friendship or anything like that. No sir, none of that bullshit. Sam's such a perfectionist, he wouldn't cast Jesus to play Christ if Jesus didn't look right for the part....

The company came to Texas. Meanwhile, Sam hadn't said much of anything to me, and I was a little puzzled by that. The first day of shooting, I was supposed to drive up to the prison at Huntsville in a chauffeured Cadillac and lay a message on [Steve] McQueen, who is playing a convict getting out. By now, I was damned edgy and nervous — nobody had said do it this way or that way, nothing. Finally, McQueen, who's a very strange guy I don't like too much, stuck his head in the window of the car and said, "Just relax, man. Remember, in your role you're a rich, influential member of the Establishment, and I'm just a little pissant convict that you couldn't care less about. Hang on to that and it'll go great." The only thing Peckinpah had ever said to me, like two weeks earlier, was something like, "Don't act. Just react...."

A few days ago, I wasn't moving right in a scene we were shooting. That was the big climactic shootout at the Laughlin Hotel. I was moving fast, but Sam wanted me to move slow, and I just couldn't seem to do it. My inclination, in the midst of all those shotguns blasting off, was to get the fuck out of the way. Sam said, "John, move slow, very slow. You're in charge, you're the big honcho in this outfit." Well, I understood, but I didn't understand. So he rode my ass all that day, and I was about ready to cut my throat by nightfall, because I wanted to do it right for him, because I really love the sonofabitch.

—Bryson, interviewed by Grover Lewis for *Rolling Stone*, 12 Oct 1972

Genevieve BUJOLD [1942-]

Born: Montreal, Canada. After studies at The Montreal Conservatory of Drama, and a few roles in Canadian films, she gained international experience working in France with Alain Resnais and Philippe de Broca. Returning to Canada, she married director Paul Almond with whom she made three films between 1967 and 1972, beginning with Isabel. In her first English language film she played Anne Boleyn opposite Richard Burton as Henry VIII in Anne of the Thousand Days (1969, Charles Jarrott):

Love is the key to life, the first brick in which everything else is built. Anne had a great gift in that she really, really loved Henry VIII....

Acting is an act of love. If you don't love the guy you're playing opposite, forget it. Acting is profound contact, deep mutual acceptance, tenderness, intimacy. Then taking off from that you can even play hatred. If you dislike the other actor it will show in the eyes, and film-making is eyes. So you've got to find something. Love his hands, maybe.

—Bujold, in *Life*, 29 May 1970

[Producer] Hal Wallis wanted me to do *Mary, Queen of Scots* [1971] for Universal. I said, "Look, Hal, I don't want to play any more queens. Give the part to some other actress who wants the job and would be very good in the part. With me, it would be the same producer, the same director, the same costumes, the same me!" Well, Hal Wallis said, "If you don't do this, they'll put you in some piece of crap!" I had innocently agreed to do three more films for Universal, and now they were suing me for seven hundred and fifty thousand dollars, and I was completely washed up in Hollywood. I had a son to support, and I couldn't work in America, so I went to Europe and did *The Trojan Women* [1971, Michael Cacoyannis] and another film in Canada [*Kamarouska* (1973, Claude Jutra)].

Then I wandered back to Hollywood, and they threatened to put me in jail, and that's how I ended up in *Earthquake* [1974, Mark Robson] and *Swashbuckler* [1976, James Goldstone]... just to erase the old debt.

I did *Obsession* [1976] because I like the director, Brian De Palma, and I'm pleased that it is a success, but I understand they've changed it a lot. When I did it, I actually married my own father [Cliff Robertson] and slept with him, then when he woke up the morning after the wedding I had gotten my revenge and disappeared.

It was fun playing a girl who was really a bitch underneath all that sweetness. Now they cut the wedding scene and the love scene because it was too shocking for the studio executives and their wives and given it a happy father-daughter ending.

—Bujold, interviewed by Rex Reed for *The New York Sunday News*, 15 Aug 1976

Peter BULL [1912-1984]

Born: London, England. On the London stage since 1933, he made his film debut in Sabotage (1936, Alfred Hitchcock). In 1963, he played one of the tutors in Tony Richardson's adaptation of Henry Fielding's Tom Jones:

I know that people are apt to say that the happiest days of their life were at school or in the war or somewhere equally quaint, but I'm not absolutely sure that my happiest days were not spent in *Tom Jones*.... The company was packed with great chums, and John Moffatt and I...were engaged over high tea as it turned out, to play Thwackum and Square, Master Jones's wildly unattractive tutors....

It was to prove unlike any film with which I had ever been associated and I gather from everyone else connected with it that they all felt roughly the same way....

One of the reasons why so many actors, myself included, are pretty keen on Mr. Richardson as a director, is that he occasionally puts his trust in one to the point of lunacy. Who else, pray, would say to Mr. Moffatt and myself during a rehearsal: "Don't think what you are saying now is very funny? Go off, dahlings, and make up something and we'll shoot it." So off we'd go and think up a lot of new lines.

—Bull, in his *Bull's Eye* (London: Robin Clark Ltd., 1985)

Billie BURKE [1885-1970]

Born: Mary Burke in Washington, D.C. Work on the London and N.Y. stages preceded her film debut in Peggy (1916, Charles Giblyn). Her first sound film was A Bill of Divorcement (1932):

George Cukor, a blessed person, went about overcoming my nervousness before the microphones.... I was afraid to move away from the camera boom and wanted to stand rooted wherever I was to speak my lines. John Barrymore, a gallant man, crossed over whenever he could so that I would not have to move. He was still magnificent, acting brilliantly, not as he was a few years later when, sick and tired but still struggling to pay his debts, he had to resort to words written on blackboards to remember his lines.

Miss [Katharine] Hepburn seemed a strange girl at first, with her hair in a tight sausage and her schoolmarm clothes; that is, until one day I saw her really act. Somehow her eyes caught fire and there was a glow....

My favorite role was in *The Wizard of Oz* [1939] directed by the great Victor Fleming, in which I played Glinda, the Good Fairy. I never played such a being on stage, but this role is as close as I have come in motion pictures to the kind of parts I did in the theater.

I recall Ray Bolger in that film. He was the Scarecrow. Day after day as the shooting went on I waited for Ray to dance. Finally I asked him when.

"Dance?" he said, amazed. "Dance? Why, I'm a professional dancer. That's what I do. I'm a dancer. So of course I don't dance."

And he didn't. My parts in pictures have been something like that.

—Burke, in her (with Cameron Shipp) *With a Feather on My Nose* (New York: Appleton-Century-Crofts Inc., 1949)

George BURNS [1896-]

Born: Nathan Birnbaum in New York City. A vaudeville performer, he teamed up with Gracie Allen in 1922, and after they were married in 1926, they performed together in vaudeville, on radio, TV, and film, until her death in 1964; they made their film debut as George and Gracie in The Big Broadcast (1932, Frank Tuttle). Burns replaced long time friend Jack Benny in The Sunshine Boys (1975, Herbert Ross) upon Benny's death:

Let me give you an example of how Herb worked. In this one particular scene he thought I was playing it too serious, but he didn't say a word to me. Between takes he went to Walter [Matthau] and quietly told him he thought I was a little tight in this scene and asked Walter to do something to loosen me up. Well, that's all he had to say to Walter. Now, this scene was a single shot of me, and Walter was standing behind the camera feeding me lines. Herb called for action so we started doing the scene. Right in the middle of it Walter dropped his pants. I'm sure it must have loosened me up a little, but I never lost my concentration. I went right on with the scene and, believe me, it's not easy to look a man in the eye when he's standing there with his pants down....

Anyway, Herb liked the scene, so Walter pulled his pants up and we went on with the picture. By using a little psychology Herb got the job done, and he didn't even have to raise his voice. All he had to do was lower Walter's pants.

—Burns, in his *Living It Up or, They Still Love Me in Altoona* (New York: G.P. Putnam's Sons, 1976)

Ellen BURSTYN [1932-]

Born: Edna Rae Gillooly in Detroit. Work as a model and dancer preceded her Broadway debut in Fair Game (1957, under the name of Ellen McRae) and her film debut in For Those Who Think Young (1964, Leslie H. Martinson). She left Hollywood, then after five years in N.Y. studying at The Actors Studio, she returned to film work, now as Ellen Burstyn.

The first day of shooting [on *Goodbye Charlie* (1964, Vincente Minnelli)] I was wearing Shirley MacLaine's old wig. I had been dressed by the wardrobe department, made up by the make-up department, I was put together by the assembly line. Vincente Minnelli did my part for me and then had me copy him. He even said the lines with me as I rehearsed so that I could get his rhythm exactly. As they were setting up for the first shot, I was sitting on the set feeling completely manufactured....

I finished the picture, packed up my furniture, dogs, cats and my kid, and moved back to New York and enrolled in Lee Strasberg's class at Actors Studio. Smartest move I ever made.

—Burstyn, in *PLAYBILL*, Dec 1978

[Cloris Leachman and I] flew to Texas on the same flight...and we discussed our characters [in *The Last Picture Show* (1971, Peter Bogdanovich)] all the way.

Once we got to Texas, we kept working on our characters, trying to put them together out of millions of clues. We would sit in the Golden Rooster cafe and kind of watch the people and their movements and say, "There's Lois" [Burstyn] or "There's Ruth [Leachman]." We tried to stay in character all of the time, even on the many long nights we spent together going over our mutual marital problems. We'd be crying and commiserating and carrying on, and we'd be doing it *in a Texas accent.*

—Burstyn, interviewed by Judy Klemesrud for *The New York Times*, 23 Jan 1972

In putting Sally [in *The King of Marvin Gardens* (1972, Bob Rafelson)] together, I asked myself, "What does she drink for breakfast?" If she drinks milk, that's a different person from one who drinks coffee. I questioned myself about her clothes because that's important to her and decided that all of her clothes are nighttime clothes, like under the fur coat it's a chiffon dress. In the day, she wore her old nighttime dresses, stuff which she wouldn't wear in the evening anymore. All of her clothes were bought at resorts, like Vegas or Palm Springs. They were all pastels or summer colors. You can see the life that starts to build. Here is a woman who has not been a prostitute, but a mistress. Maybe she was with one man for four or five years, then with another for 10. She's brought along on trips but does not necessarily live with the men who keep her. She's out for good times, and goes to nightclubs and gambling casinos and dances. She's never in anybody's kitchen.

—Burstyn, interviewed by Arthur Bell for *The Village Voice*, 3 Feb 1975

I've never seen anybody like him [Billy Friedkin directing *The Exorcist* (1973)]. He runs everything. Every single detail. He knows everything that's happening everywhere — on the set, the production, the script — and does it well, perfectly, easily and demands perfection from everybody else, nicely. There is no such thing as anybody saying, "We couldn't get what you wanted, it doesn't exist." You can't say that. He'd just say, "Well, what does that mean? Get it! I want it yesterday!"

—Burstyn, interviewed by Ann Guerin for *Show*, Dec 1972

[Martin Scorsese and I] talked about that scene [in *Alice Doesn't Live Here Anymore* (1974) when Alice returns to her motel room after a day of job hunting and yells at her son, played by Billy Green Bush], and I said that I thought that most movies don't portray mothers realistically. It's always a good mother or a bad mother — the one who never raises her voice to her children or the one who beats her kids. And I think kids get a very distorted image of what motherhood is. And I think *mothers* get a very distorted image of their own motherhood.

I wanted Alice to be a fully rounded mother. A mother who loves her kid and has a very one-to-one relationship with him. And sometimes she makes a mistake. She loses her temper and yells at her kid when she shouldn't. She takes her frustration out on the kid. That's what mothers do.

There was a very conscious decision to do that. To deal with reality, not with movie-star-as-mother. And when we did that scene I let myself go, let myself sound like a fishwife, because that's what it sounds like when you're full of hostility and anger and stupidity.

—Burstyn, interviewed by Lee Israel for *McCalls*, Aug 1975

Richard BURTON [1925-1984]

Born: Richard Jenkins in Pontrhydyfen, South Wales. Answering an ad placed by British playwright Emlyn Williams, Burton made his stage debut while still a teenager in Williams' The Druid's Rest; in 1948, he made his first film — The Last Days of Dolwyn (1948) — again under Williams' direction. His first Hollywood role was as Philip Ashley opposite Olivia De Havilland in My Cousin Rachel (1952, Henry Koster):

I was given the role in *Cousin Rachel* through George Cukor, the famous director, and I played it strictly as a stage actor, since I didn't know too much about film techniques.... I saw one day's rushes...and I thought I was miserable. It was the scene where Rachel, my village girlfriend [Olivia De Havilland] and I do a scene at the church door. It seemed to me that I practically chewed up all the scenery being hammy, doing it all in one breath to a mounting climax with the subtlety of a machine-gun blast.

—Burton, interviewed by Paul Marsh for *Silver Screen*, July 1953

[*The Robe* (1953, Henry Koster)] was a very funny film to make because we were asked, if you please, by the Head Office not to smoke on the set or drink because it was a holy picture. The stars were myself and Vic Mature and it's very difficult to stop Mature and the immature Burton from having the occasional drink.... It was rather interesting, too, because one of the supporting actors got a young girl into trouble at the time and there was a tremendous hubbub and brouhaha trying to conceal the evidence from the press because it was a holy picture.

—Burton, interviewed at The National Film Theatre, 26 Oct 1972

[Mark] Antony [in *Cleopatra* (1963, Joseph L. Mankiewicz)] is really the Roman Jimmy Porter [from *Look Back in Anger* (1959, Tony Richardson)]. He's got a most terrible father fixation for a start. A most tremendous complex about Caesar [Rex Harrison].

He lives eternally in Caesar's shadow. The great and mighty god, Caesar. Although Caesar is dead he is always talked about. Always remembered.

Antony is constantly compared with him, always to his detriment. Even to the extent of being used by Cleopatra [Elizabeth Taylor]. For this Cleopatra is incapable of ordinary love, and Antony is a very weak man.

—Burton, as told to Romany Bain for *The New York World-Telegram and Sun*, 27 Aug 1963

[Mark] Antony is a man who talks excessively to excuse his own failure. By that I mean his failure to become a great conqueror like Caesar, a great lover like Caesar — in fact, his failure to become a great man. He's extremely eloquent, but at times inarticulately eloquent. The fury is there and the sense of failure is there, but sometimes all that comes out is a series of splendid words without any particular meaning.

—Burton, interviewed by Kenneth Tynan for *Playboy*, Sept 1963

Shall Becket [in *Becket* (1964, Peter Glenville)] merely be King Henry's archbishop and obey his every whim, or shall he obey his heavenly King, defend the rights of the church under God, and face and fight Henry? He chooses the latter, and the king being possessed of a powerful, willful, muscular intelligence and being as ruthless as he is cunning — the choice inevitably means Becket's death.

Possibly there is no more brilliant or epitomal example in all history of the struggle between church and state than in the story of Becket and Henry. Here the essence of that everlasting battle is concentrated in two men....

This battle and transformation from the temporal to the spiritual in the man Thomas Becket is as fascinating to the actor as it is to the writer and as difficult to realize. It is comparatively easy to be a red, roaring man. But it is not so easy to change into a little pale man, alone, burned by the fury of his own awful and terrible belief, moving uncertainly toward unattainable and impossible saintliness. Groping quietly, preferably in silence knowing that words themselves can be seductive and devilish and tempting and dangerous and can betray with their wonderful sweetness — the gifted man of spirit must struggle to resist their lure. He must be taciturn, spare, meager and miserly in his dispensation of beautiful words. This is the writer's and the actor's problem with a part like Becket — to keep him as silent as possible and still interesting....

Initially Peter [O'Toole] and I were apprehensive about that spark that was so needed between us if our roles as Becket and the king were to come off properly. For that reason we both decided to drink absolutely nothing for the first few days of the production. We had the reputation — ill deserved, I must say — for terrible wildness. So our colleagues were quite surprised to see us hold nothing but teacups for 10 days. When it became clear that the two of us did have on-camera rapport, I put on my best Irish accent and said, "Peter, my boy, I think we deserve a little snifter." Then we drank for two nights and one day. We appeared quite blasted for the filming of the scene wherein the king puts the ring on Becket's finger, making him chancellor of England. There was no dialogue, so that was no problem. But O'Toole had a dreadful time putting that ring on me. It was rather like trying to thread a needle wearing boxing gloves....

And now that we talk of great actors, we were additionally lucky in having Sir John Gielgud to play the King of France. He had been my first idol.... In truth, from my earliest days, I modeled my acting on Gielgud's, though, because of our vast differences in temperament, voice and body, nobody has ever remarked on it.

—Burton, in *Life*, 13 Mar 1964

I think the people who really fascinate me are fellows like Shannon in *Night of the Iguana* [1964, John Huston], who was a failure, and Leamus in *The Spy Who Came in from the Cold* [1965, Martin Ritt], who was a failure, and George in *Who's Afraid of Virginia Woolf?* [1966, Mike Nichols], who was a failure. That kind of man is much more fascinating to play than the one who is always right and is golden.

—Burton, interviewed by Louise Sweeney for *The Christian Science Monitor*, 3 July 1979

[In *The Spy Who Came in from the Cold*] I play a spy — not one of the glamorous James Bond types, but the more realistic little men like civil-service clerks who do the actual work. I pretend I want to defect and the Communists take the bait, but I'm trapped finally because of the one bit of humanity I permit myself — falling in love with a mousy leftwing librarian [Claire Bloom].

—Burton, interviewed by Robert Musel for *TV Guide*, 18 Oct 1969

Q. What are some of the most interesting things you have done recently?

A. Playing those roles [of Alec Leamas] in [*The*] *Spy* [*Who Came in from the Cold*] and [George in *Who's Afraid of Virginia*] *Woolf?*. Before, I would never have dreamed of myself portraying such thin, seedy, famished men. You know, I have always acted in the bravo or panache tradition. In those two parts, logically speaking, I was supremely mis-cast. Not that I didn't like it. I did. It was immensely challenging, but it was such agony. Playing everything down, down, holding myself in all the time. The tiniest gesture, the slightest word was crucial in characterizing them. I had to watch myself constantly. I really felt like a very tensed up labyrinth. Really, would you ever think of me as a harassed has-been of a college professor [in *Who's Afraid of Virginia Woolf?*]? A couple of stars turned the role down because they felt they just couldn't get away with it. If I had played the man as being afraid of that crazed, wonderful woman [Elizabeth Taylor as Martha], the whole thing would have been a disaster. [On the set of *Cleopatra*, Burton met Taylor; in addition to *Who's Afraid of Virginia Woolf?*, they made an additional ten films together: *The V.I.P.'s* (1963,

Anthony Asquith), *The Sandpiper* (1965, Vincente Minnelli), *Doctor Faustus* (1966, Richard Burton and Nevill Coghill), *The Taming of the Shrew* (1967, Franco Zeffirelli), *The Comedians* (1967, Peter Glenville), *Boom!* (1968, Joseph Losey), *Anne of the Thousand Days* (1969, Charles Jarrott), *Under Milk Wood* (1971, Andrew Sinclair), *Hammersmith is Out* (1972, Peter Ustinov) and *Divorce His; Divorce Hers* (1974, Waris Hussein — for TV).]

—Burton, interviewed by Chandler Brossard for *Look*, 27 June 1967

[Mike Nichols] is the best possible audience. Also, he has the one thing that no other director and very few actors have — timing of a line. He knows *how* to hit the operative word. [*Who's Afraid of Virginia Woolf?*] is inevitably a tragic comedy — you must get the laugh, even to the death. And it *must* be timed perfectly.

—Burton, interviewed by C. Robert Jennings for *The Saturday Evening Post*, 9 Oct 1965

Basically, *Equus* [1977, Sidney Lumet] is a mystery, a detective story seen through the eyes of Dr. Dysart, in a series of flashbacks. But it isn't a whodunit, it's a whydunit. *Why* does the boy [Peter Firth] blind those six horses? And *why* does the analyst, Dysart, who seems so cold and remote at the outset, become so totally consumed and obsessed by this bizarre case, so driven to solve it...?

Dysart is no ordinary psychiatrist. He's an eccentric, a driven, isolated man. A doctor working in a provincial hospital who has too many patients and stays in his office seeing them 18 hours a day. He's someone who can articulate very well on the special privacy of pain. As a result, he's always questioning. I could have played Dysart as a typical shrink in a white coat, plenty of Kleenex, never raising his voice or getting involved. But to me Dysart, who's at first just plain curious about the boy, gets sucked into his patient's torment almost against his will. He envies the boy for his passion; in the end it becomes his own.

—Burton, interviewed by Patricia Bosworth for *The New York Times*, 4 Apr 1976

Gary BUSEY [1944-]

Born: Goose Creek, Texas (now Baytown). Drama studies at Oklahoma State University and with James Best in Los Angeles, and work as a drummer preceded his film debut in Angels Hard as They Come (1971, John Viola). He played the title role in The Buddy Holly Story (1978, Steve Rash):

I found a couple film clips, but both were strange. In one, he's real teed off on the Ed Sullivan show because they wouldn't turn up his amplifier and they only gave him one song, so he plays "Oh Boy" real fast and storms off. Then there's a clip from an Arthur Murray Dance Party, where he's surrounded by about 30 middle-aged women in formals. So I worked by instinct....

To find his childhood, I just sensed mine. Middle class, church on Sundays, football — or in his case, guitar. Buddy was popular at home because he played fast and furious. People who had just heard his records may have been shocked when they saw him, but he wasn't into theater at all. He was just concerned with playing his songs.

—Busey, interviewed by Susan Toepfer for *The New York Daily News*, 16 July 1978

Buddy Holly was aggressive and impatient. There was no democracy in that band. He may have been shy off stage, but he was a real monster when he went on to play....

I wasn't doing an impression of anybody — it's all Gary Busey up there, within the perimeter of Buddy Holly's life.

—Busey, interviewed by Janet Maslin for *The New York Times*, 23 July 1978

Red BUTTONS [1919-]

Born: Aaron Chwatt in New York City. Work in vaudeville and burlesque and on Broadway preceded his film debut in Winged Victory (1944, George Cukor). In 1957, he played Airman Joe Kelly in Joshua Logan's adaptation of Sayonara:

People are surprised that a Jewish boy would be picked to play the role of Joe Kelly, but it's not as farfetched as it seems. When I was a kid I grew up in a pretty rugged neighborhood like Kelly did. My pals called me Irish because of my red hair, blue eyes and ruddy complexion. So you see, Joe Kelly and I could have been brothers.

—Buttons, interviewed by John Vergara for *The New York Sunday News*, 15 Dec 1957

Kelly is a guy I know very well. He is a product of any big city, probably New York, and goes from orphanage to reform school to the Army.

He's a rough kid but he commits suicide in the end.

—Buttons, interviewed by Joe Hyams for *The New York Herald Tribune*, 24 Dec 1956

Spring BYINGTON [1893-1971]

Born: Colorado Springs, Colorado. Stage work on tour and on Broadway preceded her film debut in Little Women (1933, George Cukor).

I liked the role of Louisa [in *Louisa* (1950, Alexander Hall)] because it was gay and flippant. Louisa had lots of pep, loads of charm, a wonderful sense of humor, and, best of all, a universal problem to deal with in the film. She was an older woman with young ideas. She wanted new interests in life and found them in the persons of Charles Coburn and Edmund Gwenn. This elderly romancing disturbed her son [Ronald Reagan], who thought she shouldn't remarry....

My favorite line came when Louisa's son greeted her with, "Mother, it's a half past one and the picture show let out at eleven-thirty.... Where have you been since then?"

"We parked, son," Louisa said.

—Byington, in *The Saturday Evening Post*, 12 May 1951

C

James CAAN [1939-]

Born: Queens, N.Y. Following studies at Michigan State University and Hofstra College, he studied acting with Wynn Handman at The Neighborhood Playhouse in N.Y. and soon thereafter began working both off and on Broadway. He made his film debut in a bit role in Irma la Douce (1963, Billy Wilder). To date, he has made four films with Francis Ford Coppola, the first of which was The Rain People (1969):

[I] went to a party one night and watched men coming into the room, all of them aware of themselves, of whether their tie was on straight, their fly zipped. I went outside and walked back into that room about 15 times — as a ballsy football player, a paraplegic, a screaming fag, a grotesque, a cripple. I made a complete ass of myself. About the 16th time, when I was totally exhausted, I just walked in, completely unaware of myself, nothing going through my head. And that was it. Killer Gannon was pure, void of ego. He walked only when he had to walk, talked only when he had to talk.

—Caan, interviewed by Aljean Harmetz for *The New York Times*, 14 Jan 1973

A short time before filming began [on *The Godfather* (1972, Francis Ford Coppola)], I went to Brooklyn and spent two weeks with a couple of gangster types who were very similar to the characters in the picture.

One of the two in particular resembled what I, in my minds' eye, saw the character of Sonny to be. He had some tremendous moves. I formed many mannerisms, based partly on an osmosis from this association, partly on my own instinct.

—Caan, interviewed for *The New York Daily News*, 13 Mar 1972

There was one guy in particular who was just incredible. I used to sit up, drinking, until seven in the morning, just watching him. I became genuinely friendly with a couple of them. Nice guys. We'd go out and laugh and eat and drink. The toughest and coarsest would be the most gentlemanly. Always dressed to the teeth, the first to stand up when a girl came by. God forbid you should say a profane word if they were with a lady. I tried to get all of that into the picture....

Most actors underplay, but I put my head on the chopping block for *The Godfather*, thinking if I were bad, I would be awful, but if I were good, I'd really show them something. To me, Sonny was Damon Runyonesque, broad, bigger than life. I became him for five months; I'd go out to dinner with my mother and curse, just asking her to pass the salt....

—Caan, interviewed for an unsourced, undated article in the files of The New York Public Library for the Performing Arts

I don't idolize any actor, but if I had to pick one that I admire more than any other, it would be Brando. Marlon has always been known as a guy who is always loose when he works. He seems to have a kind of glib, nonstudied technique. In fact, he works extremely hard at his acting. It's like with a great athlete who gives the appearance of doing things effortlessly without working at it. But behind Brando's seeming effortlessness, there is a lot of effort.

Marlon sometimes sort of half studies his lines so that he will appear to be real and believable, which he always is. The other thing is that he really listens to you when you are talking in a scene. He is not locked into any physical moves or pattern of dialogue. So that if I happen to unexpectedly drop a cup while we are doing a scene, for example, he will automatically respond to it and adapt himself to it in the dialogue. Brando is just extremely aware.

I truly feel I learned something from working with Brando [on *The Godfather*]. When I very carefully watched him work, it confirmed a lot of things about my own technique, because I do work similarly to him. I think words are secondary to attitude in acting. There are certain actors who will take the script home at night and study their movements, saying to themselves: "If the other actor does such and such, I will do so and so." But I don't like this method. It is too inflexible, stilted and unreal. I think you have to be completely available to everyone around you — other actors, the director and things that may just happen during the filming. [Caan also appeared briefly in Coppola's *The Godfather Part 2* (1974).]

—Caan, interviewed for *The New York Daily News*, 13 Mar 1972

I did a comedy called *Freebie and the Bean* [1974, Richard Rush]. I played the Freebie and Alan Arkin played the Bean. I had a lot of fun with Alan; he is terrific.... Alan and I worked on this whole relationship; it was like the odd couple in the squad car. It was two ridiculous people....

In *Freebie*, I play this cop who is a real gang busters guy; he is always stomping people and shaking them down. That is why they call him Freebie, because he never pays for anything. In *Cinderella Liberty* [1973, Mark Rydell], I play a guy from the south who is a sailor, a Billy Budd-ish kind of character. He is very pure, innocent, a very gullible guy who just hangs in there. When other guys would walk away from something and say they had had enough of this, he just hangs in there a little longer — it's a love story. Finally there is this character in *The Gambler* [1974, Karel Reisz] who is completely neurotic; it's a guy who is in pain for the two hours of the movie. He is a complete neurotic with all these ticks. I've got all these twitches.... I play a college professor.... Can you imagine me a Harvard graduate? A professor of English and American Literature? We did the two classroom scenes and it was fun. I had to learn how to speak all over again. This, over the other two is the more difficult because the character is almost bigger than life; it is a very stylized kind of piece; there are these monstrous speeches. The only thing that is heroic about this guy — and he is really a prick — is that he never begs or pleads, even though he is in an awful lot of trouble.

Q. Does he turn to gambling?

A. No, he has always been a gambler.... Gambling makes him more of a rogue, a kind of guy who is going to go through life with style, with that constant life and death kind of feeling. You can only eat so many hours a day and you can only make love so much a day, but you can really gamble all the time. It's kind of based on [screenwriter] Jimmy Toback to a degree. He just does things to shock people; he says crazy things....

—Caan, interviewed by Vincent Fremont for *Interview*, Jan 1974

[*Rollerball* (1975, Norman Jewison)] was about a guy who was trained from the time he was fourteen or twenty or whatever to be this jock. And to be unemotional and be sort of led by society. It was about this one man, not a genius or political mastermind, who questioned society, and at the end of that picture you felt like there's going to be a revolution. It was like the lady who refused to get in the back of the bus down in Mississippi. She was just some old lady. She just says, "Bullshit, I don't wanna get on the back of that bus." And without her, there's no Martin Luther King. You understand. And that's how I viewed the story.

—Caan, interviewed by Ralph Appelbaum for *Films & Filming*, July 1979

[Frank in *Thief* (1981, Michael Mann)] learned to exist in jail. After he achieved the mental attitude that he didn't care about anything, they left him alone. Because if you're going to mess with him, he was willing to go the distance.

The way I work, I like to be emotionally available, but this guy is available to nothing. Pretty soon I would find myself getting angry, my personal problems...would be magnified, because this guy was in existential pain for such a long time.

For three months, I was a lunatic, I had migraines 24 hours a day, I lost about 20 pounds. And then when I looked at the movie, I couldn't stand it. My eyes were like two pieces of glass. They scared me. I said, "That guy's a killer."

—Caan, interviewed by Chris Chase for *The New York Times*, 3 Apr 1981

The guy I play [in *Gardens of Stone* (1987, Francis Ford Coppola)] is in utter despair and profound depression. You can see him in one scene wearing all the medals he won. He was a great soldier during four years of duty [in Vietnam].

But when the film begins, he's back home, hates the war and thinks it's stupid. He thinks maybe if he could just go back one more time and teach these raw kids what he knows, maybe he'd save one life. He wants to save lives that he knows are going to be wasted.

—Caan, interviewed by Gene Siskel for *The New York Daily News*, 6 May 1987

Adolph CAESAR [1934-1986]

Born: Harlem, N.Y. Drama studies at New York University, work as a voice-over announcer, in repertory and with The Negro Ensemble Company preceded his film debut in Che! (1969, Richard Fleischer). In 1983, he played Sergeant Vernon Waters in Norman Jewison's adaptation of A Soldier's Story, a role he had played on stage:

[The role] incorporates into a single black character the full spectrum of human emotions. Waters is a tragic figure in the traditional sense: his downfall is brought about by one of his noble virtues — ambition. His ambition is to improve himself and the men under him so that they do not conform to the stereotypes of black people held by the (white) powers-that-be.

—Caesar, interviewed by Donald Chase for *The New York Daily News*, 13 Nov 1983

Nicolas CAGE [1965-]

Born: Nicolas Coppola in Long Beach, California; nephew of Francis Ford Coppola. Studies at The American Conservatory Theater in San Francisco and work on TV preceded his film debut in Fast Times at Ridgemont High (1982, Amy Heckerling). In 1984, he played Al in Alan Parker's Birdy:

Birdy was part of a stage that I went through in terms of experimenting with some of the more physical sacrifices required to shoot the character, such as wearing the bandages off-screen or pulling the teeth out.

I think I did that because I was so impressed with stories about great actors who sat on a block of ice so they could feel cold in a scene, or stayed up all night so they could be tired in a scene. I just wanted to try that approach at least once. It was exhausting, and now I'm not sure how necessary that approach is to arrive at that depth of the character....

I [also] felt a little guilty about playing a guy who was in Vietnam, never having experienced anything like that, so I guess I became slightly masochistic and took it out on myself, to try to put myself through some sort of pain, to feel somewhat of a connection — even if it was only one percent.

—Cage, interviewed by Robert Morris for *The Cable Guide*, Jan 1986

I perceived the whole film [*Peggy Sue Got Married (*1986, Francis Ford Coppola)] through Peggy Sue [Kathleen Turner]'s eyes as a dream. And I thought that gave me poetic license to be as abstract as I wanted. Because in dreams, oftentimes, things are weird and distorted. So I thought, here was an opportunity for me to attempt some surrealistic acting. The reason why I come off as being weirder than the others is that no one else had the same perception as I did. So they are vertical and I'm sort of horizontal — going in a different direction....

Charlie is embittered. He did not become what he wanted to be. And I just tried to paint the history of failure on this man's face. Failure that he didn't become a rock star. Twenty years of being a commercial salesman and not a rock star.

—Cage, interviewed by Joseph Gelmis for *Newsday*, 5 Oct 1986

[Charlie Bodell in *Peggy Sue Got Married*] was a close call. Francis did stand by me on that performance. He knew I was going to do something way out, and I really laugh when I see it. A lot of people have accused me of destroying the whole movie, but I think not. I thought, "If Francis is going to paint the sidewalk pink and the trees yellow, why can't I have these big goofy teeth and gawky gestures and things that are a little bit larger than life?"

At least it struck a chord. Whether they hated it or loved it, I think they're gonna remember it.

—Cage, interviewed by Stephanie Mansfield for *GQ*, Aug 1990

Ultimately, *Moonstruck* [1987, Norman Jewison] is a happy family film for an ensemble of actors rather than a purely romantic movie and I think it frustrated Norman that I leaned toward interpreting it as a desperately romantic Beauty and the Beast fable. I didn't change my character from the way it was written, but I did try to play up the wolfish part of Ronnie's personality.

—Cage, interviewed by Kristine McKenna for *The Los Angeles Times Calendar*, 21 Feb 1988

I've often played roles that were very large and sort of manic, and I wondered how I could be that ludicrous, but in a very contained way. Sailor [in *Wild at Heart* (1990, David Lynch)] is a lot more sedate than I've been in a while in a film — he's a strong character who doesn't need to rant and rave to get attention. The challenge is to be megacool in a way that will be totally absurd.

—Cage, interviewed by Ralph Rugoff for *Premiere*, Sept 1990

[Sailor] is like an old Corvette in a snakeskin jacket. He breaks down, he starts up, he breaks down. When he's driving, he drives fast and he drives cool, but he needs a tuneup. And even though he would beg and steal — like in the Elvis song — even though he killed a man, he did it because of love. He felt he was doing the right thing, even though it was pretty screwed up. There's not a lot of rationality between his instincts and his actions.

On *Vampire's Kiss* [1988, Robert Bierman] I choreographed, more or less, everything. I was just off in my own world. With *Wild at Heart*, being that I trusted Laura [Dern] and David [Lynch] so much — I could let my guard down, and be more spontaneous, free-flowing. I wasn't blocked into anything. At *all*....

David is like a *criminal* director. He's not concerned with Establishment laws and rules. He just does what he does.... He's constantly sculpting and fishing. A scene can turn into a comedy or into heavy horror in a fraction of a second. He's very much a sculptor, a spontaneous sculptor.

—Cage, interviewed by Mike Wilmington for *The Los Angeles Times Calendar*, 12 Aug 1990

Working with David was very liberating. His set is the most open and relaxed I've been on. He's the only director I know who, the colder and later it gets during night shoots, says, "Are you ready to have some more fun?" I think that's why so many spontaneous things happen in his movies.

—Cage, interviewed by Stephanie Mansfield for *GQ*, Aug 1990

James CAGNEY [1899-1986]

Born: New York City. A vaudeville dancer brought to Hollywood in the sound boom to recreate his Broadway role opposite Joan Blondell in Penny Arcade (the film version was retitled Sinner's Holiday — 1930, John Adolfi), Cagney quickly developed into a versatile performer in a variety of genres. In 1931, he played Tom Powers in William Wellman's The Public Enemy (1931):

Two fellows, Kubec Glasmon and John Bright, had written *Beer and Blood*, a story of two young Chicago hoods who were making their presence felt with guns and beer-running during the prohibition era in Chicago. That was the basis of the film called *Public Enemy*. Warner had borrowed a good actor, Eddie Woods, from First National to play the lead, and I was set to play the second lead. Then Glasmon and Bright saw *Doorway to Hell* [1930, Archie Mayo] and said to the Warner management, "You'd better switch the two parts around." Bill Wellman, who was to direct, also held that view. They told me later that what they saw in me was a "street-gamin quality and a brashness" which they thought right for the part. They went to Darryl Zanuck, who was then head of production at Warner Brothers, and the switch was made.

—Cagney, in *The Saturday Evening Post*, 14 Jan 1956

The Public Enemy was the film that really launched my career. I played a mean, mixed-up hood, a tough kid who tried to throw his weight around and ended up dead.... It was one of the first of many chances I had to portray that kind of person, the fist-swinging gangster who becomes ruthless in order to succeed.... Each of my subsequent roles in the hoodlum genre offered me the opportunity to inject something new, which I always tried to do. One could be funny, and the next one flat. Some roles were mean, and others were meaner. A few roles among them were actually sympathetic and kindhearted, and I preferred them, but I generally did not get to do many of those parts until much later in my career, for the public seemed to prefer me as a bad guy. Since I was most frequently cast as a criminal, constantly on the prod, I rarely got to do the comedy roles I really would have preferred....

William Wellman did a good job on *The Public Enemy*, I thought, as he did on the earlier picture I did with him, *Other Men's Women* [1931], in which I played opposite Joan Blondell and Mary Astor. He let me go my way and develop my own interpretation whenever it was possible. With other members of the cast of *The Public Enemy*, such as Jean Harlow and Joan, however, he was less understanding. Having this kind of discernment makes for a good director.

It was he who suggested that I squash that half a grapefruit into Mae Clarke's face in the famous scene, and it set a precedent in the abuse of women in films. In my next film, *Smart Money* [1931, Alfred E. Green], which starred Edward G. Robinson, I again had to hit a lady in the face.

—Cagney, interviewed by Gregory Speck for *Interview*, Dec 1985

Q. Which of your leading ladies have you most enjoyed working with, and why?

A. I must answer from the viewpoint of business, and not with the involvement of personal friendship. I most enjoy working with girls like Mary Brian [*Hard to Handle* (1933, Mervyn LeRoy)] and Loretta Young [*Taxi!* (1932, Roy Del Ruth)], who are sweet, demure and charming, and who thereby strengthen my own screen characterizations by means of contrast.

Alice White was suggested for my most recent picture [*Hard to Handle*], but I preferred Miss Brian, because I feel that leading ladies such as Miss White, Joan Blondell [five films to that time: *Sinner's Holiday*, *Other Men's Women*, *The Public Enemy*, *Blonde Crazy* (1931, Roy Del Ruth) and *The Crowd Roars* (1933, Lloyd Bacon)] and Ann Dvorak [*The Crowd Roars*] are too pert to contrast properly with my own type. [Cagney and White were co-starred again on his next feature, *Picture Snatcher* (1933, Lloyd Bacon).]

—Cagney, interviewed by James Fidler for *Movie Classic*, Feb 1933

I'm sick of walking, talking, gesticulating like a tough. I'm so tired of taking cracks at women, and brow-beating them, that whenever I'm asked to do that on screen, I feel like turning to the camera and saying, "Pardon me, audience, but that's just an act. I'd much rather kiss the girl than sock her...!"

Now I don't mean that the tough guy hasn't been successful. The public has liked me tough, but I'm looking ahead. The day of the gangster, the mug, the guy who slaps the woman down, is through.... I want to take the rough edges off James Cagney, sandpaper his neck, get him out of those pinched-in suits, and put him in plus-fours...let him use his natural voice and forget these "dese" and "dems" and let him wear kid gloves instead of brass knuckles! But I'm having a devil of a time to get my studio [Warner Brothers] to see it.

—Cagney, interviewed by Katharine Hartley for *Movie Classic*, Oct 1934

Lloyd Bacon...would get a script, like the one for *Footlight Parade* [1933], and he would *never* read it. The day we'd start shooting, he'd open the script, mark out our lines for the day; he might change the setups from a long shot to a closeup, or vice versa; that was the extent of his commitment to the script. His technique was to *trust* the actors, and it worked. Bacon once said to me, "I tried for two years to make a go at acting, and I couldn't figure it out. How the hell am I going to tell you how to do it?" Sounds funny, I know, but he wasn't joking. He knew enough to keep a simple thing simple. [Cagney worked with Bacon on eight other films: *Picture Snatcher* (1933), *He Was Her Man* (1934), *Here Comes the Navy* (1934), *Devil Dogs in the Air* (1935), *The Irish in Us* (1935), *The Frisco Kid* (1935), *Boy Meets Girl* (1938) and *The Oklahoma Kid* (1939).]

—Cagney, interviewed by Timothy White for *Rolling Stone*, 18 Feb 1982

I got a message that Mr. Reinhardt wanted to talk to me. He asked me what I thought of Bottom [in *A Midsummer Night's Dream* (1935, Max Reinhardt and William Dieterle)]. I thought he was the first and best ham actor ever written. It seemed a new idea to Reinhardt but he seemed to like it....

Working with him was a joy from start to finish — as it is with any man who is an expert at his craft....

—Cagney, interviewed by Ida Zeitlin for *Movie Classic*, Dec 1935

All I'm trying to put across is realism. The idea that heroes aren't always perfect gentlemen, and villains aren't always slinking blackguards. They can come out of the same mold.

I've had people ask me to tell them about the gangsters I know. I don't know any gangsters. I'll tell you where I get those "realistic" mannerisms. Watching ordinary people, looking for odd little idiosyncrasies. That nervous shoulder hunch of Rocky Sullivan's [in *Angels with Dirty Faces* (1938, Michael Curtiz)], for example. I once knew a fellow who wore his collars too tight and got relief, unconsciously, with that mannerism. He was a shoe clerk.

—Cagney, interviewed by James Reid for *Screen Book*, Aug 1939

The ending of *Angels with Dirty Faces* has prompted a continually asked question over the years: did Rocky turn yellow as he walked to the electric chair, or did he just pretend to? For those who haven't seen the picture, I must explain that

Rocky becomes the idol of the street kids in his old neighborhood, and when he is ultimately brought to justice and condemned to die, these youngsters still hold him up as a model to emulate. Rocky's childhood pal, now a priest [Pat O'Brien] comes to him in the death house and pleads with him to kill the kids' unhealthy admiration of him by turning yellow at the last minute, by pretending cowardice as he is being led to the electric chair. Rocky scorns the request.

The execution scene is this: cheekily contemptuous of my escorts, I am being led along the last mile when suddenly, without any warning, I go into a seizure of fear, twisting and turning in the clutch of the guards as I try to prevent them from leading me into the death chamber. Or *is* it a seizure of fear? Am I not instead doing a favor for my priest pal and the kids by pretending to be yellow, thereby discouraging the youngsters from following in my convict footsteps? Through the years I have actually had little kids come up to me on the street and ask, "Didya do it for the father, huh?" I think in looking at the film it is virtually impossible to say which course Rocky took — which is just the way I wanted it. I played it with deliberate ambiguity so that the spectator can take his choice.

Outside of the little extra bits and pieces dropped in by the actors, everything about *The Oklahoma Kid* [1939, Lloyd Bacon] was cliché, even the ending — guy getting gal, kiss, fadeout....

Banal script notwithstanding, the actors went to the post set to do the best job we could with the material at hand. Bogie played a heavy in it, doing his usual expert job. By this time in his career he'd become entirely disillusioned with the picture business. Endlessly the studio [Warner Brothers] required him to show up without his even knowing what the script was, what his dialogue was, what the picture was about. On top of this he would be doing two or three pictures at a time. That's how much they appreciated him.

He came into the makeup department one morning and I said, "What is it today, Bogie?" "Oh, I don't know," he said. "I was told to go over to Stage 12." There he was fulfilling his contract, doing as required, however much against his will. We shared the same attitude: when there's a job to be done, you do it. New acting talent would come along, and the studio's idea of building them up was simply to throw them into one picture after another as quickly as possible. In this sink-or-swim situation the ones who survived were the ones with natural durability. Bogie had that kind of durability.

—Cagney, in his *Cagney by Cagney* (Garden City, N.Y.: Doubleday & Co., 1976)

I got along fine with [Raoul] Walsh [on *The Roaring Twenties* (1939)], for he took suggestions from me for script improvements and incorporated them into the scenes. I worked with him three more times, too, in *The Strawberry Blonde*, made in 1941 with Olivia De Havilland and Rita Hayworth, in *White Heat* [1949] and in *A Lion is in the Streets*, done in 1953. As for Bogey, he had a real presence as an actor, and he was able to do anything required of him.... I never really got to know the man, however, but for that matter, few people did. He seemed to have an attitude that nobody was going to like him. The way he dealt with that was to be sure that they knew that he didn't like them first. I'm not at all like that.

—Cagney, interviewed by Gregory Speck for *Interview*, Dec 1985

Before I did *Yankee Doodle Dandy* [1942, Michael Curtiz], I had seen [George M.] Cohan twice [on stage] — once in *I'd Rather Be Right* [1937] and once in *Ah, Wilderness!* [1933] — but when I finally played him I decided not to ape him 100 percent. Cohan didn't walk, he strode, and his striding was accompanied by a bobbing of the head. He had other such outstandingly strong mannerisms, not only on stage but in his daily behavior, that if I had tried to play him both off and on stage the way he really was, the result would have been top-heavy with gimmicks, and my feeling is that gimmicks should never interfere with a performance. So I decided to play Cohan with all of his mannerisms when he was on, and straight, with just a suggestion of the Cohan gestures, when he was off.

—Cagney, in *The Saturday Evening Post*, 14 Jan 1956

The original script of *White Heat* was very formula. The old knock-down-drag-'em-out again, without a touch of imagination or originality. The leading character, Cody Jarrett, was just another murderous thug. For some kind of variant, I said to the writers [Ivan Goff and Ben Roberts], "Let's fashion this after Ma Barker and her boys, and make Cody a psychotic to account for his actions." The writers did this, and it was a natural prelude to the great last scene in the picture where I commit suicide by pumping bullets into the blazing gas tank I'm standing on....

To get in the Ma Barker flavor with some pungency, I thought we would try something, take a little gamble. Cody Jarrett is psychotically tied to his mother's apron strings, and I wondered if we dare have him sit in her lap once for comfort. I said to the director, Raoul Walsh, "Let's see if we can get away with this." He said, "Let's try it." We did it, and it worked.

Not long ago a reporter asked me if I didn't have to "psych" myself up for the scene in *White Heat* where I go berserk on learning of my mother's death. My answer to the question is that you don't psych yourself up for these things, you do them. I can imagine what some of the old-timers would have said in answer to that question. They would have laughed aloud at the idea of an actor pumping himself up with emotional motivations to do a scene. The pro is supposed to know what to do, then go ahead and do it. In this particular scene, I knew what deranged people sounded like because once as a youngster I had visited Ward's Island where a pal's uncle was in the hospital for the insane. My God, what an education that was! The shrieks, the screams of those people under restraint! I remembered those cries, saw that they fitted, and I called on my memory to do as required. No need to psych up.

—Cagney, in his *Cagney by Cagney* (Garden City, N.Y.: Doubleday & Co., 1976)

The gunman I play [in *White Heat*] is an unusual kind of hoodlum. He's a diseased, psychopathic killer with a mother complex. His mother has raised him for a life of crime. He has a tremendous love for his mother and his mother has a tremendous love for him.

This guy is a pathological case. He has psychosomatic symptoms — he gets headaches and falls to the floor and writhes in agony in his tantrums. When his mother [Margaret Wycherly] is killed, a Federal "undercover" man [Edmond O'Brien] duplicates the things his mother has done for him and helps comfort him. There is a transference of affection....

The old gangsters I played on the screen were simple — they killed because it was part of their job. They rubbed out their rivals. But this guy has a streak of straight brutality — a fundamentally criminal point of view.

—Cagney, interviewed by Ezra Goodman for *The New York Times*, 12 June 1949

One of the attractions of *Kiss Tomorrow Goodbye* [1950, Gordon Douglas] was that damned good actor, Luther Adler, who taught me an acting trick I have remembered. Luther's really chilling moment in the picture came as he was sitting at a desk, just about to look up at me. Instead of lifting his face and looking at me at the same time, he lifted his face only, his eyes remaining hooded, looking down. *Then*, after his head was fully raised, he lifted his eyelids and stared slowly at me with infinite menace. Such a little thing but such a powerful thing. I had never seen an actor do that in my life, and I have been around a bit. Later I suggested that particular bit of business to Dana Wynter to use in the Irish picture we did, *Shake Hands with the Devil* [1959, Michael Anderson]. And when she whipped those big brown eyes from the ground at me it was a decided jolt.

The shooting began, and *Mister Roberts* [1955, John Ford and Mervyn LeRoy] progressed in good order. Then I realized that upcoming was a scene with Jack [Lemmon] as Ensign Pulver, that I had found so funny in the reading that I realized it would be marvelously so in the playing. The difficulty was that it was *so* funny I had serious doubts about my ability to play it with a straight face. I talked it over with Jack. I said, "We've got some work ahead of us. You and I'll have to get together and rehearse that scene again and again and again until I don't think it's funny anymore." He agreed because he had the same feeling about the scene. So we got together and did it and did it and did it. But every time I came to the payoff line in the scene, "Fourteen months, sir," I just couldn't keep a straight face. Finally, with enough rehearsal we thought we had it licked....

Now — I submit that this is one hell of a funny little scene: the commanding officer of a naval vessel finally meeting an ensign who had been ducking him during their voyage for well over a year. I used to collapse every time Jack said "Fourteen months, sir," but when we filmed it, I was able to hang on just *barely*. What you see in the film is the top of Mount Everest for us after our rigorous rehearsals.

—Cagney, in his *Cagney by Cagney* (Garden City, N.Y.: Doubleday & Co., 1976)

Jack Ford saw [my character in *Mr. Roberts*] as the most pathetic man on the ship, entirely alone and not knowing how to exert his authority. He was a lonely soul, removed from everybody and everything. I agreed.

—Cagney, in *The Saturday Evening Post*, 14 Jan 1956

What Doris [Day] has, and all the good ones have, is the ability to project the simple, direct statement of a simple, direct idea without cluttering it.

That's what she brought to *Love Me or Leave Me* [1955, Charles Vidor], which is a movie that I rate among the top five of the sixty-two pictures that I made. I played Marty Snyder, the crippled, small-time hood who sponsored and managed Ruth Etting's career. I knew the Marty Snyders of the world from the tough New York neighborhood in which I grew up. Hard-bitten, aggressive little guys, self-assertive, driven to compensate for their poverty and, in this case, for the handicap of a crippled leg. The director had some kind of iron device that he wanted to clamp on my leg to achieve the crippled effect, but I said it would only get in the way. I much preferred to play crippled as I felt it. I didn't want to imitate the real Marty Snyder any more than Doris tried to mimic Ruth Etting. It's my feeling that impersonation gets in the way of a performance and takes over. I prefer to interpret rather than imitate....

In one of the key scenes in *Love Me*, we have a slam-bang argument that culminates with me slapping Doris. We rehearsed the scene a couple of times for the camera, but each time I only feigned slapping her, stopping my hand just short of her face. That's a common movie technique, with the sound of the slap dubbed in later. But when we were playing the scene, and I felt it was going just right, I didn't pull my slap but I really whacked Doris across the cheek. I didn't want to fake anything about that scene. She was stunned, more surprised than hurt, although the slap was sharp enough to have given her face a sting — she looked at me with a stricken look on her face and tears welled in her eyes and the surprise was 100 percent genuine.

—Cagney, interviewed by A.E. Hotchner for *Doris Day: Her Own Story* (New York: William Morrow & Co., 1975)

Billy Wilder was more of a dictator than most of the others I worked with. We worked together in 1961 on *One, Two, Three*, and he was overly bossy, full of noise — a pain. Still, we did a good picture together. I didn't learn until after we were done that he didn't like me, which was fine as far as I was concerned, because I certainly didn't like him. He didn't know how to let things *flow*, and that matters a great deal to me.

—Cagney, interviewed by Timothy White for *Rolling Stone*, 18 Feb 1982

Michael CAINE [1933-]

Born: Maurice Micklewhite in South London, England. Work with The Horsham Repertory Company and other theatre troupes, on TV, and bit parts in over 30 films preceded Zulu (1964, Cy Endfield) which brought him to leading player status:

Prince Philip [The Duke of Edinburgh] walks always with his hands behind his back, and in *Zulu* I walked the whole time like that. No one found it out, but they knew unconsciously who I was, because Prince Philip is so familiar; they'd seen him on the television news. I also realized that privileged people like him speak very slowly, because they don't have to get your attention. You're already hanging on their words. They're not like some little Cockney salesman who's afraid you're going to shut the door in his face.

—Caine, interviewed by Benedict Nightingale for *The New York Times*, 26 July 1981

Alfie [in *Alfie* (1966, Lewis Gilbert)] is terribly destructive to people, but he doesn't even know it.... In order to make him acceptable to an audience, I played him with a kind of innocence that only people who do terrible things can have. If they understood the evil in the things they do, they'd go right out of their minds, off their rockers! But the whole point of the picture is that ordinary people who are not bad or immoral find themselves in dreadful situations....

No matter what kind of person you're portraying, there has to be that little bit which remains likable. As I got into Alfie's character, I kept finding more and more points in myself that I could relate to him, and the recognition of what we had in common disturbed me very much. The more you understand someone, the more you understand he is a product of his education and his environment, and the more sympathy you have for him. There came to be a kind of love-hate relationship between us.

I played the agent in *The Ipcress File* [1965, Sidney J. Furie] like an ordinary man who's caught in a terribly dangerous situation. I put a lot of myself into Harry Palmer — touches about cooking, wearing glasses. He wasn't very secure, he didn't do so good a job as he might have as a secret agent. He was sarcastic and a bit smarty-pants. I added the kind of insolence and insubordination which everyone feels some time or other, like wanting to tell the boss to take a jump in the lake, and played it cool at the same time. We kept rewriting that script every day as we went along, trying not to lose the story. Making Len Deighton's sequel *Funeral in Berlin* [1966, Guy Hamilton], I decided to change the character of Harry Palmer a little. That keeps him interesting. Harry's more confident now, more aggressive; he does a better job because he knows more....

—Caine, interviewed by Edwin Miller for *Seventeen*, Dec 1966

Caine: Like a lot of young people today, Palmer is a kind of lonely anarchist — very lonely and very anarchic....

Playboy: Is Palmer like James Bond in that sense?

Caine: Yes. In addition to being lonely and anarchists, Bond and Palmer are against government by big business. They believe in government by *small* business, and the small business is *them*. They are the judge, jury and executioner, should you come up to be tried before them. And they'll shoot you, based on their own judgment, without reference to anyone else....

I share Palmer's style of ironic *non sequitur* humor — or rather, Palmer shares mine, since I added this element to the role myself.

—Caine, interviewed by David Lewin for *Playboy*, July 1967

My nervous reaction to working with [Laurence Olivier on *Sleuth* (1972, Joseph L. Mankiewicz)] was not only out of respect for his talent, which is tremendous, but also because I knew from my own theatre experience that sometimes these theatrical giants are given to riding roughshod over some of the other members of the cast. I faced the first day with some trepidation. My worries proved to be unfounded as Larry turned out to be one of the most friendly and helpful actors I have ever worked with.

That he is a professional goes without saying, but the degree of professionalism is extraordinary and exhausting. Throughout the film he would come charging into my room to rehearse again and again, and to try new things until together we had milked the scene of every value it had.

To act with Laurence Olivier is rather like skating with Sonja Henie. The fact that you can do it is not necessarily going to do you much good. His command of his art is complete. This much you can see as an observer but it is not until you actually work with him that you experience what I used to call during the filming of *Sleuth* the "take off." This is a phenomenon which seems to overcome him when, instead of just being brilliant which is something that another artist can at least try to keep up with, he will suddenly leap into a realm of acting where it is virtually impossible to follow.

—Caine, in the foreword to *Olivier: The Films and Faces of Laurence Olivier*, ed. by Margaret Morley (Farncombe, England: LSP Books, 1978)

Mankiewicz is bloody marvelous. He knows what you should want and he also knows when you've got it. He's one of those directors who says nothing if he likes it but if he starts going on and starts questions you know you haven't got it.

—Caine, interviewed by Sydney Edwards for *The Evening Standard*, 15 Dec 1972

Q. How was it working with John Huston on *The Man Who Would Be King* [1975]? He's said to be such a terrifyingly cruel man.

A. He would be a terrifyingly cruel man if you couldn't give him what he wanted. But you see, he adored Chris Plummer, Sean Connery, and myself because the day we walked onto the set, we were exactly who he wanted us to be. And all during the picture, and for quite a long time afterwards, he called Sean and me by our character's names, Peachy and Danny....

Q. That was a very physically demanding film, since much of it was shot in mountains and snow. Do you think that physical demands on actors today are excessive?

A. Yes. You wonder where to stop. What screwed us up was the long focal lens which comes right in close up when you're on top of the mountain. Which means it's got to be you and not a stand-in.

—Caine, interviewed by Marjorie Rosen for *Film Comment*, July/Aug 1980

[Colby, in *Victory* (1981, John Huston) is] uncomfortable with himself, the sort of person who is always looking to see where others are uncomfortable with themselves, where there's an opening, somewhere for him to smack in. So I tried to play him with great watchfulness, tremendous stillness. Very, very quiet, so that the tiniest movement was a violent act.

—Caine, interviewed by Benedict Nightingale for *The New York Times*, 26 July 1981

I ran my mind through film history, all the characters I've seen, trying to think of someone who was as devious and as cunning as [Sidney] Bruhl [in *Deathtrap* (1982, Sidney Lumet)]. The only one I could come up with was Sylvester the Cat chasing Tweetie Pie. You know that terrible cunning look he gets when he comes up with this great new idea? Throughout the whole movie, the assistant director would always yell, "Get Sylvester on the set."

—Caine, interviewed by Carol Wallace for *The New York Sunday News*, 4 Apr 1982

Lewis Gilbert — who had directed me in *Alfie* eighteen years ago — said, "Would you like to do the part of Frank Bryant in the filming of this play [*Educating Rita*]?" I had already seen the play about two years before, and I'd seen the performance of Julie Walters as Rita and thought that was a helluva performance. I thought I'd like to be associated with this, and I thought I could make something of Frank Bryant. On the stage in London the part was played by an excellent actor, Mark Kingston, but on stage you don't really notice the guy. When you watch a stage play you watch whoever is talking and whoever is moving, which in *Educating Rita* means that you're watching Rita the entire time. And I remember saying to an actor friend, "I'm going to play the professor, Frank Bryant." And he said, "Whatever for? He's not in the play." I said, "I'll tell you — on the stage you're only looking at Rita because she never stops talking or moving, but in the movie you'll have to cut away to the reactions of the man she's playing with." In other words, in a movie, you cannot get away with just doing a star performance — moving and talking all the time. People become bored with you. You have to show reactions. On stage a cardboard tree is a cardboard tree, and you suspend reaction. In a movie a tree is a real tree, it loses its leaves and gets covered with snow. And that applies to everybody in a movie. Nothing is in isolation as it is in a theater — and you have to play according to the reactions of someone else to what you're doing. One of the things I'm known for in movies is not acting but *reacting*.

The part of the professor was built up and then it became a two-hander. You know, Julie had never made a movie before and on the first take — you can imagine what it's like, your first movie and your first take, your stomach is like a knot — I leaned over and gave her a little kiss, and I said, "You make 'em laugh" — which, of course, she could do — "and I'll make 'em cry" — which is what I'd figured out I could do with this role....

Q. One's first reaction to this story is that it's a reworking of *Pygmalion*. Yet it isn't. Was there a very conscious effort to stay away from that idea?

A. I've read some comments about the similarity to *Pygmalion*, but I don't see that at all.... You must have seen the performance of Emil Jannings in *The Blue Angel* [1929, Josef von Sternberg] — the unrequited love of the ugly old professor for the beautiful young cabaret dancer played by Marlene Dietrich. My performance was not based on Rex Harrison in *My Fair Lady* [1964, George Cukor], or on Leslie Howard in *Pygmalion* [1938, Leslie Howard and Anthony Asquith]. My performance in *Educating Rita* was based on man's unrequited love for a woman out of his class — and that was Emil Jannings in *The Blue Angel*. I gained the weight, chose a deliberately unattractive wardrobe, and grew that beard — which was very uncomfortable, I must say. That's the way I saw the role; I never saw her falling in love with him — I saw him as a tragic figure, a disaster, really, and that's why I liked him....

—Caine, interviewed at Judith Crist's Tarrytown seminar, 30 Sept-2 Oct 1983; repr. in *Take 22*, co-ed. by Judith Crist and Shirley Sealy (New York: Viking Press, 1984)

I'm used to doing one, two, maybe three takes. With Woody [Allen on *Hannah and Her Sisters* (1986)], it was nine or 10. He's a perfectionist. He wouldn't let any of us be less than great as he saw it....

He's interested in the basic attitude [of the characters] and evidently I'd got the right attitude. I always thought I was playing Woody's alter ego, and he seemed to like the guy.

—Caine, interviewed by Charles Champlin for *The Los Angeles Times*; repr. in *The Toronto Star*, 29 Dec 1986

Dyan CANNON [1939-]

Born: Samille Diane Freisen in Tacoma, Washington. Studies with Sanford Meisner at The Neighborhood Playhouse in N.Y. preceded her film debut in The Rise and Fall of Legs Diamond (1960, Budd Boetticher). In 1982, she played Myra Bruhl in Sidney Lumet's adaptation of Deathtrap:

Sidney is certainly the greatest utilizer of time I have ever worked with in my life. He takes two weeks before he shoots a film, and in those two weeks the actors, the cinematographer, the property master, and everyone else that's major on the set knows what they are going to do. We run through the whole thing like a play, so we have a chance to rehearse it like a play. With *Deathtrap* [1982] it was very good because it *was* a play. By the time you get on the set, he knows exactly what he wants. So he only does two or three takes of everything, which makes it *very* rough....

I had to stay pitched at hysteria. Honestly! The minute I came onto the set in the morning I had to work up the juices and *stay there* until I left at night. I'd go into my dressing room at lunch and collapse for a half hour and then come out and start again. But that's how I accomplished that part. The reason the part was so hard was that, on paper, she was the only character who didn't have any action. She didn't have any motivation. All she did was love her husband. [Cannon had previously worked with Lumet on *The Anderson Tapes* (1971).]

—Cannon, interviewed for *Dialogue on Film, American Film*, Nov 1982

Lynn CARLIN [1931-]

Born: Los Angeles. After appearing in a number of productions at The Laguna Beach Playhouse, she abandoned acting. Then, while working as Robert Altman's secretary, she was approached by John Cassavetes to make her film debut in Faces [1968].

Milos [Forman] is kind and gentle, and he always does his homework. When he came on the set [of *Taking Off* (1970)], he knew how he was going to shoot every shot, and just how he was going to cut it. We had no script at all. He'd come in and tell us what we were going to say. He said we couldn't see a script because he didn't want us to have a preconceived idea of how to play our parts. He likes spontaneity. He said if we didn't get all the ideas he wanted us to project, we'd do it over again. I *loved* working that way. I'm terribly lazy, and it's the greatest way to work. I don't ever want to learn lines again....

John Cassavetes has a much different personality. He is a madman, but a most charming and delightful person. All of our lines [for *Faces*] were learned. And where Milos would shoot a scene three or four times, John would shoot a scene 30 times. They say he can't fail to make a good movie because he shoots so much film. I was three months pregnant with my first child when we started to film *Faces* in 1964, and I was three months pregnant with my second child when he started reshooting three years later. He spent three years cutting. Three years! It's lucky I was having babies so I had something to fill up my time.

—Carlin, interviewed by Judy Klemesrud for *The New York Times*, 18 Apr 1971

Art CARNEY [1918-]

Born: Mount Vernon, N.Y. Although he made his film debut in 1941 — in a bit part in Pot of Gold (George Marshall) — it was on radio, then opposite Jackie Gleason on TV (from 1948), then on the Broadway stage (from 1957) where he found fame. His first major film role was in Harry and Tonto (1974, Paul Mazursky):

Paul came up to Ogunquit...to talk me into it.

I said I was worried. I would not do it all palsied, or whatever. I wanted dignity, with a lot of verve and drive. I was thinking of my agent, Bill McCaffrey, who started off as Albee's office boy in the Keith-Albee circuit and who's the last of the breed. William Francis Xavier McCaffrey, to give his full monicker. You can't get any more Irish than that. Anyway, Bill is that way, the way I wanted to play it.

—Carney, interviewed by Jerry Tallmer for *The New York Post*, 17 Aug 1974

Mazursky said, "Life is available to anyone at any age who wants to seize it." That's the theme of the film and that's not too unlike what I'm experiencing. I've been trying to get a good picture, and this is it.

—Carney, interviewed by Ann Guarino for *The New York Sunday News*, 18 Aug 1974

Like [Ira Wells in *The Late Show* (1977, Robert Benton)], I wear glasses and a hearing aid, the whole bit. I had a bum leg, too, because of a shrapnel wound I got back in 1944.... I'm not old — I'm only 58 — but I find that my ailments really bug me, because they seem to mean the end of me, of my work. That's why I identified with the fellow in *The Late Show*. He was so goddam *mad* about being over the hill....

No actress could have played that role [of Margo Sperling] better than Lily [Tomlin]. A lot of it came out of her ability to improvise and chatter. You can't write that kind of stuff into a script. Lily and I had a lot of fun working together, but she's a loner, not at all the gregarious person most people assume she is.

—Carney, interviewed by Guy Flatley for *The New York Times*, 20 May 1977

Leslie CARON [1931-]

Born: Boulogne-Billancourt, France. Trained in ballet at Le Conservatoire Nationale de Dance, she performed from 1946 for Roland Petit at Les Ballets des Champs-Elysées. Spotted by Gene Kelly while she was performing in La Rencontre in 1949, she was chosen to play opposite him in An American in Paris (1951, Vincente Minnelli):

All the girls from Ava Gardner to Elizabeth Taylor were doing their hair at the studio in a certain way — parted at the side and then curls, curls, curls. I refused. I kept my hair straight. They had their eyebrows plucked and all that sort of detail, which I just would not do. The day before we started shooting *An American in Paris*, I cut my hair, I cut it all off — to the dismay of the studio, I must say. They had to postpone shooting for two weeks to let *something* grow out again. Those were little things I did to keep a certain independence.

Let's face it, I certainly smiled a lot in those old films. God knows, I'm glad to have finally broken with that. I've quit smiling now and, let me tell you, it is a well-needed relief. That was the training you got at MGM. You had to be amiable. That was the number one requisite: to be pleasant, lovable — which isn't very interesting. I never liked it, but that's all there was. That's the mold I was in. I tried to break out. I was always trying. It's pathetic to say so now, but when I did *Lili* [1953, Charles Walters], people said I was taking unbelievable chances with my career, because I showed myself from not always the best angle — hardly any make-up, drab gray clothes — anything but obedient and charming and glamorous, all the things we were taught to be. It sounds almost sad now to describe that as a fist on the table on my part, but it really was.

—Caron, interviewed by Frank Pleasants for *After Dark*, Oct 1976

[*Gigi* (1958)] was my third picture with [Vincente Minnelli]. I love working with Minnelli, but one has to understand his language. He is an individualist in the way he expresses himself. He tends to go in a roundabout way, and if you ask him a direct question he won't give you a direct answer. But I find that his judgment is a marvelous thermometer, if you do something wrong he knows instinctively that it is wrong, although he cannot always tell you why it is wrong or how you should do it. [She also worked with Minnelli on *The Story of Three Loves* (1953).]

—Caron, interviewed for *Films & Filming*, July 1961

David CARRADINE [1936-]

Born: Hollywood; son of John and half brother to Keith and Robert. College dramatics at San Francisco State College, several Shakespearean roles in and around San Francisco, and work on TV preceded his film debut in a bit part in Taggart (1964, R.G. Springsteen). Following three seasons on Kung Fu, he played Woody Guthrie in Bound for Glory (1976, Hal Ashby):

Woody — that part was me.... I played him like me. He was so utterly human, so happy, always ready to get on with the next thing, uncompromising. He liked to ride trains and carry his guitar and he was restless and, well, that's me, that's me.

—Carradine, interviewed by Bernard Weinraub for *The New York Times*, 4 Dec 1976

Telling you what to do or how to do it is not really the way to direct. I think people who direct that way are primarily people who have never acted. The good directors that I've worked with — like Hal Ashby [on *Bound for Glory*], for instance — spend their time creating an atmosphere in which you will inevitably come up with something good. If a director gives you specific directions, it defocuses your own natural abilities. You turn off that part of yourself and you say, "Okay, I'll do this; you told me to do that, so I'll do it." And that's what you focus on. The director actually loses part of his actor when he does that.

—Carradine, interviewed by David Galligan for *Drama-Logue*, 12-18 Mar 1981

Q. How do you feel about *Long Riders* [1980] and Walter Hill....?

A. Walter's good; he completely accepts the existence of the system the way it is, and he works within it. And at the same time, he's very human to work with, which is very similar to the way Hal Ashby works. It's just a simple way of working, and there's a whole lot of directors who work like that. But there are differences in personality, like Hal is an older man, and very, very hip; he does not like to tell people what to do. He likes to make things grow with his hands. And Walter has great grasp of all levels of the thing, not in a hip way, and into that he infuses enormous creativity. You know, he likes John Ford. It's definitely a very positive experience.

—Carradine, interviewed by Ralph Appelbaum for *Films & Filming*, June 1980

John CARRADINE [1906-1988]

Born: Richmond Carradine in New York City; father of David, Keith and Robert [1954-]. After traveling through the South working as a sketch artist, he made his stage debut in New Orleans in 1925. Work performing Shakespeare in stock preceded his film debut in Tol'able David (1930, John Blystone). Until 1935, he appeared under the name Peter Richmond. He worked for Cecil B. DeMille on five films: The Sign of the Cross (1932), This Day and Age (1933), Cleopatra (1934), The Crusades (1935) and The Ten Commandments (1956):

Q. What was it like acting for DeMille?

A. I was very fond of him, and we became very close. Most of my early work for him was in dubbing. He also used me as an extra. Of course, he didn't call us extras. He'd say, "You wouldn't be here if you were extras." And we'd all have complete scripts. He'd quote wonderful speeches to the extras, telling us how dramatically and historically — and he was a great scholar — important our actions were. And we'd applaud him.

He didn't direct the mobs. He had twenty or thirty assistant directors who each took a group of twenty people and worked out pieces of business for every person in that group, and then he put it all together. If DeMille didn't like it, he'd raise hell. But his bark was much worse than his bite. Some actors hated him — but only the bad actors. The "hams" loathed him because he penetrated their falseness.

I had to fight [John Ford] all the way through [*The Grapes of Wrath* (1940)]. He wanted me to play Casey like a blithering idiot. And I said, "That man is not stupid, he is merely ignorant. He is not blind, he is only in the dark." I had a big scene in which Casey — who had seen the light — gives a long speech to his pals, just before he is killed.... It was all mine, and I got through and Ford said, "That was very good, John. Very good." And I said, "Well, Jack, if I had played the rest of the part the way you wanted me to, I couldn't have played this scene." It's like playing Hamlet as a madman. It works fine until you come to one of those sane soliloquies. Then you're up a tree. [Carradine also worked Ford's *The Prisoner of Shark Island* (1936), *Mary of Scotland* (1936), *The Hurricane* (1937), *Four Men and a Prayer* (1938), *Submarine Patrol* (1938), *Stagecoach* (1939), *Drums Along the Mohawk* (1939), *The Last Hurrah* (1958), *The Man Who Shot Liberty Valance* (1963) and *Cheyenne Autumn* (1964).]

—Carradine, interviewed by Danny Peary for *Focus on Film*, Aug 1979

Keith CARRADINE [1951-]

Born: San Mateo, California; son of John, half brother of David, brother of Robert; father of Martha Plimpton [1970-]. While studying acting at Colorado State College (Fort Collins), he dropped out to pursue a career in the business. Work on the stage in both the L.A. and N.Y. casts of Hair preceded his film debut in The Pink Garder Gang (1969, Jimmy Murphy). To date, he has made three films with Robert Altman (McCabe and Mrs. Miller, 1971; Thieves Like Us, 1974; Nashville, 1975) and four with Altman's protégé, Alan Rudolph (Welcome to L.A., 1977; Choose Me, 1984; Trouble in Mind, 1986; The Moderns, 1988).

Altman lets you create for yourself. You have so much freedom. He doesn't manipulate you...much. Sometimes he does and I don't know it. When I started, I knew what my obligations to the role of Tom [in *Nashville*] were. I was struggling with having to play someone I didn't like. After a day's shooting, I'd say, "My God, Bob, it's awful." He left me in trouble because he knew I was playing a guy who didn't like himself.... Clever, no?

—Carradine, interviewed by Karin Winner for *Women's Wear Daily*, 11 July 1975

Diahann CARROLL [1935-]

Born: Diann Johnson in The Bronx, N.Y. Studies at The High School of Music and Art in N.Y. and success as a singer on TV preceded her film debut in Carmen Jones (1954, Otto Preminger). In 1974, she played the title role in John Berry's Claudine:

With humanity and humor, *Claudine* told the story of a mother's determination to bring her six children safely through the perils and poverty of the Harlem ghetto. The cards are stacked against her: her fifteen-year-old daughter [Tamu] is pregnant; one of her sons has dropped out of school and become a street-corner gambler, another is so traumatized he refuses to speak. Out on her own without a husband, she has to resort to welfare to supplement her meager income as a domestic and is forced to endure all the attendant humiliations — hiding her toaster from the social worker, concealing her relationship with the new man in her life [James Earl Jones as Roop], a fiercely independent garbage collector with some money and family problems of his own. Claudine is harried and exhausted by the pressures that beset her on every side, yet she is so strong-willed and persevering, so committed to the well-being of her family, that somehow she manages to survive these adversities with her dignity intact.

I have known this woman all my life. We grew up together in the same neighborhood...we were both the same sort of verbal, highly protective mothers, and I understood all too well how her sensuality kept getting her into trouble, how more than once she had placed her trust in a man without really evaluating what she was doing.

There was so much of Claudine in me that I couldn't see anyone else in the world playing her. I felt I could give life to her humanity. I felt I could make people care about her....

The first day of shooting, John Berry decided to have me begin with a nude scene with James Earl Jones.... I think John was trying to throw me off my well-focused, serious approach to the work — that defined refinement that I always carried with me. So he scheduled the scene betweeen James and me in bed. As they called us to the set, James walked in — totally naked. Not a stitch on that body! I was absolutely stunned! My first instinct was to look the other way. But then I said to myself, "Don't be a child. You're not Diahann — you're Claudine, a mother of six (each of the kids fathered by a different man), and this is not the first time you have been to bed with this man. So relax and get into it."

—Carroll, in her (with Ross Firestone) *Diahann!* (Boston: Little, Brown & Co., 1986)

John CASSAVETES [1929-1989]

Born: New York City. Studies at The American Academy of Dramatic Arts and work in summer stock preceded his film debut in Taxi (1953, Gregory Ratoff). In 1956, he played Frankie Dane in Don Siegel's Crime in the Streets:

I found Don worked well with actors, crew, and everyone. He has an overwhelming personality and a tremendous sense of fun coupled with a disregard for authority — all of which shows in his face.

He never falls into the trap that most directors fall into: lack of preparation. When he comes on a picture he knows what he wants, but is flexible enough to accept good contributions from actors or crew.

Don doesn't set himself up as "The Director." He's not a father figure or an imposing shadow. If he tells you something, it's straight. He makes you feel at ease. If he says something should be done quickly or shot again, you know that's the way it has to be, that it's not just some sudden idea on his part.

—Cassavetes, interviewed by Stuart Kaminsky for *Don Siegel: Director* (New York: Curtis Books, 1974)

Q. *Husbands* [1970] was the first film in which you directed yourself. Were there any special problems that resulted from this?

A. Sure, a lot of special problems. It is very hard to see the scene when you're in it. But it was harder, I think, on Peter [Falk] and Ben [Gazzara] my being in the scene, because I could decide how I was going to play that scene and not worry about the direction of that scene, and they couldn't. The three of us are peers one moment, then suddenly they have to turn to me and say, "What do you think?" And they know goddam well I don't know anything more about the scene than they do, because I was in it, too. So we learned how to use our instincts. I would say to Peter, "How did it go for you?" and he'd say, "Fine" and then I'd ask Ben and he'd say, "Fine" and I'd say, "Fine" and that's the way we'd know.

—Cassavetes, interviewed by Russell Au Werter for *Action*, Jan/Feb 1970

[Peter, Ben and I] worked well together [on *Husbands*]. And we became friends on a level that's unqualified by duty or loyalty; those things don't count. The only thing that counts is that you're all doing the same thing, you're testing each other, testing yourself. In that situation, each actor is thinking, "How far up can I reach?" That's selfish — and honest. I don't think Peter and Benny were too concerned about how far I could go as a director; they were thinking about how far *they* could go as actors. And, in a realistic sense, Benny couldn't go anyplace unless

Peter was good and unless I was good. So we knew we had to work on that level, and in order to do that, we had to get tight with each other.... [Cassavetes also directed himself in *Minnie and Moskowitz* (1971), *Opening Night* (1978) and *Love Streams* (1984).]

—Cassavetes, interviewed by Lawrence Linderman for *Playboy*, July 1971

Q. What was it like to work with [Paul] Mazursky in *Tempest* [1982] as an actor?

A. Paul is very interesting. Because he's a man who doesn't really say a lot about what he's gonna do. He's always alive and vital and making statements that you can challenge. I mean, he's a dynamo! Dynamic man. Laughs in the middle of what actors would deem important scenes. And clowns around during rehearsals. And he prefers somebody to challenge his thoughts.

You know, sometimes everyone second-guesses the director. It's very simple to do and it's very normal. I'm sure when Mazursky acts he does the same thing. You know, you think, "My God, why do they have to push it in this direction, when it could be so lovely in *this* direction." That happens all the time. But Paul really likes that. He likes it in the sense that if you really know so much, *do* it. Don't sit and talk about it and conspire about it and fret about it. Put it on the screen. Who's stopping you?

And then he *might* stop you. But Paul's whole thing, not only in front of the camera, was a nice rapport between the actors.

And working with Paul wasn't, "This is the scene about the girl whom you meet for the first time," there's none of that. It's "Oh! There's Susan [Sarandon]. Gah! She looks great. Susan, you look great! Fantastic! Oh my God!" And Susan gets all embarrassed, she says, "Okay, Paul, let's do the scene," and he says, "Okay, the car is coming, *I'll* play the guy, I'll play the guy!" And off-scene Paul will play me, and he'll say, "There's no room for you, John, you get outta here!" And I found it, for everybody there, maddening, because it's a strange kind of direction. But now I miss it. And I don't want to go back to the other.

—Cassavetes, interviewed by Michael Ventura for *L.A. Weekly*, 20-26 Aug 1982

Lon CHANEY [1883-1930]

Born: Alonzo Chaney in Colorado Springs, Colorado. After work in touring shows, he found small parts in filmed slapstick comedies (50 prior to 1915). In 1915, he directed himself in 5 films for Universal then returned solely to acting. The role that made him a star was The Miracle Man (1919, George Loane Tucker):

Tucker didn't really want me for the role of the cripple in *The Miracle Man*. He wanted a professional contortionist, but the five he had already tried out in the part couldn't act it. When Tucker described the part to me I knew my whole future rested on my getting it.

Tucker explained that the first scene he would shoot would be the one where the fake cripple unwound himself before his pals. If I could do that, I got the job.

I went home to try to think it out. I'm not a contortionist, of course. It would have been easier lots of times in my subsequent work if I had been. While I was sitting, pondering over that part I unconsciously did a trick I've done since childhood. I crossed my legs, then double crossed them, wrapping my left foot around my right ankle. I caught sight of myself in the mirror and jumped up to try walking that way.

I found I could do it with a little practice. Then I rushed out to buy the right clothes.

When I came to the studio on the test day Tucker was already behind the camera. He gave me one glance and called "Camera." I flopped down, dragging myself forward along the floor, my eyes rolling, my face twitching and my legs wrapping tighter around each other....

In my pictures, I've tried to show that the lowliest people frequently have the highest ideals. In the lower depths when life hasn't been too pleasant for me I've always that gentleness of feeling, that compassion of an underdog for a fellow sufferer. *The Hunchback* [*of Notre Dame* (1923, Wallace Worsley)] was an example of it. So was *The Unknown* [1927, Tod Browning] and in a different class of society, *Mr. Wu* [1927, William Nigh].

—Chaney, interviewed by Ruth Waterbury for *Photoplay Magazine*, Feb 1928

In *The Penalty* [1920, Wallace Worsley], *Hunchback of Notre Dame* and the more recent ones such as *Mr. Wu*, *The Unknown* and *Mockery* [1927, Benjamin Christensen], I have tried to play roles that admitted of different characterizations.

I prefer these parts, not merely because I like to play with make-up but because I feel that they give me a wider scope....

Grotesqueries as such do not attract me; it is vivid characterization for which I strive. I want my make-up simply to add to the picture, to show at a glance the sort of character I am portraying. But I want my roles to go deeper than that. I want to dig down into the mind and the heart of the role. But as a man's face reveals much that is in his mind and heart, I attempt to show this by the make-up I use; and the make-up is merely the prologue.

—Chaney, in *Theatre Magazine*, Oct 1927

In *The Phantom of the Opera* [1925, Rupert Julian] people exclaimed at my weird make-up. I achieved the death's head of that role without wearing a mask. It was the use of paints in the right shades and the right places — not the obvious parts of the face — which gave the complete illusion of horror. My experiments as a stage manager, which were wide and varied before I jumped into films, taught me much about lighting effects on the actor's face and the minor tricks of deception. These I have been able to use in achieving weird results on the screen.

—Chaney, quoted in *Heroes of the Horrors* by Calvin Thomas Beck (New York: Macmillan, 1975)

Lon CHANEY, Jr. [1906-1973]

Born: Creighton Chaney in Oklahoma City, Oklahoma. Bit roles in his father's films, work as a stunt man, extra and bit player preceded his role of Lennie in Of Mice and Men both on stage and on the screen (1939, Lewis Milestone):

People sometimes have asked me how I felt playing such a "dumb" character. I never figured Lennie as "dumb." I thought of him as a kind, good-natured guy with an unfortunate mental deficiency. I have a natural understanding for the handicapped, as I was raised with grandparents, both deaf mutes, and I never thought of them as being different.

—Chaney, in *The Saturday Evening Post*, 27 Oct 1951

Charles CHAPLIN [1889-1977]

Born: Kensington, London, England. Work in music hall (from 1894) led to employment with The Fred Karno Troupe with whom he toured the U.S. In 1914, he began working for Mack Sennett at Keystone:

Ford Sterling was on one set, [Fatty] Arbuckle on another; the whole stage was crowded with three companies at work. I was in my street clothes and had nothing to do, so I stood where Sennett could see me. He was standing with Mabel [Normand], looking into a hotel lobby set, biting the end of a cigar. "We need some gags here," he said, then turned to me. "Put on a comedy make-up. Anything will do."

I had no idea what make-up to put on.... However, on the way to the wardrobe I thought I would dress in baggy pants, big shoes, a cane and a derby hat. I wanted everything a contradiction: the pants baggy, the coat tight, the hat small and the shoes large. I was undecided whether to look old or young, but remembering Sennett had expected me to be a much older man, I added a small mustache, which, I reasoned, would add age without hiding my expression.

I had no idea of the character. But the moment I was dressed, the clothes and the make-up made me feel the person he was. I began to know him, and by the time I walked onto the stage he was fully born. When I confronted Sennett I assumed the character and strutted about, swinging my cane and parading before him. Gags and comedy ideas went racing through my mind.

The secret of Mack Sennett's success was his enthusiasm. He was a great audience and laughed genuinely at what he thought funny. He stood and giggled until his body began to shake. This encouraged me and I began to explain the character: "You know this fellow is many-sided, a tramp, a gentleman, a poet, a dreamer, a lonely fellow, always hopeful of romance and adventure. He would have you believe he is a scientist, a musician, a duke, a polo player. However, he is not above picking up cigarette butts or robbing a baby of its candy. And, of course, if the occasion warrants it, he will kick a lady in the rear — but only in extreme anger."

—Chaplin, in his *My Autobiography* (London: Simon & Schuster, 1964)

The first time I wore my tramp costume was in something called *Mabel's Strange Predicament* [1914]. The scene was a hotel lobby, a rather comfortable hotel. Here was this very crummy-looking tramp. He walks in doing all the things a man of assurance would do, looking at the register — "Anyone I know?" — tips his hat to the ladies. And what he really wants to do is get anchored on a soft seat and rest awhile. Sore feet and everything else. Takes out a cigaret butt and lights it: watches the passing parade. Pretty ladies trip over his feet, and he raises his hat, says "Very sorry." I became alive, a person in a logical situation. I felt good. I felt right. The character came to me.

The idea of being fastidious, very delicate about everything was something I enjoyed. Made me feel funny. There is that gentle poverty about all the Cockneys who ape their betters. Every little draper, soda clerk wants to be a swell, dress up. So when I stumbled over some dog's leash, got my hand stuck in a cuspidor, I knew instinctively what to do. I tried to hide it. They yelled — the mere fact that I didn't want anybody to see it.

I never thought of the tramp in terms of appeal. He was myself, a comic spirit, something within me that said I must express this. I felt so free. The adventure of it. The madness. I can do any mad, crazy thing I like.

—Chaplin, interviewed by Richard Meryman for *Life*, 10 Mar 1967

Under Sennett's direction I felt comfortable, because everything was spontaneously worked out on the set. As no one was positive or sure of himself (not even the director), I concluded that I knew as much as the other fellow. This gave me confidence; I began to offer suggestions which Sennett readily accepted. Thus grew a belief in myself that I was creative and could write my own stories....

Now I was anxious to write and direct my own comedies, so I talked to Sennett about it. But he would not hear of it; instead he assigned me to Mabel Normand, who had just started directing her own pictures. This nettled me, for, charming as Mabel was, I doubted her competence as a director; so the first day [on *Mabel at the Wheel* (1914)] there came the inevitable blowup. We were on location in the suburbs of Los Angeles, and in one scene Mabel wanted me to stand with a hose and water down the road so that the villain's car would skid over it. I suggested standing on the hose so that the water can't come out, and when I look down the nozzle I unconsciously step off the hose and the water squirts in my face. But she shut me up quickly: "We have no time! We have no time! Do what you're told."

That was enough, I could not take it — and from such a pretty girl. "I'm sorry, Miss Normand, I will not do what I'm told. I don't think you are competent to tell me what to do."

The scene was in the center of the road, and I left it and sat down on the curb. Sweet Mabel — at that time she was only 20, pretty and charming, everybody's favorite; everybody loved her. Now she sat by the camera bewildered; nobody had ever spoken to her so directly before. [Chaplin and Normand co-directed 5 films later that year.]

—Chaplin, in his *My Autobiography* (London: Simon & Schuster, 1964)

You cannot beat the human equation — the things which open up a picture of humanity as it really is. One cannot do humor without great sympathy for one's fellow man. As the tramp I think I endeared myself through his terrific humility — the humility which I am sure is a universal thing — of somebody without money....

You cannot be funny without an attitude. Being without an attitude in comedy is like something amiss in one's make-up. I mean if a man walks into a situation he'll have an attitude about it, even if it's to pretend to know nothing about it. My tramp character was usually trying to be very normal and unobtrusive. When he picked up a stocking-dummy leg in a store, held it very soberly and casually, his attitude was a pretense of innocence. I used to do the most terrifically vulgar things in those days. They used to yell. The more that you hide from an audience, whatever you're thinking, the better they like it.

Perhaps because of my early environment, the comedy in tragedy has always been second nature to me. Cruelty, for example, is an integral part of comedy. We laugh at it in order not to weep. In a film called *The Floorwalker* [1916] a tremulous old man was going along like this, and I just pick up one of these little zithers lying on a counter and say, "Try it, sir." hold it up so his shaking hands strum on the strings. Cruel. And they roared.

Everything I do is a dance. [In *City Lights* (1931, Charles Chaplin)] the girl [Virginia Cherrill] extends her hand with a rose. The tramp doesn't know she's blind, says, "I'll take this one." "Which one?" He looks as though thinking, "What an incredibly stupid girl!" The flower falls to the ground, and she goes to feel where it is. I pick it up, hold it there for a moment. She says, "Have you found it, sir?" And then he realizes. He holds it in front of her eyes, just makes a gesture. Purely dance....

I had a close-up — the last scene of *City Lights*. The blind girl has recovered her sight, thanks to a benefactor she always imagined was a rich and handsome young man. And now she touches again the hands of this little tramp — and seeing through her fingers, as it were, it comes down on her. "My God, this is the man."

I had had several takes and they were all overdone, overacted, overfelt. This time I was looking more at her, interested to see that she didn't make any mistakes. It was a beautiful sensation of not acting, of standing outside of myself. The key was exactly right — slightly embarrassed, delighted about meeting her again, apologetic without getting emotional about it. He was watching and wondering what she was thinking and wondering without any effort. It's one of the purest...close-ups I've ever done.

—Chaplin, interviewed by Richard Meryman for *Life*, 10 Mar 1967

As long as I keep this character I can't talk. If I would start talking my tramp would change into a wholly different man. Talking would localize him. With the first word he would cease to be the universal creature whose joys and troubles are comprehensible to all countries.... A talking tramp would be either an American or an Englishman, someone from a specific country. This is the reason why I have resisted so far the talkies. I simply could not talk a word in this character. I would have killed my twenty years work. I may give it up, though, and it will be different then. I shall be free to talk, if I choose to talk.

—Chaplin, interviewed by A.J. Urban for *Intercine*, Oct 1935

For *The Great Dictator* [1940, Charles Chaplin] I didn't study Hitler much, I knew that he was a humorless man and I knew that a man in his position would be very fretful. And the mere fact that Hitler used those broad gestures — he'd press down, press up, cross himself with his fists, very effective — was revealing that this man was not too sure of himself. He must have a stooge at the back who says, "You're doing okay, boss. Do it again. You slaughtered them today." I'm sure he had that fat man, Goering, to lean on.

—Chaplin, interviewed by Richard Meryman for *Life*, 10 Mar 1967

Pessimists say I may fail [with *The Great Dictator*] — that dictators aren't funny any more, that the evil is too serious. That is wrong. If there is one thing I know it is that power can always be made ridiculous.

—Chaplin, interviewed by Robert Van Gelder for *The New York Times*, 8 Sept 1940

[In *Monsieur Verdoux*, (1947) I am a mass killer. I start out as a bank clerk — a respectable, dapper, middle-class Frenchman.

Then the depression of 1930 costs me my job. I have a wife and children whom I love and must support. And so I turn to the business of marrying women and killing them for their money. Actually I am a very moral man; I never let these women touch me. And I hate my new job — there is no hint of lascivious pleasure in my bearing. I hate the women. I hate their vulgarity, their little minds, their lack of aesthetic appreciation. I am in business and even though I hate it, I must do my duty after the classic, heroic model....

Von Clausewitz said that war is the logical extension of diplomacy; M. Verdoux feels that murder is the logical extension of business.... He is frustrated, bitter, and, at the end, pessimistic. But he is never morbid; and the picture is by no means morbid in treatment.

—Chaplin, interviewed by T.F.B. for *The New York Times*, 26 Jan 1947

Geraldine CHAPLIN [1944-]

Born: Santa Monica, California, to Charles and Oona Chaplin. Although she made her screen debut at age 7 in her father's Limelight (1952), her acting career did not begin until 1964 with Par Une Beau Matin d'Été (Jacques Deray). Her role as Opal in Nashville (1975) was the first of three for Robert Altman:

I don't think Opal was really a reporter at all. I think she was an American girl putting on an accent and pretending she was from the BBC so she could be near the country-music stars. The person I patterned her after was a French press agent I know. She talks with millions of commas in her sentences.

—Chaplin, interviewed by Judy Klemesrud for *The New York Times*, 21 Sept 1977

[Altman] is magic. Before shooting, there's usually a week or ten days when he's around a lot; he makes you feel very excited about your part. When you start shooting he's not around so much as *behind*, but in such control.

I adore being manipulated. An example is the whole character in *Nashville*. I really thought I wrote all those monologues in the car cemetery, and I *did* write them, but he knew what I was going to write because he gave me like six or seven things, key words or something — all that was already implanted. People say that Bob allows you the most enormous freedom and that they're creating their own part, which is an enormous lie. Everyone's lining up in the exact direction he wants them to go. He gives you the *impression* you're creating, and that marvelous ego trip, but you're the same marionette you are with other directors. [She also worked with Altman on *Buffalo Bill and the Indians* (1976) and *A Wedding* (1978).]

—Chaplin, interviewed by Jim Trombetta for *Crawdaddy*, July 1976

Q. Would you call the woman you play in *Remember My Name* [1978, Alan Rudolph] a real bitch?

A. I'd call her real tough. She's a lady who spent twelve years in jail, and she's not afraid of violence. She comes out of prison and she's out to get something. Face it. You've got to watch out for a woman like that....

Q. Is your character based on your imagination?

A. That was one of the difficulties in playing this role. I've known a lot of people who've been in jail, but that was in Spain and for political reasons. That's very different, of course, from a woman in this country charged with homicide....

I thought maybe I should visit an American prison, but I was too embarrassed to ask some poor woman what it's like to spend twelve years in jail. It just didn't seem fair.

Q. So what did you do?

A. I used something at the beginning of the film that I saw in a television interview with a boy who had just come out of jail.... This boy's face was completely paralyzed as though he was afraid of showing any emotion on his face. And he talked a little bit louder than necessary. I spoke like that for the first few reels of film, and then I dropped some of those mannerisms to show an adjustment to freedom.

—Chaplin, interviewed by Tinkerbelle for *Interview*, Jan 1979

CHER [1946-]

Born: Cherilyn Sarkasian LaPier in El Centro, California. Success as a singer with her husband and partner, Sonny Bono, preceded her film debut in Good Times (1967, William Friedkin). After success as a solo singing act and night club entertainer, she turned her attentions to acting, beginning with a Broadway debut in Come Back to the Five and Dime, Jimmy Dean, Jimmy Dean; the film version marked her return to the screen (1982, Robert Altman). In 1983, she played opposite Meryl Streep in Mike Nichols' Silkwood:

I learned something from Meryl, that if you work harder in my closeup than in your own, and I do the same thing, what we have is a great piece of work. It worked well with Eric [Stolz on *Mask* (1985, Peter Bogdanovich)]....

The woman I played in *Mask* was just a total loser, and yet she did one thing perfectly, and that was she mothered this child that a lot of Betty Crocker-Betty Furness mothers might never have had the guts to do....

The fact of the matter was that I loved this woman and these people, and he [Bogdanovich] did not. And if you look at the rest of his movie you'll see that Eric and I are better than the rest of his movie. Because Peter didn't understand them, because he didn't *like* them.

—Cher, interviewed by Harlan Jacobson for *Film Comment*, Feb 1988

Robert Altman is always willing to let you do it your way and then he might say, "Could you do this on the next one. I just want to see something." Mike Nichols will take you aside and tell you strange little stories that seem to have nothing to do with what you're filming, then later, when acting, their relevance becomes apparent. Peter [Bogdanovich] tells you how to read lines. I felt he wanted to be doing my job but had to hire me. I'm not impossible or difficult but I think I have something to contribute and I thought I knew her better at gut level.

—Cher, interviewed by Allan Hunter for *Films & Filming*, Aug 1983

I read someplace that I said it wasn't fun to work with Nicholas [Cage on *Moonstruck* (1987, Norman Jewison)], which is the truth. Nicholas is a very strange actor, he works alone and you get to work along side of him, but he's very interesting to work with, he's fascinating.

Q. Did you like working with Norman Jewison?

A. Yes, I did. He's a very strange man. Very theatrical. He's got a lot of stories; he wants to be the center of attention, but he lets you alone. He's real used to yelling but he's not used to having someone yell back, and when you do, it becomes fun for him. Also, I've never known a director who, if you're doing something funny in a scene, starts laughing. He laughed all the time when we were working, and I just...I just found that to be so bizarre, that he would just laugh.

—Cher, interviewed by Harlan Jacobson for *Film Comment*, Feb 1988

Maurice CHEVALIER [1888-1972]

Born: Paris. On the stage (from age 12), he then spent three seasons with Les Folies Bergères and ten years working with Mistinguett. While he made his film debut in Trop crédule *(1908, Jean Durand), and then worked on several occasions with Max Linder, it was in Hollywood that he made his mark as a film star. His first American film was* Innocents of Paris *(1928, Richard Wallace):*

My worries about having to play a "sophisticate" had been assuaged, because there was surely nothing sophisticated in the role of the simple Parisian rag-picker I would soon be portraying in *Innocents of Paris*. But another fear had cropped up to replace it. Except for a few already established stars, all the Hollywood actors seemed so handsome and young. I was nearly forty and I had spent enough hours making up my face to know what it looked like. I doubted that I was as youthful and dashing as I'd need to be for my Hollywood camera debut.

I had confided my fears to Emil Jannings.

"Just forget there is a camera." In his dressing room he emphasized his words with intense gestures, speaking in an almost unintelligible Teutonic accent. "Forget wrinkles and double chins and profiles. The movies need more true personalities. Less empty beauty. Forget everything except playing sincerely...."

He had offered me a valuable piece of advice and I was grateful.

Determined to practice it I faced the first night's shooting with fewer qualms than I had expected to be suffering.

[Lubitsch] was a man of strong, positive opinions delivered in a deceptively mild fashion, and I listened attentively to what he thought of my work in *Innocents of Paris*, happy to have earned this man's praise.

"I am walking around with a film musical in my head, Maurice. Now I will put it on paper." He pointed his finger at me to underline his decision. "I have found my hero."

The possibility of working with Lubitsch filled me with happy anticipation which increased when he told me that this first large-scale musical operetta the studio would be undertaking was based on a French property. There wouldn't even be the problem of trying to play a role too far removed from my own personality, I was thinking. But when he began to outline the story which would be called *Love Parade* [1929], my hopes fell down to my feet.

"The hero is a prince?" I said, dismayed. "You see *me* as a prince?"

He nodded and I shook my head in practically the same instant. "I'm sorry," I said. "I'm flattered, but it's impossible. A fisherman? Yes, that I could play or any other kind of man from a simple background. It's what I am and it's in the way I talk and the way I walk and everything I like and understand. But an aristocrat? Believe me, in a royal uniform I would make the most ludicrous-looking prince on the screen!"

Lubitsch proposed a test.... Our first port of call was the costumer's, and he steered me into a vast, crammed building where iron racks and drawers and boxes overflowed with all the trimmings needed to turn an ordinary man into a cowboy, a fire chief or a knight. But an outfit that could turn me into a prince? I seriously doubted that all the trappings of this entire establishment could pull off that trick....

Approaching Lubitsch's office the next day, certain that the still pictures would have proved me right, I was already framing a little speech of regret in my mind. Suddenly his door burst open and to the astonishment of everybody in the corridor, he rushed toward me triumphantly brandishing a batch of photos shouting in glee for all of Paramount to hear: "Splendid, Maurice! Marvelous! *You are a prince!*"

I looked at the shots and shook my head in amazement. The proof of what Lubitsch had been able to see all along was there now before my eyes. We shook hands on the deal and I grinned down at the small man whose imagination was big enough to turn me into royalty.

From the first day of rehearsal under Lubitsch's talented guidance I found him an almost magic man to work with. He was supposed to be a very difficult director with American actors, but for me he seemed the easiest person in the world to understand. Just from the expression in his eye I could see what he wanted and somehow always produce it. And that bond of creative respect and sympathy seemed to affect the rest of the company as well, including the charming young red-haired beauty named Jeanette MacDonald he had discovered singing in a Chicago musical comedy and brought out to be my partner. [Chevalier also worked on Lubitsch's *Paramount on Parade* (1930), *The Smiling Lieutenant* (1931), *One Hour with You* (1932) and *The Merry Widow* (1934).]

[The Academy Awards celebration of 1956] had been a memorable night for me, but how very much so I didn't realize till the next day when Billy Wilder telephoned.

"Maurice," he said briskly, "seeing you last night has given me an idea. Can we meet and talk about it?"

Sitting across from him that afternoon as he spoke with quick, concise gestures, I was thinking how marvelously tenacious was Billy's loyalty and affection. He had never abandoned his idea of seeing me in a Hollywood production again [Chevalier had not made a Hollywood film since 1935], and now he was offering me a part in a picture he was shooting in Paris with Gary Cooper and Audrey Hepburn to be called *Love in the Afternoon* [1957]....

I was to be the father of that adorable Audrey Hepburn.... We would be filming in Paris, and I would be doing in an American picture what I had wanted to do two decades ago — be more than cute. It was a chance to jump at, and I jumped.

But on the day that shooting began, I was wondering what I had taken on for myself. As Audrey and Gary and I listened to Billy's concept of the film that first day on the set, I suddenly began to worry about my English. Because the way I speak this language is surely a part of my personality. Yet in this role I was to put that old Chevalier aside and be someone else, a private detective who was the father of a charming, incurably romantic young girl, and if the accent were the same, could I be anything but my old self?

The combination of a marvelous dialogue coach and Billy, a great director with whom I found myself working as easily as I had once done with Ernst Lubitsch, dissolved my worries in a single day.

A cable from my agent in Hollywood intrigued me. "M.G.M. wants you for musical version Colette's *Gigi* [1958, Vincente Minnelli]. Fine part, fine songs for you. Advise."

I was remembering my visit with brilliant, enchanting Colette, dead almost three years now, and the book on the table which I had later read. Gigi — the engagingly piquant young girl who is tutored to be a courtesan only to end up marrying the rich young man. And I would be the worldly uncle of the young man, a kind of charming, rakish old fellow, wise in the ways of life and love. It was a role with zest. It was surely the one to accept....

It was to Alan Lerner that I told my philosophy of love, how in these later years I had abandoned any tempestuous romantic involvement, how I was not any more the man to play that game, and how I had no deep regrets about it.

A thoughtful expression crossed his face. "You mean you're glad it's all behind you?"

I shook my head a little unhappily. "You're never glad of it, but you can be satisfied if you have had that side of living in a beautiful way."

He said no more at the time, but later they gave me a nice tune to sing, inspired by our conversation — "I'm Glad I'm Not Young Any More." And since you can do nothing about the march of years, you might as well not grieve about it, you see?

—Chevalier, in his (with Eileen and Robert Mason Pollock) *With Love* (Boston: Little, Brown & Co., 1960)

Julie CHRISTIE [1941-]

Born: Chukua, Assam, India. After studies at The Central School of Music and Drama in London, she joined The Frinton-on-Sea Repertory Company in 1957, then worked with The Birmingham Repertory and The Royal Shakespeare Company. After a TV series and a few small movie roles (debut: Crooks Anonymous — 1962, Ken Annakin), she came to the attention of John Schlesinger who cast her in Billy Liar (1963). After that film, Schlesinger had Darling (1965) written for her:

I suppose what I really dislike about Diana [in *Darling*] is that she doesn't use her noggin. She's actually quite stupid, you know. Doesn't know what she wants. Just drifts. Just like so many of these little scrubbers today. Jumping from bed to bed, not because that's what they want but simply because nothing else occurs to them or they think it's the thing to do. Why, actually they have no interest in anything at all. Not even sex. Like Diana. She's not interested in sex. She even says so. [Christie worked with Schlesinger a third time on *Far from the Madding Crowd* (1967).]

—Christie, interviewed by Jean Antel for *The New York Times*, 21 Nov 1965

Comment on the styles of Schlesinger, Lean and Truffaut? I am terribly bad at explaining things so I will have to use the metaphor of a director guiding an actor along a path.

John almost walks along the path with the actor, but sometimes the actor runs away from him — not in a different direction but further ahead than John. They both help each other; the actor helps by maybe introducing short cuts or more interesting routes along the path. But John is ultimately the one who knows where the path ends.

David [Lean on *Dr. Zhivago* (1965)] is more liable to stalk ahead of you on the path, and you follow him pouring everything you have got into your walk because you are constantly aware of his intense, watchful eye upon you. As you are always following him there is a danger maybe of your mind relying too much on him and not enough on yourself, but although I relied intensely upon him I don't think I found this a danger. I found him enormously stimulating; his constant urging made me want to give more and more and think and find things.

François [Truffaut] is the most different. I found in *Fahrenheit 451* [1966] that there were about four paths to follow, and very often I was not told which was the one François had in mind. It was a matter of really keeping my ears and eyes open to find clues as to which path was his path, and sometimes, from something he said, I would realize I was on the wrong path, and would switch over to an other. It must make for a very jerky performance, I would think, but I am sure it is all in Truffaut's ultimate plan....

It is no wonder, I suppose, that I have gotten such a God image of directors when I have worked with three like John, David and François. I would commit myself from here to eternity, I have such faith in them. I think any good director has to be ruthless, it makes it easier if you are a subservient actress like me to be even more so. Maybe it is a sort of sado-masochistic relationship, who knows.

—Christie, in *Action*, Nov/Dec 1966

Petulia [in *Petulia* (1968, Richard Lester)] is terribly difficult to explain. She's looking for a 100 per cent man. She keeps making idols. But no one is 100 per cent, which makes it a bit sad, really. Petulia has very few inhibitions. She does things to create a violent effect. The character is evolving all the time. There's nothing hard and fast with Dick Lester.

—Christie, interviewed by Judy Stone for *The New York Times*, 7 May 1967

Robert CLARKE [1920-]

Born: Oklahoma. Beginning as a stock player at RKO, he played opposite Boris Karloff in both The Body Snatcher (1945, Robert Wise) and Bedlam (1946, Mark Robson):

Q. Can you tell us a little about working with Boris Karloff on *The Body Snatcher* and *Bedlam*?

A. He...was such the antithesis of what he portrayed on the screen: He had a very gentlemanly attitude, and in working in a scene with him he never tried to upstage you or to get the best of the scene. He was awfully kind, and his dressing room door was always open to anyone who wanted to say hello or chat with him. I never worked with any man that I had more admiration for....

Q. How about Bela Lugosi on *The Body Snatcher*?

A. Karloff used to call him "Poor Bela." And "Poor Bela" had *such* terrible problems with his back, and he was on drugs because of it. During the time that I was involved on *The Body Snatcher*, he hardly came out of his dressing room unless the assistant director called him. They had a daybed in there, and he was flat on his back on that couch nearly all the time. He talked very little to anyone, and obviously he wasn't well at all. It was very difficult for him to perform.

Q. Most of your *Body Snatcher* scenes were with Henry Daniell.

A. He was a smooth, accomplished and very professional actor. I was a bit overwhelmed, as were the other young stock players, Bill Williams and Carl Kent, by his extreme professionalism because he was a bit condescending in his attitude. The scene that we were involved with was mostly his scene — he was showing us how to perform the operation on the little girl. I had one line — "Bravo!" — and when I missed my cue, he went right by my line in his dialogue. But Bob Wise, the director, spoke up and stopped him, and said, "Wait a minute — Bobby Clarke has a line there. Now, let's go back and start again, and let Bob get his line in." Unlike Karloff, Daniell was not the type to have empathy for young actors; "aloof," I guess, would be the best word to describe him. It was *his* scene, we were just window-dressing, and he couldn't care less whether we were there or not.

Q. You had a more substantial role in *Bedlam*....

A. Mark Robson, the director, was a marvelous man; he worked so carefully with us actors.... I remember a scene where we were playing a card game called paroli and, being demented, instead of betting money I was betting dogs — whippets and bassets and such. Robson made practically every little move for me — "When you place a card here, you do *this*, and then *that*," and so forth. It's been over forty years, but I'll never forget how careful and meticulous he was. Robson...treated actors with respect, which is wonderful. I've had a couple of occasions in my career where the director would sit back near the camera and holler at you. I must give credit to Mark Robson for making my role in *Bedlam* more than it could have been; Robson gave me the kind of direction that brought out the best in me....

Q. What about working with John Carradine [on *The Incredible Petrified World* (1961, Jerry Warren)]?

A. What I remember best about Carradine is how strong his concentration was. Carradine was in the scenes we shot here in L.A., and I remember one night, in front of a garage, he had to do a long speech, almost a soliloquy, explaining some plot point. And he was so into that — right out there, practically in the street, without any setting of any kind or any actor to work with. He was just a marvelous actor.

Q. What about on a personal level?

A. I enjoyed working with him very much. He was a true professional, and he gave every bit as much working for Jerry Warren as he would working for Cecil DeMille or John Ford. He did not stint in the slightest in his performance. He was cooperative, easy to work with and he was not condescending — he was something of a star and we weren't but he treated us as equals and fellow actors. I have great respect for him.

—Clarke, interviewed by Tom Weaver for *Interviews with B Science Fiction and Horror Movie Makers* (Jefferson, N.C.: McFarland & Co., 1988)

Jill CLAYBURGH [1944-]

Born: New York City. Studies at Sarah Lawrence College and at The Williamstown Theatre Festival preceded her film debut in The Wedding Party (1969, Brian De Palma). In 1975, she played opposite Gene Wilder in Arthur Hiller's Silver Streak:

Making *Silver Streak* was a very pleasant experience. Gene is so lovely to work with, so helpful and giving. In one scene, I had to laugh over and over and over, and every time he'd think of something off-camera to make me laugh. He's generous, giving and smart.

—Clayburgh, interviewed by Judy Klemesrud for *The New York Times*, 15 Dec 1976

Erica [in *An Unmarried Woman* (1978, Paul Mazursky)] is a healthy, happy woman who is not neurotic. That's why the blow [of her husband's leaving] hits her so hard. I think she had an inkling that all was not well. But like many women who love someone and feel something is wrong, she buries her head in the sand. You daren't look in case you find a great gaping hole.

—Clayburgh, interviewed by Romany Bain for *The Magazine* (England), Sept 1978

Q. What sort of research did you do for your part in *An Unmarried Woman*?

A. For a part like Erica, you delve inside yourself a lot. Subconsciously, I think actors are always collecting and storing experiences. And somehow, in some strange, uncanny way, if you push the right button at the right time, the little computer in your brain will somehow release the right flow of information. It doesn't always happen but it happened for me. Also, Paul [Mazursky] and I talked a great deal. He had done a lot of research before writing the script. He interviewed many women and taped some meetings with his wife's consciousness-raising group — basically, they were all saying the same thing on different levels — and so all that helped. But I'm finding that the more you allow yourself to be open and not too structured in your approach to a role, the more things will be given to you.

—Clayburgh, interviewed by Samantha Dean for *LI, Newsday*, 18 June 1978

I think psychiatric scenes are usually dull. We've seen them 100 times and they can get very yawny. [For *An Unmarried Woman*] I wanted them to be unique. I had the script — but I tried not to learn my lines.... So before going to sleep,

I read them through without any intonations — no periods, no beginnings, like a wash, just so I'd know the words....

When we got to shooting the psychiatrist scenes, I said to Paul Mazursky, "Let's just put the cameras on and see." Sometimes, when something is very mysterious, you don't have to rehearse. You can always throw it out. So we started. This stuff just began happening. And the analyst [Dr. Penelope Russianoff] would add things, and that became complicated. I knew I had to get back to the script. I knew I had to help her or we couldn't finish because certain areas had to be covered. She would improvise quite a bit. She added exactly what she'd say in such a situation. "Guilt makes me livid" — she made that up.

—Clayburgh, interviewed by Arthur Bell for *The Village Voice*, 6 Mar 1978

Q. Was Paul Mazursky's method of handling actors very different from that of other directors you've worked with?

A. Paul doesn't direct in the way that a lot of other people do. He doesn't say, for instance, "That's a sad line." You can burst out laughing on it if you like so long as what you do is authentic. He doesn't try to control your emotions. You never feel pressure from him. A very relaxed feeling is what you pick up from him right away. You don't worry about anything with Paul. You don't worry about the lunch break or how many takes you're going to do. You're not thinking all the time, am I pleasing him, am I pleasing him? You can say whatever you want. In some ways you feel in charge. You can say I don't like that or let's do it this way or let's put the camera there. He won't listen to you, necessarily, but there isn't the feeling that your job is limited to merely appearing in front of the camera. Paul is not threatened by actors since he is one himself, and he doesn't have to pull a big, authoritarian number. There's never the kind of competition where you think all he's interested in is getting it his way. He's not. He's interested in getting it your way, the way you're comfortable with.

—Clayburgh, interviewed by Samantha Dean for *LI*, *Newsday*, 18 June 1978

Starting Over [1979, Alan J. Pakula] is really about the man [Burt Reynolds] and his relationship with women. It's not about my character, but I jumped at the chance of doing it. Why? Because it's a beautifully written role. Obviously Jim Brooks, the writer, fell a little bit in love with her. She's full of good qualities, and even her lesser qualities are very special and possess a certain charm.

She's a nice woman who is anything but uncomplicated. It's not often such a sweet, generous role comes along.

—Clayburgh, interviewed for *International Photographer*, Feb 1980

Montgomery CLIFT [1920-1966]

Born: Edward Montgomery Clift in Omaha, Nebraska. From age 14 he worked in summer stock, and in 1935 made his Broadway debut. After success there, he made his first screen appearances in 1948 in The Search (Fred Zinnemann) and Red River (Howard Hawks):

I didn't think I was physically right for [the role of Matthew Garth in *Red River*]; I still don't. I didn't believe I could stand up to a man as big as John Wayne, but I liked the story so much and Hawks...[gave] me the kind of contract I wanted, so I finally agreed to it....

I liked the whole company very, very much. But "Pidge" [Noah Berry, Jr.] is such a real Westerner, knows so much about horses and riding and all that, that I learned the most from him. We used to get up before dawn with the cowboys and go out on the remuda. I'm usually a late-to-bed, late-to-rise type, but that country around Tucson, Arizona, was about the most beautiful I've ever seen, particularly at sunrise.

—Clift, interviewed by Wynn Roberts for *Photoplay Magazine*, Apr 1949

The little things [Alice Tripp — as played by Shelley Winters in *A Place in the Sun* (1951, George Stevens)] did, all unconsciously, the things that were piece and parcel of her and her background would have built up — one on top of the other — until they became a mountain of irritation.

Eventually, too — inevitably — the boy I played would have fallen in love with a girl with the lovely smoothness that comes with wealth and social position. He was conditioned to do this from his childhood when he made up his mind to get away from the ugly life he then knew.

[George Stevens] got the best performances all of us were capable of giving. He never tried to make any one of us say or do anything that seemed unnatural to us.

—Clift, interviewed by Elsa Maxwell for *Photoplay Magazine*, Dec 1951

I'd lost 12 pounds to play the part [in *The Young Lions* (1958, Edward Dmytryk)]...and had my ears glued forward. I wanted to look like a rodent, that's why. Lean and slim like a rodent. Or let's say a rat passing for a mouse. But they didn't see that. Oh, no. All they saw was that my face looked different and they shrieked.

—Clift, interviewed by Roderick Mann for *The Sunday Express*, 16 Aug 1959

I have no misgivings about this character [Perce Howland in *The Misfits* (1961, John Huston)]. Someone said, "My God, it's exactly like you...." It's a wonderful part, and if I don't do it justice I'll shoot myself....

I find no value for myself in analyzing something down to some terribly finite Freudian point, because it loses its measure of relish. Wonderfully enough, [screenwriter] Arthur [Miller] is so wildly aware of the ambivalence in relations between people that for a performer it is almost an offense to dissect it. I imagine that he, as a writer, would not be able to write if he consciously tried to become clinical and symbolic. Nothing would flow....

The only line I know of that's wrong in Shakespeare is "Holding a mirror up to nature." You hold the magnifying glass up to nature. As an actor you just enlarge it enough so that your audience can identify with a situation.... The magnifying glass has been misused totally, but in this picture it has been put to the use of capturing what possibly is flitting in and out of someone's mind and one person's relationship to another and another, and that's what's fascinating.

—Clift, interviewed by James Goode for *The Story of The Misfits* (New York: Bobbs-Merrill, 1963); rep. as *The Making of The Misfits* (New York: Proscenium Books, 1986)

Glenn CLOSE [1947-]

Born: Greenwich, Connecticut. Studies at The College of William and Mary and work off and on Broadway preceded her film debut as Jenny Fields in The World According to Garp (1982, George Roy Hill):

Every character has an atmosphere or an aura.... I can tell you the aura of each character I've played and could at this moment walk across the room as that character. I know how they disturb the air. Jenny Fields of *Garp*, for example, is basically a mother and a nurse: mother it and heat it. She honestly doesn't understand lust, although she knows everything about sex because she's a nurse. And she loves her son [Robin Williams] — that's her most vulnerable point.

—Close, interviewed by Terry Materese for *The Cable Guide*, Oct 1983

[Jenny Fields] is such a strong image in people's minds. [John] Irving describes her pretty exactly — tall, long legged, slim hipped, dark hair. The opposite of me. I couldn't think of what to do so, I read it mimicking Katharine Hepburn, some of which, in a toned-down form, is still there.

I felt from the beginning that Jenny should be played as an attractive woman. I wanted her to have beautiful hair, the kind of long luxuriant hair she could braid and pin up and forget about. The thing about Jenny is she *isn't* unlucky with men — Irving has her dating in the book — she just has more important things to attend to. I wanted to communicate that choice, but convey that she's a woman of possibilities....

Although you don't see much of it in the movie, I had in my mind this image of Jenny's center being her nursing. Her day-to-day work. It gives her a base.... She wanted a child but not the nuisance of a husband, a middleman. She mounted a guy and accomplished what to her was a logical goal.... She just saw men as extraneous. My very personal opinion is men and women *are* extremely different, different animals altogether. I accept my womanness in regard to men and have a strong sense of it apart from men. That helped when I had to say, "Your father was a comatose stranger with a constant erection and I wanted a baby so I fucked him." Imagine that scene played wrong. People would be rolling on the floor.

George is a very spare director. He cast the movie, I think, to have actors with strong sensibilities, a group he could instinctively trust. If he doesn't like something he'll say so, but if he doesn't say anything, it doesn't necessarily mean you stink. That tends to make you a little crazy, not getting feedback. But when he does approve, he'll quietly say, "Oh, that was lovely," which is wonderful.

—Close, interviewed by Guy Trebay for *The Village Voice*, 3 Aug 1982

I loved the way [Jenny Fields] would look at somebody, really listen to people and really care about everything that they were telling her and be totally unjudgmental about it.

—Close, interviewed by Terry Materese for *The Cable Guide*, June 1985

[On *The Big Chill* (1983)] Larry [Kasdan] was very open to ideas and suggestions, but he *was* the writer as well as the director, and his words were pretty sacred. You'll notice that when we're all in the room together, there's no overlapping dialogue. One speaks, then the next, then the next. It's all very stylized — not at all naturalistic.

Iris [in *The Natural* (1984, Barry Levinson)] was difficult in that she was rather mythological. To make a human being out of a somewhat idealized character was the challenge, the frustration. She's the last of what I think of as my Jenny Fields cycle. You know, the centered woman, the mother, the nurturing woman, the strong woman.

—Close, interviewed by Peter Buckley for *Horizon*, Apr 1984

I worked extremely hard in developing that character [of Alex Forrest in *Fatal Attraction* (1987, Adrian Lyne)]. I did a lot of homework; I worked with psychiatrists. I went to the script and I went moment to moment.... [I considered] the thought processes that this woman would go through — and they all were incorporated into the script. An example is the moment when you see me alone turning the lamp on and off. I thought it was very important to show this character in her troubled devastation, totally alone. I always thought of her as being tragic rather than evil.

—Close, interviewed by Barbara Walters for *The Barbara Walters Special*, aired ABC-TV, 11 Apr 1988

[Alex's behavior veers] between being a total child and a femme fatale. Her sexuality has been all screwed up, and she has no sense of self-worth. She tries to provoke people to hate her as much as she hates herself.

—Close, interviewed by Cathleen McGuigan and Constance Guthrie for *Newsweek*, 12 Oct 1987

The Marquis [de Merteuil in *Dangerous Liaisons* (1988, Stephen Frears)] is such a bright and passionate woman. But she is both a product and a victim of her times, and she knows that. She has such a sense of the game, and she plays it so well — up to a point. She's a real paradox — a serious person with a lot of sadness and outrage, and ultimately tragic. But hot!

—Close, interviewed by Judy Ellis for *Life*, Feb 1989

Q. In that [final] scene in *Dangerous Liaisons*, did you force yourself into that state of frenzy?

A. To me a scene like that is worth its weight in gold. It's the only time you see the Marquise totally out of control. And you see her out of control because of grief. It makes her a human being. You have to get yourself mentally prepared, and its's a litle scary because you never know quite what's going to do it for you. I remember standing in front of that door and getting myself mentally prepared, thinking mainly of the man who was dead [Valmont/John Malkovich]. Thinking the thoughts that I thought would be in her head, the grief and anger and despair, and then you say, OK! And you go for it.

—Close, interviewed by Frank Spotnitz for *American Film*, Dec 1991

In *Fatal Attraction* and *Dangerous Liaisons* I was playing ultimately self-destructive women. [For *Immediate Family* (1989, Jonathan Kaplan] my soul needed to go on the other side. It needed to be fed by somebody who was more affirmative.

—Close, interviewed by Bonnie Allen for *Ms*, Nov 1989

Charles COBURN [1877-1961]

Born: Savannah, Georgia. Work on Broadway (from 1901) preceded his film debut in the title role of Boss Tweed (1933, a March of the Years production), followed by his feature film debut, Say It With Flowers (1934, John Baxter). In 1946, he played Dandy Gow in Victor Saville's The Green Years:

Dandy Gow...was the sort of person I would like to be. He had neither inhibitions nor prohibitions. His imagination embroidered everything it touched, taking him constantly into a make-believe land where he was a hero. Dandy had faults, of course, but they were the kind that injured no one but himself. I really think Dandy, with his cheerful philosophy and his kindness, added something to the joy quota of the world.

—Coburn, in *The Saturday Evening Post*, 13 Sept 1947

Steve COCHRAN [1917-1965]

Born: Robert Cochran in Eureka, California. Studies at The University of Wyoming, work on the Detroit stage, in stock and on Broadway (from 1944) preceded his film debut in Wonder Man (1945, Bruce Humberstone). In 1950, he played Hank Rice in Stuart Heisler's Storm Warning:

Hank was a subnormal person with a complicated set of emotions. As a frustrated egomaniac, he was easily carried away by the excitement of mob violence. He tried to compensate for his feeling of inferiority by joining the Klan, and he was unfaithful to his wife, and was a murderer, because of this same tormented ego.

Playing a character like that naturally gave me a chance to interpret just about every emotion in the book: love, hate, fear, cowardice, pride and shame. I also had to be domestically violent without hurting anyone badly, which wasn't easy. In one scene I had to hit my screen sister-in-law, Ginger Rogers, repeatedly with my doubled fist; in another I had to throw Doris Day, my screen wife, across a room. Pulling punches in a picture can be arranged without too much loss of realism, but it's hard to throw a woman across a room convincingly without damage. Doris, fortunately, was willing to collect some bruises in the cause of realism.

—Cochran, in *The Saturday Evening Post*, 8 Nov 1952

Iron Eyes CODY [1907-]

Born: Oskie Cody in Oklahoma Territory. After making his film debut as an extra in Back to God's Country (1919, Irvin Willat) when Paramount Studios rented his father's farm in Oklahoma to shoot the film, he and his father (Thomas Long Plume) returned to Hollywood with the company. His father worked for many years as a technical adviser on Western films; Iron Eyes worked both in that capacity and as an Indian extra and lead. His first speaking part — in The Wolf Song (1929, Victor Fleming) — came through the intervention of his friend, Gary Cooper. He later appeared in seven films for John Ford, the second of which was Stagecoach (1939):

"Jack" Ford and John Wayne had been friends all during Duke's Poverty Row years. We used to all go off for fishing expeditions on Ford's hundred-foot ketch....

"When you learn to act someday, I'll put you in a good picture," he would tease. Ford was the only one who could get away with remarks like that to Duke....

When we started shooting *Stagecoach* in Monument Valley, in October of 1938, he immediately started ridiculing and bullying Duke in front of the whole company. And these were real film stars, the first Duke had ever worked with: Thomas Mitchell, Claire Trevor, George Bancroft, John Carradine. He'd call him a dumb bastard, a big oaf, and say things like, "Can't you walk *normal* instead of skipping around like a goddamned fairy?" It's true that working with Jack Ford could be pure hell, and he was a sadistic man if there ever was one, but there was also a reason behind most everything he seemingly did for the sheer hell of it — at least while working.

While some could match Errol [Flynn]'s strength, I don't know of anybody who came close to his callousness. He had just about everybody either hating or fearing him, always picking fights and making corny, insulting jokes at your expense. It's solid testimony to the sheer force of his personality that most people, while hating him, still liked him very much. Suckers all, he probably thought. Including myself.

We had been on location for days shooting action sequences for *They Died with Their Boots On* [1941, Raoul Walsh]. This is the Civil War/Little Big Horn Battle opus tracing the life of General George Custer with much liberality regarding factual matters....

In one of the final moments, I was to come charging up, let out a war whoop, and leap from my horse onto Errol's back. He was then supposed to fling me off and, with me lying on my back, shoot me with his pistol. Fine, we'd done this kind of stunt dozens of times. And Errol was a true athlete. He'd know how to move, how to gracefully and harmlessly perform this kind of stunt. The only problem was that our entire time in the desert he had been drinking. I think this was his gin period, and he'd guzzle the stuff like orange juice first thing in the morning, continuing throughout the day. Every day. By the time we got to this last crucial scene, he was staggering about, bleary-eyed and dazed, waving his saber recklessly. He was the perfect Custer, half-crazy from battle fatigue, rallying non-existent troops in a hoarse, gin-soaked voice.

So there I was charging up behind him, whooping, my tomahawk in hand. I yanked back on the reins, at the same time lifting my right leg up and behind, the combined movements catapulting me onto Errol's back. Now I'm not sure at this point if he even remembered this was to occur, since he flung me off with such violence. Then he swung about and, before I even hit the ground, stuck his gun in my back and fired point blank. I had no shirt on and felt a hot, searing pain.

It must be a miracle I'm alive. That pistol, loaded with what had to be an extra couple portions of blank charge, tore a half-inch hole, narrowly missing my spinal column.

[Cecil B.] DeMille was a little dissatisfied with the horse falls in *The Plainsman* [1937] and decided we needed something more convincing. Fortunately the days of tripping up the horse with wires and ropes were over, and trained animals did sometimes set themselves down a little too delicately. What he did was instruct [Art] Rossen to use real wild bucking broncs. My brother and I complained bitterly, but no dice. If the Indians wanted to work and collect their fifteen bucks, they'd ride the horses provided. I'll say this much, it did make for realistic falls. And nobody ever said you *wouldn't* go through hell on a DeMille picture.

Women were no exception. Rossen had our leading lady, Barbara Stanwyck, jumping from railroad cars and allowing real arrows (shot by me), as well as bullets, to blast a canister of molasses over her head, which she then allowed to pour all over her. Despite what some say, though, she never let herself be chased by buffalo. That was accomplished with a process shot.

Richard Harris is not only one of the best actors I've ever worked with, he's also a genuine tough guy. Nobody messes with him, and I was happy to learn he wanted an authentic picture as much as I [in *A Man Called Horse* (1969, Elliot Silverstein)]. I spent three weeks hammering out a script with Jack DeWitt who wrote the script for *Sitting Bull* [1954, Sidney Salkow]. We decided we were going to drag Richard all over creation and, for a grand finale, hang him up for the ritualized self-torture of the Sun Dance. Richard was delighted....

—Cody, in his *Iron Eyes Cody: My Life as a Hollywood Indian* (New York: Everest House, 1982)

Claudette COLBERT [1905-]

Born: Lily Claudette Chauchoin in Paris, France. Work on the stage, including Broadway (from 1925) preceded her film debut in For the Love of Mike (1927, Frank Capra). Early in her career, she worked on two films directed by Ernst Lubitsch — The Smiling Lieutenant (1931) and Bluebeard's Eighth Wife (1938):

One of the difficulties I found on the screen, having come from the theatre, is that we didn't get enough direction. Lubitsch was not like that. Having been a comedian, he was in there himself. He would want you to do things the way he would do it, and I must say, it was very funny. I know I did things I wouldn't dare do. But he would make me laugh so much that I did them, and I was better than I would have been.

—Colbert, interviewed by Sharon Lee Dobuler for *Show Business*, 6 July 1978

I will be eternally grateful to Mr. [Cecil B.] De Mille for *The Sign of the Cross* [1932]. That changed everything. It proved I could play another kind of character.

—Colbert, interviewed by Eileen Creelman for *The New York Sun*, 26 Mar 1935

We modern women could learn a lot from Poppaea [Nero's mistress in *The Sign of the Cross*]. We go about demanding our rights, arguing with men for what we want. But Poppaea knew a trick which was far more effective. She flattered him. She let down her hair, perfumed her body and arrayed herself in her loveliest and most daring costumes for his pleasure. Then she did just whatever she pleased. He was so enchanted with her that he never noticed the things she did.

—Colbert (1932), quoted by Michiko Kakutani in *The New York Times*, 16 Nov 1979

In one scene [in *Cleopatra* (1934)], DeMille wanted Caesar [Warren William] to drop rose petals on my feet. I screamed with laughter when he told me that. I said, "He can touch my foot, he can even bite it, but if he drops rose petals on it, I'll just burst out laughing." He finally agreed — it was one of the few times I ever won an argument with him.

To us, a lot of his ideas were corny, but I don't think you can call him phony. He really believed in what he was doing. When we did the scene in *The Sign of the Cross* with the Christians being eaten by lions, he really suffered....

It was very important that everything be absolutely correct. He was very serious about giving the public what it wanted.

—Colbert, interviewed by Michiko Kakutani for *The New York Times*, 16 Nov 1979

I don't think I was right in *Cleopatra*. She was a brilliant, witty woman — even her enemies admitted that. It is in everything ever written about her. And in the picture she doesn't say or do one brilliant or witty thing....

—Colbert, interviewed by Eileen Creelman for *The New York Sunday Sun*, 26 Mar 1935

[*It Happened One Night* (1934, Frank Capra)] was really a fluke. Clark Gable was being punished by MGM, so they sent him to Columbia to make this film. All I wanted to do was get within 2 feet of Clark Gable; I never really read the script very much. But the movie started a whole new wave of comedies. Movies had about everything at that time but what they didn't have was normal-looking people who were funny.

—Colbert, interviewed by Tom Shales for *The Washington Post*; repr. in *The Bergen Record*, early 1974

Only a few days after we had started the picture [*It Happened One Night*], I was voicing my worries about it to Clark Gable. I had my doubts about the script.... The dialogue was too flip, I insisted. It was all very cute and light, of course, but that was just the trouble with it.

Well, Clark listened to about as much as he could stand. Then he said, "Oh, forget it, Claudette! What do you care? And if you do, you'd better keep it to yourself, because as far as I'm concerned, it just doesn't matter. If it's going to be a flop, it will be one. Don't forget, you and I just work here. The script isn't our business any more than the photography is...."

He absolutely scoffed me out of my worries. He suddenly made me ashamed of myself because I realized that I was annoying everyone.

I learned from Clark a thing or two about taking life in stride, and I'll always be grateful. He's so amiable, so unperturbed, that I couldn't help learning!

—Colbert, interviewed by Katharine Hartley for *Movie Classic*, Oct 1935

I didn't know anything at all about insane asylums. Before I could play a psychiatrist [in *Private Worlds* (1935, Gregory LaCava)], I did have to find out what they looked like, anyway. I thought they'd be very grim and serious. But the ones I met were charming — but really charming. They were the most delightful people, and so kind and helpful.

The doctors [at a California State institution] all wanted to know right away what kind of a story we were making. That was only natural. They said everyone had such a wrong idea about insane asylums. They thought them dreadful places, cruel and tragic. But they're not. That is what amazed me. Not these modern hospitals, anyway. And the doctors wanted us to make people realize what psychiatrists try to do....

I slicked down the bangs and tried to look more serious. I had to, you know, for the audience's sake. They would never have believed a psychiatrist could wear her hair as frivolously as this.

—Colbert, interviewed by Eileen Creelman for *The New York Sun*, 26 Mar 1935

If I hadn't seen those doctors working with their patients, my attitude would have been entirely wrong. Either I would have been too severe or I would have been too indulgent. Without my visits to that sanitarium I wouldn't have known that my attitude towards my *Private Worlds* patients should be that very nice blending of friendship and authority.

—Colbert, interviewed by Adele Whitely Fletcher in an unsourced, undated article in the files of The New York Public Library for the Performing Arts

The title [*Skylark* (1941, Mark Sandrich)] refers to a girl named Lydia Kenyon, who has been married five years to a young advertising man named Tony Kenyon [Ray Milland], and is still desperately in love with him. And he's still in love with her, but he doesn't think about it much, what with concentrating on his work. She aches to fly away with him somewhere to some place where they can escape the obligations of his success (for which *she* is partly responsible). She aches to find time for love. To her, love is more important than anything else in the world....

Skylark takes up where *Arise, My Love* [1940, Mitchell Leisen] left off. That was a comedy of courtship, against a background of foreign adventure, which ended with [Ray Milland and I] sailing for America. This is a comedy of marriage, against a background of typical American life. And the characters are completely different.

Before, Ray was a devil-may-care flier, and I was a nervy newspaperwoman, with Walter Abel for my frantic boss. Ray's only rival for my affections was my job. Now, Ray is an ambitious young businessman, with Walter Abel for a harried business associate, and I am a stay-at-home wife. My only rival for Ray's affections is his job — despite the passes that Binnie Barnes makes at him. But this time *he* has a rival: Brian Aherne.

—Colbert, as told to James Reid for *Movie Story*, 1941; in the clipping file of The New York Public Library for the Performing Arts

Ronald COLMAN [1891-1958]

Born: Richmond, Surrey, England. Studies at London University, work with The Bancroft Amateur Dramatic Society and on the London stage preceded his film debut in The Live Wire (1917, George Dewhurst — unreleased). His first released film was The Toilers (1919, Tom Watts). He came to prominence opposite Lillian Gish in The White Sister (1923) and Romola (1924), both for director Henry King:

One afternoon I came out of my stage door, a card having been sent backstage to me, and I found Henry King, the film director, awaiting me. I was told that Lillian Gish, planning to film *The White Sister* wanted an actor who looked like an Italian. Mr. King said they wanted someone with "a touch of Valentino" about him, that he had tried in vain to find his man, and that he thought he had found him — now....

Mr. King and Miss Gish were persuasive.... I was given a screen test the next day, and on the day after I found myself on the Atlantic Ocean, sitting in a steamer chair talking to Lillian Gish. She talked of acting and the answers to my questions were filled with sanity and intelligence. Lillian Gish is a very real person; wholly unspoiled by her fame, ambitious to achieve the fine ideals she has set for herself on the screen, not in any sense content to look back on *Broken Blossoms*...and so many other triumphs and rest serenely on her oars. She is genuinely, utterly sincere, and there is about her none of the manner of a film star....

[During] *The White Sister*, the cool understanding intelligence of Lillian was of unbelievable help. By this time, my picture training in England was in an old-fashioned technique. Miss Gish gave me suggestions and advice that did everything but save my life.... With Miss Gish and Henry King to help me, I found *The White Sister* the greatest acting experience I had ever been through. Whatever doubts I had about my devotion to pictures were dispelled; this was to be my field.

—Colman, in *The Newark Ledger*, 4 Feb 1930

[*Bulldog Drummond* (1929)] was a rich, slight, incredible melodrama of the old school, to be done with one's tongue in one's cheek.... There was a fine cast of stage players. We rehearsed for weeks and weeks, and then when scenarist Sidney Howard and Mr. [Sam] Goldwyn and the others decided we were ready, director Richard Jones began shooting the picture — straight through, without an hour's delay. Not a line was changed, not a scene revised. In an amazingly short time, the picture was finished....

—Colman, in *The Allentown Leader*, 25 Jan 1930

[Sydney Carton in *A Tale of Two Cities* (1935, Jack Conway)] is the psychological antithesis of the Hollywood yesman.

He never was anything else [but himself]. It was impossible for the man to make compromises with others or with himself or with problems of life. He was the most unheroic of heroes, but he had the fundamental fortitude to march to the guillotine with a smile on his lips because he was strong enough to be himself.

He utterly lacked the desire to court popularity, although he was a brilliant man. He lived his life without a thought for the impression he was making on those around him.

—Colman, interviewed for *The Brooklyn Daily Eagle*, 5 Jan 1936

Bob Conway...[in *Lost Horizon* (1937, Frank Capra)]...was an adventurer before he went to Shangri-La. Always ferreting out excitement, always jumping headlong into the thick of things, always curious, eager to try anything once. Yet when he is brought by force to Shangri-La, along with several fellow travelers, he is the first to fall under its spell. The rest hate it, fear it, as something ominous and strange. Yet from the beginning Conway falls into the peaceful pattern of the place.

Some people may find that difficult to understand. But I understand it perfectly. Because in a lesser degree I used to follow excitement around too. Of course I was never decorated for bravery or anything like that. I never made English conquests of Africa. Unlike Conway, I never did anything really noble or daring. But I did try to. Like millions of other very young men I saw zest in everything, even in war. Like the millions of others, too, I found there was nothing zestful about it. But I wasn't cured....

—Colman, interviewed by Katharine Hartley for *Movie Classic*, July 1936

As far as the movie audience is concerned, a dual role on the screen is nothing more than an engaging novelty. It is an entertaining trick, to be sure, but nothing more or less than that to the spectator. To an actor, and I speak as one who has had experience with dual roles, it is a bugaboo that directs a challenge at his ability....

However, when a part is as attractive as the one...in *The Prisoner of Zenda* [1937, John Cromwell], the dual role really holds no terrors. The two people whom I was to bring to life were strikingly similar in appearance, yet their characters were almost diametrically opposed.

Rudolph Rassendyl was the image of King Rudolph, yet his mental traits were antipodal to those of his royal cousin.

The King is the sort of light-hearted fellow who would rather make his country's songs than its laws. Not much regard for obligations, you see. He preferred the gaiety of Paris and Vienna to the duties awaiting him in his capital city of Strelsau.

Rassendyl, on the other hand, is quite a serious chap — witty enough, daring, but with both feet on the ground. Rassendyl, rather than Rudolph, was the better fitted for the throne.

—Colman, in *The New York Daily Mirror*, 9 Sept 1937

Dorothy COMINGORE [1913-1971]

Born: Los Angeles. Studies in religious philosophy and economics at The University of California, Berkeley, and work on the stage in Carmel, California, preceded her film debut in a walk-on part in Campus Cinderella (1938, Noel Smith). In 1940, she played Susan Alexander Kane opposite Orson Welles in his Citizen Kane:

Susan Alexander Kane, surrounded by a roomful of dolls, showed no growth and never grasped there really was an intellectual side to life.

—Comingore, interviewed for *The New York Times*, 31 Aug 1941

I don't know whether [Orson Welles] is a good director because he's a good actor — or the other way around, but Orson is by far the most sensitive and sympathetic director I've ever watched, and I watched plenty during my Columbia career. He seems to anticipate the actor's every move — sometimes acting out the parts himself. And he isn't tied down to any cut-and-dried Hollywood rules. Doesn't worry about camera angles and chalk marks for actors and other hallowed Hollywood traditions. He has faith in his players. And he listens to you. I had a speech to say to him which didn't ring true to me somehow. I told him so. He said, "Maybe you're right — think of another one!" Which had me right out on a limb. A bit later he said, "Did you think of another speech?" and I had to admit that I hadn't. But *he* had! All the time he'd been shooting the last scene, he'd been rewriting my speech — and thanked me for suggesting it! *That's* unusual — in Hollywood.

—Comingore, interviewed by Thomas Vaughan for *Screen Life*, July 1941

Chester CONKLIN [1886-1971]

Born: Oskaloosa, Iowa. Work as a clown with The Barnum Circus preceded his film debut in 1913 in a Mack Sennett comedy. Fame came as a Keystone Kop:

[Mack Sennett would] be there in front of the camera laughing and you'd break your neck to make him laugh. That was one secret of the Keystone's success.

—Conklin, interviewed for *The Evening Standard*, 14 May 1964

A picture called *Mabel's Strange Predicament* [1914] really started Chaplin going.... The principal players were Mabel Normand, Roscoe Arbuckle, Chaplin, Ford Sterling and myself....

During a lull in the activities, while Arbuckle and I were playing pinochle, Charlie got the idea of using his world-renowned costume. I wore baggy trousers and Arbuckle had a small derby hat, and then there was Sterling with his enormous shoes. Charlie, to amuse himself and perhaps other folk, put on my trousers, Arbuckle's hat and Sterling's footwear. Then he picked up a piece of black crepe and held it under his nose like a small, thick mustache. He looked so ridiculous that he impressed Sennett as having possibilities. They fixed the mustache on and Charlie played in this make-up. And the first thing we knew was that he had stolen the picture from us all.

—Conklin, interviewed for *The New York Times*, 6 Feb 1927

Sean CONNERY [1930-]

Born: Thomas Connery in Edinburgh, Scotland. After service in The Royal Navy and work as a body builder and model, he made his film debut in No Road Back (1956, Montgomery Tully). He made seven films as Ian Fleming's secret agent, James Bond, beginning with Dr. No (1962, Terence Young):

Playboy: There are critics of Fleming who claim that Bond's appeal is based solely on sex, sadism and snobbery; yet his defenders, most notably Kingsley Amis, find Bond a repository of such admirable qualities as toughness, loyalty and perseverance. How do you see him?

Connery: He is really a mixture of all that the defenders and the attackers say he is. When I spoke about Bond with Fleming, he said that when the character was conceived, Bond was a very simple, straightforward, blunt instrument of the police force, a functionary who would carry out his job rather doggedly. But he also had a lot of idiosyncrasies that were considered snobbish — such as a taste for special wines, et cetera. But if you take Bond in the situations that he is constantly involved with, you see that it is a very hard, high, unusual league that he plays in. Therefore he is quite right in having all his senses satisfied — be it sex, wine, food or clothes — because the job, and he with it, may terminate at any minute. But the virtues that Amis mentions — loyalty, honesty — are there, too. Bond doesn't chase married women, for instance. Judged on that level he comes out rather well.

Playboy: Do you think he's sadistic?

Connery: Bond is dealing with rather sadistic adversaries who dream up pretty wild schemes to destroy, maim or mutilate him. He must retaliate in kind, otherwise it's who's kidding who....

I must admit in all honesty that I didn't think it would take off as it did, although it had the ingredients of success: sex, action, and so forth. The only thing lacking, I thought, was humor, and luckily the director [of *Dr. No*, *From Russia with Love* (1963) and *Thunderball* (1965)], Terence Young, agreed with me that it would be right to give it another flavor, another dimension, by injecting humor, but at the same time to play it absolutely straight and realistically.

—Connery, interviewed for *Playboy*, Nov 1965

Hitherto, whenever I've tangled with a beautiful spy, have you noticed what invariably happens? Even if I know the girl is a nasty and dangerous little snake, I've still had to kiss her first and kill her later. That's the persona Ian Fleming and the film producers built up for me as James Bond. Every time I see a girl, I have to give. One of my producers, Cubby Broccoli, said to me: "It's like this, Sean. James Bond is a nut for girls. Even if he hates her, his amorous instincts die hard — and she dies soft, see?"

[*Goldfinger* (1964, Guy Hamilton)] sort of demonstrates what I believe is a subtler, more discriminating Bond than you have seen in the earlier films [*Dr. No* and *From Russia with Love*]. All the girls still want to make him, but he doesn't need to make love to all of them. It's a process of development. At first it was I who had to model myself on the James Bond that Fleming and the scriptwriters had shaped for me. But now I am making Bond more and more like me, instead of the other way round.

—Connery, interviewed by Leonard Mosley for *The New York Times Magazine*, 22 Nov 1964

My only grumble about the Bond films is that they don't tax one as an actor. All one really needs is the constitution of a rugby player to get through those 19 weeks of swimming, slugging, and necking. [His other Bond films were: *You Only Live Twice* (1967, Lewis Gilbert), *Diamonds are Forever* (1971, Guy Hamilton) and *Never Say Never Again* (1983, Irvin Kershner).]

—Connery, interviewed by Roderick Mann for *The Sunday Express*, 14 Feb 1965

I wanted to read the script [of *Marnie* (1964, Alfred Hitchcock)] before I accepted the contract, and Hitch felt it was sufficient that Grace Kelly was going to return to films in it, and therefore I should be only too happy.... As it turned out, I had a great time with Hitchcock. I adored him.... He figures that an actor should make his own contributions to the character, and observe the movements worked out by the director. [Grace Kelly bowed out of the project and was replaced by Tippi Hedren.]

—Connery, interviewed by Gordon Gow for *Films & Filming*, Mar 1974

[*Robin and Marion* (1976, Richard Lester)] was an example of "I liked the script." Here was a guy who was aging, and at the end of a myth. He's a not very intelligent guy, who's at heart a boy, and that's how I played it. Waking up with a bit of rheumatism, he goes to have a piss and realizes Marion is there, and he has to cover up and go somewhere else.

—Connery, interviewed by Ben Fong-Torres for *American Film*, May 1989

It's a long time since [Brian] De Palma had a film in which the characters are so complete. And getting [playwright, David] Mamet [to write *The Untouchables* (1987)] was a brilliant stroke, not only because he was born in Chicago and is very knowledgeable about the ethnic problems in the city, the police, the corruption and all that, he was able to go back to basics and made the story almost biblical. It's about justice. There are times when the law is enough, and times when it isn't, times when it falls over backward to be fair and favors people like Capone, and sometimes when you have almost to overstep it.

Malone is a guy who's worldly-wise, street-wise, knows the score with the crooks, is frightened for his life and had just planned on staying alive, until he met Ness [Kevin Costner].

I like contrast. Marlon Brando was one of the best examples. He was very powerful and dynamic in *On the Waterfront* and *Streetcar Named Desire*, yet there were touches which showed he had sensitivity, too. I like it when an actor looks one thing and conveys something else, perhaps something diametrically opposite. With Malone, I tried to show at the beginning he could be a real pain in the ass, so that you wouldn't think he could be concerned with such things as Ness's feelings or Ness's family, and then show he was someone else underneath, capable of real relationships.

—Connery, interviewed by Benedict Nightingale for *The New York Times*, 7 June 1987

Gary COOPER [1901-1961]

Born: Frank Cooper in Helena, Montana. Son of a Montana Supreme Court judge, he worked occasionally as a political cartoonist before entering films in 1924 as an Indian extra in The Vanishing American (1925, George B. Seitz). His first major role was in The Winning of Barbara Worth (1926, Henry King):

What Henry King had in mind was to cast me as a dispatch rider — a role that would permit me to appear now and then as Ronald Colman's messenger boy. Colman was the hero, playing the part of a smooth, sophisticated Eastern engineer out to reclaim the West by building dams. Vilma Banky, publicized as the most beautiful woman in the world, was his leading lady. Their appearance in a picture meant that it would be more than Great; it would be Colossal. Even with a small part, this was my big opportunity.

Colman was one of the actors I had studied most on the screen. Now I would have a chance to watch him work on the set, and maybe pick up a few clues to the secret of his success....

There was a third big part in *The Winning of Barbara Worth* that had been assigned to a talented actor named Harold Goodwin. That was the part of Abe Lee, a tall, slim fellow from Montana. Goodwin was to represent simple Western manhood, Colman was to represent Eastern sophistication, and it was up to Miss Banky to choose between them.

Goodwin was still busy completing a picture for Warner Brothers when Henry King was ready to roll. Rather than waste time and money by holding up production, King made a desperate move....

One morning King started running me around the studio at seven A.M. An hour later I was showing signs of strain, but he reminded me of the Marathon racers, and art for art's sake, and I kept on going. After about ten miles of this, he'd meet me about every fourth round and throw dust in my face. When I didn't seem to be sweating to his satisfaction, he'd haul out a spray gun and settle the dust with a film of water. By the time he decided I looked exhausted enough, I was staggering, completely done in. He caught me as I came around, steered me onto the set in front of the cameras, and said, "Give 'em the message."

The lights and the heat hit me full in the face. I opened my mouth mechanically, saw the camera spinning around me, and fell flat. Colman caught my head just before it hit the floor....

The second scene was the one in which I had to die in Colman's lap.... My greatest worry was whether I was emotionally up to getting through the scene with Ronald Colman, the master of emotion. I didn't want to let him down, and told him so.

"Easy does it, old boy," he said. "Good scenes make good actors. Actors don't make good scenes. My own feeling is that all you have to do is take a nap, and every woman who sees the picture is going to cry her eyes out."

I took a nap in Colman's lap, and he was right....

—Cooper, as told to George Scullin for *The Saturday Evening Post*, 10 Mar 1956

When good actors play together, the emotional give and take builds up. But when Miss [Thelma] Todd threw an emotion at me [in *Arizona Bound* (1927, Johnny Waters)], I couldn't field it. I just stood there like an iron deer.

If this had been a talkie, my career would have ended right there. As it was Waters solved the problem with semi-close-ups. He shot into my face over Miss Todd's shoulder. Then, leaning forward in his director's chair, he talked me into character. I was a love-starved cowboy back from the Indian wars.

"You're hungry, Cooper," he said. "You haven't eaten for two days. You're so hungry that you're pale and weak. Look into Thelma's eyes. What do you see? A big table full of food. Chicken. Fried chicken and gravy. Dumplings.

Virginia ham. Smile a little. Man, that's a feast in front of you. Wet your lips a little.... That's enough. Look at that pie — a big apple pie. Show us how good it looks.... Don't over do it. You don't have to eat it all.... That's it. Now lean forward for a cup of coffee.... Whoops! Hold it! Cut!

I appeared in *Wings* [1927, William Wellman] for one scene lasting exactly one minute and forty-five seconds, and in my opinion those 105 seconds were the most valuable in my life....

As a tough flight instructor, it was my job to welcome to my tent the two green cadets played by Buddy [Rogers] and Dick [Arlen]. I had to dress them down, impress them with my own superiority and imply that if they had super-human stuff, they, too — like me — might become pilots. As a bit of business during this scene, Buddy was to offer me a chocolate bar. I was to take a bite and toss the rest on my bunk as an indication that bribery would get them nowhere. Then I was to step outside, and as they stared at the tent flap, sound effects would describe the sound of my take-off, the splutter of my motor and the frightful crash.

We shot my part of the scene in one minute and forty-five seconds. Bill said "Cut," and I was through. The scene was up to Buddy and Dick, and what they did to it made me an actor. I was staggered when I saw the preview. There I was leaving the tent. Then the theater was filled with the roar of the plane taking off, the splutter and the crash. And there were Buddy and Dick, looking scared. First they looked at each other, then they looked at the chocolate bar I had tossed on my bunk, and then they looked at each other again, growing more haggard by the second. In their faces was registered all the drama of my departure from *Wings*. They were so great that the audience didn't see them at all. The audience saw only that tall, lanky pilot, the one that got killed. What an actor he was! And I wasn't even there. I was a sound effect.

—Cooper, as told to George Scullin for *The Saturday Evening Post*, 17 Mar 1956

My big picture of 1929 was *The Virginian....* It was the first major talkie ever filmed outdoors....

Aside from difficulties with our "portable" equipment, we had a battle of another kind. Victor Fleming clung to the old-fashioned notion that he was making a picture with voices. The sound director, supported by his army of electronic engineers, was convinced he was making a radio program with faces. There was little fraternizing, and nothing much in the way of a co-operative exchange of ideas....

In a way, Fleming suffered more than I did. Like all directors of the silent days, he was accustomed to talking his actors into doing what he wanted. "Do this, do that, and now smile as you turn and bow. Turn around. Take her in your arms. Bend her over a little more. Now smooch. Hold it. Ten seconds, twelve seconds. Cut. We don't want to get this scene censored." Now, with a microphone picking up sound, he was stricken dumb. No matter how he strained and sweated to reach his actors, he could not do with mental telepathy what he could do with words. Yet he was forced to remain silent. It wasn't easy.

—Cooper, as told to George Scullin for *The Saturday Evening Post*, 24 Mar 1956

[Marlene Dietrich] had just recently arrived in Hollywood after her triumph in *Blue Angel* [1929, Josef von Sternberg], the famous German-made film. *Morocco* [1930] was her first American picture, and von Sternberg was out to see that she made good. Within the first hour of shooting I could see problems ahead.... He directed almost entirely in German; I didn't understand a word.... After a couple of days, I began to feel that von Sternberg was not seeing me as the co-star, but as a camera effect — something to be thrown in now and then to help show Miss Dietrich at her best. Under this treatment what confidence I had in my acting began sinking fast....

He directed with a strong hand. A carpenter hammering while von Sternberg was thinking might be fired on the spot. And he had a habit of compelling the whole cast to stand around him in hushed silence while he coached Miss Dietrich in German. In one of those meetings I saw my chance. I opened my mouth wide and yawned. An actress gasped. Adolphe [Menjou] grinned. Von Sternberg stopped, pawed the air a minute, and then continued. I yawned again. About the fourth yawn, with von Sternberg's collar shrinking to the choking point, he let me have it in perfect English.

"Well," I said politely, "if you would speak in English all the time, I'm sure I could stay awake."

The ceiling was too high to hit, but he tried. Then he stormed off the set for the day.

The next day was much better. He even threw us underlings a word or two of English to help us along. I congratulated myself on having won a major victory. With Adolphe coaching me on the art of acting, we knocked ourselves out to make *Morocco* a success. It was too. Billboards all over the country announced its coming. Full pages were taken in newspapers and magazines. I can see them yet:

MOROCCO! MARLENE DIETRICH!

Down in the lower right hand corner of the ads was a faint line that under a magnifying glass turned out to be type. It read: " with gary cooper and adolphe menjou." Von Sternberg had had his last word, and it wasn't in German, either.

—Cooper, as told to George Scullin for *The Saturday Evening Post*, 18 Feb 1956

Thanks to a series of excellent directors, I had reached the point where I was to be co-starred with Charles Laughton and Tallulah Bankhead. Against this talented pair I'd be lucky to survive the first day of shooting.

To complicate matters for me, the picture was a submarine epic called *The Devil and the Deep* [1932, Marion Gering], and, coming from Montana, I knew nothing about submarines. So I studied books about submarines, from the Nautilus of Jules Verne to the latest models in the world's navies. The way I saw it, a submarine skipper who was surrounded by exploding depth charges would be a lot more tense than the captain of a surface vessel under shellfire.

To get the feel of it, I persuaded a naval officer attached to our unit as technical director to give me a run-through on how I should handle the controls under attack. We went to the back lot of Paramount, where cutaway sets of a submarine's vitals had been built. So it was in a full-scale mockup of the control room that Tallulah came upon me one day as I was preparing to "surface."

She saw the strain I was under. "Dahling," she said, "what in the world are you doing?"

I came up for air. "Well, if you're going crash diving with me," I said, "I thought I ought to learn how to drive."

She took a look at all those instruments and ran a gloved hand over a couple to check for dust. "What's that got to do with acting?" she asked.

"Just this," I explained. "A fast dive is a tense moment. I push this and pull that, and sort of hold my jaw like this. As the captain says, a lot depends upon the way you hold your jaw. Now, when I head back for the sunshine and fresh air, I feel better. My shoulders relax and my jaw is not so grim, and I pull this and push that. The point is, if I know what I'm doing, I don't have to act. But if I just act as if I know, the Navy might catch me in a mistake and laugh me off the screen."

"Baloney," she said with Bankhead firmness. "If you've got to be an engineer to be an actor, I'm through. I can't even flick a cigarette lighter."

With her talent and voice, Tallulah doesn't have to strike a match to warm up an audience, but the rest of us have had to come a long, hard way in making the characters we play ring true. Ever since *The Devil and the Deep*, I've made a habit of reading all the background material I can get on the characters I am to play next. Pretty soon this dusty research begins to get personal.

—Cooper, as told to George Scullin for *The Saturday Evening Post*, 25 Feb 1956

We made *Design for Living* during the summer of 1933, when the depression was beginning to lift a bit. It was a Noël Coward play dealing with a woman in love with two men at the same time, and it had to be acted as high, fast comedy. Ernst Lubitsch was the director, Miriam Hopkins was the lady, and Fredric March and I were the men she loved. Playing in a high-pressure league like that, I found myself pressing too hard to make good, rushing my lines. At last Lubitsch called me aside.

"Look, Gary," he said. "Stop trying to save film. I have lots of film. You don't have to charge through a scene in one second, like a bull. Take two seconds. Do like Freddie. He pauses. His pauses are valuable to me. They use up film, but they make a subtle point, and that's what film is for — to make a point...."

—Cooper, as told to George Scullin for *The Saturday Evening Post*, 31 Mar 1956

Like all actors I like to work for [Frank] Capra. He makes you feel important; he lets you make suggestions. Not that you have to with Capra; he senses things. If an actor seems unhappy in a scene, Frank spots it and says, "You were unhappy in that scene, weren't you?" He finds out why. Then he does the scene over and over again until you feel comfortable doing it....

I liked *Mr. Deeds* [*Goes to Town* (1936)] because I understood the chap and it offered a new twist on a small-town American character. [Cooper worked with Capra again on *Meet John Doe* (1941).]

—Cooper, interviewed by Gladys Hall for *Modern Screen*, Jan 1941

I remember my first big struggle with my responsibility to the movie-going public. Hal Wallis showed me a script called *Sergeant York* [1941, Howard Hawks], based on the real-life story of the great hero of World War I. In screen biographies dealing with remote historical characters, some romantic leeway is permissible. But York happened to be very much alive, his exploits were real, and I felt that I couldn't do justice to him. Here was a pious, sincere man, a conscientious objector to war, who, when called, became a heroic fighter for his country. He was too big for me, he covered too much territory....

By the time I got before the cameras on *Sergeant York*, I was emotionally ready. To prepare myself for the role, I visited Sgt. Alvin C. York in his own Tennessee hills, and absorbed from his faith and philosophy. He didn't smoke, or drink, or swear, and he believed that every man had a right to live in peace. But the more he had prayed for guidance, the clearer it became that peace could not be preserved by meek surrender to an aggressor. Once convinced that it was up to the strong to resist attacks on the weak, he prayed for strength, and became the fightingest soldier of the A.E.F....

With the clouds of World War II piling up fast, I saw that what had happened to Sergeant York was likely to happen all over again. In that mood, I put all I had into the role.

—Cooper, as told to George Scullin for *The Saturday Evening Post*, 7 Apr 1956

I plead guilty to a picture called *Along Came Jones* [1945, Stuart Heisler], a Western in which the cowboy couldn't hit his hat while he was wearing it. The hero wasn't too bad, I'll say that; he had won third place as a bronc rider in a rodeo. But he was all thumbs when it came to shooting, and we played that up for laughs.

The picture made money; but Cecil B. DeMille, the late producer and director, whom I admired so much, raked me over the coals for it. "You shouldn't do that sort of thing," he said. "Playing a man on the screen who can't shoot. You are the guy who is supposed to know how to do such things."

DeMille's next words made me feel better about being an institution. "Never play anything that lets the public down, your public. If you kid a Western, if you kid a hero, you are doing yourself damage. People who come to see you — they want to see a fellow who can do no wrong and can come through in tough spots." [Cooper also worked on DeMille's *The Plainsman* (1937), *The Story of Dr. Wassell* (1944) and *Unconquered* (1947).]

—Cooper, in *McCalls*, Jan 1961

When Stanley Kramer sent me the script [of *High Noon* (1952, Fred Zinnemann)], I saw in it a graphic presentation of everything dad had taught me at home. As a trial lawyer and later a judge of the Montana State Supreme Court, dad knew sheriffs all over the West, and he knew what they were up against. Law enforcement, as he taught it to me, was everybody's job: the sheriff was not a lone figure, but the representative of the people's desire for law and order. And unless he had the people behind him, he was in poor shape.

Such a man was the sheriff I was asked to portray.

—Cooper, as told to George Scullin for *The Saturday Evening Post*, 7 Apr 1956

Barbara Stanwyck and I were down in Mexico working on a picture called *Blowing Wild* [1953, Hugo Fregonese]. I was playing the part of a tough oil driller, and Miss Stanwyck was playing an even tougher oil promoter. She'd double-crossed me, the script said, and I proceed to throttle her. I got myself into character; this female oil promoter was scheming to get me murdered, and she needed choking....

"You're cheating me," Barbara said. "If you fake this choking, my face and neck will look smooth. I want the veins to swell. I want my eyes to pop. You've really got to choke me."

I could see her logic, but she was still Barbara Stanwyck, too nice to be strangled. So she stopped using logic and got into character. She began goading me — me the stupid, oil drilling sucker. She kept at me, and kept at me, until we were both seething. The director called "Action!" and I throttled her. Her veins swelled, her mouth was contorted. The director yelled "Cut!" and she slumped. We got some help around, and pretty soon we were all right, but it was two days before Barbara could talk, and three days before I could eat properly.

There are times when acting takes a lot of starch out of you.

—Cooper, as told to George Scullin for *The Saturday Evening Post*, 31 Mar 1956

Gladys COOPER [1888-1971]

Born: Lewisham, London, England. Work on the stage from 1905 preceded her film debut in The Eleventh Commandment (1913, James Welch). She made her Hollywood film debut in Rebecca (1940, Alfred Hitchcock):

They showed me what Hitchcock calls the "rushes" of my first day's work on *Rebecca* and I look GHASTLY but they say that Olivier looks very good in his scenes: I don't know what it will be like, so difficult to tell when they keep making you film it in little bits.... I don't like the Joan Fontaine girl much, she is so "cringing" in the part but if they cut her right she may turn out good: oddly enough she's quite like Daph du Maurier to look at....

I have quite a good part as Lady Nelson [in *That Hamilton Woman* (1941, Alexander Korda)], but they are making me play her very disagreeable so as not to take the sympathy away from Vivien [Leigh] as Lady Hamilton!....

I managed to get five weeks' work out of [*Now, Voyager* (1942, Irving Rapper)] which was pretty good: practically all my scenes are with Bette Davis who I couldn't have liked more.... I've been keeping up my canteen work for the Red Cross and one night I went down there and worked till midnight and then got back to the house and found a message to say they were filming three of my *Now, Voyager* scenes starting at six the next morning and of course I hadn't managed to learn any of them so I kept drying up all day which was really very embarrassing but Bette Davis was very good about it and they all pretended it hadn't happened....

—Cooper, in letters to Joan Buckmaster, repr. in *Gladys Cooper: The Biography of an Actress* by Sheridan Morley (New York: McGraw-Hill, 1979)

Lou COSTELLO [1906-1959]

Born: Louis Cristillo in Paterson, New Jersey. Work as a carpenter for MGM and Warner Brothers studios in Hollywood, as a stuntman preceded work as a comic in vaudeville where he was teamed with Bud Abbott when Abbott replaced Costello's ailing partner. Together they worked in burlesque, vaudeville, on radio and Broadway before making their film debut as a team in One Night in the Tropics (1940, Edward Sutherland).

Bud and I always read the funny papers, but we kept it a secret because we didn't want adults to think us morons. Soon we learned that Mutt and Jeff and other comic strips were popular beyond imagination. So we wondered why the two of us couldn't just become animated comic strips ourselves. Abbott could be the straight man, the wise guy, while I could be the butt of most of his jokes, turning the tables on him often enough to keep the customers amused.

Now, of course, we know that we do low and corny comedy, but apparently that's exactly what the public wants today, judging from the millions who follow the funny papers day by day. We figure one hundred million Americans can't be wrong, so as long as we keep up the wise guy and sap combination, we keep going ahead.

—Costello, interviewed by Hugh Roberts for *Modern Screen*, July 1941

Slapstick comedy has always seemed worthwhile to me — especially during the war when people needed good hard laughter to relieve their worries and tensions. But I had always hoped that someday I'd have a chance to portray a real story character rather than just play myself in a series of disrelated routines. So when Benny Miller in *Little Giant* [1946] came my way, that funny yet pathetic little guy was bound to be my favorite role.

Bud Abbott and I were lucky in having Bill Seiter as our director; he knew what he wanted and kept us always on our toes and in the right mood. In previous pictures our directors, thinking only of laughs, allowed Abbott and me to create new comedy routines right in the middle of the picture. Seiter, however, kept patiently but insistently holding us to the evolution of the characters and the story.

—Costello, in *The Saturday Evening Post*, 28 Sept 1946

Kevin COSTNER [1955-]

Born: Compton, California. Studies as a marketing major at California State University (Fullerton), work with The South Coast Actor's Co-op, in numerous student films and as a stage manager at a small independent film studio, preceded his debut in the independent film, Sizzle Beach. His feature film debut — in Frances (1982, Graeme Clifford) — was cut from the final release print, as was his role in The Big Chill (1983, Lawrence Kasdan — he was Alex, the dead friend the group gathered to mourn). In 1987, he played Eliot Ness in Brian De Palma's The Untouchables:

I saw the TV series in reruns. And I liked it. But I wanted to do the film because it was so different. I played a less knowing, seemingly less strong character. He's not on top of things — though he eventually gets on top of them. David

Mamet created the Jimmy Malone character, and in this film it's really Malone [Sean Connery] who forms the Untouchables.

Ness is just the opposite of street-smart. He has to ask for help. It's the more modern notion that a smart man takes a step back sometimes — that to be a hero you don't have to be Rambo. Mamet structured the script so that it's really about the relationship between this young guy with high ideals and this older, streetwise cop who teaches him. By the end, when Malone is gone, the student becomes stronger than the teacher.

In Mamet's script Ness has a family. That's a liberty, because the real Ness didn't have one, and that colored my performance. He becomes a really interesting man. He's not a joke teller or charismatic like Capone [Robert De Niro]. If he ever said a profanity someone would laugh. He doesn't even know how to get angry. He's fresh-faced and innocent. But by the end he's willing to lie, to manipulate, to kill. He learns that the law takes time, that the only way to get these people is to hunt them down. He sees that and it sickens him, but he's able to do it. That's a different character than the one that began.

—Costner, interviewed by Nina Darnton for *The New York Times*, 29 May 1987

Q. What was working with De Palma like?

A. Brian always had an ear for me. Never when I asked Brian something would he be irritated. Never would I ask him and he wouldn't have an answer. In the film, I have a little girl [Kaitlin Montgomery] and I'm putting her to bed and I wanted to try to develop a routine with her. You know, a Daddy routine: a kiss and then a butterfly kiss and then an Eskimo kiss, because we're going to have a scene where we're torn from each other's arms and I'm separated from my family. So I start to do it and the other actors say, "What are you doing?" But Brian totally understood. Whether he agreed with me or not, he didn't shit all over what I had to say. Maybe he didn't even like it. But he embraced it.

—Costner, interviewed by Peter Biskind for *American Film*, June 1987

There's a lot of me in Crash [Davis in *Bull Durham* (1988, Ron Shelton)]. He's not too good, not too bad, and if you can tap into his loyalty, I think Crash would be a very good friend.

There is a purity about Ray [Kinsella in *Field of Dreams* (1989, Phil Alden Robinson)]. He is truly not a confused person. He's just like us and something very unusual is happening to him.

—Costner, interviewed by Jennifer Foote for *Newsweek*, 24 Apr 1989

There is a scene in Michael Blake's book where Dunbar masturbates, and I totally understood. It is after he meets the Indians for the first time and he comes back and he is so lonely. He does it kind of unwillingly; he cried when he left the Indian camp. He was so lonely for people. I wasn't able to incorporate the scene into the film [*Dances with Wolves* (1990, Kevin Costner)], because it would have set up shock waves. But for me, it was a real clue to his loneliness.

—Costner, interviewed by George Perry for *Us*, 7 Mar 1991

Joseph COTTEN [1905-]

Born: Petersburg, Virginia. After studying at The Hickman Dramatic School of Expression in Washington, D.C., he made his acting debut on the Florida stage. In 1938, he joined Orson Welles and John Houseman's Mercury Theater, working in both theater and radio. That year he also made his screen debut in the now extinct Too Much Johnson, a short film directed by Welles for inclusion in one of his theater pieces. When Welles was invited to Hollywood, Cotten was one of the Mercury players who went with him; in 1941, he played Jed Leland in Welles' Citizen Kane:

One night I was faced with playing a drunk scene.... I thought about how to play it. The thing you don't do when faced with a drunk scene is to get drunk. But how do you avoid all the stock clichés of a drunk? Orson and I came to the conclusion that fatigue would be akin to the kind of numbness that too much drinking can bring. So we started shooting after dinner, having completed a full day's work that day. I had nothing to drink but by 3 o'clock in the morning I was drunk. I felt so heavy-footed and tired that I didn't have to act drunk at all.

I was so tired that I did a tongue-trip. I had the line: "I'd like to try my hand at dramatic criticism," but the words came out: "crammatic crimetism." The line remained in the picture.

—Cotten, interviewed for *Action*, May/June 1969

I don't know why people regard him [Orson Welles] as a difficult man. He was the easiest man I ever worked with. And the most inspiring. Contrary to what's been said, Orson as a director was very realistically aware of the limitations of his players. He would never lead them into a position of trying to achieve what they couldn't. He made the necessary compromise with your talent, or lack of it, and then demanded everything that you could give. Only then was he either cruel or demanding. The picture of Orson as this unbending tyrant is very false. [Cotten also starred in Welles' *The Magnificent Ambersons* (1942), appeared briefly (uncredited) in his *Touch of Evil* (1957), and played opposite him in Carol Reed's *The Third Man* (1949).]

—Cotten, interviewed by Derek Malcolm for *The Guardian*, 21 July 1973

Before we left for Santa Rosa, California [for *Shadow of a Doubt* (1942, Alfred Hitchcock)], I had a meeting with Hitch to discuss the role of Uncle Charlie, a man high on the most wanted list of the FBI and one with a most complex philosophy, which advocated the annihilation of rich widows whose greedy ambitions had rewarded their husbands with expensive funerals.

"What's worrying you?" asked Hitch.

"I've never played a murderer before, and here I am looking in the mirror at one who's nationally known as The Merry Widow Murderer."

"And you want me to tell you how a murderer behaves," stated Hitch.

"You're the expert," I said....

"Whenever I see a policeman, I simply go all to pieces," [he said].

"I suppose the sight of a policeman brings out a tinge of guilt in all of us," I said.

"I'm not talking about a tinge," Hitch replied. "I'm talking about real panic."

"What do you suppose Uncle Charlie feels whenever he sees a policeman?" I asked.

"Oh, entirely different thing," said Hitch. "Uncle Charlie feels no guilt at all. To him, the elimination of his widows is a dedication, an important sociological contribution to civilization. Remember, when John Wilkes Booth jumped to the stage in Ford's Theatre after firing that fatal shot, he was enormously disappointed not to receive a standing ovation."

We were driving now on Rodeo Drive in Beverly Hills. "Pull over and park wherever you can," he said. "Let's get out and take a walk." We strolled.

"Take a close look at the men you pass and let me know when you spot a murderer." I was beginning to catch on....

"How about that man there with the shifty eyes?" I pointed. "He could be a murderer."

"My dear Watson," Hitch replied, "those eyes are not shifty, they've simply been shifted...."

"What you're trying to say is, or rather what I'm saying you're saying is, that a murderer looks and moves just like anyone else," I said.

"Or vice versa," said Hitch. "That completes today's lesson...."

I mentally filed two or three gestures and stances [as Connecticut artist Robert Brackman painted Jennifer Jones for *A Portrait of Jenny* (1948, William Dieterle)]. Some weeks later, on a Hollywood stage...where Jennifer Jones was now posing for me in my New York attic, I executed one of Mr. Brackman's dramatic flourishes with the brush, then mimed what I considered a well-rehearsed imitation of one of his frequent acrobatic maneuvers.

I had noted, in his New London studio, that when Mr. Brackman felt the need of a more distant view of his canvas, it never occurred to him to walk away, turn around and look, or even simply to step back a pace or two. Instead, he kept both feet firmly planted to the floor and leaned his head back, back, back, curving his spine into a C not only defying but defeating the law of gravity.

Our production manager had engaged a technical adviser, a real artist, to be present on the set and assist my struggles in handling alien props such as brushes and palettes and, above all, to prevent any non-professional garret behavior.

On my first try at a faithful imitation of Mr. Brackman, the technical director was on his feet crying, "No, no, no, please, please — no artist was every guilty of such overacting...."

I said, "The man who painted this picture did exactly that."

"I can't believe it," said the technical director.

I looked to Dieterle, who said, "Joseph, I must admit, it looks a little broad. Although I'm sure it's authentic, it is, I am afraid, another example to prove how difficult it is for art to copy nature."

I demonstrated more of Mr. Brackman's idiosyncrasies, which drew tolerant smiles from Dieterle, sneers from the technical director, and a stony silence from the crew, most of them old friends.

Dieterle was right, it is nature that copies art, not the other way around. [Cotten had worked with Dieterle previously on *I'll Be Seeing You* (1944) and *Love Letters* (1945), and again on *September Affair* (1950) and *Peking Express* (1951)].

—Cotten, in his *Vanity Will Get You Somewhere* (San Francisco: Mercury House, 1987)

Tom COURTENAY [1937-]

Born: Hull, Yorkshire, England. Studies at The Royal Academy of Dramatic Art and work with The Old Vic Company (from 1961) and on TV (from 1961) preceded his film debut in The Loneliness of the Long Distance Runner (1962, Tony Richardson):

I had finished three years of drama school and was playing Chekhov's *The Seagull* at the Old Vic. I was trying for the traditional interpretation of Constantin, but somehow it came out different. An angry young man, in the swing, fitting the fashion — and that was what Tony wanted in *Loneliness*.

It was hard to understand and all I knew was that you had to run, run, run, without knowing why you were running, but on you went through fields you didn't understand and into woods that made you afraid.

—Courtenay, interviewed by Mike McGrady for *Newsday*, 3 Feb 1964

[*Dr. Zhivago* (1965, David Lean)] was supposed to take only 8 weeks. But production problems made it run on for months and months. That was the most unhappy time of my life.

—Courtenay, interviewed by Joseph Gelmis for *Newsday*, 2 Mar 1967

[Norman in *The Dresser* (1983, Peter Yates) is not homosexual.] He's nothing. Maybe at one time he had a boyfriend, but he's cut himself off from everything but the theater.

I based my dresser after a dresser I once employed. He was 72, petulent, his hair was always patent-leather black. My dresser was entirely a cypher.

—Courtenay, interviewed by Arthur Bell for *The Village Voice*, 27 Dec 1983

Norman goes off into his own worlds. You see, he loves all this backstage drama. It makes *him* a star as it were. I'm going to get Sir [Albert Finney] on. I think there's that element, and the relationship is quite complex. He does love Sir but he also...loves himself...

Peter was very good with me, because he soon saw that the less I rehearsed the better it was. On one or two explosive moments, there was no rehearsal. All that end scene, no rehearsal. Just running through the lines. Working out the basic position. And I said, "Will this be alright?" and he said "Don't do it now! Don't do it! Stop doing it!" Cause he didn't want to use it up then.

—Courtenay, interviewed by Lewis Archibald for *The Aquarian Weekly*, 14 Dec 1983

Peter COYOTE [1942-]

Born: Peter Cohon in New York City. Stage work, mostly in San Francisco, and work on TV preceded his film debut in Die Laughing (1980, Jeff Werner). In 1983, he played Norton Baskin opposite Mary Steenburgen as Marjorie Kinnan Rawlings in Martin Ritt's Cross Creek:

First, I read Marjorie Kinnan Rawlings' works and the two biographies on her. I called the authors of both of those biographies. Then I met with Gordon Bigelow, *the* definitive biographer of Marjorie Rawlings who had just published a lovely book of her letters. He was charming to me and very cooperative, and mentioned that Norton was alive. That blew my mind! So I called him up and we chatted! When I went to Florida, I met with him. He was *extraordinarily* generous and he actually gave me insights into playing him.

I took some aesthetic liberties with him, but it was from his photographs of parties of the '40s that I got some major ideas about body language and his inner life. No matter how much research you do, you are still answerable to the script. In the final analysis, it didn't matter who Norton Baskin was. What mattered was who he was in the script. He doesn't do anything overtly dramatic. He doesn't have the peaks in his performance that Geechee [Alfre Woodard] or Marsh Turner [Rip Torn] or Ellie [Turner/Dana Hill] has. But I made a decision that he was really an artist without a medium. That he had the creativity, perceptions and the sensibilities of an artist, and that his medium was reality, everyday life. He lived life with style and grace, with a sense of harmony, humor and wit. He put everything into his everyday life that Marjorie put onto pieces of paper.

And her everyday life was more cranky and obdurate. Unaesthetic, actually. And in that insight, I found a kind of complimentariness that explained them to me as a couple. You know how couples often act-out their blindsides in each other....

Working with Martin Ritt was a real pleasure. Most often you run into directors who are technically proficient, but empty. They don't understand story or structure, and they don't understand when an actor has a problem, how to help him or her out of it. I knew all about Martin's reputation as a director. I knew about his films and I also knew something about his background in group theater. It's very liberating to work with a very knowledgeable director because you can take risks and go places without worrying whether an inexperienced director will let it through.

—Coyote, interviewed by Charlene Krista for *Films in Review* (NY), Jan 1984

Broderick CRAWFORD [1911-1986]

Born: William Broderick Crawford in Philadelphia; son of actors Lester Crawford and Helen Broderick. Vaudeville work with his parents and work on radio and stage, including Broadway (from 1935), preceded his film debut in Woman Chases Man (1937, John Blystone). In 1949, he played Willie Stark in Robert Rossen's All the King's Men:

I liked everything about this part, the strong story, the natural drama, even the fact that Willie was largely an unsympathetic character. So often when you play a sympathetic type, you beat your brains out trying to make the audience realize you're a likable guy. Then they walk out of the theater talking about the villain.

Willie, of course, wasn't all bad. As I played him, he was a rather dull but honest man who got a taste of power and became the crooked dictator of a whole state.

—Crawford, in *The Saturday Evening Post*, 3 June 1950

I met [J. Edgar] Hoover twice. First time was at a Washington party in the '30s. I was unknown, and our conversation consisted of, "Nice day, isn't it?" Second time was five years later. I'd done *Of Mice and Men* on Broadway. Confident now, I shake his hand. And he casually names the party at which we'd first met, the day, date, hour, address, the hostess, the guest list. Spooky! Acting him [in *The Private Files of J. Edgar Hoover* (1977, Larry Cohen)], that came to me first, his diabolical memory. I was, *am*, totally awed by the guy....

Hoover was the personal police chief — he stated this himself, check it — for eight Presidents, at least six of whom longed to oust him. No way: he had the goods on them all. How else could he have held on? Edgar was an egomaniac, but no monster.... Edgar was a patriot, a hero who meant to do the best for his country. He never *consciously* used his frightening power to destroy — never.

—Crawford, interviewed by Tom Burke for *The New York Times*, 16 Jan 1977

Joan CRAWFORD [1908-1977]

Born: Lucille Le Sueur in San Antonio, Texas. Dance lessons in Kansas City, and chorus line work in road shows and on Broadway, preceded her film debut as a double for Norma Shearer in Lady of the Night (1925, Monta Bell). In 1932, she played Sadie Thompson in Lewis Milestone's Rain:

I wanted to do *Rain*. I thought I had a conception of Sadie Thompson that would present in capsule form a universal type of woman. I begged for the opportunity and it was given to me.

A few days after the picture went into production, I discovered that I was to be given little leeway in characterization, that every movement of my hands or my body, every inflection of my voice was to be in accordance with the director's conception of the play and the part. I protested — and Hollywood said I was going temperamental.

No actress worthy of the name can be a puppet in the hands of anyone. The thing that makes her an actress is her ability to dramatize an intangible figure and to inject into it an individuality. When there are restrictions surrounding an actress she automatically becomes so stilted in her performance, so unhappy in character creation, that she cannot be real.

Not only was *Rain* a disappointing picture, but it started an international controversy about the mouth make-up I used in it. It was taken for granted that I was starting a fad. All that I was doing was trying to characterize a role effectively. Sadie Thompson was a woman whose mouth would be broad and loose, so I smeared my lips. My next picture was *Letty Lynton* [1932, Clarence Brown]. Letty Lynton was a Sadie Thompson in handsome clothes. Inside they were both alike; only the backgrounds and their advantages differed. So Letty Lynton, too, had a smeary mouth. When my next picture came along [*Today We Live* (1933, Howard Hawks)] I abandoned that type of mouth make-up and returned to normalcy because the character required it.

—Crawford, interviewed by Sonia Lee for *Movie Classic*, June 1935

[Clarence Brown] didn't disturb us too much. He let us rehearse, find our way, and gave us a couple of suggestions. He never told us first what he wanted. He knew, like in the picture with Clark [Gable — *Chained* (1934)], that we had studied what we were doing, we knew our craft.... I never knew of one major suggestion or correction he made. Minor, wonderful things, which gave you a great deal of confidence. Which made you even do *better* once that camera was going, even though you had rehearsed it. [Crawford also worked with Brown on *Sadie McKee* (1934) and *The Gorgeous Hussy* (1936).]

—Crawford, interviewed by John Kobal (1965) for *People Will Talk* (New York: Alfred A. Knopf, 1985)

Clark [Gable] and I did our best work together in *Strange Cargo* [1940, Frank Borzage]. We had always been close, sometimes too close, but now we knew each other as mature persons and the chemistry was still there and it added to the fire.

We both had good parts, the kind the critics call "fully realized." The storyline was strong and the screenplay [by Lawrence Hazard and Lesser Samuels] was splendid and Frank Borzage let us take it and run. And baby, we ran. I remember — it was the second day of shooting. We were rehearsing one of the big scenes that came early in the picture, and all of a sudden Clark said, "Joan, whatever you want to do, whatever you want me to do, that's the way it is. You've become an actress and I'm still Clark Gable." I think he underestimated himself, but that's the way it played. [Crawford and Gable had previously appeared together in seven films: *Laughing Sinner* (1931, Hugh Beaumont), *Dance, Fools, Dance* (1931, Hugh Beaumont), *Possessed* (1931, Clarence Brown), *Dancing Lady* (1933, Robert Z. Leonard), *Chained* (1934, Clarence Brown), *Forsaking All Others* (1934, W.S. Van Dyke) and *Love on the Run* (1936, W.S. Van Dyke).]

—Crawford, interviewed by Roy Newquist for *Conversations with Joan Crawford* (New York: Citadel Books, 1980)

Susan and God [1940, George Cukor] — big trouble, at first. I simply didn't understand how a woman could give up her husband and her total lifestyle and everything she'd lived for to become a religious nut. I knew it had been a big success on Broadway, so obviously it had something going for it, but not until the day we started shooting, and I went to George Cukor a little hysterical, did I understand who the hell I was playing, and why. In 15 minutes George straightened me out, and from that time on I was Susan straight through the last days of shooting. It was a very difficult part, and I owe a lot to Fredric March — he played foil to me very generously. [Crawford had also worked with Cukor on *No More Ladies* (1935 — co-directed with Edward H. Griffith).]

—Crawford, in her (with Jane Kesner Ardmore) *A Portrait of Joan* (Garden City, N.Y.: Doubleday & Co., 1962)

The way [*A Woman's Face* (1941, George Cukor)] starts, I'm a shadow on the wall — that's all you see me of me, the shadow on the wall pacing back and forth while Conrad Veidt and Reginald Owen are talking in the foreground.

The shadow comes closer, bigger. It appears there in the camera like a black heart and Conrad turns and sees me, the left side of my face. I hold that into the camera. That's the side that's normal. No makeup, haggard and shiny, but okay, and the eye is big in it.

Conrad says to me, this and that...and I say, etc. Then he has to wipe something out of my eye and I offer him the left one, the good one, and he says "I once knew someone else who had beautiful eyes like you." And I say, "You did?" You know, venomously and venomously sock that right side of my face smack at his eyes. "As beautiful as this?" I say, like a snake that's been stepped on.

That right side! The cheek of it is stitched up to the eyebrow and all puffed out with scars. It looks like Lon Chaney eating a hamburger. Of course, I expect Conrad to become startled, shiver away, or look away, as every man has up to then. But he doesn't. He remains calm and begins tenderly to lift his handkerchief to my eye. "Yes," he says "quite as beautiful." And, of course, you can just imagine what that does inside the heart of this girl who never yet has met a man who could even look at her.

—Crawford, interviewed by Ira Wolfert for *The Baltimore Sun*, 11 May 1941

What worried George Cukor [on *A Woman's Face*] was my emotionalism. He anticipated that wearing a scar could affect me as wearing a cape had been known to affect some actors. To offset the possibility, he rehearsed the very life out of me. Hours of drilling, with camera and lights lined up for the opening sequence in the courtroom, *then* Mr. Cukor had me recite the multiplication table by twos until all emotion was drained and I was totally exhausted, my voice dwindled to a tired monotone.

—Crawford, in her (with Jane Kesner Ardmore) *A Portrait of Joan* (Garden City, N.Y.: Doubleday & Co., 1962)

Funny, but long after I was gone from Metro, I could actually hear [George Cukor] giving me tips when I read the script for *Mildred Pierce* [1945]. Michael Curtiz was the director, but before I began working with Mike I imagined how George would set me up for the part. In a way he did.

Mike Curtiz was a totally different director. Not subtle, not at all; he wanted scenes to come off like fireworks and they did, but he was smart enough to make the scenes believable. Confrontation was his big thing — not very subtle — but can you imagine *Mildred Pierce* without those very dramatic confrontations? No Oscar, baby.

I think I worked harder on *Possessed* [1947, Curtis Bernhardt] than on any other picture I ever made. Don't let anyone tell you it's easy to play a madwoman, particularly a psychotic. I used to think so, that you just pulled out all the stops and acted either manic or depressive and that was it. But it's the wrong interpretation of psychosis, believe me, and I realized that just as we were ready to start production. So I pulled a few strings here and there so I could actually observe what went on in psycho wards up in Santa Barbara and at hospitals in Santa Monica and at UCLA. I talked to psychiatrists; one was even kind enough to read the script and tell me how accurately it depicted a psychotic woman (for the most part it was on the nose) and how he thought I should handle the difficult scenes.... It was a heavy, heavy picture, not very pleasant, and I was emotionally and physically exhausted when we finished shooting.

—Crawford, interviewed by Roy Newquist for *Conversations with Joan Crawford* (New York: Citadel Books, 1980)

Helen [in *Humoresque* (1947, Jean Negulesco)] is a woman who drinks too much. She is not the female counterpart of Ray Milland in *Lost Weekend*, but she is a woman with too much time on her hands and too much love in her heart....

Q. This is a dressy part.

A. I guess I'll always be misunderstood. With *Mildred Pierce* released I kept hearing that all I would do would be drab roles. All I want are acting roles, and if they're dressy, okay — and if they are old ladies, okay — or if they are good girls or bad girls, I don't care, so long as they have character.

—Crawford, interviewed by Louella O. Parsons for The International News Service

Torch Song [1953, Charles Walters] was the story of an actress. This was not, as some people thought, the story of my life; but I understood Jennie and her ambitions, I felt sorry for her because she wasn't softer, sorry that she couldn't be demonstrative. Jennie had everything — success in the theater, money, a strong exterior — everything except the most important thing: the ability to give out. I understood her loneliness.

—Crawford, interviewed by Jane Kesner Ardmore for *The Woman's Home Companion*, Jan 1955

Cliff Robertson was stunning [in *Autumn Leaves* (1956, Robert Aldrich)]; very few actors could have brought that kind of credibility to such a demanding part. His mad scenes can't be topped. I'm proud to say I coached him from all the research I'd done for *Possessed.*

Sure, [Bette Davis] stole most of my big scenes [in *What Ever Happened to Baby Jane?* (1962, Robert Aldrich)], but the funny thing is, when I see it again, that she stole them because she looked like a parody of herself and I still looked something like a star. I think she tried too hard, but what the hell....

—Crawford, interviewed by Roy Newquist for *Conversations with Joan Crawford* (New York: Citadel Books, 1980)

Laird CREGAR [1916-1944]

Born: Samuel Creger in Philadelphia. Studies at The Winchester Academy in England and work at The Pasadena Community Playhouse preceded his film debut in Granny Get Your Gun (1940, George Amy). In 1941, he played Ed Cornell in H. Bruce Humberstone's I Wake Up Screaming:

In *I Wake Up Screaming*...I had two problems. In the book, the character I played was a thin man, rather short. I had to make him what amounted to a different character, so that readers of the book would not be too concerned over the change in type.

I also underplayed the role because it would have been ludicrous for me to try to be vivid when I was playing with two such vivid personalities as Betty Grable and Victor Mature. I had to suppress the role to give the proper balance to the picture.

—Cregar, interviewed by Jack Holland for *Motion Picture*, June 1942

Donald CRISP [1880-1974]

Born: Aberfeldy, Scotland. In 1906, he came to New York where he acted and directed in the theater and produced and acted in several films for Mutascope; in 1909, he joined the Biograph Company, where he assisted and acted for D.W. Griffith. In 1935, he played Burkitt in Frank Lloyd's Mutiny on the Bounty:

From the standpoint of actors...the cast was perfect. You couldn't have two more perfect people for the parts of Fletcher Christian and Captain Bligh than Clark Gable and Charles Laughton. Of course, Charles Laughton, he *was* Captain Bligh.... When I asked him about his uniform he said, "Mr. Crisp, we took that out of a British Museum glass case." He took it to a Saville Row tailor, where the original uniform had been made a hundred and some years before, and they remade the costume exactly, to fit Laughton. So when he strode down the deck he looked like a bantam cock, full of dignity. "Mr. Christian, come here! How dare you, sir, address me in such a manner!" And Gable was so offended that he hated the man because he had never heard that type of talk before, and this photographed all through the picture. It was a wonderful accident, because he just didn't like Laughton. Later though they became great friends.

Q. Does this mean that you didn't rehearse before shooting?

A. Very little. You see, we saw this conflict and Frank Lloyd just turned the cameras over and had it all taken right then.

—Crisp, interviewed for *Films & Filming*, Dec 1960

Bing CROSBY [1901-1977]

Born: Harry Crosby in Tacoma, Washington. A professional singer since 1922, he moved to Los Angeles in 1925 and with the coming of sound began appearing in short films. His first feature was King of Jazz (1930, John Anderson). In 1933, he appeared opposite Marion Davies in Raoul Walsh's Going Hollywood:

This picture was a pet project of William Randolph Hearst. He wanted his protégée, Marion, to make a musical, and since I'd had some success as a singer and a leading man, he borrowed me from Paramount....

It was the most leisurely motion picture I ever had anything to do with. It took six months to complete....

Our average day's shooting went like this: I'd show at nine o'clock, made up and ready to shoot. At about eleven Marion would appear, followed by her entourage of hairdressers, make-up ladies, secretary and — a hangover from the silent days — a five-piece orchestra. This band was not on hand to help her achieve a desired mood. It was there because she liked music, and wanted an orchestra around to keep things lively and to entertain her between shots. If a conference was coming up, they'd get a cue from Marion, take five and knock off. Otherwise they played all day....

We enjoyed the musicale until eleven-thirty; then we'd discuss the first scene with Raoul, who, up to that time, might have been leading the orchestra, or practicing driving golf balls into a canvas net on the set, or playing blackjack or rummy with a prop man and an assistant director....

Lunch dawdled on until two-thirty. Then we went back to the set. Marion's make-up would have to be re-renewed — which would take time — and I'd need a slight retread. About three the orchestra would launch into a few more *divertissements*. At five we'd be ready to shoot the scene when Marion would suggest something refreshing. Nobody was ever loath, so, thus restored, we'd get the scene shot and start thinking about the next scene.

—Crosby, in his (as told to Pete Martin) *Call Me Lucky* (New York: Simon & Schuster, 1953)

Leo [McCarey] loved oddballs, and he would spend hours with them picking their brains and pumping them for material. He was tremendously inventive — a great storyteller — and in those days when the director had an idea for a picture, he'd have to tell it to the heads of the studios and get their approval. The story he told the studio heads for *Going My Way* [1944] bore no resemblance whatever to the story he finally shot. But he made the tale so absorbing that they had to go for it. I think probably 75 percent of each day's shooting was made up on the set by Leo. The production department always demanded 20 or 30 written pages in advance of shooting. So Leo would dictate reams of stuff which he had no intention of using and then he would write what he intended to use when he came to the set in the morning. He would go immediately to the piano and play some ragtime for an hour or two, while he thought up a few scenes. This was especially tough on the actors who had already learned the lines he had sent to the story department, but it didn't bother me because I never learned by heart until I came to work. [Crosby worked with McCarey a second time, on *The Bells of St. Mary's* (1945).]

—Crosby, in *Action*, Sept/Oct 1969

[*The Country Girl* (1954, George Seaton)] turned out to be a very easy picture for me — the easiest I've ever made. It was well-prepared; we rehearsed in advance for ten days. Everything was so well coordinated we even finished the picture a week early. George had a good tight script — and the script we had at the end of the picture was the same one we started out with. That's different from big musicals — they can get pretty confusing. You try to improve on the script as you shoot. You labor and sweat, and you're all slowed down....

Working with [William] Holden...well, he paces you. He really brings you up. In a fast league like that, you've *got* to pick up the pace.

—Crosby, interviewed by Maxine Arnold for *Photoplay Magazine*, June 1955

Lindsay CROUSE [1948-]

Born: New York City; daughter of playwright Russel Crouse. Studies at Radcliffe and The American Stanislavski School, with Stella Adler and Uta Hagen and work at The Arena Theater in Washington D.C., the Yale Repertory Theater, off-Broadway and on Broadway (from 1972) preceded her film debut in All the President's Men (1976, Alan J. Pakula). In 1982, she played Kaitlin Costello Price in The Verdict, the second of three roles for Sidney Lumet:

After I did *Prince of the City* [1981, Sidney Lumet] I knew I wanted to work with him again. His sets are terribly efficient, with never a waste of time. It's also a set where rehearsal and character discussion play an important role.

Even before we started filming [*The Verdict*], I knew my character would need to wear a wig, and that she would have an Irish brogue. Knowing what you're going to do before you begin a picture saves you a lot of time. That may be Sidney's greatest strength — he always knows what he's going to do.

—Crouse, interviewed by Lorenzo Carcaterra for *The New York Daily News*, 21 Dec 1982

I had terrible flop sweats for [the courtroom scene in *The Verdict*].... I thought that if I blew it then I would have ruined David's movie [the script was by her husband, David Mamet]. I lost a lot of sleep. I've often been nervous doing other people's work that I thought was excellent, but when your husband is involved you witness the struggle, and you want it to be beautiful.

—Crouse, interviewed by Stephen M. Silverman for *The New York Post*, 10 Oct 1987

All of [Lumet's] films are political in the sense that they're about ethics. They're about what is right, but the emphasis is always on the individual, and in *Daniel* [1983] it's on an individual family. But yes, I did go back to Ethel Rosenberg since I felt I was her in the sense that it is the story of their execution. But nobody really knows if she was guilty, and while we all discussed the subject heavily, we came to the only decision: that you could play it either way. The important thing was not the guilt, but that she had a very strong belief. I was playing an ideologist, a woman who had a vision that the world could be better in some way, and when I began the film I felt, "Well, this one is for you, Ethel...." [Sidney] has all the best aspects of a mentor because basically I had my growing up in films with him. And because he is such a disciplined director, he's just spoiled me.

—Crouse, interviewed by Peter Buckley for *Horizon*, Sept 1983

I tried very hard to play [Margaret Ford in *House of Games* (1987, David Mamet)] as David wanted, pared down, very spare, like a fine jewel in a box without the cotton.

—Crouse, interviewed by Georgia Dullea for *The New York Times*, 11 Oct 1987

David and I have worked together enough before this to know that we're both strong individuals. We've bumped up against each other before. But he knows what he wants when he does a project. I appreciate that. Actually, I felt a great tenderness toward him during the filming [of *House of Games*].

But if I had a different opinion about how something I was in should be done, I'd voice it, then get off the box right away, because after all, it was his film....

David wanted [the film] to have a minimalist feel so there aren't a lot of extras, a lot of cars, a lot of people or anything like that. He wanted to concentrate on the characters rather than background, to tell their story, so he kept it simple, sparse like a work for the stage.

—Crouse, interviewed by Pat O'Haire for *The New York Daily News*, 11 Oct 1987

Tom CRUISE [1962-]

Born: Thomas Cruise Mapother IV in Syracuse, N.Y. Following high school dramatics in Glen Ridge, New Jersey, he moved to New York City to attend auditions. His film debut was a bit part in Endless Love (1981, Franco Zeffirelli), followed by his first role in Taps (1981, Harold Becker):

When you look at *Taps*, a lot of that character was my childhood. I wasn't intense like that, but the character is just fear. That's what he does when he's afraid — he fights....

Q. Did you feel you were on the ground floor of something special, working with Sean Penn and Timothy Hutton?

A. I felt like it was a chance for me, and a beginning. Me and Penn, I really don't know if we ever slept during that movie. We'd stay up all night and just talk about the film and about acting. And Hutton was working every day, so he couldn't hang out that much except on weekends. We were really scared and nervous and excited — we didn't know what was going to happen. It was a special time in my life because it was my first movie, and it was Sean's first movie. Hutton had just won the Academy Award and he was all excited. You felt that something special was happening.

Q. Whose idea was it to do the dance in your underwear [in *Risky Business* (1983, Paul Brickman)]?

A. Brickman's idea. What he did was he set up the frame of the shot. He showed it to me and said, "Let's really play it and use the whole house." We had talked earlier and he said, "Look, I want Bob Seger's "Old Time Rock & Roll" or maybe some Elvis, but if you can come up with something else, great." I went through tape after tape. In the end, nothing beat Bob Seger. So I took the candlestick, and I said, "How about making this the audience?" And then I just started ad-libbing, using it as a guitar, jumping on the table. I waxed half the floor and kept the other half dirty, so that I could slide in on my socks. As we went along, I threw more stuff in. Like the thing with the collar up, jumping on the bed. Originally, it was only one line in the script: "Joel dances in underwear through the house." We shot it in half a day....

Joel was a very internal character.... "The dream is always the same," he said. I mean, you really got to know him through seeing him dance in his underwear, alone.

—Cruise, interviewed by Cameron Crowe for *Interview*, May 1986

I like working closely with a director, and that means finding one I can trust. Paul Brickman...who directed *Risky Business*, could really listen. When I worked with Ridley Scott on *Legend* [1985], I went to script meetings and talked with the writer, William Hjortsberg.

Doing *Top Gun* [1986, Tony Scott] is probably the best example. I don't like to be at the mercy of scripts already written. This script happened to have been written with me in mind. When I met with the producers, Don Simpson and Jerry Bruckheimer, I told them I was interested in the project but that I wanted a couple of months to see where the script went and that I would commit to the film on that basis. At first, Don, who has a pretty good story sense, was a little apprehensive. But after a script meeting, he began to trust me. Eventually I spent a lot of time going down to San Diego and the air base and coming back to L.A. with information for the script.

—Cruise, interviewed by David Rensin for *Playboy*, July 1986

[For *Top Gun*] I hung out with the fighter pilots for nine months.... Duke Cunningham is a naval ace; he helped me a lot and he gave me his gold wings to wear in the film. All these guys talked to me. They're very emotional about it. When you fly in the F-14, it's one of those experiences that is bigger than life itself. It blows your shit away. These guys do it everyday and you know why they want it. Flying is so intense and emotional....

What makes my character, Maverick, want to fly? I wanted to give him a sensitivity. And I think in the dog-fights before he goes up, you see he's nervous. I mean, you're not a fighter pilot just because you want combat. It's the flying, the F-14.

Q. There's a graphic plane crash in the movie. How do you research your performance for a plane crash?

A. What I did was I looked through tapes and talked to pilots who had been in crashes. I actually saw a six-minute tape of one. They filmed some air combat maneuvers at Top Gun school. A helicopter was out there filming these jets when all of a sudden one of the engines went out. You can hear the pilots' voices. The cameras have him right in frame. They start following the jet down, and the thing is that because of the gravity, the blood is rushing to your brain. What can happen in that situation is that there is so much pressure that some pilots just die. The blood explodes through them — they can't handle the G's. They have to reach back to rip the ejection, and they're pinned so heavily that they can't reach. And you hear them trying to talk, and your heart is in your throat watching this. It's just bits and pieces...of...them...trying...to...talk, and you feel their training, trying to keep that control and knowing that, my God, this is it.

—Cruise, interviewed by Cameron Crowe for *Interview*, May 1986

In *The Color of Money* [1986, Martin Scorsese], my character [Vincent Lauria] is always showing off. I saw that as male insecurity. I find it in myself, and I know every guy has a little of that too. I wanted people to laugh and say, "I know someone like that," or, "Yeah, I'm a little like him sometimes."

—Cruise, interviewed by Ellen Hawkes for *Parade Magazine*, 8 Jan 1989

Q. What was the relationship between your character and Paul Newman's in *The Color of Money*?

A. Newman's character, Fast Eddie, is a corrupt hustler — any means justify the end. My character, Vincent, is a pure pool player. If he could just have pool, sex with his girlfriend [Mary Elizabeth Mastrantonio], a Bud in his hand, and his job at the toy store — what the hell, he's set. Newman sees this raw talent and thinks, "Man, I'm going to make a lot of money off this kid." He tries to turn Vincent into a hustler. They each act as a catalyst for the other. Eddie sees what he is missing. When you start messing with your mind it is hard to know where the purity is. You lose your perfect shot, you lose your finesse. If you are a liar, then you are going to think everyone in the room is a liar. You are not going to be able to look at someone and say, "I trust you." I believe that. Eddie gives Vince a cue and that is the bond between them. There's a great scene where Eddie says, "You don't deserve this cue," and I say, "No, you don't deserve this cue. I'm a fucking pool player." This inference being that Eddie is just a hustler.

—Cruise, interviewed by Cameron Crowe for *Interview*, May 1986

At the beginning [of *Rain Man* (1988, Barry Levinson)], there's this anger that Charlie carries with him against [his father] who wanted a perfect son and for whom nothing was ever good enough. But the film ends in his finally taking responsibility for a lot of the anger in that relationship.

—Cruise, interviewed by Donald Chase for *The New York Times*, 11 Dec 1988

Through my portrayal [of Ron Kovic in *Born on the Fourth of July* (1989, Oliver Stone)], I'd like people to see that Kovic is not simply a victim. Instead, he creates his life every day in the face of more difficulty than most of us have experienced. That was crucial for me to understand — that we have to fight back when we meet adversity. I'd like other people to see that barriers can be overcome.

—Cruise, interviewed by Ellen Hawkes for *Parade Magazine*, 8 Jan 1989

Jamie Lee CURTIS [1958-]

Born: Los Angeles; daughter of Janet Leigh and Tony Curtis. In 1978, she played Laurie Strode in John Carpenter's Halloween:

I remember John Carpenter sitting me down and saying: "I want you to make Laurie so vulnerable" and I thought vulnerability meant weakness and I didn't want to make her weak. I didn't want to play a wishy-washy weakling. He said, "She's not a weakling, Jamie. Trust me!" He said: "I want you to make her so vulnerable that when she walks across the street to the house where we all know that the two girls have been killed, people will scream out in the darkness to you, "Don't do it! Don't go in!"

[Ophelia in *Trading Places* (1983, John Landis) was] a wonderful character. A real character for once. Not just a nebulous girl on the arm of. That was my worry as to how I was going to get into big league films. I thought I was going to have to go that route. Girl on the arm of. Girlfriend of lead character. And it was really nice that Ophelia was her own specific character. It was nice to be able to get a whole character unto my own with time given to her....

[Nudity] was not something I enjoyed. It's not something that I like doing. But it was part of the job. It was part of the deal.... And it would have been wrong for Ophelia to have any sense of false modesty. Had Ophelia had any reticence to take off her clothes, you would have gone, "What?" And I wanted to make sure that I did it matter-of-factly. So that when she does it, you just go, she did it." So up until the second before the dress came off, Jamie was nervous but the moment Ophelia took off her dress, I was fine.

—Curtis, interviewed by Lewis Archibald for *The Aquarian Weekly*, 29 June 1983

Tony CURTIS [1925-]

Born: Bernard Schwartz in The Bronx, N.Y.; father of Jamie Lee Curtis. Studies at The New York Dramatic Workshop and work on "The Borscht Circuit" in the Catskills preceded his film debut in Criss-Cross (1949, Robert Siodmak). In 1959, he played opposite Marilyn Monroe in Billy Wilder's Some Like It Hot:

I don't think Marilyn was gifted at all. She was a mean little seven-year-old girl, to quote Billy Wilder. Egotistical — she felt anyone else in a movie with her was a bit player.... If you spent four months making a picture with her, you didn't want to see her again. What Billy Wilder went through to get a picture out of her!

Jack Lemmon and I had to be ready at 9 a.m. We dressed as girls and we'd have to get into these steel jocks and go through hours on our hair and make-up and she'd show up at noon...or even later. She was that erratic. Jack and I had to get it perfect every take because Wilder told us privately that whenever she was right in a take, he was going to go with that one, even if one of us was scratching himself. They were going to replace her, even halfway through the film, with Mitzi Gaynor.

—Curtis, interviewed by James Brady for *New York*, 6 Aug 1973

Cary Grant once told me that the way you judge a bottle of white wine is that when it's chilled, it tastes like a glass of cool water. It is so artful it comes out artless. Nice, isn't it? Well, I feel acting is that.

Q. In *Some Like It Hot* were you playing direct homage to Cary Grant during the yacht sequence with Marilyn Monroe?....

A. It wasn't an homage, let's say, to Cary Grant. When the film was over, Billy Wilder asked Cary Grant what he thought of my impersonating him, and Cary said [like Cary Grant], "Nobody talks like that."

Q. Did you do any preparation for playing Sidney Falco in [*Sweet Smell of Success* (1957, Alexander MacKendrick)]?

A. Never, no. I've never prepared for any movie. When I read Sidney Falco, I knew who Sidney was. I am Sidney. We are all Sidney. We'll *all* do anything for success if it doesn't look like we're going to get out of the quagmire we're in.

—Curtis, interviewed by Graham Fuller for *Interview*, June 1991

I didn't read the book or anything about the background. To me that would be confusing. I'm playing this fellow [Andrei in *Taras Bulba* (1962, J. Lee Thompson)] who lived four hundred years ago so that anybody can understand him today. A fellow loves a girl, a fellow who gets angry and wrestles with his father, there's no date on things like that. I think a guy would feel the same way four hundred years ago about these things as he does today. Jets, atom bombs, automobiles may seem to make a difference on the surface, but still the emotional things stay the same....

Taras [Yul Brynner] is a rough cossack, a little stupid, a man who can't see any farther than the horizon. Andrei, his son, is something more — he is aware of the rest of the world, of the possibilities in life. He has more imagination, more civilization....

—Curtis, interviewed by Edwin Miller for *Seventeen*, Oct 1962

John CUSACK [1966-]

Born: Evanston, Illinois. Studies at The Piven Theater Workshop in Chicago preceded his film debut in Class (1983, Lewis John Carlino). In 1990, he played Roy Dillon in Stephen Frears' adaptation of Jim Thompson's The Grifters:

You simply don't get roles, themes, or situations that are this juicy. I'm playing a guy who's got a professional mask on. A personal mask, too. He won't let anybody inside. A total loner. Inside, he's in turmoil. Outside, control. He's got his world set up. He's got his fake job. He's got his apartment. And he's got his grift. But he won't address what he really is. Because underneath all the different masks, there's him....

Q. What exactly is a grifter?

A. A grifter is a con man, a short-con operator who will get anywhere from $200 to $1,500 a week. It's dice, cards, credit cards — just money scams. The word is still used on the street today. When I was preparing for the role I met a lot of these guys. Frears dug them up somehow. We approached it like journalists and took tutorials with a couple of them.

—Cusack, interviewed by Steven Goldman for *Interview*, Dec 1990

D

Willem DAFOE [1955-]

Born: Appleton, Wisconsin. Work with Theater X in Milwaukee and with The Wooster Group in N.Y. preceded his film debut in Heaven's Gate (1980, Michael Cimino). In 1986, he played Sergeant Elias in Oliver Stone's Platoon:

We all knew that Oliver Stone's script was in some way autobiographical. We were aware that we were going to be telling his story, and that it was very important to him that this story be told. Out of respect for his vision of the film, and the message he wanted to get across, all of us developed some degree of personal involvement and responsibility.

Now as for what went into developing the *persona* of Sergeant Elias, *Platoon* was absolutely unique as film work, because the entire cast underwent an intensive field-training program for several weeks before we started shooting. This training was utterly crucial to the making of *Platoon*. It set the whole atmosphere for doing the film, for how we were going to be asked to perform as actors.

The training was done on location in the Philippines. It was actual jungle training, not boot camp where you do push-ups and jog through an obstacle course. We were under the supervision of Marine advisers who were Vietnam vets. Retired Marine Captain Dale Dye, former editor of *Soldier of Fortune* magazine, was the man actually in charge. He took the job of training us on an extremely serious level.

The idea was to parallel the actual life of a grunt. Every day we took long hikes. We received training in how to do an ambush, air navigation, how to move tactically in the jungle, to live in holes that we had to dig ourselves. We got very little sleep, and we were constantly asked to perform tasks in situations where we were completely out of our element.

The marines who were training us would then attack us at night. At night, mind you! We had to sit up all night in shifts. You would get so tired you started to imagine that you heard movement in the brush, or saw something. Certainly we weren't going to be killed, but the experience of the training was real enough.

As in a real combat situation, you unavoidably encountered tests of your character, your courage. When you didn't measure up, you had to face the other actors, and the marines who were training you. We all became engaged in the soldier's survival mentality....

We earned the respect and authority of our military advisers. And I think that in turn we also felt that we had earned Oliver Stone's respect. We now were capable of telling his story faithfully and truthfully....

Q. What about Elias as a Christ figure? In his final scene in *Platoon*, he is pursued by Vietcong as the other soldiers watch helplessly from a helicopter that has already left the evacuation area. As he is shot and dies, he stretches his arms upward toward the sky, in a gesture that is reminiscent of the Crucifixion.

A. I realize that a lot of people have picked up on this and interpreted specific things into the film as a result. Elias is a moral character, but Christ on the Cross was probably the furthest image from my mind at that moment. The gesture seemed to fit what was happening in the film, namely Elias' death under those circumstances. That doesn't mean that people viewing the film after it's been shot shouldn't read in whatever association or projections it may provoke....

I saw Sergeant Elias as the hero, the conscience of the platoon. You have the classic situation of the good guy Elias, the bad guy Sergeant Barnes [Tom Berenger], and the young kid who is being initiated into warfare, the narrator Chris [Charlie Sheen]. He starts from ground zero with those two sides influencing him.

—Dafoe, interviewed by Louis A. Morra for *Magill's Cinema Annual 1987*, ed. by Frank N. Magill (Englewood Cliffs, N.J.: Salem Press, 1987)

Q. What was that mysterious smile about when you meet Tom Berenger in the jungle?

A. I just remember we were losing light and the grin was not calculated at all. I was very clear on how they were going to shoot it. It was going to be me, him, me, him, boom, you know. And I just thought that one of the nice things about the guy was that the way he behaves is kind of fatalistic and he accepts his death a long time before it happens. So it's that weird combination of bravado and peace that comes in those moments. First he sees the guy and recognizes him and all the tension goes out and it's almost like he has a sense of humor about it. It's well, I guess this is it. It's one of those strange moments of clarity.

—Dafoe, interviewed by Lori J. Smith for *American Film*, Oct 1988

When we started shooting the climax of *To Live and Die in L.A.* [1986], William Friedkin came up to me and said, this is just too common, like a cop show. As the script was originally written, my character [Eric Masters], the artist-turned-forger, is sitting in the burning warehouse. He tries to escape when the cop [John Pankow as John Vukovich] arrives, but, just by the physics of gunplay, the cop gets the drop on him and blows him away.

Friedkin and I talked, and we came up with the ending as it now exists, in which my character is seen to be waiting, very passively. He demonstrates this odd kind of passivity in regard to the cop's arrival, which takes the viewer by surprise. It's as though he is waiting for the cop to come and take control, in order to complete the game they're both playing.

It's weird but it fits, because all throughout, the forger has shown something like a twisted spiritual side. He has a death wish that he's always flirting with. He knows he's in trouble at the end, and the fact that he's sitting in the warehouse on fire makes it quite clear that he has a hand in his own death. And since that's his choice, the moment is not entirely sad. It's kind of a glorious death. So because of his antihero status, that passivity toward dying fit. It strengthened the character.

—Dafoe, interviewed by Louis A. Morra for *Magill's Cinema Annual 1987*, ed. by Frank N. Magill (Englewood Cliffs, N.J.: Salem Press, 1987)

[Preparing for the role of Jesus Christ in *The Last Temptation of Christ* (1988, Martin Scorsese)] was incredibly intuitive and imprecise. With a role that loaded, you just try to forget about it. I just tried to put myself in a certain place where I could receive the story. A lot of the thrust of the film has a kind of human dimension to it. The basic impulse is, *this stuff happens to this guy*. I did read a lot of scholarly histories just so I could familiarize myself with what the Roman occupation was about, discover what kind of philosophies and teaching the real Jesus was privy to. I did a lot of reading that was important to me on the themes of love and forgiveness and what forgiveness means and about breaking the cycle of evil. That was really important in dealing with the relationship of Judas [Harvey Keitel] and Jesus, when they're discussing these things, because Harvey and I, as actors, would talk about this stuff....

Marty gives you whatever it is he thinks you need to do or what he needs to manipulate you into doing. He's a master of making you feel comfortable and strong. He really just fills you with a kind of confidence and also, I'm not sure to what degree it's really true, but he makes you feel like a collaborator as well.

—Dafoe, interviewed by Lori J. Smith for *American Film*, Oct 1988

[In *Mississippi Burning* (1988, Alan Parker)] I play a Kennedy-style guy from the Justice Department who's going over to the FBI. I'm the head of the investigation [into the disappearance of three civil rights workers]. Gene Hackman is one of my men. He's a Southerner and he's kind of more old-school FBI. I'm a Harvard-educated classic liberal. There's a bit of the crusader in me.... He's more pragmatic. Part of our relationship is dealing with the ethics of conducting this investigation, because a lot of people are not cooperating with us.

—Dafoe, interviewed by Kevin Sessums for *Interview*, June 1988

I play Charlie from Chicago [in *Born on the Fourth of July* (1989, Oliver Stone)], a disabled vet living down in a community in Mexico with a whole bunch of other vets. They kick back and collect disability checks and drink and whore. Charlie's a total hedonist, and he's had it with life as he knew it. And Ron Kovic, played by Tom Cruise, comes down to this community and I confront him. It's pivotal because I challenge him at the lowest point in his life...the point where he reaches absolute bottom. And I'm the guy who asks him, "How low can you go?" And he takes a good look at me and says, "Not that low!" and goes back to the States and starts to heal himself.

—Dafoe, interviewed by Bruce Feld for *Drama-Logue*, 11-17 Jan 1990

Roger DALTREY [1944-]

Born: London, England. A British rock star, he made his film debut in 1975 in Ken Russell's film of Tommy:

There were physical punishments working with Russell on *Tommy*.... I used to have nightmares and I'd wake up crying, "No, Ken, no!" Sometimes you can see what it is he wants, but he is so intent on getting it that he doesn't know how far he should go, when he should stop....

—Daltrey, interviewed by David Castell for *Films Illustrated*, Apr 1975

Q. How can a rock star portray one of the great classical music geniuses of all time?

A. Simple, Liszt [in *Lisztomania* (1975, Ken Russell)] was a very easy role for me. He was young and famous and had the original groupies following him. He actually spent most of his young life on the road touring like a pop star.

Q. But can you really compare the music lovers of the 1800s with the rabid fans that follow you and your group, The Who?

A. Of course. Women used to scream and faint and chase after Liszt.

—Daltrey, interviewed for *The Toronto Star*, 13 Oct 1975

Dorothy DANDRIDGE [1923-1965]

Born: Cleveland, Ohio. Extra work beginning with A Day at the Races (1937, Sam Wood) and work as a professional singer (mostly with Jimmie Lunceford's band) preceded her role as Carmen in Otto Preminger's Carmen Jones:

Before I was tested [for the role of Carmen in *Carmen Jones*, (1954)], Mr. [Otto] Preminger told me I seemed too sweet, too regal, that he didn't think I'd do. I said, "Look, I know I can do it. I understand this type of woman." She's primitive, honest, independent, and real — that's why other women envy her.

—Dandridge, interviewed for *The New York Times*, 24 Oct 1954

[Otto] told me that basically I was a good actress, and that I should not have dramatic training; I was uninhibited, that my natural free motions were my best performing qualities....

He told me of the Hollywood custom, how during the making of a picture so very often the people in the cast, especially producers and stars, did a two-two-two just for the duration of the picture. A coupling until the picture ended. He intimated that it was good for the picture, for the people involved. If each knows the other, if they feel all the heat of creativity, if star and director know each other heart and soul — and the rest — the spark of it all might well leap into the beauty of the film.....

That night I became his girl....

There was a limit to the professional vehicles available to me, as there was a limit to my acceptance in the white world and to white men. Whore roles were there, of course, like Bess in *Porgy and Bess* [1959], or Carmen Jones. America was not geared to make me into a Liz Taylor, a Monroe, a Gardner. My sex symbolism was as a wanton, a prostitute, not as a woman seeking love and a husband, the same as other women....

There was no way to make Bess "ladylike." I didn't know this at the time. I decided that if Goldwyn was dead set on doing the picture, he might as well do it with me. I had had cinema experience, and the film might turn out better with me in it than with someone else....

At the outset we had the services of one of the finest directors — Rouben Mamoulian. He and I got along well; he gave me many ideas on how to approach the role....

After that there was a crisis on the producer-director front. Mamoulian was taken off the picture and Otto was brought in to complete it....

When Otto entered as a director, our relationship was a professional one. His famous temper was directed as fully upon me as I had been spared it in *Carmen Jones*. The vilification he once had for some poor actor named Glennet he now heaped upon me, telling me I was doing this wrong, that wrong. Now I was the idiot. He brought up my performance in an earlier and lesser picture, *The Decks Ran Red* [1958, Andrew L. Stone]. He lit into me. "You were rotten in that," he stormed for all to hear. The old romance was now as cold as iced cucumbers....

Prejudice can show itself in many subtle ways in American movie-making. I remember an instance during the shooting of the film *Malaga* [1960, Laslo Benedek]. The scene was this: I was lying on the banks of a river in Spain; the sun was shining; a shade tree threw shadows over me.... Above me was a white man, passionate, trembling — Trevor Howard, my co-star. His face, truly an Englishman's face, was close to mine....

Trevor bent over me, his lips only a few inches from mine. I folded my arms around him, drew him close. The camera would show my fingers clutching into his back. Another instant and there would have been a bit of motion picture history — a white man kissing the lips of a Negro woman, on the screen, for the first time.

Suddenly the director's voice rang out. "Cut...!"

The next morning we resumed shooting, Trevor and I in the same position, his lips close to mine. This time the director said, "Now break."

Trevor rose; I got up. The camera shot us as we stood, without that love scene being completed. Motion picture protocol had ruled again.

—Dandridge, in her (with Earl Conrad) *Everything and Nothing* (New York: Abelard-Schuman, 1970)

Jeff DANIELS [1955-]

Born: Georgia; raised in Chelsea, Michigan. While studying at Central Michigan University, he won a role at Eastern Michigan University in a play directed by Marshall Mason. Mason then invited him to study and perform with The Circle Repertory Company in N.Y. He made his film debut in Ragtime (1981, Milos Forman). In 1985, he played a dual role in Woody Allen's The Purple Rose of Cairo:

Q. *The Purple Rose of Cairo* posed an interesting challenge — you had to play both Tom Baxter, the fictional character, and Gil Shepherd, the actor.

A. The actor character was somebody I'd always wanted to do — the guy so full of ego he can hardly tell a story without standing up. That's someone I've always wanted to spoof. Tom, the guy in the movie, was tough. I tried doing Errol Flynn but that didn't work. So Woody told me to just be honest and love the girl — just like they did back in the '30s. Whenever I found myself trying to put a lot of depth into it I just backed away from it and stuck to the simple things.

—Daniels, interviewed by Robert Morris for *The Cable Guide*, Apr 1986

Woody is very quiet on the set. He doesn't do his club routine and he doesn't come on like the nebbish he plays in his movies. He's not on parade. He may not even talk to you before he shoots a scene.

I brought my own ideas to each scene [of *The Purple Rose of Cairo*] and that's the way we'd shoot it the first or second take. Then we'd discuss what I'd done. Seventy percent of the time he would go along with me.

If my input was wrong, he would cut it in the editing room. The harshest thing he said to me was "OK, it probably won't work" or "We probably won't use it."

Woody wrote the script but told me not to treat it like the Bible. He encouraged the cast to ad lib if it felt right, but we never abused that freedom, which was great. It's hard to improve on Woody Allen dialogue.

Sometimes he seemed satisfied with a take and would say, "OK, we've got it. Now let's try to experiment a little bit." Once he scribbled some dialogue on the set and it became one of the high points of the film.

—Daniels, interviewed by Vernon Scott for *New York City Tribune*, 25 Mar 1985

I was under a lot of pressure [on *The Purple Rose of Cairo*] and it was Mia [Farrow] who made me relax. The movie wasn't life or death to her. It was very important to her to get the scene right, but it wasn't the end of the world.

Mia would sit there and knit and her kids would sometimes visit the set, and it was clear that there were things more important to her than whether this was a good career move — or any of the stuff I was going through. It was a good lesson. I got the sense that she acts because she enjoys it and she enjoys being with Woody. One of the things actors have to have is relaxation, and she's got it in spades.

From where I'm sitting, Mia's approach is very simple, very straightforward. She doesn't junk it up. It's very difficult to stay simple. I know, because I try, and then I start stuttering, doing all these gestures, so I look like a windup toy whose coil broke.

I'll tell you the sort of thing she can do like it was the most natural thing in the world — and it's not. It was the fight scene where I get beat up on the church altar [by Danny Aiello as her husband]. It was a very tough scene for me..... She comes over to me where I'm lying on the floor, and she's got to say, "Oh, Tom, poor Tom, lay your head on my chest," and then cry.

Mia's just put down her knitting and she comes over and sits down, and she does it. And then she does it again. She did it maybe ten times. Woody, after, say, number seven, would say, "Can't we just have a different lighting on that?" or "Could you just cry on the line just after the one you cried on before?" And she could do it. I was really impressed — I couldn't do that. I was doing everything I could do not to blow whatever line I had. She nailed it every time. It wasn't like the usual, "Could you give me a little more glycerin?" or whatever that stuff is that they put in your eyes to make you cry. She'd just wait about five seconds and then she'd start in, and sure enough, there'd come the tears. And finally Woody says, "OK, I think we've got it," and she goes back to her knitting.

—Daniels, interviewed by Georgia A. Brown for *American Film*, Mar 1987

Linda DARNELL [1921-1965]

Born: Monetta Darnell in Dallas. A regional winner of a "Gateway to Hollywood" contest, she made her film debut in Hotel for Women (1939, Gregory Ratoff). In 1944, she played Olga in Douglas Sirk's Summer Storm:

Olga — a selfish, designing social climber — fascinated me. I was told that such a violent change of type might ruin my career, but I insisted on taking the chance, especially since George Sanders, whom I had not played with before and whose ability I admired, was booked for the part of Fedor.

If an actor you are playing opposite doesn't bounce back, you're a dead pigeon. Sanders was never negative, never "blah," like some actors. He lived up to my expectations....

Although I got along well with Director Douglas Sirk, one day things went wrong. We made sixteen takes of one of my difficult scenes. Watching the numbers roll up on the production slate, I was tired, embarrassed, almost in tears. Finally Mr. Sirk said: "Everybody take a breather." Putting his arm around my shoulder, he urged, "Now I want you to relax." Then suddenly he yanked me across his knee, spanked me hard, and snapped, "Now you get out there and do that scene right!" That spanking — which I really felt, for I was wearing a suede hunting outfit with divided skirt — so shocked and infuriated me that I went back on the sound stage and made that scene one of the best in the picture. After that, Sirk and I got along better than ever.

—Darnell, in *The Saturday Evening Post*, 4 Jan 1947

Marion DAVIES [1897-1961]

Born: Marion Douras in Brooklyn, N.Y. A dancer in vaudeville, she received her first featured role in The Ziegfeld Follies of 1916. As a result, she was courted by William Randolph Hearst who produced her film debut, Runaway Romany (1917, Charles Lederer). Hearst then established Cosmopolitan Pictures to showcase her talents. In 1931, she played opposite Leslie Howard in Robert Z. Leonard's Five and Ten:

I had seen Leslie Howard in *Berkeley Square* in New York and I was set on having him for a leading man. He was a very fine actor. Maybe I had an audience crush on him, but I thought he was perfect....

Leslie was a great actor, yet he wasn't the type to throw himself forward. He would always try to give the scene to his leading lady, but he couldn't; he was too good. He was not a ham, and he was not pretentious. He was such an easy actor that the things he did didn't seem to be an effort at all. The lines would flow out of his mouth, exactly as if he were carrying on an ordinary conversation.

W.R. [Hearst] was after me all the time about my acting. He used to say, "I don't mean to criticize, but if you'll do it this way...." And he'd explain it. "You don't put enough drama into it. Your comedy is all right, but your voice is too high pitched."

He would coach me, and we'd go over the scripts line by line. When I'd see him with a pencil, I'd say, "Oh, Lord, don't change it. I've got it memorized."

He'd say, "This little change won't bother you."

We'd rehearse it, and it would throw me off a bit. Lots of times he'd sit on the set, which would make me a little nervous. He'd say, "You've got to do that over. You can do better."

He had a very good sense of the dramatic, and of comedy, too.

Once I was doing a scene with Louise Fazenda [in *Ever Since Eve* (1937, Lloyd Bacon)]. The dialogue wasn't very good. W.R. wanted to change it, and he said, "You're supposed to be a secretary, so when you apply for a job, Louise should ask you, 'Are you an amanuensis?'" I didn't know what it meant, but he wanted to change it to that.

I said, "Well, she probably has it rehearsed already."

"But she should change it anyway, if she knows what it means...."

The director called up the studio librarian, who told him it was okay. "All right," he said, "if you want to say a crap line like that, it's all right with me, but I don't want any part of it."

Louise said, "Well, after all, I've memorized it that way." Now she hadn't but she was quick, and since W.R. had changed it, I wanted it in.

Usually they had to admit W.R. was right. But when we'd go over the scripts after dinner, I'd think, "Oh, here we go again."

I'd say, "Don't change too much. You're driving me crazy. I won't be able to do anything tomorrow." But he'd usually insist, because he took a keen interest in our work.

But I was the one who had to face the director in the morning. I'd say, "Let's give it a little more life, be a little more literate and give it more intelligence."

—Davies, in her *The Times We Had* (New York: Bobbs-Merrill, 1975)

Bette DAVIS [1908-1989]

Born: Ruth Elizabeth Davis in Lowell, Massachusetts. Studies at The Robert Milton—John Murray Anderson School of the Theater (where Martha Graham taught her movement), stock (in Rochester, where her first professional director was George Cukor) and work on Broadway, preceded her film debut in Bad Sister (1931, Hobart Henley). Dropped by Carl Laemmle after six months in Hollywood, she was about to return to the N.Y. stage when George Arliss hired her to star opposite him in The Man Who Played God (1932, John Adolfi). That same year she appeared in Cabin in the Cotton under the direction of Michael Curtiz:

Darryl Zanuck, who was then production manager of Warners, wanted me to play the southern girl in Richard Barthelmess' *Cabin in the Cotton*, an extremely interesting screenplay by Paul Green. It was an excellent part, mine — that of a rich, vixenish belle. Aside from its literate script, it was Mr. Barthelmess' last big picture — an A production. The director, Michael Curtiz, did not want me for the part and made it clear. But Mr. Zanuck did and made it clearer. My director made my life hell every day. While Mr. Barthelmess was easygoing and kindly, I would start a scene and Curtiz would mutter behind the camera so I could hear, "God-damned-nothing-no-good-sexless-son-of-a-bitch!" which might have little taste and less syntax but a great deal of lucidity. What with Barthelmess' wife, Jessica, sitting beside the director appraising our love scenes and Curtiz' heckling, it is a wonder I made it. Richard Barthelmess had been a great silent star but his technique was utterly foreign to me. He did absolutely nothing in long shots, followed basic stage directions for medium shots and reserved his talent for the close-up....

Mr. Curtiz ignored my needs completely. During a close-up of me, supposedly kissing the star — a situation usually facilitated by the "beloved's" presence behind the camera — I was made to play the love scene into the camera, sans Mr. Barthelmess! Mr. Curtiz, with a glint in his eye that could only have been borrowed from the Marquis de Sade, made me writhe toward the camera and kiss into a vacuum. I refused to let him get me down.

Although my name was growing by leaps and bounds, I was well aware that I was not being given an opportunity to grow as an artist....

Mr. Arliss again materialized like a genie to cast me in *The Working Man* [1933] as his spoiled daughter. And again with [John] Adolfi at the helm, Mr. Arliss directed me to advantage....

He taught me always to think of what came before a scene and what was to come after. Scenes being shot out of sequence are the devil to play. "Always keep the continuity in your head. It will help." It did. One had to remember pitches of voice and mood to the fraction so that scenes when juxtaposed would blend.

John Cromwell wanted me for the part of Mildred in Somerset Maugham's *Of Human Bondage* [1934]. After seeing me in *Cabin in the Cotton* and *The Rich are Always With Us* [1932, Alfred E. Green], he felt I could do justice to the role. Besides, as a heroine she was such a disagreeable character no well-established actress would play her. The picture was to star Leslie Howard.

I told Mr. Cromwell I would give my life to be in the picture and he contacted the studio. Warners absolutely refused to lend me out. How could they? They needed me desperately for such historic milestones as *The Big Shakedown* [1934, John Francis Dillon].... I begged, implored, cajoled. I haunted Jack Warner's office. Every single day, I arrived at his door with the shoeshine boy. The part of Mildred was something I had to have. I spent six months in supplication and drove Mr. Warner to the point of desperation — desperate enough to say "Yes" — anything to get rid of me.

My employers believed I would hang myself playing such an unpleasant heroine. I had become such a nuisance over the issue I think they identified me with the character and felt we deserved each other...!

My performance in *Of Human Bondage* could make or break my motion picture career. At the outset, it was the faith Mr. Cromwell had in me that made me feel I could play it. I always did my best work when someone truly believed in me.

Mr. Maugham so clearly described Mildred it was like having a textbook to go by. However, Philip's whimpering adoration in the face of Mildred's brutal diffidence was difficult for me to believe. But that was Mr. Howard's problem and not mine. I hired an English-woman to work for me at home for two months before starting the picture. She had just the right amount of cockney in her speech for Mildred. I never told her she was teaching me cockney — for fear she would exaggerate her own accent. It is always more difficult to learn to speak a strange accent subtly. Mildred suffered delusions of grandeur and spoke, she thought, like a "liady."

The first few days on the set were not too heartwarming. Mr. Howard and his English colleagues, as a clique, were disturbed by the casting of an American girl in the part. I really couldn't blame them. There was lots of whispering in little Druid circles whenever I appeared. Mr. Howard would read a book offstage, all the while throwing me his lines during my close-ups. He became a little less detached when he was informed that "the kid is walking away with the picture."

When we were ready to do the scene involving Mildred's decline, I asked Mr. Cromwell if I could put on my own makeup. I have never understood why Hollywood actors don't put on their own makeup no matter what the part calls for. I made it very clear that Mildred was not going to die of a dread disease looking as if a deb had missed her noon nap. The last stages of consumption, poverty and neglect are not pretty and I intended to be convincing-looking. We pulled no punches and Mildred emerged as a reality — as immediate as a news-reel and as starkly real as a pestilence.

—Davis, in her *The Lonely Life* (New York: G.P. Putnam's Sons, 1962)

A love founded on artificiality or false illusions is doomed from the beginning.... Women who "put on acts" to capture their men...are shallow, stupid and selfish. I tried to put across every one of those points when I played Mildred in *Of Human Bondage*.... I tried to make audiences feel what I feel myself — that it is incredible that a man can love a woman who never risks being herself....

Instead of pretending indifference to a man — instead of using indifference as a trick, as Mildred did in *Of Human Bondage* — a woman should discover resources within herself that will make her independent and self-reliant....

—Davis, interviewed by Mark Dowling for *Movie Classic*, Feb 1936

I always felt that [Mildred] had been starved as a little girl. She was undernourished. She wasn't healthy. Her behavior was sort of mad at the world because of what she had come from. I think that people appreciated that. I think that audiences, without knowing it, felt a certain kind of honesty in the performance, rather than just going out-and-out, bang, being nasty.

—Davis, interviewed by John Culhane for *The New York Times*, 13 Apr 1980

Q. What was your feeling about working with [Paul] Muni for the first time [on *Bordertown* (1935, Archie Mayo)]?

A. Remember — I was a very young actress then, with half the experience of Muni. So number one, I was enormously thrilled to work with him. I had seen him many times and respected him. When we finished *Bordertown*, I respected him even more. And *learned* from him! *Really* learned from him..... Muni was a *star* in charge of a set. I found this a great experience. Because this was the first real honest-to-God *star* I had ever worked with. A star takes center stage. I had a scene in *Bordertown* where I wake up in the middle of the night. I put cold cream on my face and curlers in my hair. I had a fight with the studio — [Hal] Wallis came on the set and said, "You can't look like that on the screen!" I said, "That's how this woman would look in bed!"

Muni stood up for me. He also stood up for me in the mad scene in the courtroom. I think of him many, many times in my life.... *He was an actor's actor!....*

He was a genius with scripts — analyzing a script, knowing what was wrong with it. At the end of *Bordertown*, Mr. Muni said to me, "Don't ever have a director, you don't need one." I said, "Mr. Muni, the day will never come when I don't need a director! And want one!" Muni himself never trusted any director — except [wife] Bella [Finkel].... But what happened to Muni was that, in effect, he became his own director, his editor, everything. The way I feel: *you cannot do it alone.* I can be a hundred times better with a good director. Muni was brilliant. *Utterly.* Articulate. A real intellectual — but he was his own worst enemy.

—Davis, interviewed by Jerome Lawrence for his biography, *Actor: The Life and Times of Paul Muni* (New York: G.P. Putnam's Sons, 1974)

It was Hal Wallis, as head of production at Warner Bros., who raised my status as regards scripts and directors. *Jezebel* [1938] was the *real* beginning of my box office years as a prestige star. He hired William Wyler as the director; he gave me a superb cast. For the next five or six years he brought me one great property after the other. Without material there can be no progress in an acting career; next, no progress without a truly talented director. William Wyler is my all-time choice for the greatest films — directorially. Certainly he sped my career onward and upward.

It was always difficult for me to speak slowly on the screen, always difficult for me to do anything slowly. William Wyler, when he directed me in *Jezebel*, was constantly making me slow down — to say nothing of wiggling less. He forced me to get over these two very bad habits. [Davis also worked on Wyler's *The Letter* (1940) and *The Little Foxes* (1941).]

—Davis, interviewed by Whitney Stine for his (with Bette Davis) *Mother Goddam* (New York: Hawthorn Books, 1974)

Unlike some yeoman directors, [Wyler] couldn't work with the talentless. I can hear him now, dispensing with actors of no experience.

"I am not a dramatic coach. I want actors who can act. I can only direct actors, I can't teach them how to act...."

My first appearance [in *Jezebel*] was in a riding habit. As Julie entering her house, I was to lift my skirt with my riding crop. It sounds simple. Mr. Wyler asked me to take the riding skirt and the crop home and rehearse with them. The next morning, I arrived knowing he was after something special. I made my entrance a dozen times and he wasn't satisfied. He wanted something, all right. He wanted a complete establishment of character with one gesture. I sweated through forty-five takes and he finally got it the way he wanted, or at least he said so, in his very non-committal way.

I was truly upset, due to the divorce [from her first husband, Harmon Nelson], during the filming of *Dark Victory* [1939, Edmund Goulding]. So upset was I that after the first week I went to Mr. Wallis and offered to give up the part. I couldn't bear not to do justice to Judith. He had seen a week of my work on the screen. He said, "Stay upset...."

Judith's strength and courage affected me very personally. My own recent losing of my husband — plus the bravery of the character I was playing — threatened to drown Judy in sentimentality. My empathy for Judy was overwhelming. This compassion could be no part of the characterization. Judith did not know what self-pity was.

—Davis, in her *The Lonely Life* (New York: G.P. Putnam's Sons, 1962)

Judith was my kind: I respected and understood this girl who, at twenty-three, learned that she had only a few months to live. Although her background — money and the social whirl — differed from mine, I sympathized with her emotions and her way of thinking, her preference for the cold truth. She had the thoroughbred qualities we all admire.

—Davis, in *The Saturday Evening Post*, 19 Oct 1946

Mr. Goulding is a genius moviemaker, but in my opinion, he was also an extraordinarily difficult man. He was always drifting away from the story. I did [four] things with him [*That Certain Woman* (1937), *Dark Victory*, *The Old Maid* (1939) and *The Great Lie* (1941)] — and I *was* a meddler when it came to what I thought a character should be. Goulding also loved to act, so he would act out your part for you. And the way he acted out a role many times did not suit the way I thought the character should be. He *did* find me difficult, because I was very stubborn about the woman I was playing — and I didn't think he could play her as well as I did.

—Davis, interviewed at Judith Crist's Tarrytown seminar, 11-13 Jan 1974; repr. in *Take 22*, co-ed by Judith Crist and Shirley Sealy (New York: Viking Press, 1984)

[William] Dieterle has such an amazing understanding of what I'm supposed to do [in *Juarez* (1939)]. He plans all my action for me....

The really difficult thing for me was learning those formal speeches. I usually learn lines by sequence of thought and my lines follow naturally. But for Carlotta I could say them only the way they were written.

—Davis, interviewed by Nancy Naumburg for *Photoplay Magazine*, June 1939

Miriam [Hopkins] is a perfectly charming woman socially. Working with her is another story....

Miriam used and, I must give her credit, knew every trick in the book. I became fascinated watching them appear one by one [in *The Old Maid* (1939, Edmund Goulding)]. A good actress, perfectly suited to the role; it all was a mystery to me. Keeping my temper took its toll. I went home every night and screamed at everybody.

In the first place, she never looked at me. When she was supposed to be listening to me, her eyes would wander off into some world in which she was the sweetest of them all. Her restless little spirit was impatiently awaiting her next line, her golden curls quivering with expectancy.

Once, in a two-shot, favoring both of us, her attempts to upstage me almost collapsed the couch we were sitting on. She kept inching her way toward the back of the couch so that I would have to turn away from the camera in order to look at her....

The next film Miriam and I made together was *Old Acquaintance* [1943, Vincent Sherman]. We were always old somehow; everything but old friends.

Again I played the heroine and Miriam the bitch. Quite a reversal for me — but if you play the heroine you have to play it. I truly feel back of all Miriam's unhappiness and rivalry with me was this one fact. She wanted to be loved too, as a heroine. Came the scene in the script when I slap her — that's what the script said. I might add, the rafters above the stage were full of excited spectators. It was rather like a prizefight below.

Tola [Anatole Litvak] planned every move [of *All This and Heaven Too* (1940)] beforehand and the camera was his God. I thought of Willie Wyler who would get an inspiration and, on being informed that the camera was already in position, shout, "To hell with the camera. It's the slave, not me!" Tola had it all on paper. His method of directing was never to my taste. There was not the spontaneity or flexibility I found in Wyler.

I was now on my first loan-out since *Bondage*...to star in Lillian Hellman's *The Little Foxes* [1941]. Mr. Wyler was again my director. This was the first time we were not in accord with the concept of the character I played.

We fought bitterly. I had been forced to see Tallulah Bankhead's performance. I had not wanted to. A great admirer of hers, I wanted in no way to be influenced by her work. It was Willie's intention that I give a different interpretation of the part. I insisted that Tallulah had played it the only way it could be played. Miss Hellman's Regina was written with such definition that it could only be played one way. Our quarrels were endless. I was too young-looking for the forty-year-old woman and since the ladies of Regina's day had rice-powdered their faces, I covered mine with calcimine in order to look older. This Willie disagreed with. In fact, I ended up feeling I had given one of the worst performances of my life. This saddened me since Regina was a great part, and pleasing Willie Wyler was of such importance always to me. It took courage to play her the way I did, in the face of such opposition.

Margo Channing [in *All About Eve* (1950, Joseph L. Mankiewicz)] was a woman I understood thoroughly. Though we were totally unalike, there were also areas we shared. The scene in which — stuck in the car — Margo confesses to Celeste Holm that the whole business of fame and fortune isn't worth a thing without a man to come home to, was the story of my life....

The unholy mess of my own life — another divorce [from William Grant Sherry, her second husband], my permanent need for love, my aloneness. Hunched down in the front of that car in that luxurious mink, I had hard work to remember I was playing a part. My parallel bankruptcy kept blocking me, and keeping the tears back was not an easy job....

I found [Gary Merrill] an excellent actor to work with — one with integrity. Our scenes went well together. By the time we played out our story and the actress had retired to be the little woman, I had fused the two men completely. Margo Channing and Bill Sampson were perfectly matched. They were the perfect couple. I was breaking every one of my rules. I always swore I'd never marry an actor. [Merrill and Davis married in 1950.]

—Davis, in her *The Lonely Life* (New York: G.P. Putnam's Sons, 1962)

Q. On another weekend we heard from Joseph Mankiewicz that other directors warned him about what it was like to work with you.

A. Oh, yes. They said to him, "You poor thing, you'll go mad, she's a horrible creature...."

But this is interesting; Mankiewicz didn't tell me all this until we'd been working about three weeks. He said, "You just can't believe the telephone calls I've got." All of them warning him about me. But then he said he'd gotten *one* call from *one* man who said, "You're going to have the most fun you've ever had directing somebody." And I said, "Who said that?" He said, "William Wyler." I said, "I'll settle for that."

—Davis, interviewed at Judith Crist's Tarrytown seminar, 11-13 Jan 1974; repr. in *Take 22*, co-ed. by Judith Crist and Shirley Sealy (New York: Viking Press, 1984)

Tallulah herself, more than anyone else, accused me of imitating her as Margo Channing. The problem was that I had no voice at all when I started filming *All About Eve* due to emotional stress as a result of the Sherry divorce. A doctor gave me oil treatments three times a day for the first two weeks so that I could talk at all. This gave me the famous husky Bankhead voice. Otherwise, I don't think the similarity to Bankhead in my performance would ever have been thought of.

—Davis, interviewed by Whitney Stine for his (with Bette Davis) *Mother Goddam* (New York: Hawthorn Books, 1974)

I think [*The Star* (1953, Stuart Heisler)] was one of the best scripts ever written about Hollywood, about the mediocre star in Hollywood — all he or she cares about are the accoutrements of being a star.... Sterling Hayden was absolutely marvelous in it; he was perfect. I suggested Sterling for it.... I wanted him just as he was, of course, the guy who lives in dungarees and the whole thing. So, oh, God, the first day we arrive on the set there's Sterling looking unbelievably gorgeous in a tailored suit. And he was sitting there in absolute misery. I said, "Sterling, what have they done to you?" He said, "Look what they've done to me." Well, it was in moments like this that I gained my reputation. I went in...and said, "You let him go home and get those dungarees." Otherwise the whole point was lost.

—Davis, interviewed at Judith Crist's Tarrytown seminar, 11-13 Jan 1974; repr. in *Take 22*, co-ed. by Judith Crist and Shirley Sealy (New York: Viking Press, 1984)

I'd studied the script [of *What Ever Happened to Baby Jane?* (1962)]; I'd talked to Robert Aldrich. I tried out voices — accents — *zero*. Then, one day, my bleached wig and sloppy costume arrived. I put everything on, looked in the mirror — and I had Jane. She didn't spring from inward agonizing or talk about motivation. I saw Jane. It was a visual moment. The best scene I ever played is when Jane looks in the mirror and starts screaming.

—Davis, interviewed by Paul Gardner for *Action*, Sept/Oct 1974

I decided to do my own makeup for *Baby Jane*. What I had in mind, no professional makeup man would have dared to put on me. One told me he was afraid that if he did what I wanted, he might never work again. Jane looked like many women one sees on Hollywood Boulevard. In fact, author Henry Farrell patterned the character of Jane after these women. One would presume by the way they looked that they once were actresses, and were now unemployed. I felt Jane never washed her face, just added another layer of makeup each day.

I used a chalk-white base, lots of eye shadow — very black — a cupid's-bow mouth, a beauty mark on my cheek and a bleached blond wig with Mary Pickford curls. Jane always wanted to look like a baby doll....

Where the producers were uneasy about how outrageous I wanted Jane to look, they had a problem of another kind with Joan [Crawford]. It was a constant battle to get her not to look gorgeous. She wanted her hair well dressed, her gowns beautiful and her fingernails with red nail polish. For the part of an invalid who had been cooped up in a room for twenty years, she wanted to look attractive. She was wrong....

Never were there two more opposite performers in a film than Joan Crawford and Bette Davis. On the day we made our tests for *Baby Jane*, Joan came to my dressing room and said, "I do hope my color scheme won't interfere with yours."

"*Color scheme*? Joan, I haven't a speck of color in any dress I wear. Wear any color you want. Besides, it is a black-and-white film."

Gradually, Aldrich convinced Joan to make her character, Blanche, less glamorous. It took him one entire morning to talk her into removing her nail polish for a scene in which she came downstairs with her hand on the railing. She argued with Aldrich: "You have taken everything else away from me. You're not taking away my nail polish."

In her vanity she was consistent. As part of her wardrobe, Miss Crawford owned three sizes of bosoms. In the famous scene in which she lay on the beach, Joan wore the largest ones. Let's face it, when a woman lies on her back, I don't care how well endowed she is, her bosoms do not stand straight up. And Blanche had supposedly wasted away for twenty years. The scene called for me to fall on top of her. I had the breath almost knocked out of me. It was like falling on two footballs!

—Davis, in her (with Michael Herskowitz) *This 'N That* (New York: G.P. Putnam's Sons, 1987)

Everything is different now. It's all sharks and earthquakes, and they roam around the world to get scenery. Who the hell needs scenery? We never left the studios. We weren't making travelogues. *We* were the scenery....

—Davis, interviewed by Bernard Drew for *American Film*, Sept 1976

Geena DAVIS [1958-]

Born: Wareham, Massachusetts. Acting studies at Boston University, work with The Mount Washington Repertory Theatre Co. in N.H., as a model, and in TV commercials, preceded her film debut in Tootsie (1982, Sidney Pollack). In 1986, she played Veronica Quaife opposite Jeff Goldblum's Seth Brundle in David Cronenberg's The Fly:

I see *The Fly* as a tragic love story. It's about people finding each other. My character had a bad time psychologically with her editor, Stathis [John Getz], and didn't know what she wanted. He was a bad influence on Veronica's life. When she meets Seth Brundle, it's true love for the first time for both of us, the real thing. But shortly after we find love, it's taken away from us by this terrible accident.

Veronica is a demanding part. I get to go through several changes myself — *emotionally*, that is. It's exciting to evolve as a character during a limited time span. I start out as a totally different person than the one I end up as. In the beginning I'm self-confident, somewhat cocky, sarcastic and sure of myself. When all hell breaks loose, though, Veronica is terribly affected by it all.... [Davis also co-starred with Goldblum in *Transylvania 6-5000* (1985, Rudy De Luca) and *Earth Girls Are Easy* (1988, Julien Temple); they were married in 1987).]

—Davis, interviewed by Anthony Timpone for *Starlog*, Sept 1986

Muriel [in *The Accidental Tourist* (1988, Lawrence Kasdan)] somehow knows that this is it. [William Hurt as Macon Leary] is the guy.... I told myself that Muriel had figured today was different than any day in her life, and the man for her was gonna walk through the door.

Muriel has been involved with this kind of person before. The walking wounded. Muriel has had such a hard life herself, it's given her a sensitivity to that kind of thing. When she follows him to Paris on the plane, she says, "You need me. I just know that I'm good for you." Of course he resents this. But it's the truth....

I wanted to be careful not to be bitchy or kooky. She's a single mother trying to stay cheerful in the face of a lot of discouraging things in her life....

In my personal life, I get self-conscious about talking. Am I talking too long? I trail off at the ends of sentences, out of embarrassment. That's something I had to fight with this character. She thinks everything she says is worthwhile. I had to overcome my reserve about being that forward, and being able to look people in the eye. The book [by Anne Tyler] talks about how she speaks fast, and I took that as a clue.

—Davis, interviewed by Roger Ebert for *The New York Daily News*, 19 Dec 1988

Judy DAVIS [1956-]

Born: Perth, Australia. Studies at The National Institute of Dramatic Art in Sydney preceded her film debut in High Rolling (1977, Igor Auzins). This was soon followed by her role as Sybylla in Gillian Armstrong's adaptation of Miles Franklin's My Brilliant Career (1979):

In the book, Miles says something about not liking to be touched, but...Gillian Armstrong, wanted a clear decision between a husband and a career. I went along, but because I'm interested in psychological drama, I thought that Miles' statement showed sexual confusion as well. I felt I knew the importance of what she wrote because I had known what it was like to be from a family that didn't touch much....

I found her a sad character. It becomes clear in the book that she feels different, and is alienated from the society around her, but she is determined to prove that she is an important person. There is also a dichotomy in her because she is drawn to upper-class life, although Miles thought of herself as a socialist.

—Davis, interviewed by Judy Stone for *The San Francisco Chronicle*, 14 Feb 1980

David [Lean] saw [Adela in *A Passage to India* (1984)] a little differently from me and from [E.M.] Forster and he wrote her in the script differently. David said that in Forster's book Adela was a bit of a prig and he didn't want that. And I guess I liked the fact that she was a bit of a prig.

But I thought she was clearer, less ambiguous in the book. She was more vocal for a start....

[I decided] that nothing had happened [in the caves]. But I was never quite sure whether Lean agreed with me. I used to get the feeling that Lean thought something had happened. We would have these conversations and then I would think, "Does David think something happened?" So I'd try and gently say, "Of course, she's telling the truth in the court." And David would go, "Humpfff." And I would go, "Oh, he thinks she's lying in the court." But David was not...initially, he was not the easiest man to discuss that sort of thing with in depth.

—Davis, interviewed by Lewis Archibald for *The Aquarian Weekly*, 3 Apr 1985

Doris DAY [1924-]

Born: Doris Kappelhoff in Cincinnati, Ohio. After a dance career was cut short by an auto accident, she began touring as a singer with The Bob Crosby Band and Les Brown's Band before becoming a successful recording artist and radio personality. She made her film debut in Romance on the High Seas, the first of four films for Michael Curtiz between 1948 and 1951 while under personal contract to him. In 1956, she played Jo McKenna in Alfred Hitchcock's The Man Who Knew Too Much:

Alfred Hitchcock...didn't direct. He didn't say a word. He just sat next to the camera, with an interpreter on either side of him (French and Arabic), and all he did was start and stop the camera. Jimmy [Stewart] and I were left to our own devices. Hitch never spoke to me before a scene to tell me how he wanted it played, and he never spoke to me afterward. On those evenings when we all had dinner, he was chatty and entertaining but we never spoke a word about the picture we were doing. Jimmy knew Hitch very well, of course, having made *Rear Window* [1954] and *Rope* [1948] with him, but all Jimmy would say, when I asked about Hitchcock's behavior, was, "Well, that's the way he is."

I finally became so upset, broiling in that summer sun [of Marrakesh] for a director whom obviously I wasn't pleasing, that I again told [husband/business manager] Marty [Melcher] I wanted out. "I mean it, Marty. Hitchcock will probably be relieved. I'm obviously not pleasing him and he'll welcome an opportunity to get someone else...."

The first thing I did on getting back to Hollywood was to call my agent, Arthur Park.... I told Arthur that I wanted to have a heart-to-heart talk with Hitchcock before we started the difficult scenes that were scheduled for interior sets on the Paramount lot.

The meeting took place in Hitch's office with Arthur Park present. "I wanted to have a frank talk with you about the picture," I told Hitchcock. "I don't know why it is. I've gotten to know you pretty well and I like you so much, but I really feel like I'm not pleasing you."

"What makes you say that, my dear?"

"Well, you're not telling me what to do and what not to do and I just feel like I've been thrown into the ring and left to my own devices. We have all of our big scenes coming up and I want to please you, and do my best, but I just want you to feel free to say whatever you want to say to me because I want us to have a good rapport so that we can make a good movie."

"But, dear Doris, you've done nothing to elicit comment from me."

"What do you mean?"

"I mean that you have been doing what I felt was right for the film, and that's why I haven't told you anything...."

From then on, I never had an uneasy moment. My imagination had done me in — I had been reacting instead of acting.

The most difficult scene in the picture was the one in which Jimmy, who played my husband, a doctor, came to our hotel room to tell me that our son [Christopher Olsen] had been kidnapped. In the scene he first gives me some pills to sedate me, then, as the pills start to have an effect on me, he tells me about our boy. I want to rush out to try to find him but the pills are making me groggy. Jimmy restrains me but I try to fight him off. As the pills take hold, I grow progressively weaker until I can't fight them anymore and they overcome me.

"I think we should simply walk through the scene," Hitch said, "then right after lunch we'll try to get it in a single take."

I was all for that. I like to get up as high as I can for scenes that require heavy emotion, and give it everything I've got, holding back nothing. During lunch I would get myself ready, doing the whole scene, every detail, every line of dialogue in my head, which is the only place I like to rehearse. Before breaking, Jimmy and I walked through our moves for the camera and I covered our actions with a running monologue....

After lunch we assembled on the set and with no further preparation Hitch started the cameras and we did the whole scene in one take. Just like that....

Although he had verbally communicated very little to me, somehow, by some mystical process, I had learned some important things about Hitchcock movie-making that were to serve me well in the future. Certainly a lesson about confidence. And about the camera — Hitch used the camera differently from and more effectively than anyone I had worked with before. He was the most even-tempered, most organized director in my experience. Altogether a lovely man. I have had very little experience with genius but there is something about those who are touched with it that exalts everyone they work with, and I was no exception.

There was a time I shook up a studio by asking that a song be recorded as I was performing it before the camera. This is virtually never done because it's extremely difficult to get a decent sound quality on an overhead boom mike while a performer is moving around a stage. But...in *Pajama Game* [1957, George Abbott and Stanley Donen], I had to sing "Hey, There!" while crying, and in a manner that was so involved with the action (I felt it was more of a scene than just a song) that I thought it could not be properly synched if it were prerecorded in the studio in the usual way. There was the expected studio resistance to this innovation but I insisted (my seven-year indenture to Warner Brothers had ended and I had some clout by then), and from the way the song turned out in the picture, I was very glad I did.

—Day, in her (with A.E. Hotchner) *Doris Day: Her Own Story* (New York: William Morrow & Co., 1975)

Daniel DAY-LEWIS [1957-]

Born: London, England; son of poet laureate C. Day-Lewis and grandson of Ealing Studios Executive, Michael Balcon. He made his film debut in Sunday Bloody Sunday (1971, John Schlesinger). In 1986, he played Johnny in Stephen Frears' My Beautiful Laundrette:

I knew the director would have doubts about whether my background was appropriate for playing this part, so I sent him a threatening letter, saying that despite the fact that I'd had a polite education, I had some really nasty friends....

So many kids aren't able to find their own kind of morality, and it really interested me that Johnny managed to change his attitudes through a sense of guilt rather than perpetuating these appalling, unnecessary prejudices.

—Day-Lewis, interviewed by Leslie Bennetts for *The New York Times*, 21 Mar 1986

Q. How did you and Gordon Warnecke feel about your love scenes together in *My Beautiful Laundrette*?

A. Stephen was remarkably tactful. Before each scene, rather than draw us aside and having a few quiet words with us, he shouted at the top of his voice, "Who's on top?" It could have been a nightmare I suppose, but then any love scene can be a nightmare if you don't get on with the people that are involved. The most shocking thing about the relationship in *Laundrette* is that it's no different to a love that exists between anyone else.

—Day-Lewis, interviewed by Colette Maude for *Photoplay Movies & Video*, Dec 1985

Q. In *A Room with a View* [1986, James Ivory], were you very conscious of wanting to make your character likable?

A. You have to like your character yourself, regardless of whether you think he'll be liked by the audience. That's not what you're asking, I know. But it's very important to say that, regardless of how obnoxious any character you're playing might be, you have to feel sympathy or compassion or an enormous degree of empathy for that character. Cecil Vyse quite obviously isn't someone that I personally have a great deal in common with. But at the same time, I did actually like him an awful lot as well.

On the face of it, Cecil is a very black-and-white character. But I don't believe anyone is genuinely like that. It's just that some people go to a lot more trouble to disguise themselves. Cecil has a disguise.... And in the moment of his crisis, his disguise is taken away. He behaves with enormous grace in that moment, which is probably as painful as anything he's ever gone through in his life. Because he does have a genuine love for that girl [Helena Bonham Carter as Lucy Honeychurch] — even though it is a rarified, a dry and rather dusty love. And he is also able, through her criticism, to see himself for the first time. It's tremendously painful when someone forces you to look into yourself.

One of the most difficult things about the creation of any kind of life outside your own is that the more you accumulate, the more you realize what you don't have. One of the biggest things you have to do before the first shot is say, "Right, I've arrived at this point. And I'll carry on learning as much as I can. But at the same time, I must be totally unaware of everything that I *don't* know." For the sake of experience.

For example, Tomas [in *The Unbearable Lightness of Being* (1988, Philip Kaufman)] is a neurosurgeon. In the time allowed, I was able to get a kind of sensory understanding: the smell of an operation, the view of an operation. But you can't, unless you're very stupid, believe that that qualifies you to cut people's heads open. So the job is to *forget* your ignorance. Because if you're aware of your lack of understanding, that is a very short road to self-consciousness.

Q. So what did you take on with the character of Tomas.

A. He has a kind of insatiable quest which involves his attempting to conquer the world little by little by having sex with different people. There are two important women in his life [Juliette Binoche as Tereza and Lena Olin as Sabina] but the story centers around his involuntary love for one of them [Tereza], and the fact that it's inescapable, that he's almost caught in the trap of his feelings. Which is something that he's quite successfully protected himself against for a long time. And he's caught quite unprepared. The film is about how he copes with the new problem of that love, as opposed to the problem, that he hasn't really acknowledged, of having an insatiable sexual appetite....

—Day-Lewis, interviewed by Graham Fuller for *American Film*, Jan/Feb 1988

I was having lunch with [film director, Ivan Passer] and I didn't know he was from Prague but I recognized the sound that was coming out of him and asked if I could borrow him for an afternoon. He very generously came and spoke to me for some time about his experiences during the Prague Spring and the subsequent invasion and his collaboration with Milos Forman and I had those tapes during the filming [of *The Unbearable Lightness of Being*]. He was very helpful.

—Day-Lewis interviewed by Allan Hunter for *Films & Filming*, Apr 1988

Christy [Brown] gave me great license to say what I really thought [as Christy Brown in *My Left Foot* (Jim Sheridan, 1989)]. People have such firmly rooted fears of disability, of confronting something that offends our sense of order and aesthetic beauty. It's only the disabled people themselves that force us to confront that, and Christy was one of the pioneers....

I think he wanted desperately to normalize himself. That's the fascinating thing about Christy. In a very intense way, he lived out the things we do. He had to discover his sexuality and try and fulfill it. He fought with his father [Ray McAnally] and had to come to terms with a very close relationship with his mother [Brenda Fricker]. In this very intense way, he had to come to terms with everything we do.

—Day-Lewis, interviewed by Hilary DeVries for *Rolling Stone*, 8 Feb 1990

James DEAN [1931-1955]

Born: Marion, Indiana. Bit parts in a few Hollywood films in the early '50s, including Fixed Bayonets (1951, Sam Fuller), preceded his move to New York, where he worked on TV and Broadway. Upon his return to Hollywood, he made only three feature films before his untimely death.

People were telling me I behaved like Brando before I knew who Brando was. I am not disturbed by the comparison, nor am I flattered. I have my own personal rebellions and I don't have to rely on Brando's. However, it's true I am constantly reminding people of him. People discover resemblances: we are both from farms, dress as we please, ride motorcycles and work for Elia Kazan. As an actor I have no desire to behave like Brando — and I don't attempt to.

—Dean, quoted in *The Los Angeles Times*, 7 Nov 1954

Cal [Trask, in *East of Eden* (1955, Elia Kazan)] is a hero who is humanly demonic. The picture is a study of dualities — that it is necessary to arrive at goodness through a sense of the satanic rather than the puritan.

—Dean, interviewed for *The Marion Chronicle*, (May?) 1954

I didn't read the novel [John Steinbeck's *East of Eden*]. The way I work, I'd much rather justify myself with the adaptation rather than the source. I felt I wouldn't have any trouble — too much, anyway — with the characterization once we started because I think I understood the part. I knew, too, that if I had any problems over the boy's background, I could straighten it out with Kazan.

—Dean, interviewed by Howard Thompson for *The New York Times*, 13 Mar 1955

Cows, pigs, chickens and horses may not appear to be first rate dramatic coaches, but believe it or not I learned a lot about acting from them. Working on a farm gave me an insight on life, which has been of tremendous help to me in my character portrayals.

—Dean, in a press release for *East of Eden* (Warner Brothers, 1955)

Yvonne DE CARLO [1922-]

Born: Peggy Yvonne Middleton in Vancouver, British Columbia, Canada. Work as a dancer in nightclubs and on the stage preceded her film debut as a bathing beauty in Harvard Here I Come! (1942, Lew Landers). In 1949, she played Ann in Robert Siodmak's Criss-Cross:

Whatever else you might say about Ann..., you couldn't call her wishy-washy. She always knew what she wanted, and she always wanted these things — money, jewelry, furs — for Ann. When she hesitated, it was just to decide whom she could double-cross to best advantage. She was happiest while pondering the question: "What can I get out of this?"

Naturally, she wasn't a sympathetic character. But she was believable, and that's why I liked the role. Before playing this part I'd been in a long series of color fairy tales, playing princesses, slave girls, and the like....

—De Carlo, in *The Saturday Evening Post*, 19 Aug 1950

I was back in London to begin work on *Sea Devils* [1953] and my co-star would again be Rock Hudson....

Our director on *Sea Devils* was Raoul Walsh, whose specialty was action films. This film was a nineteenth-century spy story set mostly on the high seas, so the blustery Walsh with his black eyepatch was in his proper element. Walsh was the type of director who let his actors run free. I liked it fine, and didn't feel hurt when Walsh would end a take with a grunt rather than an accolade. With Rock it was more difficult. He was doing well by this stage of his career but he still wasn't the most secure actor in Hollywood, and he needed direction and personal nudges at times. Raoul started out by treating Rock almost as a son, but that situation changed. Raoul came to me one day and in his macho way said he didn't like the "birds" that were gathering around Rock.

"Birds?" I questioned.

"I don't like the birds he's traveling with," he said. "You know — birds of a feather?" We were filming in Guernsey and Jersey, the Channel Islands, and Raoul didn't care for the kind of men who followed Rock over to our location.... [De Carlo had previously worked with Hudson on *Desert Hawk* (1950, Frederick de Cordova), *Tomahawk* (1951, George Sherman) and *Scarlet Angel* (1952, Sidney Salkow).]

—De Carlo, in her (with Doug Warren) *Yvonne: An Autobiography* (New York: St. Martin's Press, 1987)

Olivia DE HAVILLAND [1916-]

Born: Tokyo, to British parents who moved to the U.S. in 1919; sister to Joan Fontaine. Educated in a convent and tutored by her actress mother (Lillian Ruse), her film career began with A Midsummer Night's Dream (1935, Max Reinhardt and William Dieterle). Early in her career, she co-starred with Errol Flynn in 8 films — Captain Blood (1935), The Charge of the Light Brigade (1936), The Adventures of Robin Hood (1938), Four's a Crowd (1938), Dodge City (1939), The Private Lives of Elizabeth and Essex (1939), Santa Fe Trail (1940 — all Michael Curtiz) and They Died with Their Boots On (1941, Raoul Walsh):

Michael Curtiz was dynamic but an extremely tense man. He cared about his films, but not for the actors. Very difficult for me to adapt to, I must say. He was so abrasive and so hostile toward actors, especially toward Flynn. [De

Havilland also worked on Curtiz' *Gold's Where You Find It* (1938) and *The Proud Rebel* (1958).]

—De Havilland, interviewed by James V. D'Arc for *American Classic Screen*, Jan/Feb 1979

It was through my sister, Joan Fontaine, that [the role of] Melanie came [in *Gone With the Wind* (1939)]. She had gone to see George Cukor, the [original] director, to read for the part of Scarlett. When he asked her to read for Melanie instead, she declined and said, "If it is a Melanie you are looking for, why don't you try my sister?" And he did. George asked me to commit it to memory and meet him at the house of the producer, David Selznick, at three o'clock the following Sunday afternoon. I did so, and dressed in a black velvet afternoon dress with a round lace collar, and short puffed sleeves. I was ushered into the great man's drawing room for one of the most significant moments of my life. But destiny had a piquant humor, and the scene that ensued was pure comedy; it was George's role to play opposite me. He was at that time portly, his hair black, curly and closely cropped, his spectacles were large and thickly rimmed. To this day, I have claimed that it was his passionate portrayal of Scarlett O'Hara clutching the portieres that convinced David that afternoon he had finally found his Melanie.

[Shortly after the beginning of filming] Vivien [Leigh] and I learned that George would be leaving the picture and another director, Victor Fleming, would be taking his place. Of all the monumental tests of strength he met during the filming of *Gone With the Wind*, there was no greater test than David Selznick met that day. In our garb of deep mourning, Vivien and I stormed his office. For three solid hours we beseeched him not to let George go. As tears rained on David, he retreated to the haven of his window seat, and when we unfurled the forlorn banners of our black-bordered handkerchiefs, he nearly fled out the window....

In spite of my confidence in the new director, however, there were moments in the months that followed when I felt the need of "the talent strained through the finer sieve." So I telephoned George Cukor and asked his help. Generously, at lunch in a restaurant or over a cup of tea in his house, George would give me black-market direction. I felt ever so slightly guilty toward Vivien about making these secret visits to George until, when the picture was finished, I learned that all during the filming, Vivien had been doing exactly the same thing.

—De Havilland, interviewed by Ronald Bowers for *The Selznick Players* (New York: A.S. Barnes, 1976)

To keep the different stages of development in *To Each His Own* [1946, Mitchell Leisen] quite clear to me, especially as armor for having to shoot sometimes out of sequence, I did the following — I selected a different perfume for each of the different Jody Norrises in her development. I thought, what shall I pick for her as a very young girl in the first scenes? I chose Apple Blossom. I thought it expressed that absolute naivety and the freshness of her personality. After the seduction, I think I chose Lilac. And then I asked my mother what was the most fashionable scent in about 1925, when Jody becomes an elegant woman, a cigarette smoking business woman, and she said she used a scent called Chypre.... Then I used Chanel No. 5 for the older Miss Norris.... I always choose a scent for each character I do so that when I come in in the morning and I put it on....

—De Havilland, interviewed for *Dialogue on Film*, Dec 1974

Q. How did you get the concept of Virginia [Cunningham] in *The Snake Pit* [1948, Anatole Litvak]?

A. By visiting the psychiatric department of [Mount Sinai] hospital in New York. There was a patient there suffering the symptoms of Virginia's guilt complex. I watched this woman; caught a vivid glimpse of her spirit; got her viewpoint of herself. I saw many other patients, but none so vividly expressed the feelings of the girl I was seeking to portray. Through my contact with her I established the character of Virginia.

There was technical information that I picked up, too, of course. I went to one of our mental institutions and observed everything. I saw an electric shock treatment, a staff meeting, a dance for the inmates, hydrotherapy — every phase of Virginia's experience — before starting the picture.

—De Havilland, interviewed by Hedda Hopper for *The Hartford Courant Magazine*, 26 Oct 1952

I believe tremendously in preparation, especially for a role of such, shall we say, specialized insight as [*The Snake Pit*] required. When I started the picture I had a good deal of luck which helped me in that preparation. I did one thing as far as reading is concerned. My first husband, Marcus Goodrich, was a very intelligent man and he told me that there was a remarkable small volume written in 1912 by a man named Bernard Hart entitled *The Psychology of Insanity*. I got that book and I read it and it helped me understand, as it were, the construction of insanity. That's an odd thing to say but it led me to believe that under certain stresses and conditions, insanity was a sort of normal occurrence in a sense. It was something that was simply bound to happen to a human being....

Anatole Litvak was wonderful help.... The character had its own life through this preparation, but he was perfectly wonderful. He's a hard worker, a faithful worker. He had very high ideals. He had two psychiatrists, a man and a woman, on the set at all times to be certain that we were accurate in every respect. I admired that, too. That was something that Litvak consistently followed. He was wonderful! It's lovely to be able to trust a director and I found I could trust him.

—De Havilland, interviewed for *Dialogue on Film*, Dec 1974

[William Wyler] is so wonderfully meticulous. I made a test [for *The Heiress* (1949)] not only with costume, but with the proper setting, and I did a real scene with dialog and gestures. Only there is no sound recording, so it comes out as pantomime. But doing it that way you get the mood of the character and environment. That gives you a head start on the picture....

—De Havilland, interviewed by Thornton Delehanty for *The New York Herald Tribune*, 13 June 1948

I wanted to play [Catherine Sloper in *The Heiress*] so much, because she embodied a deeply typical experience of all women. They have all known rejections. They have! Every single one, in some form or other. And by a male. Catherine had been rejected by both her father [Ralph Richardson as Dr. Austin Sloper] and this young man [Montgomery Clift as Morris Townsend]. She trusted, as you know, her father. She loved him and believed in his trust for her, in his love for her, but he didn't love her. He didn't even like her. For a young person to discover such a thing is an unspeakable thing, but it happens in life; it happens to women. Then, of course, for it to be compounded by Morris Townsend's attitude toward her, because he didn't value her at all; it was her money he wanted. For her to have trusted him twice! What is wonderful about Catherine is that through this she not only survives, she becomes intelligent....

There was a special preparation for *The Snake Pit* which involved all that research, but for Catherine Sloper, that meant reading the part very carefully, perhaps underlining the original material — Henry James's *Washington Square* — underlining every description of her, turning down the corner of the pages where there would be some insight of the author's into her character and her dilemma, and also, and this is always so interesting, looking up the costumes of the period, looking up the hairdressings. I got that first hairdress, the one parted in the middle and tied back so severely, out of a daguerreotype of my first husband's great-grandmother. We had that and I looked at her and oh golly, she was plain. I thought, that's it! That's the first hairdress for Catherine and it certainly worked, no question about it. Then comes this marvelous development, the subtle changes in her appearance, and the hairdress will do an awful lot for that.... You get that hairdress on and you start feeling like your hairdress. You do! It's a perfectly fascinating thing....

Q. How was it working with Ralph Richardson?

A. Oh, it was very difficult. It was very, very difficult. I thought he was so brilliantly cast, he's a marvelous performer, but he was also — shall I say this or not? — he was a wicked, very selfish man. There's a very old-fashioned expletive which I'll delete — SOB are the initials — but he really is a devil, an unnecessarily selfish artist to work with. I was in a constant state of outrage over his slick, British tricks. I had to be alert all the time to outwit him and that's no fun. I just wanted to play Catherine and enjoy doing it, just living her life, but I had to be so nimble all the time, outwitting this wicked British actor.... Oh, those gloves! There was a scene where he would slap his gloves. I had to play some agonizing scenes and it was imperative that I had the audience's attention and the proper place for the audience's attention was on Catherine, not on those wretched gloves. That sort of thing, ridiculous kind of up-staging, and then, you know, walking up and down. So I thought, "Okay, you just go on and walk up and down." Really wicked things. He wasn't thinking in terms of the scene and the characters and the audience, he was just thinking in terms of ridiculous exhibitionism and he had to be restrained all the time. I think the way he got by on the gloves was because Willy [Wyler] was afraid to talk to him about them. But he got the cameraman to frame just above the gloves, and it worked....

[Montgomery Clift] would play a scene and then look up to see what she [his dramatic coach] had to say at the back of the set and she would signal him as to whether it was okay or not. So that was really rather trying. You had to work under this. He was playing it as he had worked it out with her, very meticulously. But what I liked about him was the fact that he cared so much, that he cared enough to have a dialogue coach hidden behind the set, signalling him. *That* I liked. He was not selfish in the way that Ralph was and he wasn't out blatantly, in an exhibitionistic way. He was just tremendously interested in caring about his work....

—De Havilland, interviewed for *Dialogue on Film*, Dec 1974

Hush Hush Sweet Charlotte [1964, Robert Aldrich] was full of traps. It was a delicate tight-rope walking assignment.... I decided against it the first time, and for it the second. In the first script she was written as rude, and that's what threw me, and put me off frightfully; she depressed me deeply because she was so wicked. Then when I talked with Aldrich, he said, "You mean the ambivalence, the duality and the counterpoint of the part don't interest you?" "But that's exactly what I didn't see, that's just what she doesn't have, she's all one color which is black, solid black." I said I would read it again and then I saw the possibility of the ambivalence, duality and counterpoint, if one thing were changed — her rudeness. If you took that away and gave her the opposite, exquisite manners, exquisite courtesy, then her need to dominate becomes extremely interesting. And then she becomes really dangerous and the suspense of the story is increased because you do not suspect her.

—De Havilland, interviewed for *Films & Filming*, Mar 1966

Robert DE NIRO [1943-]

Born: New York City. Studies at The High School of Music and Art and at Stella Adler's Studio in N.Y., and work off-off Broadway preceded his film debut in The Wedding Party (1966, Brian De Palma; released 1969). In 1973, he played pitcher Bruce Pearson in John Hancock's Bang the Drum Slowly:

I went down to Georgia with a tape recorder to get the accents and the feeling. The rhythms are all different. And I learned to chew tobacco....

I didn't try to play dumb. I just tried to play each scene for where it was. Some people are dumb but they're not dumb — I guess they're insensitive, but they're not insensitive to everything....

During rehearsal — we rehearsed three weeks because Hancock is from the stage and he likes to work that way — we played ball in the mornings and did scenes in the afternoon. It was really hard for me because I never played baseball. I read a book by Del Bethel — he was the coach at CCNY — and he helped me out a lot. And I watched TV and took notes, everything....

—De Niro, interviewed by Tom Topor for *The New York Post*, 26 Aug 1973

Q. In the films you've done with Martin Scorsese, have you had much opportunity to rehearse before shooting?

A. In the few movies we've done together [*Mean Streets* (1973), *Taxi Driver* (1976), *New York, New York* (1977), *Raging Bull* (1980) and *The King of Comedy* (1982)], we've rehearsed differently. I think rehearsal is important.... There are all kinds of rehearsals. It's not like doing a play...it can also be just sitting around a table and getting familiar with each other. Sometimes you don't need more. Sometimes we videotape the rehearsals and get material that's even better than what's written and incorporate it into the scene.... [De Niro and Scorsese worked together again on *GoodFellas* (1990) and *Cape Fear* (1991).]

Coppola respects actors. In my experience [on *The Godfather Part II* (1974)], he lets them do what they want. He gives you the support. He wants you to be comfortable. I think he does that with all the people who work for him. That's the first thing — to allow people to feel that they're contributing and that they're not being held down all the time and can't express their own ideas. But he picks people who understand him, too, so they have some common ground....

—De Niro, interviewed for *Dialogue on Film*, *American Film*, Mar 1981

[For my role as the young Vito Corleone in *The Godfather Part II*] I watched a tape [of Brando as Vito Corleone in *The Godfather* (1972)] and I saw if I had done the part myself I would have done it differently. But I tried to connect him with me, how I could be him only younger. So I tried to speed up where he was slower, to get the rasp in his voice, only the beginning of the rasp. It was interesting. It was like a scientific problem.

—De Niro, interviewed by Jack Kroll for *Newsweek*, 16 May 1977

Q. Does your approach to a role change from director to director?

A. Well, I did *The Last Tycoon* [1976] with [Elia] Kazan, and we used to do "improvs" on the nature of being a studio executive. They were very simple, and he was very supportive all the time. You wouldn't feel it was laborious; it was more fun. He's very easy. It's like he takes it trippingly. If you want to do it again, he'll do it. I sometimes like to do it again and again and make sure it's right. His method of improvisation doesn't mean improvising on the screen. It means improvising behind the scenes, like on a situation to find other colors....

With Kazan we stuck very much to the script, practically word for word, because Kazan promised Harold Pinter that he wouldn't change anything. I frankly think that a script should be changed: you have to make adjustments, or it becomes something rigid....

—De Niro, interviewed for *Dialogue on Film*, *American Film*, Mar 1981

I got the idea of making Travis [Bickle in *Taxi Driver*] move like a crab. It's a hot sunny day. He's out of his cab, which is his protective shell — he's outside his element. He's all dry and hot, finally he breaks down. I got the image of a crab, moving awkwardly, sideways and back. It's not that you imitate a crab, but the image gives you something to work with. It gives you another kind of behavior.

—De Niro, interviewed by Jack Kroll for *Newsweek*, 16 May 1977

For the role of Michael [in *The Deer Hunter* (1978, Michael Cimino)] I studied how steelworkers talk and dress, how they relate to their job, their towns and their friends. It's hard to do, because it means you always have to keep looking. Some days I found nothing, other days I was inspired as I saw lots of exciting things. I go through all of this so I can feel I've prepared as well as I can. It's my job. I want to feel I've earned the right to play a person.

I like to get inside him — the character — and feel the situation as he might.... When I was preparing for this role, I spent a lot of time in Mingo Junction and Steubenville, Ohio, soaking up the environment. I talked to the mill workers, drank and ate with them, played pool. Tried to become as close to being a steelworker as possible without actually working a shift at the mill. I'd have done that too, except none of the steel mills would let me do it. They let me visit and watch but not actually get involved.

—DeNiro, interviewed for the press release for *The Deer Hunter* (Universal Studios, 1978)

Q. You gained a lot of weight for your role as boxer Jake La Motta in *Raging Bull*.

A. I ate and drank 24 hours a day. Beer, milk and so on. You can't imagine what kind of torture it was. I had to gain from 160 pounds up to 200. I couldn't breathe any more. I couldn't even close my shoes.

—De Niro, interviewed by Wolfgang Wilke for *Tempo*; repr. in *The New York Daily News*, 8 Nov 1987

I just can't fake acting. I know movies are an illusion, and maybe the first rule is to fake it — but not for me. I'm too curious. I want the experience. I want to deal with all the facts of a character, thin or fat....

I've always been intrigued by physical change, and fighters are always blowing up, right after a fight usually. They also let themselves go emotionally, so I knew all the ingredients for a film [on La Motta, the 1949 heavyweight boxing champ] were strong....

It takes a certain kind of person to be a fighter, a certain kind of anger, maybe caused by parents. A kid gets used to being whacked around — sometimes learns to get off on it. At least it's contact, some kind of human contact and better than nothing at all. A fighter gets conditioned to the pain — and to the excitement that follows. For a year I worked out daily with La Motta in there coaching me. We'd spar. He's real tough, but his rhythm's slow now....

—De Niro, interviewed by Jim Watters for *Life*, Nov 1980

[Louis Cyphre in *Angel Heart* (1987, Alan Parker) and Al Capone in *The Untouchables* (1987, Brian De Palma)] are not simply bad or evil. They are people living on the edge. I prefer the so-called evil characters because they're more realistic. Good or only positive characters always tend to be unbelievable and boring. I like to play more rounded characters. A rounded character comes into situations, into trouble, that force them into decisions. His decisions might sometimes not be the best, but his reactions show the audience they are not alone with their hopes and problems....

Q. How did you prepare for the role of Al Capone in *The Untouchables*?

A. I saw a lot of photographs. You can get a lot from the pictures. I saw the movies that have been done about him and then I did it intuitively. Everybody knows Al Capone was a robust, massive character. So I had to gain weight. I could have worn a bodysuit, but what would I have done with my face? So I did the weight thing although I didn't want to and, I promise you, I never will do it again.

—De Niro, interviewed by Wolfgang Wilke for *Tempo*; repr. in *The New York Daily News*, 8 Nov 1987

A guy I took a lot from [for the role of Leonard Lowe in *Awakenings* (1990, Penny Marshall)] was a friend of Dr. [Oliver] Sacks's who has Parkinson's disease and has really distinctive movements, and he said it's like doing isometrics — you're always in this contorted state, fighting against your muscles, and your muscles get very hard. I felt them, and they were.

—De Niro, interviewed by Fred Schruers for *Premiere*, Jan 1991

Johnny DEPP [1964-]

Born: Kentucky; raised in Miramar, Florida. Work as a rock musician preceded his film debut in A Nightmare on Elm Street (1984, Wes Craven). In 1989, he played the title role of John Waters' Cry Baby:

Because I'm on television, my image has been shoved down people's throats by people who want to see me as a product. I like the idea of making fun of that image. Otherwise, I'm any generic product in the grocery line. Also, the thought of working with John Waters was pretty great. I knew there was nobody out there doin' what he did....

[Waters] is really seductive, really charming. And at the same time, on the set, he controls it. He knows everything that's goin' on.... He's just really smart. Very calm, very composed. He gives you directions by singing the theme to *Dudley Do-right*.

—Depp, interviewed by Merle Ginsberg for *Movies*, Apr 1990

I thought, "no way that people would see me as Edward [in *Edward Scissorhands* (1990, Tim Burton)]...." Then I realized that Edward was all alone, and inside of all of us is this lonely little kid. Edward is a total outsider. I really know how that feels. And so, then, eventually I found him. And Edward — he just clicked....

I hope this won't sound completely corny, but I loved playing Edward so much, because there is nothing cynical or jaded or impure about him, nothing mean about him. It's almost a let-down to look in the mirror and realize I'm not Edward. I really miss him.

—Depp, interviewed by Glenn Collins for *The New York Times*, 10 Jan 1991

Bruce DERN [1936-]

Born: Winnetka, Illinois; father of Laura Dern. Studies at The American Foundation of Dramatic Art in Philadelphia and with Lee Strasberg at The Actors Studio in N.Y., and work on Broadway (from 1958) preceded his film debut in Wild River (1960, Elia Kazan). In 1974, he played both "Big Bob" Freelander in Michael Ritchie's Smile and Tom Buchanan in Jack Clayton's version of The Great Gatsby:

I thought my work was very honest and consistent in *Smile*, but it was very hard. The guy had to be a complete asshole throughout the movie — though I'm sure there are parts of me that are a complete asshole — but to hang in there and never budge from it, and never give Bruce Dern a chance to change the character so he'd win points with the audience, that was hard.

—Dern, interviewed by Michael Musto for *The Soho Weekly News*, 16 Feb 1978

The hardest thing for me in the making of [*The Great Gatsby*] was the fact that 18 years ago I was raised in this entire type of [Gatsby-like] environment. And I bolted and ran away from that. It was very grim. I grew up with Tom Buchanans all around me, and I probably was kind of one in a way. Although I didn't have his kind of bucks, my people had some money, and were a very prominent family in Chicago, and had a long line of old-American-bucks traditional bloodlines. And finally I realized that in order to play the role, I had to go back and dig up all this stuff that I'd been running away from for 18 years.

And it was very painful and very hard. I had to sit a different way, I had to stand a different way, I had to speak the English language — which was something I hadn't done for many years in films, because I'd been playing 'slang' people.

—Dern, interviewed by David Sterritt for *The Christian Science Monitor*, 15 Aug 1974

[Tom Buchanan]...has a sense of humor and a tremendous amount of energy. He is also charming with a certain amount of animal in him, and spoiled girls find that appealing. He's quick-witted but not necessarily bright. He's learned to think on his feet without becoming ponderous.

—Dern, interviewed by Tom Topor for *The New York Post*, 26 Mar 1977

What [*Coming Home* (1978, Hal Ashby)] comes down to is a kind of perfect triangular love story. There's the relationship between Jane [Fonda] and me, and then Jon [Voight] and Jane, and finally me and Jon. By love, I mean devotion and understanding. Jon is incapable of any kind of *physical* lovemaking, and there are no overtones or undertones of homosexuality. Our relationship is man to man. He knows what I'm going through, and he completely supports me in a lovely and touching way....

I become disillusioned with the war and with the Marine Corps, and I start collecting weapons and turning my house into one big locker room, with my wife [Fonda] serving as den mother to a bunch of veterans. I can't make it with my wife anymore, or with anybody else, and when things start piling up on me, I go into a combat flashback. I think I'm still in Vietnam, and I go off into the hills, taking some hostages with me. I don't hurt anybody, but they end up hurting me.

—Dern, interviewed by Guy Flatley for *The New York Times*, 7 Jan 1977

Laura DERN [1967-]

Born: Santa Monica, California; daughter of Bruce Dern and Diane Ladd. She made her film debut in White Lightning (1973, Joseph Sargent) in which her mother played Maggie. She then studied at The Lee Strasberg Theater Institute and The Royal Academy of Dramatic Art in London. In 1984, she played Diana, the young blind girl opposite Eric Stolz as Rocky in Peter Bogdanovich's Mask:

Because my character is blind she's the only one in the picture who doesn't have to get past Rocky's face. They're able to relate right from the beginning. That's because she is the only one who is immediately able to see him as he really is....

A woman named Betty Clark, who does public relations at the Braille Institute and who is blind, helped me and talked to me for hours. I learned about using your ears for your eyes and relating more to sound and touch. I went over different dialogue with Betty and she helped me with how I'd move....

—Dern, interviewed for the press release for *Mask* (Universal Pictures, 1984)

I was a definite daydreamer like Connie [in *Smooth Talk* (1986, Joyce Chopra)]. I lived with my mother, so I had a lot of the same fights. All kids are selfish. I wanted to do homework and do my thing and call my agent. My mother's needs weren't in my mind at that moment. So I brought up a lot of those memories when I did the film. I also brought up a lot of my quirkiness and insecurity around men as a child. Partly I related to that because I didn't have a man around the house all the time....

Joyce Chopra, being a woman, knew everything that the girl was going through without me having to relay it to her. She was also a first-time director, and I didn't feel too intimidated to tell her if I didn't agree with her about something. And she felt the same with me, because I wasn't Miss Prima Donna. We had a wonderful time collaborating. There was one scene where I was supposed to put on makeup in the bathroom. And I knew so many people who talk to themselves in the mirror. So I tried that and they kept it in.

—Dern, interviewed by Stephen Farber for *The New York Times*, 4 May 1986

What these girls [in *Smooth Talk*] are after is the bad guy, the forbidden one. Somebody they can't take home to mother....

Arnold [Treat Williams] rapes Connie. It's brutal. In the movie it's more a seduction. We leave to the imagination what actually happens, even whether she consents or not.

But the main thing is that Connie justifies to herself what she's done. I think most girls do after the first time. We all tell ourselves we're totally in love with the guy. No matter who he is.

—Dern, interviewed by Diana Maychick for *The New York Post*, 5 Mar 1986

The line I find fascinating in *Smooth Talk* — when I come out through the screen door and Treat says, "Come on, you gonna come out of your daddy's house, my sweet little blue-eyed girl?" — is when I reply, "What if my eyes were brown?" It's sort of "fuck you," in a way. It's like Connie's saying, "I'm in control of this, I'm in the driver's seat." Maybe she says it out of fear, to protect herself, but on some level she is controlling it.

—Dern, interviewed by Gary Indiana for *Interview*, Sept 1990

[For *Blue Velvet* (1986)] I had to confine myself to David [Lynch]'s vision. He's not an actor's director in the sense that you created for yourself. He's already created what he wants to see in his film, and you have to become what he has envisioned. That was challenging in a different way.
—Dern, interviewed by Stephen Farber for *The New York Times*, 4 May 1986

Connie [in *Smooth Talk*] and Lulu [in *Wild at Heart* (1990, David Lynch)] and I all share something, namely that we all want to be loved or accepted in a love relationship or family relationship, whatever; but we all bring our baggage with us in terms of how we expect that love. Connie has such a need to be found attractive by a grown-up man, and there's that feeling of wanting to break away from mother and say, "I'm a woman now...."

Q. [*Wild at Heart* is] one of the few Hollywood movies that depicts a sexual relationship that isn't infantilized.

A. From the beginning, Nicolas [Cage] and I had long talks about that. These are two people who turn each other on because they love each other. There's never a moment where one tries to turn the other on by making the other jealous. One of my favorite scenes is where he tells me about his first sexual experience. It's so great, because Lula lets herself get turned on by it. When I first tried to figure out who Lula was, I looked at that scene. In it he's talking about having sex with this chick, and it was so hot, and she says, "Did she have brown hair?" And when I saw that line, I immediately thought, she's pissed, she's saying, "Oh, a brunette, and was she better than me?" But then I realized the key to Lula is, she thinks she's got the hottest little body in the universe, that her baby loves her, and she loves her boobs, she loves her ass, she just loves doing her stuff, and she's a truly secure person in that whole area. And she's such a bubblehead, in a way, that in the middle of that conversation she just wants to picture the other girl better. She wants to know what color her hair was. Then the fact that Sailor would pick up any note of insecurity and come back with, "But gentlemen prefer blondes" — it's so beautiful, they're just madly in love....

Q. In *Wild at Heart*, it's quite uncanny to see you and your mother playing daughter and mother. The resemblance is extraordinary.

A. I think it's a little frightening, given the characters. It's always been a desire of mine to work with my parents, so this was a wish come true. The first day we did a scene together I came down the stairs and my mom pointed that finger at me: "Don't you dare talk to that boy again!" You know, I've seen that finger for twenty-three years. And I started laughing, she started laughing, then the whole crew broke up — in that moment they all knew that she and I had been there before....

I think it's interesting that there's always a dark cloud hanging over my character, in every movie.... Sandy in *Blue Velvet* is an archetype of that. David Lynch says, "If you wanted to buy a bottle of innocence as a shampoo, you'd buy Sandy in *Blue Velvet*." Lula, I guess, is a bottle of passion-flavored bubble gum.
—Dern, interviewed by Gary Indiana for *Interview*, Sept 1990

Marlene DIETRICH [1901-1992]

Born: Maria Magdalena Dietrich von Losch in Berlin. Chorus work in revues and studies at Max Reinhardt's Theater School preceded her film debut in Der Kleine Napoleon (1922, Georg Jacoby). A number of mediocre films followed until The Blue Angel (1929, Josef von Sternberg) made her an international star and brought her an offer from Hollywood. There she continued her successful partnership with von Sternberg on six more films between 1930 and 1935, beginning with Morocco:

In *Morocco*, I had a scene with [Gary] Cooper — and I was supposed to go to the door, turn and say a line like, "Wait for me," and then leave. And von Sternberg said "Walk to the door, turn, count to ten, say your line, and leave." So I did and he got very angry. "If you're so stupid that you can't count slowly, then count to twenty-five." And we did it again. I think we did it 40 times, until finally I was counting probably to 50. And I didn't know why. I was annoyed. But at the premiere of *Morocco* — at Grauman's Chinese Theater — when this moment came and I paused and then said, "Wait for me," the audience burst into applause. Von Sternberg knew they were waiting for this — and he made them wait and they loved it.
—Dietrich, interviewed by Peter Bogdanovich for *Esquire*, Jan 1973

My hair looked too dark on film. Since I refused to have my hair bleached, and since von Sternberg backed me up, the studio had to give in. In normal life I was a blond, but on the screen I turned into a brunette. This completely confused the "Big Bosses" at Paramount. A floodlight was beamed on my hair from above, from the side and, above all, from the rear so that the tips of my hair lit up, creating a halo effect....

Backlighting became very fashionable. To realize this it is enough to look at photos of that time. But backlighting also had its disadvantages. The cameraman always insisted that you never turn your head to one side, otherwise the light behind the actress would fall on her nose, which would immediately resemble W.C. Fields's proboscis.

Consequently, most of the scenes with a partner were very stiff, to put it mildly. While speaking to one another, we would stare straight ahead instead of looking into each other's eyes, even during love scenes. We all looked splendid in the circle of light emitted by the reflector in back of us, but we remained rooted to the spot. Who was at fault? The actors, of course! Of me it was said: "She never moves." One day when I timidly tried to move so as to look at my partner, the cameraman rushed over to me and insistently asked me never to do it again. I obeyed.

—Dietrich, in her *Marlene* (Frankfurt: Ullstein Verlag GmbH, 1987); trans. by Salvator Attanasio (New York: Grove Press, 1989)

I came to Hollywood for one reason — to work with von Sternberg....

I work with von Sternberg because he is touched with genius. He dares to be different. Not always does a picture turn out as he wanted it to but he keeps trying something new.

They say von Sternberg is ruining me. I say let him ruin me. I would rather have a small part in one of his good pictures than a big part in a bad one made by anyone else. After all, I have the final say in the selection of my story and director. If I prefer to work for von Sternberg that is my business.

Maybe in saying this for publication I will give greater conviction to the Trilby-Svengali fantasy. Maybe I will be further misunderstood as to my motive. But don't forget I don't mind being misunderstood. [Dietrich also worked on von Sternberg's *Dishonored* (1931), *Shanghai Express* (1932), *Blonde Venus* (1932), *The Scarlet Empress* (1934) and *The Devil is a Woman* (1935).]

—Dietrich, interviewed for *Screen Book*; repr. in *Hollywood and the Great Fan Magazines*, ed. by Martin Levin (New York: Arbor House, 1970)

It was [Joe Pasternak's] idea that I should make...*The Flame of New Orleans* [1941] under the direction of René Clair, with Bruce Cabot.

Cabot was an awfully stupid actor, unable to remember his lines or cues. Nor could René Clair, who didn't speak a word of English, lend him a helping hand. Bruce Cabot, in contrast to John Wayne [with whom she worked on *Seven Sinners* (1940, Tay Garnett), *The Spoilers* (1942, Ray Enright) and *Pittsburgh* (1942, Lewis Seiler)], was very conceited. He wouldn't accept any help....

I didn't particularly like René Clair, but I didn't hate him as much as the rest of the team did.

—Dietrich in her *Marlene* (Frankfurt: Ullstein Verlag GmbH, 1987); trans. by Salvator Attanasio (New York: Grove Press, 1989)

[Hitchcock] frightened the daylights out of me [on *Stage Fright* (1950)]. He knew exactly what he wanted, a fact that I adore, but I was never quite sure if I did it right. After work he would take us to the Caprice restaurant, and feed us with steaks he had flown in from New York, because he thought they were better than the British meat, and I always thought he did that to show that he was not really disgusted with our work.

—Dietrich, interviewed by John Russell Taylor for *Hitch: The Life and Times of Alfred Hitchcock* (London: Faber & Faber, 1978)

Fritz Lang was the director I detested most. I became conscious of my feelings toward him in 1952, when we filmed *Rancho Notorious*. In order to be able to work with Lang, I had to repress all the hatred and aversion he aroused in me. If Mel Ferrer had not been there, I probably would have walked off the set in the middle of shooting. But Mel was always near and helped to see me through those troublesome days. Fritz Lang belongs to the "Brotherhood of Sadists." He despised my reverence for Josef von Sternberg, and tried to replace this genius in my heart and in my mind....

Lang simply laid out each step, each breath, with a sadistic exactness of which Hitler would have been proud. To be sure, Fritz Lang, as a Jew, had fled to America to escape Nazism. But here he behaved like a tyrant.

Billy Wilder was a master builder who knew his toolbox and used it in the best way possible to set up the framework on which he hung the garlands of his wit and wisdom.

I spent wonderful moments with him and Charles Laughton during the shooting of *Witness for the Prosecution* [1957].

I was enthusiastic over playing this role. Naturally, the part of "the other woman" made me uneasy, and I took all conceivable pains to transform myself into a person who would be as different as possible from the person I really was. Since the film would stand or fall on this transformation, I made the most extraordinary efforts to become an ugly, ordinary woman who succeeds in leading one of the greatest lawyers [Laughton] by the nose.

Despite my many attempts I was not satisfied. I applied makeup to my nose, made it broader with massages, and called on Orson Welles — the great nose specialist — for help. In the long shot in which I'm seen going along a railroad track, I have cushions around my hips and legs. I wrapped pieces of paper around my fingers to make them look as though they were deformed by arthritis. And to complete the picture I painted my nails with a dark lacquer. Billy Wilder made no comment; like all great directors he gave his performers a free hand in the matter of costumes.

Yet there was still a major obstacle to overcome. How was I to handle the cockney dialect that this woman, sprung from my imagination, spoke...?

Charles Laughton said to me, "I'll teach you the dialect, and you will speak your lines in the purest cockney. I'll vouch for its authenticity. Nobody in Hollywood understands anything about it anyway."

I went to his house with him. His wife, Elsa Lanchester, was very nice to me. We sat around the swimming pool, and Charles Laughton began his instruction. I made rapid progress since cockney with its nasal sounds and its constant grammatical inaccuracies is quite similar to Berlinese.

But to perform in this dialect was something altogether different. Charles Laughton would remain in the studio, although his day's work was done and he could have gone home. He watched over my performance and my diction like an eagle over its prey. He assumed full responsibility for this sequence. Billy Wilder, who was not an expert in this area, readily relied on Laughton. [Dietrich had previously worked with Wilder on *A Foreign Affair* (1948).]

—Dietrich, in her *Marlene* (Frankfurt: Ullstein Verlag GmbH, 1987); trans. by Salvator Attanasio (New York: Grove Press, 1989)

Yes. I was terrific in [*Touch of Evil* (1957, Orson Welles)]. I think I never said a line as well as the last line in that movie — "What does it *matter* what you say about people...?" Wasn't I good there? I don't know why I said it so well. And I *looked* so good in that dark wig. It was Elizabeth Taylor's. My part wasn't in the script, you know, but Orson called and said he wanted me to play a kind of gypsy madam in a border town, so I went over to Paramount and found that wig.... Orson doesn't like blonde women. He only likes dark women. And suddenly when he saw me in this dark wig, he looked at me with new eyes. Was this Marlene?

—Dietrich, interviewed by Peter Bogdanovich for *Esquire*, Jan 1973

Melinda DILLON [1939-]

Born: Hope, Arkansas. Studies at The Goodman Theatre School in Chicago and work with Second City, The Arena Stage in Washington, D.C., and on Broadway preceded her film debut in The April Fools (1969, Stuart Rosenberg). In 1977, she played Jilian Guiler in Steven Spielberg's Close Encounters of the Third Kind:

Steven would tell us what things looked like and which direction they were coming from. We'd have a spot to look at. If he didn't get enough of a reaction, he would keep enlarging the image.... He talked all the way through. He had to 'cause we had nothing to react to except our imagination....

We climbed the real mountain — Devil's Tower — but then we went inside to shoot these scenes. And it was a fiberglass mountain, and we kept getting it in our hands and in our clothes — it's like glass. I had to stay within these matched shot lines which means you kept crouching — you come up a hair and they do the whole thing over. We were there for months just getting from rock to rock.

—Dillon, interviewed by Cynthia Heimel for *The Soho Weekly News*, 17 Nov 1977

Robert DONAT [1905-1958]

Born: Withington, England. Extensive touring, work with The Liverpool Repertory Co. and on the London stage preceded his film debut in Men of Tomorrow (1933, Leontine Sagan). In 1935, he played Richard Hannay in Alfred Hitchcock's The 39 Steps:

In my early pictures I made no attempt to give sincere characterizations. I turned on facial expressions as one might a tap and timed my lines very carefully, but it was all completely superficial. My emotions did not enter into it. The chief thing in my mind was that I must appear dashing. I distinctly remember in *The Count of Monte Cristo* [1934, Rowland V. Lee] pulling back my shoulders and trying to look handsome! It was Hitchcock who knocked all this out of me. When I started work on *The 39 Steps* I considered my role unreal and uninteresting. Then one day I was called upon to make a scene in which I had to pass by a window with a bread-knife in my hand and glance casually out to see whether the house was being watched. I rehearsed the sequence several times, in a manner which I considered quite adequate. Hitchcock was dissatisfied. "It's no good," he said, "for pity's sake Bob don't you realize your life depends on this glance? You must feel it in your heart." After I had rehearsed the scene several more times without success Hitch dispersed all the people standing round and himself demonstrated the sequence for me. Despite his immense weight Hitchcock is a very balanced and well co-ordinated person. He walked steadily across the set, glancing out of the window with such genuine apprehension that the whole situation assumed an entirely new significance. "You see," he said, "you must play it with your heart." For the first time in my life I tried to feel the situation. That one incident altered my whole outlook. An actor should not be content to interpret a situation as he thinks it would affect others. His business is to feel the situation himself, feel what is really happening to him and act accordingly — not with his brain alone, but with his emotions. Sympathetic sensibility is the actor's most important qualification.

—Donat, quoted by Kenneth Barrow in *Mr. Chips: The Life of Robert Donat* (London: Methuen, 1985)

Nearly all my screen parts have been romantic — *The Ghost* [*Goes West* (1936, René Clair)], *The 39 Steps*, *Monte Cristo*... Dr. Manson in *The Citadel* [1938, King Vidor] was a grand part, and something new — a chance to play entirely for character and not merely for sympathy — but still a romantic story.

Chips [in *Goodbye Mr. Chips* (1939, Sam Wood)], though, is quite different. Chips is a commonplace sort of person, never quite successful, and not in the least romantic. You have to build him up from scratch, and that's a real job.

—Donat, interviewed by Caroline Lejeune for *Photoplay Magazine*, Aug 1939

Brian DONLEVY [1899-1972]

Born: Portadown, Ireland. Raised in the U.S., he made his acting debut on the Broadway stage in 1924, and his first film — Damaged Hearts (T. Hayes Hunter) — the same year. In 1940, he played the title role in Preston Sturges' The Great McGinty:

McGinty was the kind of fellow I like best, not mushy, not mewling, a man who could take it, whatever it was....

[Preston Sturges] had a hell of a time trying to convince others I was, or could be as sympathetic a character as McGinty was. But he got me in. It is always a *person* who gives you an opportunity. Sturges gave me mine....

—Donlevy, interviewed by Gladys Hall for *Motion Picture*, Jan 1941

Paul DOOLEY [1928-]

Born: Paul Brown in Parkersburg, West Virginia. Studies in speech and drama at West Virginia University, work in regional theater (from 1951), with Second City and on and off Broadway, preceded his film debut in The Seven Year Itch (1955, Billy Wilder). In 1979, he played Mr. Stohler in Peter Yates' Breaking Away:

I had a very personal interest in the man I was playing, because 70 percent of him was my father completely — his personality. The man is a kind of gruff, blue-collar working man. He is not able to show his affection for his wife [Barbara Barrie] or his son [Dennis Christopher] directly, and his style is to sort of grumble in a kind of comic way, to sort of complain, to put his son down. It's a very subtle thing, because it doesn't seem to be mean-spirited. My father used to communicate that way, in an indirect way. You know that he cared for you, but he didn't show it directly.

—Dooley, interviewed by Lawrence Van Gelder for *The New York Times*, 23 July 1979

I like to get into a costume as soon as I arrive on a film set. It very often leads you in a direction you didn't expect.

That was very true with *Breaking Away*. I bought a hat on 14th Street in New York.... The band was too colorful so I changed that. Then I pushed my belt down under my huge stomach. I found that gave me a duck walk. As soon as I put on those wimpy shoes and hat, I knew it was the right character.

—Dooley, interviewed by Joan E. Vadeboncoeur for *The Syracuse Herald-Journal*, 2 Sept 1983

Marta [Heflin] and I are sweethearts in [*A Perfect Couple* (1979, Robert Altman)]. He is a man in his 40s, which is lucky since that's what I am. He's a wealthy Greek, divorced and back in his father's house with all the grown sons and daughters living like children. Marta is in a rock 'n' roll group and in a similar way is repressed by the leader of the group. It's a love story about repression, people being controlled.

—Dooley, interviewed by Ann Guarino for *The New York Daily News*, 11 Dec 1978

[Robert Altman] creates a wonderful atmosphere in which to work. He's very democratic and down to earth. Everybody is always thinking because, if you come up with a good idea, he'll fatten up your part. [Dooley also worked on Altman's *A Wedding* (1978), *Health* (1979), *Popeye* (1980) and *O.C. and Stiggs* (1983).]

—Dooley, interviewed by Scott Cain for *The Journal Constitution* (Atlanta), 16 Jan 1983

Kirk DOUGLAS [1916-]

Born: Issur Danielovich in Amsterdam, N.Y.; father of actors Michael Douglas and Eric Douglas [1958]. Studies at St. Lawrence University and at The American Academy of Dramatic Arts, and work on Broadway preceded his film debut in The Strange Love of Martha Ivers (1946, Lewis Milestone). In 1949, he played Midge Kelly in Mark Robson's Champion:

I've made a career, in a sense, of being an s.o.b. Look at *Champion*. The guy punched his crippled brother [Arthur Kennedy] and raped his ex-wife [Ruth Roman]. But at the preview the people cheered him in his big fight scene. People know my guy is no good but understand how he got that way. He's usually a rebel against society, and most of us would like to say, "To hell with society."

—Douglas, interviewed by Frederick Christian for *The New York Journal American*, 4 Nov 1962

The character I play [in *Ace in the Hole* (1951, Billy Wilder)] is somewhat like the fighter in *Champion*. But in this one, the muscles are in the guy's mind rather than on his body.

—Douglas, interviewed by Hedda Hopper for *The San Francisco Chronicle*, 5 Nov 1950

Before playing a newspaperman in *Ace in the Hole*...I wanted to make sure I wouldn't goof as a screen reporter once I was before a camera. I called a pal and asked, "Can you fix it so I can work for a newspaper? I'm playing a reporter in a picture. I'd like to find out how it's done."

My pal called Agness Underwood, the city editor of the *Los Angeles Herald and Express*. She asked, "Does Douglas really want to work or is he looking for a joy ride while he milks some publicity out of it?"

My pal told her, "He really wants to work."

"Have him here at seven o'clock tomorrow morning," she said....

I'll always believe that there's value in being willing to work like a horse to do a better job. Until I played the prize fighter in *Champion*, I had never boxed at all. When I started work in that picture I had three left hands, none of which could jab or throw a punch, but I trained in a gym until I became a passable fighter.

I'd never done any trapeze work before I worked as an aerialist in *The Story of Three Loves* [1953, Gottfried Reinhardt], but I trained for that, too, until I could do some real "flying." I learned to juggle for *The Juggler* [1953, Edward Dmytryk] by practicing several hours a day for weeks. I tackled the guitar in the same way for my first Western, and before going before the camera in *Detective Story* [1951, William Wyler], I spent many nights in New York's 16th precinct police station....

It could be that my willingness to work long and hard to master a new skill is just another manifestation of my hamminess — a desire to create a sensation with an unexpected accomplishment; then throw it away by saying, "It's really nothing." But I honestly don't think that's it. It's not so much exhibitionism on my part as a need to believe in those games of "Let's pretend." If I believe in them hard enough, moviegoers may believe in them, too.

During the filming of *20,000 Leagues Under the Sea* [1954], I kept trying to think up bits of business which might help my characterization. As we rehearsed each scene I would outline one of my ideas to Dick Fleischer, the director, and ask, "Is there any value in this?"

He'd say, "Let's try it," or "No, Kirk, it stinks."

Whatever he said was O.K. with me. He was the boss. But long before the picture was in the can the crew was groaning as if in pain every time I asked, "Is there any value in this, Dick?"

—Douglas, as told to Pete Martin for *The Saturday Evening Post*, 22 June 1957

Making *Lust for Life* [1956] was a wonderful but painful experience for me. The wonderful part was working with Vincente Minnelli. Minnelli was high-strung and impatient with actors. But I felt like the teacher's pet. I always seemed to do the right thing; Vincente looked with pleasure on everything I did. Was it because we had worked together successfully in *The Bad and the Beautiful* [1952]? I don't know. But it was a wonderful feeling from my point of view, to have supportive looks coming from a demanding director.

The painful experience was probing into the soul of a tormented artist....

There is no doubt that Van Gogh was an extremely complex, difficult person with self-destructive impulses. But he had a great desire to give of himself. He started out wanting to be a preacher, because he wanted to give himself to God and to humanity. What a tragic life!

We shot the movie in many of the places Van Gogh had lived and worked. It was eerie to be at the bridge that he had painted, to be at the yellow house in Arles, to be at the spots in Les Beaux. In Auvers-sur-Oise, I lay in bed in that little room above the bar where he actually lived, and looked out the window and saw what he had seen: the town hall that he had painted, with all the flags just as he had painted them.... And it was horrible to be standing in the field where he painted his last painting — the crows in the wheatfield — leaning on the same tree with a gun in my hand, to hear the noise of the shot....

Playing Vincent van Gogh shook up my theory of what acting is all about. To me, acting is creating an illusion, showing tremendous discipline, not losing yourself in the character that you're portraying. The actor never gets lost in the character he's playing; the audience does. When you're playing the role, you try to think of the thoughts of that character. When it's over, you become yourself. You must control it.

But I was close to getting lost in the character of Van Gogh. While we were shooting, I wore heavy shoes like the ones Van Gogh wore. I always kept one untied, so that I would feel unkempt, off balance, in danger of tripping. It was loose; it gave him — and me — a shuffling gait. [Douglas worked with Minnelli a third time on *Two Weeks in Another Town* (1962).]

—Douglas, in his *The Ragman's Son* (New York: Simon & Schuster, 1988)

Aside from his burning genius, the thing that attracted me to Van Gogh was his loneliness. Anyone who has experienced loneliness can understand his story. Van Gogh's tragedy was that of a man who needed other people so badly that he couldn't admit it even to himself.

—Douglas, in the press packet for *Lust for Life* (MGM, 1956)

What attracted me to the story [of *Lonely are the Brave* (1962, David Miller) was] the difficulty of being an individual today. Life gets more and more complex and convoluted. Young people are not happy with what's going on — and they're right. The character in *Lonely are the Brave* had that quality. He didn't want to belong to this day and age. It's difficult to buck the system. That's the tragedy of it all.

—Douglas, quoted in *Walter Matthau* (New York: St. Martin's Press, 1984)

In *The War Wagon* [1967, Burt Kennedy], I fought with [the producers at Universal] for the nude scene. Remember where I was walking away from the camera bare-ass? I said that's the only honest way to shoot it. I'm in the sack, see, and John Wayne's knocking at the door, and we've already established that I wear a gun at all times. So we play the whole scene at the door, me with my gun on, and when I walk back to bed you see the gun is the only thing I'm wearing! Great! You put pants on the guy, the scene isn't honest anymore.

—Douglas, interviewed by Roger Ebert for *Esquire*, Feb 1970

I knew exactly what Kazan had in mind with his hero Eddie [Anderson in *The Arrangement* (1969)]. Here was this middle-aged man who one day looked in the mirror and didn't like what he saw — the phony Madison Avenue image of the affluent advertising executive. So he tried to turn hippie — twenty years too late, and with disastrous results.

—Douglas, quoted in *The Films of Kirk Douglas* by Tony Thomas (Secaucus, N.J.: Citadel Press, 1972)

A lot of directors don't relate to the actors at all.... But Kazan is an actor's director. He feels for the actor. You sensed that he thought the actor was important. And it's because of that quality that he gets such terrific performances out of actors. He's *with* them. Sometimes a director *dares* you to give a good performance. But Kazan is the opposite; he does everything to get the performance out of the actor. The character I played in *The Arrangement*, like Van Gogh as well, called for an inner emotional and intellectual intensity. In both instances I was portraying a tormented man, who is completely twisted. To depict the different shades of that type of a person is exhausting. It's much more demanding than usual. And it needs a director who can pull all that out of you.

—Douglas, interviewed by Gordon Gow for *Films & Filming*, Sept 1972

Melvyn DOUGLAS [1901-1981]

Born: Melvyn Hesselberg in Macon, Georgia. Work in repertory and on Broadway preceded his film debut, recreating his stage role in Tonight or Never *(1931, Mervyn LeRoy). He co-starred with Greta Garbo in three films —* As You Desire Me *(1932, George Fitzmaurice),* Ninotchka *(1939, Ernst Lubitsch) and* Two-Faced Woman *(1941, George Cukor):*

She was a provocative girl.... She wasn't a trained actress — and she was aware of that herself — but she had extraordinary intuitions, especially in the realm of erotic experience.... I was a little awestruck by Garbo at first, but I found her a very easy person to be with. We talked about everything, including her awareness of how she'd never really learned to be an actress.

—Douglas, interviewed by Lillian and Helen Ross for *The Player* (New York: Simon & Schuster, 1962)

Garbo had an extraordinary face, plastic and luminous, the kind of subject sculptors adore. When she began to play, it acquired an astonishing animation. Her best work was done in love scenes; while rehearsing or even shooting with her I could not help thinking, "My God, how astoundingly beautiful! This is really *happening* somehow right here in my arms."

Her technical abilities for other kinds of scenes were not as fully developed, however. Perhaps because English was not her native language, she did not "underline," she did not pick out the most important phrases in a speech or color individual words for subtle shades of meaning. In spite of *Ninotchka*'s billing as the film in which "Garbo laughs," she was unable to articulate so much as a titter during the shooting of the restaurant scene. I never learned whether the laughter, which must have been added in the dubbing room, was Garbo or not.

The films of the thirties seem wonderfully appealing in nostalgic retrospect, but the writers who wrote them, the directors and producers who organized and supervised them and the actors who performed in them were repeating the same formulas over and over again. The work was safe and stable but finally, neither lively nor exciting.

There were exceptions, such as working with Ernst Lubitsch on *Angel* [1937], *Ninotchka* and *That Uncertain Feeling* [1941], and with Richard Boleslawski on *Theodora Goes Wild* [1936]; these directors collaborated with their actors. Lubitsch usually gathered the cast together to look at the day's shooting, and often re-did scenes which could be improved. I remember Boleslawski enlisting our aid with at least one performance problem; when Irene Dunne, as Theodora, could not manage to muster the proper amount of excitement for an important entrance, the director warned the cast and crew, then crept up behind her and fired a blank cartridge from a hand gun held just below her buttocks. If you look at the film...you will be rewarded with one of the most breathless, bewildered on-camera entrances ever recorded.

Marty Ritt was certainly not a typical film director. Although still in his early forties, he already had spent years directing for television before turning to feature films. He was sufficiently established in California to be involved in producing, as well as directing, *Hud* [1963]. A student and protégé of Elia Kazan at the Actor's Studio, Ritt in turn had had some excellent students of his own, including Rod Steiger, Joanne Woodward and the man who was to play the lead in this new film, Paul Newman. On the basis of his unusual theater background, Ritt now asked an astonishing question. Would I be willing to spend three weeks rehearsing with the cast now being assembled to delve more deeply into the role and get a sense of the continuity of the script by the time shooting started? No one in the movie industry had suggested such a practice to me since I had worked with Ernst Lubitsch...and, of course, I was delighted with the idea....

After almost a week of reading and talking, we got up and began moving around on a taped-off ground plan of the set, exactly as one might do in the theatre. Even after we traveled to our location site in the Texas Panhandle, Marty "cheated" by rehearsing a day or two extra. By the time that excellent cameraman, James Wong Howe, and his crew were ready to record our efforts, we were engrossed in what Stanislavsky might have called the "inner lives" of our characters.

The shooting went smoothly. Lubitsch used to maintain that time spent on rehearsing more than paid for itself in increased actor involvement once the cameras started to roll. That seemed to be the case with *Hud*. Beyond the ease we all felt as a result of Ritt's preparation, something intangible seemed to be happening in my own work. I liked the old man I was playing; I had sensed that in some intangible way I knew him intimately, almost from the moment I first read the script. Now I seemed to do little more than think his thoughts and the distance between the camera and me disappeared. "Ripeness is all" says Shakespeare's King Lear. In retrospect I see that I was technically and emotionally *ripe* to film this role.

The range of parts available to me during the past few years has been both broad and narrow. I have played doctors, lawyers, industrialists, politicians, good men and bad. Understandably enough, the acting problems have been similar; this man is old, this man is dying, this man is dead. Of course, death by definition means the end of life so the major performance question becomes, "what is each of these human beings made of? What are they *leaving?*" I cannot imagine a more interesting problem for an actor....

The only way I have been able to "create" a dying character is to find and get across what gives him pleasure and satisfaction, what gives him life. In Alan Alda's brilliant *The Seduction of Joe Tynan* [1979], Senator Birney, the character I played, has built a political career on the basis of a kind of honor-among-thieves to which the modern Joe Tynan does not subscribe. Without this system Birney cannot function, and he comes unraveled at a public hearing — which may throw a certain light on the late-sixties fall of President Lyndon B. Johnson. In *Being There* [1979, Hal Ashby] Benjamin Rand, the character I portrayed, has all the power, all the money, all the answers. He is nearly as bereft of needs, of questions, as the utterly opaque Peter Sellers/Chaunce Gardiner character. When Rand dies he will be succeeded by Gardiner, who lacks even the desire for companionship demonstrated by the older man....

Working on *Being There* was a joy. Jack Warden and Peter Sellers are theater raconteurs as well as wonderful actors. The two of them hardly ever left the set. Shooting on their scenes would end and they would retire to chairs in another part of the room and go on telling stories, gesturing and laughing until the tears ran down their faces....

Shirley MacLaine proved to be another sort of person entirely, intelligent and honest in her dealings with others, a woman who seems to want every effort, every moment, every contact to count. On-screen Shirley looks as if she might not have a thought in her head nor a care in the world; in person she radiates intensity. She kept pushing Hal for the reasoning behind her character's actions, and by implication, for more thorough explanations of his directorial choices. ("Why do I take Gardiner home — specifically? What *leads* me to introduce him to my husband?") Hal is passionately artistic but not always cogent or verbal. It looked to me as if Shirley's probing both bothered and stimulated him, and I suspect she had a salutary effect on the project on that account.

It was Hal himself, however, who was most responsible for making *Being There* a rich experience for me. His free-wheeling approach released a creativity, a kind of goofiness, in me.

—Douglas, in his (with Tom Arthur) *See You at the Movies* (Lanham, MD: University Press of America, 1986)

Michael DOUGLAS [1944-]

Born: New Brunswick, N.J.; son of Kirk Douglas. Studies at The University of California at Santa Barbara, the O'Neill Center's National Playwrights Conference and with Wynn Handman at The American Place Theatre in N.Y., and work as an off-Broadway actor and as an assistant film director preceded his film acting debut in Hail, Hero! (1969, David Miller). In 1988, he starred in both Adrian Lyne's Fatal Attraction and Oliver Stone's Wall Street:

I remember when I started working on [*Fatal Attraction*], all of a sudden there was this moment where it just went right through me and I closed the script and I said, "Work on what?"

Q. What moment was that?

A. Earlier, before I started the movie. I said, what's this movie about? If you take the analogy that there's two types of actors: one who sits in front of a mirror and paints on a character; and the other who's stripping away, taking it all away and getting down to the bones. It was clear to me that that was what it was about: *I* could be a lawyer; *I* could have a situation like this possibly happen. It was the closest part to me.

Q. But there's a moment where the film takes another path from what, for me, would be more interesting. About 45 minutes in, there's a conversation between your character and the Glenn Close character, where she outlines the happiness you've got and says, "So, why are you here?" The film never answers that.

A. What we tried to do was create a character who did not think. I don't think you'd think that he was a philanderer. This was — if not the first time — a very unique experience. He failed. Nobody's perfect. And at that particular moment in time, and given the fact that there was a little edge, a little problem with the wife [Anne Archer] and the house and moving to the country. And when somebody approaches you, as opposed to the stereotype about taking off your ring and pretending you're not married, and anything like this. It was, basically, in the Eighties. It was not that I was pursuing it. It was presented to me on a silver platter. I went for it. I went for it.

In *Wall Street*, I had the best part I ever had. Beautifully written, and — which people forget — I was *not* carrying the movie. Charlie Sheen had to carry it. I come in for half the movie, get those great scenes....

Q. Gekko is in theory a villain, yet enormously attractive and appealing. You had plenty of models for Gekko in the movie community.

A. If that's the choice. I wasn't trying cosmetically to make him appealing. But his talent and seduction were to Charlie, and also an audience. Listen to the greed speech and get seduced. I think there's an evil part in all of us and society teaches us to be civilized, but we all love to see villains because there's that part of us that would love the opportunity to be as dark and nasty.

—Douglas, interviewed by David Thomson for *Film Comment*, Jan/Feb 1990

Brad DOURIF [1950-]

Born: Huntingdon, West Virginia. Studies at Marshall University, at The Circle Repertory in N.Y. and with Sanford Meisner, and work on the N.Y. stage preceded his film debut as Billy Bibbitt in Milos Forman's One Flew Over the Cuckoo's Nest:

Often people who are crazy will be perfectly normal in every other way except for one specific flaw. I talked to one man for several hours and I thought he was a perfectly normal and bright conversationalist. But one day he told me that, when he got out of the hospital, he was going to become a prime minister. It was the glorifying hope of his life.

I got the impression from Jack Nicholson on the set [of *Cuckoo's Nest*] that, while he never appeared to be working, he was actually working all the time. No matter what he was doing physically, his mind always seemed to be on his role and how the role would be suited for the film.

Milos Forman believes in maintaining a sense of the company while shooting a film. Most of the cast stayed in a motel that will never become famous for its elegance. It was worthwhile for the actors because we would lose ourselves in the shooting of the film.

—Dourif, interviewed by Christopher Sharp for *Women's Wear Daily*, 21 Nov 1975

[Hazel Motes in *Wise Blood* (1979, John Huston)] is the closest I've ever come to playing a saint, and I've always wanted to play one, because they're real human beings with real problems, but very clear vision — and fanatic. The fanatic will do whatever it is he has to do.... I mean, he was a totally uneducated person, but these were *his* ideas.

—Dourif, interviewed by Carol Caldwell for *The Soho Weekly News*, 1 Dec 1981

Q. What was it like working with John Huston on *Wise Blood*?

A. I was very scared and uncomfortable. I was the lead. I was insecure. I didn't think I could act my way out of a paper bag, you know. Oddly enough, he was the one who left me alone the most....

Q. How was it working with an English director like Alan Parker [on *Mississippi Burning* (1988)]?

A. English directors believe in the director's control over the project. For instance, in *Mississippi Burning*, I gave the exact performance Parker wanted me to give. But he didn't say much, you know. He wanted it kind of thrown away and real simple.

Shoot — it wasn't just Parker, I was working with Gene Hackman, who is one of the greatest actors this country has. It's really exciting doing a scene with this guy because he becomes so involved in what's going on. He's just right there. The better you are, the better he is. And the better he is, the better you are. It just grows....

I know what it's like to feel like a piece of shit. I know what it's like to have low self-esteem. I think we all do. But I *know*. And that's the way [Deputy Pell] feels. That's why he was a bigot.

The great thing about pain is that it levels you. It makes you human, humble. If I can feel a bigot's pain then I feel more compassionate toward him....

David Lynch...is the purest, most original of all the directors I've worked with [on *Dune* (1985) and *Blue Velvet* (1986)]. His vision is so unique. His thing is truly his own. He's extremely lovable and the least defensive. Not that the others are so defensive — *I'm* defensive.

—Dourif, interviewed by Marlaine Glicksman for *Film Comment*, Nov/Dec 1989

Marie DRESSLER [1869-1934]

Born: Leila Kerber in Coborg, Ontario, Canada. A star of vaudeville and the stage, she made her film debut recreating her stage character, Tillie Blobbs, at the behest of Mack Sennett and Charles O. Bauman of The Keystone Company:

When they presented themselves in my sitting room...I discovered that the wild-eyed one was Mack Sennett, and that the spokesman for the pair was Bauman.... They wanted to make good pictures that would take them into first-rate houses. They thought they could break into first-string theatres if they had my name in the cast....

At my suggestion, we decided on *Tillie's Punctured Romance* [1914] for our first fling. The old Cinderella theme again, with plenty of tears behind the laughter. Now for actors. Instantly there leaped into my mind the name of a young chap I had seen in London several years before. I knew that boy had genius, that he would some day be acclaimed a star. I had run across him a few days before in Hollywood. Now I started a great hue and cry:

"Where is Charlie Chaplin? I want Charlie Chaplin!"

Everybody thought I was crazy. Maybe I was, but I knew what I knew. And I knew that Chaplin could act. He was an enormous success in *Tillie*.

It was not until Frances Marion wrote *Min and Bill* [1931, George Hill] that I got a part after my own heart. The moment I read the script, I knew that here was the role I had been waiting for all my life. And I was cast to play it opposite Wally Beery, to whose measure Bill was cut just as surely as Min was cut to mine.

Min, as you may recall, was the keeper of a wretched dump of a hotel on the waterfront; Bill was her man. The characters were so rich, so meaty, that we constantly had to guard against the dangers of overacting. Hitherto, in working up a role, I had first to get my teeth in it, so to speak, and then sort of roll it over and put gravy on it before it was really mine. This time, the part had everything when it was handed to me. I had only to translate Frances Marion's dream into flesh and blood.

—Dressler, in her *My Own Story* (Boston: Little, Brown & Co., 1934)

Ellen DREW [1915-]

Born: Terry Ray in Kansas City, Missouri. After several bit parts, she played her first important role in Sing You Sinners (1938, Wesley Ruggles), followed later that year by If I Were King:

"You can't just act this girl," director Frank Lloyd told me when I was assigned to the part of Huguette in *If I Were King*. "You have to *be* her. We picked you for the role because you don't know how to act. If you study and analyze the part, you'll never make it."

Fortunately, as this was only my second picture, I didn't know enough to be frightened by these instructions. As Frank pointed out, I knew nothing about acting, and, as he might have added, I didn't know I could be bad. Thus blessed by ignorance and inexperience, I sailed right into the part of this primitive and impulsive girl and played it as if I knew how. If I had to do it again today, I'd doubtless worry the role into small digestible pieces, and my performance wouldn't be spontaneous nor half so good.

Huguette was a guttersnipe, wild, ragged and completely unmoral. She walked like an animal, screamed when she talked, and heartily hated her rival in love. All this gave me a lot of acting to do, and even though I didn't know how, I thoroughly enjoyed trying....

I had a terrific crush on [Ronald Colman] at the time, and being around him in the making of the picture made me pretty breathless. As it happened, I was even more breathless when he finally kissed me. Huguette was supposed to be dead in that sad scene, so I had to receive the long-awaited kiss from Ronald Colman without the tiniest reaction. That, I suspect, was the hardest piece of "acting" I did in the whole picture.

—Drew, in *The Saturday Evening Post*, 17 Oct 1953

Richard DREYFUSS [1947-]

Born: Brooklyn, N.Y. Studies with Rosejane Landau in Hollywood and at San Fernando Valley State College, work at The Gallery Theater in Los Angeles, improv. comedy with The Session in San Francisco, and work on and off Broadway, preceded his first film work — in bit parts in The Graduate (1967, Mike Nichols) and The Valley of the Dolls (1967, Mark Robson). Success came with American Graffiti (1973, George Lucas) and The Apprenticeship of Duddy Kravitz (1974, Ted Kotcheff):

I did *American Graffiti* and in that film, the character's perception of things is so much like mine, and my experience in high school was so similar to his, that I was totally comfortable playing him because I really felt like I was just exposing myself in front of eighteen million people, that I was really just saying, "This is Rick Dreyfuss, good evening, how are you?" But Duddy Kravitz was *not* me, although I have Duddy in me. Duddy was work, hard work and it was very rare that I really got off on it. There was a lot of tension on the set that contributed to it, but the one day that I loved was the last day unfortunately. Not because it was over either, but the work I did on the last day of shooting was my favorite work on the film. It was all the billiard stuff and my conversation with Calder [Robert Goodier]. That one scene is my favorite in terms of acting, in how I enjoyed doing it. That scene is not that interesting to the audience, but to me, I said, "Let's do this forever, man! I could shoot this scene every which way! You want me to change it? (snaps his fingers) I'll change it. You want me to do this? I'll do this." And I loved it.

—Dreyfuss, interviewed by Laurinda Hartt for *Cinema Canada*, June/July 1974

There were many aspects to Duddy that are considered unpleasant, but an actor's job is to find the truth within himself that fits the character and bring it out. I realized that I was going to have to look into myself for things that weren't very pleasant — selfishness, manipulation, cruelty, narrow-mindedness, obsessiveness — those were the things I had to find to make it work. My obligation as an actor was to tell the truth.

—Dreyfuss, interviewed by Michael Goodwin for *The New York Times Magazine*, 15 Jan 1978

The way I work is very instinctual and visual. It's hard to say why I did it [his incessant scratching as Duddy].... There were reasons; he's assaulted by his environment...he's insecure and he feels a raw nerve thing about the world and himself. When I read the script, I saw Duddy Kravitz in my mind and I *knew* that he itched. It's true of him, he'd do that.

—Dreyfuss, interviewed by Howard A. Coffin for *The Philadelphia Inquirer*, 1 Sept 1974

You don't have to see [*Close*] *Encounters* [*of the Third Kind* (1977, Steven Spielberg)] to know the body of my work. If I was less lazy, I'd say it was a great challenge, but it wasn't. It was not a vehicle for a great actor. But I wanted it, and I finagled to get it. It could become the movie of the century. But I wouldn't do it again. [Dreyfuss had previously worked with Spielberg on *Jaws* (1975); he worked with him again on *Always* (1989).]

—Dreyfuss, interviewed by Paul Rosenfield for *The Toronto Star*, 7 Jan 1978

Nuts [1987, Martin Ritt] features a character who is never meant to be sexy or attractive, never meant to be anything but tired and cynical and, in a sense, an idealist. Working with Barbra [Streisand] and Marty Ritt is a very specific kind of experience. Everyone on that film was very tough, very strongminded, very willful and it was a lot of fun but very confrontational.

—Dreyfuss, interviewed by Allan Hunter for *Films & Filming*, Mar 1988

All of the physical stuff [in *Stakeout* (1987, John Badham)] was tough for me because I'm not a jock. And that's a specific thing, a way of moving so you look like you know how your body works. You have to learn how to take a gun and run down the hallway of a hotel looking like you know where you're going and how to get there without being killed.

Put a camera on that and it will look either correct or incorrect, either funny or not funny.

And I didn't know if I knew how to do it.... You gotta make sure you don't look like a fool.

—Dreyfuss, interviewed by Roger Ebert for *The New York Post*, 1 Aug 1987

Claire DUBREY [1893-]

Born: New York City. A convent education followed by work on the stage and in stock preceded her film debut:

[Thomas Ince] put this ad in the paper for society women to work in pictures. Well, I was married to a doctor; I was young; I'd been told I should be in pictures; not too unattractive, I was told, and I had time on my hands. So I went up to Inceville, and I got a job immediately. It wasn't much of a job. It was ten dollars a week, but that was the going price. And he had about thirty girls and twenty boys in what was called stock at ten dollars a piece. And one of the boys was Jack Gilbert, and one of the girls was Alice Terry. And Alice and I were great friends. So, there we were, working for Ince six days a week, and playing settlers in the morning, and possibly Indians in the afternoon....

He was using society women, as he called us, because we had independent means. We had to furnish our own clothes, make-up, etc....

Mr. Ince was absolutely charming. He never issued orders. He had a man to do that, as one should have.... He had a stooge, who was called a studio manager, and he was rude. His name was E.H. Allen. He was an Irishman, and ignorant and foul-mouthed. And he would come on the set, and bawl the director out, or the actors or anyone else. Ince issued these orders, but he, himself, was always charming, and we thought he was a dear....

Ince never, never, never directed. He just appeared on the set on rare occasions. Once or twice a week, he'd come round and smile and say, "Hello," but do nothing on his part to make himself unpleasant.

—DuBrey, interviewed by Anthony Slide for *The Silent Picture*, Spring 1972

Patty DUKE [1946-]

Born: Anna Marie Duke in New York City. A child star on television and the stage, she made her film debut as Helen Keller opposite Anne Bancroft as Annie Sullivan in The Miracle Worker (1962, Arthur Penn), recreating the role she had played on Broadway:

After doing the play all that time onstage, we hardly needed any preparation before shooting started.... And because almost everyone involved had done films before, Arthur Penn didn't have to dwell on the difference in technique involved. Occasionally he'd step in with a comment like "You know, we have to bring it down for the camera," but that was it....

The tantrum scenes were the most complex to film. The major one in the second act was shot over four consecutive days, working mornings only. I was in great shape and at an age when you can usually refuel in five minutes anyhow, so when I think about how tired I got, Annie must have felt fifty times worse. I was very quick, and God bless her, she kept up with me. There is one particular moment when I'm going hellbent for election around that table and Annie cuts me off. Now, she had longer legs, but just the breathing power to do that is not easy to come by.

And it wasn't just the actors who needed to rest, there were guys with cameras on their shoulders who were as physically involved as we were. A lot of the film was shot with hand-held equipment, with the operators sitting in wheelchairs because they were small and mobile enough to get into corners. Often we'd get half or three-quarters of the way through a complicated take and have to start all over again because one of us didn't hit a position we thought we were going to hit or the wheelchairs missed their marks or the camera tilted or was jolted in some way. That scene was just exhausting for everyone....

One of the strongest moments in the film is...the result of an accident. It happens right after the miracle, when Annie spells "teacher" into Helen's hand and Helen understands. It was a tough day for shooting; the sun was going in and out of very fluffy clouds, forcing a lot of retakes. It was getting cold and dark, there was time pressure because we would soon lose the light, and this scene was unbelievably emotional for me. Not only was it one of my strongest scenes, but I knew that pretty soon Arthur was going to say, "Cut, print" and that would be the last time I'd ever play it. My eyes were out of focus, I couldn't really see anything, but just as Annie finished spelling "teacher" I suddenly felt an amazing light and warmth on my face. Call it serendipity, God, you name it, but the blessing of having the sun move out from behind a cloud at just that moment really got me by the throat. And one tear, which was also definitely not planned, fell to my cheek. The cloud moved, the light hit the tear, the tear glistened. It was such a dog and pony show, who could believe it all happened by chance....

When the last day [of shooting] came, I tried to be professional but it was very hard. In fact I can pinpoint the scene of the chick being hatched in my hand as being shot at that time because I can see how swollen my eyes were. The heightened emotion of watching something being born, which I'd never seen before, coupled with the impending grief of being separated, made for two really beautiful faces on the screen. I don't think Annie and I look as vulnerable anywhere else in the movie as we do there.

—Duke, in her (with Kenneth Turan) *Call Me Anna* (New York: Bantam Books, 1987)

Keir DULLEA [1936-]

Born: Cleveland, Ohio. Studies with Sanford Meisner at The Neighborhood Playhouse in N.Y. preceded his film debut in The Hoodlum Priest (1961, Irvin Kershner). The following year he played David in Frank Perry's David and Lisa:

The making of *David and Lisa* was a wonderful experience. We were just like a family. We all stayed on location, and lived in a little hotel outside Philadelphia....

But for me personally, *David and Lisa* was a kind of double-edged sword. Suddenly I was hot, and my career really took off. But it also typecast me rather badly as the all-American neurotic. I was offered every killer role, every strange sort of character. I was thought of as a very intense actor. I could never get a comedy to play, which was what I wanted to do more than anything else.

Above all, what will remain memorable [about *2001: A Space Odyssey* (1968)] was working with a genius like Stanley Kubrick. He instilled incredible devotion on the part of his actors. He likes actors. I found him a very gentle director. He's a kind of benign Napoleon, in the sense that he can get actors to do things that I don't think they would do for any other director — not by exercising any kind of obvious power in the sense of being on a power-trip or screaming at people. Quite the opposite. But he is able to marshal his forces, and people tend to have allegiance to him, particularly the actors.

I find the best directors — the ones who have gotten the most out of me — create an atmosphere of safety. Stanley Kubrick was that way. Irvin Kershner certainly was that way: I think I was very lucky working with Kersh on *The Hoodlum Priest*. And Frank Perry, who directed me in my second film, *David and Lisa* is an actor's director if ever there was one.

When I talk about actors' directors, I don't mean that they all work in a certain way. Each of those three was very different in his approach, but one thing that they shared...was that they did create that atmosphere of safety. If you can do that for an actor, then the actor is not afraid to fall on his face, and you may get something far more unusual than what you think they can do. You can make them unafraid of failing. An actor's got to be able to fail if he's to create something very unusual. If an actor doesn't feel safe, then he'll fall back on things he has done in the past. He'll rely on those things. Maybe they were original when you did them first, but they become glib as time goes on. They become tricks almost — tricks of the trade.

—Dullea, interviewed by Gordon Gow for *Films & Filming*, Nov 1976

Faye DUNAWAY [1941-]

Born: Dorothy Faye Dunaway in Bascom, Florida. Studies at Boston University's School of Fine and Applied Arts and work with The Lincoln Center Repertory Company in N.Y. preceded her film debut in The Happening (1967, Elliot Silverstein). Later that year she starred as Bonnie opposite Warren Beatty as Clyde in Arthur Penn's Bonnie and Clyde:

Bonnie...and I were very much alike emotionally at that time during my life. First of all she was from the south and had the kind of frustration, the flirtatiousness which was very much a part of my background....

The script itself dealt very much with the mythic aspects of the characters. The real situation between Bonnie and Clyde and the third, C.W. Moss [Michael J. Pollard], in the film was possibly very, very different.... As Arthur once said, we were dealing very much with the mythical aspects of them and what the outlaw during that time had signified to the people — why they really became heroes to so many people during the depression.

—Dunaway, interviewed by Lewis Funke for *Actors Talk About Theater* (Chicago: The Dramatic Publishing Co., 1977)

There is a scene in the cornfield [of *Bonnie and Clyde*] when she's trying to go back to her mother. She wants to get out of this life because she doesn't know where it's going and she's getting a little nervous. She had thought she was going someplace that was free. In the middle of running across this enormous cornfield the sun went under a cloud. Anyone else would have said "Cut! The light has changed," but Arthur kept it going and in the final scene, as she's running, the shadow that happens is happening in her, so it made a wonderful counterpoint. God gave us that shadow but the scene is a mark of Arthur Penn's brilliance.

—Dunaway, in a 1981 *Guardian* lecture (England); quoted in *Faye Dunaway* by Allan Hunter (New York: St. Martin's Press, 1986)

Evelyn [in *Chinatown* (1974, Roman Polanski)] is a woman with an enormously traumatized, complex, mysterious past. She spends her life trying to rectify it and to protect her child [Belinda Palmer]. As a result, she develops neurotic behavior.

—Dunaway, interviewed by Mel Gussow for *The New York Times*, 20 Oct 1974

Evelyn Mulwray had to be played on at least two levels; on a conscious level and, as there are things that I as the actress knew that the character doesn't know, her subconscious. That subconscious then, if the character doesn't know it, can shoot through so that the character does things, as we all do I think to one degree or another, that are subconscious, that she doesn't know she's doing. She can be saying "I love you" when, if she really hates somebody, she might be twisting a ring around — doing something that she's not aware of, so that it adds to the texture in terms of characterization.

In one scene I had to deliver a lot of lines so that Jack [Nicholson as Jake Gittes] and the audience would suspect that I was a villainess and that I was guilty. At the same time I had to make that fit to the truth which was only discovered at the end of the film which was, in fact, that I was the victim. There is another moment which I think is very revealing when she says, "I don't see anyone for very long. It's difficult for me." The audience, learning that, thinks she is something of a vamp, she has difficulty making commitments to people, she's guilty. Whereas the reason she can't is because of the Oedipal relationship with her father [John Huston as Noah Cross] who had raped her.

—Dunaway, in a 1981 *Guardian* lecture; quoted in *Faye Dunaway* by Allan Hunter (New York: St. Martin's Press, 1986)

I try to do at least two things at once in any role I play. In Diane's case [in *Network* (1976, Sidney Lumet)], I tried to make her both aggressive and vulnerable. She tries to give a balance to her professional and her private life, but she isn't able to.

—Dunaway, interviewed by Christopher Sharp for *W*, 26 Nov-3 Dec 1976

Playing [Joan] Crawford [in *Mommie Dearest* (1981, Frank Perry)] was such a formidable task. I didn't want to mimic her but to inhabit her as much as I could. It was difficult because we had to trim so much from the film, but we tried to get that sense of the tenuousness of her professional existence, her drinking, her nervousness, her decorous behavior, her passion. Every scene, every moment I thought: Who was she? Why was she...?

I'm interested in women who control their own destinies — who try to form them rather than be formed by them — and what they pay for that. What softness and vulnerability — what willingness to be what you are — is lost in the person who tries and succeeds? That's a rending. A pulling both ways....

Crawford was a warrior.

—Dunaway, interviewed by Jennifer Dunning for *The New York Times*, 13 Sept 1981

Griffin DUNNE [1955-]

Born: New York City; raised in Los Angeles; son of Dominick Dunne. Studies at The Neighborhood Playhouse in N.Y. and with Uta Hagen preceded his film debut in The Other Side of the Mountain (1975, Larry Peerce). In 1985, he starred in and co-produced (with Amy Robinson and Robert F. Colesberry) After Hours (1985):

Q. *After Hours* was directed by Martin Scorsese, who has a reputation for being particularly demanding of his actors. What was it like working with him?

A. We were on the same wavelength. When Scorsese directs he inspires people to be completely free and outrageous and lets them try out a lot of different things.

He is such a good editor. We would do these long takes and he would see moments that he could put together. Actors always act very well for him, but he makes them even better in the editing room. In editing the best moments of each take he gives you tremendous freedom because you know you're working with a guy who's going to make you look great by the end of the movie.

—Dunne, interviewed by Robert Morris for *The Cable Guide*, Jan 1987

Irene DUNNE [1898-1990]

Born: Irene Dunn in Louisville, Kentucky. Vocal training in Louisville and at The Chicago College of Music led to stardom first in the touring company of Show Boat and then on Broadway, which in turn led to her film debut in Leathernecking (1930, Edward Cline). In 1936, she reprised her role as Magnolia in the film version of Show Boat:

James Whale wasn't the right director. I really shouldn't say that, but to me the picture didn't come off as well as the stage play.... There were lots of interpolations that we didn't need at all and I think the ending was stupid. It's so easy to attach blame to a man one feels was miscast as director so perhaps I shouldn't but, you see, he was more interested in atmosphere and lighting and he knew so little about that life....

Q. In those musicals, were the songs recorded after the shooting or consecutively with it?

A. Most of my numbers were dubbed, and I pride myself on that. First you record the number, then you shoot the scene and sing along to the recording. It's remarkable how you can do it. You can't really do it on the set because the sound engineers aren't happy with the result.

—Dunne, interviewed by John Kobal for *Focus on Film*, Oct 1977

I was glad of the opportunity [to play Theodora in *Theodora Goes Wild* (1936, Richard Boleslavsky)] for two reasons. In the first place, I was surfeited with what I call "martyr" roles — those that found me as the forgotten woman. Secondly, the reception of the public to my black-face and shuffle scenes in *Show Boat* convinced me that I really did have a flair for light comedy.

—Dunne, interviewed for the press packet for *Theodora Goes Wild* (Columbia Pictures, 1936)

One of the things I remember about *The Awful Truth* [1937, Leo McCarey] was Cary Grant's attitude at the beginning of the film. He could not understand Leo's improvising as he went along. I really think if Cary could have gotten out of the film at that time he would have done so.

Also my inability to do a 'bump' which I still can't do. When I came to the part in the song "My Dreams Are Gone with the Wind" where I was supposed to do the 'bump' he (Leo) said, "Just say, 'Never could do that.'"

—Dunne, in a letter to Ralph Bellamy, published in Bellamy's *When the Smoke Hit the Fan* (Garden City, N.Y.: Doubleday & Co., 1979)

Q. Which directors gave you a lot of interpretation of the characters?

A. Those were the directors I didn't like. I wanted to do my own thing. If they didn't like it, then we would do something about it, but as it turned out most times they seemed to like what I was doing, and most times they would leave it at that. George Stevens [on *Penny Serenade* (1941) and *I Remember Mama* (1948)] was especially good that way — at letting you try your own wings.

Q. Which directors discussed motivation with you a lot?

A. Michael Curtiz, for instance, in *Life with Father* [1947], because I didn't like the role very much, and he had to placate me and make it more palatable. Rouben Mamoulian [on *High, Wide and Handsome* (1937)] liked to tell you how it was to be done. Until we got together and he sort of let me have my head. No, most of the directors — the really fine directors — want to see what you will give them first. The worst kind is the frustrated actor director — the kind who gets up and shows you all the moves.... That kind of director I couldn't work with at all.

Only one argument I remember having with George Stevens — and as I look back at it he was a man of very *very* few words — was on *Mama*. He said, "I want you to come in the door and walk here, about ten steps, and then I want you to cross the room." And I said, "Why?" He said, "Do as I say. Ten steps, then cross." Well, I didn't like that. I have to know *why* I'm doing something. As it turned out, it was just for the cutting. But he wanted to be stubborn, to make me do it without telling me why. So we had a kind of upset.

Q. Stevens was slow. What took the time?

A. He was a perfectionist. He took a lot of preparation with his crew. He didn't do a lot of takes.

Q. John Stahl was slow, too?

A. Stahl [with whom she worked on *Back Street* (1935) and *When Tomorrow Comes* (1935)] was tough on his extras and bit players. He and Charles Vidor [on *Together Again* (1944)]. They treated the stars beautifully, but they were hard on the bit players. That was upsetting. Stahl would throw things around on the set.... Stahl never allowed us to see rushes.

—Dunne, interviewed by James Harvey for *Film Comment*, Jan/Feb 1980

Charles DURNING [1923-]

Born: Highland Falls, N.Y. Service in the Army, acting studies at The American Academy of Dramatic Arts, work as a dance teacher at a Fred Astaire studio, and roles off-Broadway and with Joseph Papp and The New York Shakespeare Festival (since 1963), preceded his film debut in Harvey Middleman — Fireman (1965, Ernest Pintoff). In 1977, he played President Stevens in Robert Aldrich's Twilight's Last Gleaming:

[Aldrich] was very volatile. He had a volatile temper and when he said something, he meant it. There was no bullshit about him. He was adamant about certain things and if you disagreed with him, that was your tough luck....

He said that the President became heroic through the office, not because he was heroic, but because the office *made* him heroic. He would tell me those little gems which cleared up a lot of problems for me.

—Durning, interviewed by Edwin T. Arnold and Eugene L. Miller, Jr. for *The Films and Career of Robert Aldrich* (Knoxville: The University of Tennessee Press, 1986)

The relationship between Les and Dorothy [in *Tootsie* (1982, Sydney Pollack)] didn't have anything to do with sexuality, except maybe at first. He was really attracted to her because of what she was, her dealing with life, her openness with life....

I found specific things about Dustin [Hoffman as Dorothy] that I liked — he has terrific eyes, for example — and I would play to that. And he is so immersed in the character that you find yourself swept up in the moment.

—Durning, interviewed by Will Walters for *The Cable Guide*, May 1984

Robert DUVALL [1931-]

Born: San Diego. After studying drama at Principia College, Illinois, and with Sanford Meisner at The Neighborhood Playhouse in N.Y., he began a long association with Horton Foote, eventually making his film debut as the mute Boo Radley in To Kill a Mockingbird (1962, Robert Mulligan). Further Foote projects on which he worked were Tomorrow (1972, Joseph Anthony) and Tender Mercies (1983, Bruce Beresford):

The roots of Fentry [in *Tomorrow*], especially the way he spoke, came to me from an experience I had when I was a senior in high school in St. Louis. I once went with my brother to southern Missouri to spend a few days, and went into Arkansas and we met this guy. He didn't open his mouth until he had something to say; he talked straightforward. He talked like a cow. Fentry was such a guy, a closed guy. He was no retard; he was a simple man and I wanted to keep him that way. I wanted him to be a stoic.

—Duvall, in *Tomorrow & Tomorrow & Tomorrow*, ed. by David G. Yellin and Marie Connors (Jackson: University Press of Mississippi, 1985)

I figured [Tom Hagen in *The Godfather* (1972 and 1974, Francis Ford Coppola)] was passive visually. But he had to be ready to be active, always there, like a millionaire go-fer. I tried to keep that New York speech in there and make him sound like he'd still be from the streets although he went to Fordham Law School. I knew underneath he was emotional, but he always had the control, always the control.

—Duvall, quoted in *American Film*, Sept 1981

In *Network* [1976, Sidney Lumet], everybody asked me if I was doing Barry Diller, the head of Paramount, but I didn't even know who Barry Diller was. Actually I was basing the character on a more energetic, more vicious version of President Ford. You know, a midwestern Establishment Republican.

—Duvall, interviewed by Judy Klemesrud for *The New York Times*, 6 Feb 1977

[In *Apocalypse Now* (1979, Francis Ford Coppola)], I play [Lt. Cl. Bill Kilgore] a guy in the Air Cavalry who strapped surf boards to his helicopter, and then when the battles subsided, would go surfing.... In one scene, he'd throw down napalm to clean out the enemy, and at the same time, clear the area so they can go surfing.

The irony of it is that the napalm screws up the waves and makes them all muddled, ruining his surfing. So he goes away cursing napalm. It's his savior on the one hand and his enemy on the other, but for the wrong reasons....

My last scene in the movie where the napalm screwed up everything, I take this megaphone thing, I throw it up in the air and curse, and then walk away. And [Coppola] came up and said, "You didn't do that in rehearsal, that was terrific the way you did that. That was terrific. What gave you the idea to do that — to throw that megaphone up at the end of the scene like that?" I said, "I just kind of recalled one of your tantrums." He gave me the finger and walked away.

—Duvall, interviewed by Paul Gleason for *Club*, 1978

Q. You've worked with Coppola on a few films. What's your view of him?

A. He's a maniac! Worse than an actor. No, he's very talented. I like working with him. I kid him about that. He's a high-strung, temperamental guy who wants to make his work good.... I always say Coppola works best amidst confusion. But he always has his vision. When he works with an actor, he wants to see what you can bring to the role, so he doesn't have to dictate what it's got to be. I think most good directors will see what the actor will bring — otherwise you get a robot. [Duvall also worked on Coppola's *The Rain People* (1969) and *The Conversation* (1974).]

—Duvall, interviewed by Fred Robbins for an unidentified, undated clipping in the files of the Lincoln Center Library for the Performing Arts

[Ulu Grosbard]'s one of the best damned directors around today.... He understands that things have to be lifelike. Like pauses. There are pauses in life, you see, when you and I are talking, and there are beats in scenes that really make them work. He gives his actors freedom to do things. You have to have that. I can't work with any director who doesn't let me have some say about the lines, about the shaping of the scenes, who won't let me talk to the other actors, you see? That's very important. And he's good on all these counts. [Duvall worked often with Grosbard on and off Broadway before starring in his *True Confessions* (1981).]

I drove over 600 miles of road in Texas listening to accents, watching how people held their bodies, talking to farmers. Man, I wanted my character [Max Sledge in *Tender Mercies* (1983, Bruce Beresford)] to be real. But I loved it, too. I loved talking to those people. You know, that's what all my acting is really about. Dignity. Trying to find the dignity in the man. Because the average working man has dignity that the Hollywood establishment has overlooked. The center and, especially, the South of this country have been patronized and made fun of. Things like the *Dukes of Hazard* — man, they're the worst. If I can do anything at all in my work to show what dignity is in the common man, then that's what my life is really about....

[Bruce Beresford and I] had our fights. I called him a few choice names, and he got on me.... He's a bright guy. Hell, I loved *Breaker Morant* [1980], but he has this dictatorial way of doing things with me that just doesn't cut it. Man, I have to have my freedom. Make things happen with a line change or two there. Hell, I don't change lines easily. Horton Foote, who wrote this picture is one of my favorite writers and a man I respect as a real artist. But occasionally, things have to be opened up. Bruce even flew back here and almost quit the picture. I flew back, and we had it out. But after all that happened, it helped the picture. We cleared the air. I think that once we got over it all, we ended up doing better work.

—Duvall, interviewed by Robert Ward for *Rolling Stone*, 28 Apr 1983

Shelley DUVALL [1950-]

Born: Houston. Discovered by Robert Altman, she has acted in 7 of his films to date, beginning with Brewster McCloud (1970):

I'd never acted anywhere before meeting Bob Altman; I never studied drama or speech or anything like that. I grew up in Houston, and in the high school I went to, none of my friends were interested in it.... Then one night these three guys walked into a party I was giving, and one of them asked me, "How would you like to be in the movies?" And I answered, "Oh, man, I'm not an actress!" But it all happened so fast: *Brewster McCloud* just flew by. It seemed so easy. I had no fear whatsoever, of the cameras or anything.

—Duvall, interviewed by Stephen Harvey for *Film Comment*, May 1974

[Altman] offers me damn good roles, none of them have been alike. He has a great confidence in me, and a trust and respect for me, and he doesn't put any restrictions on me or intimidate me, and I love him. I remember the first advice he ever gave me: "Don't take yourself seriously." Sometimes I find myself feeling self-centered, and then all of a sudden that bit of advice will pop into my head, and I'll laugh.

I put so much of myself into Millie [in *Three Women* (1977)], especially the parts I don't care to see, all the vanities and the mundane things, such as Millie's fondness of tuna-melt sandwiches, and Scrabble, and the color yellow. No one likes her because she's boring, and because all she can talk about is recipes. She lives in a fantasy, writing in her diary things that don't really happen to her, and totally ignoring the truth — that she really isn't popular.

—Duvall, interviewed by Judy Klemesrud for *The New York Times*, 23 Mar 1977

I wrote all my own monologues [for *Three Women*]. Bob would say, "Why don't you write a monologue just in case we can use it?" And we'd use it. He knows I always do my homework. I had been reading *Apartment Life*, *Redbook*, *Readers Digest*, and *Woman's Day*. It's easy to write. Monologues just came out in 15 minutes.

I put a lot of myself in, but I'm not a consumer like Millie. I played her like a Lubitsch comedy — people taking themselves very seriously.

—Duvall, interviewed by Cliff Jahr for *The Village Voice*, 11 Apr 1977

Once I got into the costume and the wig, I was Olive [in *Popeye* (1980, Robert Altman)]. The shoes dictated the way I walked. They were a size 14 and I wear a size seven. They made me take a longer stride and walk flat-footed and it was perfect. Olive has her own kind of grace.

Olive's voice is very musical. She exaggerates on certain notes, no matter what she says. No matter what the words are, she still emphasizes the basic note. "What! Hmmm-mmm...PHOOEY!" Musically, it's the same basic pattern over and over again.

Olive speaks very quickly, and she's always very determined and 101% woman.... She also has a very strong and long neck that she uses when she speaks.

Unlike many other people, Olive is unique. I think of her as a combination of Stan Laurel and Mae West. [Duvall also worked on Altman's *McCabe and Mrs. Miller* (1971), *Thieves Like Us* (1974), *Nashville* (1975) and *Buffalo Bill and the Indians* (1976).]

—Duvall, in a press release for *Popeye* (Paramount/Walt Disney, 1980)

I had no technical training, so you can say that [Stanley] Kubrick stretched me in every direction [on *The Shining* (1980)]. I had to cry and be hysterical for nine months without stopping. A person cannot cry for that long. I went into a state of shock and depression. I invented ways to cry I never dreamed possible before. Kubrick would only accept real tears. No glycerine or fake movie tears were used. Sometimes I cried only because I was going through such torture. "I have to cry again or I'll be here forever," I would tell myself, and that made me cry even harder. Whenever my tears dried up, I'd just think about how much I hated making that movie and it worked every time. I cried for 12 hours a day for nine months. I developed cramps, anemia, my blood sugar dropped. I lived on 30 cups of tea, 15 Coca-Colas, and hundreds of cigarettes per day as well as the horrible English food. While I was crying, Jack Nicholson was busy screwing up his face into a distorted frown. He did that until the arteries in his head got so swollen he couldn't move his eyeballs.... Kubrick is such a perfectionist that he makes you do every scene 20 or 30 times over. We'd do 50 rehearsals before we ever got before the camera, and you have to give full performances on each rehearsal or he makes you do it all over again. The hardest thing was finding the energy to get through it without having a nervous breakdown. It was like being on the front lines in a war. I'm glad I survived it, but I will never do it again.

—Duvall, interviewed by Rex Reed for *The New York Sunday News*, 20 July 1980

E

Clint EASTWOOD [1930-]

Born: San Francisco. Work as a lifeguard and lumberjack, time in the army, and studies at Los Angeles City College preceded his film debut in Revenge of the Creature (1955, Jack Arnold). His 3 roles as "The Man with No Name" in Sergio Leone's "spaghetti westerns" — A Fistful of Dollars (1964), For a Few Dollars More (1965) and The Good, The Bad and The Ugly (1966) — established him as a film star:

Q. Let's start with *A Fistful of Dollars*. How did that come about?

A. Well, at that time I'd done *Rawhide* for about five years. The agency called and asked if I was interested in doing a western in Italy and Spain. I said, "Not particularly." I was pretty westerned out on the series. They said, "Why don't you give the script a quick look?" Well, I was kind of curious, so I read it, and I recognized it right away as *Yojimbo* [1961], a Kurosawa film I had liked a lot. When I'd seen it years before, I thought, "Hey, this film is really a western...."

Sergio had only directed one other picture, but they told me he had a good sense of humor, and I liked the way he interpreted the *Yojimbo* script. And I had nothing to lose, because I had the series to go back to as soon as the hiatus was over....

—Eastwood, interviewed by Tim Cahill for *Rolling Stone*, 4 July 1985

Playboy: Was the character of the Man with No Name defined in the script, or was he somewhat of your devising?

Eastwood: I kind of devised it. I even picked out the costumes. I went into Mattsons', a sport shop up on Hollywood Boulevard here, and bought some black Levis and bleached them out, roughed them up. The boots, spurs and gun belts I had from *Rawhide*; the hat I got at a wardrobe place in Santa Monica. The little black cigars I bought in Beverly Hills.

Playboy: You don't smoke, do you?

Eastwood: No, I don't. I smoked the cigars only for those films. I didn't really like them, but they kept me in the right kind of humor. Kind of a fog.

Playboy: Did they make you sick?

Eastwood: No, they just put you in a pretty sour frame of mind. Those were pretty edgy cigars.

—Eastwood, interviewed by Arthur Knight and Gretchen McNeese for *Playboy*, Feb 1974

Q. You've said that in the original script, the Man with No Name shot off his mouth more than his gun.

A. The script was very expository, yeah. It was an outrageous story, and I thought there should be much more mystery to the person. I kept telling Sergio, "In a real A picture, you let the audience think along with the movie; in a B picture, you explain everything." That was my way of selling my point. For instance, there was a scene where he decides to save the woman and the child. She says, "Why are you doing this?" In the script he just goes on forever. He talks about his mother, all kinds of subplots come out of nowhere, and it goes on and on and on. I thought that was not essential, so I just rewrote the scene the night before we shot it.

Q. Okay, the woman asks, "Why are you doing this?" and he says....

A. "Because I knew someone like you once and there was nobody there to help."

Q. So you managed to express ten pages of dialogue in a single sentence.

A. We left it oblique and let the audience wonder: "Now wait a minute, what happened?" You try to let people reach into the story, find things in it, choice little items that they enjoy. It's like finding something you've worked and hunted for, and it's much more enjoyable than having some explanation slapped into your face like a wet fish.

—Eastwood, interviewed by Tim Cahill for *Rolling Stone*, 4 July 1985

I got on famously with Sergio Leone. To begin with, I knew no Italian and he knew no English. But we managed to communicate. And, of course, it was very agreeable filming in Spain. Sergio, by the way, while working always wears a ten-gallon hat, boots, and sideburns. I suppose it puts him in the right frame of mind.

—Eastwood, interviewed by Tony Toon for *Photoplay*, May 1969

Q. Is Leone an extremely classical director? Does he plan every shot with enormous care?

A. Leone isn't the most planned guy; he's very flexible.... Leone...has a very good concept of what he wants. He's very good with compositions; he has a nice eye. He's very good with humour, a very funny guy — his humour is very sardonic. He's not very good at directing actors, he's only as good as his actors are — but most directors aren't very good at directing actors. The most a director can usually do with actors is set up a nice atmosphere in which to work.

—Eastwood, interviewed by Patrick McGilligan for *Focus on Film*, Summer/Autumn 1976

Playboy: What's been your favorite role?

Eastwood: It would probably be *Dirty Harry* [1974, Don Siegel]. That's the type of thing I like to think I can do as well as, or maybe better than, the next guy. He's very good at his job, and his individualism pays off to some degree. What I liked about playing that character was that he becomes obsessed; he's got to take this killer [Andy Robinson] off the street.

—Eastwood, interviewed by Arthur Knight and Gretchen McNeese for *Playboy*, Feb 1974

Harry [Callahan] is a fantasy character. Nobody does what Harry does. He cuts right through the bull, tells his boss to shove it, does all the things people would like to do in real life, but can't.

Harry is a terribly honest character and I like that. He's not a political animal, and he doesn't understand political intrigue. He's like the moderator in *Network* [1976, Sidney Lumet] who goes on television and says the public has taken all the bull it can take and it won't take any more....

Harry thought that if a homicidal maniac could be sent back into the streets because of a technicality, there was something wrong with the law. The fact that you don't agree with every law in this country doesn't make you a fascist. Harry believed in a higher morality. [Eastwood also played Harry Callahan in *Magnum Force* (1973, Ted Post), *The Enforcer* (1975, James Fargo) and *The Dead Pool* (1988, Buddy Van Horn), and directed himself in that role in *Sudden Impact* (1983).]

—Eastwood, interviewed by Guy Flatley for *The New York Times*, 17 Dec 1976

Q. Is it fair to say that Dirty Harry and The Man with No Name are essentially the same character with many common qualities?

A. No. I don't think so. But they're both moved by passions. Dirty Harry is a man who is callous, seemingly hard on the surface. I think The Man with No Name is much more satiric....

—Eastwood, interviewed by Patrick McGilligan for *Focus on Film*, Summer/Autumn 1976

[Don Siegel] always worked well under pressure. He thought well on his feet, which is something I admired about him. If something wasn't working, or a set collapsed, or if something wasn't in the same direction he had planned, he could always make adjustments. And that's a very important factor for a director. I was impressed that he'd know what he wanted when he shot it. If he got something, he said, "Print that — we're moving over here now to shoot this." Some of these guys print ten takes; they don't know what it looks like, or they're not quite sure what their next setup is. Often he'd print just the one.

It wasn't that he had to have it on the first take, but he was always trying for that. He hated to see filmmakers using ten takes to warm up; that always seemed such a waste. He said, "I don't mind taking time rehearsing, but when we start shooting I like to at least try for it on the first take." It's like when you stand up to bat, you're not hoping to hit the third ball — you're hoping the first one that comes over, you can knock it over the fence....

He wasn't real heavy hands-on with actors. He'd make suggestions if he thought the actor wasn't performing right, but most of the time he depended on the ability of the people hired — as a lot of the old-time directors did....

He had a habit, whenever he was shooting a take, of crossing his fingers. A couple of times I was doing a scene and out of my peripheral vision I could see his hands there with the fingers crossed. I'd stop and walk over and uncross his fingers, and say, "Don't be superstitious, because you're making it seem like you don't think I'm going to get through this damned thing."

—Eastwood, in *Film Comment*, Sept/Oct 1991

I think I learned more about directing from [Don Siegel] than from anybody else. He taught me to put myself on the line. He shoots lean, and he shoots what he wants....

I learned that you have to trust your instincts. There's a moment when an actor has it, and he knows it. Behind the camera you can feel that moment even more clearly. And once you've got it, once you feel it, you can't second-guess yourself. [Eastwood also worked with Siegel on *Coogan's Bluff* (1968), *Two Mules for Sister Sara* (1970), *The Beguiled* (1971) and *Escape from Alcatraz* (1978).]

—Eastwood, interviewed by Tim Cahill for *Rolling Stone*, 4 July 1985

Samantha EGGAR [1939-]

Born: London, England. Studies at The Webber Douglas Academy and work on the London stage preceded her film debut in The Wild and the Willing (1962, Ralph Thomas). In 1965, she played Miranda Grey in William Wyler's The Collector:

Miranda comes into this situation as a young woman who has always been protected in her home and in her schools. Her adolescent approach and good family background make her trusting. In this cellar, where she is held captive [by Terence Stamp as Freddie Clegg], she matures.

—Eggar, interviewed by Murray Schumach for *The New York Times*, 7 June 1964

[Cary Grant] was so wonderfully generous about coaching me [in *Walk Don't Run* (1966, Charles Walters)]. "Sammy," he'd tell me, "if you want to make that line comic, first put your weight on your hips, then slowly swivel around and say it."

—Eggar, interviewed by Frank Rasky for *The Toronto Star*, 31 July 1976

Denholm ELLIOTT [1922-]

Born: London, England. Studies at The Royal Academy of Dramatic Art was interrupted by service in WWII. Following three years in a German prisoner of war camp, he made his stage debut in 1945. His film debut was Dear Mr. Prohack (1949, Thornton Freeland). In 1986, he played Mr. Emerson in James Ivory's adaptation of E.M. Forster's Room with a View:

[Emerson's] a Walt Whitman character, with a pantheistic vision of nature and of God. I love playing a role like that because I'm rather like that myself.

Mr. Emerson wouldn't see the disapproval in people's eyes — he's just saddened because people are so bound in by convention and fear that they can't enjoy life as he can.

—Elliott, interviewed by Nan Robertson for *The New York Times*, 20 July 1986

Edith EVANS [1888-1976]

Born: Pimlico, London, England. After making her stage debut in 1912, she appeared in two silent films in 1915-16 (beginning with A Welsh Singer — 1915, Henry Edwards). Disenchanted, she returned to the stage and did not make another film until 1948. In 1967, she played Mrs. Ross in Bryan Forbes' The Whisperers:

People always ask me the most ridiculous questions. They want to know, "How do you approach a role?" Well, I don't know. I approach it by first saying "yes," then getting on with the bloody thing. I read the script of *The Whisperers* and said yes in less than 24 hours. I don't do anything I don't like and this story moved me greatly. It is based on the theme of loneliness....

I'm a dreary person, really. Except when I act. Did you see me as the Mother Superior in *The Nun's Story* [1959, Fred Zinnemann] or as Miss Western in *Tom Jones* [1963, Tony Richardson]? I felt alive then. I look only for the life in any part. Then I ask, "Do I understand it? Could I be that person?" If I can, I do it. It was very daring for Bryan Forbes to send me a role of a derelict old lady rummaging about in garbage cans in a slum. But he knew I've always been daring....

—Evans, interviewed by Rex Reed for *The New York Times*, 30 July 1967

[Mrs. Ross] is NOT sad-sad. She is a touching old lady who hears voices no one else hears, whispers coming from the radiator, the bathroom pipe, anyplace. She doesn't know she is lonely. She has delusions of grandeur. A crook hides a bundle of stolen money in her cupboard and, thinking it is her inheritance, she talks about it too much for her own safety.

—Evans, interviewed for *The New York Daily News*, 23 July 1967

Madge EVANS [1909-1981]

Born: New York City. Work as a child model preceded her film debut in The Sign of the Cross (1914, William Farnum) in which she was one of the Christian children fed to the lions. In the 1930's she was part of the MGM stock company:

Q. Did you have a family feeling at MGM?

A. Yes; it was really a stock company. You're easier when you've worked with someone before; you're more relaxed. They know you, you know them.... There was no sense of caste. I think the only one that everybody stayed away from a little was Norma Shearer [Mrs. Irving Thalberg], but that was because she was the boss' wife, you know. Of course, we were all of us crazy about Jean Harlow. She was a lovely girl....

Q. An...interesting film you did on loan-out was *The Greeks Had a Word for Them* [1932, Lowell Sherman].

Q. What was Sherman like as a director?

A. I don't think he was much of a director, but he was a delightful man. I liked him enormously. He didn't take directing very seriously. That was a rather hectic picture, with him not taking the directing seriously, George Barnes falling madly in love with Joan [Blondell] so he could hardly see anybody but Joan. Ina Claire was very much in love with John Gilbert (this was before they were married) and every time she got into a costume that she thought she looked well in, particularly the bridal costume at the end of the film, she disappeared from the lot, because she had driven off to Metro to show John Gilbert how enchanting she looked. I went into that film very quickly, because Carole Lombard was supposed to do the part I played, but she became ill, and I replaced her.

—Evans, interviewed by Leonard Maltin for *Film Fan Monthly*, Dec 1972

Maurice EVANS [1901-1989]

Born: Dorchester, England. Work with The St. Pancras Theater Group in London and on the London stage preceded his film debut in White Cargo (1930, J.B. Williams). In 1968, he played Hutch in Roman Polanski's Rosemary's Baby:

Unlike most other directors, [Polanski] possessed an extraordinary knowledge of optics, normally the sole province of the director of photography. Much emphasis consequently was laid on camera and lighting tricks, which, though clever in themselves, did little to enhance the acting. It was also somewhat off-putting that, on the set, Polanski wore a cowboy outfit complete with six-shooter, which he twirled by its trigger guard while we were attempting to rehearse a difficult scene.

We very nearly had a serious falling out over one section of the script. It was an episode in which, as the character, "Hutch," talking incessantly, I was required to dish up a leg of lamb in the kitchen, carry it into the dining room, return to the kitchen for the vegetables, then back to the table with them — still talking. Now I had to carve the lamb for three persons, help them to the veg and sink into my chair precisely on cue as the dialogue ended. Polanski insisted that the action be continuous in what is known as a "tracking shot." In other words, as I moved back and forth, so did the camera. It was therefore up to me to time each move so exactly that the accompanying dialogue fitted the action to the second. Carving a leg of lamb, even at one's own table, is no mean accomplishment, but to do so by the numbers and at the same time to be a talkative master of gastronomy was a formidable challenge. A whole morning on camera, and six legs of lamb later, our whimsical director got the picture he wanted.

—Evans, in his *All This...and Evans Too* (Columbia, S.C.: University of South Carolina Press, 1987)

Tom EWELL [1909-]

Born: Yewell Tompkins in Owensboro, Kentucky. After dropping out of law school, he did a variety of jobs before starting an acting career in New York. He made his film debut in Adam's Rib (1949, George Cukor), and in 1955, co-

starred opposite Marilyn Monroe in Billy Wilder's The Seven Year Itch:

Marilyn didn't think she was any good. She suffered from a tremendous inferiority complex. It was very difficult for her to show up on a set. More difficult for her than for anyone I've ever worked with.

She wanted so desperately to be good that she found it hard to do even the smallest scene. She used to vomit before she went before the camera....

Jayne Mansfield was quite different. She was devoted entirely to her own publicity. We appeared together in *The Girl Can't Help It* [1956] for the director Frank Tashlin, who had a marvelous cartoonist's eye.

The studio was trying to create another Marilyn. I'll never forget the first day Jayne and I met, which was also the first day of shooting.

Jayne was wearing a dress which was too tight to walk in. Mickey Hargitay, who was married to her, had to carry her on to the set over his head like a suitcase! She was stiff as a board! He deposited her on the sound stage and she stood up like a shop window dummy! I'll never forget it.

She'd be looking over my shoulder in the middle of a scene. I assumed she was looking at Mickey. There was love in her eyes. Well, I snuck a glance around, and she was gazing into a full-length mirror! I couldn't believe it!

She watched herself throughout the shooting, watched herself acting....

I liked Jayne. She was sweet, devoted to her family and to animals. And yet, the stunts!

—Ewell, interviewed by Charles Higham for *Australian TV Times*; repr. in Higham's *Celebrity Circus* (New York: Delacorte Press, 1979)

F

Douglas FAIRBANKS [1883-1939]

Born: Douglas Elton Ulman in Denver, Colorado; father of Douglas Fairbanks, Jr. A stage career, including Broadway (from 1902), preceded his film debut in The Lamb (1915, Christy Cabanne). In 1920, he moved from light comedy to swashbuckling roles, typified by The Thief of Bagdad (1924, Raoul Walsh):

The reason that my biggest picture [*The Thief of Bagdad*] is a fantasy is because I believe that a beautiful fairy story is a story that everyone in the audience will feel is his own. The hero naturally starts off with great obstacles to be overcome. That is practically every man's story. Then the hero falls in love with a princess. This is also every man's dream story. He finds that in order to reach his desires he must be worthy and do more worthy things. This is what every man's spiritual side has meant at some period of his life. Then the hero goes out and surmounts innumerable barriers. He fights his way through fire; kills monsters of terrifying mien; climbs to almost impossible heights; resists seductive temptations and at the end receives the happiness he has earned, just as every man has thought of doing. We call it fantasy, but it symbolizes the very essence of life itself.

The Thief of Bagdad was very difficult to make because we had to give our story the semblance of reality and still preserve the spirit of the imaginative.

Q. Is your whole story laid in Bagdad?

A. No, it is laid in the human heart; in the Land of Fancy, where everything is beautiful and there are fairy princesses for all.

—Fairbanks, interviewed for *The Brooklyn Daily Eagle*, 9 Mar 1924

Douglas FAIRBANKS, Jr. [1909-]

Born: New York City. Son of Douglas Fairbanks, he made his film debut in Stephen Steps Out (1923, Joseph Henabery):

I have been both helped and handicapped by a famous father. He has given me a fine inheritance, but the situation has left me protected yet not protected. I feel as if a wall were around me.... When I first started in pictures they played me to look just like Dad. They were trading on his name and I resented that. I was never given credit for being an individual....

I don't look like him. I don't think like him. I love him devotedly, yet we are often constrained with each other.

—Fairbanks, interviewed by Eloise Bradley for *Photoplay Magazine*, Feb 1929

As soon as the documents were signed and sealed, Alex [Korda] and UA jointly announced his immediate production plans. The first film was to be...*Catherine the Great* [1934]. The famous German actress Elisabeth Bergner would play the young Catherine and she had insisted that her husband, Paul Czinner, be the director....

I looked nothing at all like the real [Czar] Peter III. Research reported that he was stubby with a puffy, pockmarked face. I wanted to create a real character in the part, but Dr. Czinner and Alex Korda insisted our story was essentially romantic. I took camera tests with white wig, plucked eyebrows, very white makeup, lipstick, and a few black beauty marks. My costumes were black or white satin suits, lace jabots, and knee britches. Had I not been so in love with my part and delighted with my good fortune in landing it, I might have been more objective and stubborn about my character, but was afraid I would be paid off and replaced. One of our electricians described me as "beautifully tarted up!" I agreed. When Korda saw the test he said I looked all right, but "far too young and pretty." The real Peter III of Russia was said to be rather feminine, but it was strictly against the censorship rules of that day to even hint at homosexuality. Thus I was ordered to defy the period and cultivate my mustache — well mascaraed....

Miss Bergner was charming to work with, full of special mannerisms and meticulously honed tricks of the trade. She timed her scenes to the second. To my young taste, her accented speech was too given to gooey baby talk. But, by God, she was *good*! She was technically almost unsurpassed....

Czinner directed too gently and sympathetically. It seemed he was somewhat frightened by his star-wife and the overall caliber of the cast. Therefore it sometimes became necessary for Alex to leave his producer's office, come down to the set, and take over as director. As such, he was first rate.

One evening early in 1937 I had a call from David Selznick in California. He announced that he was planning to remake the old classic *The Prisoner of Zenda* with Ronnie Colman playing the star dual role. He...offered me the part of Count Rupert of Hentzau — last played in the old silent film by Ramon Novarro.

It was clear that Selznick had chosen *The Prisoner of Zenda* as a thinly disguised reference to the Duke of Windsor's abdication and the approaching coronation of George VI in June.... I told [my father] about the offer and why I was resisting [the part was a supporting role]. He listened attentively. When I finished, he burst out with the conviction that I *had* to accept. Why? "Because not only is *The Prisoner of Zenda* one of the best romances written in a hundred years and always a success, but Rupert of Hentzau is probably one of the best villains ever written. He is witty, irresistible, and as sly as Iago...."

Before shooting began, there was some discussion about my appearance. In contrast to Ronnie I decided to have curly hair.... I tried shaving off my mustache, but then I looked too young in contrast to Ronnie, so that stayed put. The plan for costuming was that all the men were to be dolled up in the grandest of Balkan uniforms. However, I recalled my father telling me long before never to wear anything too distracting around the neck. A loud or large-figured tie always detracted from one's facial expressions. He also thought one should be as simple and in as much contrast to others as the situation allowed....

When I asked Cary [Grant] which part he intended to play [in *Gunga Din* (1939)], he answered, "Whichever one you don't want! I want us to be together in this so badly — I think the two of us, plus old [Victor] McLaglen as our top sergeant, McChesny, will make this more than just another big special." [Grant had invited Fairbanks to co-star.]

I have never so much as *heard* of another actor (usually considered a congenitally selfish breed) who proposed to a contemporary colleague, in some ways a rival, so unselfish a proposal. I later came to learn that such gestures were typical of Cary. He had always been most concerned with being involved in what he guessed would be a successful picture. If he proved right, he reckoned it could only rebound to his credit. I took this as a fine lesson. Even though I was more of a movie veteran than he, I had plenty more to learn. Since then, whenever possible I've tried to apply Cary's lesson to my own decisions. We finally settled the matter by tossing a coin! That was how I became "Sergeant Ballantyne," who wants to leave the Army for Miss [Joan] Fontaine, and Cary became the ebullient, funny cockney "Sergeant Cutter...."

George Stevens was quite unlike the conventional, overassertive director. He appeared always to stroll about with a lazy sailor's swagger instead of walking like other people. One's first impression was that he was vague, dreamy and inefficient, but actually this was an effective mask behind which his creative brain ticked at the speed of light. He confided his ideas in advance only to his cameraman, his scriptwriters, his first assistant, and his principal actors. His producers were often led to believe one thing when he really had something quite different in mind. He would look at you with a sort of dopey solemnity, only to break into a broad grin a moment later and call for a can of beer. He frankly tried to make his team feel they were his trusted partners rather than hired puppets.

—Fairbanks, in his *Salad Days* (New York: Doubleday & Co., 1988)

Peter FALK [1927-]

Born: New York City. Studies with Eva Le Gallienne in Westport, Connecticut, and at The Neighborhood Playhouse in N.Y., and work on the off-Broadway stage preceded his film debut in Wind Across the Everglades (1958, Nicholas Ray). In 1961, he played Joy Boy in Frank Capra's Pocketful of Miracles:

People are funny when convinced of the rightness of what they are saying. The guy in *Pocketful of Miracles* knew everybody else was wrong. Those kind of people are funny, especially when they are kind of dumb to begin with, which that guy was.

—Falk, interviewed by John C. Waugh for *The Christian Science Monitor*, 24 Oct 1962

During *Husbands* [1970, John Cassavetes], I was angry and frustrated because I didn't understand what was going on. I looked at John and said, "I'll work with you as an actor but never again as a director." He just laughed his ass off. After we finished, he read me the novelization and I got angry again. I said, "Why didn't you tell me these things?" It was amazingly specific. He kept you in the dark because he feared that if he articulated things clearly you might turn it into a cliché. What he wanted from you was yourself. He wanted to get some part of your feelings and emotions that were too complex and too varied to be reduced to words and then re-interpreted by you.

—Falk, quoted in *Film Comment*, May/June 1989

I was touched by this woman [Mabel Longhetti as played by Gena Rowlands in *A Woman Under the Influence* (1974, John Cassavetes)]. She was extremely moving to me. And the character of her husband, which I play, is funny — which is always good for me. He's funny, tho not too aware of what's going on. He's in over his head. He's very much in love with this woman and excited by her — he can have fun with her. But he doesn't quite know how to handle her.

There's something else about him that I like. He doesn't quit. He makes a mistake, and when he goes to fix it, he does it badly because he doesn't know quite how to do it. But there's a raw need and a raw power to get it done, and he's going to do it.

Working for John is harder than anything else I do...harder than acting in anyone else's pictures because he established a standard of reality or immediacy or spontaneity that is different from anywhere else. With other directors you can get away with very fine acting, but if you try to put that into John's pictures, it sticks out like a sore thumb — you know it just won't work. So you have to try to be effective without relying on any of those technical skills that you've acquired over the years.

—Falk, interviewed by Ben Falke for *The Chicago Tribune Magazine*, 1 Dec 1974

I don't know if you can *like* these guys [Falk as Jewish Mikey and John Cassavetes as Italian Nicky in *Mikey and Nicky* (1976, Elaine May)]. In a way, Mikey is just a worthless punk; yet, there is a residue of humanity there. I'm trying to make a connection, and Nicky is the one friend I have. An evening with Nicky is more fun than an evening with my wife. Nicky can make me laugh.

He humiliates me, and my proper response to that is rage. In real life, I can identify with being made a joke of. Not so much now, since I've become a big actor and all that, but I haven't lost the memory of what it's like when somebody tries to make me feel like I'm nothing. Nobody wants to be made a joke of, especially when that joke is made by a friend. Every friendship, every closeness, contains the potential for great rivalry.

What Nicky and I share is a past. We've grown up on the street together, knocked off grocery stores together, made deals together. We share the triumph of survival. After a certain age, you can't make new friendships like that; there is no past to share....

The toughest thing in the making of a movie is to find the right word to say to an actor. It's easy enough for a director to say "Faster" or "Slower" or "I don't believe you're doing it right," but to hit that precise phrase an actor will respond to...that's tough. The thing about Elaine is that if she can't find the phrase, she won't say anything. For that, I love her.

—Falk, interviewed by Guy Flatley for *The New York Times*, 17 Dec 1976

Elaine's known as a witty person with a satirical turn of mind, but I think what separates her from other people who are funny, the reason she has her own niche, is that she's susceptible to what is touching in people and she's looking for what is reachable in them, for what moves her. And she's always fair to her characters. She never "loads" them; in *Mikey and Nicky* everybody has two sides because she's touched by both sides.

—Falk, interviewed by D.D. Ryan for *Interview*, Mar 1977

Charles FARRELL [1901-1990]

Born: Onset Bay, Massachusetts. Studies at Boston University and work on the stage preceded his film debut as an extra in The Cheat (1923, George Fitzmaurice). He co-starred with Janet Gaynor in eight films beginning with Seventh Heaven (1927, Frank Borzage):

Both Janet and I recognize that our double-harness in pictures has unquestionably done an infinite amount of harm to me. For no two players can receive equally important roles in picture after picture. It was my misfortune to get the lesser roles — to be, after a fashion, the sacrifice to the startling charm, to the great genius that are Janet's....

Her roles were tailored for her — they were wistful, romantic — suitable to her delicate and individual talent....

But I, who had made my success in vital character parts, accepted dressed-up roles, lacking in stamina and vitality — roles that gave me nothing to do. The sad part of it is that these are the most difficult assignments, for they rarely have the redeeming virtues of telling scenes or even memorable moments.

Instead of building gradually to a climax of achievement, I found myself departing with each picture from the high standard of Chico [in *Seventh Heaven*]. I waited with growing desperation for one good picture that might take its place with *Seventh Heaven* — just one role that would help me regain lost ground....

Certainly I couldn't expect Janet to risk one bit of her prestige for me. She had worked too long and too hard for her position — no one knows that better than I do. For there exists between us not only a brother-and-sister affection, but the admiring friendship of two people who have gone through the mill together.... We have always played square with each other.

A recent incident is a case in point. When the studio was choosing the all-star cast for *State Fair* [1933, Henry King], Janet felt that it would detract from the strength of the picture if we were cast opposite each other — that it would kill the suspense in the plot. She told the studio executives so and offered to step out of the cast if they wanted me in it.... I understood her viewpoint and agreed with her. But I stepped out, instead. Lew Ayres got the part.... I want to do roles that have the flavor of a younger edition of Will Rogers — characters that are romantic in essence, but vital enough to be human, according to modern standards. [Farrell and Gaynor also worked together on *Street Angel* (1928, Frank Borzage), *Lucky Star* (1929, Frank Borzage), *Sunny Side Up* (1929, David Butler), *High Society Blues* (1930, David Butler), *Merely Mary Ann* (1931, Henry King), *Tess of the Storm Country* (1932, Alfred Santell) and *Change of Heart* (1934, John G. Blystone).]

—Farrell, interviewed by Sonia Lee for *Movie Classic*, Feb 1933

Glenda FARRELL [1904-1971]

Born: Enid, Oklahoma. On stage from age 7, she made her film debut in Little Caesar (1931, Mervyn LeRoy). In 1933, she played Florence Dempsey in Michael Curtiz' The Mystery of the Wax Museum:

Q. Is it true that the lighting of the sets [of *Mystery of the Wax Museum*] was so intense that it constantly liquidated the wax dummies?

A. Well, that's right. The figures and the people! In the days when that was made, they were still using klieg lights, and it was done in color which is, of course, much more intense and hot than black-and-white. So we were *all* almost melted! The wax figures did melt, but they put them back together again. Actually, it was such a hot set that it bothered the actors' eyes....

Q. As a director, how was Michael Curtiz?

A. He was very exacting. I liked him very much; we got along fine. But he worked people to death. We all collapsed one night on *Wax Museum*. He worked us for 23 hours! We all had hysterics and collapsed! They had to let us have the next day off to stay in bed. We didn't have union rules then.... [Farrell also worked on Curtiz's *The Keyhole* (1933) and *Little Big Shot* (1935).]

—Farrell, interviewed by Scott MacQueen for *Photon* #20, 1971

Warners never made you feel you were just a member of the cast. They might star you in one movie — I *starred* with Paul Muni in *Hi, Nellie* [1934, Mervyn LeRoy] — and give you a bit part in the next. I remember thinking, "Oh, God, I hope it's a small part this time, so I can get some rest." So you weren't Kay Francis. You were still well paid, and you didn't get a star complex.

We were a very close group — [James] Cagney, [Guy] Kibbee, Hugh Herbert, Aline MacMahon, Dick Powell and June Blondell. Of course, Bette [Davis] was *always* an outsider.

—Farrell, interviewed by Guy Flatley for *The New York Times*, 2 Feb 1969

Mia FARROW [1946-]

Born: Maria Farrow in Los Angeles, to director John Farrow [1904-1963] and actress Maureen O'Sullivan. Although she made her film debut in one of her father's films (John Paul Jones, 1959), her career was established on Broadway and TV before her starring role in Rosemary's Baby (1968, Roman Polanski):

I got on terrifically well with Roman Polanski. I thought at the beginning, "Well, he seems to spend all his time fiddling with little details about the set, without worrying about me!" But then I understood that he would stop me if I went wrong, and that he was leaving me alone because I was doing O.K. He has a marvelous, childlike enthusiasm and fantastic knowhow. And he jazzed everybody. We were on the set next to *Bonanza*, and he was leaping around all excited at this, wearing a holster and practicing his draw.

You know that scene where I'm pregnant and I have to cross Fifth Avenue in a daze? We didn't organize the traffic at all. We just *did* it. Roman said, "Nobody's going to hit a pregnant lady, not on Fifth Avenue."

—Farrow, interviewed by Mark Shivas for *The New York Times*, 23 June 1968

Tina [Vitale in *Broadway Danny Rose* (1984, Woody Allen)] was too different for me and I was scared — until I shot the first day. Then I realized I could do it. There was a woman in a restaurant we go to, and I had told Woody I wanted to play someone like her. I knew women like her over the years and so did Woody. We discussed the role before shooting and arrived at the look and voice....

I enjoy playing characters. Many people prefer being personalities. I'm not like that. I just feel more at home acting a character.

[The role of Hannah in *Hannah and Her Sisters* (1986, Woody Allen)] was hard, because it was subtle — not flamboyant like Tina or like the other two sisters [played by Barbara Hershey and Dianne Wiest]. Their parts were clearly defined. In this case, we found the character as we went along, rather than having it at the start.

—Farrow, interviewed by Georgia A. Brown for *American Film*, Mar 1987

I love working with [Woody Allen]. It's terrific because he's so sure of himself and how it ought to be — what's right, what's true. It makes it so much easier to contribute because you know the thrust of where you should be going with something. He gives me confidence. I need a little extra, anyway, and just knowing I'm in his capable hands is *so* supportive. [Farrow has also worked with Allen on *A Midsummer Night's Sex Comedy* (1982), *Zelig* (1983), *The Purple Rose of Cairo* (1985), *Radio Days* (1986), *September* (1987), *Another Woman* (1988), *New York Stories* (1989), *Crimes and Misdemeanors* (1989) and *Alice* (1990) and *Shadows and Fog* (1992).]

—Farrow, interviewed by Lindsy Van Gelder for *The New York Daily News Magazine*, 3 Mar 1985

Louise FAZENDA [1895-1962]

Born: Lafayette, Indiana. Early in her career, she worked as a Sennett Bathing Beauty:

[Bathing Beauty, Vivian Edwards] took me inside and told Mr. Sennett, "This kid needs a job." He looked me over sort of dubiously and said, "Well, I need a girl who can do stunts. Are you athletic?" I gulped and nodded. He told me I'd have to wear bathing suits — short, revealing ones. I gulped again and nodded again. He said, "If you can be back here with one at 9 tomorrow morning, I'll put you to work as a Bathing Beauty. The salary is three dollars a day...."

[In making his films] all Sennett had in mind was to add a new touch to the old vaudeville formula of comedy, in which a pretty girl was always the foil for the comic. He couldn't change the formula, because there were only six or seven different comedy plots, so he changed the girl's costume — to a flouncy bathing suit. And after a while he got the idea of introducing whole bevies of girls in flouncy bathing suits, as a sort of chorus for the comics.

—Fazenda, interviewed by Roger Carroll for *Motion Picture*, July 1942

Sally FIELD
[1946-]

Born: Pasadena, California. Studies at The Actors Studio in N.Y. and work on TV preceded her film debut in The Way West (1967, Andrew V. McLaglen). In 1977, she starred opposite Burt Reynolds in Hal Needham's Smokey and the Bandit:

I decided to take a calculated risk to do it because I knew what was going to happen to me. *Sybil* [made for TV — 1976, Daniel Petrie] hadn't been seen yet, but already the reaction was "What interesting work — she seems able to act, but she's so *ugly*. I don't think we could ever hire this girl — she's not funny, she's grim, she's very grim."

I knew I'd have to overcome that so I could get around to the kind of work I wanted to be doing. You always have to fight being pigeonholed by your last job. Burt [Reynolds] was a movie star and a sex symbol, and up to that point, I was considered about as sexy as an ingrown toenail. I thought if I was sitting across from Burt Reynolds and he looks at me and thinks I'm attractive, maybe *they'll* think I'm attractive. They'll buy it off him, so that's solely and completely why I did it.

—Field, interviewed by Darrah Meeley for *Screen Actor*, Fall 1986

Norma Rae [in *Norma Rae* (1979, Martin Ritt)] is a woman of very little education, and she really doesn't find any hope in her life at the beginning of the film. She is in a predicament where she has two children. She has no support, she has no man, and in the process of the film she grows up and learns to fight for herself, to fight for her children. It's a very mature kind of growing up. It doesn't happen through sexual events. Also, through her relationships with two men [Ron Liebman and Beau Bridges], she learns the difference between love and friendship.

—Field, interviewed for *International Photographer*, Apr 1979

Q. In the climactic scene of *Norma Rae*, when you hold up the union sign, I understand that you were using a special song to create that moment. Can you explain?

A. Part of what the Actors Studio teaches you is how to open emotional doors that you don't know are there. People who've studied acting know this. One of the really important ways is music. It helps me concentrate. I make little tapes for myself in various movies when I need to plug into an emotion.

For *Norma Rae*, I found this song that moved me. When you look at it now, it's obvious why. But at that time, I quite honestly didn't know that I was acting out something directly correlated with my own working life. It was a George Benson song called *The Greatest Love of All*. It says, "No matter what they take away from me/they can't take away my dignity." I kept hearing that song and singing it to myself. As I stood up there to do that scene, I would even beat on my leg. I kept saying, "No matter what they take away from me, they *can't* take away my *dignity*."

—Field, interviewed by Darrah Meeley for *Screen Actor*, Fall 1986

[In *Norma Rae*] all I ever worked for, was fighting for, was my own dignity, Norma's dignity, my own children, Norma's children, and you become very driven, obsessed. It's a story about a woman who learns to grow up in a way, to be more sophisticated in her anger.

—Field, interviewed by David Sheehan for *Oscar Preview*, 12 Apr 1980

Q. You said that with *Norma Rae* you had to take a poker to your heart and open up all the anger, but for Edna in *Places in the Heart* [1984, Robert Benton] you started working through love. Can you explain that?

A. The nature of the two women was so different, even though when you look at them, they were both fighters, both Southern. But Norma was compelled to reach outside herself out of anger, whereas Edna was compelled to reach outside herself simply out of love. She was not an angry person. I doubt that she ever felt very much anger in her life. She felt frightened, she felt determined, but she was never angry. Anger is such a compelling emotion. It's so easy to use anger to shoot yourself through the scene or shoot yourself through life. But to be compelled out of love is something I had never thought about, and it's so difficult to show that. It's also difficult to keep that from being sentimental, which you don't want to do....

The first part of the film was specifically difficult, because it was about Edna's containment — she was embarrassed to show her emotions....

At the beginning when she's mourning for the loss of her husband, you can't be crying all the way through that — I mean, that's boring. So I figured she had to be all cried out, drained — and there's no way to play that but to *be* drained. So the three weeks we spent shooting various scenes having to do with the death of her husband, I just cried all day long. Lindsay [Crouse], particularly, knew what I was doing, but some of them thought I had just lost my mind. Lindsay would sit beside me, in character as my sister Margaret, and say, "Oh sis, oh sis," which would bring another flood of tears. So I'd just cry some more, so that when we did the scene, I would just *be* the scene. I was tired of crying, I was emotional, swollen, too tired to cry.

—Field, interviewed by Darrah Meeley for *Screen Actor*, Fall 1986

W.C. FIELDS [1880-1946]

Born: William Claude Dukenfield in Philadelphia. Work touring the U.S. and Europe as a comedy juggler preceded his debut with The Ziegfeld Follies in 1915, the year of his first short film, Pool Sharks (Ed Middleton) based on his successful vaudeville act. In 1925, he played Professor Eustace McGargle in D.W. Griffith's Sally of the Sawdust:

Movie directors, as a whole, think of comedy in terms of stage comedy with the words left out. Griffith doesn't. Chaplin doesn't. I'm convinced the others do. They recognize comedy through their ears, not through their eyes....

Sally of the Sawdust is simply the screen version of *Poppy*, the musical comedy I played last season. I've been praised for my movie work but the credit should go to Mr. Griffith.... He is one of the greatest directors because he doesn't arbitrarily direct but lets the player feel his way through a scene. He sits by and watches and encourages. He has you do the scene over, two or three times to strengthen its weak points. The photographed one, tho, is the one you instinctively worked out, polished off. I'm doing another picture under Griffith, *That Royle Girl* [1925]. I think it is invaluable to work under him.

—Fields, interviewed by Ruth Waterbury for *Photoplay Magazine*, Oct 1925

I've been playing Micawber [in *David Copperfield* (1935, George Cukor)] all my life, under a lot of different names, and never knew it. He's the kind of a guy who is always expecting something to turn up to help him out of his present difficulties, and is always having difficulties waiting for something to turn up....

Of course, this is the first time in my life I ever played a real "character" part. At first, I always wrote my own stuff, and since I've been in pictures, I've always gone over my dialogue and made it fit my style. At first I was a little wary about playing Micawber, but as soon as I got into the part, I knew it was made to order.

—Fields, interviewed for the press book for *David Copperfield* (MGM, 1935)

Peter FINCH [1916-1977]

Born: Frederick George Peter Ingle Finch in London, England; taken to Australia at age of 10. Work on the Australian stage preceded his film debut in the unreleased Magic Shoes (1935). In the 1940's, he became a major radio actor in Australia and formed his own theatre company (The Mercury, in homage to Orson Welles). In 1948, he moved to London and got a great deal of work thanks to Laurence Olivier whom he'd met in Australia while The Old Vic Company was touring. He then made his British film debut in an episode of Train of Events (1949, Basil Dearden); that same year he appeared in Harry Watt's Eureka Stockade:

I like a performance to be as simple as possible — and for something to show from the inside. Sometimes it just doesn't happen. But in theory that's the way I like to work. Some people say that it's too gentle, that I ought to have a little bit more panache. And certainly it can be a dangerous trap — you can get too introspective. Harry Watt pointed that out to me, actually, way back when we were making *Eureka Stockade*. Because, in the Mercury group, we'd all been concentrating on working from the inside. So consequently in acting for the film, this carried over. One day I was doing a scene, thinking beautiful thoughts — marvelous things were going on inside me — and absolutely nothing was showing on the outside. And Harry Watt came up to me and said, "Would you mind breathing or something now and then, just so we can tell you're alive."

—Finch, interviewed by Gordon Gow for *Films & Filming*, Aug 1970

Jack Clayton, who I recently worked with on *The Pumpkin Eater* [1964], has his own absolutely vivid style as a director, which you could see after only 3 days' work. One was fascinated to know how that style operated, while at the same time he is really allowing your individual ideas a great freedom. But although on the surface Jack is very calm, I think he suffers enormously inside from a nervous tension — but he never lets anybody see this.

—Finch, interviewed for *Films & Filming*, June 1964

Bob [Aldrich] has a marvelous, sardonic attitude toward films. It's the baroque thing. Not realistic at all. He has a wonderful sense of irony. Sometimes he goes too far — but he knows that. I think he does it deliberately in order to say, as it were, to the public: "Look, I've gone too far. How *about* that!" [*The Legend of Lylah Clare* (1967)] is a big put-on about Hollywood. I play a corny director and Kim [Novak] plays a sort of manufactured star, and I think it's very funny. Where it failed, I suppose, was in the very corny bits, in the scenes where I was directing her, and also in her manner and in mine. Perhaps Bob went so far this time that people couldn't tell where the put-on stopped and all the overboard melodrama began. We're all terrible Gothic monsters in it. Great fun.

—Finch, interviewed by Gordon Gow for *Films & Filming*, Aug 1970

Actually, another actor had started in [*Sunday, Bloody Sunday* (1971)] — Ian Bannen — but he got nervous about it and backed out. John Schlesinger, the director, had thought of me first, but I was doing something else at the time.... I don't claim an awful lot on *Sunday, Bloody Sunday* because it was so beautifully written [by Penelope Gilliatt]. My character's tenderness; his feelings for humanity; his kind of sadness and loneliness at the end. It was all there, I just had to *do* it.

—Finch, interviewed by David Galligan for *The Advocate/Liberation Publications, Inc.*, 23 Mar 1977

[Dr. Daniel Hirsh] in *Bloody Sunday* has none of Wilde's flamboyance. But there is a basic similarity, because in both cases one is dealing fundamentally with love. I'd find it very difficult to play a homosexual in a knockabout sort of film. But I believe that love is indivisible. Wilde was full of love; there was so much in his writings to indicate that. So there [in *The Trials of Oscar Wilde* (1960, Ken Hughes)] and again now [in *Sunday, Bloody Sunday*], I didn't start off by thinking to myself, "I'm playing a homosexual!" I thought of love and tenderness.

This character is a doctor. An ordinary sensible man. Jewish, sensitive, very concerned about other people. Therefore he likes his work and he's good at it. He's not in the least self-pitying. He accepts the fact that he's a homosexual, and has no hangups about that. He's adjusted.

—Finch, interviewed by Gordon Gow for *Films & Filming*, Aug 1970

Every role you pick up looks marvelous, but then the fear sets in, and 10 minutes later they all become challenging and different. This role [Howard Beal in *Network* (1976, Sidney Lumet)] I found particularly difficult. Paddy Chayefsky and I sat in this place [Polo Lounge of the Beverly Hills Hotel] 'til 4 a.m. saying that if my character were a raving lunatic and nothing more, then he would be a bore. There had to be a suggestion that he was eminently sane underneath the madness, and that he did, in fact, have a kind of revelation. That's a very thin edge to play.

—Finch, interviewed by David Galligan for *The Advocate/Liberation Publications, Inc.*, 23 Mar 1977

Albert FINNEY [1936-]

Born: Salford, England. A scholarship student at The Royal Academy of Dramatic Art, he joined The Birmingham Repertory Company after graduation and made his stage debut in 1956 as Brutus in Julius Caesar. Following his film debut in a minor role in The Entertainer (1960, Tony Richardson), he became the quintessential British antihero, Arthur Seaton, in Karel Reisz's Saturday Night and Sunday Morning (1960):

I think Karel is very good with actors; he's very interested in the actors creating a character and not just relying on personality; he's good at encouraging actors to explore the characterization, and I think that's the kind of acting I'm interested in.

Q. Can you give me an example of what he does with actors that makes him better to work with than other directors?

A. When I commit myself to an interpretation or to a way of doing things, I like to believe that it's because I think that's absolutely the way to do it. I like to be convinced that that's the way it should be done. And I think Karel is similar. You know, very hesitant at first, but once he feels that's the way it should be done, doing it that way. We have similar temperaments in that respect.

Q. Did you find it easy acting in front of film cameras?

A. The process of acting, inside oneself, is the same. The manifestation of it is very different. What was marvelous for me at that stage, very exciting, was to work in the Raleigh factory, where certain scenes were shot. The reality of working the lathe, as an actor who'd just worked in the theater for four years before that, and trained for the theater the two years before these four, I found very exciting. When I was being photographed working at the lathe, then I could absolutely concentrate on what the character was supposed to do. There was no cheating involved, you know.

—Finney, interviewed by Ronald Bryden for BBC-2; pub. in *The Listener*, 24 Aug 1967

[*Tom Jones* (1963, Tony Richardson)] is a bizarre film. I don't feel involved. How can I be involved? Consider the book. It was written before Freud and it shows it. There's no stripping off of detail to get at the character. Now, what happens with Tom? Nothing. Everything happens *to* him. He's good-looking and nice and dashing, but what else is there? Really, it's a picture for puppets, a director's picture, all very bitty. How can you give a performance when you are one of 30 people at a stag hunt?....

Richardson has a belief that spontaneity is all. He likes things just to happen. Now, I want preparations to make everything work out so that it *looks* like an accident. If you're doing a scene well, you need more preparation, not less. I like to walk around and around the swimming pool before I dive in. In this film, I've been doing nothing but diving.

—Finney, interviewed by Donald W. LaBadie for *Show*, June 1963

Audrey [Hepburn] and I...got on immediately. After the first day's rehearsals [on *Two for the Road* (1967, Stanley Donen)], I could tell that the relationship would work out wonderfully. Either the chemistry is there, or it isn't. I find I can have very good rapport with an actress I am working with, but occasionally there's an absolute attraction. That happened with Audrey. Doing a scene with her, my mind knew I was acting but my heart didn't, and my body certainly didn't! Performing with Audrey was quite disturbing, actually. Playing a love scene with a woman as sexy as Audrey, you sometimes get to the edge where make-believe and reality are blurred. All that staring into each other's eyes — you pick up vibes that are decidedly not fantasy.... Working together was like a well-organized tennis game. I'd throw up a ball and she'd throw up a ball to match.

—Finney, quoted in *Audrey: The Life of Audrey Hepburn* by Charles Higham (New York: MaMillan, 1984)

According to the records [Hercule] Poirot is precisely five feet four inches tall. He has an egg-shaped head which he carries a little to the left on not too robust shoulders. He wears black patent shoes although in recent years he gave up carrying a cane, having recovered from the injury that made him limp back in 1920. His moustaches are waxed ferociously into points at the end and he uses a certain "tonic," not a "dye," to keep his hair perennially young looking.

The only other Poirot I have ever met was Charles Laughton, who introduced me to Agatha Christie when he played the Belgian detective on the stage. Being portly himself, Laughton was the right shape for the role, but in order to get the short, solid look I needed as Agatha Christie's elder statesman of criminologists [in *Murder on the Orient Express* (1974, Sidney Lumet)], I wore body padding, a T-shirt draped with cotton wool. I also had to have padded thighs to make me look wide so that my own height appeared less.

Facially the transformation was achieved with a false nose...and padded cheeks to achieve the egg-shaped look....

I have thought myself into him as an Edwardian. The story of *Murder on the Orient Express* is set in 1935, but Poirot made his first appearance in literature...as far back as 1920 so that the early years of the century must have had a lasting effect on his mentality.... The psychology of a murderer was more important to him than his fingerprints. He is obviously a great respector of law and order both in his work as a detective and in his private life as a neat, dapper, tidy man who would arrange all his personal belongings in perfect order before donning his pajamas, his hair net and his moustache protector, even in the temporary "bedquarters" of a wagon-lit on the Orient Express.

—Finney, interviewed for the press release for *Murder on the Orient Express* (Paramount Pictures, 1974)

The most elusive thing about film acting is giving it the breath of life. The theater is a long-distance event. You're on stage for two and a half or three hours, and the whole evening won't be one fantastic flight into the unknown. But with luck there'll be bits and passages during the evening where you really feel you've taken off. In screen acting you're doing shorter bits, so it's harder to take off. But it can happen. Working with Diane

Keaton [on *Shoot the Moon* (1981, Alan Parker)] was stimulating in this respect. Diane has a wonderful sense of spontaneity. Since I've been theatrically trained, I tend to set a performance. Once we've agreed how a theme should be played, I try and get as close to that on every take. With Diane on the other hand, if something new drifted through her mind during the third or fourth take she would try it. I would tend to censor it out. But Diane would just include everything in. And that seems to me to be the correct approach to film acting, because you can always do it again. Diane's acting has a very strong sense of the present tense. That's the most important thing in doing film.

—Finney, interviewed by Stephen Farber for *The New York Times*, 26 July 81

[In *The Dresser* (1983, Peter Yates)] I felt it was crucial not to make Sir too decrepit or far gone, to give him a touch of buried authority. I'm trying to suggest that he is a man who has flashes of greatness: that, *in extremis*, his own life coincides with Lear's and he reaches for something beyond his normal range.

—Finney, interviewed by Michael Billington for *The New York Times*, 26 June 1983

The whole Mexican experience of doing [*Under the Volcano* (1984, John Huston)] is not repeatable in my lifetime. I'm not saying I won't do another film in Mexico, but this subject, this experience, these circumstances at this time are not repeatable. One wants to relish all that, as well as the work. And, of course, it all feeds the work. So in this part, I find myself having a tequila; I had never really drunk tequila before. I'd been to Mexico before, but I never drink tequila in London or Spain. So suddenly I tried one or two kinds of tequila and mescal, just for the flavor. So that one is mildly — *mildly* — sort of savoring what the Consul *seriously* put himself through. It's not that they, or it, help; but they might help. One of the jobs is that [as an actor] you're going somewhere that's unfamiliar to you. You're trying to get yourself into unfamiliar territory in your imagination. So you help prepare the ground so you *might* get an idea you never had before. There's no guarantee. It's not to be relied on. But it might help....

Where the book [Malcolm Lowry's *Under the Volcano*] has helped me is to fill in the internal life, the subtext, the thoughts that go through my mind above and beyond what one says. Because often in life, you don't think of those things, or about what you say; you say what you say. A phrase may come out, a line may come out, but the general feeling behind it is often, in life, a sort of nonspecific area that you're preoccupied with, from which lines come out. So I thought the novel was important to me to fill in that sort of interior thought pattern. One does this anyway as an actor; that's one of the things that you're *supposed* to do. I mean, that's what one *does*: invest the undercurrent with all kinds of thoughts that may be applicable to the situation the character is in at any time. But it helped to have the novel.

The big problem as you get older is to retain the lack of self-consciousness, to retain a kind of child in your work, to be open. One of the things I love about John [Huston] is that it's your own total responsibility. John just says, "Well, show me." John thinks if he's cast it right, if the actor's got some degree of talent, he doesn't need to direct. He doesn't direct. He won't direct. In other words, he doesn't direct *a lot* — seemingly. If you say to John before a scene, "Would it be a good idea if...," he'll say, "Show me." And then you show him, and he says, "Well, maybe." So John likes to see you offer something. And then he will cajole it, nudge it, bully it, or just say, "A little less oil and vinegar — a little more lemon." Or he may say nothing. If you don't know John, you may say, "Well, he isn't giving me any direction." But when you get to know him a bit, you know that when he doesn't say anything, he's happy. [Finney also worked with Huston on *Annie* (1982).]

—Finney, interviewed by Pete Hamill for *American Film*, July/Aug 1984

Peter FIRTH [1953-]

Born: Bradford, England. High school dramatics and work on TV preceded his 1973 stage debut as Alan Strang in Equus. He made his film debut that same year in Franco Zeffirelli's Brother Sun, Sister Moon. He played Alan Strang again on Broadway, then reprised his role in Sidney Lumet's 1977 film version:

I was so instilled in *Equus*, I mean I'd been doing it so long, I knew all the different levels, I knew what came where, and I had it with me; I had it slung 'round my waist all the time.

We rehearsed in sequence even though we didn't shoot that way, and the way we shot, all the stuff that's done with the boy before he meets the psychiatrist we did before Richard [Burton] came to shoot. So, it's perfect, you see? Because he hadn't come into the story yet.

I didn't really have to pull down for the camera — I've done films before — and it's just instinctive: you know it's a camera and not an audience, you know the camera is not giving off what an audience gives off, but it does represent an audience, after all.

When we started rehearsing the play in London, we used film techniques. I certainly did. I used in my head the idea of cuts, film cuts, shifting attention from one area of the stage to another....

Mostly [Sidney Lumet] left me alone — we didn't talk about the character much, he wanted me to give him the same person I'd done on stage. But I suspect tricks. I didn't spot them when they were happening, but I suspect them.

He got results, you see, and I don't think that comes out of just leaving actors alone. Actors left alone aren't very good. So I think he's got something going on that's very clever.

—Firth, interviewed by Tom Topor for *The New York Post*, 15 Oct 1977

Alan worships a horse, Equus. To him, the horse was a god. It made more sense to him than an abstract figure in the clouds. To me, the underlying theme of the play is that we choose our own gods. Alan's, of course, is an extreme case. He went too far in his worship.

—Firth, interviewed by Ann Guarino for *The New York Daily News*, 14 Oct 1977

What Roman [Polanski, on *Tess* (1980)] most enjoyed was playing all the parts himself, so about three seconds into every take he'd call, "Cut" and then line us all up behind the camera while he leapt around playing all the parts quite appallingly. He's dreadful: totally self-obsessed, loony, very funny, unable to sustain a line of thought let alone a character for more than ten seconds, so from hour to hour you have no real idea of who you are supposed to be playing.

He sees life as a series of props for making films; actors are herded around like inconvenient cattle.

—Firth, interviewed by Sheridan Morley for *The Times*, 12 Mar 1981

Barry FITZGERALD [1888-1961]

Born: William Shields in Dublin, Ireland. While working with The Abbey Players (from 1915), he made his film debut in 1929 when their production of Juno and the Paycock was filmed by Alfred Hitchcock. He made his first American film in 1936; in 1944, he played Father Fitzgibbon in Leo McCarey's Going My Way:

All the parts I've played are patterned on someone I've seen and studied. Father Fitzgibbon is a composite of several priests I knew in Ireland. I'm not a Catholic but I loved the part as I think the kind of man represented by Father Fitzgibbon is more closely a true picture of a priest than the general idea.

—Fitzgerald, interviewed by Perry Glendon in an unsourced, undated article in the clipping file at The New York Public Library for the Performing Arts

The role of Father Fitzgibbon was the most satisfying part I ever played, and one of the easiest.... The warm and human qualities of the part were really what made me like it so much. Father Fitzgibbon mixed a fundamental kindness with the irascible temper of an elderly man....

Bing Crosby was just as relaxing to work with as his singing would suggest.

—Fitzgerald, in *The Saturday Evening Post*, 29 Nov 1947

Geraldine FITZGERALD [1914-]

Born: Dublin, Ireland. Trained for the stage, she made her film debut in the British feature, Turn of the Tide (1935, Norman Walker). Her Broadway debut opposite Orson Welles in the 1938 production of Shaw's Heartbreak House led to a contract with Warner Brothers and her role as Ann King in Edmund Goulding's Dark Victory (1939):

We used to sit around [the set of *Dark Victory*] and say, "I don't think it's going to work." A great deal was improvised, and Edmund Goulding...rewrote much of it. In fact he invented my whole character — she was not in the original stage play — as a kind of Greek chorus for the dying heroine so she wouldn't have to be complaining a lot. Do you recall the famous scene where Bette and I are gardening and we both suddenly realize that her death is imminent? Mr. Goulding said, "What would you do in real life under these circumstances?" The thought of death frightened me, so I said I'd probably run away. He told me to do just that; I did, and it's in the movie.

Q: Was Bette Davis difficult to work with?

A: Never! Well, she *could* be with directors, but only when she believed in something. I recall when it came time in *Dark Victory* for her to mount those stairs and die quietly in her bedroom, she asked Mr. Goulding, "Well, Eddie, am I going to act this or is Max?" (She was referring to Max Steiner, Warner Brothers' prolific composer of background music in those days.) She played fair with her fellow actors, never tried to turn your face away from the camera as many did. Bette's a very high-principled New Englander; she would not have thought such behavior a moral thing to do. And she knew it would be better for the film if everyone was in there pitching.

—Fitzgerald, interviewed by Doug McLelland for *After Dark*, Feb 1976

We all hated doing [*Wuthering Heights* (1939)] at the time because William Wyler, the director, was a total perfectionist and he used to make us do everything 50 times. He had no idea about how to treat actors so we were always feeling very badly about ourselves. He would ask us to do a scene and when we finished he would say, "That was awful, do it again." He would sit under the camera reading a newspaper, occasionally looking over the top of it while we did it again and again and again and again. Then after about an hour he would say, "No, it's all awful, the best thing to do would be what you did first, which was the first of a bad lot." And then we would say, "Well, we don't remember what we did...."

However, when we finally saw what he had achieved we all forgave him because that picture comes very close to being imperishable. I found out half way through making *Wuthering Heights* that his way of directing was to take hold of any little kind of lead you gave him as an actor and then apply pressure on you until you went as far as you could go in the direction you'd opened up for yourself.

—Fitzgerald, interviewed by David Galligan for *Drama-Logue*, 8-14 Sept 1983

The principal reason I so enjoyed playing the second Mrs. Woodrow Wilson in the picture *Wilson* [1944, Henry King] was that I tried an experiment and I got away with it. In most biographical films up to that time, actresses had imitated as closely as possible the dress, speech and mannerisms of the women they portrayed. It seemed to me that going through eight reels of intense copying tended to eliminate spontaneity and make for stilted, half-alive portrayals. So I concentrated entirely on making the role come alive, and didn't try to look or talk like Mrs. Wilson. I didn't study all the details of her life, feeling that too much attention to detail would prevent naturalness. And I didn't pad my costumes, although the woman I was playing, Edith Wilson, was one of the beauties of her day. I wanted to feel as attractive as I could; I knew that if I were padded I would feel unattractive and unreal. My only concession to authenticity took into account Mrs. Wilson's lighthearted laughing nature. I kept every scene buoyant, even the very serious ones.

—Fitzgerald, in *The Saturday Evening Post*, 24 Aug 1946

Louise FLETCHER [1934-]

Born: Birmingham, Alabama. After graduating from The University of North Carolina, she did summer stock then drove to Los Angeles where she studied with Jeff Corey. In 1974, Robert Altman brought her out of an eleven-year retirement to play Mattie in his Thieves Like Us (1974). This led to her role as Nurse Ratched in One Flew Over the Cuckoo's Nest (1975, Milos Forman):

The hair was "a symbol" that life had stopped for her a long time ago. She was so out of touch with her feelings that she had no joy in her life and no concept of the fact that she could be wrong. She delivered her care of her insane patients in a killing manner, but she was convinced she was right.

—Fletcher, interviewed by Aljean Harmetz for *The New York Times*, 30 Nov 1975

[Nurse Ratched] thought she was helping the men in her ward. To do that she had to control her environment because she was afraid of experiencing real feelings. I played it with repressed control and hostility.

It was a total ensemble piece. We got so involved that some of the actors actually took on the psychotic problems of the patients they played. I insisted on remaining apart from the cast and ignored the actual patients who worked on the film in the hospital scenes. I wanted to maintain the nurse's aloofness. I isolated myself.

—Fletcher, interviewed by Rex Reed for *Valentines and Vitriol* (New York: Delacorte Press, 1977)

Errol FLYNN [1909-1959]

Born: Hobart, Tasmania. An adventurer, his first contact with the film industry was as a guide to Herman F. Erben on a documentary shot in New Guinea. Erben subsequently gave Flynn the role of Fletcher Christian in In the Wake of the Bounty (released in Australia only. A stage career in England (and one film: Murder at Monte Carlo — 1934, Ralph Ince) preceded his Hollywood debut in The Case of the Curious Bride (1935) for director, Michael Curtiz. In the seventh of 12 films he made with Curtiz, he co-starred as Essex opposite Bette Davis as Elizabeth in The Private Lives of Elizabeth and Essex (1939):

There is a time when Essex comes back from Ireland. The scene occurs on an enormous set, with about 600 extras....

I have to approach her and say, "Your majesty...."

She replies something like, "Well, m'Lord Essex, what have you to say for yourself."

The dialogue goes on, about like this: "I have much to say for myself — but little for you!"

At which time, in front of the whole Court of England, she is supposed to haul off and whack Essex right over the face....

They called the first real rehearsal, and I must say that as Bette assumed her place on the throne, dressed as Elizabeth, with great big square jewels on her hands, and on her wrists big heavy bracelets, she was living the part. She *was* Queen Elizabeth.

I started the walk down through the English Court. The cameras were grinding, I reached the Queen, and then there was that dialogue that I quoted....

Then, of a sudden, I felt as if I had been hit by a railroad locomotive.

She had lifted one of her hands, heavy with those Elizabethan rings, and Joe Louis himself couldn't give a right hook better than Bette hooked me with.

My jaw went out.

I felt a click behind my ear and I saw all these comets, shooting stars, all in a flash....

In front of all these people, I couldn't say anything. Dazed, I was aware that Bette was playing the scene to the finish. I heard the director say, "All right, boys and girls, we do it again." [Flynn and Davis had previously worked together on *The Sisters* (1938, Anatole Litvak). Flynn's other films with Curtiz: *Captain Blood* (1935), *The Charge of the Light Brigade* (1936), *The Perfect Specimen* (1937), *The Adventures of Robin Hood* (1938), *Four's a Crowd* (1938), *Dodge City* (1939), *Virginia City* (1940), *The Sea Hawk* (1940), *Santa Fe Trail* (1940) and *Dive Bomber* (1941).]

I felt I was mis-cast in Westerns, but this was impossible to point out to producers when the pictures were so highly successful. It was most frustrating, it stopped my trying to act. I walked through my roles, jumped on that old horse, swung my legs over that old corral fence. My heart wasn't in it, only my limbs. What was the use? I felt I couldn't get out of my contract and couldn't get Warners to see me in other acting roles.

I am not denying that the Westerns are wonderful entertainment. I love to look at them as well as anyone. I just wanted to act, to have a chance to play a character, to say goodbye to the swashbuckler roles, to get swords and horses to hell out of my life....

Often, in these pictures, I had to alibi my accent, which was still a bit too English for the American ear. I always had to get in a couple of lines which went like this....

Heavy: Where you from, pardner?

Flynn: I happen to come from Ireland, but I am as American as you are.

That got to be a trademark in my American films.

—Flynn, in his *My Wicked Wicked Ways* (New York: G. P. Putnam's Sons, 1959)

Nina FOCH [1924-]

Born: Nina Fock in Leyden, Holland, daughter of Ziegfeld star and stage and screen actress, Consuelo Flowerton (1900-1965). Studies at The American Academy of Dramatic Arts in N.Y. and work on the stage — both in stock and on Broadway — preceded her film debut in The Return of the Vampire (1944, Lew Landers). In 1956, she played Bithiah in Cecil B. DeMille's The Ten Commandments:

I wanted to work with DeMille, but he didn't know anything about actors, so that part of him I didn't like. But I adored learning things like duty and responsibility. He taught me the beginning of a wonderful sentence. He would say, "I can't put a sign on the screen that..." You finish the sentence such as, "You weren't ready today" or "You didn't feel good today...."

I did the DeMille picture when I was very hot. What a stupid thing to do to tie myself up for 28 weeks with Cecil B. DeMille in a rotten picture. I knew it was going to be rotten — it's a terrible film.

[On *Spartacus* (1960)], Kubrick was rude to Laurence Olivier when Olivier tried to help him out in a gracious way by suggesting, "Do you think there would be any value in...." But there was Stanley Kubrick on his second day on a film he hadn't prepared (he took over from Anthony Mann) — and when Larry very sweetly suggested an idea, Kubrick just sighed and shrugged him off. Just like that. I didn't mind that he was dreadful to me — he's a tiny man, small in stature — and big tall blonds with brains don't appeal to him. That was okay — he was a male chauvinist pig before that phrase was invented. But that he was rude to Larry was too much for me.

—Foch, interviewed by David Galligan for *Drama-Logue*, 28 Aug-3 Sept 1980; amended by Miss Foch for *Actors on Acting for the Screen* (New York: Garland Publishing, Inc., 1992)

Henry FONDA [1905-1982]

Born: Grand Island, Nebraska; raised in Omaha. After studying journalism at The University of Minnesota, he joined The Omaha Community Playhouse under the tutelage of Dorothy Brando (Marlon's mother). Work with The University Players in Falmouth and a brief stay on Broadway led to his film debut in The Farmer Takes a Wife (1935, Victor Fleming):

It was easy to make the transition to movies. I started to act in the film version of *The Farmer Takes a Wife* the way I always did for a play, and Victor Fleming...told me I was mugging. And that's all it took. I just pulled it down to reality. You don't project anything for movies. You do it as you would in your own home.

—Fonda, interviewed by Lillian and Helen Ross for *The Player* (New York: Simon & Schuster, 1962)

[Fritz Lang] was too preoccupied with what everything was going to look like. Lang took a whole day to shoot a simple scene with Sylvia [Sidney] and me in *You Only Live Once* [1937]. It's the wedding supper, and the camera starts on an insert of the marriage certificate, then dollies back, sees the plates where we have finished our dinner, and finally sees us. The scene is what we say to each other, and Fritz was all day shooting it. He would dolly back and shoot, then he would stop and take the spoon from my dessert, move the ice cream round a little bit and dirty the dish, and then he would do it again, dirtying her dish a little bit, and then do it again. Then he would move the cup this way and do it, then he would tilt the marriage certificate and do it. He would do it 55 times, he would stand and blow smoke into the scene or something. Now, this is not important...this is not using an actor who's a human being, who has learned his craft, and who knows what to do. I have said it to Fritz Lang's face, and I will say it to anybody — he is a great director, but he is not for me. You must know that I love to act, that I love to build a character and have it come out of me. [Fonda worked with Lang a second time on *The Return of Frank James* (1940).]

—Fonda, interviewed by Jack Stewart for *Henry, Jane and Peter: The Fabulous Fondas* (New York: Tower Books, 1976)

Q. How was it working with [William Wyler] on *Jezebel* [1938]?

A. Great. Just great. I had been warned that it was going to be terrible, I resisted it, as a matter of fact. But he seemed to want me and he was willing to make several compromises in order to get me.... He is unlike a lot of other directors who have the reputation of doing a take and a take and a take, fifty or sixty takes until it gets monotonous. He often *does* do many takes, but there is always a reason, a reason that makes you look forward to doing it again. It is a little bit different. He may be rehearsing with film, but that's all right, because it is the same as rehearsing in the theatre as far as I'm concerned. It's getting a chance to do it again. He may say, "Why not this time reach up and swat a mosquito." There will be something each time, a reason for doing it that made it worth trying again for other effects. I was crazy about Willy, still am.

Q. Just out of curiosity, that scene in *Jezebel* where you *do* swat a mosquito on your hand as you walk down into the garden, was that in the script or was that...?

A. No. That was one of the things that occurred to him at the time.

—Fonda, interviewed by Curtis Lee Hanson for *Cinema*, Dec 1966

Q. What was it like, working with Bette Davis in *Jezebel*?

A. Oh, I loved it! I've known Bette from way back in the Cape Cod days — the playhouse in Dennis, where I worked without salary for several weeks before joining the University Players at Falmouth — and we were kind of a small romance, even in those days. Then I was very good friends with her when we were both out here, and I'm *still* a good friend of Bette's. We did two pictures together — the first was *That Certain Woman* [1937, Edmund Goulding].

—Fonda, interviewed by James Gregory for *Movie Digest*, Mar 1973

Q. *Young Mr. Lincoln* [1939] was your first film for [John] Ford, wasn't it?

A. Yes. When I was first asked to do it I was afraid of the part. I thought, "I can't play Lincoln, it's like playing Jesus." But I did a test. Without committing myself, I sat and had them put makeup on me for three hours. I went to the test stage and they photographed me, and I went back the next day and saw it on the screen. I remember sitting there and seeing this tall character with a big nose and the wart and everything, and I thought, "My God, it is!" Then I started to talk. And my voice came out. I said, "No, I'm sorry fellows." I wouldn't have any part of it. Months later they assigned Ford to the picture. He ran the tests. Sent for me. And, using all the four letter words, he shamed me into it. He said, "What's all this shit about you thinking you're playing the Great Emancipator? For Christ's sake! It's just a young jackleg lawyer from Springfield." He shamed me into it, and I am awfully glad that he did. It was the first of many happy experiences with him. He is and was certainly one of the greats. He always worked with the writer closely on the script and yet, the scripts were always very spare and economical. He would put things in as you were shooting. Whether they had been in his mind from the beginning and he just didn't put them in the script, I don't know but I don't think so. I think they are things that occurred to him driving to the studio, or driving out to the location.

Q. Lines and bits of action?

A. Sometimes lines, pieces of business. Just the other day somebody on the set here came up and said, "You know what I always remember when I see you? I remember that scene in [*My*] *Darling Clementine* [1946] where"...I stopped him and said, "When I put my feet up on the post and did the little thing." He said, "That's right." Well, that was Ford. On the set I was supposed to be lounging in this chair on the porch, in Tombstone. And there was a post holding up the roof of the porch. Ford said, "Back up so that you can put your feet up there." It was a narrow post so I could only put one foot here and one foot above it. He said, "Change your feet." And then, "Do it again. Keep doing it." It became sort of a ballet. Sitting there, enjoying doing this, until somebody comes along. It didn't really mean anything, and yet *everybody* remembers that. Another bit from *Clementine* I remember, Ford put in on the set: I had just come from the barber shop. I had had my hair cut and it was slicked down. Ward Bond came up and stood beside me and said, "Smell those desert flowers." I said, "It's me." That's all. That's one of Ford's bits that made the part memorable.

—Fonda, interviewed by Curtis Lee Hanson for *Cinema*, Dec 1966

[*Young Mr. Lincoln*] began a long romance [with John Ford].... I did *Drums Along the Mohawk* [1939], with him within days, almost, of finishing *Young Mr. Lincoln*. Within a few days of *Drums Along the Mohawk*, I did *The Grapes of Wrath* [1940]. This was three pictures in a row between March and October with Ford, and he had never worked with the same actor consecutively like that before. And it *was* — it was a *romance*.

Q. What was the genius of John Ford?

A. He hates to be *told* that it's genius, or that he has a poetic side, or a sensitive nature. But as an example — and this is typical Ford — he will usually cast actors from whom he knows exactly what to expect. He doesn't do too much direction in the sense of *talking* to an actor about his scene, and what they should do and what they should think about. But he has great *instincts*, and in casting he knows what to expect.

In one scene [in *The Grapes of Wrath*] where a group of silent hungry children was watching the Joad family eat in an Okie camp, one actor started acting up a storm. Ford just took him apart in front of everybody — *destroyed* him. "Had Theresa Helburn up to your house last night, working on the part?" he asked him. Theresa Helburn was *Miss* Theatre Guild — and to Ford it was the legitimate theater, whereas Ford instinctively knew that an emotion shouldn't be shown here.

Well, when we did the scene again, this guy had no emotion. He didn't show *anything*. It was *shamed* out of him, which was the way it *should* have been.

—Fonda, interviewed by James Gregory for *Movie Digest*, Mar 1973

[Ford is] an instinctive director like there are instinctive actors. He instinctively knows, for instance, when an actor is ready to perform. He doesn't say, "How do you feel? Are you ready? Are you up to it?" or anything like that.

An example would be the scene that people always remember of Tom in *The Grapes of Wrath* when my character, Tom, says goodbye to his mother. It was a very emotional scene. Now Jane Darwell, playing Ma Joad, certainly knew all the things that were meant in the scene. We both knew the potentials in the scene, but we didn't talk about the scene to each other. We had only gone over our lines a couple of times sitting in chairs side by side while Ford wasn't there. The camera had to follow me out of a tent, then move down a track until I sat on a bench with Ma Joad. And once we're sitting the camera moves in to us for a two shot, then we do the dialogue. It took a lot of rehearsal for the camera to maneuver the various positions and for the cameraman to know that the lights were all right. But in every rehearsal when we would sit on the bench, at which point the camera holds steady, Ford would cut the rehearsal. So Jane Darwell and I never got to play the scene in a rehearsal! As a result, after an hour and a half or so, Jane and I were both like racehorses, chomping at the bit. You know, "Hey, fellows, let us go! We got a scene to play here!" Ford knew we were like that. Not one word was said about it, but I knew Ford well enough, and I know him today well enough, to know that that son of a bitch — I say son of a bitch full of love — knew instinctively that he was leading us right up to it, then holding us back. And when he was ready, we went! And we really played that scene 'cause we *were* ready, and he got up and walked away from it. He liked to be able to do scenes, particularly that kind of scene, in one take. He wanted the spontaneity of whatever would happen the first time.

—Fonda, interviewed by Mike Steen for *Hollywood Speaks!* (New York: G.P. Putnam's Sons, 1974)

John Stahl directed *The Immortal Sergeant* [1943]. We were working in the desert in 130 degree heat, and it was brutal for everybody, but *doubly* brutal because Stahl would just say "Do it again!".... He was the kind of director that would do it 32 times, but not for a *reason*. Just "Do it again!"

—Fonda, interviewed by James Gregory for *Movie Digest*, Mar 1973

If you do have a disagreement with [John] Ford, it becomes an all-out fight. No half measures.

I've had my share of them with him, too. Total disagreements. One I particularly remember was on *The Fugitive* [1947]. It was over the way to do a scene and Ford finally said: "Okay, we'll shoot it both ways. Your way and my way!" I felt almost triumph. So first we shot it his way. With that he walked away from the whole thing and I never did get to do it my way!

—Fonda, interviewed by Peter McDonald for *Radio Times*, 2 Nov 1972

Fonda: I was not happy with the film [of *Mr. Roberts* (1955)].... [John Ford]...didn't like to duplicate anything that Josh [Logan] had done in the theater. He kept changing scenes. You can't play it for almost four years like I did and not become a purist. You don't fuck around with something that works as well as it did. We're lucky that he had his kidney attack and operation and he had to be replaced [by Mervyn LeRoy] when the picture was half finished.

Playboy: Didn't Ford actually hit you when you began to criticize his direction?

Fonda: Yeah. [Producer] Leland [Hayward] said, "Pappy wants to see you." I went in and Ford knew that I was unhappy with the way he'd handled the scene that afternoon, and so he said: "All right, what's the matter? Let's have it." So I told him in the nicest way I could that when Leland asked me who should direct this film, I said, "There's only one — John Ford. He's queer for the Navy, he's an outdoor man, and an outdoor-location director, a man's director, everything you could think of. But Pappy," I said, "you're playing around with things that worked beautifully in the theater and you're changing them." I don't know how far I got before he stood up and pushed me back over a table. It was more like a shove than a hit. Shit, I wasn't gonna fight the old man, so I just got up and left the room. A few minutes later, he came to my room to apologize, and from then on, it was almost embarrassing. He'd ask me before every scene, almost sarcastically, "Do you approve? Is this all right with you?" He stuck closer to the script from then on. [Fonda also worked on Ford's *Fort Apache* (1948).]

—Fonda, interviewed by Lawrence Grobel for *Playboy*, Dec 1981

It takes a great deal of preparation and concentration to be able to play a part and not let anyone know you're acting. Anything that gets in the way of my playing that role, my belief in that role, director or cameraman, will get me upset. First I tell them in a friendly way, but if it becomes a problem to convince him, I become less friendly. I remember fighting Dino De Laurentiis all the way through *War and Peace* [1956, King Vidor] because he saw Pierre as a leading man opposite Audrey Hepburn and I saw him as a character. I wanted him to be fatter than I was and to wear glasses. De Laurentiis came down on the set on the first day. There was a big argument and I had to take the glasses off. He was the producer so whenever he left the set for a scene I put them back on.

—Fonda, interviewed by Stuart Kaminsky for *Don Siegel: Director* (New York: Curtis Books, 1974)

Q. How was working with Alfred Hitchcock on *The Wrong Man* [1957]?

A. Very good experience. It was not one of his more successful pictures, possibly because it was unlike the typical Hitchcock. It was documentary. He bought this story, from a *Life* magazine. He filmed it where it actually happened, in the Stork Club, in the subway, in East Brooklyn. We shot in the courtroom where the actual trial was.

It was a good experience for me, working with him. He is very well organized, and all of his assistants — his production manager, his assistant director, the script girl, and so on — they know, because they have been working with him in preparation, exactly what he wants and how he expects to get it. To such an extent that he could be absent and they could set up the shot. Blueprinted practically. He knows exactly what he wants. His direction is very sparse. He hires the actors and he knows what he can get from them. He puts them in the positions that he wants them in with his camera and that's it.

—Fonda, interviewed by Curtis Lee Hanson for *Cinema*, Dec 1966

It is not possible to develop a character in a film as much as you can in the theater. The one chance I had in the cinema was with Sidney Lumet making *Twelve Angry Men* [1957] because the nature of the picture was such. We got the artists together, most of them theater actors, and we rehearsed for 2 weeks like a play. We could have opened in a theater after those two weeks; but instead of going to a theater we went onto the sound stages, and photographed it, out of continuity as you have to because of the economics of filming. But those actors had already had for two weeks the benefit and the thrill of building their parts from the beginning to the end like a graph. This you never have in films, although you might have a director who appreciates rehearsal.

—Fonda, in *Films & Filming*, Feb 1963

I was terribly impressed with [Lumet], and so were all the other actors. We had a shooting schedule of twenty-one days. Rather than shoot in sequence...when he had a certain camera setup, he would do every scene in the script that required the camera to be in that position. Say, the camera would be on two actors for a scene. After that scene was gotten, Sidney would say, "Now take their coats off, loosen the ties and put some sweat on them, and we'll shoot scene ninety-two," which is forty pages further, but requiring the same setup or camera and light position. Fonda also worked on Lumet's *Stage Struck* (1963) and *Fail Safe* (1963).

—Fonda, interviewed by Mike Steen for *Hollywood Speaks!* (New York: G.P. Putnam's Sons, 1974)

I did have a difference of opinion with Sergio Leone, for whom I did *Once Upon a Time in the West* [1968]. He sent me the script and I couldn't believe it. I'd never seen anything like it — it didn't make any sense and I turned it down. Then Leone flew to California with his co-producer, who spoke English and served as Sergio's translator. I had lunch with them at the commissary at Paramount and confessed that I had never seen any of his pictures. So they set up a screening and I saw the three Leone pictures starring Clint Eastwood. I thoroughly enjoyed myself and called my friend Eli Wallach who had been in *The Good, The Bad and The Ugly* and he said: "Pay no attention to the script. Take the picture. It's a great experience." Well I went to an optometrist and was fitted for brown contact lenses and grew and Edwin Booth mustache for the role. When I got to Spain, they were ready to shoot, and when Leone saw me, he got upset. He was buying my baby blue eyes and that's what he wanted to see.

The first scene in the picture, in which the whole family is massacred, the camera stayed behind this man as he walks up to shoot the little boy, then the camera starts to come around and the audience sees it's me. That's what Leone wanted me for, to make the audience, for that one scene, say "Jesus Christ. It's Henry Fonda."

—Fonda, interviewed by Stuart Kaminsky for *Don Siegel: Director* (New York: Curtis Books, 1974)

I enjoyed everything about [*Sometimes a Great Notion* (1971, Paul Newman)].... I'm very fond of Paul personally and as an actor, and I like him as a director. I think he'd be the first one to say you shouldn't do *both* — he didn't *want* to do both. But we had another director on the picture that didn't work out, so Paul had to take over.

Q. What do you like about his directing?

A. Well! He's an *actor's* director; because he's a good actor, he thinks like I do, like an actor *should*. The problems were *his* problems — and this is an example: We're working around a big family dinner table — actually it was a breakfast in a kitchen. Richard Jaeckel was here (indicates), and Paul was here, and I'm at the head of the table, and Michael Sarrazin is down there, and a couple of gals are here. There's dialogue going all around the table while we're eating. It's a *big* scene — a *lot* of dialogue. We rehearsed it for a long time.

Anyway, we're rehearsing this scene a *lot*. And eventually we're ready to shoot. Now, Paul is *in* the scene, and he's also the director. Here we go, "Roll 'em. Action!" The dialogue starts...goes all around the table...and then it comes to a dead stop.

It's Paul's cue, but he's wearing his other hat. He's in the scene, but as a director he's listening, thinking, and suddenly it's his cue and he doesn't pick it up. And he says, "Oh, shhh...!" In other words, at times like that he will be the first to admit, and to agree, you shouldn't try to do both.

—Fonda, interviewed by James Gregory for *Movie Digest*, Mar 1973

[Both Jane and I] were aware that in certain respects [*On Golden Pond* (1981, Mark Rydell)] was a reflection, sometimes uncannily so, of the pain we'd known in real life as father and daughter. In our big scenes together, Jane became very emotional. There's a moment when she's groping to find the right relationship with her dad, and I'm playing that I'm not sure what she's up to. When it was over, I could see Jane was proud. She pointed to the film crew — by that time everybody was crying — and whispered to me, "I guess they all had problems with their father."

—Fonda, interviewed by Richard Corliss for *Time*, 16 Nov 1981

I've never had as good a part [as that of Norman Thayer, Jr. in *On Golden Pond*, and there's a magic that everybody from the smallest grip to Katharine [Hepburn] and me feels every moment. I've never, in my 45 years of making 90-odd films, had the feeling something is so special in every scene we do....

—Fonda, interviewed by Corby Kummer for *The New York Sunday News*, 25 Oct 1981

As far back as I can remember when I started to think seriously about acting, I thought about it in terms of "Don't let it ever seem like acting. Make it real." If I feel I'm acting, I feel the audience must. So in my own rehearsals — my study of the part — I try to find a way to say the lines so it sounds as if they're coming out of me from the top of my head, so to speak — being *thought* at the moment; not a rehearsed speech. And at the same time it works the other way. When somebody's talking to you in a scene you're hearing them for the first time, so your reactions will be new and fresh and so on. These are rules of acting that I have. I don't write them down, but they're back here in my mind if I need to be reminded. But anyway, I don't like the wheels or the cogs to show. There's an awful lot of work in acting, for me, to make it look like no work.

—Fonda, interviewed by Don Shay for *Conversations* (Albuquerque: Kaleidoscope Press, 1969)

Jane FONDA [1937-]

Born: New York City; daughter of Henry Fonda. Studies at Vassar College and with Lee Strasberg at The Actors Studio, and work as a model and on stage preceded her film debut in Tall Story (1960, Joshua Logan):

I always thought that you go on and pretend the camera isn't there when you shoot a scene. But that's not so, you have to play to the camera while you act. You relate to it in a certain way, with consciousness of the lights and all sorts of technical matters. You learn such fascinating things — like the fact that audiences' eyes tend to go to the right, so you try to get over to the right side of the set.

Or you might play a scene in which you are face to face with someone; then you do it over again for a close-up and only *your* face is seen in the camera. You still have to get the same intensity of emotion, the same sincerity, even though you are acting all by yourself. Cuing Tony [Perkins], I would read my lines and really put feeling into them, but he just read his and I couldn't work up the proper reactions. When I realized that, I told him that I'd make a deal with him. If he would read my cues properly, I'd do his; otherwise I would just throw them away.

—Fonda, interviewed by Edwin Miller for *Seventeen*, May 1960

I enjoyed making *A Walk on the Wild Side* [1962, Edward Dmytryk].... People remember Kitty Twist, and how I loved that part: a girl who'd been through such hell that when she finally got into a whorehouse it was like meeting and marrying the King of England.

—Fonda, interviewed by Howard Thompson for *The New York Times*, 16 May 1965

Lee [Strasberg] somehow imparts dignity and gives you confidence in yourself. With Lee, I learned that every need has a counter-need. I also learned that somewhere inside you is an experience similar to the one you are playing. For example, if you play a murderer, you don't have to have had the experience of actually murdering someone, because somewhere inside yourself you will find some relevant experience. In one of my recent movies, *The Chapman Report* [1962, George Cukor] I play a frigid woman, a widow. To do it, I don't have to be like that woman. Instead, I call on what every woman has felt at some time in her life — doubts about herself. This feeling is enough to give me insight into the way that woman feels.

—Fonda, interviewed by Lillian and Helen Ross for *The Player* (New York: Simon & Schuster, 1962)

They Shoot Horses, Don't They? [1969, Sydney Pollack] was a turning point for me.

Q. How?

A. Well, we made it in '68, which was a turning point for *everybody*. And up until then...I had to escape being my father's daughter and being slotted into the ingenue roles. When you are asked year after year to play roles that never tap you, that are just totally on the surface and you're an earnest young actress and you try to make them seem real and penetrate these creatures that are about an inch deep, you know that there's something wrong. I was feeling very alienated. *Horses* was the first movie I had made in the United States in a long time that was about something. It also tapped my alienation: being able to play a statement that was about the manipulation of people, playing upon people's hurt and desperation. It was the first movie where I was actually asked what I thought about how the script should be. I felt that I was a part of it.

—Fonda, interviewed by Maura Moynihan and Andy Warhol for *Interview*, Mar 1984

During the filming [of *They Shoot Horses, Don't They?*], I couldn't function, I couldn't even go home at night, so I'd sleep in my dressing room. I became so unhealthily immersed in the role of Gloria I couldn't tell reality from illusion. Big black wells of loneliness and depression fell over me. I became a manic-depressive. My speech pattern changed. I even started *talking* like Gloria. And I was so uncertain about the part. It was like having a dead baby inside me and I went around wondering why I couldn't give birth.

—Fonda, interviewed by Rex Reed for *The New York Times*, 25 Jan 1970

Q. You improvised the scene in the analyst's office in *Klute* [1971, Alan J. Pakula]. What does that mean exactly? Did you have any script to begin with or what?

A. That was the last scene we shot and by that time I knew the character [Bree Daniels] very well. You find areas in yourself that relate to the character and then learn how those things are expressed differently than you would express them. By that time, I knew Bree well enough to improvise the scene. I think it worked real well. I didn't have to think about it too much, but I set myself certain tasks. Bree was the kind of woman who at a crucial point in her analysis would find an excuse, like it was costing too much or that it wasn't doing her any good, to keep from revealing another layer of herself. She would create barriers and conflicts. It was wonderful fun to do that scene. We did it real quick. We didn't do anything twice.

Q. That seems an example where the performer gets rid of the director and writer at least in one scene and sort of takes charge.

A. Not really. We all worked closely. The director and I had a lot of discussion beforehand about how the scene was going to be used and what we wanted to convey. It was his idea that the analyst be a woman and that was an important decision. Bree would not have talked the same way if it had been a male analyst.

—Fonda, interviewed by Dan Georgakas and Lenny Rubenstein for *Cineaste* 6.4, 1975

I made Bree much more vulnerable than a real prostitute would be. A real character would have been difficult to make sympathetic.... I'm not a cynical person, as Bree was. I'm not a loser. I don't get frightened. I am not somebody who needs to rely on men for my identity....

—Fonda, interviewed by Martin Kasindorf for *The New York Times*, 3 Feb 1974

Pakula is a wonderful director for women. He allows you to move around. [After *Klute*, Fonda worked with him again on *Comes a Horseman* (1978) and *Rollover* (1981).]

Q. This doesn't apply, I take it, to...[Joseph] Losey [on *A Doll's House* (1973)]?.... He's been telling everyone that the women in *A Doll's House* formed a little Women's Lib clique and were impossible.

A. In the first place — I'm so naive — when they said they were going to do the play, I thought they were going to do the play. I got to Norway and I found they had chosen an alcoholic misogynist English playwright to do some rewriting. All the men involved had decided that what Ibsen said about women didn't apply anymore. I discovered that the male characters, who are somewhat shadowy, had been built up and the women were shaved down...except Nora — if you tie Nora's tubes, you've got nothing left. There was I, another woman [Anna Wing], and Delphine Seyrig, and we were being called dykes, a gaggle of bitches.

They were supposed to give us two weeks of rehearsal, which they didn't. So there we were, and it was like the house was burning, what could you salvage. You grab your socks.... The strangest thing happened: I found I had to become Nora with Losey, bat my eyelashes, and make it seem as though it was his idea. Every day I realized how valid the play was, as Ibsen's whole thesis was being acted out.

Losey never had the guts to confront me. On the contrary, he wrote me love letters, but he attacked women in lower positions. He tried to set us against each other. Then when it was all over, he gave these interviews in which he attacked me, called me cruel....

—Fonda, interviewed by Molly Haskell for *The Village Voice*, 7 Nov 1974

I do an enormous amount of research. I try to submerge myself as much as possible in the environment and the socioeconomic context of the character. I try not to do it in a cerebral way. When I was preparing for my role of a prostitute in *Klute*, for example, I spent many, many hours with streetwalkers, with thousand-dollar-a-night call girls, madams, in after-hours clubs with pimps, trying to pick up and absorb characteristics. Then I try to forget it all. By the time I start filming, I try not to think about it. I want it to be organic.

I didn't have to do any research for the part of Jane [in *Fun with Dick and Jane* (1977, Ted Kotcheff)]. I grew up in that class, I know those people. It's part of my experience.

—Fonda, interviewed by John M. Wilson for *The New York Times*, 11 Apr 1976

I was first offered the role of Julia [in *Julia* (1977, Fred Zinnemann)], but I didn't want to play her because I was too on the nose. I'm not interested in playing committed, way-out liberated women. I think most people aren't like that, and that the value of movies is to have characters that people can identify with and relate to.

I wanted the challenge of playing this other woman, Lillian Hellman, who was so different from me. I didn't spend very much time with her — just a day and a half — but I read everything she wrote. What was particularly helpful to me were her plays. Somehow the spirit of the woman, the subconscious, was more in the plays.

I had never had the opportunity of playing a woman who thinks and who is mainly, at least at that stage of her life, motivated by ideas. [The role of Julia was played by Vanessa Redgrave].

—Fonda, interviewed by William Rademaekers for *Time*, 3 Oct 1977

I was thinking of playing the real Lillian Hellman. Then I suddenly realized I shouldn't. But I decided before I went to see her that I was going to try to draw characteristics from her that would help in building the Lillian character. Things like crossing herself when she says, "Oy veh." The way she smokes. I don't smoke and I had to learn for the film. She has mannerisms that are extremely elegant and sensual. Very feminine. Very coquettish.

—Fonda, interviewed by Susan Smith for *W*, 7-14 Jan 1977

To be able to make this movie feels very, very good. When we started shooting, I kept thinking something's different, and then the full force of it hit me.

It's about the relationship between two women. It's not neurotic or sexually aberrant, it's just about two friends who care about each other tremendously, who are interested in each other's growth. There isn't any gossip or jealousy....

The fact is that it's about a woman who is a real heroine. It's very important to make movies about women who grow and become ideological human beings and totally committed people. We have to begin to put that image into the mass culture.

—Fonda, interviewed by Judith Weinraub for *The New York Times*, 31 Oct 1976

How wonderful it is to see the face of a woman who is radiant and glowing because her mind has been introduced to Darwin, Hegel and Einstein. That is what comes across on the screen with Vanessa Redgrave.

She is unlike any actress I have ever seen before, the kind like Eleanor Duse and Kim Stanley that comes only once in a generation.

Vanessa is constantly surprising. She plays the leader of the two women, and Lillian is very much the follower. They are the same age, but Julia is years ahead intellectually.

—Fonda, interviewed by Bob Thomas for *The San Diego Union*, 9 Jan 1977

In the film the relationship [between Dashiell Hammett (Jason Robards) and Lillian Hellman] is father-daughter. Hammett helps me with my writing. It's nice. Not romantic, but there's obviously a very deep love.

—Fonda, interviewed by Susan Smith for *W*, 7-14 Jan 1977

When we shoot, I just go on instinct. With Jon [Voight on *Coming Home* (1978, Hal Ashby)] everything is up for question, everything has to be tried. It makes it hard to work with him. You could never have more than one in a crowd with his level of intensity. But it also forces everyone to grapple and struggle.

—Fonda, interviewed by Jess Cook Jr. for *The New York Times*, 29 Apr 1979

Kimberly Wells [in *The China Syndrome* (1979, James Bridges)], is a woman who is confronted with some astonishingly hard decisions about herself. She is pressured by lots of outside authoritative influences which, in former times, might have caused her to cave in. But, because of the situation she finds herself in and by virtue of the people she is surrounded by, she is forced to take tremendous risks. In the process of doing so, she grows immensely and becomes a person of heroic dimensions.

—Fonda, interviewed by Thomas Kiernan for *Cue*, 2 Feb 1979

[Hallie Martin in *The Electric Horseman* (1979, Sydney Pollack)] isn't modeled after any particular newscaster. But I did learn one thing by closely watching Barbara Walters. The trick in interviewing people is to try to throw them off balance. Do it with charm. If you make them lose their cool, you may get some good quotes.

—Fonda, interviewed for *International Photographer*, Mar 1980

It's hard to play a woman I wouldn't normally like very much. Lee Winters [in *Rollover* (1981, Alan J. Pakula)] is very rich and powerful, very manipulative. It's a part I've never played before. It was hard for me to get to a place where I could begin to accept her. I've come to like her, but it took me a while.

You have to have empathy for the character or you can't do it. It's the same problem I ran into playing Hannah in *California Suite* [1978, Herbert Ross]. I did not like the woman at all. For a week of rehearsal, I just had a very difficult time, because unconsciously I was separating myself from her. Finally, it was through her humor that I came to her.

—Fonda, interviewed by Mike Bygrave and Joan Goodman for *American Film*, Nov 1981

My dad isn't exactly Norman Thayer, but there's a lot of Dad in the part. And I guess there's a lot of Chelsea, Norman's daughter, in me. Like Chelsea, I had to get over the desperate need I once had for his approval, and to conquer fear of him. We've never been intimate. My dad simply is not an intimate person. But that doesn't mean there isn't love. There's a lot of love. *On Golden Pond* [1981, Mark Rydell] gave all of us the chance to say out loud something you could admit to yourself only at night. I can't tell you how lucky I feel that we actually got it done.

—Fonda, interviewed by Richard Corliss for *Time*, 16 Nov 1981

It's so *hard* for Chelsea to say this [to tell her father that she wants them to talk]. He tries to avoid her by saying something nasty like "You're worried about the will, huh? Don't worry, you're getting everything." I move down to sit next to him and say, "I don't *want* anything. We've been mad at each other for so long." He says, "I didn't know we were mad at each other. I thought we just didn't like each other." I reached out to take his arm — and I felt him shudder, because he wasn't expecting it. He's not an emotional actor, and everyone on the crew saw it. I took his arm and said, "I want to be your friend," and I felt him trying to keep the tears back. It was a moment of such intimacy....

—Fonda, interviewed by Corby Kummer for *The New York Sunday News*, 25 Oct 1981

It would be fast to say I don't concern myself with what the audience will think, because I do. For that reason I would never do a movie that was demeaning of a woman, or exploitative or opportunistically sexual or racist or militaristic. But that doesn't mean I'm always going to play what people perceive me as being, because if I did that, I'd retire. It'd be boring to always play yourself. I like challenges, I like to reach into areas I've never experienced before. You know, it's hard to do, and you always risk failure, and it's painful.

In fact, I found this movie [*The Morning After* (1986, Sidney Lumet)] real painful. I was really insecure and real scared that I was going to fail.

—Fonda, interviewed by Ron Base for *The Toronto Star*, 20 Dec 1986

Peter FONDA [1940-]

Born: New York City; son of Henry Fonda; brother of Jane Fonda. Work on Broadway preceded his film debut in Tammy and the Doctor (1963, Harry Keller). In 1966, he appeared in The Wild Angels, the first of two films for Roger Corman:

When we were filming *The Wild Angels*, Roger gave me a sheet detailing the budget breakdown. I studied that like mad. He let me study everything, in fact. On *The Trip* [1967], he let me shoot a few scenes and sit in on the editing. I thought that was really generous. Also, he'd answer any question that I had about filmmaking. I took my lessons very seriously. He taught me about budgeting and scheduling, the practical side of things as well as the artistic....

I don't know what other actor ever got this sort of education from making movies. It wasn't a school of hard knocks, but a school of how to learn to pick locks. When you seemed to be locked in by adverse circumstances, you found that, very often, those circumstances actually freed you to do other things. Roger was great in teaching you lessons like that. He was the example....

The only thing Roger promised all of us who wanted help (and he winds up helping just about everybody) was this: If we would give him our all, he would give us our shot. There wasn't a lot of money involved, but we were guaranteed our shot. What more could anyone ask for? Hell, I would have paid Roger for that chance....

—Fonda, interviewed by Ed Naha for *The Films of Roger Corman* (New York: Arco Publishing Inc., 1982)

Playboy: What was the message you wanted to convey as Captain America [in *Easy Rider* (1969, Dennis Hopper)]?

Fonda: I wanted to create an existential hero, and in a sense, I think I accomplished that. But the more I got into the film, the more I began to re-examine my original premise — to show the beauty of the anarchy of the individual versus the decrepit anarchy of society. And then I wondered about the beauty of this individual anarchy and what meaning it really had. I wondered, in fact, if what these guys were up to had *any* reflection of freedom. And then I found that it didn't. What I feel I [as screenwriter] shot down — which most people didn't pick up — was the idea that I represented anything that should be glorified or emulated. Well, I didn't, which is why Wyatt [Fonda] finally says to Billy [Dennis Hopper], "We blew it."

Playboy: What did that line mean?

Fonda: Many things, almost as many as you can come up with. Literally, within the story, we blew it when we went for the easy money, and then thought we could retire. And we thought that was the basis of freedom.... I promise you that when you base your life solely on economics — as Wyatt and Billy did in *Easy Rider* — you blow your life right out the window.

—Fonda, interviewed by Lawrence Linderman for *Playboy*, Sept 1970

Joan FONTAINE [1917-]

Born: Joan De Havilland in Tokyo; sister to Olivia De Havilland. In 1919, she moved with her mother and sister to Saratoga, California (Joan took her name from her stepfather, George M. Fontaine, while Olivia retained her father's name of De Havilland.) In 1935, Joan made her screen debut in No More Ladies (Edward H. Griffith). In 1939, she played Peggy Day in George Cukor's adaptation of Claire Booth's The Women:

There could have been many problems on *The Women*. Norma Shearer was queen of the lot, and Joan Crawford was very powerful at MGM then, too. Rosalind Russell and Paulette Goddard were also in the picture. Miraculously, however, there was no dissension that I could detect. All the girls kept a polite distance from each other on the set. There was not one catty word uttered off-camera by anyone within my hearing range, a testimonial to George Cukor's superb ability to run a smooth ship....

Cukor gave me the best acting advice I've ever had, and I had been to many teachers. "In films, you must think and feel, and the rest will take care of itself," he advised. The least gesture, you see, is what counts in films; thinking and feeling are what really matter up there on the screen.

—Fontaine, interviewed by Doug McLelland for *American Classic Screen*, May/June 1978

I understood Mrs. de Winter [in *Rebecca* (1940, Alfred Hitchcock)] — who had only the very best of intentions, and tried so hard to please, and encountered so many stone walls. I knew exactly how she felt. I had a crystal clear idea of how to portray her.... People wonder how I "managed to improve so, overnight as an actress." The answer is that I had a role at last that I could feel.

—Fontaine, interviewed by James Reid for *Motion Picture*, Aug 1940

Q. Was it an agreeable atmosphere [on the set of *Rebecca*]?

A. No, because Hitchcock and Selznick made it clear to me that Olivier wanted Vivien Leigh in the role, and they were taking me on some sort of tolerance....

Q. Well, whatever forces were at work, it gave you that marvelous impression of being overawed, vulnerable, shy....

A. And self-effacing and apologetic. All these things they [the British contingent — Olivier, Gladys Cooper, Nigel Bruce] actually did to me over and above the demands of the characters they were playing....

—Fontaine, interviewed by Brian McFarlane for *Cinema Papers*, June 1982

Hitch was rather intimidated by most of the cast.... I was probably the least intimidating to him, so we used to sit and talk quite a lot. And he was very dear. He would have me over to his house for dinner with his wife, Alma [Reville], whom I adored. He also used to draw what he wanted. He would draw that chair and say, "I want your face half hidden behind that chair." And that makes it much better for an actor. It gives you a visual aspect of what he wants from your performance.

—Fontaine, interviewed by Ronald Bowers for *The Selznick Players* (New York: A.S. Barnes, 1976)

When I was offered the feminine lead in *Suspicion* [1941], I had no grounds for refusing.... I had the chance to be directed by Hitchcock again. And here was a character who unquestionably had a psychological twist that I ought to be able to portray — being probably the most suspicious and jealous woman on earth, always doubting everybody's good intentions.

—Fontaine, interviewed by Roger Carroll for *Motion Picture*, Apr 1942

Q. You know that legendary remark of Hitchcock's about actors needing to be treated like cattle. What do you think about his methods of handling actors? Did you find him helpful?

A. Absolutely, though he was inclined to tear people down in front of others.... He divided and conquered; he had the habit of saying "that silly old actor over there" or "that idiot" or whatever it was, and probably did the same about me. But it was a very clever device. On both films I did for him we all ended up hardly civil because of these tactics.

—Fontaine, interviewed by Brian McFarlane for *Cinema Papers*, June 1982

Playing the part of Tessa in *The Constant Nymph* [1943] was the happiest motion-picture assignment of my career. Not only was Edmund Goulding a skillful film director, but he had also been a successful stage director. The combination was an actor's dream. Each morning the cast would arrive at the studio at 8 a.m., an unheard-of luxury, and go immediately to the closed set. Here we'd sit around a table, just like the first rehearsals of a stage play. The first day we read through the entire script, which Eddie proposed to shoot as much in sequence as possible. Each day he and the scriptwriter would adjust difficult lines, iron out dialogue problems, discuss characterization and mood with the actors. Before noon, with only the cameraman, head gaffer, and property man allowed on the sound stage, we'd "put it on its feet" and walk the scene. Before breaking for lunch, every detail of the afternoon's work would be worked out, including camera angles, props, and lighting effects.

After lunch, the actors returned in costume and makeup, now thoroughly familiar with their lines, ready for the first take, the master shot. Instead of the fifty or sixty takes indulged in by directors such as...George Stevens [with whom she worked on *Quality Street* (1937), *A Damsel in Distress* (1937), *Gunga Din* (1939) and *Something to Live For* (1952)], Eddie, because of meticulous preparation, could "Print" after the first or second. After the master shot would come the medium shots, two-shots, and finally the individual close-ups. No delays were caused by actors blowing their lines, by questions about inner meanings or motivations. All that had been thrashed out that morning around the rehearsal table....

Charles Boyer remains my favorite leading man. Charles...was a kind, gentle, helpful actor.... Above all, he cared about the quality of the film he was making, and, unlike most leading men I have worked with, the single exception being Fred Astaire [on *A Damsel in Distress*], his first concern was the film, not himself.

—Fontaine, in her *No Bed of Roses* (New York: William Morrow & Co., 1978)

You cannot battle an elephant. Orson [Welles] was such a *big* man in every way that no one could stand up to him. On the first day [of shooting *Jane Eyre* (1944, Robert Stevenson)], we were all called on the set at one o'clock — no Welles. At four o'clock, in he strode followed by his agent, a dwarf, his valet and a whole entourage. Approaching us, he proclaimed, "All right, everybody, turn to page eight." And we did it. I knew that if I underplayed — in front of the camera and off — I wouldn't get hurt.

—Fontaine, interviewed by Doug McLelland for *American Classic Screen*, May/June 1978

[Max] Ophuls was a very strict director [on *Letter from an Unknown Woman* (1948)], but most imaginative...didn't question you for a moment...didn't treat you *roughly*...and wasn't interested in the clock and making the schedule and all that sort of thing. He was a *creative* man who brought out the *creative* side of one.

Mr. Robert Wise [is] the kind of a director that wants you to pick up something on cue; say a line exactly to metronome proportions; and I think *that's* very difficult for instinctive actors. I think it's difficult for *most* actors. But he became the camera, and everything had his tempo constantly. So you could not invent, or do anything original if you wanted to. I never saw [*Until They Sail* (1957)], so I don't know how it came out.

—Fontaine, interviewed by John Kobal (1968) for *People Will Talk* (New York: Alfred A. Knopf, 1985)

Glenn FORD [1916-]

Born: Gwyllyn Ford in Quebec City, Canada; nephew to Canadian Prime Minister Sir John A. MacDonald. After stage work in Santa Monica, he made his film debut in Heaven with a Barbed Wired Fence (1939, Ricardo Cortez). In 1941, he played opposite Fredric March in John Cromwell's So Ends Our Night:

In *So Ends Our Night*, [March] did a scene where he had to cry. It was a long scene and all I had to interject was one or two words but I was so taken by his acting — he cried real tears — that I forgot my lines. So he had to do it again. I became so engrossed in his acting I kept forgetting my lines. And you know what he did? He put his hand on my shoulder and said, "Glenn, don't worry, we can do it again. Maybe we'll get it better." I felt terrible that I had let him down but he was very gentle with me and we finally got it. And it *was* better the third time. Instead of getting mad at me, he thanked me for allowing him to do it three times. I learned from that how to treat your fellow actors — people forget sometimes. He knew I was frightened.

—Ford, interviewed by David Galligan for *Drama-Logue*, 17-23 July 1986

My favorite [romantic scene] came in *Gilda* [1946, Charles Vidor] — the love scene in the bedroom where Rita Hayworth accuses me of hating her. I tell her she doesn't know, she can't know, how much I hate her. She replies, "I hate you too, Johnny. I hate you so much I think I'm going to die from it — darling." Then came the crushing embrace and kiss that shut out the world. I liked that scene because of the balanced, easy dialogue that carried us right into the mood of our story. Too, the implication was unusual — two people declaring their love by saying over and over that they hate each other.

—Ford, in *Motion Picture Story Magazine*, Aug 1947

Gilda was a sleeper. When we shot it, we didn't know how it was going to end. We had the script delivered to us each morning and did it that day. I was so fond of Rita [Hayworth].... Any affection that you saw on the screen between Rita and me was true, very true.

—Ford, interviewed by Ovid Demaris for *Parade Magazine*; publ. in *The L.A. Daily News*, 9 Nov 1986

Delmer [Daves] taught me an unforgettable lesson on a picture Van Heflin and I were doing called *3:10 to Yuma* [1957]. We'd been shooting about a week at the Western Ave. studios of 20th Century Fox. *3:10 to Yuma* was a western which all takes place in a hotel room. This particular scene was between Van and me. I was playing the heavy. So I have the handcuffs on and I'm lying on the bed. Van is going back and forth to the window, carrying this gun, very nervous like. Of course he's got to put me on the 3:10 to Yuma and eventually in jail. At our noon break, Van asked me to come across the street to a place called the Oasis and have lunch.... Well, we went over and Van says, "Glenn, have you ever had this new drink they've invented in the U.S. Senate?" I said, "No." He said, "Well, let's have one — it's called a Bullshot." I later found out it was half consommé and half vodka.

Well, it tasted damned good so we had one or two, maybe three or five, and I lost my appetite. I don't remember how many but we helped each other back across the street and got on the set. Well, Delmer knew what was going on. He said, "Gentlemen, are you ready?" And we said, "Of course we're ready." We'd already rehearsed the scene before lunch so the camera was all set up, the lights were ready and we went on the set and did the scene. During the scene, through the haze, I noticed that Van was missing the chair, missing the window and that I very nearly fell out of bed. We were acting up a storm, thinking we were the greatest things in the world. So Del said, "Cut/print. We'll wrap it up for the day." We went home feeling fairly complacent — a good day's work well done.

When we showed up the next day, Del said, "By the way, gentlemen, would you like to see yesterday's work so you can get accustomed to what follows?" We were shooting in sequence, so we said, "Why not?" Well, we go into Projection Room B and Del sits in the back of the room and Van and I sit down in the third row. What unfolds before us on the screen are the most ludicrous performances you've ever seen. Dreadful. At the end of the scene Del presses the buzzer, saying "that will be all" to the projectionist and the light comes up in the room. Del waited about five minutes before he said, "Well, gentlemen, what do you think? Perhaps you'd like to do it again?" By this time we were destroyed. He said, "All right, we're going to do it again but I want this to be a lesson to you two characters. Never, *never*, do that again. You saw an example up there of complete unprofessionalism."

—Ford, interviewed by David Galligan for *Drama-Logue*, 17-23 July 1986

Harrison FORD [1942-]

Born: Chicago. Summer stock in Wisconsin and work on stage in California preceded his film debut in Dead Heat on a Merry-Go-Round (1966, Bernard Girard). In 1973, he played Bob Falfa in George Lucas' American Graffiti:

George Lucas wanted me to get a crew cut. I suggested the cowboy hat, then it was a straw cowboy hat, and all of a sudden there was a character, and George said, "I remember those guys!" I was thinking like an actor, and the fun was realizing that people wanted to hear that kind of stuff from me. It's the first time I remember having the feeling that my wings would carry me.

—Ford, interviewed by Kenneth Turan for *GQ*, Nov 1986

I don't play characters that are immediately recognizable or even necessarily as likable.

Q. Then how would you describe the characters you've played?

A. In *Star Wars* [1977, George Lucas], Hans Solo isn't a hero; he's a mercenary who finally faces his obligations and helps a friend in a pinch — and even then his bravery is tempered by a self-deprecating sense of humor. Indy Jones in *Raiders of the Lost Ark* [1981, Steven Spielberg] is also not innately heroic. He's a scholarly man who finds himself in swashbuckling circumstances and rises to the occasion.

—Ford, interviewed by Jeff Rovin for *Moviegoer*, Mar 1982

Q. How would you describe [Rick Deckard] the character you play in *Blade Runner* [1982, Ridley Scott]?

A. He's a reluctant detective, he's forced to do a job he doesn't want to do....

Q. Do you have many discussions with Ridley about the scenes?

A. We have a lot of discussions about scenes but not about motivation. I don't ask him what my motivations are and he doesn't ask me what mine are. The discussions are usually about practical matters: what we're trying to get out of a scene, what the obligations are on him as the master of the story and me as the character. And then we'd look for common ground to accomplish the story points and the character points at the same time. And sometimes that's done without any discussion at all, and sometimes we discuss the hell out of it. But that's the process, basically.

—Ford, interviewed by Ralph Appelbaum for *Films*, Sept 1981

Q. Are there fundamental qualities you look for in a role?

A. Nothing I can set out in a list. Basically, a character is interesting to me because it *is* a character and *not* me.

Whether it's a hero or a heel, the element of likability is never as important as the likability of the project as a whole. And each part I play must also shift from even a *hint* of allowing a pattern to form in my career. I always want to compare and contrast the latest public and professional sense of who I am....

Q. Do fellow actors, writers, and directors resent it when you make suggestions concerning your character or the film as a whole?

A. Let me put it to you this way. I extend real willingness to my co-workers; in return I ask for the accommodation of a give-and-take environment. Not capitulation, but the opportunity for creative exchange. I've learned from experience that it profits everyone involved in a movie to understand everything from character motivation to why the wardrobe is the way it is. That may involve arguing, but I'd rather have that than have a character that doesn't work. On *Raiders of the Lost Ark*, Steven Spielberg and I did a *lot* of arguing, but we both profited from it. People put up with me because I'm sincere, because I don't do it for ego gratification. I may have more to say about the wardrobe than the wardrobe person wants me to, but that's the way I am about it. If things make sense to me, chances are they'll also make sense to an audience.

—Ford, interviewed by Jeff Rovin for *Moviegoer*, Mar 1982

It's not necessary for [Allie Fox in *Mosquito Coast* (1986, Peter Weir)] to be entirely likable as long as the audience can understand what he's about. You're always saying, "I know what he's talking about here," but then it's, "He's going too far. Jesus *Christ*!" Part of his irresistible charm is that he's willing to go further than anybody in the audience would have gone, he's got to outstrip them emotionally. And they've got to be by turns delighted and frightened by where he's going.

—Ford, interviewed by Kenneth Turan for *GQ*, Nov 1986

Actually, the most physically and mentally taxing film I've ever done was *Frantic* [1988, Roman Polanski] — the frustration and anxiety I had to create had a serious residual effect on me....

Q. Due to Roman Polanski's approach?

A. To a degree, yes; he's so intense! There's no question that Roman is hard to work with. He pushes actors *to the limit*. He goes over a scene again and again, maybe 20 times, before deciding how he wants to shoot it. He's got so much energy, and he exhausts you very quickly! He's 54 years old and like a rock, this little guy.... He's tough, but the results he gets makes working with him worthwhile.

Q. You endow many of your characters with subtle comic touches, but have never gone all the way with a sophisticated comedy until now [*Working Girl* (1988, Mike Nichols)].

A. Well, I'd always wanted to play comedy. Plenty of scripts are offered, but I rarely find one as ambitious, as filled with complex relationships and interesting characters as this one.... This film has a terrific dramatic structure, and I liked what it says about modern male-female relationships. There's a circumstantial equality here not often portrayed in film. It's part of the irony that this guy, relatively powerful in his world, is saved from ruin by a girl, a secretary [Melanie Griffith]....

Jack is an anomaly. To achieve success in his job, he can *only* show strength. But, we get to see him in other situations, which demonstrates his vulnerability, and creates sympathy for him.

—Ford, interviewed by Paul Freeman for *Prevue*, Mar 1989

The interesting thing is that good actors and good lawyers break all the rules. They are guys who throw out all the conventions and still win. Rusty [in *Presumed Innocent* (1990, Alan J. Pakula)] is self-contained, self-assured, controlled, which makes the relationship with Carolyn [Greta Scacchi] all the more of an anomaly in his life.

I've never experienced an obsession of such strength as Rusty Sabich does. In order to make it interesting, I thought it was important to see his resistance to the attraction so that it didn't become one-note. His attraction is not just based on a physical thing but on a relationship with this woman that is occasioned by their work together. He finds her intelligent and sensitive and a good lawyer, in addition to her more obvious physical qualities. In a way, I think he is more obsessed with the excitement of the situation than he is by the woman herself.

The naughtiness of it is something that really excites and attracts him, much to his regret.

—Ford, interviewed by Phoebe Hoban for *Premiere*, Aug 1990

Jodie FOSTER [1962-]

Born: Alicia Foster in Los Angeles. Work in commercials and on TV preceded her film debut in Napoleon and Samantha (1972, Bernard McEveety). In 1975, she played Iris in Martin Scorsese's Taxi Driver:

I'd like to say I studied and concentrated and researched, and that it all just came out of me, but I'm no method actor. In fact, I've never even had an acting lesson. If anything, what I do is by instinct. My method is to just do what I think is right. I don't think you have to *feel* the character and research it for years.

Q. How, then, do you explain the disturbingly authentic portrait of your youthful prostitute?

A. Well, I've never been one. And I've never observed or talked to a teen-age prostitute. But listen, kids aren't stupid any more, like they used to be. Everybody knows what hookers are. You see them in movies and on TV; you see them on Hollywood Boulevard. All the kids know how they act.

—Foster, interviewed by Judy Klemesrud for *The New York Times*, 7 Mar 1976

[Scorsese] was great, but for some reason he never gave me any direction. He didn't have much to do with my performance in *Taxi Driver*. Actually, De Niro did. He didn't tell me to do things, but he rehearsed with me over and over, and I knew the script so well that when we started shooting and he threw improvs at me, it was no problem.

[In *The Accused* (1988, Jonathan Kaplan)], I play a mixed-up character who is very strong yet terribly weak, very clever and smart but also uneducated and inarticulate, terribly angry and yet guilt-ridden.

The film is about the relationship between a high-powered young deputy district attorney [Kelly McGillis] who's living in a man's world, and her client, who's the victim of a very brutal gang rape. It's about how they change each other's prejudices and problems. Kelly's character is terribly cold and aloof, denying her own femininity and maybe embarrassed by it, and she looks down on this trashy girl who's all of the things she's tried to escape. What she learns is to embrace that because it's part of who she is, and that there's more to life than winning a case. And my character repossesses her will by telling her story, by being able to testify. She lives in a trailer and has a day job and moves from boyfriend to boyfriend. Kelly's character inspires a hope in her that she can achieve something better. They discover wholeness only through each other. Each of them is cut off from something the other possesses, and by becoming intimate and having someone care they become whole. It's the self-affirmation of the other in the mirror. You're my mirror and you're beautiful, then so am I.

—Foster, interviewed by Dan Yakir for *Interview*, Aug 1988

[In *The Accused*], Sarah walks into the bar at a time of strength. She's said "no" to her boyfriend and left. She's wearing a great outfit. More and more, she's becoming herself. When she plays pinball, she's one of the boys. She tells them, "I'm a winner." She feels like she's on top of things. Then her favorite song comes on.

I've been in this situation a million times. Your favorite song comes on. You feel great about yourself. You feel totally unself-conscious. There's no reason in the world why you shouldn't be allowed to do exactly as you feel, to be expressive....

Sarah's subconscious decision is: There's no danger here. And it's precisely that moment of will, of her feeling equal, being able to be a woman and one of the guys that is so incredibly anger making. Sexual violence is so much more angry than anything else. It's "How dare you think you have will over me, or that you have will over yourself. Because you don't...."

Jonathan's just the kind of director that I like. If I'm on the wrong track, he'll say, "No, no, no, no, no." But once he knows I'm on the right track, he's not afraid to be a part of my details. He'll say, "Why don't you bring that third thing up on the fourth paragraph...?"

He knows the little things that I do that I usually don't tell people and that they themselves don't see. I make certain gestures that are interpretive — he notices them all. I change dialogue in my mute ways to serve the symbolism of the piece. He understands why I'm doing that.

—Foster, interviewed by Sonia Taitz for *The New York Times*, 16 Oct 1988

[Anthony Hopkins as Dr. Hannibal Lecter in *The Silence of the Lambs* (1991, Jonathan Demme)] was in the middle of something, and then he started imitating my accent. The first time he did it, I wanted to cry and smack him. I was just so upset. You're in a scene, so you sort of feel those things, but as an actor, having somebody imitate your accent — it just killed me. It was the perfect thing for Lecter to do, because Clarice has been hiding her rural accent, trying to speak better, escape her origins in a certain way. And here's a guy who nails her.

—Foster, interviewed by James Cameron-Wilson for *Film Review*, June 1991

Michael J. FOX [1961-]

Born: Edmonton, Alberta, Canada. A Canadian TV series at age 15 — Leo and Me — led him to Hollywood and a film debut in Midnight Madness (1980, Michael Nankin and David

Wechter). Success on TV then led to starring roles in films, beginning with Back to the Future (1985, Robert Zemeckis):

Q. Christopher Lloyd's character in *Back to the Future* is so way out and crazy — did you have to discipline yourself, to hold back?

A. There are two problems doing a scene with Chris. First, is that you just want to pull up a chair, sit down and watch him, 'cause he's so much fun. The second is, if you don't keep your energy up and make sure you keep up with him, he'll blow you into the lobby. And not intentionally — he's a very giving, unselfish actor and very open to suggestion.

—Fox, interviewed by Darrah Meeley for *Screen Actor*, Spring 1986

When I first started doing the film [*Light of Day* (1987, Paul Schrader)], we were talking about wardrobe, and Paul said, "I want you to wear boots." I said, "Why boots? Does it have something to do with his height and he's insecure about it or something like that?" And he said, "No, I just want to *ground* you." I said, "Ground me?" And he said, "You don't walk — you *bounce*. I just don't want Joe to bounce."

—Fox, interviewed by Mark Morrison for *Rolling Stone*, 12 Mar 1987

[Eriksson in *Casualties of War* (1989, Brian De Palma)] was not a troublemaker. What he found in himself was that when he was pushed, he pushed back. Ultimately, you're a good guy or you're a bad guy, but you never know. In all of us there is an instinct to do what is right and not what is wrong.... This movie is about how much you will risk if you have nothing to gain....

I had humble empathy for the grunts. We weren't 18, we were in our late 20's and we were just making a movie. But it was hellishly hot [in Thailand]. We were homesick. We had insect bites, burns and sunstroke. After every take, I threw up. It certainly wasn't difficult for me to be that guy....

Sean [Penn]'s approach was that we played enemies so we shouldn't have any contact [during production]. But it was too difficult in Thailand for me to be a warrior all the time. Possibly to my detriment, I got up in the morning, put everything I was going to need that day as an actor into a "briefcase" and went to work....

—Fox, interviewed by Aljean Harmetz for *The New York Times*, 10 Aug 1989

Pauline FREDERICK [1883-1938]

Born: Beatrice Libbey in Boston. Work as a chorus girl and on Broadway preceded her film debut in The Eternal City (1915, Hugh Ford):

I was lucky from the very first moment I went into pictures. My very first director was Hugh Ford.... For both of us, it was our first pictures.

I don't think I have ever come in contact with a more extraordinary mind than Hugh Ford's. It works with electric speed; it crackles and sparks like a dynamo....

One of the characteristics he is famous for as a director is the frantic speed with which he works. When he was directing me upon one occasion we shot 22 scenes in an hour. He made the entire picture in eight working days. It may be economical and profitable for the company but it is exhausting for the actors.... I can tell you that when one has worked a day with Hugh Ford one knows that one has been doing a day's work. Rehearse? Fudge! "See here, Polly, you know what to do: you come in, walk to the table, take your gloves off, see the letter, look horrified and grab the telephone. All right! Let's take it: camera!" [She worked with Ford on four additional films, each co-directed by E.S. Porter: *Sold* (1915), *Zaza* (1915), *Bella Donna* (1915) and *Lydia Gilmore* (1916).]

Now, Mr. [Robert] Vignola's method [on *Madame Jealousy* (1917)] is the exact opposite of Mr. Ford's. He is of the school that believes in an abundance of rehearsing. Every step, every minute gesture, he wants repeated over and over again. He will try seventeen different ways of picking up an opera cloak and forty-nine variety of poses for a woman who stands at the fireplace watching for her lover to come through the door.

Quite the mildest mannered, most amiable and placid of directors in Emile Chautard. Never ruffled even by the most block-headed of the people he sometimes has to contend with — and I must admit that even actors give provocation for profanity — never excited, never in the slightest doubt as to what he wants, he always gets the best out of everybody. Of course he always continues to get actors who know their business. Himself an actor of the soundest French school, he has the craft of the drama and the art of acting at his finger-tips and he knows the camera thoroughly. [Frederick worked with Chautard again on *Fedora* (1917), *The Hungry Heart* (1917) and *Out of the Shadow* (1918).]

—Frederick, in *Photoplay Magazine*, May 1919

Morgan FREEMAN [1937-]

Born: Memphis, Tennessee. High school dramatics and acting studies at Los Angeles City College preceded his film debut as an extra in The Pawnbroker (1965, Sidney Lumet). Extensive stage work, including a 1967 Broadway debut, preceded his first major film notices as Fast Black in Street Smart (1987, Jerry Schatzberg):

[Jo Ynocenio], the costume designer called and said she wanted to go shopping with me. Fine. Whatever you say. I figure we'll be going to 42nd Street, see. But then she says, "I want to take you to Saks Fifth Avenue," and as soon as she said that, my mind was galvanized! So we went shopping at Saks. The Giorgio Armani stuff was too sedate, but we were sure at the right store! 'Cause being a pimp, it's all about lookin' good....

I've been called an intuitive actor, and I guess that's right. I go with what I feel. It doesn't do me any good to intellectualize about it. Take Fast Black. He's a real frightening guy; he's made it into an art form — intimidating people, then slacking off — but talking about it that way didn't help me. It was just getting into his *clothes* — that's when I started putting the character in place.

Sure, technique has something to do with it, knowing when to underplay, when to overplay. When you first see Fast Black, for instance, he's just a guy in a car having a conversation. Don't get all animated, don't 'act'. Then that scene on the basketball court, that was the time to go over the top.

—Freeman, interviewed by Ross Wetzsteon for *New York*, 14 Mar 1988

I just thought of the man [Joe Clark in *Lean on Me* (1989, John G. Avildsen)] as a hero. To me, he has heroic dimensions — taking on a job like this and then managing to do it. Not to confuse hero with saint. I also liked the fact that he had warts.

When you're doing a fictional person, you set all the parameters of the character. You're the shell and you fill all the spaces on the inside. When you do a living person, it's all already in place. Then you have to go and try to incorporate as much of that person as you can — dealing with the shell, the physical aspects of that person, body type, stance, how the body is used, because our body language speaks a lot more than our words.

You have to be careful about this sort of thing. The body language: that's the inner life of the character. When you're doing a live person — and Joe was right there — every time you make a mistake, you feel it and hear it....

I would just seek him out every day to get a shot of his adrenaline, and to put myself on track or make sure I was on track. If my energy level wasn't high enough, I would go find him, just touch his hand, shake hands with him or speak with him for a while.

—Freeman, interviewed by Lawrence Van Gelder for *The New York Times*, 3 Mar 1989

My father worked as a domestic when he was much younger for a lady that was crazy about him. I think that will happen, particularly with women who are left with all this.... And they hire someone to take care of it, and when they come in and start taking care of it, they're taking care of *you*. And the irony, the beauty of this piece [*Driving Miss Daisy* (1989, Bruce Beresford)] is they get this real close relationship and yet they keep that distance.

It's the servant-employer relationship. That's going to continue no matter what. It reflects the way that our society is stratified, black and white. And these are not young people — they're not going to change their way of looking at things. But still these relationships develop. My father has friends whom he's known since childhood, and they're white and he's black and they have that black-white relationship, but they still are childhood friends. And there's something that they can depend on in the framework.

I drew heavily on [my father] and the general knowledge that I have of these people.... [Hoke's] a very borderline character for black sensibilities and attitudes.... He has a real dignity to him — he's 60 years old in 1948, and it's important to stay within the social mores of the period.

—Freeman, interviewed by Myra Forsberg for *The New York Times*, 4 June 1989

G

Clark GABLE [1901-1960]

Born: William Clark Gable in Cadiz, Ohio. Pre-med studies preceded his touring in several stock companies and work on Broadway. In bit parts beginning with Forbidden Paradise (1924, Ernst Lubitsch), he then abandoned the screen for the stage in 1926. He began making films again in 1931 and was soon receiving larger roles, beginning with Dance, Fools, Dance, (1931, Harry Beaumont):

Lionel [Barrymore]...had more confidence in my ability than I did myself. "Clark," he told me, "I know that you are set for a career on the stage, but I feel that there are greater prospects for you on the screen. For me, will you take another test."

I couldn't refuse Lionel who had always been the first to help me when I needed help. So I took the test. It "took" and as a featured player I was getting along well, eating regularly and feeling quite contented. I hadn't been at MGM long when I was called to the casting office.

"Clark," I was asked, "How would you like to be Joan Crawford's leading man in *Dance, Fools, Dance*?"

I walked out, scared stiff. I had never met Miss Crawford and was still new enough to the business to be afraid of stars.

Well, Joan was swell. She showed me all about camera angles. She taught me how to make the most of close-ups, yet not overact. From her I learned a million tips about make-up, lighting, speaking lines and how to get over my awkwardness before the camera.

Dance, Fools, Dance proved a success and was my first step towards a permanent place in Hollywood. Had she wanted to, Joan Crawford could have "stolen" that picture right out from under me. Instead she bent over backwards to give me my opportunity.

—Gable, in the pressbook for *Love on the Run* (MGM, 1936)

In the beginning, it seems that this Gable stock had been going along for years in Hollywood, not doing much, when along came a manipulation called *Dance, Fools, Dance*. Up went the stock....

I've been trying to figure out ever since just what did happen. The newspaper writers called it "humanizing the heavy...."

I still hadn't got my bearings, or adjusted myself to the swing upward, when along came *Polly of the Circus* [1932, Alfred Santell] and *Strange Interlude* [1932, Robert Z. Leonard]. If *A Free Soul* [1931, Clarence Brown] was the peak of the Gable career, I should certainly rate *Polly of the Circus* as its low point — with *Strange Interlude* not doing much to improve matters....

In the first place, I don't look like a minister, nor do I look like a repressed doctor — roles which I portrayed in those two pictures, respectively. I couldn't even make myself believe that minister part. I was even more out of tune with the thwarted doctor as conceived by Eugene O'Neill in *Strange Interlude*. Naturally, this feeling was reflected in my work....

On top of that, while I was abandoning my particular type of role, other studios were developing players that were flatteringly referred to as "other Gables...." While Gable was performing as a hero, several other gentlemen were *humanizing heavies*.... It was no longer a Gable-novelty to see a gent getting rough with the heroine....

Red Dust [1932, Victor Fleming] with Jean Harlow... reinstated me in my correct medium. I had a swell story and another glamorous co-star; and for the first time since *Dance, Fools, Dance*, I figured I was once more on solid ground. I was lucky enough to get a repeat picture immediately following that in *No Man of Her Own* [1932, Wesley Ruggles] on loan to Paramount. I mean, I was repeating a role that was congenial to me, a role that was my sort of thing!

—Gable, interviewed by Nancy Pryor for *Movie Classic*, May 1933

I haven't hit nearly as many [female stars] as you think I have. There was only one who really got it — and that was a mean trick. It was Joan Crawford in *Possessed* [1931, Clarence Brown]. They wanted her to look surprised and so she had no idea what was coming. I had to let her have it. The director had two cameras grinding so we wouldn't miss it, since there would be no chance of a retake. The plan was successful. She registered surprise and how! — and then she started to cry. It took half an hour to get her calmed down. [See the Crawford entry for a complete list of their films together.]

—Gable, in an unsourced California newspaper, 23 Nov 1932, in the files of The Academy of Motion Picture Arts & Sciences Library

MGM thought it was punishing me when it pushed *It Happened One Night* [1934, Frank Capra] at me. And I thought so too.

It wasn't so much the picture itself. I hadn't seen the script. But I was loaned out to Columbia, and in those days Columbia was considered the wrong side of the tracks in the picture business.

I'd been making *Dancing Lady* [1933, Robert Z. Leonard] with Joan Crawford, and had been down with appendicitis. It bothered me for eight or nine weeks, but I guess the studio thought I was stalling. So they were going to show me how well off I was.

Eddie Mannix called me in and said, "We're sending you to Columbia" —just like that. I was so sore I turned on my heel and slammed the door as though I was trying to jam it through the frame.

I was still sore when I got a call to go over and see Frank Capra, who was going to direct the picture for Columbia. I belted down a couple of fast drinks and marched into Capra's office. He knew I wasn't happy, and he sat there with the script in his hand trying to be tactful. Frank is a gentle guy.

"Sit down, Clark," he said, drawing up a chair. "I want to tell you about the script."

I was still hopping mad. I jerked the script out of his hand and said: "Never mind, I'll tell you."

Frank only smiled and said, "I know how you feel, Clark, but read the script — it was written for you."

I started reading it and got interested in spite of myself, but it was comedy and I hadn't done comedy for the movies before and didn't know whether I could. Frank didn't think I'd have any trouble, but I wasn't so sure.

"I'll tell you what," I said. "I'll make a deal. We'll shoot four or five days, look at the rushes, and then if you want to get out of it, you can."

I didn't know how well or how badly I was doing, and when we saw the rushes, I still couldn't tell. I told Frank, "All right, what do you want me to do now?"

Capra smiled and said, "Just keep going."

I could hardly believe him, but he repeated it, and we went along.

—Gable, interviewed by Jess Stearn for *The Daily News* (L.A.), 16 July 1955

I didn't want to be in *Mutiny on the Bounty* [1935, Frank Lloyd] because it was a story about a crew of Englishmen and since I obviously wasn't English, I felt badly miscast. M-G-M had already assembled a group of all English players, with the exception of Franchot Tone, who had a Cornell accent instead of an Oxonian one. However, Irving Thalberg had cast me in the picture and while Irving was one of the most fabulously successful movie-production men who ever lived, I butted heads with him about it. "You've guided me right many times, Irving," I said, "but not this time. I can't do this. The public will never believe me as a first mate in the British Navy. I'd be more believable as the first mate on a Puget Sound scow."

For a while there was a deadlock. It was broken by Kate Corbaley, who headed MGM's story department....

Q. What did she say?

A. She said that the role called for maleness and independence, and that those two things were far more important than an English accent and knee britches and a three-cornered hat. "It's going to be a big picture," she told me, "and you'll be its hero, not its heavy. How can you lose?"

Q. Did you feel better about it as you went along?

A. Not me. I told everybody who'd listen. "I stink in it." I didn't realize I was wrong for several months.

—Gable, interviewed by Pete Martin for *The Saturday Evening Post*, 5 October 1957

My reaction to playing Rhett Butler [in *Gone With the Wind* (1939, Victor Fleming)] is both frank and simple. "The condemned man ate a hearty meal." Now don't get me wrong. As an actor, I loved it. As a character, he was terrific. As material for the screen, he was that "once in a lifetime" opportunity. But as Clark Gable, who likes to pick his spots and found himself trapped by a series of circumstances over which he had no control, I was scared stiff....

I realized that whoever played Rhett would be up against a stumbling block in this respect. Miss Mitchell had etched Rhett into the minds of millions of people, each of whom knew exactly how Rhett would look and act. It would be impossible to satisfy them all. An actor would be lucky to please even the majority. It wasn't that I didn't want to play Rhett. I did. No actor could entirely resist such a challenge....

[During production] there was only one problem but it was not an easy one to solve. Miss [Vivien] Leigh and I discussed it a hundred times. We reached the conclusion that Scarlett and Rhett, while definite and powerful characters and individualists, depended on one another for characterization. In this respect, I would like to pay tribute to Miss Leigh. She was Scarlet *every* minute and I am greatly indebted to her for her contributions to my performance.

—Gable, in the souvenir program for *Gone With the Wind* (MGM, 1939)

The problem of Rhett, to me, was that although he reads like a tough guy and by his actions is frequently not admirable, actually he is a man who is practically broken by love. His scenes away from Scarlett make him almost a weakling. My problem was to make him, despite that, a man people would respect. In that scene where Rhett has knocked Scarlett down the stairs and learns later that the baby is dead, while Scarlett hovers between life and death, Rhett has to show remorse and suffering.

—Gable, as told to Ruth Waterbury in *Photoplay Magazine*, Feb 1940

I've never played a part exactly like this fellow [in *The Misfits* (1961, John Huston)]. It interested me. As I saw it, there's not many of these fellows around. The reason there aren't is because the world has gone on. He is perfectly willing to go on doing what he always did, but the outside world has changed and it has reflected on what he does. He caught the wild horses first because he liked it, and second because they were sold as children's ponies. They decided to make dog food out of the mustangs. He didn't. They did....

Gay Langland says, "I know they can the mustangs for dog food, but that has nothing to do with me...." Gay Langland is a misfit because he hasn't kept up with the world....

This man loves the country and the excitement of rounding up the horses. He says, "I just sell them to the dealer." What bothers the girl [Marilyn Monroe as Roslyn] is that Gay is a contributor to the death of the animals....

He says to Roslyn, "I take my hat off to you." He sees sensitiveness, kindness, gentleness, that he never saw before in a woman. Basically, *he* is a very kind man, as many of these outdoor types are. He says to her, "Honey, a kind man can kill." And he also says, "I don't want to lose you but you've got to help me...."

He never does change through the whole picture. He's changed but not about the important things in his life. I think if this place was full of horses, he'd go right on catching them at the end of the picture.

—Gable, interviewed by James Goode for *The Story of The Misfits* (New York: Bobbs-Merrill, 1963); reprinted as *The Making of The Misfits* (New York: Proscenium Books, 1986)

Zsa Zsa GABOR [1919-]

Born: Sari Gabor in Budapest, Hungary. A stage debut in Vienna at age 15 and the title of Miss Hungary in 1936 preceded her move to the U.S. in 1941. She made her film debut in Lovely to Look At (1952, Mervyn LeRoy); later that year, she played Jane Avril in John Huston's Moulin Rouge:

Jane Avril fell in love as effortlessly as other women breathe, and with almost the same regularity. A singer and dancer who had Paris at her feet in the '90s, she had a vast capacity for affection and used it all. She was ruled completely by her heart, and her heart was ruled completely by a series of handsome men.

The whole point and purpose of Jane's life was highlighted by a single phrase, which she used when she appeared in a vision at the bedside of Toulouse-Lautrec [José Ferrer]. Having tried to comfort the dying artist, she said she would have to hurry away because "there is a beautiful man waiting."

There was always a beautiful man waiting for Jane, and this naturally made her a fascinating person to play. I loved her warmth and the way she looked at life with understanding humor. I liked the lines she spoke and the generous things she did. Jane was capricious and improvident, but she never was shallow or petty.

—Gabor, in *The Saturday Evening Post*, 15 Aug 1953

Greta GARBO [1905-1990]

Born: Greta Gustafsson in Stockholm, Sweden. Studies at The Royal Dramatic Theater School in Stockholm preceded her film debut as an extra in En lyckoriddare (A Fortune Hunter — 1921, John W. Brunius). Work in advertising films, then stardom in Mauritz Stiller's Gosta Berling's Saga (1924) led to a Hollywood contract:

During my first picture, Ibáñez' *The Torrent* [1926, Monta Bell], it was exactly as if I had to learn the making of motion pictures all over again. I was just beginning to learn the language. My days at the studio were long and difficult. I tried to place people and find out what they were doing. In Sweden the director is everything. Occasionally he has an assistant, and these two plan the sets, assemble the properties, select the costumes and put the story in screen form. With only a few carpenters, a laborer or two, three or four electricians, the cast and the director everything is accomplished. That is because pictures are not an industry as they are here. It often takes six months in Sweden to make one picture, here it takes six weeks....

I found that the perfected lighting at the studio here demanded a different sort of make-up. It took me longer to apply the grease-paint and powder than it did the other girls. That is but one example. I had to accustom myself in hundreds of other ways.

—Garbo, in *Theatre Magazine*, Dec 1927

After *The Torrent* I started on *The Temptress* [1926] with Mr. Stiller. But Mr. Stiller is an artist. He does not understand about American factories. He has always made his own pictures in Europe where he is the master.... He was taken off the picture. It was given to Mr. [Fred] Niblo.

How I was broken to pieces, nobody knows. I was so unhappy I did not think I could go on. I could not understand the English directions. Week in, week out from seven until six....

When I had finished *The Temptress* they gave me the script of *The Flesh and the Devil* [1926, Clarence Brown] to read. I did not like the story. I did not want to be a silly temptress. I cannot see any sense in getting dressed up and doing nothing but tempting men in pictures.

—Garbo, as told to Ruth Biery in *Photoplay Magazine*, June 1928

I don't know how I should have managed [*Flesh and the Devil*] if I had not been cast opposite John Gilbert. I had hardly met him before. He is quite a wonderful man — vital, eager, enthusiastic. He was on the set at nine each morning. He was so kind that I felt better — through him I seemed to establish my first real contact with the strange American world....

We finished *Flesh and the Devil*. I was helped by the knowledge that Stiller was getting his bearings and coming into his own.... I could see that he was getting his chance. I was happy for him, and this helped me through my own troubles.

—Garbo, interviewed by Akë Sundborg for *Photoplay Magazine*, May 1930

Andy GARCIA [1961-]

Born: Havana, Cuba. Studies at Florida International University in Miami and work in regional Florida theater and on TV preceded his film debut in Blue Skies Again (1983, Richard Michaels). In 1987, played U.S. Treasury agent George Stone in Brian De Palma's The Untouchables:

The first time I met Brian he wanted to see me for the role of Frank Nitti, the villain in *The Untouchables*, but I told him I would rather play George Stone and he was receptive to that. I had just come off of playing this character in *Eight Million Ways to Die* [1986, Hal Ashby] that had very similar colors to Nitti, so I had a very strong residue from that guy and I wanted to explore something else.... I did not want to play another dark individual and go into another movie and continue to kill people....

They had designed a lot of clothes for my character and I said, "I want this guy to have a little amount of clothes, one or two jackets that he wears all the time." And that's the way it was. For the last scene I wanted to wear a suit like the ones Eliot Ness wore, to show that my character had bought a suit, that he wanted to look like a Treasury man. The actual putting on of the costume every morning is always a ritual.... By the time I button the last button I am right in charac-

ter. It's like a spiritual thing putting on the clothes — it's a ritual like it is for the matador.
—Garcia, interviewed by David Galligan for *Drama-Logue*, 23-29 July 1987

Vincent [in *The Godfather Part III* (1990, Francis Ford Coppola) is] a young colt; he's got his own little gang. He's very bright in terms of street ethics, but he's very unpolished in terms of the civilized world — his manner and dress. And he desperately wants to protect the family and be a gangster. He's good at it: It's his destiny. A man only has one destiny, that's what the Godfather says.
—Garcia, interviewed by Guy Garcia for *American Film*, Dec 1990

Ava GARDNER [1922-1990]

Born: near Smithfield, North Carolina. After studies at Atlantic Christian College, she received a contract with MGM, making her debut in the short film, Fancy Answers (1941). In 1964, she played Maxine Faulk in John Huston's adaptation of Tennessee Williams' The Night of the Iguana:

I was determined to do my best in *Iguana*. I even made myself look awful, had lines penciled in under my eyes, because it was that kind of part. My hair was pulled back into a tight ponytail and I didn't wear anything except a sloppy serape and toreador pants. And John let me go back to my North Carolina accent, which meant that I got to say things like "cotton-pickin'" and call folks "honey," which, you can imagine, wasn't exactly a strain.

Dear John. I have only one rule in acting — trust the director and give him heart and soul. And the director I trusted most of all was John Huston. Working with him gave me the only real joy I've ever had in movies.

Take, for instance, the scene I have when Maxine goes for a romantic swim with the two beach boys she keeps around the hotel for just such occasions. I was nervous about doing it, and John, bless him, understood. He stripped down to his shorts and got into the water with me for a rehearsal, showing me exactly how he wanted it to go, then directed the scene soaking wet. That is my kind of director.

And John helped with the conceptualizing of Maxine as well. In the original Broadway production, where the role was played by Bette Davis, Maxine had been a genuine man-eater, a woman who was lonely, hard-bitten, and cruel. Shannon [Richard Burton] ending up with *her* was much more of a curse than a blessing. John, however, felt the character, especially the way I played her, was warmer, more human, a better person than Tennessee's original ending allowed, and he had the scene rewritten to emphasize the point. Tennessee was never happy with that, but anyone seeing the film knows that John's choice was the only one that fit. [Gardner also worked on Huston's *The Bible* (1965).]
—Gardner, in her *Ava: My Story* (New York: Bantam Books, 1990)

Allen GARFIELD [1939-]

Born: Allan Goorwitz in Newark, New Jersey. Studies at The Actors Studio in N.Y. led to work as an actor and director off-Broadway. Professionally, he has worked as both Goorwitz and Garfield (a name he adopted in tribute to John Garfield's performance in Body and Soul). He made his film debut in Orgy Girls (1968, Robert Canton). In 1974, he played surveillance expert, William P. Moran, in Francis Ford Coppola's The Conversation:

I think Francis's greatest gift is that he's a teacher. He's essentially a teacher because he imparts a certain kind of looseness. It's almost like a parent saying to a kid, "You can do anything you want," but also knowing that, even though the kid wants freedom, the kid wants to be told "no" too. Francis is there for that. He's there to help you when you fall, he's there to help you before you fall. He'll give you the chance to fall and he'll help you create.

In *The Conversation*, in the warehouse sequence, a lot of those lines are mine. Y'know, Francis tried to put a rein on it, but a lot of the lines were things I made up throughout the scene, which I loved his letting me do. And to show you, the most exciting thing in doing *The Conversation* was doing that warehouse scene as a Broadway play. Francis let the camera roll for twenty-five minutes and we did from coming up the elevator to the end going out the elevator in master without a stop. It was like opening night on Broadway. Of course he covered himself later with close-ups. But we did masters of twenty or twenty-five minutes — uninterrupted! I've never worked that way with any other director. Ninety percent is script. The ten per cent that fed me is improvisation. But can you imagine? A director saying, "Roll 'em, you're on," and you go for twenty or twenty- five minutes no matter what goes wrong...? You really feel like you're creating....

—Garfield, interviewed by Stuart Rosenthal for *Focus on Film*, Spring 1975

John GARFIELD [1913-1952]

Born: Jacob Garfinkel in New York City. Studies with Maria Ouspenskaya at The American Laboratory School, work with Eva Le Gallienne's Civic Repertory Group, a 1932 Broadway debut and a bit part in Footlight Parade (1933, Lloyd Bacon) preceded his first major film role as Mickey Borden in Four Daughters (1938, Michael Curtiz):

I always base my parts on specific people. Mickey Borden was based on Oscar Levant whom I had met only twice but who had made a terrific impression on me. There are some actors who do nothing but read lines. Some work from an image that is very helpful — particularly character people. It is all according to the part, or the challenge. Sometimes it doesn't come at all. I need to be driven and directed desperately. I have bad habits and I need help. I don't get it lots of times because they think I am all right, being from the Group Theatre....

—Garfield, in a lecture at The Actors Laboratory, Hollywood, 10 Dec 1945

Air Force [1943] is one of the first real examples of how Hollywood is changing. Howard Hawks told me the story one day in his office. I never saw a script. I never knew whether my role was a big one or completely unimportant. I only knew I wanted to be connected with this picture that couldn't fail to be great. Although the cast includes such people as Gig Young, Harry Carey, Arthur Kennedy, George Tobias, Jim Brown, John Ridgely, Faye Emerson, me — there's no star in the picture. The picture itself is the star. There is no magnifying of any personality. That's the right way to make a picture, I think. Subordinating the star roles to the action, to the *facts*.

—Garfield, in *Photoplay/Movie-Mirror*, May 1943

The Pride of the Marines [1945, Delmer Daves]...told the story of the boy's struggle to adjust himself and work out a romance to a happy conclusion after returning from the war incurably blind, yet hoping against hope to recover his sight.

In order to live the character honestly and with understanding, I stayed at Al Schmidt's home for a month.

I found him the kind of kid we like to think of as the wholesome American type: brave, determined, resourceful, fun loving, but not without some of the faults that are American too.

After I got to know Al well, I felt it was not only an honor to impersonate him on the screen but was also an opportunity to be of some help to the veterans like him and to their families and their sweethearts. For the problems Al faced in real life, as well as in the movie, are the problems that thousands of men face today when they come back to civilian life. It seemed to me important, first, to make the movie-going public appreciate and remember that for disabled veterans the great struggle didn't end with the coming of peace; and second, to accent the optimistic fact that the same courage and intelligence which licked the enemy can help bring these broken heroes through to the enduring happiness that they deserve.

—Garfield, in *The Saturday Evening Post*, 12 Jan 1946

Q. In *Pride of the Marines*, how did you convince yourself that you were blind?

A. I used an image.... People who are blind have certain instincts. I did speak to and watch a blind psychiatrist. They really listen because they have to depend on their hearing for so much. I found that they look up, sort of like a sparrow, as they never know exactly where the sound is coming from. On the basis of that alone, you can proceed to make a whole characterization.

—Garfield, in a lecture at The Actors Laboratory, Hollywood, 10 Dec 1945

William GARGAN [1905-1979]

Born: Brooklyn, N.Y. Work in stock and on the Broadway stage led to his film debut in His Woman (1931, Edward Sloman). In 1940, he appeared opposite Charles Laughton in They Knew What They Wanted:

Years later, Mary and I socialized with Laughton and his wife, Elsa Lanchester, in England, and off the set Laughton could be pleasant company.

On the set, he was the most difficult man I've ever worked with. An inveterate scene stealer, not at all subtle, without any of the charm of Barrymore (or his talent), he was a grubby man who fought and clawed for every inch of celluloid. He'd once played Captain Bligh [in *Mutiny on the Bounty* (1935, Frank Lloyd)]; now he kept playing Bligh. He'd become a tyrant.

On the set, while we were not shooting, he spent his time knocking the United States. Pretty soon we'd all developed a good-sized dislike for Fat Charles.

But the shooting was worse. In an early scene, Tony, the rancher, has me write a letter to the girl. He stands behind me and tells me what to write; I have to rewrite Tony to make it English and to make it romantic. The camera is up fairly close, on both of us, and as I would look down to start to write, or as I would say something, Laughton — behind me — would begin to writhe, his heavy face hanging over my shoulder like a full moon. Every line I'd speak, every time I'd bend to work on the letter, he'd growl, grimace, wipe his nose, lick his blubbery lips; he'd grovel, rub his hands, do everything but have a fit.

Finally, he had his fit as well.

So did Garson Kanin.

Kanin took it for a while, slowly burning while Laughton fiddled. He was a fine director, perhaps the best I ever worked with, showing me how to play a role both sympathetic and unsympathetic, a wife-stealer you could like, and I just placed myself in his hands. But Laughton needed no direction (Charles knew best); Laughton would take no direction (from an American!). The letter-writing scene dragged on, until Kanin's patience finally snapped and he began to let Laughton have it. Naturally Laughton answered back....

—Gargan, in his *Why Me?* (Garden City, N.Y.: Doubleday, 1969)

Beverly GARLAND [1926-]

Born: Beverly Fessenden in Santa Cruz, California. College dramatics and work on radio and stage preceded her feature film debut in D.O.A. (1949, Rudolph Maté, under the name of Beverly Campbell). Following several science fiction films, she appeared in Swamp Women (1955), the first of 5 films for Roger Corman:

Q. Did you enjoy working with him on these films?

A. The memories of working with Roger are pleasant because I got along with him very well. He was fun to be around and work with. We always did these films on a cheap budget, and people were always mad at Roger because he'd hardly feed us! And no matter what happened to you, you worked regardless. But that was all right with me because that was the type of person I was anyway — I don't like to fool around, I like to get the work done. I found Roger to be very professional — except when it came to putting us up in a good hotel or feeding us a decent meal or paying us any money! But that's how he started in the business so you can't fault him for that. After all, you didn't have to work for him. People shouldn't have complained — it was their own decision to work for Roger, no one forced them. I didn't ever bitch because I could see what he was trying to do. And he had a lot of people around him that were not particularly professional, so he really *had* to have the whip out to get the work done....

Q. In your Corman movies you yourself generally played plucky, strong-willed, sometimes two-fisted types.

A. I think that was really what the scripts called for. In most all the movies I did for Roger, my character was kind of a tough person. Allison Hayes always played the beautiful, sophisticated "heavy," and I played the gutsy girl who wanted to manage it all, take things into her own hands. I never considered myself very much of a passive kind of actress — I never was very comfortable in love scenes, never comfortable playing a sweet, lovable lady....

Q. You did all your own stunts in these films, didn't you?

A. At the end of *Swamp Women* I was killed with a spear and fell out of a tree. They got me up in this tree and Roger said, "When you're killed, you have to drop" — and this was a big tree! I'm not exaggerating when I say it was at least a twenty foot drop. I said, "Well, will somebody be there?" and Roger said, "Yes, they'll catch you." And by God, they had three guys underneath. And when they "killed" me, I just fell — dead weight on these three poor guys! [She also appeared in Corman's *Gunslinger*, *It Conquered the World*, *This Earth* and *Thunder Over Hawaii*, all 1956.]

—Garland, interviewed by Tom Weaver and Carl Del Vecchio for *Fangoria*, Jan 1986

Judy GARLAND [1922-1969]

Born: Frances Ethel Gumm in Grand Rapids, Minnesota. As a child, she performed as one of

The Gumm Sisters, making her film debut with them in The Meglin Kiddie Revue (1929). Her debut as a solo was Pigskin Parade (1936, David Butler). In 1937, she appeared opposite Mickey Rooney in Alfred E. Green's Thoroughbreds Don't Cry, the first of 8 films she and Rooney made together:

Once in *Thoroughbreds Don't Cry* they had to take a scene fifty-three times because we kept laughing. That was the scene at the dinner table in the boarding house. I was the only girl, and all the rest were boys, mostly jockeys. They all had to grab at the food, and I was supposed to get angry. But instead I had to laugh. They were so funny, Mickey Rooney and Frankie Darrow and everyone. And when I didn't laugh, someone else would. It was terrible.

—Garland, interviewed by Eileen Creelman for *The New York Sun*, 10 Feb 1938

When MGM decided to go ahead with *The Wizard of Oz* [1939, Victor Fleming], they wanted Shirley Temple for the role of Dorothy. But something went wrong with the negotiations at Fox, where Shirley was under contract.

So Metro settled for me, with a few slight changes. Slight? They tried to convert me into another person. They put a blonde wig on me and tried to change my nose, because it dipped in too much, and they put caps all over my teeth. I looked like a male Mary Pickford by the time they got through with the alterations.

Another strange thing about those days at the studio, they didn't teach me a great deal about acting. I was a trouper when I got there, but it was Mickey [Rooney] who taught me all about acting. He knew all the tricks, the important things about performing, and he taught them to me.

—Garland, in *The New York Journal-American*, 24 Feb 1964

[In *The Wizard of Oz*] I was with three very professional men, Ray Bolger, Jack Haley, and Bert Lahr. Remember that little dance we used to do down the yellow-brick road? Well, they used to crowd me out and I'd be BACK there. And Mr. Fleming, a darling man, he was always on a boom, would yell, "You three dirty hams, let that little girl in there!"

—Garland, quoted by Al DiOrio Jr. in *Little Girl Lost: The Life and Hard Times of Judy Garland* (New Rochelle, N.Y.: Arlington House, 1973)

[Billie Burke]'s giggly, and so am I. I get to laughing awfully easily in pictures. It's terrible. [During the production of *The Wizard of Oz*] something would strike us as funny, and we'd get the giggles — right in the middle of a scene.

—Garland, interviewed by Eileen Creelman for *The New York Sun*, 10 Feb 1938

[Mickey Rooney and I] worked an awful lot together. In fact, my first picture after *The Wizard of Oz* was *Babes in Arms* [1939, Busby Berkeley] with Mickey.

When we were in production, they had us working days and nights on end. They'd give us pep-up pills to keep us on our feet long after we were exhausted. Then they'd take us to the studio hospital and knock us cold with sleeping pills — Mickey sprawled out on one bed, and me on another.

Then after four hours, they'd wake us up and give us the pep-up pills again, so we could work another 72 hours in a row.

Half the time, we were hanging from the ceiling, but it became a way of life for us. [Rooney and Garland appeared together in 6 other films: *Love Finds Andy Hardy* (1938, George Seitz), *Andy Hardy Meets Debutante* (1940, George Seitz), *Strike Up the Band* (1940, Busby Berkeley), *Life Begins for Andy Hardy* (1941, George Seitz), *Babes on Broadway* (1941, Busby Berkeley) and *Girl Crazy* (1943, Norman Taurog).]

Vincente [Minnelli]...is a lovely man, but a temperamental son-of-a-gun to work with. He drives you mad, but he's a good director. [Minnelli directed Garland 5 times: *Meet Me in St. Louis* (1944), *The Clock* (1945), *Ziegfeld Follies* (1946), *The Pirate* (1948) and Garland's sequences in *Till the Cloud Rolls By* (1946, Richard Whorf); Garland and Minnelli were married 1945-1952.]

—Garland, in *The New York Journal-American*, 25 Feb 1964

I think I've become much better since then [*Summer Stock* (1950, Charles Walters)]. I know it sounds awful to say, but I never really liked myself on the screen before. But now I go to the rushes [of *A Star is Born* (1954, George Cukor)] and I actually enjoy them....

The four years [off the screen] have done me a lot of good. I...sang before live audiences. It improved my timing, and my voice is better, too. I think I look better. I don't have that "little girl" look any more.

—Garland, interviewed by Bob Thomas for The Associated Press, 9 Nov 1953, repr. in an unsourced article in the files of The New York Public Library for the Performing Arts

Teri GARR [1952-]

Born: Hollywood. Work as a dancer on TV's Shindig and in several Elvis Presley films preceded her first major role in The Conversation (1974, Francis Ford Coppola). In 1982, she played Sandy opposite Dustin Hoffman's Michael/Dorothy in Sydney Pollack's Tootsie:

When I first started making up this woman, I decided to play up her confusions and insecurities. She's sort of a statement about the times.

There are so many women out there like Sandy. Her mother told her to concentrate on getting her hope chest going, and then suddenly society changes and tells her she can be anything she wants, and she's confronted with all these choices. It's all so complicated now and Sandy is caught in the middle of all this....

In those early years I would try out for 100 parts before I'd get one job. That's a lot of rejection. I remember directors seeing me and saying, "You're good, but you're not pretty enough." And the only way I could handle it was through total denial. I'd say, "Well, you're wrong. You'll be sorry. There's no one righter than me." It's this survival tactic I made up for myself — and you see Sandy use it in *Tootsie*....

Working with Sydney is wonderful. He's so receptive to ideas. Remember Michael's birthday party scene in the movie, when Sandy gets locked in the bathroom and comes out swinging a plunger? Well, that was my idea. It occurred to me while shooting another scene at the party that my character had to get stuck in the bathroom. Sydney liked the idea and even rearranged all the cameras just to shoot the scene.

Dustin drove a lot of people crazy, but I loved it. Dustin is very brilliant — he sees 75 different ways to shoot a given scene, and he wants to try them all out before deciding which way works the best. Occasionally Sydney would let him have his own way, but that wasn't enough for Dustin. He wants you to *like* doing it his way, too. But Dustin acts that way for the good of the picture, not just to jerk people around.

—Garr, interviewed by Michele Riedel for *The Cable Guide*, May 1984

Greer GARSON [1908-]

Born: County Down, Northern Ireland. Studies at London University and repertory work in Birmingham preceded her 1933 London stage debut opposite Laurence Olivier in Golden Arrow. In 1939, she made her film debut in Remember (Norman Z. McLeod); that same year she appeared as Mrs. Chips in Sam Wood's Goodbye Mr. Chips:

I asked myself how I could do anything with that sparrow of a woman. My mother comforted me. "My dear," she told me, "the wife in this picture is not a sparrow, she's a dove. Yours will be the privilege of portraying a woman every man would like to have by his side. She is gentle and lovable. She gives out inspiration and an aura of relaxation."

—Garson, interviewed by Pete Martin for *Hollywood Without Makeup* (New York: J.B. Lippincott, 1948)

Mother said the role would reflect a side of me the public had never seen. Unfortunately, it is the side they have been seeing ever since. I am very grateful to Mrs. Chips and Mrs. Miniver [in *Mrs. Miniver* (1942, William Wyler)], but I must admit I am beginning to get a little sick of them.

—Garson, interviewed for *T.V. Guide*, 8 Apr 1955

There were many sides to Paula [in *Random Harvest* (1942, Mervyn LeRoy)]. She was, as most human beings are, capable of being several different persons — the music hall actress, gay and independent; the sympathetic, gentle girl; the adored wife, happy Mrs. Smith; the efficient secretary and finally the influential Lady Rainier. But more important even than the variety that gave color to the role was the fact that it was a sensitively written study of a woman's heart.

—Garson, in *The Saturday Evening Post*, 16 Aug 1947

I think Marie Curie [in *Madame Curie* (1943)] is the most difficult part I have ever played, yet I believe the role appeals to me more than anything I've done so far, because it is the study not only of a genius but of a warm, tender and romantic woman whose humanity was on the same high level as her great intellect.

In addition, I found the laboratory scenes engrossing, especially the handling of the complicated apparatus. It took me back to my university days, and I tried to recapture those times spent in the physics labs, even though they were a far cry from the Curies' experiments. What impressed me most about the picture was the tremendous care the producer [Sidney Franklin] and the director [Mervyn LeRoy] took in reproducing each experiment resulting in the discovery of radium. They called in Dr. R.M. Langer, physicist at the California Institute of Technology, to act as technical director and double-check on everything.

—Garson, interviewed for *The New York Herald Tribune*, 16 Jan 1944

I like Susie Parkington [in *Mrs. Parkington* (1944, Tay Garnett)] immensely. She is a fascinating person, possessing an insatiable curiosity. She is good, of course, but I try to indicate that she might, on occasion, be otherwise.

No person is completely good, or completely bad. It may be a cliché, but it's nonetheless true that there is good and bad in all of us. Motion pictures will really come of age when screen characters are permitted to be good, spiced with bad, and bad, sweetened with good....

Aging from a young girl to a spunky matriarch offers a difficult problem of make-up. My red hair photographs so light that I would have trouble aging realistically. A streak of white hair in a redhead would go almost unnoticed. Black hair was something else again. It could be changed clearly and dramatically, and I could act the various age changes not only more convincingly but with more personal conviction and ease.

Hair is such a part of personality that a change of hair color can result in a startling difference in characterization.... With dark hair I was able, I believe, to submerge my own personality and gain greater scope as an actress.

After four pictures with Walter [Pidgeon] I would know that there was something wrong if he didn't have a gag or an amusing remark before we played a dramatic scene. Trying too hard spoils more scenes than anything else. Walter's gags and jokes have a definite purpose. To ease tension. By this time, Walter and I work together automatically, by sixth sense. I know that I can depend on him, and he knows he can depend on me. That brief letdown before going into a scene makes for naturalness and spontaneity. I have checked on it, and it is amazing how many of our first takes are the best. [Garson and Pidgeon also worked together on *Blossoms in the Dust* (1941, Mervyn LeRoy), *Mrs. Miniver*, *Madame Curie*, *Julia Misbehaves* (1948, Jack Conway), *That Forsyte Woman* (1949, Compton Bennett), *The Miniver Story* (1950, H.C. Potter) and *Scandal at Scourie* (1952, Jean Negulesco).]

—Garson, interviewed for the press packet for *Mrs. Parkington* (MGM, 1944)

The role of Eleanor Roosevelt [in *Sunrise at Campobello* (1960, Vincent J. Donehue)] has intense, personal meaning for me. I consider portraying her to be a great privilege.

To me, Mrs. Roosevelt has always been the symbol of the highest ideals and integrity. No other woman in our century has accomplished more along humanitarian lines than she has.

It was in 1952 that I first had the honor of meeting Mrs. Roosevelt. We were working together in a war bond drive and I was deeply impressed with her dedicated spirit....

I think of *Sunrise at Campobello* as one of the most moving love stories ever told. It is set in 1924 — just after Mr. Roosevelt [Ralph Bellamy] was stricken with polio. Prior to that time, Mrs. Roosevelt was a shy, retiring self-effacing woman.

But, when her husband's political future was imperiled by his affliction, Mrs. Roosevelt suddenly emerged as a strong and forceful personality. She became F.D.R.'s great moral bulwark and fired him with the confidence he needed to pursue his political career.

Filming the part of a great person, especially one who is still living, is perhaps the most demanding task that any actress can have. Her performance must conform closely with the mannerisms and idiosyncrasies of the personality. She must resist the temptation to "glamorize" her character and thereby distort her role so that it no longer becomes believable.

At the same time, she must be careful not to exaggerate the distinctive characteristics of the person to the point that her role becomes a caricature. These are problems which an actress never has to consider when her role is a fictitious one.

When one is portraying such an illustrious person as Mrs. Roosevelt, she struggles to convince herself that she is keeping the role sharply in focus, giving it the dignity and stature it deserves. But I think she can never afford to be content with her performance.

To be content, she must regard the person with less respect than she regards herself. When an actress thinks in these terms, you can be sure her performance will be a poor one.

—Garson, for UPI, in an unsourced, undated article in the files of The New York Public Library for the Performing Arts

Janet GAYNOR [1906-1984]

Born: Laura Gainor in Philadelphia. Four years as a film extra at The Hal Roach Studios and a number of roles with the Western comedians Peewee Holmes and Ben Corbin, preceded her first major starring roles in Sunrise (1927, F.W. Murnau) and Seventh Heaven (1927, Frank Borzage):

Making *Sunrise* under the gentle and kindly direction of Murnau was a tremendous experience. George O'Brien and I made a pact when we started that we would do anything and everything that this man told us to do. I worked in water all day long in some of the sequences, worked until I seemed to have not a spark of life left in me. Murnau would thank me simply, and when I arrived home there would be a great bunch of red roses, expressing his appreciation.

—Gaynor, as told to Dorothy Spensley in *Photoplay Magazine*, Jan 1929

I adored doing *Sunrise* because it was my first really big step, and I learned a great deal from Murnau, who was an absolute perfectionist....

I was absolutely untrained as an actress, and he'd take twenty or even thirty takes of the smallest scene. I must say this wasn't because of me but because there'd be a glimmer of light on the wrong bullrush or something equally small. But it was wonderful training.

From there, to go to Frank Borzage, the director of *Seventh Heaven*, was almost enough contrast for a lifetime. Murnau was all mental, Borzage totally romantic — all heart....

—Gaynor, interviewed by Roy Newquist for *Showcase* (New York: Wm. Morrow & Co., 1966)

That's no *new* Janet Gaynor up there on the screen [in *A Star is Born* (1937, William Wellman)], with her silk stockings and her sex appeal and her glamour. That's the real Janet Gaynor — the real Janet Gaynor I've wanted to be on the screen ever since I went into movies; the real Janet Gaynor they've insisted on hiding under calico and cotton stockings and tatters.

—Gaynor, interviewed by Harry Lang for *Screen Book*, Aug 1937

Ben GAZZARA [1930-]

Born: New York City. Studies under Raiken Ben-Ari at Erwin Piscator's Dramatic Workshop and at The Actors Studio in N.Y., and work on Broadway (from 1954) preceded his film debut in The Strange One (1957, Jack Garfein), an adaptation of his first New York stage success, End as a Man. He worked on three occasions with director John Cassavetes: Husbands (1970), The Killing of a Chinese Bookie (1976) and Opening Night (1978):

Q. How did you start working [on *Husbands*] — did you have a script, or did you just talk about the characters?

A. Of course we had a script; it's all mystique that John improvised everything — not at all. Actually, we rehearsed. Rehearsal in John's films was to create the impression that it was happening for the first time. It was for him to hear, and look, and see, what was needed. And he would re-write right there on the floor. He'd see what was empty and where text was needed. A secretary was always taking short-hand. He loved actors, being a wonderful actor himself, and when an actor had an idea, he embraced it with great joy....

Q. Your character in *Husbands*, Harry, is the most troubled and unhappy. Was there a personal key for you?

A. [Long chuckle] Well, who doesn't have problems?

An actor uses what he can of himself, and sometimes the writer helps when the material is so good and real that you don't have to do much groping. But John was a clever devil, you know; he used a lot of things about you, without your ever knowing about it. He'd pick up clues about your personality and then use it in the character.

Q. How would he direct something if he wasn't satisfied?

A. If he was not satisfied, he never said he was not satisfied, he'd just do it again. And John was not afraid of shooting film. He would shoot it, shoot it, shoot it, until something remarkable happened. You had a lot of elbow room and felt that you could do no wrong. By the first day of shooting, you knew a lot about the characters, far more than usual.

—Gazzara, interviewed by Gavin Smith for *Film Comment*, May/June 1989

Leo GENN [1905-1978]

Born: London, England. A practicing barrister turned actor, he made his film debut in Immortal Gentleman (1935, Widgey R. Newman). In 1944, he played The Constable of France in Laurence Olivier's Henry V:

That I was able to play in *Henry V* at all was indeed one of the small improbabilities, among a very great number, which added up to the total improbability of such a film being made at such a time when shortages were at their worst, personnel unavailable, bombing continuous and every sort of difficulty to be added to those inherent in such an undertaking even at the best possible time. Larry...was by that time back from Hollywood and serving in the Fleet Air Arm at Portsmouth. On one leave he told me he was going to be released to make *Henry V* and that, if he did, I must play the Constable of France, which indeed I had done at the Old Vic, with him and directed by Tyrone Guthrie, in 1937.... I replied that it would be utterly impossible as, at the time it was suggested, I was in fact commanding a training battery and we were just starting the build-up of training gunner regiments for D-Day something like a year later. However, Larry was not prepared to take "no" for an answer from me or, as it transpired, from the War Office, who said a definite "no" when he asked for my release. After many discussions, however, he said: "Has he not got any leave due?" to which the reply was: "Yes, twenty-seven days." He said: "Very well, can't he do the work during his leave?" To this they agreed (after reference to my commanding officer) on condition that I did not do more than three days at any one time. This would have been quite enough to make anyone in his right mind say: "Well, that's impossible," and forget it, but not Larry, who chose, if you please, to so schedule things that I was able to come down overnight from Shropshire, where I was stationed, do three day's work, go back overnight and be with my battery on the following morning parade....

Incidentally, those completely crazy few days on *Henry V* provided at least two absolutely first-class examples of Larry's very special talents as, if I may refer to such a thing in these days, an "actor's director." In this particular regard he ranks in my experience with [Roberto] Rossellini [on *Era Notte a Roma* (1960)], and ahead of anybody else I have ever worked with, even including people of the calibre of John Huston [on *Moby Dick* (1956)].... The quality, in particular is that of never saying a word if a gesture or an indication would help in itself, never using one word more than is necessary to indicate what is wanted and, in Larry's case, saying: "Can I show you what I mean?" only in the last resort.

—Genn, contribution to *Olivier*, Logan Gourlay, ed. (London: Weidenfeld & Nicolson, 1973)

Chief Dan GEORGE [1899-1981]

Born: Geswanouth Slahoot in Burrard, North Vancouver, British Columbia, Canada. Chief of the Tse-lal-watt-Sioux tribe from 1947 to 1959, he then went into acting by chance, making his debut in 1963 when his actor son recommended him for a part on the TV series, Caribou County. He then made his film debut in Smith! (1969, Michael O'Herlihy); in 1970, he played Old Lodge Skins in Arthur Penn's Little Big Man:

I like Arthur Penn. He's a good director. If I had any suggestions, he listened to me, and then told me why it would be better this way and that way, and most of the time he was right. But in one particular scene, where I go up on the mountain to die, he never told me how to do it. That was my *own* song, my *own* dance, and my *own* way of talking to the great white spirit. Those things were all my idea.

I got along very good with Dustin [Hoffman], too. He's very easy to get along with, and he's a hard worker. He's what you would call a perfectionist — he likes to do his work well. If he felt he didn't do a scene well, he'd ask the director to do it over again.

—George, interviewed by Judy Klemesrud for *The New York Times*, 21 Feb 1971

Richard GERE [1949-]

Born: Philadelphia. Before working in repertory as an actor and musician (composer and performer), he studied philosophy at The University of Massachusetts. Work on Broadway preceded his film debut in Report to the Commissioner (aka Operation Undercover, 1974, Milton Katselas). In 1977, he played Tony in Richard Brooks' Looking for Mr. Goodbar:

[Brooks] didn't want to futz around spoon-feeding some actor who didn't know when to hit his marks. I told him I wanted to read the script, so what he did was go through the script, and just show me my lines. If my line started in the middle of a page, he'd rip off the top of the page, so I couldn't read any of the other actors' lines. He's a wild director, man. But after the first day of shooting, he trusted me totally. He knew I understood the character as well as he did, and I got total support. Knowing Tony wasn't the real killer made it easy to be as ugly or as outrageous as I wanted to be because I knew the audience would end up loving me. I'm not aggressive in real life. I'm very shy. Diane Keaton was shy, too. She was very nervous about the sex scenes. I was nervous about everything. I walked into a film that was already shooting and I didn't know anybody. Because of my own insecurity, I was very uptight the first day and she thought I didn't like her or respond to her as an actress, but we worked out our problems and it was a very creative experience. The set was closed, we improvised a lot. Brooks was right there, concentrating his energy on ours, so he was like an alter ego for us. Brooks was the best experience I've ever had. He told me no more than I needed and made me feel supremely confident. There was never any doubt in my mind that here was an incredible human being, working from a very clean place, with no dollar motive at all. He totally changed my ideas about filmmaking.

—Gere, interviewed by Rex Reed for *Travolta to Keaton* (New York: Wm. Morrow & Co., 1979)

It was not an easy process working with Terry [Malick on *Days of Heaven* (1978)]. The movie that was shot was not the script I read. It kept changing. Terry's a poet, and vague about what he wants. We'd set up for a scene, and Terry would say, "It's — it's like the wind coming through the window." And I'd say, "OK, I've got it." We'd do take after take, and a three-page scene might finally wind down to two or three lines.

—Gere, interviewed by Hollis Alpert for *American Film*, Oct 1979

Q. You've worked with five directors now. Who works well with actors?

A. Terry didn't really know about actors.... He knows when it's right; he knows when it's wrong, but he doesn't quite know how to make it work or why it's wrong. But he's very concerned about it. His bullshit barometer is real sensitive. He's after different kinds of things. He doesn't really care about the dramaturgy....

Q. So he wouldn't know what to tell you?

A. No, not really. He will learn that someday. I know he wants to learn how to do that. It takes time, like everything else.

Q. Does Paul Schrader know?

A. No, he doesn't really know the actor's process either. But he's very clear about what he's written and what he wants. He casts well and trusts the actor to fill it out.... [Gere worked on Schrader's *American Gigolo* (1980).]

I think as an actor I enjoyed working with Robert Mulligan [on *Bloodbrothers* (1978)] and Richard Brooks the best. They're very supportive and instil great confidence in the actor. Those films were centered around the performances.

—Gere, interviewed by Brooks Riley for *Film Comment*, Mar/Apr 1980

Q. How did you work on Jesse Lujack, your character in *Breathless* [1983, Jim McBride]?

A. Basically the root of him is music — music manifested by his moods. He uses the energy and emotions of the things around him to his own purposes. There's no guilt in him. He refuses guilt, he refuses despair. *He turns despair around.* He's a funny kind of character; he's not the kind of person you'd bring home to your mother and father. He'd be pocketing things: he doesn't see possessions as being personal. He has an outlaw mentality we haven't seen for awhile.

—Gere, interviewed by Maura Moynihan and Andy Warhol for *Interview*, Oct 1983

Edward Lewis [in *Pretty Woman* (1990, Garry Marshall)] was a pretty easy character for me to play.... I understood him immediately. As for Dennis Peck [in *Internal Affairs* (1990, Mike Figgis)], in general, the juicy, scene-stealing, crazy, out-there, energetic, charismatic character is always much easier to play than the slightly repressed one. That's been the case in all my movies. *Internal Affairs* was a very dark exploration of a personality. It was certainly a more violent film than I wanted to deal with. In the end, I did the film because it was a smart career move, because I had not had successful films for a while.... It was also a character that I was really interested in exploring.

Q. Why?

A. It was the levels of manipulation and control and how we all, on very subtle levels to be sure, because we're not psychotic — or most of us aren't — how we control and manipulate everything in our universe. Our friends, our lovers, our children, our co-workers. And on my own, outside of the career work, I'm trying to

figure out the same stuff. I found it a deeply spiritual voyage, working on this guy. It's interesting to explore how your psyche works, how your heart works, what your desires are. What the end result is. One reason I did *Pretty Woman* was to get out of that intense head.
—Gere, interviewed by David Rensin for *Us*, 30 Apr 1990

Henry GIBSON [1935-]

Born: Henry Bateman in Germantown, Pennsylvania. Work as a child actor on the Pennsylvania stage, in East Coast stock and then on Broadway (from 1962) preceded his film debut as a college student in The Nutty Professor (1963, Jerry Lewis). In 1975, he played Hamilton Haven in Robert Altman's Nashville:

It's strange for actors to be suddenly told they're not victimized by time and place and unities. Altman thinks of a script as a fluid, living, dynamic thing, not something to lock an actor into. We knew the starting point and destination of the film, but how to get there was up to circumstances. [Gibson also worked on Altman's *A Perfect Couple* (1979) and *Health* (1980).]
—Gibson, interviewed by Grace Glueck for *The New York Times*, 20 June 1975

Mel GIBSON [1956-]

Born: Peekskill, N.Y. In 1968, he moved to Australia where he later became a member of The State Theatre of New South Wales. He made his film debut in the low-budget Australian feature, Summer City (1977, Christopher Fryer). In 1980, he played the title role in George Miller's Mad Max:

Oh, that was fun, because you have your cardboard guy there. The story is comicbook style and everyone is ready to laugh at it. The images are graphic and cartoonic, so, to slot into that mould, you have to slip into that style. You can't do something totally different; it just doesn't work.

Then you have this problem of the character being a closet human being. He has to interact with other characters and yet not appear to. It is a little tricky. [Gibson played Max for Miller in two other films: *The Road Warrior* (1982) and *Mad Max: Beyond Thunderdome* (1984).]

Guy [in *The Year of Living Dangerously* (1983, Peter Weir)] had to be a journalist first, but he also had to act like a member of the audience. It is not one of those films which assaults the senses, like *Mad Max*. It actually asks you to think a little bit. And to help you along as an aid or a crutch to the process, you had Guy Hamilton, who, like a member of the audience, keeps asking, "What's going on around here? What's with this dwarf? Things are happening to me, but what?"

Guy is like an alien person coming into a situation, where he is manipulated by this dwarf, Billy Kwan [Linda Hunt]. He seldom initiates anything except in a few instances where his masculine instincts take over. But that's about it. It is his journey through this strange place [Indonesia] and around all these unusual characters....

Q. In a way, Guy is an extremely masculine man: the careerist, trying to operate in the world, and yet understanding so little.

A. Sure. He is really green and inexperienced in life. He had been in the newsroom in Sydney and all of a sudden he is in the middle of a situation that is dangerous. He is in a strange place where people don't like what he is, involved with this woman [Sigourney Weaver as Jill]. [In the end,] he screws up somebody's career just for a story. He really likes her and doesn't see it. She's crazy about him. But he does learn that he just can't step on people for his own reasons. That's what makes revolutions and wars.

But Guy does grow. That is the good thing about the character. But even then, he is not totally converted. He has just gained enough insight into things to figure, "Yeah, why not do this for a change?"

Q. What things did you learn from working with director Peter Weir on that film?

A. Peter always gives you the right dope. He would die for a friend, but he is also a pragmatist. People almost keel over about what he says at times; he doesn't mess around. Once he told me, "You were 15 per cent of what you should be in that shot. You'll get away with it, but be aware of it!"

Q. How did you get on with Sigourney Weaver?

A. We had a close friendship. It is almost impossible to work with someone you don't get on with. Linda Hunt and Michael Murphy were different in their approach; I was watching them and they were really up to it, energy-wise. They had tons of it. I usually come in from underneath some place, whereas they sort of jump on it. They work from tension — which can be good. It all depends on who you are; I can't work with that tension. If there is tension, I try and push it out and, I suppose, channel it. They handled it; if they hadn't it would be very obvious. [Gibson had previously worked on Weir's *Gallipoli* (1981).]

—Gibson, interviewed by Margaret Smith for *Cinema Papers*, Mar 1983

[In *The River* (1984, Mark Rydell)] I play a staunch, straight, basic American farmer. He's very uncomplicated: he works on the land and gets a reward for that from the land. He has his own little acreage and his dilemma is to try and hang on to it in the face of adversity — he is threatened not only by nature but by people. He has a particular kind of pride — of not having to answer to anybody, any employer. He's God-fearing, a bit hotheaded, and certainly not cynical.

—Gibson, interviewed by Dan Yakir for *Horizon*, Dec 1984

I pictured my part, Martin Riggs [in *Lethal Weapon* (1987, Richard Donner)], as an almost Chaplinesque figure, a guy who doesn't expect *anything* from life, and even toys with the idea of taking his own. He's not like the stalwarts who come down from Mt. Olympus, wreak havoc and go away. He's somebody who doesn't look like he's set to go off — until he actually does!" [Gibson reprised the role in *Lethal Weapon II* (1989, Richard Donner) and *Lethal Weapon III* (1992, Richard Donner).]

—Gibson, interviewed by Milo Mitchell & George Hadley-Garcia for *Prevue*, May/July 1987

Mac [in *Tequila Sunrise* (1988, Robert Towne)] has an unsavory profession. Yet he's honest in all his dealings and doesn't lie — an interesting combination. Hopefully, the audience will feel sympathy for him. I know that sounds terrible, but the film doesn't advocate drugs — just the opposite!

The guy is paranoid, and with good reason. He's not sure what's going on around him. Somebody might be setting him up, and all he can do is lay low while the shit flies. He's calm in a situation of extreme which makes me admire his intelligence and cool. When a character has distasteful qualities, I want the audience to know he's got *more* than one layer by finding a point of accessibility. Maybe he is a crumb, but there's a *reason* why. There's an ambiguity about Mac that's important in keeping the audience from judging him too hastily.

—Gibson, interviewed by Paul Freeman for *Prevue*, Mar 1989

John GIELGUD [1904-]

Born: Arthur John Gielgud in London, England, into a theatrical family. Studies at The Royal Academy of Dramatic Art under Claude Rains preceded his debut on the British stage in 1921. He made his film debut in Who is the Man? (1924, Walter Summers), and in 1932, he made his first sound film:

Insult [1932]...was my first 'talkie.' The director, an American named Harry Lachman, was also a painter. He had a great feeling for photography, and his arrangements of light and scenic composition were admirable — but as a director of acting he was rather eccentric. He had...a violent temper which he displayed four or five times every day. He used to go red in the face and scream at everybody, not so much from real anger, I think, as from a natural desire to ginger things up every now and again. The film was set in the East and Lachman suddenly had the idea of showing all the scenes in a certain 'sequence' through a veil of mist. Ten men would rush on to the set when all was ready for a 'take,' brandishing foul-smelling torches filled with some nauseous substance which emitted clouds of smoke. We would all begin to cough and rub our eyes, and then, just as the fog was beginning to clear, there would be shouts of delight from Lachman, and the cameras would begin to turn.

—Gielgud, in his *Early Stages* (London: Taplinger Publishing Co., 1939)

Hitchcock came to me and said that he'd got a marvelous Hamlet part for me to do in modern dress. The idea [of *Secret Agent* (1936)] was that the character, like Hamlet, had to undertake a murder. But I don't think Hitchcock had all that much confidence in me. When we came to make it, all the psychological interest was dissipated. It was quite fun to do, but it didn't really work all that well.

—Gielgud, interviewed by Michael Billington for *The Times*, 17 Apr 1967

In *Secret Agent* I played with Peter Lorre, the very striking German actor who had played "M" for Fritz Lang [in *M* (1931)]. He was a morphine addict and an expert in stealing scenes by putting in extra unrehearsed business at the take.

Joseph Mankiewicz's *Julius Caesar*, made in 1952, [released 1953], was the first film I really enjoyed making. The producers wanted to emphasize the political side of the play and Caesar [Louis Calhern] was played as a Tammany boss, so it was said, though I did not see much sign of it....

I was surprised to find that I did not have to alter my stage performance for the film to any great extent, and my knowledge of the play was a great help. Marlon Brando, on the other hand, was greatly hampered by the fact that he did not know how the scenes were placed by Shakespeare or how they progressed from one climax to another. They would photograph him for a couple of days in the taxing speeches of the Forum scene, and then he would lose his voice and be unable to work. They would fill in time by filming the extras, taking lots of shots of faces in the crowd responding, then Brando would recover and come down to the studio to do another speech....

Brando was very self-conscious and modest, it seemed to me. He would come on to the set in his fine, tomato-colored toga, his hair cropped in a straight fringe, and would look around nervously, expecting to find someone making fun of his appearance. Then he would take out a cigarette and stick it behind his ear.

—Gielgud, in his *Gielgud: An Actor and His Time* (London: Sidgwick & Jackson, 1979)

One knows that the best things in films are nearly always done by the director. Somebody told me the other day that in the film *The Chimes at Midnight* [1966] with Orson Welles, one of the most effective moments in the film is one in which I [as Henry IV] look at Falstaff [Keith Baxter]'s body, and then look at Prince Hal, and so on — there are 5 people. We never did the scene at all. On the last day Orson said: "There's a close-up I have to do of you, just look down there; now look up at me." I never even saw him made up as Falstaff, but it appears that way because of the clever cutting.... And that shows how much you owe to the cutter and the director when it comes to the screen. You can't really control your performance at all.

—Gielgud, interviewed by Derek Hart for BBC-2, Mar 1966

Orson Welles was splendid to work with, although he was always pressed for money and usually in poor health. He engaged a very fine company but he could not afford to keep us all permanently employed. I went over for a week's shooting in Spain, then Margaret Rutherford went over for a week, then Jeanne Moreau, and Orson, who was playing Falstaff, had still not done any of his own scenes. By the time he got round to them he was tired out and there was nobody left for him to act with. I never even saw him made up as Falstaff until I watched the film in the cinema. He had found a marvelous setting for the court scenes, a great empty building in the hills above Barcelona, which had been a prison at one time and had a huge hall with a stone floor. However there was no glass in the windows and the cold November air poured in. I was wearing tights and a dressing gown and practically nothing else for my death scene. I would sit on my throne with a tiny electric fire to warm my feet while Orson spent his last pesetas sending out to buy brandy to keep me going.

By far the most exciting film I have ever made was Alain Resnais's *Providence* [1977]. I was very impressed by David Mercer's script. My own part was fascinating, if somewhat alarming; a very tough, Augustus John kind of character, drunk half the time, lying in bed drinking white wine and throwing bottles about, and roaring a lot of very coarse dialogue. He is an old man trying to finish a novel and at the same time dying of cancer and confusing the novel with his own past life. His wife has killed herself by cutting her wrists in a bath and he feels he may have been responsible....

The part seemed to have wonderful opportunities, though I was afraid that I would not be sufficiently craggy for it. However, Resnais seemed to have confidence in me, and I threw myself into the work, acting scenes that would have embarrassed me dreadfully on the stage. At one point I was asked to put suppositories up my bottom under the bedclothes and play a scene in the lavatory which I confess I found somewhat intimate....

Resnais has a genius for individual groupings.... In *Providence* there is a fine shot of the static scene at the lunch table, at the end of the film. A camera on an enormous crane focused on us all [Gielgud, Dirk Bogarde, Ellen Burstyn and David Warner] as we began our meal, sitting round the table with the servants, and the big dogs sitting nearby. Then the camera went up into the air over an enormous expanse of trees and sky, and did a complete semi-circle. As it slowly came down again the servants were seen clearing away the lunch. It was a most beautiful shot and took a long time both to act and to photograph. We had to keep still for about four minutes before the camera came back to us again. Everything, every camera movement, detail, piece of furniture, was carefully thought out by Resnais beforehand.

—Gielgud, in his *Gielgud: An Actor and His Time* (London: Sidgwick & Jackson, 1979)

John GILBERT [1899-1936]

Born: John Pringle in Logan, Utah. Brief work with The Baker Stock Company in Spokane, Washington preceded his career as an extra at The Inceville Studios in Los Angeles, beginning with Matrimony (1915, Scott Sidney). In 1919, he signed a contract with Maurice Tourneur to serve as his production assistant. That year he starred in Tourneur's The White Heather. In 1920, he starred in, co-wrote and assistant directed both Tourneur's The White Circle and Deep Waters. As an actor, Gilbert starred in a fourth film for the director — While Paris Sleeps (1923). He became a leading man when he moved to MGM in 1924:

[Irving] Thalberg wanted me to play Danilo in *The Merry Widow* [1925]. Von Stroheim, the director, wanted Norman Kerry to play Danilo. Thalberg's wish was law. Von Stroheim sent for me one day and offered his hand. With guttural Austrian accent he formally explained, "Gilbert, I am forced to use you in my picture. I do not want you, but the decision was not in my hands."

"I assure you that I will do everything in my power to make you comfortable."

If you have ever sensed humiliation, you may be able to understand my reaction to the forego-ing speech. I guaranteed Stroheim that I would do my best to please him, and hated him in my heart. Throughout the first week of the picture Von kept his promise. During the second week he became a tyrant. At the beginning of the third week, I walked out. A fifteen minute session on the set had resulted in my telling him where he could put *The Merry Widow* and what he could do with Danilo. I went to my dressing room and tore off my uniform. Von followed and apolo-gized. Whereupon we had a drink. I apologized to Von and we had another drink. Then we had a drink and I returned to the set. That disagree-ment cemented a relationship which for my part will never end....

[King] Vidor did not want me to play Jim Apperson [in *The Big Parade* (1925)]. He said I was too sophisticated, and that I was hard to handle. Poor King. I had given him so much trouble during *The Wife of the Centaur* [1924] that he had reasonable cause for complaint, but what he did not know, was that I had been purged in the fires of wisdom and experience. Again Thalberg won out. A grand battle could have waged had I knocked the chip off my director's shoulder on the day he said, "Anything you have to say, say now, in Irving's presence, and keep your mouth shut after we start the picture."

My reply to King was, "In two pictures which we made together [also *His Hour* (1924)], every-thing which I said would be bad, was good; and those things which you declared would be good, were good. I will never question your judgment again." And I never did.

The day came for starting the picture. It was to be my first starring vehicle for Metro-Goldwyn-Mayer. A little six-reel movie of the war, but something more behind it. Thalberg was the first to sense an underlying greatness in our story, which imbued Vidor and the rest of us with a knowledge of our responsibility....

The gum chewing episode — with little Renée Adorée. Only a suggestion was offered in the script and no one really knew what would happen. Cameras started and away we went. Minute after minute after minute; impromptu; inspired; both Renée and me, guided by some unseen power, expressing beauty....

No love has ever enthralled me as did the making of this picture. No achievement will ever excite me so much. No reward will ever be so great as having been a part of *The Big Parade*. It was the high point of my career.

—Gilbert, in *Photoplay Magazine*, Sept 1928

For the first time in five years, I have a part [Don Antonio De la Prada in *Queen Christina* (1933, Rouben Mamoulian)] I feel I can play. It is a great opportunity. And I owe to Miss Greta Garbo a far greater debt of gratitude than I can ever hope to repay.

I have been miserable for a long time. It was terrifying to discover that overnight I had plunged from the height of popularity to almost oblivion. Now, quite as suddenly as that hap-pened, comes this amazing reversal. It is an astonishing experience.

It is a profound delight to play again on the screen with Miss Garbo. She is a great artist and a great woman. It is no secret that it was she who was responsible for my playing this part. She believed I was the victim of a terrible wrong. She simply wanted to set it right, if she could. [Garbo and Gilbert had previously worked together on

Flesh and the Devil (1926, Clarence Brown), *Love* (1927, Edmund Goulding) and *A Woman of Affairs* (1928, Clarence Brown).]

—Gilbert, interviewed by Ruth Rankin for *Photoplay Magazine*, Nov 1933

Dorothy GISH [1898-1968]

Born: Massillon, Ohio; sister of Lillian Gish. A debut in 1902 and much subsequent work on the stage with her sister and mother preceded her film debut, opposite Lillian in An Unseen Enemy (1912, D.W. Griffith). In 1918, she played the "Little Disturber" in Griffith's Hearts of the World:

Want to know where the "Little Disturber" character *really* came from? Well, she was a little Cockney girl; she's English, not French at all. Mr. Griffith saw her on the Strand one day, freshness, wig-wag walk and all. He followed her for hours — or rather, we did, and then I thought he was dreadful to make me play her. I couldn't. Besides, I didn't like her. I thought she was crazy! But Mr. Griffith insisted, and then I cried. He insisted some more.... [Gish also worked on Griffith's *The Muskateers of Pig Alley* (1912), *The Informer* (1912), *The New York Hat* (1912), *My Hero* (1912), *A Cry for Help* (1912), *Oil and Water* (1913), *The Perfidy of Mary* (1913), *The Lady and the Mouse* (1913), *Just Gold* (1913), *Her Mother's Oath* (1913), *Home, Sweet Home* (1914), *Judith of Bethulia* (1914) and *Ophans of the Storm* (1922).]

—Gish, interviewed by Julian Johnson for *Photoplay Magazine*, Aug 1918

Lillian GISH [1896-]

Born: Springfield, Ohio. On stage since the age of 6, she made her film debut in An Unseen Enemy (1912, D.W. Griffith) after visiting her friend Mary Pickford at the Biograph Studios in New York. She eventually made 36 films for Griffith:

"Gentlemen," [Griffith] said in a courtly manner that we were to discover was characteristic. "These are the Gish sisters, Miss Lillian and Miss Dorothy. We will rehearse the story of two girls trapped in an isolated house while thieves are trying to get in and rob the safe." He stared at us. "You're not twins, are you? I can't tell you apart." He strode out of the room and returned with two ribbons, one red and the other blue: "Take off your black bows, and tie these on. Blue for Lillian, red for Dorothy. Now, Red, you hear a strange noise. Run to your sister. Blue, you're scared, too. Look toward me, where the camera is. Show your fear. You hear something. What is it? You're two frightened children, trapped in a lonely house by these brutes. They're in the next room." Mr. Griffith turned to one of the men: "Elmer [Booth], pry open a window. Climb into the house. Kick down the door to the room that holds the safe. You are mean! These girls are hiding thousands of dollars. Think of what *that* will buy! Let your avarice show — Blue, you hear the door breaking. You run in panic to bolt it."

"What door?" I stammered.

"Right in front of you! I know there's no door, but pretend there is. Run to the telephone. Start to use it. No one answers. You realize the wires have been cut. Tell the camera what you feel. *Fear — more fear!* Look into the lens! Now you see a gun come through the hole as he knocks the stovepipe to the floor. Look scared, I tell you."

It was not difficult to obey. We are already practically paralyzed with fright.

"No, that's not enough! Girls, hold each other. Cower in the corner." Whereupon he pulled a real gun from his pocket and began chasing us around the room, shooting it off. We did not realize that he was aiming at the ceiling.

"He's gone mad!" I thought as we scurried around the room, looking frantically for an exit.

Suddenly the noise died. Mr. Griffith put away his gun. He was smiling, evidently pleased with the results. "That will make a wonderful scene," he said. "You have expressive bodies. I can use you. Do you want to work for me? Would you like to make the picture we just rehearsed?"

Mr. Griffith discouraged vanity in us. We were one big family, warmly united in a common goal. The films were important, not the players. If Mr. Griffith seemed to be playing chess with us, it was for an important purpose. Under his benevolent eye we came alive, stretching our talents in order to realize his conceptions.

Once the parts were awarded, the real work would begin. At the initial rehearsal Mr. Griffith would sit on a wooden kitchen chair, the actors fanning out in front of him, and as he called out the plot, they would react, supplying in their own words whatever was appropriate for the scene.

As rehearsals continued, Mr. Griffith would move around us like a referee in the ring, circling, bending, walking up to an actor, staring over his great beak of a nose, then turning away. By the time that we had run through the story several times, he had viewed the action from every conceivable camera angle. Then he would begin to concentrate on characterization. Often we would run through a scene dozens of times before he achieved the desired effect. If we still failed, he would act out the scene himself with exaggerated gestures that he would later moderate in us.

—Gish, in her (with Ann Pinchot) *The Movies, Mr. Griffith and Me* (New York: Prentice-Hall, 1969)

You know the scene in the closet [in *Broken Blossoms* (1919, D.W. Griffith)], where I spin round and round in terror as Donald Crisp is trying to open the door to beat me and kill me. I worked that out myself, and never told Griffith what I was going to do. You see, if I had told him, he'd have made me rehearse it over and over again; and that would have spoilt it. It had to be spontaneous — the hysterical terror of a child....

The smile where I just lift the corners of my mouth with my two fingers — that was all mine, too. I didn't think it out; it was automatic, instinctive.

—Gish, interviewed for *Sight & Sound*, Winter 57/8

Q. When you came to make *Way Down East* in 1920, it seems to me that you really did take your life in your hands, particularly with that ice floe sequence. Had you any idea of the dangers involved when you started that film?

A. Yes, when I heard the story I knew it was going to be an endurance test, and I started walking and taking cold baths and getting ready for it. We lost several lives, you know — the girl, Clarine Seymour, who was in *True Heart Susie* [1919, D.W. Griffith], played the part next to mine, and the exposure was too much for her.

Q. But now doesn't that suggest to you that Griffith must have been a very hard man in many ways?

A. No, not at all. He had his face frozen, he was out in the cold longer than any of us — whatever he asked us to do, he did something that was more difficult. In those days we felt the film was important, the most important thing of all — we weren't. Anything he asked, anything that we thought was necessary, we did without question....

—Gish, interviewed by Sheridan Morley for BBC-2 Late-Night Line Up; repr. in *Films & Filming*, Jan 1970

During the scene [in *Way Down East*] where I'm on the ice I had the idea to let my hair and hand drag in the water. It was so cold that it was like putting your hand in a flame. That hand still bothers me today.

Mr. Griffith was up on a little extension built out over the falls and because of the noise he could only signal by waving his megaphone so that Dick Barthelmess would know when to begin running across the ice to save me. I was facing the falls and watching them come nearer and nearer. I thought, "Well, it's too late now, I can't get up and run." So I just started saying my prayers. At the last minute Dick grabbed me, but I was too weak to help him. He wasn't a big, strong man, but in his fear he became one. He slipped and fell but he got right up with me in his arms.... Later when we saw the footage, Dick said: "There ain't enough money in the world to make me do that again."

Afterwards, Mr. Griffith and I had a quarrel when we got to the cabin scene. He wanted me to put fresh make-up on and fix my wet hair. Knowing what the girl had been through, I had a fit. He said, "You do as you're told. This film has to make money." So I did it.

—Gish, interviewed for *Horizon*, Aug 1979

Q. Did you never use doubles in those days?

A. Never. It wasn't sportsmanlike. And besides, we felt we moved in a certain way and that the audience could catch a double — they would walk differently, move differently and spoil the film. Or make them think something was wrong. And I think to this day they have that feeling when it's not the same person. [Gish also worked on Griffith's *Two Daughters of Eve* (1912), *In the Aisles of the World* (1912), *The One She Loved* (1912), *The Muskateers of Pig Alley* (1912), *The New York Hat* (1912), *The Burglar's Dilemma* (1912), *A Cry for Help* (1912), *Oil and Water* (1913), *The Unwelcome Guest* (1913), *A Misunderstood Boy* (1913), *The Left-Handed Man* (1913), *The Lady and the Mouse* (1913), *The House of Darkness* (1913), *Just Gold* (1913), *A Timely Interception* (1913), *The Mothering Heart* (1913), *During the Round Up* (1913), *A Woman in the Ultimate* (1913), *A Modest Hero* (1913), *So Runs the Way* (1913), *The Madonna of the Storm* (1913), *The Battle at Elderbush Gulch* (1913), *The Battle of the Sexes* (1914), *Home, Sweet Home* (1914), *Judith of Bethulia* (1914), *The Escape* (1914), *The Birth of a Nation* (1915), *Intolerance* (1916), *Hearts of the World* (1918), *The Great Love* (1918), *The Greatest Thing in Life* (1918), *The Romance of Happy Valley* (1918), *True Heart Susie* (1919), *The Greatest Question* (1919) and *Orphans of the Storm* (1922).]

—Gish, interviewed by Sheridan Morley for BBC-2 Late-Night Line Up; repr. in *Films & Filming*, Jan 1970

The Wind [1928, Victor Seastrom] was one of the grimmest experiences of my 105 movies over 75 years. It was also one of the most gratifying films I made at Metro-Goldwyn-Mayer.

The picture was an unrelenting view of the effects of a brutal desert environment on a delicate young woman unable to cope with it. The wind forces her into an unwanted marriage, brings about her meeting with a man [Lars Hanson] who later rapes her and helps drive her to kill him.

In the original version, the attack and murder derange the woman and she dazedly wanders into a violent sandstorm — to her death. This ending prompted vehement protests from major exhibitors, and M-G-M recalled everybody to change it.

We did all external scenes for *The Wind* in Bakersfield in California's Joaquin Valley, where the daytime summer temperature was never below 113 degrees and usually about 120 degrees....

The sun badly burned my skin and hair. Film crew members wore goggles, but actors could not, and I worked in dread of losing my eyesight....

[One day], I went to a car to get more makeup, grasped the red-hot door handle and pulled my hand away in pain. Some of my skin was on the handle.... [Gish, Hanson and Seastrom had previously worked together on *The Scarlet Letter* (1926).]

—Gish, in *The New York Times*, 1 Mar 1987

Charles Laughton went to the Museum of Modern Art and asked to see all of my old films with D.W. Griffith. Then he called and asked me to tea with James Agee and several others. He said, "When I was starting out in this business, people used to go to a movie and sit up in their seats and look at the screen. Now they go to eat popcorn. I want to sit them up in their seats again." After hearing that, I was convinced I should do [*The Night of the Hunter* (1955)] with him. Once we began work on it, we would sometimes ask him questions about what he meant by this or that, and he would exclaim, "Oh, oh, what am I doing wrong?" He had no belief in himself. If he had, he would have been a great director.

Robert Altman had no script but he came to see me and told me the story [of *A Wedding* (1978)]. It had so many characters I really couldn't make head nor tails of it, but he told me I was to die with comedy. Well, that intrigued me. It was a challenge. I had died every way except that, and I accepted the part because it would be a new experience.

—Gish, interviewed by Ronald Bowers for *Magill's Cinema Annual 1983*, ed. by Frank N. Magill (Englewood Cliffs, N.J.: Salem Press, 1983)

Scott GLENN [1939-]

Born: Pittsburgh. Work as a professional prize fighter, newspaper reporter and skin diver, acting studies at The Herbert Berghof Studio in N.Y., and work off-Broadway and on TV, preceded his film debut in The Baby Maker (1970, James Bridges). In 1980, he played Wes in Bridges' Urban Cowboy:

When I drove down to Houston to shoot the picture, I stopped off at Huntsville Prison and spent a few days there in my sleeping bag, staying over in the prison and also talking to ex- prisoners.... I got down to Houston five weeks early, so I was able to spend time with boys who made their living less than legally and also with some rodeo cowboys that I had been introduced to by the stunt coordinator, a guy named Chris Howe.

He taught me things like how a bull rider puts the glove on, how they take a leather cord and wrap it around by holding it in their teeth. I would practice that by doing it a thousand times every night before I went to bed. All the physical mannerisms I got down by sheer repetition, by doing it so much before the film that I didn't even have to think about it once the film started shooting.

I went into myself, and tried to figure out metaphors for this guy. One of them was that he should be like a snake in the zoo. People come into the snakehouse and their flesh crawls and they say, "Ooo, I hate it here," but something keeps them in there, watching the python slither around in its cage — it's a sensual fascination with something that's scary and evil but lithe and graceful at the same time.

—Glenn, interviewed by David Everitt for *Fangoria*, Dec 1983

Jim told me, when we started [*Urban Cowboy*] that the one thing I was to remember was that I was the only piece of reality in a film that is essentially about people who are living the myth of being a cowboy — to dress up like cowboys — to go to Gilley's — the great indoors rather than the great outdoors. Into all this walks my character, who doesn't live symbolically at all. He really *is* a cowboy — he really is an ex-convict — he really learned to ride by riding bulls.
—Glenn, interviewed by David Galligan for *Drama-Logue*, 29 Jan-4 Feb 1981

[For *Personal Best* (1982, Robert Towne)] my starting-off point was my own two daughters. My problem as a coach in the film is the same as my problem as a father: how do you teach someone to survive and be better, wiser if not smarter? At what point does teaching stop being profound and become manipulation? In some ways, the coach has the same qualities as a mother bear — the same combination of love and brutality. Bob and I talked about this...to some extent I play *him* in the film. The coach could appear to be cold, but to me there's a thread of love in his character that's clear all the way through. All of Bob's scripts are about love in a pressure cooker. The coach's attitude toward the girls is: if you and I have a relationship, and you come out stronger and more honorable — regardless of what I might have done to you — then our relationship has been a good one. When the coach blows up at Tory [Patrice Donnelly], it's because she wants to quit. She's been with the coach long enough to know the one rule of his life, the one thing this man is all about, is the determination to follow through.
—Glenn, interviewed by Tim Cahill for *Rolling Stone*, 15 Apr 1982

[For *The Right Stuff* (1983, Philip Kaufman)] I started thinking what kind of personality would, number one, *want* to be a test pilot, and number two, volunteer for a mission in which the odds-on chances were they *weren't* going to walk away from it.

You don't come up with squeaky-clean, button-down personalities who are willing to do those kinds of things. That image might be the window dressing, because they were all in the military, had short hair, wore suits and talked nicely. But when you think about the soul of somebody who would really do these dangerous things, you must find someone inside that exterior who's a very unconventional lunatic.

[Author] Tom Wolfe called the side of [Alan] Shepard that most of us remember the "icy commander." He was the guy who went to Admiral Farragut Preparatory School and then graduated high in his class at Annapolis. His father was a colonel and he was really American military aristocracy. But the other side, the side which Tom Wolfe termed "Smilin' Al, King of the Cape," was this irreverent, crazy adrenalin addict, the guy who made all the other astronauts laugh. I see his behavior as Smilin' Al, King of the Cape, as a way of dealing with the pressures of what he was doing.

Even before he was an astronaut, Shepard was a test pilot; he landed new fighter aircraft on carriers under minimum conditions, which was, at the time, supposed to be the riskiest test pilot's job in the world. He had another personality: José Jiménez, the Bill Dana character; he would become that character and *wouldn't* let go of it. When the NASA guys came to recruit him, he did this incredible landing on a carrier deck. He got off the plane and the ship's captain brought him over and introduced him to these two guys from NASA. They started talking and when he replied, he answered as José Jiménez. They said, "Aren't you afraid when you pilot these test flights?" And he said, "Oh no, I can *nahver* be afraid, señor." And NASA didn't want him to be an astronaut. They looked at each other and thought, "Holy cow! This guy is a candidate for the hat factory!" But he was the Navy's best aviator and they had already gone ahead and made the offer....

I spent a great deal of time down at Ames Research Lab talking to guys who had been in outer space and who designed rockets. Then, I found out the areas in which Shepard was an expert and tried to get a really crude type of workman's knowledge of ballistic acceleration. I was most concerned with what physically happens to a human being when he puts on the brakes and goes from 1800 miles per hour to 300 miles per hour inside a half-a-second.
—Glenn, interviewed by David Everitt for *Starlog*, Jan 1984

What Michael told me about Glaeken [in *The Keep* (1983, Michael Mann)] that was fascinating to me was that I was going to play a guy who had been on earth for over a thousand years. He was a semi-human who had been a voyeur of human existence for all that time because he is a sort of cosmic watchdog, put on earth to guard against the time the Devil appears. In talking to Michael about it, I realized that I was going to play a guy whose point of view, number one, was as a voyeur, a person who was dying to participate in anything, which is an interesting kind of tension to have in a character, and, number two, the perspective this character would have, rather than that of one life, would be a cyclical perspective.

From scene to scene, the way this guy reacted to life had to be invented. In terms of voice, Michael wanted Glaeken to talk in a way that was not naturalistic but, nevertheless, wouldn't be indecipherable or nonhuman. He wanted the lines to come out of a consciousness that was considering them from an experience of 2000 years. Well, how do you do that technically? It's great to sit around and talk about that, but what does that mean to an audience sitting in a theater when they see this dude with violet eyes and strange clothes. How do you go about it? Well, Michael asked me if I had ever heard Laurie Anderson, and I said, "Yeah, I've heard a couple of her records." He said, "What about her performance pieces? Listen to them, there's something about Laurie Anderson's voice that makes you feel that this woman is talking from a very deep historical perspective, talking from a past that belies the fact that the voice is also that of a young woman." It was the pauses she took in mid sentence, the cadences. To begin with, I just bald-facedly copied her patterns in rehearsals. Then, with Michael's help, I began to find my own cadence; there were pauses that I would take in the middle of sentences that would become a predictable rhythm for the character but totally unlike the way that anyone talks in real life, and yet you could believe that it was coming spontaneously out of his personality.

—Glenn, interviewed by David Everitt for *Fangoria*, Dec 1983

Danny GLOVER [1947-]

Born: San Francisco. Studies in economics at San Francisco State University and work with The Black Actors' Workshop of The American Conservatory Theatre preceded his film debut in Escape from Alcatraz (1979, Don Siegel). In 1985, he played Mr. in Steven Spielberg's adaptation of Alice Walker's The Color Purple:

There are men that exist like Mr., men who have what seems to us to be very off-center ways of perceiving women. His insensitivity is not blocked by any guilt. He is a product of old ways of looking at the world, of looking at women and their role in society.

The insensitivity comes out of a rigid, limited overview of himself and the world he has to deal with....

A lot of what Mr. does comes out of his own pain, because of a strange emotional dependency he has on Shug Avery [Margaret Avery]. He really believes that if she were around all the time, he would be happy. In his mind, she blocks whatever pain he's in.

It is only after he sees himself in a different way that he learns not to need that. After being on the planet for some 60-odd years, when he hits rock bottom, old and alone, he has to pull himself out of it. At last he begins to feel, as he says, "like a natural man."

—Glover, in the press release for *The Color Purple* (Warner Brothers, 1985)

Paulette GODDARD [1911-1990]

Born: Pauline Levy in Whitestone Landing, N.Y. Work as a model and on stage preceded her film debut in The Locked Door (1929, George Fitzmaurice). From 1933 to 1942, she was married to Charlie Chaplin and co-starred with him in both Modern Times (1936) and The Great Dictator (1940):

Usually I have to adapt myself to the parts I play in pictures. But...the part of the gamin in Charlie Chaplin's *Modern Times* was custom-built for me. I just slid into it and relaxed, because it fitted me perfectly. The gamin was an uninhibited, unselfconscious, unglamorous girl — all qualities that I admire....

The gamin...was a natural, cheerful spirit, gay and brave. She believed that people are fundamentally good....

Sometimes the gamin operated outside the law; she stole food for her two motherless sisters, yet it would have been difficult to call her dishonest.

I thought of her as very direct and perhaps more honest than most of us.

—Goddard, in *The Saturday Evening Post*, 12 June 1948

[Charlie Chaplin] *thinks* in rhyme and tempo. To the people who are to play a scene, he will describe it as though they were dancers. If they find themselves doing a bit of business awkwardly, he will say, "That's because you started on the wrong foot." Doing a scene with him is exactly like working to music that you can't help falling into.

—Goddard, interviewed by Dixie Wilson for *Photoplay Magazine*, Dec 1940

Whoopi GOLDBERG [1949-]

Born: Caryn Johnson in New York City. Work with the San Diego Repertory Company and on Broadway preceded her film debut as Celie in The Color Purple (1985, Steven Spielberg):

[Doing the turkey carving scene] was the point when I realized *The Color Purple* has no color. I'd been driving Celie to work every morning trying to get a feel on this black Southern woman who lived in the '30s and '40s. God, she was quiet. But in that scene, I realized the movie isn't about black people, it's about the power of love and cycles and relationships.

—Goldberg, interviewed by Diana Maychick for *The New York Post*, 7 Jan 1986

[Steven Spielberg] just gave me all kinds of faith. Plus, we had a lingo because he's a movie fanatic like me. He would say something like, "Okay, Whoopi, do Boo Radley right after the door opens in *To Kill a Mockingbird*." Or he'd say, "You know the scene where Indiana Jones finally finds the girl at the end? That kind of relief he has? That's what I want." He'd give me directions like that, and I could do them because I knew what he wanted.

—Goldberg, interviewed for *People Magazine*, 23-30 Dec 1985

Jeff GOLDBLUM [1952-]

Born: Pittsburgh. Studies at Sanford Meisner's Neighborhood Playhouse in N.Y. led to work off-Broadway where he was noticed by Robert Altman. Before heading to California to make two films with Altman [California Split (1974) and Nashville (1975)], he made his film debut in Death Wish (1974, Michael Winner). In 1983, he played Michael in Lawrence Kasdan's The Big Chill:

We all rehearsed for four weeks. First we all met at a party at Larry Kasdan's house in Sherman Oaks, which kicked it all off. The next day we started rehearsal, all day long, two weeks here in Los Angeles in a studio where we sat around talking about ourselves — about ourselves in terms of character — about *who* the characters were, about their backgrounds and the specifics of our history together — what our histories during the '60s might have been. We got to know each other like that by finding things in the script, constructing things about our pasts together and maybe developing some community history of our own that might be valuable in the playing of the film.

After we rehearsed those two weeks we went to a house in South Carolina.... John Bailey, the cinematographer, was there designing his various shots. So we rehearsed and went through the blocking of the scenes and how he was going to shoot it. Then we spent another week in Atlanta in this house that had been built to be the Michigan house where, in the script, we had all lived together in the '60s. We shot a flashback scene there — the Thanksgiving dinner, our senior year in college — and Kevin Costner played Alex, the fellow who killed himself.

One time, in Atlanta, Larry Kasdan left us unchaperoned and said, "Why don't you *stay* in character and kind of make dinner for yourselves? We will buy your groceries and you stay in character during the evening." And we did. It was a terrific and very valuable evening. We really felt we were in the '60s. After shooting the flashback for the first week, we said goodbye to Kevin Costner and went back to South Carolina. It served a couple of purposes. One, we acted out a real history together, back in the '60s, and left that city and moved on to another city so it seemed like we had that past together in another decade. And Kevin Costner was no longer with us, having been with us for those four weeks of rehearsal and the first week of shooting, and he was missed. Eventually, the flashback was cut out.

Larry Kasdan is a wonderful director, he loves actors and he loves acting. He knows exactly what he wants which gives him a terrific strength and then, in a masterful way, he lets you come to that point. He is very interested in what you can bring to the part; what you can show him about what has been written and what you can discover cooperatively.

—Goldblum, interviewed by David Galligan for *Drama-Logue*, 5 Dec 1985

For two weeks before production began [on *The Fly* (1986, David Cronenberg)], Geena [Davis] and I worked on the script. We got excited about running our lines. The screenplay was like a puzzle and we tried to work it out. So we rehearsed scenes and solved problems.

It's great working with someone you're fond of. You are really in touch with each other and you can work with that. It makes things easier....

[Geena] caught a fly in a Baggie and brought it to the set. We pinned the Baggie...to the wall and I spent a week observing the creature. We fed it food from the catering truck. You know the stuff — three bean-salad and yogurt — which it seemed to like....

Geena was a big help to me. It took five hours every morning for them to put on my makeup, and Geena would read aloud to me.

—Goldblum, interviewed by Vernon Scott and Richard Freedman for *The Chicago Sun-Times*, 29 Aug 1986

I loved a lot of things about the character of the Fly. The Fly is very courageous and romantic and heroic, a kind of poetic and majestic figure really.

—Goldblum, interviewed by Tina Eccarius for *The Cable Guide*, Sept 1987

Louis GOSSETT, JR. [1936-]

Born: Brooklyn, N.Y. Studies at NYU and with Frank Silvera and Lloyd Richards and work on stage (from 1953) preceded his film debut in Raisin in the Sun (1960, Daniel Petrie). In 1982, he played Sergeant Foley in Taylor Hackford's An Officer and a Gentleman:

[Sergeant Foley]'s *gotta* be that hard. He's molding men and women to protect the country. They have to be in as top a shape as they can possibly be....

This is a life and death situation. And Foley's gotta break down all the barriers. He's gotta make them men and women who are like a team that will help one another. Otherwise one day if a barrier is up and we go to war, one of those barriers will keep us from winning that war. So he has got to break them all down and pull all the covers down from them and rebuild them to men and women.

—Gossett, interviewed by Lewis Archibald for *The Aquarian Weekly*, 25 Aug-1 Sept 1982

[Sgt. Foley]...can't be nice like a college professor. Yet deep down he's got more warmth and more love for those recruits — like a father figure. And it's not until the end that the recruits realize that.

—Gossett, interviewed by Judy Klemesrud for *The New York Times*, 25 July 1982

Elliot GOULD [1938-]

*Born: Elliot Goldstein in Brooklyn, N.Y. Studies at Columbia University followed by work on Broadway preceded his screen debut in The Confession [aka Quick, Let's Get Married (1965, William Dieterle)]. In 1970, he played Trapper John in M*A*S*H, the first of four films for Robert Altman:*

I consider myself the first American jazz actor. I like to let myself go and just riff, and behave with the elements around me, not having to maintain any line or action other than those important for story continuity.... Robert Altman, my favorite director to work with, has been the one to let me have the most freedom to develop this jazz style. [Gould also worked on Altman's *The Long Goodbye* (1973), *California Split* (1974) and appeared briefly as himself in *Nashville* (1975).]

—Gould, interviewed by Danny Peary for *Bijou*, Aug 1977

I love to use colloquial words to color my performances. I can't wait for the time when I can say cunt or asshole or motherfucker as often as I please in a film. Not because I'm trying for any sensational effect but simply because that's the way people really talk. In *Little Murders* [1971, Alan Arkin], I was able to ad-lib a colloquialism that I think makes an important scene work. My father [John Randolph] and I are standing at a window. We're both snipers. He takes the first shot and he hits somebody. It's a chilling moment. Without telling Alan or [screenwriter] Jules [Feiffer], I screamed out of the window, "COCKSUCKER!" My character had gone mad by this time, and for it to be reduced to that kind of shock language was an inspiration. The word was the emotional outburst of a maniac. I was thrilled to have done it. God, I hope it's still in the film. It will be, unless we have to trade that for something else to get a decent rating.

—Gould, interviewed by Richard Warren Lewis for *Playboy*, Nov 1970

Gloria GRAHAME [1923-1981]

Born: Gloria Hallward in Pasadena, California. Work on the stage in California and on Broadway preceded her film debut in Blonde Fever (1944, Richard Whorf). In 1949, she played Laurel Gray opposite Humphrey Bogart as Dixon Steele in Nick Ray's In a Lonely Place:

[Bogart] was a great actor, of course, but also a remarkable man who helped me. One day there was trouble over the lighting and they couldn't get us both right — the movie was *In a Lonely Place* — so he simply said, not to bother about him, he'd stay in the shadows. Joan Crawford [on *Sudden Fear*] wouldn't have done that! Not many people in Hollywood would have.
—Grahame, interviewed by Brian Baxter for *Films Illustrated*, Oct 1978

As Irene Neves [in *Sudden Fear* (1952, David Miller)], a sort of junior-size Lady Macbeth, I was as changeable as March weather and often twice as nasty. Irene's main aim in life was to have a man murder his wife. In pursuance of this purpose, she was sometimes gay and charming, sometimes flirtatious, sometimes hysterical. What's more, she made these dizzying emotional shifts all through the picture.

This made the role both explosive and, to me, instructive. I learned a lot by playing Irene, and while learning it I worked harder than I ever had before. I read and reread *Macbeth* in order to try to understand Irene's basic motivation, which I felt was similar to Lady Macbeth's. I even reread *Othello*, because I felt that Iago schemed to accomplish his purpose much as Irene did.

Thus, by mixing Shakespeare with personal effort, and seasoning the whole with a great deal of helpful coaching from director Miller, I tried to make Irene real.
—Grahame, in *The Saturday Evening Post*, 16 May 1953

I dote on death scenes, or any kind of Spillane-type manhandling, because it is those scenes which linger in an audience's memory. I don't want to be typed as a woman with a face nice enough to look at, but I am interested in roles that sometimes turn a cinema-goer away in horror. So I didn't mind having my face horribly scarred [in *The Big Heat* (1953, Fritz Lang)] because my gangster boyfriend [Lee Marvin] threw a pot of boiling coffee over me. Being glamorous in movie roles all the time is not only artificial but horribly monotonous.... I'm a girl who loves to be manhandled! After all, what are a few contusions or abrasions if you get the man you love?
—Grahame, interviewed for *Silver Screen* (1953); repr. in *Suicide Blonde: The Life of Gloria Grahame* by Vincent Curcio (London: William Morrow & Co., 1989)

Farley GRANGER [1925-]

Born: San José, California. Discovered at North Hollywood High by an agent who brought him to the attention of Sam Goldwyn, he made his screen debut in North Star (1943, Lewis Milestone). His second film — The Purple Heart (1944) — was also directed by Milestone:

I had relied completely on Milestone. He was an absolute father-symbol to me. He could mould me so that I gave a very good performance.... Then Nick Ray borrowed me from Goldwyn...for *They Live By Night* (made in 1946; released in 1948).... Nick had come from the theatre in New York. And therefore his technique was different from Milestone's. I mean, at that time — because he'd never done a film before. And he was absolutely marvelous. He would take each individual performer aside in a corner, and talk very quietly and softly about a take. Never shouting "You move here" or "You go there." None of that sort of thing at all. Very subtle with each actor.
—Granger, interviewed by Gordon Gow for *Films & Filming*, Oct 1973

As Bowie, an escaped convict [in *They Live By Night*], I was supposed to have injured my foot. To make me drag the "injured" foot, director Nicholas Ray planned to have me wear an eighteen-pound shoe on it. But it wasn't necessary. Soon after we started shooting, I tore a ligament in my ankle. My actual ailment made my limp painfully authentic and the most realistic thing in the picture. But I like to think that the role was my best because of my interpretation of the contradictory character of Bowie, who was strong yet naive, sometimes tender and sometimes very hard.
—Granger, in *The Saturday Evening Post*, 23 June 1951

I remember seeing [Alfred Hitchcock] sitting in his chair beside the set on the second day of shooting [*Strangers on a Train* (1951)], and he looked very down, very sort of blue and tired. And I said, "Hitch, what's the matter?" — because I thought something was seriously wrong. And he said, "Oh, I'm just so bored." I said, "How can you be bored so early in the shooting?" He said, "I've done it all. Now all I have to do is tell you where to go, and tell the cameraman where to go." And this was true, because he has an artist sitting beside him with all the set-ups that have been drawn to Hitch's instructions. And the artist turns the pages and shows him, and Hitch follows every detail that he has figured out beforehand....

You do feel more of a prop than anything else with Hitch. But you just have to accept the way he works. [Granger had previously worked with Hitchcock on *Rope* (1948).]

—Granger, interviewed by Gordon Gow for *Films & Filming*, Oct 1973

Cary GRANT [1904-1986]

Born: Alexander Archibald Leach in Bristol, England. As a teen, he ran away from home to join The Bob Pender Troupe; when they went to New York in 1921, Grant, then a stilt-walker, stayed in the U.S. After returning to England two years later, he was spotted by a talent scout and taken back to the U.S. for a musical comedy role on Broadway. While vacationing in Hollywood in 1932, he participated in a screen test (for someone else) and as a result won a contract with Paramount Studios. His screen debut was the short Singapore Sue (1932, Casey Robinson). In 1933, he appeared opposite Mae West in Lowell Sherman's She Done Him Wrong:

I learned everything from Mae West — well not quite everything, but almost everything. She knew so much. Her instinct was so true, her timing was so perfect, her grasp of situations so right.

—Grant, in *Films & Filming*, July 1961

My theory is that if you continue to play the regular hero-type — if you get typed that way — you'll be a matinee idol for a while and then the public will find someone new....

But if you work at a lot of different characterizations, if you learn to portray strange individual characters with a trace of villainy or madness or kindliness or something very human, then your audience re-discovers you in each new role. I began it in *Sylvia Scarlett* [1935, George Cukor] and continued it in *Big Brown Eyes* [1936, Raoul Walsh].

—Grant, interviewed by Warren Reeve for *Photoplay Magazine*, June 1936

For five years I begged [Paramount Studios] to let me do something besides straight romantic leads. I said I ought to be doing light comedy. They wouldn't listen. When the five years were up, they offered me a new contract. I said, "Does choice of roles go with it?" They said, "No." So I didn't sign. I became free-lance. I was going to play some comedy or starve in the attempt.

The first picture I did as a free-lance was *Topper* [1937, Norman Z. McLeod].

—Grant, interviewed by Roger Carroll for *Motion Picture*, Feb 1941

If anybody's entitled to say anything about Katharine Hepburn, I am. I know what she's like, for I've made three pictures with her [*Sylvia Scarlett*, *Holiday* (1938, George Cukor) and *Bringing Up Baby* (1938, Howard Hawks); *The Philadelphia Story* (1940, George Cukor)] is my fourth.... As an actress, she is a joy to work with. She's in there trying every minute. There isn't anything passive about her; she "gives." And as a person, she's real. There's no pretense about her. She's the most completely honest woman I've ever met.

—Grant, interviewed by James Reid for *Modern Screen*, Dec 1940

Q. How did you happen to first work with Hitchcock?

A. He was doing a story about an English ne'er-do-well [*Suspicion* (1941)]. At that time I had become moderately popular. He sent me the script. I read it and liked it very much. That was it. I was very happy working with him. He's a remarkable man and he gives the actors a wide range. He lets us rehearse it out and then puts it all together. I was always whistling going to work.

Q. But what about all those stories about how tough he is on actors?

A. The top directors in those days were always collaborators.... They trusted actors. Some directors have tremendous power on the set, throwing their weight around. Hitch had a reputation for being reserved. On the contrary, he's very, very aware. Many people who seem distant are extraordinarily aware. He's a very imaginative man.

—Grant, interviewed by James Monaco for *Take One*, May 1976

Making comedies is serious business. You can't just say, "Well, let's be funny in the next scene." You sit right down and discuss ways and means — with each other, with the director, with the script-writer, and with anyone else who might have ideas. You read your lines this way, and you read them that way, and you try out bits of business, and you mull over toppers for the gags. You work between scenes, as well as in them. That is, you do if you've worked together as long as we [Irene Dunne and I] have and so, learned to trust each other's hunches toward possible results and audience reactions.

You'll never know how much rehearsing we did for that bathing the baby sequence in *Penny Serenade* [1941, George Stevens], and the sequence where we put the baby to bed. It was our first serious picture together and we were worried about how the public might accept it, so we wanted to do everything we could to make those two sequences funny — they were the only comedy spots in the picture. [Grant and Dunne had previously worked together on *The Awful Truth* (1937, Leo McCarey) and *My Favorite Wife* (1940, Garson Kanin).]

—Grant, as told to James Reid for *Screen Life*, Sept 1941

Acting is like playing ball. You toss the ball and some people don't toss it back; some people don't even catch it. When you get somebody who catches it and tosses it back, that's really what acting is all about. Myrna [Loy] kept that spontaneity in her acting, a supreme naturalness that had the effect of distilled dynamite. [On *Mr. Blandings Builds His Dream House* (1948, Hank Potter)] she really became the perfect wife. Melvyn Douglas and I used to talk about it.... All leading men agreed — Myrna was the wife everybody wanted.... If you haven't been married, then you can't understand what it meant to have Myrna play your wife. Even when she fed me lines off camera, I'd look over and she'd be pulling down her hem or straightening a stocking in a subconscious wifely gesture, instinctively doing the things that married women do. [Loy and Grant had previously worked together on *Wings in the Dark* (1935, James Flood) and *The Bachelor and the Bobby Soxer* (1947, Irving Reis)].

—Grant, interviewed by James Kotsilibas-Davis for *Being and Becoming* by Myrna Loy and James Kotsilibas-Davis (New York: Alfred A. Knopf, 1987)

I feel Myrna has never received sufficient acting credit.... She is the fastest study I ever saw, learning new lines so quickly on the set that I am sure her memory must be photographic. She knows instinctively when a scene is wrong, for her or the picture.

My idiocies, my moods, my fretting and fussing while working do not disturb her at all. Between takes, knowing that nothing interests me so much as travel talk, she talks travel.... I confess it never occurred to me at all during the shooting of *Mr. Blandings Builds His Dream House* that maybe Myrna wasn't as enchanted with such talk as I was. But probably she wasn't. And definitely I didn't give her a chance to discuss herself. I didn't discuss her, either. It was all I to I, with Grant starring.

That's her feminine secret. She lets you talk about you. She does not make you dream of her. She makes you dream about how terrific you are, how witty, how handsome. That is twice as potent.

—Grant, in *Photoplay/Movie-Mirror*, Aug 1948

Q. How did you get involved with *To Catch a Thief* [1954, Alfred Hitchcock]?

A. As a matter of fact, I had retired at the time. I went around the world. But the expectation of working again with Hitch was too inviting. It also gave me the chance to work with one of the best actresses I've ever worked with in my life, Grace Kelly. She made everything look easy — an extraordinary actress! [Grant also worked on Hitchcock's *Notorious* (1946) and *North by Northwest* (1959).]

—Grant, interviewed by James Monaco for *Take One*, May 1976

Grace never complained about anything. In *To Catch a Thief*, we had a scene where I had to grab her arms hard, while she was fighting me, and push her against a wall. We went through that scene eight or nine times, but Hitchcock still wanted it again. Grace went back alone behind the door where the scene started, and just by chance I happened to catch a glimpse of her massaging her wrists and grimacing in pain. But a moment later she came out and did the scene again — she never complained to me or to Hitch about how much her arms were hurting.

She isn't one of those girls who waste time by being angry. She was always patient on the set, even when hairdressers and make-up men were fussing over her between takes of a difficult scene. If a dress didn't fit, well, it just didn't fit, and that was that, with no hysterics....

—Grant, interviewed by Margaret Parton for *The Ladies Home Journal*, Mar 1956

I've worked with Bergman [on *Notorious* and *Indiscreet* (1958, Stanley Donen)], I've worked with Hepburn, I've worked with some of the biggest stars, but Grace Kelly was the best actress I've ever worked with in my life. That woman had total relaxation, absolute ease — she was an extraordinarily serene girl. Both she and Hitchcock were Jesuit trained, maybe that had something to do with it....

—Grant, interviewed at "A Conversation with Cary Grant"; reported by Maeve Druesne for *Films in Review* (NY), Jan 1987

I am getting to the stage where I have to be very careful about love scenes with young actresses. The public doesn't like to see an older man making love to a young girl. It offends them. And I must say I agree with them. I used to get furious years ago when Walter Pidgeon was making love to Greer Garson on the screen.

That's why in *Charade* [1963, Stanley Donen] I insisted on putting in so many references to my age. I anticipated a lot of people's reactions.

—Grant, interviewed by Roderick Mann for *The Sunday Express*, 7 June 1966

I must confess it's true that I modeled myself after the blasé drawing-room pose assumed by my stage idol, Noël Coward. Hand casually plunged in the pocket, you know. It took me years to get my hand unstuck and acquire the freedom to simply play myself.

We all create ourselves as we grow older and it's a pity in a way that I felt most like my true self in my next to last picture, *Father Goose* [1964, Ralph Nelson].... I felt free to perform like an unshaven old gray-haired sot in sloppy denims — the way I dress when I'm at home. The really relaxed Cary Grant.

—Grant, interviewed by Frank Rasky for *The Toronto Star*, 4 June 1976

Lee GRANT [1926-]

Born: Lyova Rosenthal in New York City. A stage debut at age 7 was followed by studies at The Juilliard School, The High School of Music and Art, Sanford Meisner's Neighborhood Playhouse and The Actors Studio in N.Y. Work on Broadway (from 1948) preceded her film debut in Detective Story (William Wyler) recreating her Broadway success. In 1970, she played Mrs. Enders in Norman Jewison's The Landlord:

Norman Jewison said, "Lee, I'm sending you this script [of *The Landlord*] but I don't think you're gonna make it *physically*." Of course *nobody* does this corny aging thing on the screen anymore: tons of lines, gray wigs. But the next night I saw *Isadora* [1968, Karel Reisz] and Vanessa [Redgrave] made those transitions from 28 to 40 *ve*-ry interestingly. Just the way she held her head, and the hard make-up colors. So I went home and did what I tend to do, getting a character: I wandered around the living room, muttering to myself. Suddenly, I thought, "Near-sighted!" Mrs. Enders *squints*, she's near-sighted, and she's much too vain to wear glasses. I looked in the mirror; squinting does something very aging to your face, takes away the innocence, the wonder, y'know? Then a voice began to come, and a walk. A character can start with something purely physical like that. I called Norman and said, "Listen, I *have* something here, and you don't have to use *me*, but let me show you, I gotta *transmit* this...."

Now, the only time I read for parts is when I don't have to. I wanted to read for this, to get beyond the physical things. I read the scene with Pearl Bailey, when Mrs. Enders is being *terribly* gracious, but doesn't quite want to *touch* anything in this tenement, or have this black lady call her by her first name. See, that's the next step, getting the *attitude*. If you have the attitude, you can play *any* age.

—Grant, interviewed by Tom Burke for *The New York Times*, 5 July 1970

The only time I was obsessed with sexual discussion in therapy was before I did *Shampoo* [1975, Hal Ashby]. Somehow it always translates in terms of my work. I have a very good thing going with my husband, but going out into another sexual situation — which is what I had to do in *Shampoo* — was like being given the job of having an affair. When you're acting, all you can use is yourself — that's your instrument. My poor doctor would get very confused when I would talk about these sexual problems which had to do with the part. He would keep asking me, "Is this a part or is this you?" And I would say, "I don't know." It opened up the area of affairs, and it was something I had to go into, because the woman I was playing [Felicia] was somebody whose whole release was through going to bed with one man after another. And my problem was to go to bed with Warren [Beatty]. And there was a real problem in that, in the story, I had been going to bed with him for *months*, so it was supposed to be very free and very uninhibited. But the fact was that as friends and fellow actors, we had *not* been going to bed. Getting into bed with a fellow actor — in front of cameras and a director — was opening up virginal feelings in me that were very wrong for this woman I played, who *did* it all the time, who was aggressive about it and simply wanted to have her sexual needs satisfied and get on with it. And I didn't know how to get to that point. So my therapist and I discussed it very much. I

would say it opened great areas of lust in me at that point, because I just found everybody who walked by me so attractive that I couldn't bear it.
—Grant, in *The Star Treatment*, ed. by Richard Seltzer (New York: Bobbs-Merrill, 1977)

Fernand GRAVET [1905-1970]

Born: Fernand Mertens in Brussels, Belgium. A child actor in films, he then took up a stage career until the advent of the talkies. His first role as an adult was in L'amour Chante (1930, Robert Florey). In 1938, he played Johann Strauss in The Great Waltz:

When I did go to Hollywood, I was under contract to Mervyn LeRoy. When an actor belonged to an individual he could be sure that it was in the latter's own interests to keep him working, and working in good films....

At one point LeRoy didn't have a script for me, so instead of waiting to find me a part he offered to lend me to MGM to play in *The Great Waltz*. This film, which was credited to Julien Duvivier, was not entirely made by him since he was obliged to return to France halfway through the shooting. When he left, Victor Fleming took over. After viewing the first part of the film and making a few changes, Fleming shot the second part, notably the scenes concerning the Vietz revolution. As for the end, that was directed by Josef von Sternberg.

You remember the departure of Johann Strauss' mistress — Carla Donner, the part played by Miliza Korjus? When she goes on to the boat and begins to sing? Well, that was von Sternberg. From the scene where Strauss composes *The Blue Danube*, including the montage with the black orchestras and the white orchestras, right up to the end, the film is Sternberg's.

I'll tell you how he set about showing *The Blue Danube* music bursting into my mind. One night he sent for me simply to have a friendly chat. We talked about all sorts of things — theatre, cinema, painting, even our private lives — for five whole hours. Finally, Sternberg said "Cut!" "What do you mean, 'cut'?" I couldn't see a camera, anything.... Well, there were three concealed cameras with 250 mm. telephoto lenses filming the whole time. And I'd actually been worrying about the time we were wasting! God knows how much film he exposed in order to get those first shots of me with the expression he wanted while *The Blue Danube* was being hatched.
—Gravet, interviewed (1970) by Rui Nogueira and Nicoletta Zalaffi for *Focus on Film*, Winter 75/6

Sydney GREENSTREET [1879-1954]

Born: Sandwich, England. Studies at The Ben Greet School of Acting and work with that company in England and on tour in the U.S. led to a long career on the stage. In 1941, he made his film debut as Kasper Gutman in John Huston's The Maltese Falcon:

Usually a movie villain role has to be played in a monotone because the menace is written in one key, emphasizing a single personal quality. In contrast, Dashiell Hammett's Kasper Gutman, the Fat Man, of *The Maltese Falcon*, is a colorful, stimulating character and, happily, John Huston, kept close to the novel in making his fine adaptation. I enjoyed the way the character became progressively more interesting with each scene — did not lose its appeal beyond a certain point, as roles sometimes do. I also enjoyed the subtlety necessary to get over the fact that while Gutman was saying one thing, he was usually thinking something entirely different.

The cameramen helped me achieve the effect of fatness. To be sure, I'm not exactly a flyweight: I weighed 285 pounds at the time. But by bringing the camera near the floor and shooting up, they made me weigh about 350.
—Greenstreet, in *The Saturday Evening Post*, 22 Feb 1947

I'm going to play some decent human beings before I take on another of those snake-blooded scoundrels. Forty two years on the stage and I never played a villain. Then I step into [*The Maltese Falcon*] and do one. And what happens? I find my whole character changed. I'm a renegade, a murderer, a cold scheming blighter who sells soul and country for a price. It is too radical a change for a man of my years.

I like these rattlesnake parts for a change of pace but not for steady playing. I mean it when I say I am going back to the path of virtue, at least temporarily. Another scoundrel like the Nazi I'm playing [in *Background to Danger* (1943, Raoul Walsh)], and I won't even be able to get anyone to play golf with me.
—Greenstreet, in the press release for *Background to Danger* (Warner Brothers, 1943)

Jane GREER [1924-]

Born: Bettejane Greer in Washington, D.C. High school dramatics and work as a singer preceded her film debut in Two O'Clock Courage (1945, Anthony Mann). In 1947, she played Kathie in Jacques Tourneur's Out of the Past:

I was believable because although Kathie was a bitch, a liar and a killer, she looked soft and innocent. She had long hair, was very glamorous and had an air of mystery about her....

Jacques was a master at creating atmosphere, but he didn't speak English very well. His direction went like this: "Do you know the word *impassive*?"

And I answered back "Yes, I know the word *impassive*."

To which Tourneur replied: "Good, that's what I want. First half of the film — *good* girl. The last half of the film — *bad* girl. OK? And no big eyes.

I knew what he wanted. But I threw in a few large eyes anyway. I couldn't resist.... Tourneur...really didn't know how to talk to actors. But he could sure talk to the camera. And he was evocative.

—Greer, interviewed by Linda Gross for *The Los Angeles Times Calendar*, 4 Mar 1984

André GREGORY [1934-]

Born: Paris, France. Acting studies with Lee Strasberg and work as a member of The Actors Studio directors unit and as artistic director of The Manhattan Project (since 1970), preceded his film debut in My Dinner with André (1981, Louis Malle) which he co-wrote with co-star Wallace Shawn:

One of the ironies about the process of making the film was that, of all the adventures I have had, the only one on which I truly learnt something about myself was making this film.

When I started rehearsing my role, I kept playing André as myself, and it tended to be self-indulgent. But I felt I had to find a character that was a distillation of myself. I had to be able to see myself the way my best friends see me, but would never tell me. It came as a shock when I finally managed to do that. But when I did, and I could see this character as manipulative, ambitious, stingy, and so on, I started having fun with the role....

André belongs to a dinner table tradition in which a framework is created for characters to reveal themselves. In the beginning, Wally hides behind silence and I hide behind words. We are both quite masked, and the film is the process of the two of us being able to open up our own feelings. In fact, that is probably one of the key dramatic tensions of the film.

—Gregory, interviewed by Tony Rayns for *Cinema Papers*, Oct 1982

Andy GRIFFITH [1926-]

Born: Mount Airy, North Carolina. Studies for the Ministry at The University of North Carolina and work as a high school teacher and on Broadway (from 1955) preceded his film debut as Lonesome Roads in A Face in the Crowd (1957, Elia Kazan):

I learned all I know about acting in making that one movie with Kazan. Now, Kazan knows people; he understands them and knows how to get the best from them....

He has a secret. He knows exactly how to keep an actor happy and excited. He treats an actor as though he had hunted all over the world to find him. He makes you feel like a very important part of what is going on. His attention was on me every second.... He taught me how to relate everything I had ever heard or ever read to what I was doing at the moment for the movie. I'd go over and tell him, "I had an experience once." And he'd say, "Yeah, tell me." Then he'd listen, and say, "Yeah, that's right, that's right." And I'd transfer that thought to what I was doing.

—Griffith, interviewed by Lillian and Helen Ross for *The Player* (New York: Simon & Schuster, 1962)

Melanie GRIFFITH [1957-]

Born: New York City; daughter of Tippi Hedren. Work as a model preceded her film debut in Night Moves (1975, Arthur Penn). In 1984, she played Holly Body in Brian De Palma's Body Double:

The parts I play help me personally to achieve something. With *Body Double*, I was getting that sexual stuff out there and saying, "Love me for it or leave me."

—Griffith, interviewed by Lisa Schwarzbaum for *The New York Daily News*, 4 Dec 1988

[Jonathan Demme and I] got together for lunch and he told me he wanted me for this part [of Lulu in *Something Wild* (1986)]. It was eight months before we started shooting so I had all this time to work on it. When he told me he was thinking about Jeff Daniels for the part, I said, "Please let me meet him, let us read together, because it's basically a two-person movie." I didn't want to be put in a situation of not getting along with someone.... Jonathan flew me to New York and I read with Jeff and by the end of the script I was sitting on Jeff's lap laughing and having fun because we were Charlie and Lulu.

—Griffith, interviewed by David Galligan for *Drama-Logue*, 4-10 Dec 1986

I think there's a little bit of Lulu in every woman. And I was saying, "It's okay to go through stuff. It's okay to be bold. But don't hurt anybody. Intentionally. Otherwise you end up getting hurt."

I couldn't say enough about [Mike Nichols'] genius [on *Working Girl* (1988)]. Something would always happen to Tess. If the scene was just to walk into the room, Mike would have me trip. At every turn, someone was trying to thwart her....

I have a brain, and I have a big heart, and I try not to lie, and I try to help people. So I try to put that into the roles I play. Because I feel for women like me who buckle under, or become self-deprecating because they're afraid to just be themselves. I want to say in the films that it's okay, whoever you are. And don't judge people on the surface.

—Griffith, interviewed by Lisa Schwarzbaum for *The New York Daily News Magazine*, 4 Dec 1988

Charles GRODIN [1935-]

Born: Pittsburgh. Studies at The Pittsburgh Playhouse, in N.Y. with Uta Hagen and Lee Strasberg, and work in summer stock, off-Broadway, TV and Broadway (from 1962) preceded his film debut in Rosemary's Baby (1968, Roman Polanski). In 1980, he played Homer in Claudia Weill's It's My Turn:

About three years ago, I began to be aware that the idea of me being the male protagonist in a story wouldn't come to someone's mind, since people's perceptions of me were entirely from things like *The Heartbreak Kid* [1972, Elaine May] and *Heaven Can Wait* [1978, Warren Beatty and Buck Henry]....

I made a conscious decision to play roles that were more of a protagonist for two reasons really: there's a kind of dead end even to being a star villain; and, two, the possibility of eventually moving to something that's going to reflect what I think is more my sensibility would be more likely if I could play a protagonist.

The role [of Homer] is of a very amusing fellow.... There's a lot of comedy in it, which was why I was particularly interested in playing it. The comedy, ironically enough, is what's wrong with the relationship [with Jill Clayburgh], because it is taking the place of real commitment....

[Claudia Weill and Elaine May are] the two finest directors I've ever worked with. They share an openness for the performer that allows the performer to make his fullest contribution before they make their directorial judgment on what they would like to have or what they would prefer not to have.

—Grodin, interviewed by Lawrence Van Gelder for *The New York Times*, 19 Oct 1980

[Jonathan Mardukas in *Midnight Run* (1988, Martin Brest)] is the closest part to me I've ever played. That is the Charles Grodin persona up there, strangely enough.... It's the best role I've ever had. It's the most dimensional, the most human, the most exciting....

It's the first part where I haven't had to sit on my own sensibilities. I've done a lot of parts where it really isn't appropriate to bring the whole person on the screen.

And for the first time, with this film, there was nothing I had to shut down in myself. My character has got a scope, intelligence, daring, compassion....

It would seem like we [Grodin and co-star Robert De Niro] are very far apart (as actors), since he's done serious stuff and I've done light comedy. But we have almost identical backgrounds — we're both members of the Actors Studio and our training is very much the same.

Both of us approach things from a reality base. And I guess you need the same reality whether you're playing opposite Miss Piggy (as Grodin has in two Muppet movies) or *Raging Bull*.... So that helped the picture, and we got to know each other and formed a friendship that evolved almost identically with the friendship formed between the characters during the course of the picture.

—Grodin, interviewed by Alan Mirabella for *The New York Daily News*, 17 July 1988

Alec GUINNESS [1914-]

Born: London, England. Studies at the Fay Compton Studio of Dramatic Art in London led to his stage debut in 1934. That same year he was an extra in Victor Saville's Evensong, but didn't make another film until he starred as Fagin in Great Expectations (1946, David Lean). In 1948, he starred in Kind Hearts and Coronets, the first of four films for director Robert Hamer:

Robert was one of the most extraordinary and idiosyncratic talents on the scene at that time, and personally I was very fond of him. He was a very curious, quirky character....

Hamer's films were often criticized for being literary, and they *were* literary. He liked that. I was a bit surprised at his almost dismissive attitude to the camera. He liked to distance things. He enjoyed the *distance* of a set-up. Of course, he used close-ups but, basically, there was always a sort of formality, a kind of very black-and-white remoteness, almost as though he wanted you to feel you were looking through an album of old photographs....

Robert certainly would let things follow their own head to see what came out. I remember on *Kind Hearts*, there was nothing written for the sermon in the church scene where I am playing the old vicar. So I assumed that when I had climbed up to the pulpit we would cut instantly away. When I got there, I looked around with a sort of wild surmise, and nobody said, "Cut!" or anything. So I just made up a string of sermonish gobbledygook, and eventually we cut. Didn't get very far, thank God.... But he had that capacity to let things roll on if he thought they looked interesting or if something useful and unexpected might emerge.... [Guinness also worked on Hamer's *Father Brown* (1954), *To Paris with Love* (1954) and *The Scapegoat* (1958).]

Very different from Sandy Mackendrick, whom I also liked working with very much. I remember the first time I worked with [Mackendrick], on *The Man in the White Suit* [1951]. I found that every set-up was already drawn out. Of course, this was fine, but I kept feeling slightly worried. Supposing something actually happens, just like that, on the set, which is better or more interesting than what you have budgeted for? [Guinness also worked on Mackendrick's *The Ladykillers* (1955).]

—Guinness, interviewed by John Russell Taylor for *American Film*, Apr 1989

I did contribute one change in *Lavender Hill Mob* [1951, Charles Crichton]. Originally the hero was a striped-pants, frozen type of banking clerk. I maintained he had no appeal. It's a bore to play a bore. Anyway, I maintained this fellow should have some silly, endearing trait, like falling over his R's. And, if you recall, he did. Incidentally, that clerk was based, at least in appearance, on one I know.

—Guinness, interviewed by Howard Thompson for *The New York Times*, 26 July 1953

Q. Do you have certain set theories about comic acting?

A. Theories about comic acting? Oh, no — I don't think I have any. First of all, though, the most important thing is the script — the comic situations have to be there. And then, in creating a comic character, it's the little touches, the subtle nuances that make the difference. One takes a fairly ordinary character and plays him slightly out of focus, like the mad criminal I played in *The Ladykillers* — it's in the incongruity between that man's actions and reactions and a normal man's actions and reactions that the humor lies. In any event, I know what comic acting *isn't* — it *isn't* arm-waving and ranting and stomping about. Playing comedy is a much subtler art than most audiences or, indeed, most actors realize.

—Guinness, interviewed by Robert Redford for *Show*, Dec 1964

I turned the part [of Colonel Nicholson in *The Bridge on the River Kwai* (1957, David Lean)] down twice. Each time it was rewritten, and finally I agreed to do it, but it was a real tight-rope to walk. I was worried constantly about Colonel Nicholson turning out to be a caricature of a British officer instead of a real person....

I pictured Nicholson as a not-very-bright Indian Army officer who would have been of much higher rank for his age if he'd really been good. He would be the sort who would soldier entirely by the book and go off and play bridge with a dull little wife at the officer's club in the evenings and who would know nothing but the book when an emergency came.

—Guinness, interviewed by Don Cook for *The New York Herald Tribune*, 15 Dec 1957

It wasn't a question of the grittiness of the voice [in *The Horses's Mouth* (1958, Ronald Neame)] so much as a question of the accent. Because it seemed to me that it had to be an educated accent and yet if you spoke with an educated accent, a lot of the lines and a lot of situations became not quite believable. If you cockneyed it up a bit, it was false to the creation of the book. So it was a compromise. I tried to find a voice in which no one would be able to detect an accent of any sort, a kind of gritty, rough...more or less like air passing out of gravel.... [Guinness also adapted the screenplay from the Joyce Carey novel.]
—Guinness, interviewed for *The Times*, 7 Aug 1971

Carol [Reed] wanted me to play the part of Wormold in *Our Man in Havana* [1959] quite differently from the way I envisaged it. I had seen, partly suggested by the name, an untidy, shambling, middle-aged man with worn shoes, who might have bits of string in his pocket, and perhaps the *New Statesman* under his arm, exuding an air of innocence, defeat and general inefficiency. When I explained this Carol said, "We don't want any of your character acting. Play it straight. Don't act." That might be okay for some wooden dish perhaps but was disastrous for me. "Mustn't act, mustn't act," I kept repeating to myself; and didn't. The director, particularly a world-famous one like Carol, is always right. Or often so. When the film was released we both received a well-deserved poor press.
—Guinness, in his *Blessings in Disguise* (New York: Alfred A. Knopf, 1986)

I meant to spend a couple of weeks in Glasgow working on the accent [for *Tunes of Glory* (1960, Ronald Neame)], but I couldn't fit it in. So I borrowed a BBC record of some street interviews up there on VJ-night and kept playing it over.
—Guinness, interviewed by Cecil Wilson for *The Daily Mail*, 1 Dec 1961

[For *Lawrence of Arabia* (1962, David Lean)] I did a lot of research about Lawrence, and in the course of it learned much about [Prince] Feisal, and his character fascinated me. He was not primarily a man of action, but a man who had action forced upon him in his revolt against the Turks.
—Guinness, interviewed by Cyrus Durgin for *The Boston Globe*, 9 June 1962

As far as the film [of *Little Dorrit* (1988, Christine Edzard)] was concerned, before it started, I felt, I don't get this man at all. I mean, I'm amused by him and despise him; I have a certain contempt for his weakness. But I don't know that I totally believe. Christine Edzard said, I think, a very sensible thing: "You must remember Dickens was first and foremost a journalist. He may have ripped into the comic characters and such, but when you get down to it, in everything that really matters, it's all journalism." And I thought, my God, she's right, and that opened a door to me, just to be *real*....

I had, a year before, been at a death bed, which I had never been at before. I was anxious, but I'm afraid my actor's self could not but note certain things. And when it came to the death scene in *Little Dorrit*, I began to think, ah yes, then that happens and then that. And I lay there doing these things, and they let the camera go on and on and on.... I was amazed that Christine let it go on like that.
—Guinness, interviewed by John Russell Taylor for *American Film*, Apr 1989

I'm never happy over any characterization until I start from the feet up. This is my personal idiosyncracy. Until I have decided how the character walks, nothing happens. This is a hangover from my student days when I didn't have much money. I spent my spare time following people to see how they walked and as I began to imitate the walk, I fancied I was beginning to know something about the person.
—Guinness, interviewed by Joan Crosby for *The New York World Telegram and Sun*, 8 Aug 1964

H

Gene HACKMAN [1930-]

Born: San Bernardino, California. Studies at The Pasadena Playhouse and with George Morrison, summer stock in Bellport, N.Y. and an off-Broadway debut in 1958 preceded his film debut in a small role in Mad Dog Coll (1961, Burt Balaban). In 1967, he played Buck Barrow in Arthur Penn's Bonnie and Clyde:

Q. Arthur Penn has spoken of the surprises you bring as an actor. He mentioned your death scene in *Bonnie and Clyde*, when he had suggested an image of a dying bull. How did you work with that image, and have you worked with other images?

A. I had seen some bullfights. In my motel room, I worked on all fours, trying to emulate the movements of a bull that has been wounded in the back of the neck and is dying.

I love animal images, but I'm so often cast as a working man, and when have we seen a working man who is, for example, a tiger...?

Q. You've made three with Arthur Penn [also *Night Moves* (1975) and *Target* (1985)] — what makes the two of you such a good combo?

A. I think it's because we both came out of theater, even though I haven't been back in a long time. Our approach is theatrical in terms of a concern for how the overall piece works. And we both have a lot of energy. I like to come on the set when I'm not in the scene just to watch him work, to see the kind of energy and enthusiasm he puts into *his* side of it.

—Hackman, interviewed by Beverly Walker for *Film Comment*, Dec 1988

John Frankenheimer and I got along famously after the first day of shooting *The Gypsy Moths* [1969]. Burt Lancaster, the star of the film, was responsible for my being cast because he'd seen me in *Bonnie and Clyde* and urged it. On the first day Frankenheimer yelled at me from across the field with a bullhorn for missing the mark. I wasn't that confident, coming from New York, and Frankenheimer was notorious for firing people, a couple of people a day is not unusual. But I was right in that case and yelled back. He thought of that role as one he could put aside and I didn't feel that way.

—Hackman, interviewed by Louise Sweeney for *The Christian Science Monitor*, 14 Apr 1971

I was uncomfortable doing the part [of Gene Garrison in *I Never Sang for My Father* (1969, Gilbert Cates)]. In terms of drama, the movie was unrelenting. Every scene was a culmination scene, and we were always taking psychological last stands. Usually an actor can find some way to play against a character, to give him some additional dimension. But it was super difficult to find an area in this guy that was different. He was always whining. I kept working at it to find ways to release that, but I never could.

—Hackman, interviewed by Roger Ebert for *The Chicago Sun-Times*, 28 Nov 1971

Q. When you made *I Never Sang for My Father*, was your personal relationship with Melvyn Douglas affected by your mutual fictional roles of warring father and son?

A. The opposite. I had admired Melvyn so much as an actor, but he didn't like me. During the filming, I inadvertently found out that he had actually wanted someone else. This hurt me, but it certainly added to the tension in the film. We kept away from each other, rarely spoke.

—Hackman, interviewed by Beverly Walker for *Film Comment*, Dec 1988

One of the things with *French Connection* [1971, William Friedkin] that was frightening to me was to open the film beating up a black guy [Alan Weeks], using the words "spick," "wop," "nigger...." You start off a film in the first five minutes, laying that out for an audience, and then you say to the audience: "You're gonna stay with this guy for two hours and you finally gotta like him, you gotta respect him, you gotta feel *something* for him." That was frightening to me, and yet it was challenging.

One thing you must do if you're gonna play a character like that is you gotta play him absolutely fucking *full*, so full that there's never any doubt that what you're saying is what you believe. If at any point in the characterization you modify him, or try to go for sympathy, *intentionally* go for sympathy, or intentionally delve into the heartstrings of the audience, you're gonna get shot down. 'Cause they're just gonna *sense* that in a second. They're gonna say, "That's dishonest. I don't know what it is, the guy lost me there somewhere." And they're often not sophisticated enough to know what it *is* that turned them off, but they'll pick it up. Just like we do in life. We pick up on people that aren't straight and honest with us, in some funny way. Just some strange way that we *know* there's something wrong there. [Hackman reprised the role in *The French Connection II* (197--, ----------.]

—Hackman, interviewed by Pete Hamill for *Film Comment*, Sept 1974

I learned a lot about movies just knowing what Billy [Friedkin] left out [of *The French Connection*] in the editing stage. He left out all kinds of character development scenes, in order to get on with the action. Yet there are enough scenes left to make the characters work. Another director might have left everything in and ruined the pace of the picture.

—Hackman, interviewed by Roger Ebert for *The Chicago Sun-Times*, 28 Nov 1971

I was interested in *The Poseidon Adventure* [1972, Ronald Neame] as a project rather than the character. I wanted the experience and the tradition of a major picture being shot in a major studio. I wanted to achieve some kind of combination of honesty and theatricality. Honesty alone isn't enough for me. I think that becomes very boring. What I like is the fusing of a real moment with a theatrical flip. If you can convince people that what you are doing is real and it's also bigger than life, that's exciting. One of the problems is to hold a professional attitude when you know all is lost, which many times is apparent early in a production.

—Hackman, interviewed by Gavin Cort for *Show*, July 1972

It's been a long, long time since I have been offered a part in such a broad, comedic vein. I'm not normally one for make-up and hair and that's what [Lex] Luthor is all about. He's a snappy dresser, wears a series of wigs — the whole works. That sort of movie is a terrific holiday for most actors, but it has the reverse effect on me. The more technical a film becomes, the more inhibited I am. Therefore the harder I have to work at it. [Hackman played Lex Luthor in *Superman* (1978, Richard Donner), *Superman II* (1980, Richard Lester), *Superman III* (1983, Richard Lester) and *Superman IV* (1987, Sidney J. Furie).]

—Hackman, interviewed by David Castell for *Films Illustrated*, Sept 1978

I never worry about learning lines. Instead, I think about the character a great deal, almost continuously. Not consciously. I just live with him. I think I'm more an instinctive than an intellectual actor. For me, to intellectualize a role is no fun. What is fun is to break a role down and find out how much I am like a character or not like that character, and to develop moments based on that.

I thought of ways I might be like [David Brice, the secretary of defense in *No Way Out* (1987, Roger Donaldson)]. He tended to be devious. Not that I'm basically devious, but I was able to call on the part of me that is and use that. I think we're all capable of a number of things in certain situations. The secretary was a guy who thought he could get away with anything.

—Hackman, interviewed by Claudia Dreifus for *Connoisseur*, Aug 1988

Q. It's possible to see your character [FBI agent, Rupert Anderson in *Mississippi Burning* (Alan Parker, 1988)] two ways — with racist tinges, or as someone who has risen above it but who understands and has compassion for these people and the problems of the region.

A. The FBI man in charge of the actual case was from Mississippi, which may have provided the movie parallel. My character did understand the regional attitudes, but he was definitely not a racist.

Q. How much of the character's background was in the script, and how much did you create for yourself?

A. There are just a few biographical-type lines. One builds the rest along with the director. As an actor, you hope that you make the character come to life and understandable, without resorting to a lot of exposition, which can be boring.

I read everything I could get my hands on about the period and the incident, including the book *Three Lives for Mississippi*. In a curious way, I got a lot of insight from a book called *The Selling of Marcus Dupree*, which paralleled the life of a black football player born on or near the day of the murders. It was done in such a way as to imply that the civil rights workers' deaths were not in vain: They died so that he could live.

There was a woman there who fought for years to get the case before the proper authorities, and she ended up losing most of what she owned. They froze her out. Everything I learned helped me shape the character in small and subtle ways. I didn't spend much time on the accent because I did not want it too strong — country rather than Southern. Otherwise it would get in the way.

Q. There's a certain ambiguity in your relationship with the deputy sheriff's wife [Frances McDormand]. Was your character coming on to her just to get information, or was he attracted as well?

A. Originally, Alan wanted me to make love to her right then, on the floor of her house. I felt that was excessive and would distract from her as a human being and from her courage in terms of what she has just revealed. She didn't do it because she wanted to make love to me but because she thought it was right.

We finally agreed that the lovemaking would be left out, but perhaps the ambiguity comes from Parker's wanting some of that feeling to remain. I never quite resolved the conflict in my own head. I felt he did care for her a lot, and in the end made a decision to just let her be, not to complicate her life further.

Q. How do you play what I'll call a double action like that? You're sweet-talking this woman, and though you may like her, you're really there to solicit information. There's something similar in *The French Connection*, when you publicly rough up a black guy who is actually your informant.

A. You cannot play a lie. You must play some kind of truth, and if you make the right choice, the audience will read it right.

Q. You mean you count on the film's montage to give the right information?

A. Yes.

Q. That takes a lot of single-mindedness, doesn't it?

A. That's right, and trust. That's why it takes most actors at least ten years to have a maturity about what they do. You have to keep separating the wheat from the chaff, so to speak, to know what's important and what isn't.

—Hackman, interviewed by Beverly Walker for *Film Comment*, Dec 1988

Tom HANKS [1956-]

Born: Concord, California. Studies at California State University at Sacramento led to work with Vincent Dowling at The Great Lakes Shakespeare Festival in Ohio. Some stage work in N.Y. then preceded his film debut in He Knows You're Alone (1980, Armand Mastroianni). Success on TV then led to his first major film role as Allen Bauer in Splash (1984, Ron Howard):

[Allen] was a potato, he was a lox, and that's what I was trying to portray, a swept-away character. If he hadn't met this girl [Darryl Hannah as Madison, the mermaid], he would have ended up in 40 years as a bitter guy sitting on a park bench who doesn't even come alive in the baseball season.

—Hanks, interviewed by Louise Sweeney for *The Christian Science Monitor*, 17 Sept 1984

[Steve Gold in *Punchline* (1988, David Seltzer) is] not a good human being, but he's an excellent stand-up comedian. I always viewed him as being trapped by this ability. It was never going to make him happy. If he goes on the Carson show and becomes a success, he is going to be just as vile and unlikable.

—Hanks, interviewed by David Ansen for *Newsweek*, 26 Sept 1988

Playboy: There were stories about Penny Marshall's eccentricity as a director. Was she difficult to work with?

Hanks: Well, one thing she did that drove me crazy was to test over and over and over again with all sorts of actors. There were scenes that I must have done two hundred times on video tape and then two hundred more in the rehearsal process. Penny just wanted to see all *sorts* of things. I would say, "I can't do this scene one more time. I don't care who it is. I cannot read these same goddamn words one more time or by the time we get to making the movie I'm going to hate it so much that I'm not going to do it at all."

Well, what happened instead was, I knew the material so well that by the time we shot it, it turned out to be the best rehearsed of all the movies that I've done....

Playboy: How does one prepare to be thirteen years old, as you did in *Big*?

Hanks: First, there were memories of my own feelings of thirteen. If there's any age that I had gone back and analyzed, even before preparing for the movie, it was those junior high years, when you can't figure anything out. You're cranky all the time; the chemicals in your body are out of whack.

I also watched the kid who played me before I got big, David Moscow. For the physical stuff.

Playboy: What do you remember about that awkward time?

Hanks: When I was thirteen I was younger than my years. I could still *play* really well. I can remember things that I loved to do, the way you could have, you know, toy soldiers or a plane, and you could sit on the couch for hours and have incredible adventures....

[And] cluelessness. Without a clue. There were times when he just didn't know what was going on. The kid was preverbal, in a way. And I remember being that way at the same age. I remember adults talking to me and just going, "Yeah, right," but not knowing *what* they were talking about.

In the movie, Elizabeth Perkins is trying to figure out our relationship — if it's serious or what. I have *no* idea what she's talking about. So I start hitting her with a rolled-up magazine and jump on top of her. It works because he's a very honest kid. He's not trying to duck anything. He doesn't know what she's asking.

—Hanks, interviewed by David Sheff for *Playboy*, Mar 1989

Oliver HARDY [1892-1957]

Born: Norvell Hardy Jr. in Harlem, Georgia. Following a stage debut at age 8 as a singer with The Coburn Minstrel Show, he then worked in stock before joining The Lubin company in Jacksonville, Florida in 1913, where he made his film debut the following year in Outwitting Dad. In 1926, Hal Roach teamed Hardy with Stan Laurel (they had appeared together in the same film on several occasions beginning in 1917); in 1927, the first official Laurel and Hardy film, Putting Pants on Philip, directed by Leo McCarey, was released. They continued to work together — in film and on stage — until Hardy's death.

Once in a while someone will ask me where Stan and I dreamed up the characters we play in the movies. They seem to think that these two fellows aren't like anybody else. I know they're *dumber* than anyone else, but there are plenty of Laurels and Hardys in the world. Whenever I travel, I still am in the habit of sitting in the lobby and watching the people walk by — and I tell you I see many Laurels and Hardys. I used to see them in my mother's hotel when I was a kid: the dumb, dumb guy who never has anything bad happen to him — and the smart, smart guy who's dumber than the dumb guy only he doesn't know it....

Q. I'm interested to know if there was ever any kind of influence over you in the creation of the particular character you play with Stan. The character was not just created on the spot, was it?

A. No, the character grew — sort of gradually. I had always worn a derby from my early days in Florida, but the Ollie Hardy character was partly based on "Helpful Henry." "Helpful Henry" was a cartoon character in Georgia newspapers when I was a boy. He was always trying to be helpful but he was always making a mess of things. He was very big and fussy and important but underneath it all, he was a very nice guy. That's very much like the character I play....

Q. I notice that in the films both you and Stan show great respect for each other when you are introducing yourselves.

A. That's right. Whenever I introduce him, it's always, "I'd like you to meet my friend, Mr. Laurel" and vice versa. These two fellows we created, they are nice, very nice people. They never get anywhere because they are both so very dumb but they don't *know* they're dumb. One of the reasons why people like us, I guess, is because they feel so superior to us. Even an eight-year-old kid can feel superior to us, and that makes him laugh....

Q. You have, of course, some traces left of your Southern accent. And, also, would it be right to say that in the pictures you still use what may be described as Southern manners — the sort of courtly or gallant way of addressing women and introducing men, and so on?

A. Yes, I guess you'd call it Southern manners. That's the way I was brought up. I was taught to be courteous at whatever cost to myself, and so in the pictures, I always am very mannerly to people because I think that's the way one should be all the time. Of course, I exaggerate for comic effect but I still mean it. It's basically the way I feel.

[On *Why Girls Love Sailors* (1927, Fred L. Guiol)] I was expecting it [a pail of water in the face], and yet in a way, I wasn't. I had a vague memory of it being part of the action coming up but as I recall I didn't expect it at that particular moment. It threw me mentally, just for a second or so, and I just couldn't think of what to do next. The camera was grinding away, and I knew I had to do *something*, so I thought of blowing my nose with my wet and sopping tie. I was raising my tie to my nose when all of a sudden I realized that this would be a bit vulgar. There were some ladies watching us. So I waved the tie in a kind of tiddly-widdly fashion, in a kind of comic way, to show that I was embarrassed. I improved on that little bit of business later on, and I used it for any number of situations. But usually I did it when I had to show extreme embarrassment while trying to look friendly at the same time....

It seems strange that so many good things for me could come out of the same film, but it's a fact that on that very set, in that very scene, just after I did the tie-twiddle, I had to become very exasperated. So I just stared right into the camera and registered disgust. The camera kept on going, and in that way my slow burn was born.

—Hardy, interviewed by John McCabe for *Mr. Laurel and Mr. Hardy* (Garden City, N.Y.: Doubleday & Co., 1966)

Jean HARLOW [1911-1937]

Born: Harlean Carpenter in Kansas City, Missouri. She made her film debut as an extra in Moran of the Marines (1928, Frank Strayer). In 1930, she played Helen in Howard Hughes, Marshall Neilan and Luther Reed's Hell's Angels:

You may remember that the final sequence of *Hell's Angels* was filmed in color. They didn't know as much about color photography in those days as they do now. They were still experimenting with it. All they knew was that several times as much light is required to shoot scenes in color. There was scarcely room for the actors to walk around, so many big arc lights cluttered up the sets.

I had a number of large close-ups to do. For these shots big batteries of light were arranged on each side of the camera. I had to face these lights, looking directly into them. The heat was terrific, but I didn't fully realize how terrific until later.

We worked for two successive days on my close-ups and each night I went home with inflamed eyes and a headache. I believed the headaches were the normal result of eye-strain. But as the days went by, my headaches became more frequent.... Soon my vision began seriously troubling me. I had always had exceptionally strong eyesight. Now it was cloudy and blurred.

Finally I went to see a doctor. His diagnosis was almost unbelievable. *My eyes were burned.*

—Harlow, interviewed by Jack Grant for *Screen Book*, 1934; repr. in *Hollywood and the Great Fan Magazines*, ed. by Martin Levin (New York: Arbor House, 1970)

My first screen lovers were Ben Lyon and Jimmy Hall, in *Hell's Angels*. It was my first picture of any importance. I was eagerly anxious. And that's why I'll never forget those two boys. If it hadn't been for Ben and Jimmy, I'd probably never have my face in the camera. I didn't know. They'd turn me around to the lens and say, "There is the camera."

Ben used to take me over to the sidelines and coach me, rehearse with me, and tell me all about how to keep the right camera angle, and all that sort of thing.... He is the most unselfish of souls, and his great spirit of helpfulness leads him to aid everybody on the set.

Then came *The Secret Six* [1931, George Hill]. It was my first lead. Johnny Mack Brown played my lover in the first part, then Clark.

Clark Gable and I were in the same boat, beginners trying to get along. And from the first day...he has not changed a bit. He is the same great person, witty, genial, sensible, a fellow who has won great success but has never let it go to his head. [Harlow and Gable worked together again on *Red Dust* (1932, Victor Fleming) and were co-starring in *Saratoga* (1937, Jack Conway), when Harlow died of a cerebral edema.]

—Harlow, in the press packet for *Suzy* (MGM, 1936)

Richard HARRIS [1933-]

Born: Limerick, Ireland. Studies at The London Academy of Dramatic Arts and work on the London stage preceded his film debut in Alive and Kicking (1958, Cyril Frankel). In 1963, he played Frank Machin opposite Rachel Roberts in Lindsay Anderson's This Sporting Life:

[*This Sporting Life*] is about the insecurities of a man and woman. The man tries to find security by playing rugby, but it destroys him and he destroys the woman.

—Harris, interviewed by Leonard Harris for *The New York World-Telegram and Sun*, 13 July 1963

[*A Man Called Horse* (1969, Elliot Silverstein)] is the story of an English lord who, in 1825, has rejected his world and gone hunting in the American West — really in search of himself. He is captured by Sioux Indians and made to prove his status as a man in their alien culture. He not only finds himself in a strange civilization but does so by a deep religious experience.

—Harris, interviewed for the press release for *A Man Called Horse* (National General Pictures, 1969)

Cromwell [in *Cromwell* (1970, Ken Hughes)] was not desiring power — like Churchill, he was a man of the moment. He had to fight incestuous corruption in the English court. England was then a bankrupt nation.... When he died 5 1/2 years later it was the strongest nation in the world. But he was not a saint, he was a very ruthless man. Cromwell finally had Charles [Alec Guinness] tried for his life. But Cromwell went to the king seven times and said, "I don't want to cut your head off; we need a king, we do need a Parliament ruling England and a king without power." But Charles believed in the divine right of kings and thought he could do no wrong. And Cromwell believed he was sent by God to make the king relinquish that. So Charles never believed Cromwell and Cromwell never understood him. Neither backed off....

I thought my own voice was too light for the role. So I went up on a mountaintop in Spain the first day we were shooting and screamed for four hours. I screamed until I broke my voice for it.

—Harris, interviewed by Louise Sweeney for *The Christian Science Monitor*, 26 Aug 1970

There is a spiritual paganism in the man [Bull McCabe in The Field (1990, Jim Sheridan)]. He's almost a force of nature.

But that's not all I saw in him. He's really Mafio-istic.... The idea is that he has a powerful sense of family — his family is all, to him.... I suppose as you get older, and nearer the finality of your life, you get more passionate about your family.

—Harris, interviewed by Glenn Collins for *The New York Times*, 16 Dec 1990

Rex HARRISON [1908-1990]

Born: Reginald Harrison in Huyton, Lancashire, England. Work on the London stage (from 1924) preceded his film debut in a bit part in The School for Scandal (1930, Maurice Elvey). In 1937, he worked with Victor Saville on Storm in a Teacup:

Victor Saville...was a lot of fun, and the director who started to relax me.... Victor was untense, and his very presence helped me to relax. He was an exceptionally easy, large, jolly man, and he made you uncare, so that you started to unwind, to speak the lines casually and naturally, and to think for the camera.

Carol Reed is another of those brilliant directors with a gift for relaxing actors.... He's careful, he's technical, he's a perfectionist, and he's marvelous with actors. In *Night Train* [aka *Night Train to Munich* (1940)] we had one scene with a lot of elderly actors. They were all German admirals, and I was a spy, dressed up as a German officer. Charlie France...kept on forgetting his lines — he must have been about 70. I had very little to do, and only a few lines, and the old man was getting rather flustered, so Carol drew me to one side and said, "Rex, *you* forget *your* line in this take. Before Charlie has his, you forget yours." So I fluffed away and apologized profusely; Carol asked me to try again, I did another take, and fluffed again. And by that time Charlie France had recovered his composure. The sight of someone else fluffing like that gave him huge confidence, and he sailed through the scene. The maneuver was typical of Carol's consideration for actors of every age and description.

David Lean was ill at ease with comedy [on *Blithe Spirit* (1945)] and his tension communicated itself to me. I remember one occasion when I had struggled through a scene in rehearsal, and Lean turned to Ronald Neame, his cameraman, and said, "I don't think that's very funny, do you?" Neame echoed, "I don't think it's very funny, no...." In those days, I suspect, Lean seemed to feel that actors were an irksome necessity who had to be tolerated until such time as he could get his hands on the celluloid and indulge his real passion, which was for editing.

We rehearsed [*My Fair Lady* (1964, George Cukor)] for 6 weeks before we turned a foot of film, and it was quite a painful business. Though I was trying to adapt the material from stage terms to film terms, I did at least know it, whereas

Audrey [Hepburn] was feeling her way through a show she didn't know....

We shot for about 4 months, which is quite a short schedule for this type of film, and I developed my own technique for doing the musical numbers.... As I knew the numbers so very well it was perfectly feasible for me to do them live on the set, as long as the director used the two-camera technique to provide for both long shots and close-ups.

In order to go right through the numbers without stopping I had to use a neck mike, a shortwave radio microphone slung around my neck under my clothes. They are used quite a lot in cabarets now, but then was the first time they had been used in a film studio.

—Harrison, in his *Rex: An Autobiography* (New York: William Morrow & Co., 1975)

William S. HART [1865-1946]

Born: Newburg, N.Y. Acting studies with F.F. Markey and work with various troupes preceded his Broadway debut in 1905. In 1914, he entered films through his friendship with fellow actor Thomas Ince. From the beginning, he wrote, directed and starred in many of his films, including The Aryan (1916):

[C. Gardiner] Sullivan wrote a story for me which I considered great. It was *The Aryan*. The star role was one of those hard-as-flint characters that Sullivan could write so well, but this man had no motive for his hardness. I wrote a beginning for the story and talked it over with Tom [Ince] and Sullivan. Sullivan gave me a great battle; his argument was that he wanted to create a character that was bad without reason. I finally convinced him that it would be stronger my way and better for the picture, and he allowed me to do it.

—Hart, in his *My Life East and West* (New York: Houghton Mifflin, 1929)

Laurence HARVEY [1928-1973]

Born: Larushka Skikne in Janiskis, Lithuania. Work on the stage with The Johannesburg Repertory Theater (from 1943), brief studies at The Royal Academy of Dramatic Art in London in 1946, and work in British repertory with The Manchester Library Theatre preceded his film debut in House of Darkness (1948, Oswald Mitchell). In 1959, he played Joe Lampton in Jack Clayton's Room at the Top:

This is the story of the northern industrial towns in England as they still exist today. It is the tragedy of an ambitious young man who doesn't understand himself or the way to get ahead and so goes about it in the most pitiful way. In the end he gets what he wants, but he is not very happy about it.

—Harvey, interviewed by Henderson Cleaves for *The New York World-Telegram and Sun*, 4 Mar 1959

Joe Lampton [in *Life at the Top* (1965, Ted Kotcheff)]...hates where he's been and figures he's really got it made running the woolen mill.

But now he's older, going into middle age and he's bored with his job, the people, his wife, everything. He takes off for London with another girl [Honor Blackman], but he finds people there are no different than in the mill town. He's trying to run away from himself and he can't.

—Harvey, interviewed by Gene Sherman for *The New York Journal-American*, 1 Aug 1965

[Elizabeth Taylor] is the nearest thing to professional perfection that I have come close to. When she says something, she says it with her face. It is filled with these wonderful expressions. Through *Night Watch* [1973, Brian G. Hutton], I relived all the marvelous impressions I had of her when we did *Butterfield 8* [1960, Daniel Mann].

—Harvey, interviewed by Christopher Sharp for *Women's Wear Daily*, 16 Aug 1973

Jack HAWKINS [1910-1973]

Born: London, England. A child actor, he travelled extensively with Sybil Thorndike's Company and performed on the London stage before making his film debut in Birds of Prey (1930, Basil Dean). In 1966, a throat operation left him unable to speak; all subsequent roles were dubbed. In 1963, he played opposite Robert Mitchum in Phil Karlson's Rampage:

Rampage...was supposed to be set in Malaya, although in fact we shot most of it in Hawaii. But for Bob, it would have been a grisly experience.

His attitude to acting is that it is a game to be enjoyed, usually on his own terms, which normally meant driving the production company to the verge of insanity. We had a running gag about losing his script, which never failed to produce a flutter of anxiety. He would come loping on to the set with an air of vagueness just before shooting was about to start.

"Am I supposed to be here?" he would drawl. "I don't know what I'm meant to do, and I've lost my script."

Immediately there would be a frantic flurry as production aides rushed about searching for a spare script, while Bob lounged sleepily in his chair. Eventually, a script would be produced and he would flip through it and say: "Oh, yes, NOW I see what I have to do." Then he would get up and play the scene absolutely word perfect down to the last comma and dot.

He is a superbly professional actor, but for some reason he tries to disguise it.

There are a few films that I cannot look back on without finding some reason for pleasure, or pride, or at least, amusement, but there is one strong exception — *Zulu* [1964, Cy Endfield]. Financially, it was a great success, and nobody can deny that it was good entertainment, but as an actor I felt let down. Indeed, in many respects I believe I was cheated out of a good performance.

The film told the story of Rorke's drift in Africa, where a hundred British soldiers fought off 3,000 Zulu warriors. I was offered the part of a Swiss Lutheran missionary, Otto Wit, which was an unusual one for me to play in a war film, for Wit was a pacifist who attempted to prevent the wholesale slaughter of the warriors. Largely because it was so unlike all the parts I was well known for, it appealed to me, and before we went to South Africa on location I discussed the role, and the way I thought it should be played, in great detail with...Endfield.

What I did not know then was that Cy is a great prestidigitator, a man who, in the kindest interpretation of the word, is a skilled conjurer. Had I realized this I might have been rather more careful but, as it was, I believed that my interpretation of the role was being taken seriously, and so I played it with this conviction.

During my scenes, Cy had arranged a number of covering shots which, for example, showed various other characters laughing at me; in other words, sending me up as a misguided buffoon. The performance that appeared on the screen bore no relationship whatever to the performance I gave in front of the cameras. When I saw it on the first night, I was so annoyed that I got out of my seat and walked out of the cinema — the only time I have ever walked out of any premiere.

—Hawkins, in his *Anything for a Quiet Life* (New York: Stein & Day, 1974)

Goldie HAWN [1945-]

Born: Washington, D.C. Studies at American University, work as a dancer and on TV's Laugh-In preceded her film debut in The One and Only, Genuine, Original Family Band (1968, Michael O'Herlihy). In 1969, she played Toni Simmons in Gene Saks' Cactus Flower:

Playboy: How was Walter Matthau to work with in *Cactus Flower*?

Hawn: He called me Goldala. To him, I was like a child.... But he was fun to play with.

Playboy: And what about Peter Sellers in *There's a Girl in My Soup* [1970, Roy Boulting]?

Hawn: I loved Peter very much. He was such a fine and delicate and, at times, neurotic spirit. It was like balancing a friend on the fine point of a needle, because he was thrown off balance by anything and everything. He also had one of the great comedy senses of all time, understanding what was funny. On this film we had terrible problems with the director. I just crossed it off as a bad day at work. But the tensions revved Peter up to the point that he was unable to function. To me, a movie is a movie and, Christ, I'm just thankful that I get to make my living this way. To him, it was more than that. He crossed into his work. He was a great master. Unfortunately, it mastered him.

—Hawn, interviewed by Lawrence Grobel for *Playboy*, Jan 1985

The Sugarland Express [1974]...was one full moment after another. And Steven Spielberg is terrific. I'd work with him again in a minute. But he's not an actor's director. He leaves you alone. He's a machine man. He loves technical kinds of objects.... He did *The Sugarland Express* because he saw the visual in the cars, the excitement, the sound, the patterns....

Shampoo [1975, Hal Ashby] was the most difficult thing I've done. I felt I was the least attractive character. "Attractive" is not the right word. That I was the least interesting of the characters, no fire, a simple person. Those people are hard to do.... She was the one that changed and had the strength to do it. In the end, he [Warren Beatty as George] didn't really get her. Everyone else is writhing in all the muck. She wasn't....

—Hawn, interviewed by Robin Brantley for *The New York Times*, 23 July 1978

What was interesting in *Shampoo* was that Julie [Christie] and I for some reason had a difficult time working with each other because we kept saying to each other, and to Warren [Beatty, the co-producer/co-screenwriter], "We're playing the wrong roles! You should have given me Julie's part and Julie should be doing my part." Because Julie has a much more puritanical sense than I do.... It was a very painful picture to do. It was as hard for her to get that character as it was for me.

—Hawn, interviewed by Andy Warhol, Bob Colacello and Barbara Allen for *Interview*, May 1976

Private Benjamin [1980, Howard Zieff] is about a protected Jewish-American princess who thinks the most important things in life are a pool, a handsome husband with a job, and going to the club. Then, it all falls apart and she ends up joining the Army, which her recruiter promises will be just like going to Lacosta for a rest cure.

After she is in, she realizes the Army's not quite like that, but she decides to take it seriously after all. To be a good soldier. And it strengthens her.

—Hawn, interviewed by John Duka for *The New York Times*, 7 Oct 1980

Sessue HAYAKAWA [1890-1973]

Born: Kintaro Hayakawa in Nancura Township, Japan. After graduating from Chicago University with a degree in political science, he moved to Hollywood. Noticed on stage by Thomas Ince, he made his film debut in Typhoon (1913):

Production on the film began as soon as the play closed its run at the Elks Hall. Mr. Ince supervised but did not direct. He assigned that task to a man named Reginald Barker. I, of course, played the role of Tokoramo. The other major characters were portrayed by Henry Kotani, Thomas Kurihara, Gladys Brockwell, Leona Hutton and Frank Borzage. Both Kotani and Kurihara were countrymen of mine. Between 1914 and 1920 they were leaders among the small band of Japanese actors who contributed to the growth of American films. After the First World War, when Japanese film-makers decided to modernize and follow the lead of Hollywood, they were called back to Japan. They both became directors, and as such introduced American techniques.

Another member of the *Typhoon* cast who became a director was Frank Borzage, with whom I became good friends during the time we worked for Ince. I found Frank a good-hearted, congenial companion. As inquisitive of life as I was, he was a man with whom I could talk seriously. He was not an educated man. Frank never got beyond grammar school. But he possessed a high degree of native intelligence and an ability to learn. From the very first, I saw he was an observer. He did not remain an actor for very long. Frank had the spark and drive which appealed to Ince, who made him a director and taught him all he could. Frank learned and developed quickly....

Ince was a perfectionist who preferred to have his ideas and inspirations beforehand, put them carefully on paper and work from them in an organized and orderly manner....

We had worked on *Typhoon* two or three days when Mr. Ince and Mr. Barker showed me a can of film they called "the rushes," the first reel of scenes taken. They invited me to see it with them.

"It's going to be great," Mr. Ince said as we filed into the darkness of his projection room.

"I shot it just the way you wanted," Mr. Barker told him. I learned this was true to the letter. Ince made a practice of laying out his picture plans in such detail that he could and would, stamp "Produce this exactly as written!" on the script, and it would be done.

My memory of Mr. DeMille as a person and a director is by far the strongest I have of making *The Cheat* [1915]. Forbidding as he appeared to be at times — and to some people all the time — Mr. DeMille was a patient and understanding man whose job fascinated him, and whose grasp of its essentials and imaginative use of them was phenomenal....

Fannie Ward was a beautiful and talented woman with a seductive voice and manner. But she was highly temperamental. Her personality and Mr. DeMille's clashed immediately....

This was her first motion picture, and one would have thought she would be co-operative. But she wasn't.... She sorely tried Mr. DeMille's patience. Her performance in *The Cheat* was all he desired. It satisfied him. However, that film was the only DeMille production she was assigned to....

As a director, Mr. DeMille was strong on having an actor understand the motive — on knowing why he must shout or laugh or cry. He liked his action to arise out of genuine emotion. He picked his people very carefully, and, once he selected them, he expressed great confidence in them. He allowed his actors to give their own best interpretations of their parts, and only stepped in to advise when it became evident what was being done was out of tune with or opposed to the sweep of the emotional and physical action as he saw it....

Actually, he did not direct me. Now and again he made suggestions, but for the most part he left me alone to go my way according to my own understanding of the role....

A professional soldier whom the vicissitudes of military life have made a martinet, Colonel Saito [in *The Bridge on the River Kwai* (1957, David Lean)] nevertheless is basically a decent man. He understands the reason of reason, but the demands of duty have deadened his understanding. Rooted in his devotion to duty are passions which are steadily consuming him. Vain, imbued with a false sense of superiority and importance, he looks upon himself as God, his camp as the world, his word as the law of it. He rules by force and fear, and is himself ruled by fear.

Time has begun to run out. With each day lost, Saito's apprehension grows. His duty is clear. He must have the bridge completed by a certain date. High military and government officials will be aboard the first train. They will expect everything to be perfect, will brook no excuses. If he fails, if the bridge is not finished, Saito knows he has no recourse but to commit hara-kiri.

It seems inevitable that self-destruction will be Saito's fate. Work on the bridge is nearly at a standstill. Saito has begun to sweat in fear of what failure will bring.

However, the plan put forth by Colonel Nicholson [Alec Guinness] is one which will solve his problem. But it compromises his honor as a Japanese and a senior officer with the Japanese Grand Army. Yet he bends, and accepts the British solution. Nicholson's mastery of the situation, almost without Saito realizing what happens, reduces, degrades and humiliates him. In a flash the hunter becomes the hunted.

Having capitulated, Saito knows the task entrusted to him will be performed. He is a beaten man. The British will succeed where he felt, in his heart of hearts, he would fail. It is as if the enemy has stripped him of his soul. Now loss of face, the grinding down of honor, refutation of what he believed to be his divine destiny — all this demands that he pay the last full measure. Alone in his quarters, he prepares to commit hara-kiri. He writes his last letter home, to Japan, to his wife and children.

As I sat before the camera in the character of Colonel Saito, at his desk in his quarters, the pictures of his beloved ones before him, a vase of white blossoms nearby, the past and the present became one. The real and the unreal fused together. Time stood still; eternity yawned. The final strokes of black ink brushes upon white rice paper conjured a memory long buried deep in my unconscious. It broke the surface like a lotus bud and unfolded as if for the first time. What was the present in Ceylon became the past in another place, in another time, more than fifty years ago, when [I as] an eighteen-year-old youth knelt in a pool of soft light from white candles and composed a poem [I] prayed would explain why, minutes later, [I] would raise an ancient dagger against [myself] in protest against [my] destiny....

—Hayakawa, in his *Zen Showed Me the Way...To Peace, Happiness and Tranquility* (London: George Allen and Unwin, 1961)

Sterling HAYDEN [1916-1986]

Born: Sterling Walter in Montclair, New Jersey. A seaman, he began working in films in order to make enough money to buy his own boat. He made his debut in Virginia (1941, Edward H. Griffith); a reluctant star, he then retired from acting until 1947. Anxious to retire a second time, he remained for financial reasons and was invited to play Dix Handley in The Asphalt Jungle (1950, John Huston):

I step on the butt, take several deep breaths, and advance toward no-man's land. Huston intercepts me, throws an arm around my shoulder, and walks me around the stage. His voice is urgent, but I'm thinking about the scene. When we stop we're next to the camera....

"Kid," he says, "play it the way it feels best. Lie down, sit up, walk around, do any damn thing you please. Wherever you go, we'll follow. Take your time. Let me know when you're ready." He drops in a canvas chair and starts to read a book. The girl [Jean Hagen] smokes, not looking at me just yet. It is absolutely silent.

Have I got the words, I wonder. Just like old times. I mess around with my shirt, trying hard to concentrate. I sit on the edge of the cot and clutch at the cage of my ribs. A minute passes, maybe more. Huston has closed the book. Our eyes meet and I nod.

—Hayden, in his *Wanderer* (New York: Alfred A. Knopf, 1963)

Dix knew what he wanted, even if he was a pretty mixed-up person from the viewpoint of accepted society. He was a hoodlum, and that's how I played him, straight. It's true I'd have gone overboard at times if it hadn't been for Huston's nice direction. Once when I was supposed to slug a cop, I had a scheme for knocking him into a fence and kicking him too. Huston did me and the picture a big favor by saying, "You're a big boy now, Sterling. Just clip the cop one."

Despite the basic grimness of the film, we clowned a lot between scenes. Huston [is] a great practical joker.

—Hayden, in *The Saturday Evening Post*, 21 Oct 1950

There is not enough money in Hollywood to lure me into making another picture with Joan Crawford. And I like money.

Her treatment of Mercedes [McCambridge, on *Johnny Guitar* (1954, Nicholas Ray)] was a shameful thing that started soon after we began work. Mercedes did all she could to get along with Crawford but it was no use.

It is hard to say how this mess began. Crawford knows Mercedes is a good actress. You can draw your own conclusions from that.

There is one thing about Crawford you must admire — her ability to create a myth, an illusion, about herself.

The great lady! Ha!

There was a lot of talk among the crew about the times Mercedes went to Crawford's cabin — five times, I understand — in an attempt to end the feud. And each time, they say, Mercedes was thrown out.

In a sense, one should be sympathetic in discussing Joan Crawford. She has so little of the things that count — peace of mind, for instance.

One night on location Mercedes won a round of applause from the entire company after she did a sensational job in a difficult scene. Crawford nearly flipped with envy and anger.

I was among those present in a motel room one night when she began blasting the director, Nick Ray. She wanted to be co-producer of the picture. I was disgusted by the whole thing.

Crawford thrives on chaos and crisis. She loves trouble. And if there is no crisis she manufactures one.

—Hayden, interviewed for *The New York Journal-American*, 3 June 1954

Kubrick at the time of *The Killing* [1956] didn't give very much. It's funny about Stanley. By the time I worked with him on [*Dr.*] *Strangelove* [1964], he'd mellowed a great deal. He was warmer. He was older and more secure. But back on *The Killing* he was like a computer. A very talented artistic computer. Very detached. Obviously he knew exactly what he was doing, but he was preoccupied with the technical aspects of it.

—Hayden, interviewed by Gordon Gow for *Films & Filming*, Oct 1973

On the first day of shooting [*Dr. Strangelove*] I found that I just couldn't handle all the technical jargon in my lines. I was utterly humiliated. Stanley told me, "The terror on your face may yield just the quality we want and if it doesn't, the hell with it, we'll shoot the whole thing over. You and I both know that is something that can happen to anyone." He was beautiful. A lot of directors like to see actors wallow. Stanley isn't one of them.

—Hayden, interviewed for *Newsweek*, 3 Jan 1972

Helen HAYES [1900-]

Born: Helen Brown in Washington, D.C.; mother of James MacArthur [1937-]. On the stage in Washington (from age 5) and in New York (from age 9), she then entered The Academy of Sacred Heart Convent at age 17. In 1925, she married the playwright and screenwriter Charles MacArthur (married until his death in 1956). MacArthur wrote her feature film debut, The Sin of Madelon Claudet (1931, Edgar Selwyn):

I have a particular sentimental attachment to the role my husband created for me, the role for which I got the Oscar, *The Sin of Madelon Claudet*. He wrote it to order; it was custom-made, and he used everything in it that he loved about me, allowing it to be shared with the world — a gesture here and a mood there. I don't know how he managed to fit everything he admired into that one role, but he did.

I played the [Grand Duchess in] *Anastasia* [1956, Anatole Litvak] under protest — I didn't want to do that at all. It was the last thing I did on the screen, and I've not been tempted to go back to do another.... I'd refused it, and they'd accepted my refusal, but they came back after Charlie died and said, "Come on, why don't you do it now?"

And all my friends...you know, after you've led an active life, and had a blow, they all get nervous and want you to plunge into something, do something...and they helped push me into it. I think I really knew, in my heart of hearts, that what I really needed to do was to sit for a while and mend, but I went off and "did something...." [She then retired from the screen, not returning until *Airport* (1970, George Seaton)].

—Hayes, interviewed by Roy Newquist for *Showcase* (New York: G.P. Putnam's Sons, 1966)

It's a sequel to *The Love Bug* [1969, Robert Stevenson] and it's called *Herbie Rides Again* [1974, Robert Stevenson]. It's about a Volkswagen with a spirit of its own. It's my car and my best friend. In the end it rallies all the Volkswagens to help me.

You see, I'm trying to save an old firehouse. It's comic but it's also about preserving our heritage. I believe in that.

My friends say I should be more selective. "You've played Queen Victoria and Mary of Scotland — why do you go about playing these dotty old women?" I have an answer to that.

As we grow older, as we grow old, we have two paths ahead. We can be very depressing or we can be amusing. I choose to be amusing with all my vagaries. My friends can't take me seriously. That's why I'm in this Disney slapstick comedy. And I'm going over to England to make another one — *One of Our Dinosaurs is Missing* [1975, Robert Stevenson] — because I've had such fun with this one.

—Hayes, interviewed by Herbert Whittaker for *The Globe and Mail*, 7 June 1974

Susan HAYWARD [1917-1975]

Born: Edythe Marrener in Brooklyn, N.Y. A fashion and photographer's model turned actress, she made her film debut in a bit part in Hollywood Hotel (1937, Busby Berkeley). In 1941, she played Hester in Adam Had Four Sons:

Roles in *Beau Geste* [1939, William Wellman] and *Our Leading Citizen* [1939, Al Santell] served to get me typed as "that sweet Susan Hayward" who couldn't be expected to play anything but doll-faced ingenues. Feeling that I'd never get far with that reputation, and hearing that Gregory Ratoff was going to direct *Adam Had Four Sons*, I asked him for the part of Hester, a remorseless character whose possibilities intrigued me. He laughed off the idea as "absurd!" But Mrs. Ratoff — Eugenie Leontovich, the actress — persuaded him....

Hester fascinated me and, as it was my first really dramatic role, also frightened me. However, Gregory's kidding and clowning soon had me relaxed. He was fun even when he got mad. I liked him so much that even when he would roar in desperation, "Susan, you are the most steenking actress I've ever seen!" I'd collapse in laughter and not be hurt. He wouldn't shrivel you with his criticism, as some directors do. He would challenge and inspire you. Then, when you got things right, he would make you glow with his "Ah, you are marvelous — wonderful!"

In addition, there was the pleasant excitement of working with Ingrid Bergman. Some actors and actresses are like blank walls, so unresponsive you can't do your best. Ingrid is just the opposite — she worked as hard for my close-ups as for her own. Finally, the role particularly appealed to me because of the physical movement which expressed Hester's nature. She was always in action, usually moving forward, constantly revealing her aggressive personality.

—Hayward, in *The Saturday Evening Post*, 6 Apr 1946

Listening [to Jane Froman], I could hear and feel in her voice how very deeply her tremendous suffering had matured her talent [she had survived a 1943 plane crash in Lisbon] — and I got so excited, so happy at the thought of playing her [in *With a Song in My Heart* (1952, Walter Lang)] that I went *ecstatically crazy*....

I remember one very long talk we had...two or three hours of girl-talk...no, it was *woman-talk* we had, about the problems and responsibilities she had to meet. Jane didn't try to hide anything from me; everything was straight from the shoulder...almost like a discussion between doctor and patient.

—Hayward, interviewed by Tex McCrary and Jinx Falkenburg for *The New York Herald Tribune*, 23 Mar 1952

I played her records at home and practiced in front of a mirror. When we began shooting, I had the sound track blare Jane's records as loud as possible, so I wouldn't miss a thing. And I would blare back with it. The first day, I was hoarse.

I was told not to copy Jane's gestures too much, a singer must move spontaneously. But I had imitated her as she did her songs, and somehow hearing them, you get the feeling, and it comes out.

—Hayward, interviewed (1952) by Margaret Elliott in an unsourced, undated article in the files of The New York Public Library for the Performing Arts

I read [Lillian Roth's] book when I had the flu. I got out of bed, called my agent, said I must have the part [in *I'll Cry Tomorrow* (1955, Daniel Mann)] — it belonged to me. I felt it was a great story of a very courageous woman, whose problem everyone should understand. And the wonderful thing is that everything went easy for me, even the drunk scenes. This had never happened to me before. Danny Mann checked every detail. He wouldn't let me cheat with lipstick or even a curl. If he thought my hair wasn't mussed enough, he put water on his hands and mashed it down.

—Hayward, interviewed for *Look*, 13 Dec 1955

It's a man's world, and women must make their way in it the best way they can. Miss Roth went into alcoholism and despair, but her spirit never completely flickered out, and she found a way to restore it. I think this is something worth saying to women, and I think women will understand what it means.... It should prove...once and for all that a person can return to normal with sufficient courage and with the help of God.

—Hayward, interviewed for the International News Service, 1954; repr. in *Susan Hayward: Portrait of a Survivor* by Beverly Linet (New York: Atheneum, 1980)

I was fascinated by the contradictory traits of personality in this strangely controversial woman [Barbara Graham in *I Want to Live!* (1958, Robert Wise)] who had had an extraordinary effect on everyone she met. She was first a juvenile, then an adult, delinquent, arrested on bad check charges, perjury, soliciting, and a flood of misdemeanors. But somewhere along the line she was a good wife and mother. I read her letters, sometimes literate, often profound. She loved poetry and music, both jazz and classical. None of this seemed to square with the picture drawn of her at the time of the trial. I studied the final transcript. I became so fascinated by the woman I simply had to play her.

—Hayward, quoted by Beverly Linet in *Susan Hayward: Portrait of a Survivor* (New York: Atheneum, 1980)

I am sure of this, that Barbara for all the bad things she did, did not have a bad heart. She wanted so terribly to be accepted and she drifted into association with the wrong people, because they were the only ones who would accept her.

—Hayward, interviewed by John Watson for *The New York Journal-American*, 30 Nov 1958

Rita HAYWORTH [1918-1987]

Born: Margarita Cansino in New York City, to dancer parents (and cousin to Ginger Rogers). In 1926, she made her film debut as Rita Cansino as part of the family act in the short film, La Fiesta. Her career as a film actress began with her second role, eight years later: The Devil's Cross (1934, Fernando de Fuentes). In 1937, she changed her professional name to Rita Hayworth. On four occasions she worked with Charles Vidor; her third was Gilda (1946):

The essence of acting is to be somebody other than yourself, yet in portraying Gilda..., I was more nearly myself than in any other role. Gilda's story was written to order for me, and her character tailored to fit me as carefully as the long black gloves which, in one wild scene, she takes off so suggestively....

Gilda herself appealed to me. It was easy to understand her fierce impulse to hurt Johnny Farrell [Glenn Ford] by pretending to be utterly rotten. The problem in portraying her was to express this flagrant abandon, yet suggest the love it camouflaged. The glove scene required dozens of rehearsals to achieve exactly the right hint of a strong passion straining to snap its controls. [She also worked on Vidor's *The Lady in Question* (1940), *Cover Girl* (1944) and *The Loves of Carmen* (1948).]

—Hayworth, in *The Saturday Evening Post*, 26 July 1947

Eileen HECKART [1919-]

Born: Columbus, Ohio. Drama studies at Ohio State University and at The American Theater Wing and work on radio and the N.Y. stage and in stock preceded her film debut in Miracle in the Rain (1955, Rudolph Maté). In Butterflies are Free (1972, Milton Katselas), she played Mrs. Baker, the mother of a blind son, a role she had played on the N.Y. stage:

Q. Did you think Mrs. Baker was one of those meddlesome mothers?

A. No, I think she has a very real point. She doesn't think this boy [Edward Albert, Jr.] is ready to go. I don't find anything malicious about her.... In the end *she's* the one who does let him go. It isn't anything he particularly does — she just knows it's *time*. And she has to sever those ties. But how hard it must be for a woman...when that moment comes.... There are certain hurts you can protect them from as a parent but there are certain things you can't — he's a man now and has to make his own way.

—Heckart, interviewed by David Johnson for *Show*, June 1972

Tippi HEDREN [1935-]

Born: Nathalie Hedren in Lafayette, Minnesota; mother of Melanie Griffith. Work as a high fashion model and on a number of TV commercials preceded her personal contract to Alfred Hitchcock who starred her in The Birds (1963):

The Humane Society was there to protect the birds but there was no one to protect me.

I was bitten and scratched, and constantly going to the hospital for repairs and tetanus shots. I never found out whether the mechanical birds frightened the real ones. They used only a few of the mechanical ones. When the assistant director told me the artificial birds were a failure and they were not going to use them, I said all right, fine; but I had no idea of what I was in for.

They built a large cage with room for the camera and five or six prop men and cartons filled with live crows and sea gulls. The men wore large, heavy gloves, picked the birds up and threw them at me at very close range. I literally had to fight them off. The birds weren't so much angry as they were unable to direct their flight correctly when tossed so close to me. The poor things were frightened and they didn't know what they were doing.

I was bitten on the lip and scratched directly under one eye. When it was all over I burst into tears, cried two hours, then went to bed for four days on doctor's orders. [Hedren worked for Hitchcock again on *Marnie* (1964).]

—Hedren, interviewed by Hedda Hopper for *The Los Angeles Times*, 14 Apr 1963

Mariel HEMINGWAY [1961-]

Born: Ketchum, Idaho; granddaughter of Ernest Hemingway; sister of Margaux Hemingway. She made her film debut in Lipstick (1976, Lamont Johnson). In 1979, she played Tracy in Woody Allen's Manhattan:

Tracy was just in love, and she knew it, and she didn't think there was any baloney about it. It was just very simple to her, and she didn't need all the excuses and the hang-ups everyone else had....

—Hemingway, interviewed by Janet Maslin for *The New York Times*, 20 May 1979

I honestly never thought it was a lesbian relationship when I read the script [of *Personal Best* (1982, Robert Towne)]. That word, *lesbian* — you hear it in some context and it sounds so perverse, so wrong. What I saw in the script were two people — and they are both innocent in some way. It is a very shaky time for them, emotionally. And that relationship seemed natural. It didn't seem morbid or sordid. Of course, I'm so innocent, and the word *lesbian* has such bad connotations that I told a friend that this relationship these two characters have wasn't really a lesbian relationship. I said that it was innocent and honest and natural, and this friend said, "Mariel, that's what lesbians think."

—Hemingway, interviewed by Tim Cahill for *Rolling Stone*, 15 Apr 1982

David HEMMINGS [1941-]

Born: Guildford, Surrey, England. At age 9, he began a singing career with The English Opera Guild, then made his film debut in Night and the City (1950, Jules Dassin). In 1966, he played Thomas in Michelangelo Antonioni's Blow-Up:

Working with Antonioni on *Blow-Up* was a tremendous experience. He's a genius. If the color of the grass doesn't suit him, he paints a park green, a street black. He doesn't like actors — I think he's afraid of them — but he can ignite you so that you blaze on the screen. I learned so much from him that it's hard to describe how much. I play the part of a fashion photographer who wants to do something more meaningful; he shoots pictures in the city streets for a book of reportage. When he makes a blow-up of a picture he shot in a park, he finds that he has completely missed the real truth of what he was seeing. In the background of a commonplace picture a murder is being committed — and psychologically he is destroyed because he can't see reality with the tools of his trade....

With the usual director you work out your characterization, then he modifies it or makes suggestions and you shape up the part as you go along. With Antonioni it's completely different. He blocks out every move for you, the rhythm with which you make every move, speak every line. If he tells you to push an ashtray in a certain way — slowly — across the tablecloth and then flick it with your finger while you're talking to someone else, and you do it in a different way, he calls for the camera to stop and demands to know why you didn't do it the way he told you to. The actor has no voice, he is manipulated. The only thing left you can work toward is a point of meaningfulness that makes your character come alive in visual terms. When I realized this, I tried to focus my characterization in relation to the plot of the film — the point the director was making with the whole movie. But Antonioni said, "Do not have the temerity to think you can understand my picture by reading the script! It's not really a script, but a notebook for a painting. Just do what I tell you to do...."

—Hemmings, interviewed by Edwin Miller for *Seventeen*, May 1967

Paul HENREID [1908-1992]

Born: Paul von Hernried in Trieste, Austria. Studies with The New Vienna Conservatory Dramatic Academy preceded his film debut in Baroud (1932, Rex Ingram and Alice Terry) made in Nice. After stage work with Max Reinhardt's theater and two roles in Austrian films, he fled the Nazi takeover in 1938. In 1940, he settled in Hollywood; in 1942, he starred opposite Bette Davis in Irwin Rapper's Now, Voyager:

There was a scene in the script of *Now, Voyager* where the author, Casey Robinson, had invented a bit of business to show the growing intimacy between Bette and me. I was to offer Bette a cigarette, take one myself, light mine, then take her cigarette out of her mouth, give her mine and put hers between my lips....

On the set the next day, I said to Bette, "Have you thought about that cigarette business?"

"Yes," she nodded. "The sharing is rather nice."

"Only it's awkward. The intimacy Casey wanted to show is good, but when we do it, there's a lot of hands and cigarettes, and I know it's going to end up on the cutting-room floor."

"Well, what do you suggest, Paul?"

"I have an idea," I told her. "First, let's try it the way the script says." We did, and then I said, "Now let me show you a better way." I took out a pack of cigarettes, took two from the pack, put them between my lips and lit them, then took one and put it in her mouth. She immediately recognized the significance and allowed her hand to touch mine. It was just right.

"Sensational!" she shouted and hugged me, then rushed up to Irving Rapper. "Irving, Paul solved it!"

"Oh? Have you?" he asked doubtfully. "What?"

"Yes. Paul, let's show him." And we did the scene for Rapper. Shaking his head, Rapper said, "I don't like it."

"You're crazy," Bette told him flatly. "This is a hundred times better than the other. Can't you see it?"

When he continued to resist the idea, insisting we should play it just as the script had it, Bette phoned Hal Wallis, the producer and asked him to come to the set. We did both versions for him, and he said, "There's no comparison, of course."

Rapper began to smile, thinking he had won the discussion, but Wallis went on, "Paul's idea is so good that I'll talk to Casey and have him put the same business in three or four more spots. It's something that's going to make an impression with the audience."

Wallis was the only one who understood what would happen. Bette and I simply thought of it as a less clumsy bit of business, but he was right. It became not only a symbol for *Now, Voyager*, to be picked up by every film critic and the public, but I myself became identified with the two-cigarette maneuver, and all over the country young lovers began to copy the gesture to show a touch of sensual intimacy. This, I believe, together with the meaty part I had and Bette Davis' intelligent acting, made a star out of me. [Henreid later directed Davis in *Dead Ringer* (1964).]

Shooting started [on *Casablanca* (1942, Michael Curtiz)] before there was a finished screenplay, in fact, before there was more than the opening scenes. Since we were shooting in chronological order, we were able to do it. The pages usually came out of the writers' typewriters the day before they were to be shot.... Nobody knew what would come next, including Mike Curtiz, the director, who did a beautiful job, especially under the wild circumstances. Mike would apologize to us, saying, "Excuse me, I don't know any more than you do about what follows or goes ahead. I'm directing each scene as best I know how!"

We all understood that the picture was being shot against time because Bogart was signed up for a role in *Sahara* [1943, Zoltan Korda], which had precedence, and *Casablanca* had to be finished first or they'd lose him....

It was all overblown melodrama and romance, but somehow it worked, even though I, as a fugitive leader of the Resistance, had to wear an immaculately clean white suit through most of the picture....

Ingrid Bergman, who played my wife in *Casablanca*, puzzled me during the filming of the picture. She was sweet and gentle in all her relationships with the other actors, seemingly a retiring, patient woman, wonderful to work with and an excellent actress, but to all of us she seemed terribly vulnerable. We wanted to take care of her, to protect her. She was so amenable to direction, never fussy over lines, never a primadonna — how had she gotten as far as she had? I wondered.

Every actress I knew who had made it had a driving vitality to her personality. If she wasn't ruthless, she was at least stubborn and aggressive. There was no other way a woman could get ahead in such a competitive field. There are too many times an actress must fight for something she wants in a script, or she must have the strength to disagree with a director or producer. Bette Davis had that strength to an inordinate degree. Ingrid Bergman showed no sign of anything like it.

The next picture I made was *In Our Time* [1944]. Ida Lupino was playing an English girl travelling in pre-war Poland who falls in love with me, a Polish count. We're married, and she teaches me "the Democratic Way." I try to change my family estate with all its serfs into a democratic enterprise, but one of my uncles, a Nazi sympathizer [Victor Francen], forces me to give up the idea. The film ends with the Nazis taking over Poland and Ida and me staying on to fight with the peasants — another piece of pseudo-historical romance concocted...in the heat of World War II.

Another uncle, a sympathetic one who was supposed to like my progressive ideas, was played in the film by Michael Chekhov. Chekhov, a brilliant Russian character actor who had set up acting schools in Berlin, London, and New York, had written a fascinating book about the stage and his beliefs about acting. When my Nazi uncle tells me off in front of him and my mother, played by Alla Nazimova, then leaves, Chekhov makes an impassioned and moving speech about how he's suffered all his life under this domineering older brother. He's glad we're fighting him and wants us to go on.

Chekhov, then in his early fifties, delivered the speech at rehearsal superbly. He did it simply, with no tears, a matter- of-fact delivery, but incredibly moving just because it was so simple. When he finished, Ida, Nazimova, and I broke into spontaneous applause.

At that point Vincent Sherman, the director, went to work on Chekhov. "Can't you take a handkerchief out and show you're moved by sniffing while you're talking?" One by one he gave him bits of business that slowly turned the impassioned speech into a terribly sentimental delivery. By the time Sherman was finished and the speech was shot, it was god-awful!

I felt that it was a devastating experience. I could hardly believe that any director could destroy such a brilliant performance by such a talented actor. The next day Chekhov and I were being driven to our location, the Warner Ranch out in the valley, and I turned to him and asked, "Why did you let Vincent Sherman do that? Your performance was so moving in rehearsal, so splendid — how could you let him destroy it?"

Chekhov was silent for a while, staring out the window. Then he sighed and turned to me, his eyes dark with a sense of pain. "Paul," he said in a tired voice, "I've played Shakespeare, Ibsen, Shaw, Goethe — I've played everything good, and I've had my time. I played my parts as I saw them, and I've had a wonderful career. Now I'm in a foreign land. I don't understand much. I'm old. I don't want any more trouble. I don't feel it's important to argue about a piece of second-rate writing. One way or the other, what difference does it make in the overall scheme of things? This script is a piece of nothing. It isn't Goethe or Schiller, and your Mr. Sherman...."

—Henreid, in his (with Julius Fast) *Ladies Man* (New York: St. Martin's Press, 1984)

Buck HENRY [1930-]

Born: Buck Zuckerman in New York City. Studies at Dartmouth College and acting work in the theatre (from 1948) preceded his film debut in The Graduate (1967, Mike Nichols), which he co-wrote with Calder Willingham. In 1971, he played Larry Tyne in Milos Forman's Taking Off:

Q. In directing *Taking Off*, Milos Forman says that he didn't give the actors the complete script. He gave it to them page by page, or scene by scene. As the star of the picture, did you ever see the screenplay?

A. No, I never had anything to read. Ever.

Q. Is that an effective way for you to work as an actor?

A. Oh, I think it's terrific. One, having been an improvisor, it's second nature. Some actors don't like it. But I think it's sensational and I think Forman's films are their own best proof of the technique. He hates acting. I mean "acting" which is why he avoids, if he can, faces that are well known; he likes for the audience to have no references, except what is happening there on the screen. He's only interested in behavior. It's interesting to go from someone like [Mike] Nichols to someone like Forman because Nichols, too, is only interested in behavior, but he can't always get it because of the structure of some of his films. There is almost no behavior in *Catch-22* [1970], which drove him crazy. The people don't behave because of the mood, because of the style, because there are so many events crammed into such a short space. His talents were stretched to their limit, I think, in finding areas for behavior. Because that's one of the things Mike does as well as any other director in the world. It's to get people to behave. But in a Forman film all you can do is behave because he constructs both the script and his system of shooting in such a way that nothing is important. Like life, the important things happen almost by accident, from moment to moment. And no one scene is the scene that says now I'm going to tell you what this is all about. I'm going to laugh, cry, or give a speech in such a way that everything is tied up in this one scene. His films are really an accumulation of every scene and every piece of behavior that happens. It's quite a different system.

Q. But he starts with a complete screenplay?

A. He starts with a total screenplay, every single word. I know this secondhand, of course, because I, being an actor, never saw the script. But I know he'll come in with it completely rewritten on the page in his own illegible handwriting or completely rewritten in his mind. Or sometimes the actors will take him in a direction that doesn't exist on the written page....

—Henry, interviewed by William Froug for *The Screenwriter Looks at the Screenwriter* (New York: Macmillan, 1972)

Audrey HEPBURN [1929-1993]

Born: Edda van Heemstra Hepburn-Ruston in Brussels, Belgium. Trained as a dancer at the Arnhem Conservatory of Music in Amsterdam and at Marie Rambert's Ballet School in London, she found work as a chorus girl on the London stage and did bit parts in several British films before being brought to Broadway to play the title role of Gigi in 1951. She made her American film debut in William Wyler's Roman Holiday (1953):

You must remember that I had just arrived in Rome and here I was making a movie with a great star like Gregory Peck and a great director like William Wyler — oh, well, it was just more than I could bear.

I must say, though, that I was enchanted with Gregory because he was so marvelously normal, so genuine, so downright *real*. There's nothing of the "making-like-a-star" routine, no phoniness in him. He's down to earth, full of real simplicity, utterly kind to everybody, a gentleman and a real professional worker.

—Hepburn, interviewed by Mike Connolly for *Photoplay Magazine*, Jan 1954

Willie [Wyler] came along and liberated me [in *Roman Holiday*]. He uninhibited me. He gave me confidence where before there was only a sort of numbed fear. He taught me what it was all about, showed me the way, and turned me loose.

We are in such close communication we hardly have to talk. I *know* when he feels it's wrong. [Hepburn also worked on Wyler's *The Children's Hour* (1962) and *How to Steal a Million* (1966).]

—Hepburn, interviewed by Peter Evans for *The Daily Express*, 1 Oct 1965

You have to refer to your own experience — what else have you got? Sabrina [in *Sabrina* (1954, Billy Wilder)] was a dreamer who lived a fairy tale and she was a *romantic* — an incorrigible romantic, which I am. I could never be cynical. I wouldn't dare. I'd roll over and *die* before that. After all, I've been so *fortunate* in my own life — I feel I've been born under a lucky star.

—Hepburn, interviewed by Michiko Kakutani for *The New York Times*, 4 June 1980

Natasha [in *War and Peace* (1956, King Vidor)] was graceful, gentle, warmhearted and of grand manner which she never lost, even in the cruel days of war.

—Hepburn, interviewed for *The New York World-Telegram*, 27 Aug 1955

Mr. Astaire is certainly the master. He works out his choreography so carefully, is a perfectionist both in rehearsal and while shooting. We rehearsed [*Funny Face* (1957, Stanley Donen)] for at least four weeks on a Paramount sound stage before going to France....

When you dance with Fred Astaire you don't dare goof. He sets up such a challenge, you must meet it...or else.

—Hepburn, interviewed by John L. Scott for *The Los Angeles Times*, 31 Mar 1957

Fred [Zinnemann on *The Nun's Story* (1959)] really does everything possible to help his actors, to create a mood, in ideal working conditions. With others — well, one's a good sport — but here, it's just not necessary.

—Hepburn, interviewed by Robert F. Hawkins for *The New York Times*, 13 Apr 1958

Many girls have lived like [Holly Golightly in *Breakfast at Tiffany's* (1961, Blake Edwards)].... I myself lived in circumstances very much like Holly. I didn't have to look far to understand and re-create the character. Just look back to my own days, back in London, as I was starting out.... Of course, I was much luckier than Holly. She was caught off base. Lost. But she was pretending just as conscientiously as we all did, and she had her identity, which was a total lack of identity.

—Hepburn, interviewed by Henry Gris; quoted by Charles Higham in his *Audrey: The Life of Audrey Hepburn* (New York: Macmillan, 1984)

Too many people think of Holly as a tramp when actually she's just putting on an act for shock effect because she's very young.

—Hepburn, interviewed by Eugene Archer for *The New York Times*, 9 Oct 1960

I read the book [*Breakfast at Tiffany's* by Truman Capote] and liked it very much. But I was terribly afraid I was not right for the part. I thought I lacked the right sense of comedy.

This part called for an extroverted character. I am not an extrovert. I am an introvert. It called for a kind of sophistication that I find difficult. I did not think I had enough technique for the part. But everyone pressed me to do it. So I did. I suffered through it all. I lost weight. Very often while I was doing the part I was convinced I was not doing the best possible job.

—Hepburn, interviewed by Murray Schumach for *The New York Times*, 16 June 1961

There have been so many fine actresses who played Eliza. Do you remember Wendy Hiller in the film *Pygmalion* [1938, Anthony Asquith and Leslie Howard]? George Cukor and I saw it before we started shooting [*My Fair Lady* (1964)] and she was wonderful. But we were doing a completely different thing.

You can't let yourself worry when you play a classic role.... If I had stopped to think about comparison with my predecessors as Eliza, I'd have frozen completely. But I loved this part. Eliza is vulnerable, but she has a beautiful inner strength. I made myself forget the problems. I threw myself into it and tried to make it me.

—Hepburn, interviewed by Eugene Archer for *The New York Times*, 1 Nov 1964

[The role of Suzie in *Wait Until Dark* (1967, Terence Young)] was a part I was very happy to be given, but it did cause some anxiety for several weeks before we even started the picture because the studio did want me to be blind in some way, and rather eager to have me wear dark glasses, or have a scar near an eye, which worried me terribly, because as I say...I don't like the technique to show, or even to be there. I also felt that this would draw attention to the fact that I'm not blind.... So, my hope was to do it from the inside out, to somehow convince the audience who knew that, thank God, Audrey Hepburn is *not* blind, but that for a fleeting moment could create an illusion of blindness. And two marvelous things happened. One was that I spent several weeks going, every day, to the Lighthouse in New York, the institution for the blind. I was blindfolded and I learned what it meant *technically* to be blind — to go up and down in elevators, to find something you throw on the floor, to make a meal, to find things in a room, but then I had another extraordinary stroke of luck, I'd say, but it was a blessing. I met a young girl who had, in fact, been blinded and in no time at all, I said, "Do something for me. Find your way around this room." And I sat on my chair and just watched. She had beautiful eyes, dark shiny eyes. There was no way of knowing that she couldn't see. So you don't need the makeup and the dark glasses....

[Ultimately], I wanted to rid myself of the technical side before I could play it, and that was being convincedly blind in my *behavior*....

With every part what has helped me a great deal...are the clothes. Because as I didn't have this technique of being able to deal with the part in however way it was, it was often an enormous help to know that you looked the part. And the rest wasn't so tough anymore. In a very obvious way, let's say you do a period picture — whether it was *War and Peace* [in which] you wear high waists and little collars and crinolines and whatever, or *The Nun's Story* when you wear a habit. Once you're in that habit of a nun, it's not that you become a saint, but you walk differently, you feel something, and it's also true if you've got rustling taffeta and a fan or whatever it is, you walk differently, you sit differently....

That is an enormous help. And also in modern day pictures, wearing Givenchys, lovely simple clothes.... [When] I was wearing a jazzy little red coat and whatever little hat was then the fashion — I felt super. And it gave me a feeling of whoever I was playing — in *Charade* [1963, Stanley Donen] or *Breakfast at Tiffany's* or walking down those stairs for the first time beautifully dressed in *My Fair Lady*. Now, actually, what you see is just a dress walking down.... The scene is set up in a glorious way, the music...and around the staircase I come in this sublime white ball dress...made up, my hair dressed to kill, diamonds everywhere.... All I had to do was walk down those stairs. The dress made me do it.

—Hepburn, interviewed by Richard Brown for *Reflections on the Silver Screen*, broadcast 10 Jan 1991 on American Movie Classics

Katharine HEPBURN [1907-]

Born: Hartford, Connecticut. A career on the NY stage preceded her 1932 film debut opposite John Barrymore in A Bill of Divorcement, the first of 10 films with George Cukor:

I learned a tremendous lot from Barrymore. One thing in particular has been invaluable to me — when you're in the same cast with people who know nothing about acting, you can't criticize them, because they go to pieces. He never criticized me. He just shoved me into what I ought to do. He taught me all that he could pour into one greenhorn in that short time.

—Hepburn, interviewed by Lupton A. Wilkinson and J. Bryan III for *The Saturday Evening Post*, 13 Dec 1941

Morning Glory [1933, Lowell Sherman] was a lovely, tricky part, in which I copied to the best of my ability Ruth Gordon, who had been doing a thing called *The Crouching Mouse*.

—Hepburn, interviewed by Gregory Speck for *Interview*, Sept 1985

When George Stevens was doing his first important picture, *Alice Adams* [1935], he was new as a director. I hadn't met him and he knew nothing about me. Early in the picture, as we shot it, there was a scene in which Alice comes home from a party.

The script said that she comes in, stops at her mother's door and tells her: "Oh, I had a lovely time!" then goes to her own room and falls weeping on the bed.

But when I came on the set that morning prepared to do the scene, George said: "Look, now, don't go to the bed. Go to the window, look out, and then burst into tears." I said: "All right." I thought it was a good idea, less hackneyed and we ought to get something. But when I went to the window, felt the glass which was cold because of the rain outside, I froze up. I suppose I was startled out of my mood by the chill. At any rate, I couldn't cry.

I tried, again and again, and the tears refused to come. I thought: "What shall I do? What shall I do? He's a new director. He'll think I'm terrible. Why can't I cry?" And the more I worried, the less I could unfreeze. I knew I'd have to do something to bring on emotion.

I blew up. I cried out: "The script says for me to go to the bed. That's the way I learned it. Why do you have me learn it one way and then ask me to do it another way!"

I knew I'd make him angry, and he shot back at me that if I could only do a scene one way, and wanted to collapse on the bed, I could go ahead. We had a hot exchange of insults and I was simply furious.

The minute I felt the emotion welling up inside I cried: "Come on, give me lights — where's the camera? — Come on, I can do it now!" I did a good scene. I could do it because I was full of emotion.

George Stevens didn't understand at first. He thought I was completely crazy. But when he saw the results he began to get my point....

That way of getting emotion may not be a good rule for anyone else. I say there are no rules that apply to everyone.

—Hepburn, interviewed by Alice L. Tyldesley for *Picturegoer Weekly*, 26 Feb 1938

Q. What role did you enjoy most?

A. Alice Adams. I had more of a hand in that than in any of the others. I feel as if I knew her better than any other character I've ever played. For one thing, I grew up in a small city, just as she did. And for another, there are so many people like her — people who have a terrific desire to create impressions, who don't realize the importance of being comfortable. Girls exhaust themselves making conscious efforts to be terribly popular with men, and they exhaust the men too. They don't let men relax or give them a chance to know them as they honestly are.

Q. How do you prepare for a role?

A. It's a long process. I have the script on my mind for weeks, sometimes months. First I read it over once — quickly. I don't attempt to remember every scene accurately. I turn my imagination loose and try to picture what each scene should be like. I build up from my hazy recollection of what I've read. I do that until it's almost time to start work. Then I read the script slowly and carefully, and find out what each scene is really like. That way, I make myself super-conscious of what the author put into each scene; and once in a while I find I've thought of something that he hasn't. That's how I did *Morning Glory*, *Alice Adams* and *Stage Door* [1937, Gregory La Cava].

—Hepburn, interviewed by James Reid for *Modern Screen*, Dec 1940

When I was very young, I used to be arrogant and — well, quite arrogant, rather like [Tracy Lord] in *The Philadelphia Story*. Phil Barry wrote that for me.... It made me a star again [on stage in 1937 and then on screen in 1940 directed by George Cukor.]

—Hepburn, interviewed by Peter S. Feibleman for *Look*, 6 Aug 1968

[As Tess Harding in *Woman of the Year* (1942, George Stevens)] I'm alive, alert, enthusiastic — and also egotistical. I love Spencer [Tracy], but I won't give up too much of myself to him.... I try to dominate him, put things over on him. I almost lose him.

The picture ought to throw some light on the problem of the modern woman who is financially independent of a man. For her the marriage problem is very great. If she falls in love with a strong man, she loses him because she is concentrated too much on her job. If she falls in love with a weakling she can push around, she always falls out of love with him!

A woman just has to have sense enough to handle a man well enough so he'll want to stay with her. How to keep him on the string is almost a full-time job.

I like one line in my picture which tells about another kind of woman.... "To a woman without talent or money, a man is as necessary as a master to a dog." This kind holds a man because she becomes a habit to him.... But who wants to be in that box?

—Hepburn, interviewed by Mayme Ober Peak for *The Sunday Star*, 2 Nov 1941

In the first scene I ever played with Spencer in *Woman of the Year*, I knocked over a glass of water. He handed me his handkerchief and I took the handkerchief and I thought, "Oh, you old so-and-so, you're going to make me mop it up right in the middle of a scene." So I started to mop it up and the water started to go down through the table. I decided to throw him by going down under the table and he just stood there watching me. He wasn't thrown at all.

—Hepburn, interviewed by Charles Higham for *The New York Times*, 9 Dec 1973

When I did *Woman of the Year*, I was very worried about being too sweet in the part. Then George Stevens, the director told me, "Katie, you get out there and be as sweet as you can be. You'll still be plenty nasty."

—Hepburn, interviewed by Theodore Strauss for *The New York Times*, 21 Feb 1943

[Spencer Tracy and I] balanced each other's natures. We were perfect representations of the American male and female. The woman is always pretty sharp, and she's needling the man, sort of slightly like a mosquito. The man is always slowly coming along, and she needles, and then he slowly puts out his big paw and slaps the lady down, and that's attractive to the American public. He's the ultimate boss of the situation, and he's very challenged by her. It isn't an easy kingdom for him to maintain. That — in simplest terms — is what we did.

—Hepburn, interviewed by Charles Higham for *Kate: The Life of Katharine Hepburn* (New York: W.W. Norton, 1975)

Spencer Tracy just *is*. He is the most remarkable actor ever born. He is one of the few people capable of total concentration. It's all based on the truth.... Spencer will read the script over and over and over again, but he doesn't decide, as some actors do, "I'm going to lift my hand and scratch my nose at this point." In the first place he wouldn't understand how you would know that you were going to reach up to scratch your nose, until you found out what the other fellow was going to do in the scene.

—Hepburn, interviewed by Roy Newquist for *A Special Kind of Magic* (Chicago: Rand McNally, 1967)

All actors are different, of course. For instance, I don't agree with the notion that the best acting comes from the first few takes. But Spencer Tracy was violent on that. He said that the first 2 takes are always the best, and I think that they were with him. But I think I can still go pretty well on that 23rd take.... And you know, it's interesting that all the times Spencer and I worked together, we never rehearsed together before shooting. Never. Not ever.

—Hepburn, interviewed by David Robinson for *The Times Saturday Review*, 24 Nov 1973

I remember only one thing about working with George [Cukor] and Spencer, and that was that George never gave Spence any suggestions *at all*. He gave them *all* to me. And George once said to Spencer, "You know, I think of a lot of things to say to you, and then I don't say them and then I go to see the rushes, and it's all there. And I've never seen you do it." With me, George obviously saw a lot of things he didn't like and he corrected me.

But George was good at making actors feel happy about themselves, creating a climate for them to work well in.... The great thing about a director is to admire an actor enough, and tell them so enough, so that the actor feels free. Because most of us build a wall of protection around ourselves. And if you think that someone thinks you're a fool, you become a fool. And if you feel that they think you're wonderful, you have a tendency to try and be wonderful and live up to what they think of you.

But that time of making *Adam's Rib* [1949] and *Pat and Mike* [1952] was a very creative and very exciting period. Spencer never used to join those conferences we had [with] George and Garson Kanin and Ruth Gordon — who wrote the scripts.... Spencer sat in a corner of the room when we had a reading of the script [of *Pat and Mike*] one night at George's house. But he didn't join in. They were written and very intimately discussed between us all, which I think was an enormous help to everyone concerned. It was very "ensemble" in spirit. And things we didn't like, or which irritated one, or you didn't understand, you were able to state it, which one doesn't always get an opportunity to do in this business. It was not just friendship, but an artistic collaboration. [Hepburn and Tracy also worked together on *Keeper of the Flame* (1943, Cukor), *Without Love* (1945, Harold S. Bucquet), *State of the Union* (1948, Frank Capra), *Desk Set* (1957, Walter Lang) and *Guess Who's Coming to Dinner?* (1967, Stanley Kramer); Hepburn's other films with Cukor were: *Little Women* (1933), *Sylvia Scarlett* (1936), *Holiday* (1938) and two films for TV — *Love Among the Ruins* (1975) and *The Corn is Green* (1978).]

—Hepburn, interviewed by John Kobal (1979) for *People Will Talk* (New York: Alfred A. Knopf, 1985)

[For *The African Queen* (1951)] we were shooting on location in Africa, way down on the Ponteville in the Belgian Congo. I had played the first scene, in which I bury [my brother played by] Robert Morley. And the next morning John Huston came waltzing up to my hut. I said, "I hope you're not planning to have breakfast with me every day, because I rather prefer to eat alone." And he said, "No, no. I'm just coming in for a minute...."

John sat down, and he just said, "Did you ever see Mrs. Roosevelt visiting the soldiers in the hospitals?" And I said, "yes, I did; I did see that movie." And he said, "Well, I think of [Rose Sayer] a little bit as Mrs. Roosevelt." Then he drifted off.

Well, it was the most brilliant suggestion. Because she was ugly so she always smiled. So I smiled. Otherwise he said very little to me on the set. But it was an awfully clever piece of direction, wasn't it? Very bright.

—Hepburn, interviewed by David Robinson for *The Times Saturday Review*, 24 Nov 1973

Bogey was a very interesting actor. He was one of the few men...I've ever known who was proud of being an actor. (I think it has upset Spencer that he's been an actor.) Bogey thought it was great, that it was a fine profession. And Bogey was quite right. Spencer has been wrong.

Bogey was totally concentrated as an actor, but he was acting. He didn't have the incredible concentration of Spencer. They were of different castes. Spencer is in a state of concentration so deep that it comes out totally simple. Bogey's work was based, a little, on Bogey's personality. I don't mean in a cute or affected way. It was an actor functioning, and Spencer is the man functioning — both in the best sense of the word, taking nothing away from either. But there was this difference.

—Hepburn, interviewed by Roy Newquist for *A Special Kind of Magic* (New York: Rand McNally, 1967)

The play [*The Lion in Winter* by James Goldman] arrived, and I read it in a morning on Martha's Vineyard.... I called Abe Lastfogel and told him immediately, "I'll do it. It's absolutely fascinating."

Then Peter O'Toole called me from London. He told me he had had a sleepless night reading the play, had fallen in love with it, and longed to play Eleanor's husband, Henry II of England. I knew Peter: he's a lovely actor! I had gone backstage when he did a play in London called *The Long and the Short and the Tall* [1959] and congratulated him on his performance. Later, I recommended him to David Lean for the role of T.E. Lawrence in *Lawrence of Arabia* [1962]. [Hepburn had worked with Lean on *Summertime* (1955)].

Peter started telling me about a director I had never heard of, Tony Harvey, and I said, "You'd better talk to me about this personally. I'll be back in Hollywood in two weeks. We can talk then."

Back in Hollywood, Phyllis [Wilbourn] and I picked him up at the Los Angeles airport.... He said, "There's a picture I want you to see playing down here at the Pan Pacific. It's a short picture, *Dutchman* [1966] about two people on a subway. It was shot by a friend of mine, Tony Harvey, in a week. Tony Harvey's the man I want to do *The Lion in Winter* [1968].

So he dragged me down to the theatre. I said, "Oh, no. I've never been to a picture at eleven o'clock at night." But he *insisted.* I thought I'd die — but when I got there, I liked the film. I thought it was very well done. But I still didn't know if Tony Harvey would be right for this picture. How in the hell're you going to tell — well done, not well done? I never know if a thing's any good. You might get a brilliant person and he'd do a bad piece of work. Well, anyway, I called Peter next morning, and I said, "If you think he's that good, I can't think of anything against him. It's fine with me." Peter flew back to London, and that's how we came to do it.

—Hepburn, interviewed by Charles Higham for *Kate: The Life of Katharine Hepburn* (New York: W.W. Norton, 1975)

I've been an admiring fan of John Wayne's for years, although we've never met. I must say he's a damn good actor and an enormous personality. He's one of our great national products. John has never been given the credit he's due. He plays with a sense of smell — like Spencer....

I've just come from doing a TV special with Larry Olivier in England, a show called *Love Among the Ruins*.

I've known Larry for years, but never worked with him. He was great of course — and I was just adorable. So sweet and lovable....[she laughs]. And now I'm working with John [on *Rooster Cogburn* (1975, Stuart Millar)]. I always feel you deserve one final enormous spree before you pass on.

—Hepburn, interviewed by Paul King for *The Toronto Star*, 5 Oct 1974

Ethel and Norman [Thayer, in *On Golden Pond* (1981, Mark Rydell)] represent the kind of couple I admire very much. They've put up with a lot. They're not quitters. There's no self-pity. They've been in love all these years, and she is satisfied to let him [Henry Fonda] be the star of the marriage. Now, that may seem old-fashioned to some, but I'm part of a generation, an era of women who saw to it that their men were not alone, who backed up their husbands against growing old and afraid, and who never lost their sense of humor. You lose your sense of humor and you might as well cut your throat. That's Ethel: a woman of deep common sense, who finds joy in life and in the beautiful things around her. She's an authentic human spirit.

—Hepburn, interviewed by Richard Corliss for *Time*, 16 Nov 1981

[Ethel Thayer] reminded me very much of my mother. She was tough, but she was infinitely kind, and brilliant. But she wasn't afraid to say, "You're a bore...."

—Hepburn, interviewed by David Hartman for *Good Morning America*; aired ABC TV, N.Y., 1981

Barbara HERSHEY [1948-]

Born: Barbara Herzstein in Hollywood, California. Work on TV preceded her film debut in With Six You Get Eggroll (1968, Howard Morris). In 1972, she played the title role in Boxcar Bertha, one of two films with Martin Scorsese:

Marty was so nervous making that movie, he was throwing up between takes. And he was very charming about his nerves and very vulnerable. That was probably the most fun I ever had with a movie. Even under all that pressure he would try things. You know, he'd shoot reflections in cars or he'd shoot into the light, into the pupil of my eye. I think his great secret as a director is he says "yes," he'll let you try anything, and if he doesn't like it, he'll cut it out. And it was back then, Marty reminded me, that I first gave him a copy of *The Last Temptation of Christ.*

Q. While you were shooting down in Arkansas?

A. Yes. It's always been my favorite book and I always thought it would be an amazing movie, and I told him he'd be great to direct it. And I don't remember saying this but he told me I did, so I must have — I said, "I've got to play Magdalene." And so years later I had lost communication with Marty, but when I read in the paper that Paramount and [Bob] Chartoff and [Irwin] Winkler were doing *Last Temptation*, to be directed by Marty Scorsese, I just screamed out loud. I remember my hands shaking as I dialed my agent. And Marty made me try out long and hard for it. I did three different screen tests because he didn't trust himself; he thought maybe he was feeling obligated.... So he made me earn that role. And I did.

—Hershey, interviewed by Ron Rosenbaum for *American Film*, May 1986

[As Nina in *The Stunt Man* (1980, Richard Rush)] I tried to show the chameleon aspect of an actor. And the child side. All the different sides and making her as varied as possible not only served me, it served the movie as well. The audience doesn't know who Nina is until the very end of the movie.

—Hershey, interviewed by Kim Garfield for *Drama-Logue*, 9-15 Oct 1980

Woody likes to define a character very carefully, through what she wears. So there'd been these long discussions we'd have about who my character Lee [in *Hannah and Her Sisters* (1986)] really was, and was she the kind of person who'd wear this or that; and I was getting very nervous because he was insisting on all these plain, toned-down clothes and I was acting without any makeup on, and I was nervous about the fact that Dianne Wiest got to wear all these funny clothes and I had to wear jeans....

He basically just said that he knew how to make me look good, and I realized that the only way to do a Woody Allen movie is to give yourself to him. From then on, if he had asked me to stand on my head, I would have.

Sometimes he'd choreograph a scene without actors, which bothered me. Sometimes he'd have an idea, like he'd want you to go to a window instead of seeing if it just happened naturally. Usually he'd let you try it and then he'd make comments on what you did, but he didn't want too much of a dialogue. I think he's afraid of actors getting too intellectual. And he'd shoot scenes without cuts; he'd shoot whole scenes beginning, middle, and end with the camera moving in and out, or actors moving in and out of close-ups. He also reshoots constantly, which is unheard of.

Q. Reshoots whole scenes, you mean?

A. Constantly. He would look at dailies and he'd come back and we'd wait for the verdict as to whether we're going to reshoot. He has it figured into his regular schedule, and so he reshot about fifty percent of it in the initial stages. Then he edits it, looks at it, rewrites, regroups the cast. Instead of cutting things short, he *rewrites* it and reshoots it shorter....

Q. What sort of things would he ask you to do in the reshoots?

A. He kept wanting me to paraphrase and put things in my own words, and I kept arguing that I liked his words better. And at the same time, if I said something in my paraphrase he didn't like he would nail it. So he'd allow freedom, but he'd really be right there to correct it.... But it was exciting. I was in actor's heaven.

—Hershey, interviewed by Ron Rosenbaum for *American Film*, May 1986

Woody blocks scenes more strictly, he's more precise in the structure of the scene. He will often shoot something in one shot. He rarely comes in for close-ups. There's a high concept on the structure of the scene, whereas Barry [Levinson on *Tin Men* (1987)] is much more free-wheeling and lets the music of the words lead you where it's natural to go. With Woody, you have to bend more to his idea.

—Hershey, interviewed by Dan Greenburg for *Playboy*, Mar 1989

I've worked with a lot of directors who feel that they have to act like they're in control and that they know. Marty says, "I don't know what I'm doing, I don't know if this is going to be any good, I don't know if I'm going to be excommunicated. I don't know if God wants me to do this movie [*The Last Temptation of Christ*]." And he means it. And it relieves me. That's all I can say. It makes me trust him.

—Hershey, interviewed for *Martin Scorsese Directs*; American Masters (PBS), broadcast 16 July 1990

Jean HERSHOLT [1886-1956]

Born: Copenhagen. Stage work in Denmark and the U.S. preceded his film debut in The Disciple (1915, William S. Hart). In 1925, he played Marcus Schouler in Eric von Stroheim's Greed:

I don't know how much *Greed* cost to make, but we worked on it steadily for nine months....

For seven months we lived in the Fairmont Hotel in San Francisco without going home once, and for two months more we worked in Death Valley. Out of forty-one men, fourteen fell ill and had to be sent back. When the picture was finished I had lost twenty-seven pounds, and was ill in hospital, delirious with fever.

We made the San Francisco scenes of *Greed* in the actual house and on the sites described by Frank Norris, the author, who had written [the novel] *McTeague* based on an actual and horrible murder in San Francisco some years previously. We rented the house where the murder had been committed, and most of the film was shot there. At the end of that time we all returned home, and then began the most terrible experience any of us has ever gone through, shooting the scenes in Death Valley. Seven car-loads went on the trip. Myself, Gibson Gowland and forty-one technicians. During the two weeks that we were in the worst part of the valley the highest temperature was 161 degrees and the lowest 91. The scorching air seared our blistered bodies, making sleep impossible....

Every day Gibson Gowland and myself would crawl across those miles of sunbaked salt, the hunted murderer pursued by the man who had sworn vengeance on him. I swear that murder must have been in both our hearts as we crawled and gasped, bare to the waist, unshaven, blackened and blistered and bleeding, while Stroheim dragged every bit of realism out of us.

That day we staged our death fight I barely recollect at all. Stroheim had made our hot, tired brains grasp that this scene was to be the finish. The blisters on my body, instead of breaking outwards, had burst inwards. The pain was intense. Gowland and I crawled over the crusted earth. I reached him, dragged him to his feet. With real blood-lust in our hearts we fought and rolled and slugged each other. Stroheim yelled at us. "Fight, fight! Try to hate each other as you both hate me!"

And that typified Von. In order to get realism he really *would* make you hate him. When he was making a film everything else was subservient to the picture, all personal feelings came last. No matter what one felt about him while under his direction, the results justified the means.

—Hersholt, interviewed for *Picturegoer*, quoted by Peter Noble in *Hollywood Scapegoat* (London: Fortune Press, 1950)

Nothing changes a person so much as the style of his hair and the cut of his whiskers.... In *Susan Lenox* [*Her Fall and Rise* (1931, Robert Z. Leonard)] it was rough and shaggy. In *Emma* [1932, Clarence Brown], it was combed with an eye to respectability. These different haircuts made different men of me. They were all subconscious imitations of men I have known or have observed....

For a part such as that of the Swiss mountaineer in *Private Lives* [1931, Sidney Franklin] with Norma Shearer and Robert Montgomery, I called upon false hair to help me out — and the mountaineer in. My own hair is curled into ringlets, my mustache was augmented and I added a curly beard to my facade. Four inches extra height were cleverly added in my boots, and my shoulders were squared and padded beyond their normal size. When I looked so big and so rough and I wore such boots and such clothes, how could I help being a mountaineer? What is an Alp to me, a giant of a man? I swaggered and I strutted, I held myself straight because I was proud of my strength and my size. I showed myself to be the hero that I looked....

[In *Beast of the City* (1932, Charles Brabin)] Al Capone [named Sam Belmonte in the film] is not an old man. He has no deep wrinkles — no marks of great age. There was no need to dress my face for this part. The expression I assumed had to make me Capone. Only the hair was arranged just so. I parted it sharply on one side, brushed it back, and glossed it with brilliantine.

A cigar between my teeth, a loose fitting suit, a gangster's insolent swagger, and Jean Hersholt existed no more. In his place was a man Walter Huston [as Jim Fitzpatrick] did very well to keep his eye upon.

—Hersholt, interviewed by Gertrude Hill for *Modern Screen*, Oct 1932

Charlton HESTON [1924-]

Born: Charlton Carter in Evanston, Illinois. His work with The Winnetka Drama Club won him a scholarship to Northwestern University where he received a degree in drama. After three years as a B-52 radio operator in WWII, he returned to acting and made his Broadway debut in 1948 with Katharine Cornell in Anthony and Cleopatra (directed by Guthrie McClintic). Having performed in two amateur productions for David Bradley in 1945 and 1949, Heston then made his professional film debut in Dark City (1950, William Dieterle). In 1952, he played Brad in The Greatest Show on Earth, the first of two roles for Cecil B. DeMille:

My role as Brad, the general manager of the circus was moonlight and roses. The part was practically actor-proof. The circus background was wonderful, and Brad himself had a single desire that motivated all his reactions and made him easy to play. He simply wanted the circus to play the next town, and the town after that, and the town after that.

—Heston, in *The Saturday Evening Post*, 18 July 1953

Moses was the greatest man who ever lived. Jesus cannot be placed in the same category because He was divine. Moses was the only man who ever talked, face to face, with God. No one can study the tremendous drama of the Exodus which Moses led and not be profoundly moved. No one can live it — as I did in the making of *The Ten Commandments* [1956, Cecil B. DeMille] — and not come out a different person. The effect was — unexplainable. The greatness of the man emerges gradually, like dawn, until in the end he towers above any other who ever lived.

Any actor worth his salt tries to *believe* in the events he is trying to portray. For instance, when I stood before the vast throng of 12,000 people and 5,000 animals, all waiting to begin their momentous journey into the Promised Land, and when I raised my arm and cried: "Hear, oh Israel, and remember this day...." I was as tight, emotionally, as it is possible for a man to be. Then, in the scene where I stood face to face with God on Mount Sinai, I was so immersed in the enormous implications of what was transpiring that I didn't have to act at all. You can't speak those magnificent lines without having your heart leap in your throat. It's like holding lightning in your hand.

—Heston, interviewed by Hyatt Downing for *Photoplay Magazine*, Dec 1956

Q. How did you like working with DeMille?

A. I found DeMille quite easy to work for — a rather formal, very intelligent man with obviously an almost flawless instinct for public response.... I found him a very decent man to work for — something of an autocrat. You can't be an absolute monarch for forty-some years and not have it mark your personality a little, but I found him very kind to actors certainly. I was enormously fortunate to have the two parts from him. As I've said more than once, if you can't make a career out of two DeMille pictures you'd better turn in your football suit.

—Heston, interviewed by Don Shay for *Conversations* (Albuquerque: Kaleidoscope Press, 1969)

February 18 [1957]: Well, we began shooting [*Touch of Evil*] with a drama I've no doubt Orson [Welles] planned. We rehearsed all day, lining up a dolly shot covering the entire first scene in Sanchez's apartment. We never turned a camera all morning or all afternoon, the studio brass gathering in the shadows in anxious little knots. By the time we began filming at a quarter to six, I know they'd written off the whole day. At seven-forty, Orson said, "OK, print. That's a wrap on this set. We're two days ahead of schedule." Twelve pages in one take, including inserts, two-shots, over-shoulders; the whole scene in one, moving through three rooms, with seven speaking parts....

March 13: Tonight in a scene with Janet [Leigh], Orson got me to use a kind of adolescent diffidence. Sort of the manner [Gary] Cooper has in scenes with women. I think he's right; if I *got* it right....

March 30: I came in after dawn this morning, too full of the exhilaration of work and watching the sun come up to go to sleep. Orson is certainly the most exciting director I've ever worked with. God...maybe it will all really begin to happen now.

—Heston, in his *The Actor's Life: Journals 1956-1976* (New York: E.P. Dutton, 1976)

Orson has a marvelous ear for the way people talk. One of the many things I learned from him was the degree to which people in real life overlap one another when they're talking. In the middle of somebody's sentence you will, in fact, apprehend what he's talking about and you will often start to reply through his closing phrase. People do that all the time. Orson directs scenes that way — to a larger degree than most directors do.

—Heston, interviewed by James Delson for *Take One*, July/Aug 1971

June 21 [1958]: Willy [Wyler] tough for me to please today [on the set of *Ben-Hur*]. My problem seems clearer: In these delicate scenes [I] must simply play with enough conviction and belief in the early takes before he fences me in with so many physical cues.... Willy beyond question toughest director I've ever worked for...but I'm inclined more and more to opinion he's also the best.

—Heston, in his *The Actor's Life: Journals 1956-1976* (New York: E.P. Dutton, 1976)

It's no fun at all doing a picture for Wyler. He's a friend of mine...and he's a charming, delightful, urbane, amusing, self-deprecating man. On the set, while not a martinet...he is so locked in his concentration on what he's doing that he really has quite a limited interest in, or trust of, actors. He doesn't particularly understand acting as an art or have much respect for the degree to which actors are capable of committing themselves to a creative end. He just knows that he has to use them and he knows how to get them to do what he wants. It's a nerve-racking process for him and God knows it is for the actor....

In terms of the way he deals with actors and his understanding of how actors work and what they need, he couldn't be more different from Welles. [Heston also worked on Wyler's *The Big Country* (1958).]

By and large, when I'm working in the studio, I prefer to look at somebody else at night. With Sam [Peckinpah, on *Major Dundee* (1964)], partly because it was a location picture and partly because of the kind of guy he is, I got very close to him. We'd go out and drink bad Mexican brandy at night and sit up talking....

I learned a lot about the character in those talks. I guess Sam directed me as much in those times as he did on the set, maybe unconsciously; I don't know, you'd have to ask Sam that. To a certain extent Sam made me into Major Dundee drinking beer and brandy in those bars at night....

—Heston, interviewed for *Dialogue on Film* #1, 1972

I think one of the responsibilities you have as an actor, in film at least, where the director is the father of us all as it were, is to fit into the way he wants to work. Frank Schaffner [on *The War Lord* (1965) and *The Planet of the Apes* (1969)] gets up at 4 o'clock in the morning and has his little model of the set and the little chess-men that he moves and the camera angles taped out. He comes in with a concept, shot by shot, which he then modifies and that's the way you work with Schaffner — or should.

—Heston, interviewed by Don Shay for *Conversations* (Albuquerque: Kaleidoscope Press, 1969)

Frank is a totally prepared and totally calm man.... He's extremely flexible.... Considering the meticulous nature of his preparation, [what's] remarkable [is] the degree of flexibility he allows himself on the set. He starts with the absolute best shot his preparation can arrive at, but he's able to keep himself open for creative developments during shooting. His prime virtue on a set is that he's a good captain...the best I've ever seen.

—Heston, interviewed for *Dialogue on Film* #1, 1972

Will Penny [1968, Tom Gries] was certainly one of the best pictures I've made. I suppose it was one of the best performances I've given; yet the part isn't very...close to me really, either to what the public seems to discern of me, or to what I deem myself to be. This illiterate drifter is not very close to the parts I've played, or to me.

Q. He's an honorable man, though.

A. Well, I was about to mention, the only thread that you can find in *Will Penny* that runs through a surprising number of my parts is it deals with the question of personal responsibility, as does *Soylent Green* [1973, Richard Fleischer], as does *El Cid* [1961, Anthony Mann], as does *Number One* [1969, Tom Gries], as does *Planet of the Apes* for that matter...*Khartoum* [1966, Basil Dearden], of course.... There are people like Mark Antony in *Antony and Cleopatra* [1972, Charlton Heston] who are destroyed because of their abdication, again the surrender, to appetite. The tragedy of Mark Antony, who was a supremely gifted leader, supremely gifted, much more gifted than the man who replaced him, Octavius Caesar...the tragic flaw in his character, which made an opening through which it all drained out, was his incapacity to control his dependence on his own pleasure.

Q. You see man as very fallible. In your roles, especially recently, are you playing a man that's fallible?

A. Yes. The man in *Soylent Green* was brutalized...the only thing that kept him at all available to human sensitivities was his experience living with the gentle old man from the past, Eddie Robinson. And thus when he was thrown into contact with this pretty girl [Leigh Taylor-Young], whom he regarded simply as sexual furniture and for whom he had no compassion whatever, somehow there was enough available raw material of humanity left in him that the death of the old man was able to trigger this....

Q. That scene with Edward G. Robinson dying, which a lot of people said was in bad taste, what do you feel about that?

A. In bad taste in what sense? Because he was in fact dying...? I think it's a very good scene. For one thing, it worked in performance.... [It] turned out to be the last scene he ever did. But while he knew he was dying, none of us in the company knew. It was clear that he was not well, but he was not a young man.... And I think Eddie did exactly what he wanted to do, what most actors would. Most actors would like nothing better than to go out on a good part, and that was certainly the best part he'd had in ten or twelve years. And he was a joy to work with. I'd worked with him before in *The Ten Commandments*. It was the ideal casting for the role, of course. He emanated a kind of callous gentleness — a callous gentility and scholarly quality that was just right for a surviving artifact from the age of reason and civilization in this inhuman world that *Soylent Green* portrayed.

—Heston, interviewed by F. Anthony Macklin for *Film Heritage*, Fall 1974

I think many film actors wearing complicated or unfamiliar period "wardrobe" make a great mistake in taking as much of it off as quickly as they can. Some will get out of it between shots. I think what you must do is wear it as much as you can. I often wear the base of it, the breeches and boots, home at the end of the day in the car. And I dress in it in the morning to come to work. It's important, you see, to feel what it's like. If "wardrobe" cannot become clothing — if it remains "costume" — then you fail with it in your work.

—Heston, interviewed by Gordon Gow for *Films & Filming*, May 1972

William HICKEY [1929-]

Born: Brooklyn, N.Y. Work as a child actor preceded his film debut in A Hatful of Rain (1957, Fred Zinnemann). After much success as an acting teacher and intermittent work on stage and screen, he played Don Corrado in John Huston's Prizzi's Honor:

During *Prizzi's Honor*, I went to dailies and was disappointed. It wasn't terrible, but gee, it wasn't that much. And I thought, "Well, I can go big, do a De Niro, or a Pacino." So I did it big once, and Huston called me over and said, "Bill, pull it back to yourself. I want to see Bill Hickey, not an imitation Italian. If I'd wanted them, I could have gotten them. I want you."

Q. What was your impression of him as a director?

A. He was very gentle with me.... He wanted a particular accent, Brooklyn-Italian, and got Julie Bovasso [noted teacher and actress] to coach me. He said, "I wanna know two things when you speak, Bill — that you were born in Italy and you never got farther than Brooklyn."

I thought, "I cannot play this one — a killer — from myself." So I asked him why he cast me. He said, "I don't know, Bill. We'll find out, won't we?" Then one day he asked if I still had my prayer beads and could I bring them with me and keep them in my pocket. He told me, "I don't want anyone to know, especially the other actors, and above all, not the public." "What will I do?" He said, "Touch them, and pray for forgiveness for killing. That's the thing he can't bear to do." Then I knew I could make it my own; from then on it was easy.

—Hickey, interviewed by Gavin Smith for *Film Comment*, Nov/Dec 1989

Wendy HILLER [1912-]

Born: Bramshall, England. Work with The Manchester Repertory Company and work on the London stage (from 1936) preceded her film debut in Lancashire Luck (1937, Henry Cass). In her second film, she played Eliza Doolittle in Pygmalion (1938, Anthony Asquith and Leslie Howard):

I was extremely lucky to have Puffin [Asquith] as the director of *Pygmalion*. I was very shy and frightened; he was most kind and patient. He encouraged me to play the role instinctively, which gave me great confidence. Anyone else might have forced me to interpret the part differently and it would have confused me. Puffin had great artistic taste and impeccable good manners. There was nothing vulgar or cheap about him....

At first it was a little baffling to find Puffin with his unique background and upbringing, the way he spoke and played the piano, and of course his fine manners, looking the way he did: he dressed like one of the electricians — if anything was less well groomed. But no one could have been more considerate. I remember I had a very bad toothache while we were shooting the ballroom scene. He was really wonderful. He noticed that I was in pain, fussed over me and did everything he could to help, and solved it in just one more take. Somehow he even managed to get on with Pascal — a lot of tact was required for that. They talked and argued far into the night.

—Hiller, interviewed by R.J. Minney for *The Films of Anthony Asquith* (New York: A.S. Barnes, 1976)

When I was offered the part of Eliza in *Pygmalion*, my husband and I were living in Bloomsbury, and we had a Cockney servant. I copied her accent for the film.

—Hiller, interviewed by Harold Hobson for *The Christian Science Monitor*, 11 May 1940

[Thomas] More [in *A Man for All Seasons* (1966, Fred Zinnemann)] married beneath him. She was a widow of a merchant from Birmingham. She couldn't read or write. More [Paul Scofield] was able to teach her to play three instruments. Everything else he taught her stepdaughter Margaret [Susannah York]. But, she could cook and sew and keep a happy house and More loved her. Of course, she never could understand why he had to go and get his head chopped off.

—Hiller, interviewed by Kathleen Carroll for *The Sunday News*, 18 Dec 1966

Gregory HINES [1946-]

Born: New York City. Work from age 2 to 22 with his father (Maurice) and brother (Maurice, Jr.) as Hines, Hines and Dad and work on the Broadway stage preceded his film debut in The Fish that Saved Pittsburgh (1979, Gilbert Moses). In 1981, he played opposite Albert Finney in Wolfen:

I got cast in a movie called *Wolfen* because I knew the director, Michael Wadleigh, from when we were hippies together. Once I got the part, I was with Albert Finney, and I was hooked. Just a small conversation with Albert Finney is like Acting 101. I remember one time when we were supposed to come through this doorway, walk through the morgue, and have some dialogue. I was back there trying to figure out how to do this thing. Wadleigh wasn't the type of director who'd really talked to you, unlike Francis [Coppola, on *The Cotton Club* (1984)]. If you even look like you don't know what you're doing, Francis will say, "Wait! What do you need?" Or he'll just start talking to you about the way you should be feeling. Anyway, Albert was sitting down, waiting for our cue, and he said to me, "If I were you, when I go through that door, I'd feel anxious because I'm late. I have someplace else to go, yet I'm intrigued by the possibility that this will be an interesting case." It was like a light bulb going off in my head. Then I knew exactly what to do....

I love to play vulnerable men. It's so rare that you get to see a black man be something other than in control of his emotions. Superfly, Shaft, now the character on *Miami Vice* — these guys are always in control. A black man gets into a frightening situation and he's not afraid. When he's with women, he's always got more experience. That's why in *The Cotton Club* it was great to play that type of character, because the woman [Lonette McKee] had so much more experience than Sandman.

Q. How did *Running Scared* [1986, Peter Hyams] happen?

A. I read the script, and I knew it was a good part. It was written for a white actor. That's what I'm up against — I have to try to make roles happen for me that aren't written black. The roles written black are the "cool guys," and I don't want to play the cool guy. I did an episode of *Amazing Stories* directed by Peter Hyams, and I knew he was allied with *Running Scared*, so I hit on him. He went to bat for me and fought for me to get the part.

—Hines, interviewed by Don Shewey for *Caught in the Act: New York Actors Face to Face* (New York: New American Library, 1986)

Alfred HITCHCOCK [1899-1980]

Born: London, England. Educated in a Jesuit school and trained as an engineer specializing in mechanical drawing, his first films as a director were made in 1925 for an English unit working in Berlin and Munich. In his third film, The Lodger (1926), he made his first of many cameo appearances; his appearance in Lifeboat (1943) proved his most challenging:

Many movie-goers think I play bit parts in the films I direct as a good-luck gesture that insures their success. That's nonsense. I've had my share of flops. Actually, I started putting myself in pictures twenty-five years ago in order to save the cost of extra players. I continued it from habit, I guess, or maybe because I was just a frustrated ham.

My favorite role was in the picture *Lifeboat* and I had an awful time thinking it up. Usually I play a passer-by, but you can't have a passer-by out on the ocean. I thought of being a dead body floating past the lifeboat, but I was afraid I'd sink. And I couldn't play one of the nine survivors, as each had to be played by a competent actor or actress.

Finally I hit on the perfect plan. I was on a strenuous diet at the time, working my way painfully down from 300 to 200 pounds. So I decided to immortalize my reduction and get my bit part by posing for "before" and "after" pictures. These photographs were used in a newspaper advertisement of an imaginary drug, Reduco, and the audience saw them — and me — when William Bendix opened an old newspaper he had picked up on the boat.

This role was a great hit. Letters literally poured in from fat people asking where they could buy Reduco, the miracle drug that had helped me lose 100 pounds. Maybe I shouldn't admit it, but I got a certain satisfaction from writing back that the drug didn't exist, and adding smugly that the best way to lose weight was to go on a strenuous diet, as I had done.

—Hitchcock, in *The Saturday Evening Post*, 12 Feb 1950

Patricia HITCHCOCK [1928-]

Born: London, England; daughter of Alfred Hitchcock and Alma Reville. Studies at The Royal Academy of Dramatic Art and work on the Broadway stage (from 1942) and as a member of the crowd in a number of her father's films, preceded her debut in his Stage Fright (1950). She later appeared in his Strangers on a Train (1951) and Psycho (1960):

Q. In *Strangers on a Train*, your role as Barbara Morton is pivotal in that you verbalize what other characters are too timid to verbalize. How did you develop this particular character; how did you perceive her?

A. The character of Barbara was seen by me as a caring supportive person to her sister [Ruth Roman]. She was very strong and blunt!

Q. Attributed to your father is a quote that actors should be treated like cattle. Whenever he was asked if he had actually said this, he seemed to delight in verbal acrobatics, neither confirming nor denying this statement. How did he work with actors?

A. My father started this as a joke with Carole Lombard on *Mr. and Mrs. Smith* [1941]. In later years he said that "I never said actors are cattle. I only said actors should be treated like cattle!" This was always said in humor. He had great respect for most actors.

—Hitchcock, in a letter to Doug Tomlinson for *Actors on Acting for the Screen* (New York: Garland Publishing, Inc., 1992)

Dustin HOFFMAN [1937-]

Born: Los Angeles, son of a prop man at Columbia Studios. Music studies at Santa Monica City College and acting at The Pasadena Playhouse, then a move to N.Y. and work in the theater preceded his film debut in The Tiger Makes Out (1967, Arthur Hiller). Later that year he played Benjamin Braddock in Mike Nichols' The Graduate. In 1969, he played Ratso Rizo in John Schlesinger's Midnight Cowboy:

I have a disagreement with some directors — I say actors shouldn't have to "act"; the scene should be constructed in such a way that you don't have to. When I did Ratso Rizo an actor told me, "Once you get the limp right, why don't you put rocks in your shoe? You'll never have to think about limping. It will be there; you won't have to worry about it." And I think that's one of the greatest things that anybody ever said, 'cause you shouldn't have to "act." It should be there, like butter — all the work should have been done beforehand — so you don't have to sit there and start jerking up emotion. It should flow.

—Hoffman, interviewed by Mitch Tuchman for *American Film*, Apr 1983

One of the things that made [*Midnight Cowboy*] successful was that Jon Voight and I knew each other. We were not close friends, but we knew each other; we were friendly. We had been actors off-Broadway for years and we've always had a little competitive thing between us. We always competed with each other in a good way....

We had this thing through the whole picture. I mean, we had electricity. The emotional scenes I did in that movie I could not have done without him. When the camera is up my schnozolla and you have about as much intimacy as being in a bathroom, here he is off-camera talking to me, moving me, getting me wherever I want to be emotionally. There was a great love between us.... I'm not from New York and I wanted a certain kind of accent. The critics drove me crazy like they always do. One critic said, "Well, he couldn't make up his mind whether he had a Jewish accent or an Italian accent." The very thing I wanted!

Unfortunately, in the movie it didn't say where the character was from. In the book the character is an Italian from a Jewish neighborhood. I worked very hard to get an Italian-Jewish accent from the Bronx.

—Hoffman, interviewed by Lewis Funke for *Actors Talk About Theatre* (Chicago: The Dramatic Publishing Co., 1977)

[Arthur Penn] wants characters to be human, rather than hero or antihero or leading man. He likes to show weak, even unattractive, sides to a character that's basically sympathetic. He gives me so much freedom [on *Little Big Man* (1970)]....

It's difficult to compare directors. When I did *The Graduate* I was always scared. I always felt I wasn't pleasing Nichols. *The Graduate* was all his; it was Nichols' film, Nichols' concept, Nichols' characters.

I think both Penn and Nichols have good taste, but in the way they treat actors they're miles apart. What Penn likes are actors who use themselves, go for broke. He'll try anything. He likes unpredictability. He's constantly trying one way, then another. You suggest something to him and he says, "Let's try it." He's open.

—Hoffman, interviewed by Bernard Weinraub for *The New York Times*, 21 Dec 1969

We were back in L.A. and we had to shoot the next day and I still did not know what to do about the voice [of the 121-year-old Jack Crabbe in *Little Big Man*]. So in a panic I went into a room, closed the door and started screaming until I got hoarse. The next day my voice was OK again. So I screamed while I got dressed, I screamed leaving the room. In the car I rolled up the windows and screamed all the way to the Sawtelle veterans' hospital. I screamed vowel sounds and different registers — screamed do, re, me, fa, trying to find a register more delicate than the others that would get hoarser.

It was a five-hour makeup job, and every half hour I'd stop and start screaming. I was just panicked because there was the camera and I knew no other way. After makeup I found a padded room with a mattress on the floor, and I went in there and screamed....

During shooting, the crew unconsciously treated me like an old person. I couldn't see too well with my contact lens cataracts, and they'd walk me over to the wheelchair they had and wheel me, and everybody was very gentle. That really helped me believe my fantasy world.

I always have a line, a very private one, that I base a character on. The line for this guy was that once I had my makeup on, all I could think of was, "I haven't had a decent bowel movement in 46 years."

—Hoffman, interviewed by Richard Meryman for *Life*, 20 Nov 1970

The reason I agreed to do [*Straw Dogs* (1971, Sam Peckinpah)] was because of the script and the potential that I thought was there. What appealed to me was the notion, on paper at least, of dealing with a so-called pacifist who was unaware of the feelings and potential for violence inside himself that were the very same feelings he abhorred in society....

The way I envisioned the character of David Sumner in the scripting stage of the production differed somewhat from what happened on the screen. I saw him as fleeing the violent campus situation in America for the peaceful English countryside on a conscious level, while on an unconscious level he would begin to set up the situation of conflict in the small town he went to. In other words, I saw the town as being completely indifferent towards him at the outset of the film, and then in snide little ways he would turn them against him because he carried his violence with him. That was the thing that I found exciting about the script. The fact that Sam and I differed over this concept doesn't mean we didn't work well together. I must say I admire his creativity and craftsmanship as a filmmaker.

—Hoffman, interviewed by Garner Simmons for *Peckinpah: A Portrait in Montage* (Austin: The University of Texas Press, 1982)

Q. In *Lenny* [1974, Bob Fosse] and in *All the President's Men* [1976, Alan J. Pakula], you played honest-to-god people. Do you find it psychologically different when you're faced with doing people instead of characters you can improvise with?

A. Yeah. I think I *prefer* fiction. *Lenny* was the first time I did a real person and it was just — painful. He was a man I had never met or seen and he had only been dead eight years. To portray someone who had been in the public eye —

an entertainer whom many people *had* seen — was a terrible disadvantage. It was just hard, and I can't say I enjoyed the experience.

In *President's Men*, I played a real character, but though I spent three-and-a-half months at the *Washington Post* talking to people, including Carl Bernstein, I found that it was *not* a character study and that I couldn't use the things about Carl Bernstein that I wanted to use, because the film doesn't focus on him. But I would prefer to do fiction, because it leaves me more open to do what I want.

—Hoffman, interviewed by Norma McLain Stoop for *After Dark*, Oct 1976

[On *All the President's Men*] the director...asked me, "What do you want to do with your character?" I said, "You really want to know? I want to look handsomer than Robert Redford." He laughed. I said, "You think I'm kidding. But that's the key to my character."

—Hoffman, interviewed by Mark Rowland for *American Film*, Dec 1988

On *Marathon Man* [1976], I did whatever I could in terms of reading up on stuff that this character was doing: a thesis on different aspects of tyranny in American history, especially the McCarthy business and the Alger Hiss business.... I started running...I found a man who trained a marathon runner and I ran with him. The research is always the best part — the most learning....

I like the acting problems that *Marathon Man* poses. I haven't played a physical part for a long time. Many times the preparations for the scenes call for a physical thing, which is a part of this emotional make-up, and I like that. Primarily, I like working with [John] Schlesinger. I worked with him on *Midnight Cowboy*, and I was sad because so many years went by before I worked with him again.

A director will say, "Just trust me, you've got to trust me." Well, I can't work that way. I either agree with you or I don't. I go by my own gut. In a film, it's a fine line, a half beat. It's meant to look effortless, but it's all worked out with such hair-splitting scrutiny. The game is to give goosebumps, then you're home. In *Straight Time* [1978], I was on it, I was doing the best work I'd ever done, and I knew the film wasn't supporting the performance. They passed rumors that I was crazy, acting irrational. Well, I wanted to go at my work meticulously and I wasn't allowed to, and so I *was* going crazy. [Hoffman began directing *Straight Time*, but was replaced by Ulu Grosbard.]

—Hoffman, interviewed by Tony Schwartz for *The New York Times*, 16 Dec 1979

[Robert] Benton is an ego-less person. He agrees with the concept I think is correct — that a film script has no integrity. It's there to be changed. It's not like a play, where the words are what it's there for. In film, it's the emotional impact and the image that counts. As Buster Keaton said, "If there's a way to say I love you without saying it — that's film...."

Oh sure, there was a lot of fighting [on *Kramer vs. Kramer* (1979)]. The kind of disagreements any marriage has. But the vision of it was never in dispute, and the desire not to exploit the material, not to go for the money but for the truth.... Benton cut out all the emotional stuff, he *dried* it out. That's what so ironic about the effect of it. I hear criticism that it's still too handkerchiefy. But Bob was going for the opposite. He was so...afraid that the women's movement could come down on him if he tilted it....

—Hoffman, interviewed by Tony Crawley for *Films Illustrated*, May/June 1980

Q. How did you get the idea for the role [of Dorothy in *Tootsie* (1982, Sydney Pollack)]?

A. It started with *Kramer vs. Kramer*. At the end of the movie, I wanted to feminize that character more. We improvised a lot in that movie — we improvised a courtroom scene, and at one point I had a good emotional thing going. The judge said, "Why should you have the child?" I said, "Because I'm his mother." And I didn't know I said it and I couldn't get Bob Benton and Stanley Jaffe to use it in the cut — they thought it was gilding the lily.

So when the film was over, I was very excited about a new feeling — what makes a woman, what is gender? I had a lot of conversations with Murray Schisgal, over what masculinity is, what femininity is, the difference between homosexuality and femininity in men. Suddenly he asked me this question: "What kind of woman would you be if you were a woman?" And I said, "What a great question."

So we started to experiment. I was so concerned with looking like a woman and not like a man in drag, and sounding like a woman and not a falsettoed camp thing, that I couldn't concentrate on the character. After a year, when the day came when I looked and sounded like a woman, then I made a crucial decision: I'm not going to try to do a character; I'm just going to be myself behind this and see what happens. And that's all

I did. I had to assume a southern voice because it held my voice up.

—Hoffman, interviewed by Mitch Tuchman for *American Film*, Apr 1983

[The working relationship between me as producer/actor and Sydney Pollack as director] was a tough marriage. I'd been with the *Tootsie* project for three years. And Sydney's the kind who is, I don't know — authoritarian. He just wanted to say, "Now I'm taking over. Now you act." I had carried the thing, and I told him, "I can't do that." So we conflicted. But in crucial areas it was very compatible. Watching the daily rushes, we never disagreed on what was the best take or what didn't work....

I couldn't have been more surprised to see that woman I played turn out that way. I would have guessed that she would wind up with a more flamboyant personality. But a kind of shy thing crept in, and I think it had to do with how self-conscious I was about the way I looked — that I wasn't as attractive as I wanted to be. No matter what sex you are, you want to be glamorous.

—Hoffman, interviewed by Stephen Schiff for *Vanity Fair*, Sept 1985

There's a lot of my mother in Dorothy — her warmth, her vulnerability, her spunk, and most of all, her outrageous sexual humor. She passed away suddenly before shooting started, and in playing the character of Dorothy, I felt I was honoring my mother's spirit.

—Hoffman, in the press release for *Tootsie* (Columbia Pictures, 1982)

When they sent me the script [of *Rain Man* (1988, Barry Levinson)] they took it for granted I'd want the [Tom] Cruise part. But I've never played someone who was legally termed 'mentally ill,' and I guess I've had a fascination with that. When I first came to New York in 1958 to study acting, I got a job at the Psychiatric Institute in New York as an attendant. I was reading *One Flew Over the Cuckoo's Nest* and thinking, "This is exactly what I'm experiencing." I was living with [Robert] Duvall in those days, and we used to 'hold court,' that was what Bobby called it, six of us in the living room of this walk-up on 109th Street. We'd share and do impressions of our experiences — and some of those people I had down.

Though this character isn't like any of them, it's still a chance to go back and do something familiar to me. Maybe it's like...you don't want to waste time. You hope that somehow before you die, you can put your experiences on the canvas.

We tried to not only duplicate [the behavior of autistics] but to understand more about them by the signals that they gave. We were self-conscious about not wanting to make a Hollywood movie that wasn't truthful to what we'd observed. To make it dramatic, but not cheat.

—Hoffman, interviewed by Mark Rowland for *American Film*, Dec 1988

I accepted the fact that in order to be authentic, Raymond [in *Rain Man*] couldn't have the dramatic arc that actors always look for in roles. And that instead of a full-scale painting, I would have to do a pencil-and-ink drawing — a poem, a haiku....

[After research] the challenge then became to do what I always try to do, which is to bring it home and not try to do a character that is not myself — to find those autistic parts of myself. Because I'm convinced that we're all a little bit autistic, just like we're all a little bit crazy.

Think of someone sitting next to you and telling you something and obviously you're not listening. Where were you? You didn't know. Or also those times where you said, "I heard what you said" and you can even repeat it — but you really weren't listening, you just recorded it....

Temple Grandon, author of *Autobiography of an Autistic*, told me: contrary to belief, autistics don't *want* not to be held and touched. But they shrink from physical contact because it's too powerful an experience; they get little jolts....

Barry was the first director who wasn't apprehensive about what I was telling him — what I wanted to do. All the other directors, to different degrees would say, "Am I hearing you right: You don't want to make eye contact with anyone in the movie? And another thing: You don't talk voluntarily?" The other directors would say, "So how can we have *scenes*?" They didn't know I was getting a lot of stuff off the people I was meeting and was moved — without eye contact. "There's a key," I would say. "We can find a code. We can discover that key and put it on paper. And the Charlie character [Tom Cruise] can be part audience and discover the key...."

[Tom Cruise and I] are both very compulsive and monk-like. When we're shooting, we both like to work out, keep up a strict diet, not go out at night. And he writes his dialogue over and over in his own handwriting — as if they're your own words, until you feel you are the writer — which is how I memorized *Death of a Salesman*.

Also, for the first time I was working with someone who was going through what I did 20 years ago — that first flush of stardom following *The Graduate*. So we were linked into each other — which allowed us to be rough with each other. There's an emotionality between us that's very difficult to act — that permitted moments to happen between us.

—Hoffman, interviewed by Donald Chase for *The New York Times*, 11 Dec 1988

William HOLDEN [1918-1981]

Born: William Beedle, Jr. in O'Fallon, Illinois. After studying chemistry at Pasadena Junior College, he had his acting debut in 1938 with the Pasadena Workshop Theater. After a two word role in Million Dollar Legs (1939, Eddie Cline), he was given the lead opposite Barbara Stanwyck in Golden Boy (1939, Rouben Mamoulian):

No one was more surprised than I when I was chosen for the title role in...*Golden Boy*. I was totally lacking in film experience and screen fame, and did not even have the curly black hair or dark complexion that went with the part of the Italian-American prize fighter, Joe Bonaparte....

From the day I was chosen I concentrated on the role day and night. Joe was a potentially fine violinist who turned prize fighter for fame and wealth. I had boxed a little, but never touched a violin. So I spent more than a week taking boxing and violin lessons all day long. During the eleven weeks that it took to make the picture, I boxed for two hours every day and practiced on the violin for an hour and a half every night. Naturally I wasn't expected to play like a young genius, but I did have to make the fingering look right.

Once, while boxing on the set with Cannonball Green, I was knocked cold. Thinking that this might make a spectacular shot, I asked whether the cameras had caught it. "Yes," the director said, "but we can't use it because it doesn't look real."

—Holden, in *The Saturday Evening Post*, 21 Jan 1950

During the first few days of work on *Golden Boy* I was so intense I found myself on the verge of a nervous collapse. Then Barbara Stanwyck, one of the stars of the movie, spent night after night, after a hard day's work, rehearsing with me, and she pulled me through. For the past twenty-two years, I've sent her flowers to commemorate the anniversary of the day that work on *Golden Boy* began. That picture was a high point for a beginning....

—Holden, interviewed by Lillian and Helen Ross for *The Player* (New York: Simon & Schuster, 1962)

[Harry] Cohn's middle name is chance. He'll take a gamble on anything. He's certainly gambled on me. One day he said: "I'm thinking about giving you a crack at a western. Can you ride a horse, Bill?" I told him, "No, but when I did *Golden Boy* I couldn't box either." He laughed and said: "Okay, You've got yourself a western." That was my first one. Then I got fairly well established in comedy after the war. So Cohn asked me if I thought I could play a psychopathic killer. I told him that I could sure try. That's how I got *The Dark Past* [1948, Rudolph Maté].

After I played the killer Cohn handed me a comedy, *Father is a Bachelor* [1950, Norman Foster and Abbey Berlin]. In that one I have the part of an amiable drifter who wants no responsibilities beyond loafing and fishing. Then he falls for a widow with six kids....

Q. You're getting typed as untyped.

A. That's what I want. I believe that an actor has two ways of tackling a screen career. He can get himself associated with a certain kind of role, so that when one comes up producers say, "That's a natural for So-and-So." Or he can spread himself thin, playing a variety of parts. And eventually he may establish himself as an actor who can handle any kind of role. The first method seems to lead to the quickest success, but I believe the second is more lasting.

—Holden, interviewed by Hedda Hopper for *The Chicago Tribune*, 12 Feb 1950

My most difficult roles have always been ones that are unlike me. Still, I've been able to find their motivation acceptable. If you're going to be [Joe] Gillis in *Sunset Boulevard* [1950, Billy Wilder], for example, you must get it across that there but for the grace of God go I. I may not be able to understand Gillis, a gigolo, but I can sympathize with him. I've found that sympathy is about all you need if you want to act a different kind of person from your real self.

—Holden, interviewed by Lillian and Helen Ross for *The Player* (New York: Simon & Schuster, 1962)

I'm sorry I had to do so many damned silly things on film. I had to shave my chest every day on

Picnic [1955, Joshua Logan] because the motion picture code said hairy chests were dirty. Do you think it's fun to stand in front of a mirror and start at your sideburns and sweep that razor all the way down to your navel every morning at 6 o'clock? I hated it. I hated anything that was phoney.

—Holden, interviewed by Jack Bond for *Marquee*, June 1978

When I look for a good part, I have two basic criteria: The character must be essentially contemporary and must reflect contemporary thinking, and there must be a sympathetic chink somewhere in his emotional armor. Perhaps I'm a coward for not ranging more widely, but these are the kinds of things I seem to do best.

In my present role [of David Ross in *The Key* (1958, Carol Reed)] I play an American tug captain working for the British. We have no armament to speak of, and we have to go out and try to bring in torpedoed merchant ships.

The person I play is unusual. He's naturally humorous in tight situations. When you're acting, it's so easy to roll with the punch — to play tense during tension. But I have to fight the punch. I have to be largely funny instead of scared. It's a real struggle to make the audience understand — and sympathize — with that sort of personality.

—Holden, interviewed for *Newsweek*, 28 Oct 1957

It's difficult to do a scene involving six characters all of whom have lines, because what you are tying to do in a master take is get everyone at their peak performance so that you can build the rest of the shooting — the close-ups and what have you — around the master, knowing you will always be able to cut back to it. Well, of course, in any given take somebody will have a high while somebody else will have a low. So the trick is always to get everyone motivated to the same degree of excellence at once.

Well, as I recall, all six of us this day had a low [on *The Wild Bunch* (1969, Sam Peckinpah)]. We had supposedly just ridden into the corral where we were meeting to divide up the silver that turned out to be washers, and the first rehearsal was just absolute chaos. It was an eight-minute scene on film, which made it long and involved. Well, Sam sat there and looked at us, and nobody knew his lines because we all had somehow felt that there would be plenty of time on the set to get sharp on the thing.

Anyway, Sam said in this very calm but menacing voice: "Gentlemen, you were hired to work on this film as actors, and I expect actors to know their lines when they come to the set. Now I'm willing to give you twenty minutes, and anyone can go wherever he wants to learn his lines. But when you come back, if you can't be an actor, you will be replaced." Well, you've never seen so many frantic people wandering off behind sagebrush and everything else, leaning against adobe walls, you name it, but getting those lines down. But Sam is a perfectionist and all perfectionists are taskmasters. Above everything else, Sam is a professional. [The other five actors were Ernest Borgnine, Ben Johnson, Warren Oates, Edmond O'Brien and Jaime Sanchez.]

—Holden, interviewed by Garner Simmons for *Peckinpah: A Portrait in Montage* (Austin: The University of Texas Press, 1982)

Actors are terribly aware of what other actors do and the point of pure dramatics as opposed to hamming it up. In...*The Wild Bunch*, Ernest Borgnine and I have this relationship going all through the film...and [in the last scene] I was shot — well, we were both wounded — but I was...fatally shot.... In the script, in the direction, it said that he just shouted "Pike," and started across this verandha to get to me and he started across shouting "Pike," then he shouted at Pike again and then in desperation he shouted at Pike again because as I was losing my life, he was losing his and it became a terribly desperate thing, and he shouted it five times crossing that verandha. And finally when he was just in his last gasps...the director yelled "Cut," and I turned to Ernie and said, "That's hamming it up, isn't it?" I mean shouting Pike all the way across the verandha. He got very indignant and said, "Well, goddam it, you're dying and after all you're my best friend" and he got a little hurt. So, the next day we saw the rushes and when I saw the whole scene put together, he was so right to do what he did because it was that final desperation kind of shouting to someone, to still relate and identify and still be alive while dying.

—Holden, interviewed by Kenneth Hufford, 5 Dec 1970, for The Arizona Historical Society Oral History Project

The Wild Bunch really started something new for me. It was the film in which I decided not to take it anymore — to use, or try to use, my liabilities as advantages: the lines around the eyes, the beer belly. I don't *look* like I can get the girl anymore, and I don't take roles like that anymore.

—Holden, interviewed by Stuart Byron for *The Village Voice*, 5 Aug 1971

Paddy [Chayefsky] writes so beautifully and he also writes long. My God, some of his speeches [for *Network* (1976, Sidney Lumet)] are fantastic. Reading them over, during our first rehearsal, I was reminded of a picture we did years ago, *Executive Suite* [1954]. It had June Allyson in it, Barbara Stanwyck, Fredric March, Walter Pidgeon, Shelley Winters, Paul Douglas and Louis Calhern. It was quite a cast. The first day we met for rehearsal, everybody knew all their lines. Robert Wise, the director, said, "I think I know what happened. You're all afraid to be bad." It was true, the standards were so high with that cast. Here it is the same thing. We're all going into the bathroom at night to try to learn our lines....

—Holden, interviewed by Kathleen Carroll for *The New York Sunday News*, 14 Mar 1976

Judy HOLLIDAY [1921-1965]

Born: Judith Tuvim in New York City. After beginning her theatrical career as a founding member of The Revuers, a New York based sketch group (whose members also numbered Betty Comden, Adolph Green, John Frank and Alvin Hammer), she made her film debut with them in Greenwich Village (1944, Walter Lang). That same year, she appeared in Winged Victory for George Cukor. Dissatisfied with films, she went back to Broadway. In 1949, she returned to Hollywood and made four films in a row for Cukor, beginning with Adam's Rib, and including the film version of her Broadway success as Billie Dawn in Born Yesterday (1950):

I took a part in *Adam's Rib* with Katie [Hepburn] and Spencer Tracy while we were fishing for the Billie Dawn deal, and the first thing I knew, Hepburn — who is terrified of press conferences — was holding them right and left, just to help me get that part of Billie Dawn. She shocked the front office at MGM like they'd never been shocked before....

—Holliday, interviewed by Tex McCrary and Jinx Falkenburg for *The New York Herald Tribune*, 17 Jan 1951

Billie was probably the dumbest dame that ever ankled onto a stage and I had to pitch my voice a lot higher to give her the proper moronic tones.

—Holliday, interviewed for *The New York Inquirer*, 18 June 1950

Everything is done for [Billie]. She doesn't have to strain a muscle, even in her head.

—Holliday, interviewed by Frank Daugherty for *The New York Times*, 10 Sept 1950

[For Billie,] I studied [my dog, Lifey] as he rested his head on my knee — his rapt way of listening to my voice, animated interest yet ignorant of what I really was saying, and his baby-eyed look while thinking of future mischief he could get away with.

—Holliday, quoted in an obituary in *The New York Herald Tribune*, Paris ed., 8 June 1965

Darla HOOD [1931-1980]

Born: Leedy, Oklahoma. A product of a determined mother, Darla began singing and dancing lessons at age 3. In New York with her dance teacher, she was spotted by Hal Roach and given the part of Darla in the Our Gang comedies. Her first was Our Gang Follies of 1936; she played the part 48 times until 1945, when she was forced by age to retire:

Except for Alfalfa [Carl Switzer], I got along well with all the kids. The troublemakers were the fathers of Alfalfa and Spanky [McFarland]. They were the real stage mothers. I mean it was just constant bickering about who got the best part and who got the most lines or close-ups. They'd complain to Mr. Roach or whoever the director was. They finally had to count lines so that each kid would get the same amount. It got to be ridiculous. After a while it got to be disgusting. Being the only girl, I didn't fare badly because I had no competition.

The worst kid in the Gang was Alfalfa. His dad told him he was God's gift to the world, and he thoroughly believed it.... He was an awful problem on the set....

—Hood, interviewed by Walter Wagner for *You Must Remember This* (New York: G.P. Putnam's Sons, 1975)

Bob HOPE [1903-]

Born: Leslie Hope in London; emigrated to the U.S. in 1908. Vaudeville, Broadway, radio, and work in short films preceded his feature film debut in The Big Broadcast of 1938:

During my early days on *The Big Broadcast of 1938*, I felt uneasy. It was one thing to make three-day musical shorts. Appearing in a big-budget musical with a bevy of stars was something else.

The director, Mitchell Leisen, was a very sensitive man, and he understood my feelings. One day when I had a musical number to do with Shirley Ross, Mitch took me to lunch at Lucey's...the Paramount watering hole.

"Now, Bob," Mitch began, "there are some things you must learn about movie acting. The important thing is your eyes. When you're thinking about what you're going to say, you will alter the muscles of your eyes. All the great movie actors do that: they say their line with their eyes before they say it with their mouths. Garbo is the best example. She can be silent for twenty minutes, yet she will tell you the whole scene with her eyes."

"Remember that: think the emotion, and it will register in your eyes."

I went back to the set determined to follow his advice.

Shirley and I were going to do a song that Ralph Rainger and Leo Robin had written, "Thanks for the Memory." Mitch Leisen did something unusual with the song....

"I'm going to make a direct recording of this one," he announced. He had the full Paramount orchestra moved onto the set, and he ordered a slower pace to "Thanks for the Memory." Robin and Rainger argued that it was meant to be a fast song, but Mitch insisted on slowing it down....

I didn't realize how Mitch's lesson at Lucey's had sunk in. When I saw the rushes, I was astonished at my galloping orbs. I did everything with them except make them change places. Even today when I see the "Thanks for the Memory" number, I cringe.

During *The Road to Singapore* [1940], Bing and I developed the system which helped contribute to the success of the *Roads*. He and I had appeared on each other's radio shows, and our writers had developed an easygoing, semi-insulting give-and-take between us. We carried that over into the picture.

Our radio writers supplied us with lines. Bing and I would go into a scene and start tossing the gags back and forth, much to the surprise of everyone. Including our director, Victor Schertzinger. But he saw that it was working, and he let us go ahead.

"You know, I really shouldn't take money for this job," he confessed one day. "All I do is say 'stop' and 'go'...."

The Crosby-Hope system was tough on Dotty Lamour. She studied her script like a good pro she is; then she got in a scene with Bing and me, and she didn't hear anything she could recognize. She felt like the judge at a tennis match.

During one long scene she finally exclaimed, "Hey boys — will you please let me get my line in?"

The system worked. The *Road* pictures had the excitement of a live entertainment, not a movie set. Crew workers at Paramount fought to be assigned to a *Road*, because they knew it would be a ball. Some stars banned visitors, but Bing and I liked to have people around. New visitors sparked new gags. Sometimes Bing and I yelled back and forth between our dressing rooms to try out new material. [Their six other *Road* films were: *Road to Zanzibar* (1941, Victor Schertzinger), *Road to Morocco* (1942, David Butler), *Road to Utopia* (1946, Hal Walker), *Road to Rio* (1948, Norman Z. McLeod), *Road to Bali* (1952, Hal Walker) and *Road to Hong Kong* (1962, Norman Panama).]

The Facts of Life [1960, Melvin Frank] was a daring picture for me. It was the story of two handicapped people who fall in love. Their handicaps were his wife and her husband.

Norman Panama and Mel Frank wrote the script — but not for Lucille Ball and me, the fools. Norman and Mel wanted to explore the adultery theme of *Brief Encounter* [1945, David Lean] with an American story that would star Olivia De Havilland and William Holden....

We shot *The Facts of Life* at Desilu Studios. Both Lucy and I were determined to submerge our own personalities in the roles we were playing. After a scene, Lucille would ask Mel Frank, the director, "Was I Lucy? Was I Lucy?" She was anxious not to play the same role that had proved so popular on television. [Ball and Hope had previously worked together on *Sorrowful Jones* (1949, Sidney Lanfield) and *Fancy Pants* (1950, George Marshall), and were teamed again for *Critics Choice* (1963, Don Weis)].

—Hope, in his (with Bob Thomas) *The Road to Hollywood* (Garden City, N.Y.: Doubleday & Co., 1977)

Anthony HOPKINS [1937-]

Born: Port Talbot, South Wales. Studies at The Royal Academy of Dramatic Art in London and the Cardiff College of Drama and work on the

London stage preceded his film debut in The White Bus (1967, Lindsay Anderson). In 1991, he played Dr. Hannibal Lecter in Jonathan Demme's The Silence of the Lambs:

When I first read the part, I thought this man was a cross between Truman Capote, Katharine Hepburn and HAL, the computer in *2001* [1968, Stanley Kubrick.] That's what I see him as — a machine, a killing machine; stark raving mad, but in control of every motion and every faculty of his being. He is, of course, a personification of the Devil. I have always perceived the Devil as very charming, witty, all clever and wise, seductive, sexual — and lethal.

—Hopkins, interviewed by James Cameron-Wilson for *Film Review*, June 1991

Dennis HOPPER [1936-]

Born: Dodge City, Kansas. Studies with Dorothy McGuire and John Swope at The Old Globe Theater in San Diego and repertory work with The Pasadena Playhouse preceded his film debut in Rebel Without a Cause (1955, Nicholas Ray):

In 1952, I saw Marlon Brando and Montgomery Clift in movies in the same week and it changed my life tremendously. *Place in the Sun* [1951, George Stevens] and [*Viva*] *Zapata* [1952, Elia Kazan]. My thinking about acting changed from this grand, classical kind of thing to trying to figure out what was an internal actor and what were these people doing....

Dean was working in areas that were way over my head. He was doing things that weren't written. He was working internally and externalizing real feelings.... He had a tremendous emotional life going on. This is at a time in the Fifties when actors only did the script. But Jimmy did the script and then some. Like in *Rebel Without a Cause*, when they arrest him for being drunk and disorderly, they start searching him and he starts laughing like they're tickling him. Or making the siren noises. There was nothing written about that.

—Hopper, interviewed by Chris Hodenfield for *Film Comment*, Dec 1986

What we really had was a student-teacher relationship, the only one [James Dean] ever had, as far as I know. When we were making *Rebel*, I just grabbed him one day and said, "Look, man, I gotta know how you act, because you're the greatest!" So he asked me, very quietly, why I acted, and I told him what a nightmare my home life had been, everybody neurotic because they weren't doing what they wanted to do, and yelling at me when I wanted to be creative, because creative people ended up in bars....

Anyway, Jimmy and I found we'd had the same experiences at home, and that we were both neurotic and had to justify our neuroses by creating, getting the pain out and sharing it. He started watching my takes after that. I wouldn't even know he was there. Two days later, he'd come up and mumble, "Why don't you try the scene this way." And he was always right.... [Hopper and Dean worked together again on *Giant* (1956, George Stevens).]

—Hopper, interviewed by Tom Burke for *The New York Times*, 20 July 1969

I had a small part in *From Hell to Texas*, in 1958, which [Henry Hathaway] directed. We argued all day and then had a wonderful time at dinner. He was a primitive director — rarely moved his camera, he'd have movement come from the actor — and he gave me line readings that were imitation Brando crap. I'd try to reason with him, and he'd snap, "Kid, that's dinner talk." I walked off the set three times.

One day, he pointed to a huge stack of film cans, and said, "Kid, there's enough film in those cans to shoot for three months, and we're gonna film this scene until you get it right." I don't know how many takes we did — I say eighty-six because I was really eighty-sixed when we were done — but Hathaway finally wore me down and got what he wanted. He said, "You'll never work in this town again." And I didn't do a major Hollywood picture for several years. [After a number of years, Hopper worked with Hathaway again on *The Sons of Katie Elder* (1965) and *True Grit* (1969).]

—Hopper, interviewed by Bill Kelley for *American Film*, Mar 1988

David Lynch is wonderful to work with. He knows what he wants. There was no improvisation on *Blue Velvet* [1986], that was all line by line stuff. The work was very demanding....

The thing I was worried about with David — but I trusted him because I really respect his films — I felt I was reaching an area there was no coming back from. I thought I got so high, and to that emotional level so quick and so soon in the movie, there's not going to be any color to the part [of Frank Booth]. It was just going to be a one-dimensional thing, just screaming, screaming, screaming, from the beginning to the end.

When I saw it put together, it didn't really work out that way. There are different colors. It's not just a one-note thing.

—Hopper, interviewed by Chris Hodenfield for *Film Comment*, Dec 1986

Lena HORNE [1917-]

Born: Brooklyn, N.Y. Work as a chorus girl and singer at The Cotton Club in N.Y., a 1934 Broadway debut, a career as a jazz and concert vocalist, and appearances in a number of short films beginning with The Duke is Tops (1938, William Nolte) preceded her feature film debut in Panama Hattie (1942, Norman Z. McLeod). In 1942, she became the first black woman to be given a long term Hollywood contract (at MGM); when she finished the contract, she turned her back on Hollywood, disgusted with their treatment of her and other black performers.

[*Cabin in the Sky* (1943)] was not only the first picture in which I was to play a real part, it was also to be the first completely directed by Vincente Minnelli, who up to that time had been employed by M-G-M only as a director of musical sequences.

I was very glad about that, because Vincente and I had drawn close in the months since I ran into him in Arthur Freed's office. [He subsequently directed Miss Horne in several musical sequences, including those in *Panama Hattie*].... It gave me a great deal of confidence that he was going to direct this picture; I knew I could trust him and lean upon him.

I knew I was going to need all the support I could get, because Ethel Waters was to be one of the stars of the picture. Long before we met I began hearing rumors around the lot that she was — to put it mildly — a rather difficult person to work with. We only had a couple of scenes together, and they were not scheduled to be shot until we were well along in production. The kids who were working in her scenes told me she was violently prejudiced against me. Miss Waters was not notably gentle toward women and she was particularly tough on other singers.... I suppose she had all the normal feminine reactions toward another woman who might be a potential rival....

Unlike Miss Waters, I was enjoying myself hugely on this picture.... For the first time I felt myself to be an important part of the whole enterprise, not just a stranger who came in for a few days to do a song or two....

While the picture was shooting, I did not see much of Vincente. Like most directors at work on a picture he used the nights to prepare for the next day's shooting. But we did talk occasionally about how I should play my scenes with Miss Waters. Up until then I had done nothing but fun comedy stuff with Rochester [Eddie Anderson] and Louis Armstrong. Now Vincente suggested that the only way to compete against Miss Waters' intensity was to be terribly helpless, almost babyish, when I confronted her. He thought it would make a good contrast with the hoydenish way I had played the comedy and musical scenes and that since she had the basically sympathetic part — the good woman trying to protect her marriage — this would be the best way to give my part a bit of complexity.

It might have worked — except for an accident. The day before our scene was scheduled I was rehearsing a big, dancing entrance into a night club with Rochester. We were to arrive in a Cadillac and make our way through a big crowd and then do this production number involving a huge number of people. Just as we started to do a full rehearsal with the music, I twisted my ankle and I heard a snapping sound.... They carried me down to the infirmary...and put me into a cast. It was painful and cumbersome and, of course, it meant extra trouble for everyone, restaging musical numbers, setting up difficult camera angles so my plaster cast wouldn't show and so on. For example, "Honey in the Honeycomb" now had to be done with me perched on a bar instead of moving through the set.

This caused a certain amount of attention to be focused on me, which was just exactly what I did not want to happen when I was working with Miss Waters. The atmosphere was very tense and it exploded when a prop man brought a pillow for me to put under my sore ankle. Miss Waters started to blow like a hurricane. It was an all-encompassing outburst, touching everyone and everything that got in its way. Though I (or my ankle) may have been the immediate cause of it, it was actually directed at everything that had made her life miserable, the whole system that had held her back and exploited her.

We had to shut down the set for the rest of the day. During the evening, apparently, some of the people at the studio were able to talk to her and calm her down, because the next day we were able to go on with the picture. We finished it without speaking. The silence was not sullen. It was just that there was nothing to say after that, nothing that could make things right between us.

It was Cab Calloway who helped me to display some sort of creditable emotion when I sang "Stormy Weather" [in *Stormy Weather* (1943)]. Andrew Stone, the director, seemed to me to represent the rock-bound coast of Maine. He simply couldn't pull any emotion out of me and I could not respond to him. Now, I supposedly sing this song when I'm grieving over having decided to leave Bill [Robinson] and go it alone on my career even though I'm still secretly breaking my heart over him. So Cab took me off in a corner of the sound stage and told me to forget all about what Mr. Stone had been telling me and to think, instead, about my own marital problems. For good measure, Cab called me a few good dirty names, just to upset me, and it worked.

—Horne, in her (with Richard Schickel) *Lena* (Garden City, N.Y.: Doubleday & Co., 1965)

Edward Everett HORTON [1886-1970]

Born: Brooklyn, N.Y. Amateur dramatics at Columbia University — beginning with the Varsity Show of 1909 — while studying at their Teachers' College, and work in stock and on the California stage preceded his film debut in Too Much Business (1921, Jess Robbins). In 1932, he played François Filiba in Trouble in Paradise, the first of five films for Ernst Lubitsch:

He always had the actor in his mind. In no part of any Lubitsch picture did he have an actor who was not just right. You rehearsed a whole week on the picture without shooting anything at all. We rehearsed in the sets. No matter what you thought or what you wanted to do, Mr. Lubitsch had gone over it in his mind and had come to a conclusion. Just as soon as you could put yourself *en rapport* with him, you were very happy. He knew these actors very well, and he wanted something from them that even they didn't know they had. [Horton also worked on Lubitsch's *Design for Living* (1933), *The Merry Widow* (1934), *Angel* (1937) and *Bluebeard's Eighth Wife* (1938).]

—Horton, interviewed by Bernard Rosenberg and Harry Silverstein for *The Real Tinsel* (New York: Macmillan, 1970)

You know, Mr. Lubitsch engaged his casts because he knew their capabilities and eccentricities and mannerisms of acting — and he knew exactly what he wanted them to do — and I loved that because I knew I couldn't help but be good in a Lubitsch film — but I also learned I would always be at my best in a Capra film for the opposite reason.

Frank Capra liked to use stage people — and I *am* basically a stage actor — and he liked to sort of teach — to help you to find the right interpretation, and he always wants you to suggest it yourself. The first movie I did for him was *Lost Horizon* [1937].... I was a fussy paleontologist stranded there with the others. Anyway, I had a scene where I was in a room all alone. And Frank wanted the suggestion of the eerieness of a different world. He said, "It seems to me if I were in a room like this I would have a feeling of fear if I felt that someone was behind the curtain and then I would look — very cautiously behind that curtain and — " and he kept encouraging me. "Do anything you like" and then he said "now make me laugh" and I sat down at the desk in the room and searched the drawers and found a Chinese lacquer box — opened it and found a mirror in the lid. None of the visitors to Shangri-La had seen their appearance since they came some time ago, and I realised I would be startled and I jumped when I saw the mirror and gasped — and Frank laughed. I worked for Frank Capra later in *Arsenic and Old Lace* [1944] and in *Pocketful of Miracles* [1961] and I just couldn't help being good in a Capra film either.

[Douglas Sirk]...was delightful and ambitious and so well-informed.

[Count Volsky in *Summer Storm* (1944)] was sort of the last gasp of aristocracy — a character reduced to his last pair of high pearl button shoes. It was the kind of part Lionel Barrymore could have played.

In one scene they brought in a huge wedding cake and I couldn't resist ad-libbing my own line. It was just right for the character. I said, "This is an old Volsky family recipe made with 300 eggs," and Mr. Sirk laughed and said he wouldn't dream of cutting it. I got along so well with Douglas Sirk. Never was a fellow so pleased with my work.

I had a feeling this film would change my career — this would be the end of all the double takes. Now I would be a real actor. This was the end of an era. But it wasn't.... I never saw Mr. Sirk again and I went right back to playing the same old fussy, nervous intellectuals.

—Horton, interviewed by Jeanne Stein for *Focus on Film*, Jan/Feb 1970

Bob HOSKINS [1942-]

Born: Bury St. Edmunds, England. A professional stage debut in 1969 and work on TV from 1972 preceded his film debut in The National Health (1974, Jack Gold). In 1982, he played Harold Shand in John MacKenzie's The Long Good Friday:

I knew a couple of little villains, but I wanted to meet the bigguns. So they introduced me and I actually walked in and said, "Teach me how to be a gangster." Everybody was real flattered, and they took on the film. "Don't say it was me," they would say. Then they'd take me around and show me the ropes. What I learned from them is their charm. They're real charmin' fellows, but they have this terrible temper.

—Hoskins, interviewed by James Verniere for *The Aquarian Weekly*, 5-12 May 1982

I couldn't allow myself a lot of research for the role [of George, the ex-convict in *Mona Lisa* (1986, Neil Jordan)] because I didn't want too rigid a structure. It had to be completely flexible. I had to create an inner something. So [me and my daughter, Rosa would] watch these birds in cages. And George became like that, a man with this incredible spirit trapped inside him by his own naiveté, by his own expectations, by the society around him. There he was, inside his own cage.

—Hoskins, interviewed by Jeff Silverman for *The Chicago Tribune*, 6 July 1986

John HOUSEMAN [1902-1988]

Born: Jacques Haussmann in Bucharest, Rumania. Work as a playwright and producer preceded his association with Orson Welles, beginning in 1936 and including their co-founding of The Mercury Theatre. He went to Hollywood in the 1940s and worked as a producer for David O. Selznick Productions and RKO. In 1965, he was appointed director of the Drama Division at The Juilliard School in N.Y. and in 1975 founded The Acting Company. A brief appearance as Vice-Admiral Barnswell in Seven Days in May (1964, John Frankenheimer) was his sole acting credit prior to playing Professor Kingsfield in The Paper Chase (1973, James Bridges):

I had a few secret misgivings over my ability (in my seventy-first year and without previous experience) to memorize the long speeches uttered by the professor. But once I realized that these presented no serious difficulty, I found playing the scholarly curmudgeon an agreeable and easy task, in which I was helped by the special circumstances of my engagement. This was no ordinary actor-director situation. Bridges and I had known each other for years in a teacher-disciple relationship that was not altogether unlike that which existed in the film between Kingsfield and Hart [Timothy Bottoms]. Since we were equally committed to making my performance a success and to justifying Jim's reckless casting of me in the part, we worked as close allies — carefully, deliberately, trusting each other and in total agreement as to what he hoped to achieve.

It felt strange, of course, after so many years of producing and directing, to find myself suddenly on the other side of the camera. But I soon got used to it, and throughout the shooting of *The Paper Chase* I found my experience and my accumulated knowledge of theatre and film a constant help to me in my performance. I was privy to the strategy by which Jim and his cameraman...were intending to heighten the initial impact of the formidable professor. Throughout my early classroom scenes I was to be consistently photographed in close-up and at angles that gave me weight and stature, in contrast to the long shots and diminishing lenses through which young Hart and my other helpless victims were introduced. I'm not sure how much my playing of those scenes was affected by this knowledge, but the use I was able to make of it unquestionably added authority and color to the relationship between the charismatic, deeply committed professor and his terrorized but worshipful students.

—Houseman, in his *Final Dress* (New York: Simon & Schuster, 1983)

Leslie HOWARD [1893-1943]

Born: Leslie Howard Stainer in London, England. A stage career preceded his film debut in the short, The Heroine of Mons (1914, Wilfred Noy). After action in WW1, he began his work in features with The Happy Warrior (1917, F. Martin Thornton), while continuing to work on the stage. In the 1930s, he worked in Hollywood, returning to England to make his directorial debut and star as Henry Higgins in Pygmalion (1938, co-directed by Anthony Asquith):

[Higgins] is more like [George Bernard] Shaw than any character the man ever wrote. For that reason it's such a hard part to play. Shaw...hates sentiment, but it comes through in spite of him.

I got to like Higgins very much.... In his curiously frustrated character you feel all the time that he would like to break away from the cerebral point of view. There is something very English about a character trying to break down the logic of reasoning. His brain tells him that the flower girl [Wendy Hiller as Eliza Doolittle] has nothing, but he wants her for an experiment.

—Howard, interviewed (1938) by Robert W. Dana in an unsourced article in the files of The New York Public Library for the Performing Arts

When we were filming *Pygmalion* at the Pinewood studio, we actually lived right there — virtually never left the place, in fact during the seven or eight weeks we were shooting. There is a beautiful big clubhouse right on the grounds and that's where we made our home. In the evenings, we would gather around and look over the day's rushes and talk over our work.

It was a most satisfactory way to do the job, really — just like the production of a play.

—Howard, interviewed by Bosley Crowther for *The New York Times*, 20 Nov 1938

Rock HUDSON [1925-1985]

Born: Roy Scherer in Winnetka, Illinois. After service in the navy, he was brought to films by Raoul Walsh in Fighter Squadron (1948). He starred in eight films directed by Douglas Sirk between 1952 and 1957, beginning with Has Anybody Seen My Gal?. In 1956, he played Bick Benedict in George Stevens' Giant:

[James Dean] and I and Chill Wills lived in a rented house together for three months while we were doing *Giant* [1956] in Texas, and although we each went more or less our own way, Dean was hard to be around.

He hated George Stevens, didn't think he was a good director, and he was always angry and full of contempt....

And he was rough to do a scene with for reasons that only an actor can appreciate. While doing a scene, in the giving and taking, he was just a taker. He would suck everything out and never give back.

—Hudson, interviewed by Ray Loynd for *The Hollywood Reporter*, 9 Aug 1968

I fell in love with [George Stevens on *Giant*]. He was like a god to me. I mean, I followed him around like a puppy.... Here was a man who had done, countless times, I felt, brilliant work.

Stevens had such a richness to him.... He read everything. He digested everything...so that when he prepared this film, he knew everything there was to know about Texas.... He so inundated himself in Texas and Texanism that whatever decision he made was absolutely right....

He did all the directing with me before the picture began, and hardly a word during shooting.... He had me so rich and so bigoted. I was Bick Benedict before we ever shot frame one.... He gave me so much power that I felt I could run the studio....

I was having lunch with him and he said, "Would you like to go down and see your house?" Which was down at the carpentry shop, being built in sections. "Oh, yeah," I said, not giving a damn about the house. That's a different department! I could walk out of a door of a modern house or a Victorian house and it didn't matter...wrong, but still that was my attitude. And I said, "Sure, sure, anything you say, sir." And there it was, in sections, the raw lumber. And he said, "What color do you want it?" And I said, "Oh...." And I realized he was serious. I was all set to make some flip joke. And I said, "Well, Victorian...I don't know. Tan with brown trim, I guess." "Okay, boys, paint it tan with a brown trim. Okay, let's go." Well, it was my house. It was mine from then on. Don't you see what he was doing? "Who would you like as your leading lady? Grace Kelly or Elizabeth Taylor?" Well! I can work with Elizabeth, and I can work with Grace, you know. And he was serious. So I said, "Elizabeth." "Fine. We'll get Elizabeth." Well, I was eighteen feet tall.

Now, what isn't being said here is that he probably had Elizabeth signed.... If I had said Grace Kelly, he would have found a way to make me think that Elizabeth would be better. That was the wonderful way of his direction, of making me think that it was my idea.

And I was rich and strong and bigoted and powerful, so I didn't have to *play* it. I didn't have to go into a scene and say, "I'm rich and strong and bigoted and powerful, and I'll do this scene from that attitude." I was there. That's good direction.

I was quite apprehensive, nervous and scared [about *Pillow Talk* (1959)], because I'd never played comedy. And in [producer] Ross Hunter's office, I met the director, Michael Gordon. Michael Gordon is very intense...he belongs behind a big tome, blowing the dust. He has these enormous eyebrows. And I thought, that man is going to direct me in comedy? Light, airy-fairy comedy? Okay! So I said, "Mr. Gordon, I am nervous about one thing: How do you play comedy?"

"Oh," he said, "just treat it like the very most tragic story you've ever portrayed." I thought about that for a minute. "That makes sense." Then he said, "If you think you're funny, nobody else will." And it's absolutely the truth....

Doris [Day] and I became terrific friends. She's a dynamo — a strong lady. And, boy, what a comedienne she is! The trouble we had was trying not to laugh. Doris and I couldn't look at each other. You know, that sweet agony of laughing when you're not supposed to. That's what we had.

The second film we made together, *Lover Come Back* [1961, Delbert Mann] was even worse. I think they added two weeks to the shooting schedule because of our laughter. We flat could not look at each other. I'd look at her forehead, her nose. And we did terrible things to each other; with our backs to the camera we'd make faces at each other.... It's perhaps acting rather juvenile in one sense, but in another, when you're shooting comedy, it isn't. What shows on the screen, I think, is what helped make those films successful. The twinkle shows in the eyes. And we had it....

—Hudson, interviewed by Ronald L. Davis for The Southern Methodist University Oral History Project, 24 Aug 1983; repr. in Hudson's (with Sara Davidson) *Rock Hudson: His Story* (New York: William Morrow & Co., 1986)

Going in, those were both playable roles. The advertising man in *Lover Come Back*, like the composer in *Pillow Talk*, was a ne'er-do-well. And playing a ne'er-do-well is terrific. I mean, you automatically like a ne'er-do-well, don't you...? The advertising executive who played around all the time, and who was bored with it until he met Miss Day and said to himself, "That would be rather interesting to toss in the hay. But I think I'll see if I can get her to go on the make for *me*" — now that's fun. And it's very playable. [Hudson and Day worked together a third time on *Send Me No Flowers* (1964, Norman Jewison).]

[Howard Hawks had] made very many brilliant films. But it was like he'd given up. And therefore it was quite disillusioning. All of the jokes and comedic sequences in [*Man's Favorite Sport?* (1963)] were repeats of things he'd done in his various other films. He would say that something was very funny in such and such a film he'd made before, and so we'd do it here.

—Hudson, interviewed by Gordon Gow for *Films & Filming*, June 1976

Barnard HUGHES [1915-]

Born: Bedford Hills, N.Y. A stage debut in The Shakespeare Fellowship's production of The Taming of the Shrew in 1934 and work on Broadway (from 1937), preceded his film debut in Play Girl (1941, Frank Woodruff). In 1969, he played Townie in John Schlesinger's Midnight Cowboy:

Q. Have you ever felt that a film director improved your performance with the control he had?

A. Yes, I've really had very good outings in film, so there's no reason for me to complain. An interesting thing did happen when I played "Townie," one of Joe Buck [Jon Voight]'s clients in *Midnight Cowboy*. John Schlesinger had the whole cast sit down and read the work together, which is something you so rarely do in film. And when it was time to shoot my scene, he said to me, "Why don't you use the script, but try improvising your way into it. Then pick up your lines and improvise your way out again." He said, "Suppose you're "Townie." Tell me about yourself." He asked me questions and I answered them as if it were an interview and I were really the character in the script. *Wonderful* things came out of it and we got so much of it on film.

But when I went to a screening of the final version, all of this material that I thought was so wonderful had been cut out of it! I was really upset. Yet I saw the film again after it had opened a few weeks later and I realized that, yes, indeed, John knew exactly what he was doing. If there had been more to my part, it could never have erupted into that violence. If there had been more of me, the audience would have felt sympathetic and the violence would have been utterly gratuitous. That would have worked against Joe Buck's character. And I thought, boy, hopefully, I'll always be in the hands of a film director as good as John Schlesinger.

—Hughes, interviewed by Joanmarie Kalter for *Actors on Acting* (New York: Sterling Publishing Co., 1979)

Tom HULCE [1953-]

Born: White Water, Wisconsin. Theater studies at The North Carolina School of the Arts and a brief apprenticeship with The New York Shakespeare Festival led to work on Broadway. He made his film debut in September 30, 1955 (1978, James Bridges). In 1984, he played Mozart in Milos Forman's Amadeus:

Milos wanted something as outrageous as I could come up with. To demystify [Mozart]. Because it's an amazingly appalling fact that someone who was such a genius was turned against by everyone at the time he was alive, and so a kind of urge to make him into some kind of reverential figure was history's inevitable desire to clean things up.

—Hulce, interviewed by Don Minifie for *Films & Filming*, Aug 1986

The particular challenge to me was to take as many risks as I could imagine and not shy away from the controversial aspect of Mozart's life. The fact that my performance was critically controversial can be attributed to the risk I took. Some of the negative critical reaction made me angry because it was as though the critics were seeing me in *National Lampoon's Animal House* [1978, John Landis]. They didn't understand there was a choice being made. It would have been easier to play something as literate as Peter [Shaffer]'s script with an English accent and to present a much more conventional picture of an artist. It's wonderful to have made the dangerous choice rather than the safe choice.

—Hulce, interviewed by Aljean Harmetz for *The New York Times*, 24 Mar 1985

What I like about working in front of a camera is that it's a machine put there to capture a moment. So you can do one moment extraordinarily, and if you do another great moment, they can put the two together and make a performance you couldn't possibly deliver all at once.... I can give you an example. In the scene [in *Amadeus*] between Mozart and Salieri [F. Murray Abraham], when Mozart is dying and dictating the Requiem, the bargain that Murray and I made was that we would not stop the scene. I would know the music well enough that anytime he, the actor, got behind, he had an invitation to stop me, to ask questions within the scene. It meant that I knew he would be with me. The scene was intricately worked out in the writing. In the doing of it, I would leave out a piece of information, so he would find out two lines later that he needed it, just to give it the messiness of life, knowing it would make him seem stupid to have to ask for something I'd already gone beyond, d'you know.

There was a moment when we were shooting the scene that I got lost. I didn't know where I was and what we were doing. I was lying in this bed, and I didn't know what was going on. So what you see in the scene is Mozart, in his condition, off someplace else in his brain for a while, and you see Salieri trying to get Mozart back on the track so he can get this fucking piece of music that he's eating himself alive to get. And because the trust and commitment between Murray and me as two people working together was great, he stuck with me, and Milos used the entire sequence. When I saw the movie put together, that was the moment when I started to cry, because it was something that could only happen in a film. It was something that could only happen with an intense connection between two people, as characters and actors and men.

—Hulce, interviewed by Don Shewey for *Caught in the Act: New York Actors Face to Face* (New York: New American Library, 1986)

Linda HUNT [1945-]

Born: Morristown, New Jersey. Studies at The Goodman School of Drama in Chicago and with Robert Lewis in New York led to a 1975 debut on the New York stage. She made her film debut in Popeye (1980, Robert Altman). In 1983, she played Billy Kwan in Peter Weir's The Year of Living Dangerously:

I was scared to death at the idea of playing a man. I was drawn to his relationship to the people of Indonesia and to his passion about injustice; to his involvement with his own size and with the whole mythology of dwarfs and the kind of power they have; to his love for Jill [Sigourney Weaver] and his inability to act that out; to his need for heroes, but in relation to Guy [Mel Gibson] and in relation to Sukarno; and to his sense of being an outsider — because of being a Eurasian and therefore a hybrid, not one thing nor the other.

I have my own version of that feeling, obviously having to do with what I've had to deal with in terms of my size. I also identified with Kwan's desire to have an effect, to create change; Kwan is one of those people who believe one person can make a difference, and at my best moments I have a sense of that about acting — that one can make a contribution.

—Hunt, interviewed by Leslie Bennetts for *The New York Times*, 12 Feb 1983

Peter [Weir] said that all the men who read for the part [of Billy Kwan] competed with the Mel Gibson character, a male-to-male thing. And he felt that Kwan would be utterly non-competitive; that this was an aspect of his being Asian. So what Peter had been looking for he suddenly got from a woman.

—Hunt, interviewed by Mary Harron for *The Times*, 4 Aug 1985

I don't do a lot of research — though there was a stage in my career when I did. I found it provided an intellectual base for a role, but there are better ways to discover your character's world: photos, paintings, music — and not only the tunes of the era. Music can stimulate me for crazy, irrational reasons. Peter Weir played the third of Strauss's *Four Last Songs* for the scene where Kwan sits alone at his typewriter. It opened me....

In film you also rely on what's around you; unlike theater, you forget it's illusion. We were in the Philippines for *Year of Living Dangerously* — it's the closest we got to Asia — and what I saw and smelled and felt gave me the material to make Kwan. We shot *Silverado* [1985, Lawrence Kasdan] in New Mexico, and I felt the vastness of that place. One isn't held by the landscape; you're adrift....

The Midnight Star Saloon [in *Silverado*] would've been the one place people in Silverado went for any kind of diversion from the crops or cattle they were trying to raise, from the sales they were trying to make. It was the one spot in town for letting go, for allowing yourself the illusion of safety. This is the feeling we have when we go to the theater: In a dark cocoon we let ourselves drift into another world away from our own business.

Think of Stella as a woman passionately committed to providing that for a community....

Stella is a lady. Elegant and refined — a feminine sensibility in a highly theatrical personality. Smart and brutally realistic. And she runs a saloon and brothel. I came to think of her as an entertainer.

—Hunt, interviewed by Marcia Pally for *Film Comment*, August 1985

The camera has a life of its own. It's observing differently at different times. *The Year of Living Dangerously* was made before I knew what the camera was seeing. I didn't know about lenses, or when they were doing a master shot of the scene. You can create a focus for yourself, but if you don't know where the bull's-eye is it's like sending an arrow into space. Peter [Weir] began to have me come up and look through the lens at the setup before we started. He did his job the way Fred Astaire danced. On subsequent films I've asked to go up and look. I *listen* now to the conversations about lenses and framing. And when they're dollying I have a pretty good idea when I'll be coming into focus. But the *camera* is the key. It doesn't enter until everything is ready.

—Hunt, interviewed by Cynthia Zarin for *The New Yorker*, 30 July 1990

Holly HUNTER [1958-]

Born: Conyers, Georgia. Studies at Carnegie-Mellon University and work in regional theater preceded her film debut in The Burning (1981, Tony Maylam). In 1987, she played Jane Craig in James L. Brooks' Broadcast News:

Jane...lacks diplomacy, is abrasive, and has a desperate need for efficiency. Hell, she's so controlled, her emotional outbursts are scheduled. She's a little obsessive, difficult, but very brave....

I followed producers around [at CBS], sat at their desks, hung around the editing booth and control room, watched people put pieces together. I boned up on "newspeak," too.

While there is no way I could really produce news, I learned enough to emulate the scrambling as a story breaks and still feel in command.

[Jane] is a new kind of heroine. Jane's an '80's woman — she doesn't have to fight for respect.

—Hunter, interviewed by Donna Rosenthal for *The New York Daily News*, 14 Dec 1987

John HURT [1940-]

Born: Chesterfield, England. Studies at The Royal Academy of Dramatic Art in London led to work on the stage and a film debut the same year in The Wild and the Willing (1962, Ralph Thomas). In 1980, he played John Merrick in David Lynch's The Elephant Man:

Q. What did you base your characterization on?

A. I thought, "Hello, here we are, it's a grotesque." Well, one thing you don't do is play it *grotesquely*. So I thought, "Let's cheat a little, and play him the opposite of grotesque." It's not much of a cheat because John Merrick was a romantic creature by nature. I gave him a kind of Victorian gentility that he would not have had if we wanted to be real for the sake of being real.

—Hurt, interviewed by Gavin Smith for *Film Comment*, Mar/Apr 1989

[*The Elephant Man* is] really a story of the tenderness of the unknown against the cruelty of the crowd.... People are always frightened of things they don't understand and real ugliness is something that not many people know much about. It's also a love story and on several levels. Firstly between the Elephant Man and the doctor Treves [Anthony Hopkins], who runs into considerable professional opposition to his plans to help what, to so many of his colleagues, is just a circus freak. Then there's the curious relationship with Bytes [Freddie Jones], the man who "owns" him and puts him on public display. Outwardly they dislike each other, but they depend on each other for their livelihood.

—Hurt, in the press release for *The Elephant Man* (Paramount Studios, 1980)

[For *The Elephant Man*] I had to rely totally on the director, David Lynch. I couldn't be sure what I was trying to do was coming across, because of the enormity of the makeup. I had to feel I was getting total honesty from him or I could not have continued. That has never been the case before — I've always been self-assured about what I was doing.

—Hurt, interviewed by Arthur Unger for *The Christian Science Monitor*, 15 Oct 1980

I think [Michael Cimino]'s an extremely talented man, but [on *Heaven's Gate* (1980)] there wasn't anybody there strong enough to say, "Come on, kid, it's only your second movie [it was his third] — you are not John Ford yet. Find yourself some humility." The technicians hated him. He was so rude to them it was unbelievable, but he was always nice to the actors, which was even more embarrassing.

—Hurt, interviewed by Marybeth Kerrigan for *Women's Wear Daily*, 25 Jan 1985

Q. The character of Stephen Ward [in *Scandal* (1989, Michael Caton-Jones)] is hard to define, contradictory.

A. I'm always fascinated by the underdog, in various different ways, from Quentin Crisp [in *The Naked Civil Servant* (1975, Jack Gold)] to Timothy Evans [in *10 Rillington Place* (1970, Richard Fleischer)] to Caligula [in *I, Claudius* (1975, for TV)]. Ward was an extremely difficult character to start playing. He seemed to have an almost metaphorical existence at the same time as the real one, in terms of where he stood in the history of Britain between the bleak Forties and Fifties, and then what happened in the Sixties.

Ward had the same background as I have. His father was a clergyman. He's...as difficult as anyone I've ever played — full of complexity, which is why he lends himself to the screen.

On the one hand Ward was a snob, on the other he was extremely kind to people and not a snob as far as Christine [Keeler/Joanne Whalley] was concerned. He was wild yet extremely conventional. He was a strange mixture.

If you're going to try to play Stephen consistently it's impossible, but then the interesting thing about a character is inconsistency really — that's when you say, God, *that's* a character.

Q. How do you play an inconsistent character.

A. From day to day. I never found him possible to plan from scene to scene — rather like Hamlet. In the sense that Hamlet is constantly surprising in every scene he plays.

There's no through line to Hamlet — or Stephen either. With all the scenes that he has to play, none of them are exactly the same. They all seem to be a slightly different person, or a different area of the same person, at any rate. You knew certain things about him...that he was upstanding until the downfall.... He lived all his life blamed for something that he shouldn't be blamed for.... When I first started playing Ward, I just thought, this man's so fucking sleazy, it's awful. I don't want to get up in the morning and do it. Yet, essentially, he was a well brought up man, in the old sense of the word.

Ward was obviously a very tactile, sexual man in many ways. He wouldn't have been an osteopath if he wasn't tactile for a start. He was also a great appreciator of beauty; adored women. Not necessarily for himself. These things are sort of facts, but it's not easy to play a fact. One just has to bump into them and see how you're going to cope with them....

Q. Why is the sexual potential between Ward and Christine unrealized? I wondered if Ward was gay.

A. It was a strange love affair altogether. I didn't go into it saying this is a love affair, but I certainly felt by the end of it that I had played one. One that never got going. It was mistimed between the two of them....

—Hurt, interviewed by Gavin Smith for *Film Comment*, Mar/Apr 1989

William HURT [1950-]

Born: Washington, D.C. Studies at The Juilliard School in N.Y., work with The Ashland Shakespeare Festival and The Circle Repertory Co. (NY), and roles on Broadway preceded his film debut in Altered States (1979, Ken Russell). In 1983, he played Nick in The Big Chill, the second of four films with Lawrence Kasdan:

Q. Was there something in the character of Nick in *The Big Chill* that particularly spoke to you?

A. With Nick, Larry paid me the infinitely great compliment of fashioning the character based on my own notes. [Ordinarily] I would never do that. I would never impose my ideas on a character. My job as an actor is to adapt myself to the characters in the piece. For me to walk around imposing my personality values on a role is ridiculous — it's *antithetical* to acting.

But after we finished doing [*Body*] *Heat* [1981], Larry was vacationing in New Jersey, and I went to visit him there. We were sitting in a car and Larry got through to me, he broke me down! I relaxed and said, "Wouldn't it be nice to play someone who blah blah blah," and I came up with these ideas. And when I read Nick, I thought: The bastard, what a remarkable compliment that he would have taken my ramblings so seriously and turned them into such a beautiful role. I loved that.

I had such a wonderful time playing Nick because it was my real opportunity to fuck around. And I did. I mean, Nick was not serious about anything.

—Hurt, interviewed by Susan Linfield for *American Film*, July/Aug 1986

[Molina']s identity of himself [in *Kiss of the Spider Woman* (1985, Hector Babenco)] is a true thing and has nothing to do with the presumptions of others, even though he has to play to them, because otherwise they'll kill him. What does a homosexual or a revolutionary, which Raul [Julia] plays, do in a society which is bent on their destruction? The minute a gay shows his hatred or contempt for society's inability to conceive of him (and for the fear and hate that the gay image breeds in society), he hates their hate. And he can't afford that. So, often, a gay's ploy is to turn society's judgment of him as trash by acting trashy — thereby showing them the worst thing about themselves. That's making your statement in a very direct way; affectation in itself and for itself may be degrading, but it can also be a useful tool. Here it's even ennobling.

Here are two characters who start from opposite poles and end up loving each other, and through their love for each other they find greater self-respect. It's beautiful.

Q. Manuel Puig, the book's author, draws a parallel between homosexuality and revolution and sees the two characters as a marriage of outcasts.

A. There's no marriage between them in a typical sense; it's a mutual-respect society they come up with, and it enables each one to go to his own destiny less afraid. You take these outcasts — and they are outcasts to each other too, because of the standards they've chosen to bear — and you find that in the destruction of their mistrust they discover that there's a much greater prison and much greater freedom, because they're humane. These two people, even if they don't know it, are looking for the liberation of their own identity. I don't think I'm degrading either homosexuality or being a revolutionary, but these conditions can be seen as an attempt to simplify their identity. It doesn't mean that their causes are an excuse for bad behavior or cruelty to others, but in this case each ends up pursuing his destiny with more commitment than before because they broke their prejudices. They were imploding on their own definitions of their identities; they were not big enough for them anymore, but through each other they do see that these identities are their choices, and they accept them....

—Hurt, interviewed by Dan Yakir for *Film Comment*, Aug 1985

Macon [in *The Accidental Tourist* (1988, Lawrence Kasdan)] is afraid of intimacy; it causes him to *feel* too much, to have to deal with himself and his weird past. But intimacy is his only hope to be free. That's where Muriel [Geena Davis] comes in. She is all of that, someone close up, intense, full of a frightening kind of hope. [Hurt also worked on Kasdan's *I Love You to Death* (1990).]

—Hurt, interviewed by John Tibbetts for *The Christian Science Monitor*, 28 Mar 1989

Ruth HUSSEY [1914-]

Born: Ruth O'Rourke in Provincetown, Massachusetts. Studies at Brown University and The University of Michigan School of Drama, work as a model, with The Aimee Loomis Stock Co., on radio and on tour, preceded her film debut in The Big City (1937, Frank Borzage). In 1940, she played Liz Imbrie in George Cukor's The Philadelphia Story:

[*The Philadelphia Story*] was no brash comedy in which everything the characters say is so odd or amusing that they seem unreal. There were hilarious moments, but there also were passages of relative seriousness that made the characters seem likable and real....

Liz was sophisticated without being world-weary. She was sardonic without being unpleasantly sarcastic and she was able to say amusing things without being smart-alecky....

The way that Liz handled her disappointment in love had a very special appeal for me. She took the bumps with a philosophical smile and a charming amount of poise.

—Hussey, in *The Saturday Evening Post*, 2 Apr 1949

Anjelica HUSTON [1951-]

Born: Malibu, California; daughter to John Huston [1906-1987] and ballerina Ricki Soma; granddaughter of Walter Huston. She made her film debut in her father's A Walk with Love and Death (1968). In 1985, she played Maerose in his Prizzi's Honor:

The temptation to fall into a caricature when you're playing comedy is sometimes irresistible. But such was the character of Maerose that it wasn't a matter of setting out to be funny. The fact that she's quite a stylishly dressed woman who takes herself particularly seriously and who talks as though she's just emerged from a fish market is inherently funny.

—Huston, interviewed by Chuck Pfeiffer for *Interview*, Sept 1985

Initially, when he is making a picture, my father searches for the key. When he came across Julie Bovasso, who played John Travolta's mother in *Saturday Night Fever*, he told us, "I've found the key — it's that voice. I want everyone to speak this way."

—Huston, interviewed by Ruth La Ferla for *Women's Wear Daily*, 4 June 1985

The Dead [1987, John Huston] is very meaningful for all of us because it's [about] Ireland. I think it very nearly broke my father's heart to leave Ireland, but he's not one to dwell on his ills. He's been brought to his knees a few times but will not lie down. He has a long cord [connected to the oxygen tank] so he can walk around, but...the fact that he goes on working, and none of this stuff stops him, is an inspiration. Everybody on the set of *The Dead* got sick except my father.... He relentlessly went on....

I've grown a lot since that first movie with him. I wouldn't say that the dynamic of our relationship has changed enormously, but *I* have changed a good deal. There is an element in me that still seeks his approval and is still disappointed if I don't win it. But I don't think I rely on that the way I used to. At a certain age, you grow up and stop feeling you have to defend yourself and provide the perfect answer every time — because that's not what he's looking for either. He's looking for me to be happy and fulfilled and, hopefully, prosperous. And *that* is what I'd like to give him.

—Huston, interviewed by Mark Morrison for *The Los Angeles Times Magazine*, 21 June 1987

Tamara [in *Enemies, A Love Story* (1989, Paul Mazursky)] is very ironic and intelligent. She comes from somewhere, is going somewhere. There's a very full center to the character. She says a lot of things that women would want said. At no point does the character not have a foundation....

Tamara never took any nonsense from Herman [Ron Silver]. She knows him better than anyone else, and she still loves him. You go through three stages of love. At first, the sun shines wherever you walk. Then there's disappointment. Finally, you make the decision to go on loving them even though you know their faults.

Despite his infidelities, he's someone that I'm bound to. Sometimes people hurt you, and you go on loving them because you understand them. Deep down there's a bond. At times he's my son, father, brother, husband. When you love someone, they might hurt you, bitterly and forever, but you don't give up on them.

—Huston, interviewed by Ben Yagoda for *American Film*, Nov 1989

You know, there's a trace of the Hedda Nussbaums [in the character of Lilly Dillon in *The Grifters* (1990, Stephen Frears)]: This is what I do; this is my boss. This is my father; this is my life. My character doesn't come through in my part of the operation — these are the rules, this is the game I play. When I mess up, that's it. It's like any dog gets its whipping. It gocs to the garbage, it pulls it apart, it can expect a whipping. But she's a bit of a coyote, this woman. She anticipates. It's not that [the burning of her hand with a cigar by her boss (Pat Hingle)] comes totally out of the blue. It's not a matter of, he burns my hand and I run off into the blue horizon. This guy's on her like a tick on a dog. Given the situation, rats will behave accordingly. Finally, the fox will eat off its own paw to get out of the trap, as will a mother kill her son to get out of the trap. We see it up in Harlem, where the seven-year-olds are selling crack to support their mothers' habit....

It's been a selfish life, what she does...

—Huston, interviewed by David Thomson for *American Film*, Nov 1990

Q. The grifter characters were all basically unsympathetic but completely compelling.

A. I found Lilly very sympathetic, very moving. It's a dark, bestial life she lives. I have this terrible theory that people are like roaches — they adapt to their circumstances. And her circumstances were pretty dire. She was human and lived in an inhuman world and finally is reduced to inhumanity. She eats her own son [John Cusack].

—Huston, interviewed by Susan Morgan for *Interview*, Dec 1991

[Morticia in *The Addams Family* (1991, Barry Sonnenfeld)] is a perfect mother, and yet she does all the things mothers aren't supposed to do. She tells her kids to kill each other; she's very wild and passionate; she wears long, form-fitting black gowns and dripping red nails. I think she's very well-bred — by way of Transylvania probably, but very well-bred nonetheless.

—Huston, interviewed by Elizabeth Drucker for *American Film*, Dec 1991

Walter HUSTON [1884-1950]

Born: Toronto, Ontario, Canada. Drama studies at The Toronto College of Music, work in vaudeville and on Broadway (from 1924) preceded his first film, the 1929 short, The Carnival Man. The following year, he played the title role in D.W. Griffith's Abraham Lincoln:

I didn't try to walk like Lincoln — to imitate the outward mannerisms which the history books tell us he possessed. No. I tried to think like Lincoln, knowing that if I captured the secret of the man's mental processes the rest would follow. I approached it the way I would approach any characterization. I said to myself: "What kind of man is this? How does his mind function? How would he act in this situation — or this one?"

—Huston, interviewed by Harriet Parsons for *Photoplay Magazine*, Dec 1930

I suppose I am *most* like the chap in *American Madness* [1932, Frank Capra)], though I might not be quite the humanitarian he was. He verged on the fanatical, and chances are that if I ever behaved that way in real life, I'd be swept up with the dust on the bank's floor. Too much charitableness is a form of self-indulgence.

But, on the whole, I figure I'm quite a bit the type of man he was, wanting from life the same things he wanted, with pretty much the same set of values and the same desire to meet my fellowmen and fellow-women with kindliness and belief.

He didn't demand too much of life. Neither do I. He believed in people and expected the best of them. So do I. He didn't worry about things he couldn't help. Neither do I. He was roused to action when there was vital and innocent need — and I would be likewise. He wouldn't have given a thought to mistakes that are done and past. I wouldn't either. He wouldn't have worried about what is to come when this life is ended. *I* don't. I am content to leave such matters to those who have control of them.

—Huston, interviewed by Faith Service for *Movie Classic*, Jan 1933

My part in *Mission to Moscow* [1943, Michael Curtiz] is really that of a sort of representative American — a kind of "Dodsworth" in a way. Although I'm playing the role of Joseph E. Davies, I don't resemble him a particle. I don't try to. The part is intended as a symbolic one — representing the American character and the typical American reaction to international events....

This picture is a recital of truth. It is like seeing history in the making and overhearing real conversations that actually happened between some of the notable figures of our time. In a way, it's a documentary picture. There's nothing emotional in it. It's a matter of observation. My problem as an actor is to avoid becoming ponderous in the role of Ambassador Davies. It's a temptation to delineate such a part in an affected way, but that's not how such people really act. They take their surroundings and their experiences for granted, and they act simply in the most formal situations.

I am therefore underplaying the part all along. It doesn't need much emphasis. The events in themselves are sufficiently dramatic to stand on their own feet. And the more you talk about big things unaffectedly, the more impressive they become. For instance, I speak to the President [Georges Renavent] very casually in this scene, without stressing the portentousness of the event. We are simply two old friends. This kind of understatement, I think is highly effective. I don't try to make too much of anything. The more you make of a situation, the less it comes to.

—Huston, interviewed by Ezra Goodman for *The New York Times*, 7 Mar 1943

Some directors tell you what to do; with others you're pretty much on your own. My son said to me in one scene [of *Treasure of the Sierra Madre* (1948)], "You're too much like Walter Huston." I knew what he meant. It's the inside spirit of the thing you have to get; if you get that you'll say the lines right.

—Huston, interviewed by Philip K. Scheuer for *The Los Angeles Times*, 12 Apr 1949

Timothy HUTTON [1960-]

Born: Malibu; son of Jim Hutton [1933-1979]. Work on the stage and TV preceded his film debut as Conrad Jarrett in Ordinary People (1980, Robert Redford):

There is some of Conrad Jarrett in me and some of me in Conrad. I know this guy. I really know him. He lost his best friend, who was also his brother. I recently lost my best friend, my father. Conrad's a loner. In some ways, I'm a loner.

But Conrad had one problem I've never had. He was hungry for love and approval from his parents. I always had plenty of both.

—Hutton, interviewed for the press release for *Ordinary People* (Paramount Pictures, 1980)

Q. How did you find working with Robert Redford as a director?

A. He was great, because although he had wonderful ideas himself he always encouraged your own spontaneity — your impulse to improvise. He was not the kind of director who would stand behind the camera and say, "All right, that's no good — do it again and do it like this!" Having worked as an actor with great directors himself, he had a strong knowledge of how to work with actors.

Q. Did he rehearse a lot?

A. Yes, quite a lot, but never so much that one grew stale.

Q. I was thinking in particular of your very strong emotional scenes with the psychiatrist [Judd Hirsch]. He let you go your own way?

A. Yes — in one of them, for instance, he said, "Take your own time. Go and sit by yourself. Do whatever you want to do and come back when you're ready." He never wanted a lot of takes — just a few to polish a scene up, tighten it a little....

Q. You have said you base your characterizations very much on observation. For your key scenes with the psychiatrist in *Ordinary People*, had you had any actual experience.

A. No, none at all, not personally — but I got permission from a doctor to attend a mental institution for a couple of days as an out-patient, under another name. I sat in at a couple of therapy sessions and generally observed what it was like. I also studied cases in books such as the *Children of Crisis* series.

—Hutton, interviewed by Ivan Butler for *Films & Filming*, Apr 1982

[Brian] Moreland [in *Taps* (1981, Harold Becker)] is a golden boy, I suppose. He excels in everything he's done, always has, probably always will. He's academically in great shape and as the cadet leader, as the regimental commander, well, that's the best you can do at a military academy. Everything he's done has always been top-notch. He's an overachiever.

[Living and training at Valley Forge Military Academy and Junior College] was really kind of strenuous at first. Everybody was complaining. You know, "Oh, God, why do we have to do this; why can't we just rehearse." But by the second day, third day, everybody was beginning to see how much it was paying off, how beneficial it was.

—Hutton, interviewed for the press release for *Taps* (20th Century-Fox, 1981)

I didn't [get in touch with Michael and Robbie Rosenberg for *Daniel* (1983)] because Sidney [Lumet] really wanted us to stay away from that line of research.

Q. Why?

A. Because [E.L.] Doctorow's book is fictional, and Sidney didn't want the direct influence of being in touch. He felt Doctorow's book was so strong in itself that he would stay with that material. It's really not about the Rosenbergs, it's about these two kids. In real life it was the two sons, but in this, one's a boy, one's a girl....

Q. Is the premise of the movie that the Rosenberg's were innocent? Is it sympathetic to them or is it neutral on that count?

A. That's the thing, Sidney didn't want to make a statement about whether they were innocent or guilty. He wanted to make the movie about *survival* when something like that happens. In the story, as Doctorow wrote it, it's really about Daniel and Susan [Amanda Plummer] and how they survive being kids of parents like that. So the movie is about getting rid of baggage, not carrying around guilt anymore, carrying on with your own life. The movie ends just as Daniel becomes involved in the movement of his own generation, instead of continuing preoccupied with the movement his parents were involved in.

Q. Anti-Vietnam —

A. That's what he becomes involved in. That is looked upon as the healthy step to survival; he's finally believing in something on his own, instead of believing so much in the past.

—Hutton, interviewed by Maura Moynihan and Andy Warhol for *Interview*, Sept 1983

I

Jeremy IRONS [1948-]

Born: Cowes, Isle of Wight, England. Studies with The Bristol Old Vic Theatre School and work with The British Old Vic Co., on the London stage and on British TV, preceded his film debut in Nijinsky (1980, Herbert Ross). In 1981, he co-starred opposite Meryl Streep in Karel Reisz' The French Lieutenant's Woman:

Q. Did Karel Reisz allow you latitude in your choices about how to play scenes, or did he tell you exactly what he wanted?

A. We talked it out before we started shooting.... The three of us talked through the journey of the film — how the characters change and develop — so when the cameras started turning, we knew what was needed. He assumed he had it cast right and let us get on with it — if he saw it going way off or didn't like a particular reaction, he'd tell us, but Meryl and I would work together the night before the scene.

Q. The chemistry is working all the time, and the understatement of feeling just makes it more intense.

A. [Harold] Pinter's dialogue is so spare that unless you find the subtext and all the layers of subtext it doesn't work. He gives you a sort of relief map of where the characters are going and you have to draw in the sky, grass and trees. Both Meryl and I work very similarly, which is extraordinary because we come from different nations. But we were both brought up in the theater. Her imagination is quite different than mine, which is exciting when you're discussing a scene and sharing your ideas. Slowly, one of us would awaken things that the other hadn't thought of, until we had a rich mixture. She's a very unconventional actress! Sometimes, I thought she was talking about a different scene than I was.

Q. That particular scene when you catch up to her after surprising her in the woods is stunning. The sexual tension you express is explosive, almost painful. There's a sense of the power she exudes all coming out in your reaction — you're quaking in your boots!

A. It's not hard when she looks as she looked, to create sexual tension. I remember that moment: she puts herself very close to him. It's nice of you to say that I did the work in that scene, but in fact you're wrong; *she* did it for me! Smithson is really a conventional man, catching up on what he thinks is a sort of servant girl who he finds attractive, but would never admit that to himself. He wants to apologize for butting in on her afternoon doze, for being so nosy. And when he finds her reacting to him not as a servant girl or as a governess, but as a full-blooded woman who believes herself to be a match for him — well, that was difficult for a Victorian man to cope with.

—Irons, interviewed by Martin Torgoff for *Interview*, Nov 1981

[Meryl] taught me what an enormously hard job [film acting] is, how much concentration it takes and how to reach emotional pitches without time to prepare. She tried something different in every take, kept throwing the ball up. I learned from her that the film actor's job is to provide raw material for the director so that when he's in the cutting room he has options.

—Irons, interviewed by Jim Baker for *GQ*, Apr 1984

Q. What was necessary for this role [as Nowak in *Moonlighting* (1982, Jerzy Skolimowski)]?

A. Well, uh, building. I knew about building and construction. I'd done that. And to try to get an understanding of what makes a Pole, what makes him different from an Englishman. I was able to look at Skolimowski for that and the other Polish actors, (Irons' three fellow workers in the film are played by actual Poles: Eugeniusz Hazkiewicz, Eugene Lipinski and Jiri Stanislav) and I also discovered a sort of parallel which I think is valid between the Irish and the Poles. My wife and I have a lot of Irish friends.

Both are poor agricultural countries, poor economy, poor soil. Both have suffered in their history *constant* conquest and colonization by other people who've walked in and walked over them. Both countries are the butt of...humor....

It seemed to me that there were similarities in those ways and also in the way they use their emotions. Both the Irish and the Poles are very near the surface. They flare up very quickly, they laugh very quickly, the Poles slightly more so. Also both nations, it seemed to me, the individuals seemed to suffer from feelings of inferiority, from feelings of being hard done by. Often rightly so as far as feelings of being hard done by but not as far as inferiority. However, they both seem to have it. But I saw things like that in Skolimowski. And yet a real canniness as well. So that's what I had to use for my character.

—Irons, interviewed by Lewis Archibald for *The Aquarian Weekly*, 27 Oct-3 Nov 1982

I don't think Nowak is a character of great intelligence, and he panics easily. But he is a man with a lot of pathos. I don't think the character is quite as funny as I wanted him to be and I wish I'd had more time to work on my accent, but I quite like the idea of playing a Pole. It's keeping one jump ahead of the audience.

—Irons, interviewed by Ron Base for *The Toronto Star*, 11 Sept 1982

Q. How do you approach a role?

A. It depends very much on what the director has in mind. One of the most difficult was *Betrayal* [1983, David Jones], because Harold Pinter's work is so exact and must be performed with attention to the minutiae of intonation. I had just done *Moonlighting* and that script gave me very little to say.... Well, it was virtually a silent film, wasn't it? And it was directed with a sense of erupting action and spontaneity. *Betrayal* was diametrically opposed to that. My performance was at the mercy of dialogue and direction, and the stylization of the psychology.

—Irons, interviewed by Karen Jaehne for *Film Comment*, Oct 1988

Although I was playing a priest [in *The Mission* (1986, Roland Joffé)], I was also playing an explorer and a man of great risk and bravery. I actually climbed the falls at Iguazu myself; I thought it would have been a great strain for him, so it should be for me. Because it was so dangerous, I was roped very well....

Working with the Indians was splendid, because they were not shop-window Indians. That helped enormously to find the character and play it in front of the camera. I learnt Waunana as a way of getting to know them. They were very flattered that here was a Westerner wanting to learn their language; it provided a great bond with them, which was almost more useful than being able to speak the language on camera.

Playing opposite Robert De Niro was a great learning experience, too, as he works very differently from me. He's a very instinctive actor, and he has an uncanny persistence in finding truthful moments.... Bob will tend to do a few takes, but within them come up with extraordinary acting choices — very real choices.... He's a very shy man, and takes a lot of getting to know. So I suppose our off-screen relationship mirrored our on-screen one.

—Irons, interviewed for *Stills*, May/June 1986

Q. What's the hardest thing about playing twins [in *Dead Ringers* (1988, David Cronenberg)]?

A. Your initial impulse is to try them as opposites, but I aimed to find out how they were similar — what made them twins instead of just the good and bad brothers....

I looked at twin films, like Hayley Mills' *The Parent Trap* [1961, David Swift] and Bette Davis' *Dead Ringer* [1964, Paul Henreid] too, but I discovered that the performances are overwhelmed by the twins business. The actors don't have the alive response, because your best stimulus as an actor is not knowing what the other person is going to do. The control becomes almost mechanical. On top of that, the audience is looking for the mechanical reproduction of the twins to slip up. It becomes a problem of production rather than art. So I tried not to respond to myself as much as to the moods.

Q. Did you find an antipathy developing between your selves? Which twin did you identify with?

A. That happened early on, as I found myself coming down on Beverly's side. His range is more subtle, and he has interesting fears. Elliot has too few anxieties about the world beyond the Mantle Clinic. He brings a claustrophobia to their relationship. In fact, I rather dislike Elliot, but he's not a very unusual man for a doctor....

Q. How do you see the relationship between the twins — physically and psychologically?

A. Well, I find their attraction fundamentally homosexual, but Platonic. It allows them the freedom to relate to other bodies — women's in their professional life, their lovers, or each other's on an unfettered physical level rather blind to emotional implications....

I wanted Beverly and Elliot to be good doctors. Good, you know, at what they do.

Q. To women?

A. Yes, I suppose. Who else really? It rather makes up for what they do to each other, which is what appalled me when I first read the script. The story was not very attractive, but an account of obsession, which David Cronenberg is inclined to do.... It offered an opportunity to explore deviant personalities in an unusual way, to say the least, which is David's stock-in-trade.... I quite like David. His mind is a constant surprise.

—Irons, interviewed by Karen Jaehne for *Film Comment*, Oct 1988

Everyone knows what [Claus von Bülow] looks like, he's 20 years older than me. Big man, Germanic, big jaw. I went to New York and worked with Dick Smith on make-up. Strange thing: once we got the hair right, I thought, "well, maybe it's possible."

Then [in preparation for *Reversal of Fortune* (Barbet Schroeder, 1990)] I watched von Bülow a lot on video. I never met him. I watched him interviewing with Barbara Walters and Donahue. I watched and watched and watched, trying to find out what was inside the man to make him behave in the way he did during those interviews. I eventually got hold of something that gave me the inner spirit of the man.

Then I looked at everything reported about him. Sort of like a detective. If he is as I think he is why would he say what he said? You have to find the spark you can attach yourself to. For me, I was looking at the screen, watching him being interviewed and I suddenly saw my father and I thought, "Let's just say that through some quirk of life he had found himself in that same situation, being accused rightly or wrongly of having attempted to murder his wife."

How would my father have reacted in an interview with Barbara Walters or through an extended television trial? He would have reacted very similarly because what he would have done is to have kept it all in, been charming, trying to ride it through, keeping everything else tucked away. Whether it be hurt at being wrongly accused or fear of being found out. Once I said, "That's how my father would react," I thought that's how I would probably react and immediately I felt at one with the character.

I had to know whether I was covering, just being mischievous, how frightened I was, how near the truth what I was saying was; if it wasn't the truth, *why* it wasn't the truth. And then I went through all the evidence, deciding why he said things that didn't make sense. He was in an emotional state. So I slowly knitted it all together, and having done that, you get a picture. It's like painting by numbers.

—Irons, interviewed by Tom Provenzano for *Drama-Logue*, 20 Dec 1990-2 Jan 1991

Q. Did you meet Claus von Bülow as you prepared for the role?

A. I could have engineered it, but I didn't want to.

Q. Why not?

A. When you're playing a character, you are that character. And it isn't very helpful to meet someone who says they are also that character. It stultifies the imagination. I watched Claus on video. I met a lot of people who knew him well, some not so well. I researched him very much as a fictional character so that I would be able to play him with freedom, without any feeling of trying to impersonate him....

Q. Whom did you talk to who knew Claus?

A. I talked a lot to John Richardson, a man who has known Claus from about the age of fourteen. I also talked to [lawyer] Alan Dershowitz, who knew Claus through the trial period. I talked to people who knew Sonny, and to people who knew them both. I also observed society people and the way they behaved by watching tapes of the trial.

—Irons, interviewed by David DeNicolo for *Interview*, June 1990

Amy IRVING [1953-]

Born: Palo Alto, California; daughter of actress Priscilla Pointer and stage director Jules Irving. Work in street theater and off-off Broadway and studies at The American Conservatory of Theater in San Francisco and at The London Academy of Music and Dramatic Art preceded her film debut in Carrie (1976, Brian De Palma). In 1983, she played opposite Barbra Streisand in Streisand's Yentl:

You know, in spite of all the things that people associate with working with Barbra and its not necessarily being a joyful experience, the crew loved her. They would do anything for her. I think as long as she's directing, then she's not taking someone else's job. The problem is that when she knows better than the director, it's frustrating for her to keep her mouth shut, and so she doesn't and it can bend people's noses the wrong way. When she was directing and producing her own film, she was a complete joy to work with. It's funny, actually, during the romantic stuff, like when we had to kiss, she was more nervous about it than I was.

Q. Really?

A. Yeah. We didn't kiss during any of the rehearsals. We'd go back in her dressing room to rehearse but we'd never kiss, and then when we finally did it, that's when she said it wasn't so bad — it was like kissing an arm. Because it wasn't real passion or anything. Also, she cut it off a lot quicker than I would have.

Q. Well, one sees that nervousness, and it rather worked for her.

A. It worked. I was the one who was supposed to be the seductress.

—Irving, interviewed by Peter Stone for *Interview*, Oct 1988

People have asked, "Would the films [*Yentl* and *Crossing Delancey* (1988, Joan Micklin Silver)] have been any different if a man had directed them?" I think they would have been different if another *woman* had directed them.

The only plus is an intimacy, something between two women I don't think men have. That ability to get close very fast. Joan was very simpatico; she knew what I was feeling. I could open my self up to her and I could let her know what was going on in a way that was comfortable because she was a woman.

I had always been just a hired hand. Joan opened me up. She didn't cast anybody without discussing it with me first. We discussed structural changes and on the set we were still working together.

—Irving, interviewed by Pat Hilton for *Drama-Logue*, 8-14 Sept 1988

J

Glenda JACKSON [1936-]

Born: Hoylake, England. Studies at The Royal Academy of Dramatic Art led to work with The Royal Shakespeare Co. After making her film debut in a small role in This Sporting Life (1963, Lindsay Anderson), she gained fame as Charlotte Corday in the London, Broadway and film versions of Marat/Sade (1966):

[I] loathed and detested doing [*Marat/Sade*]. I couldn't wait for it to end. The cast was in hysterics. One of the actors who played in a straight-jacket had rheumatism at the end of the run; another developed a permanent crossed eye and today suffers from horrible headaches. Then we all did the film for Peter Brook and it was a shattering experience. People twitching, slobber running down their chins, everyone screaming from nerves and exhaustion.

—Jackson, interviewed by Rex Reed for *The Toronto Star*, 23 Jan 1971

In one respect, Gudrun [in *Women in Love* (1970, Ken Russell)] is unbelievable. Like so many of [D.H.] Lawrence's women, she is a fabrication, a woman created to fit in with his philosophy. As a person, she would be unspeakable to be around. But Lawrence did give her something that I find fascinating — a *mysterious* element. And it was this area of mystery within herself that Gudrun wanted to explore.

—Jackson, interviewed by Guy Flatley for *The New York Times*, 7 Feb 1971

Gudrun, for all her pretensions and self-deception, had in her a genuine acknowledgment of that which is mysterious in life — not secretive, but genuinely mysterious — that gave her validity; without that she would be a petty, trendy pseudoartistic bitch.

—Jackson, interviewed by Rita Gam for Actress to Actress (New York: Nick Lyons Books, 1986)

Nina [in *The Music Lovers* (1971, Ken Russell)] was so much a victim of her lack of intelligence, her inability to control her own emotions. But she was unlikable, too, because she was a continual fantasist and — like all fantasists — dangerous and destructive. Fortunately, she was the weaker of the two fantasists. Tchaikovsky [Richard Chamberlain], after all, had a lifeline in his music. Nina had no lifeline....

—Jackson, interviewed by Guy Flatley for *The New York Times*, 7 Feb 1971

When we did *The Music Lovers*, the actors knew it was a baroque opera type of film, and therefore it was no good coming on with meaningful small moments like the people next door because that wasn't what the film was like. It had a bigness about it. The characters were people who were living on the top level of their emotions all the time. So you had to start very high and see how much higher you could go.

—Jackson, interviewed by Gordon Gow for *Films & Filming*, Jan 1977

Q. You have worked a lot with Ken Russell, during which time you tended to play a certain type of woman. Has that relationship and the particular way he saw you had any effect on the films you have made for other directors?

A. No, he had seen me in *Marat/Sade* and asked me as a result to do *Women in Love*. He was one of the young directors who had come up through television in the post-[John] Osborne era and I had always liked his work. He has tremendous energy and so much enthusiasm, but most importantly, he allows you to bring all your fantasies into play.

I've heard Liv Ullmann, talking about [Ingmar] Bergman, say that a good director creates the space for the actor's fantasies. There's an instance she cites of when she was playing a vain woman who was to walk down a passageway. Most directors would have chosen to do a panning shot, but Liv Ullmann stopped in front of a mirror in order to project her thoughts. Bergman had placed the camera exactly because he anticipated she might do just that.

Great directors have the ability to anticipate or allow innovations to occur. Ken Russell also has this ability.

Q. Have you ever had a director place you in a physically harrowing or dangerous position?

A. Ken Russell is an utter physical coward, and therefore he always has his actors doing extremely dangerous things so he doesn't look a coward himself. In one scene in *Women in Love*, Oliver [Reed] and I were in a side-car on a low loader, going along a very narrow lane in Derbyshire with deep ditches on either side. We were going at such an incredible speed that we went off the road and ended up in the ditch. Only the cameraman's protest that the speed was quite unnecessary saved us from having to repeat the scene over and over, although we actors were ready to pick ourselves up and start afresh.

On the coldest day of the coldest British winter for years, for the last shot of *The Music Lovers* in the asylum, I found myself crouched over a grating, in a disused army barracks, clad only in a thin cotton frock, no stockings or shoes. The shot was repeated over and over again during the day until I was literally blue. Eventually, my face had quite frozen — it looked perfect for the film.

For the 1812 fantasy scene in *The Music Lovers*, Richard Chamberlain and I had to run into the street in a storm. They had got an enormous wind machine with a great propeller, and it had been turned on with such force it literally lifted us off our feet and dropped us in a heap, with me on the bottom. I realized, during the moments the bodies above me were getting up, that Ken would be waiting for my comments. So I said that it was a most fantastic experience, just like flying. To which he responded by ordering that the machine be turned down by half at least. I knew if I had said how vile it was, he would have decided it had to be just like that and wanted to do it again.

—Jackson, interviewed by S. Spunner and P. Longmore for *Cinema Papers*, July/Aug 1975

[Ken Russell's] a very romantic man. Things enrage him, it's genuine. He's not doing it, thinking, "This'll bring 'em in, this'll make more money." He's exorcising demons of some kind. I was talking to Susan Sontag about him, and she thinks he may be the last great misogynist. It's probably true. I wouldn't for one minute presume to say that he beats Shirley or is a vile husband, but he does genuinely feel what's in his films.

—Jackson, interviewed by Peter Mezan for *Esquire*, May 1972

I think the ideal thing about working with [Ken Russell] is that you can surprise him as a director, and I think that is essential for actors. He gives you the sense that what you're doing is important, that what everybody is doing is important, that everyone is joined together to get the very best possible results they can. And that's a very important work atmosphere to create. [She also worked on Russell's *The Boyfriend* (1971) and *Salome's Last Dance* (1988).]

—Jackson, interviewed by Charles Marowitz for *The New York Times*, 19 Jan 1975

It is slightly disheartening that most of the scripts sent to me deal with the darker side of human nature. It's not so much that I'm being typed; it's just that we are living in an age that takes itself terribly seriously. That's why *Sunday, Bloody Sunday* [1971], the film I just did for John Schlesinger, was such a pleasant relief — for once, I was able to be singularly un-neurotic. I play a woman who has been divorced and is having an affair with a young boy [Murray Head]. The boy, however, is bisexual and is having an affair with an older man — played by Peter Finch. These characters are sane, intelligent people faced with a situation that in most films would leave them no alternative but suicide. But they *don't* commit suicide; they just go on living.

—Jackson, interviewed by Guy Flatley for *The New York Times*, 7 Feb 1971

This particular take in *Sunday, Bloody Sunday* started on a clock and then the camera came down to include Murray Head in the frame. He was standing on a ladder, hanging the clock on the wall. And then the camera panned on down to me. I was in a swivel rocking chair, and I was rocking. They picked me up from an angle that showed the back of the chair, and then I had to swing myself around towards the camera, and get up to go to the telephone and the camera had to go with me and then come back to me sitting down in the chair again.

That was the physical part. The essence of the scene was that the boy was telling me that he was going to America — something he'd neglected to mention before; and I think the reason John wanted this to be such a long take was to show two intimately involved people who were separating now in their own particular ways. The boy that Murray was playing would do something like hanging a clock on the wall while at the same time he was telling his lady that he was leaving her to go to America — and her response would be at first to simply sit and listen to this: therefore, instead of cut-cut-cut-cut-cut, John wanted consecutive action during that passage of dialogue.

—Jackson, interviewed by Gordon Gow for *Films & Filming*, Jan 1977

Q. In the context of the rest of your films, *A Touch of Class* [1973, Melvin Frank] is unusual. Why did you do it?

A. For a change it was so nice not to have to destroy anybody. I am always being such a dark lady, so gloomy. It was a lovely change to be light for a little while.

—Jackson, interviewed by S. Spunner and P. Longmore for *Cinema Papers*, July/Aug 1975

What I found curious [about playing Sarah Bernhardt in *The Incredible Sarah* (1976, Richard Fleischer)] was acting an actress; because you don't usually have to question acting in quite that way. It was actually necessary to question your own instinctive responses. One doesn't act "acting" — but in that film, one did.

Bernhardt was obviously a totally different sort of actress from me, which is why I had to go into this questioning of my instinctive responses, not to playing *her*, but to playing her *playing characters....*

Dick [Fleischer] is an immensely professional director. He's made a great many films, and he knows his business backwards. That is his pride — that he takes what he's given and he makes a film of it.

What I liked very much about working with him was that I could surprise him. I probably can't express this without sounding very rude — but it isn't, really. He's worked with a lot of actors, but he's usually worked on films where actresses were not required: what were required were female persons to fill part of the screen. And I think he's been used to a certain amount of ego-tripping in the guise of performing. It surprised him that I could work without a lot of temperamental top-dressing. That he found exciting.... I think Dick is a far, far better director than he will give himself credit for.

—Jackson, interviewed by Gordon Gow for *Films & Filming*, Jan 1977

It seemed to me her questioning of death was a questioning of life. Every time she [Stevie Smith in *Stevie* (1978, Robert Enders)] looked at death, it was a way of tasting how much she was alive. I think that is one of the brave things about this woman. The great danger is seeing her as merely eccentric. She was a highly aware, perhaps too sensitive person, who lived under no illusions about herself or the world. She asked honest questions of herself, and was prepared to accept some of the answers.

—Jackson, interviewed by Douglas C. McGill for *The New York Times*, 19 July 1981

Sam JAFFE [1891-1984]

Born: New York City. Following engineering studies at City College of N.Y. and The Columbia School of Engineering, he joined The Washington Square Players. Work on Broadway (from 1921) preceded his film debut in We Live Again (1934, Rouben Mamoulian). That same year he played the mad Grand Duke Peter opposite Marlene Dietrich in Josef von Sternberg's The Scarlet Empress:

Sternberg is a strange man. When we were first given our parts to study, the lines were completely without punctuation — without commas, periods, or even capital letters. All the words just flowed into one another. This was so the actor wouldn't get the wrong idea of the part and Sternberg could begin from scratch, as if he were using automatons.

He is famous, of course, for taking scores of shots and then using the first or second one. Once, after I had done a scene over and over in exactly the same way and it had been shot from the same angle, I told him I wouldn't do it any more, that I wasn't that interested in the movies and that I didn't care if I never came back. He appeared to be very hurt and walked me up and down the sound stage, telling me how great he was. "Why, I've got 30,000 fans in China alone," he said. Finally he agreed to take only one shot of me for future scenes and I became known on the lot as "One-Shot Sam."

—Jaffe, interviewed by Irving Drutman for *The New York Herald Tribune*, 1 Feb 1942

Q. How about Marlene?.... Tell me about her on the set.

A. She's very charming indeed. In *The Scarlet Empress*, she worked like a true trouper....

One of the most remarkable things about Dietrich is her working relationship with Von Sternberg. It's much more than a *Svengali-Trilby* act. His attitude is one of adoration for, and service to, a great artist. I felt, when they were working together on a scene, that he was forever paying her tribute — that there wasn't the slightest whim of hers that he wouldn't gratify at any cost.

As for Dietrich, she trusts his artistic judgment implicitly, almost blindly. That's why they are probably the greatest director-actress team that pictures have ever seen. Most actors, taking direction, listen to the boss with one ear and then do it their own way. Some only pretend to listen. Not Marlene. Believing whole-heartedly in her director's picture wisdom, she will do a tiny scene fifty times to achieve perfection in his eyes. And when the last shot is in the box, the result may not be perfection to the critics and the fans, but it is one-hundred percent perfect to Joe Von Sternberg!

He directs Dietrich entirely in German, calling her anything that enters his mind which ends with the affectionate German diminutive 'chen'....

It's a treat to watch him rehearse her. It's all a lot of tender cajolery.

"Putschen," he'll say, "Setzen — so! Jetzt. Bitte-augen recht, augen links! Ah, so! Aber, Putschen, mehr, bitte! So! Danke!" So they go through it — eyes right, eyes left — until Von Sternberg is satisfied. It may be once or twenty times. He checks the sound, the camera, the lights. Then he signals for a 'take' with his own copyrighted word of command: "C'MON!"

And believe me, they all 'c'mon' with everything they've got....

Q. Is she a genuine artist, or merely a synthetic product of Von Sternberg's whiplash?

A. Don't fret — she's an artist, all right. What's more, I think the screen has never made use of her greatest talent. She's a marvelous comedienne and mimic. She can put stitches in the set, imitating other people in the troupe. Some day, if they're wise, they'll let her do a spot of comedy, and she'll startle the world.

—Jaffe, interviewed by Leonard Hall for *Screenland*, May 1934

There were so many problems in connection with [the] portrayal [of the 255-year-old High Lama in *Lost Horizon* (1937, Frank Capra)], and so many angles to present him from, Mr. Capra and I spent hours conferring over an exact representation. We wanted him to show, not alone physical age, but age that expresses itself through wisdom and understanding. Make-up, of course, was of first importance, especially since, in the opening scene, the old man has to hold an audience for seven or eight minutes in speechless immobility.

They worked out a wax mask for me over which they spread a surgical rubber dressing deeply wrinkled, to give a drawn look, for with age the human frame shrinks. Then they added little pieces of paper fitted together to resemble one of those small, shrunken skulls of the head hunters.

But after some trial shots, Mr. Capra was dissatisfied. Finally he decided he could do better with lights, using certain luminous effects and shadows, to given the idea of a benign man who shows age without its emphasizing too much physical deterioration. Even so, it took two hours every morning to get my make-up on; forty minutes just for the hands.

Then I had to work out the interpretation...the small, thin voice, the trembling, unsteady movements of great age, and its philosophy....

—Jaffe, interviewed by Marguerite Tazelaar for *The New York Herald Tribune*, 16 Aug 1936

We didn't know whether to make [the voice of The High Lama] the thin, quavery voice of an old man or, because he was supposed to be still vital and well, to keep it normal. Then we decided to leave out the unessentials, the foreign accent, the quavers, all that, and try to get at the important thing, the thing behind the voice.

That is what I like to do, what I always try for. I want to get at what the man stands for, what he really is. Here we wanted the serene, kindly, prophetic, philosophic quality. I concentrated on that.

—Jaffe, interviewed by Eileen Creelman for *The New York Sun*, 2 Mar 1937

Work in pictures is just as fascinating as work on the stage, once you have mastered the technique. This I found hard in the beginning, but Mr. Capra has been a great help. He lets you alone to work out a role as you wish, not attempting to play the part himself, which some directors do, and yet acting as a kind of catalytic agent, spurring you on without destroying your mood or confidence.

—Jaffe, interviewed by Marguerite Tazelaar for *The New York Herald Tribune*, 16 Aug 1936

I like the idea of being a mastermind. I play down the criminal [aspect of Dr. Riedenschneider in *The Asphalt Jungle* (1950, John Huston)]. Like you would play Iago in *Othello*. You play *honest* Iago, not the criminal....

The first thing you get is the spine of the character. I saw in this role a man who might have been better if he had channeled his forces in a different direction. We can compare his power with that of Niagara. Unharnessed it is destructive. Harnessed it can light up the entire city of Buffalo....

Bernard Shaw showed you the existence of follies so you could laugh at them. That was effective. He didn't give you any remedies. Similarly, this film shows the existence of evils.

The Asphalt Jungle has the strong, Spinoza-like moral note that vice carries its own seeds of destruction. All those who come to grief do so through their own weakness. Their vice is that weakness.

These criminals fall, but they have good things in them. The film shows that the worst kind of vice is that which wears the dicky of morality — the policeman who corrupts his office, the pillar of society whose greed infects everyone about him....

Q. How does Huston manage to extract such uniformly fine performances from his casts?

A. John, of course, wants to make sure your design of acting is in keeping with the mural. There are two ways to go about this task. One is to force the actor to imitate you. The other is to get the desired result from within the actor's framework. To get good results, it must be *you*, the actor, who is coming through in the part.

If John feels the actor's design isn't right he talks to him. "I think the quality isn't coming through," he says. Then, if the actor has some good ideas he lets him carry them out. If not, he makes some suggestions.

The difference is in John's personality. He has the same warmth as Frank Capra. Once, in the midst of shooting a big scene, Capra discovered that someone was snoring. Capra woke the man and said, "If you want to sleep, all right, but don't snore."

If anyone ever snored while Von Sternberg was directing he would have run his sword through the man. [Jaffe also worked on Huston's *The Barbarian and the Geisha* (1958) and *The Kremlin Letter* (1970).]

—Jaffe, interviewed by Fred Rayfield for *The Daily Compass*, 21 June 1950

Dean JAGGER [1903-1991]

Born: Dean Jeffreys in Columbia Grove, Indiana. Studies at Wabash College and with Elias Day in Chicago, work in vaudeville, stock, summer theater, on radio and the N.Y. stage preceded his film debut in The Woman from Hell (1929, A.F. Erickson). In 1943, he played Rodion in Lewis Milestone's The North Star:

The characters we play in *The North Star* were so true to life that we really got so we thought we were living our parts.

That sounds pompous, perhaps, but I really mean it. Of course any actor who isn't being hypocritical will tell you there's no such thing as "living your part." But this was actually the closest I'd ever come to it. One thing that added to the illusion was that the thousand-odd extras on the lot were performing without make-up and you really seemed to be in the midst of Russian villagers going about their daily routine. Then, too, you got the "good" feeling that you were re-enacting a vital episode in history....

Then, too, Mr. Goldwyn went contrary to the general Hollywood practice in dealing with foreign background pictures. He cast all his Russian characters with American players speaking without accents. The only accents in the picture are those of the Germans. This is to give audiences here the feeling that the collective farm village in which most of the action takes place might be any typical American village or town, and to point up the fact that, in a similar situation, our people would behave with the same courage and fortitude shown by the Russians.

—Jagger, interviewed by Irving Drutman for *The New York Herald Tribune*, 5 Sept 1943

I've made more than a score of pictures since I began my film career, but [*It Grows on Trees* (1952, Arthur Lubin)] is the first time I've really felt at home and relaxed in a part. I'm a typical family man of extremely modest income who must keep his eye on the family budget.

I come home from work expecting almost anything to happen and try to keep cool when it does; I seize every opportunity to better myself and butt my head against a blank wall in doing so; I take the bitter with the sweet and hardly know the difference between the two because I'm so used to the bitter.

When my wife [Irene Dunne] plants a couple of trees in the back yard and they bear $5 and $10 bills I blow my top like any other guy would because I know in my heart it's too good to be true.

When the big blow-off comes and the money turns to dust I take it in stride and wind up the picture thankful we're not all in jail.

In *Brigham Young* [1940, Henry Hathaway], I played the title role and it goes without saying that I could hardly feel at home in the part. In *Twelve O'Clock High* [1949, Henry King] I was an Air Force officer and the only comfortable thing about the part was that I didn't have to wear a hair piece.

From then on I worked bald, as I am....

—Jagger, interviewed for *The New York Morning Telegraph*, 9 Aug 1952

Al JOLSON [1886-1950]

Born: Asa Yoelson in Srednike, Russia. A stage debut in 1899 then work with various vaudeville and minstrel troupes preceded his debut in the short film, April Showers (1926). The following year he starred in The Jazz Singer (1927, Alan Crosland):

I love this story. It is written around my life, you know. Many years ago, when I was singing in one of the music halls of San Francisco, before I had gone on the stage, a man who was there asked me why I sang ordinary jazz songs with so much sentiment. I told him it was a heritage — my father was a rabbi. That man was Sam Rafaelson [sic], author of the play.

—Jolson, in *Theatre Magazine*, Oct 1927

When I first started making pictures, I felt like one of those dolls whose strings are pulled to the right for a smile, and the left for a sad expression.... I hungered for the live sound of actual people. And just like a person who's in love, but away from his fiancée, or wife, I began to imagine my audience, with the result that after my third picture I succeeded in creating the illusion of an audience, working to it as though the end of the performance would bring down the house....

The other day I sang the song "Little Pal" for the first time under the microphone and before the cameras. I thought to myself that this wasn't much of a "first night" thrill, singing a new song that I think will be popular, with only an orchestra and a group of ice-box affairs holding the cameras in front of me. But I did remember that thousands of people were going to hear that song and see me in the picture [*Say it with Songs* (1929, Lloyd Bacon)], so I let go with all I had.

—Jolson, in *Theatre Magazine*, July 1929

James Earl JONES [1931-]

Born: Arkabutla, Mississippi; son of Robert Earl Jones [1910-]. Acting studies at The University of Michigan—Ann Arbor, The American Theatre Wing and with Lee Strasberg and Tad Danielewski in N.Y., work in summer stock and on the N.Y. stage preceded his film debut in Dr. Strangelove (1964, Stanley Kubrick). In his fourth feature film — The Great White Hope (1970, Martin Ritt) — he played Jack Jefferson, a role he had played on Broadway:

I have the advantage of playing a character... who is an American folk hero like Johnny Appleseed or Joe Louis or John F. Kennedy. The first Negro champ. They made him, then they destroyed him. America is afraid of the unusual and Jack [Johnson, the prizefighter on whom the film is based]...asserted himself and his fame as an individual, and people couldn't adjust to a Negro who didn't fit into their image.... Jack was a big success, but he had a white girl, and the world beat him down.

—Jones, interviewed by Rex Reed for *The New York Times*, 13 Oct 1968

Of course [I had reservations about the role]. Every black actor must think with two minds, an actor's mind and a black man's. I wondered how black audiences would receive the niggerisms and dialect, and I wondered how whites and blacks would receive the consorting with a white woman [Jane Alexander]....

[Jefferson] was such an individualist he was almost fascist at times. If you have to take individualism to its extreme, and America is a good example of this, you end up with something hostile and destructive. If you eliminate all altruisms, you have a killer on your hands.

—Jones, interviewed by Wanda Hale for *The Sunday News*, 11 Oct 1970

[Roop in *Claudine* (1974, John Berry)] was this big, oversized peacock. Which is a common phenomenon in minority groups, where the male is ridden with the effects of society saying he's inferior. But he doesn't feel inferior, so he has overcompensated.... He's kind of pathetic, in a way.

—Jones, interviewed by David Sterritt for *The Christian Science Monitor*, 22 May 1974

[Terence Mann in *Field of Dreams* (1989, Phil Alden Robinson) is] a black journalist from the '60's who was disillusioned about the failure of the Civil Rights Movement and other American fulfillments. He was in Boston in a Jewish neighborhood — Orthodox, because where else could he best hide so no one could find him....

Kevin [Costner] was the star but he kept it so simple. He did no star turns, he was very vulnerable. One of his talents is being so flexible.

—Jones, interviewed by Deidre Johnson for *Drama-Logue*, 25-31 Jan 1990

Leatrice JOY [1893-1985]

Born: Leatrice Joy Zeidler in New Orleans. Work in film studios in New Orleans and Wilkes Barre, Pennsylvania, preceded her move to Hollywood. In 1922, she made Manslaughter, the second of four films for Cecil B. DeMille:

As a director, Cecil B. DeMille was delightful, just delightful. I never had direction from him. He would say to me, "Leatrice, let it come from your heart, honey, and it'll be all right...."

When the morning came for me to receive my verdict in [*Manslaughter*], I thought about [convicted criminal] Madalynne Obenchain and did exactly what she did [in the courtroom]. Mr. DeMille said, "Well, when are you going to start acting, Miss Joy?"

I said, "You don't appreciate what I gathered from my experience down there because that's exactly what Madalynne Obenchain did. She just held her mouth open until I thought I couldn't watch any longer."

"Well," he said, "I'd like it a little bit more — *portrayed* is the word." So I batted my eyes, sniffed and made it just like everybody else. Every time I see that scene, I think how much more effective it would have been if I had done it the way I had originally intended. [Joy also worked on DeMille's *The Ten Commandments* (1923) and *Triumph* (1924).]

[In 1922, I did *Minnie*.... Mickey Neilan directed it. I felt so sorry for the little character I was playing. I never absorbed a character as much as I did that one. She was just a homely little girl — I had to have a great big wart on my face with hair growing out of it, a crooked part in my hair and only a little black dress.... I was so sensitive to the little thing and had such compassion for her. Of course, Mickey Neilan, being an artist and not as much of a showman, left the unhappy ending. He ended the picture with me with the warts, the straight hair and all that. When [Cecil B.] DeMille saw it, he hit the ceiling and said, "I don't know what you're going to do, but you're going to make a glamour girl out of that star of mine before that picture ends or it won't be shown." So they sent me to Paris, had surgery done, got my hair all fixed up and spoiled the picture. They killed it. Mickey never got over it, and I guess I never did either.

—Joy, interviewed by William M. Drew for *Speaking of Silents: First Ladies of the Screen* (Vestal, N.Y.: The Vestal Press, 1989)

Robert JOY [1951-]

Born: Montreal, Quebec, Canada. Studies at Newfoundland Memorial University and at Oxford College in Corpus Christi (a Rhodes Scholar), and work on the stage in Canada and on Broadway preceded his film debut; in 1981, he played Harry K. Thaw in Milos Forman's Ragtime and Dave, the drug addict, in Louis Malle's Atlantic City:

My instinct with Harry K. Thaw was to let him simmer and let it be a sort of inner-directed "film performance." Milos Forman wanted him very much out on a limb. He said, "You can't possibly be too big." He kept telling me, "More eyes, more crazy!" It was the direction some actors cringe at — "Bigger and louder!" But it made sense for the character. It was actually thrilling, because he put me in a situation where I was either going to be absolutely brilliant or a real fool. I enjoyed walking that line.

—Joy, interviewed by Don Shewey for *Caught in the Act: New York Actors Face to Face* (New York: New American Library, 1986)

[Playing Dave in *Atlantic City*] was so *easy*. I was ingratiating and superficially friendly, always smiling; but it was obvious to the audience that I had ulterior motives.

—Joy, interviewed by Eleanor Blau for *The New York Times*, 13 Aug 1982

Raul JULIA
[1940-]

Born: San Juan, Puerto Rico. Studies at The University of Puerto Rico and work on the N.Y. stage (from 1964) and on Broadway (from 1968) preceded his film debut in Panic in Needle Park (1971, Jerry Schatzberg). In 1985, he played Valentin opposite William Hurt as Molina in Hector Babenco's adaptation of Manuel Puig's The Kiss of the Spider Woman:

Bill Hurt's role is the flashier, but what I like about it is he didn't make it flashy. He wanted to be true to the part rather than use it to his advantage, which I think says a great deal about his own integrity.
—Julia, interviewed by Stephen M. Silverman for *The New York Post*, 24 July 1985

Romero [in *Romero* (1989, John Duigan)] was one of the most difficult roles I've ever had to do. [The archbishop's choices] were incredibly hard to make — they were a matter of life and death. The more involved he got, the more he knew he was going to get killed. And he could have saved his life and still have been a good priest and served the people. But he went beyond all that to really make a point and to be an example for everybody. What you begin to understand about him is that he wasn't that different. In the end he was scared like you would feel scared if you were in that situation. But he still went out and did what he did. And that's what makes him extraordinary.
—Julia, interviewed by Lynn Darling for *Newsday*, 6 Feb 1989

A good defense lawyer doesn't judge his client. He just does his best to get him off. It's not your job to question whether he is guilty or innocent. As a matter of fact, I talked to one defense lawyer [in preparation for *Presumed Innocent* (1990, Alan J. Pakula)] who told me that nobody is innocent....

Lawyers are frustrated actors. One lawyer I talked to said the production, the performance, is more important than anything else. What you wear is important, too.
—Julia, interviewed by Phoebe Hoban for *Premiere*, Aug 1990

K

Madeline KAHN [1942-]

Born: Boston. Studies at Hofstra University and work on and off Broadway preceded her film debut in What's Up Doc? (1972, Peter Bogdanovich). In 1973, she played Trixie Delight in Bogdanovich's Paper Moon:

Trixie...was such a good part. She had shine all on her own. I've never known anyone like her, but I've had similar feelings to situations, and if you use them you can bring the part home. She was a victim of the Depression, and she had to hustle to survive. She reminded me of Blanche in [A] *Streetcar* [*Named Desire*] — trying to be genteel and clinging to airs when she was down on her luck.

—Kahn, interviewed by Shaun Considine for *After Dark*, July 1973

I didn't impersonate [Marlene] Dietrich [in *Blazing Saddles* (1974)]. I think she's divine. My interpretation of the character [Lili Von Shtupp] had a lot of me and a lot of Mel Brooks in it, though Mel did want certain references to Dietrich's roles. But it's a parody of films — not of her — films in which a certain kind of lady reduces men to jelly.

—Kahn, interviewed by Robert Berkvist for *The New York Times*, 24 Mar 1974

I owe Mel Brooks so much. *Blazing Saddles* and *Young Frankenstein* [1974] gave me enormous attention and were fun to make. He could've been family, like a Jewish uncle, and from the start, he encouraged me to cut loose — be funny, bawdy, crazy. He *appreciated* me.

—Kahn, interviewed by Jack Hicks for *TV Guide*, 10 Dec 1983

Mel is involved with controlled madness. I love that. I just love it. Mel is going for *lunacy*. He gets several takes on a scene and then he says "Now do one more and *go bananas!*" — and often that's the one he likes. He is a courageous man. His humor is connected up to some main artery, like *Mad* magazine and *The National Lampoon*, and he's always on. I could never be that way: I've spent all my time and money to be respectable and dignified; to be a *lady*. I'd be afraid of just walking around and doing what I think is crazy. But Mel loves it!

—Kahn, interviewed by Vicki Hodgetts for *The Village Voice*, 16 Dec 1974

Carol KANE [1952-]

Born: Cleveland, Ohio. Work on the N.Y. stage (from 1966) preceded her film debut in Carnal Knowledge (1971, Mike Nichols). In 1975, she played Gitl in Joan Micklin Silver's Hester Street:

Gitl...was not hard to play. I felt very connected to her. Some people are completely caved in under the possibilities they are offered. Life in Russia was so structured and protected for many, that people didn't know how to handle America. It was like a new thought which can make you stronger, can also render you unable to function. I walked around the Lower East Side talking to some older Jews. I talked to my own grandmother who had worked very hard to wipe out of her mind the traditions and customs of her country because she wanted to be accepted. Even now, she is terribly reluctant to speak about her past. I read a lot about life in the *shtetl* and borrowed the *sheitel* which I was to wear in the film. They're made of horsehair and are phenomenally ugly and I felt ugly in it, something Gitl wouldn't have considered in wearing it because she felt she was serving God. I took it home and wore it around the house and in the streets so it could become a part of the way I lived.

—Kane, interviewed by Carol Wikarska for *The Village Voice*, 5 Jan 1976

There's a tremendous growth in Gitl. She starts timid and becomes strong. She gives up the man she loves [Stephen Keats] because of the pain he is causing her. She could have stayed with him and suffered the way women did in those days. But she didn't. She made a new life for herself.

—Kane, interviewed by Ann Guarino for *The New York Daily News*, 2 Dec 1975

Boris KARLOFF [1887-1969]

Born: William Pratt in Dulwich, England. Stage work in Canada preceded his film debut in The Dumb Girl of Portici (1916, Max Ratinoff). In 1931, he played the title role in James Whale's film of Frankenstein:

Manufacturing a monster is a troublesome task, as Jack Pierce and I learned in making the picture *Frankenstein*. As make-up man, Jack had to turn me into a monster once a day, an operation that required four hours. To make me appear both oversized and fabricated, he heaped me up with fifty pounds of extras, including putty eyelids and boots that weighed sixteen pounds each. The eyelids gave me a look that was something less than human. My clothes were heavily padded to increase my size, and the use of low camera angles made me seem about seven feet tall. The heavy boots made my slow, monster-like shuffle come naturally.

Acting under all this equipment was exhausting, but the role proved to be the most interesting I have ever played. Trying to portray the synthetic man in *Frankenstein* was a rare challenge. As you may remember, when the monster first appeared, his brain was just beginning to work. As the film progressed, I had to show his mental development. The monster never learned to talk, so I had to indicate all his thoughts and reactions by pantomime.

—Karloff, in *The Saturday Evening Post*, 16 July 1949

I assume that the sympathy of an audience goes out to the Monster because it is at once recognized that here is a strange creature, utterly bewildered by his surroundings. When he kills his tormentors it is only because he has no other thought or motive beyond self-preservation.

—Karloff, interviewed for *Karloff* (New York: 1969)

I had done [*The Criminal Code* (1931)] as a stage-play. The highspot was a prison scene in which I had to come on and kill a "stool-pigeon." It was a gripping scene, and you could have heard a pin drop in the theater. Yet it required no acting. The stool-pigeon was on first. He had his back to the audience. Then I came on. As I walked across the stage I was staring at the stool-pigeon. The audience couldn't see my face fully. Then I turned and had my back to them as well. There was a moment of deathly silence, then the stool-pigeon turned. Before he could do a thing I had plunged a knife into him. He flopped to the floor. The audience still couldn't see my face. But they were imagining the most terrifying expressions on it — far more spine-chilling expressions than I could possibly have achieved. I had simply provided the frame; they had filled in the picture. When we came to make the talkie, the director Howard Hawks, asked me how that scene had been played on the stage. I told him and persuaded him to film it in exactly the same way. He wanted to take one or two close-ups of me as well, but I talked him out of the idea. I knew that a single shot showing my face would have spoilt the effect. [Karloff worked with Hawks again on *Scarface* (1932).]

—Karloff, in *Film Weekly*, 18 Apr 1936

Stacy KEACH [1941-]

Born: Walter Stacy Keach, Jr. in Savannah, Georgia. Studies at The University of California at Berkeley, The Yale Drama School, and repertory work including Shakespeare for Joseph Papp in N.Y. preceded his film debut in The Heart is a Lonely Hunter (1968, Robert Ellis Miller). In 1972, he played Billy Tully in John Huston's Fat City:

Q. [Huston] claims that he likes to give the actor a lot of freedom in his creation of a role and a scene. Was this reflected in your work with him in *Fat City*?

A. Very much so. It was probably the most productive relationship that I've had with a director in the sense that we discussed the alternatives for a scene. We never made any hard and fast resolutions. I think that's an important point a lot of directors get stuck on. A lot of them think there's one and only one possible way for a scene to be done, and that can produce a feeling that's so airtight it's almost stultifying. I think it's better to give the actor alternatives so that something can happen spontaneously during a scene that is not the manifestation of a rehearsal. But Huston does rehearse a lot. He walks through the scene many times and works with the cameraman and the actors. But he sort of lets the actor stage the scene himself. He brings the camera in and lets the actor show him. Then he'll bring in his suggestions — something that might spice up a moment or change the rhythm or the tempo of a scene. It's a real collaboration in the best sense of the word.

—Keach, interviewed by Richard Fisher for *Filmmakers Newsletter*, June 1973

Buster KEATON [1895-1966]

Born: Joseph Keaton in Piqua, Kansas, into a family of vaudeville acrobats. On stage with The 3 Keatons from age 3, he was brought into films by actor/director Roscoe "Fatty" Arbuckle, making his debut in Arbuckle's The Butcher Boy (1917):

A few fan letters to Roscoe asked why the little man in his pictures never smiled. We had been unaware of it. We looked at three two-reelers we'd done together and found it to be true. Later just for fun I tried smiling at the end of one picture. The preview audience hated it and hooted the scene. After that I never smiled again on stage, screen, or TV....

The longer I worked with Roscoe the more I liked him. I respected without reservation his work both as an actor and a comedy director. He took falls no other man of his weight ever attempted, had a wonderful mind for action gags, which he could devise on the spot....

Arbuckle was that rarity, a truly jolly fat man. He had no meanness, malice, or jealousy in him. Everything seemed to amuse and delight him....

I could not have found a better-natured man to teach me the movie business, or a more knowledgeable one.

I was always puzzled...when people spoke of the similarities in the characters Charlie [Chaplin] and I played in movies. There was, to me, a basic difference from the start: Charlie's tramp was a bum with a bum's philosophy. Lovable as he was he would steal if he got the chance. My little fellow was a workingman and honest.

For an example, let us say that each wanted a suit he saw in a shop window. Charlie's tramp would admire it, search his pockets, come up with a dime, shrug, and move on, hoping he'd be lucky next day and have the money to buy it. He would steal the money if he couldn't find it any other way. If not, he would forget all about the suit.

Though my little man also stopped, admired the suit, and had not the money to buy it, he would never steal to get it. Instead he would start trying to figure out how he could earn extra money to pay for it.

In *The Frozen North* [1922]...I did a burlesque of William S. Hart, the great Western star. At one time Hart's popularity was exceeded by only three other performers — Chaplin, Fairbanks and Mary Pickford. In 1922 he was still a great drawing card. Bill, though, was not one of your handsome movie cowboys, and he took himself and his art quite seriously. In his pictures he did not sing, whistle, or yodel. Nor did he dress like some Dapper Dan of the Great Plains. As a boy he had lived on the Frontier, and he tried hard in his pictures to show the Old West as he remembered it....

If Bill didn't romanticize the Old West he sure gimmicked up his good bad man with plenty of imaginative touches. He rolled Bull Durham cigarettes with one hand. He kept his Stetson on with a leather string tied under his chin. On his gaunt eagle face this looked good. But no real cowboy ever wore one, to my knowledge. Real cowboys also didn't blaze away at human varmints with guns in both hands as Bill did on the screen. But the main thing he did in his pictures that they didn't do in real life was cry. After about 1918 there was at least one scene in every Hart movie in which Bill broke down and unashamedly let glycerine tears roll down his thin, leathery he-man cheeks.

In my burlesque of Bill Hart I got a good laugh by opening with a scene showing me coming up out of a New York subway-exit kiosk situated in the middle of frozen Donner Lake.

Like Bill, I kept my hat on with a leather string tied under my chin and I carried a six-shooter on each thigh. I made futile attempts to roll a cigarette with one hand.

But it was an action gag in this picture that burned up Bill Hart when he saw it. This showed me coming home and discovering a couple hugging. Though I cannot see their faces I am convinced it is my wife and a lover. I turn pale, then amazed, and finally am crushed. Huge glycerin tears roll down my face....

Bill's fans knew, of course, when they saw this picture that I was burlesquing their idol. As an old-time trouper Bill should have known that you can only burlesque successes, never flops. Also that if I imitated him it was only because I admired him so much that I wanted to be Bill Hart for a little while on the screen.

—Keaton, in his (with Charles Samuels) *My Wonderful World of Slapstick* (Garden City, N.Y.: Doubleday & Co., 1960)

Q. About the dream sequence in *Sherlock, Jr.* [1924, Buster Keaton], was this something that you thought of on the spur of the moment, or something that had been planned out ahead?

A. No, it was planned out ahead because we had to build a set for that one.

Q. How was that done — did you have an actual screen beforehand on which the characters were appearing?

A. No. We built what looked like a motion picture screen and actually built a stage into that frame but lit it in such a way that it looked like a motion picture being projected on a screen. But it was real actors and the lighting effect gave us the illusion, so I could go out of semidarkness into that well-lit screen right from the front row of the theater right into the picture. Then when it came to the scene changing on me when I got up there, that was a case of timing and on every one of those things we would measure the distance to the fraction of an inch from the camera to where I was standing, also with a surveying outfit to get the exact height and angle so that there wouldn't be a fraction of an inch missing on me, and then we changed the setting to what we wanted it to be and I got back into the same spot and it overlapped the action to get the effect of the scene changing.

—Keaton, interviewed by Christopher Bishop for *Film Quarterly*, Fall 1958

Diane KEATON [1946-]

Born: Diane Hall in Los Angeles. After acting in high school and college, she moved to N.Y. and studied with Sanford Meisner at The Neighborhood Playhouse School of Theater. A member of the original Broadway cast of Hair (1968), she then made her film debut in Lovers and Other Strangers (1970, Cy Howard), before teaming up with Woody Allen beginning with the stage then film production of his Play It Again, Sam (1972, Herbert Ross):

Doing *Play It Again, Sam* was a revelation of sorts for me. First of all, working with Woody, I never feel any pressure. He's like family — old hat. He respects me too much to let me sell myself out with a simple smile. And our director Herb Ross was terrific, *you'd love him.* He was so patient with me. He's the first director I've worked with that's ever asked my opinion about *anything*. It's usually "Do this, do that, Diane," and I'd just do it, never stopping to say, "Gee, how about trying it this way?" Since I had played Linda on Broadway for over a year I knew her character pretty well. But in the movie, Herb and I have tried to make her more realistic. She's really a looney neurotic, and we tried to point this up.

When I was first asked to come in and test for *The Godfather* [1972, Francis Ford Coppola], I just couldn't believe it. ME? Diane Keaton in *The Godfather*? Never. I wasn't even Italian. When I was tested they were mainly concerned about Al Pacino.... On the set no one ever knew exactly who I was. All these guys that hung around (Mafiosi?) always kept asking, "Who's the blonde broad?" And somebody would answer, "Oh, she's what's-er-name, Michael's girlfriend." Really, Al and I felt like the creepy couple all the time. Also on the set there was the added pressure of having Brando around all the time. As you can imagine, I immediately fell madly in love with the guy. He was every high school crush I'd ever had. [Keaton also appeared in Coppola's *The Godfather Part II* (1974) and The Godfather Part III (1990).]

—Keaton, interviewed by Bernard Carragher for *Show*, July 1972

Annie Hall [1977, Woody Allen]'s about a relationship, and because Woody and I know each other well and have had a relationship, there's a quality of truth in it. My real last name is Hall, for instance.

But we didn't meet on a tennis court; we met at an audition for Woody's play, *Play It Again, Sam.* I have a Volkswagen, but I'm a *slow* driver, a cautious driver, too slow. I'm a nervous wreck when I meet a man, but I don't smoke marijuana at all. I have in the past, when I was in *Hair*. But it makes me a little nervous, and I feel nervous enough without it.... My parents are not from Wisconsin, but Balboa Island, California, and they're nothing at all like the parents in the film — but they are *goyim*. I've never had spiders in my bathtub. Roaches, maybe.

—Keaton, interviewed by Lee Guthrie for *Woody Allen—A Biography* (New York: Drake, 1978)

The biggest worry I had making *Annie Hall* was whether or not I would get in my own way. I was afraid that unconsciously I might stop myself from showing the truth because it made me uncomfortable.... I wanted to do *Annie Hall* fully, without worrying what I did wrong in real life. Understand? I had to stop fantasizing about what kind of person I am. Am I bad? Was I wrong in that situation? Did I hurt Woody too much? Was I selfish? There were so many conflicts. But in the final analysis, working out my relationship with Woody was, and still is, great fun, and always a surprise and a revelation to me.

—Keaton, interviewed by Rex Reed for *The Toronto Star*, 28 May 1977

I loved the part [of Louise Bryant in *Reds* (1982, Warren Beatty)].... I felt she wasn't a talented writer — I read her stuff and it wasn't very good. But she was a fascinating woman. The part was emotionally taxing but I never lost sight of the character. Warren's feeling for the film was really passionate. How he held it together I don't know.

—Keaton, interviewed by George Perry for *The Sunday Times Magazine* (London), 18 July 1982

Q. As an actress, you've played a lot of very strong women who make big choices and throw themselves into difficult situations, dangerous situations, like in *Mrs. Soffel* [1985, Gillian Armstrong], and like Charley in *Little Drummer Girl* [1984, George Roy Hill] and Theresa Dunn in *Looking for Mr. Goodbar* [1977, Richard Brooks]. At the end of the films, however, those women are somehow subdued....

A. I don't think that Mrs. Soffel was subdued. She really defied them to the end. And — it's a true story — she got caught. She didn't say, "I'm sorry." She slapped the guy in the face and said, "Yeah, I'm going in and this is the man I love and go fuck yourself." She had to go to jail. You know she was *not* subdued.

Charley was like a total lunatic. I don't think that she was strong. I think she was always weak. And always crazy. She was an arrogant, little, selfish kind of actress who wasn't very good and who insisted on being good and trying to be good, even though she wasn't very gifted or talented. So she was going to throw herself into this terrorist world and be somebody. So she was pathetic, all ambition and no gifts. No brains. No nothing. She was not strong at all.

And Theresa Dunn was a case history, if you ask me. A lot of people view that movie as a morality tale. I never did. You know, like, "You fuck, you die." But I always viewed it as a story about a self-destructive person who was never able to find her strength, because she was on the road to killing herself. So I don't agree with you about those characters.

I think that Mrs. Soffel was positive, because she experienced real love. And for her, that made her life fuller. And at the end, she said, "You can't take that away from me if you throw me in jail for a hundred, a million years." I think she was enlarged by her experience. The other two were just sad people. I think that Theresa Dunn was really sad — sweet, because of that dichotomy in her: she could be with the deaf kids, which made her strong, but she was so crazy about men. It was more about punishment, you know, totally sadomasochistic. That she had to destroy herself that way.

Q. I get the feeling that these aren't characters you like.

A. I love them, are you kidding? I completely love Mrs. Soffel. And I felt for Theresa Dunn, because everybody has those elements in their personality. And I felt for *Little Drummer Girl* — I liked her the least because she was somebody who was so lost. But interesting, I mean, my God, all of us have so many elements in us that are so weak and strong.

—Keaton, interviewed by Marlaine Glicksman for *Film Comment*, Apr 1987

Michael KEATON [1951-]

Born: Michael Douglas in Pittsburgh. Studies in Speech at Kent State University, stand-up comedy in Pittsburgh and L.A. and work on TV preceded his film debut in Night Shift (1982, Ron Howard). In 1988, he played Daryl Poynter in Glenn Gordon Caron's Clean and Sober:

The second time through [the script], I could see that he wasn't a pig, he was just an ordinary guy who got into a lot of trouble because of cocaine and was trying to find his way out....

[In preparation for the role] I went to AA and Narcotics Anonymous meetings. I spoke with cocaine addicts and alcoholics. I wanted to observe things about their behavior. To me, the ultimate in acting is when it's like you're in your own house and the audience is looking in through the window. What I wanted to do was pick up some behavior and use it. But that was difficult because there didn't seem to be any one set form of behavior for the people I met, unless it was so inside and interior and subtle that I missed it. They're all different....

The thing that turned it around for me, after I'd been to three or four meetings, was that I discovered that every time anybody got up to speak, I'd connect with something they'd say, and I thought, I'll bet everyone connects with something. And I'd think, what is it that separates me from that man or that woman? Probably not much....

This movie...[is] about lying and fear, and how [Daryl] isn't ready yet to really level with those people [the executives from his real estate firm]. Of course, they aren't being honest with him, either. There are so many different things going on in that scene [where he tries to explain the missing money]. If you're gonna cop to something, you kinda do it and kinda don't. You think maybe he's really coming clean, but he doesn't. And he wants to think, "Aren't I great?" But he's not. He's still gotta screw up his life some more before he learns his lesson.

—Keaton, interviewed by Roger Ebert for *The New York Post*, 16 Aug 1988

When Tim [Burton] first came to me with the script [of *Batman* (1989)], I read it out of politeness. All the while, I'm thinking there's no way I'd do this. It just wasn't me. My name doesn't spring to *my* mind when somebody says, "Batman." But I read it and thought, "This guy's fascinating!" I saw him as essentially depressed. I told that to Tim, thinking he wouldn't agree, but he said, "That's exactly what I see." The choice was to play Batman honestly. So I started thinking, "What kind of person would wear these clothes?" The answer seemed pretty disturbing. This is a guy in *pain*.

—Keaton, interviewed by Bill Zehme for *Rolling Stone*, 29 June 1989

You know, Jack [Nicholson]'s role of The Joker [in *Batman*] is much more similar to what I did in *Beetlejuice* [1988, Tim Burton]. That role was so over the top that I just whaled on it. [*Batman*] is different. I keep referring to the film as a painting — Tim calls it a puzzle. I'm just sort of throwing up my hands, saying, "Paint me in, Big Guy."

—Keaton, interviewed by Hilary de Vries for *The New York Times*, 5 Feb 1989

Harvey KEITEL [1947-]

Born: Brooklyn, N.Y. Service in the U.S. Marine Corps, studies with Lee Strasberg at The Actors Studio and work in summer stock and off-off-Broadway preceded his film debut in Who's That Knocking at My Door? (1968), the first of four films with Martin Scorsese:

Q. You've worked with Scorsese a lot, and Jack [Nicholson] told me that you built the part of Sport, the pimp in *Taxi Driver* [1976], from a four-line part to that of a pimp with a big job. I also know that Scorsese wanted to give you a bigger role, but that you wanted that role.

A. That's right. It was a wonderful example of collaboration between a director and an actor. Originally the description of the character was: an Italian guy standing in the doorway. But I knew those characters from where I was living at that time, in Hell's Kitchen in New York City. I had walked by them every night for the past seven years. When I told Marty I wanted to play that role, he said, "Why? The other role is bigger." I said, "I have an idea."

Because of our previous collaboration in *Mean Streets* [1973] and before that when he was a student at NYU making *Who's That Knocking at My Door?*, he understood that if I said that, I had something in mind. Out of that collaboration grew the character of Sport. Matthew was the name he used to throw off the trade, the johns.... I had this idea for his hair, which the producer didn't want to spend the money on at the time. I had to go to Marty and say, "They won't give me the wig." He ordered them to give me what I wanted. Then I found this pimp — ex-pimp, in his words — and we spent two weeks improvising together. He would play the pimp, I'd play the girl. Then we'd switch roles.

Q. What about that scene where you're slow dancing with Jodie Foster, and as you stroke her hair the audience notices you have a three-inch fingernail?

A. Marty wanted me in another scene in the picture, so I created that scene. And along with the line producer, I wrote the lyrics for the song we were dancing to, "I Love You Baby, Come to Me...."

Q. It seems to me that you're always working behind the scenes. But not every director is open to that from actors.

A. You know, there's a common denominator among certain directors. How to define that I'm not quite sure. But it's called giving, it's called trust, it's called respect for another's work. Marty has it.... And when the ingredient of trust, encouragement, support is present on both sides, wonderful things can happen. [Keitel also worked on Scorsese's *The Last Temptation of Christ* (1988).]

—Keitel, interviewed by Julian Schnabel for *Interview*, Aug 1990

Q. A word often used about you by directors of yours I've spoken with is "prepared."

A. Well, I do my homework.

Q. You have it all worked out beforehand?

A. Absolutely. You get the script, and you analyze it. You dig into it to discover where the character is coming from, what his background is, what he does, what his desires are, what his fears are, how he lives — analyzing what the author had in mind. All that is homework....

Q. Do you feel you have to have a character's biography in your head even if it isn't in the script?

A. Absolutely. I must know what his mother and father were like together, what his childhood and home life were like. I have to know if he didn't go to college, or only stayed one year, or graduated. I have to know what his views are about many different things. And the actor creates these things; the actor creates the character's past. Most of the time all of this isn't in the script. There are indications, but a script is basically skeletal.

I saw my character [in *The Duellists* (1978, Ridley Scott)] as coming from the peasant class, someone who rose up through the ranks. I wore a *Legion d'Honneur* ribbon for that reason: to show that he had succeeded in the army through acts of bravery, not birth. I was hoping to show his disdain for the aristocracy. This is what the Bonapartists were: this was a time for the people to rise up....

I suppose I thought I was going to be able to do some things in *The Duellists* which eventually I was not able to do. Ridley saw what I wanted to do, and was very helpful. But I saw the character much more complexly than it came across in the film. It was never my intention when I got involved with the project to just play a nemesis. No way. Never. No character's just one way.

Q. How did you develop the business of humming along with your piano playing [in *Blue Collar* (1978, Paul Schrader)]?

A. From Glenn Gould, who does that when he plays. That was something I added to the character, although it was Jimmy Toback who suggested it by introducing me to Gould's work; it wasn't in the script. I thought it right for the character because I thought the character was a bit eccentric.

Q. Narcissistic?

A. Insecure as opposed to narcissistic. I felt he was propelled more by his insecurities and his quest to be loved than by any sort of narcissism. I can see where someone could be misled into thinking it's narcissism, but when you think about it, desperation can lead to very similar acts. I thought that when he was playing that piano he was living through his fantasies. I thought he was going through many sexual fantasies, many fantasies about love, fantasies about loneliness, fantasies about expressing his anger. I thought he was really going the gamut when he played that piano.

Q. How does it all tie in with his sexual obsession?

A. The acts of sex which he's substituting for love represent in his mind his only moments of feeling secure. That's why he's constantly involved with sex. He meets this girl, he runs after her, he says he loves her — and what does he know about that girl. Is that love? No. That's the act of a desperate, tormented character who thinks it's "love at first sight." But eventually he sees her in many different situations and there's nothing at all, as far as I can see, to love about that girl. He loves her because she rejects him — the way his mother's rejected him for not going into the family business.

Q. The wide-eyed look you have in the hotel room scene when Tisa Farrow is making this kind of perverse love to Jim Brown is one of the most brilliant things you do in the movie. What's supposed to be going through your head?

A. What I had in mind was: he would do anything to be loved. And he's trying to understand how this woman whom he loved could do this. He's so naive in a way that there he is trying to undo what is being done right in front of his eyes.

Q. But it seemed to me he was reacting as much to Jim Brown as to the girl.

A. Yes, he was. Here was the man who was doing this. He's saying, "How come this guy is doing this, and *I* can't do it? What does *he* have that *I* don't have. Why doesn't she love *me*? She doesn't want *me*?"

Q. And what's going through his head when he's cruised by the gay guys in the restaurant?

A. He would do anything to be loved. This is a very desperate character. This fellow would flirt with anything to get some love, and he's getting some attention from them. And finally he begins to crack up, because he's not getting any of the love he's seeking.

—Keitel, interviewed by Stuart Byron for *Film Comment*, Jan/Feb 1978

Sally KELLERMAN [1937-]

*Born: Long Beach, California. Studies at Los Angeles City College and with Jeff Corey at The Actors Studio preceded her film debut in Reform School Girl (1957, Edward Bernds). In 1970, she played "Hot Lips" in Robert Altman's M*A*S*H:*

I did *The Boston Strangler* [1968, Richard Fleischer] playing the victim who lived to tell about Tony Curtis [as murderer Alberto de Salvo].... I was the one tied to the bed with black eyes and I looked just awful, but I think it was the first time people really thought I could act.... Then I played Jack Lemmon's wife in *The April Fools* [1969, Stuart Rosenberg] but it was the same old blonde routine with only seven lines. I was so desperate after that I went to see Bob Altman about *M*A*S*H* and I said "I'll do anything! I can be funny, I can break loose, just let me *try*!" and I think I had hold of his pant legs or something because he took a long look at me and jumped up and yelled "HOT LIPS!" I was there to see about the role of Lt. Dish. I didn't know anything about any Hot Lips, but for the first time in 14 years somebody had responded to me, so I just said, "Oooh, yes, Hot Lips!" and I ran right out of the meeting and practically ripped that script apart looking for all the lines belonging to Hot Lips.... On page 40, I found one line, on page 70, another line...14 years and at the end of the rainbow a nine-line part of a soldier called Hot Lips.... I told Bob Altman I hated him, I hated his stupid script and I hated his stupid movie and most of all I hated Hot Lips and they could all take their stupid little project and go @/?*@ themselves.

Well, Bob Altman must have known what he was doing, because he said, "Don't worry, you'll have more to do than it says in the script, because I plan to make up this movie as we go along...."

From the first day, Bob told me, "If you worry about what you look like, you're fired!...." I was a stiff rigid Victorian when I got into *M*A*S*H*.... Hot Lips changed me because she was the only character in the film who was allowed to change.... She ended up *gaining* from the degradation.... She was a pill, she needed shaking up.... She was an uptight bitch, but she ended up part of the family. [Kellerman worked for Altman again on *Brewster McCloud* (1970).]

—Kellerman, interviewed by Rex Reed for *The New York Times*, 31 May 1970

Gene KELLY [1912-]

Born: Eugene Kelly in Pittsburgh. While studying at Penn State and The University of Pittsburgh, he had a song and dance act with his brother, Fred, and opened The Gene Kelly School of Dance. On Broadway since 1938, he made his film debut opposite Judy Garland in For Me and My Gal (1942, Busby Berkeley):

[*For Me and My Gal*] was a picture about things I had done in nightclubs from my old days working with my brother. I knew it well, I knew it was sleaziness and cheap clubs. I was a walking encyclopedia on this. But it wasn't translating very well. And I thought the fellow that I should go to to learn about this was Busby Berkeley, but Buzz wasn't interested in dancing per se. He was interested in film, camera, and manipulating his performers in a surrealistic way that has never been touched, never been touched. He was a genius, but not for dance.... If you came up and said, "why this solo dance, why — doesn't it work, it worked on Broadway for two years in a stage show, why doesn't it work here, the same number," he didn't know. He was not interested. He was interested in other things.

—Kelly, interviewed by Ronald Haver for *American Film*, Mar 1985

I did *For Me and My Gal* with Judy Garland, and it was very fresh and free. Judy Garland in those days was a very relaxed, marvelous person. She was a *pure* screen actress: she pitched her voice and her gestures very low, because she knew — which I didn't — that the sound track and camera pick up everything, and if you play at stage volume, it looks and sounds awful.

We had a ball. Judy and I worked out the dances so that they looked the way people would dance who weren't professionals, yet they were, of course — had to be — of the highest professional standard. It was very exciting.

—Kelly, interviewed by Charles Higham for *The Sydney Morning Herald*, repr. in his *Celebrity Circus* (New York: Delacorte Press, 1979)

Judy Garland, I think, was the most extraordinary of all. She was like a computer, that girl. She could hear a song once, and she'd know it by ear, the same with dance steps. She'd pick 'em up like that.

—Kelly, interviewed by Clive Hirschhorn for *The Sunday Express*, 1 Nov 1970

Right after I'd been jilted by Rita [Hayworth] in the picture [*Cover Girl* (1944, Charles Vidor)], there was a spot where I wandered out into the street — alone and unhappy. At this point I wanted to express what I felt in a dance. And I wanted the dance to further the plot emotionally, and not just be a musical interlude. But unless you're in a ballet, you can't just begin to dance. You have to state your "thesis" in a song, first, and then go into the dance.... So, in *Cover Girl*, what I decided to do at this point was state my thesis not in a song, but in a few words which came over the sound-track as if they were my "stream of consciousness", and then go into the dance.

—Kelly, interviewed by Clive Hirschhorn for *Gene Kelly* (London: W.H. Allen, 1974)

Joe [Brady in *Anchors Aweigh* (1945, George Sidney)] was casual, easy, without a visible care in the world, and that made him fun to play. He had the imagination of a typical American youngster plus the fast social footwork of a sailor on leave.

I also enjoyed the contrast between Joe and the sailor played by Frank Sinatra. I had known Frank for some years, and he had helped me get this part. In *Anchors Aweigh* I had a chance to help him a little by coaching his dancing. He was a quick study and had a nice sense of humor. Once, when a sequence had him racing over the tops of a long line of beds, he paused and panted, "Who arranged this number — Bing Crosby?"

—Kelly, in *The Saturday Evening Post*, 15 May 1948

Fred [Astaire] and I are very different performers. He went in for the sophisticated bit; top hat, white tie, elegant cane and tails, while with me it was just the opposite.

Instead of a dress suit, which I looked terrible in, I wore sweat shirts or sailor's gear...more easy and more casual. Only once did Fred play a part which was meant for me, and that was a result of an accident. It was when we were making *Easter Parade* [1948, Charles Walters] with Judy [Garland] and Peter Lawford, and I got hurt playing softball with a group of kids.

—Kelly, interviewed by Clive Hirschhorn for *The Sunday Express*, 1 Nov 1970

What I envied about [Douglas] Fairbanks was the way he registered his satisfaction after completing a particularly dazzling trick without in any way being smug about it. There was something in his expression that acknowledged his own excellence, and it was most engaging. I tried to acquire the same sort of nonchalance for D'Artagnan [in *The Pirate* (1948, Vincente Minnelli)], but I was never able to be as ingenuous as Fairbanks. With me it came out rather tauntingly — a sort of "come on and fight...." It was never quite the same. Fairbanks had a combination of naivety and arrogance which was unrivalled in the cinema. And although there wasn't a trick in his entire repertoire I couldn't duplicate, the "brio" with which he performed them was uniquely his. [This was Kelly's second film opposite Judy Garland.]

Chuck Walters was directing the picture [*Summer Stock* (1950)], so naturally he was worried silly, even though he had the sophistication and the grace to realize that what he was working on was a piece of crap. I, on the other hand, was in the more luxurious position of just being the leading man. So when Judy [Garland] didn't show I got together a couple of basket-ball teams and played a few games in the main rehearsal hall. It was a way of turning adversity into fun, and it helped pass the time. The thing about Judy was that she only worked when she thought she was going to be good. If she felt she wasn't up to giving her best, she didn't appear on the set. It was as simple as that.

To work successfully with kids, you *have* to have the wherewithal to make them laugh. Then you need the energy to keep them laughing, for children want you to do everything three or four times before they're satisfied — and that can be tiring. Conversely, when they do something funny, they'll repeat it over and over again — and that can be tiring as well! I've always wanted to please kids because I enjoy it when they laugh, and I'll become something of a whore, if necessary, in my desire to keep them happy — whether I have to wiggle my bottom or stand on my head. And, of course, you have to retain that child-like thing of being able to fantasize or imitate people. And not only people, but things. In "I Got Rhythm," from *An American in Paris* [1951, Vincente Minnelli], which I do with a group of French kids, I not only imitate Hopalong Cassidy and Charlie Chaplin, but an aeroplane and a train as well. I found I could generally get children to work for me if I appealed to their imaginations and had the energy to keep going. So in "I Got Rhythm," I simply did in front of the cameras what I would have done behind them, and it worked.

—Kelly, interviewed by Clive Hirschhorn for *Gene Kelly* (London: W.H. Allen, 1974)

Q. Let's take a specific number like the "Singing in the Rain" sequence [in *Singing in the Rain* (1952, Stanley Donen and Gene Kelly)]. Mechanically, how would you go about constructing that, creating it for the camera?

A. Actually, that was an easy dance to create. We had a song first. The number plainly says "I'm singing in the rain." They asked, "What are you going to do in this?" I said, "I'm going to sing in the rain." Naturally, the extension of that was dancing in the rain. It has always been my premise that a song and dance man — usually we have very weak voices — sings to state his thesis. We state what we are talking about. I say "I'm singing in the rain." After I sing it, I dance it. At the end of the song, I state, "I'm singing and dancing in the rain." And then I went on to exploit and expound on this thesis. The whole number was done very quickly. Roger Edens created that very special little vamp in the beginning which has become musically very famous; you never hear the number without it. Then Stanley Donen and myself decided to take advantage again of cinematic treatment, and we kept the dance coming into camera. I left Debbie Reynolds at her house, kissed her goodnight, told my car to go home, and started walking down a street, around a corner, down another street — in other words, I never had any weak movements. If I stopped, we would bring the camera up and cut and come sidewards so I would move back and forth. Always into the camera. Always the forces were pushing, pushing, pushing the camera....

Q. For the actual conception of the movement, would you go on the stage and literally dance around and....

A. No. I sit in a chair or pace the floor, like a writer, I guess. I get the idea before the movement. When I get the idea blocked out, I fill it in with movement. Movement, if you are a trained dancer, and especially if you have trained in more than one dance milieu, is the easiest thing of all. Like a painter. A painter should know that if he mixes blue with yellow, he gets green. He knows his trade. It is the same with dance. You have to know where you are going, just the same as a writer has to know where the story is going. You never get right up and start to shimmy and shake like you do at the Daisy club. That's for amateurs. That's for laughs. That's for kicks. We do that in the evening, after work. But professionally, you have to sit down and grind it out.

—Kelly, interviewed by Curtis Lee Hanson for *Cinema*, Dec 1966

[On *Les Girls* (1957) George Cukor would] think nothing of spending a couple of hours going over a scene which needed no explanation at all. I'm pretty conscientious myself, but there's a limit as to how long you can go on discussing a line, and every once in a while, as much as I loved him, I'd find myself interrupting and saying: "For Christ's sake, George, let's just *shoot* the goddam thing!" Then we'd all laugh and everything would be fine. Then we'd do the same bit the next time. But the women [Kay Kendall, Mitzi Gaynor and Taina Elg] loved it, and in a way there's a canny method to his madness, because by the time he's through explaining what he wants out of a scene, you feel you know everything there is to know about it, and you go out and play it with confidence. It's a luxurious way of working — but too damn time-consuming for me.

I could understand and see what Fred [March] was doing [on *Inherit the Wind* (1960, Stanley Kramer)]. He was like Olivier. A wonderful technician. You could *see* the characterization taking shape — the cogs and wheels beginning to turn. If you studied his methods closely, it was all there, like an open book. But with Spence [Tracy] it was just the reverse. He'd play a scene with you, and you'd think nothing much was happening. Then, when you saw the rushes, there it all was — pouring out of his face. He was quite amazing. The embodiment of the art that conceals art. It was impossible to learn anything from Spence, because everything he did came deep down from some inner part of himself which, to an outsider anxious to learn, was totally inaccessible. All you could do was watch the magic, and be amazed. He was also one of the most thoroughly professional men in the business. I never knew him to fluff his lines or come late. And he would remain on the set doing things his stand-in could easily have done for him.

—Kelly, interviewed by Clive Hirschhorn for *Gene Kelly* (London: W.H. Allen, 1974)

Grace KELLY [1929-1982]

Born: Philadelphia. Studies at The American Academy of Dramatic Arts and with Sanford Meisner at The Neighborhood Playhouse in N.Y., work on Broadway (from 1949) and on TV preceded her film debut in Fourteen Hours (1951, Henry Hathaway). In her second film, she played Amy Kane opposite Gary Cooper as Will Kane in Fred Zinnemann's High Noon:

I'll never be able to thank Fred Zinnemann...enough for what he did for me. He and Mr. [Stanley] Kramer were the ones who proved to me that movie making is as great a creative art as the stage, and that those on the stage who talk down the movies just haven't seen or been in the right pictures. And that Mr. Cooper!.... He's the one who taught me to relax during a scene and let the camera do some of your work. On the stage you have to emote not only for the front rows, but for the balcony, too, and I'm afraid I overdid it. Mr. Cooper taught me that the camera is always in the front row, and how to take it easy.

—Kelly, interviewed for *True Confessions*, Feb 1955

Every good dramatic coach and every good director would like you to think of the story as a whole, and not just your part in it, but Mr. Hitchcock is the first one to show me *why*, and then teach me *how*. In one telephone scene [in *Dial M for Murder* (1954)] I used all the tricks to show horror that I had ever learned in school or on television, and thought I had done particularly well with my eyes. But all he used of that scene were my hands on the telephone. I was hurt, but he flattered me by telling me my hands were good actors, too. What he meant was that acting was more than a trick of waving your eyelashes, and that to be a success, you had to learn to act with your whole body. I worked so hard after that he gave me another chance in *Rear Window*. [She worked for Hitchcock a third time, on *To Catch a Thief* (1955).]

[For *Rear Window* (1954)], Hitch asked me if I knew Anita Colby, but at that time I had only seen your photos. He suggested that I talk with some of the people who knew you when you were executive assistant to the head of Paramount.

Designer Edith Head told me that the clothes I wore should be you, that they should say: "I am a girl in the fashion world — I have money, taste and discrimination." At all times my clothes must suit the occasion.

Did you notice the little hat worn on top of my head, just as you used to wear your hats? The important earrings, and pocket-books, and the plain cut pumps? I was told that all of these were Colby touches.

—Kelly, interviewed by Anita Colby for *The American Weekly*, 26 Dec 1954

I just had to be in *The Country Girl* [1954, George Seaton]. There was a real part in it for me. An acting part.

Q. Hadn't you had acting parts before?

A. Oh, no, not like this. Sometimes I had to act, but I had beautiful clothes, or beautiful lingerie or glamorous settings to help me along.... I was just the feminine background for the male stars who carried the action and the story on their shoulders.

But this time the woman is important to the story in her own right.... You see, I'm just what the title says, a country girl, married to an actor [Bing Crosby] who has lost his grip on himself and drinks too much.... Bill Holden plays the agent who wants to make the actor the great star he should be. All I want is my real man back. I don't care if he's a star or a clerk, just so he's a man....

We live in a sleazy flat. I wear glasses, cheap skirts and sweaters, and the only make-up I use is what any housewife would use who wants to look as nice as she can afford for her husband. No rich gowns, no glamorous settings. Bing has to act. Bill has to act. I have to act. It was a wonderful challenge....

—Kelly, interviewed by George Scullin for *Motion Picture*, Mar 1955

Patsy KELLY [1910-1981]

Born: Brooklyn, N.Y. A dancer on the New York stage, she was brought to film by Hal Roach. A series of shorts at the Roach studios preceded her first feature, Going Hollywood (1933, Raoul Walsh).

[Making films at the Roach studios] was just fantastic...[especially] to be around Laurel and Hardy, who were so wonderful.... In addition to their comic genius, [they were] such sweet, kind men; they'd come in and watch us, and help, and add suggestions, so it was truly remarkable....

Stan [Laurel] was so wonderful; he'd come in and watch us shoot, and just quickly drop a suggestion that of course made the whole scene. We used to have to go see our rushes, and I can't stand myself on the screen; my voice makes me climb a wall. But I used to love to go and watch him look at his rushes, because he'd get hysterical at himself; you see, it wasn't him on the screen at all. He used to call him, like Chaplin, the Little Fellow. He'd watch it and he'd say "No, the little fellow" — even though it was funny — "wouldn't do that." Because there was a great deal of pathos, and sweetness, so he wouldn't let him do anything a little risqué or too cruel.... He'd laugh, and he'd cry at himself.

—Kelly, interviewed for *Film Fan Monthly*, Mar 1971

I had a bedside scene with poor little Miss [Mia] Farrow [in *Rosemary's Baby* (1968, Roman Polanski)]. She was black and blue after the witches' coven had pushed her, shoved her, kicked her, shook her, pinned her onto the bed at least twenty times [for the rape by the devil]. No nonsense either. She never used a double. I touched her forehead and felt a high fever. I said to them, "You'd better get this girl to a doctor," but she kept right on working.

—Kelly, interviewed for *Look*, 25 June 1968

Kay KENDALL [1927-1959]

Born: Justine McCarthy in Withernsea, England. Work in variety preceded her film debut in Fiddler's Three (1944, Harry Watt). Married to Rex Harrison in 1957, she appeared with him in both The Constant Husband (1955, Sidney Gilliat) and The Reluctant Debutante (1958, Vincente Minnelli):

I am sick, sick, sick and tired of those frothy comedies. It is tremendously hard work, and no one outside the acting profession appreciates it. The public thinks you're having a joyous time. It really is desperately difficult being light and gay at 9:00 on a Monday morning in a cold film studio. And when you've acted your heart out, people come up and say, "It's simply you, darling."

I mean, really, I don't see the point in worrying oneself to a standstill, and people turn round and say, "Darling, what gorgeous fun."

It isn't fun, believe me. Remember that scene in *The Reluctant Debutante* when I tripped down the stairs?

I told Vincente Minnelli, the director, a dear sweet man, that I couldn't do it. It was much too difficult.

I was almost in tears with frustration and anger trying to get it right. Ten times I did it. Ten times. Nothing very gay about it, is there?

—Kendall, interviewed by Peter Evans for *The Daily Express*, 16 Jan 1959

Deborah KERR [1921-]

Born: Deborah Kerr-Trimmer in Helensburgh, Scotland. Studies at The Hicks-Smale Drama School in Bristol and work with Sadler's Wells, with whom she made her stage debut in the corps de ballet in 1938, and work in repertory theater preceded her film debut in a bit part in Contraband (1940, Michael Powell). She made her U.S. debut opposite Clark Gable in The Hucksters (1947, Jack Conway); in 1949, she played Evelyn Boult opposite Spencer Tracy in George Cukor's Edward My Son:

I'm fond of character acting, and although this part was not too large, it had all the benefits of a big part, because I always came in at the right psychological time....

I tremendously enjoyed working with Spencer Tracy. He deliberately tried to play down his part so that Evelyn's role would be sharper.

—Kerr, in *The Saturday Evening Post*, 5 Nov 1949

Before we arrived in Africa preparations for making [*King Solomon's Mines* (1950)] had gone on for more than a year. Our directors, Compton Bennett and Andrew Marton, and our cameraman, Robert Surtees, had made a 45,000 mile trip to pick their locations.

The itinerary they decided on was to keep us in Africa for 5 months, taking us sometimes by plane or by boat, more often by truck, oxen-pulled wagons, horses or even by foot to the remote, fascinating lands of the Belgian Congo, Ruanda-Urundi, Kenya, and Tanganyika....

Filming on the exposed plateau at the top of [Murchison Falls] was like acting on a gigantic hot-plate. The temperature soared to 120 degrees at midday. As our boys held palm leaves over our aching heads they kept muttering in Swahili, "Bad land, very bad land." It was an understatement.

—Kerr, in *The Star*, 1-4 Jan 1951

I thought I'd got such a hell of a nerve to think that maybe I could do Karen [Holmes in *From Here to Eternity* (1953, Fred Zinnemann)]. But with Zinnemann the guidelines were right. The whole movie was a coming together of parts and personalities that together had a magic. [Frank] Sinatra's emotional life was linked up with the playing of the thing, and he was a bit on the down. His voice had left him, and he went down on bended knees to get the part. But he was born to play it. And when I watched Monty Clift...I used to feel that the day when Prewitt is shot, Monty is going to die. I'm going to feel that he's really dead. The intensity of the way that boy lived that whole part was hair-raising. He tortured himself. He suffered so.

—Kerr, interviewed by Ronald Hayman for *The Times*, 2 Sept 1972

[For Karen,] I studied voice for three months to get rid of my English accent. I changed my hair to blonde. I knew I could be sexy if I had to.

—Kerr, interviewed by Sheilah Graham for *The New York Daily Mirror*, 8 Nov 1953

[The beach scene with Burt Lancaster in *From Here to Eternity*] was just a theater thing. We worked out every move, every gesture, every kiss. It was rehearsed and rehearsed....

—Kerr, interviewed by May Mann for *The New York Herald Tribune*, 6 Mar 1956

It was Yul [Brynner] who was the solid inspiration behind the movie [*The King and I* (1956, Walter Lang)]; he knew and loved every line of the story and every note of the music, and that it came out so well was due to his insistence that this and that be done the way *he* wanted it. He could be difficult, but only because he knew he was right.

—Kerr, interviewed by Eric Braun for *Deborah Kerr* (London: W.H. Allen, 1977)

I suppose the part nearest me is Laura Reynolds in *Tea and Sympathy* [1956, Vincente Minnelli]. Of course [playwright and screenwriter] Bob Anderson didn't know that, but he wrote Laura Reynolds and Laura Reynolds happened to be me. It was the coming together of a part and an actress — the same attitude to life, a certain shyness in life, a deep compassion for people who are being persecuted for anything.

—Kerr, interviewed by Louise Sweeney for *The Christian Science Monitor*, 17 Oct 1978

The perfect person for the part [of Mr. Allison opposite my Sister Angela in *Heaven Knows, Mr. Allison* (1957, John Huston)] was Bob Mitchum, because there's a sensitivity that belies the rugged exterior, so he was able to personify the marine with this undercurrent that could make their relationship believable. They were two human beings in a perilous situation, who needed each other to exist; they needed each other's lives, and there was never any question of its being a sexual relationship. His darling, puzzled face: "But you're a woman — don't you...?" up against her absolute purity: "No, I'm married to Christ."

John's an incredible director, and so talented in many, many directions. Let's face it, he's one of the best *actors* around. Having now done three films with him [also *The Night of the Iguana* (1964) and *Casino Royale* (1967)] I say, when I get stuck, "You do it, John" and he does it impeccably, and I just mimic him in doing it.

—Kerr, interviewed by Eric Braun for *Deborah Kerr* (London: W.H. Allen, 1977)

[Cary Grant had] an eye for detail in every aspect of the movie being made, not just *his* particular part. I remember very well in the scene in *An Affair to Remember* [1957] when the ship is docking in New York and Nickie and Terry are ostentatiously keeping apart at the ship's rails, how he spotted one of the extras resting her bright red beauty-case on the rails. He at once had the case removed because, in color, on the screen, everyone's eye would automatically jump to the red case and be distracted from what was going on between the principal artists. *I* would never have thought of that — nor did anyone else — and I have never forgotten it, and in subsequent movies I have always watched out for the color RED. It's a small thing, I know, but I think it illustrates his utter concentration on detail. He was not only the king of the 'double-take', but a superb 'ad libber'. In fact, a couple of scenes in *An Affair to Remember* we just ad-libbed (mainly because either he or I had forgotten the line we were supposed to say) and our director, dear Leo McCarey, kept them in the finished product. [Kerr also co-starred with Grant in *Dream Wife*

(1953, Sidney Sheldon) and *The Grass is Greener* (1960, Stanley Donen).]

—Kerr, in a letter to Lionel Godfrey; repr. in *Cary Grant* (New York: St. Martin's Press, 1981)

[Sybil Railton-Bell], the girl I play [in *Separate Tables* (1958, Delbert Mann)] has lived for many years in a state of negativeness. I have to be careful when I play the scenes in which she reaches out for something more. I'm sure any kind of bursting forth would not be believable. It has to be very tentative, indistinct. At the end, of course, you're still not quite sure about where her experiences have left her.

—Kerr, interviewed by Richard Dyer MacCann for *The Christian Science Monitor*, 3 June 1958

I only made one movie with Jack [Clayton], *The Innocents* [1962], but we're just on the same wavelength. I used to say, "I'm skating on thin ice here. You tell me. This woman, is she quite mad or perfectly sane? Do those things really exist or are they in her mind?" The way he governed me was marvelous. I was his instrument. Which is the way I like it to be. I want to be the jelly in the mold. You're safe within the realm of what you want to do. You feel that the inner you is being used without you having to be too aware of yourself.

[Fred Zinnemann, on *From Here to Eternity* and *The Sundowners* (1960)] really brings out of me — in a completely different way — an awful lot that perhaps I'd never have the courage to lay bare, to open up. He just knows how to get you to do it, to bring out some inner quality. I always like to cut out words if I possibly can. Why do I have to say anything? You know, just look at someone and it says it....

—Kerr, interviewed by Ronald Hayman for *The Times*, 2 Sept 1972

I climbed into my dress and "wimple" and hat and gloves, etc. [for Hannah in *The Night of the Iguana* (1964)] — and John [Huston] and Ray Stark came to have a look. Ray felt it looked too elegant. And John felt it was not quite humorous enough.... After a great deal of hemming and hawing, it was decided to use it as it is. We haven't any time to change it really. And I would rather not. I don't want her to be a ludicrous figure, and I feel that although she is broke, her original taste is that of a quite good artist — individual and with a style of her own.

—Kerr, in her *Night of the Iguana* diary; publ. in *Esquire*, May 1964

[Elia Kazan on *The Arrangement* (1969)] has a kind of incredible instinct with people. He's so in sympathy with all the fears and frights of actors, through having done it himself. And he's got a personal magic that you have certain moments of feeling, "Maybe I should do that?" and he'll pull it right out of you if it's right, and yet if it's not right he'll never hurt you or embarrass you or make you feel a fool. [Kerr had previously worked with Kazan on the stage in *Tea and Sympathy*.]

—Kerr, interviewed by Ronald Hayman for *The Times*, 2 Sept 1972

[For Helen Graham in *The Assam Garden* (1986, Mary McMurray)] I wanted to look not in the least like me or the character I've played so many times. People always expect me to be the same — pretty-pretty, charming, and gentle....

I really got caught up in her incredible loneliness. There's something so vulnerable about her that I found it just heartbreaking.

—Kerr, interviewed by Marybeth Kerrigan for *Women's Wear Daily*, 11 Aug 1986

Ben KINGSLEY [1943-]

Born: Krishna Bhanji in Snainton, England. A member of The Royal Shakespeare Co. (from 1967), he made only one film — Fear Is the Key (1973, Michael Tuchner) — before playing the title role of Gandhi (1982, Richard Attenborough):

Q. What did you keep in mind in creating your portrayal of Gandhi?

A. I think what was very important was that the character, and therefore the man, had the capacity to bring out the best in people, and he made that the center of his life's work. It sounds like a very simple task. But it's an incredible gift to have political meetings that will decide the destiny of millions of people, and still to think, "Well, I'm going to bring out the best in this person and appeal to that in him which is intrinsically good." It's a marvelous way of translating one's intelligence into action, and Gandhi-ji had a staggering intelligence. He persuaded people that they were better than the petty encumbrances that cluttered their lives.

I also used various technical exercises. I did a lot of yoga, and I did lose a lot of weight. That helped me present the physical silhouette. And although it did worry my wife because she thought I was being a bit reckless, when I was doing the fasting scene, I actually refused to eat until those scenes were in the can. If you've done your preparation, the very act of fasting does release something in your brain that somehow does something to your consciousness. This isn't mystical; it's physiological. That helped me to know what it was like to maintain the character in that particular state of heat and pandemonium.

—Kingsley, interviewed by Christopher Connelly for *Rolling Stone*, 17 Mar 1983

I decided that unless I could spin, I would be missing an essential ingredient of that man's rhythm and character. It seemed to me such a central metaphor for Gandhi.

So I took on the rather arduous task of learning to spin, and initially it was pretty disastrous. But it got better, and, finally, that is me spinning in the film.... That skill involves a certain kind of concentration and has with it a certain rhythm.

That is essentially Indian; and very Gandhian.

—Kingsley, interviewed by Lewis Archibald for *The Aquarian Weekly*, 8-15 Dec 1982

[Meyer Lansky in *Bugsy* (1991, Barry Levinson)] was a patriarch in the best Judaic tradition. He was only a small step away from Henry Kissinger in terms of diplomatic panache and accuracy.

—Kingsley, interviewed by Sean Elder for *Entertainment Weekly*, 13 Dec 1991

Kevin KLINE [1947-]

Born: St. Louis, Missouri. After studies at The Juilliard School in New York City, he became a founding member of John Houseman's The Acting Company; work on and off Broadway and on TV preceded his film debut as Nathan in Sophie's Choice (1982, Alan J. Pakula):

I always thought of Nathan...as being a petty theatrical character.... Alan Pakula had seen me in *Pirates* [*of Penzance*] on stage before casting me, and it was that largeness that he wanted. This made it tricky for my film debut — I was afraid my performance would be too broad. But Alan encouraged me; he wanted it large. *The Big Chill* [1983, Lawrence Kasdan] was the first time I really explored the movie notion of "Doing Nothing" — which isn't quite true either....

What really amazed me after years in the theater is that film is a hundred times more technical, by virtue of the fact that you're doing little tiny pieces of scenes several times. You always have to hit a certain mark, and sometimes you're playing a whole scene to a little white X scrawled up near the camera. And always watching your gestures to keep the continuity straight from one shot to the next. Eating scenes are the worst — they're hell on matching, in between shots you're always thinking, "Was I eating the peas or the mashed potatoes?" On *The Big Chill*, for the dinner sequences there were eight people eating and talking and reacting to each other, and 70 ways to shoot it. So for continuity's sake, Larry Kasdan kept telling us, "I want you all to be very self-conscious of what you're doing." Which is the opposite of what actors usually are. You're certainly not concentrating on motivation at this point; it's, "Am I supposed to lift my glass to here, or out there?"

With *Silverado* [1985, Lawrence Kasdan], there was something so absurd about the idea of me playing a cowboy that I couldn't resist it. And I was intrigued by the character, this ambivalent sort of guy surrounded by people who were total absolutes of good and evil. He anticipates 20th-century man, in a way, and it was a challenge to play him as a modern man who was still of his own time....

But what most appealed to me about *Silverado* was the chance to work with Larry again. I like his taste, and I love the way he thinks about acting and filmmaking. Larry's very wise, and very funny, and I trust him. And that's from an actor who hasn't seen the final cut yet.

—Kline, interviewed by Stephen Harvey for *Film Comment*, Aug 1985

I remember someone once told me, "You can't make faces on film, that's for the stage." In the first scene we filmed for [*A Fish Called Wanda* (1988, Charles Crichton)], I pulled more faces than in any movie up to this point. [Screenwriter and co-star] John [Cleese] said, "I want this performance to make Dennis Hopper's acting in *Blue Velvet* look restrained."

—Kline, interviewed by Barry Walters for *The Village Voice*, 28 June 1988

Alexander KNOX [1907-]

Born: Strathroy, Ontario, Canada. Studies at The University of Western Ontario and work on the stage (from 1929) in Boston and London preceded his film debut in a small part in the British film, The Ringer (1932, Walter Forde). In 1944, he played U.S. President Woodrow Wilson in Henry King's Wilson:

A pianist has to develop manual dexterity into a technique, and he has to use this technique creatively to interpret his composer. An actor has to mimic a live man and then employ his mimicry to interpret the man's moods, motives and character.

In his function as mimic the actor must not only select the mannerisms which seem most significant in the man he is playing, he must also select the mannerisms which he as an actor is best fitted to bring to life in the frame of the author's conception of the man. An actor seems to me to be good if he can exercise these functions intelligently and subtly so that the audience is not conscious of the join — is encouraged, that is, to suspend disbelief and finally to accept the enactment as a human being. Both of these functions of the actor become more difficult as the character he is playing becomes more complex, less ordinary, farther from the normal experience of audiences....

Since playing Wilson, I have been asked by many people for opinions on the man and various events of his life. This brings up another difficulty. The actor has to play the character the author creates, not necessarily the character he himself conceives. Even among his intimate friends I have met no two people whose opinions about Wilson were identical — much less their emotional attitudes toward him. When the chance to play Wilson was given me I was very glad that I had done most of the essential reading about him many years before. It seemed important to me to play Lamar Trotti's Wilson and not my Wilson. Mr. Trotti's Wilson was a definite imaginative creation, with a definite dramatic impact, and it was possible to select from the vague Wilson background in my mind the facets and quirks which seemed to me to fit Mr. Trotti's conception. Whenever there was any doubt in my mind, it was easy to refer to Ray Stannard Baker's biography, but, right or wrong, I felt it wiser not to do too much study of the source materials.

—Knox, in *Hollywood Quarterly*, Vol 1, #1, 1945

Kris KRISTOFFERSON

[1937-]

Born: Brownsville, Texas. A Rhodes scholar with a Ph.D. in English literature from Pomona College, a singer/songwriter and four-time winner of the Atlantic Monthly award for short stories, he made his film debut in Cisco Pike (1972, Bill Norton):

[Bill Norton] was so preoccupied with just getting things done, getting that exposed film in the can, that he had no time at all for the cast. Which I thought was a big mistake, a case of misjudgment of priorities that in the end created an awful lot of conflict he could have easily avoided.

His idea of keeping things moving meant a policy of total inflexibility toward the actors. He wanted no ad libbing, no embellishing of parts, no extraneous business, just what was in the script. Well, okay, that was his prerogative, he was the director and the writer and he obviously knew what he wanted. But at the same time it was one of those scripts that was not really what you'd call sacred. I mean there were no long set speeches or anything, just small talk and conversations, the sort of thing where the actual words meant a lot less than the meaning conveyed.

And to be rigid about something like that and to deny the actors the chance to kind of tailor their words and their actions to themselves, was stifling to the interpretive thing that every actor goes through. It didn't make sense. There were a lot of strong, experienced actors in the cast [Gene Hackman and Karen Black, among others], people with strong personalities and the ability to project them. Norton should have tried to make use of them, take advantage of what they as individuals had to offer rather than trying to slot them into some preconceived mold.

—Kristofferson, interviewed by Bill Gray for *Impact*, Summer 1972

I was scared to death I couldn't play a guy that nice [in *Alice Doesn't Live Here Anymore* (1974, Martin Scorsese)]. Clark Gable could have done it.... I had terrible trouble with that scene at the end, in the restaurant — did it over and over again....

I didn't belong standing up in front of a bunch of people, telling some woman [Ellen Burstyn as Alice] I loved her. It was very embarrassing.

—Kristofferson, interviewed by Janet Maslin for *The New York Times*, 24 Aug 1977

I decided Hub [in *Rollover* (1981, Alan J. Pakula)] was a Kennedyesque kind of guy — effective, good at what he does, enjoying the game. Even when his rivals outplay him — which isn't often — he admires their moves. After reading the literature Jane [Fonda] gave me on banking and gamesmanship, I had dinner with several high-powered investment bankers, just to get the rhythm of the language.

I discovered that they have great peripheral hearing. They can carry on a conversation with you, overhear another one, and still answer you without breaking the flow. It's a kind of 360 degree awareness.

—Kristofferson, interviewed for *Films*, Aug 1982

L

Diane LADD [1939-]

Born: Diane Ladnier in Meridian, Mississippi; mother of Laura Dern. Work as a singer and as a Copa Girl and studies with Frank Corsaro at the Actors Studio in N.Y., and work on the N.Y. stage (from 1959) and on tour preceded her film debut in The Wild Angels (1966, Roger Corman). In 1974, she played Flo in Martin Scorsese's Alice Doesn't Live Here Anymore:

I never want to see another waitress uniform, but that doesn't mean I didn't love that character when I was playing her. When I hear people describe her as a slatternly flirt, I get hopping mad. Flo never flirted. She handled people. She made the customers want to come back. She made them feel at home. When they got out of hand, she put them in their place. She was trapped with a husband who wasn't communicative, and she was terribly tough and lonely, but she was never unfaithful. She was a good broad.

—Ladd, interviewed by Rex Reed for *The New York Sunday News*, 21 Sept 1975

Flo [is]...real because she's holding it together the best way she can — just like the rest of us. She has a kid with buck teeth as she says. And she also has a job and she has to keep her customers coming back and tipping her so she can live. So what does she use? What do we all use? *Humor...!*

When I first talked about doing the film, I told Marty I didn't want to play her as a cliché. He said: "Don't worry — this is *real.*" And he *let* me do it! He let me do what he felt I was capable of doing. So many other times, when I was working under other directors in other projects, I felt just like a doctor. A doctor with one arm tied behind his back!

They tie one arm behind your back and say, "Alright, go out there and operate!" You can't do that — as a doctor or as an actress. And Marty untied my other arm.

—Ladd, interviewed by Bill Royce for *Rona Barrett's Hollywood* (undated) in the files of The Lincoln Center Library for the Performing Arts

Christine LAHTI [1950-]

Born: Birmingham, Michigan. Studies at The University of Michigan (Ann Arbor) and at Florida State University, with Uta Hagen at The Herbert Berghof Studio and with William Esper at The Neighborhood Playhouse in N.Y., work off-Broadway, in commercials, on TV and Broadway preceded her film debut in ...And Justice for All (1979, Norman Jewison). In 1984, she played Hazel in Jonathan Demme's Swing Shift:

Hazel represents the easiest kind of woman for me to play: tough talking on the outside, vulnerable underneath.

—Lahti, interviewed by Diana Maychick for *The New York Post*, 25 Apr 1984

I think [Sylvie in *Housekeeping* (1987, Bill Forsyth) is] touched, really, by the muses. I think she has psychic ability; she has the innocence and tremendous curiosity of a child, a complete lack of vanity or self-consciousness. And I also loved the darker side of her. I think she's a tremendously complex character. I think she's bruised emotionally, suffered so much loss and abandonment in her life that she's kind of closed emotionally.

—Lahti, interviewed by Lawrence Van Gelder for *The New York Times*, 27 Nov 1987

Bill Forsyth gave us a complete space with which to do our work [on *Housekeeping*]. He was very collaborative though he didn't know a lot about technique or the craft. But he was a joy to work with. He didn't impose his ideas on mine. He didn't stifle any of my impulses.... It's the first film I've done where the work I did is on the screen in its entirety in terms of major colors of the character — the major transitions. It's all up there and it's such a joy to see. Every other film I've done things have been cut out *and* from my point of view, important things. No one else may sense that anything is missing but *I* know in terms of the character's arc.

—Lahti, interviewed by David Galligan for *Drama-Logue*, 28 Jan-3 Feb 1988

When I first saw the character of Annie [Pope in *Running on Empty* (1988, Sidney Lumet)] I thought, "I could do this in my sleep." And yet, it turned out to be an incredible challenge. I've done so many character parts where I get to be flamboyant or quirky, where I use charm. In a way, that's much easier. This time I had to go really deep, and yet keep it very simple.

—Lahti, interviewed by Katherine Dieckmann for *The Village Voice*, 13 Sept 1988

Veronica LAKE [1919-1973]

Born: Constance Ockelman in Brooklyn, N.Y. Studies at The Bliss Hayden School of Acting preceded her film debut in Sorority House (1939, John Farrow). In 1941, she played The Girl opposite Joel McCrea as John L. Sullivan in Preston Sturges' Sullivan's Travels:

Preston quickly learned a few things about me. The most important thing was that I always gave a terribly stiff reading of lines that I'd learned long in advance of the day's shooting. I've always been a quick learn. It's easy for me to pick up patter of any kind.

The first day's shooting found me going through a rigid and doltish acting job. It was terrible. I'd studied my lines over and over and knew them cold. And that was the problem.

Preston talked to me about it and allowed me to try a few days of looking at my lines just before shooting the scene. That kind of thing would be sacrilege for a stage actress — and an impossibility. But it works for me. I'd look at the script while the technicians were setting up and go out and do them. It worked much better.

"Don't ever walk on my set knowing anything about your lines or scenes," Preston told me after the first day under the new system. I didn't for the rest of the film and for most of the other films I worked in after *Sullivan's Travels*. The word got around I was better without advance preparation and most directors accepted that and worked with it....

René [Clair] was terribly nice to me despite his reluctance to use me in [*I Married a Witch* (1942)]. And he was certainly a fine director. He had everything — timing, viewpoint, appreciation of the subtle things that made good comedy....

And I hated Fredric March.

I don't believe there is an actor for whom I harbor such deep dislike as Fredric March. It's strictly personal. We all know and recognize what a fine and distinguished actor he is. But working with him gave me the feeling of being a captive in a Charles Addams tower.

He gave me a terrible time.... I'm sure that despite what René thought, March considered me a brainless little blonde sexpot, void of any acting ability and not likely to acquire any. He treated me like dirt under his talented feet....

—Lake, in her (with Donald Bain) *Veronica: The Autobiography of Veronica Lake* (New York: Citadel Press, 1971)

Hedy LAMARR [1914-]

Born: Hedwig Kiesler in Vienna, Austria. Studies at Max Reinhardt's drama school in Berlin preceded her film debut in Geld auf der Strasse (1930, Georg Jacoby). Her first American film was Algiers (1938, John Cromwell); in 1940, she played opposite Clark Gable in King Vidor's Comrade X:

The first day I started to work [on *Comrade X*], I was more afraid than usual. I suddenly realized I was playing opposite the Great Gable, and it froze me. In *Boom Town* [1940, Jack Conway], I did not have a big part and was not often on the sets; I did not have much responsibility. But this *Comrade X* was different. In this, it was Clark and myself!

He laughed at me for worrying and accused me of thinking motion pictures the most important thing in the world. He kidded me, saying, "They are not as important as all that, sister. Relax. Motion pictures will be here long after you and I are both gone." He said, "Look, baby, this is a picnic, a clambake." I did not know what he meant by a clambake, but I did know I was having fun for the first time since I had been in pictures. I did know that for the first time I relaxed when I worked....

He helped me so much by making suggestions entirely for my benefit. During the filming of a love scene that was to be shot as a large close-up of the two of us, I was supposed to lean over and kiss him quickly on the lips. It seemed rather awkward for me to do. So Clark suggested that he stay to one side, almost out of the close-up, and that I first reach over my hand and touch his cheek, then slowly draw his face to mine for the kiss. That approach was easier and gave me more confidence. It also gave me the close-up.

—Lamarr, interviewed by Gladys Hall for *Modern Screen*, Feb 1941

When Director Victor Fleming told me I was to play Dolores [in *Tortilla Flat* (1942)], I was delighted. Dolores is a completely natural girl, with no fancy trimmings. I could concentrate on creating a character without bothering how I should look for the best camera angles. I knew what I was up against. It was a real test to work with fine actors like Spencer Tracy, John Garfield, Frank Morgan and Akim Tamiroff....

Dolores is a simple little girl who worked in the Salinas bean fields before coming to Monterey to get a job in the fish cannery at $18. a week. It took me four minutes to get ready to play Dolores. A little brown make-up rubbed on, a comb run through my hair, put on a white cotton blouse, a light wool blue skirt and red sandals, and I could concentrate on acting my role without worrying about glamour.

I worked hard playing Dolores. You cannot believe how hard it is to be active in a tight fitting gown unless you have been in a straight jacket. This time, I did not have to give a thought about mussing my hair or my costume. I could let myself go, and did. Maybe I was too enthusiastic. In a scene where I threaten Garfield with a pair of scissors, they slipped from my hands and it was a close shave for Garfield. Director Fleming thought this was excellent.

"Don't put Garfield in the hospital, but don't pull any punches, Hedy," he said. "Dolores wouldn't."

—Lamarr, interviewed for the press packet for *Tortilla Flat* (MGM, 1942)

Dorothy LAMOUR [1914-]

Born: Mary Slaton in New Orleans. Miss New Orleans of 1931, she made her film debut in The Jungle Princess (1936, William Thiele). From 1940, she co-starred with Bob Hope and Bing Crosby in six Road movies:

I had always been very strict with myself about learning my lines. The night before we started *Road to Singapore* [1940], I naively studied my script like crazy. That was my first mistake. When I arrived on the set, director Victor Schertzinger was already shooting a scene with the two fellows alone. As I sat and watched, I realized that *nothing* in their dialogue sounded familiar, not even vaguely like the script I'd read. Perhaps there had been some rewrites?

At last it was time for my first scene, a three-shot with me standing between Bob and Bing. As soon as the assistant director called "Action!" ad-libs started flying every which way. I kept waiting for a cue that never seemed to come....

After the first few days, I decided it was ridiculous to waste time learning the script. I would read over the next day's work only to get the idea of what was happening. What I really needed was a good night's sleep to be in good shape for the next morning's ad-libs. This method provided some very interesting results on the screen.

—Lamour, in her (with Dick McInnes) *My Side of the Road* (Englewood Cliffs, N.J.: Prentice-Hall, 1980)

Burt LANCASTER [1913-]

Born: New York City. Vaudeville and circus work in an acrobatic act (ended by injury) and dramatic work on Broadway preceded his film debut in The Killers (1946, Robert Siodmak):

I've never had a part, including Swede in *The Killers*, that I was honestly crazy to do — except one. That part was in *All My Sons* [1948, Irving Reis]. It was a departure from the poker-faced, expressionless characters I'd done before. The part had great emotional and intellectual depth.

—Lancaster, in *Motion Picture Story Magazine*, Dec 1949

We had the good fortune to work under Danny Mann [on *Come Back, Little Sheba* (1952)], the same director who had staged the play on Broadway. It was Danny's first motion picture and my first straight drama since *All My Sons*...so we both approached *Sheba* with considerable caution....

My role as Doc gives me the best opportunity to act I've ever had. But, you know, I didn't even want to look at the script when Mr. [Hal] Wallis asked me to read it. I had been playing rough-and-tumble action roles for so long that I couldn't imagine myself as a disillusioned ex-alcoholic married to a pitiful frump [Shirley Booth]....

[Shirley is] an inspiration. This was her first picture and we expected her to be on edge, but she was so calm that she reassured all of us. She doesn't just do the stage role in front of a camera. She worked hard to adapt the part to the motion picture screen, which is anything but easy when you've grown to play a character in a certain way over months of constant association.

—Lancaster, interviewed by William H. Brownell, Jr. for *The New York Times*, 18 Jan 1953

Without exception, Monty Clift is the hardest-working actor I've ever known — perhaps the hardest worker in the business. Let me give you an example. When he was signed for *From Here to Eternity* [1953, Fred Zinnemann], he went down to see the author, James Jones, in Illinois months before we were ready to shoot. He spent days with Jones, talking about the character of Prewitt, trying to fix him in his mind. That kind of sincerity of purpose is a rarity out here. Nuts, it's a rarity anywhere.

Monty had to learn to play the bugle for *Eternity* — he studied for weeks. He had to learn to box — he worked out three months with an ex-pug named Callahan....

—Lancaster, interviewed by Richard Gehman for *Photoplay Magazine*, Mar 1957

Inferior people give [Montgomery Clift] a pain in the neck. He's always striving to get that extra dimension that gives real class into his roles. He's always out for perfection. He understands, for example, that a guy like [Clark] Gable can walk through a scene and say, "Hello baby," and get what he's saying across. He understands all that. But he wants to get complete believability into his character — realism. He is fanatically devoted to this. And he knows something that few actors know — that no actor is better than his material. That's why he will question the writing of a scene; and he won't settle for getting over only half of what's possible. He wants a scene to come fully to life. He firmly believes in everything he does.

Now three or four guys like that can drive a director out of his mind; but the real good director encourages this kind of work. Too many people in Hollywood say, "We're working on a budget; time's the element; let's get it in the can." Get what in the can? They spend six months working on a script; then the actors are to walk in and run through it and shoot it? Monty wants to find out what it's all about; see it evolve; give it a chance to grow. Few directors take that kind of trouble. Many directors, when questioned by an actor, feel they're losing control. Zinnemann encourages it.

Monty is delightful to work with. He doesn't care at all about a camera angle. In fact, if the camera's on him and he thinks it should be on you in a scene, he'll say so. He's interested in the scene as a whole.

—Lancaster, interviewed by Hedda Hopper for an article on Montgomery Clift, 9 August 1953; manuscript in the files of The Academy of Motion Picture Arts and Sciences Library

[Sandy Mackendrick] couldn't make up his mind. He'd set up shots on the stage for a scene [in *The Sweet Smell of Success* (1957)] that would play six minutes. There would be thirty-five camera moves on a dolly. The whole floor was taped. We had to hit marks like crazy. The camera moved continuously — into closeups, pulling back to here, shooting over to this person. Move in here, turn. We rehearsed all day, until 4:00 in the afternoon, just to get the technical part down. The head grip and the rest of the crew were sweating, knowing that if they missed one mark, the shot would be ruined.

But we did it. Clicked it all off. Sandy called: "Cut. Print." Then he'd stop, waiting. I'd say: "Something the matter, Sandy?" "No. It went fine. You all did it fine. Only...let's do one more." So we went through it again. Again, fine. Cut. I was delighted. Six minutes of film. A good day's work. And done in a most interesting style. But he still wouldn't be satisfied. He'd shake his head and say: "I don't like it. We've got to change it. Change everything."

—Lancaster, interviewed by Dick Lachte for *The Los Angeles Free Press*, 8 Dec 1972

Well, we got through *Sweet Smell* somehow. But when it came to the [George Bernard] Shaw film [*The Devil's Disciple* (1959)], which my company [also] produced, we realized there might be difficulties. We only had a certain amount of money and 48 days to shoot the whole thing. So we asked Sandy whether he could do it in the time. He insisted that he could, and we went ahead. At the end of the first week, we ended up with 2 days of film. It was impossible to continue like that. Let me add that what he shot turned out to be the best part of the movie, because Sandy was a very brilliant man. But we hadn't the time or the money for him. [He was replaced by Guy Hamilton.]

—Lancaster, interviewed by Derek Malcolm for *The Guardian*, 4 Aug 1972

[Richard Brooks] sent me the script [of *Elmer Gantry* (1960)]. I didn't care for it. It was terribly long, followed the book in detail. I phoned him and we got into a violent argument about it. I told him: "If you really want to do this, I'm with you. But don't start the movie with me as a 20-year-old kid in a seminary. That's not gonna play. Let's start the film later on." He gulped. For a while he wouldn't talk to me. Then his agent called and we went back together. Dick said: "I hear you play golf a lot." I told him that was correct. "Well, there's no time for that. No more golf. Instead, you come over to the studio every day and work with me on this script."

For seven months we did that. But everything — that, and the preparation — was worth it. It was a labor of love.

At the outset [of *The Young Savages* (1961), John Frankenheimer and I] had some problems. I felt his approach to his work did not get the best results because of his attitude. He was tough and arrogant and terribly demanding on the set, sometimes to his own detriment. After we settled our personal problems, we got along great, became great friends. I did five movies with him. [The four others were: *Birdman of Alcatraz* (1962), *Seven Days in May* (1964), *The Train* (1965) and *The Gypsy Moths* (1969).]

—Lancaster, interviewed by Dick Lachte for *The Los Angeles Free Press*, 8 Dec 1972

[As Ernst Jannings in *Judgment at Nuremberg* (1961, Stanley Kramer)] I am almost a symbol of the dilemma in Germany during the Nazi period. I am the man of good intentions who did things of which he did not approve. I am a man who once had a reputation for integrity and honesty; a concern for the law. But I am cynical about this trial. I doubt the ability of the judge [Spencer Tracy]. I am a man who has, in a sense, retreated into another world. At the same time I must not be a man in a cataleptic state. I must become involved in this trial.

—Lancaster, interviewed by Murray Schumach for *The New York Times*, 30 Apr 1961

The Swimmer [1968] is certainly one of my favorites. It's a John Cheever story and there was the very difficult problem of translating a literary work to the screen. Cheever speaks in the short story of how a man is walking through a lane and he smells a fire, it's an autumn fire; he describes it as the smell of autumn in the air. Well, that kind of thing in writing is lovely, especially in Cheever's phrases, but when you try to get this quality onto film, it requires some kind of approach. I'll say that I don't think Frank Perry was able to do this, and I don't know that any other director would have been. But you certainly need someone like a Fellini or a Truffaut, or someone with that kind of imagination to let the camera also tell your story. Film has its own particular life — regardless of what's actually going on in a film. And it needed some kind of strange, weird approach to capture the audience and make them realize that, in a way, they were not looking at anything real. In talking about the script we would say, "I don't know why two men in white coats don't come take this guy away." It should have been obvious that this man was going through something that was not quite real; it was all part of his imagination. But it was played in a realistic sense — so when you come to the end of that film, instead of being sympathetic and heartbroken for the man, you were surprised and shocked.

—Lancaster, interviewed at Judith Crist's Tarrytown seminar, 17-19 Oct 1975; repr. in *Take 22*, co-ed. by Judith Crist and Shirley Sealy (New York: Viking Press, 1984)

[In *Atlantic City* (1980, Louis Malle)] I'm a guy who used to be a bodyguard for a Mafia don. I turned yellow in a showdown, but they like me and they don't rub me out. Instead they set me up in a little barber shop here in Atlantic City and I handle some numbers action.

—Lancaster, interviewed by Tom Buckley for *The New York Times*, 7 Dec 1979

Elsa LANCHESTER [1902-1986]

Born: Lewisham, London, England. Studies with Isadora Duncan, work in music hall and on the London stage and in one amateur film preceded her professional film debut in One of the Best (1927, T. Hayes Hunter). She was married to Charles Laughton and appeared opposite him on both stage and screen; the second of their seven films together was The Private Life of Henry VIII (1933, Alexander Korda):

At first the film was to be about Henry VIII and Anne of Cleves. All the comedy situations appeared to be in relation to that queen and I was to play the part. I did play Anne of Cleves, but another wife came in, then another, as it became obvious that what the public knew about Henry VIII was that he had a lot of wives, and that was what they wanted to see....

Charles took a great deal of trouble to probe the period and character of Henry VIII before starting work, and while doing this he persuaded and nattered at anyone connected with the film, whom he had any contact with, to do the same. I remember him almost dragging Korda from his desk down to Hampton Court to see the architecture and pictures.... Charles read every possible book he could get on the subject, and saw innumerable paintings of Henry VIII. Gradually the character began to soak in. One day he would think he had the walk, the next day he would lose it then he would get a look in the eye and let that stew for a few days. After about a week's shooting on the picture I should say he found himself getting into the part. I myself was of course soaking up Anne of Cleves in my little way on the side. Charles and I are like a couple of sponges when we are studying; we absorb every bit of information that comes in useful, even to snatching at characteristics in our closest friends if they fit. Small mannerisms that are true to type in anyone's behavior are stored away in your mind, sometimes unconsciously, then months or years later you perhaps find yourself using this or that characteristic or expression in a new part.

—Lanchester, in her *Charles Laughton and I* (New York: Harcourt, Brace & Co., 1938)

I think James Whale felt that if this beautiful and innocent Mary Shelley could write such a horror story as *Frankenstein*, then somewhere she must have had a *fiend* within, dominating a part of her thoughts and her spirit — like ectoplasm flowing out of her to activate a monster. In this delicate little thing was an unexploded atom bomb. My playing both parts [Shelley and Frankenstein's wife in *The Bride of Frankenstein* (1935)] cemented that idea....

Apart from the discomfort of the monster makeup and all the hissing and screaming I had to do, I enjoyed working on the film. I admired Whale's directing and the waiting-for-something-to-happen atmosphere he was able to create around us. He and Jack Pierce, the makeup man, knew exactly what they wanted, so I didn't have to do many makeup tests. They had Queen Nefertiti in mind for the form and structure of the Bride's head....

A word about the screams and that hissing sound I made to show my anger and terror when rebuffing my groom. Actually, I've always been fascinated by the sounds that swans make. Regents Park in London has lots of them on the lake. Charles and I used to go and watch them very often. They're really very nasty creatures, always hissing at you. So I used the memory of that hiss.

—Lanchester, in her *Elsa Lanchester Herself* (New York: St. Martin's Press, 1983)

In *Rembrandt* [1936, Alexander Korda] our private relationship helped our acting one. Being married made it easier to act two people in sympathy, but when Charles and I came home at night we often found we had really given to the camera what we should have given to each other in our private life — like going to bed in a shop window. It was rather dangerous to our real relationship. It was a danger that we have felt before but never so strongly as in *Rembrandt*. It was as if we had mentally stripped ourselves before some other person. Very beneficial, no doubt, if you need psychoanalyzing, but I don't think we do.

Hendrickje was not such a problem for me, although not having such a wide experience as Charles it was problem enough. I represented a feminine little thing and had to be a much more fragile person than I really am. Charles had a far more difficult task in trying to show what a creative genius is, something that in the history of the screen and stage has rarely been a success — it is such an elusive and unexplainable quality in man. Charles, in trying to portray a genius, was most tentative and humble about the whole thing. But every part an actor takes should be approached humbly: if you are doing a strutting turkey you have to be humble about the strutting turkey. [Their other films together were: *Bluebottles* (1928, Ivor Montagu), *Vessel of Wrath* (aka *The Beachcombers* — 1937, Erich Pommer), *Tales of Manhattan* (1942, Julien Duvivier), *The Big Clock* (1948, John Farrow) and *Witness for the Prosecution* (1957, Billy Wilder).]

—Lanchester, in her *Charles Laughton and I* (New York: Harcourt, Brace & Co., 1938)

Martin LANDAU [1931-]

Born: Brooklyn, N.Y. Studies at the Actors Studio in N.Y. and work on stage preceded his film debut in North by Northwest (1959, Alfred Hitchcock). In 1988, he played Abe Karatz in Francis Ford Coppola's Tucker: The Man and His Dream:

I saw Abe as a loner, who sits in cafeterias in New York City, has no close friends, no family. He's a sort of seat-of-the-pants businessman who comes into contact with a Mid-western WASP [Jeff Bridges as Tucker]. The idea is there seems to be no way these guys can get together.

But Tucker's family becomes the family Abe never had, and feelings he hasn't touched in years come back, and he begins to dream again. We rehearsed for two weeks, and each day I felt him more. I sort of got a little older and a little shorter, because that's how I saw him.

—Landau, interviewed by Nina Darnton for *The New York Post*, 15 Aug 1988

Abe...loves these people. Even his own checkered past, which would have meant nothing to him in the context of his life as it was, suddenly becomes meaningful in a whole other way. He's a proud man and suddenly he's ashamed. Abe becomes a much better human being. I saw it as a kind of love story between these two very different men, between this strange couple.

—Landau, interviewed by Ian Spelling for *Starlog*, Feb 1989

Working with Francis was four months of creative joy. He gives actors a lot of room; he opened the door and let us play. I had a great creative time, and that just doesn't happen very often.

—Landau, interviewed by Kenneth Turan for *Premiere*, Sept 1988

What I had read [in the original script of *Crimes and Misdemeanors* (1989, Woody Allen)] had seemed a little too hard-edged — I mean, the man didn't do a single decent thing. He was scripted a liar, a cheat, a rich brat and a murderer. In this remote control society, it would be very easy for the audience to turn this guy off. He's a complete asshole — who wants to watch him? I told Allen that the character had to be sympathetic so that people would take the trip with him, *whoever* played the part. He hired me that day....

Its complexity and significance are an actor's dream. I've spent a lot of time playing roles that didn't really challenge me. I suppose every actor feels that way. But if you're playing a heavy, there's a certain quality to the role in action-adventure movies that isn't very demanding; you're just using a little fragment of your personality because that's all that's needed. You want roles that have dimension. And this character [Judah Rosenthal] offered me all that, as well as the opportunity to work with Woody Allen....

[Audiences] are horrified by what they see. But more importantly, a lot of people see themselves. Not that they've committed as atrocious an act, but they see those things in their own lives that they allowed to happen or things that they have done themselves that they are less than pleased with.

I wanted the audience to see themselves, and at the same time to be horrified. Any choice you make in life affects not only yourself but those around you. We've all done it in some way or another.

—Landau, interviewed by Steven Goldman for *Empire*, Aug 1990

Harry LANGDON [1884-1944]

Born: Council Bluffs, Iowa. Work backstage in an Omaha theater led to work in amateur shows and then employment at age 13 as a performer with Dr. Belcher's Kickapoo Indian Medicine Show. Work in music halls and vaudeville preceded his contract to make films for Hal Roach (on a recommendation by Harold Lloyd); before a film was released his contract was sold to Mack Sennett. There, his first release was Picking Peaches (1924, Erle C. Kenton). His most popular persona was The Little Elf:

[As The Little Elf], I must be wretched, and consequently ludicrous. When I do a part in a film, I must really suffer. In my pictures I allow myself to be a victim of Fate. But a Divine providence always carries me through.

—Langdon, in a First National press release, 15 Apr 1926

Tragedy frequently stalks behind the scenes during the making of feature comedies, more so, perhaps, than during the making of dramas, for an essential element of successful comedy is thrill, and thrills are seldom obtained without some actual physical danger....

Every man in a comedy company dreads to make thrill scenes. So often a man's life hangs on a bit of invisible wire, or his ability to conquer the instinctive fear of danger. A slip of the foot may mean actual peril to a comedian during such moments — but it is always good for a gale of glee from an audience.

During the filming of *Tramp, Tramp, Tramp* [1926, Harry Edwards], nobody in the company wanted me to hang on a fence at the edge of a steep cliff. There was no one else to do it, so I had no alternative. You can be quite sure there was not a laugh in the crowd back of the camera while this stunt was being done. The cliff dropped precipitately for several hundred yards with nothing to break the fall. When it was finished I was greatly worried about it, because there hadn't been a titter from the crew. Usually, you know, you can judge whether your stuff is funny by the reaction it gets from your impromptu audience. When I got off the fence I met nothing but blanched faces and silence....

During the filming of *The Strong Man* [1926, Frank Capra], a trick cannon exploded as I pulled the lanyard to fire the final shot of the scene. In the noise, the smoke and confusion, I didn't even know there had been an accident. When the smoke cleared away, we found that one piece of the metal cannon had grazed the back of my head, struck a musician a glancing blow in the cheek and buried itself in the wall of the stage. On the screen this scene was a scream.

The enjoyment of comedy, just like the enjoyment of tragedy, is the result of the feeling of remoteness from the situation caricatured.

—Langdon, in *Theatre Magazine*, Dec 1927

Jessica LANGE [1949-]

Born: Cloquet, Minnesota. Mime studies with Etienne DeCroux in Paris, acting classes at The Actors Studio in N.Y. and work as a model preceded her film debut in King Kong (1976, John Guillermin). In 1982, she played Frances Farmer in Graeme Clifford's Frances:

I fought Graeme although I love him dearly. On another movie, we might have a real casual, light, and friendly time of it, but not with *Frances*.... Frances took everything on as a warrior. Personally, I find that kind of combativeness too exhausting, but Frances didn't. I wish all the people so up in arms and offended by my behavior had met Frances. She tore people to pieces. I'm like a lamb compared to her.

—Lange, interviewed by Julia Cameron for *American Film*, Jan/Feb 1983

When I did *Frances*, I was delving into areas that I had never touched before. They were like wells. I'd keep tapping into a different well that would surprise me with how much rage I had or how much incredible loneliness. Something really eats away at you if you have to go in there every day and search for these emotional depths and re-create the kind of hell she was experiencing. I found she got under my skin in a very haunting way. It's draining emotionally and, of course, physically, because emotions are so connected to the body. I was quite sick when I finished making *Frances*.

—Lange, interviewed for *Dialogue on Film*, *American Film*, June 1987

On *Tootsie* [1982, Sydney Pollack], I've never been so easily directed, but then, that's Julie, my character. She lets everything slide, slugs back some wine and just gets by.

—Lange, interviewed by Julia Cameron for *American Film*, Jan/Feb 1983

The part of Jewell Ivy [in *Country* (1984, Richard Pearce)] was more familiar to me than any other part I've played. I drew from all my aunts in rural Minnesota. I wanted to convey the tremendous strength and tenacity of these women in balance with a heartbreaking vulnerability. Jewell Ivy is not the type of character you can embellish and make bigger than life. I tried to keep my performance absolutely honest, even though that was not the most showy acting choice.

—Lange, interviewed by Aljean Harmetz for *The New York Times*, 24 Mar 1985

[Patsy Cline in *Sweet Dreams* (1985, Karel Reisz)] was direct. There was nothing hidden or neurotic or withheld. Those are great qualities. Something I never played before. Tremendous ranges in emotion that last 30 to 40 seconds. Nothing harbored. Like a firecracker going off all the time....

Patsy never over-thought anything.... Things with her were fast, expedient.... If she was angry, she got angry.

—Lange, interviewed by Dena Kleiman for *The New York Times*, 6 Oct 1985

Sweet Dreams was an experience I had never even imagined. I would come home from the set exhilarated: I had a hundred times more energy at the end of the day. I believe now that it came from connecting with her songs, her voice. Patsy had somehow found in her life this tremendous release for all her sadness and her passion and her disappointments and her physical abuse and everything else she suffered through. In the course of filmmaking, it was like the energy kept mounting every day. This was the first time I had ever forced myself into a performing mode, which is unusual for me because I work so privately — I always feel that acting is this kind of sacred, secretive process. To actually get up on a stage and sing in front of the Grand Ole Opry — of course, I was lucky to have Patsy's voice piped in behind me — was thrilling.

On no film that I've worked on have we been allowed the so-called luxury of rehearsal, and I can't understand that. Even if the schedule allows for three weeks of rehearsal during preproduction, ninety percent of the time you walk in, the cast is assembled, you do a cold reading of the script, and that's it. That's all the rehearsal you have until you get in front of the camera. It just seems way out of whack to me. Can you imagine how much better the work would be if you were allowed three weeks of rehearsal, if you really worked on the relationships ahead of time, if you searched and tried things? Instead, you're expected to come on the set and hit it in the first two seconds.

Crimes of the Heart [1986, Bruce Beresford] is a case where I think we could have just gone through the roof if we'd been given an opportunity for rehearsal. As it is, it's not a *bad* film, I'm not saying that. But we could have done something extraordinary if we'd worked out the whole history of those sisters.

I suggested to Bruce Beresford once that we do some improvisational work. He got off on this thing about how he had known an actor who, in preparation for a part, liked to put on a clown suit and jump around and do bizarre things. Bruce couldn't understand how that connected with creating a character. It was at this point Sam [Shepard] said to me, "I don't think he understands what improvisation is. You might as well forget it. I don't think you're going to get any rehearsal time."

Q. Do most actors want rehearsal time?

A. It's interesting, because all actors work differently. I mean, two actors could not have worked more differently than Dustin [Hoffman] and I did on *Tootsie*. I remember one take he was doing: He had to come into camera, say one line, and then exit. That was the take. Now, the way I would have approached it is to have come prepared, said the line, and exited. End of take. But Dustin ran through it about thirty times. He was like this incredible manic energy machine that kept building and building and building. I don't know how many times I heard him say during shooting, "Keep the camera running, just keep it going!" He ran in and said the line and he ran out and then ran back in. It was amazing. But it worked beautifully for him.

—Lange, interviewed for *Dialogue on Film*, *American Film*, June 1987

Working with Costa-Gavras [on *Music Box* (1989)] was probably the best experience I've ever had as an actress working with a director because of his amazing sensitivity and kindness and intelligence. Costa creates a situation that's very productive. For the actor, he makes — at least for me he did — an environment that was very supportive and very nurturing, which allowed me to really try and experiment. He also has a certain intuition as to when to stay out of your way and when to approach you. Words can have such an impact, they can either move you positively or they can shut you down, and Costa was just amazingly intuitive and intelligent as to when to stay out of the way and when one or two words needed to be said....

Q. How important is it to you to intellectualize the film as a whole, to consider the political or social implications of the film?

A. I never think in those terms. I did an interview for *Music Box*: This man had just been talking to Costa and mentioned what Costa had said about the film, about the essence of evil and historical consciousness, and he said, "Is that what the film is to you?" And I said, "No. The only thing I know about this film is that it's a love story. It's about this woman's devotion and love and commitment to her family and to her father [Armin Mueller-Stahl]." I always have to find the simplest line, the most organic emotional thread.

-Lange, interviewed for *Dialogue on Film*, *American Film*, Aug 1990

Angela LANSBURY [1925-]

Born: London, England; granddaughter of George Lansbury, one-time leader of the British Labour Party. A scholarship student at The Webber-Douglas School of Singing and Dramatic Art in Kensington, she came to the U.S. in 1940 and studied at The Feagin School of Drama and Radio on a scholarship arranged by the American Theatre Wing. In 1944, she made her film debut as the maid in George Cukor's Gaslight:

Cukor is a man who doesn't mince words, and he told me that he wanted a very blowsy performance, rather loose. And he certainly coached me and got that out of me. I can sort of see him now, sitting there and saying, "You know, she's rather dirty and sleazy and she excites this man [Charles Boyer] because she is so young and so aware of her sexuality, and she knows that he is aware of it too." I understood that. Some men are able to describe that kind of a girl in no uncertain terms and you can imagine why: I mean, Cukor himself wouldn't have liked such a girl — she would be distasteful to him, and yet he would think she was terribly funny. George would roar with laughter at me, in everything I did in the role that appealed to him. If it was something I thought of, and he liked it, he would scream with laughter.

—Lansbury, interviewed by Gordon Gow for *Films & Filming*, Dec 1971

For a rather tense action piece like *The Manchurian Candidate* [1962], John Frankenheimer can pluck from me a whole lot of things that another director wouldn't know existed or wouldn't know how to use or wouldn't know how to challenge me to produce. Then you get into something like *The Dark at the Top of the Stairs* [1960], and you have Delbert Mann, who's an enormously sympathetic, mild man who wouldn't do a subject like *Manchurian Candidate*, but who knows how to unlock other doors with me or produce out of me facets of my abilities that Frankenheimer doesn't know about and probably wouldn't be interested in. So if you get the wrong director for the wrong film, you're in deep, deep trouble.

—Lansbury, interviewed by Ronald Hayman for *The Times*, 29 Jan 1972

Charles LAUGHTON [1899-1962]

Born: Scarborough, England. Studies at The Royal Academy of Dramatic Art in London and work on the London stage (from 1926) preceded his debut in the short film, Bluebottles (1928, Ivor Montagu). Work on Broadway preceded his American film debut in James Whale's The Old Dark House (1932), followed shortly thereafter by work as Nero in Cecil B. DeMille's The Sign of the Cross:

I was assigned the part of Nero in *The Sign of the Cross*. Cecil DeMille, the director, saw Nero as a robust, domineering personality. I visualized a type exactly the opposite — a man whose preciousness would heighten the horror of the orgies staged for his pleasure.

After a long but friendly dispute between myself and DeMille — it lasted for a week — I was ultimately permitted to play the character in my own way.

—Laughton, interviewed by Patrick Murphy for *The Sunday Express*, 3-10 Dec 1933

I prefer to act for the screen because I am not deterred by the presence of the people in front. I do not have to estimate the emphasis from moment to moment and performance to performance in relationship to them. I am able to imagine an audience and how I am making it react....

In *If I Had a Million* [1932, section directed by Ernst Lubitsch] I wished to shape the audience to a sense of expectation and make it completely ready to savour the culminating gesture — the employee's raspberry to his chief when fortune arrives.

—Laughton, in *World Film News and Television Progress*, Apr 1936

[Gary] Cooper was lighting a cigarette in front of the camera and looking up at a woman's face [in *The Devil and the Deep* (1932, Marion Gering)]. I knew in a flash then that he'd got something I would never have. I went across the set and asked him to tell me how he did it. He looked shy and bewildered and said I ought to know better than he did: I was from the stage and he was just a ham movie actor.

We act in opposite ways. His is presentational acting; mine is representational. I get a part from the outside. He gets at it from the inside, from his own clear way of looking at life. His is the right way, if you can do it. I could learn to do it, but it would take me a year to do what he can do instinctively, and I haven't the time....

—Laughton, quoted by Kurt Singer in his *The Laughton Story* (Philadelphia: John C. Winston Co., 1954)

I cannot quite say how I got my conception of Henry VIII [in *The Private Life of Henry VIII* (1933, Alexander Korda)]....

I suppose I must have read a good deal about him, but for the rest I spent a lot of my time walking around the old Tudor Palace at Hampton Court, getting my mind accustomed to the square, squat architecture of the rooms and the cloisters.

I think it was from the architecture of the houses and the rooms that I got my idea of Henry.

—Laughton, interviewed by Patrick Murphy for *The Sunday Express*, 3-10 Dec 1933

I always thought that the story of Henry was as much a saga of manners as a saga of wives — you see, in the matter of lusts, that particular Majesty was merely a temperamental child, the victim of conceit and his way of living.

If Henry had lived decently, watched his diet, exercised himself, he might have been a clean-cut, civilized fellow with a clean-cut civilized scale of values — he might have had a different attitude toward throne and bedroom. Then, too, when his story is told we have the advantage of seeing it through a retrospective glass; we can see his table lack-o'-manners from a grandstand built of knives and forks and serviettes.

Therefore when I ate anything in *Henry VIII*, I was thinking always of the progress of etiquette since that day. My mind was busy with a study in contrasts between slabs of roast in the fingers and cubes of roast impaled on a silver fork. That was what I was thinking in the final scene while I gnawed my hunk of meat.

—Laughton, interviewed by Anthony McAllister for *Photoplay Magazine*, Feb 1936

I think the elder Barrett part [in *The Barretts of Wimpole Street* (1934, Sidney Franklin)] is one of the most fascinating I've ever come across. It's the sort of thing one wouldn't want to do oftener than, say, once in several years. It's too tragic, and sinister, too unpleasantly wearing on everybody concerned. I can honestly say that I'm more glad I did this than anything else I've tried so far in pictures, though I had a much better time playing Henry or Nero.

The Barrett part is, of course, a fine study in psychology, bordering on the abnormal. Barrett is grim and sadistic, with the suggestion all the time of a relentless force driving him from outside. You have to feel that there is something deeply human about him, if one could only get the emotional balance better adjusted. He's the driving sort of leader, applying his power to parental affairs rather than to the world of finance or business.

—Laughton, interviewed for *The New York Herald Tribune*, 16 Sept 1934

Old Bligh [in *Mutiny on the Bounty* (1935, Frank Lloyd)] always fascinated me. Despite his tyrannous nature, you couldn't help admiring his "guts" when he was facing great danger.

—Laughton, interviewed by Louis Raymond for *Motion Picture*, Feb 1941

Acting is really over-acting, I suppose. A great actor, faced with the problem of suggesting an emotion, cannot possibly depict just what a character would really do under a certain circumstance. It wouldn't get over, because in ordinary life we don't portray our feelings very much through our actions. Instead, we try to cover those feelings up, we hide them because we don't want pity or sympathy from our friends, and we don't want to be laughed at....

So an actor must take that into account. He must show in his movements and on his face what is going on in the recesses of the character's heart — he must be that character without any inhibitions, defenses down....

[Take] my part in *Les Miserables* [1935, Richard Boleslavsky], for instance — when Javert was about to commit suicide. This was a man whose entire life was built around a single ideal: his belief in the law as an inviolable thing — as something more important than justice. When he found that this one premise of his life, this thing he had wasted so many years fighting for, was really wrong after all, then there was nothing left for him, and in real every-day affairs the man would probably have looked frightened or crazy or sorrowful or perhaps he would not have had any expression at all.

But subconsciously there would have been the presence of a great light in his heart — there would have been the exaltation and awe that dying men must feel at the approach of death.

So I stood against the wall with my face raised to the sky, as if God were there somewhere and I could see Him....

I don't act any one scene for the scene itself — I try to discover what mood is behind the entire story, what one definite impression the writer wanted to leave with the audience. Then every movement of mine, every word I speak, is working toward that impression.

In *Ruggles of Red Gap* [1935, Leo McCarey] the theme was that an English man-servant, steeped in the tradition of servility, should find his own individuality, a freedom of body and soul, in America. Thus there was not a moment during any part of the picture that my mind was not constantly on the climax, where Ruggles speaks the Gettysburg Address. Everything led up to that — the tones in my voice, the sissy walk, the servile attitudes — and when the Address came, it was my opportunity to thank America for what it has done for me. And I took it.

—Laughton, interviewed by Anthony McAllister for *Photoplay Magazine*, Feb 1936

Erich Pommer, the producer, and I went into business together. We formed Mayflower Pictures in London....

Instantly I split in two, like an amoeba, a herring or a frankfurter roll. From a single fat man named Charles Laughton I turned into a combination of Charles Laughton the actor, and Mr. Laughton, the businessman.

The whole thing started out very pleasantly. Erich Pommer, one of my oldest and dearest friends, produced all three pictures which we've turned out for Paramount release to date — *The Beachcomber* [1937, Erich Pommer]...*Jamaica Inn* [1939, Alfred Hitchcock] and *London After Dark* [aka *St. Martin's Lane* (1939, Tim Whelan)].... My wife, Elsa Lanchester, got the feminine lead in the first picture; in *Jamaica Inn* the cast was made up of people like Leslie Banks, Emlyn Williams, Robert Newton and others with whom I've been pals for years, and little Maureen O'Hara, whom Elsa and I have practically adopted as a member of our family. The same thing with *London After Dark*. Practically everyone in the picture, from Vivien Leigh, Ralph Richardson and Tyrone Guthrie down to the extras, has been a close friend of ours for years.

And in spite of this almost family setup, I started discovering the nasty side of this dual personality — the businessman. He has a sordidly practical nature, that Mr. Laughton, the tycoon of finance. His pockets are always filled with little pieces of paper covered with figures. He scowls constantly at anyone who suggests any idea at all which might cost a little money. He accuses directors of being too artistic and too much inclined to be dreamers. He speaks sharply to his own wife, and when that lady barks back at him with the spirit that she occasionally shows, he sulks disgustingly.

Worst of all, he has turned out to be a slave driver.

Each time we finished another picture, we returned to London. We started feeling more like ourselves. Mr. Laughton, fiend of figures, slowly started vanishing. I, his alter ego, began just as slowly to be received back into the good graces of my wife and my friends — until the time when we started the next picture, when the whole routine began over again.

And that's one of the real reasons why I'm so glad to be back in America at this time. I've come over to make a picture — not for my own Mayflower concern, but for another company entirely, RKO. While I'm here, I don't have to worry about a thing that concerns the business angles of the picture.

I know that while I'm working on *The Hunchback* [*of Notre Dame* (1939, William Dieterle)] I'll be able to be Charlie Laughton as actor all the time. My mind is perfectly at ease about that.

—Laughton, quoted by Kurt Singer in his *The Laughton Story* (Philadelphia: John C. Winston Co., 1954)

[For *They Knew What They Wanted* (1940, Garson Kanin),] I spent many days...in [the] company [of an Italian-American grape grower], studying his speech, his gestures, the way he walked. He was the very embodiment of [Sidney] Howard's character, it seemed to me, and so I patterned my role after him.

—Laughton, interviewed by Louis Raymond for *Motion Picture*, Feb 1941

[In *Young Bess* (1953, George Sidney)], Henry [VIII] is being pictured as lusty and gusty as ever, and he was quite a bum, too. But he did have his good points, even though nobody seems to pay any attention to those these days. For example, the best authorities indicate that he prided himself on a strong sense of responsibility to his kingdom and his people. They agree, too, that he was an outstanding statesman and that he started the British Navy on its way to rule the seas.

He was noted for a tremendous drive in everything he undertook and was an exceptional athlete. He excelled in tennis, archery, jousting and riding until well into his forties.

You'd never guess from the way we picture him today that he had a keen appreciation of painting and literature, or that he was extremely interested in schools. People are amazed, too, to learn that he was a skilled musician. In fact, the research for *Young Bess* revealed an old ballad written by him. It was good enough to be used in the film's music score.

He'd be the first to admit [my portrayal is] good showmanship. He was quite a showman himself — just look at the pomp and glitter he surrounded himself with.

—Laughton, quoted by Kurt Singer in *The Laughton Story* (Philadelphia: John C. Winston Co., 1954)

Stan LAUREL [1890-1965]

Born: Arthur Jefferson in Lancashire, England. A music hall performer brought to America with The Fred Karno troupe for a second time in 1912, he decided to stay in the U.S., where he made his film debut in the short, Nuts in May (1917, Robin E. Williamson). In 1927, Hal Roach officially teamed Laurel with Oliver Hardy:

[Ollie and I] never tried to use funny clothing. Of course, there were times when we would wear odd garments for a special humorous effect, but as far as our two characters were concerned, we never tried to get very far from what was real. We always wore a stand-up collar but there wasn't anything unreal about them, especially in the twenties and early thirties. Stand-up collars were formal and slightly different but never obviously so. They gave us, together with our derbies, a something we felt these two characters needed — a kind of phony dignity. There's nothing funnier than a guy being dignified *and* dumb. As far as make-up goes, I emphasized my lack of brains by making my face as blank as possible. I used very light make-up and made my eyes smaller by lining the inner lids. Babe, in keeping with his wish to obtain an even *bigger* kind of dignity, combed his hair down in a spit-curl bangs effect. This was in perfect harmony with his elegant nature and those fancy-dan gestures of his.

The only thing worth remembering about [*Get 'Em Young* (1926, Fred L. Guiol)], is that...it gave me the first real mannerism that definitely became a part of my later character when I was teamed with Hardy. In the film, I was a very timid chap, running around and reacting with horror to everything that went on around me. To emphasize this, I cried at one point, screwed my face up — and have used it ever since. Funny thing about that cry, though: it's the only mannerism I ever used in the films that I didn't like. I remember years later when we would be improvising something on the set and we came to a pause where we couldn't think of anything to do — or had a dull moment — Roach always insisted that I use the cry. It always got a laugh, and it sure became a part of my standard equipment, but somehow I never had any affection for it.

—Laurel, interviewed by John McCabe for *Mr. Laurel and Mr. Hardy* (Garden City, N.Y.: Doubleday & Co., 1966)

Q. Wasn't *The Rogue Song* [1930, Lionel Barrymore], one of your best sound pictures, originally made without you and Mr. Hardy?

A. Yes. It was made at Metro with Lawrence Tibbett, the opera star. It was a singing picture with a Russian background, and in color. After they previewed it they decided it needed some comedy — it was strictly a singing picture with romantic situations. They also realized Tibbett didn't have a name overseas. So they decided to get Laurel and Hardy to supply comedy and boost the foreign sales, and we were sent down from Roach [Studios] to fit ourselves into the picture.... Some of the sets were still up, and we studied the picture and put funny sequences into different spots. We wrote ourselves in as members of Tibbett's gang — Tibbett was a "Russian Robin Hood," you know, one of those dashing guys. After he had finished the picture he returned to New York and so had to fly back to Hollywood to shoot a scene with us — the only scene in which he and we appeared together.

—Laurel, interviewed by Boyd Verb for *Films in Review* (NY), Mar 1959

I believe that it is because we convey so much of our story in pantomime, making it understandable to most everyone that we find unusual favor with foreign audiences. A person does not have to be a linguist to know when Ollie is displeased with me on the screen, nor do they need an interpreter to explain any of the situations in which we find ourselves involved. Obviously when talkies came into popularity, pantomime became the one universal language and as this has always been our method of expression on the screen, we were not handicapped as were the dramatic actors.

We use our hands and our faces to express our feelings and emotions and we endeavor to make every body movement convey something. For instance, we can turn our backs to the camera and register dejection by dropping our shoulders. The manner in which Ollie gayly flips his tie registers his intense pleasure with himself. I often use my hands to register my helplessness or discouragement and when I scratch my head with my hand and wrist contorted in the manner of a swan's neck, there is seldom any question as to my utter bewilderment.

—Laurel, interviewed for the press book for *Bonnie Scotland* (MGM, 1935)

Piper LAURIE [1932-]

Born: Rosetta Jacobs in Detroit. Amateur stage productions in Los Angeles led to a studio contract at age 17. She made her film debut in Louisa *(1950, Alexander Hall); in 1952, she appeared in* Has Anybody Seen My Gal? *and* No Room for the Groom, *both for director Douglas Sirk:*

He was very unpleasant. He was insensitive; just like a dictator. He was all the things you hear about Otto Preminger. I was the one he picked

on. I always had trouble learning a lot of my lines because they didn't make sense to me and I was right; they didn't make sense. I remember I had this long speech, well relatively long for those days, in front of six other actors and I just couldn't get it right. Finally he got the prop department to bring in a huge blackboard and chalked the lines on it for me to read which was very humiliating.
—Laurie, interviewed by Allan Hunter for *Films & Filming*, Sept 1984

The Hustler [1961, Robert Rossen] was the best film I'd ever made, and Robert Rossen was the best director. He was also a very good friend. A lot of people didn't think we liked each other because we...hollered at each other and disagreed about things and made things difficult. Be we really liked each other....
—Laurie, interviewed by Clifford Terry for *The Chicago Tribune Magazine*, 1 Nov 1970

I got the script [of *Carrie* (1976, Brian De Palma)] and read it; I thought it was terrible. I thought they had got to be kidding, even if I never made another film I wasn't going to do this. So, I talked to my husband [film critic Joseph Morgenstern] and said, "You know, if they do it as a comedy I could see how it might work." He said, "Well, Brian De Palma's work does have a comedic approach in almost everything he does." I thought well, maybe that's what it's supposed to be.

I was working on a scene with Sissy Spacek and doing something I'd worked out very carefully that I thought was terrific. Brian said, "Wait a minute, you can't do that — it'll get a laugh." After that I never really changed my concept of the character as a comedy figure but I just knew that if I went too far he would stop me.
—Laurie, interviewed by Allan Hunter for *Films & Filming*, Sept 1984

Florence LAWRENCE [1886-1938]

Born: Hamilton, Ontario, Canada; daughter of actress, Lotta Lawrence. A stage debut at age 3 in one of her mother's productions preceded her film debut in Daniel Boone (1907, Edwin S. Porter and Wallace McCutcheon) at the Edison Studios in N.Y. She then worked for the Vitagraph Co. before moving to the American Mutoscope and Biograph Co., where she became known as "The Biograph Girl." There she appeared in 67 films directed by D.W. Griffith.

My mother heard that Mr. Edwin S. Porter, then the chief producer and manager at the Edison studio on Twenty-first street, was engaging people to appear in an historical play. I decided to see him at once. My mother accompanied me to the studio.

The news of intended activity on the part of the Edison people must have been pretty generally known, for there were some twenty or thirty actors and actresses ahead of us that cold December morning.... Everybody was trying to talk to Mr. Porter at one time, and a Mr. Wallace McCutcheon was fingering three or four sheets of paper, which I found later were the scenario.

Mr. Porter and Mr. McCutcheon conferred together and Mr. Porter announced that only twelve people were needed for the entire cast, and that some of these had been engaged....

The parts of Daniel Boone, his companion, the Indian maid and a couple of blood-thirsty savages, he announced, had been filled. That left the parts of Mrs. Boone, the Boone girls, and four Indians open. As I remember, Col. Cody's Buffalo Bill show was then in New York City and the people selected to play the parts he announced as "filled" were from the show.

Mr. McCutcheon looked at me, then at Mr. Porter, and I was told that I was engaged as one of Daniel Boone's daughters. I must have said something to mother almost instantaneously for one of them, I forget which asked, "Is that your mother?" I replied that she was, and Mr. Porter thereupon engaged her to play the part of Mrs. Daniel Boone.
—Lawrence, in *Photoplay Magazine*, Nov 1914

After *The Dispatch Bearer* [1907] was finished, I appeared in a dozen or more pictures, sometimes under the direction of Mr. [Albert E.] Smith, and sometimes under the direction of Mr. [J. Stuart] Blackton and sometimes under the direction of both, with the added help of Mr. William V. Ranous, who was then the Vitagraph studio manager and stage director.

Sufficient praise cannot be bestowed upon Mr. Blackton and Mr. Smith. It is utterly impossible for me to set down my thoughts so as to make you feel and know how high a place they have in my regard. They have achieved their wonderful success only through the hardest of work, always studying, experimenting and trying to improve their output.

When I was a Vitagraph player they would write their own stories, direct them on the stage, and, if actors who suited the parts couldn't be had, they would play the parts themselves.... Above all they were unfailingly kind and generous, always ready with an encouraging word for anyone who needed it.

Through my years at The Biograph studio I worked along this plan — a western picture, a society drama or comedy, and then a frontier or Indian picture. *The Red Girl* [1908] was the title of my first Indian picture produced by Mr. Griffith.... I was the red girl.... Nobody seemed to know how I ought to look. So I did the best I could and the result was hideous. And the strange part of it all was that Mr. Griffith did not object to my make-up in any way whatsoever.

Mr. [John] Compson was the most serious comedian I have ever known. Nothing was ever funny to him, and he never tried to be funny. When all the rest would laugh at something he had said or done he would become indignant, thinking we were making fun of him [Lawrence and Compson were teamed as Mr. and Mrs. Benjamin Bibbs in a series of films beginning with *A Smoked Husband* (1908, D.W. Griffith).]

What seemed to annoy us "Biographers" very much and hold us back from achieving greater artistic success was the speed and rapidity with which we had to work before the camera. Mr. Griffith always answered our complaint by stating that the exchanges and exhibitors who bought our pictures wanted action, and insisted that they get plenty of it for their money.

"The exhibitors don't wanted illustrated song slides," Mr. Griffith once said to us....

There was no chance for slow or "stage" acting. The moment we started to do a bit of acting in the proper tempo we would be startled by the cry of the director: "Faster! Faster! For God's sake hurry up! We must do the scene in forty feet...."

About this time [1909] the Pathé Co. imported several one reel length pictures which they called features since the leading actors and actresses of the prominent theatres of Paris appeared in them. These pictures were released under the Film D'Art brand....

Following the appearance of the Film D'Art pictures nearly all of the Biograph players asked Mr. Griffith to be allowed to do slow acting, only to be refused. He told us it was impossible since the buyers would positively not pay for a foot of film that did not have action in it.

But before I severed my connection with The Biograph Co., Mr. Griffith did commence the production of pictures employing "the close-up" and slow acting, working along the lines suggested by the French actors and actresses. And simultaneously, the American film manufacturers woke up to the fact that they were on the wrong track in producing pictures showing human beings doing things at about four times the speed of real life.

—Lawrence, in *Photoplay Magazine*, Jan 1915

Cloris LEACHMAN [1926-]

Born: near Des Moines, Iowa. Drama studies at Northwestern University, wore the crown as Miss Chicago of 1946, then studies at The Actors Studio in N.Y. and work on Broadway preceded her film debut in Kiss Me Deadly (1955, Robert Aldrich). In 1971, she played Ruth Popper in Peter Bogdanovich's The Last Picture Show:

I felt that Ruth Popper should be the woman scorned of all time. I played it with my own body, my skin, my face. I wanted that scorned look to come out through my skin rather than my mouth. As I put on those drab clothes of Ruth Popper's it just began to happen. I think by the time I was dressed I was her and I could have done anything in the world that Ruth Popper might do.

—Leachman, interviewed for *Newsweek*, 1 May 1972

Canada LEE [1907-1952]

Born: Lionel Canegata in New York City. Work with The WPA Negro Federal Theater Unit preceded his film debut in Henry Brown, Farmer (1942, Roger Barlow). The following year he was one of the shipwrecked passengers on Alfred Hitchcock's Lifeboat:

When they first handed me the part of Joe, I read it over and found "yessir, yessir, yessir," about every other word. I'd rather dig ditches for a living than act out some foolish parody of a group of people, and I pointed out to them that Joe would hardly address his shipmates like that all the time. They let me revise the part and I cut them all out.

The script had another curious twist. As the action progressed I noticed that the Negro, Joe, is always isolated from everybody else in the lifeboat. Later on the boat picks up the German captain [Walter Slezak] who sunk the ship, and he gradually fits into the community — but Joe is still more or less on the outside, and yet he has already saved two lives. I asked someone if this was being done for any special effect. The script was consulted and the answer was, "No, I guess this guy just wants to be alone." That, of course, isn't true to life at all....

When one of the characters [Gus as played by William Bendix] has his leg amputated, I was supposed to cast my eyes to heaven and 'wordlessly pray'. Nobody else prayed, so I just kept looking out to sea. When they asked me what I was doing, I just said, "I'm praying...."

I don't honestly believe that pictures are made better by all the clichés you find in them about Negroes, and that's why I criticized all the things I just mentioned. I don't see why they should always put forth a single conception of a Negro any more than of any other group, especially since this conception is usually undignified.

—Lee, interviewed by Otis L. Guernsey, Jr. for *The New York Herald Tribune*, 26 Dec 1943

Christopher LEE [1922-]

Born: London, England. Studies at Wellington College and a film debut in Corridor of Mirrors (1947, Terence Young) preceded his fame as a horror film star at The Hammer Studios. In 1958, he played the title role of Terence Fisher's Dracula:

Dracula has never been done properly. Basically it would cost an enormous amount of money. There'd have to be shipwrecks, craggy mountains, many varied locations, special effects, etc. Bits and pieces of Stoker's book *have* been presented on the screen.

With [my] first Dracula...I came fairly near it, except for the physical appearance of the character which in Hammer pix has been wrong. If I was offered Stoker's story exactly as he had written it, I'd do it again, for the last time. I've only played it 6 times in 15 years [as of 1973, he had actually played it 10 times, and played it once more after that]....

I have no intention of playing the character again because I'm increasingly disenchanted with the way he has been presented.... They write stories into which they fit the character, and that simply doesn't work. [His other films as Dracula: *Dracula — Prince of Darkness* (1966, Terence Fisher), *Dracula Has Risen from the Grave* (1968, Freddie Francis), *Taste the Blood of Dracula* (1970, Peter Sasdy), *The Scars of Dracula* (1970, Roy Ward Baker), *El Conde Dracula* (1971, Jesus Franco), *Dracula AD 1972* (1972, Alan Gibson), *The Satanic Rites of Dracula* (1973, Alan Gibson) and *Dracula and Son* (1975, Edouard Molinaro). He played a small part as Dracula in *The Magic Christian* (1969, Joseph McGrath); he also played the title role and narrated the documentary *In Search of Dracula* (1971, Yvonne Floyd).]

—Lee, interviewed by Peter Bess for *Variety*, 4 July 1973

I've made over 130 pictures and only 14 of them have been horror films. Yet those are the roles I'm remembered for and in whose image I am constantly being cast. I have nothing against the pictures themselves; I enjoyed making most of them and I believe some of them are minor classics. Certainly their popularity is enormous. But no actor enjoys playing the same sort of character over and over again and even when a film is not a horror picture, I generally play the villain.

It's too early to tell whether I'll be accepted in a wider range of parts, but the one in *Airport 77* [1977, Jerry Jameson] is a welcome start. I portray a straight, decent man and I find it quite a challenge after so many "heavy" roles.

—Lee, interviewed by Martin Malina for *Marquee*, Mar/Apr 1977

Spike LEE [1956-]

Born: Shelton Jackson Lee in Atlanta, Georgia; raised Brooklyn, N.Y. Studies at Morehouse College and NYU's Tisch School of the Arts preceded his feature film debut as director/ producer/screenwriter/editor with She's Gotta Have It (1986), in which he also played Mars Blackmon:

Q. I always wonder about that line in *She's Gotta Have It* — "It's 'cause I'm small she dogged me." I wondered if that was something you ever felt.

A. No. But I could see that happening. I really never had a complex about my height.

Q. Woody Allen makes a big deal about his weaknesses. That's the only reference in your entire film that's even like that. You play upon being skinny in the film. The biggest laugh in the entire movie is when you come out in shorts at the end.

A. The thing about it is that I don't even think my legs are skinny. People think I did that for a laugh. But in the summertime, people wear shorts. So it wasn't intentionally for a laugh like that. I think that's where a lot of comparison to Woody Allen comes in. They see me making fun of myself, letting myself be the butt of jokes. That really wasn't intentional.

—Lee, interviewed by Nelson George, 21 Nov 1986; publ. in *Spike Lee's Gotta Have It: Inside Guerrilla Filmmaking* by Spike Lee (New York: Simon & Schuster, 1987)

Q. Who is Mookie, the character you play [in *Do the Right Thing* (1989, Spike Lee)]? His relationship with Tina [Rosie Perez], the mother of his child, is unresolved. We don't really know what his hopes and his dreams are, except wanting to get paid.

A. That's all it is. Just live to the next day. He can't see beyond the next day. Mookie is an irresponsible young black youth. He gave Tina a baby. He changes, but up to that point he doesn't really care about his son or her....

What's troubling to some white critics is when Mookie throws the garbage can through the window. Because Mookie's one of those "nice black people." I've heard a lot of white friends tell me, "You're a nice black person, you're not like the rest." They really followed Mookie, they liked Mookie. He was a likable character. [Laughs.] They feel betrayed when he throws the garbage can through the window....

Q. When Mookie goes to see Sal [Danny Aiello] at the end, he just says, "Radio Raheem [Bill Nunn] is dead."

A. Yeah, but that's Mookie's character. What happened that night was tragic, but Mookie's whole character is not going to change overnight. And the reason why he's there that morning is because he wants to get paid. He's been saying that the whole movie, you know, get paid, get paid.

—Lee, interviewed by Marlaine Glicksman for *Film Comment*, July/Aug 1989

Andrea LEEDS [1913-1984]

Born: Antoinette Lees in Butte, Montana. While a student at UCLA, she was discovered by Howard Hawks and subsequently made her film debut in his and William Wyler's Come and Get It (1936). In 1937, she played Kaye Hamilton in Gregory La Cava's Stage Door:

Gregory La Cava had all of us girls come to the studio for two weeks before the shooting started and live as though we were in the lodging house itself. He had a script girl take down our conversations and he would adapt these into dialogue. He rewrote scenes from day to day to get the feeling of a bunch of girls together — as spontaneous as possible. He would talk to each of us like a lifelong friend. That gave us a feeling of intimacy. I remember he found out I was part Italian, and he was Italian, so he'd talk to me about spaghetti, pizza, and lasagna.

—Leeds, interviewed by Charles Higham for *Kate: The Life of Katharine Hepburn* (New York: W.W. Norton, 1975)

Janet LEIGH [1927-]

Born: Jeanette Morrison in Merced, California. Music studies at College of the Pacific and work as a model preceded her discovery by Norma Shearer. Her film debut was in The Romance of Rosey Ridge (1947, Roy Rowland); in 1954, she played Wally Cook in Norman Taurog's Living It Up, the first of two films opposite Jerry Lewis:

I went back to Paramount to make *Living It Up* with Jerry and Dean [Martin]....

The part of the sob-story reporter indicated a style not compatible with me. The dialogue was laced with caustic one-liners; Eve Arden manages this so effectively, but it isn't my way — glibness doesn't sit well on my shoulders. Comedy for me has to come out of a situation, not just delivering witty lines. Norman agreed completely, recognizing what was natural for me. Not much rewriting was required....

Norman understood comedy, and he knew his people. He allowed Jerry and Dean to have their heads, when that served the purpose. But he also reined in when *that* was necessary. He didn't lose sight of the balance, the overall continuity, which is so important when dealing with strong personalities who can pull away off tangent. Dean was a natural — relaxed, easygoing, open, and sexy — and it resulted in a seemingly effortless, honest, warm portrayal. Jerry came across as an inventive buffoon, and more. He's a much better actor than he has been given credit for. The die had been cast, however, and the creators and public wouldn't permit him to deviate from his familiar image. That had to wait until he directed, where he could explore through other actors.

Orson, Chuck Heston, Akim Tamiroff, Joseph Calleia, and I were involved in the prerehearsals [for *Touch of Evil* (1958, Orson Welles)]. Chuck and I were the new disciples and were absolutely fascinated. I was the court stenographer, without the skills of shorthand and typing. We would discuss the scene, explore where we wanted it to take us, improvise (each playing two characters if necessary). Then, feverishly, I would scribble down what we had done and give it to a real secretary. A lot of what we accomplished was used in the filming. Just as much was discarded. If a particular background intrigued Orson, he would alter his plan to take advantage of the virgin locals. He was always ready to extemporize....

Alfred Hitchcock sent me a book to peruse, a novel entitled *Psycho* by Robert Bloch, that was to be his next film [1960]....

The first in-person encounter was tea in Hitchcock's home on Bellagio Road, in November 1959. His deportment was cordial, matter-of-fact and academic. He outlined his modus operandi. The angles and shots of each scene were predetermined, carefully charted before the picture began. There could be no deviations. His camera was absolute. Within the boundary of the lens circumference, the player was given freedom, as long as the performance didn't interfere with the already designed move. "I hired you because you are an actress! I will only direct you if A, you attempt to take more than your share of the pie, or B, if you don't take enough, or C, if you are having trouble motivating the necessary timed motion."

I could see how this method might incur the indignation of some actors, be considered too set, hindering, confining. But I thought of it in a different light. This was the way the man worked. And since I had profound respect for his results, I would earnestly comply. As I reflected, I realized he was in actuality complimenting our profession, giving credit to our ability to inspire our own reasons behind a given movement. He was proposing a challenge, throwing down the gauntlet to our ingenuity. And I intended to be a contestant. Marion was on the screen only a short time, but she was a focal point and offered unlimited potentials in characterization....

—Leigh, in her *There Really Was a Hollywood* (Garden City, N.Y.: Doubleday & Co., 1984)

You will learn a lot from Jerry Lewis. I had a very interesting scene in a picture I did with Jerry [as director and co-star], *Three on a Couch* [1966].... You know the scene at the end, after the party, when she finds him out? They get in a cab and she starts to tell him off. Now, I started to tell him off straight, legitimately angry. Jerry said, "There's something wrong." He thought and thought, and finally said, "I've got it." He said, all through this picture you've been playing the person [psychiatrist] who said to the other three girls [Mary Ann Mobley, Gila Golan and Leslie Parrish], "Now you handle things just so," and you're very calm, and everything is under control. Now your position has been challenged because he has made a fool of you with these three girls. *They* are very calm now, they have learned to accept their position. You bawl him out, but you bawl him out because you're not thinking straight. I mean you're really angry, but you mustn't be coherently angry; you have to stammer, "How dare you...well...what...what you did was...." In other words she was no longer in control. And it was an excellent scene. It was a way of approaching that scene that had never dawned on me. It wasn't that I hadn't done my homework. I was prepared, I knew the character, but it hadn't occurred to me. That is what is so marvelous, when a director tells you to approach something in a way you hadn't even thought of.

—Leigh, interviewed by Rui Nogueira for *Sight & Sound*, Spring 1970

Jennifer Jason LEIGH [1958-]

Born: Los Angeles; daughter of Vic Morrow [1931-1982]. She made her film debut in Eyes of a Stranger *(1980, Ken Wiederhorn); in* Last Exit to Brooklyn *(1989, Uli Edel) and* Miami Blues *(1990, George Armitage), she played hookers, Tra La La and Susan:*

Playing prostitutes just sort of crept up on me. I find it an extremely complicated role to play. You're getting paid to be humiliated, so you feel this amazing power that you have. But at the same time, you know you're crawling on your hands and knees. You simply don't get that kind of power playing a clean-cut college girl.

Susan is a hooker. That's her job. But she wants to get fired. Of course, she knows that she *won't*. And it's that tug-of-war that makes the part so interesting to play. And as the events of the story unfold, she becomes more and more complex....

I don't believe that hookers have 'hearts of gold.' If they did, they'd be giving their money to charity.

—Leigh, interviewed by Eddie Murphy for *Film Review*, Dec 1990

Vivien LEIGH [1913-1967]

Born: Vivian Hartley in Darjeeling, India; educated in England, Italy, Germany and France. Studies at The Royal Academy of Dramatic Art in London preceded her film debut in Things are Looking Up (1934, Albert de Courville); in 1939, she played Scarlett O'Hara in Gone With the Wind:

I'd never have been able to get through it without the book and George Cukor [who was taken off the project and replaced by Victor Fleming]. I'd keep the book beside me and look up each scene as we filmed it to remind me where I was supposed to be, and how I should be feeling, until [David O.] Selznick shouted at me to throw the damned thing away. On Sundays, when we didn't shoot, I'd steal over to George Cukor's and discuss with him the bits we'd be working on the next week. It was probably terribly irregular, but I couldn't have finished it without him.

—Leigh, interviewed by Ronald Bryden for *The Observer*, 7 Jan 1968

I lived Scarlett for close to six months, from early morning to late at night. I tried to make every move, every gesture true to Scarlett, and I had to feel that even the despicable things Scarlett did were of my doing.

From the moment I first began to read *Gone With the Wind* three years ago, Scarlett fascinated me, as she has fascinated so many others. She needed a good, healthy old-fashioned spanking on a number of occasions — and I should have been delighted to give it to her. Conceited, spoiled, arrogant — all those things, of couse, are true of the character.

But she had courage and determination, and that, I think, is why women must secretly admire her — even though we can't feel too happy about her many shortcomings....

Perhaps the hardest days I spent, hard that is from the point of actual physical exertion, were during the time we made the scene where Scarlett struggles through the populace as it evacuates Atlanta. Naturally this could not be done all in one continuous "take," and so for what seemed an eternity I dodged through this maze of traffic on Peachtree Street, timing myself to avoid galloping horses and thundering wagons.

And between each shot, the make-up man — he seemed to be everywhere at once — came running to wash my face, then dirty it up again to just the right shade of Georgia clay dust. I think he washed my face about 20 times in one day — and dusted me over with red dust after each washing.

Here, of course, was where the tremendous task of organizing was at its most spectacular. Horses and riders had to cross certain places at just the right time — and so did I. I can assure you that it is not a pleasant experience to see a gun caisson charging down on you — even when you know the riders are experts and the whole thing planned. In fact, I was so intent on being in the right place at the right time all day that I did not realize until I got to bed that Scarlett O'Hara Leigh was a badly bruised person.

—Leigh, in the souvenir program for *Gone With the Wind* (MGM, 1939)

[Scarlett's] real emotions are throttled by a calculating worldliness. Everything she does is the result of premeditation. She is strong, capable, practical.

—Leigh, interviewed by S.J. Woolf for *The New York Times*, 9 June 1940

Larry [Olivier] directed *Streetcar* [on the London stage] with such uncanny insight. It was an early directorial effort for him, and both of us learned a tremendous lot from it. I'm absolutely convinced that my screen performance turned out well more through Larry's remembered direction than through Elia Kazan's film direction. I recall having a bit of a row with Gadge [Kazan] over Blanche's characterization. He didn't really like the character — preferred Kowalski, the Brando part. He kept robbing Blanche of her poignancy and vulnerability thus making her more and more unsympathetic. Finally we had a *very* serious talk — and luckily I won out on a good many points.

—Leigh, interviewed by John Gruen for *The New York Herald Tribune*, Feb 1967; repr. in Gruen's *Close-Up* (New York: Viking Press, 1968)

Actual beauty — beauty of feature is not what matters, it's beauty of spirit and beauty of imagination and beauty of mind. I tried in *Streetcar* [1951] to let people see what Blanche was like when she was in love with her young husband when she was seventeen or eighteen. That was awfully important, because Blanche, who needn't necessarily have been a beautiful person, but she — you should have been able to see what she was like, and why this gradually happened to her. And her sister [Kim Hunter] helps by saying, "Nobody was tender and trusting as she was," and that's a very important line.... In those two things you have to evoke this whole creature when she was young and when she was tender and trusting, as opposed to what she had become — cynical and hard, mad, and distressed and distraught.

—Leigh, interviewed by Lewis Funke and John E. Booth for *Actors Talk About Acting* (New York: Random House, 1961)

It took 3 months to make the film [of *Streetcar*], and I loved every second. I couldn't wait to get to the studio every morning and I hated to leave every night.... Brando was rather strange at first. I thought he was terribly affected. He used to say to me, "Why are you so damned polite? Why do you have to say good morning to everyone?" and I'd say, "Because it is a good morning and anyway it is a nice thing to say, so why not...?"

I got to understand him much better as we went on with the filming. He is such a good actor and when he wants to he can speak excellent English without a mumble. He is the only man I have ever met who can imitate Larry [Olivier] accurately. Larry is awfully difficult to imitate. Brando used to do speeches from *Henry V* and I closed my eyes and it could have been Larry.

Brando also has a nice singing voice; he sang folk songs to us beautifully....

—Leigh, interviewed by David Lewin for *The Daily Express*, 16 Aug 1960

Margaret LEIGHTON [1922-1976]

Born: Bart Green, Worcestershire, England. At the age of 15 she began her career with The Birmingham Repertory Theatre. She made her film debut in Bonnie Prince Charlie (1948, Anthony Kimmins); in 1971, she played Mrs. Maudsley in Joseph Losey's The Go-Between:

Joe was marvelous to me during [*The Go-Between*] because I had a bad arm and a bad leg. I was lame and halt half the time. But he never minded. I had never acted a Pinter script before, and I had to learn never to get one word wrong. Every word had a meaning. And this is what made it interesting where other films are not. The precision of the script. It had to be accurate.

—Leighton, interviewed for *The Evening Standard*, 27 Aug 1971

Jack LEMMON [1923-]

Born: John Lemmon in Boston. Studies at Harvard University, work on radio, in stock, on TV and Broadway preceded his film debut in It Should Happen to You (1954, George Cukor):

When I first went to Hollywood in 1953 to make *It Should Happen to You* with Judy Holliday, I got one of the best pieces of direction I've ever had from George Cukor. I was fresh from a successful revival of *Room Service*, and I was one of those Broadway snobs. I'd get on the set and really make it wail.

Every time we did a take, Cukor would say to me, "Less, dear boy, less." This went on for a couple of weeks. I was getting stomach aches, hearing "Less, dear boy, less." Finally, I blew up. I said to him, "Are you trying to tell me not to *act*?"

Cukor looked at me gratefully. "Yes, thank God, yes," he said. "Movie acting isn't really acting; it's *being*."

—Lemmon, interviewed by Tom Buckley for *The New York Times*, 9 May 1980

Judy [Holliday] was a consummate professional actress. She was extremely intelligent and erudite — not at all like the dumb blondes she so often depicted.

She was serious about her work and investigated all scenes and her character in great depth. She didn't give a damn where the camera was, how she looked, or about being a 'star.' She just played the scene and acted 'with,' not 'at....'

Judy was the greatest actress I've ever worked with; absolutely sensational. There isn't a superlative I can think of that doesn't befit her. [The two worked together again on *Phffft!* (1954, Mark Robson).]

—Lemmon, interviewed by Joe Baltake for *The Films of Jack Lemmon* (Secaucus, N.J.: Citadel Press, 1977)

I always felt one thing about [Ensign] Pulver [in *Mister Roberts* (1955, John Ford and Mervyn LeRoy)]: there was a naiveté about him. He was younger than the other guys, a babe in the woods in many ways, and always trying to prove himself. He wanted to be accepted by his idol and by everybody else. He wanted to be a hero and yet he'd never done a thing in his life; didn't make a football team, didn't do this, didn't do that — probably ran around the campus and got in as head of the cheerleaders. *That*, Pulver would do. He'd be out there jumpin' around like a jackrabbit trying to be accepted.

Pulver's frenetic behavior, as I saw it, came out of this tremendous drive to prove himself to [Lieutenant] Roberts [Henry Fonda], and secondarily, to everyone else — to be accepted.

A lot of people thought Billy [Wilder] was crazy to attempt such a film [*Some Like It Hot* (1959)]. Friends told me I could be ruined because the audience would think I was faggy or had a yen to be a transvestite. There was no getting around one thing; the picture was a minefield for actors. I finally decided the real trap was to ever *think* of the trap. If one began to worry about that fine line, to fret over audience reaction, it could be disastrous. The only way to play it was to let it all hang out and just go, trusting that Wilder would say, "Cut," if it got out of bounds. I saw this character I was to play as a nut from the moon who never really stopped to think once in his life. He didn't act — he reacted — to whatever was happening....

[To test our costumes and make-up] Tony Curtis and I agreed that since it was lunchtime we would, like two ding-dongs, go down to the studio commissary dressed up like broads. One of us, I forget whether it was Tony or me, got the bright idea that a true test would be a visit to the lady's room. So in we went! I mean, all the way!

Obviously, all the women were in stalls or this and that; we weren't, you know, peeking or anything. Well, we futzed around in the lounge, pursing our lips and running our fingers over our brows and whatever else we could think of that ladies would do. Do you know, not one of the girls going in or out ever batted an eyeball? They thought we were extras doing a period film on the lot.

That did it. That gave us the security we needed right there and then. We figured if those women bought it, they'd sure as hell buy it on camera....

[The scene where I reveal to Joe (Tony Curtis) that I'm engaged to Osgood (Joe E. Brown)] may well be the best scene I've ever been in, and it certainly is one of the most brilliantly written and directed scenes that I've ever seen.

When we got ready to do it, Billy handed me a set of maracas and I thought he was crazy. I'd already worked out everything at home and I could not imagine what I was supposed to do with those things. As we began rehearsing it hit me what a genius Wilder really was in coming up with those maracas. They served as a perfect — and critical — bridge; a piece of "business" that would fill the gap between my lines, providing time for audience laughter.

If Billy hadn't had me dancing around with those things in my "joy," most of the dialogue would have been lost, wiped out by laughter. From the moment I said, "I'm engaged," the uproar was almost continuous. Every time I'd read a line I'd follow it by waltzing around with those maracas while Tony was looking at me like I'm out of my mind. It was a sensational scene.

—Lemmon, interviewed by Don Widener for *Lemmon* (New York: Macmillan, 1975)

Marilyn [Monroe] drove everyone crazy [on *Some Like It Hot*], but I got along great with her....

Working with her was weird! At times, I didn't feel any contact. She might be looking me in the eyes, but I didn't really feel it. But God damn, she sure had it with that lens, on film. She had a built-in alarm clock, stopping suddenly in the middle of a scene; it would be going along fine, and the director hadn't said cut, but she would stop because something was off for her.

And she'd wring her hands, she'd say, "Just a sec, I'm sorry." She was very sweet. It was not temperament. It was just the only way she knew how to work. It was selfish to an extent, but it was not a deliberate selfish thing in a temperamental way.

—Lemmon, interviewed by Rita Gam for *Actors: A Celebration* (New York: St. Martin's Press, 1988)

[Billy Wilder] *sees* scripts. A script is to be played, not read. So if something doesn't look right in action, he'll change it.

That's the great thing about Billy; he doesn't impose himself before he sees what the actor will bring. Like the nose-spray bit [in *The Apartment* (1960)]. That was my idea.

I was working out the cold scene in my dressing room without props, when suddenly I saw my hand clench on the line: "But I *won't*!" I thought: "This is it."

I went to the prop department, because there's no point talking to the director; you have to try it first. I experimented with all kinds of sprays, punching different size holes in them, and finally used skim milk so the spray would show.

The first time I tried it on the set, the spray went low and splurted all over the script girl. Everybody broke up. [Fred] MacMurray played it exactly the way he did in the picture — just glanced at the spray, and then went on. Billy liked it, so we kept it in.

—Lemmon, interviewed by Joe Baltake for *The Films of Jack Lemmon* (Secaucus, N.J.: Citadel Press, 1977)

I've seen Billy Wilder take suggestions from a prop man, and I don't know a stronger director than Billy as far as being very definite about what he wants, especially since he's also the author. But he'll listen and let you try. That's the important thing, to at least let others try their ideas, and then say no or yes.

—Lemmon, interviewed by Steven Greenberg for *Film Comment*, May/June 1973

Q. *Days of Wine and Roses* [1962, Blake Edwards] provided a new kind of role for you, a change of pace from the comedies you had been making. How did you and Lee Remick prepare for that film?

A. We went to a lot of AA meetings, not together, individually. Also, we spent several nights in drunk tanks, just watching what really happens with these poor bastards that come in and are out of their skull with the D.T.'s. It was painful but beneficial.

Q. Valuable for that scene in the film where you're strapped down on the table?

A. I suggested that to Blake Edwards, because I had seen it happen, and he bought it immediately. I saw a guy who was strapped down come to, wondering what had happened. You're strapped down like you're a madman, and you don't know why. God, it's so degrading. But it's also terribly dramatic, as opposed to just sitting on the floor of the tank.

Q. As dramatic as the story is, you did manage to invest some humor in the character.

A. I love comedy in moments of drama, if it's legitimate. There's something perverse and wonderful if you can do it correctly. One night we were shooting the scene where he comes home and he's loaded and gets out of the cab. I just felt that the more comedy we could put in, before the dramatic part where he finally wakes the baby up and then cries and so forth, the better. Drunks can be funny, as we know. I think first of all I started to put the money in the back window of the cab, where there was no driver. Then Blake brought in the idea of having the camera behind the plate-glass window of my apartment building. But the audience didn't know there was a window there any more than I did, even though it was my own building. I was loaded. I missed the front door and walked smash into the window. It was a shock to me *and* the audience, but also funny.

—Lemmon, interviewed for *Dialogue on Film*, *American Film*, Sept 1982

Lemmon: I'd do the *phone book* with Wilder if he said he had a part in it for me. When he offered me the lead in *Irma* [*la Douce* (1963)], I signed for it without even seeing a script. I knew the plot of the Broadway musical, but I figured they might as well throw it right out the window for what Wilder would do in revising it. I was right....

Playboy: In the picture, you play a Paris gendarme who succumbs to the charms of a kookie tart — played by Shirley MacLaine — becomes her pimp, and proceeds to monopolize her trade in the guise of a well-heeled client. Did you "motivate" your part by doing any first-hand research?

Lemmon: And how, Shirley and I went to a whorehouse in Paris and talked to the madam and the girls for about five hours. The girls would say "Pardonnez-moi" about every ten minutes and go rolling upstairs. They had some pretty speedy customers, because some of the girls were back downstairs in about three minutes.

Playboy: This was your second picture with Shirley, a consummate comedienne who's stolen many a scene from her male leads. Do you work well together? [They had worked together previously on *The Apartment*.]

Lemmon: Beautifully. She's a ball to be with. I might be attracted to a woman with a gorgeous figure or a fine mind, but I only *respect* the woman who isn't a stereotype, a woman with authentic, individual qualities of her own. Shirley has all of these, and besides, she's a nut. Her sense of humor alone makes her that much easier to work with....

Whenever Wilder wants me to do another picture — in a tub, in drag, in a paddy wagon, in a Beatle wig — I'm his man. [Lemmon worked on four more Wilder films: *The Fortune Cookie* (1966), *Avanti* (1972), *The Front Page* (1974) and *Buddy, Buddy* (1981).]

Playboy: Do you think as highly of director Richard Quine and writer-director Blake Edwards?

Lemmon: All three suffer from an old theatrical disease that is kind of rare — talent. Billy's shows most of all, naturally, because he was making movies when the other two were kids. Billy has style, an individuality, which never dominates to the detriment of a picture. But all three have it....

Playboy: Do they have anything else in common?

Lemmon: Yes. I can work things out with them because with all their talents, they have security as directors. But they never, ever, arbitrarily impose their ideas on an actor. "OK," they say, "Let's read it over. Do what you want." They don't say a word more until they see what you bring. Now, all three might well know what they want, but they will not disallow the fact that the actor might add something fresh to what they had in mind already. You'd be amazed how many so-called good directors, especially under the economic pressures of getting a film done, adhere religiously to the ideas they've set up in advance. Another thing about those three: They do not give extensive, deep direction. In one sentence they can accomplish what an awful lot of guys who are sitting there motivating their grandfather's raincoat take hours to do.

Playboy: That sounds like a dig at the psychoanalytic Actors Studio technique. Is it?

Lemmon: I must admit I get griped when I see every young punk in a torn T-shirt called a Method actor. But if some guy feels he must vomit in a corner in order to get a sick feeling for a scene, and it *works*, more power to him. I just don't go for that stuff. I saw one guy spin himself around in a circle for a drunk scene and he got so off kilter that he smashed through a door and practically destroyed the whole damn set. Naturally, every actor has to have some kind of method of preparing himself for a role, but this doesn't happen to be mine. [Lemmon worked on Quine's *My Sister Eileen* (1955), *Operation Mad Ball* (1957), *Bell, Book and Candle* (1958), *It Happened to Jane* (1959), *The Notorious Landlady* (1962) and *How to Murder Your Wife* (1965); he worked on Edwards' *The Days of Wine and Roses*, *The Great Race* (1965) and *That's Life* (1986).]

—Lemmon, interviewed by Richard Warren Lewis for *Playboy*, May 1964

I've never enjoyed working with an actor more than Walter Matthau in *The Odd Couple* [1968, Gene Saks]. Many actors work at you and it can get very lonely out there with someone acting at you. But Walter's interested in making the scene work. I'll give you an example. In a scene in *The Odd Couple* I said, "I'm not so bad, you know. It could be worse." And he was supposed to say, "How?" So in rehearsal I said it and then, for the hell of it, I turned and walked out of the room, slammed the door and left him standing there with the line. He came right after me. He pushed open the door, stuck his head through — just his head — and said, "How?" It was a joy. Walter is a helluvan actor, the best I've ever worked with. [Lemmon and Matthau also worked together on three films for Billy Wilder: *The Fortune Cookie*, *The Front Page* and *Buddy, Buddy*; in 1971, Lemmon directed Matthau in *Kotch*.]

—Lemmon, interviewed by Allan Hunter for *Walter Matthau* (New York: St. Martin's Press, 1984)

Harry Stoner [in *Save the Tiger* (1973, John G. Avildsen)] is the whole middle-stream American prototype. He fought in World War Two and nobody even remembers it. If we look at our society, there is nothing left a young man coming out of that war can still believe in. We accept Watergate. We accept Vietnam. We accept cheating on our income tax and dancing around the law. We accept junkies knifing us in the streets. We accept the injustices in our courts. There are no rules, just referees. We used to salute the flag, now they're making jock straps out of it.

We live in smog and filth and pollution and we accept it because we're worried about our own personal problems. We don't react until there's a disaster. Well, I hope this film will make people more aware of what's happening. It's more than just a story of one man at the end of his rope. It's a story about the materialistic society that has made people the way they are.... It criticizes the society that turns decent men into criminals.

—Lemmon, interviewed by Rex Reed for *The New York Sunday News*, 11 Feb 1973

I did like this man [Jack Godell in *The China Syndrome* (1979, James Bridges)], but I didn't think he was beyond the average. I think that at the end of the film when he says he was the hero, I think he is correct in a way, but he is, like so many of us, might be, we don't know, an average person that under sudden exigency, under circumstances that suddenly happen, may behave in a very noble way.

—Lemmon, interviewed by David Sheehan for *Oscar Preview*; aired NBC, 12 Apr 1980

The fact is that it's much more difficult to give a good film performance than a good stage performance, particularly in something like *Tribute* [1980]. The Scottie Templeton character I play is very mercurial. He can go from tears to laughter with scarcely a beat.

On stage I had five minutes to build to such a transformation, but the way the shots are divided in a film I have to do it almost cold, and maybe do it 5 or 10 or 20 times until Bob Clark decides he has the shot he wants to print.

—Lemmon, interviewed by Tom Buckley for *The New York Times*, 9 May 1980

Q. When the role in *Missing* [1982] was first offered to you, you weren't available, so Costa-Gavras delayed production.

A. Thank God. I would be tempted to say maybe he is the greatest director I've worked for, but when I start getting wrapped up in *Missing*, I realize that some of it may be because it was the most recent. But if I had to pick only one film, I would probably pick *Missing* as the greatest experience I've had and the one film that, in the final result, is the most satisfying to me. I think it's as important as anything I've been lucky enough to be in. No question.

Q. Before filming, did you talk about the character [Ed Horman] with Costa-Gavras?

A. Not to a great extent. But enough. Fortunately, we had a good rapport going on the set. Sometimes you go a couple of weeks before you really feel that you've got the character. And other times they fall in fast. This one fell in — and thank God, because I was coming right from one film to another without a lot of time to really think. I just had certain broad strokes in mind, but they were ones that we agreed on — and other things that I thought of literally on the plane to Mexico.

Q. Like the hat?

A. Yes, and Costa happened to agree on that. Also, Costa and I love to try things in a different way. When he'd get a take and want to print it, he'd say, "That's it, I want to print that. Now, just for the hell of it, let's try another version." And he'd throw something at me absolutely different. Like I was back in acting class, you know. He'd say, "Do you want to rehearse it?" And I'd say, "Hell no. Roll it. Just let it go." I got so excited I couldn't see straight. Like going to the gym if you're an athlete and working out.

He would never throw something that wasn't legitimate. In other words, the deeper and richer the character, the more ways the same character can behave legitimately. If he's going to be predictable, then who gives a damn in the first place. A really interesting character is not predictable. I think actors or directors often assume that a character must behave one certain way, and it's a terrible trap.

Q. Did you meet Ed Horman before the film?

A. No. I didn't want to meet him before. Many actors might want to meet him because they might feel they could learn something or get something from the real Ed Horman. If you're going to play MacArthur or Truman, or anybody famous where a great percentage of the audience is going to know that person, you're locked into something. You have to speak a certain way, walk a certain way, because he's known. But Ed Horman was not known.

It's exactly what I was just talking about. If I can treat him as if he was fictional, as most characters are, then I'm not inhibited. It is unimportant that I be dead honest. It *is* important that I do not portray a totally different character, but can give my interpretation of him without the audience saying. "That's not Ed. I know Ed and that's not Ed." I want to make the character as rich as I can, not be as honest as I can. Because I don't think that dramatic reality has a damn thing to do with reality. The trick is to make it *seem* real. That's the whole thing.

—Lemmon, interviewed for *Dialogue on Film*, *American Film*, Sept 1982

[On the set of *Missing*] Costa reminded me slightly of John Ford in the sense of throwing the actor, but in a healthy way. Every now and then, he would tell somebody, but not me, that something was going to happen. The very first scene that I shot was in a garden; I'm talking with a kid who was picked up. A maid is serving tea, they're playing tennis in the background — but there's a revolution going on.

What he didn't tell me is that he was going to shoot off some guns in the distance. So nobody paid any attention, but I, naturally, reacted to it. I realized what he was doing as it happened, but he got that sense of disbelief: that disconcerting aspect to things that people who live there would take for granted but an American would be stunned by.

—Lemmon, interviewed by Peter S. Greenberg for *Rolling Stone*, 13 May 1982

Sissy [Spacek] is an immensely talented girl. A very dedicated young actress, almost too much so. She scared the hell out of me while we were working on *Missing*, because I was afraid she'd burn herself out before we got the scene. Talk about preparation — this girl would be off in a corner sobbing two hours before we ever had the lights up! Jesus, I never *saw* anybody pour themselves into it like she did! I was really worried about it. Because with all her awards and such, she still has not had all that much experience as an actress.... And I thought she was going to be emotionally exhausted before we got down to it. Well, obviously, she never was, and her performance was all you could ask for. But I think as she gets older and works more, she'll accomplish the same thing without killing herself first.

—Lemmon, interviewed by Alanna Nash for *Esquire*, Feb 1985

Eddie LEVEQUE [1896-1989]

Born: El Paso, Texas, to American/Mexican parents. Influenced by his maternal granduncle, Rito Armendariz, an impressario, mime and puppeteer, LeVeque began working with him at age 4. His first film work was for the American Film Company in Chicago. After a time of riding with Pancho Villa (as his interpreter) he skipped camp, headed for Hollywood and got a job at the Keystone Studios, eventually becoming one of the Keystone Kops:

Pretty soon Mack Sennett made a picture called *The Bangville Police* [1912], which was all about these crazy cops. It turned out to be the first Keystone Kops picture, and I played one of the Kops. Everyone at the studio played a Kop, even big stars like Fatty Arbuckle and Chester Conklin. Mack Sennett himself occasionally played a Kop. So did Bobby Vernon, who became Gloria Swanson's leading man. Another comic, Ford Sterling, usually played the chief.

We must have made forty or fifty pictures starring the Keystone Kops. And the Kops were in a lot of the other comedy pictures shot at the studio. Whenever a picture got bogged down and they needed more laughs, they'd throw the Kops in for as many sequences as possible. It didn't matter much if the Kops fit the plot of the picture....

When we started shooting a Kops picture, we never had much of a script, just a story line that more or less gave us the beginning, the middle and the end of what the picture was supposed to be about. Before a Kops sequence, the director would say, "All right, boys, do what you want, do what's funny, only don't hurt yourselves." That was the only "direction" we received.

But it was strange, once we were in the car and the chase began, there was an exhilaration that came over you. You forgot yourself, and you just took chances. I took many a fall that was unnecessary, but everyone was trying to outdo everyone else.

There was always that spirit of good-natured competition. The only thing that mattered was to make it funny.

—LeVeque, interviewed by Walter Wagner for *You Must Remember This* (New York: G.P. Putnam's Sons, 1975)

Jerry LEWIS [1926-]

Born: Joseph Levitch in Newark, New Jersey. Following solo work as a comic performer, he teamed up with Dean Martin in 1946; in 1949, their successful night club act moved to the screen beginning with My Friend Irma:

Hal Wallis acquired the rights from CBS to produce a movie version [of the CBS radio network hit, *My Friend Irma*], casting Dean and me as the boyfriends.

But first we had to take screen tests. Dean came off fine as Steve Laird, the straitlaced, handsome proprietor of an orange- juice stand. All I had to do was fill the shoes of Al, a wisecracking, blustery type, the sort of character you'd meet at racetracks, which Jack Carson used to play so successfully in Warner Brothers B movies.

I struggled with the script, but the harder I worked at it, the more frustrating it became. I wasn't Al, and I knew it....

George Marshall, the director, tried his darndest to boost me over the hurdle....

After the fourth take, he slowly shook his head. "All right, let's wrap it."

A moment later we were alone. "Jerry, I'll be honest. It's a mistake to cast you in this role. You're not making it...not even *this* close." He spread his arms wide, then dropped them helplessly to his sides....

The following morning I went to see Cy Howard at his office on the Paramount lot. We kicked the problem around and a couple of hours later created a new character named Seymour. I named him after the bike I had owned as a kid. And Seymour was the same kid Hal Wallis had caught at the Copa, the same one Cy Howard and George Marshall saw when they were at Slapsie Maxie's. What finally nailed the movie role was the scene in which I'm introduced as the eager, peripatetic nut hired by Steve Laird to help him run the orange-juice stand. Maybe you'll remember ...a million oranges squeezed in a minute and a half.

That's what made it happen. I played myself, a mischievous nine-year-old kid. And from then on, with rare exception, I was never anything other than that on the screen.

Paramount hired Frank Tashlin as director [of *Hollywood or Bust* (1956)]. He had already gone through the ringer with us the year before while directing *Artists and Models* [1955].

Tashlin, a big burly guy who carried his body around as though it was a strain to move from place to place, had a mind that moved at lightning speed. His knowledge of comedy far surpassed that of any director I had ever worked with. What I learned from him couldn't be bought at any price, because there is no college in the world where they can teach you how to think funny. But first I had to learn a painful lesson — how to behave.

I wouldn't tell Dean what I thought of him, so Frank Tashlin took all the flack. For six weeks I laid it into him, grandstanding, playing the king, reacting intemperately to his directions before each take. And during that time, through one tantrum after another, he withstood the onslaught, amazingly, with a forbearing equanimity. Meanwhile, everyone on the set became irritable....

Then the day came when Tashlin couldn't stand my antics any longer. He stopped the production cold, gathered the crew around him in a circle and accosted me.

"I want you off the set."

"Ho."

"I mean it, Jerry. Off! You're a discourteous, obnoxious prick — an embarrassment to me and a disgrace to the profession."

I looked about, the blood draining from my face. I could see a hundred or more people watching; it was a bad dream, a nightmare.

"Hey, Tish, whoa — calm down. When did you get the right...."

"Jerry, as director of this picture, I order you to leave. Go. Get your ass out of here and don't come back."

It was the longest walk of my life. I went home sobbing and spent the whole afternoon staring into myself, seeing all my efforts ending in despair, wasted, adding up to nothing but failure.

That evening I called his house. He wouldn't come to the phone. I tried reaching him again and again. Finally: "Yes, what is it?"

"Tish, I'm sorry. I can't tell you how sorry I am. I was wrong. All I ask is, please, let me come back."

A brief hesitation. "Will you behave?"

"Yes. I won't give you cause to be angry with me anymore. I promise."

"OK. Report to work in the morning. The shoot is at seven o'clock...."

I kept the lid on, doing whatever Tashlin wanted; no more hassles, everything in gear. But inside, the pressure was building, building — the vital lie, the lie that still stuck in my throat; the hostility I felt toward myself for not admitting that Dean's and my partnership was a sham. Yet a fear of what lay beyond became the knot which chafed at my dependency on Dean. I had to break out of it; otherwise, I knew it would eventually kill me. [Lewis worked for Tashlin an additional six times: *The Geisha Boy* (1957), *Rock-a-Bye Baby* (1958), *Cinderfella* (1960), *It's Only Money* (1962), *Who's Minding the Store?* (1963) and *The Disorderly Orderly* (1964).]

—Lewis, in his (with Herb Gluck) *Jerry Lewis In Person* (New York: Atheneum, 1982)

Q. You once said that your three favorite comedians were Charlie Chaplin, Stan Laurel, and Jackie Gleason. Have they influenced your work?

A. The only one that influenced me was Stan.... Stan was a teacher. I had to pay such careful attention because he established all of our discussions with, "I'm not going to be here long, so pay attention to me...." I would send him my work day by day as I wrote it. If he didn't call me in the evening, it meant I'd better rewrite it. Or if he'd call me, he'd tell me, "Good lad. Work on that. Place the camera, lad." That was his way of telling me I had to watch the placement, that the joke could hurt if I wasn't careful. But I'd then send him sketches of how I was going to shoot it. Then he'd give me marks. I didn't always agree with him, and the few times I didn't I went on my ass. I had to do it over — his way.

—Lewis, interviewed for *Dialogue on Film*, *American Film*, Sept 1977

Chaplin was both the *shlemiel* and the *shlimazel*. He was the guy who spilled the drinks — the shlemiel — and the guy who had the drinks spilled on him — the shlimazel....

My Idiot character plays both the shlemiel and the shlimazel, and at times the inter-mix. I'm always conscious of the three factors — done to, doing to self, and doing to someone else by accident or design — while playing him, but they are not in acute focus. They swim in and out of any given moment....

In each film I attempt to apply substance to The Idiot's character somewhere, sometime. The serious side of his character development cannot take place early in the film. Audiences will not accept it. But once The Idiot has made them laugh, once he is communicating clearly with them on the level of laughter, he can develop substance. Audiences then not only accept it but want it. They want him to be a little more than an idiot because in some of his entanglements he strikes awfully close to home.

—Lewis, in his *The Total Film-maker* (New York: Random House, 1971)

The Nutty Professor [1963], my fourth film as director-writer, happened out of a desire to do a comedy version of the classic horror story, *Dr. Jekyll and Mr. Hyde*. I had the whole movie envisioned, but the professor himself, Julius Kelp, took a long time to jump into my skin. Mainly because I couldn't find his voice.

Then, early in 1962, on a train going from Los Angeles to New York, while I sat in the parlor car having a drink with Jack Keller, this little guy walked up wearing eyeglasses so thick that I swear he looked like a frog peeking out of two Mason jars. He cleared his throat: "Ah, ah, ah, ah-hem, are you the show business fellow?"

I said, "Yes, I am. Who are you?"

"Haggendosh, Furnace Pipeline and Storm Window Company, Clevelend. I, ah, ah-hem, you make this trip often for shows and skits and sketches?"

"Yes, I travel back and forth."

"Oh, marvelous. Ah, say, are you going to have breakfast in the, ah, morning, or ah...the...ah, ah...my card, sir. Haggendosh, that is."

I bought him drinks for two hours; never took my eyes off him.

Then I headed to my drawing room and looked straight into the mirror: "How do you do? I, ah, ah, ah-hem, I think it's you. Ah, ha-ha, marvelous. Actually, yes. Good."

And there he was!

Many people thought the flip side of Professor Kelp — the hateful character, Buddy Love — was a vengeful attack on Dean. Untrue. No, Buddy Love was a composite of all those rude, distasteful, odious, crass, gross imbeciles whom we can spot instantly at any large gathering. We know him only too well. He's the insensitive putz who slams the door in children's faces on Hallowe'en. He's the miser who thinks Christmas is humbug, the walking time bomb who kills Presidents, the "nice boy next door" who rapes a lady in the street. He's all those things. But he isn't Dean. He's Buddy Love, infinitely for himself and disliking all other humans.

I made him a glaringly destructive force, despicable to the core, as a balance against the loving professor.

—Lewis, in his (with Herb Gluck) *Jerry Lewis In Person* (New York: Atheneum, 1982)

There are thirty ways to show a joke — insert it, cut to it, refer to it, punch it, lay back, double-cut! But why, and how?

George Marshall and I did a joke in *Hook, Line and Sinker* [1969]. We were doing a progression of scenes where a poor married man is getting his bellyful of domestic crap — weeding the plants, washing his car, sweating a broken garbage disposal. In this montage of annoyances we have The Idiot, the husband, painting on a ladder. The top of it is out of frame. The kids and dog run through the patio and knock it over. George was prepared to cut to The Idiot on his ass, paint all over him.

It was against my chemistry. I said, "George, when the kids run through and we see the ladder go over, we presume they just knocked it over. Okay, let's get another cut of the kids running further with the dog, then take them about a hundred and eighty degrees running back to where they created the trouble. They jump over the ladder, we widen a hair, and we see what was on the ladder."

I got livid to think we were going to knock this thing over, then cut to something that said visually, "Oh, I was on the ladder and they knocked me off." Certainly, it would have worked with the cut. But it was better with a sweep. It delivered better with a camera movement. [In addition to his debut, Lewis also worked on Marshall's *Scared Stiff* (1953), *Money from Home* (1954) and *The Sad Sack* (1957).]

—Lewis, in his *The Total Film-maker* (New York: Random House, 1971)

Robert LEWIS [1909-]

Born: New York City. An actor and director on both stage and screen and a co-founder of The Actors Studio, he made his film debut in Tonight We Raid Callais (1943, John Brahm):

Brahm didn't make many important films but he planned his shots — positions and movements of characters, camera angles, cuts, etc. — with great care, and I assiduously studied his handling of the actors and crew. His script was marked so meticulously that it made Bertolt Brecht's famous, detailed director's book for *Mother Courage* look sloppy by comparison.

Ultimately, Brahm also used me as an actor in one of his films. The part was a French collaborationist, and I made myself up to look like Laval, the foreign minister in the Vichy government. The picture was called *Tonight We Raid Callais* and had a cast including Annabella, Beulah Bondi, Blanche Yurka, Marcel Dalio, Howard da Silva, and Lee J. Cobb. Since the United States had entered World War II, Hollywood films concentrated on Nazis, Japanese, and collaborators. In the next picture, also about the German occupation of France, *Paris After Dark* [1943, Leonide Moguy], I was promoted to a Nazi colonel with the unlikely name of Pirosh. This one starred George Sanders who, with his clipped British delivery, naturally played the leader of the French underground. Too bored to read his dull material in advance, Sanders hardly knew the plot of the picture. He'd doze happily in his dressing room until they called him for a "take." "What do I say, luv?" he'd ask the script girl. After checking his lines, he'd deliver them in that charming way that couldn't possibly disturb whatever meaning the speech might have. This Sanders Method kept him working successfully in films, without a pause, for years.

They cast me in the role of a German officer, supporting Lassie, one of the big MGM stars, in *Son of Lassie* [1945, S. Sylvan Simon].

When I say Lassie was the star, I mean that on the way to our location in Patricia Bay, British Columbia, Canada, Lassie got the one bedroom on the train while Peter Lawford, Lassie's co-star, and I, a mere featured player, were relegated to lower and upper berths, in that order. When the script required the three of us to play a scene in the icy waters of Patricia Bay, the first one to be pulled out at the end of the shot was Lassie, who was immediately wrapped in towels and placed in front of an electric heater. Peter and I, left to fend for our shivering selves, downed several fingers of Scotch that a charitable electrician gave us in order to ward off pneumonia.

But, at least, I had an opportunity to study the remarkable acting technique of Lassie. He was the complete Stanislavskiite. Requiring an emotional memory exercise to get to a fever pitch high enough to make the dog bare his teeth and snarl at the enemy (me), Rudd Weatherwax, Lassie's personal trainer and Method coach, had only to "rev up" a motorcycle.

—Lewis, in his *Slings and Arrows: Theater in My Life* (New York: Stein & Day, 1984)

Chaplin, as a director, is superb. He only talked to me about the *interpretation* of my character as M. Verdoux's friend, Maurice, the village apothecary [in *Monsieur Verdoux* (1947)]. "He's the kind of bore who lectures when he talks," Charlie might say. Never once "Say it like this" or "Go faster or slower" or any of the kind of external manipulating to which actors are so often submitted.

Not that his directing technique is always the same. I have seen him with an amateur give every move and inflection because he had chosen the person not for his acting ability but because of a certain quality that Chaplin needed for that moment. He knows that the quickest way to get his result in this case is through imitation. Watching him direct a five-year-old child, I realized why *The Kid* [1921] was so wonderful. He makes the whole thing a game for the child, popping out from behind the camera and indulging in all sorts of shenanigans to keep the child's reactions spontaneous.

—Lewis, in *Theatre Arts Monthly*, June 1947

Lois LINDSAY

A chorus girl in several of Busby Berkeley's dance routines:

[Busby Berkeley] never made us dance. He never made anyone dance. He never chose a girl on her dancing ability. Chose 'em purely on looks....

We sat at those pianos [in *Golddiggers of 1935*] for days and day and days. We did nothing except that and just look pretty. But he would have us there for maybe two months on salary. And longer. If the front office would call and say, "What are you doing with all these people? Why do you have them there? We're paying them money and don't see any results," he'd say, "Okay, girls, come on now, the front office is coming down and [they] want to see something." He'd say, "Now when they come down, I want you all to get up and do *tour jetés* like crazy." The front office would come down and he'd say, "This is what I've been working on." They'd say, "Well, it looks pretty bad." And he'd say, "Well, I have to have the girls here to work with them in order to know what I'm going to do." In the meantime he's doing the whole thing in his head. And he would have us there and keep us on salary. All these months, and many times we would knit, play poker, tell jokes....

Q. Were you one of the water-logged girls in the pool in "By a Waterfall" [in *Footlight Parade* (1933)]?

A. Oh, sure. Of course, he'd say little half-way-dirty things like, "Okay, girls, now spread your pretty little legs." And it would get a giggle out of everybody. He didn't mean it to be disrespectful, he was doing it to have fun. On the other hand, we could kid with him, and did quite often....

Q. That "By a Waterfall" number must have been quite arduous.

A. It was, it was. But everything with Buz was more of a, not a physical activity, it was the standing and waiting while the camera and Buz did the work, really, because his work was more camera angles.

—Lindsay, interviewed by John Kobal (1976) for *People Will Talk* (New York: Alfred A. Knopf, 1985)

John LITHGOW [1945-]

Born: Rochester, N.Y.; son of Arthur Lithgow, regional theater actor, director and producer. Studies at Harvard College and The London Academy of Music and Dramatic Art, and work on the London stage preceded his film debut in Dealing (1972, Paul Williams). He then worked with The Long Wharf Theatre and on Broadway before making a second film — Obsession (1976, Brian De Palma). In 1983, he played Roberta in George Roy Hill's The World According to Garp (1982):

When I read John Irving's book, I thought I'd be the perfect Roberta, but George Roy Hill thought I was too tall. However, he relented. During preparations for the part, I became interested in transsexuals. By coincidence I'd read *Conundrum* by Jan Morris, the noted British travel journalist, who was quite well known as a man. Before his change of life, he had climbed Everest with Sir Edmund Hillary. He led quite the adventurous life as a '40s macho man, and was even more captivating as a woman. Because she seemed more content as a woman than she'd ever been as a man, Jan Morris was my model for Roberta. I played her as maternal and compassionate but not artificial.

—Lithgow, interviewed by Ellis Nassour for *Theater Week*, 30 May 1988

Wednesday May 4

I was chatting with [costume designer] Kristi [Zea] when I first caught a glimpse of Debra [Winger]. I saw a little field mouse of a woman peeking at me from behind the door of the makeup trailer, about 40 yards away, dressed in sweat pants, sneakers, and orange goosedown. Kristi introduced us....

Our first scene together in [*Terms of Endearment* (1983, James L. Brooks)] and the first to be shot, is a chance encounter in the supermarket. Sam is clearly shy, but emboldened by a crush left over from Emma's fruitless bank dealings. He comes forward to save her from a rancorous cashier who'd been humiliating her in front of the other customers and her two kids. Enter Sam Burns from the bank, her fumbling knight in tarnished armor. As he pays the difference, his heart is thundering in his chest. Unveiling the new Sam Burns [Lithgow replaced another actor after production had begun] for a crew of about forty strangers, acting with a new leading lady, half-smitten with her already, I had no trouble at all getting in touch with Sam's earnest, effortful nervousness....

Saturday May 7

In an abandoned warehouse converted to a makeshift soundstage, I did my end of a brief telephone call with Emma — the dutiful "I just had to talk to you" scene, a midpoint in the affair. This was the only scene done by my departed predecessor, the other Sam Burns, and there was lots of joking on the subject: "Ha, better do it good! You know what happened to the last guy!" I did it good all right, with Debra secretly talking dirty to me on the other end of the line.

Then, at dusk — "magic hour" they call it — we did our poignant goodbye scene, in the parking lot back at the motel. It required a lot of smiling through tears, and I privately stoked myself up by meditating on agonizing thoughts of unbearable loss. I would sit on the fender of my car, my legs dangling a little absurdly, my feet still shod in those foolish brogans, I would shake with sobs and on "action" I would grin and wave as Debra drove up — her station wagon all packed for her family's big move. I *think* the scene went well, people seemed moved and pleased with it, but it was a struggle. With the whole crew racing against the dwindling light, smelling a "wrap," and hungry for supper, and with Jim bumptiously hastening us through our paces, it was pretty hard to concentrate. Hanging on to the emotions was like keeping an erection in a dog pound. Oh well....

—Lithgow, in *Film Comment*, Dec 1983

Q. What about [*The Adventures of*] *Buckaroo Bonzai* [1984, W.D. Richter]? The plot is so complicated and your character so unusual I can't imagine even seeing that in script form. How did you decide to accept that role?

A. Well, I read it and I was intrigued. This is one of those that I turned down the first time. I understood it, alright, although there were certain things that I didn't understand. But it just seemed so far out! I was really curious about the tone of it. I spent a lot of time with Ric [W.D. Richter] just talking about just that point before I got involved. He is such a marvelous man with such a terrific imagination, and a terrific sense of humor. And in a way I needed to find out just what kind of sense of humor he had before I did get involved. I must say it was one of the most hilarious, wonderful experiences I've ever had....

—Lithgow, interviewed by David Livingston for *The Cable Guide*, Aug 1985

Movie directors tend not to direct you much at all. They're much more into staging and the camerawork. More often than not, you arrive, and you're expected to start acting immediately. The director hardly has a word to say to you. You'd be amazed. Some of them are very candid about it. I worked with Peter Hyams on *2010* [1984], and he said, "Boy, these guys who direct plays, and they have four weeks of rehearsal? I wouldn't know what to do." And he doesn't. You arrive, the camera rolls, and you start acting. It's as simple as that. The other extreme is someone like Herbert Ross [on *Footloose* (1984)], who is a stage director also, who wants two weeks of very attentive rehearsal. He really breaks down the script, stands people up, moves them around on taped diagrams. In movies, an actor has to do a great deal more, because directors aren't accustomed to worrying about it, and their ideas are usually not very concrete....

When I did *Footloose*, I went to a Baptist minister in Provo, Utah, where we were shooting, and pretended to be in a terrible spiritual crisis just so I could hear someone talk in earnest about being saved, someone who really believed it. I felt like a real hypocrite, needless to say, but it was very useful.

—Lithgow, interviewed by Don Shewey for *Caught in the Act: New York Actors Face to Face* (New York: New American Library, 1986)

Harold LLOYD [1893-1971]

Born: Burchard, Nebraska. Studies at The School of Dramatic Art in San Diego preceded his film debut in 1912 working as an Indian extra for The Edison Studios in San Diego. With Hal Roach he devised his first screen persona, "Willie Work"; later at Pathé, they developed a series based on a character they named "Lonesome Luke":

I told Roach that I had something that was an improvement on Willie Work, at least. When he saw it he approved. Later it was tagged with the name of Lonesome Luke. For it my father had found a worn pair of Number 12AA last shoes in a repair shop on Los Angeles Street, where they had been left for resoling by an Englishman on his uppers. Dad asked the cobbler if he thought five dollars would compensate the owner. The cobbler was sure of it — five dollars bought a good pair of shoes. In a haberdashery dad found a black-and-white vertical striped shirt and bought out the stock. The coat of a woman's tailored suit, a pair of very tight and short trousers, a vest too short, a cut-down collar, a cut-down hat and two dots of a mustache completed the original version of Lonesome Luke. The cunning thought behind all this, you will observe, was to reverse the Chaplin outfit. All his clothes were too large, mine all too small. My shoes were funny, but different; my mustache funny, but different.

—Lloyd, in his *An American Comedy* (New York: Longmans, Green & Co., 1928)

During the early days of my screen appearances, I played a character called Lonesome Luke. It was thought then, as now, an obvious advantage for a comedian to have an established character in a series of pictures instead of essaying a new role with a new picture. In this way, though one becomes a sort of label, one is readily recognized as one first flashes upon the screen. Chaplin, Keaton, Langdon and I get this happy recognition at once....

But though the character was readily recognized, I didn't like Lonesome Luke. He was rigid, and gave very little leeway for development. He wore a little mustache, for no reason other than that Charlie Chaplin, who was already a big success on the screen, wore one, and therefore it was thought that all comedians had to wear a mustache. My other visible distinguishing bit was a pair of very tight trousers. After more than sixty Lonesome Lukes, I loathed the get-up and the character. I had not felt this way in the beginning, for naturally I was anxious to get on and I did what they wanted without resentment....

I wanted a sincere, serious character. I wanted to be on the screen a fellow who wouldn't be ridiculous, if a romance or the ordinary story of a boy and girl came along. I wanted to wear decent or at least appropriate clothes. When I took my ideas for a new character to the company I was working for, they were not at all sympathetic. "We," they told me, "have spent a great deal of money in making and advertising Lonesome Luke, and who is Harold Lloyd anyway...?"

I kept bothering them at the studio until finally they allowed me to try the character I wanted to play [the young man with the horn-rimmed glasses].

—Lloyd, in *The Ladies Home Journal*, May 1926

I had to direct the first few glasses-character pictures myself. I didn't intend to. I didn't even intend to do the first one [*Over the Fence* (1917)]. I hired a director for it — J. Farrell MacDonald, who had directed pictures [Hal] Roach and I were extras on. He had never directed comedy. He would say, "Harold, how do you want this scene?" I had to tell him exactly how the scene should go....

As a rule, when I put on the glasses, I never did anything you couldn't believe in. It may be a little improbable, but you could figure it could happen.

We used 4 buildings [for *Safety Last* (1923, Fred Newmeyer and Sam Taylor)]. We picked out a structure we wanted for the actual building, then we chose a two story, four story, or whatever height building we needed. Then we built our own sets on top of them. We started with a one-story building and built our set right on the edge of the real building's roof. We built it so that we could put platforms out and constructed the scaffolding on the side so that the cameraman could be up there and shoot down. I remember how we had to put platforms low enough and narrow enough so that the cameraman could miss it when he was shooting down at an angle.

The platform would be 14 feet or so below us. From above it looked no bigger than a postage stamp! It was loaded with mattresses in order to break our fall if we did slip as we went through our antics. We didn't want to commit suicide just to make somebody laugh. But we were always in danger despite this precaution. Falling even a short distance was no small matter. Besides, we could easily roll off the platform because it didn't have any railings around.

In those days, we didn't want to divulge how we performed our stunts [many of Lloyd's stunts in this film were done by Harvey Parry]. We didn't want to give away any of our techniques for fear of making the public disillusioned with the thrill of it all. Looking back, it seems strange that we would have this worry, for the thrills were far from artificial. The danger, while not as great as it might appear to the public, was nevertheless still very real.

—Lloyd, interviewed by William Cahn for *Harold Lloyd's World of Comedy* (New York: Duell, Sloan and Pearce, 1964)

I made two really different types of pictures. One was a *gag* type of picture where the picture depends mostly on the comedy business — *Safety Last*...was a gag type picture. *The Freshman* [1925, Fred Newmeyer and Sam Taylor], on the other hand, is a character comedy. It starts much slower than a gag comedy. You have to condition it more, and it builds as it goes on. You have to plant your character and you get the audience completely with him; and you have to understand him and his background, and, definitely, his objective. The picture depends as much on the characterization and understanding of the boy as it does on the comedy business.

—Lloyd, interviewed by Hubert I. Cohen for *Film Comment*, Fall 1969

Carole LOMBARD [1908-1942]

Born: Jane Peters in Fort Wayne, Indiana. Discovered by Allan Dwan at age 12, she made her film debut in his A Perfect Crime (1921). In 1936, she starred as Irene Bullock in Gregory La Cava's My Man Godfrey:

For eighteen nights after I read the script I shut myself up in the house, trying to figure out how this idiotic maiden would look and sound. I wouldn't see anyone. I was a recluse...and boy, did I hate it!

I spent hours making faces and talking to myself in the mirror trying to get my character to come to life. She was out of key with the dialogue and the plot. Then I recalled what my first dramatic coach had told me: that the center of all pictorial expression lay in the lips and the eyes. By letting my lips hang open just a trifle, widening my eyes and elevating the eyebrows, I managed to get the expression of foolish expectancy to fit Irene's habit of greeting the most obvious facts of life with breathless surprise and delight.

—Lombard, interviewed for *The New York Post*, 12 Sept 1936

[*My Man Godfrey* is] the maddest picture I ever worked in, and I *love* it! Everybody here is a specialist in his or her type of madness — and with the guiding genius of Gregory La Cava for inspiration, they're out-doing themselves. Any time they let down, the keen finger of his wit stirs them up again....

Of course, Greg doesn't always know just what is coming next, because from Bill Powell's straight-faced, sharp edged kidding, Alan Mowbray's insidious wit, Gene Pallette's playfulness, Alice Brady's Alice-Bradyishness, and Mischa Auer's clowning and imitations, anything is liable to happen. And, knowing that, you realize you have to keep on your toes.

—Lombard, interviewed by William F. French for *Movie Classic*, Sept 1936

Whenever a script calls for the star to take a beating, directors immediately think of me. Whenever a girl has to be tossed about, man-handled or ducked in a pond of cold water, all minds turn in one direction. Mine....

In *Love Before Breakfast* [1936, Walter Lang], there was a scene where I went to bat with Preston Foster and wound up with a beautiful black eye. Remember *My Man Godfrey*? There was nothing exactly ladylike about that unforgettable tussle in the shower with William Powell, during which I was doused with gallons and gallons of water.

But the prize for violence went to *We're Not Dressing* [1934, Norman Taurog]. In one scene I scampered too fast for Bing Crosby and in order to catch up with me he used football tactics. A neat flying tackle brought me down. I landed with a thud and six strained vertebrae.

In *Twentieth Century* [1934, Howard Hawks] I was kicked by John Barrymore. In *Virtue* [1932, Edward Buzzell] I was knocked cold by that brute, Pat O'Brien. Who says the life of an actress is a bed of roses. I can show a few fancy scars and bruises to back up my contention that life for me has been just one hard knock after another.

—Lombard, interviewed by Eugene Schrott for *Screen Book*, Feb 1939

Q. How about playing this dramatic part in *Made for Each Other* [1939, John Cromwell]? Do you like it or would you rather continue to play film flitterbugs like Irene in *My Man Godfrey*, the loony lady in *Nothing Sacred* [1937, William Wellman] and others? Which comes easier to you?

A. They're not really so different. You know the old thing, comedy and tragedy are akin? Like lots of old things, it's the truth. Back of all comedy there is tragedy; back of every good belly-laugh there is familiarity with things not funny at all.... And Irene in *Godfrey* was, I'd say, the most difficult part I ever played. Because Irene was a complicated and, believe it or not, essentially a tragic person.

—Lombard, interviewed by Gladys Hall for *Motion Picture*, Nov 1938

Sophia LOREN [1934-]

Born: Sofia Scicolone in Rome. Her first work was as an extra in Mervyn LeRoy's version of Quo Vadis? (1951) filmed at the Cinecitta Studios in Rome (she was one of Deborah Kerr's slaves). Another dozen bit parts, work in fumetti (soap-opera photographic cartoons), and modelling preceded her first lead in the title role of Aida (1953, Clemente Fracassi — for which Renata Tebaldi did the singing). Following that role, Loren signed a personal contract with Carlo Ponti, her mentor, teacher and later her husband. In 1957, she made her first Hollywood film, opposite Cary Grant in Stanley Kramer's The Pride and the Passion; later that year, she co-starred with John Wayne in Henry Hathaway's Legend of the Lost:

After the enchantment of Cary Grant and what turned out to be the disenchantment of Alan Ladd and *Boy on a Dolphin* [1957, Jean Negulesco], I didn't know what to expect of John Wayne....

I was relieved to find that John Wayne was exactly as advertised. Big, authoritative, gruff but polite, and a pro through and through. He showed up right on the minute, knew all his lines and moves, worked hard all day long without letup, and quit right on the minute. There was no doubt that he was in command, the captain on the bridge of the ship. He did not have to exert his authority overtly because everyone automatically deferred to him. Even the director, Henry Hathaway. But he never abused his powerful position. He simply assumed his stance and kept it. With me, he was polite and pleasant, but distant. He did not show affection toward anyone but neither did he show any hostility nor make outrageous demands. But everyone was in awe of him, scared of him somewhat, and a great concerted effort was made to anticipate his needs. [The film was produced by Batjac-Hagging-Dear/UA; Batjac was Wayne's company.]

A Countess from Hong Kong [1967] had been in [Chaplin's] desk drawer for twenty years. I heard tell that he had originally written it for Paulette Goddard, and that he had gotten it out and updated it after he saw me in *Yesterday, Today and Tomorrow* [1963, Vittorio de Sica]. To be directed by Charlie Chaplin — I would never have even dreamed it.

When Charlie had finished the script he invited me and Marlon Brando, whom he had cast in the male lead, to his house in Vevey, Switzerland, for a reading.... Charlie seated us comfortably and read the script in its entirety, acting all the parts, playing my role coquettishly, then switching abruptly to the stern, befuddled American consul whom Brando was to play. Charlie even went to the piano and played a song he had composed for the film.

Through it all, Brando was half asleep, or pretended to be, his head down on his chest, his eyes closed. Charlie paid him no mind, and didn't seem the least bothered, but I found Marlon's behavior terribly embarrassing. This was Charlie's first film in almost ten years, a terribly important event for him, and Brando slept.

Marlon's behavior that night was simply a portent of his performance in the film. I liked Marlon, and still do, and I admired him enormously as one of the greatest actors who had ever performed in films, but he was obviously better suited to dramatic roles than to comedy. In all fairness, he was certainly not suited to the role he was asked to play in *Countess*; uncomfortable in it, he gave up on it soon after we started. He didn't feel right in the character's skin — that can happen, and to make matters worse, he and Charlie did not get along. There was no chemistry between them, no interplay, no carefree climate to encourage the inspiration and invention that comedy needs: they often knocked heads, and day by day the atmosphere on the set grew more tense. Marlon gave an interview in which he said, "Charlie's not a verbal man. Words at times are his bitterest enemy." Charlie's method of direction, like de Sica's was not so much to explain as to demonstrate. As a superb actor, Charlie could much better convey his intentions by acting them out, and in a few moments achieve what another director would less ably describe with a torrent of words.

—Loren, interviewed by A.E. Hotchner for *Sophia /Living and Loving/Her Own Story* (New York: Wm. Morrow & Co., 1979)

Peter LORRE [1904-1964]

Born: Laszlo Loewenstein in Rosenberg, Hungary. Theater work in Berlin with Bertolt Brecht preceded his film debut in M (1931, Fritz Lang). Fleeing the Nazi regime, he worked in France, then England where he made his English language film debut in Alfred Hitchcock's The Man Who Knew Too Much (1934). The following year, he played Dr. Gogol in Karl Freund's Mad Love:

[Dr. Gogol] is only dangerous to a person when there is reason for it. He does not hate mankind. But he is willing to ruin anyone to gain his ends. If being dangerous to a person doesn't pay, he can be perfectly kind.

[My shaven head] gives the idea that this character thinks of his science only and not of personal appearance.

I believe the low spoken villain who is absolutely blasé about what he does, who works out a murder like a mathematical problem, for instance, is much more terrifying than the human fellow who commits a murder in a fit of anger....

Some actors study real characters, but in my case this would be fatal. I can't play a role save by imagination.

—Lorre, interviewed for the press kit for *Mad Love* (MGM, 1935)

[*The Maltese Falcon* (1941, John Huston)] was one of my happiest memories, a very nostalgic one, because for a few years we had a sort of stock company, an ensemble here [at Warner Brothers]. We were a ball team....

[With] each one of those people, Claude Rains, [Sydney] Greenstreet, Bogart and so on, there is one quality in common, that is quite a hard quality to come by, it's something you can't teach, and that is to switch an audience from laughter to seriousness. We can do it at will; most people can't.

—Lorre, interviewed by Elwood Glover for "Assignment," CBC Radio, 29-31 May 1962

Bessie LOVE [1898-1986]

Born: Juanita Horton in Midland, Texas. Initially employed by D.W. Griffith, she made her film debut in The Flying Torpedo (1916, John O'Brien) for Triangle-Fine Arts before appearing in Griffith's Intolerance later that year:

[*The Flying Torpedo*] was a gigantic one for its day and necessitated three directors working simultaneously: Jack O'Brien did the dramatic story; Cristy Cabanne, one of the studio's top directors, was in charge of the modern armored battle scenes; and the McCarthy Brothers were responsible for the special effects — miniature sets for destruction, bombs and explosions. Mr.

Griffith took the last rehearsal as usual, supervising the whole finished work....

David Butler, later a well-known actor and then a director for Fox, his father Fred, Raymond Wells and Erich von Stroheim all had small parts in the film.... Lively arguments went on between [von Stroheim] and Lucille [Young] and the rest of the cast as to what constituted a villain. Mr. von Stroheim insisted there was no such thing as an all-evil villain or all-pure hero; to be real they must be a mixture of both....

The Broadway Melody [1929, Harry Beaumont] had originally been written by Eddie Goulding for the Duncan Sisters — Rosetta, nicknamed Hank, and Vivian, called Queenie in the story; but something went wrong with the negotiations...and in the end I got the part of Hank, the little one, and beautiful Anita Page played Queenie.

Sound was new to all the studios except Warner's. At MGM we would rehearse a dramatic scene and hear the play-back; the sound engineers would say, "Too much echo" (or not enough something else); and we would vacate the set, which would then be stripped of curtains, furniture, rugs — everything except the walls. Carpenters would swarm on the set and hammer, hammer, hammer all the floorboards; everything would be replaced on the set, curtains re-hung, thicker carpets laid; we would rehearse again — emotion and all; again hear the play-back, again hear the engineers' "No!" and again try something different — more curtains, gauze walls. We kept on until it was as near perfect as we could turn it out at that stage, then went on to the next scene. We improved so much as we went along that the end didn't match the beginning....

William de Mille was the soul of quiet, retiring dignity, classic wit and good taste. He always wore a battered old hat on the set — he wore it when he went fishing too. He had worn it in 1925 when he made *New Brooms* at Lasky's with Neil Hamilton, Phyllis Haver and me; and now, in 1929, he was still wearing it for *The Idle Rich* at MGM....

His attitude towards life always appeared to be sophisticated, urbane, in complete control, a bit cynical: he was a walking understatement. He was expert at exposing superficial, shallow human failing and foibles. But when it came to digging deep into an actor's emotional vitals and dragging out his innermost hidden thoughts, I'm sure William de Mille would have been most embarrassed at the very idea....

All Mr. de Mille's comedy was perfectly timed. He had every camera angle literally drawn in his script before we ever set foot on the stage. He directed the exact moment at which you would crook your finger, before, after or during a line; and we would rehearse or re-take the scene until your finger crooked at his order. One day Miss [Clara] Beranger, who wrote all his scripts, confided that she had once accused him of ruining his comedy by making it too set and lacking spontaneity. She laughed as she recalled this, because his films were considered by intellectuals to be among the most impeccable to come out of Hollywood. I thought then that she had been right: that he did restrict his actors. Now I think differently. William de Mille's style was not the naturalistic acting I was used to, but the classical comedy of manners, demanding the utmost discipline, and timing was its most important tool.

—Love, in her *From Hollywood with Love* (London: Elm Tree Books, 1977)

Rob LOWE [1964-]

Born: Charlottesville, Virginia. He made his film debut in The Outsiders (1983, Francis Ford Coppola); in 1990, he played Alex in Curtis Hanson's Bad Influence:

My character's name is Alex, and he's the bad influence. He forces James Spader, who plays Michael, this upscale yuppie, to reexamine his life. He shows Michael that there is more to life than work, work, work, and having the right car, the right date, and the right things, the right stuff.

Q. And so Alex shows Michael the dark side of the world.

A. Alex introduces Michael to the dark side of himself. Alex is a seducer. He's a manipulator —

Q. A champion of the human urge.

A. Absolutely. Alex basically has no morals. He does whatever suits the occasion and follows his whims, and the only thing that really upsets Alex is people who pretend to be something they're not, people who are hypocrites. The one thing that you can say about Alex: he is an evil character, he has no morals, but he is honest to himself....

Q. How did Rob and his Atlanta troubles translate into Alex and his bad influence.

A. I just funneled any stress or any anger or any hurt that I was feeling — I just funneled it into the performance....

Q. Did you have a new roguish feeling to draw on? For a while you were, as they say in the newspapers, an alleged perpetrator.

A. One result was that I felt it important to be brazen about what Alex is, and not to back away from it....

Alex has this speech at the end of the movie about people being hypocritical. And I guess I put all my frustration and anger and rage into that. Because what this movie says, and what I believe, is that everybody is naughty, everybody is good. Everybody is God. Everybody is the devil. And if you don't realize you have both parts, that's what really causes problems....

I'd been committed to do *Bad Influence* for about four months before the Atlanta story broke. And when it broke, I was about two weeks away from rehearsals. What I had to go through definitely made the performance. It would have been a much different performance had this not happened.

—Lowe, interviewed by Mike Sager for *Interview*, Mar 1990

Myrna LOY [1905-]

Born: Myrna Williams on a ranch near Raidersburg, Montana. As a dancer she made her stage debut in 1916 in Helena, Montana performing her own choreography; at Grauman's Egyptian Theater in Hollywood she made her professional dance debut with Fanchon and Marco. She made her film debut in Pretty Ladies *(1925, Monta Bell); the following year she worked for Ernst Lubitsch on* So This is Paris:

Lubitsch used me in *So This is Paris* as Patsy Ruth Miller's maid. I was supposed to wake her in one scene by knocking on her boudoir door. I knocked in the usual way, overhand. "No, no, this way," Lubitsch directed, turning his palm upward. "Turn your hand over and rap lightly with your knuckles. It is more *gentle* waking her up that way." Talk about the "Lubitsch touch"! He made it frightfully complicated for actors, even in a tiny part like mine, but the results justified his means.

—Loy, in her (with James Kotsilibas-Davis) *Being and Becoming* (New York: Alfred A. Knopf, 1987)

One night, the director Edward Griffith saw me doing the usual half-caste in a film, and sent for me to take a test for Evie in an Ina Claire film called *Rebound* [1931]. I got the part. Evie was a little snob from the social register, but thank goodness, not a half-caste. I owe more to Griffith than all the others. I would never have been given my role in *Animal Kingdom* [1932] but for him, and it was the picture which proved to be the turning point in my career.

—Loy, interviewed by John Barber for *Leader Magazine*, 4 Dec 1948

Rouben Mamoulian rescued me, borrowing me for *Love Me Tonight* [1932], his musical spoof of Lubitsch....

Rouben had conceived Valentine as a pent-up aristocrat hungry for life and men, so bloody bored that she'd always be sleeping — on the stairs, on the furniture, anywhere. She's napping on a little Empire sofa at one end of this huge salon when Charlie Ruggles calls, "Valentine, Valentine, could you go for a doctor?" She perks right up: "Yes, bring him in!"

—Loy, in her (with James Kotsilibas-Davis) *Being and Becoming* (New York: Alfred A. Knopf, 1987)

[In *The Mask of Fu Manchu* (1932, Charles Brabin)] I carried around a pet python and whipped a young man tied to a rack and all sorts of dreadful things. Now I had been reading a little Freud around that time, so I called the director over one day and said, "Say, this is obscene. This woman is a sadistic nymphomaniac!" And he said, "What does *that* mean?" I mean, we did it all before these kids today ever thought of it, and we didn't even know what we were doing.

—Loy, interviewed by Rex Reed for *The New York Times*, 13 Apr 1969

Manhattan Melodrama [1934, W.S. Van Dyke] was a gangster tale, but an interesting one that would be frequently retold. Two pals grow up in the streets of New York. One becomes Clark Gable, a gangster; the other becomes William Powell, the governor who must order his friend's execution — hokum, but artfully done....

In that picture...you can see a transition in the way I play my relationships with Clark and Bill. I instinctively keyed my women to the personalities of the men. Male-female relationships were much more clearly defined in those days. My job was to vivify those relationships within the framework of the script, the mores, and the abilities of the men. Clark, for instance, suffered so much from the macho thing that love scenes were difficult. He kept very reserved, afraid to be sensitive for fear it would counteract his masculine image. I always played it a little bit tough with him, giving him what-for to bring him out, because he liked girls like that.... Of course, I didn't know all this at first. It was an instinctive thing with me.

I played differently with Bill. He was so naturally witty and outrageous that I stayed somewhat detached, always a little incredulous....

They called him "One-take Van Dyke." If he could get it the first time, he wouldn't even bother with a cover shot. "Actors are bound to lose their fire if they do a scene over and over," he said. "It's that fire that brings life to the screen." He wanted spontaneity, and speed ensured it.... Woody demanded extraordinary deeds and you needed the discipline to go along with it or you couldn't work with him. He ultimately became too fast; it became an obsession. But his pacing and spontaneity made *The Thin Man* [1934].

—Loy, in her (with James Kotsilibas-Davis) *Being and Becoming* (New York: Alfred A. Knopf, 1987)

Nora [Charles, in *The Thin Man*]...was sophisticated, tolerant and gay, and she maintained the romance and glamour that first attracted Nick [William Powell]. I didn't think she took her marriage too casually, she never gave it a lot of thought. And she always played a square game, never demanding more than she was willing to give....

Nora didn't try to make her husband over. She didn't monopolize his time, and she never, never nagged. She responded to all his moods, even to hostessing his amusing but low-brow pals, and sharing in a hilarious jamboree without rebukes. They were very modern and didn't parade their devotion, yet no one doubted their complete loyalty.

—Loy, interviewed by Maud Cheatham for *Screen Book*, Feb 1938

Nora, to me, is the ideal wife.... Remember in *The Thin Man*, how she never nagged, never scolded, was always a good sport, a witty companion and a perfectly swell friend? Well, she hasn't changed a bit in *After The Thin Man* (1936, W.S. Van Dyke).

The secret of Nora's success as a wife may be summed up in one phrase, "a sense of humor." [The other films in the *Thin Man* series were: *Another Thin Man* (1939, W.S. Van Dyke), *Shadow of The Thin Man* (1941, W.S. Van Dyke), *The Thin Man Goes Home* (1944, Richard Thorpe) and *Song of The Thin Man* (1947, Edward Buzzell); they also co-starred in *Manhattan Melodrama*, *Evelyn Prentice* (1934, William K. Howard), *The Great Ziegfeld* (1936, Robert Z. Leonard), *Libeled Lady* (1936, Jack Conway), *I Love You Again* (1940, W.S. Van Dyke), *Love Crazy* (1941, Jack Conway) and briefly in *The Senator Was Indiscreet* (1947 George F. Kaufman).]

—Loy, in the press packet for *After The Thin Man* (MGM, 1936)

From the moment I read the script of *Test Pilot* [1938, Victor Fleming] which was written especially for Clark Gable, Spencer Tracy and myself, I knew that it was my greatest screen opportunity. Cast as the wife of a test pilot, I had a role of unusual range and sympathy.

Here was a woman who lived under a constant shadow of fear for her husband's safety. This shadow was with her from the time he made a forced landing on her Kansas farm, and she fell in love with him. But she refused to let her worries get her down, meeting them with cheerfulness and persiflage.

It was a challenge to me to strike the right tone in this part — to be gay without seeming callous, to make it clear that my quips in times of stress covered an inner tension. The role had much more drama than any light-comedy part I have played. Yet there were many comic touches for balance.

In my favorite scene I stood with a crowd watching my husband, Clark Gable, test a plane high above the airfield. Suddenly the plane burst into flame. Clark bailed out and, after a terrifying instant, the parachute opened. I gave a hysterical giggle and said, "Wouldn't it be funny if it started to rain and everybody but my husband got all wet? He's got an umbrella." Then I fell in a faint.

The picture was made at March Field, the big Army air base in Southern California, and this added to my enjoyment of the role. It was a privilege to meet the men who tested planes, and the women who worried about them. Like the wife in *Test Pilot*, they hid their fears under gaiety and laughter; but in their case, of course, the fear was the real thing.

—Loy, in *The Saturday Evening Post*, 1 June 1946

In *Test Pilot*, [Clark] had a moment when he talked about the girl in the blue dress — the sky.

That scene terrified him to death. He got so upset when we shot it I had to keep reassuring, comforting him. Not that he couldn't do the scene — he did it beautifully — but he was afraid it would make him appear too soft. He had this macho thing strapped on him and he couldn't get out of it. [Loy and Gable also worked together on *Men in White* (1934, Richard Boleslavksy), *Wife vs. Secretary* (1936, Clarence Brown) and *Too Hot to Handle* (1938, Jack Conway).]

Spencer Tracy and I always played well together. He was a perfectionist, aware of everything he did with a part. Those seemingly relaxed, easy-going performances were carefully thought out, structured creations. He was always so afraid he'd go too far; he knew you had to measure your distance in films. That's one of the reasons he was so good.

When he made retakes, he wouldn't let me leave. "No, no, you wait," he'd say. "You've got to tell me how I'm doing." He'd do the scene and rush back to me: "Did I ham it up? Did I do too much?" Sometimes I'd say "Yes," although it wasn't true, just because he seemed to want that challenge. [Loy worked with Tracy 3 times: *Whipsaw* (1935, Sam Wood), *Libeled Lady* (1936, Jack Conway) and *Test Pilot*.]

My only reservations about doing [*The Best Years of Our Lives* (1946)] concerned working with William Wyler, because of stories from Bette Davis and other actors about his endless retakes and bullying. "I hear Wyler's a sadist," I told Sam [Goldwyn].

"That isn't true," he replied, with a genuine Goldwynism; "he's just a very mean fellow...."

[Wyler and I] had extraordinary communication, a kind of telepathy. Willy would start to speak and I'd say, "Oh, yes, I know what you mean." Despite rumors to the contrary, if he trusted actors, he gave them a chance to be creative. We could do whatever instinctively we felt like doing. Although that is perhaps my most serious film, as moving and meaningful today as it was then, Freddy [March] and I did it with great humor....

My only trouble on [*Cheaper By the Dozen* (1950)] came from two old friends: Walter Lang and Clifton Webb. I liked Walter...but he was the kind of director that drove me crazy. After going through my scenes ahead of me, acting out every detail without giving me a chance to try it, he would call, "O.K., let's shoot!"

Look, I can't work this way," I finally protested. "How about letting *me* do it?" I have to do it myself. I have to see how it *feels*, how my body responds. It's essential. Walter and I straightened that out and we never had another problem.

Clifton's transgressions were more subtle. As a stage-trained actor of the old school, he considered scene-stealing his duty. Apparently it was kosher to do this on stage in his day. It isn't in films. You are absolutely nose to nose and cannot move or you've turned your partner around with the back of his head or some awkward angle to the camera. We were trained to consider the camera supreme, and if you turned this way or that the scene was most likely ruined. No professional film actor ever does that — ever — so I wasn't looking for it....

—Loy, in her (with James Kotsilibas-Davis) *Being and Becoming* (New York: Alfred A. Knopf, 1987)

Bela LUGOSI [1882-1956]

Born: Bela Blasko in Lugos, Hungary. Studies at The Academy of Theatrical Art and work with the National Theatre, both in Budapest, preceded his film debut in The Leopard (1917, Alfred Deesy). In 1919, he left Hungary and appeared in several German films including a small part in F.W. Murnau's Der Januskopf (1920). In the U.S. he formed The Hungarian Repertory Theater and made his U.S. stage debut in 1922; he made his U.S. film debut in The Silent Command (1923, J. Gordon Edwards). His first appearance as Dracula was in a 1927 Broadway adaptation of Bram Stoker's novel; four years later he again played the title role in Tod Browning's film version:

In playing the picture I found that there was a great deal that I had to unlearn. In the theatre I was playing not only to the spectators in the front rows but also to those in the last row of the gallery, and there was some exaggeration in everything I did, not only in the tonal pitch of my voice but in the changes of facial expression which accompanied various lines or situations, as was necessary.

But for the screen, in which the actor's distance from every member of the audience is equal only to his distance from the lens of the camera, I have found that a great deal of repression was an absolute necessity. Tod Browning has continually had to "hold me down." In my other screen roles I did not seem to have this difficulty, but I have played *Dracula* a thousand times on the stage and in this one role I find that I have become thoroughly settled in the technique of the stage and not of the screen. But thanks to director Browning I am unlearning fast.

—Lugosi, interviewed for *Hollywood Filmograph*, 18 Oct 1930

A strange thing happened to me following [*Dracula*]... I discovered that every producer in Hollywood had definitely set me down as a "type" — an actor of this particular kind of role. Considering that before *Dracula* I had never, in a long and varied career on the stage of two continents, played anything but leads and straight characters, I was both amused and disappointed.

Of course, it is true, that every actor's greatest ambition is to create his own, definite and original role — a character with which he will always be identified, but on the screen I found this to be almost fatal.

—Lugosi, interviewed for the press book for *The Black Cat* (Universal Studios, 1934)

It is my particular pride that even in the most fantastic of my film roles I do not use makeup. Instead of depending upon masks, casts, court plaster and false features, I create the illusion of a terrifying, distorted or uncanny makeup by an appeal to the imagination. An evil expression in the eyes, a sinister arch to the brows or a leer on my lips — all of which take long practice in muscular control — are sufficient to hypnotize an audience into seeing what I want them to see and what I myself see in my mind's eye. In like manner, by the way in which I use my fingers and gesticulate with my hands, I give the illusion of their being misshapen, extra large, or extra small — or whatever the part requires. And I consider it part of an actor's art to be able to shorten or lengthen his body or change its very shape by the power of suggestion, without false paddings or other artificial aids.

—Lugosi, in the press book for *The Raven* (Universal Studios, 1935)

John LUND [1913-]

Born: Rochester, N.Y. Work on Broadway preceded his film debut in To Each His Own (1946, Mitchell Leisen); in 1948, he played John Pringle in Billy Wilder's A Foreign Affair:

Making heavies of heroes is a specialty of mine, and maybe that's why the Messrs. Brackett and Wilder gave me the part of Capt. John Pringle in the film. Pringle was the nominal hero, although he committed every crime except piracy and missed that one only because he was too far inland....

As a director, Billy Wilder is the answer to a mummer's prayer. He's skillful, yet gentle. At least, he's usually gentle. Once, after I muffed a bit of business several times, then managed to bring it off after a fashion, I turned to him and asked, "How was that?" Billy simply pointed to a prop magazine, opened to an advertisement that read: "Your Future is in Air Conditioning."

—Lund, in *The Saturday Evening Post*, 29 Aug 1953

Ida LUPINO [1916-]

Born: London, England; daughter of actor Stanley Lupino and actress Connie Emerald. Studies at The Royal Academy of Dramatic Art, a London stage debut at age 12, and work as an extra in British films preceded her first role in Her First Affaire (1932, Allan Dwan). In 1936, she played Gert Molloy in Alexander Hall's Yours for the Asking:

Any laughs I get in that picture I owe to the very foggy ladies I met at bars at three and four o'clock in the morning. For I watched those ladies as they grew more and more vague until they hardly seemed to have any faces at all, until their faces became soft blobs. I watched them look right past me as they called me endearing names. Studying them I grasped the complete indifference I must show in that scene where I pick myself up after falling on my face, less concerned than you ordinarily would be if you stubbed your toe.

—Lupino, interviewed by Adele Whitely Fletcher in an unsourced, undated article in the files of The Lincoln Center Library for the Performing Arts

I like mean roles. Best of all I like roles in which I can look awful, be awful. I don't care a fig about being pretty-pretty on the screen. There's one role I want to do more than anything — that's the part of the cheap little cockney girl in *The Light That Failed* [1939, William Wellman]. Paramount wanted to borrow Bette Davis for it, but she was afraid it might be too much like Mildred of *Of Human Bondage*, so I may get it after all. [She did.] I'd rather play the meanest character part than the most entrancing ingenue.

—Lupino, interviewed by Kay Osborne for *Modern Screen*, Nov 1936

I'm playing [Ellen in *Ladies in Retirement* (1941, Charles Vidor)] for sympathy. She's merely a victim of circumstances. She killed simply because there was no other way out. Her maniacal love for her unfortunate sisters is the whole motivating influence in Ellen's life.

No, I'm not stressing her madness. Plot situations carry that element in her character well enough. Only occasionally do you see this diabolical thing grip her personality. The first time is during a short London sequence when she goes to town to bring her sisters back to the country — Ellen finds they've been put away. Her intense fury is something to behold. From then on her outward calm completely belies the inner turmoil. Only when she decides to kill do you catch baleful glances of lunacy, and again when she's roused to anger by the crafty scheming of her nephew [Louis Hayward].

—Lupino, interviewed by Harry Mines for *Screen Life*, Oct 1941

There is only one performance I ever gave that I'm proud of. It was Ellen in *Ladies in Retirement*, a role that had been played with great success on Broadway by Flora Robson....

On Broadway Flora Robson played the older sister, a woman about 60; her mad sisters were supposed to be 45 and 50.

A man called Lester Cowan — a production executive — took a chance on a 21-year-old girl — myself [she was actually 25] — to play the Flora Robson role. He and director Charles Vidor decided to have Ellen be the youngest sister — 45 — and to have Elsa Lanchester and Edith Barrett play the two older women. One was supposed to be 50, the other about 60. Actually Elsa wasn't in her fifties yet at the time; neither was Edith, but the age jump wasn't as great for them as for me....

I must admit it was difficult for me at that age to play a role in which I would give the illusion of being 45. The fact that it was a period picture helped somewhat because I could wear period hairdos which made me look older. They pulled my hair back in a very severe hairdo.

The cameraman was the late George Barnes — one of the greatest. At 21, I had a little round baby face and he said, "To make you look 45, we'll do just a few things, like running red under the eyes in the circle area...." He didn't have the makeup man add black and gray or any terrible phony lines to age me; instead he had him just shadow my face down. George Barnes said, "I will do what I can with my camera, but nearly everything depends on your performance."

—Lupino, in *Movie Digest*, Nov 1972

The moment when Junior and his mother meet in the picture [*Junior Bonner* (1972, Sam Peckinpah)] when they're outside, Sam had us ad-lib that, and it went very well. But when it came time to do the inside portion of that same scene, Steve [McQueen] had rewritten it. I had already learned what I was supposed to say, and I said that I needed more time to learn these new lines. I had loved the original but wasn't as fond of what Steve had changed it to. But I went ahead and tried to be cooperative as possible because I felt that it was necessary for a mother and a son to be motivated by a common background for the scene to work.

Then when the scene was finally shot, Steve was even ad-libbing the new stuff he'd written. And I was blowing my cues because they just weren't there the way they were supposed to be. Well, then I blew up. Sam shut down for ten minutes to let things subside, and I went over to sit down alone.

After a little while, Sam sent over one of the crew to ask if I would like a little wine.... That kind of kindness was just the right touch to bring me back into the proper frame of mind to complete the scene. The next scene, Steve made another attempt to alter my character, and I was on the verge of blowing up again. But Sam just stopped all discussion by saying: "Okay, everybody on the set. Let's make a picture." And I played it the way it was written, and it worked.

—Lupino, interviewed by Garner Simmons for *Peckinpah: A Portrait in Montage* (Austin: University of Texas Press, 1982)

M

Jeanette MacDONALD [1901-1965]

Born: Philadelphia. Work in the chorus then as a lead on the New York stage preceded her film debut in The Love Parade (1929, Ernst Lubitsch). Between 1935 and 1942, she co-starred with Nelson Eddy eight times, including Naughty Marietta (1935):

From the start I, like all other singers aspiring to a screen career, had to rely on the technical experts. I wonder now how I was able to go through with my work when I was filming *Love Parade* and some of those earlier efforts. You would hardly believe the tedious and repeated efforts which had to be made to get the voice pitched exactly so. And when the filming *did* eventually begin, one could see the sound recording people twiddling about with funny little knobs as they tried to keep everything 'okay for sound.' Too often, after long and wearying 'takes,' one would have to start all over again. It was a nerve-racking life.

Now, in *Naughty Marietta*, my voice was recorded absolutely naturally, just as it is; its full volume and strength going straight to the microphone.

I am convinced this is why my songs, as heard from the screen, seem to be delivered more pliantly.

The horribly artificial and mechanical restraints which used to worry us so much are a thing of the past.... In *Marietta* I could sing as I felt, giving my best to the mood of the song and concentrating all my attention upon interpretation and delivery.

This, for the singing actress, is like living in a new world. She may abandon herself to her part; forget the mechanics of sound, which have no rightful place in the work of an artist, and...well, just sing. The machine is no longer the master. Thank heaven it is a good servant.

I feel, too, that in *Naughty Marietta*, Nelson Eddy...and I were well balanced in the emotional as well as the musical sense. [Director] "Woody" Van Dyke, patient, painstaking and confident, did the rest.

—MacDonald, interviewed by W.H. Mooring for *Kine Weekly*, 12 Apr 1935

When I got what proved to be my most enjoyable movie role — Marsha Mornay in *Maytime* [1937] — I was known in the theater and on the MGM lot as a singer. Marsha answered my striving for a truly dramatic part, as the story ranged from the time she was an ingenuous, romantic girl all through her life until she was a magnificent grande dame of eighty, a rare opportunity for expressing varieties of feeling and character delineation.

Beyond the dramatic possibilities there was the remarkable musical scope of *Maytime*.... I sang everything from simple folksongs to arias from Wagnerian operas to songs in French, Italian, German and English. Thus the music matched the range of the acting.

There was, too, the satisfaction of working with Robert Leonard, not only one of the ablest all-around directors but one who, being a singer himself, was deft and sympathetic in his handling of the musical phases of the story. He didn't believe in the iron-handed technique, but preferred that the actors follow their own instincts at first, then redo a scene when he felt that different ideas of his own would improve it. He always kept us pliable and spontaneous. Once he relieved a period of tension by arranging for me to find, to my horror, a strange man asleep on my couch when I went to my dressing room — a man who, on closer inspection, turned out to be a dummy.

Critics say I gave my best performance in *Maytime*. If so, that was probably because the world both on the set, as I portrayed the romantic experiences of Marsha, and in my private life, was full of enchantment. Gene Raymond and I were going through all the pangs and joys of our own romance at the time; we became engaged before *Maytime* was finished.

—MacDonald, in *The Saturday Evening Post*, 7 Dec 1946

Nelson Eddy and I made a pleasant discovery the first day [of *Rose Marie* (1936, W.S. Van Dyke)]. We found that our voices were clearer and singing easier in that altitude [of Lake Tahoe] than at the heavier sea level of Culver City. I hope it's noticeable in the picture because "The Indian Love Call" and "Rose Marie" are among the most beautiful of American music. [MacDonald and Eddy also co-starred in *The Girl of the Golden West* (1938, Robert Z. Leonard), *Sweethearts* (1938, W.S. Van Dyke), *New Moon* (1940, Robert Z. Leonard), *Bitter Sweet* (1940, W.S. Van Dyke) and *I Married an Angel* (1942, W.S. Van Dyke).]

—MacDonald, in the press packet for *Rose Marie* (MGM, 1936)

Shirley MacLAINE [1934-]

Born: Shirley MacLean Beaty in Richmond, Virginia. A dancer turned actress, she made her film debut in Alfred Hitchcock's The Trouble with Harry (1956). She worked with Billy Wilder on both The Apartment (1960) and Irma la Douce (1963):

Billy Wilder's very dominating. He knows what he wants and he's absolutely certain. It's not that he leaves the actor out of it. We can discuss things with Wilder and come to some kind of an agreement. Once you get on the set the important things for Wilder are the script and the first preview. What happens on the set is unimportant compared to the other two, because the script is such a polished product that he knows exactly how it will work.

Q. Wilder then has a complete blueprint for his film before he starts shooting?

A. *Billy* yes. *Willy* Wyler, no. Willy Wyler does as much as can be done, and you think nothing more can be done with the script, but he will find something. And once you get on the set that's the beginning. He will try maybe twelve different ways. For instance, in *The Children's Hour* [1962], which I have just finished with Willy, as far as my role is concerned (and my role is the one of the guilty party), he was not sure exactly what he wanted on the screen. Or the way he wanted the audience to think. So Willy had maybe two, three or four different ways for each scene.

—MacLaine, interviewed by Robin Bean for *Films & Filming*, Feb 1962

One of the joys of being a successful actress was that I had the excuse and opportunity to explore so many levels of life. It seemed to me, sometimes, that I enjoyed the exploration more than the acting. I entered into private lives of all kinds of people — and was welcomed because they wanted to be portrayed accurately.

When I researched Gittel Moska in *Two for the Seesaw* [1962, Robert Wise], I spent a great deal of time in Greenwich Village in New York City, getting to know the life of a broken-down Jewish dancer who thinks of herself as a doormat. The Gittel I found wasn't William Gibson's Gittel, but she was enough like her and she was honest with me.

When...I made *My Geisha* [1962, Jack Cardiff] in Japan I lived in a Caburenjo (Geisha training shcool) for two weeks learning the intricacies of the tea ceremony, how to play the *samisen*, and the complexities of the Japanese dance, an art so subtle that at times the movements are barely discernible....

When I made *The Children's Hour*, I spent hours with doctors discussing latent homosexuality in women.

But the most unusual "excuse research" I ever did was after Billy Wilder asked me to play Irma la Douce. Even though I had cornered the screen market on loose women, Irma was different. She was a blatant hooker with a heart of gold (as they always are in the movies), but she was not simply a loose woman. Her body was her business, and she used it with pride and total lack of self-consciousness.

Irma was a hooker in Les Halles, one of the cheapest red-light districts in the world. Irma was the best hooker on the block, and she was proud of it. I had to find a girl, a real-life hooker, to match Irma and then get to know her.

—MacLaine, in her *Don't Fall Off the Mountain* (New York: W.W. Norton, 1970)

My compatibility with this part [of Deedee in *The Turning Point* (1977, Herbert Ross)] is nil, and this is one of the discussions I had with [screenwriter] Arthur [Laurents] and Herb in the beginning, for about a week. I would have had the baby and come back to work, it wouldn't have been any problem in my mind at all. But they made me realize that Deedee's decision had been made 20 years ago, when you couldn't even get an abortion and when the choices were very limited. I began to see that that was the way she would have felt about it then.

—MacLaine, interviewed by Janet Maslin for *The New York Times*, 22 Jan 1978

I have enough trouble understanding all the meanings of my lives. How can I possibly sit in judgment on someone else? Because I didn't judge Aurora Greenway [in *Terms of Endearment* (1983, James L. Brooks)], I could play her with a sense of love. She was never a viper or a python to me. She just loved her daughter [Debra Winger] so much she couldn't give her breathing room.

—MacLaine, interviewed by Aljean Harmetz for *The New York Times*, 1 Apr 1984

Time has not been kind to Sousatzka [in *Madame Sousatzka* (1988, John Schlesinger)] because she herself was colonized by her mother who wouldn't let her go.

On the other hand, she's not really pure because she wants to keep Manek [Navin Chowdry] for herself, as she's done with all the other students. She's basically visiting on her students what her mother, who was her own teacher, visited on her. I suppose it's probably an evolution from Aurora Greenway in *Terms of Endearment*. She's imperious, autocratic and cruel. Mostly, she's very, very manipulative, but a *very* good teacher. You *know* that. But she has this dramatic forbidding exterior because she is deeply threatened.

—MacLaine, interviewed by Leila Farrah for *Films & Filming*, May 1988

Ouiser [in *Steel Magnolias* (1989, Herbert Ross)] couldn't have a great body because she had to feel really ugly about herself. So I needed the weight, the jowels; I needed all that stuff to work with.

[In *Postcards from the Edge* (1990, Mike Nichols)] I don't play *my* character old; I play her as a very well-preserved movie star. Meryl plays her character middle-aged. Now, she doesn't play Carrie Fisher — get that out of your mind. And I don't play my character as Debbie Reynolds. Meryl plays a 38-year-old daughter who cannot get out of the house and away from her mother....

Q. And what was it like working with the great Streep?

A. She is extraordinary. You sort of don't know how it happens — what she does. It's interesting to me in terms of human identity because I would never submerge my basic and fundamental ego identity for a part. I'm just not comfortable with that. There's always a part of me in Ouiser and Sousatzka and you see it; that's why it works. But with Meryl — you're not sure what is really *her* because she totally disappears into the part. And I can't do that 'cause I'm too strong a personality.

—MacLaine, interviewed by Kim Garfield for *Drama-Logue*, 23-29 Aug 1990

Fred MacMURRAY [1908-1991]

Born: Kankakee, Illinois. A singer and saxophonist, he appeared in two small film roles in 1929 before making his Broadway debut in 1930. In 1934, he returned to films and became a leading man.

Some people seem to think there are two MacMurrays. There's MacMurray the comedian of *The Egg and I* [1947, Chester Erskine], *The Shaggy Dog* [1959, Charles Barton], *The Absent-Minded Professor* [1961, Robert Stevenson] and then the TV show *My Three Sons*. Then there's the MacMurray who played the heavy in *Double Indemnity* [1944, Billy Wilder], *The Caine Mutiny* [1954, Edward Dmytryk] and *The Apartment* [1960, Billy Wilder].

I'd say I'm a switch-hitter as an actor. If I'm playing a heavy, I don't play it that way from the beginning of a film, the way a Brando or a Sir Alec Guinness would. That's the way a *real* actor would do it. Whether I play a heavy or a comedian, I'm always the same fellow when I start out. If I play a heavy, there comes a spot in the film when the audience gets the message that I'm really a heel. I start out Smily MacMurray, a decent Rotarian type. Then I do or say something, and people know I'm a bastard.

I played my first heavy for Billy Wilder in 1943. I wasn't sure I could handle the part, but the script was so good that I finally said O.K. Billy wanted me in *Double Indemnity*. His reasoning seemed crazy. It was because I'd never done anything like that before. Billy has a thing about off casting. He counted on me to give moviegoers a shock.

If Bogart had played the part, the fans would say, "he's going to knock off her husband any minute. Just wait, you'll see." But in this picture I was just a decent insurance peddler who was hypnotized glassy-eyed by Barbara Stanwyck's sex appeal. Before she was done, I had killed her husband [Tom Powers] and had dumped him on the railroad tracks.

—MacMurray, in *The Saturday Evening Post*, 24 Feb 1962

I remember we did [the getaway scene in *Double Indemnity*] on a process stage with rear projection for the trees, y'know, the scenery behind us. Barbara and I sat in this dummy car. Just a car seat. No dashboard. No ignition key to turn. We faked it, pantomimed it. When I changed places with her and turned the key I remember I was doing it fast and Billy kept saying, "Make it longer, make it longer," and finally I yelled, "For Chrissake Billy, it's not going to hold that long," and he said, "Make it longer," and he was right. It held. It held — that was how much the audience was involved in the story. By the way, you remember that bit where I fall off the observation car platform? Where I'm pretending to be the husband with the crippled leg and the crutches? I didn't do the fall right. Wilder showed me how to do the fall. That's the only time he demonstrated an action for me by doing it. Usually he just told you what he wanted and expected you to do it.

In 1959, Billy [Wilder] came up with another pleasant-on-the-surface, heel-on-the-inside role in *The Apartment*. He said, "Your part is not the biggest — Jack Lemmon's and Shirley MacLaine's are bigger — but yours is a good motivating part." In the early scenes of that film I was once more an O.K. Joe. Shirley worked as an elevator operator in my office building. I promised her that I'd divorce my wife and marry her. The audience believed me. Then at Christmas I slipped her a hundred-dollar-bill. I tried to make it sound like a Christmas present, but the audience knew I was paying her for her love. She got it too. It was crude. It made her feel like a trollop, so she tried to kill herself. Jack Lemmon saved her — who else?

If I hadn't been a nice fellow in *The Apartment*, at least at the start, Shirley wouldn't have been in love with me. If she hadn't been in love with me, she wouldn't have tried to kill herself when I brushed her off. That was why Billy didn't want the audience to know I was a jerk until the key scene told them I was.

—MacMurray, interviewed by Maurice Zolotow for *Billy Wilder in Hollywood* (New York: G.P. Putnam's Sons, 1977)

Anna MAGNANI [1907-1973]

Born: Alexandria, Egypt; raised in Rome. Studies at The Academy of Dramatic Art in Rome preceded her film debut in La Cieca di Sorrento (1934, Nunzio Malasomma). Sixteen films later, she became an international star as Pina in Rome, Open City (1945, Roberto Rossellini). She made her first American film — Daniel Mann's The Rose Tattoo — in 1955. In 1960, she played Lady Torrance opposite Marlon Brando in Sidney Lumet's adaptation of Tennessee Williams' The Fugitive Kind:

[Brando] is great, and he's half-crazy. But to work with — impossible.

He wanted to be the big star all the time. Always the prima donna, trying to put everybody else on edge and make them feel small....

So pretentious he was. Running round playing with the lights when you wanted to discuss a scene, or suddenly stopping and staring at a hole in the wall at some big dramatic moment. Then the next minute — all over you....

The last day was terrible. By then the whole unit was reduced to such a nervous state that I turned on him and gave him such a roasting that he couldn't sleep for three nights.

After that we met at a farewell party for the film and made it up. When all the tension's over it's easy to forgive a "character" like that. I still say better a hundred Brandos any day than one nice, dull negative man.

—Magnani, interviewed by Cecil Wilson for *The Daily Mail*, 28 Apr 1961

Marjorie MAIN [1890-1975]

Born: Mary Tomlinson near Acton, Indiana. Studies at The Hamilton School of Dramatic Expression in Lexington, work in stock and vaudeville and on the New York stage preceded her film debut in A House Divided (1932, William Wyler). She played Ma Kettle in 10 films beginning with The Egg and I (1947, Chester Erskine). She was also paired regularly with Wallace

Beery — in 7 films between 1940 and 1949 — beginning with Richard Thorpe's Wyoming:

Working with Wally wasn't always easy. He'd never rehearse his lines or bits of "business," but he'd want me to rehearse mine. I've always been extremely conscientious in my work and his behavior sometimes unnerved me.

—Main, interviewed by W. Franklyn Moshier for *Films in Review* (NY), Feb 1966

Ma's character was created essentially for humor. She had fifteen children in the book — reduced for convenience, to thirteen in the film — plus a shiftless husband [Percy Kilbride] and more worries than a dozen ordinary women could stand. Thus she had to be either easygoing or crazy, and Ma wasn't one to go crazy. She was the carefree type, clothes, hair and all.

But Ma was more than just a subject for laughter. There was some pathos in her makeup, and this gave the characterization greater heart. The part had another indirect asset, too. In the fact that Claudette Colbert played Betty MacDonald, the "I" in *The Egg and I*. I thoroughly enjoyed working with her, especially in such film exchanges as the one when she asked me, as Ma, what I thought of life on a farm.

"Well," Ma replied thoughtfully, "it's all right...if it don't kill you." [The other Ma and Pa Kettle films were *Ma and Pa Kettle* (1949, Charles Lamont), *Ma and Pa Kettle Go to Town* (1950, Charles Lamont), *Ma and Pa Kettle Back on the Farm* (1951, Edward Sedgwick), *Ma and Pa Kettle at the Fair* (1952, Charles Barton), *Ma and Pa Kettle on Vacation* (1953, Charles Lamont), *Ma and Pa Kettle at Home* (1954, Charles Lamont) and *Ma and Pa Kettle at Waikiki* (1955, Lee Sholem).]

—Main, in *The Saturday Evening Post*, 12 Nov 1949

Karl MALDEN [1914-]

Born: Mladen Sekulovich in Chicago. An athletic scholarship was abandoned for a scholarship to The Goodman Theatre Dramatic School in Chicago. Work on Broadway (from 1937) preceded his film debut in They Knew What They Wanted (1940, Garson Kanin). In 1953, he played Inspector Larrue in Alfred Hitchcock's I Confess:

[In *I Confess*], I played a French-Canadian detective on location in Canada. And the first thing Hitch said was, well, what are we going to do about the accent? French-Canadian accent. And I said, well, I've decided to do nothing about it. If we were in Hollywood with all Hollywood people, I would try to achieve an accent. But you've hired people off the street who talk with the real thing, and next to them I'd be so phoney, it would be impossible. But I will try to do something for you, Hitch, and that is to create an inner feeling of these people, which I think I know and which I think I've seen, and the accent will take care of itself. If I am physically right, and look like the rest of them, and act like the rest of them, the inner temperament will emerge.

Q. Can you give us any different insights into how you might work with specific directors, once the filming is under way?

A. Yes. With Hitchcock, I wouldn't dream of going up to him and telling him how to play a scene. He knows mechanically exactly what he wants. The only thing I try to do is be so perfect in what I'm doing, and know what he wants from the over-all picture. That's the contribution in a Hitchcock film. In a Kazan film, I would go up and talk about everything and anything: "Jesus, Gadge, I think maybe you need a close-up here, don't you?" Or, "how about putting the camera here in the scene where the girl gets slapped and yet you don't want to see the physical violence?" With Kazan everybody he signs to do a picture, including the grips and the electricians, they all speak up. You don't know where it's coming from. And sometimes he'll say, "great, that's where the camera goes!" And yet other times he'll say "Jesus, that's corny, you can't say anything else, you've had it for two days!" But that's his working relationship, a happy set. [Malden worked with Kazan on *Boomerang* (1947), *A Streetcar Named Desire* (1951), *On the Waterfront* (1954) and *Baby Doll* (1956).]

With [John] Frankenheimer [on *All Fall Down* (1962) and *The Bird Man of Alcatraz* (1962)]..., I don't suggest where to put the camera.... I don't know him that well. But I would suggest how to play a scene. Or I will say I think the interpretation of the over-all scene is completely wrong. But *completely* wrong. And we'll discuss it. I may be wrong, or he may be wrong, but in other words, I can say that with him. But with Hitch I wouldn't, 'cause Hitch is set. Hitch hires professional people who should come prepared, and he hires established personalities, a certain personality for a part, which he sees in the over-all picture. And that's it.

—Malden, interviewed by Rory Guy for *Cinema*, Feb 1964

Q. What do you consider to be your best film role?

A. I enjoyed doing the priest in *On the Waterfront*. I enjoyed it because that priest was a real man and I lived with him for ten days and he made a *big* impression on me, and I still write to him. He was a Jesuit priest and quite a man. As far as a challenge is concerned, I enjoyed a picture called *Baby Doll*. The challenge of it was so strong — what Kazan wanted done with it, and what I would have liked to have done...well, I think I accomplished about eighty or eighty-five per cent of this challenge and for that I'm grateful, because it was a good challenge and I think I kind of licked it. I wish I could do it again and see if I couldn't accomplish more with it.

Q. Your Academy Award-winner's not one of your favorite films?

A. No, and I'll tell you the reason for it. You speak about challenges in the films.... The reason that *A Streetcar Named Desire* wasn't one of my favorites was because I had played the part for two years in New York, and then we laid off a year, and then Kazan hired *everybody* from the play to do the film, except Vivien Leigh and she had done it in England, you see. There was a wonderful kind of excitement because we were all together again; so for that it was a wonderful thing. But as far as starting fresh with something new, you know, it wasn't.

One-Eyed Jacks [1961, Marlon Brando] is a film that I would call and Marlon would call, because we've talked about it — it's what we call an "in-and-outer." There are moments in that film that are absolutely spectacular. And then there are some moments when it just kind of falls out. Something happened — it didn't sustain a drive. Now, one of the reasons for that might be — and I'm just guessing; this is speculation on my part — that Marlon directed it, produced it, and played the lead in it. He had *all* the headaches, and it may have been too big a burden for one man to take on his first venture [Brando took over from Stanley Kubrick]....

I'll give you a little "in" on that picture.... When Paramount took over, they did something which I think did not help the picture any.... The whole idea of *One-Eyed Jacks* that Marlon had was that you didn't know who the heavy was or who the hero was. Dad [Malden], or Rio [Brando]? So there were times in the picture when you'd say, "Well, gee, Dad is a nice guy," and he was. An then there were times when he did things really bad and you'd say, "Oh, boy...." This is what life is, really; this is true, and this is what Marlon was trying to show — that there is no such thing as a heavy or a hero. We're all human beings; we all make mistakes. So when Paramount came to putting the picture together, they insisted that Dad be the heavy. So they picked all the black things, to the extent of even rewriting a scene. Remember the scene when they meet after years, on the porch? Rio comes riding up on a horse, and Dad says: "Hiya son. Haven't seen you in a long time. Come on up on the porch and have some tequila. Let's talk this thing over." And they get up on the porch and talk. Well, the way Marlon did it was that he had Dad tell the truth of what happened to him. The truth was: "Son, I did steal the money, and I gambled it away. I spent it on women. I drank it away up to the point where it didn't mean a thing to me anymore. And it made me sick. I caught tuberculosis — consumption. And I was dying — I was dying when this woman saw me, brought me to my feet and gave me this Bible. I've got religion now, boy. I'm a different man. I made a mistake, but I'm a different man." He was telling the truth, and all the while Marlon was saying, "Jesus, is that the truth, or isn't it?" You don't know really, do you? Now Paramount insisted that they rewrite the scene and in the scene that you see in the picture, he's lying and you know he's lying. That's the difference in the concept of the picture.

—Malden, interviewed by Don Shay for *Conversations* (Albuquerque: Kaleidoscope Press, 1965)

Q. Have you any comment about some of the greats you've worked with? Cooper? Colbert?

A. It was a great honor to work with Coop. For years, I heard that this "Yep" man didn't know anything about the business. Well, don't kid yourself. Coop knew and Coop could act. He knew his limitations. There were times, even in *The Hanging Tree* [1959, Delmer Daves] when he tried to stretch and do things that he somehow instinctively said, geez, I can't do them. But he had the courage to try something. I know, because I directed a couple of scenes. And he tried. He had sheer instinct. A part of acting, in films, especially, is not the dialogue so much as who do you look at when you say the dialogue? I might be saying the dialogue to you, but actually it's meant for him. Coop was great at this. Coop knew exactly where to focus, he could do it with his eyes. That's instinct....

I don't know much about Claudette Colbert. I did do *Parrish* [1961, Delmer Daves] with her, and it was wonderful working with her. A real pro. Prepared, knows what to do, how to do it, wants to work day and night on scenes to perfect them. Which is what I don't find in the younger people as much. They get tired too fast. Or if they're too young and they're embarrassed about saying "I'm tired," they say, when we start to re-shoot a scene, I'm afraid I'll lose some of the spark, the firstness, the oneness quality. Which means to me he doesn't know how to work. I'd put Rosalind Russell in the same category as Claudette. These people have energy, they work. They didn't get where they are because they were lucky, they worked! They worked hard, and they're still working. And that is why they're still in the business. [Malden worked with Russell on *Gypsy* (1962, Mervyn Le Roy).]

—Malden, interviewed by Rory Guy for *Cinema*, Feb 1964

John MALKOVICH [1953-]

Born: Christopher, Illinois. Drama studies at Illinois State University and work with The Steppenwolf Theatre Company in Chicago and New York preceded his film debut in The Killing Fields (1984, Roland Joffé). In his second role, he played Mr. Will in Places in the Heart (1984, Robert Benton):

I went to the Dallas Lighthouse for the Blind to observe blind people, but I try never to do any more research than is absolutely necessary. For me, research is boring. I became an actor to exercise my imagination, not my research skills. In the end, I could never possibly know what it was like to be blind, so why pretend I could?

—Malkovich, interviewed by Marjorie Rosen for *The Sunday News Magazine*, 16 Sept 1984

Q. Valmont, the character you play in...*Dangerous Liaisons* [1988, Stephen Frears], plans elaborate emotional games to seduce women.

A. Well, the thing about Valmont, I think, that's widely misunderstood is that he's perceived to be a misogynist. But of course he's really a victim. He is completely obsessed with women, in all ways and not just sexually, which is not really a major theme for him. For him it's a kind of battle for the soul — it's a battle that, as a man, he's not equipped to win.

Q. One of the central conflicts or tensions in the film is the schism between love and sex. Valmont is always playing for sex. What eventually undoes him is that he falls in love.

A. Yeah. The reason I think it's such a seminal novel about men and women is that it's very much about self-delusion. He and Merteuil [Glenn Close] have deluded themselves into thinking that love is not a possibility on this planet. Not a real thing. And when he finds out that's not true, it destroys him because it destroys his self-image, and he dies.

—Malkovich, interviewed by Becky Johnston for *Interview*, Mar 1989

Dorothy MALONE [1925-]

Born: Chicago; raised in Texas. Discovered by an RKO talent scout in an SMU production, she made her film debut as a book store clerk in Warner Brothers' The Big Sleep (1946, Howard Hawks):

Howard Hawks saw me at a western party where I was the only one dressed as an Indian. I had on a really short costume, black shoe polish in my hair and dark makeup all over me. Hawks asked to be introduced, and then called me in for an interview. He liked to act outrageous. He liked to throw people off, so you had to be very sharp and a little contrary. He preferred you to be a little contrary.

But on the picture, we stopped at 3 o'clock and had tea, with the crumpets and the pinafores. We were treated royally, and Hawks let me do what I wanted in the scene, like pulling down the shade. And Bogart was a lovely man. I hate to use the word, but that's what he was — lovely.

—Malone, interviewed by Gerald Peary for *The Chicago Tribune*, 13 May 1985

Fredric MARCH [1897-1975]

Born: Ernest Frederick Bickel in Racine, Wisconsin. While studying commerce at The University of Wisconsin, he worked in amateur theater. His first film work was as an extra in Paying the Piper directed by George Fitzmaurice at the Astoria Studios in N.Y. in the early 1920s; with the coming of sound his experience on Broadway brought him to Hollywood where he made his debut in The Dummy (1928, Robert Milton). In 1929, he played Martin Boyne in The Marriage Playground:

I learned about the importance of relaxation when I started making pictures. The director of *The Marriage Playground*, Lother Mendes, was the first person to mention it to me. He said,

"Freddie, when I say 'Camera,' all it means is — relax."

—March, interviewed by Lillian and Helen Ross for *The Player* (New York: Simon & Schuster, 1962)

Q. What was the most unpleasant role you ever played in pictures?

A. *Jekyll and Hyde* [1932, Rouben Mamoulian] purely because of the makeup problems involved. I had to get up every morning at 5 o'clock to be at the studio at 6. Wally Westmore would start work immediately on my eyes. First he'd put collodion under my eyes, so that no perspiration would come through. Then he'd weigh the underpart of the eye with pieces of surgical cotton to force open the eyeball. The idea was that every time I talked the eyes would open in an unnatural leer. To accomplish this, he'd attach threads from the cotton down the cheeks and tie them under my chin. As a result, every time I opened my mouth the lower eyelid would be dragged down an inch.

—March, interviewed by Ed Sullivan for *The New York Herald Tribune*, 14 June 1938

I conceived Mr. Hyde as more than just Dr. Jekyll's inhibited evil nature. I saw the beast as a separate entity — one who could, and almost did, little by little, overpower and annihilate Dr. Jekyll. And I tried to show the devastating results in Dr. Jekyll as well. To me, those repeated appearances of the beast within him were more than just a mental strain on Jekyll — they crushed him physically as well.

—March, interviewed by Potter Brayton for *Motion Picture*; repr. in *Hollywood and the Great Fan Magazines*, ed. by Martin Levin (New York: Arbor House Publishing, 1970)

I know I couldn't help imitating John Barrymore during the early years of my movie career. It took me a long time — what with *The Royal Family of Broadway* [1930, George Cukor and Cyril Gardner] and *Dr. Jekyll and Mr. Hyde* to live that reputation down. Still, he's no unworthy fellow to imitate.

—March, interviewed by Irene Thirer for *The New York World Telegram*, 1939

[Norma Shearer] was a tremendously gifted actress.... I always felt she was every bit as naturally talented as Garbo, and with a greater range; there was a sweetness and a sincerity about her that came across with a wallop on-screen, but she was also a strong person with the true artist's discipline and perseverance....

She had a wonderful sincerity and poise, and she was deeply emotional but she knew how to filter that emotion with discipline so that it came off the screen as deeply felt rather than merely sentimental. She had some very strong scenes with me in *Smilin' Through* [1932, Sidney Franklin]; I especially recall one in which we were to part as I went to war; she got across her agony in truly eloquent terms. I heard how perfectionist she was supposed to be, but if she gave her best, she expected everyone else around her to give theirs along with her, and as I have always tried to set the highest standards for myself, I could hardly fault her for that.

Yes, she did fuss around with Lee Garmes about "white" lighting and all that, but there was a reason for it as she had a rather peculiar face, beautiful as it could be, with eyes smaller than normal, and it took a combination of the right lighting and the right eye makeup to get her looking at her best. I don't think vanity had a thing to do with it — she just wanted to give — and look — her absolute best, and how can one fault an entertainer for *that*? [March and Shearer also worked together on *The Barretts of Wimpole Street* (1934, Sidney Franklin).]

Garbo was all instinct. She wasn't a trained actress and her love scenes were the best, because she believed them totally and something radiant and wonderful came over her and she was totally true to the mood. She could be awkward at times, and worried a great deal about her looks and her performance — but that kind of instinct and camera magic are so rare that she was in a class by herself. She was a *natural* actress, and followed her own special laws, and they *worked*. [March played opposite Garbo in *Anna Karenina* (1935, Clarence Brown).]

—March, interviewed by Lawrence J. Quirk; repr. in Quirk's *Norma: The Story of Norma Shearer* (New York: St. Martin's Press, 1988)

I detested the part I played in *Anna Karenina*.... I'm stuffed into one uniform after another, thrown from the arms of one lovely screen star to those of another and I have to give myself a mental flogging to work up any enthusiasm at all. So I worry and complain and argue about the significance of the role.... Besides I never see myself as romantic. If I can do anything on the screen, it's light comedy. *The Royal Family of Broadway* [and] *Laughter* [1930, Harry D'Arrast]. They suited me.

—March, interviewed by Janet Howell for *Screen Guide* 1.4, 1936

Certainly, Anthony [in *Anthony Adverse* (1936, Mervyn LeRoy)] has his affairs here, there and everywhere. Woman after woman gives him her favor, and Anthony takes and moves on. And yet — he's not a philanderer. He's a real lover, a sincere lover, a complete romanticist, and women can't help but love him.

I played the role straight. I didn't try to "play down" to the twenty-year-old level. That would have been a mistake. I let the twenty-two-year-old Anthony Adverse be an adult. A romantic adult, but an adult nevertheless. But I did let his bewilderment remain — not because that bewilderment is a necessary part of being twenty-two years old, but because it was a necessary part of Anthony Adverse. You see, that is the whole story of Anthony.

He is an illegitimate child. He knows it. He is deeply conscious of it. And so he goes through life and the world, seeking, questing, always hunting for some unnamed something, the lack of which he feels. In that quest, he turns most naturally to women for the solace and the surcease from bewilderment which he craves. And that is why he has these affairs....

Anthony is the irresponsible, "lost" type of good-looking young man for whom every woman in the world finds affection. It's not the mother-instinct you hear so much about. It's something different. Every woman instinctively feels responsible for every man she comes in close contact with. Let's say, instead of feeling she wants to "mother" him, that she has the instinctive and subconscious desire to reform him. Every woman is, at heart, the potential reformer of the man she loves.

With all his charm, Anthony Adverse has one other ingredient in his make-up that stimulates this instinct in women. That is a fundamental weakness. The reason is his knowledge of his illegitimacy. He feels incomplete, unsound. Women, intuitively, sense that. And they try to reform him, to make him strong. And so they go about it in the ages-old unchanging way of women with men through time and place. They love him, they try subconsciously to give him the sense of conquest and of power. And all the time, the truth is that instead of women "falling for" him, he is in reality "falling for" them. He is not the Don Juan, the conqueror , the philanderer, at all. He is still the befuddled, bewildered seeker.

And the strangest part of it all is that Anthony always returns love in full measure. He gives himself completely — until he moves on and a new woman takes the place of the old. He believes himself, with each successive affair, finally and utterly in love and so gives himself completely to his flame of the moment.

In short, to resort to the colloquialism of today, it's not that women are pushovers for Anthony — it's rather that Anthony's a pushover for any woman.

—March, interviewed by Harry Lang for *Movie Classic*, May 1936

[The fight with Carole Lombard in *Nothing Sacred* (1937, William Wellman)] is one of the comedy moments of the picture and by far one of the most difficult jobs I have ever encountered. I had to graze Carole's chin by less than a quarter of an inch to make it look real. The slightest bit of misjudgment and — well....

I had to measure off against a swaying target, none too steady myself at the same time, and swing with all my might past Carole's jaw. We rehearsed the scene for hours, then made it in long shots, medium shots and close-ups, with an extra rehearsal preceding each take.

You can well imagine the strain, the fear in the back of my mind that I might stretch my arm just a fraction of an inch too far....

I'll say this for Carole: she has nerves of steel. Not once did she wince or move back, and I must have thrown two dozen punches in the taking of that one knock-out blow.

—March, interviewed for the press book for *Nothing Sacred* (Selznick International Pictures, 1937)

The role of Al Stephenson in *The Best Years of Our Lives* [1946, William Wyler] was an honest role in a fine picture. It dramatized the problems of the returning veteran in a down-to-earth way — at a time when servicemen were coming back by the thousands to every town and city. I felt more at ease in the part because I had been a lieutenant in the artillery in World War I and had made 33,000 miles of overseas tours with the USO in the last war.

I especially enjoyed working with Harold Russell, a naturally fine actor with a grand sense of humor. I also enjoyed the fact that the part of Al Stephenson showed how veterans' problems could be handled with humane understanding; and this gave me the feeling that I had made a tiny contribution toward the solution of one of our biggest postwar tasks.

—March, in *The Saturday Evening Post*, 3 Apr 1948

[Admiral George Tarrant in *The Bridges at Toko-Rio* (1955, Mark Robson)] is a kind of compassionate iconoclast. He knows that no war is good to be in, and that it almost always has to be fought in the worst possible place in the world. But he also knows that you can't hate the people that aren't in it.

Here is this re-tread, this younger fellow, played by Bill Holden, who doesn't see why he has been sent off to war a second time. But the captain has had some troubles of his own — lost two sons, and his wife a mental case. He keeps right on going, no matter how many people ask him, "What's the use?"

—March, interviewed by Richard Dyer MacCann for *The Christian Science Monitor*, 2 Mar 1954

The truth is, I enjoyed making *Inherit the Wind* [1960, Stanley Kramer] too much. I remember the rehearsals; I had already learned the whole script, the way you do in the theater, and Spence [Tracy] was still using the script. One day he called Kate [Hepburn] on the phone and said, "That s.o.b. March knows his whole part already." "Of course, he does," Kate said, "that's his *theatuh* background." "Well, thank you, Mrs. Shakespeare!" Spence said and hung up.

—March, interviewed by Guy Flatley for *The New York Times*, 27 May 1973

Mae MARSH [1895-1968]

Born: Mary Marsh in Madrid, New Mexico. While her older sister, Marguerite, was working for D.W. Griffith and Mack Sennett, Mae was cast as an extra in a Sennett film starring Mabel Normand then sent to Griffith who used her as an extra in The Lesser Evil (1912). Later that year, she appeared in Man's Genesis, the third of fifteen films for Griffith:

When Mr. Griffith began rehearsing a picture called *Man's Genesis*, I got my first chance for a lead role. In the film a girl had to wear a grass skirt which would show all her limbs. Mary Pickford didn't want to do that. "Give the part to the little girl. She doesn't mind showing her limbs." In those days, they wore skirts down to the ankles. You couldn't show the calf of your leg. And I said, "Oh, yes, I would like to do it." It was immaterial to me whether I showed my limbs or not.

I received $5 a day when I worked on *Man's Genesis*. Mr. Griffith would tell me exactly what to do. On the first day, he explained, "I want you to sit on that rock wall over there. The boy you're sitting next to, you're very, very much in love with him. Have you ever been in love?" And I said oh yes, which I hadn't. He said, "Just think that you're terribly in love and look up at him shy-like." So I did, and then he said, "Look up at him again and then put your head down," which I did. Then he said, "Now get up and run away." So I got up and ran away. That was my first acting part. I loved it. I said to Mr. Griffith, "When am I going to do it again?" He said, "You've done it once. You can't do it again. That was fine. Maybe you can do something else tomorrow."

—Marsh, interviewed by Bernard Rosenberg and Harry Silverstein for *The Real Tinsel* (New York: Macmillan, 1970)

I have been told that one of the sweetest and, at the same time, most pathetic scenes done in motion pictures occurred in *The Birth of a Nation* [1915, D.W. Griffith] where I, as Flora Cameron, the little sister of the Confederate soldier, trimmed my cheap, home-made dress in preparing to welcome home my big brother....

You will remember the situation. The Camerons, an old and distinguished Southern family, had been impoverished by the war. They were preparing for the return of the big brother — played capitally by Mr. [Henry B.] Walthall — with the mixture of emotion to be expected under the circumstances. I, as the youngest member of the family, was least affected by our cruel poverty. The joy of being about to see my big brother again overcame any other feeling.

I begin to dress. The sadness of my stricken family cannot affect my holiday spirit. I have but one dress. It is of sack cloth. I find that its pitiful plainness is not in keeping with my happiness or the importance of the event. Looking about for something with which to trim that dress I find some strips of cotton — "southern ermine," as it was called. With these I trim that homely old dress, spotting the "ermine" with soot from the fireplace, in a manner that I think will be pleasing to my big brother.

Mr. Walthall suggested the "southern ermine" and it was Mr. Griffith, always kindly in the matter of accepting a suggestion, who built the drama about it....

In *The Birth of a Nation*, by the way, all of us were forced to do a great deal of research work upon our costumes. This is a good thing. It gets one into the spirit of the drama that is to be played.

I am often asked many questions regarding Mr. Griffith's manner of directing. Wherein is it different from other directors? Wherein does it excel...?

Mr. Griffith is extremely human. There is no unnecessary flourish, or blowing of trumpets, about his manner of direction. That has the simplicity of true greatness. He never lords it over his players as I have seen some directors do. He is kindly, sympathetic and understanding.

Perhaps we are about to do a very vital scene. Mr. Griffith tilts back in his chair — he has a manner of directing while seated — and may say to the actress:

"You understand this situation. Now let us see what you would do with it."

Here is a direct challenge. The actress is put upon her mettle. After giving the matter careful consideration she plays the scene after her own idea. If she does it well no one is quicker in his praise than Mr. Griffith. If otherwise, no one is more kindly in pointing out the flaws.

In other words, Mr. Griffith gives the actress a chance....

In this way Mr. Griffith draws out the best that is in his players, and, by seeming to depend upon them to stand upon their own feet, maintains an enthusiasm among his players....

I hope no one understands me to say that the actress, under Mr. Griffith, has the say of how she shall act. Quite the contrary! No one has a way of bringing a player more abruptly to his or her senses when he or she is unqualifiedly in the wrong.

And no matter how well we think we have outlined a scene Mr. Griffith may entirely change it. When he does change it we know it is for a reason other than a fondness for showing authority. In other words, he has built up among his artists a great and abiding faith in his ability to do the right thing at the right time, or, as importantly, have it done.

For another thing, Mr. Griffith is big enough not to be small about receiving suggestions....

To illustrate:

In *The Birth of a Nation*, when the Cameron house was being mobbed by frenzied negroes and the family had barricaded itself in the cellar it was a matter of some moment how the little sister...would be affected.

I can hear your average director:

"Roll your eyes," he would say. "Cry! Drop to your knees in terror."

In other words, it would be the same old stuff. It is this same old stuff that makes so many pictures positively deadly. The least that can be said about this conventional style of doing things is that, if it cannot be criticized, neither can it be applauded.

Mr. Griffith, when we came to the cellar scene, asked me if there had ever been a time in my life when I had been filled with terror.

"Yes," I said.

"What did you do?" he inquired.

"I laughed," I answered.

He saw the point immediately.

"Good," he said. "Let's try it."

It was the hysterical laugh of the little girl in the cellar, with the drunken mob raging above, that was, I am sure, far more effective than rolling the eyes or weeping would have been. [She also worked on Griffith's *The Old Actor* (1912), *Sands of Dee* (1912), *The New York Hat* (1912), *Brute Force* (1912), *Fate* (1913), *The Battle of Elderbush Gulch* (1913), *Judith of Bethulia* (1914), *The Escape* (1914), *Home Sweet Home* (1914), *The Avenging Conscience* (1914), *Intolerance* (1916) and *The White Rose* (1923).]

—Marsh, in her *Screen Acting* (Los Angeles: Photo-Star Publishing Co., 1921)

Dean MARTIN [1917-]

Born: Dino Crocetti in Steubenville, Ohio. Work as an amateur boxer, in a steel mill, and as a croupier preceded his show business career. Beginning as a singer with Ernie McKay's Band, he then teamed up with Jerry Lewis, with whom he worked in clubs, radio and TV until 1956. He made his film debut opposite Lewis in My Friend Irma *(1949, George Marshall), the first of 16 films together:*

Why do you think that I split with Jerry? Cause I was doin' nothin' and I was eatin' my heart out. I sang a song and never got to finish the song. The camera would go over to him doin' funny things, then it would come back to me when I'd finished. Everthin' was Jerry Lewis, Jerry Lewis, and I was a straight man. I was an idiot in every picture.... And everybody says, "Oh, that poor Martin, he's gonna die." And for the first year, I did die. Then my friend Frank [Sinatra] gave me the role in *Some Came Running* [1958, Vincente Minnelli]. Two of the greatest turnin' points in my career were: First, meetin' Jerry Lewis; second leavin' Jerry Lewis. [Their other films together include: *My Friend Irma Goes West* (1950), *At War with the Army* (1951), *That's My Boy* (1951) and *Sailor Beware* (1952, all Hal Walker), *Jumping Jacks* (1952, Norman Taurog), *The Stooge* (1953, Norman Taurog), *Scared Stiff* (1953, George Marshall), *The Caddy*

(1953, George Marshall), *Money from Home* (1954, George Marshall), *Living It Up* (1954, Norman Taurog), *Three Ring Circus* (1954, Joseph Pevney), *You're Never Too Young* (1955, Norman Taurog), *Artists and Models* (1955, Frank Tashlin), *Pardners* (1956, Norman Taurog), *Hollywood or Bust* (1956, Frank Tashlin).]

I did *The Young Lions* [1958, Edward Dmytryk] with [Montgomery Clift], and nobody wanted him around, nobody would eat with him. So I took him to dinner, or I would have a drink with him, or I would put him to bed cause he was always on pills, you know. He was such a sad, sad man, and he was like a boy, so unhappy, and rejected, and so I'd say: "Come on, Clift, let's go." And I'd bring him with me everywhere, and I'd say: "If you don't want him, you don't want me." And we'd leave the party. But first I'd spit in their faces for him.

—Martin, interviewed by Oriana Fallaci for *Look*, 26 Dec 1967

Steve MARTIN [1945-]

Born: Waco, Texas; grew up near Disneyland. Studies in theater arts at UCLA and work in nightclubs preceded his success on TV, first as a writer — notably for The Smothers Brothers Comedy Hour — then as a comedian. He made his film debut in the short, The Absent Minded Waiter (1977, Carl Gottlieb — which Martin co-wrote); his first feature was The Jerk (1979, Carl Reiner), which he co-wrote with Michael Elias and Carl Gottlieb. In 1984, he played Roger Cobb in Carl Reiner's All of Me:

There were two important things I wanted to avoid. The first was, don't just be effeminate, the swishy cliché. It has to be that this other person [Edwinna Cutwater/Lily Tomlin] is really inside you. The second was, don't be a mime. Mimes show you a wall that isn't there, but it's still not real. I don't want to show artifice; it wouldn't be useful. I don't want to get applause off being extremely clever. It wouldn't be right.

—Martin, interviewed by Kenneth Turan for *Rolling Stone*, 8 Nov 1984

[For *All of Me*] I rehearsed by walking with my body entirely like [Lily Tomlin], and then subtracting her from half my body, rather than trying to add her. It was just a working process, really. You need something, and out of desperation you try to figure it out. [Martin also starred in Reiner's *Dead Men Don't Wear Plaid* (1982) and *The Man with Two Brains* (1983).]

—Martin, interviewed by Tim Appelo for *Entertainment Weekly*, 22 Feb 1991

My first thought was that C.D. [in *Roxanne* (1987, Fred Schepisi)] would be a policeman. But then I felt that a fighting policeman would be too hostile. Yet, to parallel the play [*Cyrano de Bergerac*], C.D. needed men. Later I realized that fireman was the proper metaphor. C.D. is constantly quenching fires in his heart.

The most important thing to me in writing and playing C.D. was that I avoid self-pity. In the play, Cyrano's self-pity is noble. Today self-pity turns people off. The most dangerous scene was when Dixie [Shelley Duvall] asks why I don't get a girl, and I see my shadow on the wall. My line was melancholic, and it was important that I say it matter-of-factly.

—Martin, interviewed by Aljean Harmetz for *The New York Times*, 12 July 1987

Strother MARTIN [1919-1980]

Born: Kokomo, Indiana. Studies at The University of Michigan and with The Stage Society headed by Arthur Kennedy and work as a swimming extra in several films between 1948 and 1950 preceded his first non-swimming part in The Asphalt Jungle (1950, John Huston). In 1967, he played the Captain of the work farm in Stuart Rosenberg's Cool Hand Luke:

When I was first reading the script of *Cool Hand Luke*, I knew this could be a big one. The Captain is sitting there reading off [Paul] Newman's record: "Lucas Jackson, maliciously destroying municipal property while under the influence. What was that?" "Cuttin' the heads off parking meters, Captain." "Oh? We never had one o' them before...."

In *Luke*, that singsong sadness that a Southerner gets, well, it comes out when the Captain gets under pressure. He really didn't want to hit Luke, he didn't want to use violence. But Luke mimics him, and the Captain says, "You'll be used to wearin' these chains after a while." And then trying to justify this violence to himself as well as to the prisoners he says: "What we have here is a failure to communicate." I like the ring of sadness in the word "failure." The way I like to think of it, this Captain — who probably had a sixth-grade education — read a sociological tract once, and this was the one phrase he remembered. It is practically the only intelligent thing he says. He was embarrassed to show violence to the men. He wanted them to see him as a gentle, good man. To me, it was the key to the character.

—Martin, interviewed by Digby Diehl for *Show*, 9 July 1970

On *The Wild Bunch* [1969], Sam [Peckinpah] was getting acquainted with the low-brow side of my acting abilities. It was the kind of role he had never cast me in before. [Martin had previously been in Peckinpah's *The Deadly Companions* (1961).] He saw Coffer as somewhere close to psychotic. Gordy Dawson, Sam's wardrobe man on the film, had made up this really seedy looking outfit with a sanded-down, greenish-colored hat that really looked weather-beaten. And Sam had looked at me and said: "I want to see him with a piece of jewelry. What would his vanity be?" And I said: "You know how priests have a black wooden cross? I think my character might collect those." So Gordy got me this cross and we went back up before his eminence, his holiness, the horseshit-marvelous Mr. Peckinpah, and Sam, who has an eye like Picasso for the West, looked at the cross and said, "Too clean!" So Gordy said: "Strother, come here. We'll fix that son of a bitch!" And Gordy went and wired a bullet onto the cross, and we went back to Sam who gave a crooked little grin and said, "Terrific...!"

I had my ass chewed on every shot in *Wild Bunch*. But don't get the wrong idea, I have more respect for Sam than almost anybody else in the world. He was keeping me in this frenetic state for a purpose: he wanted me to portray this psychotic character as if I were on the edge of a nervous breakdown, not that that's any great struggle. But Sam is like a dirty psychiatrist — he gets inside your head and probes around with a scalpel....

In that opening sequence where we were up on the roof waiting in ambush, I said to Sam, "Could I wink at L.Q. [Jones]?" And Sam growled back at me, "Why don't you kiss him?!" And I said, "Well, he's too far away." Then a little later he demanded that I kiss my rifle, which I didn't want to do because I thought it had been done many times before. I remember saying, "I don't want to!" and Sam shouting, "Kiss it!" And I remember how hard my pulse was racing as I kissed that rifle. So a trembling guy kisses a gun. Well, I have to admit that when I finally saw that on the screen.... Sam had managed to get a different kind of a kiss of a rifle than anybody else has ever gotten. He got it, of course, because I was scared shitless and mad at the same time, but then that was exactly right for Coffer at that moment....

Sam will help you develop a character, but he expects you to bring something of your own. He insists on it....

What's more, Sam will allow you — even expect you — to improvise certain scenes as you go along to give them spontaneity. For example, after the shooting stops and the bounty hunters come down into the street to check the bodies, Sam had L.Q. and I 'winging' the dialogue because it wasn't very full at that point. That whole thing where I called L.Q. a "liar!" and then a "black liar!" was all improvised. I remember I was very pleased with "black liar!" And I remember Sam saying to me, "That's your worst line in the picture," which, of course, means he loved it!

—Martin, interviewed by Garner Simmons for *Peckinpah: A Portrait in Montage* (Austin: The University of Texas Press, 1982)

I've worked with Duke [John Wayne] six times. Always find it exciting; also always know it's going to be a kind of baptism of fire. I see John Wayne as an extension of John Ford, and especially more so as he gets older. Ford was a super perfectionist and I think our greatest director. And I think there's a lot of Ford in everything Wayne touches....

I think Duke respects hard work, especially in action scenes — and I'm sure he got this from John Ford. He's ready to bust his ass. And he expects everybody else to bust his ass. That's where you get in trouble with Duke, if you try to loaf through something. There's never any lethargy on a John Wayne set, so I'm always excited when I'm going to work with John Wayne because I know it's going to be exciting.... To be on a set with John Wayne is an electric experience.... [Martin made six films with Wayne: *The Horse Soldiers* (1959, John Ford), *The Man Who Shot Liberty Valance* (1962, John Ford), *McLintock!* (1963, Andrew McLaglen), *The Sons of Katie Elder* (1965, Henry Hathaway), *True Grit* (1969, Henry Hathaway) and *Rooster Cogburn* (1975, Stuart Millar).]

—Martin, interviewed for *Film Heritage*, Summer 1975

I've always known honestly that I was not a leading man type, so I've played the characters that I could make money doing. But I've always tried to play them the way the playwright N. Richard Nash taught me: by justifying the character on the highest level possible. That is, always trying to say the most you can for human beings. I might be playing a killer, but I want to give a bicycle to my little boy. The trouble with most scripts is that they are so one-dimensional in their characterization, the actor has to find this higher justification for himself and hope its plays across.

Where you *find* characters like that in yourself is another question. Once Lee Marvin said to me, "You know, as character actors, we play all kinds of sex psychos, nuts, creeps, perverts and weirdos. And we laugh it off saying what the hell, it's just a character. But deep down inside, it's *you*, baby." And he's right: these characters are one part of you, and the hardest part of acting such roles is letting the audience see that part of you.

—Martin, interviewed by Digby Diehl for *Show*, 9 July 1970

Lee MARVIN [1924-1987]

Born: New York City. After receiving the Purple Heart for Marine duty in the South Pacific, he enrolled at The American Theater Wing under the G.I. Bill of Rights. Work on Broadway and TV preceded his film debut in You're in the Navy Now *(1951, Henry Hathaway). In 1956, he played Colonel Bartlett in* Attack!, *the first of three films for Robert Aldrich:*

Aldrich always rehearsed a film, which not many directors do because the time element is so costly. But we'd sit around a table for days, sometimes even weeks, and we'd read a script over and over again. And, of course, when you're sitting there, reading it, if he had any doubts prior to the reading, he would suggest changes, cuts. You would iron out the rough spots at those readings. The actors would contribute and he would listen to any comments the actors had and consider them....

Robert was a very tough man. He was definitely a man you listened to, and you had to weigh your answers. He was enamored of discipline. After all, it is the discipline of life that flows over into your work....

Having been a P.F.C. in the Marine Corps, I was aware of officers that didn't come up to the standards and respect of the common man — the dogface. I did know this colonel who had that attitude, browbeating the guys at poker games to win, just covering his own tracks, and I just looked forward to playing that kind of little bastard.

—Marvin, interviewed by Edwin T. Arnold and Eugene L. Miller, Jr. for *The Films and Career of Robert Aldrich* (Knoxville: The University of Tennessee Press, 1986)

In essence [Bill Tenny in *Ship of Fools* (1965, Stanley Kramer)] is The Ugly American. Stanley Kramer sent me the first 47 pages of the script, knowing it would interest me. I thought I understood that character. He's an ex-ballplayer, a has-been, a wash-out, a drunk who's spent his life pursuing Mexican whores — there's a load of them aboard ship. He's a childlike adult, a little afraid, trying to work out values in his own way. A little like me.

—Marvin, interviewed by Howard Thompson for *The New York Times*, 23 May 1965

[Aldrich would] play with you and tease you and put you in a personal jeopardy with the other actors, which I thought was good.... I remember the first day [on *The Dirty Dozen* (1966)] that he said, "All right, let's put it on its feet. First of all, let's line up for the first inspection when Reisman [Marvin] comes in to check the men." So he's calling off names and positions.... Aldrich is calling off the list of the men in the order they should be standing in line, so he said, "Clint Walker," who is about 6'7" or something, and then he said, "Charlie [Bronson], you're next." Then he got Donald Sutherland, who's about 6'4" or 6'5", on the other side of Charlie. So Charlie's standing there, looking straight forward; and then he looks up to his left and he sees Sutherland about a *foot* over his head and then he looks over to his right and there's Walker about a *foot and a half* over his head. So he just stepped out of line and walked towards Bob and said, "Fuck this!" Well, the whole joint fell down because that's a funny bit. Of course, it took Aldrich about ten minutes to quit laughing. He was just hysterical over this.

Because this was the type of test that he put guys through, which I found to be very advantageous to the film. It's people taking advantage of each other at playing THE GAME. He knew, at least by that exercise, that if there was ever a scene with Charlie standing up next to these guys that it'd be in Charlie's favor, that something was going to happen. These are the kinds of nice, little in-house games that you like to watch. [Marvin also worked on Aldrich's *Emperor of the North* (1973).]

—Marvin, interviewed by Edwin T. Arnold and Eugene L. Miller, Jr. For *The Films and*

Career of Robert Aldrich (Knoxville: The University of Tennessee Press, 1986)

I've made some mistakes I wish I hadn't. One of them was workin' with Michael Ritchie on *Prime Cut* [1972]. Oh, I *hate* that sonofabitch. He likes to use amateurs because he can totally dominate them. One night I wanted to rehearse a scene and he didn't want to, so he pretended to be sick. I said, "Shitfire, Michael, I'll get you a fuckin' doctor." *Nothin'* worked with that guy, and the picture just fell apart before we even got started.
—Marvin, interviewed by Grover Lewis for *Rolling Stone*, 21 Dec 1972

Groucho MARX [1890-1977]

Born: Julius Marx in New York City. With brothers Chico (Leonard Marx, 1887-1961) and Harpo (Adolph Marx, 1888-1964), he had success in vaudeville and on Broadway before Paramount Studios brought the trio to the screen beginning with The Cocoanuts (1929, Robert Florey and Joseph Santley). From 1929 through 1933, a fourth brother, Zeppo (Herbert Marx, 1900-1979) was co-starred; Margaret Dumont played Groucho's foil in seven films, beginning with The Cocoanuts:

[Margaret Dumont]...didn't understand half our jokes. She always kept saying to me, "What are they laughing about....?" A wonderful dame and a great foil. I never had a foil like her. She took everything so seriously.... She was practically the fifth Marx Brother....

I remember when we made *Duck Soup* [1933, Leo McCarey], we had a battle scene at the end of the picture. Shells were coming through the windows so I rushed over and pulled the shade down as if that would stop a shell. Maggie yelled, "Rufus, what are you doing?" And I said, "Fighting for your honor, which is more than you ever did!" She didn't understand that joke either.... [Marx and Dumont were also teamed in *Animal Crackers* (1930, Victor Heerman), *A Night at the Opera* (1935, Sam Wood), *A Day at the Races* (1937, Sam Wood), *At the Circus* (1939, Edward Buzzell) and *The Big Store* (1941, Charles Reisner).]

McCarey had a wild sense of quality. There's a mirror scene in *Duck Soup* where Harpo and Chico are dressed like me. McCarey devised that scene.... He was the only first class director we had.

We met [Irving] Thalberg for lunch one day. He said that he had been impressed with the Marx Bros. films and said he'd like to do pictures with us. But, he said, "Not lousy pictures like *Duck Soup*." I was a little annoyed by this, as I thought *Duck Soup* was a very funny picture and I told him so. "Yes," he said, "That's true, but the audience doesn't give a damn about you fellas. I can make a picture with you that would have half as many laughs as your Paramount films, but they will be more effective because the audience will be in sympathy with you...."

Q. How involved was Thalberg with the shooting of [*A Night at the Opera*]?

A. Completely. He was on the set every morning, going over the previous day's shooting and if he didn't like what he saw, he had it shot again. I remember once I said, "Why do you allow Sam Wood to shoot this picture? He's a lousy director." He said, "It suits my purpose because if he shoots a scene and I don't like it, I can call Wood into my office and say, 'Sam, shoot that scene again. I didn't like the way you handled it,' and he will do it." We never worked with Wood before, but we did so because that's what Thalberg wanted. Politically, Wood was impossible. He was a fascist. We all disliked him intensely. But we respected Thalberg....

[Thalberg's] death affected the brothers personally. We had nobody to look up to after he died. When he died, at that moment I knew that the Marx Bros. wouldn't make any more good pictures because the people who would replace Thalberg were second-rate talents. Yeah, he was good. He was the only first-class producer Hollywood ever had.
—Marx, interviewed by Richard J. Anobile for *The Marx Bros. Scrapbook* (New York: Darien House, 1973)

Playboy: Tell us about some of the other great comics you knew. How about Buster Keaton?

Marx: He used to put in gags for Harpo when we were at MGM.

Playboy: In which films?

Marx: *A Night at the Opera*, *A Day at the Races*, *Go West* [1940, Edward Buzzell]. He was washed up by then, but he was good for Harpo. Harpo was always looking for a good piece of business. He didn't talk, he didn't need lines, but he did need good business, and Keaton was a hell of a comic in silent films.
—Marx, interviewed by Charlotte Chandler for *Playboy*, Mar 1974

Here I am on Stage 18 waiting to shoot some retakes [for *The Big Store*]. I had some dialogue with three models that wasn't particularly funny at the last preview so they brought in a little man to write some jokes to replace it — the result will be that these jokes will be six times as unfunny when they reach the screen....

We previewed the picture twice — the first time, it went fairly well; then they took out 900 feet, previewed it again and it flopped. They are now straightening out the story (this they do with every picture after a preview) — they imagine the audience hasn't laughed because the plot wasn't understood. The fact of the matter is, the audience hasn't laughed because they didn't understand the jokes! However, this is my farewell, and regardless of what the future holds in store for me, I'm happy to escape from this kind of picture, for the character I'm playing I now find wholly repulsive....

Acting in the movies no longer interests me, and unless I were to get something that I was crazy about, I don't think I'll be seen again in any of the local studios. [Marx did not return to the screen until 1946].

—Marx, in a letter to Arthur Sheekman, 23 June 1941; repr. in *The Groucho Letters* (New York: Simon & Schuster, 1967)

James MASON [1909-1984]

Born: Huddersfield, Yorkshire, England. An architecture graduate of Cambridge University, he began his stage career in 1931 and made his film debut in Late Extra (1935, Albert Parker). Success in British films and work on Broadway then preceded his first Hollywood film — Caught — the first of two for Max Ophuls in 1949:

I was invited to play the part of the heavy who was a fictionalized version of Howard Hughes, the eccentric multi-millionaire.... I did not want to play the...part because I was determined to smash my villainous image.... There was a role for a nice guy in the script [Dr. Quinada] — that was the one that I would like to play, even though it was clearly not so effective....

My latent hostility to producers showed itself at one point. There was a scene in which Dr. Quinada, the pediatrician, seated at his desk in the office, is given a report on a patient's condition by the nurse-receptionist. He takes it in and seems to be thinking about what she has said for a moment or two, then suddenly he stands up, picks up his bag and moves to the door. He has considered the symptoms, put two and two together and has recognized an emergency. Max chose to shoot this in medium long shot, that is to say that when I stood up, my full figure, including my feet, would be in the frame. Then he panned me to the door. It was not a situation in which you needed to see the actor's face especially; in this case it was the action that told the story. Max asked me if I felt that I needed a close-up, I said no. What could I do with my face that was not adequately told in the full shot? He was happy because, he said, there was nothing that he hated more than what he described as 'the rabbit shot.' He meant whenever a surprising event took place conventional movie-makers always felt obliged to cut to a close-up of one of the actors registering 'surprise.' So we did not cover what we had done with any further set-ups. But the next day, as we had half expected, word came from the producer's office to say that a close-up would be needed. Max and I were both disappointed. I suggested that we just take no notice of the message because surely a shrewd director's choice of set-ups should clearly indicate the manner in which the sequence should be cut together.

Max said that he would talk to the producer about it. And he did. And he did not give in until the end of the following day when he figured that he had expended more than enough energy on something that was not more than an academic point. And after all, he said, our cutter was a man of taste. He himself was a survivor and he had learned a long time ago that to put your foot down rarely got results.

—Mason, in his *Before I Forget* (London: Hamish Hamilton Ltd., 1981)

Carol Reed has always been one of my two or three favourite directors. I admire him and I adore him personally. He was always a director who got as much out of actors as could possibly be gotten.... And he could stage individual scenes as well as they could possibly be staged. If he had a weakness, which I admit he has, it was that he didn't have a sufficiently keen story sense, and [*The Man Between* (1953)] was a story which could have been told much more effectively by Alfred Hitchcock, who is not a director that I admire and adore on the same level as Carol Reed, because Carol Reed is a human story teller and Hitchcock, as we know, is ice-cold as a director. [Mason also worked on Reed's *Odd Man Out* (1947).]

—Mason, interviewed by Rui Nogueira for *Focus on Film*, Mar/Apr 1970

[George] Cukor is at the head of a short list of directorial elite with whom I worked in Hollywood....

During those early days when I started to work with him [on *A Star is Born* (1954)] I found it rather hard going. He was nervous in the same way that practically everyone on a sound stage is nervous on the first few days of a new movie. I was feeling not quite on the top of my form because of the lingering dizziness [of an inner ear infection], and here was George talking at me, talking, talking. I was trying to assemble myself in the pattern that I had prepared and at the same time to incorporate the drift of his suggestions. Although I hope he would agree that we did in fact communicate and share our ideas effectively, in the long run I was left with the regret that I could not do just what he had wanted of the character in the first place. I fancied that the Norman Maine whom Cukor had in mind had all the colors of John Barrymore, whereas I was putting together an actor who resembled much more closely some of my own drunken friends. In fact this was the best that I could offer him. Stylistically a Barrymore figure might have been preferable but I had never liked what I saw of Barrymore.

—Mason, in his *Before I Forget* (London: Hamish Hamilton Ltd., 1981)

[Philip Vandamm in *North by Northwest* (1959, Alfred Hitchcock)] was a pretty straightforward part, and I was expected to do pretty straightforward things in it. Except in the last scene when Hitchcock wanted me to get a laugh, which I just couldn't deliver. Otherwise there were no problems and we got on well together, even though he isn't my ideal director. For example, Hitch never expects an actor to help him. And he seldom diverges from his blueprint, regardless of what the human circumstances might be. One can't complain since it is such a skilful and amusing blueprint.

—Mason, interviewed by Clive Hirschhorn for *The Films of James Mason* (London: LSP Books, 1975)

Q. Do you like to improvise, and does the opportunity often occur?

A. Yes, I do — and no, it doesn't. The film in which I was able to improvise the most was Stanley Kubrick's *Lolita* [1962]. We did this strictly at rehearsal level, to explore and get intimately acquainted with the significance of various scenes. Kubrick first hit upon the idea because he became aware of the fact that Sue Lyon, who played Lolita, knew the script back to front, and front to back but really needed to be induced to think of the lines in a particular scene as something that came out of the feeling of the character in that scene. So we started improvising during rehearsals — forgot the lines we'd learned and got to grips with the situation instead, finding that this helped us to understand much more quickly what each scene was basically about. Sue Lyon made a considerable contribution to many of the scenes because she spoke the same language as the character she was playing. This opportunity doesn't often occur.

—Mason, interviewed by Ivan Butler for *The Making of Feature Films* (Harmondsworth, England: Penguin Books, 1971)

Kubrick had become a director of enormous sophistication when it came to handling our group. I can think of only one minor criticism. He was so besotted with the genius of Peter Sellers that he seemed never to have enough of him....

Come to think of it though, you could not fault Peter Sellers. He was the only one allowed, or rather encouraged, to improvise his entire performance. The rest of us improvised only during rehearsals, then incorporated any departures from the original script that had seemed particularly effective during rehearsal. Sellers told us that he did not enjoy improvising, but I think that he was referring to the occasional necessity to think on his feet when giving a live performance. He was painstaking and meticulous in his preparation. He had told Kubrick that in order to play Quilty with an American accent he must find a model, since he needed always to be specific. Together they decided that the ideal voice for Quilty was that of Norman Grantz, the jazz impressario.

The sequence in which Sellers impressed me most was when Quilty is shot by Humbert Humbert. Kubrick's set for this sequence looked like the main hall of a Victorian mansion, complete with grand staircase, chandeliers, etc. He asked me if I could think of any items that could be introduced which would suggest the bizarre lifestyle of Quilty, its present occupant. I said that a ping-pong table beneath the principal chandelier might look nicely incongruous. But I certainly did not imagine that he would ask us to play on it. Then, in order to suggest that a wild party had taken place the night before, he had the property man distribute wine glasses and tumblers on the table. So when we came to play the scene which now incorporated a game of ping-pong, Peter, while keeping the score, would insert little wisecracks relative to the hits or misses scored by the ping-pong ball as it careened among the glasses.

—Mason, in his *Before I Forget* (London: Hamish Hamilton Ltd., 1981)

An actor is a man who by his very nature can understand many people's points of view and sympathize with them. People, for instance, often say or refer to some role I have played as being a *heavy*...which sometimes gives me a shock, because I haven't played it or even been aware when I was playing it that it was a heavy. In order to be able to play [a part], I have gotten to understand so well the reservations of the man and the nature of the man I am playing that I am, as it were, behind the character, and motivating the actions of this man.

Take for instance, Humbert Humbert.... You couldn't refer to him as a heavy, he was just a man who had this unfortunate perversion, taste, obsession — call it what you like. Another one is the man in *The Seventh Veil* [1945, Compton Bennett] who is a possessive, dominating man given even to outbursts of violence, because he was a passionate man and couldn't always control his passions. I do find myself playing characters who are torn between conflicting loyalties, shall we say.

—Mason, interviewed by Louise Sweeney for *The Christian Science Monitor*, 3 Feb 1981

Marlon Brando...is quoted as saying that when he is playing opposite another actor he has no need to draw anything at all from him.... Brando would rather look into space, and use his own imagination to feed him. I, on the contrary, like to receive whatever is available from the actors around me: I find the personal exchange very often of the greatest possible help. In *The Seagull* [1968, Sidney Lumet], for instance, not only did I receive the most wonderful assistance from Vanessa Redgrave's speaking of her lines and from the way she reacted to mine, but also she was entirely unpredictable herself, constantly expressing thoughts with her eyes or her manner of speaking to which I could react in an altogether fresh way myself.

—Mason, interviewed by Ivan Butler for *The Making of Feature Films* (Harmondsworth, England: Penguin Books, 1971)

My model for Watson [in *Murder by Decree* (1979, Bob Clark)]...was your former President, Gerald Ford. When I think of both of them, the first word that comes to my mind is "decency." Both are perfectly capable and intelligent men in their own lines, but they lack to some extent, the creative imagination that makes Holmes, say, a genius.

—Mason, interviewed by Tom Buckley for *The New York Times*, 9 Feb 1979

Concannon [in *The Verdict* (1982, Sidney Lumet)] is a star lawyer.... When he is center stage in a courtroom, he is in command, not a blustering type showman but calculating and assured. Behind the scenes he has influence and doesn't hesitate to use it — but quietly, subtly.

—Mason, interviewed for the press release for *The Verdict* (20th Century-Fox, 1982)

[Concannon's] low moral standards were the result of his desire to win. It's subtly ambiguous and crystal clear at the same time. He's a full human being, with failings. Compared to some of my other roles, Concannon was a mild scoundrel....

Sidney and I got on famously because he believes in movie rehearsals. We were in an actual courtroom for two weeks *before* we started shooting. That way your lines have a chance to grow on you. You're not memorizing, you're refining. [Mason had previously worked on Lumet's *The Deadly Affair* (1966), *The Seagull* and *Child's Play* (1973).]

—Mason, interviewed by Diana Maychick for *The New York Post*, 28 Dec 1982

I would say that, on a point of style, [Sir Randolph Nettleby in *The Shooting Party* (1985, Alan Bridges)] was *not* very eccentric. He may have had a few odd thoughts. But, as an Edwardian aristocrat, his general behavior was fairly conservative: How could it have been anything else? What he was, though, was a man of the future — a man not exclusively of his times: He was capable of seeing and feeling what other people felt. And that's what is important about the film for a modern audience: that the story forces them, in a lighthearted, attractive way, to think a little about the values of our life — to look at our habits and ask ourselves where this is leading and whether we're on the right track. Should we be smug about these habits, or should we try to change them? In effect, the film is a combination of a rather affectionate portrait of a disappearing age and a rather critical view of it.

—Mason, interviewed (Dec 1983) by Nick Roddick for *Magill's Cinema Annual 1986*, ed. by Frank N. Magill (Englewood Cliffs, N.J.: Salem Press, 1986)

Marsha MASON [1942-]

Born: St. Louis, Missouri. Following college, she made her film debut in Hot Rod Hullabaloo (1966, William T. Naud). Work in commercials and on day-time TV, on the off-Broadway stage and with The American Conservatory Theater in San Francisco preceded her second film, Blume in Love (1973, Paul Mazursky). Later that year she played Maggie in Mark Rydell's Cinderella Liberty:

[To prepare] I went out and talked with the topless dancers in Seattle. Gorgeous, 18 years old.... They were trapped. I mean one girl talked about doing television commercials! They just didn't know anything else.

Also [the role] was very difficult because Maggie is an unsympathetic character to many men. Jimmy [Caan as John Baggs, Jr.] found her unsympathetic.

I liked her. I found myself defending her. I mean they call her a terrible character, a whore, a prostitute, a terrible mother. She wasn't!

—Mason, interviewed by Jerry Tallmer for *The New York Post*, 2 Feb 1974

The Goodbye Girl [1977, Herbert Ross] was based on the dynamics between Richard [Dreyfuss] and me as we rehearsed for a film Neil [Simon] wrote called *Bogart Slept Here*. That film never worked out, but Neil went home and decided to write about the chemistry between us.

—Mason, interviewed by Charles Salzburg for *The New York Daily News*, 18 Dec 1983

[Working with Richard Dreyfuss on *The Goodbye Girl* was like] hitching myself to a skyrocket. He carries most of the comic thrust of the movie. I'm the one who had to root the movie in reality. I was always stirring spaghetti and telling the kid [Quinn Cummings] to go to bed, and what I really wanted to do was act crazy, too.

—Mason, interviewed by Rex Reed for *The New York Daily News*, 20 Nov 1977

The role of Georgia [in *Only When I Laugh* (1981, Glenn Jordan)] was difficult because she's not that sympathetic. Her alcoholism is shrill and strident. But she's pretty spunky. I started reading books about women alcoholics who are different from men alcoholics. Society judges women alcoholics much more severely. It makes no allowances for a woman drunk. The guilt and pain is enormous.

The daughter [Kristy McNichol] is a strong, healthy person. Her perseverance and drive for the relationship gives her mother strength. Neil [Simon] really wanted to write about the fact that you have choices and don't have to be a victim.

—Mason, interviewed by Beverly Stephen for *The New York Daily News*, 22 Sept 1981

Raymond MASSEY [1896-1983]

Born: Toronto, Ontario, Canada. Studies at The University of Toronto and work on the London stage as both an actor and producer preceded his film debut in The Old Dark House (1932, James Whale). In 1936, he played both John and Oswald Cabal in William Cameron Menzies' adaptation of H.G. Wells's Things to Come:

This was the biggest and most difficult film I ever worked in. I had read Wells's novel, fascinated by its humor and the earthy humanity of its characters. It was a huge canvas of adventure. I was thrilled by the news that I was to play the two roles of John Cabal and his grandson Oswald, and so travel through the whole century of Wells's prophecy, the next war, the age of dark frustration and anarchy, the new world of science.

But when I saw Wells's script I was appalled. Every trace of wit, humor and emotion, everything which had made the novel so enthralling, had been cut and replaced with large gobs of socialist theory which might have been lifted from a Sidney Webb tract. Although Wells often declared he was not a teacher or political theorist, this was exactly what he had become....

The picture was fantastically difficult to act. Wells had deliberately formalized the dialogue, particularly in the later sequences. The novel's realism had vanished from the screenplay in which we delivered heavy-handed speeches instead of carrying on conversation. Emotion had no place in Wells's new world....

[In *Action in the North Atlantic* (1943, Lloyd Bacon)] there was some pretty good acting by a typical Warner Brothers cast. From Bogart, as always there was the matchless performance. In a picture like *Action* you were lucky if the character you played was sufficiently defined to be recognizable. Bogie did not have much to go on in this respect. But he knew enough to trust his own understated style to get him through. Most actors, especially those with a stage background, are inclined to overstress a thin role. Not Bogie. He understood the why and the wherefore of underplaying better than most screen actors of his time.

The character of Cal [in *East of Eden* (1955, Elia Kazan)], the "bad" son, was an early example of the anti-hero. Gadge [Kazan] had wanted Marlon Brando for this role and when he proved unavailable, had chosen a young actor, James Dean. Regardless of his inexperience, James Dean was a good choice. In every respect he was the Cal of Steinbeck's novel....

Jimmy had only to act himself. But that is a difficult role even for an experienced actor to play. A rebel at heart, he approached everything with a chip on his shoulder. The Method had encouraged this truculent spirit. Jimmy never knew his lines before he walked on the set, rarely had command of them when the camera rolled and even if he had was often inaudible. Simple technicalities, such as moving on cue and finding his marks, were beneath his consideration.

Equally annoying was his insistence on going away alone once a scene was rehearsed and everything ready for a take. He would disappear and leave the rest of us to cool off in our chairs while he communed with himself somewhere out of sight. When he was ready we would hear the whistle Gadge Kazan had given him and he would reappear. We would assemble to our appointed spots and the camera would roll.

Gadge did nothing to dissuade Dean from these antics. Most directors would not have tolerated such conduct, myself included; but Gadge knew his boy and he must have figured that his only course was to pamper him and winnow the grain from the chaff as we went along....

He said to me one morning as I waited near my camera marks for that damn whistle to blow, "Bear with me, Ray. I'm getting solid gold!"

I remember a scene at a big ice-house which had been built on the Warner back lot. The key moment of the scene was Jimmy in a rage pushing huge blocks of ice from the cool storage loft down a long chute to melt quickly in the sweltering California sun. This was Cal's senseless attempt to destroy the refrigeration experiment. The action was simple. Jimmy just had to push the blocks down the chute as Burl Ives and I looked up at him. It was a set-up favoring us in the foreground, Jimmy being up on a platform and not in clear focus.

Everything was ready for the take. But nothing happened. Jimmy just continued to pace up and down glaring at the blocks of ice.

"What the hell goes on?" I said.

Burl Ives looked at his watch. "Jimmy's got to get to hate the ice," he muttered. "It takes time."

It was nearly five minutes before Dean signalled his readiness to perform.

—Massey, in his *A Thousand Different Lives* (Boston: Little, Brown & Co., 1979)

Marlee MATLIN [1965-]

Born: Morton's Grove, Ill. Work in children's theater with the Chicago's Center for Deafness from age 7, and work on the Chicago stage, preceded her film debut as Sarah in Randa Haines' 1986 adaptation of Children of a Lesser God:

I learned how to smoke for the movie. The director said to me [at the audition], "Sarah needs to smoke." I said, "Oh." She said, "Well, you'll have to smoke....you'd better start smoking, in case you get the part." I said, "I don't smoke. If I get the part, then maybe we can change the script," and she said, "No, you have to smoke."

I said, "Wait a minute, I'm playing Sarah, not you."

She said, "I'm the director, and I decide."

I said, "Well, wait a minute. I'm working with you."

She said, "Sarah's smoking is part of Sarah."

At first, I disagreed with her completely, and we fought about it. Then I got the part and still fought over that point, and finally I said, "I accept this," and I smoked. She told me to start smoking two months before the making of the film. I didn't start until one week before the filming started. She doesn't control my life, I don't control hers.

—Matlin, interviewed by David Blum for *New York*, 6 Oct 1986

Working with the cast and crew and director, I learned about Sarah. She didn't trust anyone, not even herself. Sarah grew up fast.

—Matlin, interviewed by Lou Ann Walker for *Parade Magazine*, 22 May 1988

Walter MATTHAU [1920-]

Born: Walter Matuschanskayasky in New York City. Work as a child actor in the New York Yiddish theater, studies at The New School for

Social Research Dramatic Workshop under Irwin Piscator and work in summer stock and on Broadway preceded his film debut in The Kentuckian (1955, Burt Lancaster). In 1966, he played Whiplash Willie Gingrich opposite Jack Lemmon's Harry Hinkle in Billy Wilder's The Fortune Cookie:

I always play Wilder. Wilder sees me as Wilder — a lovable rogue full of razor blades. To Wilder actors are a necessary evil. I think he wishes there were some way he could make pictures without actors. He once told me that he envied Walt Disney. Donald Duck and Mickey Mouse didn't make trouble. [Matthau also worked on Wilder's *The Front Page* (1974) and *Buddy, Buddy* (1981); both also co-starred Jack Lemmon.]

—Matthau, quoted by Allan Hunter in *Walter Matthau* (New York: St. Martin's Press, 1984)

People say, "Walter, you stole *The Fortune Cookie*." No I've got to reply, I was given *The Fortune Cookie*. It was given to me by Billy Wilder...and Jack Lemmon. If an actor steals a scene, he's not doing well by the show. It's no good. It all goes akimbo.

—Matthau, interviewed by Donald Freeman for *The San Diego Union TV Week*, 12-18 Nov 1967

Horace Vandergelder [in *Hello Dolly* (1969)] isn't much of a part. I took it because I wanted to work in a musical. A lot of things about it were rather painful. There is a tremendous amount of work one must do to become proficient in song and dance. Acting is easier for me. I always enjoy working with Gene Kelly, who also directed me in *A Guide for the Married Man* [1967], because he is charming, intelligent and has an inordinate amount of patience.

—Matthau, interviewed by Judy Stone for *The New York Times*, 8 Sept 1968

There was a strange kind of attraction to the fact that I was going to work with Streisand [on *Hello Dolly*]. I almost knew that I was going to blow up at her.

I tried very hard, very hard to be civil, but it's extraordinarily difficult to be civil to her. See, she's a soloist, and she likes to tell the conductor when the flutes come in, when the violins come in.

When she acts — and I say that in quotes — she likes to tell the director when the other actors should come in. She pretends as tho she's asking, but she's overstepping her boundaries. She should simply be the instrument of the director, and not be the conductor, the composer, the scene designer, the costume designer, the acting coach, et cetera.

—Matthau, interviewed by Gene Siskel for *The Chicago Tribune*, 24 Dec 1972

[On *Pete 'n' Tillie* (1972, Martin Ritt), Carol Burnett and I] worked overtime to make each other laugh.

I wouldn't have dreamed of trying it on some of my leading ladies...but with Carol Burnett or Lucille Ball [in *A Guide for the Married Man*] or any other comedienne, yes! It's a show-business compulsion.

I broke up Carol every chance I got during filming. I let up when we got to our dramatic scenes, of course. That wouldn't have been fair. But whenever we went back to comedy, I had to make her bust out laughing in the middle of a speech.

—Matthau, quoted by Allan Hunter in *Walter Matthau* (New York: St. Martin's Press, 1984)

Sure I loved working on *Casey's Shadow* [1978, Martin Ritt]. It was a character part. I'm a character actor, and when they give me something I can bite into I like it better. It's better than the easy stuff you just phone in.

Q. You just phone in your performance?

A. Yeah, just phone it in.... [On *California Suite* (1978)], I just came to phone it in and the director got angry. Herbie Ross. Started picking on me. I bawled him out. He bawled me out. We had a terrific fight for a week. He was right. I've grown lazy being a successful actor and a movie star. I've grown very lazy so I come in with an absolute *surface* performance and the guy's gotta really rile me up.

—Matthau, interviewed by Cynthia Heimel for *The Soho Weekly News*, 23 Mar 1978

Victor MATURE [1915-]

Born: Louisville, Kentucky. Military and business training preceded his film debut in The Housekeeper's Daughter (1939, Hal Roach). In 1947, he played Nick Bianco in Henry Hathaway's Kiss of Death:

Nick wasn't everyone's dish. He was a thief and a stool pigeon, yet I had to make him a sympathetic character. I had to show him as a man full of faults, but one strong enough to face misfortunes without self-pity. Nick's partners in crime double-crossed him. One of them made love to his wife while he was in prison, and finally she killed herself. But Nick didn't crack up. This trait, plus his genuine courage and his great love of children, furnished me with the only ammunition I had to win audience sympathy for Nick.

—Mature, in *The Saturday Evening Post*, 10 Sept 1949

Virginia MAYO [1920-]

Born: Virginia Jones in St. Louis, Missouri. Drama studies as a child and work on stage from age 12 (Broadway from 1941) preceded her film debut in Jack London (1943, Alfred Santell). Early in her career, she played opposite both Bob Hope and Danny Kaye:

Q. Did you like playing opposite Bob Hope and Danny Kaye, or did you resent being their stooges?

A. I wasn't considered a stooge, not really. People probably said it, but I never heard it or felt it. I was their straight man and that wasn't easy — it requires, if I may say so, impeccable timing and a good sense of humour. I never tired of playing with Danny Kaye or Bob Hope because they were wonderful talents....

Working with Bob Hope on *The Princess and the Pirate* [1944, David Butler] was a fun, fun thing. He was always trying to make me laugh, trying to tickle me or make me break up during a scene. And I was a good audience for him. And it was fun working with Danny Kaye because he was the same way — only Danny was a bit more moody. Bob Hope never displayed any moodiness.... [Mayo also worked with Kaye on *Wonder Man* (1945, Bruce Humberstone), *The Kid from Brooklyn* (1946, Norman Z. McLeod), *The Secret Life of Walter Mitty* (1947, Norman Z. McLeod) and *A Song is Born* (1948,Howard Hawks.]

Q. How was it working with William Wyler [on *The Best Years of Our Lives* (1946)] who, of course, many actresses considered a taskmaster?

A. It went so smoothly, I couldn't believe it....

There was only one time we disagreed about anything, and even that was minor. We were doing a close-up of me being angry at Dana Andrews. And Wyler said to me, "Now, look, in this scene, I want you to *rip* off your eyelashes because Marie's not being allowed to go out this evening!" I didn't want to rip off my eyelashes on camera and said, "Oh, no. I don't want to do that." But he persisted, "O.K., let's do it." But I still wanted to get out of it and made up an excuse: "You know I won't be able to put them back on again today because that'll take too long." But he wouldn't let me get away with that, and told me, "We'll do one take, and if you don't like it, we'll cut it out; or if we don't need it, we won't use it." So I did the scene, and ripped off my eyelashes in a huff. It turned out pretty good, and Wyler used it in the picture.

I had heard that William Wyler was just so difficult to work with but, for *me*, acting for him turned out to be easy, like a dream....

Q. Can we talk about *A Song is Born*, and working with Howard Hawks?

A. Hawks's method was entirely different than Wyler's. Willie would plan ahead; he was thorough and analytical about everything, much more so than Hawks who loved to work off the cuff and change things as we went along. Hawks loved to improvise according to how he *felt* things were going.... I loved making that picture with him.

Hawks wanted his women to have a unique "angle." He loved his women to be sexy and antagonistic. Lauren Bacall was exactly his dish: slim, sexy, and tough with that low voice of hers. I don't think he liked my type at all. He wanted me to lower my voice. At the time I was quite young and voices are always higher when you're young. So he wanted me to go, on my free time, to a soundstage and scream in order to make my voice sound lower and sexier — like Bacall's. I did what he wanted, but all it did was make my voice weak and tired.

I loved playing the gangster's moll in *White Heat* [1949, Raoul Walsh]. Jimmy Cagney...stimulated me to such an extent, I must say that I didn't have to act very much; I just had to react to him because he was so powerful. His acting ability was so strong that you could feel him radiating all these wonderful sensations. Jimmy is a very friendly person, but very retiring, and was not very social on the set. He just wanted to do his acting and leave.... He made a lot of suggestions to Walsh as to what he wanted to do with his part, and he was always right, always 100% accurate....

There is no doubt that [Walsh] was my *favourite* director with whom I worked.... He could make his actors perform at their peaks. He felt that I was a good actress, and liked me to try gutsy things that he would inject into his films. So he opened a whole new style for me, a wonderful new avenue, and that was a great break for me. He didn't try to teach me anything, but just by being with him I learned to be more dramatic, more exciting, and more interpretive. He gave me a lot as an actress.

—Mayo, interviewed by Danny Peary for *Focus on Film*, Mar 1981

Mercedes McCAMBRIDGE [1918-]

Born: near Joliet, Illinois. Work as an actress on radio and on Broadway (from 1945) preceded her film debut as Sadie Burke in Robert Rossen's All the King's Men (1949):

I got there [Hollywood] on Sunday, went to work the same day at Suisun, where the company was on location.... A cameraman shook hands with me and said, "Good luck." A stand-in told me, "Broderick Crawford is going to make a speech. All you have to do is get on the platform and take notes." I didn't even know where the camera was, but I followed instructions.

Next thing I know, Broderick Crawford and I were being pelted by some antisocial persons armed with singularly loose-skinned tomatoes, mixed with soft lettuce and, I believe, some radishes.

"If this is the movies," I said to Broderick Crawford, "I don't want any part of it. I'm going back to Broadway."

But I didn't go back to Broadway, in spite of this unhappy start. And, once I got into the role, I loved doing Sadie Burke. One reason why I liked the part was that Robert Penn Warren had made the character so clear in his novel. Everything she felt and did and said was in the book, which I used as a constant guide. Too, Sadie never was a hypocrite. She couldn't be dishonest; she couldn't fool herself, and she always would be lonely, which made her easy to play.

—McCambridge, in *The Saturday Evening Post*, 8 Sept 1951

[On *All the King's Men*] Robert Rossen told me the secret of any great film is that at the very top there has to be one whose word is law. One god. It has to be his conception, and if people don't agree, that's too bad.

—McCambridge, interviewed for *Cinema Texas*; in the clipping file at The Museum of Modern Art

There was no point in spending an entire afternoon of "color tests" with Joan Crawford staring me in the face. It was a farce, and a cruel one, because she had already decided that I would wear nothing but a heavy black, slightly modified nun's habit throughout the whole film [*Johnny Guitar* (1954, Nicholas Ray)]. She knew that she would be costumed in finest gabardine jodhpurs, silken shirts, and, best of all (and most unbelievable), a diaphanous white chiffon gown which she would wear in the scenes on her horse and in the sequence where I was supposed to hang her. She had also already decided that my hair had to be dyed jet-black to contrast with her warm russet-brown, also a dye job.

The film was a western...shot in Oak Creek Canyon.... Red dust in your teeth and ears...wind that ground the sand into your flesh...everybody looked like Margo in *Lost Horizon*...everybody but Joan....

For the scene in which I died...my fall was done by a great stunt man, Chuck Wilcox. He looked so funny in a copy of my dreary costume with a frizzy indigo wig.... However, until the moment of the fall, the person on the balcony is me. It is even me crashing backwards through the wooden railing. I did the fall onto a mattress on the ground just a few feet down. Then the camera discovers Chuck, careening crazily to *my* death way down there in the bottom of the gorge. The reverse angles of that sequence — i.e. Miss Crawford's footage — were all shot inside, back at the studio, in the San Fernando Valley. The lighting crew painted the lustrously sunny light and shadows on the constructed indoor balcony against a canvas sky, and when all was set, Miss Crawford was escorted from her lavishly decorated dressing-room trailer....

—McCambridge, in her *The Quality of Mercy* (New York: Times Books, 1981)

[Linda Blair's] vocal performance [on *The Exorcist* (1973, William Friedkin)] was laughable!

I have nothing against the child. I've never met her. But if people had heard her saying some of those obscenities, they would have fallen over laughing.... No, it's not true that some of her words were blended with mine on the final track. All of the devilish vocality is mine — all of it. Every word....

Doing the sound track was a terrible experience. I didn't just do the voice. I did all of the demon's sounds. That wheezing, for instance. My chronic bronchitis helped with that. I did it on one microphone, then on another, elevating it a bit, then a third and fourth, two tones higher each time, and they combined them, as a chorus.

The wailing just before the Demon is driven out, that's the keening sound I once heard at a wake in Ireland.... For the groaning sounds, I pulled a scarf around my neck, tight, and almost strangled.

I had to imagine Lucifer. I had to imagine the incredible, bottomless agony — the eternal agony of a lost soul. I drew on memory for that. I've been an alcoholic, saved by A.A., and I've seen people in state hospitals, vegetables in straitjackets, the hopeless, abysmal, bottomless groaning and screaming. I used imitations of those hellish cries. I've been through hell, and I thought, who better than I would know how the Devil feels? I'm out of hell, he's there forever. To be on Death Row for eternity has got to be some kind of sentence.

So I cried out from my remembered hell. And when I spoke the scene in which the little girl spits out green vomit, when I made the ugly sounds of violent expectoration, I swallowed eighteen raw eggs, with a pulpy apple. To convey the feelings of the Devil being trapped, I had the crew tear up a sheet and bind me hand and foot. Sometimes I was so exhausted and my circulation so sluggish that I wasn't able to drive home; I stayed in a motel near the Burbank Studios. My voice was ruined. For weeks, I couldn't talk above a whisper....

—McCambridge, interviewed by Charles Higham for *The New York Times*, 27 Jan 1974

Joel McCREA [1905-1990]

Born: South Pasadena, California. Studies at Pomona College and work as an extra in the mid-20s led to his first role in The Fair Co-Ed (1927, Sam Wood). Early in his career, he worked three times for both Preston Sturges and Gregory La Cava:

I think the two most interesting men I worked with were Sturges [on *Sullivan's Travels* (1941), *The Palm Beach Story* (1943) and *The Great Moment* (1944)] and La Cava [on *Bed of Roses* (1933), *Private Worlds* (1935) and *The Primrose Path* (1940)], because they were original guys. They had an idea for a film they wrote with the writer, and they did it according to who they cast for it. If La Cava had gotten [Robert] Montgomery for *Private Worlds*, he would have done it differently. He always wanted me *not* to be the nice "All-American Boy" that Mr. [William Randolph] Hearst called me [Hearst was instrumental in McCrea's receiving leading roles]. And so he made me do things in *Primrose Path*, where I turned Ginger [Rogers] upside down and called her a tart and everything, and the same thing in *Private Worlds*. That's when Goldwyn said, "Oh, I thought he was just a nice, easy-going boy, but I saw some sparks fly there." I didn't have sense enough to know to do that, but La Cava took it upon himself if he was interested in you. The two people he liked the best among actors were [Katharine] Hepburn and me. And Richard Dix, of course....

Actors really loved working with him. Because everything was kind of tailored for you. He wanted *you*. No one forced you on him, it wasn't a commitment, it was what he wanted. And when he wanted it, he saw that he got it. Hepburn hung around his office all the time. Because she needed a La Cava at RKO....

A director like Sturges helps you tremendously because he gives you confidence. You get confidence the day he comes to you and says, "Here's a script that I've written, and I want you to play the director...."

He told me that he wrote *Sullivan's Travels* from watching me around Paramount, working there with DeMille and Wellman and different people. I knew him as a writer for a long time before he even became a director. I told him, "Well, Preston, that's very flattering that you said you wrote it for me. No one writes things for me. They write them for Gary Cooper, and if they can't get him, they use me." "Well," he said, "That isn't the instance here. I could have gotten anybody; I could have gotten Gable, Cooper, anybody for *Sullivan's Travels* and I wanted you. I wrote it for you. You're the one." Well then, right away, a fellow who's not real cocksure of himself, like me, I needed that kind of compliment, because then I would cut loose and do things and live up to what was expected of me.

We rehearsed very little with Sturges because he would talk it over with us and he was so articulate.... Some of the better directors even...are not articulate, so they'll rehearse and rehearse and rehearse, and then they'll take many takes.... Preston Sturges was particularly articulate, because he wrote the thing as well as directed it, so he could tell you exactly what to do, and he never superimposed things that would be different from your character. And very seldom would he change anything....

He wrote dialogue that I could remember; I mean, he'd give long speeches and different things, but it was very easy to remember it because he'd talk it out. If you get somebody who types it out but doesn't say it, sometimes it doesn't flow so easily, you know; it's often kind of difficult.

[William Wellman] was a wild little bastard but I liked him. If you were professional, he really worked fine with you.... He would raise hell with actresses sometimes, if they were a little phoney. He loved actresses like Stanwyck, who was his favourite, and Carole Lombard, another of his favourites; people like that. But if the actress was a little prissy or a little synthetic or phoney, why, then he would ride hell out of them.

He never made more than three or four takes if he didn't have to, because it bored him. He was a vigorous, virile, gutty little guy and I liked him. But he could be tough on people, yes. He didn't like one of the actors in *Buffalo Bill* [1944], and boy, he just rode him. He was a good actor too, Tommy Mitchell.... I knew him and I liked him, but Wellman thought he was hamming it up too damn much. He wasn't playing the character, Ned Buntline; he was playing Tommy Mitchell. So Wellman rode him, to cut him down. He could be tough....

[Raoul Walsh] was a wonderful director because he never let a thing die. [On *Colorado Territory* (1949)] he would have me rolling the brown-paper cigarettes in a scene. I didn't smoke and I wasn't very good at it, but I could roll those brown-paper cigarettes. He had me doing that, because he never let a scene be static. Every minute, I was moving. I was getting on the horse; I was doing something else; Virginia [Mayo] was coming in; some guy was coming up from behind. Everything was always fluid, so there was never a dull moment when you say, "Oh hell, is anything ever going to happen?"

I always felt so much more comfortable in the western. The minute I got a horse and a hat and a pair of boots on, I felt easier. I didn't feel like I was an actor anymore; I felt like I was the guy out there doing it. When I was doing Wyatt in *Wichita* [1955, Jacques Tourneur], I believed it. I even went back to the period, because I had read "Frontier Marshal," the Stuart N. Lake book, and I knew all the things Earp was thinking and it gave an authenticity to it. The audience believed in it, and I believed in it....

I never pretended to be a great actor; I didn't try to create a character the way Muni did with Zola and Pasteur, which I gratefully admired. I didn't feel qualified to do it and I didn't try to do it. I tried to be Joel McCrea as Wyatt Earp, how I would have been if I'd have been there in that day. Because I thought the worst thing you could do — in my day...was to make a pretense of being something you weren't....

Whether it was Wyatt Earp or Buffalo Bill or when I played Sam Houston in a picture called *The First Texan* [1956, Byron Haskin], I tried to rehearse for them and make them as authentic as I could. To me, it was not only a responsibility to show things as nearly as they were, rather than some kooky modern idea of the thing, but also to make it more easy for me to play it, because once I'd researched it, I knew everything about Buffalo Bill, I knew what he would do....

It's very important to me to be historically authentic. [McCrea also worked on Tourneur's *Stars in My Crown* (1950) and *Stranger on Horseback* (1955).]

—McCrea, interviewed by Patrick McGilligan for *Focus on Film*, June 1978

I read [*Ride the High Country* (1962, Sam Peckinpah)] and said, "I'll do it...but only if I do Steve Judd. I don't want to do the other part. I want to be the guy with integrity, because that's what I've been working at for forty-seven years, and I might as well just finish it out that way. But Randy [Randolph Scott] is the one who found the story, and so he should have first choice." So he said, "We'll ask him." So he called Randy up and said, "Joel wants to do the picture with you, but he wants you to say which part you want to do." So Randy said, "Well, ordinarily they'd think of me for Steve Judd, the guy with honesty, but I've done it so many times that I'd like to do something different. I'd like to do the sonofabitch that wants to steal and go away. It would give me a little color." So I said, "Okay, you've got a deal." And that's the way we did it. He was the most charming Southern gentleman.

—McCrea, interviewed (1983) by John Kobal for *People Will Talk* (New York: Alfred A. Knopf, 1985)

Hattie McDANIEL [1895-1952]

Born: Wichita, Kansas; raised Denver, Colorado. Work in minstrel shows, including her father's (The Henry McDaniel Minstrel Show), as a singer and dancer with Morrison's Orchestra, on radio and as a songwriter preceded her film debut as an extra in 1931. In 1939, she played Mammy in Gone With the Wind:

Every actor and actress is possessed of the absorbing passion to create something distinctive and unique. He or she desires a role which will challenge his capabilities and send him searching for new mannerisms, and latent dramatic power. Such a role was given Louise Beavers in *Imitation of Life* [1934, John M. Stahl], and the veteran actress Madame Sul te Wan in *Maid of Salem* [1936, Frank Lloyd].... In playing the part of Mammy, I tried to make her a living, breathing character, the way she appeared to me in the book. There was an opportunity to glorify Negro womanhood; not the modern, streamlined type of Negro woman who attends teas and concerts in ermine and mink, but the type of Negro woman which gave us Harriett Tubman, Sojourner Truth, and Charity Still; the brave, efficient, hard-working type of womanhood [who] has built a race, mothered our Booker T. Washington, George W. Carver, Robert Moton, and Mary McLeod Bethune.

So you see, the mothers of that era must have had something in them to produce men and women of that caliber.

—McDaniel, on "Wings over Jordan", TV broadcast, Cleveland, Ohio, 7 July 1940; repr. in *Hattie: The Life of Hattie McDaniel* by Carlton Jackson (Lanham, Maryland: Madison Books, 1990)

[I was proud to play the role of Mammy, a black woman] who was fearless, who cringed before no one, who did not talk in whispers, walk on tiptoe, who criticized a white woman's morals, and who showed real emotion.

—McDaniel, quoted in *Hattie: The Life of Hattie McDaniel* by Carlton Jackson (Lanham, Maryland: Madison Books, 1990)

Malcolm McDOWELL [1943-]

Born: Malcolm Taylor in Leeds, England. Studies at The London Academy of Music and Art, work in provincial repertory (from 1963), with The Royal Shakespeare Theatre, and on TV preceded his film debut in Poor Cow (1967, Ken Loach). His part in that film was deleted, making Mick Travis in If... (1968, Lindsay Anderson) his first realized role:

A good actor might do one pure performance in a lifetime. I had mine in *If...* Don't ask me how I did it, because I haven't got a clue. It was totally intuitive, and it was never like that again. Everything that came after that was tainted by technique. And once you begin to have technique, there's nothing to do but develop more and more, to make it so good that it begins to erase itself. That's the central paradox of an actor's life. I go through hell now to achieve through technique what used to happen automatically.

—McDowell, interviewed by Laurence Shames for *Esquire*, Apr 1981

It was extraordinary making [*If...*] because we were shooting the sequences up on the roof with sten guns. Then we'd read *The Times*, and there would be pictures of students with sten guns on the roof of the Sorbonne. It was an amazing period. We felt we were pioneers.

—McDowell, interviewed by J.P. Benson for *The Face*, Mar 1987

We didn't start shooting [*A Clockwork Orange* (1971, Stanley Kubrick)] till September, and I went out to [Kubrick's] house pretty well every day from June on, played about a million games of table tennis.... We talked a lot about costume. I'd bought some makeup and lashes to try and find the futuristic bit. I was putting on one pair, and he said, "Let's just take a still of that." Saw the still and that was it. I said, "That's all Alex wears, none of the colors, that, only that." He said, "Oh, would you like black lips or something?" I said, "No, just the one eye, 'cause when they see the face, there's something wrong, and they're not quite sure what it is at first." I was very pleased with that.

The "Singin' in the Rain" sequence was extraordinary. We had come to the set, looked at it, sat down for the whole day, said nothing, did nothing, nothing happened. The next day, the same. On the third day Stanley said, "You come in, kick the feller down, can you dance?" So I came in, kicked the feller down the stairs, suddenly went into..."Doobie-do-dah-bah-doobie-do...I'm Singin' in the Rain...Just singin' in the rain." And it just went through, like that on a rehearsal, right the way through to the end....

There was quite a lot of ad-libbing in the film. The psycho test, where they show you the ink-blots and ask you to do the first thing that comes in your head. What you heard on the film were the first genuine things that came to mind.

—McDowell, interviewed by Andrew Bailey for *Rolling Stone*, 2 Aug 1973

Alex enjoys life very much, especially when he's raping and pillaging and "singing in the rain." It's the most euphoric kind of image one gets. He's not angry. I felt my job was to get some form of sympathy for him without being too obvious. So I tried to give the character a happiness for living life on his *own* terms.

—McDowell, interviewed by Greg Vellner for *The Cable Guide*, Jan 1985

Alex in *A Clockwork Orange* is a motivator, a mover of events. What happens is caused to happen by him. But Mick in *O Lucky Man!* [1973, Lindsay Anderson] is a reactor — things happen to him. Both performances were stylised in a sense but from there on they were not alike at all. Working for Kubrick and working for Lindsay is of course very different, too. Yet both are obsessives — they have to be or they would never have got what they wanted on to the screen.

But where Stanley is the absolute satirist, Lindsay is the absolute humanitarian. Both are able to build up an atmosphere where it is possible to create. Neither treats you like a puppet. They don't ask you to do what they tell you. Everything happens on the set. No pulling of strings, just bloody hard work and thought. [McDowell worked with Anderson a third time on *Brittannia Hospital* (1982).]

—McDowell, interviewed by Christopher Ford for *The Guardian*, 16 May 1973

Dorothy McGUIRE [1918-]

Born: Omaha, Nebraska. Broadway success in Claudia took her to Hollywood to recreate her role in the film version (1943, Edmund Goulding). In 1945, she played Katie in Elia Kazan's A Tree Grows in Brooklyn:

Katie was a woman who had been battered by poverty and hardship. Therefore her basically tender nature was heavily coated with hardness....

The part of this picture that frightened me most came when Katie was to have a baby. I was totally unrehearsed by experience for anything like that, and I was afraid I couldn't make it look real. I was so disturbed that Elia Kazan, the director, took me aside to help me. He probably could have soothed me, but he was too wise for that. He let me get all worked up, and in the end I was nearly as hysterical as Katie was supposed to be in the story.

—McGuire, in *The Saturday Evening Post*, 31 Dec 1949

It took me a whole picture [*Friendly Persuasion* (1956)] to figure [William Wyler] out, but I would love to work with him again today. He is difficult and enigmatic. I remember for one whole day he had me kneading bread and I thought, "Why?" But he wanted me to be very familiar with the set. It may have been frivolous to have spent a whole day kneading bread. I am sure I would have felt just as at home without spending all that time, but I learned what he was driving at. He was not articulate about giving you direction. I had to poke around and explain the character for myself and he would simply wait. Then he would add something here and there and wait some more.

—McGuire, interviewed by Ronald Bowers for *The Selznick Players* (New York: A.S. Barnes, 1976)

Victor McLAGLEN [1886-1959]

Born: Tunbridge Wells, England; father of director Andrew McLaglen [1920-]. Work as a prize fighter, in vaudeville and with the circus preceded his film debut in The Call of the Road (1920, A.E. Coleby). His U.S. film debut was in The Beloved Brute (1924, J. Stuart Blackton); in 1926, he played Captain Flagg in What Price Glory?:

I had seen the play on the stage and had realised immediately that if I was born for nothing else I was at least born to play Captain Flagg in that full-throated yarn of the American Marines....

I immediately went to see Raoul Walsh who was to seal his reputation with the direction of the picture, and I asked him for the leading part.

"You're English," he said, as though that finished it.

I admitted it, but argued that my nationality did not matter twopence. Walsh would not agree. He said that I could not possibly portray the prototype of the American Marine. I knew nothing of the American service, or of the mentality of its troopers, he maintained.

Arguing very fiercely with him, for I was dead keen on that part, I told him that there were no soldiers in the world tougher than the men in my own old Middlesex Regiment. A soldier was a soldier all the world over, I said, and if a man could handle the tough Cockneys of the Middlesex he could act the part of handling equally tough men in the American Marines.

—McLaglen, in his *Express to Hollywood* (London: Jarrolds Publishers, 1934)

I have no illusions about acting, and certainly I have none about myself. Long ago I came to the conclusion that actors are victims of luck and circumstance. If the role you are in fits the size of your head and some inherent quality in yourself, you do it well.

If the picture is a box-office winner, then, through reflection, you are considered a great actor. Too many elements have to reach perfection at the same time to boost you into the elect class. Merely doing a job well is of no great advantage to you unless the story, the presentation, the writer, and the director are equally inspired at the same time.

Luckily for me, these various elements in picture-making reached this perfection I speak of in the production of *The Informer* [1935, John Ford]. Because mine was the principal and only important role, the honours piled in on me....

—McLaglen, in *The Sydney Morning Herald*, 28 Dec 1937

The thing about being an actor that teaches a man is the chance to play different types. Now when I was in the army if anybody'd told me that one day I'd sympathize with and understand a fellow who betrayed his comrades, I'd have taken him apart the hard way. Yet when I studied the part of Gyppo and played it in *The Informer*, I grew to know just what went on in that poor dog's tortured intellect. In the end, I actually felt sorry for him.

—McLaglen, in *The New York Daily Mirror*, 30 Apr 1937

Gyppo Nolan in *The Informer* was a weak, unintelligent and unresourceful man. In contrast, MacChesney [in *Gunga Din* (1939, George Stevens)] was physically and mentally virile; he had humor, and even his faults were delightful.

—McLaglen, in *The Saturday Evening Post*, 13 Apr 1946

Butterfly McQUEEN [1911-]

Born: Thelma McQueen in Tampa, Florida. Dance studies with Katherine Dunham and work on Broadway preceded her film debut as Prissy in Gone With the Wind (1939, Victor Fleming):

I'll tell you. I was the only unhappy one in that film. [Producer David O.] Selznick understood. He was a very understanding man. He knew it was a stupid part and I was an intelligent person and he thoroughly agreed with me that it wasn't a very pleasant part to play. However, I did my best. My very best. And Mammy [Hattie McDaniel] said, "You'll never come to Hollywood again. You complain too much...." [She did, however, including Selznick's production of *Duel in the Sun* (1946, King Vidor).]

Q. Can you tell us some things about Clark Gable and Vivien Leigh?

A. One day he said to me, "What's the matter, Prissy?" As if to say, "If they're not nice to you around here, I have some pull." But I was just generally unhappy. I didn't want to be that little slave. I didn't want to play that stupid part. I was just whining and crying.

Q. Well that was a terrible thing that you did to poor Scarlett O'Hara, telling her you knew about birthin' babies when you didn't.

A. But I was a stupid girl. That's what Prissy was.

—McQueen, interviewed by Tinkerbelle for *Interview*, Nov 1974

Steve McQUEEN [1930-1980]

Born: Terence Steven McQueen in Indianapolis. Studies at Sanford Meisner's Neighborhood Playhouse on the G.I. Bill and with Lee Strasberg at The Actors Studio in N.Y., and work on TV and stage preceded his film debut in a small role in Somebody Up There Likes Me (1956, Robert Wise).

[On television] I usually played a killer or a delinquent, and I did a lot of snarling. Producers would tell me I had "mean" eyes. That's when I began to sweat over being pegged as a heavy. Once they hang that label on you, it can knock out your chances for a lot of other stuff. So I began looking for something to improve my image — and what I got was *The Blob* [1958, Irwin S. Yeaworth]. The main acting challenge in this one consisted of running around, bug-eyed, and shouting, "Hey, everybody, look out for the Blob!" I wasn't too thrilled when people would tell me what a fine job I'd done in it.

—McQueen, interviewed by William F. Nolan for *McQueen* (New York: Congdon and Weed, 1984)

Adolphe MENJOU [1890-1963]

Born: Joseph Adolphe Menjou in Pittsburgh. Studies at Cornell University and work as a manager of one of his father's restaurants preceded his film debut in The Man Behind the Door

(1914, Wally Van). In 1923, he played Pierre Revel in Charlie Chaplin's A Woman of Paris:

At first I had no great faith in the story. To me it was simply a job and a good part. Not until we started shooting did I begin to realize that we were making a novel and exciting picture. It was Chaplin's genius that transformed the very ordinary story. Aside from his own great talent as an actor he had the ability to inspire other actors to perform their best. Within a few days I realized that I was going to learn more about acting from Chaplin than I had ever learned from any director. He had one wonderful, unforgettable line that he kept repeating over and over throughout the picture. "Don't sell it!" he would say, "Remember, they're peeking at you."

It was a colorful and concise way to sum up the difference between the legitimate stage and the movies — a reminder that in pictures, when one has an important emotion or thought to express, the camera moves up to his face and there he is on the screen with a head that measures 6 feet from brow to chin....

From my early days in the movies I had been schooled in the exaggerated gestures and reactions that were thought necessary to tell a story in pantomime. But when I, or any other actor, would give out with one of those big takes, Chaplin would just shake his head and say, "They're peeking at you." That did it. I knew that I had just cut myself a large slice of ham and had tossed the scene out the window.

Since then I have never played a scene before a camera without thinking to myself, "They're peeking at you; don't sock it."

Another pet line of Chaplin's was, "Think the scene! I don't care what you do with your hands or your feet. If you think the scene, it will get over."

And we had to keep shooting every scene until we *were* thinking it — until we believed it and were playing it with our brains and not just with our hands or our feet or our eyebrows.... There were days when we rehearsed the same little scene time after time and then shot and reshot it until we thought we would go crazy. But Chaplin was satisfied with nothing less than perfection, or as close to it as we could come....

Each morning the whole company — including electricians, grips, anybody who wanted to watch — was invited to the projection room to see the rushes of the film that had been shot the day before. We would all sit there and express our opinions. Chaplin listened to everybody's ideas and evaluated them with unerring instinct for those that were good....

After watching the rushes in the morning we would discuss them at some length and then we would usually go back to the stage and shoot some of the scenes over again. There was no worry about a production schedule; no effort was too great if 1 foot of the picture could be made better. One day, after watching the rushes of a scene, Chaplin expressed approval and asked me how I liked the scene.

"I think I can do it better," I told him.

"Great!" he replied. "Let's go." So we spent the rest of the day shooting the scene over again....

He insisted on our learning dialogue and saying it exactly as it was written, something that none of us had ever done before in pictures. This was because he felt that certain words registered on the face and could be easily grasped by the audience.

Lubitsch, as a director, had the same regard for realistic and subtle touches as Chaplin, but his methods were entirely different. Lubitsch planned everything very carefully in advance; he knew the content of every scene before he began shooting, and he acted out every part in rehearsal. I discovered in [*The Marriage Circle* (1924)] that all I had to do to make Lubitsch happy was to step before the camera and mimic every gesture he gave me.

The Lubitsch method produced some very good pictures, for he was a fine director; but Chaplin taught me much more about my business.

The character of Walter Burns [in *The Front Page* (1931, Lewis Milestone)] was supposed to talk like a machine gun, bang-bang-bang. In his first big scene he gave many rapid-fire orders, grabbed a telephone, dictated a story, hung up, and delivered an oration about the newspaper business. I had never played that sort of a part before, so it was difficult for me. When we started this first long take, I kept blowing lines and forgetting speeches, thus ruining the scene. I got so upset that I begged Milestone to cut the scene up into shorter takes.

"You say you're an actor," Milestone finally taunted. "Well, prove it! Real actors go through two hours on the stage without blowing any lines. Can't you do a six-minute scene?"

That stopped me. I went back at it and finally we got the scene right. After the first one, the others were not so difficult. Later I was glad that Milestone had made me play those long scenes in one take, because they looked terrific to Hollywood directors.

—Menjou, in his (with M.M. Musselman) *It Took Nine Tailors* (New York: McGraw-Hill, 1948)

I've played with a lot of actresses, and I've had to learn how to defend myself. You know, troupers who step on your lines and steal your scenes. But this child [Shirley Temple on *Little Miss Marker* (1934, Alexander Hall)] frightens me. She knows all the tricks. She backs me out of the camera, blankets me, crabs my laughs — she's making a stooge of me. Why, if she were forty years old and on the stage all her life, she wouldn't have had time to learn all she knows about acting. Don't ask me how she does it. You've heard of chess champions at eight and violin virtuosos at ten. Well, she is an Ethel Barrymore at six.

—Menjou, quoted by Gene Ringgold in *Screen Facts* #12, 1965

Ethel MERMAN [1909-1984]

Born: Ethel Zimmerman in Astoria, N.Y. Work in vaudeville and on Broadway (from 1930) preceded her film debut in We're Not Dressing (1934, Norman Taurog). Mainly a Broadway star, she occasionally made films of her stage successes:

Anything Goes [1936, Lewis Milestone] had been a spectacular success as a Broadway show. I ought to know. I'd been in it, hadn't I? So what happened? When Paramount decided to make a film out of it, they changed it as much as possible. In New York I'd sung "I Get a Kick Out of You" to Billy Gaxton, standing perfectly still at a bar, as a sort of prologue to the rest of the show. But in the movie version I was strung up on a crescent moon on wires and I had whole birds of paradise in my hair, not just feathers. I was smothered in a big chiffon gown, and I was flown around the stage with 300 extras chasing along under me. Naturally that killed it. On Broadway it had been staged simply, with a bow to the way in which Fanny Brice stepped out and sang a song all by herself. Yet there were gents with pointed heads in the studio who wondered what happened to the movie version of the song. Then and there I promised myself — I'll never come back to Hollywood again unless I'm certain I can do something worthwhile.

That's why I love Walter Lang. Walter is a nice fellow anyhow, but the way he directed the two movies, *Call Me Madam* [1953] and *There's No Business Like Show Business* [1954] won my foolish heart. Other directors had told me I was too "brassy," "too bouncy," "too gusty"; that I "projected too much." When I was in a picture I had to underplay it. But when Walter was ready to direct *Call Me Madam*, he told me, "Get out there and be as brassy and as full of bounce and gusto as you know how. That's what zillions of people who saw you in the theater paid to see." [Between 1936 and 1953, Merman made only four movies].

—Merman, (as told to Pete Martin) in *The Saturday Evening Post*, 5 Mar 1955

Bette MIDLER [1945-]

Born: Paterson, New Jersey; raised in Hawaii. High school dramatics and work with a female folk trio preceded her film debut in Hawaii (1966, George Roy Hill). On the mainland, she worked both on and off Broadway before becoming a recording and performing artist. She returned to the screen in the title role of The Rose (1979, Mark Rydell):

There is a certain superficial resemblance between "The Rose" and Janis [Joplin], but nothing is intended. She was so spectacular, I really didn't think I could imitate her. She sang in a much higher key, where I'm an alto. Her range was miles higher than mine, and she had a falsetto that I don't use much. Also, she was a white Southern girl, and my experience was so alien to that....

[Janis] was so free, so energetic. I'd never seen a performer that powerful. I'd never seen anyone chew the scenery that way — and it definitely rubbed off.

Q. Where does "The Rose" end and Miss Midler begin?

A. I am "The Rose." I made her up. She was on the page, but I made up that voice. I made up that outlook. Most of it is an alcoholic's outlook, which tends to have a narrow perspective. But there is also a little-girliness, which is probably the thing I have most in common with her. That childlike quality, that naiveté, that determination to go on and plow through the bad times, are me.

—Midler, interviewed by Judy Klemesrud for *The New York Times*, 11 Nov 1979

Q. Let me ask you about working with...Lily Tomlin on Big Business (1988, Jim Abrahams)...?

A. Well, Lily is *really* a perfectionist. I kept saying, "Lily, this is the Bette Midler School of Mugging, you just have to mug your way through this. Lil, it's very light, look, I'm singing with a cow! How deadly can it be? "But she just wouldn't buy it. I couldn't talk her into it. She really struggled with that material, she was determined to get her message across. Her heart was in the right place, she wanted to make it better.
—Midler, interviewed by Lawrence Grobel for *Movieline*, Dec 1991

Sarah MILES [1942-]

Born: Ingatestone, Essex, England; sister to director Christopher Miles. Studies at The Royal Academy of Dramatic Art in London and work with The Worthing Repertory led to her film debut in Term of Trial (1962, Peter Glenville). Following Blow-Up, (1966, Michelangelo Antonioni) she took a four year absence from the screen.

There was this scene in *Blow-Up* where I'm supposed to be making love to somebody in bed and David Hemmings comes in. I asked Antonioni if the man were my husband or my lover and he said, "Does it matter?" Well, if that didn't matter then what did? I got fed up with the whole thing.
—Miles, in a press release for *The Hireling* (Columbia/Warner Brothers, 1973)

Vera MILES [1930-]

Born: Vera Ralston in Boise City, Oklahoma. Studio talent scouts brought her to Hollywood as a result of her third place finish in the Miss America pageant of 1948 (as Miss Kansas). She made her film debut in For Men Only (1952, Paul Henreid). Alfred Hitchcock signed her to a five year contract; she worked for him on two films — The Wrong Man (1957) and Psycho (1960) — a third appearance (as Judy/Madeleine in Vertigo) was thwarted due to a pregnancy:

I found him difficult to work with because he had a preconceived image of me which made it hard for us to communicate.

Q. What was wrong? Did Hitch think you were another Grace Kelly?

A. Along that line. Over the span of years he's had one type of woman in his films — Ingrid Bergman, Grace Kelly, and so on. Before that it was Madeleine Carroll. I'm not their type and never have been. I tried to please him but I couldn't. They are all sexy women but mine is an entirely different approach.

I had a wonderful time working with all those tall, handsome males [in *The Man Who Shot Liberty Valance* (1962, John Ford)]. They are John Ford's ideal types. He wouldn't let me wear anything but Mary Janes because he wanted me to look 4 feet tall. He's terrifying to work with, so bright, fast, and keeps you busy....

He talks in a kind of shorthand. When we started, he explained he wasn't English, was no Hitchcock. "Just old Jack Ford, old Gentle John, and you can be natural with old Gentle John."
—Miles, interviewed by Hedda Hopper for *The Los Angeles Times*, 24 June 1962

Ray MILLAND [1905-1986]

Born: Reginald Truscott-Jones in Neath, Wales. After studies at King's College and The University of Wales, service with His Majesty's Household Cavalry and work in provincial repertory companies, he entered films at the encouragement of Estelle Brody. His debut was in The Informer (1929, Dr. Arthur Robinson). His first Hollywood film was Way for a Sailor (1930, Sam Wood). In 1945, he played Don Birnam in Billy Wilder's The Lost Weekend:

One of the things I had to do in preparation...was lose about eight pounds so that I could have the drawn and haggard look required for the end of the tale, because they intended to shoot the picture backward, do the last half first.

When we first arrived in New York I wanted desperately to spend one night in the psychiatric ward of Bellevue Hospital.... Up until now, what little knowledge I had about drunks I had got from watching my friends. I had never seen anyone with d.t.s.... Without much trouble the evening was arranged. I was taken to the hospital and, after much conspiratorial goings-on, stripped, was given some hospital pajamas and a threadbare terrycloth bathrobe and assigned to a narrow iron bed....

For most of the work in New York the cameras were hidden. Holes were cut in the canvas tops of delivery trucks, or from the inside of a huge piano packing case strategically placed on the sidewalk before dawn or from the inside of a vacant store front. Therefore, nobody paid any attention to the unshaven bum staggering along Third Avenue looking for a pawnshop for his battered typewriter, an instance of protective coloring. To them I was normal....

After a month in New York the company returned to Hollywood. Now the real work started, the cerebral part, the part where the thought processes become vocal, where the camera comes so close that nothing can be hidden and fakery isn't possible. Thank God for Wilder and [screenwriter Charles] Brackett, Wilder with his prying, probing, intuitive touch of genius, and Brackett with his kindly calm and sociological insight. There was also Charles Jackson, the author of the book, like a bright, erratic problem child, telling me of the horrors he had been through that had led to the writing of it, which only served to increase my morbidity.

—Milland, in his *Wide-Eyed in Babylon* (New York: William Morrow & Co., 1974)

Ann MILLER [1923-]

Born: Johnnie Lucille Collier in Houston, Texas. A child dancer, she travelled to Hollywood with her mother in 1934 and signed with Central Casting, making her debut as an extra in The Good Fairy (1935, William Wyler). Three years later, she returned to Hollywood, and lying about her age (adding four years), began her film career with New Faces of 1937 (Leigh Jason). The following year she played Essie Carmichael in Frank Capra's You Can't Take It With You:

When I was testing for the role, I was asked if I had ever done any toe work in ballet. Of course I had taken those ballet lessons as a child, but I had never done toe work. I lied again (by now I was accustomed to lying about my age) and said I had. So they brought me a pair of toe shoes to put on and gave me a wad of white lamb's wool which any ninny knows you're supposed to stick in the hard toe shoes....

But since I'd never handled toe shoes before, when they gave me this wad of stuff, I thought it was something you put in your hair...and I tossed it aside.

I got there and danced on my toes and did what I was supposed to do, all right. I was supposed to be rotten anyway, in the picture, and I was in such pain that it was easy enough to play the role of a lousy ballet dancer. But what it did to my toes! It almost crippled me. All my toenails were pushed up into my feet, and by the time I finished work my feet were a bloody mess....

I was bleeding and in great pain most of the time but naturally I wouldn't tell anyone. I remember how Jimmy Stewart sometimes caught me crying. He didn't know why. He thought I was frightened about doing the role and he always gave me a candy bar to cheer me up. He kept his dressing room well stocked with candy bars because he was so painfully thin.

—Miller, in her *Miller's High Life* (Garden City, N.Y.: Doubleday & Co., 1972)

Patsy Ruth Miller [1904-]

Born: St. Louis. Discovered by Nazimova, she made her film debut in a small part in Camille [1921, Ray C. Smallwood]. In 1923, she played Esmeralda opposite Lon Chaney as Quasimodo in The Hunchback of Notre Dame:

Lon Chaney was extremely kind. Indeed Mr. Chaney directed much of the picture, although Wallace Worsley was the nominal director. I wasn't so aware of it then, but as I look back, I realize poor Mr. Worsley had been put in a very, very unhappy spot because Lon did take over a lot — he really did....

Mr. Chaney was very helpful to me. He was directing me in this big dramatic scene where I was being tortured. I was struggling and carrying on when he took me aside and explained to me that acting was making people feel what you wanted them to feel. It was not necessarily doing what you wanted to do or feeling the way you wanted to feel. It was making the audience feel. So if you wasted yourself in all these dramatics, you might not have any effect on the audience at all. You might think you're being frightfully dramatic and terribly forceful, but it might not be affecting the audience, so control yourself. Acting is not just feeling — it is acting the feeling, so be in control of yourself at all times and make the audiences do the suffering for you....

— Miller, interviewed (1983) by William M. Drew for *Speaking of Silents: First Ladies of the Screen* (Vestal Press, N.Y.: The Vestal Press, 1989)

Sir John MILLS [1908-]

Born: Felixstowe, Suffolk, England; father of Hayley [1946-] and Juliet [1941-]. A London stage debut in 1927 and work in repertory preceded his film debut in The Midshipmaid (1932, Albert De Courville). He made five films with David Lean beginning with Lean's debut, In Which We Serve (co-directed by Noël Coward):

In Which We Serve was one of the best scripts I'd ever had in my hands, and by a strange coincidence Noël, having been responsible for launching me on my career, twelve years later was providing me with a golden opportunity to restart it with a part that he had written especially for me. Able Seaman Shorty Blake was a superbly drawn character....

An entry in my diary of 5 Feb 1941 reads, "First day's work on *In Which We Serve* with Noël Coward. This is the only way to make pictures — efficiency, drive, enthusiasm and a perfect script. Actors also word-perfect." The Master had blown into the studios like a whirlwind bringing with him all his dedication and excitement from the theatre. With a play everyone feels totally involved: he managed to achieve this state of affairs in the studio.

On 5 March 1969, I found myself in front of the camera in southern Ireland about to shoot the first take of *Ryan's Daughter* [1970] with my old friend David Lean once again directing me. I looked right, and felt right, because it had taken me three months of study and work to prepare for that moment. I had watched hours of film showing patients with brain damage to the left side of their heads. From them I'd built up a composite picture — Michael. The walk, the posture, the angle of the head were all as real as I could make them.

I worked on the make-up for two months with a man who was a master of his craft, Charles Parker. Charlie was as thrilled as I was at the challenge. We wanted to get the maximum effect with a minimum amount of actual make-up. We worked by a process of elimination. We started with everything and ended up with practically nothing — a small, upturned tip on the end of my nose, horrific uneven teeth which he made to clamp on to my own, with a slight bulge in the top set to distort my face, and a small piece of plastic behind one ear to push it forward. He then gave me what was undoubtedly the worst haircut that has ever been seen. He shaved the back of my head and allowed long pieces of hair to fall over the bald patches. The whole make-up was so simple I was only in the make-up chair for fifteen minutes every morning, and the result...was staggering. [Mills also worked on Lean's *This Happy Breed* (1944), *Great Expectations* (1946) and *Hobson's Choice* (1954).]

—Mills, in his *Up in the Clouds, Gentlemen Please* (London: Ticknor and Fields, 1981)

Liza MINNELLI [1946-]

Born: Los Angeles; daughter to Judy Garland and Vincente Minnelli. Although she appeared on the screen as Judy Garland's daughter at the end of In the Good Old Summertime (1949, Robert Z. Leonard), it was a Broadway career following studies at The Sorbonne in France and at The Herbert Berghof Studios in N.Y. that preceded her first role as Eliza in Charlie Bubbles (1967, Albert Finney):

It was fun making my first movie in England with Albert Finney. It's not a starring role for me or anything. It's about a girl who doesn't feel anything too deeply or for too long, but very intensely.

—Minnelli, interviewed by Sheilah Graham for *The New York Post*, 16 May 1967

Why should an actor take so much credit when a role — Pookie [in *The Sterile Cuckoo* (1969, Alan J. Pakula)] is so realized to begin with? Not to mention the fact that we had four really intensive weeks of rehearsal before shooting. Alan was very smart. By the time we got up to location, at Hamilton College, he had Wendell Burton and me doing only improvisations. We already knew the scenes; so by then, we could be just riding in a car with Alan, or anywhere, and he would say to us, "Okay, go, improvise," and we would become the characters. We knew them that well.

And there was this point that my character sort of stepped from *here* to *here*. And once that happens, it keeps on happening, at the right times. For instance, when Alan got me together with the four college girls, there at Hamilton, who were going to play the girls in Pookie's dorm, he wanted us to get to know each other, just as ourselves, so each girl started talking about her background. The first girl said, "Well, my mother collects antiques, my father's a minister," and so on. So I thought, what am I gonna say? That I come from a show business family, my mother was really a groovy chick no matter what you read about her, my father is a director? And they're not gonna know what I'm talking about. And at that moment, Pookie moved in. And when I had to talk, I told *her* background, just automatically. Alan said, "Good, that's it." He did lots of things like that, he let us take our time. His feeling is that you are asking an actor to find out about a character what it would take a person, say, five years of analysis to discover, and he doesn't hurry. Now, of course, Otto Preminger — Otto has a different philosophy [on *Tell Me That You Love Me, Junie Moon* (1970)]....

Otto's theory is that an actor is hired to act, and must be ready at all times. He wants the work done immediately, and perfectly. You get the impression with Otto that you don't have time to ask questions, and you come in and don't ask, and if you do it wrong, you get yelled at. It's like teachers. There are some who correct you by saying, "It would be better this way," and others who just say, "That's wrong!" And Otto is, uh, the latter.

—Minnelli, interviewed by Tom Burke for *The New York Times*, 7 Dec 1969

In the beginning Sally [Bowles in *Cabaret* (1972, Bob Fosse)] was hard for me. She is just so wildly self-destructive — that lunge toward death she's taking — it wasn't that I didn't understand her, but there is a whole difference between understanding something and getting it out.

Bob Fosse was a great help. He talks to you like maybe you're *all right*. He makes you feel secure, and he works with you. He doesn't give orders which is important because when you are acting, you are like an open wound almost. Everything is ready to go one way or another and if someone shouts directions at you, it's like pouring lemon on a cut. It all closes if you do that. A director has to sort of gently guide the action, make it go the way he wants it to, and that's what Bob did. I trusted him completely.

—Minnelli, interviewed by Fred Robinson for *Show*, Mar 1972

Bob Fosse wanted the cabaret set to be authentic, and authentic meant smoky. So he built a completely enclosed set, 4 walls, no walls down for the camera to shoot from or anything phony. We almost got acute asphyxiation every time we did a number.

I had to do my own makeup for *Cabaret* — there wasn't much money, so we had to do everything ourselves and it's fantastic. Fosse made us dress for every rehearsal. Nothing slapdash about it, I can tell you. We rehearsed for 3 or 4 weeks before we ever saw a camera. That picture is really authentic. I mean Fosse wouldn't even let the girls shave under their arms, and they just hated it! That's how you can tell I'm the star, because I'm the only one who doesn't have hairy armpits.

—Minnelli, interviewed by George Anthony for *Impact*, Mar 1972

My mother gave me one great acting lesson. I was up for a TV show, Ben Casey or something, and the part was a pregnant girl who had had an abortion that had gone wrong and she's in the hospital. I knew how I wanted to see it, but not how to be it. So I sort of gingerly took the script to Mom, and said, you know "Mama, help me." We sat down on her floor, and she said, "Now, read me your lines, and the doctor's lines, both." His line was, "Did you want to have the baby?" I read it and Mama said, "All right, he's a doctor, he isn't getting personal — but how *dare* he intrude on you, how *dare* he ask you that, how *dare* he be there, how *dare* you be in the hospital, if only you could have married the father, if only he'd loved you, which he *didn't*. Now, *did you want to have the baby*?!!" All I had to say was, "No," but it came out right. Because she had given me thoughts — the pause, not the line. Then she said, "Read me his line again," and I did, and she said, "Now this time you are going to concentrate on *not crying*. That's all you have to worry about, not letting him see you cry. Your baby is dead, your life is ruined, but you're not gonna cry, you're a strong girl, your parents have told you, your teachers have told you, you *know* it, you *know* it, *you're not going to cry*." And my "No" came out even better. She taught me how to — fill in the pauses. And if there's a way I act, that's the way. From that one day there on the floor. And now, if maybe another actor will say, "What are you using in that scene," I'll say, "Well, I'm playing that I'm not gonna cry." They say, "Whaat?" But *I* know!

—Minnelli, interviewed by Tom Burke for *The New York Times*, 7 Dec 1969

Robert MITCHUM [1917-]

Born: Bridgeport, Connecticut. Acting with The Long Beach Civic Theater, an organization for which he also worked as writer and producer, and writing for radio, preceded his film career.

After working as an extra, his first role was Rigney, the heavy in the Hopalong Cassidy film, Hoppy Serves a Writ (1943, George Archainbaud). In 1955, he played Harry Powell in Charles Laughton's Night of the Hunter:

[Laughton] was very fond of me and he didn't want people dragging their children in off the streets so he kind of introduced a sort of fairy-tale atmosphere, a children's book atmosphere in the film just so that people wouldn't think too unkindly of me. That was really contrary to my thought because I thought that the "mother" should be a solid strangler all the way.
—Mitchum, interviewed by Clive James at The National Film Theatre (London), 7 Sept 1972

Robert Wise couldn't find his way out of a field without a choreographer. Bobby even times a kiss with a stopwatch. He marks out the floor at 7 o'clock in the morning, before anybody gets there. Lays it all out with a tape measure. True. It's very difficult to work that way. I worked with him and Shirley MacLaine on *Two for the Seesaw* [1962] and Shirley said, "Why doesn't he go home? He's just in the way." [He had previously worked with Wise on *Blood on the Moon* (1948).]
—Mitchum, interviewed by Roger Ebert for *The New York Times*, 1 Sept 1969

[*Cape Fear* (1961, J. Lee Thompson) is] about the failure of reason in an extreme situation. The [Gregory] Peck character is as guilty of "doing wrong" in the sense of bending the law to suit his ends as my man is. I had to believe that — in fact, I had to believe that my man was *right* in order to be convincing in the part.
—Mitchum, interviewed by Donald Chase for *Horizon*, Jan/Feb 1983

With *Secret Ceremony* [1969, Joseph Losey] they sat around discussing who they could get with the right accent [to play Albert]. Finally Elizabeth [Taylor] suggested me. They didn't want an actor whose accent was so English it would bring Elizabeth's into relief. So Losey called me in Mexico and asked if I could do an English accent. Hell, yes, I could. What do you want? North Country? Lancashire? Cockney? He asked for an indifferent accent, so that's what I gave him. Then I read a review asking what in hell Mitchum was trying to do if he thought that was an English accent. They should write the director's instructions on the edge of the screen....

After my 10 days were finished they took two scenes that I was in and recast them with Elizabeth. You know that bathtub scene? In the script, I was in the bathtub with Mia [Farrow]. The scene where she was rubbing Elizabeth's back. Licking her back. In the script that was *my* back....

Joe Losey has an architectural fetish. Sometimes you think he'd be happy to clear the actors out altogether and just photograph the rooms. He never says a word. Not one word. He walks into a room and engineers and choreographs and then the actors go through it. Then he prints it, and that's that.
—Mitchum, interviewed by Roger Ebert for *The New York Times*, 1 Sept 1969

I was in Ireland shooting *Ryan's Daughter* [1970] for nine months, although I was committed for only six. David Lean has a great visual sense — he spends days waiting for the right conditions. He defies the weather. Once we were shooting inside for four days in the schoolroom, with the sun shining outside — very precious sunlight. When we finally moved back outside, we didn't get a shot for four days. David is very meticulous. You stand there with a 75 mph gale blowing from a wind machine, rain from a hose pelting your face, blowing sand, and David says: "Now look anxious." But you can't do anything....

It's a lot different than the old days. I remember the way Raoul Walsh used to work [on *Pursued* (1947)]. He'd set up a shot, then as the camera started, he'd turn his back and roll a cigarette. Then he'd ask, "Is it over? Anything happen?" "Yes, a lamp fell on the set." "Well," he'd ask "did it look natural? O.K. print it," and he'd rip another page of the script out.
—Mitchum, interviewed by Deac Rossell for *Boston After Dark*, 4 May 1971

Marilyn MONROE [1926-1962]

Born: Norma Jean Baker in Hollywood. A photographer's model, she made her first screen test in 1946 and played her first bit in Dangerous Years (1947, Arthur Pierson). Her first significant role was as Angela Phinlay in The Asphalt Jungle (1950, John Huston):

When I first read for him I was so scared I shook. I'd studied my lines all night but when I came in to read I just couldn't relax. He asked me to sit down but there were only straight-backed chairs all around the room so I asked him if I could sit on the floor — just to get comfortable. But I was still nervous so I asked if I could take off my shoes. "Anything, anything," he said. Then I read for him — and I was sure I was awful — but before I had a chance to say anything he kind of smiled and said I had the part. Then he said I'd probably turn into a very good actress — which is really what I want to be. I want to grow and develop and play serious dramatic parts — my dramatic coach, Natasha Lytess tells everybody that I have great soul — but so far nobody's interested in it. Someday, though, someday.

[On the set of *Gentlemen Prefer Blondes* (1953, Howard Hawks)], Jane [Russell], who is deeply religious, tried to convert me to her religion and I tried to introduce her to Freud. Neither of us won.

—Monroe, interviewed by Barbara Berch Jamison for *The New York Times*, 12 July 1953

[Director] Sir [Laurence] Olivier tried to be friendly [on the set of *The Prince and the Showgirl* (1957)], but he came on like someone slumming. He upset me a lot by telling me to "Look sexy, Marilyn." It sounded condescending to me.... I started being bad with him, being late, and he hated it. But if you don't respect your artists, they can't work well. Respect is what you have to fight for.

—Monroe, in conversation; reported in *Conversations With Marilyn* by W.J. Weatherby (New York: Mason/Charter, 1976)

Nobody would have heard of me if it hadn't been for John Huston. When we started *Asphalt Jungle*...I was very nervous, but John said, "Look at [Louis] Calhern, see how he's shaking. If you're not nervous, you might as well give up." John has meant a great deal in my life....

Working with John ten years later [on *The Misfits* (1961)] is very good. He's helpful in a personal way as well as professionally. He's a different kind of director than the people I've been working with. The thing that's wonderful that he does — he's an artist with a camera — he sees it like a painter. He watches for the reality of a situation and he leaves it alone, and he waits until he needs less or more before he comes in....

As far as I'm concerned, I play a girl — a contemporary young woman who is searching, probably yearning, but she doesn't know it, and she doesn't know what for.

—Monroe, interviewed by James Goode for *The Story of The Misfits* (New York: Bobbs-Merrill, 1963); reprinted as *The Making of The Misfits* (New York: Proscenium Books, 1986)

Robert MONTGOMERY [1904-1981]

Born: Henry Montgomery in Beacon, N.Y. Work on stage, including Broadway, preceded his film debut in College Days (1926, Richard Thorpe). In his fourth film, he played opposite Norma Shearer in Their Own Desire (1929, E. Mason Hopper), the first of four films together:

I was only twenty-five and I was still green in films, and she was the soul of kindness and helpfulness. But she was very strong-minded and wanted her way in certain things. I remember she was always arguing with Bill Daniels about camera setups and she told me privately that she thought the script was terrible and that actors could only manage to be as good as the script and direction allowed. She didn't care for our director, either, considered him a hack, said he didn't understand the new sound medium....

My chief impression of Norma was that she was a very ambitious woman with a definite plan for her career, and she wasn't letting anything or anybody get in the way of it. To give her credit, she did help me to look good; I can't say she wasn't generous to other players, but I felt her attention was always on herself. She didn't seem so much vain as worried. I got the distinct feeling that career success was an obsession with her — certainly she had the industry and discipline to bring *that* off, all right....

There was a new feeling on *The Divorcée* [1930, Robert Z. Leonard]. The project screamed *success* from the word go. Everyone was feeling positive. I knew Norma was happy with her role; they had given her something she could really get her teeth into, and I could sense her elation. [Montgomery and Shearer also worked together on *Strangers May Kiss* (1931, George Fitzmaurice) and *Private Lives* (1931, Sidney Franklin).]

—Montgomery, interviewed by Lawrence J. Quirk; repr. in Quirk's *Norma: The Story of Norma Shearer* (New York: St. Martin's Press, 1988)

[The studio bosses at MGM] insisted that it was a mistake for me to play the part of Danny, a murderer [in *Night Must Fall* (1937, Richard Thorpe)]....

Happily, in this picture, the audiences supported my beliefs. One young newsboy pleased me especially by saying, "I thought *Night Must*

Fall was a swell picture, and that Danny might have been a better guy if he'd gotten better breaks." That last statement pretty well explained why the role became my favorite. It made you understand the forces that had molded Danny's character. Without straining for effect, it showed his bleak childhood, his lack of training, the fact that he had no parents.

This role opened up areas of acting I had never touched before. The story was dramatic, of course, but it was the strange complexity of Danny's character that gave it real depth. He was a schizophrenic, sometimes gay, sometimes angry, often sinister, yet women found him charming. It was necessary for me to play the part so this could be understood, and I was helped greatly by the fine performance of Rosalind Russell, who played Olivia.

One nice touch was Danny's habit of whistling Mighty Lak a Rose when he was concentrating on some new deed of violence. But the line I liked best came after he finally was arrested and handcuffed, "You know," Danny said then, "I want something now I've never wanted before — a long walk all by myself."

—Montgomery, in *The Saturday Evening Post*, 22 May 1948

Colleen MOORE [1902-1988]

Born: Kathleen Morrison in Port Huron, Michigan. She entered the movies when her uncle, Walter Howey, claimed a favor owed him by D.W. Griffith. Under Griffith's sponsorship, she made her debut in Bad Boys (1917, Chester Withey). In 1923, she played Pat in John Francis Dillon's Flaming Youth:

I read Warner Fabian's sensational best-seller, *Flaming Youth*, and when First National bought it, I knew that here was my chance for stardom. Sweet young thing I was not. Pat, the heroine of *Flaming Youth*, I was.

I begged for the role, but the New York office said I wasn't the type. I was a dramatic actress, better in costume parts....

It was my mother who came up with the answer. She said, "Why don't you cut your hair and then make [Earl] Hudson give you a test for the part?"

I was elated.

She picked up the scissors and, whack, off came the long curls. I felt as if I'd been emancipated. Then she trimmed my hair around with bangs like a Japanese girl's haircut — or, as most people call it, a Dutch bob.

It was becoming. More important, it worked.... Five days later I had the part.

We started shooting at once. Never had I been so happy in a movie role before. I loved every scene. After six years of treacle, it was heaven to be given a little spice.

With *Flaming Youth*, a new word entered the American vocabulary — flapper. She was the new American girl, Colleen Moore her prototype.

We didn't laugh — and neither did anybody else — when my first talking picture was released in 1929....

It was surely the longest, slowest, dullest picture ever made.... Bill [Seiter] made some very fine talking pictures later on, but when we made *Smiling Irish Eyes* [1929] he didn't know a thing about the new medium of talk.... We made it the only way we knew how — like a silent film.

In silent pictures the actors anticipated the title by pantomiming it in action. For instance, if the title coming up was, "I'm going to leave you," I would make a broad nod or gesture toward the door and then toward the character the line was intended for. Then I would mouth the line verbatim. After I'd said the first couple of words, the film would be cut and the title inserted. When the picture flashed back on the screen I would be saying the last word, and the action would continue with a little more pantomime about leaving before I actually went out the door.

That was how we did *Smiling Irish Eyes*, the actors pantomiming every sentence, then speaking it, then pantomiming it again. The obvious solution would have been to edit out the repetition. Obvious, but unfortunately, impossible. The sound system we used was the old disc one [Vitaphone]. Since the film was matched to the record, and there was no known way to cut the record, we couldn't cut the film.

—Moore, in her *Silent Star* (Garden City, N.Y.: Doubleday & Co., 1968)

Dickie MOORE [1925-]

Born: Los Angeles. He made his film debut playing John Barrymore as a baby in The Beloved Rogue (1927, Alan Crosland). Throughout the 1930s, he appeared in several feature films as well as many of the Our Gang shorts. In 1936, he appeared in The Story of Louis Pasteur, the first of three films for William Dieterle:

Three times I worked for director William Dieterle. In *The Story of Louis Pasteur*, I played the boy that Paul Muni — Pasteur — cured....

Dieterle wore immaculate white gloves at all times.... He was very German, screamed a lot.... A large exuberant man, he played all the parts for you and wanted you to imitate him.

When Muni finished a scene, he would glance quickly at his wife, who sat behind the camera, and she would nod or shake her head almost imperceptibly. Paul Muni would then tell the director whether or not he wanted to do the scene again. Dieterle never indicated how he felt about this. He gave no sign of noticing. [Moore also appeared in Dieterle's *The Life of Emile Zola* (1937) and *A Dispatch From Reuters* (1940).]

By the time I worked with Shirley [Temple] in *Miss Annie Rooney* [1942, Edwin L. Marin], both of us were teenagers....

Before each of Shirley's scenes, Mrs. Temple positioned herself behind the camera just before the action started, and called softly, "Sparkle, Shirley!" to help focus her daughter's concentration. She had done this since Shirley was a tot.... [Moore gave Temple her first on-screen kiss in this film.]

—Moore, in his *Twinkle, Twinkle, Little Star* (New York: Harper & Row, 1984)

Dudley MOORE [1935-]

Born: Dagenham, Essex, England. Studies in music at the Guildhall School of Music in London and at Oxford University and work as a jazz pianist and as an actor on the London stage preceded his film debut in The Wrong Box (1966, Bryan Forbes). In 1981, he played Arthur Bach in Steve Gordon's Arthur:

I spent a lot of time in Scotland watching people get drunk. I've seen it so many times, the pain of trying to talk distinctly when you can't, of trying to be graceful when your body's collapsing. I think Arthur is nice and kinda lonely. That's why I was attracted to him....

John Gielgud was an easy man to work with. There's basically a glorious relationship between Hobson and Arthur and that made it easier....

In *Arthur* we stuck to the script very tightly; the order of words was very paramount with Steve.

—Moore, interviewed by Carrie Rickey for *The Village Voice*, 15 July 1981

Mary Tyler MOORE [1936-]

Born: Brooklyn, N.Y. Work as a professional dancer preceded her film debut in X-15 (1962, Richard D. Donner). Following success on TV, she returned to the screen in Thoroughly Modern Millie (1967, George Roy Hill). In 1980, she played Beth Jarrett in Robert Redford's Ordinary People:

[Beth's] an enigma, a shadowy, negative force, and you never quite know why she's that way. She's also an achiever, with a real zest for winning. In one scene that was cut from the film, you see Beth playing tennis. She is terribly charming until she puts away a shot at net, and her teeth are bared and you see that animal instinct. And then she is charming again....

She loves [Conrad/Timothy Hutton], she just has an inability to communicate with him. She felt her first son, Buck, was threatened by the existence of her second son. She put all of her hopes in the first son, and saw him as an extension of herself, and then he dies in a boating accident, and Conrad survives....

I asked [my psychiatrist] if it could be true that a woman can't express feelings for a son. He said it was true, and he cited some examples. I just wanted to make sure that what Beth had was a valid reaction.

—Moore, interviewed by Judy Klemesrud for *The New York Times*, 24 Sept 1980

[Redford's] as kind and considerate to the man who sweeps the cigarettes off the floor as he is to the principals. He has a wonderful sense of humor and is dear and *I love him madly*. What he does especially well is shoot a lot of takes — what we've rehearsed — and then come in and say, "Okay, now, throw out everything we've discussed and just do whatever the hell you feel like doing." That's how he gets those wonderful mood changes and unexpected line readings and reactions. There's a very loose atmosphere, filled with mutual respect. He really listens to each one of us.

—Moore, interviewed by Clifford Taylor for *The New York Times*, 27 July 1980

Victor MOORE [1876-1962]

Born: Hammonton, New Jersey. Work in vaudeville preceded his film debut in Snobs (1915, Oscar Apfel). In 1937, he played Barkley Cooper in Leo McCarey's Make Way for Tomorrow:

Make Way for Tomorrow...was frankly and unashamedly a tear jerker. It was about an old couple who lost their home after fifty years of married happiness and found that none of their children had room for both of them; finally Barkley had to go to California and live with a daughter while his wife [Beulah Bondi] entered an old ladies' home in the East. Adolph Zukor, who was on the set most of the time, tried to persuade Director Leo McCarey to make the ending a happier one. But McCarey...insisted that the parents must part to make the story effective....

I felt my role so keenly that sometimes I couldn't prevent tears from coming to my eyes. "Barkley mustn't feel sorry for himself," Leo would say....

—Moore, in *The Saturday Evening Post*, 11 Jan 1947

Agnes MOOREHEAD [1906-1974]

Born: Clinton, Massachusetts. Musical stock with The St. Louis Municipal Opera (from age ten) and studies at The University of Wisconsin, Columbia University and The American Academy of Dramatic Arts preceded her association with Orson Welles, first with The Mercury Theater on radio and Broadway and then in her film debut, Citizen Kane (1941):

Orson believed in good acting, and he realized that rehearsals were needed to get the most from his actors. That was something new in Hollywood: nobody seemed interested in bringing in a group to rehearse before scenes were shot. But Orson knew it was necessary, and we rehearsed every sequence before it was shot.

—Moorehead, in *Action*, May/June 1969

Jeanne MOREAU [1928-]

Born: Paris, France. Studies at The Conservatoire National d'Art Dramatique preceded her four years as a member of Le Comédie Française (1948-1951) and her screen debut in Le Dernier Amour (1948, Jean Stelli). Her first English language film was Five Branded Women (1960, Martin Ritt):

That was a different experience for me. [Ritt] would cover everything — closeups, medium shots, long shots; very few tracking shots. It took ages and ages to make a sequence; and I was used to working with people who did a sequence — and covered four pages — in one movement. So, I learned a new way of shooting.

—Moreau, interviewed by Michael Buckley for *Films in Review* (NY), Dec 1983

Q. How is it to work with Orson Welles?

A. It's an experience, all right. Working with him is invention all the time. In the middle of filming, he might decide he needs to write a new scene. He sets the camera, he gives you the words. He tells you to turn your head or to walk or to sit down, and though it may sound unnatural, a most difficult situation for an actor, there is an incredible magic. You're spellbound, and something unpredictable comes alive. Invention, invention, all the time. And that sureness — the choice, the way he sets the camera. There's no hesitation. [Moreau worked on Welles' *The Trial* (1962), *Chimes at Midnight* (1966) and *The Immortal Story* (1968).]

—Moreau, interviewed for *Dialogue on Film*, *American Film*, July/Aug 1984

Frank MORGAN [1890-1949]

Born: Francis Wupperman in New York City. Work on Broadway (from 1914) preceded his film debut in The Suspect (1916, S. Rankin Drew). In 1940, he played Mr. Matuschek in Ernst Lubitsch's The Shop Around the Corner:

The Viennese merchant in *The Shop Around the Corner* was my first departure from the comedy parts in which I had been typed. Director Ernst Lubitsch wanted me to have the role and he put the project over despite strong opposition from studio executives....

Mr. Matuschek, the merchant, was a delightful combination of faults and virtues — he might have been a shopkeeper in any town, and the familiarity and plausibility of the character made portraying him an unusually pleasant task. Another endearing aspect of the work was that we followed the natural continuity of the scenes from beginning to end, rather than what some of us call the "cart-before-the-horse and vegetables-in-the-middle" sequence of most movie-making. And the scenery was very simple, just one or two sets, not those elaborate setting which often obscure both the story and the actors.

To give the final perfect touch, I found it was a treat to work with Margaret Sullavan and Jimmy Stewart, neither of whom I had met before. One always gets a lift from working with a truly fine actress like Miss Sullavan. Jimmy turned out to be just what you think he is — natural, easygoing, never indulging in flights of temperament. Everything about *The Little Shop* came out right, including its reception by the public and after that Metro didn't argue against my playing dramatic roles.

—Morgan, in *The Saturday Evening Post*, 30 Nov 1946

Chester MORRIS [1901-1970]

Born: John Chester Morris in New York City, to actor parents. He made his film debut in An Amateur Orphan (1917, Van Dyke Brooke). In 1930, he played Morgan in George Hill's The Big House:

I guess all actors like roles that let them wear a beard or have their heads shaved. My head was shaved for the role of Morgan in *The Big House*. This was just one phase of the special attention paid to realism in filming this story of a man who committed a robbery, then atoned for his mistake by serving his prison sentence and deciding to go straight thereafter....

On the first day of shooting, our director, the late George Hill, lined the cast up in a cell block, strode up and down like Patton reviewing troops and thundered, "The first person that acts gets canned!" It made us feel important as he kept shooting our natural actions, ordering, "Play those lines the way you feel them." If someone overacted, he had the scene done over, scoffing, "You played that like an actor in New York!"

—Morris, in *The Saturday Evening Post*, 19 Jan 1946

Paul MUNI [1895-1967]

Born: Muni Weisenfreund in Lemberg, Austria (now Lwow, Poland) to actor parents who emigrated to the U.S. via London in 1902. Work in burlesque, Yiddish stock and on Broadway preceded his film debut as Dyke in The Valiant (1929, William K. Howard):

We had completed one reel and a half of it, when William Fox arrived in town. The next day, I was notified that the picture had been halted. I learned later that Fox looked at the rushes and tore out his hair: "Who hired that actor?" he demanded. "He has no sex appeal; the girls won't accept him as a lover." Not that I blamed him. I was rugged, rather than handsome, the movies were in the half zone between silent pictures and talking pictures, and leading men had to be Adonises. I didn't qualify.

—Muni, interviewed by Ed Sullivan for *The New York Herald Tribune*, 9 Apr 1937

When we made [*I am a Fugitive from a*] *Chain Gang* [1932, Mervyn LeRoy], ex-convicts worked hand in chain with us. Not Hollywood actors simulating convicts but men who had been chained to gangs themselves. The men who played the parts of some of the guards had been guards in real life. I *became* a prisoner working, suffering, sweating.

When I played *Scarface* [1932, Howard Hawks] there were gangsters working right along with us. We became a part of the gangster mind, not from second hand information, not from books or highly colored newspaper accounts, but from the men who had come up from the underworld to meet and mingle with the world of Hollywood....

There were miners from the Pennsylvania coal fields in [*Black Fury* (1935, Michael Curtiz)]. I came to know them well. I absorbed their methods of working, the conditions under which they work. I became intimate with their problems....

—Muni, in *Movie Classic*, Nov 1936

In *Bordertown* [1935, Archie Mayo] I think I succeeded in portraying a real human being and getting right into the very soul of that particular character. That's why I liked it. It wasn't perhaps, in the theatrical sense, the most effective work I ever did, but it was nearer to truth than anything else I ever did.

—Muni, interviewed by W.H. Mooring for *Film Weekly*, 25 Sept 1937

In [*The Story of Louis*] *Pasteur* [1936, William Dieterle] there were bacteriologists from other countries conferring with us, working with us. These were men who were carrying on the work Pasteur had begun. Men who spoke his language, who were familiar with his methods, who worked with his precision, were infused with his passion. I knew these men. I worked with them. I read the books Pasteur had read. I was able to follow, a little way at least, the road Pasteur had pioneered. I handled the same kind of implements Pasteur had handled. I was enabled, thus, to enter into the body, the life and spirit and hopes and dreams of Pasteur.

—Muni, in *Movie Classic*, Nov 1936

Q. I'd like to come back to the historical characters. You were saying that you do a lot of reading about them.

A. Yes. The most interesting part to me is the research. I enjoy that because I find out things that otherwise I would not have known.

Q. Could you give us a sort of count-down on how you did the research for one particular role?

A. I couldn't give you a count-down in order of the way it was, but.... For instance, when I was working on *The Story of Louis Pasteur*, I read most everything that was in the library — in the studio, where they have their own library — and most everything I could lay my hands on that had to do with Pasteur, with Lister, with his contemporaries.... I immediately brought up or had someone lend me books, and I would for months on end continue to read.... I read everything. I mean, characters that had nothing — I mean, a fellow like Ehrlich, who had no connection with Pasteur, actually any contact with him, but he also dealt in the same field. I read up everything I could on Ehrlich and others like that....

Q. Do you study photographs, too?

A. I study photographs, but not so much.

Q. What does all this do for you?

A. I don't know. I don't pretend to — I don't want to know.... It's one of those things. You become saturated with some kind of psychological images, if you can use that term at all. It's one of those things that you do not — you do not methodically work out. It's one of those things that you throw yourself into, a kind of, if you can call it that, miasmic thing that is just a conglomerate business, and you just pick out whatever instinctively seems to fit into the pattern of what you — what you're looking for.

Q. Did you ever go to the Pasteur Institute, for instance, outside of Paris?

A. I went there....

Mrs. Muni: Before he did *Bordertown*, in which he also played a Mexican, all of a sudden, out of a clear sky, Muni came home with a Mexican flower boy that he had found down in Los Angeles. And he brought him home and he put him to work in the garden.

Muni: He became a gardener and I worked with him.

Mrs. Muni: And then he spoke to him and got his rhythm.

Muni: I got his — the feeling of his character, of his accent and his general moods.... In other words, what I'm trying to get over is that there wasn't any specific method. There wasn't any arithmetic arrangement there. It was a catch-as-catch-can business....

Mrs. Muni: During *The Good Earth* [1937, Sidney Franklin] he brought home a Chinese fellow from San Francisco.

Muni: Yes, yes. I had a Chinese person with me for quite a long time. I talked to him; I listened to him.

—Muni, interviewed by Lewis Funke and John E. Booth for *Actors Talk About Acting* (New York: Random House, 1961)

[O-lan and Wang in *The Good Earth* (1937, Sidney Franklin)] worked with such animal-like martyrdom, wresting their difficult sustenance from the soil, suffering the loss of wheat crops by rain, suffering, through drought, the loss of all their merciless, menial labour.

We have, all, I think, entered into the arduous spirit of our roles. The studio, the director, the cast, everyone has laboured mightily. This location set; these growing fields of wheat, these garden patches — all were sown and planted and tended especially, and only, for this picture.

—Muni, in an unsourced, undated article in the files of The New York Public Library for the Performing Arts

When First National assigned me to the role [of Emile Zola in *The Life of Emile Zola* (1937, William Dieterle)] I began collecting all the material bearing on Zola's life and times that I could lay hands on. I read the man's own books; I read personal reminiscences of him by friends and fellow authors; I read half a dozen biographies.

When I felt sure of my background, I began to study the physical appearance of the man. I looked over innumerable portraits, some of them life-size, some mere sketches. Out of them I got a good mental picture of what Zola looked like and then I began several weeks of experiments with makeup until I approached that appearance as closely as it was possible.

For the voice part, I used a dictaphone arrangement. I would read the lines several ways, then play them back so I could judge what was the most effective way of delivering them. And I practiced walking with a stoop as Zola himself did. I found it exhausting often, because I had to hold it....

—Muni, interviewed for the press book for *The Life of Emile Zola* (Warner Brothers, 1937)

Do you realize how the lives of these two men [Louis Pasteur and Emile Zola] paralleled each other? Both were French, each lived in the same period, knew many of the same people, neither was appreciated until after his death. They even looked alike. I had to be sure that my makeup as Zola was different enough from that of Pasteur so as not to confuse the theatre-going public.

Q. Well, you certainly succeeded in making them two different individuals.

A. It was largely a matter of makeup. We broadened the face, created a higher hairline and added to my own beard. We usually spent three and a half hours getting the right effect which even included adding skin to the face.

—Muni, interviewed by Louella O. Parsons for *The New York Evening Journal*, 11 July 1937

I found *Zola* tremendously easy to do — one of the easiest I've ever done, in fact — despite the changes in make-up, long speeches and everything else. It was the only picture I ever finished — that and *Pasteur* — not completely worn out. And the reason is — I liked it. It was close to me.

You see, when an actor has to work into a role which he doesn't feel or understand, he must work just that much harder giving it decoration and elaboration. But with *Zola* and *Pasteur*, I was portraying characters I almost knew. A message? Yes, there is undoubtedly a great message in the stories of these two men. But when I was doing them I had no consciousness of delivering a sermon. I simply felt a strong sympathy with my characters.

—Muni, interviewed by Bosley Crowther for *The New York Times*, 24 Oct 1937

When I did a film — which was not a successful film, it was an unfortunate affair — on the life of Juarez [*Juarez* (1939, William Dieterle)], I went to Mexico, traveled around various cities there, wherever Juarez was known to have had any influence of one sort or another, where other characters were in some way or another connected with Juarez. And I made every possible exploration and investigation that I could at the time, as the time allowed.

—Muni, interviewed by Lewis Funke and John E. Booth for *Actors Talk About Acting* (New York: Random House, 1961)

Before we left for Mexico [for filming of *Juarez*] I had already devoted some eight months to the study of [emancipator, Benito] Juarez.... Here was a man much like Lincoln, who rose by the brilliant powers of his own mind to save the nation that had given him birth. It was this man we sought to know.

—Muni, in *Film Guide* Vol III, #9, 1939

To me, this story [*The Last Angry Man* (1959, Daniel Mann)] has the stability and morality of an old, bygone day — about a nonconforming man who went his own way. In a way, this is a means of getting something off my chest.

—Muni, interviewed by Howard Thompson for *The New York Times*, 23 Nov 1958

Don MURRAY [1929-]

Born: Hollywood; raised East Rockaway, N.Y. Studies at The American Academy of Dramatic Arts in N.Y. and work on Broadway (from 1948) preceded his film debut opposite Marilyn Monroe in Joshua Logan's Bus Stop (1956):

Buddy Adler was the head of [Twentieth Century-Fox] when I got there. It's funny because some of the studio vice presidents — as the rushes came in on *Bus Stop* — they didn't like what I was doing. They thought it was too big for the movies. They called it an outlandish performance.... Well, it was an outlandish performance — rightfully outlandish, I think. *Bus Stop* is just bordering on farce comedy and it has to be played very big and very fully. If it isn't, I think it would be very dull and so there were arguments. Logan...stood by the way I was playing it and Buddy Adler agreed, but he had a lot of arguments with the other executives at the studio.

Q. There was a lot of print coverage of the difficulties you were having with Marilyn.... I've read that of all her leading men she was supposedly meanest to you.... In one book it is said she never wanted you for the part and it was also reported that she humiliated you on the set.

A. The first part is untrue and the second — well, that was accurate but that only happened one day. It wasn't so much humiliation as...I'll tell you what happened. It was a scene in the night club. I was supposed to grab her and I ended up grabbing a piece of the dress....

Q. ....and she is supposed to turn on me and say, "You ain't got the brains, you big monkey" and she is supposed to bawl me out and say, "Give me back my tail" and run out. This was the first film she made after studying at the Actors Studio and she was using her own emotions for the first time honestly in films. So she got very emotionally worked up for that scene.

Q. And so the outburst was a result of that?

A. Well, it was a result of several things. She was emotionally worked up and what happened is that as she yelled at me, she charged into me, hitting me, which was fine because she was just hitting me on the chest.... But what she was doing was knocking us out of the lights and the camera view so Logan came up and he finally said, "Well, look, I'm afraid to talk to her because I don't want to destroy what she has going emotionally. Now even though she is not doing what is in the script, I like it. I want to get whatever is there so you just hold your ground. Don't let her push you backwards." Well, anyway so I braced myself and she came running up and she bounced off my chest and fell flat on her back. I immediately thought she might be hurt. I broke character, picked her up and started talking to her like my own self with my own Eastern accent, without the western drawl, and Arthur O'Connell did the same thing. Then she got up and was a little dazed at first. When she came around she kept on going with the scene. Logan always gave orders whenever Marilyn acted: "Never cut unless I say cut because you have to take whatever you can of Marilyn and put it together in little pieces...."

So they kept rolling while all this was going on... She ran up to Logan and said, "Is that all right? Can we use that...?" So he turned to the cameraman and said "Is it usable?" The cameraman said, "It's all right for us...." So Logan said, "Okay, print it." Now I said "Wait a minute. It might be all right for you. It might be all right for Marilyn, but it's not all right for me and I'm sure it's not all right with Arthur." I broke character because I was concerned about her as a person. I said "you can't use any of that because it's totally unfair to me. I was not in character," and so she turned around and said "Oh, my God, can't you AD LIB?"

—Murray, interviewed by Guy Trebay for *Interview*, Oct 1973

N

Nita NALDI [1899-1961]

Born: Donna Dooley in New York City. Work as a model and chorus girl preceded her film debut in Dr. Jekyll and Mr. Hyde (1920, John S. Robertson) on the recommendation of the film's star, John Barrymore. She played opposite Rudolph Valentino in both Blood and Sand (1922, Fred Niblo) and Cobra (1925, Joseph Henabery):

[Valentino] isn't a wild animal. He's a sweet, adorable charming boy — not the least spoiled or conceited; at least he wasn't when I played with him in *Blood and Sand.* In his love scenes he's great because he's perfectly natural. He doesn't have any of those pap formulas for love-making that a lot of our steam-heated lovers have. He walks on the set and acts as a human being would act in the situation. When he embraces me I don't feel as though I were going to swoon or anything like that...but I do feel that he is behaving efficiently and that he isn't going to pop out his eyes at me or do any of the strange things that most screen lovers do. I've seen them where they looked as though they were strangling — that passionate, you know. After all, love is nothing to catch fire and burn up about.

—Naldi, in *Photoplay Magazine*, June 1924

Patricia NEAL [1926-]

Born: Packard, Kentucky. Acting studies as a child and later at Northwestern University, work on Broadway and further studies with George Shdanoff and at The Actors Studio preceded her film debut in John Loves Mary (1949, David Butler). In 1963, she played Alma in Martin Ritt's Hud:

I had known Marty [Ritt] from the early days at The Studio. "I'd like to send you a script," he said. "I hope you won't think the part is too small." The thought of working in a film again fired my engines, and if Marty was involved, I was sure there was something good up his sleeve. The script was titled "Hud Bannon...."

Marty was right, it wasn't a large part, but it was the only woman in the picture, which was a plus. And although Alma was a brief role, it was strong. She was an earthy, shopworn gal who had been handled badly by life, which had made her wise and tough but not invulnerable.

Alma had no real highs, no dramatic monologues, and she played mostly in the background to the other characters. But I knew her in my bones. I had thought the days when I would be offered a part like Alma were over....

Paul [Newman] and I worked together beautifully. On the set he was an ace, thoroughly professional and completely in character at all times....

Halfway through *Hud* is an important scene between Paul and me. Alma is straining curds through cheesecloth at the sideboard when Hud comes up behind her and begins to fondle her shoulder and kiss her neck. Just as Paul moved in, a huge, furry green horsefly began to crawl up the porch screen. I couldn't take my eyes off it. "I've done time with one cold-blooded bastard," Alma says. Instinctively I grabbed a dishtowel. "I'm not looking for another." And zap! That bug went flying.

"Cut! Print!" called Marty. "Perfect. The fly was great!"

—Neal, in her (with Richard DeNeut) *As I Am* (New York: Simon & Schuster, 1988)

My best bit, and the thing I loved most about Alma, hit the cutting-room floor. It was a scene where the young boy [Brandon De Wilde] comes out to her cabin and asks Alma what life is all about anyway. "Honey, she tells him, you'll just have to ask someone else."

—Neal, interviewed by Howard Thompson for *The New York Times*, 26 Jan 1964

I loved the character of Nettie [in *The Subject Was Roses* (1968, Ulu Grosbard)]. I understood her frustration with her husband [Jack Albertson] and her maternal struggle for her child [Martin Sheen]. She was a woman with calluses on her ego. I knew I could play her. I knew it would be a good thing to do. I just did not have any confidence that I would be up to it [after suffering a series of strokes]....

I liked my co-stars...but I couldn't thaw out that [first] day [of rehearsals]. My stroke had put me in another rhythm for the past three years, and my clumsy body was out of the acting habit. Jack and Martin were repeating their stage roles and were letter-perfect in their lines....

But by the time we got into the actual filming, something else was at play. There was such appreciation from Jack and Martin, I began to realize I was doing it for them, too. And for Ulu, a director of great considerateness who made me feel that everything I did came from the soul of Nettie Cleary, and all we had to do was select the treasures....

—Neal, in her (with Richard DeNeut) *As I Am* (New York: Simon & Schuster, 1988)

Q. On the screen you are often aloof, or seem remote.... I guess I'm trying to say that you give a very independent effect, more so than most players.

A. Perhaps I give that impression because I am rather like that myself. I always feel I can take care of myself. And I have an adventurous streak.

—Neal, interviewed by Hedda Hopper for *The Chicago Sunday Tribune*, 10 June 1951

Paul NEWMAN [1925-]

Born: Cleveland, Ohio. Undergraduate studies in economics and drama at Kenyon College and graduate studies in directing at Yale University, work in repertory, TV, and on Broadway (from 1953) preceded his film debut in The Silver Chalice (1955, Victor Saville).

I had fun with that comparison thing between Brando and me. When I first went out to Hollywood and everybody was referring to me as the "road-company Brando" and things like that, I found it was kind of interesting, 'cause that's what I consider lazy journalism.... [Journalists] didn't have the vaguest idea of what Marlon's focus is, which is eruptability. Eruptability is always in the potential of the masses-type hero. And the quality that I carry is Ivy League — Shaker Heights and like that.

—Newman, interviewed by Grover Lewis for *Rolling Stone*, 5 July 1973

Before I did *Somebody Up There Likes Me* [1956], I almost *lived* with Rocky Graziano for two weeks. I'd meet him at ten o'clock in the morning and I wouldn't get home until four o'clock the next morning. We went down to his old neighborhood, went up to Stillman's gymnasium. But I could see he didn't want to talk about his family. So one night at the Embers, Bob Wise, the director, and I tried to get Rocky stoned so that he'd loosen up and talk about himself. The fact is that Rocky loosened *us* up. We told him *our* life stories. He poured us into two taxicabs. It was a funny evening. Anyway, I never did really absorb the character; though I certainly sponged a lot, I wound up being *a* Graziano rather than *the* Graziano.

—Newman, interviewed by Richard Warren Lewis and Roy Newquist for *Playboy*, July 1968

Gore Vidal wrote a screenplay I did, *The Left-Handed Gun* [1958, Arthur Penn], where his concept was Billy the Kid as gay. In the '50s, we couldn't do that, and so my friend Gore's concept went by the wayside.... Actually, if I ever did a character who might have been inherently gay — but of course wasn't allowed to be on screen — then it was Brick in [Tennessee Williams's] *Cat on a Hot Tin Roof* [1958, Richard Brooks] and also Chance Wayne in [Williams's] *Sweet Bird of Youth* [1962, Richard Brooks]. In my opinion, those two men were gay no matter how you slice or edit it.

—Newman, interviewed by Boze Hadleigh for *The New York Native*, 30 Apr 1990

In working with Elizabeth Taylor [on *Cat on a Hot Tin Roof*], I was astonished to find that she was a real pro. She's not afraid to take chances in front of people. Usually, stars become very protective of themselves and very self-indulgent, but she's got a lot of guts. She'd go ahead and explore and risk falling on her face.

—Newman, interviewed by Lillian and Helen Ross for *The Player* (New York: Simon & Schuster, 1962)

A plus about making pictures is that you learn something new on every one, whether it's a good one or a stinker. If nothing else, you meet new people. I didn't want to do *Exodus* [1960, Otto Preminger], for example. I thought it was too cold and expository, and actually I tried to get out of it. But I did get to know Preminger.

He's got the reputation of being such a fascist asshole, when he is on the set. I mean, he can pick out the most vulnerable person and then walk all over him, you know. He could walk down a line of 200 people at a fast pace and pick somebody out and make lunch out of him. Off the set, though, I found him articulate, informed, funny, absolutely lovable....

Good scripts are damn scarce. I recall I wanted to do *The Hustler* [1961] with Bob Rossen from the word go. That picture was something special for Rossen, who was already terminally ill, because he was familiar with the world of pool and that whole hustler era, and he just pulled himself together to do the film, and he was incredible. I blame the blacklist in part for Rossen's death. I think the second he succumbed to that, he hurt his pride to a fatal extent.

There was one scene in *The Hustler*, though, that I always had a big quarrel with — the scene on the hillside where Eddie tells the girl [Piper Laurie] what it's like to play pool, right? Well, the way it was originally written, I thought it was a nothing scene — it just wasn't there, it had no sense of specialness. So I told Rossen he ought to somehow liken what Eddie does to what anybody who's performing something sensational is doing — a ball player, say, or some guy who laid 477 bricks in one day.

Well, we were shooting on 55th Street in New York, and Bob listened to what I said, and we walked into his office, and it couldn't have been 6 minutes later that he came out with the 4-page scene that was in the film. He was that type of artist. He did the whole goddam thing.

—Newman, interviewed by Grover Lewis for *Rolling Stone*, 5 July 1973

For God's sake, *Sweet Bird* [*of Youth*] is a morality play. I understand this guy. I don't like him but I understand him. What Tennessee [Williams] was trying to say was if you want to know this guy, understand whatever there is of you in him. You have to trace the corruption. It started early with Chance. He was raised believing you had to be IT, that finishing second was no good. You had to be first. And so Chance had to sell his strong point which happened to be his beauty and his sexuality. That seed of corruption is in all of us — to sell and capitalize on whatever we have that people want to buy. Look, this guy isn't just a big swordsman. He did a lot of "mercy" work. He was just selling what they were buying and in the end, when he stays and takes his beating, he's paying off. He's expiating his sins. He's saying to you...all of you..."look at me and recognize whatever there is of me in you."

—Newman, interviewed by Al Morgan for *Show Business Illustrated*, Feb 1962

Newman: To me, *Hud* [1963, Martin Ritt] made the simple statement that people sometimes grow up at tragic expense to other people. It was a wide study of a particular dilemma of our time. I tried to give Hud all the superficial external graces, including the right swing of the body. I took out as many wrinkles as possible. I indicated that he boozed very well, was great with the broads, had a lot of guts, was extraordinarily competent at his job, but had a single tragic flaw: He didn't give a goddamn what happened to anyone else. That tragic flaw simply went over everybody's head — especially the reviewers' — and he became a kind of antihero, especially among teenagers. One review I'll never forget: It said that *Hud* was quite a marvelous picture. "The only problem" the reviewer wrote, "is that Paul Newman is playing the part, because basically, he has a face that doesn't look lived in." But Jesus Christ, that's exactly what made the bastard dangerous. The whole point of the character is that he has a face that doesn't look lived in. [Newman also worked on Ritt's *The Long Hot Summer* (1958) and *Hombre* (1967).]

Playboy: How do you feel about the kind of campaign [Bobby] Kennedy's been conducting?

Newman: I don't think it accomplishes anything to run a campaign based on innuendo and cutting people up and getting your shots in. I also think he might have entered the race a little more gracefully; and there is something a little too theatrical about Bobby's oratorical technique — even about his presence. But I suppose I should be grateful for that. Did you know I stole the character of *Harper* [1966, Jack Smight] from Bobby Kennedy? The way Bobby listens, at least the one time I've been with him, is very peculiar; there's an odd quality about it. He seems almost inattentive. If you didn't watch him very closely, you'd think he wasn't listening. It's not that there isn't contact; he's really honed in and sharp. But it's not just listening. It's mulling and evaluating; while you're talking you can see him preparing his rebuttal. It kind of puts you off until you get used to it. I thought that was a nice bit of business for a private detective.

I'm great at writing voluminous notes to myself on the back of a script. It all breaks down to the way the character walks or uses his hands, his motions and his movements. I think that once you get the physical quality of a character, the inner person comes by itself. In *The Secret War of Harry Frigg* [1968, Jack Smight], for example, I got the guy's walk down because a fellow in my squadron during the War used to walk a special way, and all of a sudden it occurred to me that Private Frigg should walk that way. You see, the actor's got to come to the part; the part doesn't come to the actor.

—Newman, interviewed by Richard Warren Lewis and Roy Newquist for *Playboy*, July 1968

Q. You are known for preparing very carefully for roles — for *The Sting* [1973, George Roy Hill] you watched William Powell play the Thin Man.

A. Well, I watched about fifteen of his movies.

Q. To observe how a con man plays a con man?

A. No, what I did with that, particularly, was just watch the movies, with no idea of creating that character or anything anywhere near it.... I think there are certain things that happen by osmosis, and that's what I depended on, for that part at any rate....

George [Roy Hill] and I have quite a marvelous relationship. He is, I think, an extraordinarily gifted man, he really has a concept of what a movie should be like. He has a great musical sense. He is loyal, affectionate, gifted....

When I took over the direction of *Sometimes a Great Notion* [1971, in which he also starred], and was really in bad shape because I did it involuntarily, he was the first guy to call up and say, "How are you?" I said, "I'm terrible." He said, "I'll be up." He got in his airplane and flew up to Portland and said, "What do you want me to do." I said, "I've got fifteen thousand feet of silent footage and I don't even have time to look at it." So he sat in the cutting room up there for three days, put the sequence together, and I said, "What do I need?" He said, "You need twenty setups, you need a point of view of the kid, you need his walking shot away, and so forth." And then he got in his airplane and left. [Newman also worked on Hill's *Butch Cassidy and the Sundance Kid* (1969) and *Slap Shot* (1977).]

The Drowning Pool [1975, Stuart Rosenberg] is really a continuation of the Harper character. I simply adore that character because it will accommodate any kind of actor's invention. He can do the most outrageous things. He can put people on, he's got a great sense of humor, so I can horse around. It's just lovely to get up in the morning, it's great to go to work, because you know you're going to have a lot of fun that day.

Q. Is that character close to you personally?

A. I think it is because he's funny, but my wife says he isn't.

—Newman, interviewed by Leonard Probst for *Off-Camera* (New York: Stein & Day, 1975)

Robert Altman is less restrictive than any other director I've ever worked with. He demands and depends a great deal on the actor outside of the confinements and construction of the script.

He is very much a community man. Artistically he's a community man. He's not a tyrant and he's not an egoist. His gift comes from being able to let somebody else father something without putting his imprint on it. It's a great gift to be able to use power and talent gracefully and he has that. The thing about Altman is that he deals in concepts, not linear story lines, although [*Buffalo Bill and the Indians* (1976)] is one of the most linear stories he's told. He's also one of the best casting agents I know. He casts to character rather than worrying about the commercial aspects of a performer. [Newman also worked on Altman's *Quintet* (1979).]

—Newman, interviewed by Philip Anderson for *Showbill*, June/July 1976

Q. When you decided to do *Absence of Malice* [1981, Sydney Pollack], did you think of it as a "statement" film, as one that summarized your feelings about the press?

A. The film, as far as I was concerned, had a very narrow focus. It was simply a frontal attack on *The New York Post*. It's tragic when a newspaper with *The Post*'s heritage is turned into a garbage can. For instance, an incident occurred during the shooting of *Fort Apache* [*: The Bronx* (1981, Daniel Petrie)] as I came out of a camper. There were some photographers there, and a lady production assistant who was with me simply explained, "Come on, guys, we're late." Three days later, there's a picture in *The Post* captioned,

"Paul Newman looks on in horror as production assistant tries to ward off protesters."

There were also other times when they fabricated incidents that simply didn't take place. The idea, I suppose, was that if they could create a riot where there wasn't any, they'd sell a lot of newspapers. So, when I started *Absence of Malice*, I still had that taste in my mouth.

—Newman, interviewed by Andrew Horton for *Cineaste*, Vol 12 #1, 1982

[*The Verdict* (1982, Sidney Lumet) is] a story about the redemption of a human being. It's not an attack on the legal system or the Catholic Church or hospitals. These institutions are a springboard for the development of his character. They're metaphors for what seem to be insurmountable obstacles all around him.

There are a million ways Galvin can lose the case. But whether he wins it or loses it isn't the point. His victory is that he fights it through all the way to the end. This emotional progression from a down-and-out alcoholic to a whole person again is tied in with his ability to find the strength to keep fighting. And he's battling more than just institutions: he's scratching and clawing to save his life.

It's a very interesting character for me because he's unlike Cool Hand Luke or Butch Cassidy or some of the others who were the cool, collected types. He's frightened. He's living on the edge and he's panicked. There are people who really do find their lives in a shambles and they decide they don't like it. Some just continue to degenerate and some, like Galvin, can pick themselves up.

Every person is vulnerable in certain ways, at certain times in their lives. This guy, Frank, is not exactly a pillar of strength. But he's a believable, fallible, human being....

—Newman, interviewed for the press release for *The Verdict* (20th Century-Fox, 1982)

[Frank Galvin] becomes unglued not because he's bad — he's no worse than most people — but because he can't help himself and he can't be helped by those who see what's happening to him. It's such a relief to play something like this, instead of those strong, stalwart guys. This guy is ordinary; he's no better than he should be.

—Newman, interviewed by Don Shewey for *American Film*, Dec 1982

When Marty Scorsese and I were planning *The Color of Money* [1986], we went through lists of actors, but we never seriously considered anyone else [besides Tom Cruise]. Why? I'd only seen *Risky Business* [1983], but you wouldn't have to see a lot more to know that Tom is a bold, ingenious actor with a lot of actor's courage. He's willing to try *anything*....

Scorsese and I were maniacal. We were always rehearsing, working on the script, looking for a way to do it. More than he'd been able to in his earlier films, Cruise was getting his feet wet in the communal effort. I don't think he showed his hand so much. He watched a lot, which is smart....

—Newman, interviewed by Jesse Kornbluth for *Vanity Fair*, Jan 1989

[Tom and I] worked well together. In some ways it was the most compatible experience I've ever had on a movie. The whole film was a wonderful, collaborative experience. I insisted on two weeks rehearsal beforehand, which is something Cruise had never experienced, and it worked....

It's a very personal film for me. A film about the rekindling of passion, about the competition between youth and old age. Of course, it's not really a sequel to *The Hustler*, which was made 25 years ago. It's an extension of the character of Eddie examined from a different angle....

There are sequences in the movie that any actor would kill to play. The dialogue is so sharp and original. It's like, in another way, a film I did called *Slap Shot*, which offended many people. Actually I think [*Slap Shot*] is probably my most original work, thanks to the screenplay. But for many people it was too blasphemous.

—Newman, interviewed by Brian Baxter for *Films & Filming*, Mar 1987

[Mr. Bridge in *Mr. and Mrs. Bridge* (1990, James Ivory) is] a very shy person. We have that in common, I guess. He's very purposeful. He cares about his work. He has very old-fashioned ideas about how to behave. And I think he's quite a noble guy.

—Newman, interviewed by Graham Fuller for *Interview*, Nov 1990

I like [Walter Bridge] very much. The fact is, he was a man of basic honor, given what he knew in his time. He performed his function as he saw it: He raised a family. He reached out as best he could, given his basic shyness.

—Newman, interviewed by Maureen Dowd for *McCall's*, Jan 1991

Q. Are you bored with the charismatic superstar status?

A. No...I'm not bored by it. You can't be bored by it. You can be plenty embarrassed by it, though, because what they're applauding has nothing to do with me. They're applauding Harper, Hombre, Hud — all of those celluloid manifestations of what I'm supposed to be like. But those characters were created by writers. They were interpreted by me as an actor, but they were created by writers, and they have nothing to do with me. That's why it's embarrassing, because people don't seem to be willing to separate the allure of the character and the actor who plays him.

—Newman, interviewed by Grover Lewis for *Rolling Stone*, 5 July 1973

Jack NICHOLSON [1937-]

Born: Neptune, New Jersey. Acting studies with Jeff Corey in Los Angeles and stage work with The Players Ring Theater preceded his film debut in The Cry Baby Killer (1957, Jus Addiss). In 1960, he played Wilbur Force in Roger Corman's Little Shop of Horrors:

That was the low-budget production of all time. A two day shooting schedule. I was in a sequence which was 13 pages long; six and one half pages before I came in and six and one half afterwards. Another actor played a dentist and I played the guy who comes into the dentist's office. Before I get there, the dentist is killed. A friend of mine was playing the dentist, an actor named John Shaner, and we went down together to pick up our scripts. When we got in there Roger took one script and he gave John the first six pages and he took the seventh page and ripped it in half and gave him the top half and gave me the bottom half and the next six pages. That was it. That's all we knew about it. I didn't know what the picture was or anything like that....

My whole sequence was shot in an hour and ten minutes: seven pages. The actors went in and Roger figured out where he was going to set the camera and where he was going to put the lights. We rehearsed it for two or three hours, but Roger never much directs the actors. He'll tell you if you're doing something too cute or too much. I did *The Raven* [1963] with [Peter] Lorre and [Boris] Karloff and [Vincent] Price and I wanted to be as funny as they were. It was too many funny people in one movie. The kind of direction you get is: "You can't be as funny as they are." That's the interpretation of the role from Roger.

—Nicholson, interviewed for *Dialogue on Film* #1, 1972

Playboy: Is it true, as one interviewer reported, that you smoked 155 joints during *Easy Rider*'s campfire scene [1969]?

Nicholson: That's a little exaggerated. But each time I did a take or an angle, it involved smoking almost an entire joint. We were smoking regular dope, pretty good Mexican grass from the state of Michoacan. Now, the main portion of this sequence is the transition from not being stoned to being stoned. So that after the first take or two, the acting job becomes reversed. Instead of being straight and having to act stoned at the end, I'm now stoned at the beginning and have to act straight and then gradually let myself return to where I was — which was very stoned. It was an unusual reverse acting problem. And [director and co-star] Dennis [Hopper] was hysterical off-camera most of the time this was happening. In fact, some of the things that you see in the film — like my looking away and trying to keep myself from breaking up — were caused by my looking at Dennis off-camera over in the bushes, totally freaked out of his bird, laughing his head off while I'm in there trying to do my Lyndon Johnson and keep everything together.

Playboy: We've heard you were equally into the part for the scene in *Five Easy Pieces* [1970, Bob Rafelson] in which you're confronted with a sullen waitress [Lorna Thayer].

Nicholson: Yeah, the one where the waitress says, "No substitutions," and I end up having to ask for a chicken-salad sandwich on wheat toast — hold the butter, lettuce, mayonnaise and chicken salad — just to get an order of wheat toast. Finally, boom, I sweep the table clear of glasses, silverware and dishes. Actually, something like that scene had occurred in my own life. Years ago, when I was maybe 20, I cleared a table that way at Pupi's, a coffee shop on the Sunset Strip. Carole Eastman, the screenwriter of *Five Easy Pieces*, and an old friend of mine, knew about that incident. And Bob Rafelson, the director, and I had gone through something like the bit with a "no substitution" waitress, although that time I hadn't dumped the dishes. So, knowing me, Carole and Bob just put the two incidents together and into the script.

I moved Jonathan [in *Carnal Knowledge* (1971)] a great deal toward me. Mike Nichols and I agreed that this guy must not become a lascivious character, because that's not really what's being said. Jonathan is the most sensitive character in the picture. He's the one who doesn't recover from the original sexual triangle. He's never able to really trust girls after that. He winds up in a very ritualistic but honest sexual relationship with a professional [Rita Moreno], which is the best thing — not the worst — he can do for himself. He's a person with sexual problems who's never been fortunate enough to make a genuine contact, probably largely through his own doing. He's in a position where he truly doesn't want to go on rifling women's cunts. By paying for it, he gets it off with no muss, no fuss. Nobody's pissed off. Nobody's concerned that he's fucking them over.... He hasn't solved his problem positively, but he's given himself the best negative answer that he can come up with.

—Nicholson, interviewed by Richard Warren Lewis for *Playboy*, Apr 1972

Q. Is the character you play in *The King of Marvin Gardens* [1972, Bob Rafelson] the antithesis of your previous roles?

A. This character is sort of what I call a one-roomer. He's Kafkaesque. He lives alone. He's a radio monologist. He's an intellectual, and he's been institutionalized. He has a brother [Bruce Dern] who's very colorful; he is not. He's involved strongly in the absurdities of life. He's not really in with society; he's like a bystander. He's very laid back. Most of his thinking and verbosity relate to his work and not to his life. He's a watching character in life.

—Nicholson, interviewed by Robert David Crane and Christopher Fryer for *Jack Nicholson: Face to Face* (New York: M. Evans & Co., 1975)

[On *The Passenger* (1975), Michelangelo] Antonioni's basic approach to his actors is "Don't act, just say the lines and make the movements." He doesn't make dramatic constructions, he makes configurations. And the simpler you can be, the clearer will be the configuration. If you mess the interior up, and so break up the interior part of your character, you will in fact be working at cross-purposes with him, because he is looking for clarity in that area, so that the configuration can be seen. If you break that up, you are working against the style in which he is working.

—Nicholson, interviewed by John Russell Taylor for *Sight & Sound*, Summer 1974

Antonioni doesn't want you to overintellectualize the role to pieces. That doesn't mean that he looks down on you. It does possibly imply that he exploits you within the framework of your own possibilities.

He approaches each scene as if it were a reality that he wants to capture; each scene is a document he wants to give an account of. No preconceived opinions!

Polanski [on *Chinatown* (1974)] is different. He too is in charge, but in a different way: he listens to arguments, comes up with counter-arguments — but he doesn't yield. He is always on the go; he discusses things and waxes enthusiastic. Everybody's intellectual capacity is increased in Roman's presence. He pushes us further than we are conscious of being able to go; he forces us down into the subconscious — in order to see if there's something better there.

—Nicholson, interviewed by Lars-Olof Lothwall for *Chaplin*, #8, 1974; trans. by Barry Jacobs for *Actors on Acting for the Screen* (New York: Garland Publishing Inc., 1992)

The secret to [*One Flew Over the*] *Cuckoo's Nest* [1975, Milos Forman] — and it's not in the book — my secret design for it was that this guy's a scamp who knows he's irresistible to women and in reality he expects Nurse Ratched [Louise Fletcher] to be seduced by him. This is his tragic flaw. This is why he ultimately fails.... That's what I felt was actually happening with that character — it was a long, unsuccessful seduction which the guy was so pathologically sure of.

—Nicholson, interviewed by Ron Rosenbaum for *The New York Times Magazine*, 13 July 1986

What I liked about [Jack Torrance in *The Shining* (1980, Stanley Kubrick)] was that he was so nuts that even before he was doing anything, he liked scaring people.... I liked that quality in him. Grand Guignol was that story's classification for me. [For] a lot of scenes in the rehearsal period we'd do other horror scenes from other movies just to get on to or into the dialogue.

—Nicholson, interviewed by Lewis Archibald for *The Aquarian Weekly*, 30 Nov 1983

I played *The Postman Always Rings Twice* [1981, Bob Rafelson], let's say, in a much less romantically attractive way than it had ever been done before. I mean, this *is* a murder. That's why in the first scene, I steal cigarettes from the guy who's giving me a free meal, without even thinking about it.

Rafelson kept trying, which everybody does, to slim me down for that part. But I found it interesting to break the cliché of the gaunt, Depression-deprived man of the road. Because if this guy gets hungry for five minutes, he'll just steal your food. He might be a bum, but he didn't miss no meals. He wolfed his meals down, and next thing, give me your wife.

—Nicholson, interviewed by Fred Schruers for *Rolling Stone*, 14 Aug 1986

The fact of the matter is [Frank Chambers in *Postman* is] a sadist who solved every problem he ever had in his life with violence. And in the earlier film [directed by Tay Garnett in 1946] he was kind of a severely worried man when John Garfield played him because in those days the style was likability, likability, likability. No matter what the character was.

But my keys are different from that. I don't particularly want a guy who murders a man and then fucks his wife on top of her husband's body to be all *that* charming.

—Nicholson, interviewed by Lewis Archibald for *The Aquarian Weekly*, 30 Nov 1983

One of the things that motivated me with [Garrett Breedlove in *Terms of Endearment* (1983, James L. Brooks)] is that everyone was starting to make a total cliché out of middle age. Everybody was supposed to have a middle-age crisis. They were dissatisfied, they hated their job. I just went against the grain of the cliché. I just wanted to say, "Wait a minute, I happen to be this age and I'm not in any midlife crisis. I'm not an object of scorn and pity by anybody 10 years younger than me. There's got to be other people like me, so I'd like to represent that in this movie."

—Nicholson, interviewed by Ron Rosenbaum for *The New York Times Magazine*, 13 July 1986

John [Huston] camera cuts. If you only do one take you don't really know what you did. You don't get to refine it. You come home and think of the 35 things you might've thrown in the stew. When a director shoots several takes, you eventually find his rhythm and try to come up to the boil together. But with John Huston everybody's got to be ready to go right away. But there were never any problems [on *Prizzi's Honor* (1985)]. Everyone had such respect for him that no one wanted to be the fly-in-the-ointment, so to speak.... I did more one-takes on this picture than anything since my Roger Corman days...!

Q. What kind of dialogue did you have with Huston about your character, Charley Partana?

A. I was down in Puerto Vallarta for a week but about all we did was watch the boxing matches on the Olympics twelve hours a day. The business talk was very brief. After I found out it was a comedy, I went back to my room and read it over a few more times, and then came back and this is what he said to me: "It seems, Jack that everything you've done until now has been intelligent. We can't have any of that in this film. And I've got an idea, I hesitate to say what it is, but something to let people know immediately that *Prizzi's Honor* is...different...from anything else you've done. I hesitate to say it, but I think you should wear a wig."

Now I've got comedy...and dumb...and a wig to deal with. I went to bed.

Q. What kind of wig did he have in mind?

A. A bad one. I've never worn a wig except in *Carnal Knowledge* for the teenage stuff, but I've always thought of it as an aging device rather than the reverse. If you do it just a little wrong, it makes you look older. So, while I was ready to wear this wig John had in mind, I was definitely searching for something else to make the same point.

Some friends of mine who grew up in Brooklyn took John and me out and about in the "environment" there, and one day I came up with this little device...[curls his lip as he does throughout the film]...which helped me talk funny, too. One small thing like that can give you the spine of a character....

The opaqueness of *Prizzi's Honor* took me by surprise. But I used it. I put my not understanding the material together with the character's dumbness into a kind of dynamic on how to play him. I let the character's limitations keep me happy.

For example, I did not want to know what period the film was set in and I didn't try for the same kind of dialogue with John that I do with other directors. When you bring him an idea, he doesn't say he don't like it. He just goes [big tooth-gnashing grimace]...and that's all he has to do. You never bring up the idea again. You drift off like smoke.

So I said to myself, "Okay, I've got one of the most commanding people I've ever known with his hand on the helm; the producer's an old friend of mine; I'll just do my own simple job like a dummy and that's it."

—Nicholson, interviewed by Beverly Walker for *Film Comment*, June 1985

Q. In *Heartburn* [1986, Mike Nichols], your portrayal of "the Carl Bernstein character" seems fully rounded. But if I ask how much of the real-life Bernstein is in there, I suppose you'll tell me not much.

A. I'm gonna tell you — *nothing*. I was specifically hired *not* to play him. Mike and [screenwriter] Nora [Ephron] and Meryl [Streep] were very anxious to move the film into fiction. And since I had no desire on a couple of days' notice to do a biographical portrait, that suited me just fine.

Q. Still, you must have had to cram a lot of preparation into less than a week.

A. I was working three days after I read the script...never read the book until partway into the shooting. This is my third film with Mike [also *The Fortune* (1971)], and I'd always wanted to work with Meryl, and that made me want to do it — maybe a part I might not have done under other conditions. They kind of held their hands under my chin while I treaded water. [Nicholson worked with Streep again on *Ironweed* (1987, Hector Babenco).]

—Nicholson, interviewed by Fred Schruers for *Rolling Stone*, 14 Aug 1986

The degree of difficulty varies from role to role rather than with the type of role. The main difficulty in playing the devil [in *The Witches of Eastwick* (1987, George Miller)] or The Joker [in *Batman* (1989, Tim Burton)] is that those roles are more physically demanding. They require movement, action, big sets and space....

A conventional approach to character can lead to a sameness in the work. I played The Joker short-wired. I'd do anything that came into my mind....

—Nicholson, interviewed by Aljean Harmetz for *The New York Times*, 18 June 1989

What I like about the Joker is that he has no taste in his humor.

—Nicholson, interviewed by Jack Kroll for *Newsweek*, 23 Jan 1989

David NIVEN [1910-1983]

Born: James David Niven in Kirriemuir, Scotland. After walk-on parts in 27 westerns and numerous other bit parts, he landed his first major role in Splendour (1935, Elliott Nugent). The following year, he played Captain Lockert in William Wyler's Dodsworth:

[Sam] Goldwyn decided that I was ripe to appear in one of his own super-pictures and cast me as Captain Lockert in *Dodsworth* with Walter Huston and Ruth Chatterton. Walter had created the role on Broadway and had now moved to California. His son, John, then a scriptwriter, also worked on the picture. He and his father were wonderful to me; so was Ruth Chatterton. William Wyler, the director, was not.

Willie Wyler, as his record all too plainly shows, is one of the world's all-time great directors...but in 1936 he was a Jekyll-and-Hyde character.

Kind, fun and cozy at all other times, he became a fiend the moment his bottom touched down in his director's chair.

Some directors, especially those touched by the Max Reinhardt school, believed in breaking actors down completely so that they became putty in their hands. As practiced by Willie, he even managed to reduce the experienced Ruth Chatterton to such a state that she slapped his face and locked herself in her dressing room.

I became a gibbering wreck.

Whenever I was working, it was perfectly normal for Willie to sit beneath his camera reading *The Hollywood Reporter* and not even look up till I had plowed through the scene a couple of dozen times. "Just do it again," he'd say, turning a page.

—Niven, in his *The Moon's a Balloon* (New York: G.P. Putnam's Sons, 1972)

The problem of my imperturbability is something my agents, managers, directors and fellow actors might like to avoid. My reputation for being imperturbable under pressure goes back twenty years or more, when Warner Bros. was casting *Charge of the Light Brigade* [1936], a picture starring a newly discovered swashbuckler named Errol Flynn. By coincidence, this new star was also my roommate, and he suggested that I try out for the important supporting role of the young captain. There were a dozen candidates for the job and Michael Curtiz, the great director, glossy in a silk scarf and smooth riding boots, was running the tryouts. After listening to the first seven pros skillfully try the scene, each reading the same lines, I knew I'd never make it.

I was No. 8, and as I stepped up before the camera Curtiz asked, "Where's your script?"

"I know my part," I said, hoping I did.

"Where's your script?" he repeated impatiently.

"I left it in the make-up tent," I said.

"Run and get it!" he snapped. "And I do mean run."

My wool costume was hot and sticky, and the sun that morning would have tanned a Ubangi chief.... I boiled over, "You can damn well run and get it yourself!" I said.

The cameraman froze, the assistant director paled and groped for support, and Mike Curtiz looked as though he'd been hit by a Kansas twister. I was dead, dead, dead, when suddenly he began to laugh.

"Dismiss the others," he roared, "and give him the part!"

Imperturbable? Ah, yes, indeed. The picture was big box office, incidentally — no thanks to me — but Mike and I have been good friends ever since.

—Niven, as told to Dean Jennings for *The Saturday Evening Post*, 26 July 1958

Lubitsch once said to me: "You can't play comedy unless a circus is going on inside you," and I suppose I try to remember that. [Lubitsch directed Niven in *Bluebeard's Eighth Wife* (1938).]

—Niven, interviewed by Michael Maslansky for *The Newark Sunday News*, 28 June 1970

My big scene [in *Wuthering Heights* (1939)] came toward the end of the story — when Cathy lies dead on her bed and Edgar, her husband, stands over her and, according to the script, "breaks down and sobs." Merle Oberon was lying on the bed, waxen-faced and looking very gone, when director William Wyler called for silence.

"All right, David," he said, "Start crying."

I screwed up my face, blinked my eyes and concentrated on sad things — the bills I couldn't pay, the beautiful girl who dumped me for Errol Flynn, the leaky radiator in my car, and so on. But it was no use.

"Willie," I said, "I can't cry. I've never been able to cry. Not even when I was a little boy."

Wyler stalked out from behind the camera, and his eyes panned around the room, as though he were the D.A. asking the jury to send some poor slob to the electric chair.

"Ladies and gentlemen," he said tartly, "here is an actor who says he can't act. Well, when there are actors who can't act, we just have to help out a little."

First, they tried the sad-music-and-sliced-onion routine. Nothing. Then Wyler sent for what I call the "duct hunters" — makeup men who stand by with a sort of spray gun and shoot at your face with an irritating menthol mist.... It only made me cough, and my sensitive nose dripped steadily on the corpse....

Half an hour later, I was still dry-eyed, but Wyler solved the crisis. He turned me away from the corpse and the camera focused on my back while I groaned, heaved my shoulders and rocked back and forth.... When *Wuthering Heights* was released, the critics were almost unanimous in predicting a fine future for me, with some saying: "Niven was superb...Most touching deathbed scene in years...Niven pulls at heartstrings." And so on....

—Niven, as told to Dean Jennings for *The Saturday Evening Post*, 19 July 1958

[Sam] Goldwyn talked me into having my hair bleached white for the last scene [of *The Bishop's Wife* (1947, Henry Koster)] instead of wearing a wig. He examined the result of several trips to a women's beauty parlor, ignored the fact that my own dog had attacked me on sight the night before, and said, "It looks good. Now we have to slow down your movements as the old man."

So saying, he ordained that sixty pounds of lead should be distributed in the soles of my shoes and about my clothing. When he called me again to his office to inspect the result of his brainstorm, I arrived like a heavily handicapped race-horse.

An argument developed over the physical fatigue that I stoutly held would prostrate me during the long, hot hours of shooting. During this altercation I sprang from my chair to make my point and strode briskly about his office, but Goldwyn was right: My spring had become a rheumaticky rise, and my stride a stately totter.

—Niven, in his *Bring on the Empty Horses* (New York: G.P. Putnam's Sons, 1975)

[Cantinflas and I] had great times together on *Around the World* [*in 80 Days* (1956, Michael Anderson)], but he has the age-old instinct of the comic to top everything.... I didn't mind, except for one scene in which we were on the boat, tearing up everything and tossing it into the boiler. I had the idea to toss in my top hat and umbrella when there was no fuel left. I took off my hat, threw it into the furnace — and something fluttered past my face — it was Cantinflas' tie! I said: "This is my idea — and to hell with your tie!" It was the only time we had heated words — and all in French! He said, "But I'm your servant and want to help — my tie is important!" Well, we did it over without the tie.

—Niven, interviewed by Hedda Hopper for *The New York Daily News*, 19 Jan 1959

I hope you didn't think I was imitating [Eric] Portman [in *Separate Tables* (1958, Delbert Mann).]

Q. Had you seen him in it?

A. Yes, but at the London opening three years before. I saw the play again when it came to Hollywood, but left purposely to avoid watching Portman's part. I didn't want to be influenced.

Q. It was remarkably close. Not just the role. It was sort of uncanny.

A. There's an explanation, I think.... The character was written that way — it was [Terence] Rattigan's most clearly written play — and if you know those British officer characters the way I do, and the way Portman does, you have to follow the same path. For instance, suppose two American actors were asked to portray a St. Paul's-Princeton advertising executive character. If they knew that type, they'd come up with something pretty similar without conferring with each other, wouldn't they? The British officer type is unmistakable.

Q. It seemed to me that it was a little more than that. You had always been so uniquely your self, no matter what the role. This time I was startled to see those little Portman gestures.

A. You have to know these officers. They're exactly the same. You know I had 12 years of looking at them, 18 months at Sandhurst, four years in the Army, then six and a half years in the war.... I've [also] played that same British officer before — [in *Enchantment* (1948, Irving Reis)]. I'm smarting under your accusation.

Mind you, I take direction. Delbert may have told me to do certain things, and these may be the same things he had told Portman to do in the play. The way the character averts his eyes.

Q. Yes. Portman did do that noticeably in the play....

—Niven, interviewed by Archer Winsten for *The New York Post*, 19 Jan 1959

The Guns of Navarone [1961] was a long and physically very arduous picture culminating with five weeks in England in November simulating a storm at sea by working nine freezing hours a day in a huge tank full of filthy water.

After nine months, Gregory Peck and I were left alone with two weeks of exhausting night work still to do, shooting from dusk to dawn, filming the actual finale of the picture — the blowing up of the guns. As my character had been built up as "a genius with explosives...the only man who can do it," it will readily be appreciated that without my presence during those crucial last two weeks, the colossal $7,000,000 epic could never be finished. With only three days to go, I picked up a fearsome infection via a split lip and at two o'clock one morning was carted away with what in the grim times before antibiotics was known as general septicemia. I lay dangerously ill for days while the experts from Guys Hospital struggled to identify, isolate and eliminate the bug that had struck me down.

The picture ground to a halt amidst general consternation. The big brass of the company arrived posthaste from America. They called a meeting with Carl Foreman, the producer, Lee Thompson, the director, the head of the finance department, representatives of the banks and insurance companies and various assistants.

One of those present reported the scene to me later.

Foreman read out the latest ominous bulletin from the sides. After a suitable pause, the biggest brass spoke. "We gotta problem here, fellers...so David is very, very sick...That's tough on him...and we all love him...but wadda *we* do if the son of a bitch dies?"

"The son of a bitch," pumped full of drugs, went back to work against the doctor's orders far sooner than was prudent, completed the crucial three days' work, and suffered a relapse that lasted seven weeks.

The big brass never even sent me a grape.

—Niven, in his *The Moon's a Balloon* (New York: G.P. Putnam's Sons, 1972)

Nick NOLTE [1940-]

Born: Omaha, Nebraska. An aspiring football player, he then began to study acting with Stella Adler disciple Bryan O'Byrne and acting in repertory, stock, and dinner theater. Work on TV preceded his film debut in Return to Macon County (1975, Richard Compton). In 1978, he played Ray in Karel Reisz's Who'll Stop the Rain?:

Robert Stone, who wrote *Dog Soldiers*, the novel that *Who'll Stop the Rain?* was based on, knew [Neal] Cassady. In fact, that scene at the end of the movie of me walking down the railroad tracks was kind of inspired by Cassady. Bob and I talked about Cassady a lot, and when I began asking about him, it seemed that everybody in Topanga Canyon had a story to tell about him.

I tried to find out what created the mythology of this man [Cassady, who he then played in *Heart Beat* (1980, John Byrum)]. I came to the conclusion that he was kind of a magician. That he could seem different at different times.

—Nolte, interviewed by Tom Buckley for *The New York Times*, 3 Aug 1979

Elliott [in *North Dallas Forty* (1978, Ted Kotcheff)] is a man caught in his bubble-gum card days. He operates from childhood desire. It's not the money and it's not the glory — he's hooked on football because it's the only thing he knows how to do, and he does it well. He doesn't realize that kind of thing is transferable to other things.

—Nolte, interviewed by Geraldine Fabrikant for *The New York Times*, 2 Aug 1979

With [reading Dostoyevsky's] *The Gambler* and hanging out with the painter [Chuck Connelly, whose paintings are used in the film — *New York Stories* (1989, section directed by Martin Scorsese)], I understood both the obsession our painter has and the artistry. This character has his art down to the point that he needs a relationship, a younger woman, to get his painting started.

—Nolte, interviewed by Alan Mirabella for *The New York Daily News*, 26 Feb 1989

Q. How long do you research a role?

A. About two or three months. For *Cape Fear* [1991, Martin Scorsese], where I was playing a lawyer, I first went to a small country lawyer in West Virginia and ran the situation in the movie by him. Then I went down to Atlanta and sat in on a lot of plea bargains and deals. I followed cases all the way through with the prosecution.

Q. It all sounds so calculating, especially for an actor who often plays characters who seem on the verge of losing control.

A. That's the point. You want to get it up there on the screen so it seems spontaneous and natural. Sticking a camera on somebody is not a normal, natural situation. We all know, we've had snapshots taken of us. So you have to figure out how to make it look spontaneous. If you're going appear out of control, you've got to know why. What is the dilemma that creates this? It takes time to discover how a character moves. Some characters are extremely still. How do you get to that stillness? You can't get in front of a camera and pretend you're still....

Q. Was it apparent after working with Martin Scorsese on *Cape Fear* why many consider him the great American director of the day?

A. He makes films from the inside out. Martin has to tell a story as honestly as he knows it. The original *Cape Fear* sanitized the whole question of good and evil. It didn't entertain any possibility there was an interrelatedness between good and evil. Martin knows full well it's a great, gray world.

Q. Did you ever feel that as an actor you were subordinate to Scorsese's preoccupation with working out his themes?

A. No. But the thing with Marty is he has a complicated vision of the film, so you have to understand how he sets up shots, the technicalities of the shots. You have to get on his track and get on his train and go along....

Q. Scorsese and your co-star, Robert De Niro go back twenty years. Did you ever feel like you were a fifth wheel?

A. Just the opposite. Bobby and Marty go out of their way not to allow their friendship to become a thing that makes anyone else feel excluded. Bobby is one of the politest actors around. He's very conscious of other people's feelings....

Barbra Streisand was the first female director you've worked with [on *Prince of Tides* (1991)]. Did it make a difference?

A. I'd wanted to work with a female director for maybe five years. I knew you'd get a different kind of insight. With a male director, there's always an agreement about how far a conversation about emotions can go. It's analytical. You lay out the emotions a character would feel and the two men sit there and say, "Yeah, that's it. Fine." With a female, it's never "it."

Q. Why what happens?

A. You get into a lengthy discussion of feelings. One thing about Barbra, there is not going to be a leaf unturned. We spent many days before we shot discussing masculinity, femininity, women, men, relationships, love, mothers, fathers, That's the process I wanted to get into. I wanted to follow it through and see what the female aspect of it was because that's what Tom Wingo's problem is. He's trying to figure out the women in his life.

—Nolte, interviewed by Trip Gabriel for *Us*, Jan 1992

Kim NOVAK [1933-]

Born: Marilyn Novak in Chicago. Studies at Wright Junior College in Chicago and work as a model in both Chicago and Hollywood preceded her film debut in The French Line (1954, Lloyd Bacon). In 1957, she played the title role in George Sidney's Jeanne Eagles:

On *Jeanne Eagles*, I had more notes — filed and cross-filed — than I could hold. The notes folder was bigger than the script! I learned my lines early, so that each morning I could pore over my notes to get the feeling for the scene ahead, not just the words of the dialogue. Jeanne's favorite songs were "Elegy" and "The Prisoner's Song." Every morning on the set, we'd play a Caruso recording of "Elegy." I learned to sing it in English. Before the death scene, I read and re-read a poem written about Jeanne, tender and sad. "God made thee with broken wings...."

—Novak, interviewed by Hildegarde Johnson for *Photoplay Magazine*, June 1957

Q. Did you like working with Hitchcock [on *Vertigo* (1958)]?

A. It was totally different working with him because he was not somebody that talked to you about the script. You couldn't say, "Tell me a little more about the character." He didn't want to communicate on that level. He did his communication through the camera and his direction. Tempo, he wanted everything a certain rhythm.

Q. Tempo?

A. Oh yes, tempo was his thing. During the rehearsal of one scene, he used a metronome. He wanted my pace to increase. He said, "I want you to get it done and hear that metronome going in your head," and I said, "God!" I could barely get out all those lines.

—Novak, interviewed by John Calendo for *Interview*, Mar 1981

Ramon NOVARRO [1899-1968]

Born: Ramon Samaniegos in Durango, Mexico. Work in Los Angeles as a singing waiter and vaudeville performer preceded his film debut as an extra in 1917. By 1922, he was cast as a "Latin lover," a character he abandoned in the wake of Valentino's success. In 1932, he played Lt. Alexis Rosanoff opposite Greta Garbo in the title role of George Fitzmaurice's Mata Hari:

The instant she begins a scene, her whole being seems to change. At once she was Mata Hari and not Greta Garbo. It is a great pleasure to work with so magnificent an artist. You find yourself living the role, not merely acting it. The energy she expends in her work is amazing. She is not satisfied with only pleasing the director.

Often after a scene is okayed, she will plead for a chance to make it again, believing her performance inadequate.

When we began work together I discovered Miss Garbo did not care to rehearse. It was her habit to walk into her scenes and go right through with them.

She knows the story, the dialogue by heart before production begins.

But it is difficult for me to work that way. I need rehearsals to make myself certain I understand exactly how a scene should be played. I like to rehearse with the lights, camera, microphones, just as it will be when it is actually filmed. When Miss Garbo realized my method of working differed from her own, she graciously offered to rehearse.

Often, while the new camera angles were being lined up on the set we would sit in her little portable dressing-room and go over the lines together. Other times she would prefer to walk outside and run through the dialogue as we strolled the streets between the stages.

During our conferences with Mr. Fitzmaurice on the set, Miss Garbo never was arbitrary in making demands. Her ideas are sound and studied. She has a comprehensive knowledge of picture technique and nothing is too much trouble for her if it means anything to the picture. If a point tended to bring a discussion to the borderline of disagreement, she always managed to smooth it over with a joke....

Her emotional intensity is genuine. Her role acts as a complete metamorphosis. It is an inspiration to work with her.... It was the happiest experience of my entire career.

—Novarro, interviewed by Ralph Wheelright for *Photoplay Magazine*, Feb 1932

O

Jack OAKIE [1903-1978]

Born: Lewis Offield in Sedalia, Missouri. Work on stage (beginning in the chorus of a George M. Cohan musical in 1922) preceded his film debut in Finders Keepers (1928, Wesley Ruggles). In 1940, he played Napaloni opposite Charlie Chaplin in The Great Dictator:

Chaplin offered me the part of Mussolini in his first talkie, *The Great Dictator*.

"Why not get an Italian actor to play Mussolini?" I asked him. "Why me with my Irish face?"

"What's funny about an Italian playing an Italian?" Chaplin said.

He had me there....

Playing Mussolini — Napaloni in the picture — was easy. Chaplin played Hitler — Hynkel — and I figured they were both disappointed ham actors, so I played Napaloni with his chin sticking out. Napaloni was always trying to steal the show from Hynkel and Hynkel was always trying to steal it back.

—Oakie, in *The Saturday Evening Post*, 6 Nov 1948

Merle OBERON [1911-1979]

Born: Estelle Merle O'Brien Thompson in Tasmania; moved to India at age 7, later to England. Work as a dancer using the name Queenie O'Brien preceded her film debut in Alf's Button (1930, Will P. Kellino). In 1936, she played opposite Miriam Hopkins in William Wyler's These Three:

Q. There's been so much said about poor Miriam, about her temperament and everything else. You had to work closely with her in *These Three*; did you have any problem with her?

A. Yes, you couldn't not, and I never had problems with anyone. Poor Miriam, I think she did these things automatically. But that's where I got an education — I learned how to play to a gobo. Because at the beginning, when she would be standing beside the camera to give me my lines — instead of giving me my lines, she would be looking at me critically, you know, then giving lines. So I said to Willie, quietly, "Let Miss Hopkins rest and I will do my scenes to the gobo."

—Oberon, interviewed (1973) by Al Kilgore and Roi Frumkes for *Films in Review* (NY), Feb 1982

During the early days of the shooting of *Wuthering Heights* [1939, William Wyler], Larry [Olivier] had unnecessarily acquired athlete's foot. We were shooting the film in sequence, and had filmed three days with Larry as the stable boy in our initial scenes. Sam Goldwyn strode on to our set on this particular day, and called cast and crew around him. Larry was on crutches because of the athlete's foot, and it took him somewhat longer to gather around than most. As Larry put it, he made a splendid picture of "the show must go on" — the brave actor coming to work despite discomfort and crutches.

The attention he expected was at least a pat on the shoulder for his courage. Instead Sam, with a face puce with fury, and pointing an accusing finger at Larry, cried out in a voice that undoubtedly carried to Sunset Boulevard, "Thees ector es the ogliest ector in pictures, thees ector will ruin me."

Larry's mimicry of Sam's voice and manner were hilarious. What had caused this panic in the hierarchy was Larry's makeup, and appearance in general. He had insisted on looking like an authentic and very grubby stable boy. Coming from the Old Vic, where he had an enormous success, he didn't agree that he should tone down his makeup and performance for the magnifying screen. He was finally convinced by seeing the rushes of the first few days. It is really interesting to look back and realize we were witnessing a great actor adapting his art from stage to screen, even though we all suffered a bit from the growing pains. [Oberon had previously played opposite Olivier in *The Divorce of Lady X* (1938, Tim Whelan).]

—Oberon, contribution to *Olivier*, ed. by Logan Gourlay (London: Weidenfeld & Nicolson, 1973)

[*That Uncertain Feeling* (1941)] was probably the happiest picture I ever made, because Lubitsch was such a funny man. Such a darling man. He played the piano between every take and there would be laughs. Then I'd always ask him to do the scene for me before I did it only to have a laugh. I remember when Alex [Korda] came from England and he saw the picture, I said, "Alex, how is it, and how am I?" and he said, "Oh, fine. You played it beautifully, like a little Jewish girl." Apparently Ernst had been doing the mannerisms, you know, and then I did them.

—Oberon, interviewed (1973) by Al Kilgore and Roi Frumkes for *Films in Review* (NY), Feb 1982

Edmond O'BRIEN [1915-1985]

Born: New York City. Studies at Fordham University and at The Neighborhood Playhouse, and work with Orson Welles' Mercury Theater preceded his film debut in The Hunchback of Notre Dame (1939, William Dieterle). In 1954, he played Oscar Muldoon in Joseph L. Mankiewicz's The Barefoot Contessa:

As soon as I read the script of *The Barefoot Contessa*, I began to admire Oscar Muldoon. Not that Oscar was a person you'd fall in love with at first sight, or even second or third sight. He wasn't; he had some very unpleasant characteristics.

But this part held a great deal of humor and — this above all — it seemed very real to me. I'd far rather play a believable heel than an unrealistic hero.

Certainly Oscar was human enough, and in making the most of his bad points I borrowed heavily from other humans I knew. Oscar was a very nervous person; when he wasn't perspiring, he was anticipating a worried sweat. So, when I talked as Oscar, I held a handkerchief in my hand, ready to wipe my brow. From another very human person, I borrowed the habit Oscar had of talking with his hands. From a third I took his sickly sweet smile.

—O'Brien, in *The Saturday Evening Post*, 11 June 1955

George O'BRIEN [1900-1985]

Born: San Francisco. Work as a camera assistant, extra, and stuntman preceded his film debut in White Hands (1922, Lambert Hillyer). In 1927, he played the husband in F.W. Murnau's Sunrise:

Murnau...decided he wanted me after he saw *The Man Who Came Back* [1924, Emmett Flynn]....

[Murnau] had, as they said then, far-out ideas on camera techniques.... I would sit for hours while [Murnau and his cinematographers Charles Rosher and Karl Struss] were lining up a shot.... In order to help me with my mood, Murnau would explain each situation....

Q. You worked with a legendary character, Michael Curtiz, on *Noah's Ark* [1929].

A. Yes, indeed. Some said he was a madman, but I don't think so. But I lost both my big toenails in the flood scene; he had me tied up. Then, when I was to be blinded with a hot poker, he said, "George, I want to come very close, my boy. I want the audience to scream." And I'll tell you, I could feel the heat of that thing. I screamed bloody murder. Dolores Costello, who was in the picture, was out of it for two months; she caught pneumonia from all the water.

—O'Brien, interviewed by Leonard Maltin for *Film Fan Monthly*, May 1971

Pat O'BRIEN [1899-1983]

Born: William Joseph Patrick O'Brien in Milwaukee. Studies at Sargent's School of Drama in N.Y. preceded his film debut in Shadows of the West (1921, Paul Hurst). Following his debut, he began performing on the stage and did not make another film until 1929. In 1930, he played Hildy Johnson in Lewis Milestone's The Front Page:

In 1930, [Howard Hughes] had purchased *The Front Page* and was seeking someone to play Hildy Johnson. The director, Lewis Milestone, saw me in a play called *The Up and Up*, in which I used a rapid, staccato delivery, playing a bookie. He never even came backstage, but contacted Hughes, saying, "I've seen some young fellow who would be right for the role...."

Q. Was it Hughes or Milestone that decided to move the camera around the actors...?

A. Hughes made suggestions, but he never did any direction. Milestone wouldn't allow it. The shots of [Adolph] Menjou and me around the table were Milestone's innovation. He said, "I'm the director. Don't tell me they can't be done." The camera was set up in the flies, and it worked.

—O'Brien, interviewed by Karyn Kay and Gerald Peary for *The Velvet Light Trap*, Fall 1975

Those familiar with the plot of *The Front Page* on stage know it had an explosive curtain line, used by the editor on the phone to keep his reporter from leaving town with his girl [Mary Brian]. "The son-of-a-bitch stole my watch!"

Menjou said to Milestone, "Just seems criminal that we can't use the line in the film [1931]."

Milly answered, "Who said we weren't going to use it?"

Menjou's famous eyebrows stood at attention. "But can you use *that* epithet on the screen? The Hays Office would run us all out of the picture business! They even frown on 'bum'"

"Look, when you pick up the phone from the desk to make the call, just before you read the s-o-b tag line, plant your fanny next to the typewriter. As you say that word, nudge the Underwood, so the carriage will release itself and ring the bell."

"You think it will work?"

"Sure. No one will hear you actually utter the word — the bell will drown it. But the audience will be fully aware that you have said it."

"You think so?"

"We'll do *take* and *retake* until the synchronization is perfect." It was. After a lot of nerve-fraying takes.

Mike Curtiz was shooting *Angels with Dirty Faces* [1938] in the railroad yards of downtown Los Angeles. He failed to tell the engineer of a moving train what the full action of the scene was to be. The two boys who were playing the roles Cagney and I were doing as adults were supposed to be running away from the police, and were to cross the tracks in front of an onrushing train. Someone forgot to check the train speed. The train barely missed hitting the two boys, who leaped aside like salmon. The shaking engineer clambered down out of his cab; he looked like death at bargain prices.

Mike, a true Hungarian, just smiled at him. "*Very* good. This was part of the action of our story. I purposely did not tell the two boys before you go so fast."

It was only the quick action of the crew on the picture that prevented this engineer from killing Mike Curtiz.

Mike later shook his head and, in his mangled English, said, "How do you get realism if not take chances?"

—O'Brien, in his *The Wind at My Back: The Life and Times of Pat O'Brien* (Garden City, N.Y.: Doubleday & Co., 1964)

There's no need for me to eulogize Knute Rockne; I suppose his influence in American sports is appreciated by just about everyone. For my part, I was a worshiper of the immortal Notre Dame football coach long before I got into the movies. I first met him when the Marquette football team, of which I was a member, played the Fighting Irish, and I've seldom been so moved by anything as I was by a talk he gave at the banquet after the game. I heard him speak many times after that, and each occasion deepened my conviction that here was a truly great man.

When I heard that Warner's was thinking of a picture based on his life, I wanted to play the part [in *Knute Rockne, All American* (1940, Lloyd Bacon)]. It was more than a matter of desiring a fine role; I wanted to do it as a tribute to Rock. So when I got the assignment I was delighted...and scared. Who was I, a gabby Irishman, to play Rockne, with his quiet, profound Norwegian nature...?

So before going to work, I steeped myself in the Rockne legend. I went back to Notre Dame. I talked with charming Mrs. Rockne and with the wonderful family. I talked with faculty members who had worked with him and adored him. I questioned kids coached by him. I chinned with bench sitters. The more I prepared myself, the more humble I felt about the job ahead. Then I tackled that job, and I gave it everything I had.

—O'Brien, in *The Saturday Evening Post*, 15 Dec 1945

Rockne...was a difficult assignment to me, as he had been alive so recently. He was killed in an air crash in 1931 and in 1939 most people still remembered him from newsreels and radio interviews. There were hundreds and hundreds of thousands of people who had their own vivid image of Rockne. I was uncomfortable with the thought that many would be quick to say, "*That* isn't Rockne — he wouldn't talk like that — he never made that kind of gesture. It's just some Hollywood ham...."

I played Rockne not just as a sports figure, but as a man dedicating his life to the cause of youth — a great humanitarian. I had his recording of a locker-room speech. I played it over and over again, trying desperately to absorb his voice intonation, his unusual delivery and vocal attack....

I have been fortunate to have played many biographies. I think, probably more than any other actor, even Paul Muni, but I leave it open for challenge. *Oil for the Lamps of China* [1935, Mervyn LeRoy] was actually the life of Alice Tisdale Hobart's husband.... I was Father Duffy in *The Fighting 69th* [1940, William Keighley]; Major Cavanaugh in *The Iron Major* [1943, Ray Enright]; another priest in *Fighting Father Dunne* [1948, Ted Tetzlaff]; Colonel Paddy Ryan (founder of the Bombardier School in New Mexico) in *Bombardier* [1943, Richard Wallace]; Forman in *The Last Hurrah* [1958, John Ford]; and — best, to some — Knute Rockne.

—O'Brien, in his *The Wind at My Back: The Life and Times of Pat O'Brien* (Garden City, N.Y.: Doubleday & Co., 1964)

[John] Ford was the genius of them all. He was an artist drawing a portrait in oil, with [Frank] Capra [with whom he worked on *American Madness* (1932)] a close second. I made *Air Mail* for Jack Ford in '32, and he was wonderful with me, but he got a little prickly over the years. He was always a very rough disciplinarian; I remember on *The Last Hurrah* he'd go nuts about the littlest things, like marks on the floor. But after the storm, he'd be the same old Jack. He would never talk the part you were playing, he'd just tell you what he wanted. "I hope you can get it," he'd say, chewing on that handkerchief he always had. When you failed, he'd say, "That wasn't what I wanted. Try to get what I wanted. We're going to take another whack at it and it better be good." After you finally got it, he'd come over and put his arms around you. "Why the hell didn't you get it in the first place?" he'd say.

—O'Brien, interviewed by Scott Eyman for *Films & Filming*, Apr 1982

Donald O'CONNOR [1925-]

Born: Chicago. Work as a member of "The O'Connor Family" circus and vaudeville act preceded his film debut in Melody for Two (1937, Louis King). In 1952, he played Cosmo Brown in Gene Kelly and Stanley Donen's Singing in the Rain:

I ad-libbed all sorts of stunts. I'd done the somersault off a wall before in two other pictures. Gene gave me the bit where I scrunch up my face after running into the door. We began to rehearse the number and I'd get very tired. I was smoking four packs of cigarettes a day then and getting up those walls was murder. I'd roll around the floor and get carpet burns. They had to bank one wall so I could make it up and then through another wall. My body just had to absorb this tremendous shock. So finally we filmed it straight through, and I went home and couldn't get out of bed for three days. On my return Gene comes up to me and asks if I could do it again. "Sorry," he says, "Hal Rosson fogged out the negative by mistake and ruined the footage." So I did it again and went to bed for three more days.

—O'Connor, quoted in *Film Comment*, May/June 1978

Maureen O'HARA [1920-]

Born: Maureen FitzSimons in Milltown, Ireland. Studies at The Abbey Theatre School in Dublin, The Guildhall School of Music in London and The London College of Music, and work on both radio and stage preceded her film debut in My Irish Molly (1939, Alex Bryce). In 1941, she played Angharad Morgan in How Green Was My Valley, the first of five films directed by John Ford:

I enjoyed tough directors who didn't waste time with politeness and that sort of nonsense.... Ford was a tough taskmaster. He did not direct you in detail. He did not say, "Now turn your arm, now turn your head." He put you in a corner of the room and forced you to act your way out of it. He didn't like to do more than one or two takes. Practically every time you'd do a scene you'd hear, "Cut! Thank you. Next set-up." It never dawned on you that you should do more than one or two.

Ford was brilliant in his sense of what was right and what was wrong, a fine portrait painter with lights. He framed a scene. I never could leave the set, because watching how he would move his camera, and what he would take into the picture — it might be a shaft of light — made you realize that he was creating mood by how he placed his camera, how he moved his performers, and how he asked his cameraman to light the set. In *How Green Was My Valley* I came down the steps in my wedding dress and Walter Pidgeon was way up in the background — a tall, dark figure — and my wedding veil blows up, straight up in a spiral in the sky from the back of my neck. A noted Hollywood director said to me how lucky Ford was to have the wind blow my veil like that. I told him it was not luck. Ford used three wind machines to get that effect. He wouldn't allow actors to stop in the middle of a scene if they made a mistake. We all knew that no matter what happened, we had to use the accident and continue going in the sense of the scene until he said cut. Very often in the finished movie you saw all of those impromptu scenes and they were marvelous.... The one thing about him — he let you be you, and made you feel proud of yourself....

He would occasionally attack a particular performer and that was called by us "being in the barrel." Every day we would say, "Who's in the barrel today?" If it was you, it meant you were going to have a terrible, miserable day because he would never let up nagging you, and insulting and hurting you. But it didn't mean that he was necessarily mad at you. It meant that out of the corner of his eye he was watching somebody else until he got him in the mental condition he wanted him in and then he would shoot the scene.

Only one time on *How Green Was My Valley* was I put in my place. We were doing a scene in which we had to use baskets. And the prop man brought in baskets which were very modern Kraft Cheese baskets. I said, "Oh, Mr. Ford...these are totally out of character. They belong to another era. They're too modern." And he said, "Well, you don't have to worry about that. You're not in the scene anymore, so you go and sit on the hill." Which meant, "Why don't you mind your own business, I'm the director, not you." So I swallowed my pride and went up and sat on the hill. Oh, about fifteen minutes later there was a beckoning arm and he called, "Come down here." So I went down and he said, "I've changed my mind." It taught me a lesson and I never again brought up that kind of thing. He was an old devil, but a fabulous and wonderful man to work with, and we all loved him dearly. [O'Hara also worked on Ford's *Rio Grande* (1950), *The Quiet Man* (1952), *The Long Gray Line* (1955) and *The Wings of Eagles* (1958).]

—O'Hara, interviewed by Kevin Lewis for *Films in Review* (NY), Apr 1990

I never met [Mary Maher]. She died five years ago. For the part [in *The Long Gray Line*], I just copied a bit from my mother and from several other people I know. I always do that. In *Sitting Pretty* [1948, Walter Lang] I copied Mrs. Bob Crosby who lived across the street from me. I needed someone with a bunch of kids. She has five.

—O'Hara, interviewed by William Peper for *The World Telegram*, 26 Feb 1955

Dan O'HERLIHY [1919-]

Born: Wexford, Ireland. Work with Dublin's Abbey Players and work on Irish radio preceded his film debut in Hungry Hill (1946, Brian Desmond Hurst). In 1954, he played the title role in Luis Bunuel's The Adventures of Robinson Crusoe:

[*The Adventures of Robinson Crusoe*] was a strange and wonderful experience, working under one of the world's great directors, watching this dedicated man handle a classic everybody already knows, piecing it together in the most primitive conditions imaginable — partly in Mexico City and in the Manzanillo jungle on the coast.

Crusoe, after all, isn't just an adventure yarn. As Bunuel reminded me the day we met, it's more a psychological study of a man with an aging, crumbling mind. Suddenly he meets Friday [Jaime Fernández], as an eccentric, and the mind rights itself. Oddly enough, we never used the script after the first week of shooting. I'm not a Stanislavsky man, just an instinctive actor, so I'd say to Bunuel, "What happens now?" Luckily, Bunuel's even more instinctive as a director.

He always knew what was supposed to happen — and how.

—O'Herlihy, interviewed by Howard Thompson for *The New York Times*, 11 July 1954

Dennis O'KEEFE [1908-1969]

Born: Edward James Flanagan, Jr. in Fort Madison, Iowa, to the vaudeville team of Flanagan and Edwards. Stage work with his mother preceded his film debut under the name of Bud Flanagan in Reaching for the Moon (1930, Edmund Goulding); his first film as Dennis O'Keefe was Bad Man of Brimstone (1938, J. Walter Ruben). In 1947, he played Dan O'Brien in Anthony Mann's T-Men:

I was completely sold on the role of T-Man Dan O'Brien. Dan started out as the hero of a second-rate cops-and-robbers story.

But director Anthony Mann and I thought that if the script were pulled down to earth and made honest, the picture could be both sound and exciting. To help make it authentic, I went to Washington at my own expense and studied Treasury Department methods in connection with counterfeiting....

Back in Hollywood, we tried to duplicate real Treasury Department techniques and to discard all the phony material. In the original script, for example, one T-Man taps out a message to another in Morse code on a punching bag. That was a good twist for a comic strip, but it had no place in a picture that was trying to reflect reality, so I refused to do the scene....

This was typical of the whole picture. Almost everyone seemed eager to make it as nearly as possible a documentary record of how T-Men combat counterfeiting. [O'Keefe worked with Mann again on *Raw Deal* (1947).]

—O'Keefe, in *The Saturday Evening Post*, 26 Aug 1950

Gary OLDMAN [1958-]

Born: New Cross, South London, England. Studies at The Rose Bruford College of Speech and Drama in London and work in provincial repertory preceded his film debut as Sid opposite Chloe Webb as Nancy in Sid and Nancy (1986, Alex Cox):

The only way that Sid could express himself, his love, was to carve Nancy's name on his chest, because he couldn't really say it with words. It was "Let's show the world."

—Oldman, interviewed by Richard Christiansen for *The Chicago Tribune*, 19 Oct 1986

[Joe Orton in *Prick Up Your Ears* (1987, Stephen Frears)] is a highly articulate, very witty man. Not like Sid. But I do see certain similarities in them in the way they were both out to shock the world.

—Oldman, interviewed by Victoria Balfour for *The New York Daily News*, 12 Oct 1986

I don't see great connections between Sid [Vicious] and Joe [Orton] and Jackie [Flannery in *State of Grace* (1990, Phil Joanou)], but they are all outlaws in one shape or form. And, of course, Sid and Joe were setting trends. They both, in their own way, were pioneers. And Jackie is just his own creature, isn't he? He's his own animal....

He's the wild man, he's emotional, he's volatile, he's spontaneous, and he's very loyal. Even though Terry [Sean Penn] is connected only emotionally — not in a blood sense — he treats him like a brother....

I found Jackie to be, in many respects, an innocent. There's a lot of lovely things about Jackie. To some extent, I found him rather charming and rather sweet and rather a tortured spirit. But nothing a big cuddle and a lot of love wouldn't cure.

—Oldman, interviewed by Robert Seidenberg for *American Film*, Oct 199Q

You are so adept at physicalizing and internalizing all of these various characters. Do you want to go into that at all or do you just want to say, "It's what I do?" Let's take [Lee Harvey] Oswald [in *JFK*, 1991, Oliver Stone], for example.

A. I sort of don't know what I do. I did the homework for Oswald. I had tapes of him speaking on the radio, and of course there is the footage of him in the corridor at the press conference in Dallas. There is about twelve or fifteen minutes of him on tape. That's all I had but it was enough, because it was Oswald talking, walking...and I studied it for hours, for months, because there were sections of it that were going to be in the movie. I thought, I have the guy here — I should try to make this as I possibly can.

The most interesting thing about it was that only ten percent of the role was actually written, and the other ninety percent I had to fill. So I had to improv most of it, which meant I read as many books as I could, talked to as many people who knew him as I could. I met Marina; I met his two daughters, June and Rachel; I met people who knew him in New Orleans. One guy in particular, Ron Lewis who was a very good friend of Oswald's, helped me enormously. Where books just led to dead ends, he went beyond that. He would say, "You know that why that says that in that book there? They are confused about this. I'm not, because I can tell you where Oswald was that day...."

Q. Did you come away with the feeling that Oswald did it by himself?

A. No.

Q. Do you think he was involved in a conspiracy?

A. I don't think he fired a gun. I think he was innocent. He was what he said he was. He was a patsy, and they set him up....

Q. I think Oliver Stone is, in a sense, creating our history....

A. Oliver wants truth, and he's like a bulldozer getting in the way of truth. He would give me a situation where I'd read in a book, that Oswald got arrested in New Orleans and asked to see an FBI agent. I'd go to one book, then I'd go to another book. Then I'd ask my friend Ron Lewis what he thought and then someone else. Then I'd have my theory about it. I'd get to the set, "What do you think the scenes about, Gary? What went down here?" And I'd give my opinion and he'd go, "Right." Well, let's improv. Do one. Show me."

—Oldman, interviewed by Dennis Hopper for *Interview*, Jan 1992

Lena OLIN [1955-]

Born: Stockholm, Sweden. Studies at The Royal Dramatic Theater School in Stockholm and work there upon graduation preceded her film debut in The Adventures of Picasso (1978, Tage Danielsson), followed by Ingmar Bergman's After the Rehearsal (1980 — she has also worked with Bergman on the stage.) In her first English language film — The Unbearable Lightness of Being (1988, Philip Kaufman) — she played Sabina; in her second — Enemies, A Love Story (1989, Paul Mazursky) — she played Masha:

I don't think they are alike. Sabina is more comfortable with herself. There is a sadness deep in her heart, but she's much less destroyed than Masha — her soul is still in one piece. For Sabina, sex is a way to confirm herself. For Masha, sex is a way of escaping. She doesn't get a break anywhere — except making love.

—Olin, interviewed by Susan Linfield for *Rolling Stone*, 8 Mar 1990

[Masha] is like an open...[embrace]...like jumping into the ocean and you have to swim. She's so rich. I love her.

It's Masha's joy that really makes her interesting. She doesn't dive into pain and sorrow, though she has all the reason in the world. But she has made up her mind to live. She takes every possibility she has — sometimes she's a little too much, she cannot take it easy. Masha understands that this time on earth is like...borrowed time.... Life can't be taken for granted. Masha feels that life is so precious that she has to use every minute of it. That's why she can't sleep at night.

—Olin, interviewed by Ben Yagoda for *American Film*, Nov 1989

In the filming [of *The Unbearable Lightness of Being*], Phil and [producer] Saul [Zaentz] created a warm and giving atmosphere, it was a very happy set, and this made it easier for me to do some very difficult scenes, like the nude scenes with Daniel Day-Lewis and the episode where Juliette Binoche and I are photographing each other in the nude — I'd never done nude scenes before. I found that something grows between these two women, that they begin to like and respect each other; even though they both know they are sharing the same man, Tomas, it's not a question of two rivals. Daniel was such a help on the set to Juliette and myself, coaching us; he's so English, so polite and considerate, most generous to work with.

I was most astonished by Phil Kaufman, because I did not know what to expect from my first American director. In many ways working with Phil is like working with Bergman, they both make everyone feel so safe, so much at home in the studio, like a family.

—Olin, interviewed for the press release for *The Unbearable Lightness of Being* (Orion, 1988)

Laurence OLIVIER [1907-1989]

Born: Dorking, Surrey, England. Acclaimed performances while a schoolboy at All Saints Choir School in London (his debut was as Brutus in Julius Caesar), studies at Elsie Fogerty's Central School of Speech Training and Dramatic Art, and work on the London stage (from 1924), preceded his film debut in Murder for Sale (1929, Gustav Ucicky). In 1935, he played Captain Ignatoff in Moscow Nights, the first of two films for Anthony "Puffin" Asquith:

Puffin was a very polite, extremely gentle creature. He spoke very quickly but not more quickly than he was thinking. He was witty. He made you laugh and he laughed at your jokes. But you felt there was a strong layer of nervousness there. He seemed to be in very much awe of Alexander Korda, who produced the film. On one occasion while we were on the set right in the middle of a shot being taken, some production manager came up and put his hand gently on Puffin's shoulder and said very softly: "Mr. Korda wants to see you." Puffin leapt up as if someone had shot him.... That sounds as if he was a coward. He wasn't. The most you could ascribe to him was anxiety to please.

—Olivier, interviewed by R.J. Minney for *The Films of Anthony Asquith* (New York: A.S. Barnes, 1976)

Looking back at it, I was snobbish about making films. Then I had the good luck — but what hell it seemed at the time — to be directed in a film by William Wyler, *Wuthering Heights* [1939]. He was a brute. He was tough. I'd do my damnedest in a really exacting and complicated scene. "That's lousy," he'd say, "we'll do it again." At first we fought. Then when we had hit each other till we were senseless we became friends.

Gradually I came to see that film was a different medium, and that if one treated it as such, and tried to learn it, humbly, and with an open mind, one could work in it.... It was for me a new medium, a new vernacular. It was Wyler who gave me the simple thought — if you do it right, you can do anything. And if he hadn't said that, I think I wouldn't have done *Henry V*.

—Olivier, interviewed by Kenneth Harris for *The Observer Review*, 9 Feb 1969

When Jane Austen wrote her romantic comedy [*Pride and Prejudice*, made into a film of the same name by Robert Z. Leonard in 1940], she was poking fun at a period in English history when family pride, wealth and position were considered all that mattered. Darcy, in his love scenes with Elizabeth [Greer Garson] is constantly torn between two impulses. One is his pompous synthetic pride in family, the other is attraction for the heroine. So, while my love scenes with Miss Garson are in a serious vein, there is an underlying comedy element to them.

—Olivier, in the press release for *Pride and Prejudice* (MGM, 1940)

By the time I made my next film, *The Demi-Paradise* [1943] with [Asquith] I was in a position to be allowed to work on the script.... Quite frankly it was a propaganda film. I daresay it was unnecessary propaganda. The purpose of the propaganda was to make the English love the Russians who had just come into the war. Again I had Penelope Dudley Ward as my leading lady....

And again we had a marvelous time making the picture. And here again one was conscious of his strange, seeming mixture of reserve and yet — I wouldn't call it kitten claws, for there was always some admirable strength somewhere...and fondness...and charm...and wit...and delight...delight.

—Olivier, interviewed by R.J. Minney for *The Films of Anthony Asquith* (New York: A.S. Barnes, 1976)

I have been luckier than most because I was ultimately given the opportunity to take Shakespeare from the "wooden O" and place him on the silver screen. "Not possible," I was told. Initial attempts to do this had been absolutely appalling [Olivier had starred in *As You Like It* (1936, Paul Czinner)]. The audiences had stayed away in their multitudes. But I had the good fortune to be something of a movie star; I already had a following, so whatever I did was looked upon with curiosity. [Olivier directed himself in *Henry V* (1945), *Hamlet* (1948), *Richard III* (1955), and starred in *Othello* (1965, Stuart Burge).]

I'd played Richard III so often on stage, I'd let ham fat grow on my performance. This I had to rid myself of before the cameras got me. So for two weeks I hid myself away and studied the text and my inflections anew, hacked off the extra flesh and broad gestures I needed on stage to reach the back row of the upper circle some fifty yards away, made myself lean and austere in my expressions, and changed the phrasing, because Richard would be flirting with the camera — sometimes only inches from his eyes — and would lay his head on the camera's bosom if he could.

I took Richard's misshapen body and his sardonic smile, but I wanted to convince the audience of the mind behind the mask. A demonic mind, a witty mind. But there's something of the flirting, calculating witch about him, so I kept the long black curls to insinuate this femininity. I made his nose and hump smaller than for the stage, but the nose was big enough to have the effect of concentrating the focus on the eyes: the only way to the mind when the speech is sardonic or false.

Shakespeare's genius fills the play with images of eyes — "Out of my sight! Thou dost infect mine eyes." "Thine eyes, sweet lady, have infected mine" — of looking glasses, shadows, the sun. What a gift to the cinema! When an actor gets his eyes right on film, he's reached a peak in his professional life.

—Olivier, in his *On Acting* (London: Wheelshare Ltd., 1986)

Q. You worked with [Marilyn Monroe] on *The Prince and the Showgirl* [1957]. What was she like? How do you remember her?

A. She was a most extraordinary mixture — two very clearly demarked people. One was the most enchanting girl I've ever met, and I'm not alone in that, I know. I thought this is going to be terrible, I'm going to fall in love with this girl so much. What shall I do? It's going to be awful. And then gradually, although not very gradually, very very quickly it became obvious to me that when she was working she was an entirely different person, given that she was thoroughly ill-mannered, always, always late. She kept our wonderful Sybil Thorndike sitting bolt upright in an iron corset for three hours while she dithered around in front of the makeup mirror. It certainly took more understanding than I could find in myself. She was so terribly rude to me.... I was the director, the producer [and star]. It was so utterly humiliating. It was dreadful. She put me through the most dreadful time. I've never been so glad when anything was over. She had no resistance to being a great star, a great world figure, to being a great model. It's not the same. Being a star and being an actress is not necessarily the same thing.

—Olivier, interviewed by Barbara Walters for *The Barbara Walters Special*; aired ABC TV, 17 June 1980

Archie Rice [in *The Entertainer* (1960, Tony Richardson)] is a tragic figure. Archie was an entertainer who also acted parts in his real life, which was unreal — making him even more real and tragic.... He was a loathsome person, but I felt sorry for him.

—Olivier, interviewed by Curtis Bill Pepper for *The New York Times*, 25 Mar 1979

I watch all my colleagues very carefully, admire them all for different qualities. I think the most interesting thing to see is that an actor is most successful when not only all his virtues but all his disadvantages come into useful play in a part. The man who, I think, gave me the best sort of thoughts about acting was my friend Ralph Richardson. I watch Rex Harrison for timing. I watch all my colleagues for different qualities that I admire, and I imitate them and copy them unashamedly....

Of all the people I've ever watched with the greatest delight, I think, in another field entirely, was Sid Field. I wouldn't like anybody to think that I was imitating Sid Field when I was doing *The Entertainer*.

Q. Well, there were little things in it.

A. Little things, but Sid Field was a great comic and Archie Rice was a lousy one. But I know when I imitate Sid Field to this day, I still borrow from him freely and unashamedly....

Q. Now let's talk about *Othello*.... What was there in your conception of the part that made it different from the conventional Othellos that we're used to seeing?

A. Well, you know that very rough estimate of the theme of Shakespearean tragedy. It's constantly said that Shakespearean tragedy is founded by Shakespeare upon the theme of a perfect statue of a man, a perfect statue; and he shows one fissure in the statue, and how that fissure makes the statue crumble and disappear into utter disorder. From that idea you get that Othello is perfect except that he's too easily jealous; that Macbeth is perfect except that he's too ambitious; that Lear is perfect except that he's too bloody-minded, too pigheaded; that Coriolanus is too proud; that Hamlet lacks resolution; and so on. But there seems to me, and there has grown in me a conviction over the last few years, that in most of the characters, not all, but in most of them, that weakness is accompanied by the weakness of self-deception, as a companion fault to whatever fault may be specified by the character in the play. It's quite easy to find in Othello, and once you've found it I think you have to go along with it; that he sees himself as this noble creature. It's so easy in the senate scene for you to present the absolutely cold-blooded man who doesn't even worry about marital relations with his wife on his honeymoon night, to reassure the senate that he's utterly perfect, pure beyond any reproach as to his character, and you can find that, and trace it, constantly throughout. He's constantly wishing to present himself in a certain light, even at the end, which is remarkable. I believe, and I've tried to show, that when he says "Not easily jealous" it's the most appalling bit of self-deception. He's the most easily jealous man that anybody's ever written about. The minute he suspects, or thinks he has the smallest grounds for suspecting Desdemona [Maggie Smith], he wishes to think her guilty, he wishes to. And the very first thing he does, almost on top of that, is to give way to the passion, perhaps the worst temptation in the world, which is murder. He immediately wants to murder her, immediately. Therefore he's an extremely hot-blooded individual, an extremely savage creature who has kidded himself and managed to kid everybody else, all this time, that he's nothing of the kind. And if you've got that, I think you've really got the basis of the character. Lodovico [Kenneth Mackintosh] says it for us: "Is this the noble Moor...whom passion could not shake...I am sorry that I am deceived in him."

Q. There is also a sense of a caged animal in your performance. I remember writing that you communicate more than almost any actor I know a sense of danger, you feel at any moment that the great paw may lash out and someone's going to get hurt. Are you conscious of this power you have over audiences — and over other actors for that matter?

A. I'm not very conscious of the workings of it. I feel consciousness of the desirability of having that ingredient in my work, very much so. *Othello*, of course, screams for it. It's the only play in the whole of Shakespeare in which a man kills a woman, and if Shakespeare gets an idea he goes all out for it; he knows very well that for a black man to kill a white woman is a very big thrill indeed to the audience, and he doesn't pull any punches. As an alchemist Shakespeare gets hold of that one all right. Therefore, if you feel that thing in yourself, that sort of easily released or closely guarded animal inside you, you must use it in this part of all parts.

—Olivier, interviewed by Kenneth Tynan for the BBC; repr. in *The Tulane Drama Review*, Winter 1966

Through the rehearsals [for *Sleuth* (1972)] I found Michael Caine wonderfully good company, ceaselessly funny and a brilliant actor. Two days or so before shooting, Joe Mankiewicz, who was directing us, said privately he was a bit worried about me; I seemed to lack the essential authority for Andrew Wyke's stature in the relationship. It did not take me very long to work out why. I had developed a habit of being an audience to Michael, a foil for him. This was disastrous to the enterprise; if the character of Wyke does not completely dominate the younger man there is no dramatic peak when the positions are reversed. Moral: Be religiously firm on a character even at possible risk to personal relationships. Joe also asked me, a little wistfully, whether I couldn't possibly do something to make myself look a little more attractive. "Nothing easier," I said. Since I was twenty-four in Hollywood I have had recourse to one panacea to which I always fly should a little beautifying be required. I stick on, if there is not time to grow it, a Ronald Colman mustache; I appeared with this adornment on my upper lip next day and the shock of the transformation ran through the studio. Everyone thought that now they had a certain success on their hands, as indeed they had. It seems almost too simple.

—Olivier, in his *Confessions of an Actor* (London: George Weidenfeld & Nicolson, 1982)

Edward James OLMOS [1947-]

Born: East Los Angeles. Work as a night club entertainer and on TV preceded his film debut in Hit Man (1972, George Armitage). In 1988, he played Bolivian born, East Los Angeles math teacher, Jaime Escalante in Ramon Menendez' Stand and Deliver, which he also co-produced:

I really tried to re-create Jaime in a mirror image. I literally went to the full extent of parting my hair on the opposite side, so when he saw me he'd be seeing a reflection of himself. I tried to emulate and imitate, become him on film. A very difficult chore, which I made even harder by putting a set of pressures on myself that I felt were mandatory for this type of role.

He was with me all the time on the set, except when he had to go teach his kids, so people were looking at him while they were looking at me being him. That kept me at a constant high pitch, which is ridiculously difficult....

He has a huge sense of pride and ego about his job. He's a true teacher; that's his calling, like my true calling was to be an entertainer. He told me he had a tremendous love of seeing the light bulbs go on, of hearing someone say, "Oh, I get it." Any great teacher will tell you that's food for the soul.

—Olmos, interviewed by Bob Strauss for *The Chicago Sun-Times*, 17 Apr 1988

When I was studying the man, I realized that one of his biggest attributes is his confrontational style. How can he do this to streetwise kids? Why aren't they punching his lights out?

The answer, I discovered, was that he was laughing at himself as much as they were laughing at him. He was not a threat....

—Olmos, interviewed by Brian Moss for *The New York Daily News*, 20 Mar 1988

Maureen O'SULLIVAN [1911-]

Born: Boyle, County Roscommon, Ireland; mother of Mia and Tisa [194-] Farrow. A convent education in Ireland, England and France preceded her film debut in So This is London (1930, John Blystone). She played Jane to Johnny Weismuller's Tarzan six times, beginning with Tarzan the Ape Man (1932, W.S. Van Dyke):

They put me in the first Tarzan film, which was really rather fun to do — all that swinging through trees. But after that it was decided to make several more, and the whole thing became a chore because they took such a long time as the bloody animals had to be especially trained.

Anyway, I couldn't feel much sympathy for Cheetah, the chimp, who was really rather queer, I'm afraid. Didn't like girls at all. But he adored Johnny Weismuller and was terribly jealous of me! [She also appeared as Jane in *Tarzan and His Mate* (1934, Cedric Gibbons and Jack Conway); *Tarzan Escapes* (1936), *Tarzan Finds a Son* (1939), *Tarzan's Secret Treasure* (1941) and *Tarzan's New York Adventure* (1942), all directed by Richard Thorpe.]

—O'Sullivan, interviewed for *The Sunday Express*, 2 Dec 1973

Woody Van Dyke used to get very spontaneous performances out of people because he would take it and he'd say, "O.K. Print it." If you said, "Oh, please, can we do it again? I wish I had done it different," he'd say, "Well, you should have thought of it sooner." He would go ahead and print it anyway, and consequently there was a great spontaneity in his films — perhaps I was a better actress than I thought I was, or perhaps we all were, because the results were always very fresh and good. [In addition to *Tarzan, the Ape Man*, she also worked on Van Dyke's *The Thin Man* (1934) and *Hide-Out* (1934).]

Ann Harding, with whom I had to play a rather difficult scene in a film called *The Flame Within* [1935, Edmund Goulding]...said: "Remember one thing — that an emotion released is an emotion lost." In other words, always keep something back for the imagination of your audiences.

I did not have very much contact with Garbo during the making of *Anna Karenina* [1935, Clarence Brown]. I liked her; she was nice, very beautiful. As an actress, she gave you very little. In other words, it was a love affair between her and the camera. In fact, when working with her, one felt she was doing nothing really, that she wasn't even very good, until you saw the results on the screen and you realised the love affair she had with the camera. The camera with her was quite extraordinary. I think she was just a natural. And, of course, she always had marvellous cameramen who photographed her divinely.

—O'Sullivan, interviewed by Kingsley Canham for *Focus on Film*, Summer 1974

Peter O'TOOLE [1932-]

Born: Connemara, Ireland. Studies at The Royal Academy of Dramatic Art, work with The Bristol Old Vic Co. and on the London stage (from 1959) preceded his film debut in Kidnapped (1959, Robert Stevenson). In 1962, he played the title role in David Lean's Lawrence of Arabia:

Q. You said something about *Lawrence of Arabia* once: that you went to see it for the first time and you were shocked when it cut from a shot of you at one age to a close-up of you two years older.

A. What happened was David, at the end of the film, said, "Pete, believe it or not, I'm missing about four close-ups. I think it would help the film." So having been in the wilderness of Zin we find ourselves in the relative wilderness of Hammersmith [England] in a tiny little room with an old blue wall and a bit of dry ice: "Look there," or "Look there...."

Do you remember the scene with a mirage? Which was not an optical, it was *there*. He wanted another close-up to help build the tension of that amazing entrance of Ali [Omar Sharif]. He showed me it and it was extraordinary, for I was 27 in the first shot; cut to the figure coming through the mirage; 29 in the second shot; and 27 in the third. The difference was astounding, it really was. I'd lost the bloom of youth.... It *was* a shock. But don't forget, attitudes change as the years change. It doesn't bother me now. We're in a strange situation, film actors. We can watch the process of decomposition of the flesh.

—O'Toole, interviewed by Joseph McBride for *Film Comment*, Mar/Apr 1981

Playboy: You've made your name in films playing tormented heroes who end up more or less martyred. Do you enjoy being "on the cross"?

O'Toole: No, but I know what you mean.... *Lawrence of Arabia*? Yes, I suppose he was a martyr of sorts. Henry II in *Becket* [1964, Peter Glenville]? Well, he ended up being whipped for his sins, but he didn't enjoy it. He accepted it because it was politically expedient, and he loathed every second of it. As for Lord Jim [in *Lord Jim* (1965, Richard Brooks)], he certainly chose to die, but I played him not for that reason but because it was the only chance I'd ever had of doing a Western — or an Eastern, if you like. He was a simple, silent, guilt-ridden fellow who rides into town like Shane; I just fancied the idea.

—O'Toole, interviewed by Kenneth Tynan for *Playboy*, Sept 1965

[*How to Steal a Million* (1966, William Wyler)] is one of those sophisticated comedies.... I've been running lots of Cary [Grant]'s old films. Not so that I can imitate him — just to watch his superb technique. I did the same thing before [*What's New*] *Pussycat* [1965, Clive Donner]; ran some old W.C. Fields comedies.

—O'Toole, interviewed by Roderick Mann for *The Sunday Express*, 1 Aug 1965

My trick [in preparing a film role] is to vanish for two weeks. Be alone. And I have a set routine of reading the script and working on it that seems to work...the script perks you. You get such perks constantly. They lead me on to my own loves which are archaeology and history. I play Henry [II in *The Lion in Winter* (1968, Anthony Harvey)] and that leads me to histories of Henry and Eleanor, and that leads me to where he lived and was born, and that leads me to the groundworks about him and his influence upon other people of the time....

—O'Toole, interviewed by Lewis Archibald for *Show*, Jan 1973

In *Becket*, Henry was foxy and shrewd. In *Lion*, he is wise and more the master tactician. Both Henrys have mad rages. They are passionate men.

—O'Toole, interviewed by Bruce Bahrenburg for *The Newark Evening News*, 21 Sept 1968

The point for me of doing *The Ruling Class* [1972, Peter Medak] was that I found that a great deal of the '60s, the more obvious manifestations of thought, were silly. Daffy. Goofy. Its frivolous aspects, its pleasurable aspects were *great* fun. And its ideas were imperishable, and are imperishable. The first time middle class young men and women were being hit on the head by the forces of law and order. All right, so 99 percent of them gave it up and became whatever they became. But they can't kill the ideas that happened. You cannot. And in a way the more relevant parts of the Bible were reinforced. So the idea was to make a sort of pyrotechnic metaphor of the '60s within *The Ruling Class*.

—O'Toole, interviewed by Lewis Archibald for *The Aquarian Weekly*, 4 May 1983

Q. Whom did you have in mind when you were playing the director [Eli Cross in *The Stunt Man* (1980, Richard Rush)]? A lot of people thought it was John Huston.

A. Yes, I've heard John Huston. I've heard Orson Welles. I've heard [Sam] Peckinpah. I've heard the Devil. I've heard God. I've heard all sorts of things. I hope he's a complete original. If there is any influence, it's through the pores and it would be David Lean. I was two years and three months with David [on *Lawrence of Arabia*] and it was as though he'd given me a course in how to be a director. At every shot I looked through the viewfinder. I was with him viewing takes of other performers watching his complete involvement....

Q. He's not so flamboyant as Eli Cross though, is he?

A. No, he's not, but he's always beautifully tired. And a very handsome man, diabolical in appearance. *Lawrence of Arabia* was a great adventure, one of the great adventures of my life. I learnt more from David than from anybody else in theater or cinema. He's my master. Standards are set by David Lean.

—O'Toole, interviewed by Joseph McBride for *Film Comment*, Mar/Apr 1981

If there were any idiosyncracies in the character [of Eli Cross] at all, I took them from David Lean, his way of looking, crouching, his sense of empathy. But the dress, that was all Richard Rush, the very soft corduroy loose trousers, the bluish velour shirt, and the pouch around the waist, in which he carries his cigarettes.

—O'Toole, interviewed by Judy Klemesrud for *The New York Times*, 9 Jan 1981

I don't know where [Alan Swann in *My Favorite Year* (1982, Richard Benjamin)] came from. He took me by surprise. I liked the piece, wanted to do it, knew that something could be made of it, enjoyed the rehearsals, but the moment the camera turned over, I can't explain it and I don't even want to try. I have no idea, I don't know where that drunk came from. For when I was ridiculously drunk, I rolled around, I fell over. But this amazing sort of dignified gentleman. It wasn't conscious. The subconscious was saying, "That's what you do."

—O'Toole, interviewed by Lewis Archibald for *The Aquarian Weekly*, 4 May 1983

Q. Did you model the character of Alan Swann after the late Errol Flynn?

A. Not entirely. I think he's somewhere between Barrymore, Flynn, Rathbone, Fairbanks, Gilbert, the *swashbucklers*. My own idol is Barrymore, but from the moment I began to study the part, it became Alan Swann.

—O'Toole, interviewed by Judy Klemesrud for *The New York Times*, 8 May 1983

P

Al PACINO [1940-]

Born: South Bronx, N.Y. Studies at The High School of Performing Arts, at Herbert Berghof's Studio and with Lee Strasberg at The Actors Studio, and work off-off and on Broadway preceded his film debut in Me, Natalie (1969, Fred Coe). In 1972, he played Michael Corleone in Francis Ford Coppola's The Godfather, a role he reprised in The Godfather Part II (1974) and The Godfather Part III (1990):

Playboy: What were you trying to capture when you played Michael?

Pacino: In the first *Godfather*, the thing that I was after was to create some kind of enigma, an enigmatic-type person. So you felt that we were looking at that person and didn't quite know him. When you see Michael in some of those scenes looking wrapped up in a kind of trance, as if his mind were completely filled with thoughts, that's what I was doing. I was actually listening to Stravinsky on the set, so I'd have that look. I felt that that was the drama in the character, that that was the only thing that was going to make him dramatic. Otherwise, it could be dull. I never worked on a role quite like that. It was the most difficult part I've ever played.... With Francis, although I had personality differences with him, those were his performances, he *made* them. And he knew it. He'd say, "I created you — you're my Frankenstein monster...."

Playboy: In fact, you did walk and move differently as Michael didn't you?

Turner: I had to move in a different way than I've ever moved before. All *heavy*. Especially in *II*.

—Pacino, interviewed by Lawrence Grobel for *Playboy*, Dec 1979

[Music] can change my state of being. I did a simple scene in the boathouse [in *Godfather Part II*] when I tell Tom Hagen [Robert Duvall] about what's going on and what he has to do. It was a six-minute scene of exposition. Michael is talking about what's going to happen. I mean, impossible stuff. How do you make it active? How do you act it? Well, I knew that I was stuck with that. I'm not somebody who just goes up there and mouths things. And I'm not using Shakespeare's dialogue, either, to say it. Something has to be happening inside me to make me say these things. And I found I didn't have that much time to research, to work to find these things — so I used music.

Q. I don't know what you mean when you say, I used music.

A. Music would put me in a state. It would work on my subconscious, subliminal state. And I would come in with that state, so that was going on inside me, whatever that was.... Then I would talk, and that would be ringing in my ears. Michael had a lot of stuff going on in the back of his head and I didn't know what it was. So I found something commensurate with it....

Q. There's a change that comes over you in *Godfather I* and *Godfather II*, you're not the same person. You become more a monster.

A. I'm more alienated.

Q. Did those scenes bother you, the restaurant scene in *Godfather I*, where you kill two men.

A. Drove me crazy. Drove me crazy. *Godfather II* put me in the hospital. It was doing this character, the loneliness of him. I couldn't be that guy and have a good time. I wanted to have a good time doing it but I couldn't. And I couldn't go through that stuff inside. We were working twenty weeks on that film. I was living with that weight all the time, and it was suffocating, it was hurting....

Q. Why was *Godfather II* so oppressive?

A. I became physically exhausted and got bronchial pneumonia. It was frightening. This had to do with a combination of nervous exhaustion and my own need to get away, to pull out. I'm not very fond of doing films — it's wear and tear on me. I have a very strong musical sense in me. In a movie, there's not a chance for that rhythm to build.... That's why I fear doing things in translation, because words are notes to me and I play them. This is an area of myself nobody knows about. Michael Corleone didn't have many words....

Q. Did you want the audience to dislike you?

A. I knew that was going to be a problem, but no, I didn't.... I wanted people to like Michael but like him in the sense that I wanted them to see him, to understand him and his dilemma, without asking them to identify with him. That's what I was after. It's a difficult thing to do....

Q. What was Michael's dilemma — the losing and winning?

A. Yes, that balance of losing and winning, his struggle to be a person he couldn't be. He became a non-person. When you start that lie, that pretense, no matter how noble your intentions...he didn't know who he was anymore.... Michael didn't know where he was way back in the '40s when he was going to school and moving away from "the family," in one sense, but also moving away from his destiny. In *Godfather II*, his problems are manifest more and more. There's such a dichotomy in this guy, he's so ambivalent.... Michael...is unpredictable but he's very intelligent. This dichotomy finally leads to his madness. He is lost at the end of this film. He's a beaten man. He is a desperately sad person.... If you notice at the end of *Part I* there's a kind of bounce to Michael. There's that ever subtle joy of what he's doing, that newness and that kind of taking it on, but when we pick him up in *II*, he's been doing it for five years, and that's gone. And that's what I went for.

—Pacino, interviewed by Leonard Probst for *Off Camera* (New York: Stein & Day, 1975)

Everything [Marlon Brando] does seems so effortless. His pacing is absolutely perfect, and he's incredibly inventive. I couldn't get over the way he aged in [*The Godfather*] — jutting his belly forward and accentuating his jowls. Brando does those little things with great concentration. And how about the way he died in the picture with that slice of orange in his mouth! That was his own idea.

—Pacino, interviewed for *Pictorial Living Coloroto Magazine*, *The Chicago Tribune*, 23 July 1972

In the dailies [for *Dog Day Afternoon* (1975, Sidney Lumet)] I came into the bank wearing glasses. And I thought, *NO*. He wouldn't be wearing glasses.

Q. Why?

A. Because he wants to be caught. Subconsciously he wants to be caught. He wants to be there.

—Pacino, interviewed by Ron Rosenbaum for *Vanity Fair*, Oct 1989

Bobby Deerfield [1977] was a move away from anything I had done before. I'm very grateful to Sydney Pollack for having wanted me to do it....

Playboy: It was reported that you and Pollack didn't get along very well.

Pacino: We didn't. It's because we're different. Sydney had a genuine idea for the movie, it meant something to him. We had different views, and in a movie like that, you need to be together on it. It was a very delicate subject. On that film, it was necessary to be in sync with each other and we were just a mess. Maybe we would have been better off had I listened to him more; it would have been consistent. I didn't quite understand his point of view....

Playboy: What were you after in *Deerfield*?

Pacino: I was after the other side of narcissism. That something that happens to a superstar who is left and is idolized, and a kind of loneliness I was after, narcissistic detachment, depression. That's what it was about — about breaking that depression, that self-absorption; opening like a flower. In my own life, I have not gone into or resolved many things; many things I've avoided. That is what *Bobby Deerfield* is about. About avoiding — knowing when to duck, when to move, when to hide, when to go in, when to roll with the punches.

Playboy: What made you decide to do [*...And Justice for All* (1979, Norman Jewison)]?

Pacino: Norman came to me with it. I said, "Norman, why don't I get some actors together and read it for you? Then I will see how I feel after I hear it." We read it aloud and after I finished, I said I'd do it. I thought it had a nice structure to it. It's an unusual film because it is so verbal; you really have to pay attention to it.

Playboy: How much research did you do for the part?

Pacino: I researched it a lot. I did a lot of work with lawyers before filming began, so I felt kind of close to the courts. At one point recently, a friend said to me he was having trouble with a contract and I just instinctively said, "Let *me* see that." You get the feeling that you are able to *do* these things. It is crazy. I literally took it from him and began to give him a legal opinion. Can you imagine that?

Playboy: Didn't you also do something like that when you played *Serpico* [1973, Sidney Lumet]?

Pacino: Yeah, I tried to. It was a hot summer day and I was in the back of a cab. There was this truck farting all that stuff in my face. I yelled out, "Why are you putting that crap in the street?" He said, "Who *are* you?" I yelled, "I am a *cop* and you are under arrest, pull over!" I pulled out my *Serpico* badge. It was a fantasy for a moment. I told him I would put him under citizen's arrest, but then I realized what I was doing.

Playboy: Don't you feel a responsibility for some of the issues the movie [*Cruising* (1980)] raises, since it's an Al Pacino movie?

Pacino: You're turning this into an Al Pacino movie? Al Pacino is an *actor* in this movie. The way the press focuses attention on something like this is by throwing my name into it. Responsibilities are relative. My responsibility is to a character in a script, to a part I'm playing — not to an issue I'm unqualified to discuss.

Playboy: But aren't we all ultimately responsible for what we do? Isn't what you're saying something of a cop-out?

Pacino: I don't think the film is anti-gay, but I can only repeat — I'm responsible for giving the best performance I can. I took this role because the character is fascinating, a man who is ambiguous both morally and sexually; he's both an observer and a *provocateur*. It gave me an opportunity to paint a character impressionistically — a character who is something of a blur. I also took the role because Billy Friedkin is one of the best directors working today.

—Pacino, interviewed by Lawrence Grobel for *Playboy*, Dec 1979

Q. Who thought of turning [*Scarface* (1983, Brian De Palma)] into a modern story?

A. At first, I was caught up with the idea of recapturing the Thirties. But when I talked to some writers, we found it was very hard, because it was so melodramatic. I didn't want to do a copy of it. I was looking for a style. You see, what [Paul] Muni had done was a base for me to start from; he gave such a solid foundation to the role, it was like a canvas. I knew it was a characterization I wanted to continue....

I thought De Palma was an interesting choice. He brought a definite style to it, almost Brechtian in a way. He knew what he wanted to do with it right from the start.

Q. How did you "get" this particular character? It's really unlike anything you've done before, playing a Cuban with a heavy accent.

A. At first, it was almost a potpourri, using everything I knew: coming from the South Bronx, being, in a sense, Latin myself, I have a certain connection to the Latin feeling, although the Cuban thing is different. I didn't do it alone; I had a lot of help.

When I started, I met with the lady doing the costumes, and the makeup person, the hair person. We would have long discussions out at my house about what the guy I was going to play would be like. It was the first time I opened the character up to a lot of people, which was helpful for me. I worked with my friend Charlie Laughton on the part, and with Bob Easton, the dialect coach, intensively. I worked with an expert in knife combat, with a phys. ed. guy who helped me get the kind of body I wanted for the part.

Q. Did anyone in real life inspire you?

A. Well, I used Roberto Duran a little bit. There was a certain aspect of Duran, a certain lion in him, that I responded to in this character. And I was very inspired by Meryl Streep's work in *Sophie's Choice*. I thought that her way of involving herself in playing someone who is from another country and another world was particularly fine and committed and... courageous.

—Pacino, interviewed by Larry Grobel for *Rolling Stone*, 2 Feb 1984

Keller [in *Sea of Love* (1990, Harold Becker)] is coping with a midlife crisis. He's headed toward retirement, his wife has left him for another cop, he's lonely and intensely vulnerable — completely swallowed up in [the character played by Ellen] Barkin. His need for her love is *immense*. He's craving it....

The *danger* of investigating the woman he's in love with is turning him on. The chance of getting murdered by her is titillating — and self-destructive....

He senses that time is running out. He has a one-way ticket, the train is coming out of the tunnel and he sees, in the distance, the big mountain of his mortality. And he wants to make his time here count.

—Pacino, interviewed by Glenn Plaskin for *The New York Daily News*, 12 Sept 1989

[Michael Corleone] is much older when we pick him up in [*The Godfather Part III* (1990, Francis Ford Coppola)], and I am too. The saga was a long, complicated journey for Francis and Mario Puzo. They made it *together*. And for me they came up with a character that is credible in the sense that he seems to be a continuation of Michael, only he's different in a way that seems organic. It was all very interesting to think about what happened in the ensuing years, to speculate on what could have happened to a person like this. They didn't lose the continuity. He's different, but as different as a person like that would be in order to survive the kinds of things that happened to him. And I don't mean because somebody was gonna knock him off. Just to live with what he's —

Q. Done.

A. I mean, this is a person who had another destiny — at least he thought he did — who had another way to go, who had a desire to do something else and was taken off his course and put on another course. The moment when he made the decision to go in that direction has been the thing he has dealt with his entire life.

—Pacino, interviewed by Julian Schnabel for *Interview*, Feb 1991

When [Francis Ford Coppola] theorizes, all you have to do is listen for 10 minutes and you've been given a wealth of imaginative, stimulating insights and images. I've read where people compare him to the Don, but he's more an *emperor*sario — maybe we've found a new word — than a Don. He's intense, preoccupied, doesn't miss a trick. He's a maestro....

Francis views Michael as a prince. There is the King, who is the Don [Marlon Brando], and there are his sons and his kingdom. The Don's life is threatened, he knows he is going to die. Which son will defend him? He loses one Sonny [James Caan], and the other, Fredo [John Cazale], is inadequate. And then there's the third one, who comes to his aid and takes over the kindgom, even though he never wanted it....

—Pacino, interviewed by Lawrence Grobel for *Entertainment Weekly*, 21 Dec 1990

["Big Boy" Caprice in *Dick Tracy* (1990, Warren Beatty)] is greedy. Very, very greedy. What's big about him is that he's the world's largest dwarf....

—Pacino, interviewed by Ron Rosenbaum for *Vanity Fair*, Oct 1989

Geraldine PAGE [1924-1987]

Born: Kirksville, Missouri. Studies at The Goodman Theatre Dramatic School in Chicago led to her film debut in Out of the Night (1947) made in Chicago by The Moody Bible Institute. After some stage work, she made her only Hollywood film of the 1950s — Hondo (1953, John Farrow):

I didn't know what I was doing at all [in *Hondo*], the work was so unlike what I'd learned for the stage. I had lots of help and direction from [John] Wayne, really, not from that horrible man who was called the director. He's really terribly bright, John Wayne. He has a marvelous mind. He always reminds me of a nice guy who got in with the wrong crowd. He was so different alone from what he was with those creeps he has around him.

—Page, interviewed by Lynn Tornabene for *Cosmopolitan*, July 1963

Off-Broadway, I had one skirt and two blouses to play the whole show in. When I went to Paramount [for the movie of *Summer and Smoke* (1961, Peter Glenville)], Edith Head opened these big double doors and there were 12 mannequins with these exquisite gowns on them. I said, "Now we must be doing the life of Lillian Russell." Then I had to make the adjustment, so I said, "Well, I guess papa's moved to a better parish." I was supposed to be a real wallflower dog, and they put me in a blonde wig and eyelashes and I looked like a Barbie Doll.

—Page, interviewed by Michael Musto for *The Village Voice*, 3 Sept 1985

[Big Sister in *The Day of the Locust* (1975, John Schlesinger)] is a popular revivalist in Los Angeles. I listened to the voice of Aimee Semple McPherson on a record, and I used some of that in my characterization. But I didn't copy her.

—Page, interviewed by Emory Lewis for *The Sunday Record*, 27 Oct 1974

Most of the directors I've worked with have allowed me to see the dailies. It's a general policy that actors are not allowed, because most people get shook and upset and then they start nagging about things that aren't essential. They get self-conscious and freeze up. So I can see why directors are against it. But I have proved to director after director that I am very good and I'm quiet and I don't then start telling them how to do things. I just learn for myself. And contrary to shaking my confidence, I always feel better. I say, "Oh. It wasn't as bad as I thought. Oh, I know what to do about that...." But Woody [Allen on *Interiors* (1978)], who is...well, he *is* paranoid. He would not allow it. I thought I'd finally persuaded him and he did say, "Okay, you can look at the rushes. They'll be Saturday morning." I couldn't believe it. He's finally going to let me see some! Then on Friday he said, "Well, it's so close to Christmas and the projectionist doesn't want to come in...." I never did see any of it.

Q. Did you find that a particularly difficult role?

A. Well, in a way. I felt I understood the character; that part didn't bother me so much. But the execution of it was extremely difficult because of pleasing Woody. I would do a scene a particular way and he would say, "That's too...I just don't believe that." Me, the specialist in realism? Then we'd go back and do it again and he'd say, "Ah, it's just...." He doesn't have any of the Method's verbiage or even the non-Method director's vocabulary at all. All he'd ever say is, "Well, I don't like it...."

Q. In other words, he didn't tell you in any specific way what he wanted?

A. Yeah, he'd say, "It's still like somebody you see playing an interior decorator in the movies. I just want the woman to come in and put down her handbag." It was exasperating and very difficult; I kept trying to simplify and simplify and take all the theatrical things out. But still he'd say, "No, that's like on the stage. Just come in and put the bag down." He didn't even go so far as to say, "Don't put the bag down like...." He would just shake his head. I'd say, "What's wrong with that? How much simpler can I be?" I'd go back and do it again.

But what was wonderful was that I agreed with his taste. When he said he didn't like it, I believed it; I knew that if I saw it, I would agree with him. That's wonderful because you can't always trust those decisions, yet in this case, I knew. When people tell me it's some of my best work, I'm very inclined to believe they must be telling the truth. God knows, every director I've ever worked with has tried in various ways to get me to simplify, especially in the movies....

Q. Do you carefully plan out what the character is thinking?

A. No. I used to, but over the years I have learned that if I preconceive what the character is thinking, it's not going to be as interesting or as varied as if I just go along and see what the character turns out to be thinking at the moment. Usually, if a line of inner thought seems to be working well, I keep it in. But if something happens to change, then I explore it. And it's wonderful with a role like Eve in *Interiors*; she's reminiscent of a character in a Chekhov play whose inner life is much more complicated than her outer life; it's just not expressed overtly. While she has very deep, complex inner thoughts, all she's doing is serving tea or something, yet her strong feelings come through even in that very simple behavior.

One of my favorite moments is at the birthday party when I'm sitting there but can't allow myself to show how straining it is to be surrounded by my family. When my son-in-law [Richard Jordan] pours the champagne, I love the way it comes across how I disapprove, how I'm suffering through this; just the merest, tiniest fraction of a drop spills on my hand, but I wipe it off with such long suffering. I like that.

—Page, interviewed by Joanmarie Kalter for *Actors on Acting* (New York: Sterling Publishing, 1979)

I used to hate acting in films. I could not cope at all. I thought they were all nuts, doing everything backwards. But after many, many years now I've calmed down. Now I know what to expect and I've found a way to really enjoy it. I like films equally as well now. The thing that bothers me the most is when you're onstage, unless you stand behind the furniture all the time, you are seen from your toes up so if you're standing on stage and you get some bad news or something you just turn your ankle over a little and everybody goes (she makes a gasping sound). But if you try that in a movie and the camera's only here (she demonstrates with a hand to her waist) then the ankle is useless. In movies you always have to change what you're doing, depending on what they're seeing....

Interiors was Mary Beth Hurt's first movie and she was in the state of being appalled at the process. I said, "Listen, Mary Beth, the thing you have to learn about movies is to say to yourself all the time 'nothing is my fault' and have a good time." She said, "But we played it this way and he printed it and when we did it again he asked us to do it the opposite way and we did it completely different and he said print it. Now what's going to happen when they shoot the scene that takes place after this? We don't know whether we were *this* way before or *that* way." I said, "It's up to them, they have to make sense out of it. You just ignore all that." That any movie makes any sense takes a compendium of miracles.

—Page, interviewed by David Galligan for *Drama-Logue*, 19 Dec 1985-1 Jan 1986

Q. What's so wonderful about your performance [in *The Trip to Bountiful* (1985, Peter Masterson)] is that you spare yourself nothing. You are touching, tragic, and annoying at the same time.

A. Horton Foote is a wonderful writer. It's *in* there if you want to use it. There's that speech where Carrie says, "I don't want to be that person." So you have to show that she's become someone she doesn't want to be, show the abrasive side. I worked hard on that. I didn't want to make it very obvious, but I wanted that to be *shown*. And the wonderful humor...that argument between Carrie and the daughter-in-law [Carlin Glynn] is so marvelously funny.

—Page, interviewed by Quentin Crisp for *The New York Native*, 10-16 Feb 1986

What I *really* like about Mrs. [Carrie] Watts is her self-dramatization — "I'll walk those 12 miles." She sees herself as going up to Mount Everest. Of course, she doesn't stop to think about what will happen when she gets there. Whether anybody will be there.

—Page, interviewed by Myra Forsberg for *The New York Times*, 22 Dec 1985

Jack PALANCE [1920-]

Born: Vladimir Palanuik in Lattimer, Pennsylvania. Studies at The University of North Carolina on a football scholarship and at Stanford University (English major; amateur dramatics) and work on Broadway preceded his film debut in Panic in the Streets (1950, Elia Kazan). In 1953, he played Stark Wilson in George Stevens' Shane:

The very brevity of my part allowed me to put a high shine on it.... If the part had been longer, I couldn't have played it in that flat, completely unemotional way....

—Palance, in *The Saturday Evening Post*, 1 May 1954

[As Wilson] I was trying to get the feel of a hooded cobra.

—Palance, interviewed by Archer Winsten for *The New York Post*, 9 Jan 1956

Lili PALMER [1914-1986]

Born: Maria Lilli Peiser in Posen, Germany (now Poznan, Poland). Work on the German stage (from 1932) preceded her film debut in the British film, Crime Unlimited (1935, Ralph Ince). In 1946, she played Gina in Fritz Lang's Cloak and Dagger:

I quickly made friends with my fellow actors and the stage crew. [Gary] Cooper, the star, didn't behave like one. He sat around with us and listened, said "Yup" now and again, and fell asleep several times a day, a sign that he felt comfortable.

Not so Fritz Lang. He never ate with us and became more unapproachable every day. Any attempt to talk to him and "break down the barriers" was greeted with an icy look and a curt reply. One day during a break, my chair happened to be next to his, so I tried German on him. I told him of the unforgettable impression his film *The Nibelungs* had made on me and my classmates....

He looked at me without a word. Perhaps he didn't believe me. To prove it, I sang the still unforgotten Siegfried motif from the silent film, and, when he still didn't react, the Hagen motif. Delighted at this sudden discovery of an unsuspected musical archive in my memory, I began the Volker motif.

That was too much for him. He got up and brusquely interrupted me, in English. "None of that interests me anymore."

In England I had worked several times with famous directors, including Hitchcock [*The Secret Agent* (1936)]...and Carol Reed [*A Girl Must Live* (1939)]. Every one of them, though occasionally strict, was anxious to have a relaxed, friendly climate in the studio. Fritz Lang was anxious to have the opposite. He was one of the few German refugee directors who were able to continue their illustrious careers without a break in a new country and a new language, a tribute to the quality of his direction. Perhaps he needed tension and an electrically charged atmosphere. I certainly didn't. The moment the clapperboard announced the first take and I heard him bark "Action!" my heart dropped into my boots. What's more, I had the feeling that he wasn't quite so gruff with the other actors and spoke to Cooper in quite a civilized tone. Only when I was alone on camera was he on the warpath.

What impressed me most about [Clark Gable on *But Not for Me* (1959, Walter Lang)] was his sturdy "pro" mentality. Every morning on the stroke of 9 he entered the set, knew his lines to perfection, nodded to the director's suggestions, never disputed them, and carried them out. His contract stipulated that he could go home at 5:00. At 5 minutes to 5 he would glance at his watch and call out a calm, firm, "Five more minutes, boys!" into the air, not caring if anybody heard him or not. On the dot of 5 he would get up and leave. Sometimes we were in the midst of a take, and I pleaded with him to let us finish, but he shook his head. "If I stayed on for a couple of minutes just one single time, that would be the thin edge of the wedge. I work eight hours a day, like everybody else. No more."

The Pleasure of His Company [1961] apparently gave pleasure to a lot of people, and I was signed for a third film by the same team [director George Seaton and producer William Perlberg], by now my friends. I was to play the part of a German resistance fighter during the Hitler years in a film called *The Counterfeit Traitor* [1962], a good story. What's more, a true one.

It seems that in 1942, when the tide of war had turned in favor of the Allies, they managed to blackmail a Swedish businessman named Ericson into doing some all-important spying for them, a task for which his yearly business travels inside Germany fitted him perfectly. His "contact" in that country was a devout Catholic girl called Marianne von Mollendorf. Inevitably they fell in love. In the end Ericson, played by William Holden, could escape, but Marianne was executed in the infamous Moabit prison in Berlin....

Old Ericson, by now in his seventies, a red-faced giant of a man, stayed with us during the shooting to make sure that the details were correct....

The old prison in Moabit, Berlin, is still in use. Some three thousand major criminals live there, a lot of them for life. Our action shots of Marianne's execution were to be filmed at the very spot where she died, in the center courtyard, entirely surrounded by the main cell blocks. The inmates had been told what we were to do during our three-day schedule, and were allowed to watch from behind their barred windows, provided they kept quiet.

I was handed a piece of clothing that the frugal Germans had preserved from the days when it had been "in use," one of the many colorless old garments that had not been destroyed by blood. But I thought I detected stains, and I thought I found bullet holes. I put it on. I was to be "executed" with two other traitors, all in similar outfits. I walked out into the cobbled courtyard and watched while the cameras were being set up. There was the wall against which I was to stand. It was scarred by hundreds of bullet holes. They were the real thing. The wall was the real thing. Marianne had stood in front of it early one morning, had been snuffed out in a few seconds — and then somebody had hosed down the wall and the courtyard.

I looked up. Hundreds of faces were watching me from behind their iron bars. The assistant director called "Ready" and I walked across to the wall. My knees were shaking, my hands dripping wet. I said to myself almost audibly, now don't be a bloody fool. *She* faced the SS firing squad. *You* face the cameras!

No scene was ever easier to act. It played itself. I did nothing — just let myself go. The only difficulty, the usual one, was doing it several times over. In the end I had stopped shaking and had become an actress again.

—Palmer, in her *Change Lobsters — and Dance* (New York: Macmillan, 1975)

Gail PATRICK [1911-1980]

Born: Margaret Fitzpatrick in Birmingham, Alabama. Studies at Howard College preceded her film career begun through a Paramount talent contest. Her debut was in "The Clerk" one of Ernst Lubitsch's sections of If I Had a Million (1932). In 1936, she played Cornelia in Gregory LaCava's My Man Godfrey:

[LaCava] told me I should suck on lemons and beat up little children to prepare as the nasty sister Cornelia. And at first I felt so way out of my league because Carole [Lombard] and Bill Powell knew exactly what they were doing....

LaCava was a madman — he worked between takes to get us to come up with bits of business. He borrowed me again for *Stage Door* [1937] where I was never nastier and told me to underplay — [Katharine] Hepburn and [Ginger] Rogers were having temperamental tifts and I just purred and talked slow in my scenes to get attention.

—Patrick, interviewed by James Bawden for *Films in Review* (NY), May 1981

Katina PAXINOU [1900-1973]

Born: Katina Constantopoulos in Piraeus, Greece. Studies at The Geneva Conservatoire and work with The Greek National Theater and on Broadway preceded her film debut as Pilar in the screen adaptation of Ernest Hemingway's For Whom the Bell Tolls (1943):

Sam Wood waited beside the camera to see me for the first time as Pilar. It was the most difficult moment of my life. Everything was left to me since I had refused to consider the sketch of the character that was shown to me and the responsibility was entirely on my shoulders. The sketch they showed me resembled the Golem dressed up to look like a Mongolian gypsy.

"This is not Pilar," I told them.

"How would you have her look?" I was asked.

"Like a woman who has seen better days, and whose bravery and devotion to the cause leaves no time for fancy dresses," I answered. "Hemingway wrote that 'many men loved her,' so she must give some impression of a past charm and fascination. He also wrote that 'she was all woman.'" "Therefore," I added, "she couldn't have been this Frankenstein."

—Paxinou, interviewed by Terence Kennedy for *Motion Picture*, June 1944

Gregory PECK [1916-]

Born: Eldred Gregory Peck in La Jolla, California. Studies at St. John's Military Academy, The University of California — Berkeley (medicine), and San Diego State U. preceded his entrance into The Neighborhood Playhouse School of Dramatics in N.Y. There, he was noticed by Katharine Cornell and Guthrie McClintic who invited him to join their touring company and later gave him his Broadway debut in 1942's Morning Star. Disqualified from World War II service due to an earlier spinal injury, Peck became one of the new leading men in Hollywood; his debut was Days of Glory (1944, Jacques Tourneur). That same year, he played Father Chisholm in John M. Stahl's adaptation of A.J. Cronin's The Keys of the Kingdom:

It was wonderful to have Dr. Cronin say he liked the picture. I felt he wanted to say something in it that was important to him, about Catholicism, about tolerance, about a man who was always something of a rebel, always in trouble in spite of his good intentions, always unorthodox and yet, in the end, much the best Catholic of them all....

We had a great help on *The Keys* from a Catholic missionary, Father O'Hara, who spoke Chinese and had lived eight years in China. I remember particularly, in one scene where I had to preach in Chinese, how Father O'Hara was persuaded to act out the scene for me. I hadn't been able to catch the feeling of it somehow. I couldn't feel natural. So we asked him to try it. And he did it, walking through that crowd of Chinese extras ringing a little silver bell and talking to each one, in Chinese, after first bowing with the greatest courtesy. He did it as he must have done it a thousand times in real life. Then I realized what I had missed in the scene, that grave courtesy and respect for each person as an individual.

—Peck, interviewed by Eileen Creelman for *The New York Sun*, 27 Dec 1944

I like to be in films that stir up some emotional response in the audience — something like *To Kill a Mockingbird* [1962, Robert Mulligan] or *Roman Holiday* [1954, William Wyler] for instance, or a film that I did when I was very young and green, *The Keys of the Kingdom*, which was the kind of film that an audience responded to emotionally. That's one of those films that I would love to do over because it was such a wonderful part and I was so green that I couldn't really do it justice. All I could do was to invest all the sincerity that I could in it, which I did. That's *all* I was able to do, because I simply wasn't skillful enough to do more.

—Peck, interviewed by Don Shay for *Conversations* (Albuquerque: Kaleidoscope Press, 1969)

I think that Hitchcock knows how to make good copy. And if he said that the preparatory work is all, and the filming is merely a matter of driving the cattle into the corral, I think that is part of his public relations talent. The fact is that he treats actors with great affection, great delicacy. I've never seen him browbeat or put down or humiliate an actor on the set. He's far too wise and too human to do a thing like that. But, of course, he does put great store in preparation, and has every foot of film in his head before he begins. This means that if an actor has been trained in the Stanislavsky system as I was, where the external aspect is theoretically all right if the inner feeling and the thinking is straight — the facial expressions and the bodily attitudes take care of themselves, because they come out of truth: you're recreating a moment that's truthful and therefore the externals are right, that's all well and good, but Hitch knows the facial expressions and the attitudes that he wants. He's already seen them in his mind's eye. So if your inner truth produces a different facial expression, or if you feel like standing differently, or sitting down in another place, then, of course, you do have a bit of a clash with Hitch, because he doesn't like to readjust his thinking in that sense.

With him, given his long record of success, you don't quarrel. You do it his way. I don't think I was at my most effective with him [on *Spellbound* (1945) and *The Paradine Case* (1947)] — not because I didn't like him as a director, but because I wasn't quite flexible enough, nor indeed professional enough yet — it was quite early in my film career, to do everything that he wanted me to do and at the same time to provide my own inner truth. Because it's quite possible to act the other way about, from the externals *in*. Many, many great actors do this. But I wasn't experienced enough to do that.

—Peck, interviewed by Gordon Gow for *Films & Filming*, Sept 1974

[David O. Selznick] took the saint from *The Song of Bernadette* [1943, Henry King] and the noble priest from *The Keys of the Kingdom* and turned us loose in a wild untrammelled sex story [*Duel in the Sun* (1946, King Vidor)] — I think he got a kind of perverse kick out of seeing St. Bernadette [Jennifer Jones] and Father Chisholm going at each other like that. He was chuckling all the time in the background.

—Peck, interviewed by Michael Freedland for *Gregory Peck* (New York: Wm. Morrow & Co., 1980)

What is [Jennifer Jones] really like? Artist and girl? I agree with my friend John Huston, who directed Jennifer in *We Were Strangers* [1949].... John, full of admiration for Jennifer's sensitive performance...commented, "As an actress, Jennifer knows all the things she doesn't know as an individual."

I'll never forget a routine color test she did for *Duel in the Sun*. It was the first time we had met. Jennifer came on the stage wearing a simple cotton dress and flat heeled shoes, her hair hanging girlishly down her back. I thought her lovely and unusual-looking, but when the director gave the down-beat, the girl in the flat heels and cotton dress disappeared. In her stead, there was a sexy creature who looked out of the side of her eyes and walked with a stealthy glide.

—Peck, in *Photoplay Magazine*, June 1949

[In comparison to Hitchcock,] a director like Kazan [on *Gentleman's Agreement* (1947)] would have given one some clue as to what the character was supposed to be thinking. After all, what Bogart said about screen acting is basically true: if you think right, then you look right.

—Peck, interviewed by Michael Billington for *The Times*, 9 Nov 1968

I remember the back projection that was used on *The Snows of Kilimanjaro* [1952, Henry King]. They don't use that now because audiences are too sophisticated. You'd find yourself acting in front of a screen, with flickering images. There was one scene where Ava Gardner and I were supposed to be in a crocodile-infested river. We were paddling along with some Los Angeles black extras done up in African costumes — and on the screen behind us was a river with crocodiles. And when I had to shoot a rhino, it'd be on the screen. I'd be standing there, feeling foolish. A red light would flash just off camera and that meant the rhino was about to go down — so you went "Bam!"

—Peck, interviewed by Michael Buckley for *Films in Review* (NY), May 1984

I think I did some of my best work for Henry King, who I just seemed to have a good rapport with. Henry was a man's man, warm, humorous, strong, an expert technician, prepared. He didn't always direct me meticulously, in great detail. He'd sort of sit back and see what I had to offer, and then he'd make little adjustments and changes on what I brought to the part. You wanted to come in well-prepared and well-studied with him, because he went at his work that way; you felt you were performing for a friend who wanted you to be your best. So, the working atmosphere was warm. I think I made more pictures with him than with any other single director. [Peck also worked on King's *Twelve O'Clock High* (1949), *The Gunfighter* (1950), *David and Bathsheba* (1952), *The Bravados* (1958) and *Beloved Infidel* (1959).]

—Peck, interviewed by Ron Haver for *American Film*, Mar 1989

For my own part I was unable to overcome the feeling that Ahab [in *Moby Dick* (1956, John Huston)] was an old lunatic. Whether you take it on the level that he's pursuing a dumb brute who chewed off his leg, pursuing purely for revenge — on that level it's an adventure tale, or

you take it on the level that the white whale represents a malevolent deity, toying with creatures of his own creation and visiting them with pestilence and suffering, he's still an old lunatic.
—Peck, interviewed by Gordon Gow for *Films & Filming*, Sept 1974

[John] Huston was not that great an actor's director. When people were perfectly cast, like Bogart and Lorre and Greenstreet, he was great with them. But he was not very good at helping actors to find a performance. I think that John really didn't have that much respect for the craft of acting. Writers and directors were people who made the movies, and actors were the people to be dealt with. Certainly, he had his gifts, but I don't think it was in the direction of helping an actor to find the center of the role and get to it.
—Peck, interviewed by Ron Haver for *American Film*, Mar 1989

Here's the real plot of [*The Guns of Navarone* (1961, J. Lee Thompson)]. David Niven really loves Tony Quayle and Gregory Peck loves Anthony Quinn. Tony Quayle breaks a leg and is sent off to hospital. Tony Quinn falls in love with Irene Papas and David Niven and Peck catch each other on the rebound and live happily ever after.
—Peck, interviewed by Michael Freedland for *Gregory Peck* (New York: William Morrow & Co., 1980)

To Kill a Mockingbird is a special memory. It was so easy for me to do. It was just like putting on a comfortable well-worn suit of clothes. It was never any strain. I identified emotionally with everything that happened in that story. With the character I played and with the children in the small-town life. There was something about it. It was as if I were born to do it.... Yet, it was more like a gift from Harper Lee — the author. I feel I was lucky to be there at the right time. And to be her idea of the best man to play it.
—Peck, interviewed by Clive Denton for *Marquee*, June/July 1976

I don't like the parallel — it's too easy — but this man [Manuel Artiguez] in *Behold a Pale Horse* (1964, Fred Zinnemann)] is really like an aging matador who feels compelled to make a last comeback. It is a peculiar obsession of the Spanish to restate the simple fact of their manhood — and to restate it regularly.

The guerrilla fighter and the matador are both specialists. Many of the exiles had been fighting for 10 years. They joined the French resistance during World War II — and knew no other trade. When the fighting ended, they were cast-offs.

I tried to convey a man with a spiritual canker gnawing at him, a man who feels he has been put on the shelf, who sees the exile movement eroding.
—Peck, interviewed by Leonard Harris for *The New York World-Telegram and Sun*, 17 Aug 1964

When I first thought of doing [General Douglas] MacArthur [in *MacArthur* (1977, Joseph Sargeant)], I disliked him. No. That isn't right. I didn't dislike him, I just had a natural old-time Democratic liberal suspicion that he was willing to start World War III in Korea to — as he saw it — rid the world of the menace of Communism.

But I couldn't reconcile the contradictions in MacArthur. The more I studied, the many myths about him turned out to be just gossip. The truth is, his career is almost unblemished, a total success. Militarily, he was right in Korea, the Russians weren't about to have World War III start there.

When MacArthur ran head-on into [President] Truman [Ed Flanders] over war policy, he was wrong, of course, constitutionally. But the man was 72 years old. He was brought up on Army posts in the West while his father was still fighting Geronimo. He was indoctrinated at West Point in the idea that his job was to win wars. He was a 19th-century man. To ask him at this point in his career to fight to a stalemate in Korea was shortsighted and ill advised....

I had a talk with Laurence Olivier after he'd heard I was going to do MacArthur. He reached over and poked me in the solar plexus, and asked, "How is your breath control?" He knew that MacArthur wrote with flair and spoke in grand, rotund phrases. In that kind of speech, you have to have the breath to carry through to the end of the phrase. You just can't gasp for breath in the middle.

[Olivier also said] "No matter how heavy the drama, you must always look for the foibles of the character, and exploit them in tragedy." I did my best to take this advice.... MacArthur was absurd, pompous and egotistical. There was never any attempt to glorify him. I wanted the warts and the foibles and the vanities. That's part of him. [Peck and Olivier co-starred in *The Boys from Brazil* (1978, Franklin J. Schaffner).]
—Peck, interviewed by William P. Luce for *The New York Times*, 11 July 1977

Anthony PERKINS [1932-1992]

Born: New York City; son of actor Osgood Perkins (1892-1937). Studies at Rollins College and Columbia University and work on the stage (from 1946) preceded his film debut in The Actress (1953, George Cukor). In 1956, he played Gary Cooper's son, Josh Birdwell, in William Wyler's Friendly Persuasion:

I think Gary Cooper is a great actor. A *very* great actor. I studied him every minute of the time we were working together on *Friendly Persuasion*. Not just because I wanted to mimic him and to increase the feeling that I was really his son, but because he's *good*.... If people want to say I'm like him, why that's fine.

—Perkins, interviewed by Laura Lane for *Photoplay Magazine*, Jan 1957

Q. What was it like working with William Wyler in *Friendly Persuasion*?

A. Well, I'd only met him twice before we started the picture and the first thing we did was to read the script through, and we were all very nervous. We came to my first scene, my first sentence which was "Hurry up or you'll be late to church." Something of that nature. And I said it and he said, "Nope that's not it. That's not the character at all." Everyone was sitting around this table and I was feeling, you know, getting smaller and smaller and he outlined the character in about three minutes. And it was beautifully done, very concise, exactly what he wanted. And that was just the explicit and specific information I had from him. We had a marvelous relationship, or at least I felt that we did. It was fun. I used to come in in the morning with four different ways to play every scene that we were to shoot that day. And we'd get off in the corner and I'd run them down, and he'd sit there kind of biting his knuckle and I'd do the first thing. He'd say, "No." The second one, "No." The third one, he'd say, "Hold on to that." He'd say, "let's see the fourth." And I'd do the fourth one. He'd say, "Do the third one again." And he'd say, "That's the one." And we'd film it that way. Willy...oh, there are so many terrific things about him. Much has been made about his lack of articulation with actors, that he'll just come up and say, "I think it should be more, uh...kind of less..." and then back away. Well, actually I think he does it on purpose, it makes *you* think, "What the hell is he talking about?" and it makes you think you're not quite so instructed, you're not quite so dictated to. In other words, you don't become so passive and you're kept thinking every minute. One great thing he told us once. We were doing a scene — we'd done about four takes and there'd been technical difficulties. He said, "All right, we'll do it once more." The cameras are rolling. He said, "Please, no better." It seemed a strange thing to say at the time but I realized that the natural urge an actor has to improve every take which finally will lead to pressing and pushing and making things unnatural, overstated. And Willy's statement, "No better," once more but no better, was a very rich two words.

—Perkins, interviewed for *Cinema*, Mar/Apr 1965

I think the role [of Norman Bates] in *Psycho* [1960, Alfred Hitchcock] is one of the greatest gambles I've taken because if that picture hadn't worked, if the public's acceptance of the role hadn't been as complete as it was, it might have been a very disadvantageous thing for an actor to play. I discussed this question very frankly with Hitchcock. He agreed that it was a gamble...but he suggested that I give it a try anyway.

—Perkins, interviewed by Robin Bean for *Films & Filming*, July 1965

Of course [Hitchcock's] been quoted many times either correctly or incorrectly, that he thought of actors as cattle. When we started [*Psycho*] I had actually never met him but once, and I was very apprehensive about making any statements about what I thought, what I felt about the character and about different scenes. But, even as the first day proceeded I could see he wanted to know what I thought and what I wanted to do and I was really very surprised by this. I kind of tentatively made a small suggestion about something I might do. He said, "Do it." And later I suggested changing a "but" to and "and." He said, "Go ahead." I got to relaxing more with him and making more and more suggestions and ideas. At the end of the picture, I realized I'd worked with THE director who had been more open to the actor's suggestions and ideas than any I'd ever worked with before, with the possible exception of William Wyler. Since that was the reverse of what I'd expected of Hitchcock, it came as a great surprise....

Q. Did you, on your own, add much to the action of the character you played?

A. No...the only thing I added, and I added it a little bit late in the picture so I don't know how clear it is, but that is my eating of the candy corn which is always in my pocket. I kept nibbling on it through the whole picture. I came to him one morning and said, "What about if Norman is always chewing on candy? If in all his pockets he's got candy?" "Fine, fine." He didn't even think, he didn't have to stop to think if it was right or wrong. He has the kind of mind that can instantaneously accept or reject a suggestion. Sometimes I would say, "Hitch, why don't we try....?" Before I said it, he knew. "No, that's not right. Forget it." You know, to many directors you may make a suggestion, and the next half hour is spent in great, soul searching, agonizing reflection on whether it's right or not. Finally you lose enthusiasm for it because you're afraid you're holding the picture up. But with Hitchcock no matter what you said he had the answer almost before it was out of your mouth.

—Perkins, interviewed for *Cinema*, Mar/Apr 1965

It was one of those crazy unplanned things that I came to do *The Trial* [1963, Orson Welles]. I got a call from [Anatole] Litvak [for whom he had made *Aimez-vous Brahms*? (1961)] saying, "Orson Welles wants to get in touch with you.... He acted as a kind of go-between between Welles and myself....

The biggest problem for me on that film was the simple technical one that I don't like to work at night, and I do my best work, my best scene or shot is always before noon and from then on till 6 I'm all right but...the earlier the better. Orson doesn't really feel like doing it until after dinner and from then on until dawn. He himself has told me many times that he doesn't really like to go to sleep until he can see the outlines of buildings against the sky as morning is breaking. This to me is a horrifying idea and it was very hard to stay with it all night — we frequently shot through all night long.

Q. How was Welles to work with?

A. Absolutely great. He'll listen to any suggestion, he'll take it very seriously, he's extremely patient with the actors, he never loses his temper, never becomes impatient. Even with the greatest problem — it may be a financial one — on the picture where the assistant director tells him, "We've got to be out of here in half an hour," and we have still 4 setups to do, if the actor needs something Orson will always, always, supply it.

He can speak to the actor in any way that the actor responds to — if it's a physical, mental, Stanislavski, personal or emotional way, Orson will direct the actor in the vocabulary that the actor responds to. It is a very distinct trait which few directors have: Hitchcock has it, so does Wyler, Bob Mulligan [with whom he worked on *Fear Strikes Out* (1957)], and Jules Dassin [on *Phaedra* (1962)]....

Q. How many of the actors did Welles in fact dub himself?

A. I can hear at least a dozen. Orson probably dubbed more than that.

Dubbing is a fantastic art. In *The Trial* there wasn't one line of original track. Orson's theory, and it's one I wholeheartedly subscribe to, is that the very least you can expect in dubbing is as good as the original. I hated dubbing until I did *The Trial*; then I realized the possibilities of it.

—Perkins, interviewed by Robin Bean for *Films & Filming*, July 1965

Q. How was it playing opposite [Welles]?

A. I didn't have that pleasure because we were running out of something...I don't remember what it was, it was money, or film, or time on me, or time on him, but we shot all my scenes with him from my angles. Then later, when the picture was all finished, he just came back with a skeleton crew and shot his angles, working from a moviola and what I did. So I didn't get to work with him as an actor. But there's not a day of that entire picture that I would hesitate living over. It was a very eye-opening experience.

—Perkins, interviewed for *Cinema*, Mar/Apr 1965

Valerie PERRINE [1943-]

Born: Galveston, Texas. Work as a show girl and lead dancer in Las Vegas preceded her film debut in Slaughterhouse Five (1972, George Roy Hill). In 1974, she played Honey Bruce in Bob Fosse's Lenny:

Q. What was it like having to play a real person as opposed to playing a character made up by a screenwriter?

A. I think Honey Bruce was very close to being made up by a screenwriter, not that close to what she's really like. She was really sweetened up and cleaned up and events were switched around to make it look as though Lenny had talked her into doing certain things, when she had as much to do with it as Lenny did...from what I hear....

Q. Was the lesbian scene challenging for you?

A. I didn't think I'd be able to do it. I kept going up to Fosse saying, "I can't do it! You may as well cut it! I just can't do it! I don't know it, what am I going to do?" You know? Not that I have anything against it whatsoever at all, but I just had nothing to fall back on, no experience to use, and I was scared to death. But Kathy Witt, the girl they used, turned out to be very sweet and very nice and *super* scared. I mean *shaking* when I first met her. So I became like a big sister, you know. All of a sudden I had to be brave because she wasn't! And it turned out to be a very easy thing to do because Bob did it like a dance number. It was choreographed. It was a movement here and a movement there and there was slow music playing and it became a very technical thing we were doing. It wasn't emotional at all....

Q. Did your experience as a showgirl help you at all with the scene in *Lenny* where you do the strip?

A. As a matter of fact I had brought in my costume from the Lido shows to have it copied. That was my Lido make-up.... And that was definitely my Lido strut!

—Perrine, interviewed by George Abagnalo for *Interview*, Jan 1975

Joe PESCI [1943-]

Born: Newark, N.J. Following work on TV as a child and later in regional theatre, he made his film debut in The Death Collector (1976, Ralph DeVito). In 1980, he played Joey LaMotta in Martin Scorsese's Raging Bull:

Somebody asked me the other day which I'd rather do — comedy or drama — since I've done both, and I said, "What you said: Both." I have a tendency to make you laugh when I'm serious. Sometimes it's wisecracking or sometimes it's just flippy, but it helps. There is that place where you can do drama and still make people laugh. Some of it was in *Raging Bull*. Martin Scorsese has a great flair for this.

[The real Joey LaMotta] thought I portrayed him too violently, beating people up, things like that, but I don't think so. Actually, I painted a nice picture of the guy. He was a loyal brother, and you can't ask for more than that....

—Pesci, interviewed by Harry Haun for *The New York Daily News*, 16 July 1989

I don't think any of the guys I play are really sleazy. They all basically change, except for Tommy [DeVito in *GoodFellas* (1990, Martin Scorsese)], and he dies. He was just a victim of his own environment. I don't think of him as a a bad person totally. He was a little on the edge; I mean, no doubt about it. But he loved his mother [Catherine Scorsese]. He didn't, like, mug old ladies on the subway and beat them up and take their money. If he killed somebody, it was somebody who thought they were a tough guy or who was in the wrong. He was playing by that law, and that's it. I tried to make him charming in a way, interesting, fascinating, funny. He was very passionate about whatever he did. He just had this one little quirk.... He liked to kill people....

[As an actor] I try to go all the way. I identify with the roles I play. Tommy could not back down in any situation. If he wanted to uphold a certain place in that society, he had to let everyone s--- when his name was mentioned or when he walked in the room. No one would ever stick him for money. No one would ever try to f--- him because of the way he was, which is the way you have to be in *that* business. What people really understand is fear. What they respect is fear, quicker than kindness.

Marty, as great as he is, allows things to happen without getting in the way. People want to know what makes him such a great director. Because he leaves actors *alone*. He knew how to guide me; he gave me the setup; he gave me the space; and I came up with the stories. When I had an idea that he thought was great, he made the spot for it. And working with De Niro is fantastic. He's very giving. You never have to worry about getting a false beat from him. He just worries about the scene. If he had to shut up during the scene and let you go, he does that. There's a thing especially with Scorsese and De Niro. Right after the scene, you all look at each other and Marty will go, "What do you think, does it feel right to you?" And if one of us said, "Well, I don't know," we explore it.

—Pesci, interviewed by Phoebe Hoban for *New York*, 4 Mar 1991

Michelle PFEIFFER [1958-]

Born: Santa Ana, California. Work in beauty pageants and commercials preceded her film debut in Falling in Love Again (1980, Steven Paul). In 1988, she played Madame de Tourvel in Stephen Frears' adaptation of Dangerous Liaisons:

[Playing Madame de Tourvel in *Dangerous Liaisons* (1988, Stephen Frears)] was emotionally demanding and very draining.

I remember sometimes sitting in my trailer as they were setting up for a scene and knowing I had to go in there and cry again and just not wanting to do it, just sitting there and saying, "I don't want to do this."

Because my work was condensed into a short time, every scene was some kind of a heavy scene; there were no sort of light days, and doing a period film is very difficult; you're corseted for 12 hours and some days longer than that. You can't ever just relax, and it's really draining. Usually, you do a movie and you have one or two scenes that scare you, that you're not really looking forward to doing. But in this script I had quite a few of them.

—Pfeiffer, interviewed by Robert Lindsey for *The New York Times*, 1 Jan 1989

The description of [Frankie in *Frankie and Johnny* (1991, Garry Marshall)] is that Frankie is an attractive woman if she'd just put a little effort into how she looks. So that's basically the way I played her. I consider myself an attractive woman, and I can be not-so-great-looking if I don't put any effort into how I look. But more important, the core of the character is someone who has given up on love, and that could be any age, any size, any form of beauty. That could be anybody.

—Pfeiffer, interviewed by Cyndi Stivers for *Premiere*, Oct 1991

I was excited about the opportunity of just playing an ordinary person, with everyday fears, everyday struggles, everyday sorrows. There's a fantasy that beautiful people can't look unattractive or aren't lonely or aren't hurt. It's all fantasy that if you're considered attractive you have a perfect life and there's no dark side. Everybody goes through shutting down and being hurt and being frightened. Everybody.

The heart of the character, the heart of the movie, is about loneliness. You know the amazing thing about human beings is that when it comes to love, no matter how beat up you think you are, no matter how scarred or wounded or down you've become, when it comes to love you can somehow manage to muster up the courage to open yourself up one more time. It doesn't matter what you look like and how old you are. That's not relevant.

—Pfeiffer, interviewed by Bernard Weinraub for *The New York Times*, 6 Oct 1991

Mary PICKFORD [1893-1979]

Born: Gladys Marie Smith in Toronto, Ontario, Canada. Work on the stage (from age 5) preceded her film debut in Her First Biscuits (1909, D.W. Griffith); between 1909 and 1912, she acted in 75 of Griffith's two-reelers.

I went into pictures in 1909. I refused to exaggerate in my performances, and my brother Jack wouldn't either. Nobody ever directed me, not even Mr. Griffith. I respected him, yes. I even had an affection for him, but when he told me to do things I didn't believe in, I wouldn't do them. I would *not* run around like a goose with its head cut off, crying "Oooooh...the little birds! Oooooh...look! A little bunny!" That's what he taught his ingenues, and they all did the same thing.

"I'm a grown girl. I'm sixteen years old. I won't do it!" I said....

But he taught me a lot. For instance, in one picture I was a poor little girl, and I had this miserable little coat on, with a moth-eaten fur collar, and a funny little hat with a bird on it. I came into my room, threw the hat on the bed, and threw my coat on top of it. Griffith stopped the camera.

Now to stop the camera in those days, with film costing something like two cents a foot, was unheard of. He walked over to the set and said, "Pickford, you'll never do that again. You'll never come in and throw your hat on the bed and put your coat down without shaking it. You must take care of your clothes. No heroine is untidy."

I said, "Yes, sir."

"Now, Pickford, you go back and come in again. Camera, Bitzer."

I thought, "Mr. Griffith's right." So I went outside and came back in, took my coat off, shook it, brushed the fur, fixed the little bird on the hat, put it down on the chair, and put my coat carefully on the back.

Mr. Griffith said, "Very good."

That was the way he directed me. He once said that he could sit back of the camera, think something, and I'd do it.

—Pickford, interviewed (1965) by Kevin Brownlow for *The Parade's Gone By* (New York: Alfred A. Knopf, 1968)

I was twenty-two years old when I played that unforgettable little eleven-year-old from Sunnybrook Farm [Rebecca in *Rebecca of Sunnybrook*

Farm (1917, Marshall Neilan)]. But I enjoyed the part as if I were still a child myself....

Another child's role that I played when I was an adult was Sara Crewe of *The Little Princess* [1917].

I was supposed to look like a girl of eight or ten. In order to create the illusion of a small child everything I touched had to be a third bigger than life.... If I touched a glass it would be a third larger than any actual glass. Knobs of doors were both larger and higher, and of course the people I worked with were selected for their abnormal height. I believe the men averaged six feet three or four. Of course there was the initial advantage of my being rather small myself.

It was in *The Little Princess* that my director Marshall (Mickey) Neilan began using off-stage tricks to get me into the right humor for a scene. Zasu Pitts was playing a scullery maid in that film.... There was one scene where it was important to catch the slow spread of laughter on my face as I turned suddenly and caught Zasu going through a comical routine of being a grand lady. Mickey wanted to photograph the laughter being born in my eyes, from the first blank surprise to the final hilarious outburst.

In the midst of that crescendo of mirth out pranced Charlie Chaplin and my brother Jack, draped in mounts of artificial flowers and pieces of old lace and ribbon; Jack with a hideous hemp wig which he had on backwards. Safe from the eye of the camera, but within the range of my own, they proceeded to do a spring dance — cavorting about with trouser legs rolled up, while Mickey whistled Mendelssohn's "Spring Song"!

I think Mickey was satisfied with the results....

If reincarnation should prove to be true, and I had to come back as one of my roles, I suppose some avenging fate would return me to earth as Pollyanna — "the glad girl."

While making the film in 1919 [directed by Paul Powell] I remember I got so sick of Pollyanna in the seventh or eighth week of production that I finally rebelled. I decided the saintly little creature was just too good to be true. There was nothing in the script to indicate the slightest lapse from saintliness in the intolerable weeks ahead. I was appalled at the prospect of unrelieved goodness. My chance to revolt finally came. While the cameras were grinding away one day, I caught a fly on the table, scooped it up and said, "Little fly, do you want to go to heaven?" With that I smacked my two hands together and said, "You have!" That fly in the ointment of Pollyanna's purity was definitely not in the script, but it remained in the picture. Sickening as I found *Pollyanna*, the public did not agree with me. It proved to be one of my most successful pictures.

I was twenty-seven years old when I played one of my most successful children — Little Lord Fauntleroy [in *Little Lord Fauntleroy* (1921, Adolph E. Green and Jack Pickford)]. In this film I also portrayed Little Lord Fauntleroy's mother. Nowadays trick photography, trick sets, and parallel takes are a commonplace, but in those days every new device was an adventure, every new camera angle a discovery.

People were baffled that I looked nine inches taller as a mother than I did as the boy.

Three of those inches came from an elevated ramp on which I walked whenever Little Lord Fauntleroy was beside me. I got my idea for the remaining six inches from a practice adopted centuries ago by some enterprising young ladies of Venice. I had read that they used to wear shoes that gave them a height they thought more appropriate to their rank. So I had a pair of these "platforms" made....

—Pickford, in her *Sunshine and Shadow* (Garden City, N.Y.: Doubleday & Co., 1956)

Walter PIDGEON [1897-1984]

Born: East St. John, New Brunswick, Canada. Studies at The University of New Brunswick and The New England Conservatory of Music in Boston and work with The Copley Players in Boston and on the London and New York stages, preceded his film debut in Mannequin (1926, James Cruze). In 1941, he played The Reverend Gruffydd in John Ford's How Green Was My Valley:

The Reverend Gruffydd, with his rumpled clothes and loosely knotted ties, was a welcome change from the well-groomed men of the world I had been portraying. More than that, he was a profoundly appealing character, with a message I could thoroughly believe in.

His entire life was motivated by idealism and self-sacrifice. He strove unceasingly to improve conditions in his little Welsh mining village. He did not believe that a minister's duties ended with the preaching of sermons, but tried instead to make his sermons come true in the lives of the people around him.

He renounced his love for Angharad [Maureen O'Hara] because he could not bear to have her share the life of poverty he had chosen.

Angharad married another man and went to South Africa, but she was unable to get along with her husband and came back. She and Gruffydd seldom even saw each other, but vicious gossip about them spread over the village. The minister's faith in basic human goodness was severely tested. He delivered a challenging sermon, which was the scene I liked best.

"Why do you come here?" he rebuked his congregation. "Why do you dress your hypocrisy in black and parade it before your God on Sunday? You have proved that your hearts are too withered to receive the love of the Divine Master."

It was one of the most outspoken moral lessons the movies have ever dared to convey: that going to church means nothing unless we put its teachings into practice in our daily lives.

—Pidgeon, in *The Saturday Evening Post*, 27 Apr 1946

I'd never worked with John Ford before. It comes under the heading of a profound experience. So far I've been fortunate in always having good directors in Hollywood....

But I'd never known a director like Ford. After making *How Green Was My Valley*, I've been forced to the conclusion that the man operates by telepathy. He smokes a pipe constantly. I doubt if he removes the pipe from his mouth except to eat. He never removes it merely to talk. Furthermore, when Ford speaks, he mumbles. There's no kinder expression for it. He definitely mumbles. I listened to his instructions, and five intelligible words out of seventy-five were a good hearing average.

With most directors, the result of such obscurity would be helpless confusion. With Ford, no. You go out on the set and find yourself following orders you haven't heard. Readily and naturally you act exactly what Ford had in mind, and, only later, with a perceptible shock, do you ask yourself how you did it. The only answer is telepathy.

But do you want to know the biggest bouquet I can toss to John Ford? It's this. When an actor has to get up at 6, and his scenes for the day are over at, say, 11 in the morning, most of us rush off for home and bed as fast as we can. But in *How Green Was My Valley*, for the first time in my Hollywood record, I stayed in the studio all afternoon, simply to watch Ford work. The man generates inspiration. He really hypnotizes his cast, so all of them are held by a sort of beneficent spell....

—Pidgeon, interviewed for *The New York Herald Tribune*, 2 Nov 1941

The beard helped my characterization of Pierre [in *Madame Curie* (1943, Mervyn LeRoy)] immeasurably. Without the beard, I would have been handicapped. I would have been undeniably Walter Pidgeon and not Pierre Curie.

Acting is the art of being what you are not. Pierre was a quiet, sensitive sincere scientist. I tried to give an honest performance of the man, and make him believable. I made a careful study of him and adopted mannerisms and a way of speaking that seemed to me best suited to his character. But the beard was a major factor in my interpretation of Pierre. It gave me the feeling of actually walking in his shoes.

—Pidgeon, interviewed for the press book for *Madame Curie* (MGM, 1943)

Joan PLOWRIGHT [1929-]

Born: Scunthorpe, England. Studies at The Laban Art of Movement Studio and at The Old Vic Theatre School and work on the London stage preceded her film debut in The Entertainer (1960, Tony Richardson). In 1977, she played Mrs. Strang in Sidney Lumet's version of Equus:

As a parent, there is a part of me that identifies with the mother in the play. I can imagine her bewilderment at being blamed for her son's grotesque behavior. A lot of parents feel that they give their children all they can in the way of education and love, and yet they can't finally account for what that child [Peter Firth as Alan Strang] does, what he becomes. Maybe what the play is saying is that we are all born alone and we all die alone, and somewhere in the middle we become individuals, something which is not made up of what our mothers and fathers gave us, but a unique soul. That's what the mother says — "Every soul is itself."

—Plowright, interviewed by Guy Flatley for *The New York Times*, 29 Oct 1976

Sidney POITIER [1924-]

Born: Miami, Florida, to Bahamian parents on a tomato selling venture. Leaving home at 15, he eventually settled in New York where he worked as a dishwasher before studying at The American Negro Theater. He made his Broadway debut in an all-black production of Lysistrata (1946); his commercial film debut was in No Way Out (1950,

Joseph L. Mankiewicz). In 1957, he played Rau-ru in Raoul Walsh's Band of Angels:

Martin Baum struck a deal with Warner Brothers Studios that sent me off to Baton Rouge, Louisiana, to appear in a picture, *Band of Angels*, starring Clark Gable and Yvonne De Carlo. I had a featured role as Clark Gable's son (would you believe)....

Watching Clark Gable play the principal role in that picture turned out to be a lesson in professionalism. He came to work each day knowing every word of his dialogue — every word. When director Raoul Walsh called for a rehearsal, Gable would play the scene exactly the way he was going to play it in front of the camera. Exactly. Impressed with his ability to commit to memory ten or more pages of dialogue, and on a moment's notice execute them without a single fluff, I set about picking his brain, trying to ferret out how he did it. That he studied his scripts aggressively and that he sometimes put his lines on tape to be played back while he slept was about all he would allow me to unearth. But there had to be more, and I wondered what the missing elements could be. If I hadn't been so young and flip, I would have recognized them easily. I would have seen an old, tough professional who had been pounded into shape by the grueling regimen of the proving ground that was the American film business in the vibrant thirties, where one could learn only by doing — doing — and doing.

Everyone in the cast [of *Porgy and Bess* (1959)] anticipated some difficulty with Otto Preminger because of his notorious reputation for being harsh on actors; we had all heard the many stories about him chewing up actors and spitting them out.... Mr. Preminger had worked with blacks before. Having made a picture with Harry Belafonte and Dorothy Dandridge called *Carmen Jones* [1954], he was not entirely new to us as a group, and word came down suggesting that he was a liberal on the question of race. And it was soon established that he *was* indeed a liberal when it came to racial questions, but he was also a tyrant whose monster within surfaced frequently on his bad days. At our first meeting I looked for telltale signs to confirm the presence of furies lying dormant somewhere in the strong, muscular, bald-headed director. Unless I missed something, no sign appeared, he was as charming as a minister, and checked out normal — he was sweet, kind, loved to tell stories, laughed a lot and was fun to be around. During rehearsal time he never once raised his voice, and was very patient and considerate with each actor, even those who were slow in getting to what he was attempting to convey. All went very nicely indeed....

It happened, I think, on the first day I started to work. Otto Preminger jumped on Dorothy Dandridge in a shocking and totally unexpected way. She had done something that wasn't quite the way he wanted it. "What's the matter with you, Dorothy?" he exploded at her. "You're supposed to be an actress. Now what kind of an actress are you that you can't do such a simple thing?" I thought: Well, he's a little irrational now and it looks like it's not going to be a smooth day, but I never anticipated events moving so quickly to the next level. After a brief pause during which he seemed to be calling his monster to heel, he said, "All right, we're going to do it again and I want you to give it to me the way you did it in rehearsals. Okay, let's take it from the top." Dorothy Dandridge, visibly shaken, started the scene again, hoping to recapture the missing ingredient and save herself from further embarrassment. She hadn't proceeded very far before he exploded again. "No, no, no — what's the matter with you? You can't even do a simple thing like that? That's stupid, what you're doing — you don't have any intelligence at all. What kind of a dumb way for a girl to behave! You don't even know who Bess is. You call yourself an actress — you get paid to perform, not to do stupid things." And on he went. Well, I heard it — watched it — analyzed and categorized it — because one day sure as hell my turn was to come.

Nobody went to Dorothy's defense. The rationale was, since he was not abusing her physically, since his attacks remained verbal, no matter how brutal, it was still an "artistic dispute" between the director and his actress....

—Poitier, in his *This Life* (New York: Alfred A. Knopf, 1980)

I liked playing Homer [in *Lilies of the Field* (1963, Ralph Nelson)] because he is a nice man. Just a nice man. I was tired of playing villains and those other roles.

—Poitier, interviewed by Wanda Hale for *The New York Daily News*, 28 Oct 1963

As actors, well — I tell you [Katharine Hepburn and Spencer Tracy] were giants. It wasn't easy for me to work opposite them [in *Guess Who's Coming to Dinner?* (1967, Stanley Kramer)]. I wasn't able to get this out of my head: I am here playing a scene with Tracy and Hepburn! It was all so overwhelming I couldn't remember my lines. With the other actors I was fine. The long, tough father/son scene with Roy Glenn, in which I had page long speeches to make, went smooth as silk without a hitch — no stumbling, no bobbling, we sailed right through it, and it turned out to be a terrific scene, a highlight of the picture. But when I went to play a scene with Tracy and Hepburn, I couldn't remember a word. Finally Stanley Kramer said to me, "What are we going to do?" I said, "Stanley, send those two people home. I will play the scene against two empty chairs. I don't want them here because I can't handle that kind of company." He sent them home. I played the scene in close-up against two chairs as the dialogue coach read Mr. Tracy's and Miss Hepburn's lines from off camera.

—Poitier, in his *This Life* (New York: Alfred A. Knopf, 1980)

I have never met a producer who was not interested in my concept of the "blackness" of a script. However, "blackness" has changed in concept over the last twenty years. What was of particular value to us in terms of our priorities twenty years ago was antiquated five years later; and what was important ten years ago is today quite old hat. I have to speak in the context of what was at that time. I sought to present as forceful an image as I could, counter to the prevalent one.

The prevalent image in those days was that "the niggers" were lazy, shiftless, screwed around a lot. I tried — if you will examine the films — to present that which was most lacking: a guy with a job other than the ten menials. So, I played a lot of doctors, a lot of lawyers. I played a psychiatrist for Stanley Kramer [in *Guess Who's Coming to Dinner?*]. That was *that* time, and it was, to my mind, a very interesting period. Many of those films are certainly heavily dated today, but I believe in the historical evolution of things: Those of us who are black here are in this room partly because of that history. I've had job opportunities partly because there were black actors before me who died and never had a shot, you see. I am here partly because of the dues they paid — and I am talking about Frank Wilson, Canada Lee, Rex Ingram, Hattie McDaniel, Louise Beavers.

—Poitier, interviewed for *Dialogue on Film*, *American Film*, Sept 1976

Eleanor POWELL [1910-1982]

Born: Springfield, Massachusetts. A child performer in Atlantic City clubs, she made her Broadway debut in 1929. Known for her tap style, she made her film debut in George White's 1935 Scandals (George White). In 1937, she played the title role in Rosalie, directed by W.S. Van Dyke:

I had to train with real cadets for *Rosalie*; they had about thirty-four West Point cadets. They embellished the rest with the chorus boys. The head man from West Point came down and taught me that drill.

The drum number was my own idea. We went on the backlot at night to shoot that and it was slippery because the dew had settled on the drumheads.... We had to stop production and put corking on top of each drum because we'd forgotten about the dampness....

It was very dangerous, they were big drums. They didn't use a double for me. I had to learn how to do a line of turns down those drums — turn and dip a little bit but not break the flow of the turn. Oh, that was hard! The top drum was about 75 feet high and they had to hoist me up there. I could have done that number better but I was just holding back a little bit because I was afraid of the dew.

—Powell, interviewed by John Kobal for *Focus on Film*, Spring 1975

William POWELL [1892-1984]

Born: Pittsburgh. Studies at The American Academy of Dramatic Arts, work on Broadway (from 1912) and in stock preceded his film debut in Sherlock Holmes (1922, Albert Parker). In 1923, he played Tito in Henry King's Romola:

Tito in *Romola* was an ambitious man. He married the woman he loved and because he found her cold, he took the little peasant girl [Dorothy Gish] and had with her the simple peasant-like life he craved. But he didn't go around making fools of women just because it was easy, or he could.

—Powell, interviewed by Marie House for *Screenland*, Apr 1931

In *The Bright Shawl* [1923, John S. Robertson] and *Romola*, the villain's character was defined clearly. He had characteristics and motives....

This isn't true in the average movie. In a picture like Aloma [*of the South Seas* (1926, Maurice Tourneur)], the villain is there for artificial reasons. The playwright sat down to write before he really had a play. All he had was the central character of the island girl [Gilda Gray], which he desired to show in various emotional climaxes.

Therefore he required a menace. The menace must be a villain and [the author] must run the heroine into certain difficulties and dispose of the villain promptly when the time comes.... He has no place in the scheme of life and is required to indulge in the most fantastic behavior, with only rickety motivation for his actions. Such a part is handed the man who plays the villain.

It is up to the man playing that part to make his character seem possible and real. To justify faulty motivation the actor must add such eccentricities to the superficial part of the character as will convince the audience this particular man might be erratic enough to want to marry a woman whether she loved him or not, and all the rest of it. When the author sends him to walk into the obvious trap of a savage's canoe on a shark-infested lagoon the fellow playing the villain must somehow make you think he is sufficiently befuddled and sufficient of a fool to go. That is not always easy.

—Powell, interviewed for *The Kansas City Star*, 29 Jan 1927

I went along for years, playing heavies, the villain of the piece. During all that time the public's 'care' for me was certainly not remarkable. Then I made *Interference* [1929, Lothar Mendes and Roy Pomeroy] with Clive Brook and Evelyn Brent. It was my first talking picture and instantly my status changed. There was that sympathetic reaction.... It was just because I had played a sympathetic character, you see, a raffish fellow with a heart of gold.

—Powell, interviewed by Gladys Hall in an unsourced, undated article in the files of The New York Public Library for the Performing Arts

Q. Don't you think Jamie Darricott of *Ladies Man* [1931, Lothar Mendes] was a villain?

A. Never! He was just weak. Passive. He had to be. He hasn't any of the characteristics of the parts I like to play, that I feel I can play best. No mentality. None of those sparkling facets of character which make personality....

—Powell, interviewed by Marie House for *Screenland*, Apr 1931

Manhattan Melodrama [1934, W.S. Van Dyke] is melodramatic in its intent; it is a story with a great deal of action. But the best scenes, I think, are those of small compass: scenes in which the district attorney talks with his life-time friend [Clark Gable], whom he must prosecute for murder; scenes in which Myrna Loy, as the district attorney's wife, visits Gable, her old sweetheart, in the death cell.

The camera was literally breathing down our necks when these scenes were made. We had little space for movement. The ideas had to be expressed with comparatively little motion, with great sincerity and with the repression that is, to my way of thinking, the greatest form of dramatic art.

—Powell, interviewed for *The New York Evening Post*, 28 Apr 1934

Even my best friends never fail to tell me that the smartest thing I ever did was to marry Myrna Loy on the screen.... We were married in thirteen pictures, including *Libeled Lady* [1936, Jack Conway], and I never saw Myrna go into a temperamental tantrum, rave and rant, or walk off the set in a huff. She never lets her emotions come too near the surface, and remains calm and posed in the most difficult situations....

When we did a scene together, we forgot about technique, camera angles, and microphones. We weren't acting. We were just two people in perfect harmony. Many times I've played with an actress who seemed to be separated from me by a plate-glass window; there was no contact at all. But Myrna, unlike some actresses who think only of themselves, has the happy faculty of being able to listen while the other fellow says his lines. She has the give and take of acting that brings out the best.

The Thin Man [1934, W. S. Van Dyke] would never have been the success it was without her. When the bed rolled beneath her in the hangover scene and she looked up at me with the ice bag on her head and said, "You pushed me," she became every man's dream of what a wife should be: beautiful and glamorous with a sense of humor, provocative and feminine without being saccharine or sharp, a perfect gal who never lost her temper, jumped at conclusions, or nagged a guy.

—Powell, interviewed by James Kotsilibas-Davis for *Being and Becoming* by Myrna Loy and James Kotsilibas-Davis (New York: Alfred A. Knopf, 1987)

Nick and Nora [in *The Thin Man* series], represent the sort of friendly and happy-go-lucky marriage any two people would like. Neither is perfect, but each has a perfect understanding and is all-forgiving, and as long as that relationship lasts so long will Nick and Nora. [See Loy's entry for a complete list of their films together.]
—Powell, interviewed by Edward Axford for *The Argus* (Melbourne), 1 Dec 1937

Probably no one ever lived who was like Godfrey [in *My Man Godfrey* (1936)]. But [Gregory] La Cava, the director made the man seem quite plausible.... Every morning he'd give us some dialogue that he'd written during the night.... Working with someone like [W.S.] Van Dyke or La Cava is a great help to an actor. You have confidence in them.
—Powell, quoted by Charles Francisco in *Gentleman: The William Powell Story* (New York: St. Martin's Press, 1985)

The smart star, as any other smart businessman, realizes his assets for what they are worth and does everything he can to enhance their value. For instance, Philo Vance, Nick Charles, the gentlemen's gentleman I played in *My Man Godfrey* and in *The Baroness and the Butler* [1938, Walter Lang] had, in common, certain qualities of urbanity, of taking life in their stride. Recognizing this I observed that, when men seem to be sure of themselves, when they have poise, they command our liking. Very well, then, these characters I've played most successfully must command liking, I figured, because they have poise. But what is poise? It was up to me to find out. Poise indicated, I concluded, clear thinking. People with poise are people who think straight, who are not all cluttered up and clacking about like ducks. Poise comes from having really digested life.
—Powell, interviewed by Gladys Hall in an unsourced, undated article in the files of The New York Public Library for the Performing Arts

It probably required a certain flexibility of imagination for movie-goers to accept The Thin Man as Father in the picture, *Life with Father* [1947, Michael Curtiz]. But I found the transition from modern detecting to 1880 paternalism quite easy to make.

I always was in complete sympathy with Father. I recognized in him traits I felt I could delineate; I knew his various moods, which ranged from naiveté to pomposity to tyranny, but I also knew that basically he was a man of gentleness. He had a flash temper, and I have always suspected there was a little Irish in the Day family. I am half Irish myself, so I could easily match Father's temper, although mine is of a slower type. Father's outbursts came and went so quickly that if anyone had accused him of being angry, he probably would have said, "Angry? Me? Why, I never lost my temper in my life!" And he would have believed it.
—Powell, in *The Saturday Evening Post*, 31 July 1948

Robert PRESTON [1918-1987]

Born: Robert Preston Meservey in Newton Highlands, Massachusetts. Work with The Pasadena Playhouse preceded his film debut in King of Alcatraz (1938, Robert Florey). The following year, he played Dick Allen in Cecil B. DeMille's Union Pacific:

I'll never forget that first day on the set. It was the toughest sequence in the entire script, and I couldn't understand why Mr. DeMille wanted to shoot it first, me being so jittery and more apt than not to set the whole company off on the wrong foot when the camera began to grind. Somehow I managed to go through my part well enough to satisfy Mr. DeMille. The reason he selected the toughest sequence first, he explained to me when he finally okayed the shooting, was because he knew I was as high-strung as a fiddle string, a state of mind and of nerves demanded of me by the sequence, and he was afraid I'd never be able to whip myself into this particular tension later on. Which was pretty slick of him, don't you think?
—Preston, interviewed for *Screenland*, Oct 1939

I played opposite Barbara Stanwyck in *Union Pacific*. I broke in with the greatest girl in the world. She was so generous. We were in production six weeks — we knew each other quite well — but we hadn't had any of the intimate scenes yet. One was coming up and she said to me, "I don't know how many years you've seen me on the screen and who you think I am but I've *got* to be Molly, this little girl, and you've got to be Dick, and you're going to have to woo me. I've got to be pursued. You've got to do it; you've got to carry the ball." With that she took me over to the corner of the stage and said, "Have you ever seen Lunt and Fontanne on stage?" I said, "Since I was 10." She said, "Well, the difference between Lunt and Fontanne and the leads in the high school play is just as simple as this" — and she took me and pressed her body right against mine, all the way down and said, "*That's* an embrace."

Doing *The Music Man* on Broadway brought me back to Hollywood's attention. I would have stayed with the show, because I was still having fun and I played it for two years, but Warner Bros. offered me the film of *The Dark at the Top of the Stairs* [1960, Delbert Mann], which was a worthwhile property and I wanted to do it. Then they said, "We want you to sign a three picture deal. You can't do the film unless you sign for three pictures." Well, I did, because I knew they'd bought *The Music Man* — and I also knew they wanted anyone in the world to play it *except* me. That was the standard procedure in those days. The actor who created the role never played the part. Eventually I wore them down. Actually, Cary Grant got the part for me. Jack Warner wanted Cary to play it. I knew Cary had seen the show 12 times, to my knowledge, and he told Warner not only would he not play it but if Preston doesn't play it he wouldn't even go and see it. That's what cinched it for me. I said to Jack Warner, "I know what you want. You're going to spend five million on it, which was a lot of money then, and you want a star to guarantee your property." But I said, "We have just spent the last two years making a star for you and it's called *The Music Man*." He wouldn't buy that line of reasoning but he took all the credit for the marvelous casting. [The film version was directed by Morton Da Costa in 1962.]

—Preston, interviewed by David Galligan for *Drama-Logue*, 25-31 Mar 1982

Julie [Andrews] and I were in England a full month before production started [on *Victor/Victoria* (1982, Blake Edwards)] because of the song and dance numbers and prerecording. And we got to know who those two characters were.

That's the best way to find out who the hell you're playing: To have to get ready for prerecording. Because what you do you're stuck with for the rest of the picture. And when you find out how a guy moves on the dance floor, you find out how he walks down the stairs, out on the street....

You get a strange kind of rehearsal with Blake.... Blake says "Now, I wasn't quite sure when I wrote this that this was the way it was gonna be. Let's kick it around!" And that's how you become part of the creative process on a Blake Edwards' picture. Anything funny happens, it's gonna be in. The improvisation starts with the first rehearsal. And by the time the picture's through, you forget what was originally there and what you put in. And you're having such fun....

You know what was even more fun? The Gay Paree number: Because of the audience that Blake got me. They were such a strange group that to this day I cannot tell you legitimately which were male and which were female.

I said to them before they even heard the number, I said, "This is the first time in a long career that I am ever going to do a number in front of an audience every one of whom could do it better." And they loved it. We had a lot of joking and camaraderie so that by the time we got ready to do the scene, I could use anyone of them for anything I wanted. I could touch them. I could get a leer from some. The laughter and applause was live and sure, it made it. Instead of being an actor playing a number, it became what Toddy did for a living. God, it was fun!

And then to have almost that same crowd back in that same little café when we did "You and Me." That's what made that number. The laughter at our little ad libs.... The whole thing was done right off the cuff. Blake never let us rehearse. He said, "I want it to look impromptu. It's got to be a little impromptu thing...."

So Julie and I would sneak around behind the set and practice little things so we wouldn't step on each other while we were doing it. We did plan one thing, too. It comes from Barbara Stanwyck. I made a picture with her called *The Lady Gambles* [1949, Michael Gordon] and we had a scene in a restaurant where we're dancing and I had to say to her every once in a while during the rehearsal, "Missy, you're leading again." And she would say, "I am not."

—Preston, interviewed by Lewis Archibald for *The Aquarian Weekly*, 5-12 May 1982

Vincent PRICE [1911-]

Born: St. Louis, Missouri. Studies at Yale University and The University of London and work on both the London and New York stages preceded his film debut in Service de Luxe (1938, Rowland V. Lee). His second film role was Sir Walter Raleigh in The Private Lives of Elizabeth and Essex (1939):

This was a frightening experience. I was still very new to the movie business, a greenhorn, and I walked into an atmosphere on that film that you could cut with a knife. [Bette] Davis objected to [Errol] Flynn playing Essex, she had wanted Olivier, and Flynn was at the height of his success and charmingly cavalier — to the extent of not bothering to learn his lines. Every time Errol would blow a line when I was on the set, the director, Michael Curtiz, would point to me and say in his hideous Hungarian accent, "I get this boy to play part." I had done Essex on the stage with Mildred Natwick as Elizabeth, and Curtiz used me as a stick to wag in Flynn's face, which did nothing to endear me to Errol. But his part called for him to despise me anyway — Raleigh was a rival suitor for the Queen's favor.

—Price, interviewed by Tony Thomas for *Cads and Cavaliers* (New York: A.S. Barnes, 1973)

[Shelby Carpenter in *Laura* (1945, Otto Preminger)] was a wonderful character — a real upper-class scum! He was really elegant. Everything about him was charming, but he was a *schmuck*. He was a terrible man and he was such fun to play because he didn't know that. Most villains don't know they're villains at all.

—Price, interviewed by Graham Fuller for *Interview*, Dec 1990

Roger [Corman] has an extremely ambivalent attitude toward actors. Even on those tight schedules he'd make sure we rehearsed the film. We would come in on our own, you know, without pay or even a fixed starting date, and read it and then walk through it. This was terribly important. But on the other hand, he hasn't the slightest interest in makeup, which is a key factor is some of these [Edgar Allen] Poe films. In [*The House of*] *Usher* [1960], I bleached my hair white and wore pure white makeup with black eyebrows — I don't think anybody had done that since Conrad Veidt [in *The Cabinet of Dr. Caligari* (1919, Robert Weine)] — there was this whole extraordinary thing that [Usher] was ultrasensitive to light and sound, so I tried to give the impression he'd never been exposed to the light, someone who had just bleached away. Now Roger dug this entirely...he found it very exciting that the actor could bring it to a visual creation that complemented his. And again makeup was so vital in *Tales of Terror* [1962], the collection of 3 short stories. I was the only actor to appear in all 3, so I had to change the looks, change the characterization, in each one. Well, Roger couldn't have cared less about this aspect, it was my problem, but then he would come to you with all these deep and profound things which he feels underlies the stories. Personally, I think that Roger only three-quarters believes in them, and one-quarter uses them to prod the actor. I must confess that it's very stimulating and inventive to work with him. [Price also worked on Corman's *The Pit and the Pendulum* (1961), *Tower of London* (1962), *The Raven* (1963), *The Haunted Palace* (1964) and *The Tomb of Ligeia* (1965).]

—Price, interviewed by David Austen for *Films & Filming*, Aug 1969

Q

Dennis QUAID [1954-]

Born: Houston, Texas. Brother to Randy Quaid [1950]. Drama studies at The University of Houston preceded his film debut in Crazy Mama (1975, Jonathan Demme). In 1983, he played astronaut Gordon Cooper in Philip Kaufman's The Right Stuff:

It's like a gold mine when you portray a real guy. Gordo Cooper lived about five miles from here. I spent around fifteen hours with him over a period of weeks and picked his brain. With Gordo it all had to do with his walk — well, it wasn't a walk, really; it was a march. He was a marine before he was in the air force. That stuff helps out a lot. Same with Jerry Lee [Lewis in Great Balls of Fire (1989)]. As an actor, I start with the outside and work inward. Let's say a guy has a bum leg and limps — well, what kind of pain is that guy in, not only physical, but emotional? These outside things tell you how a person has to get around in the world. It gives you some eyes, the character's point of view. You don't create the inside; you're led there.

Q. You circled back around to work with Jim McBride again on *Great Balls of Fire*. He had directed you in *The Big Easy* [1987]. You two seem to have an easygoing working relationship.

A. Jim is a great director. We've got a kind of shorthand worked out between us. I like directors to be helmsmen, because film is a director's medium. If you have a real strong director everything else will fall into line. I like a director to work harder than I do — and I work really hard. When there is conflict I think it can be good. Creation comes from chaos. But the director has the final say. Through argument I might find out that I was mistaken, or maybe the director will make that same discovery. I'm not talking about fighting — I'm talking about argument.

—Quaid, interviewed by Kevin Sessums for *Interview*, June 1989

Anthony QUINN [1915-]

Born: Chihuahua, Mexico. Brief work on the stage preceded his film debut in Parole (1936, Louis Friedlander). In 1952, he played Eufemio in Elia Kazan's Viva Zapata!:

I was born in Mexico during Zapata's revolution and spent my first few years hiding in the hills with my mother to avoid being shot. This precaution not only kept me intact so that, many years later, I could play the part of Zapata's brother, Eufemio, in the film *Viva Zapata!*, but also gave me a definite feeling of kinship for the part.

Eufemio was no man of vision, no revolutionary do-gooder. He accepted the revolution as a great thing simply because his brother said it was; he grabbed the spoils of war at every opportunity. However, I enjoyed playing him because he had a sense of humor, a zest for life and a lot of explosive passions.

—Quinn, in *The Saturday Evening Post*, 27 Mar 1954

Q. When you played Paul Gauguin in *Lust for Life* [1956, Vincente Minnelli], how did you get inside of him?

A. I was just about to turn 40. I had four children. I had to ask, "Have I really been honest with myself? Am I happy with my whole existence?" This is the kind of soul-searching Gauguin must have gone through to leave his five children and wife to be honest with himself and his painting. I couldn't just do an interesting characterization. I had to plead Gauguin's case.

—Quinn, interviewed by Dick Schaap for *The Saturday Evening Post*, 13 Jan 1962

We live in a world of false values, surrounded by hypocrisy, with little honesty or respect. We have come to the stage where representation has become more important than the thing it represents. I hope Zorba [in *Zorba the Greek* (1964, Michael Cacoyannis)] is seen as a kind of liberation. He's very American because he's a pioneer, he sets his own values. Each man must find his own values, not accept predigested ones. But while anybody can show you the way, you have to have the strength to walk it yourself.

—Quinn, interviewed by Melton S. Davis for *The New York Times*, 21 Mar 1965

Q. As an actor, do you find that you sometimes have to adapt your own performance to allow for the personality of other actors?

A. I recently made *The Shoes of the Fisherman* [1968, Michael Anderson] in which I played the pope, and I had actors like Larry Olivier, John Gielgud and Oskar Werner to work with. It depends on the part, but here, being the pope, I have to convince them to treat me like a pope. It must have been difficult for them, and it wasn't only convincing them in the scene that I was a pope, but off-stage I had to create a certain kind of atmosphere for them, to help them treat me like a pope.

I felt rather sorry for them because, you know, they had to kneel before me, they had to kiss my ring so to speak. I could hardly finish telling some story before the take and then expect them to kiss my ring with any reverence....

Besides, with a camera, to me it's a great love affair. I happen to be an actor who loves the camera. The camera has such a personality of its own and you cannot lie to it, especially when you have to look at it and it looks into your eyes. When those eyes are enlarged a hundred times on screen, it sees everything. So for their sakes I had to be almost a pope off-stage.

—Quinn, interviewed by Robin Bean for *Films & Filming*, Feb 1970

R

George RAFT [1895-1980]

Born: George Ranft in New York City. Work as a boxer and as a dancer both in vaudeville and on Broadway preceded his film debut in Queen of the Night Clubs (1929, Bryan Foy). He often played gangster roles on film while fraternizing with the Capone Gang:

Owney [Madden] had backed a Broadway show called *Diamond Lil*, and I went to the theater every Saturday night to collect his share of the investment from the star and her managers. Her name was Mae West, and I admired her unique talents.

Eventually, when I was starred in a picture called *Night After Night* [1932, Archie Mayo] and was allowed to choose my own leading lady, I sent for Mae West.

It was her first screen appearance, and her cleverness on stage was a new kind of thievery to me. She stole everything but the cameras, and I never made another picture with her. I knew she had me licked.

—Raft, in *The People* (London), 17 Nov 1957

Why did [Howard] Hawks pick me for a big role in *Scarface*, the film biography of Al Capone, when Hollywood was full of experienced young actors? I asked him that question once, and he said, "You were the type." Well, that's a trick answer. All I know is that they asked me a lot of questions — how Capone dressed, how he walked and talked, what kind of guns he used, and so on.

They wanted me in the role of Capone's bodyguard — his name was Frankie Rio — and they wanted realism....

In 1932, *Scarface* made me a movie star overnight and changed my whole life. If you saw the picture you may recall that I was a cool, icy-veined character who was constantly tossing a coin — a little bit of stage business which later became my trade-mark. The reviews...said that the fade-out, in which [Paul] Muni shoots me, was the finest dying scene they had ever seen.

I have never admitted until now that this so-called great acting was sheer accident. In doing the fall after the shooting, I slipped and hit my head on the door. The pain made my eyes roll, and the cameras were on. They shot the scene only once, and I couldn't have done it again without another crack on the head. After that, they had me typed. In film after film the script writers had me killed in the last reel, hoping I would come up with another great death scene.

—Raft, as told to Dean Jennings for *The Saturday Evening Post*, 19 Oct 1957

Q. You like to play the villain....

A. The half-villain.... I don't like to play a yellow rat any more than I'd like to play Little Lord Fauntleroy....

It's the mixture of good and bad in people that gets me. After all, nobody in the world is all-black and probably nobody is all-white....

The kind of part I like is the one I had in *The Glass Key* [1935, Frank Tuttle]. Now there was a real guy. He might have been a little bit on the shady side in some of his dealings. But he was loyal and he had "plenty of what it takes." He didn't have much to say either but when he did talk, it registered.

—Raft, interviewed by James Fletcher for *Movie Classic*, Apr 1936

Luise RAINER [1910-]

Born: Vienna, Austria. A stage debut at age 16 in Düsseldorf, and work with Max Reinhardt's company in Berlin preceded her film debut in the short film Ja, der Himmel über Wien (1930). A three year contract with MGM began with Escapade (1935, Robert Z. Leonard); despite success in The Great Ziegfeld (1936, Robert Z. Leonard) and The Good Earth (1937, Sidney Franklin), MGM did not renew her contract in 1938. She made only one more film.

It is always a great happiness to an actress to play a character she loves, and I loved O-lan from the first moment I read *The Good Earth*. She was strange to me, for I knew little of Chinese women, but she was so intensely human that one could not help absorbing a sort of inspiration from her.... She was a peasant, with knowledge of only a few words. She was stoical, the heritage of centuries. She was almost a clod. Still in her heart was every emotion a woman could have: love, fear, joy, suffering, pride, and a devotion that passes understanding. True, to project these to an audience and still retain the lack of apparent emotion of a stoical race, frightened me a little at the outset. The actress essaying such a part has nothing but her eyes and toneless syllables to work with. The secret, I believe, in such a case is to think the meaning — and think it hard.

—Rainer, in the souvenir program for *The Good Earth* (MGM, 1937)

One day [the bosses at MGM] decided I should be glamorous. "Oh, my god," I cried, "don't make me glamorous." There are so many lovely girls here, so many, I tell them. Please just let me act from the heart and pay no attention to the outward. But after *Good Earth* they were afraid the public might think I am homely and can play only such roles.

So for *The Emperor's Candlesticks* [1937, George Fitzmaurice] they wanted me to be glamorous — which is something I can't be. It weighed me down more than the character of O-lan in *The Good Earth*. I was unhappy....

—Rainer, interviewed by Sara Hamilton for *Photoplay Magazine*, June 1938

Claude RAINS [1889-1967]

Born: William Claude Rains in London. Work on the London stage (from age 11) led to a 1926 tour with the British Company of The Constant Nymph. Rains decided to stay in the U.S., where he made his U.S. film debut with The Invisible Man (1933, James Whale). In 1934, he played Lee Gentry in Crime Without Passion:

I have always enjoyed playing the part of a heel rather than a fine, upright individual. It acts as a safety valve for the primitive urges most of us occasionally feel....

Lee had some scruples, but did not indulge them; he really behaved in a thoroughly shabby fashion.

He was a criminal lawyer, yet he got into the worst type of jam and came to believe he had committed the crime. Then, worried sick for fear he would be caught, he lost his nerve and committed a real crime, for which he paid the penalty....

Ben Hecht and Charles MacArthur asked me to take the part of Lee Gentry.... After hearing the script, I said, "It's beautifully written and it has everything an actor could ask for." I said many more things that evening, mellowed by the genial atmosphere of the Helen Hayes-Charles MacArthur household, and apparently they remembered them all. When I next heard the script, I found they had spread some personal icing on the part for me, and I liked it even better.

—Rains, in *The Saturday Evening Post*, 12 July 1947

The technical language [of *White Banners* (1938)] wasn't so hard, but when Director Edmund Goulding insisted that I really learn something about machinery — valves, compressors, reduction coils and such, I — well, profanity being unprintable, let's say that I did learn, and now know how to operate a compressor and hook up a reduction coil, although what to do with this particular 'know-how' remains, to this day, beyond me.

—Rains, interviewed by Gladys Hall for *Silver Screen*, Dec 1947

When I started *Notorious* [1946], my first scene was a highly dramatic one with Ingrid Bergman. Thinking about it gave me the willies. I didn't think I could do that scene properly. And just before we started to shoot I got as nervous as a cat in a dog pound. Alfred Hitchcock saw the condition I was in, so he took me aside and said: "Listen, Claude, don't ever do anything you don't want to do. If you think it best, we'll shoot around you till you get yourself straightened out." That was all I needed. If Hitchcock didn't take a possible failure on my part seriously, why should I? So I went into the scene and did all right.

I need the confidence of people with whom I work.

—Rains, interviewed by Hedda Hopper for *The Chicago Tribune*, 28 Sept 1947

In *Notorious*, I, standing five foot, seven and a half inches, performed upon a carpet-covered elevated platform in order to be within eye-level of five foot, eight Ingrid Bergman. This bit of contriving, Alfred Hitchcock...called "The Shame of Rains."

—Rains, interviewed by Gladys Hall for *Silver Screen*, Dec 1947

Esther RALSTON [1902-]

Born: Esther Worth in Bar Harbor, Maine. Following work with the family's travelling show, she made her film debut in The Deep Purple (1915, James Young). In 1922, she appeared with Lon Chaney in Frank Lloyd's adaptation of Charles Dickens' Oliver Twist:

I worked with Jackie Coogan and Lon Chaney in *Oliver Twist*. Mr. Chaney was so marvelous and he taught me more than I think I have learned from anybody else. We were sitting together on the set one day and I was seated on the edge of my chair. Mr. Chaney said, "Relax, Esther, relax, they'll get to you soon." I said, "But if they call me, will I be ready?" "You'll be ready. I want to show you how to relax." He took a little dinner bell out of his pocket and put it on his stomach. Then he dropped one leg out front, then the other leg out front, then one arm, then the other arm, then he bowed his head on his chest and went to sleep. After about a minute, the bell fell from his stomach onto the floor, rang and woke him up. He said, "That one moment of relaxation was all I needed. You need to learn to sit back and relax until they're ready for you." Well, I used that technique during my whole career.

I was co-starred with Clara Bow, the "It" Girl, in *Children of Divorce* [1927, Frank Lloyd].... I don't know if Clara thought I was a prude or not. I've always been more or less reserved and yet I'm sure there's nothing prudish about me. But she was a little minx and if she could shock me by what she said, or did, her day was made....

Gary Cooper was fired from *Children of Divorce*. We did two or three scenes and evidently he was so stiff that they felt he couldn't do it so they fired him and put Douglas Gilmore or somebody in his role. Then one day, Mr. B.P. Schulberg came down and said to me, "You know something — I think we ought to put that big Montana cowboy back in again. He's got a face — there's something about him, but he's just so stiff. Esther, can't you do something with him? Can't you ease him up a little bit? Isn't there something you can do?" I said, "Just what did you have in mind?" He said, "Well, you know, take him to lunch, talk to him or something. He's afraid to touch you for fear you'll break." So I said, "Yes, I'd be glad to...."

The Case of Lena Smith [1929] directed by Josef von Sternberg was the greatest. He believed that I was an actress and I was being wasted as a comedienne. He said, "Let me have her in this really great role and I think I can make an actress of her...." Well, by golly, he had mud dumped all over me, I climbed barbed-wire fences and I went through the period of the young girl into the old lady.... It certainly was my best role in the silents. As a director, Mr. von Sternberg was very, very subtle and very sensitive. He would bring out exactly what he wanted. He just worked very sensitively and quietly until you felt you could do anything he wanted.

I worked in *Sadie McKee* [1934, Clarence Brown] with Joan Crawford. When I arrived on the MGM lot, she jumped out of her car, came rushing over to mine and said, "I'm Joan Crawford and I'm so glad you're going to be with me." So we really got along pretty well for a little time but then, we had a couple of little disagreements because she didn't like the way I did my eyes. They were made up the same way she did hers. I said, "Well, I've always done that — I find I photograph best that way." She wasn't quite as cordial to me from then on but otherwise we got along beautifully....

—Ralston, interviewed by William M. Drew for *Speaking of Silents: First Ladies of the Screen* (Vestal, N.Y.: The Vestal Press, 1989)

Basil RATHBONE [1892-1967]

Born: Johannesburg, South Africa; educated in England. Stage work in England and the U.S. (on tour with Benson's Shakespearean Company) preceded his British film debut in Innocent (1921, Maurice Elvey). In 1925, he made his U.S. film debut in Christy Cabanne's The Masked Bride. In 1937, he played Lord Arthur Dilling opposite Norma Shearer in the title role of Sidney Franklin's The Last of Mrs. Cheyney:

[Norma] was disciplined, hardworking, totally dedicated, and had a distinctive, very intriguing voice — unlike any I had ever heard.... She was very anxious to please Irving [Thalberg], wanted him to be proud of her. I think she had a great deal of determination — a tremendous will to succeed, and that is particularly important in acting.

I got tired of hearing that she was Galatea to Irving's Pygmalion; she was a very strong character on her own, very much of a self-starter, with true self-sufficiency. I was Tybalt in her *Romeo and Juliet* [1936, George Cukor] at MGM years later, and her command of the Shakespearean rhythms and cadences astonished me — she spoke Shakespeare so naturally. And I was not at all surprised when some of her finest performances came in the years after her husband's death, when she was very much on her own.

—Rathbone, interviewed (1954) by Lawrence J. Quirk; repr. in his *Norma: The Story of Norma Shearer* (New York: St. Martin's Press, 1988)

[Q. Which actress have you learned the most from?]

A. Miss Garbo in *Anna Karenina* [1935, Clarence Brown], gave me economy. She is the screen's greatest economist. Yet she never economizes to the extent of defeating an emotion. She has a manner of expression which enables her, with the slightest possible means, to convey any emotion. Miss Shearer has two things — a beautiful rightness and the same unconscious ability to act that children have. With all this she has the wisdom of simplicity. Miss Dietrich [on *The Garden of Allah* (1936, Richard Boleslavsky)] has the most restless imagination in pictures. It is vivid and tireless. Her ability to help a fellow player — if she wants to — is remarkable. Her mind moves like a flash.

—Rathbone, interviewed by Charles Darnton for *The New York Herald Tribune*, 15 May 1938

Karenin is a human being — a man whose point of view you can see even though you don't wholly sympathize with it. To me he's an even more tragic figure than Anna [Greta Garbo] — for there's no greater tragedy than that of the person who feels, but is so bound by convention that he can't give expression to his feeling.

—Rathbone, interviewed for *Motion Picture*, Aug 1935

I was to play the cold, cruel Mr. Murdstone [in *David Copperfield* (1935, George Cukor)], and one morning at MGM, I thrashed the living daylights out of poor little Freddie Bartholomew as David Copperfield.

It was a most unpleasant experience, for I was directed by Mr. George Cukor to express no emotion whatsoever — merely to thrash the child, to within an inch of his life! I had a vicious cane with much whip to it, but fortunately for Freddie Bartholomew and myself, under his britches and completely covering his little rump, he was protected by a sheet of foam rubber.... As Mr. Murdstone, I tried to make my mind a blank, thrashing Freddie as hard as I could but like a machine. From time to time, George Cukor would call for another "take." Basil, he would say, "You were thinking of something. Please don't — all right, let's try again."

When the picture was released, I received good reviews and a very heavy fan mail — all of it abusive....! For some considerable time I was to become a victim of one of motion pictures' worst curses — "typing." I was now typed as "a heavy" or villain....

—Rathbone, in his *In and Out of Character* (Garden City, N.Y.: Doubleday & Co., 1956)

[On *David Copperfield*], I even hated George Cukor at times — childishly, illogically — for the things he made me do. And this I want to say. Whatever credit's due belongs not to me, but to him. I know it's the fashion to say pleasant things about one's director, but believe me, this has nothing to do with fashion. He can get anything out of anyone — the tenderest sentiment, the bitterest cruelty. He wanted cruelty from me and he got it. He was the whip. He stood over me like a circus-master over a trained seal.

—Rathbone, interviewed for *Motion Picture*, Aug 1935

[In *Romeo and Juliet*,] Tybalt kills Mercutio [John Barrymore]. This may make an audience dislike him, still he has many human qualities.

Shakespeare knew perfectly well that no man is 100% bad or good.

—Rathbone, in the press packet for *Romeo and Juliet* (MGM, 1936)

Actually, I used very little make-up [for the role of Louis XI in *If I Were King* (1938, Frank Lloyd)]. A few lines in the face, a little oil on my hair to make it hang in scraggly wisps around my head and careful attention to my eyes was about all I needed. It is surprising what an effect of senility you can get by just letting your tights wrinkle about the legs.

Most of my attention was devoted to getting just the right expression about the eyes. And that I finally achieved by using the eyebrows of Frank Lloyd, the director. That is, I copied his. They're the kind that hang over and droop — you know. Later I discovered that Charlie Laughton had also used them in *Mutiny* [*on the Bounty* (1935, Frank Lloyd)] and Bob Burns had lifted them for his make-up in *Wells Fargo* [1937, Frank Lloyd].

—Rathbone, interviewed by Bosley Crowther for *The New York Times*, 25 Sept 1938

As I imagine [Sherlock Holmes in *The Hound of the Baskervilles* (1939, Sidney Lanfield)], was not a neat man in his personal habits. He was careless in this respect, inattentive to minor details of dress and deportment. As we put it here, he just "wouldn't be bothered." But he was a man of tremendous powers of concentration, completely absorbed in whatever happened to engage his professional mind. Very properly, then, he never associated with women, evinced no interest in them. Imagine what a hell being his wife would have been.

There is no other character in English literature quite like him. While, of course, there have been other great detectives in fiction, somehow they have never been able to get hold of the popular imagination as Holmes has done. There is, for instance, Philo Vance.... I played him once for the screen [in *The Bishop Murder Case* (1930, Nick Grinde and David Burton)], but somehow I had the feeling he was a little too smart, that he belonged to Park Avenue rather than to Main Street. He didn't have the common touch which Sherlock, in spite of his erratic brilliance, manages to convey. [Rathbone played Holmes in 13 more films over the next 9 years: *The Adventures of Sherlock Holmes* (1939, Alfred Werker); *Sherlock Holmes and the Voice of Terror* (1942, John Rawlins); *Sherlock Holmes and the Secret Weapon* (1942), *Sherlock Holmes in Washington* (1943), *Sherlock Holmes Faces Death* (1943), *The Spider Woman* (1944), *The Scarlet Claw* (1944), *The Pearl of Death* (1944), *The House of Fear* (1945), *The Woman in Green* (1945), *Passage to Algiers* (1945), *Terror by Night* (1946) and *Dressed to Kill* (1948), all directed by Roy William Neill.]

—Rathbone, interviewed by Charles Darnton for *The New York Herald Tribune*, 26 Feb 1939

Ronald REAGAN [1911-]

Born: Tampico, Illinois. Work as a sports radio announcer preceded his film debut in Love is in the Air (1937, Nick Grinde). In 1940, he played George Gipp in Lloyd Bacon's Knute Rockne: All American:

Usually when a person is being tested for a role, some contract player is given the chore of playing the other part in the scene. You can imagine my gratitude when I arrived on the set and found that my assistant, complete with make-up, was Pat O'Brien, who already had signed for the Rockne part. It was a half day's work he wasn't required to do, but he was there to give me all the tools possible to help me get the part he knew meant so much to me. I really didn't have to learn any lines; I had known Gipp's story for years. My lines were straight from Rock's diary....

I got the part. It occupied only one reel of the picture, but in that reel it was a nearly perfect part from an actor's standpoint. A great entrance, an action middle, and a death scene to finish up. By way of frosting on the cake, in the last reel of the picture Gipp is recalled to the audience when Rock asks the team to win one for the Gipper, and reveals for the first time that this was Gipp's dying wish.

The entire picture was a sentimental journey and a thrilling experience.... For inspiration Rockne's widow Bonnie was on the set every day as technical advisor. Between scenes most of our time was spent listening to reminiscences and stories of that great era when Notre Dame was the scourge of the football world.

I discovered I would again be playing a biographical role [in *Santa Fe Trail* (1940)], but with less attention to the truth this time. I was playing the young Lieutenant Custer and [Errol] Flynn was playing J.E.B. Stuart, the great cavalry leader of the Confederacy, in a pre-Civil War epic that was in reality the story of John Brown [Raymond Massey]....

Errol was a strange person, terribly unsure of himself and needlessly so. He was a beautiful piece of machinery, likable, with great charm, and yet convinced he lacked ability as an actor. As a result, he was conscious every minute of scenes favoring other actors and their position on the screen in relation to himself. He was apparently unaware of his own striking personality. [Reagan and Flynn worked together again on *Desperate Journey* (1942, Raoul Walsh)]....

Mike Curtiz was properly cast to direct the story of the madman John Brown.... When he was shooting a picture, Mike — who was normally a kind, good-natured soul — became a ruthless tyrant, as hard on himself as anyone else. It was a strange character quirk. In that hanging scene he was setting up his shot, looking through the viewfinder and motioning to a very elderly actor who played the minister, to move first to the left, then to the right; finally he kept motioning him to move back. The poor old fellow moved back one step too far, and fell twelve feet from the scaffold, breaking his leg. Mike walked across, looked down where he lay on the ground, turned to his assistant, and said, "Get me another minister."

MGM was sort of the Tiffany of Hollywood, so I was duly impressed when a loanout was arranged. The picture was the old Broadway play, *The Badman*, being refilmed for its umpteenth time [1941, Richard Thorpe]....

Wallace Beery was the "Badman," Lionel Barrymore my crotchety uncle, and the very nice Laraine Day the love interest. I was warned that Beery was an inveterate scene-stealer and would even get his face in the camera when it was a closeup on other players, with the camera shooting over his shoulder. The director briefed me on all that would happen, and assured me of closeups, to cover all stolen scenes. I gathered that I was not only being assured but warned against protecting myself, lest it anger Mr. Beery who might just disappear in mid-picture.

If I had any ideas about protecting myself I forgot them when I saw Wally operate. In one "two-shot" I thought I had him. He was standing beside his horse and I was at the horse's head. We were both profile to the camera, facing each other. With him anchored in place by a thousand pounds of horse, and me free to move around the horse's head, I didn't see how he could maneuver upstage and thus get the back of my head in the camera — but he was Wally Beery. He must have sprung that horse's ribs. By the scene's end he was full face to the camera, which was virtually shooting over my shoulder. Like the old adage about forced romance: when it's inevitable, relax and enjoy it.

I'd been warned about Beery but no one had said anything about Barrymore. Let me make one thing plain — it was a great honor to work with him, and I'm glad I had the opportunity. Wally never rehearsed a line the way he would say it in the scene, so you were always on edge trying to anticipate a cue for your own line. Lionel was, of course, theater through and through, and you were made better by his great ability — providing you kept from being run over. He was confined to his wheelchair at the time and he could whip that contrivance around on a dime. It's hard to smile in a scene when your foot has been run over and your shin is bleeding from a hubcap blow.

My key scene [as Drake McHugh in *King's Row* (1942, Sam Wood)] was to be played in a bed. This environment was the result of the plot which had me injured in an accident in the railroad yards. Taken to a sadistic doctor (who disapproved of my dating his daughter and felt it was his duty to punish me), I recovered consciousness in an upstairs bedroom. I found that the doctor [Charles Coburn] had amputated both my legs at the hip.

It was the portrayal of this moment of total shock which made the scene rough to play. Coming from unconsciousness to full realization of what had happened in a few seconds, it presented me with the most challenging acting problem in my career. Worst of all, I had to give my reaction in a line of no more than five words.

A whole actor would find such a scene difficult; giving it the necessary dramatic impact as half an actor was murderous. I felt I had neither experience nor the talent to fake it. I simply had to find out how it really felt, short of actual amputation.

I rehearsed the scene before mirrors, in corners of the studio, while driving home.... I consulted physicians and psychologists; I even talked to people who were so disabled, trying to brew in myself the caldron of emotions a man must feel who wakes up one sunny morning to find half of himself gone....

I appeared wan and worn on the sound stage, still not knowing how to read the line. Without hope, without make-up pasted on and in my nightshirt, I wandered over to the set to see what it looked like. I found the prop men had arranged a neat deception. Under the gay patchwork quilt, they had cut a hole in the mattress and put a supporting box beneath. I stared at it for a minute. Then, obeying an overpowering impulse, I climbed into the rig. I spent almost that whole hour in stiff confinement, contemplating my torso and the smooth undisturbed flat of the covers where my legs should have been.

Gradually the affair began to terrify me. In some weird way, I felt something horrible had happened to my body. Then gradually I became aware that the crew had quietly assembled, the camera was in position, and the set all lighted. Sam Wood, the director, stood beside me, watching me sweat.

"Want to shoot it?" he said in a low voice.

"No rehearsal?" I begged. Somehow I knew this one had to be for real.

God rest his soul — fine director that he was, he just turned to the crew and said, "Let's make it."

There were cries of "Lights!" and "Quiet, please!" I lay back and closed my eyes, as tense as a fiddlestring. I heard Sam's low voice call, "Action!" There was the sharp *clack* which signaled the beginning of the scene. I opened my eyes dazedly, looked around, slowly let my gaze travel downward. I can't describe even now my feeling as I tried to reach for where my legs should be. "Randy!" I screamed. Ann Sheridan...burst through the door. She wasn't in the shot and normally wouldn't have been on hand until we turned the camera around to get her entrance, but she knew it was one of those scenes where a fellow actor needed all the help he could get and at that moment, in my mind, she was Randy answering my call. I asked the question — the words that had been haunting me for so many weeks — "Where's the rest of me?"

There was no retake. It was a good scene and it came out that way in the picture. Perhaps I never did quite as well again in a single shot. The reason was that I had put myself, as best I could, in the body of another fellow. [Reagan and Sheridan had previously worked together on *Naughty But Nice* (1939, Ray Enright), *Angels Wash Their Faces* (1939, Ray Enright) and *Juke Girl* (1942, Curtis Bernhardt).]

—Reagan, in his (with Richard G. Hubler) *Where's the Rest of Me?* (New York: Elsevier-Dutton Co., 1965)

Robert REDFORD [1937-]

Born: Charles Robert Redford, Jr. in Santa Monica, California. After attending The University of Colorado on a baseball scholarship, he travelled around Europe living off his art (painting). Returning to the U.S., he studied at Pratt Institute and then The American Academy of Dramatic Arts. Work on Broadway (from 1959) preceded his film debut in War Hunt (1962, Denis Sanders). In 1966, he co-starred with Natalie Wood in Robert Mulligan's Inside Daisy Clover:

[Natalie and I] were on a boat doing a scene in *Inside Daisy Clover* and somebody asked her to do something and she said, "I can't do that, I'm a star!" and then she just roared with laughter. That kind of self-effacement was tremendously impressive to me. [Wood and Redford also worked together on *This Property is Condemned* (1966, Sydney Pollack).]

—Redford, interviewed for *Natalie*; aired station KCOP, Channel 11, Los Angeles, Aug 1982

[Sheriff Cooper in *Tell Them Willie Boy is Here* (1970, Abraham Polonsky) is] a loner who cannot make the adjustment to modern society. He was raised with Indians, but around 1909 the Indians were beginning to be squelched. He has no respect for the white community, for the attitude of "I think I'll go out and kill me a few Indians," but he has to maintain law and order. In the process of the chase he discovers a lot about himself.

In the beginning, he's an uncommitted man; at the end of the film you should feel he is a man committed. He learns, he grows. I was attracted by the idea of playing a simple man who grows.

—Redford, interviewed by Joan Barthel for *The New York Times*, 6 Oct 1968

Playboy: *Butch Cassidy and the Sundance Kid* [1969, George Roy Hill] is the kind of film that looks as if the actors had fun making it. Did you?

Redford: No film is a laugh a minute, because you always have problems. But for the most part, it was the most consistent fun of any film I've ever done. Paul Newman is a very generous, giving actor who was at his happiest when the whole thing was working. Not just his part, but everything....

Playboy: You said you felt comfortable playing the Sundance Kid. Why?

Redford: I had a strange identification with him that I can't quite put my finger on. There was a time when I was very young that I didn't think it would be so bad to be an outlaw. It sounded pretty good to me. The frontier wouldn't have been a bad place to be in the 1880s, it seemed to me.... One reason I liked *Butch Cassidy* was that it pointed out the fact that a lot of those people were just kids, doing what they did — robbing banks, holding up trains — as much for the sheer fun of it as for anything else.

—Redford, interviewed by Larry Dubois for *Playboy*, Dec 1974

George Roy Hill is a crazy bastard. And a *military* goddam director. Oh, you can fight with him, you can have an idea about something, but you'd better have about four reasons to back it up, and be able to fight for it, because he will fight like hell. [Redford also worked on Hill's *The Sting* (1973) and *The Great Waldo Pepper* (1975).]

—Redford, interviewed by Laurence Luckinbill for *Esquire*, Oct 1970

Jeremiah Johnson [1972, Sydney Pollack] was my project. That was one that was really close to me; it took place where I live. The reason Sydney was so good on it was that he understood how I felt. He went through a lot of anguish on that picture. It went on for months. We'd talk and talk and argue and we could never articulate what we wanted. Choices were made by both Sydney and myself that just weren't explainable. The crew didn't know what we were doing. It was just me wandering through the mountains and then suddenly it was put together and there it was. The idea was about a man who decides he doesn't want to live by someone else's code. He wants to create his own. He happens to go where the Indians were. It wasn't that he was attracted to the Indian way of life. He just wanted to go off by himself.

—Redford, interviewed by Patricia Erens for *Film Comment*, Sept/Oct 1975

I never thought of myself as a glamorous guy, a handsome guy, any of that stuff. Suddenly there's this *image*. And it makes me very nervous, because it keeps people from judging you on performance. When I made *The Candidate* [1972, Michael Ritchie], people said, "Yeah, sure, slick, handsome guy, the part's just right for him." When I made *The Way We Were* [1973, Sydney Pollack], they said, "Yeah, Ivy League WASP jock. The part fits him like a glove." But I had to fight to get *Jeremiah Johnson* because it didn't fit the *image*.

And I think a lot of the knocks I took for [*The Great*] *Gatsby* [1974, Jack Clayton] were because of image. Critics said Redford was too good-looking, Redford was awkward with the language.... *Fitzgerald* never said Gatsby wasn't good-looking. He said Gatsby was a fine figure of a man, an elegant young roughneck. He said Gatsby's language *was* awkward, bordering on the absurd. That was a key to the character. That was a quality I *worked* for. I mean, didn't they read the *book*?

—Redford, interviewed by Martha Weinman for *The New York Times Magazine*, 7 July 1974

The Watergate break-in was spawned by political procedures, but getting the story and investigative reporting didn't have much to do with politics. What Woodward and Bernstein were after was a story, they were not out to get Nixon.... I'm sure the idea that this might lead to the Oval Office and involve the head of our country had a lot of impact.

These guys were frightened by that notion, but they were doing their job, and working very hard. The anatomy of how a job is done interested me.... [In *All the President's Men* (1976, Alan J. Pakula)] we depicted these characters not as knights on horseback, but as reporters who would use dubious techniques at times to get information.

—Redford, interviewed by William Wolf for *Cue*, 17 Apr 1976

Am I using any of Woodward's characteristics? His shoes; he wears round shoes.

Q. Anything else?

A. Yeah, he has an interesting attention span. He'll stay with you as long as you interest him, then he becomes very polite. The turnoff point is sometimes very transparent...some reporters are just plain rude. He tends to maintain a relationship, but it's sort of clear you cease to interest him in terms of what you're saying, what you can provide. That's a trait I find interesting. Also he has a tenacity that's unbelievable.

—Redford, interviewed by Louise Sweeney for *The Christian Science Monitor*, 17 June 1975

I wouldn't mind moving away from the role of, uh, a glamour figure of cartoon proportions. I've felt tremendously reduced by that. I've been grateful for a lot of it — no complaints — but I *have* felt reduced.... I look at directing as a natural step. I've been frustrated for many years in wanting to have total control of something. It's like doing a painting. I started out to be an artist, and the one thing I always missed as an actor was that when you painted a picture, it was *yours*. No one came in and changed anything for you — altered the diagonal or put sienna in there. In making a film, you have directors and producers and editors and sound people who want to alter your performance. No question, it's a collaborative medium....

I guess the directors I respond to the best are the older ones, from the days when there weren't any cinema schools — the pioneers with fresh approaches who didn't spend a lot of time over-analyzing their craft but who operated strictly from their gut. I've always been impatient with directors who overintellectualize. Sitting around and talking about a scene interminably is like standing on the edge of a high dive. The longer you stand, the tougher it is to dive. Constipation sets in. No one wants to do anything.

—Redford, interviewed by Clifford Terry for *The New York Times*, 27 July 1980

Q. Why did you decide to direct *Ordinary People* [1980]?

A. Well, since I've always had a sociological-political interest in the country, I was interested in the family unit and what's happening to it — the changing mores in this country. That seemed to me a good subject. I liked the book [by Judith Guest] because it dealt with feelings and behavior, which are two things that have interested me most as an actor. And it also had something I had felt about my own upbringing — the camouflage of feelings, the inability of people to get in touch with themselves.

—Redford, interviewed for *Penthouse*, Dec 1980

[Denys Finch-Hatton in *Out of Africa* (1986, Sydney Pollack) was] the most purely symbolic character I've ever played and the least satisfying as an actor. The toughest. He isn't given any purpose, really, any professional purpose, other than to exist like a bird would.

—Redford, interviewed by Neal Gabler for *New York*, 10 Dec 1990

Lynn REDGRAVE [1943-]

Born: Chiswick, England. Studies at The Central School of Speech and Drama in London and work with The Royal Court Theatre and The Dundee Repertory Co. (Scotland) preceded her film debut as the girl who yelled "Rape" in Tom Jones (1963, Tony Richardson). In 1966, she played the title role in Silvio Narizzano's Georgy Girl:

Q. What were your feelings undertaking the role of the tall, gawky, unloved girl hungering for the affection she feels she never will receive?

A. From start to finish of the picture I did something I intensely dislike in a professional. I lived the part of Georgy. I've always felt a good actor parks his part when he removes the make-up. But not for one moment could I shake Georgy — at home, with my family, my friends. I was really quite impossible to be with — just as Georgy is impossible, trying to hide her true nature.

—Redgrave, interviewed by Dorothy Manners for *The New York World Journal Tribune*, 18 Dec 1966

Michael REDGRAVE [1908-1985]

Born: Bristol, England; father to Lynn, Vanessa and Corin Redgrave [1939]. Studies in modern languages at Cambridge University, stage work with The Liverpool Repertory Theatre and at The Old Vic in London preceded his film debut in The Lady Vanishes (1938, Alfred Hitchcock):

I have learned nearly all of the little I know about films through my directors. From Hitchcock who directed my first film I learned to do as I was told and not to worry too much. Hitchcock, being the brilliant master of the technical side of his script that he is, knew that he could get a performance out of me by his own skill in cutting. He knew that mine was a very good part, that I was more of less the right type for it, that I was sufficiently trained to be able to rattle off my lines and that mercifully, since I was aware that not even the cleverest cameraman in the world could make me look like Robert Taylor, I was never particularly camera-conscious. But he also sensed that I thought the whole atmosphere of filming was, to say the least, uncongenial compared to that obtaining in the theatre....

One of Hitchcock's tricks which he works on the psychology of the public is to cast actors against their type, a trick he has managed often with great success; he also uses shock tactics on actors and besides his famous practical jokes he likes to 'rib' his actors, believing, sometimes but not always correctly, that actors, who have an infinite capacity for taking praise, are jogged into a more awake state if humorously insulted. I well remember him saying 'Actors are cattle!' I can see now that he was trying to jolt me out of my unrealistic dislike of working conditions in the studios and what he thought was a romantic reverence for the theatre....

The method of my second director, Paul Czinner [on *Stolen Life* (1939)], was in most ways the complete reverse. He overwhelmed me with subtle praise in order to make me feel that I was a good enough actor to play opposite my adored Elisabeth Bergner. He further explained to me that whereas there was never time for what stage actors would call proper rehearsals, the camera was often able to catch the artist's emotions or reactions when these were still in their early, improvisatory states. He printed all the takes, and there were usually a great many, of all the shots. 'Rushes' each day frequently ran for three quarters of an hour or more. He explained that by frequent close cutting and the selection of a look from one take, a line from another and a particular though perhaps quite irrelevant expression from the third, a performance was often very much richer than the actor felt it to be even in his 'best' take. He personally directed the editing of the film over many months, and no editing was begun until the shooting of the film was completed.

This of course is a very expensive method and has gone completely out of fashion. The tendency now is to use less 'cross-cutting' and a great number of tracking shots, and much work is done from 'dollies' and cranes. In a way this would seem to be preferable from the actor's point of view for it allows him to build up a scene, to know how he is going to make his effects more or less on his own. But some of these moving shots are extremely tricky for the technicians as well as for the actor and it is very galling for the actor to find that the take which he has felt to be unquestionably the best from the acting point of view has to be scrapped because someone fancies he could see a mike shadow. After a time the actor learns to be philosophical about this and to realize that it puts a further onus on him to be as good as he can be all the time....

It is perhaps from Carol Reed, with whom I made my third film [*Climbing High* (1938)], and with whom I was to make two more [*The Stars Look Down* (1939) and *Kipps* (1941)] that I learned for the first time how intimate the relationship between actor and film director can be. Reed understands the actor's temperament perhaps as well as any director alive. The theatre and acting are in his blood and he is able, with infinite pains and care, to give the actor the feeling that everything is up to him and that all the director is doing is to make sure that he is being seen to his best advantage. A very warm and friendly feeling prevails, not only on the set, and the actor is encouraged to feel that he has also assisted in the preparation of the film. Indeed Reed frequently did ask my opinions and I think on several occasions adopted suggestions of mine.... He is enormously considerate of other people's feelings but underneath this gentle velvet glove is an iron will which eleven times out of ten will have its own way in the end. I find this entirely admirable.

—Redgrave, in his *Mask or Face: Reflections in an Actor's Mirror* (London: Billing and Sons, 1958)

I confess that many of the pictures I have made I have accepted because the money they brought me helped me to choose in the theater only the parts I liked. *Dead of Night* [1945] is one of the films that many people, oddly enough, seem to remember me for. I played the role of a mad ventriloquist. The director of my sequence in the film was Alberto Cavalcanti, and something happened, the kind of thing that happens when a particular actor meets a particular director who excites his invention in a particular part and works with him on a give-and-take basis. Perhaps it's too easy an answer, but I've always believed to a certain degree that the effectiveness of a film part depends on whether you can say in one sentence, or on a postcard, what the part is. For example, about my part in *Dead of Night* you can say, "It's about a ventriloquist who believes his life is controlled by his dummy."

—Redgrave, interviewed by Lillian and Helen Ross for *The Player* (New York: Simon & Schuster, 1962)

It was Jean Gabin, I believe, who answered when someone asked him what he looked for in a film, *L'histoire! L'histoire!*. I might have done well to consider this before accepting *Secret Beyond the Door* [1948]. It had a strong story, to be sure, a mystery of sorts, pseudo-pathological and pretentious. But it was to be directed by Fritz Lang, a hero of mine since those far-off students days when I watched the *Niebelungen* [1924] in a dingy, smoke-filled cinema in Heidelberg. And it was to be made in Hollywood....

"Take in the church, Joan honey. Give a glance at the ceiling. You're waiting for Michael — be a little apprehensive!"

We were shooting our first scene in a Mexican church. Joan Bennett seemed a little distressed, I thought, as Fritz kept up a continual running commentary from behind the camera.

"Don't close your mouth, Joan. No, *don't* close your mouth! I said *don't*. Cut! Do you think you could leave your mouth a little open, Joan honey?"

"He treats me like a puppet," muttered Joan as she walked off the set to her caravan after the shot. But he must know what he's doing, I thought. In his two previous films [*The Woman in the Window* (1944) and *Scarlet Street* (1945)] she had given very polished performances.

—Redgrave, in his *In My Mind's Eye* (London: George Weidenfeld & Nicolson Ltd., 1983)

It is impossible for anybody who knew Puffin [Asquith] to escape the word "charm." One loved even his extreme mannerisms, like his habit of ducking his head on one side, rather like a bird, and clasping his hands and saying with a sweet smile, "Oh, thank you! Do you think you could? Oh, that would be so good, I think that would be fine...."

I remember particularly the scene [in *The Browning Version* (1951)] in which Crocker-Harris, the villain-hero of the play, has to digest the fact that he is known as Himmler of the Lower Fifth. The set for that scene — the classroom — was a very big one with two people in it.

Puffin said: "Where do you feel like going? Where would you like to be for that bit?" And I said: "I would like to walk away from the camera, with my back to it — away — away to the end of the long classroom, take in the names carved on the walls, the initials and so on. Then come back again and come into close-up." I wanted to do this great circumambulation in this scene for my very long speech.

Puffin said: "Fine! Fine!" But the sound people said, "We are going to pick up quite a lot of noise...."

"I can either do it your way," said Puffin, "and put the sound on afterwards — or I can follow you with the camera." I said: "No. I will dub what I am saying afterwards." Not many directors, especially of Puffin's magnitude, would say to the actor: "Where would you like to go? What would you like to do?" and be able to accommodate the actor's wishes with his own concept of how it should be done. He could afford to give one those bits of latitude. He was so humble and truly modest as really good artists usually are....

I remember especially the arrangements Puffin made for Lady Bracknell's first entrance [in *The Importance of Being Earnest* (1952)]. Very carefully he explained to Edith [Evans] that chalk marks had been made on the floor to indicate where she should stand when she came in, with a corresponding mark for the camera; then she should move on a certain word while speaking her line, on to the second chalk mark...and so on.

It had been worked out and rehearsed very thoroughly for the camera movements and the artist's movements. It worked splendidly at the rehearsal. But Edith, who is her own mistress, would almost invariably come through the door saying: "Ah, Mr. Worthing!", or whatever her line was, and go right past the first chalk mark and straight on to the second one.

Puffin with his...er...I cannot avoid using the words "elfin charm," said: "Dear Dame Edith. If you go straight on to the second mark the camera isn't with you any more." And Edith said: "Well, I don't know what it is about me but I always feel the camera should come to *me* instead of me go to the *camera*." I shall never forget Puffin crumpling up with laughter, because he understood the actor's side extraordinarily well. He gave the minimum of direction. [Redgrave also worked on Asquith's *The Way to the Stars* (1945).]

—Redgrave, interviewed by R.J. Minney for *The Films of Anthony Asquith* (New York: A.S. Barnes, 1976)

Vanessa REDGRAVE [1937-]

Born: London, England; daughter of Michael Redgrave and Rachel Kempson; sister of Lynn and Corin. Studies at The Central School of Speech and Drama in London and work on the London stage preceded her film debut opposite her father in Behind the Mask (1958, Brian Desmond Hurst). In 1966, she played Leonie in Morgan!, the first of two films for Karel Reisz:

[Karel] explained to me that in filming each individual scene is a whole unit, and its own value must be found, unlike a play which has a single value and climbs to it from start to finish. I'm sure he used clearer words than that, but however he said it I understood him.

We rehearsed a bit too. I was very nervous and I overacted terribly, which was what he wanted me to do, to clean myself out. Of course, working with David Warner was marvelous. He was smashing. I hate to use words like this but he was, how else can I say it? Sensitive.

Morgan! changed a lot as we went along because of the people in it. Karel let it grow. He had to tell me an awful lot of things — technical things and things about acting. But electricity did happen among the three of us. David's interpretation of Morgan, for instance, was so delightful and charming that I became sure that Leonie had to have a side that loved him deeply, always would love him, in spite of not really understanding him.

—Redgrave, interviewed for *Radio Times*, 30 Sept 1971

Some people see [Isadora Duncan] as a sort of pioneer hippie but she wasn't that at all. I have a fantastic admiration for her. She believed in free love at a time when such ideas were taboo, so, of course, all the right people had to pretend to despise her....

Isadora's most treasured possessions were her children. When she lost them she lavished her love on all the children of the world. During her life she adopted more than 30 children and tried to give them what she would have given her own....

She was utterly fearless. Look at the way she tells those Russian politicians off, and it's only 1921, just four years after the revolution. She did what she wanted without worrying much what people thought, and I'm fond of that. She fought for so many of the freedoms women are still fighting for, without in any way being a suffragette. Of course, she was hell sometimes; I suppose we all are. She was just *more* so.

Even trying to keep up with her in make-believe is exhausting. But I'm crazy about this role [in *Isadora* (1968, Karel Reisz)]. It gives me a great chance to do *big* things in a *big* way, something you don't often get on the screen. The picture covers more than 30 years and I'm in every scene but two. And it gives me an opportunity to dance, which I love.

—Redgrave, interviewed by Warren Hall for *Sunday News*, 21 Jan 1968

I didn't think of Julia [in *Julia* (1977, Fred Zinnemann)] as being like a god, but it was Lillian's idealization of her that made her bigger than life. There are people in every time whose principles set them higher than the people around them. That was the case with Julia, a least with how Lillian Hellman saw her.

—Redgrave, interviewed by Mary Rourke for *Women's Wear Daily*, 19 Sept 1977

Q. Are there overtones of lesbianism in [*Julia*]?

A. No. I don't think so, not at all. There is no hint of it in the way Lillian Hellman writes of their friendship. In fact, in the book where Lillian views Julia's body in the funeral parlor, she says something like, "It wouldn't matter if I said I never even kissed her. So I just touched her face." There was a certain element of teacher and student to it, with Julia the teacher and Lillian the student. Julia often told Lillian [Jane Fonda] what to do, and that was obviously a certain source of strength and steadiness for Lillian.

—Redgrave, interviewed by Judy Klemesrud for *The New York Times*, 2 Oct 1977

I feel that all I've done [in *The Bostonians* (1984, James Ivory)] is play the lady Henry James wrote about, a lady who really existed. My own bluestocking spinster great cousin was one of the first women undergraduates admitted to college in London. Girls of a certain background were treated with contempt if they tried to do anything with their lives except marry for the right amount of money. Socially, there were enormous pressures to give in. They were proud women who were ridiculed, who were living in a milieu that treated them with scorn. Henry James wrote with an intense attraction and intense revulsion toward all those women. I don't share James's cynicism about those women, but none of us tried to change what James wrote. The one really basic danger for all of us actors is to try to make the characters we play as we would like them to be and not as they really are. Every woman would like to be courageous and not to be jealous or have ignoble petty feelings, but James traces in Olive the pettiness all of us would like to avoid portraying and I try scrupulously to show characters in all their unlikable moments.

—Redgrave, interviewed by Aljean Harmetz for *The New York Times*, 24 Mar 1985

Some time after the fact, I read reviews of [*The Bostonians*]. Only one review mentioned Olive as being potentially lesbian. Proving, again, that people see what they want to see. When I'd read the script, I found it quite clear that she was a woman-loving woman, but — in that time and era — not one who had acted upon her sexuality. Many women like Olive would have been virgins, in that era. Sexuality of a sort was not encouraged or condoned in women. But to me it was clear that the story was in its essence a romantic triangle....

—Redgrave, interviewed by Boze Hadleigh for *The New York Native*, 30 Apr 1990

Oliver REED [1938-]

Born: Robert Oliver Reed in Wimbledon, England. Work as a nightclub bouncer, boxer and cab driver preceded his film debut in The League of Gentlemen (1960, Basil Dearden). In 1971, he played Father Grandier in The Devils, the third of four films for Ken Russell:

Q. All that pain and torture in *The Devils* — was that simulated?

A. No, it was quite painful. I had a little buzzer thing to use when I couldn't take any more.... They had these flames all around, gas flames, which could be turned up. They shaved my hair off, but that scene they saved until last in case I died. It's true! They built Loudon, the city, but they didn't account for the wind — and on this particular day, every time the flames went up high Ken would go completely mad and run up with buckets of paraffin and throw them on the fire. He went a bit strange. It got very, very tense, but I think the violence was quite effective. The trouble is I think sometimes one couldn't see the woods for the trees — there was so much calculation and abuse that Grandier, my character, got lost.

—Reed, interviewed by Linda Merinoff for *Penthouse*, Jan 1976

When [Ken Russell] gets volatile I usually shout back at him and take him quietly aside and tell him he's being unreasonable. Usually he then comes back and says in front of people "I'm sorry...." He's one of these incredibly talented people who lives off nervous energy and he needs to be understood — that is he needs people around him who understand his moods.... There are very few times when I need direction from him now so he can get on with other things and not have to worry about me. For him that's one problem out of the way.

A lot of directors like to work closely with actors and actresses, but Ken likes working with the camera, concentrating on movement, the way you move, the way the light falls. [Reed also worked on Russell's *Dante's Inferno* (1967 — for TV), *Women in Love* (1970) and *Tommy* (1975).]

—Reed, interviewed for *The Story of Tommy* by Richard Barnes and Pete Townshend (Middlesex, England: Eel Pie Publishing, 1977)

Christopher REEVE [1952-]

Born: New York City. Studies at The Juilliard School in NY, and work on TV and Broadway preceded his film debut in Gray Lady Down (1978, David Greene). To date, he has played Superman in four films beginning with Superman (1978, Richard Donner):

Before we started filming, we met with the guys who do the comic books — bright guys. We sat around a table and they said there are two things you have to remember about Superman:

A) He's an orphan, and that governs his emotional behavior;

B) He's an alien, and what makes him super is he's got the wisdom to use his powers well.

The 'Man of Steel' aspect is totally exaggerated. He's only super because he happens to come from another planet. If he'd grown up on Krypton he might have been a plumber. But here he's a symbol, a fantasy. For me, that limits him, because there isn't enough to do with the part. Even physically, there are only three or four poses he takes.

People want to see Superman a certain way — you have to honor that expectation. So I give them that and then take it one step further with Clark Kent. We take away the makeup that strengthens Superman's features. I shrink — Clark actually walks about three inches shorter than Superman. My voice becomes flatter, more Midwestern — Clark has asthma.... I see Clark as a deliberate put-on by Superman. Clark's a tongue-in-cheek impression of who we are.

—Reeve, interviewed by Dan Carlinksy for *The New York Times*, 10 Dec 1978

Clark [is]...a little nervous; he has a stutter, and asthma in the winter. The prescription in his glasses is wrong, so he walks into things. He has a bad habit of dropping his coat when he's trying to hang it up. There's an eagerness to him, an eagerness to please that I've gotten from Harold Lloyd and Cary Grant in some of those Thirties comedies; perhaps a little Jimmy Stewart is thrown in, too. Now while I'm not modelling my performance on any of them, there's an influence there from that kind of comedy.

—Reeve, interviewed by Sharon Hammond for *Interview*, Dec 1978

Richard Dreyfuss said about doing *Close Encounters of the Third Kind* [1978, Steven Spielberg] that a lot of the time he was standing in the middle of the soundstage having to fake a flying saucer going over, which would be put in later by the animation department with model work. So often, particularly in the flying sequences in *Superman*, there was nothing to look at except some weird machines on the studio floor and an English crew sitting around drinking cups of tea. But it challenged you to find it inside. [Reeve also starred in *Superman II* (1980, Richard Lester), *Superman III* (1983, Richard Lester) and *Superman IV* (1987, Sidney J. Furie, which was based on a story by Reeve, Lawrence Konner and Mark Rosenthal).]

—Reeve, interviewed by David Galligan for *Drama-Logue*, 28 Jan-3 Feb 1988

[Sidney Lumet — on *Deathtrap* (1982)] knows how to talk techical language — he knows how to talk Method, he knows how to improvise, and he does it all equally well. Michael Caine had his part nailed from day one, so Sidney left him alone; they just cracked jokes and had a good time. Irene Worth brought a lot of ideas; Sidney's job was to refine and edit the wealth of material she brought him. My way is improvisation as a process of finding out what I *don't* want in order to get what I *do* want. Then during shooting Sidney would often come up at the last minute and give me a new idea I'd never throught of — not a major change, but something fresh to put on my plate. That, combined with the work we'd done in rehearsal, made for spontaneous work.

—Reeve, interviewed by Don Shewey for *American Film*, Dec 1982

I loved playing Superman. People would say to me, when I did *The Bostonians* [1984, James Ivory] or *The Aspern Papers* which I did on stage in London, "Well, I suppose after Superman it must be incredibly difficult to play Henry James." Actually the reverse is true because in *Superman* you're standing out there without the support of real actable material. It is much easier to act with a Henry James script to lean on, with the details it provides and the truth it shows about behavior; whereas, if you're playing somebody from outerspace, where do you go for *that*? What do you base the part on...?

—Reeve, interviewed by David Galligan for *Drama-Logue*, 28 Jan-3 Feb 1988

Lee REMICK [1935-1991]

Born: Quincy, Massachusetts. Ballet studies with Mme. Ruth Swoboda and modern dance with Charles Weidman and work in summer stock and on Broadway preceded her film debut in Elia Kazan's A Face in the Crowd (1957):

Before I did any filming, Kazan sent me to Arkansas to live with a family there for about two weeks, until the unit arrived to shoot the scenes I was in. He knew I was a city girl, so he wanted me to absorb that atmosphere which was quite new to me, and also he wanted me to get accustomed to the accent. It was a fairly painful experience. The family were sweet people but I had absolutely nothing in common with them.... By the end of the fortnight, when the unit turned up, I must say I was hungry for someone to talk to....

Anatomy of a Murder [1959, Otto Preminger] wasn't all that difficult, really. As I saw it, the girl's sexuality was innocent, in a sense. She was sweet and simple and dumb. Of course she knew what she was doing, but she wasn't a tart. She just enjoyed the sheer pleasure of knowing that she was attractive to men. She held a position of strength in the most instinctive way.

I had heard, of course, that Preminger is ferocious with actors. And he can be. But he was charming to me always, both on the set and off it. He could have chopped me in little pieces if he'd chosen. In fact he did start in on me one day and I replied in kind, and after that he didn't do it any more. I was married by then and I'd just had a baby, and I think this must have awed him. Probably he was impressed by that feminine mystique thing — the vulnerability of a woman at such a time....

—Remick, interviewed by Gordon Gow for *Films & Filming*, Feb 1971

My part in [*Wild River* (1960, Elia Kazan) was] of a raw mountain girl, warm and loving, who isn't satisfied with her life and who chooses to follow her own desires instead of what her family wants for her.... Working with Kazan on that part was a revelation. He has been an actor himself, and he knows how actors feel. He knows that anyone who is fool enough to get up on a stage or go before a camera is exposing himself in so many ways, and needs someone to give him support and confidence. Kazan always made me feel that I was the only person in the world who could do my part. There's so much to Kazan. He knows how to listen to actors; most actors love to talk, and never have a chance to say enough. He's observant of everything relevant to the actor. He's eloquent, and he knows how to extract the best performance from an actor. Actors confide in him. They tell him things they'd never tell another living soul. Then, whenever it's needed for your performance, he pulls something you've told him out of a hat and hands it back to you, and you know what to do in the performance. My interpretation of the role in *Wild River* was the truest in my experience, and it was Kazan who enabled me to make it true. In one scene, for example, it's raining outside, and I'm in my house waiting for Montgomery Clift, the man I'm in love with. Kazan suggested that I have a towel in my hands while waiting. He wanted me to give the towel to Monty in a certain way. Kazan kept telling me, "It's wet outside, wet and muddy, muddy and wet, wet, wet, and as soon as Monty comes in you'll want to give him the towel." Then, when Monty came in, I don't remember how I did what I did, but somehow I was feeling Monty's wetness. There was a certain feeling in it that couldn't have been there without Kazan.

—Remick, interviewed by Lillian and Helen Ross for *The Player* (New York: Simon & Schuster, 1962)

[Montgomery Clift] was not very well at the time when we were working together, but he did inspire such love from everybody. He was really like a wounded bird, he really was. He cared an awful lot about what he did, he was meticulous, absolutely, but I mean meticulous to the point of, if he had a scene to play sitting in this chair and he would finally settle himself in and he'd say, "That okay?" He was convinced that everybody hated him and he was hopeless and awful and he would fall apart if you said, "No, it's not quite right at all." "Why isn't it all right?" and he'd shuffle himself around, "Now, there, is that okay?" Every little move was so carefully, painfully, and painstakingly worked out. I adored him, I really did love him.

Days of Wine and Roses [1962, Blake Edwards] called for a kind of research...so, [Jack Lemmon and I] went off to A.A. meetings, and I, of course, had the general idea that a lot of people have, that A.A. meetings are all a lot of sort of derelict drunks sitting around looking red eyed and shaking in awful hovels in the Bowery in New York. So the author of the piece, J.P. Miller, took us to a meeting...on 64th and Park Avenue where all these lovely people were drinking coffee, shaking a bit, to be sure, but it was a marvelous experience in a strange way.... Anyway, we watched that one, then went down to see another sort on the Bowery in California. I went to a few, to listen to these people talk and tell why they did what they did, what it meant to their lives and then I also went unhappily to the jails in Los Angeles, to the drunk tanks and things, late at night watching them bringing in people they would have picked up off the street from doorways and things and that was very upsetting, revealing and helpful in so far as the way people looked physically...the way they talked, it was very depressing.

Paul Newman is a director with whom I hope I will work again [having worked with him on *Sometimes a Great Notion* (1971)]. He's an absolutely marvelous director. He's worked with Kazan and so he and I had that sort of common language to refer to. He would say, "Y'know what Gadge would say in this kind of instance?" and we would both think, "Well, what would Gadge say?"

—Remick, interviewed at The National Film Theatre, London, 15 June 1972

Burt REYNOLDS [1936-]

Born: Waycross, Georgia. Following studies at Florida State College (he was quarterback of their football team) and Palm Beach Junior College, he won a scholarship to The Hyde Park Playhouse in N.Y. Work on Broadway preceded his film debut in Angel Baby (1961, Paul Wendkos). In 1972, he played Lewis in John Boorman's Deliverance:

Boorman...called me and said, "I want to see you about this film...." I flew back to Los Angeles, went in to see him, and asked what he'd seen me in. He said, "I saw you on the *Tonight* show." And I said, "How could you think of me for this picture because of the *Tonight* show?" He said, "Because there were five people there and you were in control. I want a guy who's in control." I turned around and Jon Voight, whom I'd never met, walked in. Voight, who's always very much into the character he plays, had already been in rehearsal a couple of weeks and he was doing a southern accent. I started talking with him — in a southern accent — and we immediately got into an improvisation together, about going up to this river — which later turned out to be the improvisation over the opening credits. We did it first in that office. I was there maybe a total of an hour; I got up to leave and Voight shook my hand. I liked him immediately. I turned to John Boorman and Boorman said, "You've got the part." I was stunned....

Anyway, [novelist and screenwriter James] Dickey said to me, "Have you read a book called *Zen and the Art of Archery*?" I said no, and he said, "You must read that book, boy, otherwise you'll never be Lewis." I said I didn't have the book and he said, "*I* have the book. What it says is that *you* don't release the arrow — the *arrow* releases you, and it goes where you want it to go."

We got to rehearsing every day. The four of us [Reynolds, Voight, Ned Beatty and Ronny Cox] became so close. We would rehearse all morning and then go get in the canoes in the afternoon. In the original script there was a scene where we're shooting targets — in fact I talk them into going on this trip while we're shooting targets. And supposedly I never miss. We went out to shoot and I couldn't hit anything — I was hitting my feet or hitting the trees or hitting the mountain. But when I got the character, when Lewis started coming to me, we were rehearsing one day and I knew I had him. We got into this scene with the bows and arrows and I picked up the arrow and I shot seven arrows into the bull's-eye about forty yards away. And *I* didn't release the arrow; *it* released me....

Q. I want to know how the other actors learned how to run the rapids? I know you've been a stunt man and could do things like that....

I must tell you that at least ten times I — and the other guys on the picture — were almost killed. Without exaggeration. We were lost, didn't have a chance. But we somehow managed to get ashore. We just did it, but I don't know how we did it. I'd never attempt to do it again, I *couldn't* do it again....

There is a certain genre of film — like *Wages of Fear* [1952, Henri-Georges Clouzot] — that represents terror, real terror, man against the elements, man testing himself.... I stole from the film, unabashedly, the idea of the broken bone sticking out of my leg. It was a pork bone that I bought at a butcher shop and broke in half and then tied around my leg.

—Reynolds, interviewed at Judith Crist's Tarrytown seminar, 21- 23 April 1978; repr. in *Take 22*, co-ed by Judith Crist and Shirley Sealy (New York: Viking Press, 1984)

I'm sure when *Deliverance* came out, ninety percent of the people who saw it...thought that character was me. They probably said, "How brilliant John Boorman was to cast this brutish Marlon Brando-type of musclehead." But that character wasn't me. He was a guy totally into himself with, I think, a lot of homosexual tendencies, which you see in his relationship with Jon Voight. He had the whole psychological thing of killing somebody in the act of saving him, which was definitely an orgasm for him. We played it that way.

—Reynolds, interviewed by Joseph McBride and Brooks Riley for *Film Comment*, May/June 1978

I loved making [*The Longest Yard* (1974, Robert Aldrich)]. It's closer to me than anything I've ever done. It is the only script I've ever done that was written for me — the whole kind of self-deprecating, egomaniac humor.... There's a line I ad-libbed in the picture which sums up my whole life: "I've always felt that I always had my shit together. I just couldn't carry it."

—Reynolds, interviewed by Andy Warhol for *Interview*, Feb 1976

The Longest Yard had an atmosphere of fun. Also, Bob kept the game very competitive. The members of the two [football] teams didn't socialize during filming, just as they wouldn't have socialized in the fictional setting. We would run plays the defense knew. Then I would call plays that they didn't know about and those takes were generally what ended up in the movie because they looked so much more real.... We discussed my character a lot, and, fortunately, completely agreed. He was [to be] a combination of Joe Namath and Bobby Lane. Bob wanted me to have fun with the role and to feel free to improvise — an actor's dream. Bob and I both felt that this All-Pro, All-American had learned nothing in his life, but a rag-tag band of convicts finally taught him a lesson about humanity.

—Reynolds, in a letter to Edwin T. Arnold and Eugene L. Miller (1 May 1984); repr. in *The Films and Career of Robert Aldrich* (Knoxville: The University of Tennessee Press, 1986)

Debbie REYNOLDS [1932-]

Born: Mary Francis Reynolds in El Paso, Texas. Miss Burbank of 1948, she made her film debut in June Bride (1948, Bretaigne Windust). In 1950, she played Melba Robinson in Two Weeks with Love:

Many of the mannerisms of Melba Robinson, the unquenchable fourteen-year-old in *Two Weeks with Love* were grafted onto her character because they were the things I normally did.

Director Roy Rowland arranged this because I still was very new to pictures and didn't have the experience necessary to sustain a characterization. His rough idea...was to help me relax and be myself. I was seventeen at the time, and though I had no trouble looking three years younger, Roy knew it would be hard for me to act like a fourteen-year-old.

Thus, when he discovered I played the French horn, he arranged to have Melba play it. When he found eating was one of my favorite hobbies — I regularly consumed two lunches then and had a hearty afternoon snack — he made Melba a marathon muncher. Melba even developed a fondness for dill pickles because they were a favorite of mine.

—Reynolds, in *The Saturday Evening Post*, 7 Mar 1953

I got along very well with Louis B. Mayer. He was always very kind to me. It was at his insistence that I do *Singin' in the Rain* [1950, Gene Kelly and Stanley Donen]. Gene Kelly didn't want me.... I was only eighteen, and I wasn't a professional dancer. I still feel my performance in *Singin' in the Rain* is just adequate. Any thanks for my dancing must go to Gene. He taught me the routines over and over again.

—Reynolds, interviewed by Shaun Considine for *After Dark*, June 1973

Gene would put me in a rehearsal studio with either Carol Haney or Jeannie Coyne, his assistants, and a tap teacher called Ernie Flatt, and he wouldn't let me leave until I was step perfect. Sometimes I danced for eight to ten hours a day and, perfectionist that he is, he'd come in and say, "Okay, show me what you've learned." And I was so petrified of him because of the temper I knew he had, that whenever he came in, I'd do everything wrong, and he'd say "Back!" and slam the door again. He would work me so hard that at times my feet bled — literally. But I wanted to prove to him that I could do it, so I just worked and worked. He makes you feel you're capable of more than you are, and I didn't want to let him down. Well, this torture went on for months, and I remember, Fred Astaire was in the rehearsal room next to mine, (where he was making *The Belle of New York* [1952]), and he would come in and pacify me. "It'll all work out," he'd say. "So don't get so discouraged." And I'd burst into tears and say, "But I'll *never* learn to dance. Never!" And he'd say, "Debbie, if you want to be a great dancer, you'll have to keep trying and sweat it out for as long as it takes. It's the only way." And he was right. It *was* the only way. But it was sheer agony for me. Everyone else seemed to be having lots of fun but me. I had too much to learn, and in too short a period. There was just no time for fun. To be thrown into the Gene Kelly type of class was too formidable for fun....

Gene taught me discipline, and he taught me how to slave. And today, if I don't drop dead from exhaustion after a rehearsal, I feel I haven't accomplished a thing....

One of the things I remember most vividly about Gene was that he never liked to be proved wrong. On the "Good Morning" number, we were all doing a step around a stool at the bar counter, and suddenly Gene stopped and insisted that Donald [O'Connor] was doing it wrong. In fact, Donald was doing it right and Gene was the one who was wrong. And both Donald and I *knew* Gene was wrong. But all Donald did was to say he was sorry. Well, Gene became very angry and said, "You should know this by now. We've worked long enough on it." I looked at Donald, because I expected Donald to say something back, but he didn't. He adored and worshipped Gene Kelly and wouldn't have dared answer back. Besides, Donald was younger than Gene, and being the very respectful type of person he is, he just kept quiet. So we did it again and again. Finally Gene stopped and said, "*I'm* doing it wrong! Why the hell didn't you tell me?" Then he was madder than ever at us for not pointing it out to him. And I said to him, "But Gene, you can't win for losing with you."

—Reynolds, interviewed by Clive Hirschhorn for *Gene Kelly* (New York: W.H. Allen, 1974)

You learn when you work with Bette Davis. We had a scene together [on *The Catered Affair* (1956, Richard Brooks)], mother and daughter, where she's cooking fish and talking to me. We rehearsed that bit for two weeks. Everything had to be timed. Turn on the gas jets on one line. Pick up the spatula on another. Put it down on the third. It had to look very natural. It's very tricky working with props in movies because the different shots have to match. In the end it just looked like the two of us having a conversation. Davis is a perfectionist, and brilliant. To this day I am grateful for her many lessons.

Ernie Borgnine also worked with me, rehearsing me in my scenes with him. When it came to actual shooting, the director worked hard with me too. But he intimidated me throughout the production and I hated it.

Shelley Winters is wildly bananas. I'll say that from here to China, because she is. It's not that she's not funny, provocative, and all those other things, but when she's working on a film, she's unpredictable, to say the least. I called her "Killer" on the set [of *What's the Matter with Helen?* (1971, Curtis Harrington)]. To this day I call her Killer. She gets so into the role she becomes it. In this case she was playing a murderess.

When we first got together to read the script, she said, "My psychiatrist told me not to do this picture because it would probably flip me over the edge...."

It started out very well because she liked rehearsing. She can be quite brilliant. We got along fine, although Shelley likes all the attention....

She had the habit of constantly changing her lines *during* the scene. If you don't know that's what's coming, it is very difficult. When Shelley first did this, Curtis Harrington very diplomatically stopped everything and read her the correct lines.

"I don't learn words; I learn thoughts," she snapped. And she went on doing it her way....

—Reynolds, in her (with David Patrick Columbia) *Debbie: My Life* (New York: William Morrow & Co., 1988)

Thelma RITTER [1905-1969]

Born: Brooklyn, N.Y. Studies at The American Academy of Dramatic Arts in N.Y. led to work in vaudeville and stock. In 1944, she emerged from retirement to act on the radio. She made her film debut in Miracle on 34th Street (1947, George Seaton). In 1949, she played Sadie in Joseph L. Mankiewicz's A Letter to Three Wives:

Sadie is the kind of person I admire, maybe the kind I'd like to be. Nothing disturbed her; she was practically indestructible.

Besides admiring her toughness, I loved her impudence. She said the things we all wish we could say at times, but don't have nerve to. She happened to be a maid, which made this more amusing, but she could as well have been an elevator girl or a clerk. The important thing about Sadie was that she was a character. And once you encountered her, you knew it.

—Ritter, in *The Saturday Evening Post*, 11 Oct 1952

That [Bette] Davis! She's the most conscientious actress in the world, to say nothing of one of the most talented. [In *All About Eve* (1950, Joseph Mankiewicz)]...she pitched her lines so that mine would be heard to best advantage.

—Ritter, interviewed by Hedda Hopper for *The Chicago Sunday Tribune*, 4 Feb 1951

[Screenwriter, Arthur] Miller's given me a thing to work with [on *The Misfits* (1961, John Huston)]. In one speech, for instance, Isabelle, with no vanity, naive, innocent, no animosity, no bitterness, tells a perfect stranger she got drunk and fell down and broke her arm. She's a nice woman. She lives vicariously — involved with Roslyn's life. You're quite sure she doesn't read or knit. Her feeling for Roslyn [Marilyn Monroe] is maternal. She has no envy. A little sadness too. She's uncomplicatedly complicated. If she ever went to a psychiatrist, she'd drive him out of his mind....

The picture is a little unlike any I've done before, because it depends on the personalities and the relationships of the actors. There would be no room in this script for a run-of-the-mill personality. I don't remember a picture that depends quite so much on oddity.

—Ritter, interviewed by James Goode for *The Story of The Misfits* (New York: Bobbs-Merrill, 1963); reprinted as *The Making of The Misfits* (New York: Proscenium, 1986)

Jason ROBARDS [1922-]

Born: Chicago; son of Jason Robards, Sr. [1896-1963]. After service in the Navy during WWII, he studied at The American Academy of Dramatic Arts in N.Y. and with Uta Hagen. Work on radio and on the Broadway stage preceded his film debut in The Journey (1959, Anatole Litvak). In 1965, he played Murray Burns in Fred Coe's A Thousand Clowns:

There's more of me in *Clowns* than any of the O'Neill plays I've done. For one thing, I've been involved with the script for six years now — as play and film.

There's [also] a lot of him in me. And I love to explore New York like him, particularly around six in the morning when the streets are empty. It's good to get off and be alone, don't you think?

—Robards, interviewed by Frances Herridge for *The New York Post*, 17 Dec 1965

Q. Over the years, your films seem to have been a weird mixture. What determined your choice of film roles?

A. I went through a long period of time where I got strapped financially and alimony determined! I just had to get some extra money, somehow. That period was really detrimental to me creatively.... The one thing that saved my life through all that was staying in the theatre. That was my anchor to reality. Nevertheless, I couldn't meet all the financial demands, so I would go do a film and I did some really rotten ones....

Q. Were there any films that you enjoyed.

A. Yes. I liked working with Karel Reisz on *Isadora* [1968] because we rehearsed a lot and Vanessa Redgrave and I could play out our scenes.... And, oddly enough, I liked working with Roger Corman [on *The St. Valentine's Day Massacre* (1967)]. He said, "How many days can you get in?" I told him I had to be in Mexico in 11 days, so he said, "Right, we'll shoot it in 11 days." He was quick and to the point and we got to play out the scenes.

Q. Did you know [Ben] Bradlee?

A. Yeah. I knew him slightly from the days when I used to hang out with newspapermen.... I had met Ben through some guys I knew, but I didn't know him too well. I still don't think I know him too well, but he was very gracious and gave me a whole run-down on the [*Washington*] *Post* and invited me over to dinner, but we didn't talk about the movie [*All the President's Men* (1976, Alan J. Pakula)] very much.... Our job was to make what we had dramatic and interesting and human. That's the hardest thing, you know, to make these people into human beings that people sitting in a theatre will care about. As far as copying is concerned, Pakula said to me, "If I wanted any of that rubbish we would have got Rich Little," who is an impersonator....

Q. How about Dashiell Hammett? You knew him, didn't you?

A. I'd met him — the same way like Ben, in a way. I was doing Lillian [Hellman]'s play [*Toys in the Attic*] and he came up to Boston to see it. We met after the show one night. [Robards played Hammett in *Julia* (1977, Fred Zinnemann).]

—Robards, interviewed by Jenny Craven for *Films & Filming*, Sept 1978

They couldn't have cast anyone else as Howard Hughes [in *Melvin and Howard* (1980, Jonathan Demme)]. Robards was his middle name, and he had cousins named Loomis, which was the maiden name of one of my grandmothers. I figured I didn't have to do any preparation for the part. It's all built in genetically....

—Robards, interviewed by Tom Buckley for *The New York Times*, 18 May 1979

Eric ROBERTS [1956-]

Born: Biloxi, Mississippi; brother of Julia Roberts [1967-]. Training and work under the direction of his father — Walter Roberts — at The Actors and Writers Workshop in Atlanta, studies at The Royal Academy of Dramatic Art in London and The American Academy of Dramatic Arts in N.Y. and work off-Broadway preceded his film debut in King of the Gypsies (1978, Frank Perry). In 1983, he played Paul Snider in Bob Fosse's Star 80:

I went after that role, because a chance to work with Bob Fosse was a chance of a lifetime. As it turned out, it was the last movie he made. So God bless me, I'm lucky. But I had no affinity for that role. And I told him that. He saw me as a tool he could work with. And he did....

Fosse gave me the greatest direction I ever got. Once, I was having terrible trouble doing a scene, and I stopped and got very frustrated. I said, "I don't know what the *fuck* I'm doing here!" Fosse grabbed me, the way he would do — he was a very physical guy — and he said, "Look at me! If I were not successful — this is what you fuckin' play!" I understood it after that.

Q. Did it disturb you, playing Snider?

A. Yes. To play a loser is one thing. To play a loser who has lost before he's started is quite another. And that's what Snider was.

—Roberts, interviewed by Patrick Merla for *Theater Week*, 4 July 1988

Cliff ROBERTSON [1925-]

Born: La Jolla, California. Navy service during WWII, studies at The Actors Studio in N.Y. and work in repertory, on TV and on the N.Y. stage preceded his film debut in Picnic (1955, Joshua Logan). In 1963, he played John F. Kennedy in Leslie H. Martinson's P.T. 109:

President Kennedy had requested 3 things only about the movie. That it be historically accurate...that any money due to him from added sales of the book, film rights and so on, be given to the crew (or their dependents) of the P.T. 109...and finally that he be allowed to select who would play him.

They tested a lot of actors at the Warner's studio, and sent on the better tests to Washington. And whenever he had 2 minutes free, the president would stick his head into his cinema and look them over.

Emotionally, I'll always be terribly grateful that President Kennedy chose me for the role. That's the sole reason I played it.

—Robertson, interviewed for *Photoplay*, July 1969

Q. You obviously have a mobile, expressive face. But in the first part of the film [*Charly* (1968, Ralph Nelson)] did you have some special makeup to look more jowly? It was remarkable how the contours of your face changed.

A. No, no special makeup. I worked from the inside — but I'd had seven years of digesting the character. I can't explain it. I still think acting is one of the more mysterious art forms. I'll give you an example: the night before the first day's shooting my wife [Dina Merrill] and I were preparing for bed and she said, "How're you going to play him?" That sort of stopped me. I said, "What do you mean by that?" She said, "*Physically* — how will you play him?" I said, "I don't know." She looked at me and said, "You've had this property for seven years — you've been to all these workshops, and you can't tell me how you see him?" I said, "No, at this minute I can't tell you." I went to work the next morning and Ralph asked me if I wanted a run-through, and I said, "No, crank 'em up." That's what is called "going with the instrument," I guess — I just went with it. But I had seven years of osmosis — normally an actor doesn't have that privilege. So when you have that kind of background you *can* go with the instrument.

I'll tell you a story about the actor's sensibility, as opposed to that of someone like a technician.... Geraldine [Page] had flown out from New York, exhausted after being on several short flights to get there. She arrived on the set [of *J.W. Coop* (1971)] at eight o'clock while I was on another location, and about nine the first assistant came to me panicked and said, "She's here — but she's just sitting there, she hasn't touched her makeup or anything." I told him to relax. At about nine-thirty I went over to her and she said, "Hi, Cliff honey, how are ya?" And we started talking about Rip — Rip Torn, her husband — and the old days. Now, it's about ten o'clock. And about ten-thirty she started to put a little bit of makeup on — we're talking about the character, but not too much, just a little bit, just easing into it. Finally, she said, "What about lipstick?" I said, "Maybe you could put it on like you hadn't looked in a mirror — sort of smeared around. And why don't you wear some white bobby socks and some curlers in your hair. It would look sort of sad." Very casually, very easily, what we were trying to do was become related. After all, she was playing my mother — and she could be my sister. We were not *saying*, "Let's get related," it was just a reflex of an experienced actor, just like an old race horse — you *know* those things.... At noon Geraldine and I were still in the dressing room.... At two-fifteen we cranked up the camera, and we finished a two-day shooting with Geraldine half a day early. Once we got started it just *worked*. She's that kind of actress.

—Robertson, interviewed at Judith Crist's Tarrytown seminar, 26-28 Nov 1976; repr. in *Take 22*, co-ed. by Judith Crist and Shirley Sealy (New York: Viking Press, 1984)

Paul ROBESON [1893-1976]

Born: Princeton, New Jersey. After studies at Rutgers University and while pursuing a law degree at Columbia University, he began acting at the Harlem YMCA. Admitted to the N.Y. Bar in 1923, he continued to pursue an acting career, and made his film debut in Body and Soul (1925, Oscar Michaux). In 1933, he played the title role in Dudley Murphy's adaptation of Eugene O'Neill's Emperor Jones, a role he had played on the stage:

Why was the film version of *Emperor Jones* a failure? Partly because scenes in it were changed around from the proper psychological order of the play and partly because the big episode, the long monologue in the forest, which had been built up in the theatre by the use of drums, was not played in the same way in the film. On the stage a drum became an actual character in the scene. The lines I spoke were dialogue addressed to the drum and answered by it. Only in that way could I get the necessary feeling to play the scene as O'Neill's writing of it deserved. We engaged an expert drummer for the part. But in the film, which I started with enthusiasm, I was told that of course we couldn't play the scene that way. We couldn't use the drum in the dramatic emotional way that was essential for me.

—Robeson, interviewed by Sidney Cole for *The Cine-Technician*, Sept/Oct 1938

Q. Well, about *Sanders of the River* [1935, Zoltan Korda]. This picture in which you played the leading role was a slanderous attack on African natives who were pictured as being well-satisfied with the "benevolent" oppression of English imperialism. You, yourself, played the role of selling the natives out to the imperialists. Such a role is inconsistent with your professed love for the Soviet Union and what that country represents.

A. The twist in the picture which was favorable to English imperialism was accomplished during the cutting of the picture after it was filmed. I had no idea that it would have such a turn *after* I had acted in it....

Q. As evidence of your good faith, Paul, that explanation may be acceptable, but good faith alone is not enough. The picture was an out and out betrayal of the African colonials, whatever may be said of your good intentions, and the imperialist twist came about in more than the cutting of the film. You became the tool of British imperialism and must be attacked and exposed whenever you act in such pictures and plays.

A. You're right and I think all the attacks against me and the film were correct. I was roped into the picture because I wanted to portray the culture of the African people in which I have the greatest interest. I wanted to show that while the imperialists contend that the Africans are 'barbarians and uncivilized,' that they have a culture all their own and that they have as much intelligence as any other people.

Nothing would hurt me more than to have the African natives think that I have betrayed them.

—Robeson, interviewed by Ben Davis, Jr. for *The Sunday Worker*, 10 May 1936

I thought I could change [*Tales of Manhattan* (1942, Julien Duvivier)] as we went along, and I did make some headway. But in the end it turned out to be the same old thing — the Negro solving his problem by singing his way to glory. This is very offensive to my people. It makes the Negro child-like and innocent and is in the old plantation tradition. But Hollywood says you can't make the Negro in any other role because it won't be box office in the South. The South wants its Negroes in the old style.

—Robeson, interviewed for *The New York Times*, 24 Sept 1942

Edward G. ROBINSON [1893-1973]

Born: Emmanuel Goldenberg in Bucharest, Rumania; emigrated to the U.S. in 1902. Studies at Columbia University and The American Academy of Dramatic Arts and work on the N.Y. stage (from 1913) preceded his film debut in The Bright Shawl (1923, John S. Robertson). This was not followed by another screen role until the coming of sound when Robinson was one of the many stage actors recruited to 'talk.' Beginning with The Hole in the Wall (1929, Robert Florey), he became identified with the gangster films of the classical period:

In late 1930 Hal Wallis asked me to his office to discuss my playing the role of Otero in *Little Caesar* [1931, Mervyn LeRoy] — the best-seller by William R. Burnett....

Yes, I said Otero. Not Rico, the lead, but Otero, a minor part.

To this day I think it was a ruse. I think Hal had always meant for me to play Rico, and his ploy was to soften my rigid backbone.... In his cool, offhand and peremptory manner he handed me the script of *Little Caesar*, pointing out that the part of Otero was exactly right for me. I took the script back to my dressing room, read it, and decided not only that the part of Otero was exactly wrong for me but that the script itself was a literal and undramatized rendering of the novel....

So I went back to Wallis and announced pompously: "If you're going to have me in *Little Caesar* as Otero, you will completely imbalance the picture. The only part I will consider playing is Little Caesar."

Hal listened carefully to my ravings, made a few notes, then reminded me that my contract gave me no approval of roles.... Hal then said he would take the matter up with Mr. Warner, and within a matter of hours I was cast as Little Caesar.

—Robinson, in his *All My Yesterdays* (New York: Hawthorn Books, 1973)

In treating Little Caesar in the most favorable light possible, I was able to get in a powerful, back-handed slap at criminals. I made people feel sorry for him even when they hated him. When prospective criminals saw what a cringing, crawling thing this big-time killer really was, underworld glamor lost a lot of allure. They couldn't help but see that crime doesn't pay even the smartest crook. I could put my heart into something like that because it might help keep young men out of crime.

—Robinson, interviewed by George S. Kullen for *Screen Book*, June 1939

[Johnny Blake in *Bullets or Ballots* (1936, William Keighley)] was a hard part — I had to play it differently from those gangster roles, play it down, make it quieter. After all, he was a detective, and not a crook. Even so, in that scene where I had to convince the audience as well as the gang that I was turning racketeer, I could see a trace of Little Caesar....

—Robinson, interviewed by Eileen Creelman for *The New York Sun*, 16 June 1936

It is impossible to portray the reactions of a character you are creating in the movies or on the stage unless you are thoroughly familiar with his mental and emotional reflexes, and have determined in your own mind what his reaction will be to any given circumstances.

For instance, when Jack Warner tossed me a script of *Kid Galahad* [1937, Michael Curtiz] I re-lived the entire life of Nick Donati until he, to me, became a factual instead of a fictional personage. I reconstructed his life, quite literally, from the cradle to that big moment in his boxer's dressing room at Madison Square Garden. I knew all his doubts and complexes, his strength and his weakness, his passions and his powers. I knew he was a fellow of terrible, quick temper, kept in control only by the self-discipline which enabled him to rise to the top of his own peculiar profession....

He wasn't a bad guy, did the best he could according to his code. That it was a savage, remorseless code wasn't his fault. It was the fault of his heritage and environment.

—Robinson, interviewed by Regina Crewe for *The New York Journal-American*, 23 May 1937

Of all the gangster pictures in which I've played, *The Last Gangster* [1937, Edward Ludwig] gave me the most pleasure. It has everything an actor might desire — plot, action, romance, plus a definite noteworthy moral message. The message is so indelibly scored that I am quite certain even the most unmindful will derive from it some psychological benefit.

In this picture, the lead character, after having fattened on his nefarious machinations, after participating in gruesome assaults and killings, comes out of it all unscathed and wealthy. But he is a miserable human, haunted by fears and phobias, in a piteous pathological condition. There is certainly nothing in the script to indicate that such a calling, if it may be dignified by that title, is the least bit attractive.

—Robinson, interviewed by Regina Crewe for *The New York Journal-American*, 11 Dec 1937

[Dr. Clitterhouse in *The Amazing Dr. Clitterhouse* (1938, Anatole Litvak)] is an entirely different kind of criminal from the average type. He really is a psychopathic case, a man driven by peculiar mental impulses [he joins a criminal gang in order to study their mental processes and finds that in order to truly succeed in his study he must commit a crime himself]. That is what makes him interesting to play on the screen. It is more an exposition of his mental processes than of action.

—Robinson, interviewed by Hollis Wood for *The Richmond News Leader*, 9 Aug 1938

You can't imagine the pleasure I got out of doing [Dr. Ehrlich in *Dr. Ehrlich's Magic Bullet* (1940, William Dieterle)]. So far, most of the rats, detectives, prosecutors and editors I've played were two-dimensional characters, and it was up to me to round them out, give them flesh and blood and the qualities of human beings. But Ehrlich is a different matter altogether. The character is there...and all an actor has to do is to play it honestly and simply.

—Robinson, interviewed by Michael Mok for *The New York Post*, 16 Feb 1940

[*Dr. Ehrlich's Magic Bullet*] was made when the world was reading banner headlines about Hitler and Mussolini and the bullets which they were releasing so horribly against humanity. At such a moment it was particularly dramatic and gratifying to do the biography of a great humanitarian who sought to release magic bullets into bloodstreams to save life rather than destroy it. Most people remember Doctor Ehrlich as the man who developed salvarsan, the magic bullet with which to kill syphilis. Actually he was the father of chemotherapy, and conceived the idea of fighting disease with chemicals introduced into the body. A master scientist, he was also a rare personality — simple, sincere, honest, courageous, possessed of a timeless vision. It was inspiring to try to make people appreciate his greatness.

—Robinson, in *The Saturday Evening Post*, 16 Feb 1946

Fritz [Lang] was a hellion on the set [of *Woman in the Window* (1944) and *Scarlet Street* (1945)]. He was autocratic, dominating, and extra-precise. He knew exactly what he wanted and he was going to get it, no matter what....

In spite of Fritz's manner and method, which did not always make for a happy set, it was a comfort for an actor to have a director with good taste. If Fritz okayed a take it was all right. If he thought it was fine, I could relax. I was in good hands. There was never any real problem of interpretation of a role with Fritz. First, he was as meticulous as it was possible to be under the old system in choosing actors. He was also very careful with externals, which is very important. You could also talk to Fritz about the whole film and he would take the time to tell you what he was doing.

He was part of everything, not just in the direction of actors, but to the point of doing the make-up. He would even sweep the floor of the set. During *Scarlet Street*, the light wasn't hitting the floor exactly the way he wanted it to, so he had it washed. It still wasn't right, so he put dust all over it and then swept it himself. Once during *Woman in the Window* he spent a whole hour rearranging the folds in Joan Bennett's negligee so that she would cast a certain shadow he wanted. That kind of perfectionism seems great now, and it helps the film when you see the finished picture, but at the time, well....

Fritz was an innovator, of course, and that scene in *Woman in the Window* in which [my] character seems to die, then the camera comes in for a close up and immediately pulls back to reveal him just asleep in a different costume in a different room was extraordinary. There was no cut at all. I was wearing a second costume under the first which grips pulled away as the camera came in, and the entire room also split in half and was pulled away to reveal a second set. No cut. Extraordinary. He was a superb director.

—Robinson, interviewed by David Overby for *Take One*, May 1978

[Sol Roth], the character I play [in *Soylent Green* (1973, Richard Fleischer)] is symbolic of the weakness of liberal intellectuals who aren't doing enough to stop the rot in our society. He is a brilliant man, a close friend of a policeman played by Charlton Heston, who has foreseen the worst, but, in common with many others like him, has done nothing. Finally, he submits to euthanasia....

Soylent Green is...a harrowing projection of our existence 50 years from now. It shows very clearly what may well become of us if we don't look out. It is set in Manhattan, a city of 40 million people living miserably and horribly in a depersonalized Orwellian state.

—Robinson, interviewed by Charles Higham for *The New York Times*, 5 Nov 1972

Ginger ROGERS [1911-]

Born: Virginia McMath in Independence, Kansas. After work in vaudeville and on tour as a dancer, she made her feature film debut with Young Man in Manhattan (1930, Monta Bell). She co-starred with Fred Astaire in ten films between 1933 and 1949, beginning with Thornton Freeland's Flying Down to Rio:

[Astaire] is a perfectionist, a passionate perfectionist. We'd be rehearsing a scene and I'd say, "Oh boy, it's hot, very hot in here," and he'd say, "Well, come on, let's do it again." And so we'd do it again. If I would say, "I think I'll go change my shoes and put on some fresh ones" because I'd wear shoes out just rehearsing, you'd just wear them out. He would say, "Oh, no, no, that's fine, that's good enough." He didn't know that I needed a new pair of shoes because my feet were hurting.... He loves his craft, he loves everything about it. You can tell when you watch him in action. He's quite a guy.

—Rogers, interviewed by R. Couri Hay for *Interview*, Oct 1972

I am always asked if someone is just as he or she seems to be in the movies. In this case, [Edward Everett] Horton was exactly the same as he appeared on the screen. He loved comedy, and behaved in a comical manner all the time. Consequently, we couldn't take our eyes off him, for fear of missing the topper to whatever he was doing. He had our undivided attention. [Rogers and Horton co-starred in *The Gay Divorcee* [1934], *Top Hat* [1935] and *Shall We Dance* [1937].]

[Kitty Foyle in *Kitty Foyle* (1940, Sam Wood)] was the daughter of a proud Irishman and had to look and act like one. Dark hair, blue eyes, a quick wit, and a stinging tongue...that was the way Mr. Foyle saw his offspring. She could take care of herself, "come hell or high-water...."

Sam Wood was friendly, but firm in his direction. However, I found him very receptive to little suggestions along the way. He knew how to hold a film together and bring out the nuances in the script. We had very few disputes, though I remember one minor incident. There was one scene with which I had trouble; it takes place in the hopspital just after Kitty has given birth. I had asked Sam if I might have a few minutes to go to my dressing room to listen to some sad music to get into the mood. Sam okayed the request and off I went to the portable dressing room to hear Tchaikovsky's "Romeo and Juliet." Tears were ready to well up in my eyes when I returned to do the scene. Sam had a bad habit of jingling the coins in his pocket just before a scene. I never thought to speak to him about this very disturbing habit, especially before this scene, which would turn the audience to their hankies....

At that moment, he jingled his coins in his pockets. It was all I could do to keep a straight face, let alone think of a baby I'd just given birth to only minutes before. The take was a disaster.

I went back to my dressing room to hear my sad music again, earnestly trying to get myself into the mood. When I came back to the set, I got back into the hospital bed and prepared for the new take. This time Sam omitted his "excited

and happy" remark. Thank heavens some sensitive friend got to him and told him to stop jingling his coins. The scene proceeded without a hitch, and the rest of the picture followed suit.
—Rogers, in her *Ginger: My Story* (New York: HarperCollins, 1991)
I can assure you that my tits were absolutely *not* taped down, not even a tight brassiere [on *The Major and the Minor* (1942, Billy Wilder)]. Don't know why Ray Milland and Billy Wilder say those things. They're out of their cottin-pickin' minds. I am an actress. I just acted a twelve-year-old girl in a middy blouse. Yeah, and I also played me as a mature woman — and as my mother. I played three generations in *The Major and the Minor*. Don't give me this drivel about strapping down tits, old boy.
—Rogers, interviewed by Maurice Zolotow for *Billy Wilder in Hollywood* (New York: G.P. Putnam's Sons, 1977)

Note: See the Astaire entry for a listing of their ten films together.

Roy ROGERS [1912-]

Born: Leonard Slye in Duck Run, Ohio. After working as a singer with various groups, he made his film debut with The Sons of the Pioneers in The Old Homestead (1935, William Nigh). Three years later, he made his debut as an actor in Under Western Skies (1938, Joe Kane). From 1938, he co-starred with Trigger:

I realized that in many respects the film cowboy was the same as the range rider — he was only as good as his horse.

That was when I decided to take the advice of old-time horsemen in the Western movie business and get myself a good horse — not just one with a sleek coat and showy style, but one with conformation, brains and ability....

It took a lot of doing, but I finally owned Trigger. That was in 1938, and it was the cheapest $2500 I ever spent — though I didn't know it at the time....

In addition to being a good all-around cow horse, Trigger today is considered the most versatile horse star in the motion picture business. He does eight distinct dance steps, dressage maneuvers uncommon to most horse actors and thirty to forty acting routines. Strangely, he rarely if ever confuses his routines or takes the wrong cue, despite the fact all cues are strictly by hand motions. He has a reputation for getting his acting job done letter-perfect, so to speak, the first take — a fact that has made him plenty popular with producers and directors.

In the early days of our movie career, I worked the whole picture from start to finish with Trigger — the close-ups, trick shots, running shots and all. And believe me, we covered a lot of miles in three or four weeks of that kind of shooting. But Trigger was always ready to go. In fact, he seemed to enjoy the long runs — even at the end of a tough day before the cameras....

I have no illusions about our popularity. Just as many fans are interested in seeing Trigger as they are in seeing me. In fact, he does a pretty good job of packing them in all by himself at personal appearance shows when picture work keeps me at the studio. We have to hire a guard to keep people from pulling out his mane and tail — or there wouldn't be a hair left in either; but I have yet for an admirer to ask for a hair out of my head.
—Rogers, in *The Hollywood Reporter*, 31 Oct 1940

Will ROGERS [1879-1935]

Born: Cologah, Oklahoma. Work as a lasso artist and rough rider, in vaudeville and on the Broadway stage (from 1912, and including many appearances with The Ziegfeld Follies) preceded his film debut in Laughing Bill Hyde (1918, Hobart Henley). His popularity increased greatly with the coming of sound:

Sure, [sound] is just up my alley, for talk is the way I've put over my gags. In the silents I'd do a scene and say what I thought was the right thing, but they'd always change it in the titles. For instance, in *A Texas Steer* [1927, Richard Wallace] I was a congressman, and one day I'm walkin' along a street in Washington — we shot it there — when I met a white wings cleanin' the street. I said to him: "Is yours a political job?" He looked at me in contempt. "No," he answers. "Civil Service. We have to pass examinations!"

That gag had meanin'. What do you think they changed it to? I say to the fellow: "One-horse town, what?" and he answers, "You wouldn't think so in my job." Smart crack instead of satire, and an old smart crack at that.

No, the best part of the talkies is that when I say somethin' I say it, and it sticks. There's no way of changin' it without cutting the whole sequence....

Furthermore, Frank Borzage, who's directing *They Had to See Paris* [1929], has a good subtle sense of humor. He doesn't make me do such broad comedy as I have had to do in most silent pictures. Also he lets me ad-lib, and that helps, for some of my best gags come to me durin' the action.

—Rogers, interviewed by Rob Wagner for *Screenland*, Oct 1929

Howard E. ROLLINS, Jr. [1950-]

Born: Baltimore, Maryland. Studies at Towson State University and at The Player's Workshop in N.Y., and work on the stage in Baltimore, Washington and N.Y., and on TV preceded his film debut as Coalhouse Walker in Milos Forman's Ragtime (1981):

I'd like Coalhouse to be seen not just as a terrorist, but as a man of principle and action. He has exhausted every legal means at his disposal and is left with no other choice.

—Rollins, interviewed by Dan Yakir for *American Film*, Dec 1981

The book [by E.L. Doctorow] was never discussed on the set, but I used it to get some wonderful clues as to how I would portray Coalhouse. For instance, the book at one point says that one of the interesting things about Coalhouse Walker was that he didn't particularly see himself as a black man. That told me he saw himself as a human being. Not a black man, not a white man, but a human being.

—Rollins, interviewed by Lorenzo Carcaterra for *The New York Daily News*, 9 Dec 1981

I went to see Mr. Cagney [on the set of *Ragtime*] who was a damn dream, and I said, "Mr. Cagney, I don't know what to do. I've got this scene where I've got to die and I've never died before." And he just went, "Heh, heh, heh, just die, kid, just die."

—Rollins, interviewed by Anna Quindlen for *The New York Times*, 15 Nov 1981

[Captain Richard Davenport in *A Soldier's Story* (1983, Norman Jewison)] is written very simply and very straightforwardly and that is often deceptive. Davenport must contend not only with racism but the fears and skepticism of the black troops.... From the moment you see Davenport, it's clear that he's a forerunner. His type was not known at that time. I like that.

—Rollins, interviewed for the press release for *A Soldier's Story* (Columbia Pictures, 1983)

Mickey ROONEY [1920-]

Born: Joseph Yule, Jr. in Brooklyn, N.Y. Work on the vaudeville circuit with his parents preceded his film debut in the short Not to Be Trusted (1926, Thomas Buckingham). Between 1927 and 1934, he appeared in several short films billed as Mickey Maguire. In 1935, he played Puck in William Dieterle and Max Reinhardt's adaptation of Shakespeare's A Midsummer Night's Dream:

How can a thirteen-year-old play Shakespeare? Or more correctly, how can a thirteen-year-old who has never previously read Shakespeare play Shakespeare? There is no precise answer. Something in the wild and gentle Puck struck a chord of understanding within me, within a youth who if not yet wild, was no longer truly gentle. Same vitality Shakespeare had infused into a character four centuries earlier stirred a corresponding vitality in me.

—Rooney, in his *I.E.: An Autobiography* (New York: G.P. Putnam's Sons, 1965)

As the rehearsals began [on *A Family Affair* (1937) — the first movie about the Hardy Family], I froze. I just couldn't get any life in the part of Andy Hardy — I was stiff and self-conscious.

The trouble was: Andy Hardy, the boy I was trying to be, was an ordinary fellow from a small town. And I was a stage kid. *I was appalled to discover I had no idea how kids behaved outside the theater!* After all, I had started in show business at the age of four.

So, creating a personality for Andy Hardy stumped me. I still remember how the other folks in the cast tried to get me to *relax* in the role. They'd clown between scenes, buy me ice cream cones, coach me. But nothing worked.

Then one day I got into a game of baseball with some other kids around the lot. Trying to win the game became so important to me that I forgot all about rehearsals. I finally got back to "The Hardy Family" set an hour late.

Still breathless, with my hair mussed and my shirt tails hanging out, I tried to explain to the director [George Seitz]. My arms flew in all directions — to straighten my clothes, smooth my hair, grab the script.

Instead of scolding me, the director shouted: "*That's it, Mickey. Now you're Andy Hardy!*"

In a flash I realized I'd been trying to make Andy Hardy an artificial, stuffy fellow. But Andy was *natural* and I had to be that way, too.

—Rooney, in *Parade*, 25 May 1952

In the year 1937, I appeared in six pictures.... In 1938, when I was even hotter, I made nine pictures. Three were Andy Hardys....

Andy Hardy was a phenomenon. He wasn't handsome, because I wasn't. He wasn't any bigger than I, either. But somehow he struck an image that flared all across the country among young people who told themselves, "I'm like that," and among parents who said, "Hey, that's my boy." Andy was a super-typical young man who lived in a super-typical small town called Carvel. He had both schemes and dreams, which always caused complications a few minutes into the picture and always produced general happiness at the end. Andy had a sister [Cecelia Parker], with whom he squabbled about the use of the telephone plus dates who were to include Lana Turner, Esther Williams, Kathryn Grayson, Donna Reed, Judy Garland and Ann Rutherford. He had a father [Lewis Stone] who was a small-town judge as honest as Abe Lincoln, and a mother [Fay Holden] who was as sweet as my own.

When Judy [Garland] came into the Hardy series, performing talent was all she had going for her. She couldn't wiggle like Turner, swim like Williams, purr like Donna Reed or (maybe) hit as high a note as Kathryn Grayson. All Judy could do was entertain....

I don't think I knew how good Judy was until I played opposite her. Her timing was like that of a chronometer. She could deliver a comic line with just the right comic touch, or say a poignant line slowly enough for the poignancy to hit hard but still stay short of schmaltz. She could turn on intensity, as I could turn on intensity, memorize great chunks of script, as I could, ad-lib, as I could....

When I was acting with someone like Esther Williams, who was struggling, I played everything straight. Clown, fiddle with timing, ad-lib, and you rattle a novice and ruin a scene. With Judy, it was the other way. We actually tried to rattle each other. Take a scene of tenderness, where the script called for me to whisper something sweet. With a novice, I really would whisper something sweet. With Judy, I might whisper, "Are you wearing a green garter belt today?" Then Judy, when it came time for her to whisper something to me, would hit back the same way....

We were a couple of teen-age kids, proud of our talent and our poise, trying to make each other lose that poise on camera. I couldn't rattle Judy and she couldn't rattle me. God, we had fun. [Rooney appeared in fifteen more Hardy films, all but three of which were directed by George Seitz: *You're Only Young Once* (1938), *Judge Hardy's Children* (1938), *Love Finds Andy Hardy* (1938), *Out West with The Hardys* (1939), *The Hardys Ride High* (1939), *Andy Hardy Gets Spring Fever* (1939, W.S. Van Dyke), *Judge Hardy and Son* (1939), *Andy Hardy Meets Debutante* (1940), *Andy Hardy's Private Secretary* (1941), *Life Begins for Andy Hardy* (1941), *The Courtship of Andy Hardy* (1942), *Andy Hardy's Double Life* (1942), *Andy Hardy's Double Trouble* (1944), *Love Laughs at Andy Hardy* (1946, Willis Goldbeck) and *Andy Hardy Comes Home* (1958, Howard W. Koch).]

—Rooney, in his *I.E.: An Autobiography* (New York: G.P. Putnam's Sons, 1965)

An actor in the movies can appear taller or shorter at will, once he gets the hang of it. Take Lionel Barrymore, looking so frail and small in *Grand Hotel* [1932, Edmund Goulding] as compared to the ship captain he played in *Captains Courageous* [1937, Victor Fleming]. I talked to him a good deal about it on the set [of *Captains Courageous*]. He tells me it's not so much a matter of clothes or make-up as of posture and thinking the character.... It's the way you feel that makes you get over to your audience what you wish them to feel. [Rooney and Barrymore also co-starred in *A Family Affair*.]

—Rooney, interviewed by Hollis Wood for *The Richmond News Leader*, 10 May 1938

The best thing that ever happened to me was going back to Boys Town three years ago [for *Boys Town* (1938, Norman Taurog)].... I saw things that made me appreciate my own good luck. Knowing Father Flanagan and meeting his boys gave me the determination to make the most of my opportunities. I realized what it meant to have swell parents, a good home and a chance to make good in the world.

Don't misunderstand me. I didn't look down on those boys because they were less fortunate than I was. They didn't need my sympathy. They didn't ask for anybody's sympathy. I never saw a happier bunch of boys. They couldn't learn much from me. But I learned a lot from them.

Many of them were younger than I. They seemed older, more serious and more sure of themselves. Most of them had known plenty of trouble. They were glad to be at Boys Town. It was the best life they had ever known. They took pride in doing their jobs well. They worked hard at trying to improve themselves. I had so much more to be thankful for than they that it made me think. They were so thankful for so little and I was taking everything that had come to me for granted.

I worked harder playing Whitey Marsh, the Mayor of Boys Town, than at any role in which I had appeared. I enjoyed it more, too. For one thing, I felt that I had to do my best because I was representing the boys of Boys Town. They deserved all I could give....

When I knew Metro-Goldwyn-Mayer was going to make *Men of Boys Town* [1941, Norman Taurog] giving me another chance to be with Spencer Tracy in a picture, I couldn't have been happier. I think all of us were.... It was like being away and then coming home again.

—Rooney, in *The New York Morning Telegraph*, 10 Apr 1941

I should have done [*Babes in Arms* (1939, Busby Berkeley)] for nothing. It wasn't work. It was fun. I do everything in it that I've wanted to do all my life. Playing piano to me is like, well, eating ice cream. I love it. I'm crazy about dancing....

There's only one thing that bothers me. That's the singing. I was teamed with Judy Garland and Betty Jaynes. That's real competition. Especially when I never sang in a picture before....

I'm also a little nervous about those imitations, too. After all, I've got to live in Hollywood with the people I'm going to imitate....

—Rooney, interviewed for the press packet for *Babes in Arms* (MGM, 1939)

No actor could ask for more than was offered by the role of Homer Macauley in *The Human Comedy* [1943, Clarence Brown]. Homer was a boy with all the usual teenage tendencies, with all the bright hopes and all the sharp disappointments of adolescence. Yet he matured in the picture and accepted adult responsibilities. It wasn't easy to show Homer as a youngster, and at the same time show him reacting to his growing responsibilities. But I enjoyed trying....

Homer saw a lot of things in the small town he served as messenger boy during the war years. His job took him to homes that reacted with bright joy to good news, and to other homes, dark with sorrow because they had suddenly received a telegram from the War Department, beginning, "The Secretary of War desires that I tender his deep sympathy...."

The picture, we all thought, carried a message of hope to America....

—Rooney, in *The Saturday Evening Post*, 27 Sept 1947

Diana ROSS [1944-]

Born: Detroit. Lead vocalist for The Supremes, she left the group for solo status as a recording artist and actress, making her film debut as Billie Holliday in Lady Sings the Blues (1972, Sidney J. Furie):

Shall I tell you how insecure I was about this role? I was frightened of it. People advised me not to do it, or to start with something a little less challenging. But I had people around me who encouraged me, too....

The preparations started in 1969.... I started listening to her records, started reading everything that had Billie Holliday's name on it — her book, record jackets. I went to the library and read clippings. Then I'd play the records over and I'd try to co-ordinate. Find out when she recorded a certain song and then figure out what was going on in her life at the time she was singing that song.

The most important thing for me was reading between the lines, because I know a lot was left out of what people wrote about her. A lot of things have been written about me, but just a few people really know me. I just had to guess, so I made a person; I made a Billie Holliday of what I thought she would be like.

—Ross, interviewed by Jerry Parker for *Newsday*, Jan 1973

I had to learn the facial expressions that junkies have for my role as Billie Holliday — like the way they keep nodding off all the time. I learned that by watching the way a child will suddenly nod when he's very sleepy but doesn't want to fall asleep.

—Ross, interviewed by Ray Connolly for *The Evening Standard*, 3 Apr 1973

Isabella ROSSELLINI [1952-]

Born: Rome; daughter of Ingrid Bergman and Roberto Rossellini. A film debut as a walk-on in A Matter of Time (1976, Vincente Minnelli) and work as a professional fashion model (from 1980) preceded her first major film role as Dorothy Valens in Blue Velvet (1986, David Lynch):

I completely loved the character. I understood immediately who she was and why she had to be seen nude.... I saw one image that I actually imitated as I came out of the bushes nude. It was of that little girl hit by a napalm bomb in Vietnam. She had skin hanging off and she walked like that, completely naked down the street. The only thing you could see was pain. I think David had imagined the scene that way. He told me that when he was a child, as he was walking home from school one day with his younger brother, they saw a woman walking down the street and she was naked. The younger brother started to cry, and David became very frightened and ran away with the child. There was no indication that the woman was harmful. Everybody's always trying to look at naked women; why was it frightening all of a sudden? I understood that scene....

The hardest [scene was when Frank (Dennis Hopper) rapes me].... We did try to do the scene with underwear, but it didn't work very well. So David came and said, "Could you do it without underwear?" I said we had to reduce the number of people around.... I was very thankful because Dennis was extremely funny. He was completely irreverent.... We had to try to make it as dramatic and violent — psychologically violent — as we could. That was the focus, and that helped. It was very choreographed, with David actually counting as we moved....

A good director...makes you feel that you can trust him. You can make a fool of yourself, but he's going to embrace you and laugh and say, "That was such a mistake — ha, ha, ha." They should never make you feel bad. You'll do anything for David Lynch because he's always there, playful, supportive, naive, kind. You do all sorts of strange things without a second thought because he's so candid. David has a wonderful tenderness toward the characters and toward humanity. He also has a big sense of sadness, and he's very quiet. A friend of ours, Eve Arnold, always asks, "How's the choirboy?" — meaning David. He's very much like that. Maybe that's why he can go into these very dangerous roles with his fantasy....

Blue Velvet was extremely violent and alienated some people — and I understand and respect that. [*Zelly and Me* (1988, Tina Rathbone] came to me, and it was almost the same story, of how little by little somebody becomes his own murderer. The child starts hurting herself, the same way Dorothy in *Blue Velvet* allows Frank to torture her. Half the pleasure is that she feels it's like a ritual through which, in the strangest, craziest way, she becomes purified. She feels she deserves to be punished.

It's really about how violence and rage can turn and you start hurting yourself. This was not the theme of *Blue Velvet*, but it was the theme of my character. Here, instead, it's the theme of the film. It reveals how a child does it, and it tells you how step by step she is led into burning herself.

—Rossellini, interviewed by Peter Stone for *Interview*, Apr 1988

David [Lynch] has developed his very personal brand of surrealism even more.... In *Wild at Heart* [1990], that mood impregnates the whole film. It's about the reality of the unconscious, of your emotions, of how you remember things — and not the reality of a fact. When he puts a wig on me and makes my eyebrow very hairy, it's part of that perception of the brain.

—Rossellini, interviewed by Ralph Rugoff for *Premiere*, Sept 1990

Mickey ROURKE [1950-]

Born: Schenectady, N.Y. An amateur boxer, he then studied at The Actors Studio. Some stage and TV work preceded his film debut in Fade to Black (1980, Vernon Zimmerman). In 1983, he played Motorcycle Boy in Francis Ford Coppola's Rumblefish:

I was so nervous on that film. I thought I was going to get fired the first day. I thought I was going to get fired every day for the first two weeks. You know, working with Francis isn't like working with other directors. There's this kind of big daddy professor thing about him. Everytime he walks on the set it's like this grand arrival: "OK, boys, his majesty is with us, the genius has arrived...."

The great thing for me about that role was that no one really knew where it was going. Francis just handed me these books, some novels by Camus and a biography of Napoleon, and asked me to think about them. So the Motorcycle Boy became like a general without an army, in a land full of enemies he knows he can't defeat. But at the same time he doesn't care, because he knows it's all illusion anyway.

When we were doing those scenes of me walking down the street and I wanted a thought that would make me smile I would imagine that my troops had finally arrived. I could see thousands of warriors. All I would have to do is make a little gesture and they'd come down and kill all the fucking asshole producers on the set. And that would put me in a good mood.

—Rourke, interviewed by James Truman for *The Face*, May 1985

I thought [*The Year of the Dragon* (1985, Michael Cimino)] was a challenge. Because I had very few moments when I could make Stanley likeable and show a side of him that cared. As an actor it was a challenge because Michael brings a certain level of truth to his films, in a humanistic way, much stronger than other directors.... I spent three months in L.A. with Stanley White. I went on twenty-eight actual homicides with him. I had a beeper and it would go off at 3 or 4 o'clock in the morning and I'd show up at the scene of the murder. I watched the way he would detach himself so that he could be almost scientific about it. And to see the young cops all standing around eating up this knowledge because they wanted to be like him.

—Rourke, interviewed by Curtis Hutchinson for *Films & Filming*, Jan 1986

[John in *9 1/2 Weeks* (1986, Adrian Lyne)] was such an unlikely part for me to play that the character really interested me. But I can't say I enjoyed doing it. Adrian Lyne is the most meticulous motherfucker I've ever met. He was always afraid that I was getting too fat for the part. So he'd weigh me. He'd lift up my fucking shirt to see if my belly looked bigger. And he'd have people following me to make sure I didn't stay out too late. There would be people stationed in phone booths around my hotel, calling in reports to him. I mean, God bless him, he's immensely gifted, but he's the most conniving, sneaky, paranoid son-of-a- bitch I've ever met.

—Rourke, interviewed by James Truman for *The Face*, May 1985

Q. Given your mental state at the time [Rourke had suffered a near nervous breakdown while working on *A Prayer for the Dying* (1987, Mike Hodges)], why did you choose to play a character as complex as Henry Chinaski [in *Barfly* (1987, Barbet Schroeder)]?

A. Well, he's a character who was battered down by life and the realities of it. I don't know if I could mentally or physically have gotten it up to portray anything else but this particular type of character.

Q. What kind of research did you do for the part?

A. I had no time to do any research, nor did I care to do any. Mentally, I wasn't able to. Psychologically, I really didn't give a f—k. Artistically, I didn't want to make the character clichéd. I wanted to give him sort of a life of his own.

I was drawing stuff off the fact that I really didn't care if I stunk or not. That gave me a certain freedom to go all the way with the character. To me, that was growth in itself: It may have been a little self-destructive, but it gave me the sense that I really didn't have anything to prove....

When *Year of the Dragon* came out and the critics slaughtered it to pieces and ripped Cimino a new asshole, I was taking a drive with him and he says, "Let me tell you a story: I know a director who made a movie once, and as soon as the reviews came out, he got a bottle of whiskey and went to bed and didn't get out of bed for the rest of his life." Michael says, "That's what they want you to do." And to me, *Barfly* is about people who've given up....

Q. Where did the voice come from?

A. That was as close to Bukowski as I could come. Whiny. It was a choice I made moments before we went out to do the first scene.

—Rourke, interviewed by Margy Rochlin for *American Film*, Nov 1987

Henry [in *Barfly*] doesn't deal with his feelings, he cuts them off — that's where the drinking comes from. And that's part of the reason I didn't like the character to begin with.

Q. He is not just the dull drinker type.

A. No, no. He's the drinker who doesn't like to get drunk — the overly sensitive type who drinks and cuts himself off to a degree. He doesn't really care what he looks like, or what people say about him or if he gets beaten up, you know. He's lost a lot of his self-image. But I like playing a character like that because it represents the way I feel about the industry I'm in.

—Rourke, interviewed by Gisela Martine Getty for *Interview*, Jan 1988

Gena ROWLANDS [1934-]

Born: Virginia Rowlands in Cambria, Wisconsin. Studies at The American Academy of Dramatic Arts, work in stock at The Provincetown Playhouse, and on live TV preceded her film debut in The High Cost of Loving (1958, José Ferrer). In 1954, she married John Cassavetes; he directed her in seven films beginning with A Child is Waiting (1962). They co-starred in three of those seven films. Here Rowlands and Cassavetes discuss her approach to performance:

JC: In directing her, I found her to be a mean actress, one who is totally aware of the other actors' deficiencies and takes every opportunity to cash in on some other actor's failings. She's easy to play with but difficult to top. Her outwardly calm, sweet nature belies the hysterical animal underneath.

GR: What do you mean — a *mean* actress? Why I'm the sweetest, easiest... John, I don't like the word "mean" and if you say it again I'm going to punch you. I don't have to take that. I don't give out interviews like that on you. Why, I totally resent, that, John. You have to take that part out.

JC: Well, Gena, what do you think about actors you're working with?

GR: Why, I don't think about them at all. I never think about them. I think about my character and try to get her through hard situations. She's always in a hard situation. I think about the other actors only as my character relates to their character. Why, I can hardly remember to say good morning to them when I come in. I don't think about them until we're acting.

JC: She's a person who feels so deeply about the character she plays that she protects her the way a mother does a child.

GR: Of course I'm protective about my character. I feel so protective about my character that I *become* her, but that doesn't mean you have to carry me off afterward with a net over my head. I still know who I am. It's temporary schizophrenia. All actors have that.

—Rowlands, interviewed by John Cassavetes for *The New York Times*, 13 Feb 1972

It's fascinating to me how [John] uses different personalities directing different actors. I asked him about it once. With some actors, he said, you have to show them they have someone to be afraid of, more afraid than of themselves.

Q. What does John do directing you?

A. With me, he says, "I leave you alone. Your instincts are always right until you get tired, and then, with you and your kind of actor or actress, I have to watch for that tired, let-down spell and then I get mean and that gets you angry and that anger gets your energy up."

—Rowlands, interviewed (1967) by Wolfson for 20th Century-Fox release to Sidney Skolsky (in the Skolsky collection at The Academy of Motion Picture Arts & Sciences Library)

When I first read the script for *A Woman Under the Influence* [1974, John Cassavetes] I was awestruck. Not only by the part, which was *marvelous* for any actress, but the fact that John saw these things and was able to write about them with such compassion.

I loved Mabel so much that I wanted to do right by her. I never loved a character more than this one. That's why, above all, I pleaded with John: "Please, let's not romanticize her martyrdom." Consequently, we tried to put a lot of pep and humor into the part, in an effort to lessen the emphasis on sorrow and suffering, which the storyline projects. Throughout the film I believe that you have a sense of the valiance of her struggle, however ineffectual.

As fond as I was of Mabel, I couldn't quite grasp how to play her. Something was missing — something that would trigger the interpretation. I read and reread the script, trying to recall incidents from my own childhood. But it was after a visit from an old friend that I got my clue: an actress of some reknown in the '50s, who gave up her career after a nervous breakdown and who now lives in virtual seclusion. Totally vulnerable and giving, she had no sense of her own worth, and was completely mirrored in the eyes of men. Now, they didn't ask her to be that way. But then, they didn't ask her *not* to.

There's a little of Mabel in all of us, I believe. The raw, primitive and uneducated part of a woman that longs to love and be loved — with abandon and without condition, without games or devices. I know too well what that is. I also know what it is to hear the silence of that house once our husband has left for work and your children are off to school. That's enough to drive you crazy! The things that you've given your whole life to that suddenly disappear — even though you know it's temporary. I believe that women specialize in their own disaster films: buses crashing and husbands dropping over in offices. I think that every woman in the world has terrible anxieties, because our whole life is based on emotion.... But unlike Mabel, I know how to cope with my emotionalism: how to go off to the Actors Studio for a workout where, with a group of other actors, I can do it — act it out, perform it and discharge it. If it weren't for acting, I think that I would be a lot crazier than Mabel.

Everyone — the doctor [Eddie Shaw], the mothers-in-law [Katherine Cassavetes and Lady Rowlands], the husband [Peter Falk], want to do right by Mabel. Which is why Peter's depiction of Nick is so touching. How he tries to get through to this woman, because he loves her and knows how delicate the balance is. But he gets bored. He gets sick of her nuttiness — picking up strange guys in bars — and he's embarrassed by her in front of his friends. A lot of things that shouldn't have anything to do with love. And for a period there he doesn't love her, and that, in my opinion, is what makes her 'wacko', as he calls her — pushing her off the deep end. Sensing that love's gone, sensing betrayal, precipitates her breakdown. Because until this time she is okay — a little 'flaky' perhaps, but a lot closer to the normal state of women than most people would like to admit.

—Rowlands, interviewed by Sandra Shevey for *New Times*, 7 Mar 1975

Q. How on earth did you ever get under the skin of the mixed-up Mabel?

A. First of all, I went out and found the kind of clothes Mabel would wear. Cheap clothes, out-of-date clothes, the kind you can still find hanging in some shops. I bought everything off the rack because if they'd been made by a dressmaker, someone would have noticed. We never cheat.

I wore Mabel's clothes and mussed my hair the way hers would be mussed. Also, I knew many girls who had had breakdowns. I drew little touches from each of them, and a lot from myself. I don't mean I'm really going mad. But I'm a little crazy, we all are, and sometimes I let things go. It was a question of taking that small, wild, desperate feeling we all get sometimes and raising it to the highest pitch.

John told me to go 'all out' in my playing, because Mabel is someone without inhibitions. She's freer than 'normal' people, she doesn't have restrictions on what she may do, she's trying to please, she's trying to be human and open in a mechanical society, and she's trying to be perfect, to be totally pleasing to her husband in every way, and it destroys her.

—Rowlands, interviewed by Charles Higham for *The New York Times*, 6 Apr 1975

I don't know where that gesture came from [the pphffftt and the cock of the thumb that Mabel uses]. The thought breeds the outer expression. I think actors who play crazy people — and anyway I don't happen to think Mabel is all that crazy — too often make the mistake of doing research, talking to specialists, working inward from a pattern of recognized behavior rather than working outward from inner feelings. After all, even crazy people retain their individuality.

—Rowlands, interviewed by Bridget Byrne for *The Los Angeles Herald Examiner*, 15 Dec 1974

I've never before played an actress playing an actress. It's a strange feeling. At first I thought I'd have to overemphasize the onstage woman, make her gestures broader in contrast to the offstage woman. But it hasn't worked out that way [in *Opening Night* (1978, John Cassavetes)]. Whether onstage or off this woman's problems are similar, very similar, to those of every working woman.

—Rowlands, interviewed by Dorothy Manners for *The Los Angeles Herald Examiner*, 19 Feb 1977

John and I talk about scripts all the time. Some we've done, dozens we haven't; but we've been married 26 years, and it's our pleasure, as some people play bridge. He'll say to me, "What would you like to do?" To that question, he wants a very sparse answer.

When he asked me that two years ago, I replied, "I'd like to work with a child." Because I noticed, especially during *Woman Under the Influence* that in all my scenes with children, I felt, as an actress, a special excitement, a real challenge. Children don't have any preconceived ideas; their natural honesty puts such a demand on you for total honesty.

People think I have this secret input into the scripts John writes. I'd love to claim I do, but if I want to go to heaven, I have to say no. We never talk about a script while he's working on it. When he's finished, and I've read it, we talk a lot. If there's something I feel I can't play, I tell him; John's strangely without ego when it comes to his writing being criticized. He listens to everybody — me, you, the bartender. He may not accept what you say, but he'll always consider it.

I was stunned by *Gloria* [1980]. It's so far from anything I'd played! Also, it worried me that she's so mean to him [John Adames]; until the last scene, she's rotten to him the whole time. She knows nothing of kids. She expects this little boy who's had his family wiped out by the mob to behave like an adult; she won't even allow him grief. And every actress knows, the first year of drama school, you can't be mean, on the stage or in films, to old people, people shorter than you are, or kids!

I thought, "If I'm going to act this, I'm not going to hedge, for the sake of the audience or commercialism, and say, 'Well, Gloria really likes this child underneath.'" Because she doesn't. She's stuck with him, and when she defends him against the gangsters, she's doing so only because she lives by a firm code of what's right. She's tough, but she's totally courageous. I'm not Gloria. I'm not nearly that strong. When she's scared, she steps forward, not back, and in a movie script, that's an unusual attitude for a woman. In her world, you can't sit and cry, or you don't survive.

As for her shooting people, John and I never discussed whether or not she's a sympathetic character. I certainly never thought she would be. I don't like violence on the screen, but the movie doesn't revel in it. There's no blood-lust feeling. Defending herself is what Gloria does, how she lives. She shoots only when she must, and the men she shoots are monsters. If you like her by the time she draws her gun, then you don't expect her to do so. You expect people you like to do things you like them to do. It's very hard to take their sudden, unacceptable behavior, and that's true when you're acting a character. Yet it's people's contradictions that are fascinating. I mean, just when you've got them nailed down, right?

—Rowlands, interviewed by Tom Burke for *The Chicago Tribune*, 12 Oct 1980

Q. How do you explain who and what Gloria was supposed to be?

A. Well, I tried very hard not to make her appear to be a hooker, even though from what we've seen of tough women like that all of our lives, we've been conditioned to think they are prostitutes. My own background for her was something like Virginia Hill, if you know who that is. She was what used to be called a bag woman, someone who carries illegal money from Las Vegas; someone who'll go to prison and won't talk when she's caught. She's a working part of the mob. And maybe she was a chorus girl when she was young, and because nightclubs are a hangout for gangsters, the chorus girls can make these alliances with the mobsters; they may fall in love with one of them, and suddenly find themselves in a new line of work.

—Rowlands, interviewed at Judith Crist's Tarrytown seminar, 28-30 Sept 1980; repr. in *Take 22*, co-ed. by Judith Crist and Shirley Sealy (New York: Viking Press, 1984)

When I read the script [of *Gloria*] I knew I wanted a walk for her. I wanted something that from the minute you saw me, you would know I could handle myself on the streets of New York. So I started thinking about when I lived in New York — how differently I walked down the street when there was nobody but me. It was a walk that said, "They'd better watch out."

—Rowlands, interviewed by David Galligan for *Drama-Logue*, 6-12 Nov 1980

Gloria is the closest I've come to comedy in a long time. I like heavily dramatic roles, portraying women at an extreme point of stress.

—Rowlands, interviewed by Miles Beller for *The Los Angeles Herald Examiner*, 23 Oct 1980

John's theory is that if there's something wrong, it's wrong in the writing. If you take actors who can act in other things and they get to a scene they've honestly tried to do, and if they still can't get it, then there's something wrong with the writing. Then you stop, you improvise, you talk about it. Then he'll go and rewrite it — it's not just straight improvisation. I'm asked a lot about this, and it's true, when I look at the films and I *see* that they look improvised in a lot of different places where I know they weren't. But I think it's because it's the way John shoots, and the lighting. It's not in the script at all. John uses a general lighting so that you are freer to move than in most pictures. In most pictures, honestly, there are marks on the floor that you have to hit or you'll be out of focus. And that's very hard for an actor — to be thinking about your part and about hitting your marks — and you can't look at them either. But John doesn't believe in that — being an actor himself, John realized how hard that is. So instead of lighting in spots, he lights the whole thing. Then he gets a very good cameraman and a very good focus. And if, in a scene, you feel like going across the room — then go. Usually the cameramen will stop you; you have to fit into their way. With John, the actor is first, so that all the rest of the crew has to follow the actor. We wear battery microphones a lot which are pretty well perfected now; a few years ago they were awful. So, sometimes, I think it's not the actual dialogue that makes John's pictures look improvised — it's the fact that people are moving freely on the film.

—Rowlands, interviewed at Judith Crist's Tarrytown seminar, 26-28 Sept 1980; repr. in *Take*

22, co-ed. by Judith Crist and Shirley Sealy (New York: Viking Press, 1984)

I'll tell you that if any actor doesn't like to work with John Cassavetes, I would truly have to question his motivation. To work with him is what you dream of when you just enter this business, when your hopes are pure. To work with him is to be loved by a director who is an actor, who understands your problems, who understands that the reason you're being difficult and dumb and clumsy and obtuse is because you're panicked and don't know what to do. He encourages you, and he believes in you to the point where you're able to push yourself into areas that you fear to risk with other directors because of the possible censure involved, because of the embarrassment. But he is not afraid for you to make something very funny one moment, or conversely, to make something very serious, and then something ridiculous the very next minute, and then something.... [Rowlands also worked on Cassavetes' *Faces* (1968), *Minnie and Moskowitz* (1971) and *Love Streams* (1983); in 1982, they co-starred in Paul Mazursky's *Tempest*.]

—Rowlands, interviewed by Ted Allen for *On Stage*, Premiere Issue, 1978

Charlie RUGGLES [1886-1970]

Born: Los Angeles; brother of director Wesley Ruggles [1889-1972]. Work with The Alcazar Theater in Los Angeles (from age 15), in stock and on the NY stage preceded his film debut in Peer Gynt (1915, Oscar Apfel). He was co-starred eleven times with Mary Boland:

In my pictures, especially the ones in which I've been teaming lately with Mary Boland — mama loves papa too much. She can't leave him alone. After him from morning till night — with talk, talk, talk, and nag, nag, nag!

You remember how she kept after him in *If I Had a Million* ["The China Shop" segment directed by James Cruze (1932)]? Always trying to improve him — making his life practically unbearable? In my screen life, there's too much mama for papa! [Ruggles and Boland also appeared as husband and wife in *The Night of June 13* (1932, Stephen Roberts), *Mama Loves Papa* (1933, Norman McLeod), *Six of a Kind* (1934, Leo McCarey), *Melody in Spring* (1934, Norman McLeod), *The Pursuit of Happiness* (1934, Alexander Hall), *Ruggles of Red Gap* (1935, Leo McCarey), *People Will Talk* (1935, Alfred Santell), *Wives Never Know* (1936, Elliott Nugent), *Boy Trouble* (1939, George Archainbaud) and *Night Work* (1939, George Archainbaud); in addition, they co-starred in *Evenings for Sale* (1932, Stuart Walker) and *Early to Bed* (1936, Norman McLeod).]

—Ruggles, interviewed by Hilary Lynn for *Photoplay Magazine*, Sept 1933

Harold RUSSELL [1914-]

Born: Sydney, Nova Scotia, Canada. Wounded in training, he was seen in an army documentary — Diary of a Sergeant — by director William Wyler who then cast him for the pivotal role of disabled vet, Homer Parrish in The Best Years of Our Lives (1946):

From the outset Director Wyler took an unusual interest in my career. When he found out I had been going to Florence Enright's acting classes because Goldwyn had ordered it, he was furious.

"I don't care who tells you, stay away from acting coaches. Why do you have to learn how to sit down? Any acting lessons given on this set, I'll give them....!"

I was flattered by Wyler's insistence that acting lessons would destroy the naturalness he felt I'd project in front of a camera. He told me I was a natural actor, that I had an innate ability.... He was determined to preserve this innocence in my delivery....

Because he was such a perfectionist, it wasn't unusual for him to lose his temper. An actor could suggest anything he wanted, and sometimes Wyler would accept it; but once he had made up his mind how a scene was to be done, he would have it done his way....

As...the first day of shooting came nearer, I felt less sure I could handle playing Homer. I still wasn't convinced an inexperienced actor could deal with such an important role. What was worse, I had heard what other producers were telling Goldwyn and Wyler about using me in the role....

But Goldwyn and Wyler stuck to their belief that audiences would not be turned off by seeing my real-life injury on the screen. They felt that skillful direction could lead me to substantiate the part perfectly. Using me as Homer would assure his not being dismissed as merely pitiful; my Homer would give audiences crucial information about veterans' disabilities. Eventually I understood what Wyler had seen in me: that I was *already* playing the part of Homer Parrish. Wasn't that the whole point of all my two years' learning that constituted "rehabilitation?"

Like me, Homer was extremely concerned about his homecoming because of the loss of both hands. Specifically, how his girl friend [Cathy O'Donnell], family and friends were going to react to his startling new appearance. There were a multitude of such emotional hang-ups, and what made the film was that Homer reconciled his physical mangling easier than the men Fredric March and Dana Andrews played managed with their merely emotional wounds.

—Russell, in his (with Dan Ferullo) *The Best Years of My Life* (Middlebury, Vermont: Paul S. Eriksson, 1981)

Jane RUSSELL [1921-]

Born: Ernestine Russell in Bemidji, Minnesota. Acting studies at Max Reinhardt's Theater Workshop and at Maria Ouspenskaya's school in L.A. preceded her film debut in The Outlaw (1943, Howard Hughes). In 1953, she co-starred with Robert Mitchum in Josef von Sternberg's Macao:

Q. What about von Sternberg whom [Howard] Hughes hired to work with you on *Macao*....

A. I thought he was just a nasty old man. I don't mean dirty. I don't mean that. He just was crabby. He came on a small lot, which RKO was, where we were like family. There was Bob Mitchum and myself, and we all knew and adored each other, the whole cast and crew. He immediately laid down all kinds of rules: You can't have any food on the set, no drinks on the set. He'd make nasty little remarks to people about other people...kind of putting everybody down.... So, the first day, after we'd gotten this announcement of the new rules, Bob Mitchum came in with a huge picnic basket and laid out a cloth in the middle of the floor of the set, sat down and invited all the crew guys to have a sandwich and eat and have a drink.... No, von Sternberg just didn't go over.

Q. Do you suppose he was just trying to break you all down so you'd be more malleable for his vision?

A. He went about it in the strangest way. It didn't work....

The studio was working on the Jane Russell and Bob Mitchum team. We had first done *His Kind of Woman* [1951, John Farrow] and *Macao* followed.... Our teaming came about just because we were both under contract and Howard Hughes also thought that we'd be a good combination.... [Hughes] cared about the combination of people; he cared about the way I was photographed. When I was loaned to another studio, Harry Wild was still the cameraman, and Harry always went to the other studio, no matter how they screamed or said that they had their own cameraman or anything. Harry and all of my crew always went with me. Howard Hughes was always very meticulous and very careful about those kinds of things. But as to what the story was really saying, he didn't care.... [Russell and Mitchum were not teamed again.]

—Russell, interviewed by John Kobal for *Films & Filming*, July 1984

Darryl Zanuck, the head of Twentieth Century-Fox, had just bought *Gentlemen Prefer Blondes* [1953] for Marilyn Monroe. This was to be her first big picture, and he wanted Howard Hawks to direct it. Hawks wanted me to play Dorothy, Lorelei's best friend, and he made sure both parts were equal. After all these years Hawks and I were finally going to do a picture together. He had been so wonderful to me when I was still wet behind the ears, so with him at the helm, I knew it would be great. So my whole crew and I went to Fox for the first time....

We started dance rehearsals with Jack Cole, and Gwen Verdon, his assistant. Jack was every dancer's idea of a genius, and many people were terrified of him, but I adored him madly. Jack worked dancers to death, but with Marilyn and me he was patience itself. He knew we didn't know our left foot from our right, but he stayed tirelessly with us. I worked until I got fuzzy headed and said, "Ol' Jack, I'm not learning." He'd say, "Go baby. Tomorrow." Marilyn would stay for an hour or two after I left, and he'd stay with her. She was worried and determined. Jack said she wouldn't really learn anymore during that time, but he understood her insecurity....

I had a ball on that picture, but I don't think Marilyn did altogether, because she was torn between the front office, who was calling her a cheap, dumb blonde, and Natascha Lytess, her drama coach who worked with her every night. It started going wrong when Natascha began directing her on the set. Marilyn's eyes would turn immediately to her when a scene was finished. Howard Hawks, who was trying to direct the picture, wasn't pleased at all. He was a director that even producers didn't interfere with. He was lord of the set.

Finally, Hawks threw Natascha off the set, but things continued to be strained. Marilyn started coming to the set late and that didn't go over too well, so I talked to Whitey [Marilyn's make-up man]. He told me she came in long before I did and was really ready, but she'd stay in her dressing room and putter. "I think she's afraid to go out," he said. So from then on I'd stand in her doorway and say, "Come on, Blondl, let's go," and she'd say, "Oh, okay," in her whispery voice, and we'd go on together....

—Russell, in her *Jane Russell: My Path and My Detours* (New York: Franklin Watts Inc., 1985)

Kurt RUSSELL [1951-]

Born: Springfield, Massachusetts. As a child actor, he made his film debut in It Happened at the World's Fair (1963, Norman Taurog). In 1981, he played Snake Pliskin in Escape from New York, the third of four for John Carpenter:

There are things about Pliskin that all of us have felt. His anguishes, desires, fears. But when he walks down the street, he's in *control*, an island, totally alone.

Whatever it was that ruined him, out in Siberia, left him a shell. It's a kind of ultra-punk attitude. Total alienation. He's a psychiatrist's nightmare. [Russell also worked on Carpenter's *Elvis* (1979 — for TV), *The Thing* (1982) and *Big Trouble in Little China* (1986).]

—Russell, interviewed by Guy Trebay for *The Village Voice*, 8-14 July 1981

Q. What made you decide to accept the role [of Drew Stephens in *Silkwood* (1983, Mike Nichols)]?

A. Before I read for Mike, I read about 35 pages of the *Silkwood* script and although it didn't jump out at me, I thought it would be interesting to work with people like Mike Nichols and Meryl Streep and see if they work any differently than I do. They seemed different somehow to me, different from the people that I had been working with.

Q. Were they?

A. Yeah, they were. I was surprised to see and very happy to find that the way they worked was the way I really like to work. They were just smart as hell. It was a matter of learning that really talented people go with their instincts. These people would say, "I don't know, maybe it doesn't work, but it's the way it looks right now to me." That happens to be exactly the way I am. It was simple to me because it was just a matter of looking at something and saying, "Do you see the same thing on this page I see? Is this the way it goes?" Mike Nichols was especially that way. His philosophy was try to be inventive and be confident in your own instincts....

Q. Did playing Drew Stephens require any special preparation?

A. If you read a script and get a strong idea of how to play the character, that's a script that has really done a good job. It does the work for you. All you have to do is play. You don't have to find things. I spent three days with Drew, but I wasn't researching the character. I wanted to see what he was like as a person. It turned out the people who had written the script [Nora Ephron and Alice Arlen] had him right.

—Russell, interviewed by David Livingston for *The Cable Guide*, Dec 1984

Rosalind RUSSELL [1911-1976]

Born: Waterbury, Connecticut. Studies at Marymount College and The American Academy of Dramatic Arts, work in summer stock, with E.E. Clive's company in Boston and on Broadway preceded her film debut opposite William Powell in Evelyn Prentice (1934, William K. Howard), the first of three films together:

The occasion of our first get-together was my first picture, *Evelyn Prentice* — in which I played the second feminine lead.... I learned more from him than from anyone else I've encountered in Hollywood....

I was a hopeless novice — I had never been on a movie set before, and I just didn't know what it was all about. He took time out to give me some tips.

I'll never forget one scene in which I was on the witness stand, and he was cross-examining me. "Where were you on the night of August 15th?" he thundered. "Why, I was at home," I said. Several more lines flew back and forth. After the take, I told Bill, "You nearly threw me in that scene. You never looked at me." He laughed again. "I was too busy, looking at the camera," he said. "You'll learn, you'll learn...." And I *did* learn, thanks to him. [Russell and Powell worked together again on *Reckless* (1935, Victor Fleming) and *Rendezvous* (1935, William K. Howard).]

—Russell, interviewed by James Reid for *Modern Screen*, Oct 1941

I liked working with Ronald Colman [on *Under Two Flags* (1936, Frank Lloyd)].... He was charming but he never would kiss you on the mouth. He always got over on the corner of your mouth because of the better camera angle. He knew the camera better than any actor I have known. He also played a little bit to your ear, never looking you in the eyes, so that his face would be more turned toward the camera. That was always a little disconcerting....

Q. Do you think he was just being aware of how he should be photographed, or was that his way of trying to steal the scene?

A. No, that was the way he worked with everyone. He couldn't have been more polite. He was the essence of good manners.

Q. But I suppose you have had experiences when somebody tried to steal the scene.

A. Oh, that's useless with me, kid! No, no. Those people are easy to put down. Anybody starts to upstage you, you simply turn your back to the camera, then the director has to come around to take a close-up of you. It's a technical thing. The director *must* do it.

—Russell, interviewed by Mike Steen for *Hollywood Speaks!* (New York: G.P. Putnam's Sons, 1974)

I thought I really understood Christine [in *The Citadel* (1938, King Vidor)]. One way I tried to express her character was through clothes. I did that with *Night Must Fall* [1937, Richard Thorpe], too. Remember that costume? I had only one. It's terribly important, you know. You can tell a lot by clothes.

For instance, with Christine, we had to show her first as a rather drab little school teacher in a mining-town. She couldn't afford good clothes but she had good taste. So instead of buying cheap clothes, as she would have had to do, I bought expensive clothes — to get the good lines, and then spoiled them, by letting them out, making them too big, a little sloppy. That gave the same effect.

Later when Andrew [Robert Donat] makes his big success in London, and Christine is so unhappy and bewildered, she had to have expensive clothes. So I tried to show her a little uncomfortable in the lovely clothes, as though she really didn't like them. At least that was my idea. I don't know whether I succeeded or not.

—Russell, interviewed for *The New York Sun*, 2 Nov 1938

I was blissful until we actually began work on [*The Women* (1939)] and [George] Cukor stopped me right after my first few lines. "No, no," he said, "do it like you did it in the test."

"Isn't this what I did in the test?" I said.

He said, "No, the very, very exaggerated version is the one I want."

I was horrified. "Oh," I said, "Mr. Cukor, I can't do that, the critics will murder me...."

"In this picture Sylvia's breaking up a family, and there's a child involved, and if you're a heavy, audiences will hate you. Don't play it like a heavy, just be ridiculous."

He was a hundred-percent right. I was frightened to death, but from then on, I did what he said, and everything that came to me from *The Women* — namely, my reputation as a comedienne — I owe to George.

He was marvelous to work for, he could think of a hundred bits of business for every moment. In one scene, where I was in a powder room with some other women, he said to me, "After they leave I want you to look at your teeth."

"What?" I said.

"Yes," he said. "When you girls make up in front of people, you make up one way, and when you're alone, you make up another."

So I waited for the others to leave, then bared my teeth at myself in the mirror, and eventually got credit for an inspired moment, courtesy of George Cukor....

One day...Norma Shearer and I were running over our lines, when Cukor said, "All right, all right, quiet, clear the set, we're going to make a take." Hazel started toward me with a piece of Kleenex to wrap around my chewing gum, and Cukor stopped her. "I want Miss Russell to chew gum in this scene. I've been watching her, and that's just what I want...."

Norma Shearer...couldn't believe her ears. "Just a minute, dear," she said to Cukor. "Is she going to knit and talk and chew gum and let those glasses hang down on the end of her nose in a scene with *me*?"

"Yes, she is, Norma," said Cukor. "Now let's go."

"Who can compete with that?" Norma said somewhat sharply, and I completely understood her irritation. "I don't blame you, kid, it's rough," I said, but I went ahead joyfully with my work....

After the knitting scene Norma and I had a scene in a dressing room, and all the time she's being fitted in a dress, I'm talking a mile a minute.... As Norma turns around, there I am buzzing, buzzing, buzzing. "Just think of it like a bee," Cukor had told me. "Get in her ear, and if she turns away, get into her other ear."

After the second day [of shooting *His Girl Friday* (1940, Howard Hawks)] I went to Cary Grant. "What is it with this guy? Am I doing what he wants?"

"Oh, sure, Ross," Cary said.... "If he didn't like it, he'd tell you."

"I can't work that way," I said. I went over to where Hawks was sitting. "Mr. Hawks," I said, "I have to know whether this is all right. Do you want it faster ? Slower? What would you like?"

Unwinding himself like a snake, he rose from his chair. "You just keep pushin' him around the way you're doin'," he said. I could hardly hear him but I could see those cubes of eyes beginning to twinkle.

He'd been watching Cary and me for two days, and I'd thrown a handbag at Cary, which was my own idea, and missed hitting him, and Cary had said, "You used to be better than that," and Hawks left it all in. It's a good director who sees what an actor can do, studies his cast, learns about them personally, knows how to get the best out of them. You play the fiddle and he conducts....

Grant...was terrific to work with because he's a true comic, in the sense that comedy is in the mind, the brain, the cortex....

Cary loved to ad-lib. He'd be standing there, leaning over, practically parallel to the ground, eyes flashing, extemporizing as he went, but he was in with another ad-libber; I enjoyed working that way too. So in *His Girl Friday* we went wild, overlapped our dialogue, waited for no man. And Hawks got a big kick out of it....

Hawks was a terrific director; he encouraged us and let us go. Once he told Cary, "Next time give her a bigger shove on the couch," and Cary said, "Well, I don't want to kill the woman," and Hawks thought about that for a second. Then he said, "Try killin' 'er."

—Russell, in her (with Chris Chase) *Life is a Banquet* (New York: Random House, 1977)

To date, the picture I've enjoyed most, is *His Girl Friday* — and the main reason is: I had to try to keep up with that human dynamo named Grant. He hits a terrific pace. When he isn't using his eyes or his mouth or his hands to get a reaction, he's using his feet. He's a *terrific* ham, but he gets results no one else gets.

—Russell, interviewed by James Reid for *Modern Screen*, Oct 1941

Q. About this time [1941] you got into your career-woman era.

A. Yes. Those parts went on and on! I played 23 different career women. If you need an operation, I am capable, you know! I have played a doctor, a psychologist, a newspaperwoman, a nurse, a head of an advertising firm, an actress, a professional pilot, a lady judge, and so on....

Q. Most of your career-women pictures were made at Columbia, right?

A. Right. I had the same office set in I don't know how many pictures! Ten or fifteen! The same cameraman, Joe Walker, and the same propman named Blackie. The opening shot was always an air shot over New York. Then it would bleed into my suite of offices on the fortieth floor of Radio City. I would have the same desk and the same side chairs and bookcase. Out the window behind me was always a view of the Empire State Building, in order to identify the setting. I used to say to Joe Walker, "Joe, where was the Empire State Building in the last picture?" which had only been a couple of months before. He would say, "I had it a little to the left." I'd say, "Well, this time throw it over on the right."

—Russell, interviewed by Mike Steen for *Hollywood Speaks!* (New York: G.P. Putnam's Sons, 1974)

Clark [Gable] is one of the most effective actors in the business — and for a very good reason. No matter how disappointed he is in a scene, he plays it with enthusiasm and vitality. I've worked with actors who don't do this, and it makes all the difference in the world. What you feel when the camera records a scene is what is recorded. I'll argue that point till Doomsday.

To carry off a scene, you have to attack it with authority, and that's what Clark does every time. It has nothing to do with his being six-feet-one and built in proportion....

He gets a great boot out of everything he plays. The idea that he walks casually through his scenes is a canard. He's an easy-going man, but that's truer of his private life than of his work. He's always at ease in front of a camera, but he's a terrifically hard worker. Very conscientious....

He isn't satisfied to *look* like a man of action. He has to *be* one. That's something else I found out about him. Remember that sequence in *They Met in Bombay* [1941, Clarence Brown] where he did a Sergeant York, and climbed an embankment and wiped out some machine-gun nests, single-handed? Clark insisted on doing that entire sequence himself, even in the long shots, when the camera couldn't tell the difference.

[Russell and Gable also worked together on *Forsaking All Others* (1934, W.S. Van Dyke) and *China Seas* (1935, Tay Garnett).]

—Russell, interviewed by Carol Craig for *Motion Picture*, Nov 1941

To know and have Sister [Elizabeth] Kenny's friendship is a constant source of inspiration and strength. And making [*Sister Kenny* (1946, Dudley Nichols)] was the most exciting, the most strenuous and the most wonderful thing that ever happened to me.

I could go into superlatives for hours, extolling Sister Kenny's noble qualities, her great work, and the happy recourse of her great mind and generous personality. To me, however, the fact that she rests not on Mount Olympus with her laurels, but that she is a down-to-earth woman, with human virtues and frailties, one who gives of her indomitable and unsinkable spirit, and who is entirely approachable and understandable, is all important. She's no sainted mystic legend to be revered and 'salaamed' from afar. She is the stalwart, dependable Kenny who fights back and wins because she is right — something all of us need a little more of, to stabilize our purpose and add persistency to our initiative. Some people call it 'backbone.' Some people call it having the courage of one's convictions or some may call it strength of character.

Sister Kenny's inner repose and her ability to live with herself in harmony, is far reaching. To her a complicated life or a lie would be sheer stupidity. She does not plague herself with confusion and intrigue. The simplicity of her belief, and her faith in humanity, and her courage is a lesson to anyone....

Her quality of unselfish giving will be an inspiration, I believe, to everyone who sees her on the screen.

But don't mistake me, Sister Kenny is anything but a long-faced pious individual. Her spark of wit and humor makes her an entertaining person.

—Russell, in *Screen Stars*, Dec 1946

The ebullient lady I portray [in *Auntie Mame* (1958, Morton Da Costa) — which she also played on Broadway]...offers a characteristically offbeat quip during the course of the comedy. Life is a banquet, she says, and rails at those who are starving themselves....

Auntie Mame is not a selfish woman, you know. She doesn't mean that life should be a banquet for her alone. A banquet, remember, always includes others. It's a sharing, a spilling out of goodwill, a consideration for others, a spirit of graciousness. To make life lovely, it's sometimes a matter of who speaks first. Auntie Mame is the lady who speaks first. Hello, stranger, won't you join the banquet?

Mame has real, not surface, manners. A snub never bothers her; she has no false self-importance. She is not led by convention. She is not a victim of life; she takes life by the hand.

There's kindness beneath that scatter-brained exterior. She's nobody's fool. She may be wacky, but she's so wise. She possesses naiveté: she doesn't have a vicious bone in her body. She can be taken in. Rather, she pretends to be taken in. But Mame is never really victimized. She enjoys life too much to worry about such negative matters.

—Russell, in *Cue*, 29 Dec 1956

[Auntie Mame] is so contemporary. She is a woman who never clings to the past and never looks back. She has no time for regrets. She takes up the challenge and forges ahead.

This is a healthy quality. So many people resist change — they are afraid of it but Auntie Mame is always ready to try something new because she knows it can bring new interests and a new personality....

I think every woman could profit by acquiring some of Auntie Mame's attitude of not being too influenced by what people will think of any change she wants to make in herself.

—Russell, interviewed by Lydia Lane for *The Los Angeles Times*, 30 Nov 1958

Gertrude Berg was divine in the role of Mrs. Jacoby on Broadway [in *A Majority of One*] — but I'm not Gertrude Berg, so I had to bring something else to it [in the film version (1961, Mervyn LeRoy)]. That's why I walked around, listening and observing. I wanted to see how the women dressed — how they set their hair. It was the little things I was after, like the use of hands. I use mine when I talk, but I keep them high. Their hands are lower and busy — always moving.

And I discovered something about the so-called Yiddish accent. It's not so much an accent as a cadence — a rhythm from inside. The Jews are the only people in the world who react first, and then speak. It's complicated as hell with nineteen thoughts in five lines, all flowing together. When I went home I tried to put down my recollections of speech on a tape recorder, and found I was speaking too fast. So I bought a metronome, set it at a leisurely, housewifely tempo, and practiced the dialogue. It still didn't come off. Something was missing. I was missing the movements. You have to see the movements with the speech to get the feeling. So I worked on that.

Then I tried to get some of the religious background. Mrs. Jacoby follows the dietary laws. Dore Schary [who produced and directed the play on Broadway] sent me books he had written, and Mervyn LeRoy has been a darling. He told me lots of stories from his background. They all talk about their relatives. It was the same in *Auntie Mame*. Everyone knew a Mame, just as everyone knows a Mrs. Jacoby.

—Russell, interviewed by Joe Hyams for *Theatre Arts*, June 1961

Theresa RUSSELL [1957-]

Born: Theresa Paup in San Diego, California. Acting studies at The Lee Strasberg Institute preceded her film debut in The Last Tycoon (1976, Elia Kazan):

Q. What kind of experiences did you have early on, with *The Last Tycoon* and *Straight Time* [1978, Ulu Grosbard]? You had De Niro and Dustin Hoffman as co-stars.

A. On *The Last Tycoon*, De Niro played a very intense character and his thing was to be very reclusive, which I didn't find difficult at all. He was very giving and, whenever I wanted to rehearse, he was willing.

Hoffman was wonderful too, once he got it all pinned down. It takes a long time to get to the core of what he's doing, to establish the character.

Straight Time was hard for me, because I'd only done *The Last Tycoon*, where the script was sacred. You couldn't change a line, which was fine by me; I like that — and I had to go from that and from Kazan directing to the complete opposite. It was total improvisation, which I've never done since. You'd come to the set and shoot the shit until you figured it out. It was very scary, but in the end I had fun. And I learned a lot.

—Russell, interviewed by Dan Yakir for *Interview*, Nov 1985

[Milena in *Bad Timing/A Sensual Obsession* (1980, Nicholas Roeg)] is simply a creative person who has no release for her restless imagination. She is searching for her identity. She isn't ready to commit herself emotionally to only one man. That was the 'bad timing.'

—Russell, interviewed by Frances Herridge for *The New York Post*, 18 Sept 1980

Q. What actor were you happiest to work with? Who was the most stimulating?

A. Mickey Rourke was really good to work with. I guess he has a similar kind of feeling about acting.... We only had a couple of things together in *Eureka* [1982, Nicholas Roeg]....

Q. How do you work with Roeg? What does working with someone you're close to mean? Does the personal infringe on the professional?

A. I hope it doesn't. In *Eureka*, for instance, there was a big dinner scene, where all the characters were present and the other actors were a little bit nervous about whether I was going to get more attention or more direction. I can only say that this was not the case. It never is. I go and learn my lines and make my humble choices about what I think is happening in the scene. After that scene in *Eureka*, the other actors put their apprehensions to rest. I was one of them.

I know more about the financial side of the film, because I speak with him about it. But as far as the character goes, that's completely separate.

Q. Do you sometimes wish he were more partial?

A. A couple of times I tried to pick his brain, but he said, "I'm not going to talk to you about it." And that was that. Normally, I don't do that. And I don't want special treatment. Still, when he explains something, I know what he's talking about without having to complete the sentence. When you know a person that intimately, you do have an advantage. [Russell has also starred in Roeg's *Insignificance* (1985) and *Track 29* (1988); they were married in 1986.]

—Russell, interviewed by Dan Yakir for *Interview*, Nov 1985

Ann RUTHERFORD [1922-]

Born: Therese Ann Rutherford in Vancouver, British Columbia, Canada, to theatrical parents. Stage work as a child in San Francisco and work on Los Angeles radio preceded her film debut in Student Tour (1934, Charles F. Reisner). She played Polly Benedict — Andy Hardy's girlfriend — in the MGM series:

I wasn't in the first of the Andy Hardy films [*A Family Affair* (1935, George Seitz)]. But they decided to recast the series. Lionel Barrymore, who was having trouble with arthritis, was out, replaced by Lewis Stone. And I was the new Polly. Frankie Thomas was almost set as Andy until the studio decided it would be funny if Andy were shorter than his girlfriend.

My whole subsequent career was colored by the Hardy films. I got taller but Mickey [Rooney] remained the same height. Soon I was acting in my stocking feet and mostly in close-up. Once they built a trench for me to walk in. There were very few long shots.

The trouble is, I remained 15 although I was growing up. I'd be up for another film and the director would say, "Oh, but she's Polly: she can't do this!" When I was 18, I went to New York on a tour and I wasn't allowed to be seen smoking or be near night clubs. MGM assigned five people to keep me in tow.

—Rutherford, interviewed by J.E.A. Bawden for *Filmograph* Vol 4.1, 1974

[The Hardy pictures] were big, big moneymakers. They made these things in four weeks, for peanuts. So Mr. Mayer thought, "Aaah, we will give it the 'A' picture treatment." He called in Woody [W.S.] Van Dyke, a very prominent and very expensive director. They stretched the schedule out to about double the original length of shooting time. The only thing that they did not take into consideration was the fact that Mickey Rooney was the prime motivating factor in these pictures. He was so creative, so instinctive. He was totally responsible for the success of those first three pictures.... We now have this big hot-shot director, who's a lovely man, except he was a speed demon. You know, just (clap!) "First print out...!" He wouldn't give anybody a chance to do anything. Dear Mickey Rooney, who normally after we would finish rehearsing a scene, would tug on the sleeve of George Seitz, our original director, and say, "Uncle George, I've got an idea." He would then very modestly come up with a bit of business that would have us all on the floor.... It would wind up that the scene they printed was always totally different than the one that George Seitz started to direct. All right. Now we're doing this thing with Woody Van Dyke. Dear Mickey would say, "Mr. Van Dyke, I have an idea." Mr. Van Dyke would say, "Sssh, quiet kid, you're bothering me. All right. Light 'em. Roll. Print it." The whole thing. As a result, after three weeks of shooting, they closed down production. They say they had absolutely nothing. The spark was gone. They scrapped it, called back George Seitz. Put it back on our old schedule.... So, you see, an actor can contribute something.

—Rutherford, interviewed by Edward Ashley for *Screen Actor*, Summer 1981

Besides playing Polly Benedict, I was also doing a series with Red Skelton, *Whistling in the Dark* [1941], *Whistling in Dixie* [1942], *Whistling in Brooklyn* [1944, all S. Sylvan Simon]. You name it, we whistled in it. In order to make those I sometimes had to be written out of the middle of the Hardy pictures. In the beginning I'd go away on vacation with my family or leave for school. That would give Mickey the chance to have his dalliance with Lana Turner or Judy Garland, but I always got him back in the end....

—Rutherford, interviewed by Walter Wagner for *You Must Remember This* (New York: G.P. Putnam's Sons, 1975)

Note: See the Mickey Rooney section for a list of the Andy Hardy films.

Margaret RUTHERFORD [1892-1972]

Born: London, England. Acting studies at The Old Vic in London and work in repertory and on the London stage preceded her film debut in Dusty Ermine (1936, Bernard Vorhaus). In 1945, she played Madame Arcati in David Lean's adaptation of Noël Coward's Blithe Spirit:

My part in Noël Coward's new play, *Blithe Spirit* was to be Madame Arcati, a spiritualistic lady whom Noël Coward had vaguely based on Clemence Dane, the author. He did not write the play with me in mind, but once it was completed he thought of me and added extra dialogue....

Noël Coward vividly remembers the night he came to Exeter to tempt me.... The way Noël acted out the various parts and told me how helpful mediums can be to people in distress was quite magnificent....

I hesitated to give my decision then and there. I simply hate hurting people's feelings and though I do not entirely understand spiritualism, I feel that as many people take it seriously I had no right to make fun of sincere professional mediums....

For this very reason, I played Madame Arcati straight and for real.... I played [her] as if I had been a professional medium. She was a wholesome woman who got down to business and worshipped fresh air.... I was so concerned to get my stage business correct that I went to several seances to observe the professional at work....

Noël Coward was very particular about one thing: he wanted the play translated on to the screen exactly as it had been interpreted in the theatre, and this is what was done....

The film seemed to go on for ever. In fact instead of taking twelve weeks it took six months — something to do with the color film, which was then fairly new, having to be sent to America to be processed and then returned each time to match up. We all became very tired of it towards the end....

I never wanted to play Miss Marple in the Agatha Christie films.... It was several years in fact before I finally consented. It was simply that I never found murder amusing. I don't like anything that tends to lower or debase or degrade....

Possibly the person who did most to convince me that Miss Marple was in fact a very fine woman and definitely on the right track was the director, George Pollock. George is a sweet man and full of integrity. He finally told me that he was having a script prepared so that I could see it, and at least I would know what we were talking about. He sent it to me and we talked on the phone together. There is nothing bombastic about George and, looking back, it was his very gentleness and sincerity that finally won me.

He persuaded me that Miss Marple was not so much concerned with crime, even though she was an indomitable sleuth always one stage ahead of the police, but that she was more involved in a game — like chess — a game of solving problems, rather than of murder....

Two years later I was to make another Agatha Christie film, *Murder at the Gallop* [1962], with George Pollock once more. Once more I had that dear man Robert Morley working with me. *Murder Most Foul* [1963] and *Murder Ahoy* [1964] complete the Miss Marple quartet.

I completely overcame my first tentative prejudices about Christie crime and became most fond of Jane Marple. She was of course so right for the period when directors like George Pollock were producing low-budget, light-weight comedies that sent people home from the cinema feeling warm and happy with life....

When I was first shown the script of [*The V.I.P.s* (1963, Anthony Asquith)] and asked if I would play the role of the Duchess of Brighton I turned it down completely. I knew that this film was going to create quite a stir in the film world puddle, with that handsome couple Elizabeth Taylor and Richard Burton topping a list of stars which included Orson Welles, Maggie Smith, Louis Jordan and Elsa Martinelli, but I felt it was definitely not for me....

The Duchess of Brighton had been forced to leave England because of crippling taxes and had taken a job as social director of a Miami Beach Hotel. On the surface it looked all right until I realized that this part had no background and I simply cannot say funny lines without this. I have to find something in common with the character and in this case the character of the Duchess had no beginning, middle or end. There was simply nothing there for me to get my teeth into....

Here Anthony Asquith stepped in. Knowing that I would have given my decision a lot of thought, and not made it lightly, he said that they would have another look at the part. Over the weekend he, the producer Anatole de Grunwald and Terence Rattigan, who had written the script, got together and the result was that they gave the character more substance....

Having accepted the role of the Duchess of Brighton there came the question of what she would wear. And once again I was firm. I decided that I would not have 'funny' clothes, instead I would chose the kind that my Duchess of Brighton, which I now believed in, would wear in her normal life had she been travelling on that plane. So along with my fur-trimmed travelling coat I chose a perfectly ordinary squashy green felt hat — the kind that country ladies have worn for many years.

I decided that this hat would make my part credible. I was determined that the hat would become almost alive — magical — and therefore a prop of some consequence. I wore it as I thought any self-respecting duchess would. When I was agitated I jammed it down hard, all the time inventing my own little bit of 'hat business'. In the end the hat became for me as much a character as the boat in *The African Queen*....

For years I had a very splendid crocodile [handbag] in which things were inclined to get lost. I always felt like a terrier ferreting down a rat hole with paws scurrying fast and fur flying everywhere. And this of course was exactly how the duchess travelled. When she mislaid her tranquilizers all hell was let loose until she found them snuggling wickedly in the far corner of her bag....

It was almost as though Mr. Rattigan had in fact travelled with me and knew by instinct the things that I do. These he had seized on and made them just a little larger than life. I felt very much at home in the part.

—Rutherford, in her (with Gwen Robyns) *Margaret Rutherford* (London: W.H. Allen, 1972)

Robert RYAN [1909-1973]

Born: Chicago. Work in stock in Chicago, acting studies at Max Reinhardt's school in L.A. and work on the N.Y. stage preceded his film debut in Pare Lorentz's unrealized Name, Age and Occupation. His first screen credit was Golden Gloves (1940, Edward Dmytryk); in 1949, he played Stoker Thompson in Robert Wise's The Set-Up:

As Stoker Thompson, I was trying to mirror the fighting game as 99 per cent of the fighters really find it. Stoker was no near-champion, no crowd pleaser. He was a tenth-rater, getting slower, getting knocked out more often, with only a few modest hopes and a loyal wife to support him.

In this film, however, Stoker's wife [Audrey Totter] never cheered him to victory with helpful shouts from the ringside. I doubt very much if a man who's busy fighting has time to look around for a loyal wife or to pick out her treble voice from the roar. Anyway, we dropped this phony mechanism.

I liked the character of Stoker. I liked his decency in a pretty grim business. I've known fighters all my life; at Dartmouth I managed to win the collegiate heavyweight title, and even thought briefly of becoming a fighter. But to play Stoker I had to learn to fight like a professional instead of an amateur, and that took months of training.

—Ryan, in *The Saturday Evening Post*, 15 July 1950

[Thor Storm] the character that I play [in *Ice Palace* (1960, Vincent Sherman)] is the son of a missionary, and, as such, is governed more by rules of fair play than his partner — Sib Kennedy [Richard Burton]. As the years pass, Storm becomes more and more concerned with the spoiling and plundering of Alaska by large American commercial interests and also the fact that Alaska has no representative in the U.S. congress. The latter part of his life is spent in fighting for Alaska's recognition as a state and also the protection of Alaskan resources from the depredations of large companies who come up, as he says, to take everything out of Alaska and put nothing back. As an acting part it is very interesting, because I go from the age of 27 or 28 to 74 or 75. Also, the character is one of extreme sympathy, which is something I don't always do.

Q. How do you like doing a sympathetic part, as opposed to the heavy?

A. I don't have any preference, really. I think it's good for business to be liked by the audience every few years; but as far as playing the part, I, or any actor, I think, don't care just as long as it's a good part. The trouble with most sympathetic parts is that they tend to be wishy-washy. And the main thing you have to do is just stand there and be good. The villain or the heavy is much more interesting, and, for that reason, is sought after by actors.... This particular part involved portraying what you might call a practical saint, and this is a very unusual experience for me. For that reason, I am getting a great kick out of it.

—Ryan, interviewed by Sidney Skolsky (1960), in an unsourced, undated article in the files of The Academy of Motion Picture Arts and Sciences Library

I think the hardest part I did was Claggart [in *Billy Budd* (1962, Peter Ustinov)] for there was no reason for what he did — he didn't do it for money, for fame, to get a girl, he just did it. That made it very hard to give it any credibility.

—Ryan, interviewed by Allan Eyles for *Films & Filming*, Sept 1967

Peter [Ustinov — on *Billy Budd*] gives you a form of education as well as direction. His terms of reference are enormous. For instance, he once told me to play a scene "like the third act of *Don Carlos*...."

—Ryan, interviewed by Gideon Bachmann for *Film* (London), Winter 1961

[Colonel Everett Breed in *The Dirty Dozen* (1967, Robert Aldrich)] is a West Point officer, a very obnoxious character who feels that this whole operation is very irregular, besides having a great dislike for Major Reisman [Lee Marvin] personally. There are no subtleties at all...he becomes as close as anyone...to being the villain of the piece.

—Ryan, interviewed by Allan Eyles for *Films & Filming*, Sept 1967

[Michael Winner] creates a really electric atmosphere on the set because he's an unpredictable man and that's good because the repetition and boredom of making movies can have its effect on the whole picture and I'd say that nothing like that ever happens when he's around.... His approach [on *Lawman* (1970)] is radically different. Every other director I've worked with followed more or less the usual pattern — they film the whole scene in what we call master shots with all the actors involved and then move to medium shots, close-ups and so forth. Winner doesn't work that way. In fact, I've never shot a master in this picture. He does something we call cutting with the camera.... Cutting with the camera means you only shoot what you're going to use. It has one disadvantage, at least to the older ones of us. We, in this case, have to rely on [Winner's] camera technique to give what we call a sustained performance; but I'm perfectly willing to see the results.

—Ryan, interviewed for *Films & Filming*, Mar 1971

Winona RYDER [1971-]

Born: Winona Horowitz in Rochester, Minnesota. Studies at The American Conservatory Theatre in San Francisco preceded her film debut in Lucas (1986, David Seltzer). In 1990, she played Charlotte in Richard Benjamin's Mermaids:

What I related to about Charlotte is that she's inconsistent. One day she'll be obsessed with Catholocism, but the next day she'll be obsessed with Joe the gardener. And the *next* day she'll want to be an American Indian. I had really been going through stuff like that. I would think, I'm going crazy! I don't know what I want! I don't know who I am...!

A song the Replacements sing really inspired my performance in *Mermaids*.... To me, the song [Sixteen Blue] is about inconsistency. It's about thinking you are crazy — that's how you feel when you're sixteen. There's this incredible guilt that Charlotte carries around with her: "I don't know who I am. If I want to be a nun, why am I horny?"

—Ryder, interviewed by Jeff Giles for *Interview*, Dec 1990

S

Eva Marie SAINT [1924-]

Born: Newark, New Jersey. Studies at The Actors Studio and work on radio and stage in N.Y. preceded her film debut as Edie Doyle in On the Waterfront (1954, Elia Kazan):

Gadge [Kazan] gets to know you and your capacities better than you do, and brings them out. He gets what he wants but he encourages you to contribute on your own. Little improvisations which can mean so much were considered and often used. And Marlon [Brando]. I'd heard some disquieting things about working with him, but just the opposite happened. He helped me, encouraged me, showed me things he'd learned about movie acting. He was gentle and considerate.

—Saint, interviewed by Oscar Godbout for *The New York Times*, 1 Aug 1954

Kazan worked internally, and Hitch [on *North by Northwest* (1959)] externally — "lower your voice, don't use your hands (I tend to use my hands a lot), just look at Cary [Grant]." What he would direct was different from what Kazan would choose to direct. With a Hitchcock film, you just jumped in and had a hell of a good time. I mean, who doesn't want to play a sexy spy?

To me, Kazan was the finest. I just loved working with him. Since I came from the Actors Studio, I understood him.... He seemed to understand the actors, he was very private with them — and I really appreciated that. I learned many things from him — such as how to conserve my energy. He taught me to think of myself as an hourglass with just a certain amount of sand....

Hitch was a big bear. He didn't like the wardrobe that Helen Rose had designed. So, he brought me to New York; and, as the mannequins came by, I'd say, "Oh, Hitch, I love that black dress with the red roses." He'd snap his fingers and say, "We'll take that for Miss Saint, please!" He was my one and only sugar daddy! Hitch was so meticulous, he knew what he wanted from every shot.

—Saint, interviewed by Michael Buckley for *Films in Review* (NY), May 1983

Chris SARANDON [1942-]

Born: Beckley, West Virginia. Studies at Catholic University of America and work in regional theater, TV and on Broadway preceded his film debut as Leon, the suicidal, transsexual "wife" of Al Pacino in Dog Day Afternoon (1975, Sidney Lumet):

It was important to me to play the character with a dignified femininity rather than stereotyped swishy. I wanted to approach it positively, as a woman trapped in a man's body, which is what a transsexual is. So I said to myself, "Play a woman." So I spent a couple of days at home alone floating around in loose, flowing clothing and wearing clogs. I wanted to get the feeling of how women sit, and how they move. So often, the way women move is caused by what they wear....

I refused to make Leon into some sort of screaming queen.... I think characters are much more memorable if they're not clichéd, if there is a surprise. Usually that's the thing that is remembered most.

—Sarandon, interviewed by Judy Klemesrud for *The New York Times*, 23 May 1976

Susan SARANDON [1946-]

Born: New York City. Following studies at Catholic University of America, she accompanied her husband, Chris, to an agent audition; she was also signed despite this not being her intention. After some summer stock in Washington, she made her film debut in Joe (1970, John G. Avildsen). In 1975, she played Janet Weiss in Jim Sharman's The Rocky Horror Picture Show:

Every time I look at *The Rocky Horror Picture Show*, I think I must have had a great time. Actually I had pneumonia through most of it because I ran around wet in my underpants and bra in this cold house in London in November and December. They were constantly spraying me, and it wasn't until the second half of the movie that I dry off. By that time I was already sick, and then I jump in the pool. It was really excruciating....

—Sarandon, interviewed by Stephen Saban for *The Soho Weekly News*, 20 Apr 1978

You choose clothing to enhance your personality and hide your faults, and suddenly there you are. If you're naked, it's necessary to have something to play, so that you're not thinking about the fact that you're naked....

In *Pretty Baby* [1978, Louis Malle], I take my top off because she's a whore. It would be kind of coy to go around tricking with your clothes on. Yet there is nothing in the way it's filmed that I feel was exploitative. As I said to Brooke [Shields] when she was going to be naked: ultimately, if you're going to do it, and you've said you'll do it, and you think it's necessary for it to be done, and you trust the cameraman and the director, the only thing you can do wrong is make the audience uptight by you seeming to be uptight, so you might as well find some way to seem relaxed, because it'll draw more attention to it if you seem very uncomfortable.

—Sarandon, interviewed by Peter Knobler for *Crawdaddy*, May 1978

Playboy: The scene a lot of men say they'll never forget is in *Atlantic City* [1981, Louis Malle], when you rub lemon juice on your body in front of a window as Burt Lancaster looks at you.

Sarandon: Well, I guess voyeurism is always erotic. But, for me, that scene wasn't particularly erotic. Anyone who would rub lemons on her chest is completely insane. Believe me, it's very uncomfortable. I just tried to be as matter-of-fact as possible about it. I remember saying to Louis, "This scene should be shown as *ordinary*. It should be done only because she wants to get the smell of fish off her body."

Playboy: If *Witches [of Eastwick* (1987, George Miller)] has been your worst professional experience, what has been your best?

Sarandon: *Bull Durham* [1988, Ron Shelton]. Without question. Working on that movie restored my faith in passion, poetry and team playing. In the past few films I had done before that, I'd been pretty badly treated. On *Bull Durham*, the team worked together and refused to become susceptible to manipulation from the outside. Everyone was treated as an equal. We were respected. We were generous to each other.

Playboy: Why do you think that was?

Sarandon: Perhaps it had to do with the mentality of the project itself. In *Witches*, there was the Devil [Jack Nicholson] and then there were these three gals [Cher, Michelle Pfeiffer and myself], who, put together, made one leading lady. *Bull Durham* was about full, actualized people. I *loved* that movie. Ron Shelton...really trusted me with a lot of his heart. Annie Savoy, my character, is a composite of a lot of the real women in Ron's life.

Playboy: Annie Savoy was considered a movie breakthrough. She is an older heroine — already unusual — and she is aggressively sexy without being punished for it. In the old movie cliché, the sexy woman pays for her sexiness with some kind of punishment.

Sarandon: Yeah, it's strange. I've read that Annie is every man's fantasy. But I think she is a female fantasy, too. I mean, it has always been my fantasy to be everything — sexy, smart, fun-loving and fragile — at the same time. The way I saw Annie was as a...high priestess. She is as straightforward as any guy. At the same time, she is fragile, because she really wants to believe.

Playboy: Believe what?

Sarandon: In everything from the Church to baseball to love. Annie is someone who always keeps looking.

Playboy: Of the characters you've played in your twenty-four movies, is Annie the closest to your own character?

Sarandon: I'd love to think so. Yes, she's certainly the first character I felt was large enough for me to just jump in, fill her up and let her take me somewhere. What I usually have to do is take a smaller person and put in a lot of myself to expand her....

Playboy: Those sex scenes with Kevin Costner turned a lot of viewers on.

Sarandon: That's what we had in mind. They are not Kevin and me futzing around, groping each other. We *knew* what we were trying to say. That's why I touch his bruise and that's why I kiss his face and that's why he doesn't rip my clothes off. What we're saying is, "These people have really found each other."

We put the sex into an emotional context. There's a wonderful scene in the kitchen. Kevin and I eat together, we laugh together, we read together. He carries me upstairs and then he starts to undress me. At one point in the filming, Ron thought maybe we should do all the sex scenes downstairs, because we were under incredible time pressures to finish the movie. At first it was suggested we stay downstairs and that Kevin should just throw me on the floor. But God bless Kevin, he said, "No, no, no. This has to be romantic." He was completely right. Kevin will make a great director some day. His instincts are wonderfully on target.

Playboy: Actors often say sex scenes are actually boring to do.

Sarandon: Well, these *weren't* boring.... Kevin's a fairly modest guy, so it wasn't easy for him. But no, it never got boring, because we were doing a lot more than just rolling around on the bed. What's wrong with most movie sex scenes is that they are not scripted; they have no purpose. Actors are just photographed in embarrassing positions. But we were really *acting* — and what we were doing was important in the context of the story.

—Sarandon, interviewed by Claudia Dreifus for *Playboy*, May 1989

The beauty of [Annie Savoy] is that she is literate *and* lusty. That's fabulous. You're usually not allowed to be both on screen. She's not a fragile Tennessee Williams heroine. This woman is sexual. And she's strong.

—Sarandon, interviewed by Alan Carter for *The New York Daily News*, 12 June 1988

I put on 15 pounds, which is a lot for me, because I thought Nora [in *White Palace* (1990, Luis Mandoki)] was a big, centered earthy kind of woman, which I'm not. Linda Ellerbee would be perfect. Of course, the night before shooting started, I found myself doing situps. Everyone thinks De Niro's such a great actor for putting on weight, but nobody mentioned that I did it. I don't know if they think women are in bad shape anyway or what....

[*White Palace*] was [test-marketed] right after *Pretty Woman* hit, and everything had to have a feel-good, fantasy ending, no matter what happened before.... We were shooting new endings up until two weeks before the opening. It's frustrating. You put your guts out there on the line; then finally somebody takes your entrails and puts them before the public.

—Sarandon, interviewed by Ben Yagoda for *American Film*, May 1991

Telly SAVALAS [1925-]

Born: Aristotle Savalas in Garden City, N.Y. Studies at Columbia University, a purple heart in WWII and work with ABC News preceded his career as an actor, first on TV, then in films, beginning with Mad Dog Coll (1961, Burt Balaban). In 1967, he played Maggot in Robert Aldrich's The Dirty Dozen:

I play the part of Maggot. The name is ugly enough. I think the part is even uglier. I play a Southerner and for the most part he's a bigot, a religious fanatic, a sexual deviate.... He has been convicted of murder and rape but he thought he did it with justification because he was a representative of the Lord. He's on the side of the Redeemer and to him the other eleven are all evil sinners and should be punished....

As an actor you have to bring another dimension into it, otherwise you get the stereotyped Southern bigot and it doesn't mean anything, but if the man seems charming and if he seems logical — except for every once in a while you have to suggest the psychosis — he becomes frightening because he can be anybody — and that's exactly how I'm playing it, away from the Southern accent and on a very practical basis. He's precise, almost makes sense....

—Savalas, interviewed by Allen Eyles for *Films & Filming*, Sept 1967

Roy SCHEIDER [1932-]

Born: Orange, New Jersey. Pre-law studies and work with The Theater Company at Franklin & Marshall College, The Theater Guild and The Shakespeare Festival preceded his film debut in The Curse of the Living Corpse (1964, Del Ten-

ney). In 1971, he played Buddy Russo opposite Gene Hackman as "Popeye" Doyle in William Friedkin's The French Connection:

Playboy: *The French Connection* was an extraordinarily realistic film. It is rumored that while preparing for that movie, you and Hackman actually went on busts with Egan, Sonny Grosso and the rest of the dope squad.

Scheider: Absolutely true. Hackman and I went up into Harlem with those cops every night. We were busting into shooting galleries and.... Don't get me wrong, Gene and I weren't the first and second ones through the door. We were maybe the fifth and sixth ones through. But we were there all right, without guns, scared shitless. And the tableaux we'd see were incredible, like they'd been staged for us. There'd be burners going. Guys with needles in, guys with needles out. One guy lying on the bed, dead, overdosed. I kept thinking, Jesus, this is too perfect. It's *too much* like a movie. Gene and I would see all that, listen to the cops talk, then rush down to the car and write it all down. Because Friedkin had told us from the beginning that we'd be free to improvise a lot of the incidental conversation and we were intent upon making it as realistic as possible.

Playboy: So you had that part of Sonny Grosso — Russo in the film — down pretty well in your mind by the time you began shooting.

Scheider: Actually, I didn't have the part figured out at all for the first two weeks Gene and I spent with them. I kept wondering what the relationship between Egan and Grosso was really about. What held it together? I mean Egan fashioned himself the Lone Ranger, a one-man fight for law and order in Harlem. Grosso was shy, reserved, sensitive. Nobody liked Egan, everybody liked Grosso, and the two of them seemed to have nothing in common. Yet they were a terrific team. One night, I said to Grosso, "Jesus, Sonny, that Eddie is really tough to take, isn't he?" And Grosso said, "Look, if I didn't like Eddie Egan, who would?" Well, that was it. I'd found the center of the character. It took me two weeks to get that out of Grosso, but as soon as I heard it, I knew exactly where I was going with the role....

Playboy: Did Hackman...discover the center of his role that way?

Scheider: No, Gene's interpretation was really Billy Friedkin's idea, and the two of them fought bitterly about it every day. Although, as I've said, I think Billy has certain problems as a director, and although I think Gene is absolutely one of the greatest actors in the world today, in that case, Gene was wrong and Billy was right. Gene kept wanting to humanize Egan, but Billy would say, "No, this man is a pig. He's as rotten as the criminals he's chasing." Billy molded an unbelievable performance, a character who was so outrageous you could laugh at him, yet you were still behind him because he believed so strongly in what he was doing. He was a man possessed.

Scheider: The most important direction any actor ever receives is "as if." And if you or the director can find the right "as if" for that moment, you've got it. Because the child in you will make you do it right.

Playboy: Which brings to mind a reaction shot you did in *Jaws* [1975, Steven Spielberg].... You were on the boat and you suddenly saw the shark for the first time. You expressed abject horror with utter blankness. A hundred million viewers shrieked with terror, but you never made a sound — and it worked.

Scheider: The key to that scene, to that game of "as if" was that *no* reaction would work. It was *too* extraordinary. So it had to be just, "Ah." Mouth drops, facial muscles relax, silence. It was the most frightening reaction, because it was the most real.

Playboy: Was that your idea or...Spielberg's.

Scheider: It was mine, and the most difficult thing about shooting it was that I didn't have the benefit of the goddamn shark, which was broken most of the time. When Steven said, "Now you see it," there was nothing in front of me but the lens.

Playboy: You had a terrific death scene in *Marathon Man* [1976, John Schlesinger], a picture you made with your old friend Dustin Hoffman.... People say he's hard to work with. Sometimes impossible.

Scheider: He can be difficult, but the difficulties always come out of Dustin's efforts and frustrations in trying to do what he thinks is best for the movie. They'll never come out of vanity or ego or personal bullshit. I told that to Robert Benton when they were starting *Kramer* [*vs. Kramer* (1979)]. I said the only problems you'll ever have will be the result of Dustin's obsession for attacking a role in as fresh a way as possible....

Playboy: Many people in the industry were surprised when you took that part.... You'd already done *Jaws* and were being offered a lot of starring roles, but you took a much smaller one as the third lead. Why?

Scheider: It's true that I took that part against the wishes of a lot of people. But it was the best part around, which is all I ever go for. I mean, it's a tremendous part. The guy was fouled up sexually and felt guilty about it. He was a double agent who was lying to his brother [Hoffman], had run away from his father [Allen Joseph] and was a killer besides. Just layer on top of layer. Now, all of that is great fun for an actor to work on. All that, plus I even got to die.

Playboy: What more could you want?

Scheider: Nothing. So I took it. But the ultimate indignity was that the director, John Schlesinger, then said he didn't think Dustin and I could be brothers because we didn't look alike. So he asked me to do a test. My first reaction was, fuck him, I'm a star who has gallantly condescended to play third lead, and now they want me to test for it. But I calmed down and Dustin and I worked out this little improvisation of the two of us meeting in which we dance around and spar with each other and end up embracing. We shot it and Schlesinger liked it, so I got the part. And that little screen test turned out to be very important. Because later, when [Laurence] Olivier, Dustin and I were rehearsing, we all realized there was something missing from the script — a scene to cement the bond between the two brothers. Without that, the remainder of the movie wouldn't hold together. So we called in the author, William Goldman, but he said, "The kind of scene you two guys are talking about is not one I can write. I mean, I could, but it probably wouldn't be very convincing because it wouldn't come out of my experience. You'd be better off just winging it, finding something there for yourselves." But we didn't have to look very far. We already had the scene we needed; my screen test.

—Scheider, interviewed by Sam Merrill for *Playboy*, Sept 1980

Bob [Fosse] and I got along well [on *All That Jazz* (1979)] because we both have the same acting technique. It's called the Yugoslav total immersion into absolute make-believe reality. What it boils down to is: Don't get caught acting. Bob demands great verisimilitude in his films. He will always point out what was for him a great scene in Kazan's *On the Waterfront*, when Brando and Steiger are in the back of the car, and Brando simply says, "Wow!" Bob loves that because it's so absolutely real, and that is his criterion in movies: It has to be real.

Everyone knows about Bob's great eye, but they don't know about his ear, which is just as strong. He is not only concerned about the words people utter, but the sounds they make when they're tired, bored, lovesick. He can hear those rhythms, and after finishing a scene, instead of talking to the actors, he'd go to the sound box, close his eyes, and listen to how the scene played.

When we started, the most difficult thing for me as an actor was to convince myself that I could portray a choreographer who tells all the top-flight dancers Fosse used what to do. So, in those early stages, when Bob and I were still feeling each other out, he would tell me about his personal experiences in his own life, so that I could better relate to the character. But as the picture went on and I gained confidence, he gave me more freedom. So I was able to use my own instincts.

—Scheider, interviewed by Bernard Drew for *American Film*, Nov 1979

What I was trying to show [in *All That Jazz*], which I felt was in the script was the possession [Joe Gideon] was under, the state he was in. He's a guy who thinks that his talent is not as good as everyone thinks it is. As he says, he doesn't think he's funny enough, rich enough, deep enough, or philosophical enough, but he *is*, of course he is, he is as much as anyone else is. What I had to do was find Bob Fosse and Joe Gideon within me...there are aspects of him, the womanizing aspects, the drinking aspect, the workaholic aspects, the artistic drive. I mean I have all those things, you have all those things. I had to find them within me and put them into the part.

—Scheider, interviewed by David Sheehan for *Oscar Preview*; aired on NBC, 12 Apr 1980

Maximilian SCHELL [1930-]

Born: Vienna, Austria; brother of Maria Schell [1926-]. On stage (from age 11), he made his film debut in Kinder, Mutter und eine General (1955, Laslo Benedek). His first English language film was The Young Lions (1957, Edward Dmytryk). In 1977, he played both Stransky in Sam Peckinpah's Cross of Iron and Johann in Fred Zinnemann's Julia:

I liked making *Cross of Iron* because Sam Peckinpah is one of the few directors who has a true sense of poetry. That may sound odd, when you consider his reputation for violence, but I think he is a great poet in his heart. However, I must say that I hate playing Nazis. I can't stand the uniform; it's not me. The role I played in *Julia* was much closer to me — an ordinary human being, lost in Paris during the rise of Hitler. I could identify with that, with somebody who is half-resigned, half-hopeful, a person who rises to do just a little something that is courageous. That is much more intriguing to me than an extraordinary personality.

—Schell, interviewed by Guy Flatley for *The New York Times*, 16 Sept 1977

Joseph SCHILDKRAUT [1895-1964]

Born: Vienna, Austria; son of Rudolph Schildkraut [1862-1930]. Following his film debut at age 13 in The Wandering Jew, he studied at The Imperial Academy of Music in Berlin and The American Academy of Dramatic Arts in N.Y. He then worked on the Berlin stage, with Max Reinhardt and on Broadway prior to his U.S. film debut as the Chevalier de Vaudry in D.W. Griffith's Orphans of the Storm [1921]:

The agent informed me that the great D.W. Griffith was producing and directing the film and wanted me for the leading part.... Lillian and Dorothy Gish were the orphans and the storm was the French Revolution. Griffith had me in mind for the part of the Chevalier de Vaudry, a nobleman at the Court of Louis XVI....

A fanatical perfectionist, Griffith was at the same time one of the most patient directors I have ever worked with. There were scenes between Lillian Gish and me on which we worked for six weeks at a stretch before he was satisfied. And he never lost his temper; in all those eighteen months he did not raise his voice once. Tall, lean, kind, soft-spoken, Griffith was the typical Southern gentleman, so different from the flamboyant and extravagant directors whose showmanship was the trademark of Hollywood. He was a genius without ever attempting to prove it — except in his work....

[In] *The King of Kings* [1928, Cecil B. DeMille], the story of Christ...[my father] was the high priest, Caiaphas, and I was Judas....

As a director, [DeMille] was the opposite of Griffith. A great showman, he always went for the spectacular — mass scenes with thousands of extras, earthquakes, train wrecks. I think he turned to the Bible for his most famous films, not out of a deep religious feeling but primarily because biblical figures have the larger-than-life dimensions, because primitive emotions and violent passions can be splashed on the screen in a grand manner. DeMille is always aiming at sweeping theatrical and pictorial effects, and not only in his work. On the set he is never merely the director guiding the actors; he *performs* the role of a director, sitting on his chair in a Caesarian pose, shouting through the megaphone, every word, every gesture calculated to impress onlookers and invited guests with his importance and power....

Although he is at times tyrannical, willful, and impatient, DeMille has one thing in common with D.W. Griffith: a generous heart and a great kindness which he hides behind an aloof and sometimes unapproachable attitude. [Schildkraut also worked on DeMille's *The Road to Yesterday* (1925), *Cleopatra* (1934) and *The Crusades* (1935).]

—Schildkraut, in his (as told to Leo Lania) *My Father and I* (New York: Viking Press, 1959)

I really feel that [*The Life of Emile*] *Zola* [1937] has done for me in the films what *Liliom* did for me in the theater. Frankly, I've had a terrible time in Hollywood for the last two years, because nobody wanted to work with me. "Sure, he's a good actor," they would say, "but he's hard to get along with and he'll act all over the place."

The sad part of it is that it took me so long to discover they were right. I did act all over the place and I was hard to get along with.... It wasn't until William Dieterle, who directed *Zola* pointed out to me that the secret to screen acting, like drawing is "leaving away" as much as possible, that I stopped overacting....

Jack Warner thought it might be bad for a Jew to play the part of a Jew in the film, but [Paul] Muni insisted that I should be allowed to do it. At first, Dieterle and I were pretty antagonistic, but now we're the greatest of friends. When he first saw the tests he told me quite frankly that in his opinion nobody wanted to see Joseph Schildkraut having an actor's field-day in the role of Dreyfus, but someone they could believe.

He was right about that, just as he was about screen acting. He rehearsed me in the scene where Dreyfus is released from prison for two weeks at his home, and it was he who insisted that it should be done in pantomime, because he felt that no words in the English language could express just such an emotion.

—Schildkraut, interviewed by William Boehnel for an undated, unsourced article in the files of The New York Public Library for the Performing Arts

Paul SCOFIELD [1922-]

Born: David Paul Scofield in King's Norton, Warwickshire, England. On stage (from age 14), he then studied with The London Mask Theater before joining The Birmingham Rep in 1942. He made his film debut in That Lady (1955, Terence Young). In 1966, he played Sir Thomas More in A Man for all Seasons, a role he had created on the stage:

Sir Thomas More...is a very difficult man to show because he was a family man and he liked good living, but at the same time he was a lawyer and an aesthete and he had spiritual and intellectual length which I couldn't really understand....

I had to use a special voice...an accent that was a bastard thing of my own. His dryness of mind I thought led him to use a dryness of speech, so I would flatten or elongate vowels in a certain way to get the effect I wanted.

—Scofield, interviewed by Alex Harvey for *The People* (London), 12 Feb 1967

[Filmmaking is] all very baffling yet fascinating too. In one sense it is not entirely satisfactory at times. One wants to take the full responsibility, because that is what one is used to. I like depending on myself, but in films one has to strike a balance because it is — and I accept this — primarily a director's medium. Fred Zinnemann is wonderful because he not only tells me what he is doing but why. He never leaves me in the dark about his intentions as I've known directors to do — and I've suspected it was because they were not entirely sure of themselves. I've often been at a loss as to whom I was supposed to be.

—Scofield, interviewed by Stephen Watts for *The New York Times*, 24 July 1966

George C. SCOTT [1927-]

Born: Wise, Virginia; father of Campbell Scott [1961-]. Journalism studies at The University of Missouri, work in stock and on the N.Y. stage (from 1957) preceded his film debut in Anatomy of a Murder (1959, Otto Preminger):

Preminger had seen me on Broadway in *Comes a Day* [1958]. He called me in and wanted me to play the bartender in his movie — the role Murray Hamilton ended up playing. I read the script and said I wanted to play the state's attorney. That was that. Otto never opened his mouth.

Q. It was that easy?

A. Sure was. All I did was ask for it. I was tickled to death. It was a big step for me. A big, big break for me in films, that picture. Good part — well-written as far as it went — a showy part, a flashy part. A lot of work, but it was very worthwhile doing. I like working for Otto. We've been friends a long time. Not close friends, but I respect Otto.

Q. How would you rate him as a director?

A. I don't think he's an exceptional director. I think he's a magnificent producer and promoter. Otto is really too emotional to be a terrific director. But he is competent.

—Scott, interviewed by John Weisman for *Penthouse*, May 1973

Playboy: When you talked earlier about being a subtle actor, did you have in mind your role in *The Hustler* [1961, Robert Rossen]?

Scott: That was the whole idea. To underdo it. Restrained.

Playboy: You never raised your voice until the end —

Scott: That one line.

Playboy: "You owe me money!" A frightening moment. Is it true that Rossen wanted you to whisper it?

Scott: That's correct. We argued about it for a couple of days. He wanted me to play it both ways and I wouldn't. I knew he wouldn't print it. He would print it his way and not my way and I refused. He got very angry with me.

Playboy: Why did you want to shout it?

Scott: I just had a feeling. The scene had flattened out and was going to be dead and it was the most important scene in the film, because it was the climax, and I just hung in there. He finally gave up and did it my way. I don't think he ever regretted it, frankly.

Scott: We rewrote [*Dr. Strangelove* (1964, Stanley Kubrick)] every day. I don't take any more credit than anybody else. Stanley Kubrick, of course, gets all the credit and Peter [Sellers] gets the rest. But Stanley is very meticulous and hates everything that he writes or has anything to do with. He's an incredibly, depressingly serious man, with this wild sense of humor. But paranoid. Every morning, we would all meet and practically rewrite the day's work. He's a perfectionist and he's always unhappy with anything that's set.

Playboy: Weren't you unhappy, as well, with the ending?

Scott: It bothered me a lot, but there was a very bad problem there. Stanley was right.

Playboy: The original ending was to be a pie-throwing scene involving the President and all the top brass. What was the problem?

Scott: The assassination of President Kennedy was the problem, and that was a *bitch* of a problem! Peter Sellers gets hit with a pie and he swoons in my arms and I say, "Gentlemen, our beloved President has been struck down at the prime of life." What the fuck, you couldn't use the line and you couldn't use the rest of it either; there was nothing Stanley could do about it. He had to find some other way to end the movie. It would have been so distasteful.

Playboy: Didn't you pattern General Buck Turgidson after a real person?

Scott: Yes, a business acquaintance of my father's. He was like Buck exactly. Had he been in the Armed Forces, that's what he would have been. He was frightening. Those people are frightening, obviously. And to make them funny is a good thing, because they're scary people.

Playboy: Do you often pattern your characters after real people?

Scott: I used to do it much more than I do it now. That's the loss of observation. Dickie Burton said it one time, too, and I noticed it to be very true. He said, "I can't observe as well as I used to." When you're so concerned about yourself being observed, you cannot observe. It robs the actor of one of his great tools, which is the nondescript personality that can observe. It's just like writers who listen to dialog. Actors do it, too. I did it for years. But I certainly don't do it very much anymore. I'm so self-conscious in public. I can't go anywhere and sit down in the corner of a barroom and listen to the guy talking for an hour; no way. That's one thing fame does for you.

—Scott, interviewed by Lawrence Grobel for *Playboy*, Dec 1980

[John Huston] is not a maker-over of actors. He is not an imposer upon actors. He is not a man who would tell you how to act. In the first place, he doesn't hire you if he doesn't respect you; in the second place, he won't work with you if he doesn't respect you. And he's the easiest man, the best man in the world to lose a point to. Because we can disagree at any time — and have many times — but there is always a grace about him, and a charm about him, when he defeats you. Many times you win; you impose your viewpoint on him. Now, he may take three days to adapt to an actor's ideas, three days to make a change in *his* concept — which is rather remarkable — and he'll say, "Yeah, kid, I see what you gotta do, kid," and he will go out of his way to make that change. There are very few directors who are even intelligent enough to do this. [Scott also worked on Huston's *The List of the Adrian Messenger* (1963) and *The Bible* (1966).]

I didn't know what the hell was going on in *Petulia* [1968, Richard Lester], and I don't think Lester gives a damn about actors as much as he does about camerawork, but I really liked him. He makes it so much fun, you don't worry, somehow. I can't ever recall having a close-up on *Petulia*. They were all from fifty feet away. None of that bullshit about a master, then a reverse, then a medium shot. If I were going to emulate anyone it'd be him. [Scott worked for Lester again on *Firestarter* (1984).]

—Scott, interviewed by Rex Reed for *The New York Times*, 29 Mar 1970

[General George S. Patton] was a professional, and I admire professionalism. And whatever else he was, good or bad, he was an individual, and that's what's most important to me today when everybody else around seems to be some kind of ostrich.

—Scott, interviewed by Allen Harbinson for *George C. Scott* (New York: Pinnacle Books, 1977)

From the beginning [of shooting *Patton* (1970, Franklin J. Schaffner)] all I asked was that we show him as multi-faceted as he really was. It caused trouble. Conflicts grew out of trying to serve too many masters. We had to serve the Pentagon, we had to serve General Bradley and his book, we had to serve the Zanucks. If you ride that many horses at the same time, you're going to have problems.

I simply refused to play George Patton as the standard cliché you could get from newspaper clips of the time. I didn't want to play him as a hero just to please the Pentagon, and I didn't want to play him as an obvious, gung-ho bully, either. I wanted to play every conceivable facet of the man. There were three basic scripts and several revisions before I got the character I wanted. We re-worked it the whole time we were shooting, and I kept screaming a lot.

I ran 3,000 feet of film here at home and really studied the man. I watched the way he moved and talked. Some of it I absorbed, some I threw out. For instance, he had a high, squeaky voice, like a football coach. The more excited he got, the higher it got. I didn't use that. People are used to my gravel voice and if I tried to use a high little voice it would be silly. I tried not to editorialize about his beliefs or the things he said. Hell, you get paid for acting, for giving the *illusion* of believing, not for *actually* believing. For chrissakes, no, I didn't believe in what he did any more than I'd believe in the Marquis de Sade or Frank Merriwell! This is a schizoid business to start with. The biggest mistake an actor can make is to try to resolve all the differences between himself and the characters he plays.

Patton actually believed what he was doing was right. So did Hitler. The face slapping scene? Hell, he really struck *two* men. We only had time to put *one* in the movie. But he wasn't a hypocrite. Even though war was all he cared about, it was what he did for a living. It was a profession. Patton's war was unavoidable, not like Vietnam, which is an obscenity. At least he had no political ambitions, which is more than you can say for our generals today. I told Frank McCarthy, the producer, "I don't want to play another 'Strangelove.' I already played that goddam part. But on the other hand, I rejected the glory-hunter cliché. Patton was a mean sonofabitch, but he was also generous to his men. Now that it is over, I feel we did right by the man. There are still things about him I hate and things I admire — which makes him a human being, I guess. On the whole, it was one of the best working situations I've ever had and it came wholly from my interest in Patton.

—Scott, interviewed by Rex Reed for *The New York Times*, 29 Mar 1970

[Dr.] Bock [in *Hospital* (1971, Arthur Hiller)] was an interesting character, a sweet character, but sad. I think he symbolizes a kind of middle-aged frustration that happens to all of us — unhappy with himself and unhappy with the way he had conducted his life. I believed his problems. He was credible to me.

—Scott, interviewed by John Weisman for *Penthouse*, May 1973

Jean SEBERG [1938-1979]

Born: Marshalltown, Iowa. An unknown, she was chosen, amidst great publicity, to be directed by Otto Preminger in Saint Joan (1957):

I think I was a better actress on the first day I auditioned for Preminger than at any time since. I mean better in the sense of being spontaneous. Otto has a special gift for inspiring terror in people. What he never came to realize after all the time we worked together was that if someone yells at me I simply hide, I go into a shell. At first I thought he'd rescue me; I saw him as my father, my savior — he did teach me certain heel-clicking rules of professionalism, although I'm not sure how much they're really worth — being on time, being nice to the press, that kind of thing.

I remember the day of my screen test; he went at me and I fought him back. I still had a lot of Midwestern strength. I really sometimes think that's why he took me; unconsciously, he saw a spirit to break. It would have been the best thing in the world if I'd gone on fighting Preminger, but I got so that I never dared to open my mouth to him.... In an odd way, of course, I suppose I wouldn't have it any other way than it happened. If it weren't for him, I wouldn't be here at all. But I don't think I've still pulled out from the shadow of those years. When *Bonjour Tristesse* [1958, Preminger] was finished, I turned off the faucets and withdrew.

—Seberg, interviewed by Donald LaBadie for *Show*, Aug 1963

It was Warren Beatty who advised [Robert Rossen] to see me [for *Lilith* (1964)]. At the start, Rossen and he had a relationship which was strangely fraternal, very intimate, very like accomplices even. Oddly, this relationship of intimacy stopped at the first day of filming, and from then on, it did nothing but deteriorate more and more....

The indications [Rossen] gave the actors were never literal, but aimed at helping them psychologically and intellectually, at steeping them more in their roles. In the picnic scene of *Lilith*, he did not indicate to me by gestures what I should execute, but he explained to me how I should be fascinated by the water, by reflections.... His patience was exemplary, and did away with every external worry for the actors....

One of his constant concerns was to try to avoid falling into a too easily fairy-like aspect of the character; it was too easy to do the mad Ophelia, and I entirely shared his reticence in this respect.... He wanted the part of Lilith to be strongly characterized as feminine and virile at the same time.

—Seberg, in *Cahiers du Cinéma*, Apr 1966

George SEGAL [1936-]

Born: New York City. Studies at Columbia University and work as a jazz musician and on the

N.Y. stage (from 1956) preceded his film debut in The Young Doctors (1961, Phil Karlson). In 1970, he played Brooks Wilson in Irvin Kershner's Loving and Gordon Hocheiser in Carl Reiner's Where's Poppa?:

[1970] was the year I was really an actor, the year that will never come again. I will never make a film better than *Loving*. It was so almost perfect on every level that its flaws were irrelevant. That was a very personal film, a collaboration between Irvin Kershner and me, and there was a lot of me in that, the me of 1970. And there will never be a more original film on mother love, or a funnier one, than *Where's Poppa?* A beautiful collaboration also, a moment in Carl Reiner's life, and mine, the actor I was then, the man I was then, working together. I worshipped Carl. Remember, I grew up on *The Show of Shows*.

I must tell you that my contribution to *Who is Killing the Great Chefs of Europe?* [1978, Ted Kotcheff] is somewhat less than it was in *Loving* and *Where's Poppa?* This is an expensive picture, a project all set up before I came into it. This is in no way a personal film. Today, they are buying a known quantity in me, and I am giving them that. I learned how to be a commercial actor in *A Touch of Class* [1974, Melvyn Frank], and now that is what I give them, because that is what they want. It's a whole new ball game.... Like a taxi driver, I drive a clean taxicab; I can turn on a dime. I am a personality now....

—Segal, interviewed by Bernard Drew for *American Film*, May 1978

[Ted Kotcheff] *loves* to shoot film. It becomes almost a test of wills after awhile. "All right, go again. I'll show you something you haven't seen before." I hate doing all those takes, but I'd still work with him. I enjoyed the experience. Ted's a perfectionist, but he understands what an actor is trying to do. He'll accept and print it, but he also wants what he sees *in his head*, and he'll go 20, 30 times till he gets it. [Segal also worked on Kotcheff's *Desperate Hours* (1967, for TV), *Of Mice and Men* (1968, for TV) and *Fun with Dick and Jane* (1977).]

Q. Is [Burt] Reynolds a very inventive director, or does he come to the set knowing exactly what he wants [on *Stick* (1985)]?

A. He's very disciplined, much like Melvin Frank, with whom I did *Touch of Class* and *The Duchess and the Dirtwater Fox* [1976]. Burt's very organized, which gives him incredible freedom on the set. He's delighted when someone develops a new bit. And he's an incurable re-writer. The clap board claps, and he says, "Let's do it this way. Say...," and he'll spout a *new* line. It adds real spontaneity to the scene, giving the actors a line they've *never* rehearsed before. That's a way of really keeping actors on their toes, and Burt knows who he can do it with. He's got a very strong sense of his actors and their capabilities....

Q. What is Reynolds' technique for directing himself?

A. He trusts himself, and he brings his own camera crew with him. They know what he looks for, and they get it when he's playing a scene. Plus, Burt has the good sense of when he gets it right, and of what he'll need in the editing room.

—Segal, interviewed by Steranko for *Prevue*, Nov/Dec 1984

Peter SELLERS [1925-1980]

Born: Southsea, England. Work in vaudeville (from age 5) and an appearance in the low-budget short, Let's Go Crazy (1951), preceded his first feature film, Penny Points to Paradise (1951, Tony Young). Work on radio, particularly The Goon Show, furthered his film career. In 1959, he played Fred Kite in John Boulting's I'm All Right, Jack:

Oh, I know the Kites of this world. They're just there. Little Hitlers in the factory, forgotten men at home. They're tragic, in a way. Wonderful people living in the...ummm...look around and you find them.

—Sellers, interviewed by Joe Morgenstern for *The New York Herald Tribune*, 24 Apr 1960

In *Lolita* [1962], Stanley [Kubrick] wanted me to speak with a New York accent. He said, "Listen, a friend who's a jazz impresario, Norman Granz, has a really perfect sound. So he put this tape on, and it was hysterical. You heard a voice, speaking too loud, saying (in a lisping Clare Quilty voice), "Hi there, Stanley, this is a whole script, for God's sakes. I mean, you really do ask for some strange things." Then you hear some rustling of paper, and he starts reading the *Lolita* script. And that's where Quilty came from.

Q. How did you first meet Kubrick?

A. It was right before *Lolita*. He came straight to me and asked me to play Quilty.... To me, that was an enormous honor. I said I'd do anything he wanted to make — film the phone book, anything. The greatest directors I've worked with are him and Hal [Ashby, on *Being There* (1979)].

While I sat on the plane to Rome [to begin production on *The Pink Panther* (1963, Blake Edwards)], I had some thoughts about Clouseau. Suddenly, something came to me — Captain Webb matches. That's an old British brand of safety matches. On its package is a guy in a long, straight, striped, old-fashioned bathing costume, with a big stiff mustache standing out on his face. I thought that one of the things some Frenchmen have is this sort of ostentatious show of virility.

So I think Clouseau will have a nice big mustache and I shall play him with great dignity because — I feel *he* thinks he is probably one of the greatest detectives in the world. From what I gather from the script, he is a complete idiot, but he would *never* want anyone else to know that....

Q. And the clumsiness was just something you worked up?

A. The clumsiness was part of what Blake wanted him to be. Because of this dignity, Blake wanted him to be, shall we say, *accident-prone*. That's why when something happens to him, like he falls over something, he gets up from the floor and says to his assistant, who's been completely silent, "What was that you said?" The assistant says, "Nothing, sir." And he can only say, "Eh, yeah, I see." That's how his mind works.

—Sellers, interviewed by Mitchell Glazer for *Rolling Stone*, 17 Apr 1980

Q. What about that scene at the billiard table with George Sanders [in *The Pink Panther*] where you play with all these cues that are the wrong shape? Was all this written or did you work that out with the director?

A. Well, as with all Blake's things, they are partly written and the rest we sort of improvised, you know. That was mainly written.

—Sellers, interviewed by Clive James at The National Film Theater, 19 Oct 1972

Clouseau is an absolutely devoted policeman, fearless, bold, and serenely confident that in the end he will triumph. In that he is like a [Buster] Keaton character. He also has Stan Laurel's qualities of purity and simplicity, mixed with Oliver Hardy's pomposity. But if I had to define his outstanding trait in one word, it would be purity. [Sellers also played Inspector Clouseau in *A Shot in the Dark* (1964), *The Return of the Pink Panther* (1974), *The Pink Panther Strikes Again* (1976), *The Revenge of the Pink Panther* (1978) and *Trail of the Pink Panther* (1982), all directed by Blake Edwards.]

—Sellers, interviewed by Tom McMorrow for *The Sunday News*, 25 May 1975

Q. Terry Southern [who wrote the screenplay of *Dr. Strangelove* (1964, Stanley Kubrick)] was telling me a *Strangelove* story. He said you were originally going to do the Slim Pickens role [as Major T.J. "King" Kong], as well as [Captain Mandrake and President Muffley].

A. Yes, I was. In fact, I was going to do them *all.* Stanley Kubrick was convinced I could. I could do no wrong, you see. Some days Stanley used to be sittin' outside my front door saying, "What about Buck Schmuck (Turgidson, played in the film by George C. Scott)?! You've *got* to play Buck Schmuck."

And I'd say, "I *physically* can't do it! I don't like the role anyway, Stan. And I'll try and do the Slim Pickens thing, but I mean, I think that's *enough....*"

I'll tell you how Strangelove's voice came about. On the set, we had a special stills guy called Weegee, who is now dead. He was very famous, and he took a lot of pictures for *Life* magazine in the old days.... He used to talk in a strange little voice like (mimics Weegee's adenoidal speech), "Hey, Peter, I really have an idea for a shot here." So I put a German accent on top of Weegee's.

—Sellers, interviewed by Mitchell Glazer for *Rolling Stone*, 17 Apr 1980

If I were a leading man, a tall, good-looking sort of chap, you know, a chap who has a way with him, who gets parts tailored for his personality, like Cary Grant, then there would be a Peter Sellers film just as there were Cary Grant and Clark Gable and Rock Hudson films. However, I'm not a star because I have no personality of my own.

With each role I play, I try to develop a completely different voice, a completely different walk, a completely different make-up and so on. Thus, though I may have five films released in one year [in the U.S.], I consider that there is one "Clare Quilty" picture, the "General Fitzjohn" film [*Waltz of the Toreadors* (1962, John Guillermin)] and so on, not five Sellers films.

My current film, for example — *The World of Henry Orient* [1964, George Roy Hill] — is to me a Henry Orient film. When I first read the script, I didn't say, "Now how do I fit Orient's personality to mine?" Instead, I tried to analyze the character of this rascally, lecherous concert pianist, who has his mind more on keyholes than the keyboard. Having been a radio actor by training, I always try to get the voice first. In the case of our friend Henry, I decided that, being involved in the concert field, he would somewhere along the line have picked up a, excuse the phrase, bastard "Continental" accent to impress the ladies.... As for his looks, a fine line mustache was de rigueur, topped by a wig of wavy, uncut hair....

I am grateful that producers seldom call me to say that a particular character is a "Peter Sellers role." If they tell me it is an odd, challenging, bizarre, whimsical or even revolting role, I am interested. But faced with a character who has been carefully glued together to fit my personality — or, rather, what some producer thinks is my personality — I am disinterested.

—Sellers, in *The New York Herald Tribune*, 18 Aug 1963

Q. From what I've heard, the film version of *Being There* was a long time coming.

A. Yes. You see, I read the book nine years ago, when Hal Ashby was in London. I had just seen his *Harold and Maude* [1971], which absolutely blew me out.... I sent him the book with a note saying, "Need to see you, read this." He saw everything it had to say. We then started our quest.

Q. I could tell on the *Being There* set that you often were unusually focused.

A. Shirley MacLaine couldn't figure me out at all; she just couldn't. But Jack Warden did; we were great buddies. And Melvyn Douglas, jeeze, I found myself in scenes with him where I was so carried away with the force of his acting that I forgot my lines. Almost by just looking at him. The whole experience of making *Being There* was so humbling, so powerful. And I'd often say, "Cut." And people would come running, saying, "Is anything wrong? Don't you feel all right?"

And I'd say — and I know this is a bit Chance-like to say a thing like this — but I'd say (in a guileless monotone), "Oh. No, no. I've just never seen anything quite like this film before."

—Sellers, interviewed by Mitchell Glazer for *Rolling Stone*, 17 Apr 1980

A lot of actors have been asked in their careers: "What is your ambition in life. Do you want to play Lear in Shakespeare, do you want to do this in *Richard III*, do you want to do Ibsen? What do you want to do?" I can tell you quite simply — the ambition in my life has been to play Chance the gardener in *Being There*.

—Sellers, interviewed by David Sheehan for *Oscar Preview*; aired on NBC, 12 Apr 1980

Omar SHARIF [1932-]

Born: Michael Shalhoub in Alexandria, Egypt. Studies at British Victoria College in Cairo preceded his film debut in Sera's fil Wadi/Struggle in the Valley (1953, Jusef Shadine). He made his English speaking film debut as Sheriff Ali in David Lean's Lawrence of Arabia (1962):

When they work in the studio, actors are hidden behind the masks of the characters they're portraying. The day's work over, they split up until the next day. They seldom have a chance to get to know one another.

We, on the other hand, were living out in the middle of the desert. We were forced to watch ourselves live, listen to ourselves talk....

Peter O'Toole showed me tricks of the trade and the very next day I'd try to put them into practice. Arab film actors use lots of mime and grandiose gestures that come more from silent movies than talkies.

David Lean curbed my Middle Eastern temperament mercilessly. "He who can do the most can do the least," he told me by way of encouragement....

A great deal has been said about the nature of the Lawrence-Ali relationship and countless articles have been written about it. The screenwriter [Robert Bolt] did not expressly define their intimacy. He presented their complicity. It revealed itself throughout the film in affectionate behavior, which was actually a reflection of the everyday life that Peter O'Toole and I were living. The moviegoers must have been aware of this. I'm convinced that the fraternal feeling that sprang up between Peter and me was one of the great things to come out of the film, just as it made those two years in the desert two years of joy, two full years.

—Sharif, in his (with Marie-Therèse Guinchard) *The Eternal Male* (Paris: Editions Stock, 1976; Garden City, N.Y.: Doubleday & Co., 1977 — trans. by Martin Sokolinsky)

[On *Behold a Pale Horse* (1964), Fred Zinnemann] does a scene, then he discusses it with you. He lets you bring out your own ideas which he later incorporates into his final instructions. When it's all over, you realize that he has really guided you into expressing his own ideas, but he has done it so subtly, and with such respect for his actors, that we think we have done it ourselves. He has a marvelous rapport.

—Sharif, interviewed by Oscar Barnes for *The New York Herald Tribune*, 9 Aug 1964

I made a mistake, for a reason that was understandable but unforgivable: I betrayed [Robert Bolt] the scenario writer [of *Dr. Zhivago* (1965, David Lean)]. I did it unconsciously, of course, but I did betray him. Dr. Zhivago is an omnipresent character who looks on, watches, feels some emotions, but never expresses anything.

The picture was made in little sections, like all the others. Every day I would shoot different scenes with one actor, then another, and day after day I faced them — actors who acted. I wasn't supposed to do anything but look on, watch, never show a reaction....

I followed those instructions for two months, but the day came when this apparent self-effacement began to disturb me, and gradually I let more emotion creep in than I should have, an inner emotion but one that revealed itself by certain looks or by mime (spontaneous but superfluous).

I let my emotiveness get the upper hand. I couldn't resist the lines that my co-stars spoke. I should have had complete trust in the scenario writer and the director; instead, I let myself fall into the trap. I know that an impassive Zhivago would have been more convincing than Omar Sharif's emotiveness.

[While making *Funny Lady* (1975, Herbert Ross)] I wanted to get back to Austria, to another part, to a new movie adventure, with a new co-star. I'd picked her. She was Karen Black....

I went off confidently to Zurs, a little ski resort in the Arlberg region of Austria, and...met [Ivan Passer] a real movie maker in the proper sense of the word, a leader of actors, a man who brought me out of myself....

[Passer] helped me find total freedom of expression. I did *Crime and Passion* [1976] without holding back. For the first time I let myself be expressed. It was fantastic.

—Sharif, in his (with Marie-Therèse Guinchard) *The Eternal Male* (Paris: Editions Stock, 1976; Garden City, N.Y.: Doubleday & Co., 1977 — trans. by Martin Sokolinsky)

Wallace SHAWN [1943-]

Born: New York City. Studies at Harvard and Oxford and work as an academic preceded his career as a playwright. His first play was produced in 1975. He made his acting debut on the stage in 1977. His film debut was in Woody Allen's Manhattan (1979):

Working with Woody — it's as if you're a little boat on a big lake, and he just gives a very gentle push to the boat, setting it off in a vague direction, and you have to sail it from then on. He doesn't want to be drawn into telling people what they should do. He wants to create an atmosphere, a very quiet happiness that I think everybody, including himself, enjoys working in. Woody doesn't want to see actors straining and struggling and choking with hard work. I think he finds that unappetizing on screen. Mia [Farrow, with whom he worked on *Radio Days* (1987)] obviously knows how to follow her instincts in that atmosphere and she trusts that he'll say something if she starts floating in the wrong direction. She seems, to put it mildly, extraordinarily unpretentious about acting. Whatever the process she uses to achieve what she achieves, she doesn't burden her fellow actors with it. I suspect that she derives quite a bit of what she does from the way she's feeling at that individual moment — how she feels about other actors, the set, and just how she feels at that moment of life. Because the moment you're being filmed is also a moment of life.

I also feel she enjoys the fantasy of playing someone not herself and dressing up in a costume the way a child or an adolescent enjoys it. She acts with a certain light touch that they have when they act, when they dress up and pretend. You can see the child enjoying it, and I felt I was seeing this in her.

—Shawn, interviewed by Georgia A. Brown for *American Film*, Mar 1987

Norma SHEARER [1900-1983]

Born: Edith Norma Shearer in Montreal, Quebec, Canada. Following her film debut as an extra in The Flapper (1920, Alan Crosland), she appeared in several small roles before being signed by MGM in 1923, where she then became a leading lady and in 1927, the wife of producer Irving Thalberg.

I can't do the Garbo or Dietrich thing. I admire them both greatly and wish that I could play such characters as they interpret, but I have to go through a transition to become worldly.

Hence I have to begin by being very nice, and then about the middle of the picture I am likely to go all haywire. That's when things really grow interesting....

I enjoyed tremendously portraying the roles in *The Divorcée* [1930, Robert Z. Leonard], *Strangers May Kiss* [1931, George Fitzmaurice] and *Free Soul* [1931, Clarence Brown] because they had the flash I speak of. *Strange Interlude* [1932, Robert Z. Leonard] is even better because it's more psychological....

[Nina Leeds in *Strange Interlude*] is a wonderful character to interpret, because of the many transitions that she goes through.... [She] is all bad right at the beginning of the story, and then goes through a sort of regeneration, when she confesses to Charlie [Ralph Morgan], her friend, the various indiscretions of which she has been guilty.

Then she has a setback again morally when she discovers the hereditary influences in her husband [Alexander Kirkland]'s life. She becomes hard and cold after this and decides to take as much out of life as possible.

—Shearer, interviewed by Edwin Schallert for *The Los Angeles Times*, 10 July 1932

Q. What are the two most widely diverse parts you have ever played — from the angle of sex appeal?

A. The girl in *He Who Gets Slapped* [1924, Victor Seastrom] — my first role at MGM — and Jan Ashe in *A Free Soul*. Of course, that is what makes every part individual — the angle of sex-appeal. In the first, the boy and girl were two children in love. It was a fresh, dawning kind of love, with timorous gropings and shy responses. But with a very definite undercurrent of young sex. The *Free Soul* girl was as close to the primitive, elemental sex-urge as any I have ever played. She was wasting no time to build up a romance with Clark Gable.

In *The Barretts* [*of Wimpole Street* (1934, Sidney Franklin)] Elizabeth Barrett was an invalid simply because she had no vitality. She was not ill. I tried to make her vital only from the moment she first saw Robert Browning [Fredric March]. From that moment was the urge to walk, to see him. He brought her warmth and life — sex-interest. Yet this is certainly not a role that could ever be named "sexy."

—Shearer, interviewed by Ruth Rankin for *Photoplay Magazine*, Dec 1934

There have been so many exquisite Juliets created on the stage that I was fortunate to have the opportunity of playing her on the screen instead [1936, George Cukor]. As ours is a completely different medium, I feel that it has given us the privilege of disregarding a great deal of the traditional Shakespearean style of acting....

I didn't attempt to play the role as it was played four centuries ago. I tried rather, to interpret the part of Juliet in a manner that would make it believable and entertaining to modern audiences. To my mind, acting is good if it convinces, delights and pleases the audience of the particular moment or period in which it is presented.

—Shearer, in the press release for *Romeo and Juliet* (MGM, 1936)

Marie [in *Marie Antoinette* (1938, W.S. Van Dyke)] was the original glamour girl. She had all the female characteristics. The story...takes Marie from the young and eager Austrian princess to the reckless, extravagant queen and then to the disillusioned woman who died courageously on the guillotine....

Marie's main object in living was to be amused. She had no caution. She hated unwisely; loved too well. Her greatest fault was that she had a passionate desire for happiness, and under other circumstances I think she might have been a very fine queen.

—Shearer, interviewed by Bosley Crowther for *The New York Times*, 21 Aug 1938

Marie Antoinette was a very human person. Her virtues and faults were no different from those of any modern woman. It was this discovery that first interested me in playing the last Queen of France on the screen.

To me, Antoinette has become more real, fascinating and understandable since reading the intimate details of her life as revealed by MGM research workers. She was outspokenly frank and impatient of ceremony. She never could hide her feelings. Hating her royal robes and ornaments, she exclaimed when freed from then, "Thank heaven I'm out of harness...!"

According to Antoinette's contemporaries, she was gay, witty, generous, considerate, courageous and dependable so far as her husband, King Louis XVI [Robert Morley], was concerned, but frequently liked to ridicule others....

During the weeks we have been making *Marie Antoinette*, Director W.S. Van Dyke II and I have tried our best to work the little and perhaps relatively unimportant, but definitely humanizing things about Antoinette into the picture.

Antoinette's sheer joy of living, for one thing. I believe that, despite her tragedy, she had a greater capacity for happiness than any woman in all history.

—Shearer, in *The New York Daily Mirror*, 21 Aug 1938

It was wonderful to have Tyrone Power play opposite me [as Count Axel de Fersen in *Marie Antoinette*]. He is born to the costumes of the period. And in addition, he is a very fine, a really great actor. He reminds me singularly of Irving [Thalberg]. He has that same fineness and sweetness — you might even call it sensitivity. He has the same coloring, and at times, almost the same cast of features. I found it very inspiring to work with him.

—Shearer, interviewed by Sonia Lee for *Screen Book*, Sept 1938

Mary, the character I am playing in *The Women* [1939, George Cukor], was the one more or less normal character in the play, and, therefore, she somewhat suffers by comparison to all the other eccentric and more amusing women surrounding her, but I feel she gives strength and meaning to the story. She is like the Christmas tree and they the trimmings which provide the glitter.

—Shearer, interviewed for *The New York Post*, 23 Sept 1939

I have always played roles before where I followed another actress, and while that is often a handicap, because of a lack of freshness in the characters when seen a second time, still it does give one something to go on. For example, in both *The Women* and *Idiot's Delight* [1939, Clarence Brown], Margalo Gilmore and Lynn Fontanne had already familiarized audiences with their heroines, which left me a pattern to follow. But in *Escape* [1940, Mervyn LeRoy], I felt I was really sticking my chin out, because I was playing the countess for the first time and also because of the challenging character of the woman. She is intriguing, mysterious, yet altogether feminine, so that in order to catch her many-sided personality I had to create not only one woman but several. It was this unpredictable quality in the countess which captivated the many readers of the story....

—Shearer, interviewed for *The New York Post*, 17 Aug 1940

It was such fun to be doing something light and happy and gay again [*We Were Dancing* (1941, Robert Z. Leonard)]. And I couldn't have had a more expert partner in gaiety than Melvyn Douglas. His sense of fun is delicious, very subtle and very infectious. Playing comedy with Melvyn, when you haven't played it for a long time, is like dancing with Cesar Romero when you are out of practice. You can't miss when he leads.

—Shearer, interviewed by Gladys Hall for *Motion Picture*, Apr 1942

Martin SHEEN [1940-]

Born: Ramon Estevez in Dayton, Ohio; father of Emilio Estevez [1963-] and Charlie Sheen [1966-]. Work on the London stage and off-Broadway plus numerous roles on TV preceded his film debut in The Incident (1967, Larry Peerce). In 1979, he played Captain Willard in Francis Ford Coppola's Apocalypse Now:

I have a lot of mixed feelings about Francis. I am very fond of him personally. The thing I love about him most is that he never, like a good general, asked you to do anything he wouldn't do. He was right there with us, lived there in the shit and mud up to his ass, suffered the same diseases, ate the same food. I don't think he realizes how tough he is to work for. God, is he tough. But I will sail with that son of a bitch anytime. There is only one other director I would go that far with, and that's Terry Malick [with whom Sheen worked on *Badlands* (1972)]. You bet your ass. I won't get to work with a Malick or a Coppola too many times in my life and, my God, I consider it an honor.

—Sheen, interviewed by Jean Vallely for *Rolling Stone*, 1 Nov 1979

Q. Was Brando intimidating?

A. The image of Brando I brought with me [to the set of *Apocalypse Now*] certainly was, but the reality proved to be one of the sweetest professionals you could meet. A man with a mischievous sense of humor, easiest in the company of actors and least at ease in public.

—Sheen, interviewed by Alexander Walker for *The Evening Standard*, 15 May 1979

[Bob Dylan is] the most powerfully spiritual composer since Bach.... I carry around his themes in my head while I'm working. You know, "Tambourine Man" was the theme for

Private Slovik [in *The Execution of Private Slovik* (1974, Lamont Johnson — for TV)], "Desolation Row" was the theme for Kit Carruthers in *Badlands*. Everything I did had a Dylan theme. "My Back Pages" was for Mitch Snyder [in *Samaritan: The Mitch Snyder Story* (1986, Richard T. Heffron — for TV)]. It's all a rhythm. I gave each character a theme, a rhythm, and Dylan was the basis of every single character since I first heard him in 1964. That continues today, absolutely. I still grab a theme. I still grab a phrase. For *Apocalypse Now*, there was a lot of music from *Billy the Kid*, and the *Desire* album. "Knockin' on Heaven's Door," that was *Apocalypse*. "Mama, take these guns offa me, I can't use them anymore." That's the only scene in the movie had anything to do with me. There you saw me wrestling with devils on-camera. When I'm lying in that bed, that's what I'm hearing. "Mama, take these guns offa me." I can hear it playing in my head while you're watching me, I'm singing it, it's bringing tears to my eyes, it moves me in the spirit.

—Sheen, interviewed by Stephen Schiff for *Vanity Fair*, Aug 1987

Ann SHERIDAN [1915-1967]

Born: Clara Lou Sheridan in Denton, Texas. After winning a "Search For Beauty" contest, she was given a Paramount Studios stock contract, and then made her film debut in Search for Beauty (1934, Earle Kenton). In 1949, she played Lt. Catherine Gates opposite Cary Grant as Capt. Henri Rochard in Howard Hawks' I Was a Male War Bride:

Q. I've...wondered for some time whether much of the dialogue between you and Grant wasn't ad-lib?

A. Oh, it was. Cary did it. The scene where we're in front of my commanding officer and she said, "There's a hitch," and he said "Itch? Do you itch, Catherine?" and I said, "No, I don't itch" — this was all Cary, all ad-lib. He was right; he'd say, "People don't wait for somebody else to finish a line, they talk over each other."

Q. You talked over each other a lot in that picture.

A. Well, that was Cary. We would sit and work for hours.... Remember that scene in the haystack — "Oh, you think a French girl can kiss better than I can?" That was all Cary.

Q. Well, it was the two of you.

A. No. Howard Hawks would sit on the set and he'd say, "Well, I'm not quite satisfied with this scene. What would you say in a situation like this?" So we'd sit and think, and it was invariably Cary. He would tell you what to say. Howard is a very clever man. He picks brains. And he had a very clever brain to pick with Cary Grant, believe me.

—Sheridan, interviewed by Ray Hagen for *Screen Facts* #14, 1966

Talia SHIRE [1947-]

Born: Talia Coppola in Lake Success, N.Y.; daughter of arranger/composer Carmine Coppola and sister to Francis Ford Coppola. Studies at The Yale School of Drama and work on the Los Angeles stage preceded her film debut in The Dunwich Horror (1970, Daniel Haller). She played Connie Corleone in her brother's The Godfather (1972), The Godfather Part II (1974) and The Godfather Part III (1990):

Q. Didn't Francis create a family attitude with his actors off the set [of *The Godfather*] before filming?

A. Yes. He comes out of a theatrical tradition with a tremendous respect for actors and dramaturgy, which is why his writing is so brilliant. He knows what actors need to do their best. Brando and Francis got along magnificently because of that. You see, Francis always rehearses before his movies, which most directors hardly ever do. But, he began by getting the boys — Brando, Pacino and Duvall — and me together at an Italian restaurant, to start developing our relationships. Very gradually, what formed that night was a family.

—Shire, interviewed by Steranko for *Prevue*, May/July 1987

I was the baby girl in an Italian family of gifted dynamic men. I was programmed to be a woman who devotes her life to a man. That's understandable if you know how Italians feel about the man-woman relationship and if you were raised with the giants in my family.

I was the ultimate sister. [My role in *The Godfather Part II*] was a natural for me to play. I loved my brothers and father and admired them tremendously. I still do. But I lived in the wings while my family was on stage. I was the observer to the vitality and accomplishments of the men....

As for my role in *Rocky* [1976, John G. Avildsen], now that I've seen it twice I can say I'm proud of my work. The dynamics are all very subtle. If you are playing the piccolo, as I was, against a drum, which Sylvester Stallone was, you can be blown off the screen.

But I loved resonating off Sylvester's largeness. I played a shy girl and I had to do it forcefully. That's not an easy thing to accomplish. [Shire also co-starred with Stallone in *Rocky II* (1979), *Rocky III* (1982) and *Rocky IV* (1985) — all directed by Stallone — and *Rocky V* (1990, John G. Avildsen).]

—Shire, interviewed for UPI; repr. in *The Toronto Star*, 4 Mar 1977

As far as my character, Connie [in *The Godfather Part III* (1990, Francis Ford Coppola)] goes, I was very careful to make sure that she was designed correctly and authentically from the first timid victim that we saw [in *The Godfather*].

There was a scene that Francis wrote which we never shot, but it was a hook for me: Connie is continually dreaming of her father [Marlon Brando]. Obviously she is out of time. I mean, she's had enormous tragedies surrounding her. She must feel Sonny [James Caan]'s death in a guilty way. Her husband [Gianni Russo] being killed. Her brother, Fredo [John Cazale], being killed. So what do you do? You go into a kind of fantasy or obsession with your father. That was my hook.

I decided she was a strange kind of character out of time, obsessed with her father, and making sure she would preserve the father's dream.

I took [costume designer Melena] Canonero the tape of *Sunset Boulevard* [1950, Billy Wilder]. Because that woman, Norma Desmond, fascinated me. There was something in her out-of-timeness I connected with. We went through the costumes and started to find a way to build Connie correctly.

But the main point is that Connie does go from victim to power. The Corleones are a dynasty. As Francis portrays it, they are Shakespearean and they must do these things.

—Shire, interviewed by Bruce Feld for *Drama-Logue*, 31 Jan-6 Feb 1991

Sylvia SIDNEY [1910-]

Born: Sophia Koscow in The Bronx, N.Y. Studies at The Theater Guild Acting School in N.Y. and work on the stage (from 1926) preceded her film debut in Through Different Eyes (1929, John Blystone). In 1932, she played Joan Prentice in Dorothy Arzner's Merrily We Go to Hell:

Dorothy doesn't care about clothes for herself, but she has a great appreciation of their dramatic values.... Every morning I would sweep on to the set in a new dress. And Dorothy would be delighted. She would insist that we take a long shot of every scene just so that the dress would be shown to its full advantage....

I don't think I've ever laughed so much in my life. Either Fredric March was terribly funny or I just thought he was. Anyway, I just laughed all the time. He plays a drunkard whom I, as his fiancée, try to reform. Then I go all to pieces myself....

—Sidney, interviewed by Eileen Creelman for *The New York Sun*, 9 June 1932

The important thing [in British cinema] is the production as a whole — not the particular stars. Not that the stars are neglected, but the atmosphere of the studio is one that makes every actor have a feeling of the whole production rather than of his or her part alone.

[On *Sabotage* (1936)] I've seen Alfred Hitchcock spend as much effort on getting perfection in one small sequence, which at the moment might seem unimportant, as he would on a scene with the two leading actors. There is no sliding over the minor incidents to get the big moments in the picture and the whole mood is catching. We were all intensely interested in how the whole thing would turn out.

One might think that such a method would lead to less effort on the part of the individual actors and particularly of the leading members of the cast, to perfect their own roles. It doesn't. We all slaved over our own parts. But no one was out to 'steal' the picture.

—Sidney, interviewed for *The New York World-Telegram*, 3 Sept 1936

You know, I'd always wanted to be in a Lang picture. When I heard he was going to do *Fury* [1936] I was determined to be in that. There wasn't any girl in the story when they offered me a part, but they said if I'd accept they'd see to it there was a girl. So I accepted.

People said I was crazy. Another studio had offered me a big part in an important picture and for much more money. But I just wanted to have Fritz Lang as a director, so I took a chance. Afterwards I was glad.

—Sidney, interviewed by Eileen Creelman for *The New York Sun*, 21 Dec 1936

I think it was general knowledge at the time that Fritz Lang was basing [*You Only Live Once* (1937)] on the lives of Bonnie and Clyde. Except the parts that Henry Fonda and I played were romanticized. We were two people in love on the run, victims of circumstances, rather than creators of our own circumstances.

—Sidney, interviewed by Arthur Bell for *The New York Times*, 17 Dec 1972

I like working with [George] Raft [on *You and Me* (1938, Fritz Lang)] for many reasons, and one of them — of all things — is that when I'm playing opposite him I do not have to wear high heels. In roles with tall boys like Gary Cooper [on *Madame Butterfly* (1932, Marion Gering)] and Fred MacMurray [on *The Trail of the Lonesome Pine* (1936, Henry Hathaway)] the studio has had to build me up so that I could be within reach of these romantic stars. But even with high heels, I've gotten cricks in my neck gazing up at Gary and Fred.

—Sidney, interviewed by Bland Johaneson for *The New York Daily Mirror*, 31 May 1938

I didn't agree with the death scene [in *Summer Wishes, Winter Dreams* (1973, Gilbert Cates)], so I called a heart specialist to give me an appointment for a consultation. I showed him the script and he gave me all the variations of a heart attack. I showed the report to Gil, an then he agreed with me. It's not the intake of breath that hurts, it's the outtake. That's why there's that gasping.

—Sidney, interviewed by Ann Guarino for *The New York Sunday News*, 11 Nov 1973

Simone SIGNORET [1921-1985]

Born: Simone Kaminker in Wiesbaden, Germany. Work as a typist preceded her film debut as an extra in Le Prince Charmant (1941, Jean Boyer). In 1948, she made her first English language film with Charles Crichton's Against the Wind. In her second, she played Alice Aisgill opposite Laurence Harvey as Joe Lampton in Jack Clayton's Room at the Top (1958):

One of the more fascinating aspects of the story was [Joe's] affair with a lady who was no longer quite young (she was then in her forties), whose name was Alice. Alice Aisgill. Alice was intelligent, generous, understanding, maternal, sexually liberated and socially without prejudice. Alice was a character who had everything going for her, including her death before the end of the novel. Alice was a piece of cake to play. (I almost forgot: on top of it all, Alice was married to a complete cad)....

In the novel, Alice was English. To justify my temporary immigration, she became a Frenchwoman married to an Englishman....

I arrived in Bradford, Yorkshire, the wool capital. There I met the people who were to become my mates for three and a half months and my friends for life: Jack Clayton, Laurence Harvey, Heather Sears, Jimmy Woolf, Freddy Francis, the cameraman, and all the others who breathed life into a story that caused so many English and American tears to flow — between fits of giggles.... Once again the location miracle took place. If you want to start a family, you move in together under one roof. A film unit, if it's to work well, must be a family. If you begin a film by going out on location, it's the best way of cementing your foundations....

Bradford is a busy industrial city. Factory smoke mingles with local fog and great wealth nudges great poverty. This is part of what Clayton wanted to show in his film. So to tell the story well, it was better to be right there. And once there, all might just as well live under the same roof....

The friendship and reciprocity between Jack Clayton and his cast grew and grew. Our working days in the studio ended as they had in Bradford. We separated with regret. We generally ended the day in a little pub, where we had a snack before going to bed early....

I was happy because I had a marvelous director. Without throwing his weight about, and without pretentious explanations, he made us do exactly what he wanted. And as the rushes showed us that what he wanted was true and right, I was happy....

Furthermore, my leading man, about whom I had been told every possible variety of tale, was someone I got along with very well.

—Signoret, in her *Nostalgia Isn't What It Used To Be* (Paris: Edition du Seuil, 1976; New York: Harper & Row, 1978)

The woman I play [in *The Seagull* (1968, Sidney Lumet)] — this Arkadina — she's a bitch, the kind of woman I detest. But bitchery is something I know about. I'm no saint. I also know how to play older women. I *am* one. And I've lived, my friend....

—Signoret, interviewed by Rex Reed for *The New York Times*, 12 Jan 1969

Jean SIMMONS [1929-]

Born: Crouch Hill, London, England. Studies at Aida Foster's School of Dancing preceded her film debut in Give Us the Moon (1944, Val Guest). In 1948, she played Ophelia opposite Laurence Olivier in his Hamlet:

[Olivier] sat down and explained to me his conception of what Ophelia really is: a young girl, well brought up in a secluded way, who loses her reason when faced with all the scheming intrigues of the Danish court. Then he told me something about the great Ophelias of the past...Mistress Saunderson, the first female Ophelia; Mistress Mountford, who went crazy herself but was allowed to continue in the part despite her dementia; the immortal Ellen Terry, Lillian Gish, Vivien Leigh and others.

What large footsteps to follow...!

Many of the [Shakespearean] words and phrases were beyond my understanding. So [my coach] Molly [Terriane] and Mr. Olivier would patiently explain the psychological metamorphosis which changes the sweet and love-struck Ophelia into a woman so mad she takes her own life.

—Simmons, in *Seventeen*, Sept 1948

[On *The Actress* (1953)] George [Cukor] ...played my role absolutely beautifully. I'd just sit there and watch — it was so marvelous to watch him — it was a great help. The best bit of direction I had from George was a scene I had involving my walk. He was very worried about it. I had a long walk to do in a very tight skirt. George said, "Why don't you walk as though you're dying to go to the bathroom?" And it worked for that scene.

—Simmons, interviewed by David Galligan for *Drama-Logue*, 24-30 Mar 1983

I was scared of Marlon [Brando] when I first worked with him in *Desirée* [1954, Henry Koster]. I knew, as everyone did, that Marlon wasn't anxious to do the picture. I don't believe I spoke twenty-five words with Marlon outside the scenes...except the customary greetings.

Q. That's an odd relationship. It probably made the acting difficult.

A. Well, I'd say my line, and Marlon would say his. There wasn't any playing off each other. Yet some of the scenes came off better than I expected. There's so much to Marlon inside. He couldn't keep it from coming through.

Q. It must be different with *Guys and Dolls* [1955, Joseph L. Mankiewicz]. Marlon appears relaxed, seems to be having a good time.

A. Marlon's having a ball. He's more fun. This hasn't lowered my opinion of his talent. If anything, it's increased. In rehearsing a scene with Marlon, I'd watch him do a piece of business ten or twenty different ways. Like picking up a plain water glass. I'd say to myself, "What the hell is he doing?" Then we'd do the scene for the camera. Marlon'd pick up the glass differently than he did during the many rehearsals. I'd be so fascinated, I'd forget I was acting....

Q. What about the Lead Out bit?

A. Joe started it. During our initial cast meetings, Joe took me aside and told me: "I think you and I will get along fine. Just one thing — don't try and play the part like Desirée or Ophelia. Sarah Brown is a plain girl. Get the lead out of your pants.

That's how Lead Out started. Often, when I'm a little tense in a scene, Marlon whispers in my ear: "Get the lead out of your pants."

—Simmons, interviewed for *Motion Picture* (undated); in the files of The New York Public Library for the Performing Arts

Frank SINATRA [1915-]

Born: Hoboken, New Jersey. A career as a singer (from 1935), including work with Harry James and Tommy Dorsey and appearances as a singer in several films preceded his first major role in Higher and Higher (1943, Tim Whelan). In his third starring role he appeared opposite Gene Kelly in Anchors Aweigh (1945, George Sidney):

The picture was *Anchors Aweigh*, and the producer was saying, "Gene Kelly, meet your costar, Frank Sinatra."

Gene flashed that twinkly Irish smile and said, "I've got a five-tube radio, so I know you can sing. The important thing is, can you dance?"

I pointed at my feet and issued a pronunciamento: "These here babies can do anything I tell 'em to do!"

"Good," said Gene. "Tell 'em to do this!"

He popped straight up like a champagne cork, did a mid-air somersault, came down in a leg-split, and segued into a tap routine that sounded like a nest of angry machine-guns.

Suffice it to say, I was impressed, and fool that I was, when Gene volunteered to be my dance instructor, I accepted — with humble gratitude yet!

Cut to eight weeks later. I've got seven hundred torn ligaments, compound fractures in every bone in my body, and I've lost vitally needed weight.... But my wild Irish slave-driver paid me the ultimate compliment.

"Francis," he said, "You've worked your way up from lousy to adequate — I'm ready to dance on camera with you...."

If Gene was endowed with total talent, so too, was he endowed with total integrity. His fierce urge for perfection, his almost fanatical need for success, have always been matched by his need for justice for the less gifted, or less advantaged, whose paths crossed his.

—Sinatra, in the foreword to *Gene Kelly* by Clive Hirschhorn (London: W.H. Allen, 1974)

Maggio [in *From Here to Eternity* (1953, Fred Zinnemann)] is like a lot of kids I knew in Hoboken, and he's not unlike myself — not entirely like me, but in spasmodic periods of my life. Some people say that Maggio is me and vice versa. Well, I don't know. Maybe. Could be.

—Sinatra, interviewed by Norton Mockridge, in an unsourced, undated article in the files of The New York Public Library for the Performing Arts

I'm quite limited as to what I can do. I'm not a matinee idol or a leading man. The director who got the best out of me was Otto Preminger in *The Man with the Golden Arm* [1955]. I'd like to do a musical once in a while, if I could find one — that's my basic talent.

—Sinatra, interviewed by Jack Hamilton for *Look*, 31 Oct 1967

I've known Joe [E. Lewis] since 1938.... To me, [*The Joker is Wild* (1957, Charles Vidor)] has got to have some reason. His life is a really tragic tale, a story of a terribly lonely man....

You see him on the stage at El Rancho, you think what a ball this guy has. He's with Lili St. Cyr, he's drinkin' it up and playin' the tables, and all he's got to do for this is stand around on a stage and talk about the tough life he leads.

It's not that pat. This is a lonely man. And that's the way the story has to be.

—Sinatra, interviewed by George Laine for *The Pasadena Independent Star*, 4 Nov 1956

Joey Evans [in *Pal Joey* (1957, George Sidney)] is probably the best-known lady-killer in show business history. He's a heel — a real likeable heel.

Naturally, he's an expert on broads. They all go for him and he knows all about them. He even has his own special language for them.

This gave me an idea. When we started the picture, I decided to work up a list of the various types of broads. In other words, compile sort of a dictionary of Joey's jargon.

The way I figure it, broads can be divided into eight different classifications: There's the 'Mouse,' the 'Tomato,' the 'Beetle,' the 'Quim,' the 'Twist and a Twirl,' the 'Gasser,' 'the Barn Burner,' and the 'Mish Mash.'

It's really very simple. A 'Mouse' is a cuddly broad. A 'Beetle' is a flashy broad. One who makes with sharp clothes.

A 'Quim' is a loose broad, one who's easy to pick up. A 'Twist and a Twirl' is a broad who likes to dance.

Of course, I suppose, everybody's heard of the word 'Gasser.' Well, in broadsville talk that means a dame who's a real looker, a knockout.

Now take the 'Barn Burner' — that's a broad with real polish and class. Who wouldn't dig her the most?

As for the 'Mish Mash,' she's a broad who's all mixed up. Of course, the one to really watch out for is the 'Tomato.' She's a broad who's ripe for marriage.

—Sinatra, in *Photoplay Magazine*, Jan 1958

When I first started singing, I used to study the singers I admired. I took what I liked from Bing, and what I liked from this singer and that singer. I took the best from the best, but I made it fit into how I wanted to sing a song.... I did the same thing with acting.... Anyway, I studied those actors I admired. Spencer Tracy — I see all his pictures once or twice. And working with good actors, that helps. You can't work with someone like Monty Clift [on *From Here to Eternity*] without some talent rubbing off on you whether you know it then or not. It might be nothing more than his attitude toward a role or toward work....

Q. How do you study a role? How do you learn a part — like Dave Hirsh [in *Some Came Running* (1958, Vincente Minnelli)] for example?

A. I don't deliberately learn a part. I have my own — I hate to use the word method — system. I read the whole script through first. I think about the story...about my part...about the other parts. I read the script through about five times that way. By then I have a pretty good idea of my part and the lines.... I never memorize my lines. By the time we get to the set I must have read the script or my part at least 30 times.... The night before we're to film a certain scene, I don't memorize my lines, as most actors do. I don't even look at the script.

On the set in the morning, I say to the script girl, "What are my jokes here?" I always call my lines the jokes. She starts reading a line, and the whole speech comes back to me. I remember what I read 30 times or more. Sometimes I change a few words, but the same idea is there....

—Sinatra, interviewed by Sidney Skolsky for *The New York Post*, 16 Jan 1959

Originally, I was to play the role of François [in *Can-Can* (1960, Walter Lang)], a playboy-lawyer, with a French accent. Shirley [MacLaine] politely reminded me of the last time I tried an accent — in a Technicolor wide-screen epic called *The Pride and the Passion* [1957, Stanley Kramer] in which I played a Spanish guerrilla with bangs and which I'd like to forget. I realized the girl had a point. François is being played straight — or at least as straight as I can play him.

—Sinatra, in *This Week Magazine*, 21 Feb 1960

My role [in *The Manchurian Candidate* (1962, John Frankenheimer)] is very difficult. What with the brainwashing, it borders on neuroticism. I'm not a trained actor and so it takes a lot of doing....

—Sinatra, interviewed by Don Ross for *The New York Herald Tribune*, 11 Feb 1962

Tom SKERRITT [1935-]

Born: Detroit. Acting at Wayne State University, with The Dearborn Players and in stock, led to his film debut in War Hunt (1962, Denis Sanders). In 1977, he played Wayne Rodgers in Herbert Ross' The Turning Point:

In *The Turning Point*, I was saying, "Here's a guy who's really in charge of who he is and has confidence that the wife he dearly loves [Shirley MacLaine] will come back to him — no matter what kinks she has to work out in herself. The only way she was going to get rid of the kinks was for my character to allow her to do whatever she had to do." My point was to set up an example like that, where other men would not suppress their women, where they will be willing to let them have their way. It's one reason I have loved playing second lead to a woman in features. If you're a strong man with a strong woman in films, it says to the other guys that they don't have to be threatened by a strong woman. They can do nothing but make you better. It's that simple. Too many men feel a strong woman will take away from them and make them look or seem less than they are. It's not true. Strong women will never do that to a strong man.

—Skerritt, interviewed by David Galligan for *Drama-Logue*, 5-11 June 1986

Walter SLEZAK [1902-1983]

Born: Vienna; son of Leo Slezak [1873-1946]. Discovered for films by Michael Curtiz, he made his debut in Curtiz' Sodom und Gomorra (1922). In the U.S., he made his Broadway debut in 1930, but did not make his first American film until Once Upon a Honeymoon (1942, Leo McCarey). In 1943, he played Major Erich von Keller in Jean Renoir's This Land is Mine:

Jean Renoir has a wonderful sly way with actors. After a scene has been shot, he is full of praise, embraces you, makes you believe that you have surpassed yourself, that the scene was flawless and inspired, that you cannot possibly fail to win the Academy Award this time. Then he will say: "Shust for de luck — we shoot it again!"

Working with Alfred Hitchcock [on *Lifeboat* (1943)] was a great experience. He knows precisely what he wants to say and show in each shot. He pinpoints the essence, the core. During the scene when I amputate William Bendix's leg, he kept the camera outside the boat, behind the helmsman's back. I asked him why, because usually operations are shown in close-ups, with the action of scalpel, sutures, and the masked faces of the doctors and the nurses' frightened eyes showing. "All that has been done," he explained. "I want to show the hazard of doing an operation in an open boat, against the background of an oncoming storm."

The young actress who played the nurse [Mary Anderson] had trouble with a very emotional scene. Hitchcock waited for her to get into the mood, then he said: "Look, child, we haven't got that much time! First of all you will drop your voice about three notes. You will then take one long deep breath and begin talking. At that and that line your breath will give out — but you *will keep on talking*, even if I can't hear a word of what you are saying! Let's shoot!"

They did the scene in one take. At the exact line where Hitchcock had predicted, her breath gave out, but she kept on mouthing the words. And suddenly you had a feeling, that there was a girl who was completely spent; her parched lips, after forty-two days on the open sea, quivered and trembled. She didn't have the strength to make them heard, but you understood everything she said.

—Slezak, in his *What Time's the Next Swan?* (Garden City, N.Y.: Doubleday & Co., 1962

Charles Martin SMITH [1955-]

Born: Van Nuys, California. While a student in the drama department at California State University at Northridge, he made his film debut in The Culpepper Cattle Company (1972, Dick Richards). In 1973, he played Terry "The Toad" Fields in George Lucas' American Graffiti:

George let us ad lib, practically whenever we wanted; changed dialogue at will; let the scenes run on and on. We did many, many takes on every scene in *American Graffiti*, and printed lots of them — we would maybe do 12 takes and print half a dozen of them. And we felt as though we weren't being directed, a lot of the time. But when we saw the finished product, it became obvious that what he was doing was collecting all this raw material and editing it into a picture. Without saying anything to the actors at the time — letting them do whatever they would.

—Smith, interviewed by Alexander Stuart for *Films & Filming*, Oct 1979

I wanted this guy [Tyler in *Never Cry Wolf* (1983, Carroll Ballard)] to be like all those guys I knew in college. My brother was in the science department and I knew a lot of those guys. Who were strictly book-learned guys. And that's a lot of what our society turns out certainly. Very educated.... Tyler, is a highly educated guy and he's very self-sufficient in the world that he's used to. He's damned good with a microscope and a bunsen burner. But he's never been out in the field.

The difference between Tyler and most of those other guys, I think, is that he really feels that there's something wrong with this. He wants to go out. He wants to find something else for his own good. He's an idealistic guy. He really thinks that the experience is going to be good for him and that he'll find something in himself.

Which we kept trying to get into the narration. And we finally got it in, last draft. He's got to be a different person by the end of the film. And the thing is, I wanted to show that. Not just tell the audience that he's different. One obvious manifestation of that is the different appearance, the long hair and beard.

Okay, that tells you that he's different, but it's also the way he behaves, the way he moves. I found a different way of running during the final scenes than I did during the early sequences. When the guy is up there in the beginning, he's kinda clumsy, he looks out of place. Whereas everything I did by the time of the caribou hunt was a different kind of run, a new kind of movement. Trying to make it look like he was one of the animals now. The way he stands and postures and all that stuff.

I wanted to make it seamless. I wanted to make it gradual so that the guy changes so steadily and carefully that the audience is not aware that he's changing. That was my hope. And it's only when he meets the bushpilot [Brian Dennehy] for the second time, he scoots over the rocks like a lizard the way he's zippin' around and sees the pilot and the pilot says, "You've changed." Then the audience should realize. "That's right. This guy really is a lot different than he was in the beginning." But I didn't want for it to come in steps.

—Smith, interviewed by Lewis Archibald for *The Aquarian Weekly*, 24 Nov 1983

Maggie SMITH [1934-]

Born: Ilford, England. A stage debut with The Oxford University Dramatic Society and work on the London stage and on Broadway (from 1956) preceded her film debut in Nowhere to Go (1958, Seth Holt). In 1969, she played the title role in Ronald Neame's The Prime of Miss Jean Brodie:

The whole film business seems a bit weird to me, actually, though I'm slowly getting used to it, and *The Prime of Miss Jean Brodie* has been a bit different. For a start, we had 10 days of rehearsal and we actually got to know everybody who's in it. On most of the films I've done, you just walk in one morning, and you're told that this is X and you've never seen him before. But, tough bananas. I didn't meet anyone on *The V.I.P.s* [1963, Anthony Asquith] except Rod Taylor and Richard Burton. Somebody said, "You're in an airport and Elizabeth Taylor is meant to be over there and Orson Welles over there," and you were making them all up. I was whizzed in and whizzed out....

—Smith, interviewed by Mark Shivas for *The New York Times*, 21 July 1968

I was fortunate to have so little time for the usual sort of shilly-shallying [on *Travels with My Aunt* (1972, George Cukor)] that goes before a big part. If there had been time to sit around mulling the role over, the whole thing would have been quite terrifying. A great deal came out of the kind of energy that is produced by panic....

There was some talk of using a rubber mask for the aging process, but it would have been too restricting, and the sheer eccentricity of the old lady was a help. To play a straight *old* lady would have been very hard, but Augusta is so excessively dotty that her age becomes irrelevant. I was very fond of her you know. With Aunt Augusta you just can't help it.

—Smith, interviewed by John Sandilands for *The Observer*, 21 Jan 1973

The easiest thing about this role [of Aunt Augusta] is that it doesn't matter if my eyes are bloodshot or I have bags around my ankles. The constant worry of what you look like is removed when you play an old woman. George has directed so many of those elderly film stars who were like the crazy aunt I play that his stories helped. Everything fell into place. Besides, I didn't have time to work on a characterization or a voice. I only had ten days to think about it. [She replaced Katharine Hepburn].

—Smith, interviewed by Rex Reed for *The New York Daily News*, 25 June 1972

[Diana Barrie in *California Suite* (1978, Herbert Ross)] was much nearer to me than anything else I've done. It was a wonderful part to have. Except that it was kind of weird because you were playing yourself.... I was saying things that were absolutely accurate. It sort of was quite near the truth. To be an actress playing just *that*.

Then when I did get nominated actually, it was to-tally odd. TOTALLY odd. Like boxes within boxes. I went to the awards that year.... I had absolutely *no* idea that one would *get* it. In the film of course I didn't get it. Got very grumpy and drunk instead....

—Smith, interviewed by Lewis Archibald for *The Aquarian Weekly*, 17-24 Mar 1982

Gale SONDERGAARD [1899-1985]

Born: Edith Sondergaard in Litchfield, Minnesota. Work on the stage preceded her film debut as Faith in Anthony Adverse (1936, Mervyn LeRoy):

[My husband, Herbert J. Biberman] took me to see Mervyn LeRoy and they were looking for somebody, a new face for Faith in *Anthony Adverse*. They really wanted someone quite new for it because it was an unusual role and they didn't want it stamped by any sort of established person....

—Sondergaard, interviewed by John Kobal for *Films & Filming*, Nov 1985

I don't mind playing a villain. Eugenie [in *Juarez* (1939, William Dieterle)] is a fascinating character, even though she does everything she can to balk what the picture stands for — the cause of democracy. I'm proud to play Eugenie because she shows up the side of dictatorship in its true colors.

—Sondergaard, interviewed by Nancy Naumburg for *Photoplay Magazine*, June 1939

The Letter [1940, William Wyler] had me as a Eurasian woman and people have a tendency to think that...an oriental, or perhaps any other color, is perhaps a wicked person. I came up against this when we were discussing how to play the role [of Mrs. Hammond] in *The Letter* and later the role [of Lady Thiang] in *Anna and the King of Siam* [1946, John Cromwell]. I had to argue for the characters of both these women and say, "Why should you consider them lesser human beings than the white woman, who *was* the adulteress, who *was* the murderer?" And I won out, and I was allowed to play her with dignity. [In *The Letter*] my point was that this man [who Leslie Crosbie (Bette Davis) shoots at the beginning of the film] had married her, that she was a woman of dignity, and there was no reason for making her cheap in any way because he had gone to her; and she was able to see the real wickedness of the other woman [Davis]. It was a fascinating discourse we had on how to show her.

Q. What was Bob Hope like to work with? Did he try to break you up?

A. He did. Yes, he did, of course, all the time, off the set too.

I did four pictures with Bob. The first one was called *Never Say Die* [1939, Elliott Nugent].

Martha Raye was also in it. And I never would come home from that studio without absolutely being in agony from laughter.... Bob was such fun; he was always full of such quips and always terribly, terribly funny. [Sondergaard also worked with Hope on *The Cat and the Canary* (1939, Elliott Nugent), *My Favorite Blonde* (1942, Sidney Lanfield) and *The Road to Rio* (1948, Norman Z. McLeod).]

—Sondergaard, interviewed by John Kobal for *Films & Filming*, Nov 1985

Paul SORVINO [1939-]

Born: New York City. Studies at The Academy of Musical and Dramatic Arts and work on Broadway (from 1964) preceded his film debut in Where's Poppa? (1970, Carl Reiner). In 1990, he played mob boss Paulie Cicero in Martin Scorsese's GoodFellas:

As far as displaying an Italian-American from Brooklyn's speech and mannerisms, that's not difficult. That's what I am. The lethality, remorseless and sociopathic nature, along with the love and nurturing qualities he shows his family and Henry [Ray Liotta] — well, this was a job indeed.

My preparation was all internal. I didn't have to find a voice, a speech, a walk. I knew all of that instantly. What I didn't know, and what I wasn't sure I would find was that kernel of coldness and absolute hardness that is antithetical to my nature except when my family is threatened. And that took two months, and I never thought I'd get it. Then one day I passed a mirror and startled myself.

—Sorvino, interviewed by Lawrence Van Gelder for *The New York Times*, 12 Oct 1990

Sissy SPACEK [1949 -]

Born: Mary-Elizabeth Spacek in Quitman, Texas. Work as a background singer preceded her film debut as an extra in Trash (1970, Paul Morrisey), produced by Andy Warhol. In 1973, she played Holly Sargis in Terence Malick's Badlands:

From Terry Malick I learned how to approach a character.... With Terry you feel an incredible intimacy. [On *Badlands*], we spent a lot of time just talking about our lives, remembering things that help you tie the character into your own life.

Terry never hits anything on the head — he goes against the grain. He taught me that to make a point sometimes you throw it away. Terry is lyrical, romantic. He likes to work under pressure. Bob Altman [on *Three Women* (1977)] is the opposite — he absorbs all the pressure. You never feel it. With Bob, if a scene goes differently than the way it was conceived, then that's the right way....

Bob works by bringing elements together, not expecting anything — he brings things together to capture the unexpected.

Brian [De Palma] approaches films more like a science project. With Brian [on *Carrie* (1976)] I learned how to work with the camera. With Bob you didn't really prepare that much. With Brian everything was storyboarded. Brian knows what the camera can do. You can act your guts out and the camera can miss it. But one little look, if you know how it's going to be framed, can have a thousand times more impact.

—Spacek, interviewed by Howard Kissel for *Women's Wear Daily*, 4 Apr 1980

You'd be surprised how easy it is [to play a character like Carrie]. We all have a little of that in us. We've all been rejected by others on some level. Basically I decided that I should not fraternize with the other actors. I stayed in my dressing room a lot and studied the research material I'd acquired, absorbing the information Carrie would draw on.... I wanted her to be more than a scapegoat, more than just a stereotyped reject, because every school has those people and to an extent we've all been that person. The least important thing about Carrie was her telekinetic power. She wanted to be accepted, she wanted to be normal.

There was such a close rapport between the three of us [De Palma, Spacek and her art director/husband, Jack Fisk] and that gave me another dimension on the film. We talked and talked, back and forth until we all had the same vision.

—Spacek, interviewed by Susan D'Arcy for *Films Illustrated*, Mar 1977

The shower sequence [at the beginning of *Carrie*] was very tricky. I knew it had to be horrendous and bigger than life.... I used an etching from the *Bible* of a guy getting stoned to death. The Doré facial expressions are *so* intense and so much *larger* than life....

Jack rebuilt the gymnasium in the sound stage, as it had to burn.... I had to stand on that stage while everything was on fire! I got all the hair on my body practically singed off! I got so involved in it! "Fire?! What do you mean? It can't hurt *me*! I'm Carrie, I'll flex!" While I was on the platform, my cue was: "Leave the stage only when you can't stand the heat anymore. But walk *slowly*!"

—Spacek, interviewed by Mike Childs and Alan Jones for *Cinefantastique* #1, 1977

Before I met [Loretta Lynn] I was frightened about doin' a film about someone who was living and performing and vibrant. [For *Coal Miner's Daughter* (1980, Michael Apted)] I thought "Do you try and look like her? Do you try not to?" But then I met her and that was that....

She's had an enormous effect on my life — just her attitude about things. She's fearless and trusting. I've watched her and I've copied her a lot since I've been workin' on the film. I've put myself out just as I've seen her do — signin' autographs and things, just to get the feel of her. And it works! You know, I never had a sister and it's almost like we're sisters. It's sorta like we know each other's insides.

—Spacek, interviewed by Martha Hume for *The Sunday News Magazine*, 9 Mar 1980

There's such an intimate thing that happens on a set between actors and director, and it's something Jack [Fisk] and I always wanted to experience together. I've found that when I work with any director, the first bit of time I have to get to know him. But with Jack [on *Raggedy Man* (1981)] there wasn't that barrier; I wasn't self-conscious. He knows all the buttons to punch, when to talk to me, when not to talk to me. As an actress, you use things from real life, and Jack knows all those things about me, so we can get to them real fast....

This movie reminds me of my mother a lot: the kind of women in the 1940s or the '50s who were probably smarter than anybody in the whole family, but when the men relatives were talking business, they would say, "Oh, I'll just go out and get y'all some coffee." They were self-effacing women who always seemed to rise above circumstances, who had a lot of integrity and dignity — and hope, even though they'd always been kept under a big giant thumb. Feminists, even if they didn't know it, but real feminine.

My mother was the key to the whole thing. I did all the things I remember her doing. I remember her coming in at night and putting the covers up around us and feeling our foreheads — I always remember her cool hands on my face. She was always reassuring. We'd say, "Is something going to happen?" and she'd say, "No, honey, I don't think so — it'll be all right." Nita reminded me of my mother in that she always put her children first. The reason she wanted to move up in the world was because she wanted something better for her kids.

—Spacek, interviewed by Leslie Bennetts for *The New York Times*, 13 Sept 1981

I thought [*Missing* (1982, Costa-Gavras)] was a very important statement, and I loved the character of Beth and the way her relationship with her father-in-law [Jack Lemmon] slowly changes and strengthens. But I was also scared because I worried about how people would take this film. Finally, though, I felt I had to work with my own conscience.... Once I knew about Charlie Horman [an American residing in Chile allegedly murdered by the American military, played in the film by John Shea], I couldn't stick my head back in the sand. But there's no way I would have done *Missing* had I not thought it *very* pro-American, even in the sense that only in America could we do a film that is so revealing and at the same time so critical....

The women [Joyce Horman (Charlie's widow) and her friend Terry, played in the film by Melanie Mayron] came to the set and we spent some time talking and looking at stills. It was a real cleansing for them, and there was a very moving moment when we all cried. They said they'd been carrying the weight of Charlie Horman's murder on their shoulders for so long, and suddenly they were able to share it with people who understood. It was a moment I'll never forget.

—Spacek, interviewed by Marjorie Rosen for *Ms.*, Mar 1982

Mae Garvey [in *The River* (1984, Mark Rydell)] was a very silent, loving woman who didn't need to take credit for being strong.

—Spacek, interviewed by Aljean Harmetz for *The New York Times*, 24 Mar 1985

Babe [in *Crimes of the Heart* (1986, Bruce Beresford) is] a great character. She just lets the chips fall where they may. She's very impulsive and doesn't worry about the consequences until later. [Playwright and screenwriter] Beth Henley once told me that Babe is the kind of person who has a dinner party, gets her hair and nails done, gets a new dress and a gorgeous centerpiece and forgets to put in the roast.

—Spacek, interviewed by Rex Morgan for *The Cable Guide*, Dec 1986

Diane [Keaton], Jessica [Lange] and I first got to know each other — through these characters [in *Crimes of the Heart*].

I mean, I had met Diane very briefly years ago, and I knew Jessica a little bit better than Diane. But these characters made us friends, brought us much closer. The characters really cared for one another, so we were nurturing that kind of relationship....

So often you never really get to know other actresses. There are just not that many films where there is more than one lead actress.

So it was quite an experience. I loved seeing how they work, just bein' a voyeur. The other thing was, no one was afraid to speak up, say what they thought. But I don't ever remember an argument. There was discussion, there was collaboration, and there was *passion* about the work. But there was never anything, uh, weird. Everyone fully expected it, but there wasn't.

—Spacek, interviewed by Ron Base for *The Toronto Star*, 21 Dec 1986

[Miriam Thompson in *The Long Walk Home* (1990, Richard Pearce)] does all the right things for all the wrong reasons: she becomes involved driving her maid [Whoopi Goldberg] during the bus boycott not because she was an activist, but she wanted her maid to clean her house.

—Spacek, interviewed by Michael J. Bandler for *McCalls*, Feb 1991

Robert STACK [1919-]

Born: Los Angeles. The All-American world record holder in skeet shooting at age 17 (364 straight hits), he made his film debut opposite Deanna Durbin in First Love (1939, Henry Koster). In 1954, he played Sullivan in William Wellman's The High and the Mighty:

[John Wayne] was the star of *The High and the Mighty*, and he was its co-producer....

An unwritten law says that a big star will appear eighty per cent of the time in any scene he plays with a younger actor. This is ensured by taking close-ups of the star after the scene is shot. When I had finished my big scene with Duke, he said he thought it was swell.

"Okay," Director William Wellman said. "Let's shoot those cover shots now."

"No," Duke said. "I think the scene went okay."

"But we have to...." Wellman began.

"I'm tired," Duke said and walked off the set. "Go on to something else."

Those close-ups were never shot. Duke wasn't tired. It was his way of telling me that he had liked the scene and that he wanted me to have an equal chance in it on the screen.

—Stack, in *Photoplay Magazine*, Apr 1955

I was told to go to Sam Fuller's office. There I met a man who was short in stature and long on whiskers. He hadn't shaved for a week, and had a long Havana cigar pointed at me like a .45-caliber pistol. He thrust his lantern jaw aggressively in my face when he talked. But even the smoke screen of rich Havana leaf couldn't hide the glint in his blue eyes. He didn't know me from a hot rock, but in five minutes, he cast me as the lead in *House of Bamboo* [1955], a high-budget, Cinemascope gangster movie set in Japan. He had the little-boy enthusiasm and controlled craziness that usually goes with big talent, as well as the courage to do all the things directors of lesser talent wouldn't touch for fear of getting in trouble with the brass....

The Japanese were obviously sensitive regarding displays of weapons. The war had ended not too long before, but Sammy behaved as if he were preparing for World War III. He prowled about the streets of Tokyo like a latter-day Wyatt Earp, with two .45s strapped to his sides. Instead of saying "roll'em," Sammy's signal to the cameraman to start shooting was a couple of shots from his blazing .45s. Sammy was undaunted by the panic he caused; he was like a kid playing cowboys and Indians.

Filming *Written on the Wind* [1956] proved to be one of those rare experiences when everything came together all at once. Our director Douglas Sirk was wonderfully talented and, for some reason, showed constant faith in me....

But Sirk was also demanding. There was no way to get by with "good enough" when he wanted a scene to be "good." He was a perfectionist. He worked my tail off....

The film called for me to express emotions I had never felt or even thought about before. It was the kind of part an actor dreams of getting before the fears set in, when he wonders if he'll cut it or make a fool of himself....

Written on the Wind was like a parachute jump. Every day, I prayed my chute would open. When it came time to prepare for my delirium-tremors scene, I literally had nothing but my imagination on which to depend. I didn't want to go to a drunk tank.... I wanted this to be my character, not a copy of an anonymous unfortunate. Finally, my old friend George Shdanoff came up with the answer.... He gave me the key in one brilliantly visual sentence.

"You're in a coffin," he said, "the lid is being forced down on you. You are trying to push your way out...."

Dorothy [Malone] and I had most of the intense and dramatic scenes. Rock [Hudson], a gentleman as always, and one of the nicest people in our business, let all our juiciest histrionics remain on film, not on the cutting room floor. Since I was a loan-out actor and Universal was his home base, he could have used his influence to have the heart cut out of my part. But he let the script run exactly as written. I can't tell how many others in this survival profession would have done things differently.

—Stack, in his (with Mark Evans) *Straight Shooting* (New York: MacMillan, 1980)

Sylvester STALLONE [1946-]

Born: Michael Sylvester Stallone in New York City. Drama studies at The University of Miami, work off-Broadway, a series of small parts including his debut in the porno flick, Party at Kitty and Studs (1970), and his first commercial film, Bananas (1971, Woody Allen) preceded his 'overnight' success as screenwriter and star of Rocky (1976, John G. Avildsen):

Playboy: How long did it take before you got an offer for *Rocky*?

Stallone: I got my first real bite by August first [1975]. United Artists wanted to pay me $75,000, which is a good price for a first script. I was broke by then — I mean, I didn't even have $100 to my name — but something in the back of my mind told me I could play that role. So when Herb [Nanas] brought me the good news about the $75,000, I turned to him and said, "Don't sell it." And, oh, were they shocked back at UA! Their next offer was $100,000 and a guarantee that they'd get a celebrity to play Rocky. They said it would make an excellent film and that I could come by and visit the set....

I remember the day I learned about all the actors they were considering. I was in Herb's office, and after he told me their names, I said, "Hey, this is not going to work." Herb said, "*What's* not going to work, Sly? They're up to $150,000, which is more money than you and I have ever seen." I told him, "Look, my friend, they can go to $500,000, they can go to $1,000,000 or $2,000,000 or $5,000,000 or $10,000,000, take your choice. Under the threat of death, I'm telling you not to sell that script unless I play Rocky."

So Herb went back to UA with that. They came back with an offer of $175,000, and then $210,000, and then $250,000, and a final offer of $315,000. I kept saying no until they gave in and said, "Oh, Jesus, let's forget all this and let him have a shot at it...."

For *Rocky* I purposely altered my diet so that it would severely change my intelligence level, which it did. I went on a strict shrimp-and-shellfish diet, with no carbohydrates whatsoever, and eventually, my intelligence level dropped to the point where I'd want to listen to country-and-western music, which is really bizarre for me. Your brain can't function without carbohydrates, and if I'd kept it up much longer, I probably would've wound up in a hospital. Plus, of course, I was walking like Rocky and sniffing and shadow-boxing and talking like Rocky. I *became* Rocky. [Stallone starred in and directed *Rocky II* (1979), *Rocky III* (1982) and *Rocky IV* (1985); he starred in *Rocky V* (1990, John G. Avildsen).]

Now, maybe this dietary stuff works and maybe it doesn't, but it helps me get into a character, so, in a sense, it *does* work. For *F.I.S.T.* [1978, Norman Jewison], I gained 35 pounds eating bananas and water, which wasn't a laugh riot, by any means. In fact, it left me bordering on lunacy, but bananas contain potassium, which stimulates the nerve synapses, those little tissues that transmit the brain's electrical impulses up and down the spine. As Johnny Kovac became older and more physically ponderous, I wanted him to look suspicious and to be ready with a wisecrack for everything.... Thank God that in my next movie, *Paradise Alley* [1978], I play a...guy very closely aligned to my normal state. For that role, I got into energy foods — nuts, fruits, juices and things that go through your system very easily, like pulverized chicken.

—Stallone, interviewed by Lawrence Linderman for *Playboy*, Sept 1978

Rambo is considered this violent psycho, which I've never understood. Rambo is a disenchanted, disenfranchised American who lives abroad; America's waif looking for an answer. He has no family, no country, no sense of self.

He's the kind of guy I would like to throw my arm around and say, "Hey, tell me about it. Where do you want to go? What do you want to do?" Because he has no dreams, he has no aspirations for the future. He lives for the moment. He likes to serve....

Rambo is a humanitarian, he is self-sacrifice all the way. He doesn't have a great sense of self-worth, so he is looking to gain peace of mind. He dedicates himself to doing something above and beyond the call of duty. He doesn't want any part of war, yet there is something nagging him. He needs to be involved in a cause. [Stallone has starred as John J. Rambo in *First Blood* (1982, Ted Kotcheff), *Rambo* (1985, George P. Cosmatos) and Rambo III (1988, Peter MacDonald).]

—Stallone, interviewed by Candace Burke-Block for *The New York Times*; syndicated in *The Courier News* (Central New Jersey), 17 May 1988

Terence STAMP [1939-]

Born: Stepney, London, England. Studies at The Webber- Douglas Drama School in London led to work on the stage. Noticed by Peter Ustinov in the play Why the Chicken?, he made his film debut in Ustinov's version of the Herman Melville novel, Billy Budd (1962):

I would always go out of my way to do something for Ustinov because if there were just a few more people like him the world would be a better place. I would like to be like him. I always have. He should have played Billy Budd. He chose me for it because I looked the part.... I got a lot of my ideas for Billy Budd from the way [Ustinov] lived, not the things he says. He lives that life, that's why he's a happy man. He's nice to people, and what you put out you get back. He is an optimist, he tries to believe the best of people, not the worst.

Once having made peace with myself about playing [Freddie Clegg in *The Collector* (1965, William Wyler)], I then had to find a way to make it believable. The main thing that worried me was the impotence of the character, and impotence is something that the public normally associates within very vague terms with the kind of bloke who creeps about watching girls through binoculars, wearing macs, seeing dirty films and going in dirty book shops, which in the book the character did. He was a kind of *voyeur*, he did have all these kind of pornie photographs. The thing I realized was that people's outward appearance isn't any kind of barometer to their potency.... Then I decided to make him as near normal as possible, to widen the effect of the character, so that there were moments in the film...when there would be a certain amount of empathy, where people would be able to see themselves in the character. I figured that most men at some time in their life had had this kind of fancy about having a girl to themselves in a room, a house or in a cellar, and it was just that he'd got stuck on that particular fancy....

When I started making the film it became apparent to me that Wyler didn't want to tell the same story as the book, and right until the last week he was undecided about having a happy ending. So really the only thing you can do as an actor is just to forget the book completely, and try to go along with what the director is doing. It wouldn't have been *my* way of doing a picture ideally, but that was his way. I think he saw it in terms of a modern love story which was a difficult situation for me to function inside.

—Stamp, interviewed by Robin Bean for *Films & Filming*, Dec 1968

[Freddie] has a boy's dream. I had those kinds of fantasies about girls when I was 14 or 15. But part of his mind has never matured. He doesn't really believe he is doing anything wrong. What really saves his character is that he believes the girl [Samantha Eggar] will really fall in love with him.

—Stamp, interviewed by Murray Schumach for *The New York Times*, 7 June 1964

Poor Cow [1967, Ken Loach]...turned out great. It was very satisfying and is one of the things I've done that I was pleased I did.

Ken Loach is a guy who has good taste. A lot of directors ask you to do things and it's not that you can't do them, but they don't come naturally to you. Whenever Ken Loach directed me it was in impeccable taste. A good director's hand is never apparent in a performance, he just knows how to get that extra little bit out of you at the moment. He knew how to make me tick. He didn't bully me, he didn't make me feel up-tight, he just gave me very good ideas at exactly the right time, and that can be any time. It could be halfway through a "take" and he would realise that if he cut and went again immediately it would be exactly right for me. There was a love scene I was doing with Carol [White]. Love scenes are always very embarrassing; they are not a thing that I do very well....

But on *Poor Cow* there was a scene where Carol and I had to get under the blankets, and I remember Ken saying, "When you get under the blanket, sort of hold the blanket up for her to get under.... I'm sure that a lot of directors don't think like that, but Ken was thinking of that. And he was completely right, and it was one of the things that made her love Dave, although she probably wasn't conscious of it. That was one of the things that was indicative of his attitude towards her. I mean he wouldn't know about the things that "gentlemen" are supposed to know, like walking on the outside of a girl on the pavement because the horse-drawn carriage was going to splash mud over her stockings.... He wasn't that sort of guy, but he would help her get into bed for the first time he was going to make love to her, because he didn't look on her as a scrubber. She was the girl that he was in love with. And that's the kind of director Ken Loach is.

—Stamp, interviewed by Robin Bean for *Films & Filming*, Dec 1968

Kim STANLEY [1925-]

Born: Patricia Reid in Tularosa, New Mexico. Studies at The Pasadena Playhouse and with Elia Kazan and Lee Strasberg at The Actors Studio in N.Y. preceded work on the N.Y. stage and her film debut in The Goddess (1958, John Cromwell):

Q. What was it about the experience of making *The Goddess* that discouraged you from a more active movie career?

A. *The Goddess* is my least favorite of any work I've ever done. I had read the script [by Paddy Chayefsky], which was really a much better script than it was a movie. And I was promised three weeks' rehearsal, which turned out to be me standing in front of a camera while they set positions. No other actors there. That isn't a rehearsal. And, of course, the film wasn't shot in sequence. That's the reason I like the theater.

It was a terrible experience because I was an amateur in the medium. The director, John Cromwell, was wonderful. John was the last of the great gentlemen. But Paddy Chayefsky didn't let him do his work, until way into the film, when I said I would not act if Paddy was on the set. He was really very disruptive and destructive to his own work....

After I saw it I never wanted to do another film.

—Stanley, interviewed for *Dialogue on Film, American Film*, June 1983

[Myra Savage in *Seance on a Wet Afternoon* (1964, Bryan Forbes) is] a real, true medium, not a fake. And she's also schizophrenic — whether that helps or not I don't know.

Q. What techniques of "immersion" in the character did [you] employ?

A. None at all. I just tried to 'dig' her — to understand her as the writer [Bryan Forbes] had conceived her, to *feel* her and make her believable.

—Stanley, interviewed by Stephen Watts for *The New York Times*, 8 Sept 1963

I still find it very difficult to do films. You see, you have *no* control over what is seen on the screen. None. On *Frances* [1982, director] Graeme Clifford had to cut about forty-five to fifty minutes that Jessie [Jessica Lange] and I had done on why these two women, mother and daughter, are so inextricable. Now, of course, the film doesn't make any sense. Why should Frances keep coming back to this woman who keeps having her locked up...?

What is the hook between these two women? It was not in the script, and it was very difficult for both Jessie and me to find it, and we did find it. Boy, she is some gal! Such a good, hard worker, and very talented. I loved working with her. So that part of doing the film was wonderful. But then to have it all cut...!

—Stanley, interviewed for *Dialogue on Film, American Film*, June 1983

Barbara STANWYCK [1907-1990]

Born: Ruby Stevens in Brooklyn, N.Y. A show business debut at age 15 as a chorus girl at The Strand Roof night club in NY, and Broadway work preceded her film debut in Broadway Nights (1927, Joseph C. Boyle). In 1930, she played Kay Arnold in Ladies of Leisure, the first of five films for Frank Capra:

I enjoyed everything I ever did with Frank. He was a gentle, understanding man who loved actors, which not all directors do.

Q. How did he work with you?

A. I don't really know because I can't remember him really directing me. He gave you the feeling that you were directing yourself. He allowed you to express yourself. Then, and only then, if you were wrong, would he tactfully suggest something else. But he was never didactic. [Stanwyck also worked on Capra's *The Miracle Woman* (1931), *Forbidden* (1932), *The Bitter*

Tea of General Yen (1933) and *Meet John Doe* (1941).]

—Stanwyck, interviewed by Bernard Drew for *Film Comment*, Mar/Apr 1981

Frank Capra taught me that if you can think it, you can make the audience know it. You can make them know what you are going to do. On the stage, it's mannerisms. On the screen, your range is shown in your eyes.

—Stanwyck, interviewed by Paul Rosenfield for *The Toronto Star*, 5 Apr 1987

Stella Dallas [1937, King Vidor] was a part which showed a woman moved primarily by unselfish motives.

The role was a challenging one for me because it had once been beautifully played by the late Belle Bennett in the first version [1925, Henry King]. In fact, it was a double challenge because the role had to be played on two levels, almost making Stella two separate women. On the surface, she had to appear loud and flamboyant — with a touch of vulgarity. Yet while showing her in all her commonness, she had to be portrayed in a way that audiences would realize that beneath the surface her instincts were fine, heartwarming and noble. Part of her tragedy was that while she recognized her own shortcomings, she was unable to live up to the standards she so painstakingly set for herself.

The story of her life was a study of mother love and of devoted sacrifice. Her ambitions for her daughter, Laurel [Anne Shirley], were so great and yet so utterly unselfish that she finally cut herself completely away from her child so that Laurel could attain the kind of life Stella wanted for her. She realized that she would be a discordant note in any attempt Laurel could make to achieve that kind of life.

Stella's tastes were cheap, her clothes loud, her manners crude. It was only as she grew older that she faced the realization that what she had thought were smiles of appreciation were actually smiles of tolerance, pity or contempt. To spare her daughter the humiliation of a mother with such surface commonness, Stella deliberately planned an affront which would leave Laurel free of any feeling of responsibility for her....

My favorite scene in the movie was the one where Stella Dallas stands by a rail outside a church as Laurel is being married to her well-born fiancé [Tim Holt]. I had to indicate to audiences, through the emotions shown by my face, that for Stella joy ultimately triumphed over the heartache she had felt. Despite her shabbiness and loneliness at that moment, there was a shining triumph in her eyes, as she saw the culmination of her dreams for her daughter.

—Stanwyck, in *Movie Digest*, Jan 1972

Q. Did you find King Vidor helpful on [*Stella Dallas*]?

A. King was very nice. But there wasn't any great affinity there.... King did his job and I did mine....

Q. What about Rouben Mamoulian on *Golden Boy* [1939]?

A. He was like [Howard] Hawks [on *Ball of Fire* (1941)], technically fine, you couldn't ask for more, but again, there was no affinity there, no joy. To me, the essence of a good director is not to say, "Walk to the table, then turn around and face to the left." The good director will walk you through gently and give you some air. Let me put it this way. I'd rather have made a bad picture with Frank Capra, Billy Wilder, Preston Sturges, and Wild Bill Wellman than a good one with John Ford [with whom she did *The Plough and the Stars* (1937)], Howard Hawks, and some of the others. Because I had to have the feeling that the director was with me because I sure as hell was with him. [Stanwyck worked on Wellman's *Night Nurse* (1931), *So Big* (1932), *The Purchase Price* (1932), *The Great Man's Lady* (1943) and *Lady of Burlesque* (1944).]

Q. What about Preston Sturges?

A. Well, he wrote *Remember the Night* [1940] which Mitch Leisen directed, and Sturges came on the set one day and said, "You know, you're funny." And I said, "I am?" And he said, "I'm going to write a comedy for you." Well you know how people are. Over the years they say a lot of things to you and they never do anything about it. But a couple of months later, he gave me the script of *The Lady Eve* [1941], which even in script form was brilliant. He directed it himself....

—Stanwyck, interviewed by Bernard Drew for *Film Comment*, Mar/Apr 1981

As the story of *Meet John Doe* [1941, Frank Capra] opens, Ann is a cynic all right. She has a gift for writing. She can think up such beautiful, inspirational things for John Doe [Gary Cooper] to say that people will believe them blindly, gladly. But all the time she is thinking these same people are suckers to fall for "that stuff." The money in it is all she wants, Ann thinks. Oh, yes, Ann is a fine cynic — until her benevolent Frankenstein creation turns on her and calls her to account. Then, suddenly, she sees those who have embraced the "messages" from her facile pen as they really are — better off and happier than she has ever been.

—Stanwyck, interviewed by Marian Rhea for *Photoplay-Movie Mirror*, Mar 1941

[Phyllis Dietrichson in *Double Indemnity* (1944, Billy Wilder)] was the most hard-boiled dame I ever played. I had never played an out-and-out killer. When Billy Wilder sent me the script — the most perfect script, bar none, I ever read — I was a little frightened of it. Back in his office, I said, "I love the script, and I love you, but I am a little afraid after all these years of playing heroines to go into an out-and-out cold-blooded killer." And Mr. Wilder — and rightly so — looked at me and he said, "Are you a mouse or an actress?" And I said, "Well, I hope I'm an actress." He said, "Then do the part."

—Stanwyck, interviewed by Ralph Nelson for *Portrait: Barbara Stanwyck*; quoted by Ella Smith in her *Starring Miss Barbara Stanwyck* (New York: Crown Publishers, 1973)

When I mention 'atmosphere' in *Double Indemnity* — that gloomy, horrible house the Dietrichsons lived in, the slit of sunlight slicing through those heavy drapes — you could smell that death was in the air, you understood why she wanted to get out of there, away, no matter how. Can you imagine that picture being *colorized*? My God! And for an actress, let me say that the way those sets were lit, the house, Walter [Neff/Fred MacMurray]'s apartment, those dark shadows, those slices of harsh light at strange angles — all that helped my performance. The way Billy staged it and John Seitz lit it, it was all one sensational mood. Color? How dare they?

—Stanwyck, interviewed by Robert Blees for *American Film*, Apr 1987

Anatole Litvak was the director [of *Sorry, Wrong Number* (1948)] and a very fine director and a marvelous person to work for. I had twelve days of terror in bed. And he very kindly...asked me did I want to do those twelve days all at once or spread them in between continuity. And when I thought it over, I thought it would be better if I could do the twelve days at once so that I myself might have continuity. And he very graciously fixed his schedule as such. And I did twelve days — consistently.

—Stanwyck, interviewed by Ralph Nelson for *Portrait: Barbara Stanwyck*; quoted by Ella Smith in her *Starring Miss Barbara Stanwyck* (New York: Crown Publishers, 1973)

[In *Clash by Night* (1952, Fritz Lang)] I play a woman who for reasons which she feels are justified, commits adultery. The audience may sympathize with me to an extent, for I am a woman who has a lot of good reasons for doing what is contrary to accepted social behavior.

My entire role is written and acted, I hope, along the line of the European realistic approach to a situation which is not uncommon among people everywhere. But don't mistake the story's theme. Adultery is not upheld. In the end adultery is shown to be definitely wrong, as it should be. But what I am trying to stress is that the approach to this situation is off-beat, at least by Hollywood standards, and it is this, if anything, that sets it apart, as a distinctive, adult motion picture.

—Stanwyck, interviewed by Lowell E. Redelings for *The Hollywood Citizen-News*, 31 Mar 1952

[Marilyn Monroe] was awkward [on *Clash by Night*]. She couldn't get out of her own way. She wasn't disciplined and she was often late, and she drove Bob Ryan, Paul Douglas and myself out of our minds...but she didn't do it viciously, and there was a sort of magic about her which we all recognized at once. Her phobias, or whatever they were, came later; she seemed just a carefree kid, and she owned the world.

—Stanwyck, interviewed by Clyde Gilmour for *The Toronto Telegram*, 1965

I had never seen Elvis Presley in a picture. But I had worked for Hal Wallis, the producer, many times. And when he called me and said he had a part in a picture [*Roustabout* (1964, John Rich)] and mentioned Elvis Presley — I thought, well, for heaven's sakes, what would I do in an Elvis Presley film? I liked [the part]. And the idea of working with Mr. Presley intrigued me.... Mr. Wallis said he was a wonderful person to work with...and he is. His manners are impeccable, he is on time, he knows his lines, he asks for nothing outside of what any other actor or actress wants.

Q. That's an interesting comment.

A. Yes, it is. Because so many people expected the other — the swelled head and all that sort of thing. As a matter of fact, very honestly, so did I. It is not the case.

—Stanwyck, interviewed by Bill Hahn for WNAC (Boston); repr. in *Starring Miss Barbara Stanwyck* by Ella Smith (New York: Crown Publishers, 1973)

Maureen STAPLETON [1925-]

Born: Lois Maureen Stapleton in Troy, N.Y. Studies at The Actors Studio and with Herbert Berghof preceded work on the N.Y. stage and her film debut in Lonelyhearts (1958, Vincent J. Donahue). In 1960, she appeared opposite Marlon Brando in Sidney Lumet's adaptation of Tennessee Williams' The Fugitive Kind:

Marlon can take great pauses and fill them, but if you're the actor acting with him and you can't fill that pause, you're up the creek. So after we rehearsed [a particular scene] once or twice, I said, "Marlon, you're a genius actor, I'm not, I'm just an actor actor and I don't know what the hell to do when you're taking those pauses — I could write my will, wash the dishes, write a book...." So the next time we went through it, he went like lightning, and then he said, "OK, is that fast enough for you?" But then, we reached a compromise.

—Stapleton, interviewed by Claudio Masenza for *The Rebels: Marlon Brando* (Aida United Video, 1983)

[*Airport* (1970)] was directed by George Seaton — a sainted man. The film was in CinemaScope, and I was supposed to look around at the airport. After the first take, he took me aside and said, "Maureen, you have to understand that this is wide screen, and when you come in and look from right to left, on the screen you look crazy. Pick a point, look, count two beats; pick a next point, count two beats."

—Stapleton, interviewed by Annette Insdorf for *The Los Angeles Times*, 8 July 1987

Emma [Goldman in *Reds* (1981, Warren Beatty)] was like all fanatics. They have no life in them, no humor; it's always, "I'm going to help you if it kills me."

—Stapleton, interviewed by Melody Kimmel for *Films in Review* (NY), Feb 1982

Mary STEENBURGEN [1953-]

Born: North Little Rock, Arkansas. Waitressing and studies with Sanford Meisner at The Neighborhood Playhouse in N.Y. preceded her film debut in Goin' South (1978, Jack Nicholson). In 1980, she played Linda Dummer in Jonathan Demme's Melvin and Howard:

Q. Did it bother you to do a nude scene in *Melvin and Howard*?

A. Oh, yeah. But you must remember, I had a great deal of faith in Jonathan Demme. He is such a wonderful director. I wondered for a year what my parents were going to think about it. When I told my mother, she was quiet for a long time, and then she said, "Well, what kind of shape were you in?" I said, "I think I looked OK." She said, "Well, all right." In the scene, I'm at a strip joint and I quit. I rip off what I'm wearing, throw it in the air, and walk naked out of the place. The night before the scene, I thought, "Who is going to be there tomorrow?" There's going to be a skeleton crew. I didn't sleep that night, but I thought I was prepared for what was going to happen. I had totally forgotten there were going to be about sixty guys — extras from Central Casting — sitting around.

I did it OK for about the first eight times, but I started to lose it. I was becoming upset because these guys kept making comments. I called [my husband] Malcolm [McDowell], and he said, "Listen, you've done it. You have already put it on film. Do it one more time, and just try and do it real well." I had lost sight of that. I was so busy worrying about my clothes I had forgotten about the moment of it. I knew it was a moment of bravery and freedom, and he reminded me of that. So I went back and I did it really well. As I walked out, I flipped off the construction hat of the guy at the bar and I waved goodbye to all the other dancers on the stage. That is the one they used.

Ragtime [1981, Milos Forman] was a very strange experience for me because I had grown up in film being ushered into the dailies from the first day. Milos Forman doesn't let you see any dailies at all. There is no use arguing about it; that is his way of making a film. It was weird.... But I have a great deal of respect for Milos and his talent.

Q. Who do you play in *Ragtime*?

A. I play Mother, a woman who starts off in the film asking her husband [James Olson] permission to speak and ends up defying him, the FBI, and everybody else for something she believes in. I always look in a script for a journey of a character, and she had quite a wonderful one. That's why I wanted to do it. She's also not a bubble brain, and I had got a little tired of reading how stupid I am.

—Steenburgen, interviewed for *Dialogue on Film, American Film*, Oct 1981

It's difficult to portray an "artist." There's the risk of looking self-indulgent, or the other extreme, not expressing anything. [Marjorie Kinnan] Rawlings [in *Cross Creek* (1983, Martin Ritt)] was a bit prickly and spinsterish; she was unsentimental and didn't ask anybody to like her. But I think inside, she wanted to be loved and she had her appetites — for drink, and, I strongly suspect, for sex.

—Steenburgen, interviewed by Fred Schruers for *The New York Daily News*, 18 Sept 1983

The truth of [Marjorie] is that she was somewhat emotionally constipated — everything was on ice until she felt she could write. It was difficult for her to have warm, loving relationships; she had to write before those things could come out.

—Steenburgen, interviewed by Howard Kissel for *Women's Wear Daily*, 27 Sept 1983

Rod STEIGER [1925-]

Born: Westhampton, N.Y. Service in the U.S. Navy was followed by acting studies at The New School for Social Research, the American Theater Wing (on the G.I. Bill) and The Actors Studio. Work on the N.Y. stage preceded his film debut in Teresa (1951, Fred Zinnemann). His next role was as Charley Molloy opposite Marlon Brando as Terry Molloy in Elia Kazan's On the Waterfront:

I don't know what made [the taxi scene] as good as it was. Maybe because it was made under peculiar circumstances. We were supposed to have back projection. It didn't happen. The director was forced to find a way to shoot in the cab. One of the stagehands said, "I was in a cab the other day — had a venetian blind." Kazan, who is no coward, said, "Get a goddamn venetian blind." So the scene became two close-ups, more or less. You never cut outside the cab because you couldn't. You had to keep going.

—Steiger, interviewed by Ronald Hayman for *The Times*, 31 Oct 1970

I don't like Mr. Brando. I'll never forget, or forgive, what he did to me on [*On the Waterfront*]. We were doing that now-famous taxi scene. I did the take with him, when the camera was on him, but when it came for the camera to be on me — he went home! I had to speak my lines to an assistant director. It must have just burned him up that we came out even in that scene — despite what he did.

—Steiger, interviewed by Roderick Mann for *The Sunday Express*, 31 Oct 1965

One of the greatest disasters that can hit an actor is for him to make a judgment of his character rather than let the audience do it. He can fall into this trap all too easily. He plays somebody who is no good. He puts on a gruff voice, or acts tough. He tries to make sure the audience's judgment will be exactly what his was. If you do that, it becomes a sterile piece of work for the audience, because then they have no reason to be there. A film is a window that the audience looks through, and it is for them to judge whether the character is good or bad. Stanley Hoff in *The Big Knife* [1955, Robert Aldrich] was one of the most challenging things I have ever tried to do. I was 30 years old at the time, and Hoff was supposed to be in his middle forties. I couldn't find, as that wonderful actor Vladimir Sokoloff said to me once, *the raisin for the part*. The raisin meaning an expression among Russian actors — they have a drink called kvass, and in the bottom of the kvass is a raisin that adds flavor. They say, find the raisin and the whole bottle is good. The same thing with acting.

So I kept reading the script and rereading it. Then I noticed that Hoff attacked women continuously. And I had a hunch. There is a game I play sometimes when I am stuck. I go through a department store, and seeing all the merchandise through the eyes of the character, I try to relate to every object. What would this object mean to this particular character?

I was walking through the men's department, and I passed a bunch of tie clasps. Just as I was about to go by, I saw a sterling silver question mark. And I said, this man is a question-mark man. He is a latent homosexual. He doesn't know it. He despises women. He can't stand them. He uses them. He degrades them. And that one aspect opened up the whole part for me. In fact, I bought the tie clasp and wore it in the film. You can't see it on the tie because it is such a little thing, but I used it to remind myself during rehearsals, to clarify my point of view and concept.

But, then, to hate the people around me, I didn't know what to do. And I happened to see a newsreel that had to do with Nazi concentration camps, and I said to myself, what if all these people around me were Nazis? It was, strangely enough, a Fascistic character but the actor had to pretend that the people around him were Nazis in order to hate them! But in these elements I found my raisin.

—Steiger, in *Cinema* (Beverly Hills), Winter 1967

Fred Zinnemann's original idea [for *Oklahoma* (1955)] was to use Montgomery Clift and Eva Marie Saint; he wanted a whole new approach to the musical. He was going to use more trained theatrical actors than singers, but [composer] Richard Rodgers was against it....

After I got the role of Judd, Agnes de Mille — who was choreographing the film — told me she was having trouble getting someone to dance my part, because I looked too big from the back. She couldn't find a dancer who was as broad-shouldered as me.... Finally [she said she had] found someone. I asked her who, and she said..."You."

I told her she had to be kidding! I couldn't dance with those accomplished artists, who had better discipline than any actor had....

She was very funny. She said, "Can you count to four? That's all you have to do — let's start the music...!" Thank God Judd's choreography was lumbering and grotesque; otherwise, I never would have been able to do it.

Al Capone [1958, Richard Wilson] came off the way I'd hoped — as a personality study, rather than an indictment — I exposed the man's character, but didn't judge or glorify him....

I originally didn't take the film because I wanted nothing to do with that type of person. They made two different offers, but I told them I didn't like the script. One of the producers got a little uppity and said, "If you don't like it, why don't you take it home and re-work it?" I worked on it for a month and a half, brought it back with a cast list, then told them I wanted ten days of rehearsal — which was *unheard* of in those days...! They called me back the following Monday and said, "We can't give you ten days, but we'll give you seven!" I said, "Well, I'll be a son of a bitch! I had four aces, and you've dealt me five!"

—Steiger, interviewed by K.H. Johnson for *Prevue*, Nov/Dec 1984

When I played a shrink in *The Mark* [1961, Guy Green], I adopted my own psychiatrist's short-sleeved shirts and his chronic fatigue. He also smoked a pipe constantly, so I made the character a nervous chain smoker, too — all to get away from that terrible cliché of the calm, quiet psychiatrist with the deep voice. I tried to play that part very well and humanly as a token of appreciation for the patient endeavors of my doctor.

—Steiger, interviewed by Richard Warren Lewis for *Playboy*, July 1969

[*The Pawnbroker* (1965, Sidney Lumet) was] the most challenging part I've played, and the challenge in that part was that Nazerman was a man who tried to exist in the world without participating, which means he was, in a sense, an amoeba, a walking dead man. How do you play that? You can't try to be too exciting, because if you do they'll say, "Well, what the hell; he's participating." I cut a lot of my lines in three-quarters of the film, and if you'll notice in the beginning, I did what they tell me you're not supposed to do in movies — I didn't look up until somebody said something *really* important. I never looked up because I didn't want to have any connection with the world.... I tried to hide, and it's very hard to play a person who hides.

—Steiger, interviewed by Don Shay for *Conversations* (Albuquerque: Kaleidoscope Press, 1969)

I felt that if a man like Nazerman doesn't aspire to anything more than merely existing in society, then he wouldn't want to have contact with people.... One of the most revealing moments in the picture is when a customer says, "You Jew!" and Nazerman doesn't even change his expression. He says, "What's your address?"

—Steiger, interviewed by Richard Warren Lewis for *Playboy*, July 1969

In *The Pawnbroker*, according to the script, I was to look at a dead boy's body, then throw back my head and scream. While the camera was running, I opened my mouth, and suddenly remembered Picasso's *Guernica* — the woman with the sharp tongue. Even though it's only a painting, it's one of the loudest screams I've ever heard — so, I didn't make a sound. Several people told me to scream, but I made $100 bets that my version would work, and I think it did. That may be as close as I've ever come to the highest level of acting, which only happens two or three times in a career — the poetic presentation of life at a high point of pain.

—Steiger, interviewed by K.H. Johnson for *Prevue*, Nov/Dec 1984

Komarovsky in [*Dr.*] *Zhivago* [1965, David Lean] is an interesting part. He's basically weak. He's intelligent enough to realize his mistakes but he can't resist being a bigshot. I see him as a sort of Dorian Gray: at the very end he's old and broken.

David Lean is good to work with; very thorough, very considerate....

—Steiger, interviewed by Michael Kuh for *The New York Times*, 6 June 1965

Steiger: In *Zhivago*, I added something when Julie Christie slapped me in one scene. Nobody slaps Komarovsky; he doesn't give a shit *who* you are. She hauled off and belted me and I spontaneously belted her right back; it wasn't in the script. David Lean said, "Cut," and left it in.

Playboy: You certainly touched on something unique as Mr. Joyboy in *The Loved One* [1965, Tony Richardson], which *Time* called the epitome of your obvious fascination with the deviate character.

Steiger: First of all, I resent that crack. I am fascinated with *people* — not deviates. All of us are deviates in one way or another. Who dares define the norm? Mr. Joyboy was delightful because it was an exercise in acting for me. Before I went to talk to Tony Richardson about it, I passed a statue of Apollo in white plaster and I got the idea of wearing the bleached hair and curls. I saw him as a chubby Apollo.... Aside from the hair and the effeminacy, I came completely equipped for that part. I was already so chubby that I didn't have to gain any weight to play Mr. Joyboy.

Playboy: Aren't some of your dramatic innovations a bit too subtle to be noticed by most people in the audience?

Steiger: They're not *supposed* to be noticed. If they were, they would come off as affectations rather than as natural character traits. When I did *In the Heat of the Night* [1967, Norman Jewison], for instance, I chewed gum constantly and wore oversized chukka boots to give the sheriff a shambling walk.... My normal girth wasn't enough for Norman Jewison and Sidney Poitier.... Norman kept saying, "I'd like to see your stomach over that belt." That's all I had to hear. I gladly sacrificed myself to art. If I had only two pieces of pecan pie, they went mad. So I gorged myself.

—Steiger, interviewed by Richard Warren Lewis for *Playboy*, July 1969

Jan STERLING [1923-]

Born: Jane St. Adriance in New York City. Studies at Fay Compton's Drama School in England and work on Broadway (from 1938) preceded her film debut in Johnny Belinda (1948, Jean Negulesco). In 1951, she played Lorraine Minosa in Billy Wilder's Ace in the Hole (aka The Big Carnaval):

Lorraine Minosa...was a pretty deplorable person, judged by any standards. She had overbleached hair, a strident voice and practically no ethics. She happily capitalized on a cave-in accident that threatened the life of her husband [Richard Benedict], and her reaction to churchgoing was "I never go to church, because kneeling bags my nylons."

Despite these things, the role appealed to me more than any other I've played.... It was a difficult, important and interesting part. I couldn't make Lorraine a sympathetic character, but I tried hard to make her an understandable one. Instead of hating her, I wanted audiences to walk out after the show wondering what they might have done if, like Lorraine, they had been in poverty and repeatedly disappointed by life.

Getting Billy Wilder as a director was like winning a sweepstakes to me, and working with Kirk Douglas was pure pleasure. Kirk and I agreed that in the scenes of violence we would dig right in and make it as real as possible, which was fine except in the scene where he was supposed to choke me with a fur stole. He suggested that I say, "Kirk" if he pressed too hard, and I thought this a good idea — until the choking started. Then I discovered I couldn't say a word, so I just turned purple and passed out.

—Sterling, in *The Saturday Evening Post*, 1 Mar 1952

Stella STEVENS [1938-]

Born: Estelle Egglestone in Yazoo City, Mississippi. Studies at Memphis State University preceded her film debut in Say One for Me (1959, Frank Tashlin). In 1960, she played Jess Polanski in John Cassavetes' Too Late Blues:

John can carry on like a madman but on the set, he's very quiet. You were never aware of being told what to do or of being pushed into giving any other reaction than your own out of the character. John would never instil his own reaction into you; you were hardly ever aware that he was directing but every second he was....

The difficulty of the part lay in the fact that there wasn't much the girl said or did. It was by her being there and looking, by her feeling what was going on that she showed things. Sometimes the best thing would be to do nothing at all. If the camera is running on you, you feel you have to do something. In the last scene when I was just standing there watching all this apologising going on, it was hard for me to reach the point — it's real and honest now but it was hard to get there — that the girl would do nothing. Finally John said, "Just do what you feel" and he put the camera on a close-up of me. I stood there with my head on the piano, and did absolutely nothing, then I started singing. It's very hard to get to that, that nothing may be the best thing to do.

—Stevens, interviewed for *Film* (London), Spring 1962

James STEWART [1908-]

Born: Indiana, Pennsylvania. Architecture studies at Princeton University and work on the Broadway stage preceded his film debut in The Murder Man (1935, Tim Whelan). In 1939, he played Jefferson Smith in Frank Capra's Mr. Smith Goes to Washington:

When an actor has a chance to do not only a remarkably interesting character but one whose story...has something really important to say, he's apt to find it an exciting experience.

Frank Capra, who taught me a lot about acting while we were making *Mr. Smith*, refused to build synthetic Washington street scenes at the Columbia lot or use process shots; he took the cast to Washington and caught scenes at the exact moments when natural settings dovetailed with the story. In order to get a certain light, we made a shot at the Lincoln Memorial at four in the morning. To catch me getting off a streetcar, a camera was hidden in some bushes. I got on a regular car, paid my dime and, to the motorman's amazement, departed two blocks later — in front of the bushes. For shots of me going up the Capitol steps, I sat in a car and, at a given secret signal, went trudging up through the swarming lunch-hour crowd. This search for absolute realism, plus the superlative work of the supporting actors, had a great deal to do with "making" the picture....

The scene I liked best was the filibuster in the Senate — well, what actor wouldn't enjoy doing practically all of the talking for a theoretical twenty-three hours? We worked on it for four weeks. When my throat finally got tired, my simulated hoarseness sounded like natural speech; so I went to a doctor and asked him for something that would give me a sore throat. Having pulled himself together, he painted my throat with a mercury solution that felt bad. After that, he came to the set and whenever I'd say, "Doc, I'm beginning to feel pretty well again," he'd rush out and swash on another sore throat.

—Stewart, in *The Saturday Evening Post*, 26 Oct 1946

Q. How does Capra direct? Does he talk to you a lot? Or does he kind of leave you to yourself to work things out?

A. Well, he's *so* prepared. He has the story, and he has all these values. He has these things that he knows he wants to get up there on the screen. He doesn't talk to you much, but he talks a lot to the cameraman.... In *Mr. Smith*, we had six cameras in the Senate scene....

Frank planned. He had it all on film any way he might need it. That came from his conversations with the cameraman. He'd say, "Let's try this...." He worked that way with actors, too. He didn't say, "I want you to do this," he'd say, "Let's try it this way." [Stewart had previously worked on Capra's *You Can't Take it with You* (1938).]

—Stewart, interviewed by Leonard Maltin for *The It's a Wonderful Life Book* by Jeanine Basinger (New York: Alfred A. Knopf, 1986)

Q. How did you find working with so formidable a pair [as Katharine Hepburn and Cary Grant in *The Philadelphia Story* (1940, George Cukor)]?

A. A joy. Because when you work with Grant and Hepburn, you *work*! You let up for a second and they'll steal the movie from under your nose! They're the best sort of competition an actor can have. Talent like that keeps you on your toes.

I recommend a dose of it regularly.

—Stewart, interviewed by Clive Hirschhorn for *The Sunday Express*, 30 Mar 1975

By the time of *It's a Wonderful Life* [1946]...Frank [Capra] could just say to me, "Now go in and do the scene." We all felt, "Now it's up to us. This is what we're being paid for. Go in and act." I never remember his saying..."Now what is your feeling about the motivation in this scene?" No, no, he didn't.

Q. Any rehearsal before shooting?

A. Mostly for the cameraman. To see if the camera could get everything, if the camera should be moving. If there was more than one camera working on the thing, he wanted to coordinate the two. Then he would give us one [rehearsal] if we were having a little bit of trouble with timing or something. He'd give us a couple and then always say, "Is everybody ready? Shall we try it?" Sometimes he got what he wanted after a lot of takes, sometimes the first time. But he always knew what he wanted....

Q. Did he change much after you got to the set? Did he get ideas for changing things in a scene — dialogue, anything?

A. He wasn't one to stick strictly to the dialogue. You could go off and get a little dialogue-wise, get him to change things. He didn't mind that. But he didn't do very much scene changing, because he was just so well prepared. He had this *complete* idea, right up here....

I remember the scene in which all the banks closed and everybody who'd invested in the Building and Loan came to get their money. This is when Donna Reed and I were on our way to our honeymoon. I came up and decided that we could give just so much to each person, and we should ask the people how much they needed. And I had a speech when all the people were there. I said, "Please don't take all of your money, and then we can keep going." So I got the money, and one by one they would come past and I would say, "How much do you want? How much do you want?" "I'll have seventy-five dollars." "How much do you want?" "I'll have sixty dollars, that's enough." And then comes Ellen Corby. Frank told her what to say, but he didn't tell me that she was going to say it. You know, she's about this tall, and she could barely see over the counter, and she said, "Twelve dollars and eighty cents." And this threw me completely! I reached over the counter and kissed her on the cheek. That's how Frank Capra worked. That's how he created things, by letting us all help him....

This was another quality Frank had. He just hits the right note as far as casting is concerned. There couldn't have been anybody better than Henry Travers for Clarence.... His timing and his looks and the way he played it straight. You could see him absolutely guarding himself against anything that would be a comic-strip type of thing.... It was just a joy to see him work and to work with him. In that scene where we're drying off after being in the water, I kept hearing these things that he was saying. Frank had said, "Let's not rehearse it. Let's keep it natural. Just go ahead with it and we'll see how it plays, but do the whole darn thing no matter what...."

Frank once told me that when he said to himself, "Who will I get for the angel?," Henry Travers came right into his mind.

—Stewart, interviewed by Leonard Maltin for *The It's a Wonderful Life Book* by Jeanine Basinger (New York: Alfred A. Knopf, 1986)

When I got *The Stratton Story* [1949, Sam Wood], I was determined to get as much instruction (as possible), to get myself physically ready — so I'd look right pitching a ball. Two months before the picture started, Monty Stratton came up. Everyday, for three hours, back in the backlot of MGM, I just threw the ball. And Monty kept after me and after me. He'd say, "You're not using your wrist at the right time." It paid off.

—Stewart, interviewed by Michael Buckley for *Films in Review* (NY), June 1991

I still can't play a note on the trombone. My music teacher quit because he said the sounds I made were so terrible he went home and yelled at his wife. So we plugged up the trombone and he taught me how to breathe and spit, and then he stood behind the curtain and played all the old Glenn Miller arrangements [on *The Glenn Miller Story* (1954, Anthony Mann)].

—Stewart, interviewed by Rex Reed for *Travolta to Keaton* (New York: William Morrow & Co., 1979)

When I was making *The Man Who Knew Too Much* [1956, Alfred Hitchcock] there was this big climax in the Albert Hall in which I had one helluva speech which more or less explained the plot.

Well, suddenly Hitch told me to cut all the talk and act with my hands and face because, he said, the words were drowning out the playing of The London Symphony Orchestra. And the orchestra, he said, was more pleasant to listen to than my voice!

—Stewart, interviewed by Clive Hirschhorn for *The Sunday Express*, 30 Mar 1975

Doris [Day] surprised a lot of people with her acting in *The Man Who Knew Too Much*, but she didn't surprise Hitch, who knew what to expect from her. A singer's talent for phrasing, the ability to put heart in a piece of music, is not too far removed from acting, in which the aim is to give life and believability to what's on paper. It all has to do with the center of thrust — the ability to find that which can make a song, or a scene, work.

I knew Hitch pretty well, from having made *Rear Window* [1954] and *Rope* [1948] with him. He didn't believe in rehearsals. He preferred to let the actor figure things out for himself. He refers to his method as "planned spontaneity." Of course, this is confusing to an actor who is accustomed to a director who "participates" in the scene. In the beginning, it certainly threw Doris for a loop. Hitchcock believes that if you sit down with an actor and analyze a scene you run the danger that the actor will act that scene with his head rather than his heart, or guts.

—Stewart, interviewed by A.E. Hotchner for *Doris Day: Her Own Story* (New York: William Morrow & Co.,1975)

There is always such discipline on a Hitchcock set, he is always so completely prepared for what he wants to do, that he makes the job of directing look easy, and that makes the job of acting seem easy too. Some people suppose that he must have a bad reputation with actors, because of some of the provocative things he has said....

I don't see how the reputation, if he has such a reputation, for being bad to actors came about. I have never worked with anyone who was more considerate, more helpful, more understanding of actors than Hitchcock. He expects you to know your job and do it. He has no patience with people who insist on a sort of group analysis of a scene before, or a long private conversation with Hitchcock about a line or a certain feeling the actor may or may not have. This sends Hitchcock right up the wall. He expects a lot of actors, he expects them to know their job, he expects them to take the direction he gives, to use the talent they are being paid for, and they're supposed to have, to interpret that and put it on the screen.

If there is some genuine problem for an actor Hitch can be very helpful. I remember Kim Novak, whom I like very much and think is an excellent actress, had never worked with Hitch before *Vertigo* [1958]. At one point Kim came up, early in the shooting of the film, and said, "Mr. Hitchcock, in this scene I don't feel that Madeleine, the way she's written here, shows that she's engrossed enough in the relevant aspects of the scene itself. Perhaps to show a little more vigor in the writing...." And Hitch said, "Kim, this is only a movie. Let's not go too deeply into these things. It's only a movie." Now I don't say that he has not gone more deeply into things beforehand, in his preparation. But he takes the responsibility for all that off the actor's shoulders. He immediately put Kim Novak at ease, she relaxed and never again questioned anything throughout the whole movie. And of course she was just fine.

He has this absolute fetish about telling a story visually, he has very little respect for the spoken word, and these are all good things for an actor to have, because he occupies himself with his sphere, and leaves the actor completely free in his. He will tell you what effect he wants a particular scene or moment or line to have on the audience, and then leave it up to you to make it your own way. He isn't about to baby anybody through a role; he is a professional and expects to work with professionals. But when you come down to it, that is the best and most valuable sort of respect an actor can receive.

—Stewart, interviewed for *Take One*, May 1976

I wanted to watch [50,000 feet of 1927 newsreel footage of Charles Lindbergh] because while it would be impossible for my face to look exactly like Lindbergh's [in *The Spirit of St. Louis* (1957, Billy Wilder)], I wanted to catch his mannerisms. For instance, I noticed he has a very distinctive walk. He has a habit of swinging his left arm in front of him, even when he only takes three steps; I tried to imitate that. Then I went through the horrible ordeal of having my eyebrows dyed reddish-blond like Lindbergh's, and my hair colored the same.

The other half had to do with actually flying Lindbergh's little monoplane — so that I'd know exactly how it reacted, and so that closeups showing my hands on the controls would reveal the muscles working correctly. Maybe this kind of aviation fussiness isn't important to the average moviegoer. But it's important to me.

I'll never forget a transatlantic flight I made after *Strategic Air Command* [1955, Anthony Mann] was released. The pilot told me, "The picture was great except toward the end. You had an overcontrolled rudder." I saw the movie again, and he was absolutely right.... So I was determined to really fly the Lindbergh plane ahead of time.

—Stewart, interviewed by Eleanor Harris for *The Los Angeles Examiner*, 1 Jan 1956

Q. *Two Rode Together* [1961, John Ford] had one very long sequence of you and [Richard] Widmark on a log by the river, in which the dialogue seemed "awkward," almost as though it were improvised! Was this completely intentional on Ford's part?

A. Yes, it was just all one take. It was early in the morning and he was sort of grouchy and he walked out and for some reason put the camera in the river. He didn't have to put the camera in the river, but I think he did it because that meant that all the crew had to walk out up to their waists in the river — he's like that — and it was terribly cold. Widmark and I did this, it was a long, long scene, we did it and left....

John Ford has no respect for the spoken word. He loves to tear pages out of scripts, he likes to cut sentences down to phrases, and phrases to words. He'll spend an hour getting the wind at the right force, so that it blows the sand in the background just right. But if you don't have the dialogue right immediately when he is ready, he is completely impatient. [Stewart also worked on Ford's *The Man Who Shot Liberty Valance* (1962), *How the West Was Won* (1963, co-directed by George Marshall and Henry Hathaway) and *Cheyenne Autumn* (1964).]

[Frank Towns in *The Flight of the Phoenix* (1965, Robert Aldrich) is]...a sort of a sad man in a way.... I felt he was a man who had been passed by, by the modern jet airplane and the computerized systems and automation. He doesn't want it that way. He wants to run the machine, he doesn't want the machine to run him....

Mr. Aldrich rehearses all the time evidently. I'd never worked with him before. But we rehearsed for a week, actually part of the week just as in a play, just reading the script around a table, getting familiar with the script. Then we got on our feet in a blocked-out area of the crashed airplane. Which is very helpful for this type of picture.

—Stewart, interviewed for *Films & Filming*, Apr 1966

Q. You have been described as having the ability to be extraordinarily ordinary through all of your 75 films.

A. Do you know how difficult that is? Very difficult indeed. Those stars like John Wayne are stars because they have the ability to do just that, to keep their own natures intact through any script that might come along. That's what I've tried to do. And that's what audiences pay to see, I guess.

—Stewart, interviewed by Tom Hutchinson for *Radio Times*, 31 Aug 1972

Dean STOCKWELL [1936-]

Born: Robert Dean Stockwell in North Hollywood, to actor parents; brother of Guy Stockwell [1938-]. On Broadway (from age 7), he made his film debut in Anchors Aweigh (1945, George Sidney). In 1950, he played John Humperdink Stover in William Wellman's The Happy Years:

[*The Happy Years*] was based on the stories Owen Johnson wrote about the Lawrenceville school and the fights were a pretty important part of it. So the studio hired Johnny Indrisano, a famous boxer, to train me and make me fight convincingly....

There were more than thirty boys in the cast with me, some of them actors and others real students from Lawrenceville.

We all got along fine with Mr. Wellman. He knows how to handle kids; he has six of his own. So he never fussed at us. He talked to us as if we had some sense, and he wasn't always worried for fear we'd make mistakes and spoil a scene. He told us to be natural and if we slipped up he'd just leave the mistake in the film. One time I accidentally hiccuped during a scene, but Mr. Wellman said it sounded like a perfectly natural hiccup to him and it stayed right in the picture.

—Stockwell, in *The Saturday Evening Post*, 23 Sept 1950

Q. You worked with [Erroll Flynn] on *Kim* [1950, Victor Saville], the adaptation of the Rudyard Kipling novel.

A. He treated me as an equal.

Q. How was that expressed? I know that when you were working on *Kim*, he walked up to you and said, in front of your mother and your schoolteacher, "Had your first fuck yet, kid?"

A. He didn't say "kid." He said, "Have you had your first fuck yet?" And from that moment I loved him. He was not in awe of a teacher or a mother, or of any stricture whatsoever. So it was as perfect a relationship as possible between an adult and a child. He was leading me into the world, or opening up the doors to the world for me. And no one had done that.... The guy was solid, whole, impervious to everything. He was a romantic, intellectual stud.

—Stockwell, interviewed by Greg Goldin for *Interview*, Oct 1988

There was a lot of good fortune involved [in *Long Day's Journey into Night* (1962, Sidney Lumet)]. The way the film was cast, the four people who were to do it...had kind of a similar relationship in flavor, that fit the characters they played. Not the disastrous things — Kate Hepburn is certainly not addicted to morphine, but Ralph Richardson was just like the figure of the Father of all Time.... We just all blended together very nicely and we didn't get too involved in discussions of the play, as far as interpreting it before we did it. We all seemed to have the same point of view, and just began to act in it and tried to rehearse it. There are always times when you discuss interpretations, you know, and you like to backtrack a little bit in order to find out how to overcome the flaws. Other than that we just tried to let it flow. We rehearsed it well though. We rehearsed it for three weeks....

Q. Did you rehearse on sets?

A. All three weeks? No, we started in just a hall...where a lot of television shows are rehearsed. It's a great big hall which is taped out — like you do for television, tape the set right out on the floor — made a diagram of it and then acted in the framework of that, so that the camera shots could be worked out.

Q. With camera?

A. No, well, Sidney was functioning as the camera as he watched. He didn't have to bring the camera in and he didn't have to have the set. Then we did move into the set and each thing we started to film we would rehearse extensively again and go over to make sure that everything worked right....

—Stockwell, interviewed for *Cinema* (Beverly Hills) Vol. 1 #3, 1963

When I first read *Blue Velvet* [1986, David Lynch], here was...Frank Booth [Dennis Hopper], so unforgivably black and psychologically villainous. And now he's going to visit *my* character, who is someone that he looks up to. So it occurred to me that this Ben had to be fucking stranger than Frank.

—Stockwell, interviewed by Pope Brock for *Rolling Stone*, 4 May 1989

I had no model for [Ben].... But I've been around all sorts of weird scenes and stuff, sure. You know, it's a long life; you run into things like that. One of the things I was playing was heroin. People ask, "Was that junk you were on?" What else could you possibly be on where you fall asleep standing up? But the character really just came out of my imagination and out of a desire to make him more extreme than Dennis' character....

Q. The murderer sees the degenerate as the poet.

A. And thinks he is suave.

—Stockwell, interviewed by Julian Schnabel for *Interview*, Mar 1990

I sort of knew what David Lynch wanted, what his vision is. I feel a sympathy for it; there is a weird correspondence there. I was always confident that the direction my intuition took me in was in line with what he was after for that sort of role. [Stockwell had previously worked on Lynch's *Dune* (1984).]

Q. That character was your invention.

A. Yeah, everything. The makeup, the wardrobe, everything.

—Stockwell, interviewed by Greg Goldin for *Interview*, Oct 1988

David [Lynch] and Dennis [Hopper] share a certain facet of their vision — although I'm not sure either one would agree with me. Both of them have at least a streak of surrealism in their souls, and I have always been very partial to surrealist art, to surrealist thought, to surrealist being. I think *Blue Velvet* is surrealistic, and Dennis' film *The Last Movie* [1971] is definitely surrealistic....

—Stockwell, interviewed by Patrick McGilligan for *Film Comment*, Aug 1988

I rely mostly on my imagination when I do a role. I did Howard Hughes in *Tucker: A Man and His Dreams* [1988, Francis Ford Coppola], and I didn't go read about him. I've seen Howard Hughes enough. I've seen pictures of him, newsreels of him, and I've read a few things about him. I just use my imagination about where the guy would be coming from and what he'd be like.

—Stockwell, interviewed by Greg Goldin for *Interview*, Oct 1988

No character has ever come to me as clearly, as easily, and as fully as Tony "The Tiger" [in *Married to the Mob* (1988, Jonathan Demme)]. It was almost as though I had done it before in another life. I don't know whether it is because I'm half-Italian, or that I've never had the opportunity to do this type of role before — a woman-chasing, amoral, top dog Don. But I just lit up the minute I read it and I didn't have to touch it. There! Solid. Completely.

Q. But I get the idea that, in *Married to the Mob* at least, acting isn't work any longer, it's fun for you.

A. It should be fun. It wasn't for years and years and years. Now, in this third stage of my career, all that has completely turned around and good luck is still with me. Now, I am finally able to enjoy it.

—Stockwell, interviewed by Patrick McGilligan for *Film Comment*, Aug 1988

I'll always be grateful to Jonathan for taking this step, because before *Married to the Mob*, no one had ever thought of me for this type of role. It's a romantic comedy, and I play a charismatic guy who chases after women and who people are afraid of, and it's charming and funny. Prior to that, everyone always thought of me as this serious actor who plays psychotics and neurotics and sensitive people. In fact, my real nature is more in the direction of this character in *Married to the Mob.* Demme was able to see that — without a reading. I'll forever be indebted to him.

—Stockwell, interviewed by Greg Goldin for *Interview*, Oct 1988

Lewis STONE [1879-1953]

Born: Louis Stone in Worcester, Massachusetts. Work on tour and on the N.Y. stage preceded his film debut in Honor's Altar (1916, Thomas Ince). He starred as Judge Hardy in 15 films beginning with You're Only Young Once (1938):

In many ways the Judge and I are alike. Like myself, the Judge is not one to retire and take his ease. He has worked hard all his life as I have worked hard all my life. And neither of us could be happy away from his chosen profession. I feel that the Judge loves his work and I love mine....

The Judge, too, I feel, is the type of man who does his work conscientiously, to the best of his ability. And then lays down his gavel and goes home. Similarly, I lay down my script and go home....

Nor would the Judge be half the man he is without his family. Nor would I....

Yes, I believe I can say that I shrug into the Judge's slightly worn coat easily. The Judge is a straight-line character. No quirks in it. Possibly nothing of extraordinary interest in it, either. He has no mannerisms, no tricks of personality, no complexities, no neuroses....

—Stone, interviewed by Gladys Hall for *Photoplay Magazine*, June 1939

Note: See the Mickey Rooney entry for a complete list of his films as Judge Hardy.

Meryl STREEP [1949-]

Born: Mary-Louise Streep in Summit, New Jersey. Studies at Vassar, the Yale School of Drama and work with Joseph Papp's Public Theater in N.Y. preceded her film debut in Julia (1977, Fred Zinnemann). The following year, she played Linda opposite Robert De Niro as Mike in Michael Cimino's The Deer Hunter:

[De Niro]'s very kind, very generous — and extremely careful. Every little thing is eloquent to him. He's a minimalist. A really thoughtful performer. He's got a concentration level that goes into the stratosphere. He comes on the set just shimmering with the energy of the character. If you go deep into a character Jack Nicholson is playing, sooner or later Jack will pop out. But no matter how deep you go into a character Bobby is playing, it will be that character all the way through. He's really pure. He just *loves* acting. He's a pure actor acting. Acting is his Zen. When you look into his eyes, it's like looking into the fathomless deep.... His face can be a mask, with *nothing* showing. Yet *everything's* emanating from it. He just looks with a completely straight face and you know *everything* he's feeling. That's what I meant by minimalism. [Streep and De Niro worked together a second time on *Falling in Love* (1984, Ulu Grosbard)].

—Streep, interviewed by Brad Darrach for *Life*, Dec 1987

When they came to my part [in *Kramer vs. Kramer* (1979)], [Robert] Benton and Dustin [Hoffman] both, would just kind of draw a blank. Really the film is the story of a father — mothering a child — and they didn't know what Joanna felt. They asked, could I speak from that very subjective point of view? I said, Sure...but I don't know if you'll use it.

What happened was I had a few days off in the shooting and went to Indiana to visit my husband's family. On the way back...a whole speech came to me. I just wrote it on one of those yellow legal pads — I'm very professional! I showed it to Benton, and sort of did it for him. He took out two words and otherwise used it verbatim.

And on the last scene, we went through a similar thing. We hit a snag. Everybody went off into their cubicles and tried to write what I should say at the end. Dustin wrote his, the producer [Stanley R. Jaffe] wrote his, Benton wrote his and I wrote mine. And...(big laugh) they used mine!

—Streep, interviewed by Tony Crawley for *Films Illustrated*, May/June 1980

I thought [Sarah in *The French Lieutenant's Woman* (1981, Karel Reisz)] was maddening. John Fowles gets a kick out of the fact that a lot of people picked up the book as some kind of banner for women's liberation, but in fact, I found her a character I would not like to emulate. She doesn't seem liberated to me. She was very manipulative in a very old-fashioned feminine way, leading Charles [Jeremy Irons] on in a flirtatious manner. She was mendacious.

—Streep, interviewed by Mel Gussow for *Horizon*, Oct 1981

For Sophie [in *Sophie's Choice* (1982, Alan J. Pakula)], I had a dual task: to immerse myself in the character, the kind of woman I thought she was, and at the same time to learn the language — Polish — and to figure out how a Polish refugee would mangle English. At least I wanted to make sure that what came out of my mouth didn't sound like New Jersey!

As much as you depend on the script, you have to come up with the goods on the day of shooting, yourself. So I thought about the character, but then I remained blank, letting her evolve, because I think Sophie is a character who is written upon by her circumstances. She's engraved by her past and her present and her ability to forget, to leave things behind when she can. She remains imprinted, but a lot depended on how Alan cast the other characters. That was and is the key. You never know what's going to be until the day you walk onto the set and look into the other actors' eyes.

—Streep, interviewed by Michael J. Bandler for *American Way*, Dec 1982

While they were working on the script [of *Silkwood* (1983, Mike Nichols)], I was in Yugoslavia shooting *Sophie's Choice*. I only had two and a half weeks off between projects. So I kind of backed into *Silkwood*. I was afraid about that, but actually, in an odd way, it served the script. Mike spoke of the film as being about people being asleep in their lives and waking up: "How did I get here?" And that's exactly how I felt. One day I was in Yugoslavia and the next I found myself in a plant with a light flashing and a siren going, "Woop, woop woop," thinking, "How did this happen?"

Q. At the beginning of the film, Karen is shown prowling around the plant, teasing, flirting. She comes off as a kook — was that intentional?

A. Absolutely. She was on the prowl in a lot of ways. She wasn't settled. She was always looking for trouble. There are people who are always exploring possibilities, looking around, making waves. That was the way she seemed to me.

Q. Not only is she kooky, but she's cocky, especially with the men in the plant.

A. I do think Karen had a chip on her shoulder, but I don't think it had to do with her being a woman. I think hers was a very personal crusade.

Q. When Karen cheats on her boyfriend, Drew [Kurt Russell], and has an affair with a union official in Washington, don't you think she runs the risk of losing sympathy with the audience? Aren't people going to say, "Now, wait a minute—"

A. I *want* them to say that, because Karen spelled trouble — not only to the people she worked for, but the people she lived with. She was a difficult person.

—Streep, interviewed by Thomas Wiener for *American Film*, Dec 1983

I thought [*Out of Africa* (1986, Sydney Pollack)] was a great script, but there was this one line that I thought was just preposterous, and I didn't know how I was going to get it out. I didn't want to say it. I didn't mind being proprietary about "my" Africans, or Karen Blixen's other sort of grande-dame pretensions; but when Denys [Robert Redford] suggests taking their young friend along on one of his flights and she rises up from her chair and says, "I won't *allow* it, Denys," I thought it sounded like a mother admonishing her child, which did not reflect their relationship at all. It felt to me like something you have the woman say to give him a reason to walk out.... When we came to do the scene, I said, "All right, you know, I'm a good sport. I'll *say* it, and I'll *try* to make it work, but it won't." And, *of course*, when we played it, it was the easiest and freest thing she said in the scene, because all the reason had been used up; there was nothing left to argue with but her desperation, and it was so preposterous and pathetic, that it was *right*. It was a key to the woman.

—Streep, interviewed by Wendy Wasserstein for *Interview*, Dec 1988

A lot of people thought Bob [Redford] was wooden in *Out of Africa*. I didn't. I thought he was subtle — and just right. But then I'm the worst one to ask. I had a big crush on him. He's the best kisser I ever met in the movies. Anyway, Sydney [Pollack] had the idea that Redford's essence lined up with Denys Finch Hatton's and I agree. Redford *is* that kind of guy. He's an adventurer and loves to put himself in danger. He cares about the disappearing wilderness. He likes to be alone. He likes a good story. And good wine. And he's a heartthrob, you know. Even the old-time Africans said Finch Hatton had that same aura. A lord. Redford walked on the screen with that — with size. He just *has* it. That old movie-star stuff. Other actors would need five scenes to make that happen. With Redford, the work's done when he appears in the doorway.... [In this movie] he fulfills what's usually the woman's part...the roles are flip-flopped. The woman is central, the man is unattainable. Bob felt that was the balance, and he very generously played it that way. He's a lovely black Irishman.

My image for Helen [in *Ironweed* (1987, Hector Babenco)] was the sign of the treble clef. It expressed for me her passion for music and her inner grace, and it gave me the sad, drooping line of her body....

For Helen I had a lot of things to prepare. Secret things that no one else would know. And that intrigued me because that's how we encounter people who live on the street. We don't know anything about them except how they look. So I see Helen as a shadow, like a lot of those people are. They're just souls, stripped of all the things that most of us carry around. And they drift around like souls in purgatory. All these people have are their dreams. That's their real world. And their past, which they change into dreams, to make it better. They illuminate their ruins, because ruins are all they have. And drink comes into this. Alcohol is the fuel for these stuttering engines.

Helen has none of the things most people covet — possessions and accomplishments and children. All she has are the purest impulses — fidelity and pride and resilience. I liked playing a stripped-down character. Even her age was a mystery. I located one for purposes of reality but then I threw it away. People who live on the edge don't *know* how old they are.... Helen is sort of an ember.... We just get the last glow, and then she goes.

Jack [Nicholson] is an extraordinary being.... He's got a voracious appetite for the work and for the quality of the work. He's never satisfied, he's always churning. Energy! Fire in the belly...! But the character in *Ironweed* is different from anything else Jack's done. Jack's tendency is to take a character and blow it through the roof. But this time he shows us a life that's just trickling quietly out, like sand. This was a tough role for Jack. He turned 50 on the project. Most of the time he looked 70. It was a descent into the hell we all have somewhere inside.... [Streep had previously worked with Nicholson on *Heartburn* (1986, Mike Nichols).]

—Streep, interviewed by Brad Darrach for *Life*, Dec 1987

The Australian press was dying to know when [Lindy Chamberlain and I] were going to meet [in preparation for *A Cry in the Dark* (1988, Fred Schepisi)]. I invited Lindy to my house for supper. She travels by night in unmarked cars, by the way, with other people driving....

I spoke to her about this story, and she said, "Oh, I knew it. Now you're getting a taste of what it's like." And I said, "I deal with this at home too." I was bitching and moaning to her about being a famous person, and she said, "Yes, Meryl, you're famous and I'm infamous, and there's a *real* difference...."

As an actress, I'm fascinated in how we judge each other on the TV and how much how you look and sound has to do with what you're saying in terms of legitimizing it, making it palatable.... Lindy was judged based on how she communicated. I'm real careful to make it right — to reproduce exactly how she looked and sounded — so that you can look beyond that.

—Streep, interviewed by Sonia Taitz for *The New York Times*, 6 Nov 1988

Q. Is there a difference between playing a role that is fictional and one that actually exists or has existed?

A. Well, you know, nobody really exists when you start the movie but yourself. I hope that I was close to portraying Karen Silkwood or Isak Dinesen.... I imagine that I was not. I was more like me with somebody else's clothes on.

The role of Lindy Chamberlain in *A Cry in the Dark* was the only case where I was really trying to replicate somebody. I was really trying to get that thing that people disliked about her. I was trying to get whatever it was that came out in her eyes.

Q. Is it always in the eyes?

A. Almost always.

—Streep, interviewed by Rod Lurie for *The West Side Spirit*, 18 Sept 1990

Barbra STREISAND [1942-]

Born: Barbara Streisand in Brooklyn, N.Y. Winning an amateur singing contest in Greenwich Village in 1961 quickly led to work on TV and Broadway. She made her film debut as Fanny Brice in Funny Girl (1968, William Wyler), having previously done the role on Broadway:

I just played Fanny Brice as a part — I never studied her whole life. I felt that we were so instinctively alike that I didn't have to work to get her.

I love Willy Wyler.... He's not eloquent. He'll sit there and he won't know when it's quite right. He's not like a director who says "Print!" and that's it and on to the next. He'll print 5, 6 of them even when the first one was right. But he always knows in the end, d'ya know what I mean, and will always pick the right piece. And that's really what counts, because I guess that's what makes him a better director than most. I think he's tremendous, but he's not what I thought a director would be like.

—Streisand, interviewed by George Perry for *The Sunday Times Magazine*, 12 Nov 1969

I have very little in common with a character like Dolly [in *Hello Dolly!* (1969, Gene Kelly)] who fixes people up and lives other people's lives. I do share the fun she gets in bargaining and buys, and can understand her experience as a woman who has loved and lost. But I really didn't respond to the Broadway show — a piece of fluff. It's not the kind of thing I'm interested in. I'm interested in real life, real people. In playing Medea. Dolly takes place in an age before people realized they hated their mothers — the whole Freudian thing. So it wasn't something I could delve psychologically into too deeply.

—Streisand, interviewed by Jack Hamilton for *Look*, 16 Dec 1969

Streisand: What interested me most about [*A Star is Born* (1976, Frank Pierson)] was the woman issue. In the old version, the characters never fought or disagreed; the female character was willing to give up her career for her man; she used his name at the end. I wouldn't do that. I don't think women should do that. I was interested in being more sexually aggressive in this film — a different character than I've ever played before. I wanted to portray her as taking what she wants, something that's a big thing for women today, especially sexually. So many women you hear about never have orgasms. It's a matter of asking for your own pleasure. In our first love scene, I wanted to be a sort of Clint Eastwood — you know, the guy always takes his belt off. That's why I have her being on top [of Kris Kristofferson]. Why should a man always be the one shown opening his pants first....?

Playboy: Why did Frank Pierson single *A Star is Born* out as being such a nightmare?

Streisand: It *was* a nightmare. The experience of making this film was a nightmare for all of us. One time I was a little sharp with him and I apologized. I said, "I have a problem with tact, I only know how to be direct. I'm sorry, I don't know how to shmeikle you, I don't know how to go around the bush, I just tell you what I feel." He said, "That's OK, I agree with you and then behind your back I do what I want anyway." So we had two different styles, you see. When things got worse, I had to assume more responsibility [as executive producer].

But, look, maybe he's right. Maybe he's this terrific director. Maybe it was the combination of our chemistries that didn't click. In my opinion, he didn't know how to deal with actors. When I asked him one day what he thought of the difference in playing a scene in one of two ways, he said, "I'm neutral." I said, "Frank, if you ever want to be a director, you can never be neutral — lie, make it up, explore your feelings, anything — because the actor has to have some feedback, some mirror, some opinion, even if it's wrong." What I was trying to tell him was that he's got to communicate with the actors, use all their talents, improvise. He didn't try to talk to the actors, give them a sense of their characters, a sense of their importance in this film. Every extra is important! Every detail!

—Streisand, interviewed by Lawrence Grobel for *Playboy*, Oct 1977

Although it's set in Eastern Europe in the early 1900s, *Yentl* [1983, Barbra Streisand] is a love story as contemporary as any made today. It's more than a story about the love between a man and a woman — it's about the love between parent and child, between friends, and ultimately the love we should have for ourselves.

Yentl is someone with a dream who's not afraid to take chances.

—Streisand, interviewed for the press release for *Yentl* (United Artists/Barwood, 1983)

Q. Are you like Yentl?

A. Yentl is like *me*, Liz! No — of course I'm like Yentl. She existed. I didn't invent her. But I *do* serve the material! In the Yeshiva of Brooklyn in Williamsburg, whether the teacher called on me or not, I'd always answer. I'd ask "Why?" like Yentl.

—Streisand, interviewed by Liz Smith for *The Sunday News Magazine*, 13 Nov 1983

Donald SUTHERLAND [1934-]

*Born: St. John, New Brunswick, Canada; father of Keifer Sutherland [1967-]. Studies at The University of Toronto and The London Academy of Music and Dramatic Art, and work on the British stage preceded his film debut in the low-budget Italian horror film, Castle of the Living Dead (1964, Luciano Ricci). In 1970, he played Hawkeye in Robert Altman's M*A*S*H:*

On *M*A*S*H,* I repeatedly tried to force Robert Altman into giving me an overall concept of the film; to verbalise what was in his own head. He couldn't and I refused to accept that. I thought it meant he had no overall concept. Of course he had, but he couldn't verbalise it. That's why he was making the picture.... Altman...[was a] marvellous director to work with, but at the time I was too dumb to realise it.

—Sutherland, interviewed by Jenny Craven for *Films & Filming*, June 1978

Sutherland: When I'm acting, I'm kind of a concubine to the director. I mean that, quite seriously. My job is to understand the character and give the director what he wants. What I have to do is satisfy him. It is very intimate, very sensuous, very loving to do that. The director ends up liking you because you satisfy him and you end up loving him because it is very satisfying making someone else happy. It's like being a good lover to someone — wonderful. With Nick Roeg [on *Don't Look Now* (1973)], with Federico Fellini [on *Fellini's Casanova* (1976)], with John Schlesinger [on *The Day of the Locust* (1975)], with Bob Redford [on *Ordinary People* (1980)], I think I've been a very good lover.

Playboy: Did you always have that attitude about acting?

Sutherland: Oh, no. I used to think the actor was all-important. The truth is that film making is about directors. When I made *Klute* [1971] with Alan Pakula, there were real problems. I had a specific way I wanted the character to be — a different way from Alan's. I wanted Klute to go to New York with a Pennsylvania Dutch accent and I wanted him to be more shocked by the decadence of the place — the shopping-bag ladies, the poverty, the extreme wealth. Well, all of that made for big problems between Alan and me. It was, after all, *his* movie and my ideas were outside the context of the film....

Playboy: When did your attitude about acting change?

Sutherland: I began to understand that the actor is not important with Nick Roeg and *Don't Look Now*.... Roeg had sent me the script for the movie and then telephoned me. On the phone, I said, "Well, the character should do this and that." Roeg said, "No, we're not making *any* changes. The script is going to be what I want it to be. Take it or leave it." So I thought to myself, Why not try this? Let's find out what it's like to not interfere. That conversation changed my life — changed my whole attitude about acting. Now I think of myself as the director's plaything. Film acting, basically, is about the surrender of will to the director. Francine and I named our first son after Nick Roeg — *that's* how important the lesson was.... I love that movie.... But making it was *perilous*. We filmed in Venice.... I had this premonition that I was definitely going to die in Venice.

Playboy: Which is what the movie is about — a man who has visions of his own death.

Sutherland: And that's what I was having every minute I was there. A lot of my own life was paralleling the movie. I mean, I was death-obsessed.... I've always been convinced that I was going to die by drowning — and there I was in Venice, with water everywhere....

—Sutherland, interviewed by Claudia Dreifus for *Playboy*, Oct 1981

I have found gradually over the years that there is more truth in getting as close to the center of myself as I can. All the characters I've played were based on emotion, really gut-raw emotion. What I would like to achieve is moving them to an intellectual base. There's not much difference (for audiences), but there is for me as a performer. The center of it is different. The center is somewhere just behind the eyes, as opposed to just below the rib cage; more in the brain than in the diaphragm.

I started doing it in *Don't Look Now*, but that was really Nick Roeg more than me. [*The Invasion of the*] *Body Snatchers* [1978, Philip Kaufman] is where it started for me. He was a *lot* like me. The character was straight on what I thought, straight on rationality, straight on observing people in crisis situations. I would like to develop that character and examine him further.

—Sutherland, interviewed by Jordan Young for *The New York Times*, 23 Sept 1979

Sutherland: *Ordinary People* was a completely wonderful thing to have been part of. Redford, he's a genius. Every note in that film was right. The fact that the movie moved my image to something more like what I wanted made the whole experience even better.

Playboy: Yet you were ambivalent at first about doing the movie, weren't you?

Sutherland: Well, originally, they had wanted me for the psychiatrist. I wanted to play the father. I knew Bob Redford would be a terrific director — it would be impossible for a man as sensitive as he not to be.... Usually when I start a film I'm always awkward with the director the first few days. But with Bob, the first few days were much easier. He surrounds actors with a great deal of affection. And I knew things would be right from the first rehearsals at Bob's house in Chicago....

You know, after we had shot that last scene where Calvin Jarrett tells Beth [Mary Tyler Moore] through his tears, "I'm not sure I love you anymore," I felt that the way I had done it just wasn't right for the character, for what happened to him next. Bob didn't agree. The film editor didn't agree. They thought the take was terrific. I wanted Calvin to be calmer, less hysterical. Well, Bob had enough faith in my sense of it to later hire a complete studio, reconstruct the set and reshoot the scene. By that time, Mary Tyler Moore was already in New York, playing in *Whose Life Is It Anyway?*, so we reshot the scene with Bob off-camera delivering Mary's lines. And that's what Bob went with — that's what you see in the movie.

—Sutherland, interviewed by Claudia Dreifus for *Playboy*, Oct 1981

Grady SUTTON [1908-]

Born: Chattanooga, Tennessee. As a teenager, he made his film debut in The Mad Whirl (1925, William D. Seiter). He played opposite W.C. Fields in The Pharmacist (1933, Arthur Ripley), the first of four films together:

I worked with him in a two-reeler at Mack Sennett's — *The Pharmacist*, and from then on he would ask for me, or write a part especially for me. He'd say, "Grady's got to do it." I remember when he did *The Bank Dick* [1940, Eddie Cline] they wanted someone else, I don't know who it was, but the powers-that-be wanted this other guy. Fields said, "No, I want Grady. I like to work with him; I like the way he reacts to me...."

Q. Did he ad-lib a lot?

A. All the time; you never knew. The first feature I did with him, *The Man on the Flying Trapeze* [1935, Clyde Bruckman], there was a dining-room scene.... He's going on a like a wild-man, and a few minutes later I hear the director yell "Cut." And Bill says, "I didn't give the boy a cue. Leave him alone — I never give cues!" He got me over to one side and he said, "Now look, son, we'll work it this way. When you think I've said enough, well you just butt in." [Sutton also worked with Fields on *You Can't Cheat an Honest Man* (1939, George Marshall).]

—Sutton, interviewed by Leonard Maltin for *Film Fan Monthly*, Oct 1969

Gloria SWANSON [1899-1983]

Born: Gloria Svensson in Chicago. Film work in Chicago, including her debut in The Fable of Elvira and Farina and the Meal Ticket (1915, Richard Foster Baker), preceded her work with The Keystone Company in Hollywood. In 1919, she made the first of six films for Cecil B. DeMille:

Under Mr. DeMille, the actors never used a script. Mr. DeMille told us very carefully what the story was about and what each scene meant, but he never gave specific instructions. One day shortly after I started work [on *For Better For Worse* (1919)], a young actor asked Mr. DeMille if he would explain to him how he wanted him to play such and such a scene.

"Certainly not!" Mr. DeMille bellowed. "This is not an acting school. I hired you because I trust you to be professional. *Professional!*" he thundered. "When you do something wrong, *that* is when I will talk to you."

—Swanson, in her *Swanson on Swanson* (New York: Random House, 1980)

I acquired my expensive tastes from DeMille. When the script called for diamonds, he bought or borrowed real gems. If he needed flowers for a set, he sent fleets of trucks through lower California buying up hothouses. If you were supposed to wear an ermine wrap in a scene, it was ermine, not rabbit. [Swanson also worked on DeMille's *Don't Change Your Husband* (1919), *Why Change Your Wife?* (1920), *Something to Think About* (1920) and *The Affairs of Anatole* (1921).]

—Swanson, interviewed for *The Saturday Evening Post*, 22 July 1950

Allan [Dwan] said he tried to direct as much in New York and as little in Hollywood as possible because in Hollywood he felt trapped in the glamour system, whereas in the little studio in Astoria he had to cut corners and force himself to be truly creative....

Zaza [1923] turned out to be the fastest, easiest, most enjoyable picture I had ever made. Allan and I worked together like Mutt and Jeff one day, like Maggie and Jiggs the next, but we both loved every second of it. If anything we needed didn't exist, Allan invented it. He was a tinkerer, a fixer, a doer. When the New York summer heat hit us, nobody wilted. Allan simply ordered giant blocks of ice, placed huge fans behind them, and created his own cool air. He prepared everything with such a care that the first take was often the best one, and he had the confidence to know that and shoot a whole long sequence at once....

Allan used a script like a blueprint. The best things in the picture we made up as we went along. We were always stretching, always trying to improve the scene up to the last minute before we shot it. Watching the rushes, I could see that the energy level of *Zaza* was higher than in any other film I'd made in years. Allan had found some mysterious way of unleashing me. There was a long, elaborate fight scene in the picture, for instance, and he made Mary Thurman and me do it in one take. We had to make it good just by our acting. We couldn't depend at all on sets and costumes. And Allan convinced us we could. In a minute, he could push the most phlegmatic member of the cast to peaks of excitement. He was extraordinary. [Swanson also worked on Dwan's *A Society Scandal* (1924), *Manhandled* (1924), *Her Love Story* (1924), *Wages of Virtue* (1924), *The Coast of Folly* (1925), *Stage Struck* (1925) and *What a Widow!* (1930).]

—Swanson, in her *Swanson on Swanson* (New York: Random House, 1980)

[Billy] Wilder called [concerning *Sunset Boulevard* (1950)]; I was rude to him. I said what the hell do you have to test me for? You want to see if I'm still alive, do you? Or do you doubt I can act? And I asked him to send me some goddam pages of script. So far all I heard was talk. So he sent some pages, I don't know, about twenty pages. I liked what I read. I was intrigued by the character, yes, but I was also horrified by this element of it being anti-Hollywood. I took it as an attack on the movie industry....

Then I got a phone call from darling George Cukor. Oh, he is so persuasive, charm the birds out of the trees, that dear man. He said this was the greatest part of my career and I'd be remembered for this part and that Billy Wilder had become the number one director of Hollywood. He swore that Mr. Wilder would do justice to me. He said I had to come out and test for it and I did and we started shooting without a completed script and sometimes we were working only one day ahead. And Mr. Wilder shot in continuity and it was the first time in my many years in pictures, the very first, I was in a film done like this.

—Swanson, interviewed by Maurice Zolotow for *Billy Wilder in Hollywood* (New York: G.P Putnam's Sons, 1977)

The script [of *Sunset Boulevard*, by Charles Brackett, Billy Wilder and D.M. Marshman, Jr.] described my character, Norma Desmond, very sketchily: "She is a little woman. There is a curious style, a great sense of high voltage about her." The tone of the piece was a mixture of gothic eeriness and nostalgia for the old Hollywood of the twenties....

Edith Head and I together created perfect clothes for my character — a trifle exotic, a trifle exaggerated, a trifle out of date. For my scene with Mr. DeMille, I designed a hat with a single white peacock feather, remembering the peacock-feather headdress everyone was so superstitious about when Mr. DeMille and I made the scenes with the lions in *Male and Female* [1919]....

In April, Erich von Stroheim arrived from France. We had long since reconciled our differences over *Queen Kelly*, but I hadn't seen him in eight or nine years.... He looked grand, and we reminisced for hours when Billy Wilder showed us a print of *Queen Kelly* and asked me if he could use a scene from it for a scene in *Sunset Boulevard*, where Norma and Joe [William Holden] are watching one of her old pictures. Of course I didn't mind, I said; it was a brilliant idea because almost no one had ever seen *Kelly*....

Mr. DeMille took direction like a pro. Erich von Stroheim, on the other hand, kept adding things and suggesting things and asking if scenes might not be reshot — very much in his grand old manner of perfectionism regardless of schedule or cost. Billy Wilder always listened patiently to his suggestions, and took some, but more often he would say that he really didn't see how this or that change would improve the scene or further the story, and therefore he thought we should leave it alone. In one scene Erich, as Max...drives [Norma] and Joe to Paramount in her old Isotta Fraschini with leopard upholstery. Erich didn't now how to drive, which humiliated him, but he acted the scene, and the action of driving, so completely that he was exhausted after each take, even though the car was being towed by ropes the whole while.

—Swanson, in her *Swanson on Swanson* (New York: Random House, 1980)

In 1923, when I was making *Manhandled* in Astoria, in between scenes one day, I picked up a walking stick and just began impersonating Chaplin for the fun of it. The director, Allan Dwan, saw me and said, "We'll put that in the picture" — in those days they were always adding something to the script, or taking something out. The studio didn't know there was a law then that said you couldn't impersonate anyone, so the first release of the picture is the only one with my Chaplin impersonation in it — after that, it was deleted.... 27 years after *Manhandled*, I did my Chaplin impersonation again, in *Sunset Boulevard*, because Billy Wilder asked me as Norma Desmond to do some impersonations to amuse Joe.... Mr. Wilder suggested Doug Fairbanks and I said, "Why don't I just do my Charlie Chaplin?" He said fine and he had the wardrobe department bring in 50 derbies for me to choose from.

Q. Has anyone ever done an impersonation of you in a film?

A. I tried to do myself in two pictures — *Sunset Boulevard* and *Airport 1975* [1975, Jack Smight] — and I discovered that I didn't know how to do myself — how I walked, how I talked, what my gestures were, anything. You know, it's the most difficult thing in the world to do yourself.

—Swanson, interviewed by Steven M.L. Aronson for *Interview*, Feb 1981

Blanche SWEET [1896-1986]

Born: Sarah Sweet in Chicago. After two films for the Edison Co. (both 1909), she joined the Biograph Company where, between 1909 and 1914, she appeared in more than 50 films for D.W. Griffith beginning with A Corner in Wheat.

I can remember *Oil and Water* [1913] because Griffith was trying for something, a characterization. You didn't usually have time for characterizations in pictures those days, because you got through as quickly as you could do it adequately. I mean you did the best you could, but you couldn't take time.

We had a system, if anything could be called a system in those days. For instance, we were supposed to do exteriors, and it was raining or snowing, and we couldn't do them. Then, we would take that day to stay inside and rehearse several ideas, not just one but several, so that we would have a backlog on which to draw when something happened like inclement weather. Then we could go right into shooting in the studio. I don't know if other directors did that or not, but that was his way of doing it.

—Sweet, interviewed by Anthony Slide for *The Griffith Actresses* (London: Tantivy Press, 1973)

I doubt if any of us wanted to leave because we were all devoted to [Griffith]. There wasn't a member of that company, male or female, who didn't love that man. It's difficult to explain this devotion. We had great respect for his ability and understanding as a director. He opened up vista after vista. He was a marvelous actor himself, although he didn't make good as an actor. One minute he was discouraging to you, and the next minute he was inspiring you. I say "discouraging to you" because if you weren't getting the scene as he felt you should, he would show you how it should be done. He'd show you so beautifully that you felt, "Oh, I'd never be able to do it that way...."

He was a one-man show. He had to do everything himself: develop the original idea, carry it through, do it his own way, spend what he wanted on it. He was never good at working with anybody else — except [cameraman] Billy Bitzer. They were like fingers on a hand, and they got along beautifully. But that was different because Billy wasn't in a position of control. He would have ideas and then bat them back and forth with Mr. Griffith — you couldn't really know whose idea it was. Often they didn't know themselves.

—Sweet, interviewed by Bernard Rosenberg and Harry Silverstein for *The Real Tinsel* (New York: Macmillan, 1970)

T

Constance TALMADGE [1899-1973]

Born: Brooklyn, N.Y.; sister to Norma Talmadge [1897-1957]. Work as an extra at The Vitagraph Studio preceded her starring role in a series of short films either as "The Vitagraph Tomboy" or "Connie." In 1916, she played "The Mountain Girl" in D.W. Griffith's Intolerance:

I went to see Mr. Griffith in New York one day with Norma. Right away he exclaimed, "The Mountain Girl." I was a bit angry and puzzled. Mountain Girl, indeed! I glanced down at my smart new tailored suit, at my modish shoes and gloves. Then I decided it must be my hat — that it probably wasn't on straight. I was pretty mad, but of course I didn't say anything. He kept looking at me, and by and by he asked us to go for a ride in his new car. We went, and he dashed around corners and across streets at a terrible rate. I sat with him and enjoyed it hugely. And when I laughed with joy when we dashed through the throngs — two policemen stopped us at different times — he again said, "The mountain girl." I guess he was testing me out to see if I were really as daring as I looked. I'm glad he found out that I was....

My two pet aversions were forced upon me in *Intolerance*. I had to drive horses — and drive them like mad; and I loathe onions — and I had to eat them. As the scene wasn't satisfactory — I guess an awful face or something — I had to eat them again. And then as they wanted another picture of the scene anyhow, why I had to eat them again.

It wasn't an easy matter getting used to the horses. First I fed them lumps of sugar to get on the good side of them. Then I drove them slowly around the studio lot attached to a light wagon. Next they were taken to San Pedro, where there is a big expanse of country, and I drove them fast, and then faster. Of course, there were sentinels posted about the field to see that no harm came to me....

About milking the goat?.... How did I happen to bite her ear in that scene? Why Mr. Griffith called out to me just then, "Do something funny!" I had been dying all along to bite Nanny's ear, just to see her jump. So I did that.

—Talmadge, interviewed by Grace Kingsley for *Photoplay Magazine*, May 1917

Never again shall I work with Douglas Fairbanks. I nearly died when I was his leading woman. Of course I like him. Every one loves Douglas, but I cannot stand the strain. A hundred times during the filming of a picture he risks his life. Why, in *The Matrimaniac* [1916, Paul Powell], he stood in front of an express train until it wasn't ten feet from him and then he jumped. One woman fainted and I didn't get over the shock for a day. He never fakes anything even when it would do just as well. He seems to like taking the risk, but I used to tell him that dead men make no pictures.

—Talmadge, interviewed by Harriette Underhill for *The New York Tribune*, Oct 1917

One of the hardest things to learn [for the role of Ming Toy in *East is West* (1922, Chester Franklin)] was to walk and stand naturally in those funny flat heeled shoes. After wearing high heels for so long, I felt all the time as though I were tipping over backward. Wearing these shoes, however, makes it easier to learn the queer little walk that all Chinese women use. It is hard for me to explain just how you do it: you just have to do it, that's all. You take very short steps, of course, but there's more to learn about it than just short steps....

When we began to make the picture, the director was afraid that the audience would see by my lips that I was speaking English, so I had to get another Chinese tutor and learn to speak the right words in Chinese. I am terribly conceited about this accomplishment. I spring my vocabulary on my adoring family until they cry for help.

—Talmadge, interviewed for *Motion Picture Classic*; undated clipping in the files of The New York Public Library for the Performing Arts

Akim TAMIROFF [1899-1972]

Born: Baku, Russia. Studies at The Moscow Art Theatre and work on the Moscow stage preceded a 1923 tour to the U.S. to appear in two Chekhov plays. Remaining in the U.S., he made his film debut in Okay America (1932, Tay Garnett); in 1936, he played General Yang in Lewis Milestone's The General Died at Dawn:

A good script has characters, not just words. An actor must know his part. He must be at home with the character because it has a head, a heart, arms, legs, everything, just like a human being.

That is why it is harder to be a great actor on the screen than on the stage. You must know who you are and how you will act, because here the scenes are not shot in sequence. Sometimes they shoot the last scene in the picture first, and you must know.

I remember in *The General Died at Dawn*, we had the big scene, the last scene in the picture first, and everybody said, "Akim, you're overacting. It is too much." I was worried. But director Milestone said, "Don't listen to them, Akim. It was just right. Just what we need."

—Tamiroff, interviewed for *The Chicago Daily News*, 4 Jan 1941

I've been a sinister villain representing all nations including the Chinese and excepting my native Russia in six years of pictures, and I was overwhelmed with delight when Mr. [Cecil B.] DeMille offered me a comic character in *The Buccaneer* [1938].

I suppose now that I've played comedy, I'm destined for it forever. But I'm happiest in it. It's the sort of thing I always did on the stage.... I have no true feeling for heavies. I like to make the public laugh.

—Tamiroff, interviewed for *The New York Post*, 19 Jan 1938

I admire DeMille for many things, of course, but most for one thing. Whatever he wants he gets. It does not matter what it is, he gets it. That shows in his pictures. He decides what he will do, and no matter how impossible others say it is, he does it.

Now I do a great deal of study at home. I work on a part a long time ahead. In *Union Pacific* [1939], I had to use a bull whip. Mr. DeMille suggested I learn how to carry one around — not to use it, of course, that would be too difficult; but just to get used to handling it.

I had four months before the picture started. I got a teacher and I learned to use that bull whip. You should see me. I am an expert. I can whip cigarettes out of your mouth. I can handle that whip as though I were in a circus. DeMille could not believe it. But that is the way I like to work.

—Tamiroff, interviewed for *The Milwaukee Journal*, 5 Jan 1943

Jessica TANDY [1909-]

Born: London, England. Studies at The Ben Greet Academy of Acting and work on the London stage (from 1927) and on Broadway (from 1930) preceded her film debut in the British feature, The Indiscretions of Eve (1932, Cecil Lewis). In 1989, she played Daisy Werthan opposite Morgan Freeman as Hoke in Bruce Beresford's adaptation of Alfred Uhry's Driving Miss Daisy:

[Daisy is] a very spiky lady, fiercely jealous of her independence. She was the product of her time and she had the prejudices of her time. But she *does* grow. She learns. By the end of the film she's really changed....

Even in the nursing home, where Daisy is down to her absolute basics, I don't think she would have given up. It's just that she suffered what we all come to as we get older — less ability, physically, to do things.... Those scenes [after her stroke] were painful for Daisy, and therefore painful for me. I know people who skip a beat now and then. I know how angry it makes them — they say a word and it's not the one they mean. It's frightening.

—Tandy, interviewed by Glenn Collins for *The New York Times*, 8 Feb 1990

[Morgan Freeman] was so sure about everything. I just had to go along with him. I could ask him a lot of things about it. After all he grew up in the south; he would know what it was like...he would have greater knowledge than I of how people behaved.

—Tandy, interviewed by Tom Provenzano for *Drama-Logue*, 21 Dec 1989-3 Jan 1990

Elizabeth TAYLOR [1932-]

Born: London, England; raised in California from age 7. A child star, she made her debut at Universal Studios in Man or Mouse (1940) opposite Carl "Alfalfa" Switzer. In 1951, she played Angela Vickers in George Stevens' A Place in the Sun:

The first time I ever considered *acting* when I was young was in *A Place in the Sun.* I was...thrilled to be in the film because it was my first kind of adult role. It was a tricky part, because the girl is so rich and spoiled that it would have been easy to play her as absolutely vacuous. But I think she was a girl who could care a great deal.

That was when I first met Montgomery Clift.... I watched how much time he spent on concentration — which has since become the key to my kind of acting....

My next big opportunity didn't come until I was married to Michael Wilding and heard about *Giant* [1956, George Stevens], which was going to be done by Warner Brothers. The role I wanted started at the age of eighteen and ended up a very pedicured, manicured, well-coiffed, well-dressed fifty....

George Stevens' first choice was Grace Kelly, but they couldn't get her, and M-G-M didn't want to let me go. So I had to stamp my flat feet for quite a while...pleading to be given a chance to do a film I considered good. I had to go almost on a sit-down strike....

I had been working on *Cat on a Hot Tin Roof* [1958, Richard Brooks] for two weeks when [husband] Mike [Todd] died, and having that to finish saved me in a way. I couldn't tolerate what I was, and it gave me somebody else to become. When I was Maggie was the only time I could function. The rest of the time I was a robot. When they said, "Cut," I would go back to my dressing room, and I don't remember much what I did....

But it was a cruel film to be making at that time — all about death. There was one line Judith Anderson [as Big Mama] had to say to me: "I guess things never turn out the way you dream they are going to turn out." Mike and I had planned our lives up to age one hundred. The one thing neither of us planned on was death.

—Taylor, in her *Elizabeth: An Informal Memoir* (New York: Harper & Row, 1965)

It's a terribly mean thing they've done to me. Sol C. Siegel, head of MGM production, insists I appear in a picture called *Butterfield 8* [1960, Daniel Mann]. I refused for two reasons. First, it's the most pornographic script I've ever read, and secondly I don't think the studio is treating me fairly. They have the power to keep me off the screen for the next two years unless I agree to do *Butterfield* and it looks as if that's what they're going to do. I've been with the studio seventeen years. During that time I never was asked to play such a horrible role as the one in *Butterfield.*

The leading lady is almost a prostitute. When I pointed this out to Mr. Siegel, he said he would clean up the script. But she's still a sick nymphomaniac. The whole thing is so unpalatable I wouldn't do it for anything — under any condition.

—Taylor, quoted by Dick Sheppard in his *Elizabeth* (Garden City, N.Y.: Doubleday & Co., 1974)

I really could have done without *Cleopatra* [1963, Joseph L. Mankiewicz] except for meeting Richard [Burton]. I think it was a little like damnation to everybody. Hume Cronyn, when he was told that it was his last shot, was on top of the barge — maybe three stories up. With his gray wig and beard and his sandals and his long smock, he yelled "Hallelujah!" and leaped overboard in the most perfect swan dive.

Hume was the only one who really went out with style. For the rest of us, *Cleopatra* just sort of dribbled off. After my last shot, there was a curiously sad sort of aching, empty feeling — but such astronomical relief. It was finally over. And then it wasn't finally over. Months later I had to go to Paris and do some more. It was like a disease, shooting that film — an illness one had a very difficult time recuperating from.

Richard and I went through a whole set of qualms over taking the roles of [George and Martha in *Who's Afraid Of Virginia Woolf?* (1966, Mike Nichols)]. Let's face it, we were not obvious casting and a lot of people hooted at the idea. For me, the age thing was wrong. I had never played a part like that. I couldn't imagine myself as Martha, and I couldn't imagine myself dominating Richard. It was the most difficult part I had ever read and made me feel as though in my whole life I'd never acted, never interpreted a line....

I wanted to create my own Martha who had nothing to do with anybody else's Martha. I think she is a desperate woman who has the softness of the underbelly of a baby turtle. She covers it up with the toughness of the shell, which she paints red. Her veneer is bawdy; it's sloppy, it's slouchy, it's snarly. But there are moments when the facade cracks and you see the vulnerability, the infinite pain of this woman inside whom, years ago, life almost died but is still flickering.

Mike Nichols...and Ernie Lehman, the producer [and screenwriter], decided I should be about forty-five. And then we did eight different make-ups, and we all chose the same one. I liked it immediately. Once I got all the trappings on, Martha just happened without anybody discussing it, without my even thinking much about it.

In the wardrobe tests, assuming Martha, taking her on gradually, it was the walk that happened first. I can't describe it. It's a state of mind; it's Martha's walk. Then came the voice. It's in a much lower key than my own, much more bawdy, much more raucous. I've done something with my accent, I don't know exactly what. The hardest thing was the laugh. Martha's laugh is mostly vulgar. There are only one or two times that she laughs genuinely, from inside, and that's quite a different one.

It was very exciting. I had to keep on generating other things every day, because in the film as the evening wears on, there is the drunkenness, the disintegration. It's not static. Martha goes slowly down until at the end there is a new, different element in both Martha and her husband, George. It's like a patient's chart in a hospital.

Though it was such a hard part, because it was such a complete change from anything else, it was strangely one of the easiest things I've ever done. It was stepping into somebody else's skin who was so remote from my own skin that it was like wearing a mustache and beard and old long wig and cloak.

—Taylor, in her *Elizabeth: An Informal Memoir* (New York: Harper & Row, 1965)

Robert TAYLOR [1911-1969]

Born: Spangler Arlington Brugh in Filley, Nebraska. Studies at Doane College, Pomona College and The Neely Dixon Dramatic School in Hollywood preceded his film debut in Handy Andy (1934, David Butler). The following year, he played Bobby Merrick in John Stahl's Magnificent Obsession:

I started out with terrific enthusiasm. I know I was a trial to...John M. Stahl.... I acted all over the place. Enthusiasm is highly important to an actor, just as it is to anyone who wants to make progress in his work, but in an inexperienced actor, it will always make him overact till he learns better.

—Taylor, interviewed by Rosalind Shaffer for *Screen Book*, Sept 1937

John Stahl...approached the responsibility of a director...with infinite care and painstaking slowness. It was not uncommon for us to do 30, 40, 50 takes on a relatively simple scene.

—Taylor, in *Variety*, 1966; repr. in *Film Fan Monthly*, June 1969

Garbo is probably one of the most misunderstood women anywhere. I met her for the first time when I walked on to the set to make *Camille* [1937, George Cukor]. She said, "How do-you-do?" Then she went to work. She wasn't rude or condescending. She's naturally shy....

There's something about Garbo's silence and her concentration that gets you, way down inside. The woman is one of the most powerful personalities in the world. She wears a sort of flat, colorless make-up that gives her a suggestion of something out of this world, and that's just what she is. There's a radiation from her when you're playing an intense scene that makes you play up to it, whether you have the stuff in you or not. She simply makes you find it and give.

—Taylor, interviewed by Dugal O'Liam for *Modern Screen*, Mar 1942

Miss Garbo is unhurried. Her own sure poise is infectious. By her own manner of perfect assurance she imparts confidence to those around her. I felt it constantly....

This experience is the most interesting I have encountered, not only because *Camille* is such a splendid story for the screen and because Miss Garbo was so pleasant in our professional relationship, but also for the remarkable opportunity

I have had to study the dramatic power of restraint, for which I have to thank Miss Garbo.

—Taylor, interviewed for the press packet for *Camille* (MGM, 1937)

Shirley TEMPLE [1928-]

Born: Santa Monica, California. After her debut at age 3 in The Runt Page (1931, Roy La Verne), she went on to featured roles beginning with Stand Up and Cheer (1934, Hamilton MacFadden). Later that same year, she was cast as Shirley Blake and sang "On the Good Ship Lollipop" in Bright Eyes, the first of four films for David Butler:

I like Mr. Butler.... He is nice to get along with because he calls me "One-Take Temple," and he lets me off every night at five so I can go home and play with the kids on the block. But I wish Mother would speak to him and make him say "please." I would like him a lot better then, and then I wouldn't mind saying "please" myself.

Then, I am going to ask Mr. Zanuck to make the print larger on my scripts. I don't like small type because it is hard to read and I can't read very well yet. I have just finished the Fourth Reader, and the letters are so big in that I don't have to squint. I would like to have glasses to read the scripts Mr. Zanuck gives me, but Mother says glasses wouldn't look good on me. I don't know why, because other people wear glasses to read small print — and I'm smaller than they are.

But sometimes I fool Mother and don't read the script at all. I say, "Mother, I can't read that big word," or I say that I am very tired and can't learn any more. Then Mother takes the script and reads it to me. I can learn faster doing it that way. She reads my speech and I remember it pretty well. [Temple also worked on Butler's *The Little Colonel* (1935), *The Littlest Rebel* (1935) and *Captain January* (1936).]

—Temple, in *Liberty Magazine*, Dec 1935

Damon Runyon's classic lines for *Little Miss Marker* [1934, Alexander Hall] were riddled with insolence, as captivating to adult audiences in a theatre as they would have been infuriating in real life. Smart-aleck behavior was not my normal style, but I plunged into my task with something more than professional verve. One of my early rehearsals was with Dorothy Dell, the warm-hearted blond gun moll called Bangles. Stuck as my foster mother on behalf of her mob, Dell was attempting to get me to eat breakfast and behave like her version of a lady....

I felt treated like an equal.... Time and again during the film she turned out to be a splendid foil for my energy and exuberance. My special affection for her was based on this positive attitude, one which made me feel inches taller than I was.

Adolphe Menjou's film character was a hard-bitten, lovable gambler who liked Marky, but off-camera he treated me with the reticence adults commonly reserve for children, sometimes staring at me fixedly without comment.... He spent little time directly with me, always preferring to watch me from a distance.

Like Dorothy Dell...Carole Lombard [on *Now and Forever* (1934, Henry Hathaway)] was a prankster, a lovely, funny, generous lady. Easily dropping down to her knees, she echoed my jubilant yelps about all sorts of nonsense, her great expressive eyes crinkling at the corners....

Menjou's earlier allegation concerning my competitive attitude obviously was well remembered. Before many days passed other actors on the film were fiercely crowding me at every turn with confounding new tricks. However, I was not without a strong ally. Perched quietly on her stool apart from the main activity, knitting unobtrusively but keeping track, Mother was a superlative auditor of events. Privately we tried to devise ways to obstruct each theft....

[Bill "Bojangles" Robinson was] a superlative teacher, imperturbable and kind, but demanding. Although bubbling with energy, his physical motions were so controlled and fluid, they came out looking relaxed. He made it look easy, but was not one to pick his way gingerly. I must be guided solely by muscular memory. I must visualize my own sounds, not think about them. It must all be reflexive and unthinking, the sound of my taps telling me how I am doing, setting the pace and controlling the sequence. Every one of my taps had to ring crisp and clear in the best cadence. Otherwise I had to do it over.

That sort of repetitive rehearsal lay behind our familiar staircase dance in the southern plantation mansion in *The Little Colonel*. We made an unusual couple. A raggedy urchin with tousled curls paired with a regal black man in striped vest and brass buttons and patent-leather shoes. Every sound matched, every gesture, the scuffle, the staccato tap, a sharp-toed kick to the stile, a trip-time race up and down the staircase, tapping as we went. The smile on my face was not acting; I was ecstatic.

—Temple, in her *Child Star: An Autobiography* (New York: McGraw-Hill Publishing Co., 1988)

Alice TERRY [1899-1987]

Born: Alice Taafe in Vincennes, Indiana. After working as an extra at Inceville, and playing a few larger roles, beginning with Not My Sister (1916, Charles Giblyn), she retired from acting and took a job in the cutting room at Lasky's. Returning to acting, she won a minor role in The Day She Paid (1919) directed by Rex Ingram; later Terry and Ingram were married and Terry became the leading lady in thirteen of his features, including The Four Horsemen of the Apocalypse (1921), the first of two in which she co-starred opposite Rudolph Valentino:

We had a wonderful time making that picture. A spirit of camaraderie enveloped the whole company and I'll never forget how good they were, each trying to help me. Mr. Ingram took infinite pains to explain what he wanted brought out; Miss [June] Mathis sat on the set and told me the thousand and one things a woman sees in a role such as mine; while Rudie encouraged me every minute....

[Valentino] always suggested more than he gave. He underacted always.... I always had the impression that I was playing with a volcano that might erupt at any minute. It never did, but that was the secret of his appeal.... [She also starred opposite Valentino in Ingram's *The Conquering Power* (1921).]

Ramon [Novarro]...was the best actor of all.... I think that Valentino was so much a type that he couldn't have played certain scenes.... Ramon, though, I could have seen in almost any part outside of an American boy. I think he had more ham in him — I don't like to use the word ham. Maybe it's nerve or confidence to get up and try something where someone like Ronald Colman, for instance, wouldn't try because he would feel silly. But Ramon would attempt anything — comedy, drama, crazy scenes, everything, and he could do it. I always thought he was capable of doing better than almost anyone except possibly John Barrymore who had the same thing. [Terry and Novarro worked together on Ingram's *Trifling Women* (1922), *The Prisoner of Zenda* (1922), *Where the Pavement Ends* (1923), *Scaramouche* (1923) and *The Arab* (1924); Novarro also had a bit part in *The Four Horsemen of the Apocalypse*. Terry also worked on Ingram's *Hearts are Trump* (1920), *Turn to the Right* (1921), *Mare Nostrum* (1925), *The Magician* (1926), *The Garden of Allah* (1927) and *The Three Passions* (1929).]

—Terry, interviewed by Liam O'Leary for his *Rex Ingram: Master of the Silent Cinema* (Dublin: Academy Press, 1980)

Danny THOMAS [1914-1991]

Born: Amos Jacobs in Deerfield, Michigan. Work as a radio singer and as a nightclub MC/comedian preceded his film debut in The Unfinished Dance (1947, Henry Koster). In 1951, he played Stanley in Lloyd Bacon's Call Me Mister:

Some comedians are most successful when scattering sunshine all over the place. But not me. I'm at my best when things are at their worst. The more I suffer and complain, the more laughs I get....

Therefore, the part of Stanley in *Call Me Mister* had a built-in appeal for me. With Stanley, things invariably were terrible. He was married to the pots and pans in the Army and wanted a divorce. On the other hand, he'd have liked to be a lot more cozy with Betty Grable, who played Kay Hudson, and he couldn't get to first base with her.

These and other tribulations gave me plenty to complain about in the picture, and made me as happy as a well-fed lark.

—Thomas, in *The Saturday Evening Post*, 12 Apr 1952

Sybil THORNDIKE [1882-1976]

Born: Gainsborough, England. Considerable work on the British stage preceded her film debut in Moth and Rust (1921, Sidney Morgan). In 1957, she played the Queen Dowager in Laurence Olivier's The Prince and the Showgirl:

When I was in that film version of *The Prince and the Showgirl* with Larry [Olivier] and Marilyn Monroe I couldn't hear a word she was saying as I watched her doing her first scenes. I said to myself: "Is this the great young star from Hollywood? I think she's awful." I said as much to Larry and he said: "Come and see the rushes, darling." Well, I did and everything she'd done that I'd thought was a muck-up came over beautifully on the screen. *I* was the old ham. I'm afraid I've never mastered the movie technique. It always looks underplayed to me — a bit careless.

—Thorndike, interviewed by Logan Gourlay for *Olivier* (London: Weidenfield & Nicolson, 1973)

Gene TIERNEY [1920-1991]

Born: Brooklyn, N.Y. Work on Broadway preceded her film debut in The Return of Frank James (1940, Fritz Lang). In 1944, she played the title role of Laura, the first of four films for Otto Preminger:

Otto had gotten his way with [Darryl F.] Zanuck in casting two of the major roles: Dana Andrews and Clifton Webb. Both were regarded as gambles. Andrews was unproven as a leading man. Webb had...spent [most] of his career on Broadway and had an image that was, well, prissy....

It was pleasant to observe at close range the professional respect between Clifton and Preminger. The role of the acid-tongued Waldo Lydecker was the most demanding of all, with long stretches of dialogue.

There was a wonderfully brittle edge to Clifton, his manner, his speech, the way he moved. Part of what came across on the screen, the impression of a man very tightly strung, was true in person. After we finished filming, he suffered a nervous breakdown....

I never felt my own performance was much more than adequate. I am pleased that audiences still identify me with Laura.... Their tributes, I believe are for the character — the dream-like Laura — rather than any gifts I brought to the role....

—Tierney, in her (with Mickey Herskowitz) *Self-Portrait* (New York: Wyden Books, 1979)

Ellen [in *Leave Her to Heaven* (1946)] was an abnormal person — a woman who loved her husband [Cornel Wilde] so jealously that she killed his brother [Darryl Hickman] and her own unborn child....

It was hard to make Ellen's complex personality understandable to movie audiences let alone sympathetic. John Stahl's direction helped me very much. He has the knack of making you feel attractive, and capable of meeting any acting demand. He gives you so much confidence....

I felt she illustrated a moral important to women. We are inclined to be too possessive. Ellen's case showed the dangers of this attitude. Her possessiveness unbalanced her completely.

I particularly enjoyed playing the scene in which Ellen confessed her crimes to her husband. Here, at last, she was revealed as not merely a cruel woman but a pitiful one, hopelessly twisted mentally.

—Tierney, in *The Saturday Evening Post*, 15 June 1946

When no one else in Hollywood would offer me an opportunity, Otto Preminger did. A friend, genuine and unafraid, Otto signed me in 1962 for the all-star cast he was assembling for *Advise and Consent*. I was to play Dolly Harrison, the Washington hostess who has an affair with the Senate majority leader [Walter Pidgeon]. It was my first film since *The Left Hand of God* [1955, Edward Dmytryk], and I immediately ran into a problem unrelated to my ability to act. I was considered uninsurable because of my mental history [she had been in and out of sanitoria in the interim]. Otto told the insurance company flatly that, if they rejected me, he would cancel his coverage with them for this and any future productions. They caved in. That was quite a risk for Preminger to take. I could have fallen ill again. Thankfully, I didn't....

My part was less than major, but it had glamor.... I enjoyed playing a mature woman in a film that dealt with mature subjects. In my youth, my taste had always run to what I called cut crystal and champagne pictures; deep rugs, chandeliers, and gay weekends. Swimming to the side of a pool and stretching out a hand for a glass of champagne. Pictures that made life seem secure, when everything else in the world is insecure. [Tierney also worked on Preminger's *Whirlpool* (1949) and *Where the Sidewalk Ends* (1950).]

—Tierney, in her (with Mickey Herskowitz) *Self-Portrait* (New York: Wyden Books, 1979)

Kenneth TOBEY [1919-]

Born: San Francisco. Pre-law studies at The University of California were abandoned for a scholarship to The Neighborhood Playhouse in N.Y. Classmate Gregory Peck convinced Tobey to try films; his debut was in a Hopalong Cassidy film, Dangerous Venture (1947, George Archainbaud). Howard Hawks hired him for I Was a Male War Bride (1949), then starred him in The Thing (1951):

Q. Who really directed *The Thing*?

A. Howard Hawks. Technically, of course, Chris Nyby directed it and is given screen credit for it.... He was new at directing and Mr. Hawks maintained a kind of overseeage on the picture.

Q. Was a lot of ad-libbing done on the set?

A. Howard has a wonderful ear. He can hear reality a mile away. He'd listen to a scene during a rehearsal and, if it didn't sound normal or if it sounded a little stilted, he'd say: "Let's do that again. Let's just listen to it and see what happens." So we'd do it again and he'd say: "What you're saying there doesn't seem to fit somehow. Can you think of anything you'd like to say instead?" We went on like that a good deal....

Q. The cast in *The Thing* worked beautifully together.

A. Well, it helped that Howard used a lot of not-too-well-known people. We all kind of fell in love with his style and, as it happens in dramas, you get a camaraderie and an essence of jollity and fun that comes across very clearly, I think. This happens more on the stage, because you rehearse more. Of course, we rehearsed a great deal on this picture.

Q. It's amazing that you say you rehearsed so much when the film looks like it was a first take all the way through.

A. Actually, it takes a lot of rehearsal to get that unrehearsed quality.

—Tobey, interviewed by Mark Frank for *Photon* #22, 1972

Lily TOMLIN [1939-]

Born: Mary Jean Tomlin in Detroit. Studies with Paul Curtis and work in coffee houses and on TV (notably Rowan and Martin's Laugh-In) preceded her film debut in Nashville (1975, Robert Altman):

I'm so used to deciding what my characters are going to do and say that I do have some problems with movies, but I'm getting more used to it. *Nashville* was a special case, because we were encouraged to improvise. I had relatively little screen time and Altman was very freewheeling. Since then I have tried to bring as much creativity to my roles as possible. But it can be confusing because as I understand a part, I try to make the best selections I can to bring the role to fruition, and whenever people don't agree with my choices I get confused.

[Working on *The Late Show* (1977, Robert Benton)] I didn't think I was being lit properly. I have very black hair, and we were shooting in small spaces and they were bouncing a lot of light off the ceilings. So I wanted more fill light because it affects everything. It affects your character and your performance...everything. And of course if you're a woman, they just think you're being vain. And all these guys on the crew would pat my hand and patronize me and say things like, "Oh, you're a pretty girl. I'd marry you." Ha! So I started carrying a mirror on the set, and I would refuse to shoot the scene until they changed the lighting.

When the script [of *All of Me* (1984, Carl Reiner)] first came to me there were all sorts of unconscious things in it...things against women and stuff like that. You see, it's the consciousness that influences me most about material, and very often people just have blind spots. In the initial draft of the film [by screenwriter Phil Alden Robinson], whenever someone crossed Edwinna she'd slap them because she was so arrogant. Now, I allowed a certain amount of that because the character was emotionally immature. But then later, the slapping carried over into the sex scenes and that wasn't OK, see? But they changed it to my satisfaction. The image of a man in bed with a woman and him slapping her was just gone, as far as I was concerned, that was a real bottom line for me in accepting the role. But if you're going to print any of this you have to say how open they were to discussing these things and to making the changes I wanted. They weren't so invested in any of it to the degree that they weren't willing to change it.

—Tomlin, interviewed by Vito Russo for *The Advocate/Liberation Publications, Inc*, 18 Mar 1986

Spencer TRACY [1900-1967]

Born: Milwaukee, Wisconsin. Studies at The American Academy of Dramatic Arts in N.Y., work on the N.Y. stage, and a film debut in the short, Taxi Talks (1930, Arthur Hurley), preceded his feature film debut, Up the River (1930, John Ford). In San Francisco (1936, W.S. Van Dyke), he played Father Mullin, the first of three roles as a priest:

I had a tough time deciding whether or not to get myself out of the part. I thought of how my father wanted me to be a priest, and I wondered if it would be sacrilegious for me to *play* a priest. All of my Catholic training and background rolled around in my head, but then I figured Dad would have liked it, and I threw myself into the role.

—Tracy, quoted by Bill Davidson in his *Spencer Tracy: Tragic Idol* (New York: E.P. Dutton, 1987)

Why shouldn't I use the popularity I've earned or had manufactured for me, whichever way you look at it, for something better than putting on a buck and wing or doing a parlor, bedroom and bath farce?

People will listen to us — the Gables, the Munis and the rest of us because we have captured their interest and imagination. We should use that interest, not only for ourselves, but to do good, the kind of good that will live after us....

From now on and insofar as it is within my power, I'm only going to give those character portrayals with which I can do some good. I believe that my part as the priest in *San Francisco* did the kind of good I'm talking about. I think that *Captains Courageous* [1937, Victor Fleming] did good also. I think *Fury* [1936, Fritz Lang] did some good.... Anything that shows up the cruelties men inflict upon their fellow men does good, whether it be the cruelty of grown-ups to kids or the cruelty of the mob to one trapped wretch or the cruelty of those of us who just don't bother.

—Tracy, interviewed by Gladys Hall for *Photoplay Magazine*, Mar 1938

Once before I played the part of a priest. It was as Father Tim in *San Francisco*. I fought against taking that part.... I still think no one can properly portray such a character without having lived as one. Maybe I'm not a real actor but I do know that one can be confronted with a particular role that demands more than is in one's power to give.

This time [in *Boys Town*], instead of putting a fictitious person on the screen, I played the part of a great man who is still alive.... It's difficult to play the part of a living man, but Father Flanagan has given me sound advice and has helped me with the little personal touches which made the role much simpler.... He told me many things which helped a lot in making him real on the screen. [Tracy played Father Flanagan again in *Men of Boys Town* (1941, Norman Taurog).]

—Tracy, in the press release for *Boys Town* (MGM, 1938)

If [*Dr. Jekyll and Mr. Hyde* (1941, Victor Fleming)] turns out to be any good it will be because of that Bergman girl. Watch her. She's one of the finest actresses I've ever seen. It's the way she reacts to Mr. Hyde that will put the character over with the audience. Her own acceptance of the character will be the only thing that could make him credible. It was the same thing in *Captains Courageous*, when I was playing that Portuguese. Well, I didn't know how to speak the language. I didn't even know what a Portuguese accent should be like. I spoke all kinds of crazy jargon, but the thing that made it real to the audience was the way Freddie Bartholomew made it seem real to him. That's what Bergman is going to do with *Hyde*.

—Tracy, interviewed by Thornton Delehanty for *The New York Herald Tribune*, 9 Mar 1941

Woman of the Year [1942, George Stevens] is a welcome, and I think, a timely change of pace for me. I was impressed at first reading with the legitimacy and honesty of the story. It was interesting because it was about understandable people of today and their problems, particularly the readjustment of a man and woman genuinely in love but poles apart in their outlook on life and marriage.

I am not much for farce comedy. Besides the best comedy is that which does not have to be strained for, when laughs come as the result of situations that parallel those that happen every day. They are the best kind and the most believable. Kate [Hepburn] and I both tried to play our comedy scenes as simply and straight as possible.

—Tracy, in the press packet for *Woman of the Year* (MGM, 1942)

Making a film with Katharine Hepburn — it's as if one was acting in the midst of an endless auto accident. [Tracy and Hepburn co-starred in eight subsequent films. See the Hepburn entry for the full list.]

—Tracy, quoted by Bob Bergut in *Les Exquis Mots de l'Entracte* (Paris: Editions Pierre Horay, 1964)

I'll tell you when it all started. I was making that goddam *Plymouth Adventure* [1952, Clarence Brown] and the ulcer was kicking up. I looked lousy and I felt worse and one day I found myself out there in front of a great big process screen. I felt particularly fat that morning, and about 94. I'd seen myself in the mirror and thought I was like an old beat-up barn door. My face looked like it could hold three days of rain. Anyway, there we stood playing the scene and this lovely kid, Gene Tierney, had to look up and say to me, "I love you, John. I love you." And all of a sudden, I was embarrassed. I don't mean for myself. I was embarrassed for *her*.... Later on I began to think, "What the hell will the audience make of this idiocy? This sensational young beauty looking up at this cranky old man and saying all this bullshit." It just didn't make any sense. The only reason she was saying it to me was because I was a big Metro star playing the lead in the picture. That was the moment I decided I ought to begin to think of packing it in as an actor.

—Tracy, quoted by Garson Kanin in *Tracy and Hepburn* (New York: Viking Press, 1971)

It's an odd rule of mine never to discuss a director because, if you can't say something bad about them, few people want to listen. But I want to say something good about one director I've worked with...Stanley Kramer. He's directed me in two pictures, *Inherit the Wind* [1960] and now *Judgment at Nuremberg* [1962].

He approaches an actor — and I mean every actor in the cast — on the basis that the performer is first an intelligent human being, secondly that he has an understanding of the part and thirdly that he is doing his best. And I find that pretty refreshing.

Kramer takes the view that an actor thinks, reflects, reacts and has a feeling about the part he's playing. That's all for the good. It establishes something strong and warm between an actor and his director. It suggests to me that Kramer is willing to concede that there are actors who understand what the script is trying to say.

He is not arbitrary about his interpretation of a role; but he is willing to discuss the characterization and to listen to the ideas of others. All of that is rare. And all of it suggests the kind of guy Kramer really is. When he is dissatisfied with a take and asks for another he explains that he thinks a performer missed something, and his reasons are sensible and to the point. [Tracy's two final films — *It's a Mad, Mad, Mad, Mad World* (1963) and *Guess Who's Coming to Dinner* (1967) were also directed by Kramer.]

—Tracy, in *Films & Filming*, Jan 1962

John TRAVOLTA [1954-]

Born: Englewood, New Jersey. Studies at The Actors Studio Workshop in N.Y. (from age 12) and work on stage and in commercials preceded his success on TV as Vinnie Barbarino in Welcome Back, Kotter. He made his film debut in The Devil's Rain (1975, Robert Fuest). In 1977, he played Tony Manero in John Badham's Saturday Night Fever:

I got the *Fever* script, I read it that night, frowning all through it. I wondered if I could give it enough dimension. Diana [Hyland] took it into the other room, and in about an hour she burst back in. "Baby," she shouted, "you are going to be great in this! This Tony, he's got *all* the colors! First, he's angry *about* something; he hates the trap that Brooklyn and his dumb job are! There's a whole glamorous world out there waiting which he feels only when he dances. And he grows, he gets *out* of Brooklyn!" She went on like that a long time. "He's *miles* from what you've played, and what isn't in the script, you're going to *put* there!" I said, "He's also king of the disco. I'm not that good a dancer." Diana said, "Baby, you're going to *learn*...!"

I never really find a lot of things about a character when I'm reading a script, and that was doubly true with Tony. Even after Diana talked to me, I still saw the negative in him; he read flat to me, and not sympathetic, the way he treats women, and so on. I had to find his vulnerability, so you cared about him, so that *I* cared about him.

—Travolta, interviewed by Tom Burke for *Rolling Stone*, 15 June 1978

Playboy: How many hours did you spend rehearsing the dance routines?

Travolta: I trained about three hours a night for five months in a studio with Deny Terrio, who was with The Lockers. Then, after the lessons, we'd go to the discos and I'd try out my stuff....

Playboy: How else did you prepare?

Travolta: I'd go out to discos and watch the people. I'm very good at absorbing situations and duplicating people. I spent a couple of days in Brooklyn with Norman Wexler, the [script] writer, and I spent a lot of time talking to some of the kids I met. It gave me confidence in what I was doing.

Playboy: Give us an example.

Travolta: A couple of times I went incognito. Sort of sat in the back and watched. And I picked up two or three things right off the bat. The guys at the bar, they all stood like this (stands with his shoulders back, legs about a foot apart, hands clasped in front of his groin, face expressionless). And they all played with their rings. Well, those are two things I did a lot during *Saturday Night*

Fever. Just kind of hands in front, real cool, playing with the rings, checking it out.

I used that in the scene where I went to Stephanie [Karen Lynn Gorney]'s house and I met her boyfriend. I'm sort of awkward; I'm in that purple shirt and black-leather jacket. So when you're awkward, what do you do? You put your hands together in front and you ground yourself — trying to remain cool and solid. It worked perfectly.

—Travolta, interviewed by Judson Klinger for *Playboy*, Dec 1978

Claire TREVOR [1909-]

Born: Claire Wemlinger in Bensonhurst, N.Y. Studies at Columbia University and The American Academy of Dramatic Arts in N.Y., work in stock and on Broadway and performances in two Vitaphone shorts preceded her feature film debut in Life in the Raw (1933, Louis King). In 1937, she played Francey in Dead End:

Q. Did you have the experience with William Wyler on *Dead End* of doing take after take, or did his reputation for that come about later on?

A. William Wyler to me was pure gold. I *loved* working with him. Bear in mind I'd made fast pictures with directors, some who were new and didn't know really what they were doing, and he was a real pro and a genius, a man of taste. The night before I was supposed to shoot he said, "You better come down to the studio about eight o'clock." But I had no wardrobe, so we went through the wardrobe department together, those racks and racks of thousands of clothes that they gather through the years, and he picked out a sleazy looking black satin dress. He said, "Try that on." I put it on, he said, "Yeah, I like that, that's good." Maybe it needed a little fitting. I had long blonde hair then, and he said, "A hat, we'll get a hat." We looked through the hats, picked out a hat, and he said, "I want you to wear stockings because I want them to have runs in them, and high-heeled broken down shoes, an old purse." We got shoes and an old purse, and he said, "When you go to bed tonight, get up in the morning and *don't* comb your hair. Come to the studio exactly as you get up out of bed." I wore no makeup, just some eye makeup and some lipstick, that was it. I felt dirty and run-down and awful, and it was marvelous. He told me explicitly what he wanted. He gave me a wonderful feeling of the whole thing. I wished that scene had gone on forever. I could have worked with him for weeks. It only took a day and a half.... I was through at twelve the next day. I was so disappointed.

—Trevor, interviewed by John Gallagher for *Films in Review* (NY), Nov 1983

During our own scenes [in *Stagecoach* (1939, John Ford)] the actors didn't get any feeling of great drama; the scenes were too fragmentary. But it was all shaping up in Ford's mind. He knew how all the pieces were going together.

There was one scene I was looking forward to. It was the one where Duke [John Wayne as The Ringo Kid] finally says that he'd like to see me after the whole thing was over. Up to that time, Ford had set up the romance merely by looks that Duke and I had exchanged. At last I came to my chance to be romantic!

When I came on the set, Ford looked at the page and a half of script and said, "Too mushy!" He threw everything out but two lines of dialogue. I was crushed.

Later I saw Ford at Goldwyn Studios when he was cutting the picture.

"It's going to be great," he said. "And you're so good that they're not even going to notice it. It'll go right over their heads."

He was right. *Stagecoach* made Duke Wayne, but it didn't do much for me. There are certain parts that command attention.... I had mine in *Dead End* and *Key Largo* [1948, John Huston]. But not *Stagecoach*. It was too subtle.

—Trevor, in *Action*, Sept/Oct 1971

Q. Was [John Ford] tough on Wayne?

A. Yeah, very tough on Wayne, very tough. I felt sorry for him; I felt sorry for Duke because he wanted to succeed so badly, and this was his big chance. Ford and he had been friends, of course. But Ford would take his chin in his hand and he'd shake his head, and say, "What are you acting with? You're not acting with your chin and your mouth, for God's sake, it's up here," and he'd tap his head. Right in front of everybody, but Duke took it. He took it like a soldier. Because he knew he was helping him.

Q. What kind of director was [William] Wellman [on *My Man and I* (1952) and *The High and the Mighty* (1954)] compared to Ford?

A. I think they were quite different. Wellman had eye-to-eye enthusiasm with you and he'd say, "We'll do this." Ford never did that. Never. Wellman was the old style director, building up enthusiasm in his people.

Q. At Metro you did two pictures with Jack Conway, a director nobody ever talks about, *Honky Tonk* [1941] and *Crossroads* [1942].... What was Conway like?

A. He was very easy-going, a social kind of guy, sweet and nice, amusing. I thought he was kind of lightweight compared to a lot of other directors. I don't think he was a big talent. He had the facility for doing things well. *Honky Tonk*...Gable was fun, Gable was a sweet man and like a young boy you know, he was like a young boy, but unpretentious, real. I really liked him.

—Trevor, interviewed by John Gallagher for *Films in Review* (NY), Nov 1983

To me, Gaye [in *Key Largo*] symbolized the lost dreams of many persons. At one time she hoped to become a great singer. Then she listened to the bright promises of a gangster, and when they proved empty, she turned to the bottle.

The climax of the role came in the hotel scene, when Gaye literally sang for a drink. A hurricane was approaching, and she was nervous and frightened. Edward G. Robinson, who played the gangster, promised her a drink if she would sing; so, although Gaye knew she had lost her voice, she struggled through the song.

—Trevor, in *The Saturday Evening Post*, 24 Dec 1949

Q. How did you prepare for the scene in which...you sing for a drink in front of Bogart, Bacall, and [Lionel] Barrymore?

A. This was Huston's brilliance. First of all, I had no idea I was going to sing it myself, because I can't sing. I thought they were going to have a recording and I was going to mouth the words to the recording, and have a singer do it. I wanted the music department to rehearse me and train me in the gestures of a singer, a nightclub singer. I wanted to get that look of a *passé* nightclub singer.

Q. The Helen Morgan torch style?

A. Exactly. You know. I wanted to get something like that, so each day I'd say to John, "When can I get to the music department and rehearse, when are you going to shoot the song?" "Oh, we've got lots of time." This went on and on and on. I began to really pester John, "I want to go to the music department and rehearse, I've got to get the gestures."

So we came back from lunch one day. He said, "I think I'll shoot the song this afternoon." I said, "WHAT? Where's the recording? I haven't heard it." He said, "You're going to sing it." I said, "I can't!" and that's what he did to me. He stood me up there with the whole cast and the whole crew looking. You think that's not embarrassing? And off-stage is a piano, and they hit one note. Start. (laughter) No time for anything except pure embarrassment and torture and that's what came through....

—Trevor, interviewed by John Gallagher for *Films in Review* (NY), Nov 1983

François TRUFFAUT [1932-1984]

Born: Paris. Work as a film critic for Cahiers du cinéma and Arts preceded his debut as a film director with Une visite (1955). He appeared as an actor in three of his own films, beginning with The Wild Child (1969) and made his acting debut in a film by another director with Close Encounters of the Third Kind (1977, Steven Spielberg):

Q. How do you prepare for a role? Do you become the character?

A. I've never become the character. I do very little things — I remain myself. Even for Spielberg. The character of Claude Lacombe in *Close Encounters* is a cartoon character. Before the shooting, [Spielberg] showed me the storyboard, which was enormous — almost 2000 drawings — and I understood that I had to "enter" them. That's all.

—Truffaut, interviewed by Dan Yakir for *Film Comment*, Feb 1985

Tom TRYON [1926-1991]

Born: Hartford, Connecticut. High school dramatics, studies in Fine Arts at Yale University and work in stock and on TV preceded his film debut in The Scarlet Hour (1956, Michael Curtiz). He was signed to a three picture deal by Otto Preminger, but completed only two films — The Cardinal (1963) and In Harm's Way (1965):

Otto was a real bully. He only picked on people who were either frightened of him or couldn't fight back. Ohhh, if I had known then what I know now, which is once you get two weeks of film in the can you can tell him to go fuck himself and walk off the set. But the powers that be came to me and said, "Tom, don't fight back. He'll stop eventually. See if you can take it."

That was a lot of bullshit. I was so frightened he was going to scream that I didn't give a shit about what my acting was like. I simply wanted to get through the take and get a print. I wanted the experience to end.

When we did a scene for *The Cardinal*...there was a priest who was being played by Grady Sutton. Well, I walked in and Otto was screaming and Grady was shaking like a leaf; his voice had gone real high. We were in this little room and by 10 o'clock it was sweltering. [After lunch], I came back on the set to finish the scene and there was Chill Wills in a clerical collar. I said, "Good God! What are you doing here?" He said, "They let Grady go." Well...it was a four-page scene which he did in two takes, okay?

Now jump to two years later and Otto's getting ready to start *In Harm's Way* and he says, "Ve must have Chill. Chill is our lucky symbol. Ve vill have him. Chill vill play the admiral." I'll never forget it. There were hundreds and hundreds of people on the set and Chill said, "Mr. Preminger, my name is Chill Wills and I'm an actor. I've been in 144 movies; I have been acting for 42 years and you are making me shake."

Preminger turned on him saying, "You are fired." He threw him off the set, sent him home and closed down the production. The next morning Henry Fonda was in the admiral's uniform. Now, here was Chill Wills, a wonderful actor who had helped him out of a spot on the first movie and he destroys him on the second one....

He started on Paula Prentiss during *In Harm's Way* and got her screaming. She was jumping up and down on the bed and he turned to me with a diabolical look and said, "How does it feel to see somebody else getting it for a change?" Another day he got her so upset she tried to kick him and missed and kicked the bed and broke her ankle. Otto screamed to bring the script in and went through it and tore out all her scenes. He sent her home and then patched the film.

In the whipping scene in *The Cardinal*, they literally flayed the skin off my back and shoulders. Otto kept saying, "He's got enough skin left. Ve do one more take...!"

I never would have gotten through a third film with Preminger.

—Tryon, interviewed by David Galligan for *Drama-Logue*, 29 Jan-4 Feb 1987

Kathleen TURNER [1954-]

Born: Springfield, Missouri. Drama studies at Southwest Missouri State University and The University of Maryland, stage work with The Manitoba Theatre Company and in daytime soap opera TV preceded her film debut as Matty Walker in Body Heat (1981, Lawrence Kasdan):

Playboy: What about Matty's sex scenes? She put so much passion into her scenes with Ned Racine [William Hurt], the man she later betrayed, that it was hard at the end of the movie to believe she'd been faking it. *Was* it all an act? Did she love him?

Turner: Yes, yes, yes! I think she was in love. The sex was great. It was a bonus. I don't think she had ever had the freedom of a beautiful young lover like that. She loved it.

Playboy: Then how could she betray him?

Turner: Love and sex ain't necessarily the most important thing. That's what Matty believed....

Playboy: Can you fake that intensity of sex? Is it possible to make that kind of love on the set and not get turned on?

Turner: Part of it is very mechanical. Larry [Kasdan] and Bill and I would block out the moves in advance and know what we were going to do in front of the camera, so we would be comfortable with it. And the three of us became close through the work. But you have to get over this hump — at some point, you have to kiss the other person and hug the other person. It was easier to get over that when we were alone than with the crew standing there. So we just walked through the scenes, not performing the actions, not acting them out, but exploring them. Then, when the tension got real heavy, we'd have races up and down the lawn — stuff like that. We'd jump into the water, just to get comfortable with each other....

The truth is, you can act sexuality to a certain extent, but if you are actually being touched, actually touching someone, there is a gray area there, because your body is responding even though your mind is saying, "OK, now the camera is there; I have to kiss at three quarters...." So you're thinking that stuff but you are also having physical reactions, because nobody can be petted, touched and kissed without feeling something....

Playboy: So what do you do? You can't take cold showers every ten minutes?

Turner: Actually, "Cut!" is a very good cold shower.

Playboy: Then you have to get turned on enough without getting too turned on?

A. I'm not really sure you can get too turned on. I think there's an automatic safety valve that is simply your responsibility technically as an actor. If you get too turned on, you start rolling around and you're out of the shot....

Q. What was it like working with Hurt, who is obviously a gifted actor but has a reputation for being somewhere on the edge?

A. Maybe he is a little bit. I think he sometimes is difficult to deal with personally, because he doesn't proceed in a linear fashion. His actions don't progress in any sensible shape or form. However, he never brings that stuff on camera. We'd go to dinner and I would spend all evening completely unable to understand what the hell he was talking about. I mean, it got a little scary sometimes, like spending the whole night talking about your preferred mode of death, for instance. He said he would like to be sucked up into a jet engine and immediately atomized — and I'm saying, "Oh, my God, OK, here I am, sitting with this man I have to work with tomorrow who wants to die by being atomized in a jet engine." Uh-huh. But the next day, there's none of that. I think Bill is one of those people who are afraid that if they find a form of contentment or stability, they will lose the gift of their work. I don't agree, but I think that is part of his behavior....

Playboy: Were you at all wary of playing such a nasty character?

Turner: When you're doing a character, you never think the character is evil. You find all the sympathetic things that touch you and move you.... The biggest challenge was to make the audience believe her. I was always terrified that they would stop believing. The challenge was to...to suck them all in. Everybody. At the same time, you had to leave clues all the way down the line, so when they looked back, they wouldn't suddenly say, "Wait a minute! When did she go from good to bad?" There had to be little notes that sounded wrong in every scene. Why did she hesitate to say that word? What was that look? There had to be clues in every scene that she wasn't what she seemed to be, but you couldn't see them until you knew.

—Turner, interviewed by David Sheff for *Playboy*, May 1986

How does she walk? Does she wear high heels? The shoes you wear really affect the whole attitude. Matty wears high heels, a tight skirt; she's a woman who's always touching herself, touching her hair, checking her face, touching her thigh. In *Crimes of Passion* [1984, Ken Russell], Joanna wears flat shoes and jackets and ties, so you've always got constriction in the neck and nothing to push you forward in a feminine manner, which is what heels do; so she's always a little lumpy. China Blue [Joanna's alter ego], on the other hand, wears five-inch heels, so I made her real loose at the hips; her legs kind of swing. You get the feeling of "screw you" — because that's what her body's doing. So I find that first, and then the voice that the body produces. Joanna's is pretty tight and talks-like-this (very clipped, run-together syllables); China Blue is "like, oh, yeah...." So I find the body and the mental attitude that body creates.

—Turner, interviewed by Christine Doudna for *American Film*, Nov 1984

I was up against a lot to do *Crimes of Passion*. [My husband] Jay [Weiss] was very concerned about my doing it. My mother was absolutely appalled by the idea. Even my agent had very mixed feelings about my doing it. I was doubtful. I was afraid of the sex, but I got contractual approval on the way everything would be shot.... It was an acting tour de force, and you don't get offered too many of those, especially if you are becoming a commercial Hollywood leading lady. Studios don't want you going out on a limb and risking your reputation with these kinds of roles, because then you might lose audience. As time goes on and you become more popularly successful, the odds are you start to be limited in your choice of roles. So I really thought it was a good time to grab it, to go for that kind of stretch and because I thought I would act my ass off it in. And I think it was a correct decision. I think *Crimes* is my best work. I'm very pleased with it. I'm not pleased with the film. It's not as good as I wanted it to be, but I like the work very much....

Joanna is so angry and so hurt! To me, the background story on Joanna comes through in one scene when she sort of jokes with Anthony Perkins and says, "When I was in the kitchen trying desperately to make my husband's favorite casserole, he was in the bedroom with my best friend, making her." I envision that Joanna was trying to be Superwoman. She was carrying this job and this marriage, and when they were breaking up, her husband turned around and said something like, "You're not a real woman." It's a problem for so many women today. What do you do? Do you spend your time making sure your man is all right or pursuing your career? Does he feel neglected? Ahh! It's very hard! And Joanna got burned! He used her expertise and confidence against her and attacked her femininity. I envision that one night she went out and bought that wig because it was her idea of absolutely grotesque, absurd, and she went out to see if any man was going to pay attention to her. She got into the control thing and liked it. She was completely irresponsible. She could go fuck anybody she wanted to and pull any trip on him, play any kind of game, and then go back to her other life and not have to pay the price. It was obviously a very destructive way to use this anger, but it was her first access to it.

—Turner, interviewed by David Sheff for *Playboy*, May 1986

Joan [Wilder in *Romancing the Stone* (1984, Robert Zemeckis) and *Jewel of the Nile* (1986, Lewis Teague)] is probably the closest to me I've ever played.... She's got that mixture of cockiness and being afraid. She's certainly brave. She'll say, "I'll try," even if she can't handle it....

—Turner, interviewed by Nancy Mills for *Stills*, Mar 1986

Romancing the Stone was well done, but it wasn't a huge personal triumph for me. *Prizzi's Honor* [1985, John Huston] was. After working with Jack [Nicholson] I'm finally beginning to believe myself rather an expert on film acting. Jack has that ability to fulfill all the physical requirements of acting — hit that mark, be at that depth of focus, don't change your rhythm at the end of the scene because it's going to have to match the beginning you shot two months ago. Do all of those things without thought, then you're acting. It's the old saying about the stricter the boundaries, the greater the power. Jack has that power, and that's what I want too. I think I'm getting it.

—Turner, interviewed by Louise Bernikow for *Moviegoer Magazine*; repr. in *The Toronto Star*, 1 Mar 1987

Irene [in *Prizzi's Honor*] was just a working girl who happened to earn her living by shooting people. Because of easy money and disguises, she made herself look like a very glamorous woman. I caught a touch of Matty in her. It was the closest I've come to repeating any of my characters.

—Turner, interviewed by Nancy Mills for *Stills*, Mar 1986

Playboy: The sex scenes in *Prizzi's Honor* are of a different order from the ones in your other movies.

Turner: Oh, sure. The love scene on the bed was just a gas to do. I think that's one of the secrets of doing good sex on film, actually. I think that just having intense, intense kissing or touching is really kind of boring and archaic. I think the real joy is finding joy. I always try to laugh, always try to put in a gurgle of joy, because that touches people much more than watching someone pant. I mean, when we hit the headboard and it's banging the wall — there isn't a person in the world who doesn't know that sound.

—Turner, interviewed by David Sheff for *Playboy*, May 1986

I loved Peggy Sue [in *Peggy Sue Got Married* (1986, Francis Ford Coppola)] because she's a woman who, unlike me, grew up in one place and had the same friends from childhood. The movie is life-affirming; she starts out unhappy, believing she never should have married her high school sweetheart [Nicolas Cage], then she finds the choices she made were right, were inevitable.

—Turner, interviewed by Joseph Gelmis for *Newsday*, 5 Oct 1986

Barbara [in *The War of the Roses* (1989, Danny DeVito)] is someone fresh in terms of film. She has no rules to keep her contained, no boundaries, so she can't say she should not do this. Once she makes up her mind, *whoosh*....

The couple in the film has seventeen years of marriage behind them. You take a man for granted after that, and as well as Michael [Douglas] and I know each other, we can act with that ease. Associations are important in this work.... Michael and I are finding that in this film, repetition adds richness. [Turner and Douglas had previously co-starred in both *Romancing the Stone* and *Jewel of the Nile*.]

—Turner, interviewed by Malcolm MacPherson for *Premiere*, Nov 1989

Lana TURNER [1921-]

Born: Julia Turner in Wallace, Idaho. Following studies at Hollywood High, she made her film debut as an extra in A Star is Born (1937, William Wellman). Under contract to Mervyn LeRoy, she played her first character — Mary Clay, the teenager who is raped and murdered, in his They Won't Forget — later that year:

When I learned more about filmmaking, I understood what director Mervyn LeRoy had done.

He had emphasized my sexiness to fix me in the viewers' minds. He gave me what they call "flesh impact," to let a tight sweater imply what couldn't be said on the screen. But that walk down the street of a Southern town would completely change my life.

That image clung to me for the rest of my career. I was the sexual promise, the object of desire. And as I matured, my facade did too, to an image of coolness and glamour — the movie star in diamonds, swathed in white mink. [Turner worked with LeRoy again on *Johnny Eager* (1942), *Homecoming* (1948) and *Latin Lovers* (1953).]

In *Calling Dr. Kildare* [1939, Harold Bucquet], I had the opportunity to work with Lionel Barrymore. An incredible man! How I admired and feared him. But at the same time I couldn't help liking him. Everyone on the set paid him deference, and he would shrug it off as though he were just a fellow actor. He would be wheeled onto the set because of his bad knee, and he would pretend to be crotchety and cantankerous, but in playing a scene with me he'd look up from under his brows with an adorable twinkle in his eyes. He enjoyed teasing me because I blushed easily. But he kept me on my toes, and I loved doing scenes with him.

—Turner, in her (with Hollis Alpert) *Lana: The Lady, The Legend, The Truth* (New York: E.P. Dutton, 1982)

The more I thought about [Sheila Regan in *Ziegfeld Girl* (1941)], the more I realized I knew nothing about Ziegfeld girls — except what I had read in the Sunday supplements, about their glamour and how they wore diamonds and were courted by millionaires. I didn't know what they were like inside: what they thought and felt, how they looked at life. I had to have the emotional background of this girl, Sheila, because her downfall was her own fault. I had to understand what made her as she was....

The first thing I did was to walk into the office of Lillian Burns, the studio dramatic coach — who, before that, used to shake her head about me, I think. I said, "Look, we've got to go to work. I don't know anything. I want to start from scratch."

And I did start from scratch. I worked harder than I'd ever worked in my life, frantically trying to make up for lost time — time I'd spent not learning anything. But if any credit is being passed out for my performance as Sheila, a lot of it should go to Burnsey and to Pop [Robert Z.] Leonard, who directed. Working with him was like taking a course in navigation. They drew the lines and I followed....

But I still didn't know Sheila Regan — or Sheila Hale, as she became. We talked over everything she did, and why she did it. We analyzed her in terms of ourselves. We compared situations in her life to situations in my life and in Burnsey's. They weren't exactly similar situations, but they had emotional parallels. Remembering how I had felt, and realizing how Burnsey must have felt, in those situations, I began to understand how Sheila felt. We grafted our emotions onto her, and her character began to unfold like a pattern. Every scene was another step in her development.

It was like climbing a flight of stairs, without ever having climbed stairs before. It was monumental work. But by the time I got to the last step, I knew Sheila's every thought, every movement. I didn't even have to practice her walk. I knew how she would walk, because I knew everything else about her.

It was the first time I ever got inside of a character. It was the first time I ever had the *urge* to get inside of one.

—Turner, interviewed by James Reid for *Motion Picture*, Nov 1941

When I read the script for *The Three Musketeers* [1948, George Sidney], I found that Lady de Winter was not a starring role. Surprised that my agents had signed me for it, I went straight to Mr. Mayer and refused the part....

There were meetings and negotiations; they rewrote the script to give me more to do, and finally I agreed to make the picture.

Am I glad I did! I enjoyed the filming enormously.... It was my...first chance to play a truly villainous lady....

My equal in villainy was Vincent Price as Cardinal Richelieu. He was a master of high camp. I had been playing Milady straight, but Vincent was stealing every scene. I studied him, and it challenged me, and I began to try things I never knew I could do. I found my own little touches — a certain sly look, the flap of a glove, a tilt of the head. I began to stylize my role. In my prison scene June Allyson replaced one of my regular guards, because a woman wouldn't fall for my feminine wiles. With lightning flashing outside the window, I played cat-and-mouse with her and let my eyes go crazy. They were things I'd never been *allowed* to do before, things that were not in the pages of the script. June told me later that I terrified her.

As MGM's glamour star I wouldn't have had a chance at the dramatic role of Georgia Lorrison [in *The Bad and the Beautiful* (1952)] except that John Houseman and Vincente Minnelli, the film's producer and director, respectively, had asked for me....

When the script reached me I knew right away that I understood the character — a film star who is seen at first as a soggy mess and then is resuscitated by an unscrupulous producer [Kirk Douglas as Jonathan Shields]. I could believe in her. Moreover, the screenplay was a much better one than those I usually received. The atmosphere of the film was totally familiar to me. The sets were the very sound stages where I had spent so much of my working life. The conferences in executive offices, the nerve-racking sneak previews — all of them had a familiar ring. Even the Hollywood party scenes were true to life....

When production closed down, the scene I had thought most important to my role had not been shot. As Georgia, I took an emotional drive through a blinding rain after discovering that Jonathan, the man I loved, had betrayed me. Minnelli told me that the special effects for the scene were still being developed, so he would shoot it separately later on....

[Eleven] weeks were to pass, in fact, before the call came to report to the sound stage for the wrap-up of *The Bad and the Beautiful*. The script gave me almost no clue about how to play the scene. There was no dialogue. I was sure Minnelli would run the previous scene for me so I'd be able to pick up the mood again. But as it turned out, the rest of the film was in its final editing stages. Still I didn't fret. After makeup and hairdressing I got into costume and went to the sound stage. There the sight of what they'd been workng on all those weeks sent me right through the floor. The chassis of a car, with its trunk and fenders missing, sat on gigantic springs on top of some planks. Standing around it was a group of men dressed in the heavy yellow slickers deep-sea fishermen wear. They had big buckets of water, huge sponges, and hoses with fine spray nozzles. Pipes hung from the rafters above the car....

[Minnelli] asked my stand-in, Alyce May, to get into the car while crew members alongside pushed the planks this way and that, making the chassis sway, or dipped sponges into the buckets and sprayed water on the windshield. I watched goggle-eyed, wondering how I was supposed to be able to act a scene in that contraption....

I went to the set, climbed over the paraphernalia, and got into the chassis. I tried to re-create the shock of finding Jonathan with another woman, the scene I had filmed nearly three months earlier. I dug for it, dug deeper into my own feelings, into my own bitter experiences with love. God knows, I had enough by then to call upon. After a few minutes I decided I was ready and caught Vincente's eye.

The car moved and threw me from side to side. I concentrated on my hysteria, building with each movement of the car. *It's my big night, my premiere, and meanwhile he's with another woman....* Emotions welled up inside me and tears sprang to my eyes.

I don't like to cry but once I am in tears, the more I try to fight them, the more they come. They came gushing now and were echoed by the gush of water against the windshield.

"Cut!" Vincente called. He explained that they had to change lenses for a new set of camera angles. I told him I didn't think I could take any more.

"Yes, you can, darling," he said.

Now they removed the door, and the camera came in closer. Water spattered the top of the car, and the men with the sponges kept splashing it onto the windshield. I had to concentrate on Georgia and not see them. I went through the scene again, and yet again. It took the whole day. After each time he said, "Cut," Vincente would come to me and take my hand and kiss it. Then another angle. The mike was pushed into the cab, and in my hysteria I sobbed and the mike picked up the sobs. The agony by then was genuine. Too much was coming back to me, too much of my own life: the bitter marital disappointments, the babies I had fought to keep and had lost — and that crushing last meeting with Tyrone [Power], the man I had loved most of all. When Vincente said, "Cut. That's it," for the last time, I was totally drained.

—Turner, in her (with Hollis Alpert) *Lana: The Lady, The Legend, The Truth* (New York: E.P. Dutton, 1982)

Ben TURPIN [1874-1940]

Born: New Orleans. Work as a burlesque comedian preceded his film debut — in 1907 — with the Essanay Co. in Chicago. His first film success came as foil to Charlie Chaplin in 1915. In 1917, he joined Mack Sennett and became a leading slapstick comedy star:

It's a great life. I've been in the hospital twenty-five times. I've had my teeth knocked out four times. Once they got me up on a rope over a canyon and somebody let go the rope, dropping me about the distance you fall out of a balloon. I've been hit by a peevish lion and chased by temperamental actors. In one of the Mack Sennett comedies, the villain was to hit me with a trick statuette. He grabbed up one made out of solid marble by mistake. I just remember everything turning black.... Another time, I was acting in Mack Sennett's comedy, *The Battle Royal* [1918]. There was a scene where a fellow was to swat me with a club padded on the end with a boxing glove. The glove slipped off and hit me on the top of the head so hard that I went down through the floor....

—Turpin, interviewed by Harry C. Carr for *Photoplay Magazine*, Dec 1918

John TURTURRO [1957-]

Born: Brooklyn, N.Y. Studies at SUNY/New Paltz and The Yale Drama School and work in regional theater and Off-Broadway preceded his film debut in Raging Bull (1980, Martin Scorsese). In 1988, he played Heinz Sabantino in Tony Bill's Five Corners:

I liked that role. There was some depth to work with. I'm not that interested in playing heavies — I prefer comedy. I think if you do that well, you can do anything. I have no interest in exploitive parts — violence for violence's sake. And I don't want to wind up my life doing psychos. But Heinz is in love with that girl [Jodie Foster], their relationship is totally chaste. I feel he's more like King Kong than anything else.

—Turturro, interviewed by Patricia O'Haire for *The New York Daily News*, 27 Jan 1988

Q. What's it been like [working with Spike Lee — on *Do the Right Thing* (1989), *Mo' Better Blues* (1990) and *Jungle Fever* (1991)] and Joel and Ethan Coen — on *Miller's Crossing* (1990) and *Barton Fink* (1991)]?

A. You can improvise more with Spike. Joel and Ethan, I improvise ideas. Spike is jazz and the Coens are classicists. The Coens, you've got to do in on the language. With Spike you can do it on the language or off. I've seen people take the freedom that [Spike] gives and make the material worse. People would push him to make it a little more sentimental. I don't like that.

—Turturro, interviewed by Paul Minx for *The Village Voice*, 19 June 1990

Q. Your character in *Miller's Crossing* is a juicy one: a low-life criminal and killer, but very human and somehow likable. What turned you on about the role?

A. The thing that really turned me on was his wits — how he was a hustler, how he got himself out of these situations, how he lived moment to moment, always on the move, intellectually, emotionally, in every way. Sexually — I mean the guy would probably have sex with anybody. And I had never played a very Jewish character — they made him Jewish because it made him more of an outsider and because of the history of always being persecuted and always having to move to survive.

Q. Bernie seems amoral and yet sincere, real. You get the sense that there's no line he won't cross.

A. A total '80s character. Doing him, I realized that he doesn't have any moral or emotional residue. For the moment, yes, he could agree with you, but when you're gone he's off to something else. There are people like that. They're really in tears, they really feel terrible, but a moment later they're fine. It doesn't stay with them. The trap about doing something like that was that you could overintellectualize it. But he's looking for the moment. That moment could be really full and really heartfelt, but when it's over, it's over. People might see me as more visceral here, but I was able to use my intelligence probably more than in many other roles. Those transitions he can make with his brain — I actually do that, not act that, but do that.

Q. The Coen brothers' films seem to gloss over the characters.

A. Everybody starts from different things. They started more from the other side, more visual. But they're moving more toward character development. Certainly whenever I came up with stuff that they thought was funny, I made it more human.... This other cartoon kind of funny is good for a sketch, but that's it. They're trying to move away from that.

—Turturro, interviewed by Gavin Smith for *Interview*, Sept 1990

Susan TYRRELL [1946-]

Born: Susan Creamer in San Francisco. Work with The Lincoln Center Repertory Company preceded her film debut in The Steagle (1971, Paul Sylbert). In 1972, she played Oma in John Huston's Fat City:

Ordinarily I don't like loud women who wallow in self-pity. I tread lightly around them, but Oma was something different. Originally the cliché was there, a 35-year-old woman with a broken nose and a drinking problem. I saw a little more coming from Oma than the cartoon drunks have become on the screen. No matter how freaky, there was something basic. Oma had roots. Drinking for Oma takes the place of fucking.

I guess I brought this understanding to the role. I'm not an actress who studies and analyzes a character. The less I do, the more the character takes over because I don't work from upstairs. I work from the gut and I need great margins for it to happen. John Huston gave me space to breathe, and when I got in front of the camera, wearing the clothes of Oma, things started to come.

Huston and I didn't get along at first. It was like two circuses colliding. During the early filming there were some moments when he had me weeping, but out of the fighting came a great love and respect for each other.

—Tyrrell, interviewed by Arthur Bell for *The Village Voice*, 10 Aug 1972

Cicely TYSON [1939-]

Born: East Harlem, N.Y. After making her debut in the unrealized independent film, The Spectrum, she studied at The Actors Studio and with Lloyd Richards and Vinnette Carroll. Work off and on Broadway and on TV preceded her first major role as Rebecca in Sounder (1972, Martin Ritt):

Sounder really *is* significant for the black woman. She has always been the strength of our race, and she has always had to carry the ball. During the days of slavery, her husband was likely to be lynched or castrated. She was maybe taken in the back and raped, but she was always the one to hold the family together, like Rebecca....

But there has never been a positive image of her. You get women like Sapphire in *Amos 'n' Andy*, who are always fighting with their husbands, but *never, ever*, a positive image of a full home life with both mother and father figures, and with warmth, beauty, love and understanding. We *do* have that. It *does* exist....

I patterned the part of Rebecca after my mother and also on Nana, a woman who took care of us while my mother worked. There aren't many blacks who haven't had some sort of hardship, you know. If you're raised in poverty, you know what it is to want a piece of bread. When I was 9 years old, I was selling shopping bags on the street. I know what it is to be without. My parents did everything they could to make things meet, but they were still on welfare. But we never went raggedy, and we never went without things to eat. Mother would whip up some potatoes and put a little salt pork in them, and we would have a meal.

—Tyson, interviewed by Judy Klemesrud for *The New York Times*, 1 Oct 1972

U

Peter USTINOV [1921-]

Born: London, England, to Russian parents. Studies at The London Theatre Studio and work on the stage preceded his film debut in Hullo Fame (1940, Andrew Buchanan). In 1951, he played Nero in Mervyn LeRoy's Quo Vadis:

I met Mervyn LeRoy 24 hours before we started shooting. I'd never seen the poor man before. We met on a sound-stage in Rome. I said to him, "Mr. LeRoy, do you have any ideas how I should play the part?" And he said, "Son-of-a-bitch, yes, son-of-a-bitch." I said, "Pardon me?" He said, "Nero, you know what he did to his mother?" I said, "Yes, I do, is there any other point you would like to make?"

He suddenly started tap dancing. I looked at his feet. He said, "I used to be a hoofer." I said, "Fantastic but apart from that?" He said, "Just give me those big eyes, Peter. Other than that I think Nero's the kind of guy who plays with himself at night." I thought that was ridiculous. Now, of course, I think he was exactly right.

—Ustinov, interviewed by David Galligan for *Drama-Logue*, 6-12 Oct 1983

Of the films I have had the pleasure of making in my short career, [*We're No Angels* (1955, Michael Curtiz)] was the one which gave me the most pleasure, and the one which I wish could have gone on for longer.... It is to the credit of all those who could have turned the making of this film into a solemn affair that they did no such thing, but allowed a spirit of gentle enjoyment and free rein....

And there can certainly be no better traveling companion than Bogie [Humphrey Bogart] when it comes to delving into the latent possibilities of a shooting-script.

Much as it may displease him, I feel bound to say that I know of no more generous actor, nor one who is more liable to break himself up by suddenly seeing the funny side of things. In short, an object lesson in how to be professional and light hearted at the same time.

—Ustinov, in *The New York Herald Tribune*, 10 July 1955

[*Lola Montes* (1955, Max Ophuls)] was an incredible production, costing something like 700,000 pounds — it ran, I think, some three months over schedule. I began work the day before I was due to finish.

It was actually shot in three versions (French, German and English) which was rather incredible. One only had a vague idea of when a character (speaking say in German) had finished (by some flicker of the eyes or something). Phonetically learned dialogue was spoken in a very relaxed, natural way and scenes were often shot through curtains and screens which made it all very difficult. In fact it was a difficult film. An ordinary commercial story overloaded with ideas. Ophuls is something of a Toscanini. He has his orchestra assembled and going through the motions but he prefers the music he hears in his head. Directors recognize this trait in each other and perhaps that is the reason why a number of them wrote in defense of the film after its premier.

Personally I got on very well with Max. He has a sense of humor and there's no bluffing him....

The whole production was conceived on a scale that even Hollywood would not have sanctioned. Locations were at Nice, Paris and

Bavaria. They built at Munich one of the largest sets I've ever seen, for the circus sequences....

But the whole film reveals, apart from the story, an almost neurotic preoccupation with ideas.... Many of the sequences have special color significance — everything is blue — literally everything — or green. In another circus sequence there are dwarfs going up and down ropes in rhythm to the music. A number of the dwarfs were in fact just small men and the harnesses that they were wearing kept slipping up to their necks. At one time one of the hands thought it advisable to let them down to avoid strangulation. I can still hear Max calling — "Keep ze dwarfs hanging — keep ze dwarfs hanging."

—Ustinov, in *Continental Film Review*, Sept 1956

[Ophuls] was not easy to work for, he was even more difficult to work under, but he was infinitely rewarding to work with. Dispute and argument he enjoyed almost as much as laughter, and although he was a bit of a dictator, he disliked and mistrusted servility.

—Ustinov, in *Sight & Sound*, Summer 1957

Q. Your participation in *The Sundowners* [1960, Fred Zinnemann] and in *Spartacus* [1960, Stanley Kubrick] was similar insofar as you provided a comic relief with something substantial and sensible beneath it.

A. Working in *The Sundowners* was rather different from working in *Spartacus*. I think that acting is the imitation of the imaginary: you imagine what you are going to do and then put it into motion. There's a degree of imitation in all acting.... People have a tendency to think that mimicry is a second-rate thing which bases itself entirely upon something else and tries to copy it. But even babies when they imitate something in their own way *comment* upon it. Sometimes you get a bitter criticism from a three-year-old of the mannerism of a grown-up, a distortion which is a satire in itself. And unless we had the capacity to imitate we wouldn't even be able to speak a language now, because we all started imitating others and getting the music of it in our heads. So there *is* a difference in interpretation between *Spartacus* and *The Sundowners*. In *Sundowners* you have the living example of certain Englishmen who behave like that because they are embarrassed, professionally, and by nature, permanently, slightly embarrassed.

When you are dealing with a Roman gentleman, as I was in *Spartacus*, you haven't got any Romans to imitate. You've got Italians but that isn't the same thing. You can't adapt a vocabulary of Italian manual gestures to a Hollywood film about Romans. So you have to imagine a modern parallel, a man who would perform the same kind of function, somebody who deals in gladiators and supplies them for contests. Quite frankly I thought of a theatrical agent, a minor agent who doesn't belong to any large organisation, but the kind about whom many people say, "I will go to him because he looks after me personally." And with that in mind I did it in a way that I hope is not too aggressively modern, but at the same time is recognisable as a type who must have existed then.

—Ustinov, interviewed by Gideon Bachmann for *Film* (London), Winter 1961

What makes a character like [Batiatus in *Spartacus*] interesting is that he is obviously reprehensible, odious, but convinced that he's right.... In modern parlance, I'm a retired technical sergeant who has invested money in a gym and has a piece of a few wrestlers.

—Ustinov, interviewed by Joseph Morgenstern for *The New York Herald Tribune*, 21 Aug 1960

Spartacus was [Kubrick's] first enormous picture and Charles Laughton refused to perform the script he'd been given so I had to write those scenes I did with him, with the approval of Universal. We rehearsed them very often at his place or mine during the night and then in the morning came in to Stanley and said, "We want to show you something," did it, and invariably he would say, "Let's shoot it."

—Ustinov, interviewed by David Galligan for *Drama-Logue*, 6-12 Oct 1983

What I am doing in *The Sundowners* is quite a different character and I think that it is probably the most difficult, in a way, that I've ever tried. It is a sort of Don Quixote of the outback who has a mysterious past. It becomes clear that he's been cashiered from some cavalry regiment and that he has probably also been fired from various other posts....

There is also a side of him which is not terribly reassuring, and that is that he likes leading women up the garden path and then leaving at dawn because he cannot face settling. By now, at the age of fifty, the wanderlust has become a sort of habit. So there you have a contradiction, the fact that you have to cover up a man's inherent loneliness by a show of brightness all the time. And that is what makes it fun to play, especially when you have a director of the kind of quality who first of all knows what you are trying to do, and secondly can contribute along those lines.

Fred Zinnemann is very easy to work with, and very rewarding. Because quite apart from being very far-seeing, very sensitive and instinctive, he's at the same time perfectly functional as well. If you say, "Yes I know the kind of effect that we all want here, but if we leave this one word in it ruins it all" he understands immediately why. I don't have to do more than tell him and he understands. He puts himself in an actor's shoes and looks at it from their particular viewpoint.

—Ustinov, interviewed for *Films & Filming*, May 1960

Q. What about other actors and actresses? Have you had any particular favorites among those with whom you've actually worked?

A. Yes. There are certain actresses who are so good that you almost come out of your own character in appreciation. Maggie Smith has that sort of pointed quality which makes it very difficult to keep a straight face, because she's so intent on being what she is that she practically forces you out of what you're trying to be. But I think she's probably the most palpably gifted woman I've ever worked with. [Ustinov worked with Smith on *Hot Millions* (1968, Eric Till), *Death on the Nile* (1978, John Guillermin) and *Evil Under the Sun* (1982, Guy Hamilton).]

—Ustinov, interviewed by Walter Harris for *Game*, Mar 1975

I find Poirot a very engaging character, although he's quite awful, really. I should hate to know him. He's very vain, self-contained and finicky. People have asked me why he never married — because he couldn't solve it, of course. An ancillary reason is that he's very much in love with himself. He has probably been quite true to himself. I don't think he's ever cheated on himself. [Ustinov played Hercule Poirot in the adaptations of Agatha Christie's *Death on the Nile* and *Evil Under the Sun*.]

—Ustinov, interviewed by Leslie Bennetts for *The New York Times*, 7 Mar 1982

Q. Several actors have played [Charlie] Chan before you — Warner Oland, Sidney Toler, Roland Winters, and J. Carroll Naish among them. Did you take another look at their work, to study their methods [before making *Charlie Chan and the Curse of the Dragon Queen* (1981, Clive Donner)]?

A. No, I remembered the old films pretty well. And I knew the most important thing is to keep as placid and serene as possible. Everyone does this in his own way — mine is "stiff upper lid." The whole secret is, Chan doesn't react to anything. He sees the most absurd murder, and he says, "Most interesting...!"

In the long run, you realize that he's the steadying sail of this absurd craft. The fun comes from all the horrible things that happen around him, which he hardly takes notice of. There's a great contrast between reality and his endless politeness.

Once you've caught on to that, everything becomes enjoyable: Charlie Chan knows that any arrow or German shepherd aimed at him will miss its mark, because of some — who knows what? And even if he does get flapped, he doesn't show it....

—Ustinov, interviewed by David Sterritt for *The Christian Science Monitor*, 19 Feb 1981

V

Rudolph VALENTINO [1895-1926]

Born: Rudolpho Guglielmi di Valentina d'Antonguolla in Castellaneto, Italy; emigrated to the U.S. late in 1913. While working at The Vitagraph Studio in Brooklyn as an assistant to a set director, he made his film debut as an extra in My Official Wife (1914, James Young). Moving to Hollywood, he then worked as a dancer before securing further film roles. June Mathis negotiated his role in The Four Horsemen of the Apocalypse (1921, Rex Ingram), the film which brought him a career as a romantic lead:

I told [Emil Jannings] how I read the book [*The Four Horsemen of the Apocalypse*] by Ibáñez, and then simply lived the character for the weeks preceding the actual filming of the story. We agreed that the finest results are obtained by an actor entering into the very skin of the role he is about to interpret. Thinking, philosophizing, acting just as the character would act were he actually flesh and blood. In such wise, one can almost take on the physical habiliments, the lineaments of the personality. And only in such wise can one really be convincing in a part that would otherwise be an extemporaneous bit of acting.

I try, have always tried, NOT to be Rudolph Valentino in the various roles I have played. To do that would be like playing the same tune over and over on the same instrument. However marvelous the piano, or the violin, however exquisite and consummate the tune played, an audience would soon tire of it. Adaptability...versatility...pliability...sensitivity ...all of these things are important in the make-up of the artist who must give birth to successive personalities.

—Valentino, in his *My Private Diary* (Chicago: Occult Publishing Co., 1929)

You have to experience emotions actually in order to give them realistic expression, particularly on the screen. Although I felt little in common with the Sheik [of *The Sheik* (1921, George Melford)], there was much in the character and experience of Julio [in *Four Horsemen*] and El Gallardo [in *Blood and Sand* (1922, Fred Niblo)] that I understood intimately and sympathetically.

—Valentino, in *Photoplay Magazine*, Apr 1923

I don't know what is going to happen to me. I shall have to try something *different* from the things I have done before. I feel as though I should begin all over again...make a new start....

I can't go on playing Great Lover roles, even if this picture [*Son of the Sheik* (1926, George Fitzmaurice)] is a success. The public grew tired of me in that type of thing before. They will tire of me again. I know it.

You see, with the sort of success I have had, this is what happens. You are publicized as a Great Lover — a "thrilling" personality. After a time, the male portion of your public begins to resent that with a very real and active resentment. "So *that* is the Great Lover!" they sneer. Then the feminine portion of your audience begins to challenge you. "All right — if you're so exciting — let's see you excite *me*!" they say, in effect, when they come into the theatre. They challenge you and dare you. It is absolutely impossible, of course, to live up to any such reputation. The whole thing is false and artificial — actually accidental. You can't go on and on with it.

I've just begun to realize that — that *I can't go on with it.* No one can, year after year, sell a mere type of personality. Especially, a type as definite as the one I have acquired by some strange fluke....

They *have* to let me try some other type of thing! Otherwise, I shall be through — finished — washed up — very soon, I know it! [This was his final film; he died later that year.]

—Valentino, interviewed by Helen Louise Walker (1926) for *Motion Picture Classic*, Mar 1933

Conrad VEIDT [1893-1943]

Born: Berlin. Studies with Max Reinhardt and work with his company in Berlin (from 1917) preceded his film debut in Der Spione (1917, Karl Heiland). His first English language film was The Beloved Rogue (1927, Alan Crosland), upon invitation by John Barrymore:

[After he realized I was 6'3"], I was surprised when Barrymore still wanted me in his picture. I played the part of Louis XVI, a short, wizened man, a feat that I managed by wearing a tremendous robe, which hid the fact that I was walking around in a squatting position.

After that I signed with Universal where I played a varied assortment of men without souls. The high spot was the title role of *The Man Who Laughs* [1927, Paul Leni] in which I played a tortured human being made horrible by a permanent grimace. I think that might have led somewhere. But talkies came in and I couldn't speak English well. I went back home.... [Bob Kane, the creator of *Batman*, modelled The Joker after this character.]

[In *A Woman's Face* (1941, George Cukor)] I play [Torsten Barring] the greatest meanie in the world. I befriend a girl [Joan Crawford] who has never had a friend, and then, when she falls desperately in love with me, I try to make her the instrument of a terrible vengeance against my fate. If only I can make people feel that this man, this spirit of evil, is an unhappy human being. Sick with unhappiness, the unhappiness of Lucifer, the angel cast out of heaven....

A villain can be very phony, if he's villainous just for the pleasure of being villainous. If he isn't compelled to villainy by something beyond his control — some illness, mental or physical; some abnormality; some supernatural force. I always try to find an excuse for any villain I play. Something that will make the audience sympathize with him even as they hate him....

There is a strange satisfaction purely from an acting standpoint in being able to play a demonic character convincingly. To make an unreal character real. It's the hardest kind of role to do, because it's the easiest kind to over-do.

—Veidt, interviewed by Betty Harris for *Modern Screen*, June 1941

In *Escape* [1940, Mervyn LeRoy], I tried to suggest that the General had little use for the Nazis, but was compelled to do what they would expect him to do — that he was a villain only because of that.

—Veidt, interviewed by Carol Craig for *Motion Picture*, Sept 1941

Jon VOIGHT [1938-]

Born: Yonkers, N.Y. Studies with Sanford Meisner at The Neighborhood Playhouse in N.Y., work both on and off Broadway and with The San Diego Shakespeare Festival preceded his film debut in Fearless Frank (1967, Philip Kaufman). In 1969, he played Joe Buck opposite Dustin Hoffman's Ratso Rizzo in John Schlesinger's Midnight Cowboy:

John Schlesinger [was] good for me because [he] gave me lots of room. And they also gave me lots of help. Because you need to know when you're off. I like to be criticized when I work, but I don't like to be told what to do. But I like to be helped because I can't see myself. I can't see what I'm doing.

I'll give you a good example. There was a terrific scene in [*Midnight Cowboy*], the crux of the film, really, when I come back with some stuff. I've just had a good night with that girl that I picked up [Brenda Vaccaro]. I made some money as a stud. I come back with all this stuff — pills, and soup and clothes. I come back and Dusty's sitting on the bed. He's sick. And I come in and I'm real happy. I'm on top of it. Now, the way the scene was written, it was, "See, I've got some stuff for you, got this thing for you, Ratso, goddam, we're gonna make it, man." Then Dusty says, "I ain't feeling good, Joe," and I say, "Oh yeah, what's the matter?" We played the scene a couple of times. It was so sentimental, something was wrong. We were acting it well but something was wrong.

John couldn't figure it out. He called up Waldo Salt, the screenwriter. Waldo was asleep, but he says, "Yes, I'll be down." He comes down to the studio in an hour; we've closed it; we've rehearsed it every kind of way. Waldo comes in. We go through the scene and he says, "You've got to remember that Joe is very selfish. He wants to leave Ratso." Bing! Here we go. So I changed a few lines. I said, "Well, then I'll say, 'I've got some stuff in there for you too.'" I pulled out this stuff — I've got some socks. "Look at them socks, see? Ratso, I got some stuff in there for you too, boy; you're gonna be all right." But I'm thinking, "I'm getting out of here in a couple of days because man, I'm tough stuff." I find him sick and it makes me angry.

—Voight, interviewed for *Dialogue on Film*, June 1973

What moved me so deeply [about the scene on the bus at the end of *Midnight Cowboy*] was that Joe was like a dumb animal; here's a person who has lost his family and adopted Dusty...as his mother. At the end he knows that's not appropriate and people are staring at him; he feels he is defending the relationship some way. He has amazing dignity there — he loves his Ratso who has died in his arms and he's angry and upset and he's deeply, deeply lost and trying to function.

—Voight, interviewed by David Galligan for *Drama-Logue*, 24 Feb-2 Mar 1983

[Milo] Mindbender [in *Catch-22* (1970, Mike Nichols)] is a perverse character. He's got to be a number of different things, depending on the situation he finds himself in. He can be nice, tell jokes, manipulate the base commander [Bob Newhart]. In one scene he's funny, in another he's like a head-waiter — I even play him with that kind of stance, slightly bent forward, eager to please — in another he's as persuasive as an automobile salesman. But when he's fully himself, when he comes on ornery like a beast, he's got to make the others afraid when they look at him. He's got to be able to get that across. Then you suddenly realize, why, this guy is a fascist! In tonight's scene he's reached the height of his villainy. He is so interested in money, and in trading everything for money, even on a human level, that nothing means anything to him except as a commodity. Basically, I think, that's what fascism is, the absence of a human viewpoint. Milo is the antithesis of everything I believe in. I myself am fighting the spirit of Milo, and I hope that everyone who sees the picture will react and see what he's all about, perhaps even see a little of themselves in him and say, "Oh, my God!" in recognition of where that kind of thing can take you. I hate to sound pretentious, but that's the statement I'm trying to make. It's a simple-minded beginning, but you have to make a start somewhere....

I was uncertain whether I could really play the part, and in the beginning I guess I didn't trust Mike Nichols enough to rely on him. One day Mike said to me, "I'm getting some flak from your direction. What's wrong?" We talked. I said, "Tell me what you want from me, what quality you want in each scene, then give me time to figure out a character who can make all those points and still be a person. I've got a methodical mind. Working on a part, I like to figure it all out step by step; then when I've got the center worked out, as that character, I can do anything, handle anything that comes up. But I just can't do that without preparation." So he told me what he wanted, and I broke my back and worked it out.

—Voight, interviewed for *Seventeen*, Sept 1969

What we didn't get to [on *Deliverance* (1972, John Boorman)] was completion, in a sense. It wasn't complete work but it was good work. I didn't feel I completed it but I did what I had to do under the circumstances well and [Boorman] did what he had to do well. The best thing in the movie is the scene with the guitar. He was in top form.... Then he gets to the end of the script and he's worked so hard and he just gets impatient.

I'll give you an example. We're on this river. There's this dam up above and the river is dry. We turn the dam on, open two gates; the river becomes a river — a huge roaring river....

So John says, "Let's get this shot." And usually we try to test the river. It takes four minutes for the gates to open and it takes so many more minutes for the river to fill up and then get to full height. He's looking at the sun and he's saying, "Open it up to 4. Open the gates up to 4!" I'm saying, "John, four is a lot of gates. How do you know what four is today?" We hadn't tried the river that day and 1 could be the same as 4 depending on the rainfall and stuff. But John's yelling, "Let's get it on. Jon, let's go!" He gets the megaphone. This is the scene where we're floundering around and Louis [Burt Reynolds] has gotten his leg broken. So the water starts coming down. We're making a lot of noise — boy, we're in trouble here. Vilmos Zsigmond is down there and the crew is there and they have nets to catch us from going over the 70-foot waterfall. And I'm standing there watching this crazy guy and he's got this dopey hat on. He's wearing this hat and glasses and he's looking and the water's starting to come and he's yelling, "Okay, just about ready to shoot! Camera rolling! Sound!" and the water's coming up and up and up and finally it goes right over the camera and he says, "This is filmmaking!"

—Voight, interviewed for *Dialogue on Film*, June 1973

Jane [Fonda] and all the members of this group — [screenwriter] Waldo Salt and [producer] Jerry Hellman and [director] Hal Ashby — came to me with this script for *Coming Home* [1978] and asked me if I was interested in doing the part that Bruce [Dern] ended up doing — the Captain.

This was heaven to me. The Captain's part was very well written, but I felt that I really wanted to make a statement with the other character [Luke]; I knew what the problem was. I knew exactly what I wanted to change.

I was really feeling very fragile.... I felt down at the bottom of the totem pole in terms of viable commercial personalities, and I was. In other words, I couldn't get a film made. That these people wanted me was just a great gift, and I was very appreciative. [His last film had been in 1974.]

I took a meeting with Hal, and in that meeting I really understood why I felt like the character, because I felt damaged and I felt lots of rage, and I felt also a sense of dignity about myself.... I wanted the role very badly.... I said, "This part is the part of a lover," and as it was written, it was not. I said the part should be played by a lover; and that's what I am. Despite the pain, the anguish and the anger, there was also a certain quality in this man as the lover....

For *Coming Home*, I stayed in a wheelchair as long as possible. I slept in a hospital seven nights a week, most nights. I had my little room there. I was all alone — I wasn't with anybody else. It was good for my head to be relating to the experience of the guys, and it was the kind of thing that once I was in the chair with the guys, I just didn't want to get out. It was like I didn't feel I was a walker. I wasn't relating to walkers very much; I was really relating to the paras; I was just one of the paras, you know. It's a very funny kind of thing, you know; it sounds like it's a little schizophrenic or something, but it really isn't. It's just that if you're with a group of people, you see things their way.

—Voight, interviewed by Mara Purl for *Rolling Stone*, 31 May 1979

Jane [Fonda]...has a tremendous ability to commit herself totally to the moment and not think about the past or any ramifications in the future. On *Coming Home* she came to the set totally prepared, dropped the mother role she played that morning getting her kids to school, worked as a professional actress, then during the lunch break she would make all of her phone calls to set up her projects for solar energy or whatever else she was into. Then when she left the set, she would go on to the next person she is. She has total energy. I've never been able to do that. I go from job to job, pulling all of these loads behind me, trying to figure out who I am.

—Voight, interviewed by Rex Reed for *Travolta to Keaton* (New York: Wm. Morrow & Co., 1979)

Hal Ashby is the kind of guy who stays very much in the background yet he's extremely sensitive and encourages a kind of playfulness on the set. He's a very bright, intuitive director, not at all manipulative of his actors. It's not that he doesn't control the set, it's just that he chooses to stay apart when the processes are going on. He doesn't interfere — he tries to follow what the actors want and encourages that.

—Voight, interviewed by David Galligan for *Drama-Logue*, 24 Feb-2 Mar 1983

When [Andrei] Konchalovsky offered me the film [*Runaway Train* (1986)], I first found it quite shocking to my sensibilities. I couldn't figure out how I could approach this character. But then I decided that Andrei was too great a director not to work with him.

The role, Mannheim, is a kind of mythical character, but the elements that I've put into him are real. I tried to connect with as many convicts as I could, and I met people who were very helpful. I shaped my character from real people, and Manny is mostly scars. He's very tough and very alone and isolated. Prison does that to people. It's a very demoralizing existence.

But Manny cannot be defeated, that's what we sense about him. This is a man who has digested all the ugliness that a man can possibly digest, and he still stands up and says, "You cannot beat me down. I will not die here. You do not have control over me."

—Voight, interviewed by Candace Burke-Block for *The Chicago Sun-Times*, 12 Jan 1986

Erich von STROHEIM [1885-1957]

Born: Vienna, Austria, emigrated to the U.S. around 1906. Work as an extra preceded his association with D.W. Griffith with whom he worked as actor, assistant director and military advisor, beginning with The Birth of a Nation (1915). In 1921, he starred in and directed Foolish Wives:

Iris Barry, the Curator of the Museum of Modern Art in New York, appointed herself as supreme censor and in the shuffle my character of the American ambassador [in *Foolish Wives*] became of all things a travelling salesman! All the scenes of pomp and splendour, such as the ambassador's arrival in Monaco, or on the U.S. cruiser, with all the accompanying etiquette and ceremony were deleted, as also were the scenes of the ambassador's arrival under military escort at the Palace with the Prince of Monaco, and all the sequences showing the receptions of the ambassador by the Prince.

This, of course, weakened the story because Count Sergius in the film used the wife of the American ambassador to put the counterfeit money into circulation. Nobody would have believed that the ambassador's wife would ever do such a thing, whereas the wife of a commercial traveller would have been immediately suspect. Thus the point which I made — of selecting as a medium for the distribution of the counterfeit money a person of incontestible integrity — was lost, as were many many other significant scenes and incidents.

In [*Three Faces East* (1930)] I had a run-in with Constance Bennett as well as with the director [Roy del Ruth]. After I had read the screenplay I made some suggestions to producer Darryl Zanuck pertaining mostly to my own scenes. He liked them very much and asked me to write them out in scenario form. I did so, but when Roy del Ruth was handed the changed script he was furious. However he had to obey Zanuck, though he never forgave me. As some of the scenes included Constance Bennett, she too was incensed by the fact that a mere actor had had the audacity to change some of her action and dialogue. What she and the director both forgot was that I was not only an actor but the writer of all the stories of my own films, as well as many others, and that I was a director also. They could not see that I did not look at a scenario only from an actor's standpoint, but that I developed the faculty of visualizing the finished film after reading the scenario only a few times. It is that striving for perfection which has caused me some other minor and major frictions with producers in whose pictures I worked as an actor....

Stories about my changing the script and the dialogue before I accepted a scenario in which a part was offered to me were told many times in Hollywood. Disgruntled screenwriters and additional-dialogue hacks who had come to believe that every word they had written was a diamond set in platinum told stories about my being "difficult." But real artists, such as James Cruze [on *The Great Gabbo* (1929)], and particularly Jean Renoir, for whom I made *La Grande Illusion* [1937], not only accepted my suggestions willingly, but in fact asked me for my opinion before shooting the script. Directors with small minds, e.g., the aforesaid Roy del Ruth, never have, and never will, create anything important, because in order to do so you have to have an open and flexible mind and not believe that you are omnipotent.

—von Stroheim, in a letter to Peter Noble; repr. in *Hollywood Scapegoat* (London: Fortune Press, 1950/New York: Arno Press, 1971)

My outfit [in *Sunset Boulevard* (1950, Billy Wilder)] is the correct one for morning schedule housework. I designed it myself. I work well with Billy Wilder. He takes suggestions. Some directors I have worked with in the past do not take suggestions from a director of thirty years ago. It's heartbreaking....

—von Stroheim, interviewed by Ezra Goodman for *The New York Times*, 3 July 1949

Max von SYDOW [1929-]

Born: Carl Adolf von Sydow in Lund, Sweden. Work with The Stockholm Royal Dramatic Theater preceded his film debut in Bara en Mar/Only a Mother (1949, Alf Sjoberg). His long association with Ingmar Bergman — 11 films between 1957 and 1970 — began with the role of Antonius Block in The Seventh Seal. He made his first English language film — George Stevens' The Greatest Story Ever Told — in 1965:

I didn't decide to play Christ for the money. George Stevens did not raise his first offer, which was large by our modest Swedish standards. But I was scared. It meant going to Hollywood, out of the security of our stock-company type of filmmaking.

It meant playing a whole role in English, and what a role! Not that I am against representing Christ in the flesh. But not being a deeply religious man, I felt I must show Him as a man of worldly powers before He had divine ones attributed to Him; and this carries a big risk. My Christ was a kind of cross-country preacher prepared to live, if need be, on the iron rations of his faith....

Unfortunately, the film had to take account of the sensitivities of Lutherans, Catholics, and Jews. That is what went wrong with it, I think. That and the fact that the characters in it behave as if they had read the Bible in advance....

—von Sydow, interviewed by Alexander Walker for *The Evening Standard*, 2 Sept 1966

W

Christopher WALKEN [1943-]

Born: Astoria, N.Y. A child actor, he briefly attended Hofstra University before dropping out to work in musical theater. Studies with Wynn Handman and at The Actors Studio, and work off Broadway and in musical revue preceded his film debut in The Anderson Tapes (1971, Sidney Lumet). In 1978, he played Nick opposite Robert De Niro as Michael in Michael Cimino's The Deer Hunter:

When I look at a role, I try to find the equation that makes it true in the context of the film just as it would be true in real life. People always talk about *The Deer Hunter*, for instance. It became a very political movie. I saw nothing political about it. What is it that happens to real men with romantic notions about war? They think it's adventure, that it's fun. Then they go out and get their legs blown off. I'm sure that the equation there has been the same since the beginning of time. It has nothing to do with Vietnam, Russia, America, anything. It has to do with real men and the illusions of young men about war. That's what it was about for me.

—Walken, interviewed by Chuck Pfeifer and Mark Matousek for *Interview*, Mar 1988

My admiration for [De Niro] is one of the things that shows in the film, but it [also] had some bearing on the characters. They're supposed to have been friends for 20 years; there's a powerful feeling between them. I think my feelings about his work helped create an impression of warmth, of friendship.

—Walken, interviewed by Janet Maslin for *The New York Times*, 17 Dec 1978

Eli WALLACH [1915-]

Born: Brooklyn, N.Y. Stage work at The University of Texas, studies at The Neighborhood Playhouse in N.Y., summer stock, and a 1945 Broadway debut preceded his entry into The Actors Studio. He then made his film debut in Elia Kazan's Baby Doll (1956). In 1961, he played Guido in John Huston's The Misfits:

Guido is a man wrapped up in himself, [who's] had enough of getting laid. [He's] just about right for a woman who stands behind him one hundred percent, and is as uncomplaining as a tree.... He's restless as hell. Every girl suffers comparisons to his wife. He has terrible dreams about the past and he can't understand how quickly people forget the war. When he talks about dropping the bombs, this is a mere recitation of war deeds, on a one-dimensional level. On another level, it is [screenwriter, Arthur] Miller's absolute brilliance in having him say this at the moment he wants something else, Roslyn [Marilyn Monroe].

—Wallach, interviewed by James Goode for *The Story of The Misfits* (New York: Bobbs-Merrill, 1963); reprinted as *The Making of The Misfits* (New York: Proscenium Books, 1986)

A fine director like Huston...guides you. For example, in *The Misfits* I had a scene with Clark Gable where we were supposed to be drunk. We sat around a table, and I kept drinking and all that stuff.... We did it several times: didn't work. While they were setting up and changing lights, Huston walked over and said, "You know the drunkest I've ever been?" and I said, "No." He said "Yesterday" (there was a camel race in Virginia City, and he raced on a camel and won the race), "that was the drunkest I've ever been." I said, "I had no idea you were drunk." "Oh," he said, "it's the worst I've ever been." I said, "Nonsense, John, I was there at the race." He said, "So help me, that's the drunkest I've ever been in my life." The technicians said, "We're ready, Mr. Huston." He got up and walked away from the set and I realized he's telling me you can be so drunk that no one knows it, you see. That was direction by indirection. And it's the sweetest way to elicit a performance from someone.

—Wallach, in *Films & Filming*, May 1964

Julie WALTERS [1950-]

Born: Birmingham, England. Studies at Manchester Polytechnic and work with the Everyman Theatre in Liverpool and on the London stage and TV preceded her film debut as Rita in Educating Rita (1983, Lewis Gilbert), a role she had created on the London stage:

I was starting over in a role I already knew very well, but I needed some encouragement....

Michael Caine gave me the best advice. "Remember the camera. Be fresh. Don't leave your performance in the dressing room." He taught me how to restructure my concentration. He's a great bloke!

I can't tell you what playing Rita on film means to me. It meant that I could perfect her — for me, for [playwright] Willy [Russell], for all the Ritas out there. She is a very valid character, believe me. I know she's really Willy, but there's a lot of me in her, too, and there's a lot of the '80s in her....

I identify with Rita's struggles, especially with her decision to change her life. Rita decides to go off to an open university. I decided to become an actress when I was already well into my studies of nursing. So I know what it means for her to make a momentous decision....

The movie is about this little person overcoming obstacles. That's lovely. Who couldn't identify with that or love it?

—Walters, interviewed by Joe Baltake for *The New York Daily News*, 24 Oct 1983

Jack WARDEN [1920-]

Born: Newark, New Jersey. Work on the stage preceded his film debut in The Asphalt Jungle (1950, John Huston). In 1982, he played Mickey Morrissey in Sidney Lumet's The Verdict:

[Mickey Morrissey is] an ambulance chaser. I imagine at one time he had great ideals, as most young lawyers do, but now he's getting old and doesn't have any illusions or great expectations with regard to his place in the legal world.

He sees a lot of himself in Galvin [Paul Newman]. They were partners and at one time I think he recognized the great potential Frank had and identified with that. Now, even though he sympathizes with Galvin's bitterness, his drinking and carryings on, he's trying not to let the guy wallow in it. He looks at Galvin sort of as the son he never had. He has that kind of paternal protectiveness. He wants Galvin to accept his limitations in the way that he's done. He wants him to make peace with that instead of drowning himself in booze.

[*The Verdict*] is the fourth picture I've done with Sidney. He still amazes me. He's so organized and, being an actor, he understands what you have to do.

Everything I've ever done with him, we've rehearsed for at least ten days and it pays off. There are fewer breaks and retakes and that makes it easier for an actor to sustain, to concentrate. This is an especially intense film and Sidney's pace helped tremendously in allowing us to develop that necessary momentum. [Warden also worked on Lumet's *Twelve Angry Men* (1957), *That Kind of Woman* (1959) and *Bye Bye Braverman* (1968)].

—Warden, interviewed for the press release for *The Verdict* (20th Century-Fox, 1982)

Leslie Ann WARREN [1946-]

Born: New York City. Studies at The Actors Studio and work on Broadway (from age 16) preceded her film debut in The Happiest Millionaire (1967, Norman Tokar). In 1982, she played Norma in Blake Edwards' Victor/Victoria:

The character of Norma is all bosom and hips. I literally had to be sewn into those costumes. Norma was a platinum blonde because Jean Harlow was the most popular movie actress of 1934, and Norma wanted to be a movie star. I ran *Dinner At Eight* [1933], and carefully copied Harlow's makeup and mannerisms.

Q. Did you visualize Julie Andrews as a man in the scene where she closes the door and starts to disrobe?

A. I had to. When Julie came at me, I thought, "Oh, my fuckin' word, what's she going to do? Am I going to be raped?" It was Blake Edwards' idea for me to say, "Lock the door." It came to him when we were rehearsing. He does that a lot — all of a sudden, he'll throw something at you. His direction allows for spontaneity and quick decisions, and you never have the sense of being rehearsed.

I'm comfortable improvising within character. When Edwards found this out about me, he'd keep the camera rolling after a scene would end. For instance, that scene in the train where I open my coat and the guy falls down in surprise? After we shot it, I asked the actor, "Are you okay?" The camera rolled on and the dialogue's in the film.

The set was unbelievably harmonious. Edwards knows what he wants and he's in total control, but there's laughter along with the hard work. You want to give him your all.

—Warren, interviewed by Arthur Bell for *The Village Voice*, 30 Mar 1982

Individually, and as a unit, the two of them [Blake Edwards and Julie Andrews] are phenomenal towards other actors. They are generous, supportive; there is no sense of competition. They are totally gracious and dear and funny.... They are so in love with each other. They adore each other and that feeling pervades the set. I mean I've never been on such a happy set in my life.

—Warren, interviewed by Robert Hayes for *Interview*, Oct 1982

Denzel WASHINGTON [1955-]

Born: Mount Vernon, N.Y. Studies at Fordham University in the Bronx and at The American Conservatory Theatre in San Francisco, and work on the New York stage preceded his film debut in Carbon Copy (1981, Michael Schultz). In 1987, he played the role of Stephen Biko in Richard Attenborough's Cry Freedom:

[Biko] was an intellect first of all, a very intelligent young man. He was a very complex, very compassionate, very humble man. All the tapes I've listened to, all the people talk about [is] how soft-spoken he was. He had a very pure, analytic mind.

He was a really unique individual who didn't appear to have hatred in his heart. It's almost hard to imagine a black South African not having some kind of hatred for his enemy. This was a compassionate man, who felt that South Africa could work for black and white alike if they would let it work. Sad to say his enemies weren't as optimistic in their thinking as he was. So he paid the price.

—Washington, interviewed by Lawrence Van Gelder for *The New York Times*, 1 Aug 1986

It was difficult to break myself down and become a primitive man [for the role of Trip in *Glory* (1989, Edward Zwick)]: that was the challenge of this part.... He's a man who says words like onliest. Onliest! I've played a lot of the clean-cut roles, the intelligent parts. Not that Trip isn't intelligent. He's very cunning, a brilliant survivor. And then, one day, he finds himself in a place where he can make a difference....

Trip's an instigator — wild, rebellious, angry. He's a product of racism who's *become* a racist. He hates all white people. Confederates most of all. But finally in the end, when he sees the white officers make the maximum sacrifice, he's the most patriotic one in the bunch.

Q. Is Trip a 20th-century man in a 19th-century drama?

A. There were a lot of black soldiers like Trip and he's not a 20th-century invention. They were rowdy, they spoke out when they could, and some of them were killed, and some of them went on to be loners. They lived in the woods, in caves, and did whatever they could to stay away from the reach of their masters. Some of them later became scouts. The job was perfect for them.

—Washington, interviewed by Glenn Collins for *The New York Times*, 28 Dec 1989

[Spike Lee on *Mo' Better Blues* (1990) is] more quiet than most directors I've worked with. He didn't have a lot of things to say while we were shooting. We kinda hashed it all out in rehearsal. We communicated, but there wasn't a lot of theater-type directing going on. He's more on the technical side of it. He expects you to come in and hit it. But he'll leave the camera on to allow things to happen. We would set up shots some time where he'd just set the camera up and say, "OK, start talking." In that regard, there was a lot more freedom to be spontaneous. He might just leave the camera on and see. So you got used to knowing that that was what was going to happen in certain circumstances. So you freed up that way. And probably some of the most interesting and funny stuff comes out of those times.

—Washington, interviewed by Thulani Davis for *American Film*, Aug 1990

Ethel WATERS [1900-1977]

Born: Chester, Pennsylvania. On the stage (from age 17), she made her film debut in On with the Show (1929, Alan Crosland). In 1943, she played Petunia Jackson in Vincente Minnelli's Cabin in the Sky:

[When I] made *Cabin in the Sky* there was conflict between the studio [MGM] and me from the beginning. For one thing, I objected violently to the way religion was being treated in the screenplay.

Eddie (Rochester) Anderson, Lena Horne, and many other performers were in the cast. But all through that picture there was so much snarling and scrapping that I don't know how in the world *Cabin in the Sky* ever stayed up there.

I won all my battles on the picture. But like many other performers, I was to discover that winning arguments in Hollywood is costly. Six years were to pass before I could get another movie job.

I had always loved John Ford's pictures. And I came to love him, too, but I was frightened to death working for him. He'd never seen me on the stage and he used the shock treatment while directing me. That system has worked with a great many other performers, but it didn't work well with me. I almost had a stroke working for John Ford.

After four weeks, though, John Ford's doctor told him he'd have to quit directing for a while as he had overworked himself. Elia Kazan came in and replaced him [on *Pinky* (1949)]. He remade the picture from the beginning. Kazan...had been an actor himself and he understood my problems. Mr. Kazan, God love him, was able to bring out the very best in me. I was able, through his help, to let myself go and live the part of Granny as I moved before the cameras.

Elia Kazan gave me credit for intelligence. Together we'd walk through the sets while discussing my role.

—Waters, in her (with Charles Samuels) *His Eye is on the Sparrow* (New York: Doubleday & Co., 1950)

Sam WATERSTON [1940-]

Born: Cambridge, Massachusetts. Studies at Yale University and work on Broadway (from 1963) preceded his film debut in the low budget independent film, The Plastic Dome of Norma Jean (1967, Juleen Compton). In 1980, he played Sydney Schanberg in Roland Joffé's The Killing Fields:

Q. *The Killing Fields* had as its center the theme of friendship (between Sydney Schanberg and Dith Pran). How did you approach recreating the friendship on screen with Haing Ngor?

A. Roland gave us an extraordinarily long time to get to know each other and arranged things so that we would get to know each other in somewhat the same way that Sydney and Dith Pran did in real life.

They rushed us [Haing Ngor, John Malkovich, Julian Sands and myself] all out to Thailand in a great hurry and then they said there really isn't anything for you to do, why don't you go up to the Golden Triangle. It was all so disingenuous, because the idea was for us to go off and form a unit on our own, so we went up there and Haing became our guide. Haing speaks at least a half-dozen languages apart from English — he speaks all the languages of Southeast Asia really — he speaks some Thai, he speaks Cambodian, he speaks several dialects of Chinese.

We found out as Sydney must have found out, as all the journalists in Southeast Asia must have found out, that your life depends, or certainly the ease of your life depends, upon the person who lives there, who knows how to get around, knows how much to pay for things, knows where the best restaurants are....

We had nothing to do except get to know each other. We sat around at night after we'd been tourists during the day, and told each other the stories of our lives. Haing's story is an incredible story, full of courage, sadness, tragedy. It's an unthinkable story for a nice boy from the Northeast of the United States — an unbelievable story.

That was the first thing that we did, and then we went to the refugee camps where Haing had been a refugee, and had worked as a doctor and he told us that whole part of his story. Then we went and visited a Khmer Rouge camp, a newly set up camp. Haing had been tortured and nearly killed several times at the hands of the Khmer Rouge. He served as our guide through this camp — one unforgettable experience on top of another.

We then went back to Bangkok, and he served as my guide in town. Roland sent us out to do newspaper stories together and we did. So by the time we started shooting we knew each other really rather well, certainly in movie terms we knew each other extraordinarily well, because you usually don't get any rehearsal at all, or this kind of background....

Q. The role of Dith Pran was Haing's first acting role. Did you reciprocate as his guide during filming? Did he learn the trade from you?

A. He was a natural actor.... We all improvised together, and he was as good at it as any of the rest of us. Another thing that Roland did which was wonderful was that he made all of the technical questions of making the movie — hitting your mark, getting your face in the light and being turned just the right way for the camera — entirely the responsibility of the camera crew, not the responsibility of the actors. So that thing which very often takes a little part of your concentration even if you're very used to it was removed for all of us. I think it caused enormous headaches for the camera crew, but it was a great burden off us.

—Waterston, interviewed by Terry Materese for *The Cable Guide*, Mar 1986

Usually audience response to a character comes out of real sympathy for the guy. [In *The Killing Fields*] we didn't court sympathy, didn't make him cuter or make him get cozy with the audience. That's an opportunity you don't get very often in big parts in movies because sympathy has to go to the leading character....

I spent an intense three days with Sydney Schanberg over a period of a few weeks. It made the preparation of the part easier, made it easier to nail down the specifics of the character. But it was hard for him. There was no fencing around or feeling each other out. He poured himself out. It's a tremendous act of trust to put your life story in someone's hands.

—Waterston, interviewed by Aljean Harmetz for *The New York Times*, 24 Mar 1985

John WAYNE [1907-1979]

Born: Marion Morrison in Winterset, Iowa. A football scholarship to The University of Southern California (Los Angeles) preceded his film debut as a double for Francis X. Bushman in the football film, Brown of Harvard (1926, Jack Conway). Over the next five years he had numerous bit parts and worked as a set director until he landed his first major role in The Big Trail (1931, Raoul Walsh), on John Ford's recommendation. In 1928, Wayne had met Ford while working as a set director and extra on Ford's Mother Machree. Between 1928 and 1930, Wayne played bit parts in four Ford films; in 1939, he played The Ringo Kid in Stagecoach, the first of sixteen leading parts for Ford:

I played a tough youngster who really was decent at heart. My father had been shot to death and I was blamed for it. I had broken out of jail in pursuit of the real criminals. In my opening scene I enter the stage and the passengers ask me who I am, and I say, "The Ringo Kid. That's what my friends call me. But my right name's Henry."

Those three sentences were my passport to fame.

But I didn't know that on the first day of shooting. Ford yelled, "Don't you know how to walk? You're as clumsy as a hippo. And stop slurring your dialogue and show some expression. You look like a poached egg."

The first two days I had to take the worst ragging of my career, but on the third day Ford nudged me and whispered, "Don't worry, Duke — you're good. Damn good."

Years later he explained why he had deliberately bullied me. He had two reasons. First, he knew if he could arouse my anger, it would mobilize all my emotions and I would give a better performance. He wanted to help me shake off the bad habits of 10 years of mechanical acting in quickie westerns. Secondly, he was afraid the other actors, who were all big stars, would resent the fact that Ford had placed one of his protegés in an important role. By taking the offensive against me, Ford suspected he could get the rest of the cast on my side. His tactics worked beautifully.

—Wayne, as told to Maurice Zolotow in *The American Weekly*, 28 Nov 1954

Working with Jean [Arthur] in *A Lady Takes a Chance* [1943] which [her husband] Frank

[Ross] produced, has been a real experience for me. This is the first time I was ever in a comedy. If it hadn't been for Jean, I might not have made it. She is an amazing person to work with. No matter how I read my lines, she always suited hers to match my tempo — which is, at times, eccentric to say the least. I have never met any actress who has such perfect timing....

Jean is a retake artist. She never does the same scene twice in the same way. She makes each new shot a refreshing and better one than the last. To say that she keeps her cast on the jump is putting it mildly. William Seiter, our director, was also impressed with her work, but I didn't think so at first. Several times after Jean had done a perfect take, he would make her shoot it over again. One day I asked him why he did this. He replied, "Jean may do something new that will be even better and I want to see what it will be."

She nearly threw me on the first day, though. I was a little surprised when I saw her jumping up and down and yelling just before we did our first scene. I looked at her strangely. She smiled and said, "Oh, I'm just relaxing." Since then, I have found that this gymnastic exercise is part of Jean Arthur at work.

—Wayne, in *Screenland* (undated), in the files of The New York Public Library for the Performing Arts

Nobody seems to realize...I was playing [Charles] Laughton's part in *Mutiny on the Bounty* [1935, Frank Lloyd] in *Red River* [1948, Howard Hawks]. It's just the story of *Mutiny on the Bounty* put into a Western, and the guy that wrote it [Borden Chase] did it in that way.

—Wayne, interviewed by Anthony Macklin for *Film Heritage,* Summer 1975

You've got to project a code of ethics that the audience respects. My code, for instance, is that I stick to what I believe is right, no matter what happens. An audience respects that, and it's respect that creates manliness.

You have to create an image that's always pulling for you. I've played plenty of heavies, but ethics always pull you through....

While I was making *Red River*...I was supposed to be frightened in one scene, and the director told me it was a good chance to do some "acting."

I guess some of the younger guys today would have used the chance to go all to pieces, but I couldn't. I acted frightened all right, but I played it out. The difference is, you just don't yellow out. You don't ruin the illusion.

No matter how much of a man you are, you can look pretty silly sometimes if you go exactly by what's in a script. You've got to remember a script is written by a typewriter on a piece of paper — it's not entirely human.

My feeling about movie acting is that it's like sitting in a room with somebody. The audience is with you — not like the stage, where they're looking at you — so you've got to be careful to project the right illusion.

—Wayne, interviewed by UPI; repr. in *The New York Herald Tribune*, 7 June 1959

Maureen O'Hara is a big lusty, wonderful gal. My kinda gal.

She doesn't care if she's messed up if it'll help the picture along. We did a scene together [in *The Quiet Man* (1952, John Ford)] where I had to drag her through a lotta pig manure.

I looked at her, laughed and she said, "You're not going to do anything else are you? How dare you?"

Well, I aimed to take a playful kick. She yelled. "You wouldn't. You couldn't." But I did.

And she went sprawling in the manure. The cameras were still rolling and Jack Ford, the director, said, "We'll use it."

—Wayne, interviewed for *News of the World*, 30 June 1974

Q. Why did you assume that Harry Carey pose holding your arm at the end of *The Searchers* [1956, John Ford]?

A. Jesus, you noticed that! You know why I did this at the end of the picture — Harry Carey had died and his widow was playing the mother of [John] Qualen's wife [Vera Miles]. In the last scene they had taken the girl [Natalie Wood] in, and as they went by the camera the wind was blowing on me and I saw them turn around. She and I had talked about Harry in that stance on other occasions, and I saw her looking at me and I just did it. Goddam, tears just came to her eyes. I was playing that scene for Ollie Carey....

—Wayne, interviewed by Anthony Macklin for *Film Heritage*, Summer 1975

While they're lighting a set [John Ford] talks to the actors very quietly, puts them through a scene. Now he calls the cameraman over. He watches them go through the scene. He talks to them. "Do you think you can go down over there instead of here?" "Yeah, sure." Now, when you start to do the scene you're at complete ease. You've walked through it, and as you're setting your lines you're in the right position. Some directors line the whole scene up the night before and say, "You stand here and you stand there and when you say that line come over here." Well, when you say "Come over here on that line," instinctively it affects your performance. The other way, you're eased into it so beautifully you're where he wants you for composition but you're also where you want to be for the lines. Ford wants the action to come out of the actor in a manner that is comfortable to him. After that's done, then he gives you the little touches that he wants. But he gets you at ease first. [Wayne also worked on Ford's *The Long Voyage Home* (1940), *They Were Expendable* (1945), *Fort Apache* (1948), *Three Grandfathers* (1948), *She Wore a Yellow Ribbon* (1949), *Rio Grande* (1950), *Rookie of the Year* (1955 — for TV), *The Wings of Eagles* (1957), *The Horse Soldiers* (1959), *The Man Who Shot Liberty Valance* (1962), *Flashing Spikes* (1962 — for TV), *How the West Was Won* (1962, co-directed with George Marshall and Henry Hathaway) and *Donovan's Reef* (1963).

Q. What about William Wellman?

A. He's a wonderful old sonofabitch. Really wild. He had a metal plate in his head from some old accident and he'd go around belting all these big, tough guys and they'd be afraid to hit him back for fear they'd kill him. Wild Bill Wellman — a wonderful old guy!

Q. Fine director?

A. Fine director. He didn't delve into characters as much as some. I'll tell you the difference between directors: Hawks [with whom Wayne also worked on *Rio Bravo* (1959), *El Dorado* (1967) and *Rio Lobo* (1970)] has tremendous patience with people. He'll keep working on a fellow, even if he's not cutting the mustard. Ford won't hire you unless he knows he can get it out of you. Wellman figures you're a pro and doesn't bother you much as an actor. If you don't deliver, he'll simply cut the part down. It's that easy. [Wayne also worked on Wellman's *College Coach* (1933), *Island in the Sky* (1953), *The High and the Mighty* (1954) and *Blood Alley* (1955).]

—Wayne, interviewed by Scott Eyman for *Focus on Film*, Spring 1975

[Historian Frank] Dobie gave me the key to the character of Crockett in *The Alamo* [1960, John Wayne] — that he [Crockett] never ate on an empty stomach, nor drank on a full. And that kind of tells his character and gives you an attitude of how to make a human being out of the great hero.

—Wayne, interviewed 29 Apr 1970 by Kenneth Hufford for The Arizona Historial Society Oral History Project

The Western...it's an American art form. It represents what this country is about. In *True Grit* [1969, Henry Hathaway], for example, that scene where Rooster shoots the rat. That was a kind of reference to today's problems. Oh, not that *True Grit* has a message or anything. But that scene was about less accommodation, and more justice....

I like so many things about the movie. The dialogue, for one. It's the authentic stuff, the way people talked. The last time I had dialogue of that style was in *She Wore a Yellow Ribbon* when John Ford had the integrity to use dialogue that fit the period. Mostly, nobody gives a damn....

But to get back to *True Grit*, the thing that makes me happy is that Henry Hathaway is getting some credit. For years, Henry got the thankless jobs at Fox. They'd give him the problem pictures.... Henry was known as a craftsman, but his stature as a director wasn't recognized. On this picture he did a hell of a job....

Hathaway did a wonderful thing. He used the backgrounds in such a way that it became almost fantasy. Remember that one scene, where old Rooster is facing those four men across the meadow, and he takes the reins in his teeth and charges? That's Henry at work. It's a real meadow, but it looks almost dreamlike. Henry made it a fantasy and yet he kept it an honest Western.

—Wayne, interviewed by Roger Ebert for *The New York Times*, 29 June 1969

A. Hathaway is a fine, instinctive creator....

Q. I've heard that he's been known to make grown actors cry.

A. Well, there's a legend built up around this man. I never saw him yell. He treats you very gently as an actor. He'll put down green boughs for you to walk on so you'll walk softly. Unless you are careless or not interested. Then he can be a sonofabitch. He treats a little mistake the same as a big one. He's a bludgeon on all mistakes. Ford, on the other hand, uses a rapier zinging in and out. Hawks never lets anything perturb him: he's the coldest character I've ever met in my life. [Wayne also worked on Hathaway's *The Shepherd of the Hills* (1941), *Legend of the Lost* (1957), *North to Alaska* (1960), *How the West Was Won*, *Circus World* (1964) and *The Sons of Katie Elder* (1965).]

—Wayne, interviewed by Scott Eyman for *Focus on Film*, Spring 1975

You know that old buzzard Rooster Cogburn.... Well, he was the same character I played years ago in *Yellow Ribbon*. I played him exactly the same way and it worked both times.

—Wayne, interviewed by Lorraine Gaugin for *Views and Reviews*, Sept 1973

One of the people from Warner Brothers at first said I didn't have to die in *The Cowboys* [1972, Mark Rydell]. But I said that the picture is no good if I live. The whole idea of it is what this Mr. Chips teaches the kids. If I'm alive and they recapture the herd of cattle from the rustlers, it doesn't mean as much.

—Wayne, interviewed by P.F. Kluge for *Life*, 28 Jan 1972

[*The Shootist* (1976, Don Siegel)] is one of the best pictures I've ever been in. And I seldom brag about a picture. Sometimes there's a scene that's pretty good, and the fact is I made a fair number of pretty damn good pictures for Ford and Hathaway and Hawks...but this is a good one. I knew it from the beginning. Ron Howard is the best young actor I've ever worked with.... The idea is that Ron will go on to be a better man because he's known the Shootist, who represents values that have become pretty scarce.

—Wayne, interviewed by Roger Ebert for *The Chicago Sun-Times*, 12 Sept 1976

I have found that you take your ah, ah, ahs in the middle of a sentence. You say, "I think I'll...." Now they're looking at you, and you can stand there for twenty minutes before you say, "go to town." If you say it normally, "I think I'll go to town. Um [pause]. Then we can go over and see something," the audience would have left you. But if you say, "I think I'll go [pause] to town, and I'll [pause] see those three broads," now they're waiting for you. You can take all the goddam time you want if you choose your time for the hesitation. So that's where these bastards that try to imitate me...they don't know what I've done to establish a thing where I can take all the time I want.

—Wayne, interviewed by Anthony Macklin for *Film Heritage*, Summer 1975

I just can't understand the theory that you're trying to put those words in my mouth that I play myself, which is a lot of crap. In one role, I'm a guy with a sense of humor. In another I'm a mean old man. In others, I'm a romantic or a tough character. Each of those characters is different. And he's different to the people around him. You don't see that, do you?

—Wayne, interviewed by Joe McInerney for *Film Comment*, Sept 1972

Seems like nobody remembers how different the fellows were in *The Quiet Man* or *The Sands of Iowa Jima* [1949, Allan Dwan] or *Yellow Ribbon* where I was 35 playing a man of 65. To stay a star, you have to bring along some of your own personality. Thousands of good actors can carry a scene, but a star has to carry the scene and still, without intruding, allow some of his character into it.

—Wayne, interviewed by Roger Ebert for *The New York Times*, 29 June 1969

Dennis WEAVER [1924-]

Born: Joplin, Missouri. Studies at The University of Oklahoma and at The Actors Studio in N.Y. and work on stage and TV preceded his film debut in Dragnet (1954, Jack Webb). In 1958, he played the Motel Clerk in Orson Welles' Touch of Evil:

I accepted a small part described only as the caretaker of a motel. The call for the first day was eight AM and I wasn't used until four PM. Sitting around the set is an important part of the actor's craft. On this day it turned out to be a real blessing. I began to bring ideas for the character to Orson. He always weighed them and usually said something like, "Hey, that's good, but on top of that what if...?" giving me a stimulating thought that spurred me on, making me feel that nothing was being imposed but that I was creating.

I was playing Chester in *Gunsmoke* at the time. Orson's first words to me were wonderful. He asked me what were some of the outstanding characteristics of Chester. I mentioned that he was a follower. Whereupon Orson said let's make this character totally different. Never let anyone get in front of you. This made me walk with a quick step always glancing from side to side to see if anyone was making a move beside me.

While most directors would have played safe and asked me to do what they knew I could, Orson's impulses wouldn't allow it. He wanted something fresh and new. We decided that the character should be tremendously attracted to women but at the same time, totally scared of them. I had a scene with Janet Leigh in a motel room. I told Orson I was having trouble staying in the room.... I had an impulse to run and he asked what was stopping me. I said according to the script I've got to stay in the room. He told me that the script must yield to the truth...so run! The rest of the scene was played peeking at her from behind trees with a good fifty feet between us.

—Weaver, in *American Cinematographer*, Apr 1975

Sigourney WEAVER [1949-]

Born: Susan Weaver in New York City; daughter of actress Elizabeth Inglis [aka Elizabeth Earl] and TV executive Sylvester (Pat) Weaver. Studies at Stanford University and The Yale School of Drama, and several collaborations with playwright Christopher Durang preceded her film debut in a walk-on part in Annie Hall (1977, Woody Allen). In her next film — Alien (1979, Ridley Scott) — she starred as Ripley:

[On *Alien*], I worked terribly hard under conditions I did not think were terribly pro-actor. The lighting was the most important thing, then the special effects, and somewhere way down the list was acting. Our assistant directors were incredibly surly...for some reason. Even John Hurt, I remember him crying in the office of one of the producers. Everyone said it was the toughest film they'd ever made. I never wanted to make another film again.

—Weaver, interviewed by Teresa Carpenter for *Premiere*, Oct 1988

I often worked with shorter actors, and much taller ones, and only one really minded my height — Chevy Chase [on *Deal of the Century* (1983, William Friedkin)]. I'd come on the set with my high heels, and he'd say, "Should I get up on a box?" I think his wife is really tiny, so he wasn't used to a tall woman. It made him uncomfortable.... You know Mel Gibson? When I tell people I'd love to work with him again [after *The Year of Living Dangerously* (1983, Peter Weir)], they say, "Oh, you're so much taller than he is!" But he didn't mind and I didn't mind. I would have minded if he had minded. That film was a huge experience for me, a turning point. I just adore Mel. I think he's the sexiest man I ever met.

—Weaver, interviewed by Dotson Rader for *Parade*, 25 Sept 1988

This kind of script [*Aliens* (1986, James Cameron)] gives you the opportunity to do something you'd only do in classical theater, which is to play a warrior. And it's kind of an opera, in that all the emotions are very big-scale.

I tried to work on it the way I would if I were playing a Prince Hal or something like that; not to heroize myself, but to get back in touch with those bigger values of finally being willing to take the power and use it for good, and all those sorts of classical demands. Like the women warriors in China. I was thinking more along those lines than about Arnold Schwarzenegger or something like that....

There were things in Ripley's situation — in the script you realize she's outlived her own daughter, that she's a prisoner in this modern time, the fact that no one believes her — very haunting things that to me as an actor I'd never been asked to deal with.

—Weaver, interviewed by Michael Healy for *The New York Post*, 21 July 1986

There had been talk about making [*Gorillas in the Mist* (1988), Dian Fossey's] descent into madness. But [director] Michael Apted and I felt that that was not the story. What we try to tell is the story of a woman with an obsession. She got over there and started making huge discoveries. She ended up being quite isolated. She did become fiercely single-minded about what she thought could save them — it became a very personal thing with her. To me that's not madness.

—Weaver, interviewed by Teresa Carpenter for *Premiere*, Oct 1988

I had read Fossey's book a long time ago and had been very interested in her, but I didn't think it would make a good movie. I thought that she was very difficult to understand and that a movie would sort of flatten that out about her and make her too understandable. But I don't think this film did. There is a lot of controversy over what happened. Was she a racist or not? Was she raped during the civil war in the Congo?

I did a lot of research. I found she had real highs and lows, and I certainly know what I consider to be the truth. For instance, I don't believe she was raped. But even if you disagree with what we think are the facts, the character still has a kind of energy that could easily get someone into terrible trouble — yet also keep one out of trouble. There's almost nothing you can say about Dian that doesn't have a good and a bad side to it.

Q. In what way would she have been considered a racist?

A. Anyone who threatened the gorillas in any way, she would capture.... She went to violent extremes to make her point. She was completely pro-animals. Not that she didn't like human beings, but most people think that animals are third-class citizens. Very few people really see animals as "the others" with whom we inhabit this planet. They have equal rights with us.

Q. So her racism wasn't necessarily anti-black; it was anti-human.

A. It was anti her enemies. The gorillas' enemies were her enemies. She was very clear about that and, therefore, I think, was a very irrational, unpopular person.

—Weaver, interviewed by Christopher Durang for *Interview*, July 1988

A sci-fi picture should be easier for an actress than the story of an amazingly complex woman. But as it happened, the *Alien* movies were much harder. With Dian, I had so many facts. I didn't have to do it all in my head. And I'd finally learned what Peter Weir had tried to teach me — it's O.K. to do all the background work, and it's also O.K. to leave it at home. The important thing is to let things come out that are right for the part....

—Weaver, interviewed by Jesse Kornbluth for *Vanity Fair*, Aug 1988

If feminists are going to object to me playing a ruthless woman sympathetically, all I can say is I don't care. I'm interested in human nature, not whitewashed human nature, and there are people like Katherine [Parker in *Working Girl* (1988, Mike Nichols)] *out* there. It's not my responsibility if certain others don't like that fact....

[Katherine is a person who] sees the world as her oyster, who's been brought up, in the most privileged circumstances, to believe that everything would come her way.

—Weaver, interviewed by Charles Leerhsen for *Savvy Woman*, Jan 1989

Chloe WEBB [1959-]

Born: New York City. Studies at The Boston Conservatory of Music and Drama and work on the stage in Boston, Chicago, Los Angeles and N.Y., preceded her film debut as Nancy Spungen in Alex Cox's Sid and Nancy (1986):

I wanted to meet someone who had something nice to say about Nancy. When [Nancy's sister Susan Spungen and I] finally got together, she didn't think I looked a bit like Nancy. She brought lots of photographs of her and Nancy when they were little and you could really see Nancy's need to be loved in those pictures.

The thing about Nancy was that she was so strong. If only she could have channeled her strength into something positive, she could have been anything she wanted. But the thing she wanted was to be a rock star's girlfriend and she got what she wanted: she became the most famous groupie in the world.

—Webb, interviewed for the press release for *Sid and Nancy* (The Goldwyn Co., 1986)

Clifton WEBB [1891-1966]

Born: Webb Hollenbeck in Indianapolis. Work with Palmer Cox's Lyceum's Children's Theatre (from age 9), in opera, and as a dancer and actor on Broadway (from 1913) preceded his film debut in Polly with a Past (1920, Leander de Cordova). In 1948, he played Mr. Belvedere in Sitting Pretty (1948, Walter Lang), the first of three films as this character:

I always enjoy doing something unexpected.... So, when I was given the part of an unsuccessful writer turned baby sitter, I decided to play it right against type. Instead of making Belvedere a long-haired, carelessly dressed and not-too-clean Bohemian, I gave him a crew hair-cut, neatly pressed clothes and a precise manner. I also made him supercapable, yet kind and a complete gentleman. You just couldn't help but like a character like that. [He also starred in *Mr. Belvedere Goes to College* (1949, Elliott Nugent) and *Mr. Belvedere Rings the Bell* (1951, Henry Koster).]

—Webb, in *The Saturday Evening Post*, 19 Nov 1949

Tuesday WELD [1943-]

Born: Susan Weld in New York City. As a child she worked as a photographer's model and appeared on TV; she made her film debut in Rock, Rock, Rock (1956, Will Price). In 1968, she played Sue Ann Stepanek in Noel Black's Pretty Poison:

[*Pretty Poison*] was the least creative experience I ever had. Constant hate, turmoil and dissonance. Not a day went by without a fight. Noel Black, the director, would come up to me before a scene and say, "Think about Coca-Cola." I finally said, "Look, just give the directions to Tony Perkins and he'll interpret for me." I don't care if critics like it; I hated it.

—Weld, interviewed by Rex Reed for *People Are Crazy Here* (New York: Delacorte Press, 1974)

The sonuvabitch [Frank Perry] wanted to test me [for *Play It As It Lays* (1972)]. I said no way, that's highly insulting. He was testing *models*. We had this huge argument. "I wouldn't do this part if you paid me a million dollars if I have to test." I said, "I've done twenty-two movies, you've done *four*. But make up your mind *quick*." He's such a liar. I wasn't nuts to do the part anyway. Who'd want to play *that* lady? It represents a great deal of pain having to get into the character. My life is depressing enough. Anybody jumping up and down for it has to be a masochist. It's very removed from me, as well as a very different part for me. It's a *character* part. And I was past the point of exhaustion doing it. The identification is in the pain rather than the incidents. If you took it word for word, Maria never *was* really an actress — she made one gang-bang picture. But if you take what I've been through and *that* character has been through, it's very similar emotionally. Pain is pain.

—Weld, interviewed by C. Robert Jennings for *Cosmopolitan*, Oct 1972

[Richard Brooks] was wonderful to work with [on *Looking for Mr. Goodbar* (1977)] because he's fast. He knows exactly what he wants and, of course, he writes it, so that's a great help. If there's any problem, he doesn't have to go to the writer, he'll sit down and do it. I respect that. He also had this crew together. He'd just set up a shot in fifteen minutes and he'd do it — bang. That was it! I like that, because I guess my greatest problem is impatience. I just don't like doing it around and around.

—Weld, interviewed by Tony Crawley for *Films Illustrated*, Sept 1978

Mel WELLES [1930-]

Born: New York. Work on the stage preceded his film debut in Appointment in Honduras (1953, Jacques Tourneur). In 1960, he played Gravis Mushnik in Little Shop of Horrors, the second of three films for Roger Corman:

Q. Did Corman give you creative freedom in shaping your characters?

A. Generally, yes — he was really busy with the actual filmmaking process, and he didn't have time to tell you much about them! That's why he kept a repertory company and always used the same group, because he could rely on them to do a competent or adequate job under any conditions....

Q. Dick Miller told us that practically everything you did and he did in *Little Shop* was ad-libbed.

A. Absolutely none of it was ad-libbed. Dick Miller and I used to talk to each other in accents all the time, and use Jewish expressions in conversation. But every word in *Little Shop* was written by Chuck Griffith, and I did ninety-eight pages of dialogue in two days.

Q. Is it difficult to maintain a sense of humor when you're under pressure to make a movie in two days?

A. No, we weren't under pressure. We got together and rehearsed the lines for about three weeks before we got on the set, so we were all very well prepared and we did it like a play. Roger had two camera crews on the set — that's why the picture, from a filmic standpoint, really is not very well done. The two camera crews were pointed in opposite directions so that we got both angles, and then other shots were "picked up" to use in between, to make it flow. It was a pretty fixed set and it was done sort of like a sitcom is done today, so it wasn't very difficult. And sense of humor? Hell, that was a real love project — everybody on that film knew each other and was having a good time. Jackie Joseph, Jonathan Haze, Dick Miller, Chuck Griffith and myself were all very good friends; the first patient in the dentist's chair was Chuck Griffith's father, and Myrtle Vail, the woman that played the mother to Seymour Krelboined [Haze], was Chuck's grandmother.... Even the extras on *Little Shop* were friends! It was an exercise in love....

The best part I ever had was in *Little Shop of Horrors*, but it wasn't really because of Roger; it was because Chuck Griffith created the character based on things that I would say when I talked with an accent. The character was written for me, and there was no question about the fact that I was going to play it. [Welles also appeared in Corman's *The Attack of the Crab Monsters* (1956) and *The Undead* (1957).]

—Welles, interviewed by Tom Weaver and John Brunas for *Fangoria*, Oct 1986

Orson WELLES [1915-1985]

Born: Kenosha, Wisconsin. Work as an actor and director with The Gate Theatre in Dublin, Ireland (1931-1934), as an actor with Katherine Cornell's company — both on the road and on Broadway — and on the radio, preceded his formation (with John Houseman) of The Mercury Theatre Group in N.Y. His work as an actor and director with that group both on the stage and radio led to his contract to direct and act on the screen. He co-directed his first film — a 4 minute short — in 1934; he made his feature film debut as a director with Citizen Kane (1941), which he also co-wrote and in which he starred as Charles Foster Kane:

Kane is selfish and selfless, an idealist, a scoundrel, a very big man and a very little one. It depends on who's talking about him.

—Welles, in *Friday*, 14 Feb 1941

Q. There is a line spoken by [Kane] to his banker [Mr. Thatcher (George Coulouris)] which we would like very much to hear you explain: "I could have been a great man, if I hadn't been so rich."

A. Good, the whole story is in that. Anything at all may destroy greatness: a woman, illness, riches.... If he had been poor, Kane would not have been a great man but one thing is sure and that is that he would have been a successful man. He thinks that success brings greatness....

It isn't because everything seems easy to him. That is an excuse he gives himself. But the film doesn't say that. Obviously, since he is the head of one of the biggest fortunes in the world, things become easier, but his greatest error was that of the American plutocrats of those years, who believed that money automatically conferred a certain type of stature to a man. Kane is a man who truly belongs to his time. This type of man hardly exists any more. These were the plutocrats who believed they could be President of the United States, if they wanted to. They also believed that they could buy anything....

Q. Did you make any suggestions as to the way of handling [your scene as Father Mapple in *Moby Dick* (1956, John Huston)]?

A. All we did was discuss the way in which it would be shot. You know that my discourse is very long. It goes on throughout a full reel.... I arrived on the set already made-up and dressed. I got up on the platform and we shot it in one take. We did it using only one camera angle. And that is one of Huston's merits, because another director would have said, "Let's do it from another angle and see what we get." He said, "Good," and my role in the film ended right there.

—Welles, interviewed by Juan Cobos, Miguel Rubio and J.A. Pruneda for *Cahiers du Cinéma*; trans. by Rose Kaplin for *Cahiers in English* #5, 1966

It's a mistake to think that [Hank] Quinlan [in *Touch of Evil* (1958)] finds any favor in my eyes. To me, he's hateful. There's no ambiguity in his character. He's not a genius: he's a master of his field, a provincial master, but a detestable man. The most personal thing I've put in this film is my hatred of the abuse of police power. And it's obvious: it's more interesting to speak of the abuse of police power in connection with a man of a certain size — not only physical but also with regard to his personality — than with an ordinary little cop. So Quinlan is better than an ordinary cop, which doesn't prevent him from being hateful.... But it's always possible to feel sympathy for a son of a bitch. Sympathy is a human thing, after all.... Quinlan is sympathetic because of his humanity, not because of his ideas. There's not the least particle of genius in him.... Quinlan is a good technician, he knows his job: he's an "authority." But because he's a man of certain breadth, a man of courage, you can't prevent yourself from feeling sympathy for him. In spite of everything, he's a human being. I believe that Kane is a detestable man, but I have a great deal of sympathy for him so far as he's a human being.

Q. And Macbeth [in *Macbeth* (1948)]?

A. A similar case. More or less voluntarily, you know, I've played a lot of unsavory types. I detest Harry Lime [in *The Third Man* (1949, Carol Reed)], that little black market hustler, all these horrible men I've interpreted. But these aren't small men, because I'm an actor for characters on a grand scale. You know, in the old classic French theater, there were always some actors who played kings and others who did not. I'm one of those who play kings. I have to be, because of my personality. So naturally, I always play the role of leaders, men of some unusual breadth; I always need to be bigger than life. It's a fault of my nature. So it's not necessary to believe there's anything ambiguous about my interpretation.... Certainly Quinlan is a "moral" character, but I detest his morality.

Q. Isn't this feeling of ambiguity reinforced by the fact that at the end of the film Quinlan has been right in spite of everything, since the young Mexican [Victor Millan] is guilty?

A. Despite everything, he's wrong. It's only an accident. Who cares about knowing whether he was mistaken or not?

Q. Isn't it important?

A. That depends on your point of view. Personally, I believe in everything that's said by [Vargas] the character played by [Charlton] Heston. I'd be able to say everything Vargas says. He speaks as a man of dignity, according to the tradition of classical humanism, which is absolutely my tradition as well. So this is the angle from which you have to understand the film: whatever Vargas says, he says as my mouthpiece. It's better to see a murderer go free than for a policeman to abuse his power. If you have a choice between the abuse of police power and letting a crime go unpunished, you have to choose the unpunished crime. That's my point of view. So, let's accept the fact that the young Mexican is really guilty. What exactly is his guilt? That does not really concern us. The subject of the film is elsewhere.... *The truly guilty one is Quinlan....*

Quinlan does not want to submit the guilty ones to justice so much as to assassinate them in the name of the law, using the police for his own purposes; and this is a fascist scenario, a totalitarian scenario, contrary to traditional law and human justice as I understand them. Thus, for me, Quinlan is the incarnation of everything I struggle against, politically and morally speaking. I'm against Quinlan because he wishes to arrogate the right to judge; and that's what I detest above all, men who wish to judge by their own authority.... But I have to like Quinlan because of something quite different I've given him: the fact that he's been able to love Marlene Dietrich [as Tanya], that he's taken a bullet intended for his friend [Joseph Calleia as Menzies], the fact that he has a heart. But what he believes in is detestable. The possible ambiguity is not in the character of Quinlan, it's in the betrayal of Quinlan by Menzies. Kane too is a man who abuses the power of the popular press and sets himself up against the law, against the whole tradition of liberal civilization. He too holds cheap what I consider the very basis of civilization and tries to become the king of his universe, a little like Quinlan in his border town. It's at this level these men come together. And they also come together with Harry Lime, with his contempt for everything, who tries to make himself king of a world without law. All these men are similar, and each in his own fashion stands for the things I most detest. But I like and I comprehend — I have a human sympathy for — these different characters I've created. Morally I find them detestable — morally, not humanly....

Q. You won't have us believe that such consistency in the choice of "detestable" characters doesn't imply more than just sympathy on your part. You're against them, yet you serve them better than an advocate! You'll have a hard time convincing us that at the same time you condemn them, you do not feel an admiration that is, in spite of everything, a way of bailing them out and giving them a chance for salvation....

A. All the characters I've played, and of whom we've been speaking, are versions of Faust, and I'm against every Faust, because I believe it's impossible for a man to be great without admitting there is something greater than himself. This might be Law, or God, or Art — it doesn't matter what the concept, but it ought to be greater than man. I have interpreted a long line of egotists, and I detest egotism — that of the Renaissance, that of Faust, every egotism. But obviously an actor is in love with the role he plays. He's like a man who embraces a woman, he gives her something of himself. An actor is not a devil's advocate, he's a lover, a lover of someone of the opposite sex. And for me Faust is like the opposite sex. It seems to me that there are two great human types in the world, and one of them is Faust. I belong to the other camp, but in playing Faust I want to be true and faithful to him, to give him the best of myself, and the best arguments I can find, for we live in a world that has been made by Faust. *Our world is Faustian.*

—Welles, interviewed by Andre Bazin and Charles Bitsch for *Cahiers du Cinéma*, June 1958 and by Andre Bazin, Charles Bitsch and Jean Domarchi for *Cahiers du Cinéma*, Sept 1958; trans by Terry Comito for *Touch of Evil* (New Brunswick, N.J.: Rutgers University Press, 1985)

Oskar WERNER [1922-1984]

Born: Oskar Bschliessmayer in Vienna, Austria. Work with The Vienna Burgtheatre (from age 18) and at The Salzburg Festival preceded his film debut in Der Engel mit der Posaune/Angel With the Trumpet (1948, Karl Hartl). His first English language film was Decision Before Dawn (1951,

Anatole Litvak); in 1965, he played Dr. Schumann in Stanley Kramer's Ship of Fools:

[Simone] Signoret and I had the phoniest parts in the world — a dope addict and a doctor with heart disease. We had to create everything ourselves. I told Stanley Kramer I had a bad reputation for being difficult and he said, "When you get to Hollywood, everyone will tell you I have a bad reputation, too," so we got along. I changed the role completely. They even had a business suit and tie for me to wear and I refused. I said, "No Nazi ship's captain would ever wear a suit," and I ended up wearing an officer's uniform designed for one of the extras.

[François Truffaut and I] used to speak, but no more. During *Jules and Jim* [1961] I gave him advice, tried to teach him something, and he listened. Whole scenes, whole pages of dialogue came from me. But when I went to England to make *Fahrenheit 451* [1966] he thought he had learned it all. He destroyed that film. It had nothing left of Ray Bradbury in it. It was ridiculous to cast Julie Christie in two parts. He only did that to save paying an extra salary. Nothing was worked out. The dramatic plot was completely lost. He refused to accept any of my suggestions. I was 15 when Hitler came to power and I saw the *real* book burnings. Truffaut's film was child's play compared to that. Every time I had to register an emotion that was true to my character, Truffaut would cut away with his camera. That's the trouble with these *nouvelle vague* directors. They care nothing about actors.

—Werner, interviewed by Rex Reed for *The New York Times*, 2 June 1968

Mae WEST [1892-1980]

Born: Brooklyn, N.Y. Work as a child entertainer (from age 8), on Broadway (from age 11), and in vaudeville and nightclubs preceded her film debut in Night After Night (1932, Archie Mayo):

In 1932 I was doing a play called *The Constant Sinner* on Broadway. We'd closed down for the summer and were planning to reopen in the fall — when I got an offer from Paramount. They wanted me for a picture [*Night After Night*], minimum of ten weeks at $5,000 per week. I didn't want to do it without seeing the script, but it hadn't been written yet. My agent felt it was foolish to turn down good money like that, script or no script, so I went.

When I got there, I sat around for a few weeks, doing nothing and collecting my salary. They do things like that out here, you know. The waste is unbelievable. Anyway, the script finally came through - and my part had absolutely nothing going for it! It was unimportant to the story and flatly written. I got very upset and offered to give them back all the money they'd paid me if they'd let me out of the contract.

William LeBaron, a fine man whom I'd known back in New York, was the producer. He saw I was quite serious and said I could rewrite the part any way I wanted — which is exactly what I did. So I made the picture; it wasn't easy to get things the way I wanted them. Archie Mayo, the director, was all right, but he didn't know theater, pauses, the value of timing, that sort of thing. My first line in the film was in response to a remark about my jewelry. Someone said, "Goodness, what beautiful diamonds," and I was supposed to say, "Goodness had nothing to do with it, dearie."

I wanted the camera to follow me as I spoke the line, as I walked away from the person and up a stairway. I knew it was a great line, that it would break up the audience; it had to be protected with footage. There was a big row about that. Mayo wanted to cut away right after the line. It got so bad that they called in Emanuel Cohen, who was in charge of production at the studio. He told Mayo to shoot it my way, and if it didn't work at the preview they could take it out. So we shot it, and the preview audience went wild....

—West, interviewed by Scott Eyman for *Take One*, Sept/Oct 1972

I wrote *I'm No Angel* [1933, Wesley Ruggles]...it's about this girl who lost her reputation but never missed it.

—West, interviewed by C. Robert Jennings for *Playboy*, Jan 1971

You know, it never would do to let a man see in Lady Lou [in *She Done Him Wrong* (1933, Lowell Sherman)] or Ruby Carter [in *Belle of the Nineties* (1934, Leo McCarey)] the sweet young thing that had made a sucker out of him or to let a woman see in either of them a fair picture of herself as she is preparing to shake down her boy-friend. That's why my characters have to be different — and a little exaggerated — so that neither man nor woman can resent them and can get laughs.... My girls' morals may be a little off-center — but they're human, with human faults and human kindnesses. I don't mind if my characters gold-dig a little, so long as they mean well and keep what they get in circulation — and as long as they aren't hypocrites. I won't have my women characters selfish and mercenary, because hardness kills appeal. I don't care how physically fascinating a woman may be on the screen, as soon as men see that she is grasping and selfish, her appeal flops cold. Yes sir, selfishness and hardness can make any woman look like a dose of poison to a man. In real life, a selfish woman can keep her victim from seeing farther than her physical charms, but when she is exposed on the screen, her lure falls away like a rotting tunic.

On the other hand, weakness builds appeal. You know how the men eat up that clinging vine, "I'm so weak" act. That's why my gals have their weaknesses, and why I write faults and weaknesses into their characters....

My characters must have old-time background for two reasons. First, so that they can be more effectively burlesqued; second, so that no man in the audience can see too close a resemblance in Mae's girl to someone who has recently taken him for a buggy-ride.

—West, interviewed by William F. French for *Movie Classic combined with Screen Star Stories*, Dec 1934

My Little Chickadee [1940, Eddie Cline] was all right; I think it's a good picture. But Bill [W.C.] Fields got co-script credit, which was a farce. He wrote one scene, between himself and another guy in a barroom. One scene! I liked Bill and all that, but he could be miserable when he wanted to be. I guess he hounded them and hounded them until they gave him screen credit just to get rid of him.

—West, interviewed by Scott Eyman for *Take One*, Sept/Oct 1972

Oh, I'm never dirty, dear. I'm interestin' without bein' vulgar. I have — *taste*. I *kid* sex. I was born with sophistication and sex appeal, but I'm never vulgar.... In the script [of *Myra Breckenridge* (1970, Mike Sarne)] I have a line, "I've got the judge by the..." but I never say the word, just make the motions (cupping her hand).... I don't like obscenity and I don't have to do it at any time. They thought I might be willing for *Myra*, because it's in vogue now, but I won't. I just — suggest.

—West, interviewed by C. Robert Jennings for *Playboy*, Jan 1971

Pearl WHITE [1889-1938]

Born: Greenridge, Illinois. Circus work and extensive touring in stock preceded her 1910 film debut at The Powers Studio in N.Y. She achieved significant success in several serials — beginning with The Perils of Pauline (1914, Donald Mackenzie) for Pathé:

When I started to work in *The Perils of Pauline*, I took unto myself quite a task. I spent a week before I started learning to play a fairly decent game of tennis. There is no danger attached to this sport, but you can certainly get a big collection of sore muscles when you start learning. I have also learned to drive a motor car and stand a smashup. During the filming of the first episode I had to spend three or four hours each night in a swimming pool learning to swim and dive. And so it has been ever since, even up to the present time. I'm always learning to do something new for each picture. I've even learned to fly an aeroplane, a feat that took me many months. If I have to jump off a moving train, automobile, etc., I always take myself out and try it several times until I get to be pretty sure of myself before they take the picture. If I have to do a big struggle or a fight the next day, I very often go into a gymnasium the night before and do a lot of work....

—White, in her *Just Me* (New York: George H. Doran Co., 1919)

Richard WIDMARK [1914-]

Born: Sunrise, Minnesota. Work as a drama instructor at Lake Forest College and work on radio (from 1938) and the Broadway stage (from 1943) preceded his film debut as Tommy Udo, the ultra-villain with the piercing laugh, in Henry Hathaway's Kiss of Death (1947):

I was doing straight romantic leads for George Abbott and the Theatre Guild when the Tommy Udo test came along. I threw everything I had, or could dredge up, into it....

Tommy Udo was a composite of scores of characters I've spotted at one time or another. You don't realize how many impressions are stored away in your subconscious until suddenly you get warmed up on a character, and they begin to creep out — a slant of the eye, a twist of the neck....

—Widmark, interviewed by Myrtle Gebhart for *The Boston Post Magazine*, 26 Dec 1948

The laugh partially came out of nervousness.... And then, too, part of the laugh came from the fact that I've always had a goofy laugh. As kids, my brother and I used to go to the movies in Princeton, Illinois, where we grew up, and if it was a comedy, people in the audience would always say, "Uh-oh, the Widmark boys are here."

Before I tested for the part, I went out and bought a wide-brim hat, black shirt, and white tie. George Raft always dressed like that....

—Widmark, interviewed by Gene Siskel for *The Chicago Tribune*, 10 June 1973

Q. As an actor, which directors have you found most rewarding to work with?

A. I think that from an actor's standpoint, there are people who make better movies per se than this man, but the greatest actor's director I have ever worked with, because he himself is an excellent actor, is [Elia] Kazan. I've only made one movie with him [*Panic in the Streets* (1950)]. I did one play with him years ago, and I used to act with him on the radio many years ago. I think almost every actor that's ever worked with Kazan feels this way about him because he's so in tune with an actor. He's a great, great, great rarity. You find very few directors that have his quality.... From a real moviemaker's standpoint, there's nobody like [John Ford]. It's different. Ford is the complete autocrat. Nobody says anything but Ford, that's *it.* Whereas Kazan, he'll ask a guy up in the rafters, "What do you think, Sam? How do you think this scene ought to go?" He'll collect information from everybody, sift it out, use what he wants to. But he's still the man in power. He asks questions like this, but everybody knows why he's asking the questions. It's for a purpose. He uses everybody. And he gets what he wants out of it. But with Jack it's, "This is it. This is it. You do this, you do that." And no questions. And if you ask a question you'll get your head pounded in. Unlike a good many of the younger directors who have a tendency to talk a situation to death. They'll analyze it from every psychological angle, thought, theme, and mood, till the time you get to do it you know it's out the window. They'll just talk it to death. Unlike that, Ford won't tell you anything, he won't tell you what you're going to do twenty minutes from now. You might be doing the end, or the beginning. It keeps you constantly alert. Nobody on a Ford picture ever lets down for a minute. You have to follow him around, literally, physically, to know what's going on. Or you're going to get lost and he'll embarrass you. [Widmark worked on Ford's *Two Rode Together* (1961), *How the West Was Won* (1963, co-directed with Henry Hathaway and George Marshall) and *Cheyenne Autumn* (1964).]

—Widmark, interviewed by James R. Silke for *Cinema*, Mar/Apr 1965

[Gary Cooper] was a true professional. Earthy, no phony star attitude — always prepared — knew exactly what he was going to do — always on time — a perfect work mate....

His concentration was remarkable, and he really *talked* to you in a scene. In fact I was taken aback in the first scene we did together [in *Garden of Evil* (1954, Henry Hathaway)], for it can be so rare for an actor to work with someone who is really *talking* to you. It's what separates the men from the boys — and it's difficult to do. And above all he really *listened.*

—Widmark, interviewed by Stuart Kaminsky for *Coop* (New York: St. Martin's Press, 1980)

[Spencer] Tracy's brilliance as an actor pulled *me* up as an actor. I had gone into *Broken Lance* [1954, Edward Dmytryk] with bad feelings. It was my last picture at Fox. Darryl Zanuck was teed off at me, so he put me in this picture.... He was angry because I didn't want to re-sign with the studio. I didn't want to do the movie and tried to get out of it. So I wasn't in a very good frame of mind when I was forced to go to the location in Nogales, Arizona. My inclination was to just walk through the picture, collect my money and get out.

But all that changed as soon as I began to work with Tracy. He was so brilliant, even in this unimportant little film, that I couldn't just walk through it. I had to call on all my acting skills and work my ass off, just to keep up with him. It was so enjoyable working with him. We'd really go at each other, and he gave me so much to make me come out at my best.

—Widmark, interviewed by Bill Davidson for *Spencer Tracy: Tragic Idol* (New York: E.P. Dutton, 1987)

In my adult years, the man I have admired most in acting is Spencer Tracy. What an actor should be is exemplified, for me, by him. I really like the reality of his acting. It's so honest and seems so effortless, even though what Tracy does is the result of damn hard work and extreme concentration. Actually, the ultimate in any art is never to show the wheels grinding. The essence of bad acting, for example, is shouting. Tracy never shouts.... When I'm in a scene with Tracy, I play to him. He's the greatest listener in this business. It's a very elusive thing. Somebody can be looking you in the eye and he's in Timbuctoo. You can only *feel* it; you can't know it intellectually. Tracy plays Judge Dan Haywood in *Judgment at Nuremberg* [1961, Stanley Kramer], and I play Colonel Lawson, an attorney. I look at this guy, and something goes. He doesn't talk much about acting, but he knows it all.

—Widmark, interviewed by Lillian and Helen Ross for *The New Yorker*, 4 Nov 1961

Cornel WILDE [1915-1989]

Born: New York City. Studies at The Theodora Irvine School of Drama and with Lee Strasberg, and work on Broadway preceded his film debut in The Lady with Red Hair (1940, Curtis Bernhardt). In 1945, he played Chopin opposite Paul Muni as Joseph Elsner in Charles Vidor's A Song to Remember:

Working with Paul Muni in *A Song to Remember* was interesting because he was a very fine actor and a great technician. It also was a bit disturbing because I admired him so much. When we started working on *A Song to Remember*, I asked him to rehearse some of the scenes with me. I wanted to sit down in the dressing-room and go over the lines so we would know what each one would sound like. How he would do his role meant a lot to me as to how I would respond....

Much to my amazement, he refused to do it and said, "I don't care how you do your role or what you sound like. I have my own concept of Chopin and that's all. So you do anything you like, it doesn't matter to me." It left me a little wounded.

—Wilde, interviewed by Joel Coen for *Film Comment*, Spring 1970

In preparation for the role [of Chopin], I had a concert pianist to help me. We worked...at my house. I had a silent piano and he had a sound piano. He would play two bars and then show me the fingering, and then he'd play again and I had to go right along with him on the silent piano. We expanded in this way, on and on and on, piece after piece, until finally I could keep up with him.

—Wilde, interviewed by Gordon Gow for *Films & Filming*, Oct 1970

Oddly enough, although I had fenced in national and international competitions for many years [Wilde was an olympic sabre contender], the fights I find most dangerous are those involving swords, spears, lances, etc., especially if the combats are on horseback. I have been hurt several times in sword fights, generally because my opponent had to learn fencing for the first time in his life and then memorize a difficult routine which had to be done at considerable speed to look good. For me, the routines were easy, like learning dialogue, because I already knew the moves and the terminology. I was cut on the eyeball in one film and spent ten days in the hospital with my eye bandaged, hoping that it would heal with no damage to the eye. I was lucky and it did. I have been pierced and cut many times on various parts of the body. In *A Thousand and One Nights* [1945, Alfred E. Green], one of the prop men gave my opponent the wrong sword for a rehearsal — a sword which had been sharpened for a special stunt involving cutting a stool in half, and I almost lost a finger as a result. It could just as easily have been my neck.

—Wilde, interviewed by Stuart Kaminsky for *Film Reader* #2, 1977

Gene WILDER [1935-]

Born: Jerome Silberman in Milwaukee, Wisconsin. Studies with Herman Gottlieb in Milwaukee, at The University of Iowa, The British Old Vic Theatre School, and at The Herbert Berghof and Actors Studios in N.Y., and work on the N.Y. stage (from 1961) preceded his film debut as Eugene Grizzard in Bonnie and Clyde (1967, Arthur Penn):

[In the Broadway play, *The Complaisant Lover* (1961)] the audience was seeing a prototype for a lot of films that I was to do later where I was a victim. I was innocent, I was in deep trouble and I was wriggling to get out of it and in that wriggling process the audience was laughing because they knew how they would feel in that situation.

In *Blazing Saddles* [1974, Mel Brooks] or *Young Frankenstein* [1974, Mel Brooks] or *The Producers* [1968, Mel Brooks], maybe I got more hysterical, I went higher, I had fireworks go off. But still that essential ingredient was there. Even in *Bonnie and Clyde* that was still the basic situation.

There I'm a simple guy, not that bright, kissing my girl [Evans Evans] on the back porch. And a desperate gang of killers steals my car and I'm tough and brave and all that till we find out who they are and then we get caught and then I'm an innocent boob again and how am I going to get out of this? With those people who could kill me. It seems that whenever there's a threat they could kill, I get funny.

—Wilder, interviewed by Lewis Archibald for *The Aquarian Weekly*, 16-23 June 1982

[In *Bonnie and Clyde*] I decided that the funniest thing was not to cower but to pretend that I was not afraid. Humor comes in how you hide, not how you show, feeling.

—Wilder, interviewed by Mel Gussow for *The New York Times*, 5 Jan 1976

Q. You certainly looked satisfactorily neurotic in *The Producers*....

A. Yes, I suppose I did. I had a lot of hysteria going for me at the time. A lot of people remember that scene where I'm afraid that Zero Mostel is going to jump on me. Well, having a vivid imagination, I let myself respond fully to the thought of Zero Mostel pouncing on me and, wow, what a thought that is....

Q. I've always wondered about some of the *little* things in *The Producers*. Like when Mostel sits down heavily on the floor next to the safe filled with bills, and he reaches out and pats them and says, "Hello, boys."

A. That scene, and a lot of the bits in the movie, [Mel] simply made up on the spot. He told Mostel to sit down and pat the dollar bills. Mostel asked him, "What should I say?" Brooks said, "Say? I dunno. Say hi. No...say, Hello boys!"

—Wilder, interviewed by Roger Ebert for *The Chicago Sun-Times*, 11 July 1971

Mel is the only genius I've ever had the opportunity to work with. He made me a lot braver than I ever was before in learning to go all the way with humor. I was inclined to think of something that was funny and logical, but Brooks taught me that you could be funny and crazy. If you go for a banana-peel comedy situation, Brooks would have five peels. He is willing to take a chance.

—Wilder, interviewed by William Wolf for *Cue*, 8 Nov 1975

I'm really Candide in [*Stir Crazy* (1980, Sidney Poitier)] — someone who only sees the good side of things and believes that if you give people a chance, they'll come through, because they need love, affection, understanding...until Richie [Pryor] and I get the shit kicked out of us. But it's a good character and one that bounces off well with what Richie does — to always be street smart, never trust a guy, because the minute you turn your back he'll stab you. It's the pessimist and the optimist, the realist and the dreamer.

Q. How did you work with Richard Pryor?

A. There was a peculiar magic, which I never had with any other actor I've worked with. Our artistic instincts are so close that we might break out in a song during an improvised scene — at the same time — because the same funny nerve clicked in both of us that moment. We haven't done a single take together without improvising, which is strange because I don't improvise as a rule. I believe that if you've worked a year and a half on a script, there should be a pretty good reason to depart from it. But we didn't have a director who told us to stick to the script. Sidney said, "If you hold back one impulse, one line that pops into your mind, you're doing yourselves — and the author and me — an injustice, because what we want is for you to take off." [Wilder and Pryor had previously co-starred in *Silver Streak* (1975), and were teamed again in *See No Evil, Hear No Evil* (1989), both directed by Arthur Hiller, and *Another You* (1991, Maurice Phillips.]

—Wilder, interviewed by Dan Yakir for *In Cinema*, Feb 1981

Sidney [Poitier] is meticulous; you can rest assured that when he comes on the set, he's prepared for everything. And if something goes wrong, he's ready; nothing's going to throw him....

We worked together on this script [of *Stir Crazy*] — he and I — after the author had finished his draft and a writer was brought in to change the structure of the second half. I worked with Sidney every day for six weeks, six days a week, going over the script to make certain it was going to be right for us. [Wilder was directed by Poitier a second time, on *Hanky Panky* (1982).]

—Wilder, interviewed by Ralph Appelbaum for *Films*, July 1981

Billy Dee WILLIAMS [1937-]

Born: Harlem, N.Y. A stage debut at age 7, studies at The National Academy of Design, and work on television preceded his film debut in The Last Angry Man (1959, Daniel Mann). He then studied acting with Sidney Poitier and Paul Mann at The Actors Workshop in Harlem. He played Lando Calrissian in both The Empire Strikes Back (1980, Irvin Kershner) and The Return of the Jedi (1983, Richard Marquand):

Lando is a charming man, and I've been known to have a little bit of charm. I tried to bring enough of that to the role so audiences would be sympathetic to him. But, I also wanted to show his vulnerability — which is very important.

With a character like Lando, he should always appear to be stumbling through life. That's *my* idea of a great hero, anyway — guys who walk into doors and walls, tripping over things — yet they manage to succeed in *spite* of themselves.

Han Solo [Harrison Ford] is similar to Lando in that respect. Neither of them ever really *know* what they're doing, like when they're flying their spaceships. My character will try to pilot a ship and screw it up, but always take the position that he *knows* what he's doing. Of course, it's played off Princess Leia [Carrie Fisher], because she always makes little cracks like, "You really know what you're doing, don't you?" The same thing happens with Han Solo....

Lando Calrissian was created by George Lucas, who knows exactly what he wants. I worked with him to prepare myself for the role. We discussed the ideas he had for costumes, and I worked out a hairstyle that I wanted to use. Though Han and Lando are mercenaries, he was the one who settled in Cloud City. As he was originally written in the script, he was a governor there, but he was also a businessman. He *is* lucky, but he also uses his head — he's not as impulsive as Han Solo....

[In terms of directors], Marquand is a quiet person, while Kersh is much more energetic. They both have good ideas about what they want, but George is the one who makes the major decisions. When he hires a director it's not someone he can manipulate or control. He hires people who are competent, who have input he can use. Primarily, though, they execute his ideas.

—Williams, interviewed by K.H. Johnson for *Prevue*, Dec/Jan 1984

Robin WILLIAMS [1952-]

Born: Chicago. Studies with John Houseman at The Juilliard School in N.Y., work as a stand-up comedian and on TV preceded his film debut in the title role of Popeye (1980, Robert Altman):

[Popeye]'s a simple man. He's kind of bittersweet, he's got a lot of pain, and he's been through a lot. He's kind of an outsider — nobody you'd notice until he turns on his talent when he really has to prove himself.

—Williams, interviewed by Dave Hirshey for *The New York Sunday News Magazine*, 7 Dec 1980

[For *Moscow on the Hudson* (1984, Paul Mazursky)] I studied five hours a day every day for three months. It was just like a Berlitz course. I learned how to write it and I learned how to read it. My teacher, David Gomburg, was a director in Russia, and he was always on the set, and he'd help me get back into the language or the accent if I started to fall out of it....

—Williams, interviewed by Judy Klemesrud for *The New York Times*, 15 Apr 1984

I found [*Good Morning, Vietnam* (1987, Barry Levinson)] easier than my other films. But it's also harder than anything else I've ever done. It's not that far away from who and what I am.

—Williams, interviewed by Hank Gallo for *The New York Daily News*, 20 Dec 1987

[In *Good Morning, Vietnam*] I'm trying to do comedy like jazz. I'm trying to stay with things. I'm trying to get more of a jazz feel, more of a free form, where you can connect things up, like a jazz riff, like a scat riff, to the moment before. The object is to expand the time.

—Williams, interviewed by John Culhane for *The New York Times*, 20 Dec 1987

[Barry Levinson] has that Baltimore cool. He's so fucking easygoing that it puts a lot of people off, I guess. They're looking for someone to tell them everything and he's just, like, "Hey, let's see what happens."

—Williams, interviewed by Dan Greenburg for *Playboy*, Mar 1989

The character [of Dr. Oliver Sayer in *Awakenings* (1990, Penny Marshall)] is him [Dr. Oliver Sacks, on whose work the film is based], and it isn't. Originally it was his name in the script, and we changed it because it has many of his qualities but some of mine. Performing for me is just a full-out frontal attack, and Oliver is a man who absorbs and then formulates this kind of aikido attack.

He reacts to a lot of things and is basically absorbing them — it's cerebral. He is cocooned in his own way. Somebody who saw the movie described [Sayer and Leonard (Robert De Niro as Leonard Lowe)] as being two similar characters: he is a cocooned intellectual; Leonard physically is cocooned. Suddenly there's an in-

terchange. And I think the patients did that for Oliver. They brought him out in a certain way.
—Williams, interviewed by Fred Schruers for *Premiere*, Jan 1991

Lois WILSON [1894-1988]

Born: Pittsburgh. Work as a teacher and success as a Universal Studios beauty pageant winner preceded work for that studio. In 1921, she made Miss Lulu Bett, the fourth of six films for William C. deMille:

I feel I learned more from William deMille and Edward Everett Horton than anyone else I ever worked with. It was William deMille who taught me to be glad that I was a good character actress.... He directed me in my best picture, *Miss Lulu Bett*, in 1921 in which I worked with Milton Sills and Theodore "Daddy" Roberts. I had a character lead and I just loved it....

To play serious scenes against that Daddy Roberts, who was a comedian of the first water, was sometimes heartbreaking because I thought, "He'll get the laughs I might not get." I went to William de Mille — I was almost in tears — and I said, "Look, this scene's coming up. This is my scene. Don't let Daddy Roberts..." because he used to do bits with his cigar all the time.

William said, "He's an actor. He has a right to do whatever he interprets, and you're an actress. This is your scene; you'll make it your scene."

And I did, so he was right. He taught me that I don't ever ask another actor not to do something. [Wilson also worked on deMille's *What Every Woman Knows* (1921), *The Lost Romance* (1921), *Only 38* (1923) and *Icebound* (1924).]
—Wilson, interviewed by William M. Drew for *Speaking of Silents: First Ladies of the Screen* (Vestal, N.Y.: The Vestal Press, 1989)

Debra WINGER [1955-]

Born: Mary Debra Winger in Cleveland, Ohio. Studies at California State University (Northridge), and work on TV preceded her film debut in Slumber Party '57 (1977, William A. Levey); in 1980, she played Sissy in James Bridges' Urban Cowboy:

Most people think I was most naked in that love scene I did in *An Officer and a Gentleman* [1982, Taylor Hackford], but actually I felt more raw and naked in a scene in *Urban Cowboy* [1980, James Bridges]. It's the scene (in a Western bar) where I ride that mechanical bull real slow to make my husband [John Travolta] more jealous. Now, every review mentioned how sexual it was, but that didn't even occur to me.... I had worked so hard on it gymnastically; I never intended for it to be sexual. All I thought was that I was making him jealous by how good I was on the bull.

But the specific shot that I thought was so raw was a shot right after I finish riding the bull. I stand up and [Travolta] says, "We got to get out of here." And it's a long shot, and you can't see that I'm crying. But that's okay. It's the most vulnerable moment I've ever had in a film, both visibly and in my experience of it. I'm crying because I'm in love with this man and we're breaking up, and everyone in the bar around me is applauding and yelling, "Yea, Sissy!" But instead of feeling good I know then that I've succeeded in doing what I wanted to do — I've hurt him. And you have to be pretty messed up to feel good about hurting someone.
—Winger, interviewed by Gene Siskel for *The New York Daily News*, 8 Jan 1984

The mothers of young children, the middle-class mother, that's who [*Terms of Endearment* (1983, James L. Brooks)] was inside of me. I've always had this deep resentment of how the middle class is treated.... Some of the worst psychic abuse is on the middle class. So here was this perfectly middle-class girl who turned into a housewife with children, and I really felt the responsibility, it was very important to me, to make a hero out of this class of woman.
—Winger, interviewed by Diana Maychick for *The New York Post*, 2 Oct 1984

Shelley WINTERS [1922 -]

Born: Shirley Schrift in St. Louis, Missouri. Studies at The New Theater School in N.Y., and work in nightclubs, summer stock and on the N.Y. stage preceded her film debut in What a Woman! (1943, Irving Cummings). In 1948, she played Pat in George Cukor's A Double Life:

Pat was a waitress who tried awfully hard to please Anthony John [Ronald Colman] and was murdered for her pains. This was my first important role, and I was very anxious to put it over. In fact, I even took a job as a waitress in a Hollywood delicatessen to get the "feel" of being a waitress. It felt awful. I quit after four evenings. But at least it gave me an understanding of what a waitress means when she says her feet are killing her.

I'd never even met Ronald Colman before, and in the first love scenes I was so much in awe of him that I was scared even to touch him. Then he took me to lunch, talked away my nervousness and gave me some very helpful advice.

—Winters, in *The Saturday Evening Post*, 8 July 1950

[In] *A Double Life*, during a scene in which Ronald Colman enacted Othello and strangled me as his fantasy Desdemona, everyone on the set had to sit down and wait an hour. The Breen Office came down to the set and gave us a decision as to how the scene could be shot so that it would be acceptable in the 48 states. After another hour of discussion with the director George Cukor, Mr. Colman, the president of the studio and a couple of the stagehands...it was decided that if we pasted my nightgown close to my chest, *above* my bosoms, and the camera saw one of Mr. Colman's feet on the floor, the implications of the scene would probably be acceptable.

I never did understand why one foot was better than no feet or two feet. But maybe there's something about sex the Legion of Decency knows that I don't. In retrospect, it seems funny, but in reality it was terrifying, costly and certainly artistically stultifying to the writers, director and actors.

—Winters, in *The New York Times*, 5 Aug 1973

Q. You don't memorize the lines, you first have to understand what the character is about?

A. Yes. The first person I got this from was George Stevens. He didn't mention it this way, but the first time when we started on *A Place in the Sun* [1951], I said, "Now, what do I do in this scene?" And he said, "I don't know. Let's find out." And he said, "If you were such-and-such, would you do this?" Then I did a scene — you remember the abortion scene in the picture when I go and ask the doctor? He sprang that on me one morning.... I did the scene and I was crying, and I thought I was great, and he sat and thought for a while and then he said, "Now, Shelley, let me ask you something about this girl. What is she here for?" And I said, "She's desperate to get the doctor to help her." And so he said, "What she wants in this scene is for the doctor to help her." And I said, "Yes." And he said, "If she does what you just did, would he help her?" And I said, "No, she would scare him." But I was angry at him, because you know, I thought it was so great if I started crying away like crazy. And so he said, "Then the problem in the scene is for her not to cry." And I said, "All right." "Now let's do it again. And you get this doctor to help you." I started the scene, and I wanted to cry, and I had to wait — I don't know whether you remember it, but there were long waits while I got myself under control, and I just sat there and looked at him. Well, it was 90 times more effective than the other.... His favorite trick is to rehearse you with the lines and then take the lines away and say, "Now, do the scene — just looking at each other." And in some ways, it's more powerful because you communicate thoughts....

He has a thing that's just wonderful — I wish there was a way to use it in the theater. You know, he's from silent pictures and he has a kind of thing — it's a gadget that's next to his chair, and he knows what music works on you, and he pushes the button and he finds the kind of music you respond to; and in preparation for a scene, when he says, "Roll 'em," before you start acting, he will play that music, sometimes he'll play it during the scene. Like when I was doing a scene [in *The Diary of Anne Frank* (1959)] where I was being very courageous, he turned on a thing with German boots marching and Hitler talking, and he said, "You are not scared, you are courageous" — he gave me something to push against, you know.

—Winters, interviewed by Lewis Funke and John E. Booth for *Actors Talk About Acting* (New York: Random House, 1961)

Dixie [in *The Big Knife* (1955, Robert Aldrich)] was a pretty, sad Hollywood call girl. She was uneducated but not stupid, and she was very courageous and cunning. Although in the scene she is threatened, she will not shut up. She tells everybody off.... My agent didn't want me to do this role for financial and artistic and maybe political reasons, even though the gifted Robert Aldrich was producing and directing the film. But I did it anyway.

The Big Knife is about a fine actor from New York, a movie star. He commits suicide at the end of the film when the powerful studio, which had developed and protected him and built him into a superstar, suddenly decides to throw him to the wolves — to accommodate the terrible witch-hunt going on in Hollywood at that time....

As I started to prepare for the role of Dixie, I was haunted by the sense of having lived through the actual events with John Garfield....

The filming of *The Big Knife* was very strange and difficult. Robert Aldrich insisted that I be smart-ass, terrified, and courageous, all at the same time. I decided to seek Lee Strasberg's help, and when we finished rehearsing, on a Friday, I flew to New York....

I told Lee how I was having difficulty communicating the nameless fear of this courageous little actress within the limitations of the scene in the film script. Rod Steiger is trying to keep me from blabbing about what I have overheard, especially that Steiger has threatened the film star with blacklisting and physical violence. Blacklisting then as now was supposedly illegal. Dixie won't shut up because she knows how unjust this persecution is. She doesn't know it consciously, but squealing on one's friend is against every moral code that good men live by.

I couldn't seem to communicate Dixie's courage while enacting her fear. I was trying to do two opposite things with the same thoughts and words. When I arrived in New York midday Saturday, I went right to Paula and Lee Strasberg's apartment. Lee watched me do the scene. He of course knew that the script was based on John Garfield's life and death. When I finished, he thought about it quietly for a long while and then said, "Act her courage. Shelley, just be afraid of the furniture, as if it could come to life and hurt you." It was inspired direction. I knew exactly what he meant....

Lee had helped me be funny and brave and at the same time communicate "nameless dread," that feeling of trying to function without knowing where or how your doom is going to strike.

—Winters, in her *Shelley II: The Middle of My Century* (New York: Simon & Schuster, 1989)

I played a Dutch housewife [Mrs. Van Daan, in *The Diary of Anne Frank*]. I was very concerned with the Dutch aspect of it. And I studied it. In the character it is indicated her father was a rich farmer, and I did some investigating into Dutch agriculture. And did you know that in Holland a man starts to make a field a hundred years before it's going to be used.... It's a process that goes on for a hundred years. Now, a woman who has watched her father do that is a special kind of woman. What I tried to achieve in it was a woman who is scared, who's had a bourgeois life, who's namby-pamby. But when the chips are down, the strength that is inherent in her background comes out. I played that — the fear, and then through danger, the courage comes out, as a kind of crucible.

—Winters, interviewed by Lewis Funke and John E. Booth for *Actors Talk About Acting* (New York: Random House, 1961)

I once asked George Stevens what the difference between film acting and stage acting was and he said, "Shelley, in films you talk soft and think loud...." Stevens always felt that what was really in the actor's eyes and face was what was really important. [She also appeared in Stevens's *The Greatest Story Ever Told* (1965).]

—Winters, interviewed by Jim Haspiel for *Films in Review* (NY), June/July 1980

Q. Are you supposed to look glamorous in the picture [*Lolita* (1962)]?

A. Stanley Kubrick wants me to, but I'm fighting it. The author, Vladimir Nabokov, said I was ideal for the role, and I think I should play it looking a bit dowdy. It's easier, you know, when you don't look so good.

—Winters, interviewed for *The Sunday Express*, 27 Nov 1960

I've always found something to like in the characters I've played. But not this time.

I really hate this woman [Rose-Ann D'Arcey in *A Patch of Blue* (1965, Guy Green)]. She blinds her daughter [Elizabeth Hartman] by accident when she was trying to blind her husband. And when the girl grows up she beats her....

It's instinctive for an actor to make his character likable, even when the role is villainous.... But the woman I play hasn't a single redeeming feature. She's just horrible.

—Winters, interviewed by Vernon Scott for *The Newark Evening News*, 28 Apr 1965

Q. How is *Alfie* [1966, Lewis Gilbert] going?

A. Great, they say. Everyone thinks the "rushes" terribly funny. To me they just look licentious. All I do is wear nightgowns.

And it's not easy. Half the time I don't understand what Michael Caine is talking about. It's that Cockney accent of his. It's worse than acting with an Italian. I just wait until he pauses and then say my bit....

I'll tell you something about Michael Caine, though. He's very bony. I had to lie on him in one scene, and what with my waist-pincher sticking into my ribs and his bones, it was darned uncomfortable.

So the props man laid a whole line of tiny pillows on him to make it easier for me. I thought that was very nice. I suppose they felt they must make the visiting artist from America comfortable.

—Winters, interviewed by Roderick Mann for *The Sunday Express*, 11 July 1965

In my first scene with my teenage sons in *Bloody Mama* [1970, Roger Corman] I had to give them a bath in an outdoor washtub. I have never been particularly good at filming nude or sexy scenes — in color you always see me blush. Bobby De Niro made it easy for me by pretending very realistically to be a baby; it seemed as if I was bathing an infant and not a grown man. I can't say the same for his film brothers; they kept teasing me and saying, "Use it!" I refused to bathe Don Stroud.

Bloody Mama was one of Robert De Niro's first films and he played a boy who becomes a junkie in the course of the film. Bobby stayed in character twenty-four hours a day, losing forty pounds and getting scabs all over his body. Toward the end of the film when he OD's and the Barker family must bury him hurriedly, Bobby insisted on getting into the grave so the camera could record the dirt covering his face. In the scene I was hysterical with grief, and I didn't realize until he was almost completely covered that it was Bobby and not a dummy in this grave. I immediately stopped the scene and pulled him out, saying, "For Christ's sake, Bobby! Even Marlon [Brando] has never pulled such a dangerous stupid trick in a movie. This is not real life, it's only a film."

His soft answer has puzzled me for years. "But Shelley, for actors, aren't the movies our only real life?"

—Winters, in her *Shelley, Also Known as Shirley* (New York: William Morrow and Co., 1980)

I was reading the script [of *The Poseidon Adventure* (1972, Ronald Neame)]...trying to get to know this Belle Rosen, former super-star, I would be playing, so I could get into the heart of this fearless woman. I went to the source for help. I called [novelist] Paul Gallico at his home...and talked with him about it.... He gave me very good advice....

[Belle is] a former Olympic swimmer who weighs 300 pounds.... Ronald Neame had to be satisfied with 193. I actually swam under water for a minute at a time, helping the survivors of the sinking ship make their way through the propellor shaft tunnel. There is small hope of rescue, but we tried.

I wasn't frightened doing the underwater scenes, but I wasn't too comfortable, either. But when I saw the film, watching myself do it, I was almost scared out of my wits — I kept saying, "I couldn't have done that. I would have been out of my mind." I was so scared I couldn't watch.

—Winters, interviewed by Wanda Hale for *The New York Sunday News*, 10 Dec 1972

Natalie WOOD [1938-1981]

Born: Natasha Gurdin in San Francisco. A child star from age five, her first three appearances, beginning with Happy Land (1943) were for Irving Pichel. In 1955, she played Judy in Nick Ray's Rebel Without a Cause:

All of us who worked on [*Rebel Without a Cause*] — Jimmy Dean, Nick Adams, and so on — we threw ourselves into it heart and soul, because it was just as if the story belonged to us. In many ways, it's the story of all teen-agers. And all through it, Nick Ray...kept asking us, "How would *you* feel if this happened to you? Do the scene the way *you* feel it would be." He was wonderful.

—Wood, interviewed by Barbara Henderson for *Filmland*, July 1956

For the first time I had a director, Nicholas Ray in *Rebel Without a Cause*, who actually encouraged me to have ideas and opinions. I kept learning about the Method, and just about everybody on the set was carrying a copy of [Michael] Chekhov's book *To an Actor*, and using phrases like "sense memory," and "emotion memory."

I started dropping in at the Actors Studio, and found it basically the way I'd been working all along. "Emotion memory" is recalling something sad when you have a sad scene to do, and very early on I used to get myself in the right mood by thinking of a pet dog that died. Nobody told me how to do it. It just came naturally.

—Wood, interviewed by Philip Oakes for *The Sunday Times*, 28 Dec 1969

In *The Searchers* [1956, John Ford] I was a very young teenager, isolated on a Utah Indian reservation and surrounded by much older people. Mr. [John] Wayne seemed to sense my loneliness and tried to include me in as many location activities as possible. I was into the Method at the time and he of course is a spontaneous actor. I thought I was quite sophisticated, while he probably viewed me as a silly teenager. Yet he always treated me with respect as an individual and as an actress, and he allowed me to work my way.

—Wood, interviewed for *Radio Times*, 11 July 1974

[John Ford is] not as patient, I found, as Nick Ray.... Their approach to the performer is so different. Ford says, "I want you to do this!" Ray says, "Now, how would you do this?" — and we discussed the scene.

—Wood, interviewed by Irene Thirer for *The New York Post*, 24 Oct 1955

Q. You worked with Warren Beatty in his first film; what was that like?

A. Warren and I didn't get along very well when we did *Splendor in the Grass* [1961, Elia Kazan]. I wouldn't say that I enjoyed working with Warren. I like Warren socially and I got to like him after the film but at that time we really didn't get along, we didn't have a terrific rapport.

Q. You couldn't tell from the way it turned out.

A. I know but people were very worried. They said "Oh, these two hate each other. How are the love scenes going to work?" Well, it's very odd. There doesn't seem to be any particular rule. Sometimes you can all love each other and get along absolutely great and the picture's a flop or you hate each other and it's a hit.

—Wood, interviewed by Jeff Freedman for *Interview*, Oct 1978

Working on [*Splendor in the Grass*] with Kazan was like being reintroduced to that golden world that Nick Ray had given me a glimpse of. There was nobody an actress could want to work with more than Kazan in the 1950s and '60s. He was God. Nick was sort of his disciple. So here I was with Kazan, the real number one director.

Working with Kazan was different than I'd expected. I thought he would teach me everything. I expected him to teach me how to cry. Instead, I got a different kind of lesson. He tried to demonstrate to me that crying on cue wasn't so all-fired important....

Kazan taught me other things that were very important — about being bold, not being afraid. I was very inhibited, actually. I found it very hard to utilize rehearsal. Normally, I didn't like to rehearse. I would always hold back because I felt I only had one or two takes in me, especially if the scene was emotional.

Kazan showed me different ways to play a scene. He said, "Try things, risk it, don't worry about making a fool of yourself; be bold; be brave; don't be afraid; don't play it safe. What's the worst that can happen?" he said. "Suppose you make a complete fool of yourself; we'll do the scene again." He was trying to get me to be free. To loosen up. His teaching was a wonderful gift.

—Wood, interviewed by Dick Moore for *Twinkle, Twinkle, Little Star* (New York: Harper & Row, 1984)

[Kazan is] like a psychologist. There's a scene in a bathtub in *Splendor* where my mother [Audrey Christie] is talking to me and I go hysterical.... Kazan and I talked a long while and then he had Audrey stand offstage and say a line which would set me off.

It wasn't the line in the script. But it was a line which, when I was little, used to drive me crazy. You know that mothers' tone, so sweet: "Darling, is there something bothering you? Is there something I can do to help...?" Audrey just said that line in that sweet tone and I went off the way I always used to and they shot it and that was it. With Audrey he used to have me stand off camera and thumb my nose at her. She didn't get it at first; she looked at me and said, "What are you doing that for?" But it did get her mad.

—Wood, interviewed by Murray Kempton for *Show*, Mar 1962

In most films I've tried to create a character, but in *Bob & Carol & Ted & Alice* [1969, Paul Mazursky] I've used more of myself. It's one of the things I've enjoyed doing most. For one thing we shot it in sequence, and for another thing we shot it pretty quickly. Ten weeks from start to finish.

—Wood, interviewed by Philip Oakes for *The Sunday Times*, 28 Dec 1969

Alfre WOODARD [1953-]

Born: Tulsa, Oklahoma. Acting studies at Boston University, stage work in Washington, D.C. and work on TV preceded her film debut in Remember My Name (1978, Alan Rudolph). In 1983, she played Geechie in Martin Ritt's Cross Creek:

Marty Ritt...has such good taste and judgment that he kept it from being sentimental. After I met him, after we talked, I knew if I paid attention to him and trusted him, he would be a good marker for me.

A lot of times you can lose your bearings.... If you get someone like Marty, who is focused on the work and getting to the truth of it, then you give up all responsibilites of trying to watch yourself while you're trying to create.

Marty worked us as an ensemble. He said, "I want everybody on the set every day because I don't know what I might shoot that day." He might say, "Alfre, I've decided to do the coming back scene — oh, no, it's going to rain — cut that and let's start with the pig scene." So it was actually like an acting pool.

—Woodard, interviewed by David Galligan for *Drama-Logue*, 20-26 Oct 1983

James WOODS [1947-]

Born: Vernal, Utah. Studies in political science and acting at MIT, work in stock and performances both on and off Broadway preceded his film debut in The Visitors (1972, Elia Kazan). In 1979, he played Greg Powell in Harold Becker's The Onion Field:

Powell has been depicted in reviews as a psychotic killer, but a psychotic killer is somebody who kills people because it's Monday or because they don't like the color red. If you listen to Greg Powell's explanation of why he does things, it is, from his point of view, completely rational. What makes it irrational is the way he perceives the universe about him.

The trick with Greg Powell was making it clear that everything he did within his framework of understanding made sense, while at the same time making it clear how he could misconceive what the framework of life really was.

—Woods, interviewed by Barry Brennan for *Evening Outlook*, 14 Mar 1980

I hate [Richard Boyle,] the guy I played in *Salvador* [1986, Oliver Stone] — I think he's a total asshole. I don't hate him; I'm indifferent to him — the kind of guy who is a drunken, boring, disgusting fool who's always gypping people with money and lying and bullshitting and all the other wonderful things that compulsive obsessives do — but I loved the story. And I found a way of turning that character into a fictional amalgam of what he is and what I hoped he could be in his life....

Q. I hear Oliver Stone is pretty intense.

A. Well, he met his match the day he walked on the *Salvador* set in Mexico with me. But our arguments were over the right stuff. They were about interpretation, balancing the picture, not making it a polemic. Not making the character too heroic, which Oliver didn't want. And not making him such a loathsome scumbag that the audience would be so turned off that they wouldn't get any of it, which was my point of view. And so we had two very antithetical points of view that resulted, I thought, in a very constructive synthesis. And I like to work that way. If it's all peaches and cream, you're in trouble, believe me. It's a cardinal rule of filmmaking that if everybody's happy at the dailies every night, you've probably got a piece of junk on your hands. We struggled through that thing like a war. We're great friends now.

—Woods, interviewed by Eve Babitz for *American Film*, May 1987

What's so intriguing about Boyle is that he was a seeker of the truth who is an inveterate liar himself.

—Woods, interviewed by Sean Mitchell for *The Los Angeles Herald Examiner*, 22 Mar 1987

Joanne WOODWARD [1930-]

Born: Thomasville, Georgia. Studies with Sanford Meisner at The Neighborhood Playhouse in N.Y., plus work in stock and on Broadway preceded her film debut in Count Three and Pray (1955, George Sherman). In 1957, she played the title role in Nunnally Johnson's The Three Faces of Eve:

I'm often asked which was the most difficult of the three roles in *The Three Faces of Eve*? It was, without a doubt, the normal woman.

—Woodward, quoted by Bob Bergut in *Les Exquis Mots de l'Entr'acte* (Paris: Editions Pierre Horay, 1964); trans. for *Actors on Acting for the Screen* (New York: Garland Publishing Inc., 1992)

Q. What first interests you in a character — that idea of getting into a character's mind or finding things you like about a character?

A. I'm afraid I work backward — especially for someone trained as I have been. Mine is an odd way to work; I work from the outside in. I always have to know what a character looks like because to me, having studied with Martha Graham, so much that goes on inside is reflected outside; it has to do with the way you move. So I generally start with the way a character moves. I'm not very intellectual, so I can't go to find very specific things until I find them, as Paul would say, viscerally. I took Rachel's movements [in *Rachel, Rachel* (1968, Paul Newman)] from my child, Nell. She's very pigeon-toed, so I just took the way Nell looks and grew it up. And somehow, when you move like that — all sorts of things happen to you.

—Woodward, interviewed at Judith Crist's Tarrytown seminar, 12-14 Apr 1974; repr. in *Take 22*, co-ed. by Judith Crist and Shirley Sealy (New York: Viking Press, 1984)

Rachel was Paul's directing debut. Who could direct better than the person you live with? He knows all there is to know about you. Paul is an actor's director in that he is very specific, clear; he talks to me in shorthand.... We rehearsed for two weeks.... I really knew who that character was.

—Woodward, interviewed by Iain F. McAsh for *Films and Filming*, June 1984

[When Paul was directing me in *The Effect of Gamma Rays on Man-in-the-Moon Marigolds* (1972)] I came close to sheer insanity. The role had an effect on me both during the shooting and afterwards. At home, I was a monster and Paul and I avoided each other as much as possible. There was something ugly about the character of Beatrice that got to me. Such putrefaction inside. I understood her all too well. You know, if you're rejected and you reject yourself, then the goodness gets swallowed up by the ugliness. [Woodward has also starred in Newman's *The Shadow Box* (1980 — for TV), *Harry and Son* (1984) and *The Glass Menagerie* (1988); they have also co-starred in *The Long Hot Summer* (1958, Martin Ritt), *Rally 'Round the Flag, Boys* (1958, Leo McCarey), *From the Terrace* (1960, Mark Robson), *Paris Blues* (1961, Martin Ritt), *A New Kind of Love* (1963, Melville Shavelson), *Winning* (1969, James Goldstone), *WUSA* (1970, Stuart Rosenberg) and Newman's *Harry and Son*.]

—Woodward, interviewed by Arthur Bell for *The Village Voice*, 1 Nov 1973

As far as other actors are concerned, I think one of the most fun people I've ever worked with, once I caught on how to work with him, was Orson Welles [on *The Long Hot Summer*]. I loved him because he was so there — everything was just coming at you. George Scott [in *They Might Be Giants* (1971, Anthony Harvey)] is the same. I was terrified of George Scott but he was enormously exciting because it's like acting with an erupting volcano. I hated working with Marlon Brando [on *The Fugitive Kind* (1960, Sidney Lumet)] — because he was not there, he was somewhere else. There was nothing to reach on to. And this is not saying anything behind his back because it has already been reported that after that picture, the only way I'd work with Marlon Brando is if he were in rear projection.

—Woodward, interviewed at Judith Crist's Tarrytown seminar, 12-14 Apr 1974; repr. in *Take 22*, co-ed. by Judith Crist and Shirley Sealy (New York: Viking Press, 1984)

Q. Give me the adjectives that describe her [India Bridge in *Mr. and Mrs. Bridge* (1990, James Ivory)].

A. She's vulnerable, she's repressed, and dominated. Not by him [Paul Newman as Walter Bridge]. Actually she is dominated by the society which tells her you must be dominated by your husband. So that she falls into it and yet there is an element with her that says, "No, this isn't right. There is something else there...."

Q. Is she not to some extent intimidated by him?

A. Well, I think she's intimidated only because she's told that she has to be. I really always thought that India Bridge would, in another life, have been a feminist. But she doesn't understand that. There is a certain way things are done. There are certain things that she should do and not do. And she doesn't know anything beyond that.

—Woodward, interviewed by Spencer Christian for *Good Morning America*; aired ABC TV, 11 Mar 1991

I felt a great kinship with Mrs. Bridge. I am just one generation removed from her. I still have in my drawer white kid gloves which we wore whenever we left the house in the '60s, and I wore a girdle straight through my 30s. I had no sense of politics until I came north to study. I was told, at home "Honey, whatever you do, don't discuss religion or politics with anyone."

The things that were important to my mother were the things Mrs. Bridge thought were important. You know, "Waste not, want not." Good manners. When my mother had a bridge party, I had to be introduced and go around to all the tables. "Hello, Mrs. Smith," "Hello, Mrs. Brown." Not that there wasn't something lovely about those sorts of manners. But the story of Mrs. Bridge is a tragedy....

[The character] really is an example of the roles women were forced to play out of a lack of knowledge and ability, and the men in their lives who would not encourage them to have any other thoughts.

—Woodward, interviewed by Maureen Dowd for *McCalls*, Jan 1991

Q. Did James Ivory give you much room to maneuver with the script [of *Mr. and Mrs. Bridge* (1990)]?

A. Well, he has a clear idea of what he wants. I'm not sure that when you have a problem he's...er, helpful, because he sees it all pictorially, as an artist — which he is. And I found that difficult, simply because it was not fun. So I don't think I enjoyed making this film. I like to explore, I like to experiment, and because we were using a different *vocabulary*, that wasn't possible. It didn't make either of us right or wrong. It just made us different. [laughs] I think Jim's feeling is, I have actors — they're supposed to know what they're doing, right? But sometimes an actor wants a director to say, "Let's find this little nugget here together." I didn't have a sense of being part of the creative process. I felt like I was being told, "Do your job and mind your manners. No talk."

—Woodward, interviewed by Graham Fuller for *Interview*, Nov 1990

Fay WRAY [1907-]

Born: Cardston, Alberta, Canada. Her film debut was in the short, Gasoline Love (1923); in 1928, she played Mitzi Schrammel in Erich Von Stroheim's The Wedding March:

[Von Stroheim] paced up and down and told me the story of *The Wedding March* and asked me if I could play Mitzi, and I told him I could. So he held out his hand and said "Goodbye Mitzi...." I was so thrilled that I just began to cry, and from that moment on he seemed very secure about me.

Q. He had never seen you in a film?

A. No. Just that one meeting.

Q. You were not frightened of him as a person or as a director?

A. Oh, no. There was something quite different than I would have expected about him. He was very real. He had great energy. He was personable. He was dressed very casually, and there was none of that austere raiment that you might expect.

Q. Can we talk a little bit about Von Stroheim's working methods?

A. He had written the story, and, as you know, he played it. He did all things. He was all things. There was a total creative quality about him. I don't remember much about his auditory direction, but he certainly talked me through the scenes. Of course, there was music on the set; it was his music, the music of Vienna. It was very stimulating.

—Wray, interviewed by Anthony Slide for *Magill's Cinema Annual 1982*, ed. by Frank N. Magill (Englewood Cliffs, N.J.: Salem Press, 1982)

I tried on clothes one evening [for *The Wedding March*]. They had been brought from Mr. Powers's Western Costume Company. Every detail was important to von Stroheim. There was no mirror but I could see my reflection in his expressive face. When he was certain, it was certain he was right. All flowed along with a precision as though he were dressing the Mitzi character from memory and loving the remembering. She must have been in his life because he knew so much about her. But what was wonderful was that he didn't pour me into the mold of that memory or make an arbitrary shape for me to fill. He watched me, observing my mannerisms, and would say, "Keep that. Do that." For instance, shyness made me sometimes bite my lower lip. "Do that!".... He was making a blend, coloring the character with his own rememberings and what he was seeing in me. He had loved that Mitzi and so there was that feeling of his love surrounding the character and that was the best garment of all.

When it came time for the seduction scene in the orchard, I was glad that I had seen the film, *The Sea Beast* [1926] with John Barrymore and Dolores Costello. In a full-figure shot of those two embracing, she had let her arm suddenly fall, a gesture of complete surrender. I knew that was right for the moment when Nicki embraced Mitzi just before he picked her up to take her to the carriage; but I didn't tell von Stroheim I had "borrowed."

—Wray, in her *On the Other Hand: A Life Story* (New York: St. Martin's Press, 1989)

Q. You can't say that [that it was stimulating] about Josef von Sternberg and *Thunderbolt* [1929]?

A. No. I think it was an awkward time for him because he was trying to find his way in sound films, and I didn't feel comfortable about being a gangster's moll. It just didn't feel right, and he was not the communicator that Von Stroheim was. There was a distance, as though he was a painter, painting from a distance. He was a cold person.

—Wray, interviewed by Anthony Slide for *Magill's Cinema Annual 1982*, ed. by Frank N. Magill (Englewood Cliffs, N.J.: Salem Press, 1982)

[*The First Kiss* (1928, Rowland V. Lee)] was not a good one for [Gary Cooper] or me. He would have done better with a more — aggressive is not the word — someone who did not have the same temperament and style. He did better with more vigorous and aggressive ladies.

—Wray, interviewed by Stuart M. Kaminsky for *Coop* (New York: St. Martin's Press, 1980)

I knew two very fine producers — Merian C. Cooper and his partner Ernest B. Schoedsack — and I admired the work that they had done. Mr. Cooper said to me that he had an idea for a film in mind. The only thing he'd tell me was that it was going to have the "Tallest leading man in Hollywood." Well, naturally, I thought of Clark Gable hopefully, and when the script [of *King Kong* (1933)] came I was absolutely appalled! I thought it was a practical joke. I really didn't have much appetite for doing it, except that I did admire these two people...and I realized that it did at least have scope...a good imagination.

—Wray, interviewed for NBC Television

The hand and arm in which my close-up scenes [in *King Kong*] were made were about eight feet long. Inside the furry arm there was a steel bar and the whole contraption (with me in the hand) could be raised and lowered like a crane. The fingers would be pressed around my waist while I was in a standing position. I would then be raised about ten feet into the air in the ape's hand but then his fingers would gradually loosen and begin to open. My fear was real as I grabbed onto his wrist, his thumb, wherever I could, to keep from slipping out of that paw! When I could sense that the moment of minimum safety had arrived I would call up imploringly to the director and ask to be lowered to the floor. I would have a few minutes rest, be re-secured in the paw and then the ordeal would begin all over again....

—Wray, in *The New York Times*, 21 Sept 1969

Teresa WRIGHT [1918-]

Born: Muriel Teresa Wright in New York City. Work in stock and on Broadway (from 1938) preceded her film debut as Alexandra Giddens in The Little Foxes (1941, William Wyler), a part she was recommended for by playwright/ screen-writer, Lillian Hellman. The following year she played Charlie in Alfred Hitchcock's Shadow of a Doubt:

I was terrified of Hitch, of course. There was that myth about him not liking actors. It was a pose, I think, and it made good copy. Hitch was really a remarkable storyteller. He could see the whole film in his mind's eye, frame by frame.... Hitch was very articulate, which Willy Wyler was not....

Sometimes I think Willy was not articulate on purpose. He hated actors to *act*. He wanted you to do it instinctively. Not because you were told to.

—Wright, interviewed by Paul Rosenfield for *The Los Angeles Times*, 18 Jan 1982

I'd seen Willy be very hard on other people in the two previous pictures we did together [*The Little Foxes* and *Mrs. Miniver* (1942)]. He could wear people down with the amount of takes he'd make. But there was less of that on *The Best Years of Our Lives* [1946]. It was more spontaneous because he really liked his cast. He seemed to be sitting back and enjoying himself. He just got a terrific kick out of watching Myrna [Loy] and Freddy [March] together....

They shared the same easy rapport off the set.... When he asks her to dance in the bar scene, they began to kid and ad-lib, contributing texture that wasn't written in the script. Willy liked it, so that's what you see in the film. Myrna is just exactly the kind of actress Willy loved. He never liked things that seemed too theatrical, overstated. She exudes powerful yet quiet femininity. It's so inner. The subtlety of what goes on within her amazes me. You feel her sensual quality, her deep womanliness, while underneath there is always this little laugh lurking. She would look at Fred, and the distance caused by months and months of separation just vanished. It was a lovely thing to watch in rehearsal and in the actual scenes. You seldom realize during shooting when a scene is very, very special, but I was always aware of it in their scenes.

—Wright, interviewed by James Kotsilibas-Davis for *Being and Becoming* (by Myrna Loy and James Kotsilibas-Davis) (New York: Alfred A. Knopf, 1987)

Every one of the roles [in *The Best Years of Our Lives*] except mine seemed credible. I just could not concentrate on the part. I never really liked the girl I played (nor me) in the film. You must be able to understand and believe the character. And I just didn't believe. How could that supposedly sensitive, intelligent girl be capable of turning on her parents in such an adolescent manner with the charge, "You've forgotten what it's like to be in love."?

—Wright, interviewed by Bea Smith for *The Newark Sunday News*, 11 Dec 1955

I made...*The Men* [1950, Fred Zinnemann] with Marlon Brando. It was his first film.... He had worked a long time, ahead of time, with Fred Zinnemann and he had prepared himself for the film by going out to the Veteran's Administration Hospital and really getting to know the fellows he was going to work with — the paraplegics — learning how to become like them and learning how they thought and felt and joked. And he'd go out to bars with them, and really lived in the hospital for a while with them. So he came to the film with a great deal of physical preparation for the role.

—Wright, interviewed by Claudio Masenza for *The Rebels: Marlon Brando* (Aida United Video, 1983)

Jane WYMAN [1914-]

Born: Sarah Jane Fulks in St. Joseph, Missouri. At age 18, she made her film debut as a Goldwyn Girl — using her real name — in The Kid From Spain (1932, Leo McCarey). In 1936, she changed her name, but continued to do bit parts and work as a chorus girl for the next few years. In 1948, she played the title role in Jean Negulesco's Johnny Belinda:

Johnny Belinda, from the successful Broadway stage play by Elmer Harris, is the story of a waif, an uncultured little animal, denied speech and hearing from birth, dwelling among the simple fishing and farming people of Prince Edward Island. A sympathetic young doctor [Lew Ayres] from the "outside world" penetrates the girl's world of silence by teaching the sign language and lip reading by which she can attempt to communicate her thoughts to those around her who previously had been denied, or failed to attempt, any contact whatsoever due to her affliction.

It's an utterly absorbing characterization, an emotional challenge to any actress, particularly to this one who prefers character roles any day to leading women. I wholeheartedly accepted the challenge.

Elizabeth Gesner, who has devoted years of energy and her brilliant talents to teaching and working with the deaf, was assigned as technical advisor.... She taught me sign language and lip reading.

Mrs. Gesner also found a young Mexican girl, who had been born deaf, to serve as my model for emotion. The girl came to my home and to the studio, and we made innumerable tests of her in 16 and 35 mm. for me to study. I spent hours with the youngster — a cheerful, delightful little thing despite her handicap — watching her every move and reaction.

What I fought most to get in my characterization was what I call the "something quality" that I saw in her eyes. How may I describe that expression? An "anticipation light" possibly. Anyhow, it was the look of one who wanted eagerly to enter in, to share. With all deaf people, you'll observe this expression — inquiring, interested, alive — as they watch you, to understand by lip reading or by our actions and expressions what you want to impart to them.

Weeks of tests followed. Desperation gripped me whenever I viewed these tests. Something was missing, something intangible. Then, one day, I realized what was wrong. I could hear. Small wonder I was missing out on that vital key to a realistic portrayal of a deaf girl.

So I had plastic, wax and cotton ear stops made for my ears to block out all sound and conversation. I wore these throughout shooting to give me the necessary quality of indecision, of faltering. Negulesco and I were put to evolving a sign language of our own so he could direct me when I had my ears plugged. The cast and crew, as well, developed their own set of signals in order to speak to me.

I completely altered the timing of my acting to where I was always one beat late; never reacting squarely on the line or cue. And having, for the sake of my career, been trained to walk gracefully, with correct posture and to display clothes to the best of my ability, I had to overcome the problem of Wyman entering into Belinda's physical appearance. Wyman had to be ruled out.

So, whenever I walked in the scene, I began with my left foot instead of my right and used my left hand to get over the feeling of an unsureness. In other words, it was a reversal of Jane Wyman who had worked all these years to make herself into a positive personality.

—Wyman, in *The Hollywood Reporter*, Oct 1948

[Q. How did you grow old so gracefully in *The Blue Veil* (1951, Curtis Bernhardt)?]

A. I put a lot of research in it. First of all, I started studying old people — at the club, on the lot or in restaurants.... I would just sit and stare.

Then I went to the library and read up on the subject.... I found out that as people age, their bone structure changes. That's why they stoop and walk the way they do.

Next, [makeup artist] Perc Westmore and I spent many nights...sketching the various postures of old people.

—Wyman, interviewed by James R. Bacon for *The Oregon Journal*, 14 Oct 1952

To play the club-footed character [Laura Wingfield] of *The Glass Menagerie* [1950, Irving Rapper], I spent much time with a little crippled girl. I discovered then, even as I discovered from a blind companion who assisted me with the technical advice on *Magnificent Obsession* [1954, Douglas Sirk], that my greatest problem would be the tendency to overact.

The blind do not careen around rooms knocking over vases and lamps nor do they grope wildly at the air in front of them. With this type of handicap, as with all the others I learned, the importance was knowing how blind persons feel inside.

—Wyman, in *The New York Times*, 29 Nov 1953

Y

Michael YORK [1942-]

Born: Fulmer, Buckinghamshire, England. Studies at University College, Oxford and work with various stage companies including The National Theater Company preceded his film debut in The Taming of the Shrew (1967, Franco Zeffirelli). In 1972, he played Brian Roberts in Cabaret:

My friends warned me to turn it down [*Cabaret* (1972, Bob Fosse)]. Thank God, we rehearsed in Germany. Every day I sat and rewrote the script with Bob Fosse, the director and Hugh Wheeler, the writer trying to make the guy more than just the human camera [Christopher] Isherwood wrote of in his stories. It killed me when they played it on network television recently, cutting the lines where Liza Minnelli says she slept with the German millionaire, and I reply, that I did, too. His bi-sexuality made the man a human being, and slashing those lines made his character totally incomprehensible.

— York, interviewed by Richard Townsend for *The Sunday News*, 4 July 1976

Susannah YORK [1939-]

Born: Susannah Fletcher in London, England; raised in Ayrshire, Scotland. Studies at Marr College in Troon, Scotland and at The Royal Academy of Dramatic Art in London, and work in repertory preceded her film debut in Tunes of Glory (1960, Ronald Neame). In 1962, she played Cecily Koertner in John Huston's Freud:

John Huston saw *Greengage Summer* [1961, Lewis Gilbert] and was one of the few people imaginative enough to offer me a totally different kind of part — which was what *Freud* was. He had nothing else, really, to go on, and I think that was remarkable. But I must say I fought quite bitterly with John on the making of the film, and found it a very painful experience — but one I wouldn't have missed for anything in the world. There again, some of my difficulties arose on occasions when I was asked to do something and I didn't believe in it. One of the troubles was that constantly we had re-writes: we would have done a scene, and then seven or eight days later we would be given a new lot of pages of the same scene to read, around which we'd subsequently built work. So it often seemed to throw one's previous work to rubbish. I was about four or five test cases all rolled into one, I had so many complexes — it was terribly confusing.

I felt [Alice "Childie" McNaught in *The Killing of Sister George* (1968, Robert Aldrich)] was a girl who was basically heterosexual and who's had two or three rather unfortunate love affairs in which she'd been the one who'd been left as flotsam on the shore, and not being a very strong character or having any really very strong principles she couldn't say, when things didn't work out, "O.K. It doesn't matter, I'm going to try again." I always had the feeling about her that she'd probably been abandoned pretty early by her mother, and that George [Beryl Reid] represented a sort of rock to her, and that the sexual side (to her) just happened. I would say she was an amoral person as opposed to immoral. But there *was* real affection there, and a sense of guilt; but also that she'd found in her life the easiest way to get by. I thought in her early life there'd been rows, rows, rows, and that she had a horror of violence and rows; and since the bullying side of George was very strong, in her own little and rather weak way she revolted and just simply lied, because she couldn't really face up to it. One has to take into account that this was the equivalent of a seven-year marriage, when you *are* irritated by your partner, frequently, they *do* bore you sometimes, you know, you could just scream at them. And when Alice saw that her rock, which was George, was foundering — was not the strong rock — that was a shock.

—York, interviewed by Derek Elley for *Focus on Film*, Spring 1972

I was fed up with the sweet young things I'd generally been playing, and I was willing to take any role that would get me out of the goo and treacle I was sinking into. Even in *Tom Jones* [1963, Tony Richardson], that lusty film about life in 18th Century England, they had me play a candy box girl — the sweet young thing with the morning dew still on her face at bedtime. I figured the role of Childie...would change my virginal film image for all time. It did....

—York, interviewed by Jack Shafer for *The Sunday Star-Ledger*, 4 June 1972

Originally, Alice [LeBlanc in *They Shoot Horses, Don't They?* (1969, Sydney Pollack)] was much more hysterical. There were just a few attributes like nymphomania and starletism, but no character floating around, no human being. Then we created the Harlow-figure, the dress, the care about her cleanliness and make-up, and the way she looks. The shower scene was my last day — they filmed all through the night to get that....

—York, interviewed by Derek Elley for *Focus on Film*, Spring 1972

Loretta YOUNG [1914-]

Born: Gretchen Young in Salt Lake City, Utah. Work as a Hollywood extra from age four preceded her first featured role opposite Lon Chaney in Laugh, Clown, Laugh (1928, Herbert Brenon):

Laugh, Clown, Laugh was directed by one of the top directors of that time. I knew beforehand that he was brilliant, temperamental and a harsh taskmaster, and I learned the hard way why he was called a tyrant. He shattered all the young self-confidence I had and I was terrified throughout the picture. No matter how hard I tried, he ranted and raved and once even threw a chair which fortunately missed its target and didn't hit anyone else either. He'd storm at me: "You're not an actress. You know nothing about acting — absolutely nothing."

He was right. I did have everything to learn, but telling me in front of everybody absolutely killed me.

—Young, in her (as told to Helen Ferguson) *The Things I Had to Learn* (New York: Bobbs-Merrill Co., 1961)

Working with Mr. Chaney was the finest thing that could happen to any youngster. He was so kind, so considerate, so helpful, so happy to tell you what he knew. And he knew all there was to know about pictures.... To all who had the privilege of knowing him, he was a true friend and splendid teacher.

—Young, in an unsourced undated article in the files of The New York Public Library for the Performing Arts

[On *Platinum Blonde* (1931)] you [Frank Capra] signaled for a rehearsal and my brain obediently clicked your instructions back to me. At the end of the rehearsal you walked to where I was standing and your voice was so low no one else could hear what you said.

"Whatever do you think of the character, Loretta?" You asked me.

"Think?"

I hastened to reassure you.

"Oh, I never *think*, Mr. Capra. I *never* think about the characters I play — I just try to do what the director says."

You gave me a look I've never forgotten. There was tenderness, understanding and — well, there was sadness in it, too. I stood very still.... Even my heart stood still, waiting for some kind of awful thing to happen. Like being fired, maybe.

You spoke in such a gentle voice. You said, "Loretta!" A smile sort of whispered across your face. "Little Loretta, you must learn to think. Nothing in your acting is more important than what you think. Acting isn't doing just exactly what the director says! It's thinking yourself into the character you're playing. It's deciding what the character would do — and then it is doing just exactly that."

—Young, in a note addressed to Frank Capra in her (as told to Helen Ferguson) *The Things I Had to Learn* (New York: Bobbs-Merrill Co., 1961)

Mr. Zanuck was very frank when he first told me of his decision to assign me this part [of Meg in *Clive of India* (1935, Richard Boleslavsky)]. He even mentioned the fact that most of his associates were quite dubious about his plan to give me the role. Well, so was I until I had read the book and the script over many times. I realized immediately, though, that I wanted to play this role....

So many things she did were so foreign to our conventional ideas. But still I was forced to admire her...because she had the strength and the honesty to live her life as she thought best, without particular regard to the copy-book version....

In the early part of the film, she shows a strong sense of adventure, when she comes to India to meet Clive [Ronald Colman], whom she has never seen in her life. He has fallen in love with her photograph and written her asking her to come. She marries him. She has led a quiet, sheltered life, but there was something in Clive's letters, some undercurrent of real love that causes her to ignore the conventionalities under which she had been brought up.

I can't help but think that there was something of that same feeling of adventure in my own romance and marriage four years ago. Of course, mine was not the daring adventure of going to a strange country to marry a man I had never seen before. But, in a way, it was a stupendous adventure to me. I, too, had been brought up conservatively, sheltered in the heart of my family. It was a terrific step in my life to run away, cut myself off from my mother's guidance at seventeen — for what I thought (just as deeply as did Meg) must be true love....

Meg loved her husband with an almost maternal love. He was a child to her....

Later in the story, when [Clive]...puts adventure and duty before love and home...she does not think he has really failed her. She knows Clive too well. She knows it is merely a matter of waiting, waiting until his little-boy world of glamor and military uniforms crashes before him. She has infinite patience with him.

—Young, interviewed by Walter Ramsey for *Modern Screen*, Apr 1935

[As] a little girl I used to fancy myself as the persecuted Ramona; I'd wear a lace curtain for a mantilla and hang over the banister in lieu of a balcony. My affection for the half-Scotch, half-Indian girl never waned. When I was under contract to Fox, I talked so much about Ramona that the studio finally bought the book and cast me in the title role [of *Ramona* (1936, Henry King)].

That was a dream come true. The part had the magic of childhood make-believe as well as the inspiration of a character rich in courage, intelligence and spirituality.

—Young, in *The Saturday Evening Post*, 20 Apr 1946

Robert YOUNG [1907-]

Born: Chicago, Illinois. Studies with and work at The Pasadena Playhouse and brief touring preceded his film debut in The Black Camel (1931, Hamilton MacFadden). In 1941, he played the title role in King Vidor's H.M. Pulham, Esq.:

We didn't play the elder Pulham simply with gray hair and make-up. As King Vidor pointed out, a man does not change appearance greatly in twenty years or so. To have used "old man" make-up would have been incongruous.

So as a young man, I went clean-shaven at Harvard, wore a rather ragged mustache in the World War sequence, one neatly trimmed during the New York sequence with Hedy Lamarr. In the forty-five-year-old period, the mustache was iron-gray and a little untrimmed.

The principal thing Mr. Vidor wanted to bring out was the man's demeanor, not make-up. At forty-five he had changed after years of a hum-drum routine existence. He had become a creature of habit, smug and stolid. These were brought out in gesture, deportment, manner of speech. Dozens of little details went into the action.

Both Miss Lamarr and myself, in the final sequences, had to give the impression of maturity, but at the same time seem perfectly capable of a romance that we'd come to realize could not be rekindled.

—Young, in the press packet for *H.M. Pulham* (MGM, 1942)

APPENDIX

NOMINATIONS AND AWARDS OF THE ACADEMY OF MOTION PICTURE ARTS AND SCIENCES, AND THE AWARDS OF THE BRITISH ACADEMY, THE FOREIGN PRESS ASSOCIATION, THE LOS ANGELES FILM CRITICS, THE NATIONAL BOARD OF REVIEW, THE NATIONAL SOCIETY OF FILM CRITICS, AND THE NEW YORK FILM CRITICS CIRCLE

THE ACADEMY OF MOTION PICTURE ARTS AND SCIENCES NOMINATIONS AND AWARDS

F. MURRAY ABRAHAM	1984	AMADEUS*
NICK ADAMS	1963	TWILIGHT OF HONOR#
ISABELLE ADJANI	1975	THE STORY OF ADELE H
	1989	CAMILLE CLAUDEL
BRIAN AHERNE	1939	JUAREZ#
DANNY AIELLO	1989	DO THE RIGHT THING#
ANOUK AIMÉE	1966	A MAN AND A WOMAN
EDDIE ALBERT	1953	ROMAN HOLIDAY#
	1972	THE HEARTBREAK KID#
JACK ALBERTSON	1968	THE SUBJECT WAS ROSES#*
NORMA ALEANDRO	1987	GABY - A TRUE STORY#
JANE ALEXANDER	1970	THE GREAT WHITE HOPE
	1976	ALL THE PRESIDENT'S MEN#
	1979	KRAMER VS. KRAMER#
	1983	TESTAMENT
WOODY ALLEN	1977	ANNIE HALL
SARA ALLGOOD	1941	HOW GREEN WAS MY VALLEY#
DON AMECHE	1985	COCOON#*
JUDITH ANDERSON	1940	REBECCA#
JULIE ANDREWS	1964	MARY POPPINS*
	1965	THE SOUND OF MUSIC
	1982	VICTOR/VICTORIA
ANN-MARGRET	1971	CARNAL KNOWLEDGE#
	1975	TOMMY
ANNE ARCHER	1987	FATAL ATTRACTION#
EVE ARDEN	1945	MILDRED PIERCE#
ALAN ARKIN	1966	THE RUSSIANS ARE COMING, THE RUSSIANS ARE COMING
	1968	THE HEART IS A LONELY HUNTER
GEORGE ARLISS	1929/30	DISRAELI*
	1929/30	THE GREEN GODDESS
JEAN ARTHUR	1943	THE MORE THE MERRIER
DAME PEGGY ASHCROFT	1984	A PASSAGE TO INDIA#*
FRED ASTAIRE	1974	THE TOWERING INFERNO#
MARY ASTOR	1941	THE GREAT LIE#*
MISCHA AUER	1936	MY MAN GODFREY#
MARGARET AVERY	1985	THE COLOR PURPLE#
DAN AYKROYD	1989	DRIVING MISS DAISY#
LEW AYRES	1948	JOHNNY BELINDA

HERMIONE BADDELEY	1959	ROOM AT THE TOP#
MARY BADHAM	1962	TO KILL A MOCKINGBIRD#
FAY BAINTER	1938	WHITE BANNERS
	1938	JEZEBEL#*
	1961	THE CHILDREN'S HOUR#
CARROLL BAKER	1956	BABY DOLL
MARTIN BALSAM	1965	A THOUSAND CLOWNS#*
ANNE BANCROFT	1962	THE MIRACLE WORKER*
	1964	THE PUMPKIN EATER
	1967	THE GRADUATE
	1977	THE TURNING POINT
	1985	AGNES OF GOD
GEORGE BANCROFT	1928/9	THUNDERBOLT
IAN BANNEN	1965	THE FLIGHT OF THE PHOENIX#
MARY-CHRISTINE BARRAULT	1976	COUSIN, COUSINE
BARBARA BARRIE	1979	BREAKING AWAY#
ETHEL BARRYMORE	1944	NONE BUT THE LONELY HEART#*
	1946	THE SPIRAL STAIRCASE#
	1947	THE PARADINE CASE#
	1949	PINKY#
LIONEL BARRYMORE	1930/1	A FREE SOUL*
RICHARD BARTHELMESS	1927/8	THE NOOSE and THE PATENT LEATHER KID
MIKHAIL BARYSHNIKOV	1977	THE TURNING POINT#
ALBERT BASSERMAN	1940	FOREIGN CORRESPONDENT#
ALAN BATES	1968	THE FIXER
KATHY BATES	1990	MISERY*
ANNE BAXTER	1946	THE RAZOR'S EDGE#*
	1950	ALL ABOUT EVE
WARNER BAXTER	1928/9	IN OLD ARIZONA*
NED BEATTY	1976	NETWORK#
WARREN BEATTY	1967	BONNIE AND CLYDE
	1978	HEAVEN CAN WAIT
	1981	REDS
WALLACE BEERY	1929/30	THE BIG HOUSE
	1931/2	THE CHAMP*
ED BEGLEY	1962	SWEET BIRD OF YOUTH#*
BARBARA BEL GEDDES	1948	I REMEMBER MAMA#
RALPH BELLAMY	1937	THE AWFUL TRUTH#
WILLIAM BENDIX	1942	WAKE ISLAND#
ANNETTE BENING	1990	THE GRIFTERS#
TOM BERENGER	1986	PLATOON#
CANDICE BERGEN	1979	STARTING OVER#
INGRID BERGMAN	1943	FOR WHOM THE BELL TOLLS
	1944	GASLIGHT*
	1945	THE BELLS OF ST. MARY'S
	1948	JOAN OF ARC
	1956	ANASTASIA*
	1974	MURDER ON THE ORIENT EXPRESS#*
	1978	AUTUMN SONATA
ELISABETH BERGNER	1935	ESCAPE ME NEVER
JEANNIE BERLIN	1972	THE HEARTBREAK KID#
CHARLES BICKFORD	1943	THE SONG OF BERNADETTE#
	1947	THE FARMER'S DAUGHTER#
	1948	JOHNNY BELINDA#
THEODORE BIKEL	1958	THE DEFIANT ONES#
KAREN BLACK	1970	FIVE EASY PIECES#
BETSY BLAIR	1955	MARTY#
LINDA BLAIR	1973	THE EXORCIST#
RONEE BLAKLEY	1975	NASHVILLE#
JOAN BLONDELL	1951	THE BLUE VEIL#
ANN BLYTH	1945	MILDRED PIERCE#
HUMPHREY BOGART	1943	CASABLANCA
	1951	THE AFRICAN QUEEN*
	1954	THE CAINE MUTINY
BEULAH BONDI	1936	THE GORGEOUS HUSSY#
	1938	OF HUMAN HEARTS#
SHIRLEY BOOTH	1952	COME BACK, LITTLE SHEBA*
ERNEST BORGNINE	1955	MARTY*
CHARLES BOYER	1937	CONQUEST
	1938	ALGIERS

	1944	GASLIGHT
	1961	FANNY
LORRAINE BRACCO	1990	GOODFELLAS#
ALICE BRADY	1936	MY MAN GODFREY#
	1937	IN OLD CHICAGO#*
KENNETH BRANAGH	1989	HENRY V
KLAUS-MARIA BRANDAUER	1985	OUT OF AFRICA#
MARLON BRANDO	1951	A STREETCAR NAMED DESIRE
	1952	VIVA ZAPATA!
	1953	JULIUS CAESAR
	1954	ON THE WATERFRONT*
	1957	SAYONARA
	1972	THE GODFATHER*
	1973	LAST TANGO IN PARIS
	1989	A DRY WHITE SEASON#
EILEEN BRENNAN	1980	PRIVATE BENJAMIN#
WALTER BRENNAN	1936	COME AND GET IT#*
	1938	KENTUCKY#*
	1940	THE WESTERNER#*
	1941	SERGEANT YORK#
JEFF BRIDGES	1971	THE LAST PICTURE SHOW#
	1974	THUNDERBOLT AND LIGHTFOOT#
	1984	STARMAN
ALBERT BROOKS	1987	BROADCAST NEWS#
LESLIE BROWNE	1977	THE TURNING POINT#
YUL BRYNNER	1956	THE KING AND I*
GENEVIEVE BUJOLD	1969	ANNE OF THE THOUSAND DAYS
VICTOR BUONO	1962	WHAT EVER HAPPENED TO BABY JANE?#
BILLIE BURKE	1938	MERRILY WE LIVE#
CATHERINE BURNS	1969	LAST SUMMER#
GEORGE BURNS	1975	THE SUNSHINE BOYS#*
ELLEN BURSTYN	1971	THE LAST PICTURE SHOW#
	1973	THE EXORCIST
	1974	ALICE DOESN'T LIVE HERE ANYMORE*
	1978	SAME TIME, NEXT YEAR
	1980	RESURRECTION
RICHARD BURTON	1952	MY COUSIN RACHEL#
	1953	THE ROBE
	1964	BECKET
	1965	THE SPY WHO CAME IN FROM THE COLD
	1966	WHO'S AFRAID OF VIRGINIA WOOLF?
	1969	ANNE OF THE THOUSAND DAYS
	1977	EQUUS
GARY BUSEY	1978	THE BUDDY HOLLY STORY
RED BUTTONS	1957	SAYONARA#*
SPRING BYINGTON	1938	YOU CAN'T TAKE IT WITH YOU#
JAMES CAAN	1972	THE GODFATHER#
ADOLPH CAESAR	1984	A SOLDIER'S STORY#
JAMES CAGNEY	1938	ANGELS WITH DIRTY FACES
	1942	YANKEE DOODLE DANDY*
	1955	LOVE ME OR LEAVE ME
MICHAEL CAINE	1966	ALFIE
	1972	SLEUTH
	1983	EDUCATING RITA
	1986	HANNAH AND HER SISTERS#*
LOUIS CALHERN	1950	THE MAGNIFICENT YANKEE
DYAN CANNON	1969	BOB & CAROL & TED & ALICE#
	1978	HEAVEN CAN WAIT#
HARRY CAREY	1939	MR. SMITH GOES TO WASHINGTON#
LYNN CARLIN	1968	FACES#
ART CARNEY	1974	HARRY AND TONTO*
LESLIE CARON	1953	LILI
	1963	THE L-SHAPED ROOM
DIAHANN CARROLL	1974	CLAUDINE
NANCY CARROLL	1929/30	THE DEVIL'S HOLIDAY
PEGGY CASS	1958	AUNTIE MAME#
JOHN CASSAVETES	1967	THE DIRTY DOZEN#
SEYMOUR CASSEL	1968	FACES#
RICHARD CASTELLANO	1970	LOVERS AND OTHER STRANGERS#
GEORGE CHAKIRIS	1961	WEST SIDE STORY#*
JEFF CHANDLER	1950	BROKEN ARROW#

CAROL CHANNING	1967	THOROUGHLY MODERN MILLIE#
CHARLES CHAPLIN	1927/8	THE CIRCUS
	1940	THE GREAT DICTATOR
RUTH CHATTERTON	1928/9	MADAME X
	1929/30	SARAH AND SON
MICHAEL CHEKHOV	1945	SPELLBOUND#
CHER	1983	SILKWOOD#
	1987	MOONSTRUCK*
MAURICE CHEVALIER	1929/30	THE LOVE PARADE
	1929/30	THE BIG POND
JULIE CHRISTIE	1965	DARLING*
	1971	MCCABE AND MRS. MILLER
DIANE CILENTO	1963	TOM JONES#
CANDY CLARK	1973	AMERICAN GRAFFITI#
JILL CLAYBURGH	1978	AN UNMARRIED WOMAN
	1979	STARTING OVER
MONTGOMERY CLIFT	1948	THE SEARCH
	1951	A PLACE IN THE SUN
	1953	FROM HERE TO ETERNITY
	1961	JUDGMENT AT NUREMBERG#
GLENN CLOSE	1982	THE WORLD ACCORDING TO GARP#
	1983	THE BIG CHILL#
	1984	THE NATURAL#
	1987	FATAL ATTRACTION
	1988	DANGEROUS LIAISONS
LEE J. COBB	1954	ON THE WATERFRONT#
	1958	THE BROTHERS KARAMAZOV#
CHARLES COBURN	1941	THE DEVIL AND MISS JONES#
	1943	THE MORE THE MERRIER#*
	1946	THE GREEN YEARS#
JAMES COCO	1981	ONLY WHEN I LAUGH#
CLAUDETTE COLBERT	1934	IT HAPPENED ONE NIGHT*
	1935	PRIVATE WORLDS
	1944	SINCE YOU WENT AWAY
PATRICIA COLLINGE	1941	THE LITTLE FOXES#
PAULINE COLLINS	1989	SHIRLEY VALENTINE
RONALD COLMAN	1929/30	BULLDOG DRUMMOND
	1929/30	CONDEMNED
	1942	RANDOM HARVEST
	1947	A DOUBLE LIFE*
BETTY COMPSON	1928/9	THE BARKER
SEAN CONNERY	1987	THE UNTOUCHABLES#*
TOM CONTI	1983	REUBEN, REUBEN
GARY COOPER	1936	MR. DEEDS GOES TO TOWN
	1941	SERGEANT YORK*
	1942	THE PRIDE OF THE YANKEES
	1943	FOR WHOM THE BELL TOLLS
	1952	HIGH NOON*
GLADYS COOPER	1942	NOW, VOYAGER#
	1943	THE SONG OF BERNADETTE#
	1964	MY FAIR LADY#
JACKIE COOPER	1930/1	SKIPPY
ELLEN CORBY	1948	I REMEMBER MAMA#
VALENTINA CORTESE	1974	DAY FOR NIGHT#
KEVIN COSTNER	1990	DANCES WITH WOLVES
TOM COURTENAY	1965	DR. ZHIVAGO#
	1983	THE DRESSER
JEANNE CRAIN	1949	PINKY
BRODERICK CRAWFORD	1949	ALL THE KING'S MEN*
JOAN CRAWFORD	1945	MILDRED PIERCE*
	1947	POSSESSED
	1952	SUDDEN FEAR
DONALD CRISP	1941	HOW GREEN WAS MY VALLEY#*
HUME CRONYN	1944	THE SEVENTH CROSS#
BING CROSBY	1944	GOING MY WAY*
	1945	THE BELLS OF ST. MARY'S
	1954	THE COUNTRY GIRL
RUPERT CROSSE	1969	THE REIVERS#
LINDSAY CROUSE	1984	PLACES IN THE HEART#
TOM CRUISE	1989	BORN ON THE FOURTH OF JULY
QUINN CUMMINGS	1977	THE GOODBYE GIRL#

TONY CURTIS	1958	THE DEFIANT ONES
JOAN CUSACK	1988	WORKING GIRL#
WILLEM DAFOE	1986	PLATOON#
DAN DAILEY	1948	WHEN MY BABY SMILES AT ME
JOHN DALL	1945	THE CORN IS GREEN#
DOROTHY DANDRIDGE	1954	CARMEN JONES
BOBBY DARIN	1963	CAPTAIN NEWMAN, M.D.#
JANE DARWELL	1940	THE GRAPES OF WRATH#*
BETTE DAVIS	1935	DANGEROUS*
	1938	JEZEBEL*
	1939	DARK VICTORY
	1940	THE LETTER
	1941	THE LITTLE FOXES
	1942	NOW, VOYAGER
	1944	MR. SKEFFINGTON
	1950	ALL ABOUT EVE
	1952	THE STAR
	1962	WHAT EVER HAPPENED TO BABY JANE?
GEENA DAVIS	1988	THE ACCIDENTAL TOURIST#*
JUDY DAVIS	1984	A PASSAGE TO INDIA
BRUCE DAVISON	1990	LONGTIME COMPANION#
DORIS DAY	1959	PILLOW TALK
DANIEL DAY-LEWIS	1989	MY LEFT FOOT*
JAMES DEAN	1955	EAST OF EDEN
	1956	GIANT
OLIVIA DE HAVILLAND	1939	GONE WITH THE WIND#
	1941	HOLD BACK THE DAWN
	1946	TO EACH HIS OWN*
	1948	THE SNAKE PIT
	1949	THE HEIRESS*
ROBERT DE NIRO	1974	THE GODFATHER PART II#*
	1976	TAXI DRIVER
	1978	THE DEER HUNTER
	1980	RAGING BULL*
	1990	AWAKENINGS
VITTORIO DE SICA	1957	A FAREWELL TO ARMS#
BRANDON DE WILDE	1953	SHANE#
WILLIAM DEMAREST	1946	THE JOLSON STORY#
SANDY DENNIS	1966	WHO'S AFRAID OF VIRGINIA WOOLF?#*
GÉRARD DEPARDIEU	1990	CYRANO DE BERGERAC
BRUCE DERN	1978	COMING HOME#
MARLENE DIETRICH	1930/1	MOROCCO
MELINDA DILLON	1977	CLOSE ENCOUNTERS OF THE THIRD KIND#
	1981	ABSENCE OF MALICE#
RICHARD DIX	1930/1	CIMARRON
ROBERT DONAT	1938	THE CITADEL
	1939	GOODBYE, MR. CHIPS*
BRIAN DONLEVY	1939	BEAU GESTE#
KIRK DOUGLAS	1949	CHAMPION
	1952	THE BAD AND THE BEAUTIFUL
	1956	LUST FOR LIFE
MELVYN DOUGLAS	1963	HUD#*
	1970	I NEVER SANG FOR MY FATHER
	1979	BEING THERE#*
MICHAEL DOUGLAS	1987	WALL STREET*
BRAD DOURIF	1975	ONE FLEW OVER THE CUCKOO'S NEST#
LOUISE DRESSER	1927/8	A SHIP COMES IN
MARIE DRESSLER	1930/1	MIN AND BILL*
	1931/2	EMMA
RICHARD DREYFUSS	1977	THE GOODBYE GIRL*
OLYMPIA DUKAKIS	1987	MOONSTRUCK#*
PATTY DUKE	1962	THE MIRACLE WORKER#*
FAYE DUNAWAY	1967	BONNIE AND CLYDE
	1974	CHINATOWN
	1976	NETWORK*
JAMES DUNN	1945	A TREE GROWS IN BROOKLYN#*
MICHAEL DUNN	1965	SHIP OF FOOLS#
IRENE DUNNE	1930/1	CIMARRON
	1936	THEODORA GOES WILD
	1937	THE AWFUL TRUTH
	1939	LOVE AFFAIR

	1948	I REMEMBER MAMA
MILDRED DUNNOCK	1951	DEATH OF A SALESMAN#
	1956	THE BAD SEED#
CHARLES DURNING	1982	THE BEST LITTLE WHOREHOUSE IN TEXAS#
	1983	TO BE OR NOT TO BE#
ROBERT DUVALL	1972	THE GODFATHER#
	1979	APOCALYPSE NOW#
	1980	THE GREAT SANTINI
	1983	TENDER MERCIES*
JEANNE EAGELS	1928/9	THE LETTER
SAMANTHA EGGAR	1965	THE COLLECTOR
DENHOLM ELLIOTT	1986	ROOM WITH A VIEW#
HOPE EMERSON	1950	CAGED#
STUART ERWIN	1936	PIGSKIN PARADE#
DAME EDITH EVANS	1963	TOM JONES#
	1964	THE CHALK GARDEN#
	1967	THE WHISPERERS
PETER FALK	1960	MURDER, INC.#
	1961	POCKETFUL OF MIRACLES#
RICHARD FARNSWORTH	1978	COMES A HORSEMAN#
JOSÉ FERRER	1948	JOAN OF ARC#
	1950	CYRANO DE BERGERAC*
	1952	MOULIN ROUGE
SALLY FIELD	1979	NORMA RAE*
	1984	PLACES IN THE HEART*
PETER FINCH	1971	SUNDAY, BLOODY SUNDAY
	1976	NETWORK*
FRANK FINLAY	1965	OTHELLO#
ALBERT FINNEY	1963	TOM JONES
	1974	MURDER ON THE ORIENT EXPRESS
	1983	THE DRESSER
	1984	UNDER THE VOLCANO
PETER FIRTH	1977	EQUUS#
BARRY FITZGERALD	1944	GOING MY WAY
	1944	GOING MY WAY#*
GERALDINE FITZGERALD	1939	WUTHERING HEIGHTS#
LOUISE FLETCHER	1975	ONE FLEW OVER THE CUCKOO'S NEST*
NINA FOCH	1954	EXECUTIVE SUITE#
HENRY FONDA	1940	THE GRAPES OF WRATH
	1981	ON GOLDEN POND*
JANE FONDA	1969	THEY SHOOT HORSES, DON'T THEY?
	1971	KLUTE*
	1977	JULIA
	1978	COMING HOME*
	1979	THE CHINA SYNDROME
	1981	ON GOLDEN POND#
	1986	THE MORNING AFTER
JOAN FONTAINE	1940	REBECCA
	1941	SUSPICION*
	1943	THE CONSTANT NYMPH
LYNN FONTANNE	1931/2	THE GUARDSMAN
HARRISON FORD	1985	WITNESS
FREDERIC FORREST	1979	THE ROSE#
JODIE FOSTER	1976	TAXI DRIVER#
	1988	THE ACCUSED*
ANTHONY FRANCIOSA	1957	A HATFUL OF RAIN
MORGAN FREEMAN	1987	STREET SMART#
	1989	DRIVING MISS DAISY
LEONARD FREY	1971	FIDDLER ON THE ROOF#
BRENDA FRICKER	1989	MY LEFT FOOT#*
CLARK GABLE	1934	IT HAPPENED ONE NIGHT*
	1935	MUTINY ON THE BOUNTY
	1939	GONE WITH THE WIND
GRETA GARBO	1929/30	ANNA CHRISTIE
	1929/30	ROMANCE
	1937	CAMILLE
	1939	NINOTCHKA
ANDY GARCIA	1990	THE GODFATHER PART III#
VINCENT GARDENIA	1973	BANG THE DRUM SLOWLY#
	1987	MOONSTRUCK#
AVA GARDNER	1953	MOGAMBO

JOHN GARFIELD	1938	FOUR DAUGHTERS#
	1947	BODY AND SOUL
WILLIAM GARGAN	1940	THEY KNEW WHAT THEY WANTED#
JUDY GARLAND	1954	A STAR IS BORN
	1961	JUDGMENT AT NUREMBERG#
JAMES GARNER	1985	MURPHY'S ROMANCE
TERI GARR	1982	TOOTSIE#
GREER GARSON	1939	GOODBYE, MR. CHIPS
	1941	BLOSSOMS IN THE DUST
	1942	MRS. MINIVER*
	1943	MADAME CURIE
	1944	MRS. PARKINGTON
	1945	THE VALLEY OF DECISION
	1960	SUNRISE AT CAMPOBELLO
JANET GAYNOR	1927/8	SUNRISE*, SEVENTH HEAVEN* and STREET ANGEL*
	1937	A STAR IS BORN
MICHAEL V. GAZZO	1974	THE GODFATHER PART II#
LEO GENN	1951	QUO VADIS#
CHIEF DAN GEORGE	1970	LITTLE BIG MAN#
GLADYS GEORGE	1936	VALIANT IS THE WORD FOR CARRIE
GIANCARLO GIANNINI	1976	SEVEN BEAUTIES
JOHN GIELGUD	1964	BECKET#
	1981	ARTHUR#*
JACK GILFORD	1974	SAVE THE TIGER#
LILLIAN GISH	1946	DUEL IN THE SUN#
JACKIE GLEASON	1961	THE HUSTLER#
JAMES GLEASON	1941	HERE COMES MR. JORDAN#
PAULETTE GODDARD	1943	SO PROUDLY WE HAIL#
WHOOPI GOLDBERG	1985	THE COLOR PURPLE
	1990	GHOST#*
THOMAS GOMEZ	1947	RIDE THE PINK HORSE#
DEXTER GORDON	1986	'ROUND MIDNIGHT
RUTH GORDON	1965	INSIDE DAISY CLOVER#
	1968	ROSEMARY'S BABY#*
LOUIS GOSSETT, JR.	1982	AN OFFICER AND A GENTLEMAN#*
ELLIOTT GOULD	1969	BOB & TED & CAROL & ALICE#
GLORIA GRAHAME	1947	CROSSFIRE#
	1952	THE BAD AND THE BEAUTIFUL#*
CARY GRANT	1941	PENNY SERENADE
	1944	NONE BUT THE LONELY HEART
LEE GRANT	1951	DETECTIVE STORY#
	1970	THE LANDLORD#
	1975	SHAMPOO#*
	1976	VOYAGE OF THE DAMNED#
BONITA GRANVILLE	1936	THESE THREE#
GRAHAME GREENE	1990	DANCES WITH WOLVES#
SYDNEY GREENSTREET	1941	THE MALTESE FALCON#
JOEL GREY	1972	CABARET#*
HUGH GRIFFITH	1959	BEN-HUR#*
	1963	TOM JONES#
MELANIE GRIFFITH	1988	WORKING GIRL
ALEC GUINNESS	1952	THE LAVENDER HILL MOB
	1957	THE BRIDGE ON THE RIVER KWAI*
	1977	STAR WARS#
	1988	LITTLE DORRIT#
EDMUND GWENN	1947	MIRACLE ON 34TH STREET#*
	1950	MISTER 880#
JOAN HACKETT	1981	ONLY WHEN I LAUGH#
GENE HACKMAN	1967	BONNIE AND CLYDE#
	1970	I NEVER SANG FOR MY FATHER#
	1971	THE FRENCH CONNECTION*
	1988	MISSISSIPPI BURNING
JEAN HAGEN	1952	SINGIN' IN THE RAIN#
GRAYSON HALL	1964	THE NIGHT OF THE IGUANA#
TOM HANKS	1988	BIG
ANN HARDING	1930/1	HOLIDAY
TESS HARPER	1986	CRIMES OF THE HEART#
BARBARA HARRIS	1971	WHO IS HARRY KELLERMAN AND WHY IS HE SAYING THESE TERRIBLE THINGS

		ABOUT ME?#
JULIE HARRIS	1952	THE MEMBER OF THE WEDDING
RICHARD HARRIS	1963	THIS SPORTING LIFE
	1990	THE FIELD
REX HARRISON	1963	CLEOPATRA
	1964	MY FAIR LADY*
ELIZABETH HARTMAN	1965	A PATCH OF BLUE
LAURENCE HARVEY	1959	ROOM AT THE TOP
GOLDIE HAWN	1969	CACTUS FLOWER#*
	1980	PRIVATE BENJAMIN
SESSUE HAYAKAWA	1957	THE BRIDGE ON THE RIVER KWAI#
HELEN HAYES	1931/2	THE SIN OF MADELON CLAUDET*
	1970	AIRPORT#*
SUSAN HAYWARD	1947	SMASH-UP - THE STORY OF A WOMAN
	1949	MY FOOLISH HEART
	1952	WITH A SONG IN MY HEART
	1955	I'LL CRY TOMORROW
	1958	I WANT TO LIVE!*
EILEEN HECKART	1956	THE BAD SEED#
	1972	BUTTERFLIES ARE FREE#*
VAN HEFLIN	1942	JOHNNY EAGER#*
MARIEL HEMINGWAY	1979	MANHATTAN#
JUSTIN HENRY	1979	KRAMER VS. KRAMER#
AUDREY HEPBURN	1953	ROMAN HOLIDAY*
	1954	SABRINA
	1959	THE NUN'S STORY
	1961	BREAKFAST AT TIFFANY'S
	1967	WAIT UNTIL DARK
KATHARINE HEPBURN	1932/3	MORNING GLORY*
	1935	ALICE ADAMS
	1940	THE PHILADELPHIA STORY
	1942	WOMAN OF THE YEAR
	1951	THE AFRICAN QUEEN
	1955	SUMMERTIME
	1956	THE RAINMAKER
	1959	SUDDENLY, LAST SUMMER
	1962	LONG DAY'S JOURNEY INTO NIGHT
	1967	GUESS WHO'S COMING TO DINNER?*
	1968	THE LION IN WINTER*
	1981	ON GOLDEN POND*
CHARLTON HESTON	1959	BEN-HUR*
WILLIAM HICKEY	1985	PRIZZI'S HONOR#
WENDY HILLER	1938	PYGMALION
	1958	SEPARATE TABLES#*
	1966	A MAN FOR ALL SEASONS#
JUDD HIRSCH	1980	ORDINARY PEOPLE#
DUSTIN HOFFMAN	1967	THE GRADUATE
	1969	MIDNIGHT COWBOY
	1974	LENNY
	1979	KRAMER VS. KRAMER*
	1982	TOOTSIE
	1988	RAIN MAN*
WILLIAM HOLDEN	1950	SUNSET BOULEVARD
	1953	STALAG 17*
	1976	NETWORK
JUDY HOLLIDAY	1950	BORN YESTERDAY*
STANLEY HOLLOWAY	1964	MY FAIR LADY#
CELESTE HOLM	1947	GENTLEMAN'S AGREEMENT#*
	1949	COME TO THE STABLE#
	1950	ALL ABOUT EVE#
IAN HOLM	1981	CHARIOTS OF FIRE#
OSCAR HOMOLKA	1948	I REMEMBER MAMA#
MIRIAM HOPKINS	1935	BECKY SHARP
DENNIS HOPPER	1986	HOOSIERS#
BOB HOSKINS	1986	MONA LISA
JOHN HOUSEMAN	1973	THE PAPER CHASE#*
LESLIE HOWARD	1932/3	BERKELEY SQUARE
	1938	PYGMALION
TREVOR HOWARD	1960	SONS AND LOVERS
ROCK HUDSON	1956	GIANT
TOM HULCE	1984	AMADEUS

JOSEPHINE HULL	1950	HARVEY#*
ARTHUR HUNNICUTT	1952	THE BIG SKY#
LINDA HUNT	1983	THE YEAR OF LIVING DANGEROUSLY#*
HOLLY HUNTER	1987	BROADCAST NEWS
KIM HUNTER	1951	A STREETCAR NAMED DESIRE#*
JOHN HURT	1978	MIDNIGHT EXPRESS#
	1980	THE ELEPHANT MAN
WILLIAM HURT	1985	KISS OF THE SPIDER WOMAN*
	1986	CHILDREN OF A LESSER GOD
	1987	BROADCAST NEWS
RUTH HUSSEY	1940	THE PHILADELPHIA STORY#
ANJELICA HUSTON	1985	PRIZZI'S HONOR#*
	1989	ENEMIES: A LOVE STORY#
	1990	THE GRIFTERS
JOHN HUSTON	1963	THE CARDINAL#
WALTER HUSTON	1936	DODSWORTH
	1941	ALL THAT MONEY CAN BUY
	1942	YANKEE DOODLE DANDY#
	1948	TREASURE OF THE SIERRA MADRE#*
TIMOTHY HUTTON	1980	ORDINARY PEOPLE#*
MARTHA HYER	1958	SOME CAME RUNNING#
JOHN IRELAND	1949	ALL THE KING'S MEN#
JEREMY IRONS	1990	REVERSAL OF FORTUNE*
AMY IRVING	1983	YENTL#
BURL IVES	1958	THE BIG COUNTRY#*
GLENDA JACKSON	1970	WOMEN IN LOVE*
	1971	SUNDAY, BLOODY SUNDAY
	1973	A TOUCH OF CLASS*
	1975	HEDDA
RICHARD JAECKEL	1971	SOMETIMES A GREAT NOTION#
SAM JAFFE	1950	THE ASPHALT JUNGLE#
DEAN JAGGER	1949	TWELVE O'CLOCK HIGH#*
EMIL JANNINGS	1927/8	THE LAST COMMAND and THE WAY OF ALL FLESH*
GLYNIS JOHNS	1960	THE SUNDOWNERS#
BEN JOHNSON	1971	THE LAST PICTURE SHOW#*
CELIA JOHNSON	1946	BRIEF ENCOUNTER
CAROLYN JONES	1957	THE BACHELOR PARTY#
JAMES EARL JONES	1970	THE GREAT WHITE HOPE
JENNIFER JONES	1943	THE SONG OF BERNADETTE*
	1944	SINCE YOU WENT AWAY#
	1945	LOVE LETTERS
	1946	DUEL IN THE SUN
	1955	LOVE IS A MANY-SPLENDORED THING
SHIRLEY JONES	1960	ELMER GANTRY#*
KATY JURADO	1954	BROKEN LANCE#
MADELINE KAHN	1973	PAPER MOON#
	1974	BLAZING SADDLES#
IDA KAMINSKA	1966	THE SHOP ON MAIN STREET
CAROL KANE	1975	HESTER STREET
DIANE KEATON	1977	ANNIE HALL*
	1981	REDS
LILA KEDROVA	1964	ZORBA THE GREEK#*
CECIL KELLAWAY	1948	THE LUCK OF THE IRISH#
	1967	GUESS WHO'S COMING TO DINNER?#
SALLY KELLERMAN	1970	M*A*S*H#
GENE KELLY	1945	ANCHORS AWEIGH
GRACE KELLY	1953	MOGAMBO#
	1954	THE COUNTRY GIRL*
NANCY KELLY	1956	THE BAD SEED
ARTHUR KENNEDY	1949	CHAMPION#
	1951	BRIGHT VICTORY
	1955	TRIAL#
	1957	PEYTON PLACE#
	1958	SOME CAME RUNNING#
GEORGE KENNEDY	1967	COOL HAND LUKE#*
DEBORAH KERR	1949	EDWARD MY SON
	1953	FROM HERE TO ETERNITY
	1956	THE KING AND I
	1957	HEAVEN KNOWS, MR. ALLISON
	1958	SEPARATE TABLES

	1960	THE SUNDOWNERS
BEN KINGSLEY	1982	GANDHI*
SALLY KIRKLAND	1987	ANNA
KEVIN KLINE	1988	A FISH CALLED WANDA#*
SHIRLEY KNIGHT	1960	THE DARK AT THE TOP OF THE STAIRS#
	1962	SWEET BIRD OF YOUTH#
ALEXANDER KNOX	1944	WILSON
SUSAN KOHNER	1959	IMITATION OF LIFE#
MILIZA KORJUS	1938	THE GREAT WALTZ#
JACK KRUSCHEN	1960	THE APARTMENT#
DIANE LADD	1974	ALICE DOESN'T LIVE HERE ANYMORE#
	1990	WILD AT HEART#
JOCELYN LAGARDE	1966	HAWAII#
CHRISTINE LAHTI	1984	SWING SHIFT#
BURT LANCASTER	1953	FROM HERE TO ETERNITY
	1960	ELMER GANTRY*
	1962	BIRD MAN OF ALCATRAZ
	1981	ATLANTIC CITY
ELSA LANCHESTER	1949	COME TO THE STABLE#
	1957	WITNESS FOR THE PROSECUTION#
MARTIN LANDAU	1988	TUCKER: THE MAN AND HIS DREAM#
	1989	CRIMES AND MISDEMEANORS#
HOPE LANGE	1957	PEYTON PLACE#
JESSICA LANGE	1982	FRANCES
	1982	TOOTSIE#*
	1984	COUNTRY
	1985	SWEET DREAMS
	1989	MUSIC BOX
ANGELA LANSBURY	1944	GASLIGHT#
	1945	THE PICTURE OF DORIAN GRAY#
	1962	THE MANCHURIAN CANDIDATE#
CHARLES LAUGHTON	1932/3	THE PRIVATE LIFE OF HENRY VIII*
	1935	MUTINY ON THE BOUNTY
	1957	WITNESS FOR THE PROSECUTION
PIPER LAURIE	1961	THE HUSTLER
	1976	CARRIE#
	1986	CHILDREN OF A LESSER GOD#
EVA LE GALLIENNE	1980	RESURRECTION#
CLORIS LEACHMAN	1971	THE LAST PICTURE SHOW#*
PEGGY LEE	1955	PETE KELLY'S BLUES#
ANDREA LEEDS	1937	STAGE DOOR#
JANET LEIGH	1960	PSYCHO#
VIVIEN LEIGH	1939	GONE WITH THE WIND*
	1951	A STREETCAR NAMED DESIRE*
MARGARET LEIGHTON	1971	THE GO-BETWEEN#
JACK LEMMON	1955	MISTER ROBERTS#*
	1959	SOME LIKE IT HOT
	1960	THE APARTMENT
	1962	DAYS OF WINE AND ROSES
	1973	SAVE THE TIGER*
	1979	THE CHINA SYNDROME
	1980	TRIBUTE
	1982	MISSING
LOTTE LENYA	1961	THE ROMAN SPRING OF MRS. STONE#
JOHN LITHGOW	1982	THE WORLD ACCORDING TO GARP#
	1983	TERMS OF ENDEARMENT#
SONDRA LOCKE	1968	THE HEART IS A LONELY HUNTER#
GENE LOCKHART	1938	ALGIERS#
ROBERT LOGGIA	1985	JAGGED EDGE#
CAROLE LOMBARD	1936	MY MAN GODFREY
SOPHIA LOREN	1961	TWO WOMEN*
	1964	MARRIAGE ITALIAN STYLE
JOAN LORRING	1945	THE CORN IS GREEN#
BESSIE LOVE	1928/9	BROADWAY MELODY
PAUL LUKAS	1943	WATCH ON THE RHINE*
ALFRED LUNT	1931/2	THE GUARDSMAN
ALI MACGRAW	1970	LOVE STORY
SHIRLEY MACLAINE	1958	SOME CAME RUNNING
	1960	THE APARTMENT
	1963	IRMA LA DOUCE
	1977	THE TURNING POINT

	1983	TERMS OF ENDEARMENT*
ALINE MACMAHON	1944	DRAGON SEED#
AMY MADIGAN	1985	TWICE IN A LIFETIME#
ANNA MAGNANI	1955	THE ROSE TATTOO*
	1957	WILD IS THE WIND
MARJORIE MAIN	1947	THE EGG AND I#
MAKO	1966	THE SAND PEBBLES#
KARL MALDEN	1951	A STREETCAR NAMED DESIRE#*
	1954	ON THE WATERFRONT#
JOHN MALKOVICH	1984	PLACES IN THE HEART#
DOROTHY MALONE	1956	WRITTEN ON THE WIND#*
JOE MANTELL	1955	MARTY#
FREDRIC MARCH	1930/1	THE ROYAL FAMILY OF BROADWAY
	1931/2	DR. JEKYLL AND MR. HYDE*
	1937	A STAR IS BORN
	1946	THE BEST YEARS OF OUR LIVES*
	1951	DEATH OF A SALESMAN
COLETTE MARCHAND	1952	MOULIN ROUGE#
JOHN MARLEY	1970	LOVE STORY#
LEE MARVIN	1965	CAT BALLOU*
JAMES MASON	1954	A STAR IS BORN
	1966	GEORGY GIRL#
	1982	THE VERDICT#
MARSHA MASON	1973	CINDERELLA LIBERTY
	1977	THE GOODBYE GIRL
	1979	CHAPTER TWO
	1981	ONLY WHEN I LAUGH
DANIEL MASSEY	1968	STAR!#
RAYMOND MASSEY	1940	ABE LINCOLN IN ILLINOIS
MARY-ELIZABETH MASTRANTONIO	1986	THE COLOR OF MONEY#
MARCELLO MASTROIANNI	1962	DIVORCE-ITALIAN STYLE
	1977	A SPECIAL DAY
	1987	DARK EYES
MARLEE MATLIN	1986	CHILDREN OF A LESSER GOD*
WALTER MATTHAU	1966	THE FORTUNE COOKIE#*
	1971	KOTCH
	1975	THE SUNSHINE BOYS
MERCEDES MCCAMBRIDGE	1949	ALL THE KING'S MEN#*
	1956	GIANT#
KEVIN MCCARTHY	1951	DEATH OF A SALESMAN#
PATTY MCCORMACK	1956	THE BAD SEED#
HATTIE MCDANIEL	1939	GONE WITH THE WIND#*
MARY MCDONNELL	1990	DANCES WITH WOLVES#
FRANCES MCDORMAND	1988	MISSISSIPPI BURNING#
ELIZABETH MCGOVERN	1981	RAGTIME#
DOROTHY MCGUIRE	1947	GENTLEMAN'S AGREEMENT
VICTOR MCLAGLEN	1935	THE INFORMER*
	1952	THE QUIET MAN#
MAGGIE MCNAMARA	1953	THE MOON IS BLUE
STEVE MCQUEEN	1966	THE SAND PEBBLES
KAY MEDFORD	1968	FUNNY GIRL#
ADOLPHE MENJOU	1930/1	THE FRONT PAGE
VIVIEN MERCHANT	1966	ALFIE#
MELINA MERCOURI	1960	NEVER ON SUNDAY
BURGESS MEREDITH	1975	THE DAY OF THE LOCUST#
	1976	ROCKY#
UNA MERKEL	1961	SUMMER AND SMOKE#
BETTE MIDLER	1979	THE ROSE
SARAH MILES	1970	RYAN'S DAUGHTER
SYLVIA MILES	1969	MIDNIGHT COWBOY#
	1975	FAREWELL, MY LOVELY#
PENELOPE MILFORD	1978	COMING HOME#
RAY MILLAND	1945	THE LOST WEEKEND*
JASON MILLER	1973	THE EXORCIST#
JOHN MILLS	1970	RYAN'S DAUGHTER#*
SAL MINEO	1955	REBEL WITHOUT A CAUSE#
	1960	EXODUS#
LIZA MINNELLI	1969	THE STERILE CUCKOO
	1972	CABARET*
THOMAS MITCHELL	1937	THE HURRICANE#
	1939	STAGECOACH#*

ROBERT MITCHUM	1945	THE STORY OF G.I. JOE#
ROBERT MONTGOMERY	1937	NIGHT MUST FALL
	1941	HERE COMES MR. JORDAN
RON MOODY	1968	OLIVER!
DUDLEY MOORE	1981	ARTHUR
GRACE MOORE	1934	ONE NIGHT OF LOVE
JUANITA MOORE	1959	IMITATION OF LIFE#
MARY TYLER MOORE	1980	ORDINARY PEOPLE
TERRY MOORE	1952	COME BACK, LITTLE SHEBA#
AGNES MOOREHEAD	1942	THE MAGNIFICENT AMBERSONS#
	1944	MRS. PARKINGTON#
	1948	JOHNNY BELINDA#
	1964	HUSH...HUSH SWEET CHARLOTTE#
RITA MORENO	1961	WEST SIDE STORY#*
FRANK MORGAN	1934	AFFAIRS OF CELLINI
	1942	TORTILLA FLAT#
CATHY MORIARTY	1980	RAGING BULL#
NORIYUKI "PAT" MORITA	1984	THE KARATE KID#
ROBERT MORLEY	1938	MARIE ANTOINETTE#
CHESTER MORRIS	1928/9	ALIBI
PAUL MUNI	1928/9	THE VALIANT
	1932/3	I AM A FUGITIVE FROM A CHAIN GANG
	1936	THE STORY OF LOUIS PASTEUR*
	1937	THE LIFE OF EMILE ZOLA
	1959	THE LAST ANGRY MAN
DON MURRAY	1956	BUS STOP#
J. CARROL NAISH	1943	SAHARA#
	1945	A MEDAL FOR BENNY#
MILDRED NATWICK	1967	BAREFOOT IN THE PARK#
PATRICIA NEAL	1963	HUD*
	1968	THE SUBJECT WAS ROSES
PAUL NEWMAN	1958	CAT ON A HOT TIN ROOF
	1961	THE HUSTLER
	1963	HUD
	1967	COOL HAND LUKE
	1981	ABSENCE OF MALICE
	1982	THE VERDICT
	1986	THE COLOR OF MONEY*
HAING S. NGOR	1984	THE KILLING FIELDS#*
JACK NICHOLSON	1969	EASY RIDER#
	1970	FIVE EASY PIECES
	1973	THE LAST DETAIL
	1974	CHINATOWN
	1975	ONE FLEW OVER THE CUCKOO'S NEST*
	1981	REDS#
	1983	TERMS OF ENDEARMENT#*
	1985	PRIZZI'S HONOR
	1987	IRONWEED
DAVID NIVEN	1958	SEPARATE TABLES*
JACK OAKIE	1940	THE GREAT DICTATOR#
MERLE OBERON	1935	THE DARK ANGEL
EDMOND O'BRIEN	1954	THE BAREFOOT CONTESSA#*
	1964	SEVEN DAYS IN MAY#
ARTHUR O'CONNELL	1955	PICNIC#
	1959	ANATOMY OF A MURDER#
DAN O'HERLIHY	1954	ADVENTURES OF ROBINSON CRUSOE
MICHAEL O'KEEFE	1980	THE GREAT SANTINI#
LENA OLIN	1989	ENEMIES, A LOVE STORY#
EDNA MAY OLIVER	1939	DRUMS ALONG THE MOHAWK#
SIR LAURENCE OLIVIER	1939	WUTHERING HEIGHTS
	1940	REBECCA
	1946	HENRY V
	1948	HAMLET*
	1956	RICHARD III
	1960	THE ENTERTAINER
	1965	OTHELLO
	1972	SLEUTH
	1976	MARATHON MAN#
	1978	THE BOYS FROM BRAZIL
EDWARD JAMES OLMOS	1988	STAND AND DELIVER
NANCY OLSON	1950	SUNSET BOULEVARD#

RYAN O'NEAL	1970	LOVE STORY
TATUM O'NEAL	1973	PAPER MOON#*
BARBARA O'NEIL	1940	ALL THIS, AND HEAVEN TOO#
PETER O'TOOLE	1962	LAWRENCE OF ARABIA
	1964	BECKET
	1968	THE LION IN WINTER
	1969	GOODBYE, MR. CHIPS
	1972	THE RULING CLASS
	1980	THE STUNT MAN
	1982	MY FAVORITE YEAR
MARIA OUSPENSKAYA	1936	DODSWORTH#
	1939	LOVE AFFAIR#
AL PACINO	1972	THE GODFATHER#
	1973	SERPICO
	1974	THE GODFATHER PART II
	1975	DOG DAY AFTERNOON
	1979	...AND JUSTICE FOR ALL
	1990	DICK TRACY#
GERALDINE PAGE	1953	HONDO#
	1961	SUMMER AND SMOKE
	1962	SWEET BIRD OF YOUTH
	1966	YOU'RE A BIG BOY NOW#
	1972	PETE 'N' TILLIE#
	1978	INTERIORS
	1984	THE POPE OF GREENWICH VILLAGE#
	1985	THE TRIP TO BOUNTIFUL*
JACK PALANCE	1952	SUDDEN FEAR#
	1953	SHANE#
ELEANOR PARKER	1950	CAGED
	1951	DETECTIVE STORY
	1955	INTERRUPTED MELODY
LARRY PARKS	1946	THE JOLSON STORY
ESTELLE PARSONS	1967	BONNIE AND CLYDE#*
	1968	RACHEL, RACHEL#
MARISA PAVAN	1955	THE ROSE TATTOO#
KATINA PAXINOU	1943	FOR WHOM THE BELL TOLLS#*
GREGORY PECK	1945	THE KEYS OF THE KINGDOM
	1946	THE YEARLING
	1947	GENTLEMAN'S AGREEMENT
	1949	TWELVE O'CLOCK HIGH
	1962	TO KILL A MOCKINGBIRD*
ANTHONY PERKINS	1956	FRIENDLY PERSUASION#
VALERIE PERRINE	1974	LENNY
JOE PESCI	1980	RAGING BULL#
	1990	GOODFELLAS#*
SUSAN PETERS	1942	RANDOM HARVEST#
MICHELLE PFEIFFER	1988	DANGEROUS LIAISONS#
	1989	THE FABULOUS BAKER BOYS
RIVER PHOENIX	1988	RUNNING ON EMPTY#
MARY PICKFORD	1928/9	COQUETTE*
WALTER PIDGEON	1942	MRS. MINIVER
	1943	MADAME CURIE
SIDNEY POITIER	1958	THE DEFIANT ONES
	1963	LILIES OF THE FIELD*
MICHAEL J. POLLARD	1967	BONNIE AND CLYDE#
WILLIAM POWELL	1934	THE THIN MAN
	1936	MY MAN GODFREY
	1947	LIFE WITH FATHER
ROBERT PRESTON	1982	VICTOR/VICTORIA#
RANDY QUAID	1973	THE LAST DETAIL#
ANTHONY QUAYLE	1969	ANNE OF THE THOUSAND DAYS#
ANTHONY QUINN	1952	VIVA ZAPATA!#*
	1956	LUST FOR LIFE#*
	1957	WILD IS THE WIND
	1964	ZORBA THE GREEK
LUISE RAINER	1936	THE GREAT ZIEGFELD*
	1937	THE GOOD EARTH*
CLAUDE RAINS	1939	MR. SMITH GOES TO WASHINGTON#
	1943	CASABLANCA#
	1944	MR. SKEFFINGTON#
	1946	NOTORIOUS#

MARJORIE RAMBEAU	1940	PRIMROSE PATH#
	1953	TORCH SONG#
ANNE RAMSEY	1987	THROW MAMA FROM THE TRAIN#
BASIL RATHBONE	1936	ROMEO AND JULIET#
	1938	IF I WERE KING#
ROBERT REDFORD	1973	THE STING
LYNN REDGRAVE	1966	GEORGY GIRL
MICHAEL REDGRAVE	1947	MOURNING BECOMES ELECTRA
VANESSA REDGRAVE	1966	MORGAN!
	1968	ISADORA
	1971	MARY, QUEEN OF SCOTS
	1977	JULIA#*
	1984	THE BOSTONIANS
JOYCE REDMAN	1963	TOM JONES#
	1965	OTHELLO#
DONNA REED	1953	FROM HERE TO ETERNITY#*
LEE REMICK	1962	DAYS OF WINE AND ROSES
ANNE REVERE	1943	THE SONG OF BERNADETTE#
	1945	NATIONAL VELVET#*
	1947	GENTLEMAN'S AGREEMENT#
DEBBIE REYNOLDS	1964	THE UNSINKABLE MOLLY BROWN
BEAH RICHARDS	1967	GUESS WHO'S COMING TO DINNER?#
RALPH RICHARDSON	1949	THE HEIRESS#
	1984	GREYSTOKE: THE LEGEND OF TARZAN, LORD OF THE APES#
THELMA RITTER	1950	ALL ABOUT EVE#
	1951	THE MATING SEASON#
	1952	WITH A SONG IN MY HEART#
	1953	PICKUP ON SOUTH STREET#
	1959	PILLOW TALK#
	1962	BIRD MAN OF ALCATRAZ#
JASON ROBARDS	1976	ALL THE PRESIDENT'S MEN#*
	1977	JULIA#*
	1980	MELVIN AND HOWARD#
ERIC ROBERTS	1985	RUNAWAY TRAIN#
JULIA ROBERTS	1989	STEEL MAGNOLIAS#
	1990	PRETTY WOMAN
RACHEL ROBERTS	1963	THIS SPORTING LIFE
CLIFF ROBERTSON	1968	CHARLY*
FLORA ROBSON	1946	SARATOGA TRUNK#
MAY ROBSON	1932/3	LADY FOR A DAY
GINGER ROGERS	1940	KITTY FOYLE*
HOWARD E. ROLLINS, JR.	1981	RAGTIME#
MICKEY ROONEY	1939	BABES IN ARMS
	1943	THE HUMAN COMEDY
	1956	THE BOLD AND THE BRAVE#
	1979	THE BLACK STALLION#
DIANA ROSS	1972	LADY SINGS THE BLUES
KATHARINE ROSS	1967	THE GRADUATE#
GENA ROWLANDS	1974	A WOMAN UNDER THE INFLUENCE
	1980	GLORIA
HAROLD RUSSELL	1946	THE BEST YEARS OF OUR LIVES#*
ROSALIND RUSSELL	1942	MY SISTER EILEEN
	1946	SISTER KENNY
	1947	MOURNING BECOMES ELECTRA
	1958	AUNTIE MAME
MARGARET RUTHERFORD	1963	THE V.I.P.'S#*
ROBERT RYAN	1947	CROSSFIRE#
EVA MARIE SAINT	1954	ON THE WATERFRONT#*
GEORGE SANDERS	1950	ALL ABOUT EVE#*
CHRIS SARANDON	1975	DOG DAY AFTERNOON#
SUSAN SARANDON	1981	ATLANTIC CITY
TELLY SAVALAS	1962	BIRD MAN OF ALCATRAZ#
DIANA SCARWID	1980	INSIDE MOVES#
ROY SCHEIDER	1971	THE FRENCH CONNECTION#
	1979	ALL THAT JAZZ
MAXIMILIAN SCHELL	1961	JUDGMENT AT NUREMBERG*
	1975	THE MAN IN THE GLASS BOOTH
	1977	JULIA#
JOSEPH SCHILDKRAUT	1937	THE LIFE OF EMILE ZOLA#*
PAUL SCOFIELD	1966	A MAN FOR ALL SEASONS*

GEORGE C. SCOTT	1959	ANATOMY OF A MURDER#
	1961	THE HUSTLER#
	1970	PATTON*
	1971	THE HOSPITAL
MARTHA SCOTT	1940	OUR TOWN
GEORGE SEGAL	1966	WHO'S AFRAID OF VIRGINIA WOOLF?#
PETER SELLERS	1964	DR. STRANGELOVE
	1979	BEING THERE
OMAR SHARIF	1962	LAWRENCE OF ARABIA#
ROBERT SHAW	1966	A MAN FOR ALL SEASONS#
NORMA SHEARER	1929/30	THE DIVORCÉE*
	1929/30	THEIR OWN DESIRE
	1930/1	A FREE SOUL
	1934	THE BARRETTS OF WIMPOLE STREET
	1936	ROMEO AND JULIET
	1938	MARIE ANTOINETTE
SAM SHEPARD	1983	THE RIGHT STUFF#
TALIA SHIRE	1974	THE GODFATHER PART II#
	1976	ROCKY
ANNE SHIRLEY	1937	STELLA DALLAS#
SYLVIA SIDNEY	1973	SUMMER WISHES, WINTER DREAMS#
SIMONE SIGNORET	1959	ROOM AT THE TOP*
	1965	SHIP OF FOOLS
JEAN SIMMONS	1948	HAMLET#
	1969	THE HAPPY ENDING
FRANK SINATRA	1953	FROM HERE TO ETERNITY#*
	1955	THE MAN WITH THE GOLDEN ARM
LILIA SKALA	1963	LILIES OF THE FIELD#
MAGGIE SMITH	1965	OTHELLO#
	1969	THE PRIME OF MISS JEAN BRODIE*
	1972	TRAVELS WITH MY AUNT
	1978	CALIFORNIA SUITE#*
	1986	ROOM WITH A VIEW#
CARRIE SNODGRESS	1970	DIARY OF A MAD HOUSEWIFE
GALE SONDERGAARD	1936	ANTHONY ADVERSE#*
	1946	ANNA AND THE KING OF SIAM#
ANN SOTHERN	1987	THE WHALES OF AUGUST#
SISSY SPACEK	1976	CARRIE
	1980	COAL MINER'S DAUGHTER*
	1982	MISSING
	1984	THE RIVER
	1986	CRIMES OF THE HEART
ROBERT STACK	1956	WRITTEN ON THE WIND#
SYLVESTER STALLONE	1976	ROCKY
TERENCE STAMP	1962	BILLY BUDD#
KIM STANLEY	1964	SEANCE ON A WET AFTERNOON
	1982	FRANCES#
BARBARA STANWYCK	1937	STELLA DALLAS
	1941	BALL OF FIRE
	1944	DOUBLE INDEMNITY
	1948	SORRY, WRONG NUMBER
MAUREEN STAPLETON	1958	LONELYHEARTS#
	1970	AIRPORT#
	1978	INTERIORS#
	1981	REDS#*
MARY STEENBURGEN	1980	MELVIN AND HOWARD#*
ROD STEIGER	1954	ON THE WATERFRONT#
	1965	THE PAWNBROKER
	1967	IN THE HEAT OF THE NIGHT*
JAMES STEPHENSON	1940	THE LETTER#
JAN STERLING	1954	THE HIGH AND THE MIGHTY#
JAMES STEWART	1939	MR. SMITH GOES TO WASHINGTON
	1940	THE PHILADEPHIA STORY*
	1946	IT'S A WONDERFUL LIFE
	1950	HARVEY
	1959	ANATOMY OF A MURDER
DEAN STOCKWELL	1988	MARRIED TO THE MOB#
LEWIS STONE	1928/9	THE PATRIOT
BEATRICE STRAIGHT	1976	NETWORK#*
LEE STRASBERG	1974	THE GODFATHER PART II#
ROBERT STRAUSS	1953	STALAG 17#

MERYL STREEP	1978	THE DEER HUNTER#
	1979	KRAMER VS. KRAMER#*
	1981	THE FRENCH LIEUTENANT'S WOMAN
	1982	SOPHIE'S CHOICE*
	1983	SILKWOOD
	1985	OUT OF AFRICA
	1987	IRONWEED
	1988	A CRY IN THE DARK
	1990	POSTCARDS FROM THE EDGE
BARBRA STREISAND	1968	FUNNY GIRL*
	1973	THE WAY WE WERE
MARGARET SULLAVAN	1938	THREE COMRADES
JANET SUZMAN	1971	NICHOLAS AND ALEXANDRA
GLORIA SWANSON	1927/8	SADIE THOMPSON
	1929/30	THE TRESPASSER
	1950	SUNSET BOULEVARD
RUSS TAMBLYN	1957	PEYTON PLACE#
AKIM TAMIROFF	1936	THE GENERAL DIED AT DAWN#
	1943	FOR WHOM THE BELL TOLLS#
JESSICA TANDY	1989	DRIVING MISS DAISY*
ELIZABETH TAYLOR	1957	RAINTREE COUNTY
	1958	CAT ON A HOT TIN ROOF
	1959	SUDDENLY, LAST SUMMER
	1960	BUTTERFIELD 8*
	1966	WHO'S AFRAID OF VIRGINIA WOOLF?*
LAWRENCE TIBBETT	1929/30	THE ROGUE SONG
GENE TIERNEY	1945	LEAVE HER TO HEAVEN
MEG TILLY	1985	AGNES OF GOD#
RICHARD TODD	1949	THE HASTY HEART
LILY TOMLIN	1975	NASHVILLE#
FRANCHOT TONE	1935	MUTINY ON THE BOUNTY
TOPOL	1971	FIDDLER ON THE ROOF
RIP TORN	1983	CROSS CREEK#
LEE TRACY	1964	THE BEST MAN#
SPENCER TRACY	1936	SAN FRANCISCO
	1937	CAPTAINS COURAGEOUS*
	1938	BOYS TOWN*
	1950	FATHER OF THE BRIDE
	1955	BAD DAY AT BLACK ROCK
	1958	THE OLD MAN AND THE SEA
	1960	INHERIT THE WIND
	1961	JUDGMENT AT NUREMBERG
	1967	GUESS WHO'S COMING TO DINNER?
HENRY TRAVERS	1942	MRS. MINIVER#
JOHN TRAVOLTA	1977	SATURDAY NIGHT FEVER
CLAIRE TREVOR	1927	DEAD END#
	1948	KEY LARGO#*
	1954	THE HIGH AND THE MIGHTY#
TOM TULLY	1954	THE CAINE MUTINY#
KATHLEEN TURNER	1986	PEGGY SUE GOT MARRIED
LANA TURNER	1957	PEYTON PLACE
SUSAN TYRRELL	1972	FAT CITY#
CICELY TYSON	1972	SOUNDER
LIV ULLMANN	1972	THE EMIGRANTS
	1976	FACE TO FACE
MIYOSHI UMEKI	1957	SAYONARA#*
MARY URE	1960	SONS AND LOVERS#
PETER USTINOV	1951	QUO VADIS#
	1960	SPARTACUS#*
	1964	TOPKAPI#*
BRENDA VACCARO	1975	ONCE IS NOT ENOUGH#
JO VAN FLEET	1955	EAST OF EDEN#*
DIANE VARSI	1957	PEYTON PLACE#
ROBERT VAUGHAN	1959	THE YOUNG PHILADELPHIANS#
JON VOIGHT	1969	MIDNIGHT COWBOY
	1978	COMING HOME*
	1985	RUNAWAY TRAIN
ERIC VON STROHEIM	1950	SUNSET BOULEVARD#
MAX VON SYDOW	1988	PELLE THE CONQUERER
CHRISTOPHER WALKEN	1978	THE DEER HUNTER#*
JULIE WALTERS	1983	EDUCATING RITA

JACK WARDEN	1975	SHAMPOO#
	1978	HEAVEN CAN WAIT#
H.B. WARNER	1937	LOST HORIZON#
LESLIE ANNE WARREN	1982	VICTOR/VICTORIA#
DENZEL WASHINGTON	1987	CRY FREEDOM#
	1989	GLORY#*
ETHEL WATERS	1949	PINKY#
SAM WATERSTON	1984	THE KILLING FIELDS
LUCILLE WATSON	1943	WATCH ON THE RHINE#
JOHN WAYNE	1949	THE SANDS OF IOWA JIMA
	1969	TRUE GRIT*
SIGOURNEY WEAVER	1986	ALIENS
	1988	GORILLAS IN THE MIST
	1988	WORKING GIRL#
CLIFTON WEBB	1944	LAURA#
	1946	THE RAZOR'S EDGE#
	1948	SITTING PRETTY
TUESDAY WELD	1977	LOOKING FOR MR. GOODBAR#
ORSON WELLES	1941	CITIZEN KANE
OSKAR WERNER	1965	SHIP OF FOOLS
STUART WHITMAN	1961	THE MARK
JAMES WHITMORE	1949	BATTLEGROUND#
	1975	GIVE 'EM HELL, HARRY
DAME MAY WHITTY	1937	NIGHT MUST FALL#
RICHARD WIDMARK	1947	KISS OF DEATH#
DIANNE WIEST	1986	HANNAH AND HER SISTERS#*
	1989	PARENTHOOD#
JACK WILD	1968	OLIVER!#
CORNEL WILDE	1945	A SONG TO REMEMBER
GENE WILDER	1968	THE PRODUCERS#
CARA WILLIAMS	1958	THE DEFIANT ONES#
ROBIN WILLIAMS	1987	GOOD MORNING, VIETNAM
	1989	DEAD POETS SOCIETY
CHILL WILLS	1960	THE ALAMO#
PAUL WINFIELD	1972	SOUNDER
OPRAH WINFREY	1985	THE COLOR PURPLE#
DEBRA WINGER	1982	AN OFFICER AND A GENTLEMAN
	1983	TERMS OF ENDEARMENT
SHELLEY WINTERS	1951	A PLACE IN THE SUN
	1959	THE DIARY OF ANNE FRANK#*
	1965	A PATCH OF BLUE#*
	1972	THE POSEIDON ADVENTURE#
NATALIE WOOD	1955	REBEL WITHOUT A CAUSE#
	1961	SPLENDOR IN THE GRASS
	1963	LOVE WITH THE PROPER STRANGER
PEGGY WOOD	1965	THE SOUND OF MUSIC#
ALFRE WOODARD	1983	CROSS CREEK#
JAMES WOODS	1986	SALVADOR
JOANNE WOODWARD	1957	THE THREE FACES OF EVE*
	1968	RACHEL, RACHEL
	1973	SUMMER WISHES, WINTER DREAMS
	1990	MR. AND MRS. BRIDGE
MONTY WOOLEY	1942	THE PIED PIPER
	1944	SINCE YOU WENT AWAY#
TERESA WRIGHT	1941	THE LITTLE FOXES#
	1942	THE PRIDE OF THE YANKEES
	1942	MRS. MINIVER#*
MARGARET WYCHERLY	1941	SERGEANT YORK#
JANE WYMAN	1946	THE YEARLING
	1948	JOHNNY BELINDA*
	1951	THE BLUE VEIL
	1954	MAGNIFICENT OBSESSION
ED WYNN	1959	THE DIARY OF ANNE FRANK#
DIANA WYNYARD	1932/3	CAVALCADE
SUSANNAH YORK	1969	THEY SHOOT HORSES, DON'T THEY?#
BURT YOUNG	1976	ROCKY#
GIG YOUNG	1969	THEY SHOOT HORSES, DON'T THEY?#*
LORETTA YOUNG	1947	THE FARMER'S DAUGHTER*
	1949	COME TO THE STABLE
ROLAND YOUNG	1937	TOPPER#

NOTES: The first awards were given in 1927/8; supporting awards were added in 1936. Winners are indicated by an *; supporting nominations are indicated by a #. There were ties for Best Actor in 1931/2 and for Best Actress in 1968. Beginning in 1927/8, performers could be nominated and win for more than one film; beginning in 1929/30, performers could be nominated for more than one film, but only win for one; beginning with 1930/1, performers could only be nominated for one film per category. Children were awarded special Oscars until 1960, after which time they became eligible for regular competition. One anomoly: Barry Fitzgerald was nominated in both categories for the same role in 1944.

SPECIAL OSCARS FOR JUVENILE PERFORMANCE

BOBBY DRISCOLL 1949
The outstanding juvenile actor of 1949.
DEANNA DURBIN 1938
For her significant contribution in bringing to the screen the spirit and personification of youth, and as a juvenile player setting a high standard of ability and achievement.
JUDY GARLAND 1939
For her outstanding performance as a screen juvenile during the past year.
PEGGY ANN GARNER 1945
Outstanding child actress of 1945.
IVAN JANDL 1948
For the outstanding juvenile performance of 1948 in *The Search.*
CLAUDE JARMAN, JR. 1946
Outstanding child actor of 1946.
HAYLEY MILLS 1960
For *Pollyana*, the most outstanding juvenile performance during 1960.
MARGARET O'BRIEN 1944
Outstanding chld actress of 1944.
MICKEY ROONEY 1938
For his significant contribution in bringing to the screen the spirit and personification of youth, and as a juvenile player setting a high standard of ability and achievement.
SHIRLEY TEMPLE 1934
In grateful recognition of her outstanding contribution to screen entertainment during the year 1934.
JON WHITELEY 1954
For his outstanding juvenile performance in *The Little Kidnappers.*
VINCENT WINTER 1954
For his outstanding juvenile performance in *The Little Kidnappers.*

SPECIAL OSCARS FOR SPECIAL CONTRIBUTIONS

G.M. "BRONCHO BILLY" ANDERSON 1957
For his contributions to the development of motion pictures as entertainment.
FRED ASTAIRE 1949
For his unique artistry and his contributions to the technique of musical pictures.
JAMES BASKETTE 1947
For his able and heart-warming characterization of Uncle Remus, friend and storyteller to the children of the world.
RALPH BELLAMY 1987
For his unique artistry and his distinguished service to the profession of acting.
EDDIE CANTOR 1956
For distinguished service to the film industry.
CHARLES CHAPLIN 1927/8
For versatility and genius in writing, acting, directing and producing *The Circus*.
1971
For the incalculable effect he has had in making motion pictures the art form of this century.
MAURICE CHEVALIER 1958
For his contributions to the world of entertainment for more than half a century.
GARY COOPER 1960
For his many memorable screen performances and the international recognition he, as an individual, has gained for the motion picture industry.
DOUGLAS FAIRBANKS 1939
Recognizing the unique and outstanding contribution of Douglas Fairbanks, first president of the Academy, to the international development of the motion picture.
HENRY FONDA 1980
The consummate actor, in recognition of his brilliant accomplishments and enduring contribution to the art of motion pictures.
GRETA GARBO 1954
For her unforgettable screen performances.
LILLIAN GISH 1970
For superlative artistry and for distinguished contribution to the progress of motion pictures.
CARY GRANT 1969
For his unique mastery of the art of screen acting with the respect and affection of his colleagues.
ALEC GUINNESS 1979
For advancing the art of screen acting through a host of memorable and distinguished performances.
BOB HOPE 1952
For his contribution to the laughter of the world, his service to the motion picture industry, and his devotion to the American premise.*
DANNY KAYE 1954
For his unique talents, his service to the Academy, the motion picture industry, and the American people.
BUSTER KEATON 1959
For his unique talents which brought immortal comedies to the screen.
GENE KELLY 1951
In appreciation of his versatility as an actor, singer, director and dancer, and specifically for his brilliant achievements in the art of choreography on film.
STAN LAUREL 1960
For his creative pioneering in the field of cinema comedy.
HAROLD LLOYD 1952
Master comedian and good citizen.
GROUCHO MARX 1973
In recognition of his brilliant creativity and for the unequalled achievements of the Marx Brothers in the art of motion picture comedy.
PAUL NEWMAN 1986
In recognition of his many memorable and compelling screen performances and for his personal integrity and dedication to his craft.
LAURENCE OLIVIER 1946
For his outstanding achievement as actor, producer and director in bringing *Henry V* to the screen.
1978
For the full body of his work, for the unique achievements of his entire career and his lifetime of contribution to the art of film.
MARY PICKFORD 1975
In recognition of her unique contributions to the film industry and the development of film as an artistic medium.
EDWARD G. ROBINSON 1972
Who achieved greatness as a player, a patron of the arts and a dedicated citizen...in sum, a Renaissance man. From his friends in the industry he loves.
MICKEY ROONEY 1982
For fifty years of versatility in a variety of memorable film performances.

HAROLD RUSSELL 1946

For bringing hope and courage to his fellow veterans through his appearance in *The Best Years of Our Lives.*

BARBARA STANWYCK 1981

For superlative creativity and unique contribution to the art of screen acting.

JAMES STEWART 1984

For fifty years of meaningful performances, for his high ideals, both on and off the screen, with the respect and affection of his colleagues.

ORSON WELLES 1970

For superlative artistry and versatility in the creation of motion pictures.

NOTE: Bob Hope was awarded three additional honorary citations for his devotion to the film industry (1940, 1944, and 1965).

THE AWARDS OF THE BRITISH FILM ACADEMY

JENNY AGUTTER	1977	EQUUS#
ANOUK AIMÉE	1967	A MAN AND A WOMAN*
ROSANNA ARQUETTE	1985	DESPERATELY SEEKING SUSAN#
DAME PEGGY ASHCROFT	1985	A PASSAGE TO INDIA
FRED ASTAIRE	1975	THE TOWERING INFERNO#
RICHARD ATTENBOROUGH	1964	THE GUNS AT BATASI and SEANCE ON A WET AFTERNOON
STEPHANE AUDRAN	1973	THE DISCREET CHARM OF THE BOURGEOISIE and JUSTE AVANT LA NUITE
DANIEL AUTEUIL	1987	JEAN DE FLORETTE#
ANNE BANCROFT	1962	THE MIRACLE WORKER*
	1964	THE PUMPKIN EATER*
	1987	84 CHARING CROSS
INGRID BERGMAN	1974	MURDER ON THE ORIENT EXPRESS#
BETSY BLAIR	1955	MARTY*
DIRK BOGARDE	1963	THE SERVANT
	1965	DARLING
CORNELL BORCHERS	1954	THE DIVIDED HEART*
ERNEST BORGNINE	1955	MARTY*
MARLON BRANDO	1952	VIVA ZAPATA!*
	1953	JULIUS CAESAR*
	1954	ON THE WATERFRONT*
BORA BRYAN	1961	A TASTE OF HONEY
ELLEN BURSTYN	1975	ALICE DOESN'T LIVE HERE ANYMORE
RICHARD BURTON	1966	WHO'S AFRAID OF VIRGINIA WOOLF? and THE SPY WHO CAME IN FROM THE COLD
MICHAEL CAINE	1983	EDUCATING RITA
LESLIE CARON	1953	LILI*
	1962	THE L-SHAPED ROOM
SALVATORE CASCIO	1990	CINEMA PARADISO#
JULIE CHRISTIE	1965	DARLING
JOHN CLEESE	1988	A FISH CALLED WANDA
PAULINE COLLINS	1989	SHIRLEY VALENTINE
SEAN CONNERY	1987	THE NAME OF THE ROSE
VALENTINA CORTESE	1973	DAY FOR NIGHT#
JAMIE LEE CURTIS	1983	TRADING PLACES#
JUDY DAVIS	1980	MY BRILLIANT CAREER
DANIEL DAY-LEWIS	1989	MY LEFT FOOT
JUDI DENCH	1986	ROOM WITH A VIEW#
	1988	A HANDFUL OF DUST#
BRAD DOURIF	1976	ONE FLEW OVER THE CUCKOO'S NEST#
RICHARD DREYFUSS	1978	THE GOODBYE GIRL
ROBERT DUVALL	1979	APOCALYPSE NOW#
DENHOLM ELLIOTT	1983	TRADING PLACES#
	1984	A PRIVATE FUNCTION#
	1985	DEFENSE OF THE REALM#
DAME EDITH EVANS	1967	THE WHISPERERS
PETER FINCH	1956	A TOWN LIKE ALICE
	1960	THE TRIALS OF OSCAR WILDE
	1961	NO LOVE FOR JOHNNY
	1971	SUNDAY, BLOODY SUNDAY
	1976	NETWORK
LOUISE FLETCHER	1976	ONE FLEW OVER THE CUCKOO'S NEST
HENRY FONDA	1957	TWELVE ANGRY MEN*
JANE FONDA	1978	JULIA
	1979	THE CHINA SYNDROME
JODIE FOSTER	1976	TAXI DRIVER and BUGSY MALONE#
EDWARD FOX	1971	THE GO-BETWEEN#
	1977	A BRIDGE TOO FAR#
JOHN GIELGUD	1953	JULIUS CAESAR
	1974	MURDER ON THE ORIENT EXPRESS#
WHOOPI GOLDBERG	1990	GHOST#
ALEC GUINNESS	1957	THE BRIDGE ON THE RIVER KWAI
GENE HACKMAN	1972	THE FRENCH CONNECTION and THE POSEIDON ADVENTURE

ROHINI HATTANGADY	1982	GANDHI#
AUDREY HEPBURN	1953	ROMAN HOLIDAY
	1959	THE NUN'S STORY
	1964	CHARADE
KATHARINE HEPBURN	1968	GUESS WHO'S COMING TO DINNER? and THE LION IN WINTER
	1982	ON GOLDEN POND
DUSTIN HOFFMAN	1969	MIDNIGHT COWBOY and JOHN AND MARY
	1983	TOOTSIE
IAN HOLM	1968	THE BOFORS GUNS#
	1981	CHARIOTS OF FIRE#
BOB HOSKINS	1986	MONA LISA
TREVOR HOWARD	1958	THE KEY
JOHN HURT	1978	MIDNIGHT EXPRESS#
	1980	THE ELEPHANT MAN
WILLIAM HURT	1985	KISS OF THE SPIDER WOMAN
GLENDA JACKSON	1971	SUNDAY, BLOODY SUNDAY
BEN JOHNSON	1972	THE LAST PICTURE SHOW#
CELIA JOHNSON	1969	THE PRIME OF MISS JEAN BRODIE#
KATE JOHNSON	1955	THE LADYKILLERS
DIANE KEATON	1977	ANNIE HALL
BEN KINGSLEY	1982	GANDHI
DIANE LADD	1975	ALICE DOESN'T LIVE HERE ANYMORE#
BURT LANCASTER	1962	BIRD MAN OF ALCATRAZ*
	1981	ATLANTIC CITY
CLORIS LEACHMAN	1972	THE LAST PICTURE SHOW#
VIVIEN LEIGH	1952	A STREETCAR NAMED DESIRE
MARGARET LEIGHTON	1971	THE GO-BETWEEN#
JACK LEMMON	1959	SOME LIKE IT HOT*
	1960	THE APARTMENT*
	1979	THE CHINA SYNDROME
SOPHIA LOREN	1961	TWO WOMEN*
ARTHUR LOWE	1973	O LUCKY MAN!#
SHIRLEY MACLAINE	1959	ASK ANY GIRL*
	1960	THE APARTMENT*
ANNA MAGNANI	1956	THE ROSE TATTOO*
LEE MARVIN	1965	CAT BALLOU and THE KILLERS*
MARCELLO MASTROIANNI	1963	DIVORCE, ITALIAN STYLE*
	1964	YESTERDAY, TODAY AND TOMORROW*
WALTER MATTHAU	1973	PETE 'N' TILLIE and CHARLEY VARRICK
RAY MCANALLY	1986	THE MISSION#
	1989	MY LEFT FOOT#
VIRGINIA MCKENNA	1956	A TOWN LIKE ALICE
LIZA MINNELLI	1972	CABARET
YVONNE MITCHELL	1954	THE DIVIDED HEART
KENNETH MORE	1954	A DOCTOR IN THE HOUSE
JEANNE MOREAU	1966	VIVA MARIA*
PATRICIA NEAL	1963	HUD*
	1965	IN HARM'S WAY*
PAUL NEWMAN	1961	THE HUSTLER*
HAING S. NGOR	1984	THE KILLING FIELDS
JACK NICHOLSON	1974	CHINATOWN and THE LAST DETAIL
	1976	ONE FLEW OVER THE CUCKOO'S NEST
	1982	REDS#
PHILIPPE NOIRET	1990	CINEMA PARADISO
LAURENCE OLIVIER	1955	RICHARD III
	1969	OH! WHAT A LOVELY WAR#
PETER O'TOOLE	1962	LAWRENCE OF ARABIA
AL PACINO	1975	DOG DAY AFTERNOON and THE GODFATHER PART II
GERALDINE PAGE	1978	INTERIORS
MICHAEL PALIN	1988	A FISH CALLED WANDA#
FRANÇOIS PERIER	1956	GERVAISE*
MICHELLE PFEIFFER	1989	DANGEROUS LIAISONS#
SIDNEY POITIER	1958	THE DEFIANT ONES*
ROBERT REDFORD	1970	TELL THEM WILLIE BOY IS HERE and BUTCH CASSIDY AND THE SUNDANCE KID
RALPH RICHARDSON	1952	THE SOUND BARRIER
RACHEL ROBERTS	1960	SATURDAY NIGHT AND SUNDAY MORNING
	1963	THIS SPORTING LIFE
	1979	YANKS#

KATHARINE ROSS	1970	TELL THEM WILLIE BOY IS HERE and BUTCH CASSIDY AND THE SUNDANCE KID
PAUL SCOFIELD	1967	A MAN FOR ALL SEASONS
HEATHER SEARS	1957	THE STORY OF ESTHER COSTELLO
PETER SELLERS	1959	I'M ALL RIGHT, JACK
SIMONE SIGNORET	1952	CASQUE D'OR*
	1957	THE WITCHES OF SALEM*
	1958	ROOM AT THE TOP*
LIZ SMITH	1984	A PRIVATE FUNCTION#
MAGGIE SMITH	1969	THE PRIME OF MISS JEAN BRODIE
	1984	A PRIVATE FUNCTION
	1986	ROOM WITH A VIEW
	1988	THE LONELY PASSION OF JUDITH HEARNE
MAUREEN STAPLETON	1982	REDS#
ROD STEIGER	1966	THE PAWNBROKER*
	1967	IN THE HEAT OF THE NIGHT*
MERYL STREEP	1981	THE FRENCH LIEUTENANT'S WOMAN
JESSICA TANDY	1990	DRIVING MISS DAISY
ELIZABETH TAYLOR	1966	WHO'S AFRAID OF VIRGINIA WOOLF?
SPENCER TRACY	1968	GUESS WHO'S COMING TO DINNER?
JULIE WALTERS	1983	EDUCATING RITA
COLIN WELLAND	1970	KES#
BILLIE WHITELAW	1968	THE TWISTED NERVE and CHARLIE BUBBLES#
JOANNE WOODWARD	1974	SUMMER WISHES, WINTER DREAMS
SUSAN WOOLDRIDGE	1987	HOPE AND GLORY#
IRENE WORTH	1958	ORDERS TO KILL
SUSANNAH YORK	1970	THEY SHOOT HORSES, DON'T THEY?#

NOTES: The first awards were given in 1947. The first performing awards were not given until 1952, when two awards were instituted within each category (i.e., Best British Actor and Best Foreign Actor), a practice which was dropped in 1968 (winners in the "foreign" category are indicated with an *; supporting awards were added in 1968; winners in this category are indicated with a #). There were no supporting awards in 1980; in 1981, only one supporting award — Best Supporting Artist — was given. All those listed won awards. There were ties for Best Actor in 1983 and for Best Supporting Actress in 1982 and 1983.

THE AWARDS OF THE FOREIGN PRESS ASSOCIATION (GOLDEN GLOBES)

F. MURRAY ABRAHAM	1984	AMADEUS (D)
ANOUK AIMÉE	1966	A MAN AND A WOMAN (D)
JUNE ALLYSON	1951	TOO YOUNG TO KISS (M/C)
JULIE ANDREWS	1964	MARY POPPINS (M/C)
	1965	THE SOUND OF MUSIC (M/C)
	1982	VICTOR/VICTORIA (M/C)
ANN-MARGRET	1971	CARNAL KNOWLEDGE#
	1975	TOMMY (M/C)
ALAN ARKIN	1966	THE RUSSIANS ARE COMING, THE RUSSIANS ARE COMING (M/C)
DAME PEGGY ASHCROFT	1984	A PASSAGE TO INDIA#
FRED ASTAIRE	1950	THREE LITTLE WORDS (M/C)
	1974	THE TOWERING INFERNO#
RICHARD ATTENBOROUGH	1966	THE SAND PEBBLES#
	1967	DR. DOLITTLE#
ANNE BANCROFT	1964	THE PUMPKIN EATER (D)
	1967	THE GRADUATE (M/C)
KATHY BATES	1990	MISERY (D)
ANNE BAXTER	1946	THE RAZOR'S EDGE#
WARREN BEATTY	1978	HEAVEN CAN WAIT (M/C)
RICHARD BENJAMIN	1975	THE SUNSHINE BOYS#
TOM BERENGER	1986	PLATOON#
INGRID BERGMAN	1944	GASLIGHT (D)
	1945	THE BELLS OF ST. MARY'S (D)
	1956	ANASTASIA (D)
KAREN BLACK	1970	FIVE EASY PIECES#
	1974	THE GREAT GATSBY#
LINDA BLAIR	1973	THE EXORCIST#
SHIRLEY BOOTH	1952	COME BACK, LITTLE SHEBA (D)
ERNEST BORGNINE	1955	MARTY (D)
STEPHEN BOYD	1959	BEN-HUR#
KLAUS-MARIA BRANDAUER	1985	OUT OF AFRICA#
MARLON BRANDO	1954	ON THE WATERFRONT (D)
	1972	THE GODFATHER (D)
GENEVIEVE BUJOLD	1969	ANNE OF THE THOUSAND DAYS (D)
ELLEN BURSTYN	1978	SAME TIME, NEXT YEAR (M/C)
RICHARD BURTON	1977	EQUUS (D)
RED BUTTONS	1957	SAYONARA#
MICHAEL CAINE	1983	EDUCATING RITA (M/C)
DYAN CANNON	1978	HEAVEN CAN WAIT#
CANTINFLAS	1956	AROUND THE WORLD IN 80 DAYS (M/C)
ART CARNEY	1974	HARRY AND TONTO (M/C)
LESLIE CARON	1963	THE L-SHAPED ROOM (D)
GEORGE CHAKIRIS	1961	WEST SIDE STORY#
CAROL CHANNING	1967	THOROUGHLY MODERN MILLIE#
CHER	1983	SILKWOOD#
	1987	MOONSTRUCK (D)
RONALD COLMAN	1947	A DOUBLE LIFE (D)
SEAN CONNERY	1987	THE UNTOUCHABLES#
GARY COOPER	1952	HIGH NOON (D)
ELLEN CORBY	1948	I REMEMBER MAMA#
TOM COURTENAY	1983	THE DRESSER (D)
BRODERICK CRAWFORD	1949	ALL THE KING'S MEN (D)
TOM CRUISE	1989	BORN ON THE FOURTH OF JULY (D)
BRUCE DAVISON	1990	LONGTIME COMPANION#
OLIVIA DE HAVILLAND	1949	THE HEIRESS (D)
ROBERT DE NIRO	1980	RAGING BULL (D)
GÉRARD DEPARDIEU	1990	GREEN CARD (M/D)
KIRK DOUGLAS	1956	LUST FOR LIFE (D)
MELVYN DOUGLAS	1979	BEING THERE#
MICHAEL DOUGLAS	1987	WALL STREET (D)
RICHARD DREYFUSS	1977	THE GOODBYE GIRL (M/C)
OLYMPIA DUKAKIS	1987	MOONSTRUCK#
PATTY DUKE	1969	ME, NATALIE (M/C)
FAYE DUNAWAY	1976	NETWORK (D)

ROBERT DUVALL	1983	TENDER MERCIES (D)
SAMANTHA EGGAR	1965	THE COLLECTOR (D)
DAME EDITH EVANS	1967	THE WHISPERERS (D)
TOM EWELL	1955	THE SEVEN YEAR ITCH (M/C)
JOSÉ FERRER	1950	CYRANO DE BERGERAC (D)
SALLY FIELD	1979	NORMA RAE (D)
	1984	PLACES IN THE HEART (D)
PETER FINCH	1976	NETWORK (D)
ALBERT FINNEY	1970	SCROOGE (M/C)
PETER FIRTH	1977	EQUUS#
BARRY FITZGERALD	1944	GOING MY WAY#
LOUISE FLETCHER	1975	ONE FLEW OVER THE CUCKOO'S NEST (D)
HENRY FONDA	1981	ON GOLDEN POND (D)
JANE FONDA	1971	KLUTE (D)
	1977	JULIA (D)
	1978	COMING HOME (D)
GLENN FORD	1961	POCKETFUL OF MIRACLES (M/C)
JODIE FOSTER	1988	THE ACCUSED (D)
ANTHONY FRANCIOSA	1959	CAREER (D)
MORGAN FREEMAN	1989	DRIVING MISS DAISY (M/C)
JUDY GARLAND	1954	A STAR IS BORN (M/C)
GREER GARSON	1960	SUNRISE AT CAMPOBELLO (D)
JOHN GIELGUD	1981	ARTHUR#
HERMIONE GINGOLD	1958	GIGI#
WHOOPI GOLDBERG	1985	THE COLOR PURPLE (D)
	1990	GHOST#
RUTH GORDON	1965	INSIDE DAISY CLOVER#
	1968	ROSEMARY'S BABY#
LOUIS GOSSETT, JR.	1982	AN OFFICER AND A GENTLEMAN#
JOEL GREY	1972	CABARET#
MELANIE GRIFFITH	1988	WORKING GIRL (M/C)
ALEC GUINNESS	1957	BRIDGE ON THE RIVER KWAI (D)
EDMUND GWENN	1947	MIRACLE ON 34TH STREET#
	1950	MISTER 880#
JOAN HACKETT	1981	ONLY WHEN I LAUGH#
GENE HACKMAN	1971	THE FRENCH CONNECTION (D)
TOM HANKS	1988	BIG (M/C)
RICHARD HARRIS	1967	CAMELOT (M/C)
REX HARRISON	1964	MY FAIR LADY (M/C)
GOLDIE HAWN	1969	CACTUS FLOWER#
SUSAN HAYWARD	1952	WITH A SONG IN MY HEART (M/C)
	1958	I WANT TO LIVE! (D)
EILEEN HECKART	1956	THE BAD SEED#
AUDREY HEPBURN	1953	ROMAN HOLIDAY (D)
DUSTIN HOFFMAN	1979	KRAMER VS. KRAMER (D)
	1982	TOOTSIE (M/C)
	1988	RAIN MAN (D)
PAUL HOGAN	1986	CROCODILE DUNDEE (M/C)
JUDY HOLLIDAY	1950	BORN YESTERDAY (M/C)
EARL HOLLIMAN	1956	THE RAINMAKER#
CELESTE HOLM	1947	GENTLEMAN'S AGREEMENT#
BOB HOSKINS	1986	MONA LISA (D)
JOHN HOUSEMAN	1973	THE PAPER CHASE#
JOSEPHINE HULL	1950	HARVEY#
KIM HUNTER	1951	A STREETCAR NAMED DESIRE#
JOHN HURT	1978	MIDNIGHT EXPRESS#
JOHN HUSTON	1963	THE CARDINAL#
WALTER HUSTON	1948	TREASURE OF THE SIERRA MADRE#
TIMOTHY HUTTON	1980	ORDINARY PEOPLE#
JEREMY IRONS	1990	REVERSAL OF FORTUNE (D)
BURL IVES	1958	THE BIG COUNTRY#
GLENDA JACKSON	1973	A TOUCH OF CLASS (M/C)
BEN JOHNSON	1971	THE LAST PICTURE SHOW#
JENNIFER JONES	1943	THE SONG OF BERNADETTE (D)
KATY JURADO	1952	HIGH NOON#
DANNY KAYE	1951	ON THE RIVIERA (M/C)
	1958	ME AND THE COLONEL (M/C)
DIANE KEATON	1977	ANNIE HALL (M/C)
GRACE KELLY	1953	MOGAMBO#
	1954	THE COUNTRY GIRL (D)
KAY KENDALL	1957	LES GIRLS (M/C)

ARTHUR KENNEDY	1955	TRIAL#
DEBORAH KERR	1956	THE KING AND I (M/C)
BEN KINGSLEY	1982	GANDHI (D)
SALLY KIRKLAND	1987	ANNA (D)
ALEXANDER KNOX	1944	WILSON (D)
SUSAN KOHNER	1959	IMITATION OF LIFE#
KRIS KRISTOFFERSON	1976	A STAR IS BORN (M/C)
JOCELYN LA GARDE	1966	HAWAII#
BURT LANCASTER	1960	ELMER GANTRY (D)
ELSA LANCHESTER	1957	WITNESS FOR THE PROSECUTION#
MARTIN LANDAU	1988	TUCKER: THE MAN AND HIS DREAM#
JESSICA LANGE	1982	TOOTSIE#
ANGELA LANSBURY	1945	GASLIGHT#
	1962	THE MANCHURIAN CANDIDATE#
JANET LEIGH	1960	PSYCHO#
JACK LEMMON	1959	SOME LIKE IT HOT (M/C)
	1960	THE APARTMENT (M/C)
	1972	AVANTI (M/C)
PAUL LUKAS	1943	WATCH ON THE RHINE (D)
ALI MACGRAW	1970	LOVE STORY (D)
SHIRLEY MACLAINE	1960	THE APARTMENT (M/C)
	1963	IRMA LA DOUCE (M/C)
	1983	TERMS OF ENDEARMENT (D)
	1988	MADAME SOUZATSKA (D)
ANNA MAGNANI	1955	THE ROSE TATTOO (D)
FREDRIC MARCH	1951	DEATH OF A SALESMAN (D)
LEE MARVIN	1965	CAT BALLOU (M/C)
JAMES MASON	1954	A STAR IS BORN (M/C)
MARSHA MASON	1973	CINDERELLA LIBERTY (D)
	1977	THE GOODBYE GIRL (M/C)
DANIEL MASSEY	1968	STAR!#
MARCELLO MASTROIANNI	1962	DIVORCE ITALIAN STYLE (M/C)
MARLEE MATLIN	1986	CHILDREN OF A LESSER GOD (D)
WALTER MATTHAU	1975	THE SUNSHINE BOYS (M/C)
MERCEDES MCCAMBRIDGE	1949	ALL THE KING'S MEN#
ETHEL MERMAN	1953	CALL ME MADAM (M/C)
BETTE MIDLER	1979	THE ROSE (M/C)
RAY MILLAND	1945	LOST WEEKEND (D)
JOHN MILLS	1970	RYAN'S DAUGHTER#
SAL MINEO	1960	EXODUS#
LIZA MINNELLI	1972	CABARET (M/C)
MILLARD MITCHELL	1952	MY SIX CONVICTS#
MARILYN MONROE	1959	SOME LIKE IT HOT (M/C)
RON MOODY	1968	OLIVER! (M/C)
DUDLEY MOORE	1981	ARTHUR (M/C)
	1984	MICKI AND MAUDE (M/C)
MARY TYLER MOORE	1980	ORDINARY PEOPLE (D)
AGNES MOOREHEAD	1944	MRS. PARKINGTON#
	1964	HUSH, HUSH SWEET CHARLOTTE#
RITA MORENO	1961	WEST SIDE STORY#
J. CARROL NAISH	1945	A MEDAL FOR BENNY#
HAING S. NGOR	1984	THE KILLING FIELDS#
JACK NICHOLSON	1974	CHINATOWN (D)
	1975	ONE FLEW OVER THE CUCKOO'S NEST (D)
	1983	TERMS OF ENDEARMENT#
	1985	PRIZZI'S HONOR (M/C)
DAVID NIVEN	1953	THE MOON IS BLUE (M/C)
	1958	SEPARATE TABLES (D)
EDMOND O'BRIEN	1954	THE BAREFOOT CONTESSA#
	1964	SEVEN DAYS IN MAY#
DONALD O'CONNOR	1952	SINGIN' IN THE RAIN (M/C)
LAURENCE OLIVIER	1948	HAMLET (D)
	1976	MARATHON MAN#
PETER O'TOOLE	1964	BECKET (D)
	1968	THE LION IN WINTER (D)
	1969	GOODBYE, MR. CHIPS (M/C)
AL PACINO	1973	SERPICO (D)
GERALDINE PAGE	1961	SUMMER AND SMOKE (D)
	1962	SWEET BIRD OF YOUTH (D)
MARISA PAVAN	1955	THE ROSE TATTOO#
KATINA PAXINOU	1943	FOR WHOM THE BELL TOLLS#

GREGORY PECK	1946	THE YEARLING (D)
	1962	TO KILL A MOCKINGBIRD (D)
BERNADETTE PETERS	1981	PENNIES FROM HEAVEN (M/C)
MICHELLE PFEIFFER	1989	THE FABULOUS BAKER BOYS (D)
SIDNEY POITIER	1963	LILIES OF THE FIELD (D)
LYNN REDGRAVE	1966	GEORGY GIRL (M/C)
VANESSA REDGRAVE	1977	JULIA#
JULIA ROBERTS	1989	STEEL MAGNOLIAS#
	1990	PRETTY WOMAN (M/C)
KATHARINE ROSS	1976	VOYAGE OF THE DAMNED#
GENA ROWLANDS	1974	A WOMAN UNDER THE INFLUENCE (D)
ROSALIND RUSSELL	1946	SISTER KENNY (D)
	1947	MOURNING BECOMES ELECTRA (D)
	1958	AUNTIE MAME (M/C)
	1961	A MAJORITY OF ONE (M/C)
	1962	GYPSY (M/C)
MARGARET RUTHERFORD	1963	THE V.I.P.'S#
MAXIMILIAN SCHELL	1961	JUDGMENT AT NUREMBERG (D)
PAUL SCOFIELD	1966	A MAN FOR ALL SEASONS (D)
GEORGE C. SCOTT	1970	PATTON (D)
GEORGE SEGAL	1973	A TOUCH OF CLASS (M/C)
PETER SELLERS	1979	BEING THERE (M/C)
OMAR SHARIF	1962	LAWRENCE OF ARABIA#
	1965	DR. ZHIVAGO (D)
RAY SHARKEY	1980	THE IDOLMAKER (M/C)
JEAN SIMMONS	1955	GUYS AND DOLLS (M/C)
FRANK SINATRA	1953	FROM HERE TO ETERNITY#
	1957	PAL JOEY (M/C)
MAGGIE SMITH	1978	CALIFORNIA SUITE
	1986	ROOM WITH A VIEW#
CARRIE SNODGRESS	1970	DIARY OF A MAD HOUSEWIFE (M/C)
ALBERTO SORDI	1963	TO BED OR NOT TO BED (M/C)
SISSY SPACEK	1980	COAL MINER'S DAUGHTER (M/C)
	1986	CRIMES OF THE HEART (M/C)
MAUREEN STAPLETON	1970	AIRPORT#
MARY STEENBURGEN	1980	MELVIN AND HOWARD#
ROD STEIGER	1967	IN THE HEAT OF THE NIGHT (D)
JAN STERLING	1954	THE HIGH AND THE MIGHTY#
MERYL STREEP	1979	KRAMER VS. KRAMER#
	1981	THE FRENCH LIEUTENANT'S WOMAN (D)
	1982	SOPHIE'S CHOICE (D)
BARBRA STREISAND	1968	FUNNY GIRL (M/C)
	1976	A STAR IS BORN (M/C)
GLORIA SWANSON	1950	SUNSET BOULEVARD (D)
AKIM TAMIROFF	1943	FOR WHOM THE BELL TOLLS#
JESSICA TANDY	1989	DRIVING MISS DAISY (M/C)
ELIZABETH TAYLOR	1959	SUDDENLY, LAST SUMMER (D)
MEG TILLY	1985	AGNES OF GOD#
TOPOL	1971	FIDDLER ON THE ROOF (M/C)
SPENCER TRACY	1953	THE ACTRESS (D)
KATHLEEN TURNER	1984	ROMANCING THE STONE (M/C)
	1985	PRIZZI'S HONOR (M/C)
TWIGGY	1971	THE BOY FRIEND (M/C)
LIV ULLMANN	1972	THE EMIGRANTS (D)
PETER USTINOV	1951	QUO VADIS#
BRENDA VACCARO	1975	ONCE IS NOT ENOUGH#
JON VOIGHT	1978	COMING HOME (D)
	1985	RUNAWAY TRAIN (D)
JULIE WALTERS	1983	EDUCATING RITA (M/C)
DENZEL WASHINGTON	1989	GLORY#
JOHN WAYNE	1969	TRUE GRIT (D)
SIGOURNEY WEAVER	1988	GORILLAS IN THE MIST (D)
	1988	WORKING GIRL#
CLIFTON WEBB	1946	THE RAZOR'S EDGE#
RAQUEL WELCH	1974	THE THREE MUSKATEERS (M/C)
OSCAR WERNER	1965	THE SPY WHO CAME IN FROM THE COLD#
JAMES WHITMORE	1949	BATTLEGROUND#
ROBIN WILLIAMS	1987	GOOD MORNING, VIETNAM (M/C)
SHELLEY WINTERS	1972	THE POSEIDON ADVENTURE#
JOANNE WOODWARD	1957	THE THREE FACES OF EVE (D)
	1968	RACHEL, RACHEL (D)

JANE WYMAN	1948	JOHNNY BELINDA (D)
	1951	THE BLUE VEIL (D)
GIG YOUNG	1969	THEY SHOOT HORSES, DON'T THEY?#

NOTES: The first awards were given in 1943. Beginning in 1950, there were two awards in both the Best Actor and Best Actress category: one for best performance in a drama, one for best performance in a comedy or musical. There is no such division in the supporting categories; supporting awards are indicated by a #. All those listed won awards. There were ties for Best Actor in 1983 (drama), for Best Actress in 1977 (musical or comedy), 1978 (musical or comedy) and 1988 (drama — a three way tie), and for Best Supporting Actress in 1970. (D) is used to signify (drama) and (M/C) is used to signify (musical or comedy).

THE AWARDS OF THE LOS ANGELES FILM CRITICS

F. MURRAY ABRAHAM	1984	AMADEUS
DANNY AIELLO	1989	DO THE RIGHT THING#
DAME PEGGY ASHCROFT	1984	A PASSAGE TO INDIA#
FLORINDA BALKAN	1975	A BRIEF VACATION
SANDRINE BONNAIRE	1986	VAGABOND
LORRAINE BRACCO	1990	GOODFELLAS#
GENEVIEVE BUJOLD	1988	DEAD RINGERS and THE MODERNS#
ADOLPH CAESAR	1984	A SOLDIER'S STORY#
GLENN CLOSE	1982	THE WORLD ACCORDING TO GARP#
DANIEL DAY-LEWIS	1989	MY LEFT FOOT
ROBERT DE NIRO	1976	TAXI DRIVER
	1980	RAGING BULL
MELVYN DOUGLAS	1979	BEING THERE and THE SEDUCTION OF JOE TYNAN#
RICHARD DREYFUSS	1977	THE GOODBYE GIRL
OLYMPIA DUKAKIS	1987	MOONSTRUCK#
ROBERT DUVALL	1983	TENDER MERCIES
SHELLEY DUVALL	1977	THREE WOMEN
SALLY FIELD	1979	NORMA RAE
ALBERT FINNEY	1984	UNDER THE VOLCANO
JANE FONDA	1978	COMING HOME, COMES A HORSEMAN and CALIFORNIA SUITE
MORGAN FREEMAN	1987	STREET SMART#
BRENDA FRICKER	1989	MY LEFT FOOT#
JOHN GIELGUD	1981	ARTHUR#
	1985	PLENTY and THE SHOOTING PARTY#
ALEC GUINNESS	1988	LITTLE DORRIT#
TOM HANKS	1988	BIG and PUNCHLINE
DUSTIN HOFFMAN	1979	KRAMER VS. KRAMER
DENNIS HOPPER	1986	BLUE VELVET and HOOSIERS#
BOB HOSKINS	1986	MONA LISA
LINDA HUNT	1983	THE YEAR OF LIVING DANGEROUSLY#
HOLLY HUNTER	1987	BROADCAST NEWS
WILLIAM HURT	1985	KISS OF THE SPIDER WOMAN
ANJELICA HUSTON	1985	PRIZZI'S HONOR#
	1990	THE GRIFTERS
TIMOTHY HUTTON	1980	ORDINARY PEOPLE#
JEREMY IRONS	1990	REVERSAL OF FORTUNE
BEN KINGSLEY	1982	GANDHI
SALLY KIRKLAND	1987	ANNA
CHRISTINE LAHTI	1988	RUNNING ON EMPTY
BURT LANCASTER	1981	ATLANTIC CITY
JOHN LITHGOW	1982	THE WORLD ACCORDING TO GARP#
ANDIE MACDOWELL	1989	SEX, LIES AND VIDEOTAPE
SHIRLEY MACLAINE	1983	TERMS OF ENDEARMENT
STEVE MARTIN	1987	ROXANNE
ROBERT MORLEY	1978	WHO IS KILLING THE GREAT CHEFS OF EUROPE?#
JACK NICHOLSON	1983	TERMS OF ENDEARMENT#
	1987	IRONWEED and THE WITCHES OF EASTWICK
AL PACINO	1975	DOG DAY AFTERNOON
JOE PESCI	1990	GOODFELLAS#
MICHELLE PFEIFFER	1989	THE FABULOUS BAKER BOYS
VANESSA REDGRAVE	1977	JULIA#
JASON ROBARDS	1977	JULIA#
SISSY SPACEK	1980	COAL MINER'S DAUGHTER
MAUREEN STAPLETON	1978	INTERIORS#
	1981	REDS#
MARY STEENBURGEN	1980	MELVIN AND HOWARD#
MERYL STREEP	1979	KRAMER VS. KRAMER, MANHATTAN and THE SEDUCTION OF JOE TYNAN#
	1981	THE FRENCH LIEUTENANT'S WOMAN
	1982	SOPHIE'S CHOICE
	1985	OUT OF AFRICA

KATHLEEN TURNER	1984	CRIMES OF PASSION and ROMANCING THE STONE
CATHY TYSON	1986	MONA LISA#
LIV ULLMANN	1976	FACE TO FACE
JON VOIGHT	1978	COMING HOME
MONA WASHBOURNE	1978	STEVIE#
DIANNE WIEST	1986	HANNAH AND HER SISTERS#

NOTES: The first awards were given in 1975; supporting awards were added in 1977 (indicated by a #). All those listed won awards. There were ties for Best Actor in 1984 and 1987, for Best Actress in 1987 and 1989, and for Best Supporting Actress in 1978 and 1986.

THE AWARDS OF THE NATIONAL BOARD OF REVIEW

ISABELLE ADJANI	1975	THE STORY OF ADELE H.
ALAN ALDA	1989	CRIMES AND MISDEMEANORS#
HARRY ANDREWS	1965	THE AGONY AND THE ECSTACY and THE HILL#
DAME PEGGY ASHCROFT	1984	A PASSAGE TO INDIA
SABINE AZEMA	1984	A SUNDAY IN THE COUNTRY#
MARTIN BALSAM	1964	THE CARPETBAGGERS#
ANNE BANCROFT	1962	THE MIRACLE WORKER
	1977	THE TURNING POINT
VICTOR BANERJEE	1984	A PASSAGE TO INDIA
RICHARD BASEHART	1951	FOURTEEN HOURS
	1956	MOBY DICK#
MARISA BERENSON	1972	CABARET#
INGRID BERGMAN	1958	INN OF THE SIXTH HAPPINESS
	1978	AUTUMN SONATA
CHARLES BICKFORD	1955	NOT AS A STRANGER#
KAREN BLACK	1970	FIVE EASY PIECES#
RONEE BLAKLEY	1975	NASHVILLE#
JOAN BLONDELL	1965	THE CINCINNATI KID#
SHIRLEY BOOTH	1952	COME BACK, LITTLE SHEBA
ERNEST BORGNINE	1955	MARTY
KLAUS-MARIA BRANDAUER	1985	OUT OF AFRICA#
YUL BRYNNER	1956	THE KING AND I, ANASTASIA and THE TEN COMMANDMENTS
DAVID CARRADINE	1976	BOUND FOR GLORY
JULIE CHRISTIE	1965	DARLING and DR. ZHIVAGO
GLENN CLOSE	1982	THE WORLD ACCORDING TO GARP#
SEAN CONNERY	1987	THE UNTOUCHABLES#
TOM CONTI	1983	MERRY CHRISTMAS, MR. LAWRENCE
JOAN CRAWFORD	1945	MILDRED PIERCE
BING CROSBY	1954	THE COUNTRY GIRL
DANIEL DAY-LEWIS	1986	MY BEAUTIFUL LAUNDRETTE and ROOM WITH A VIEW#
RUBY DEE	1961	A RAISIN IN THE SUN#
OLIVIA DE HAVILLAND	1948	THE SNAKE PIT
ROBERT DE NIRO	1980	RAGING BULL
	1990	AWAKENINGS
PAUL DOOLEY	1979	BREAKING AWAY#
MELVYN DOUGLAS	1963	HUD#
MICHAEL DOUGLAS	1987	WALL STREET
OLYMPIA DUKAKIS	1987	MOONSTRUCK#
CHARLES DURNING	1975	DOG DAY AFTERNOON#
DAME EDITH EVANS	1959	THE NUN'S STORY#
	1964	THE CHALK GARDEN#
	1967	THE WHISPERERS
RICHARD FARNSWORTH	1978	COMES A HORSEMAN#
MIA FARROW	1990	ALICE
SALLY FIELD	1979	NORMA RAE
PETER FINCH	1967	FAR FROM THE MADDING CROWD
ALBERT FINNEY	1961	SATURDAY NIGHT AND SUNDAY MORNING
NINA FOCH	1954	EXECUTIVE SUITE#
HENRY FONDA	1981	ON GOLDEN POND
PAUL FORD	1967	THE COMEDIANS#
JODIE FOSTER	1988	THE ACCUSED
PAMELA FRANKLIN	1969	THE PRIME OF MISS JEAN BRODIE#
MORGAN FREEMAN	1989	DRIVING MISS DAISY
GREER GARSON	1960	SUNRISE AT CAMPOBELLO
LILLIAN GISH	1987	THE WHALES OF AUGUST
JACKIE GLEASON	1961	THE HUSTLER#
WHOOPI GOLDBERG	1985	THE COLOR PURPLE
JOEL GREY	1972	CABARET#
HUGH GRIFFITH	1959	BEN-HUR#
ALEC GUINNESS	1950	KIND HEARTS AND CORONETS
	1957	THE BRIDGE ON THE RIVER KWAI
GENE HACKMAN	1971	THE FRENCH CONNECTION

	1974	THE CONVERSATION
	1988	MISSISSIPPI BURNING
REX HARRISON	1963	CLEOPATRA
SESSUE HAYAKAWA	1957	THE BRIDGE ON THE RIVER KWAI#
JOHN HOUSEMAN	1973	THE PAPER CHASE#
LINDA HUNT	1983	THE YEAR OF LIVING DANGEROUSLY#
HOLLY HUNTER	1987	BROADCAST NEWS
WILLIAM HURT	1985	KISS OF THE SPIDER WOMAN
ANJELICA HUSTON	1985	PRIZZI'S HONOR#
WALTER HUSTON	1948	TREASURE OF THE SIERRA MADRE
GLENDA JACKSON	1970	WOMEN IN LOVE
	1981	STEVIE
BEN JOHNSON	1971	THE LAST PICTURE SHOW#
CELIA JOHNSON	1947	THIS HAPPY BREED
SHIRLEY JONES	1960	ELMER GANTRY#
RAUL JULIA	1985	KISS OF THE SPIDER WOMAN
DIANE KEATON	1977	ANNIE HALL#
GRACE KELLY	1954	THE COUNTRY GIRL
BEN KINGSLEY	1982	GANDHI
FRANK LANGELLA	1970	DIARY OF A MAD HOUSEWIFE and THE TWELVE CHAIRS#
ANGELA LANSBURY	1962	THE MANCHURIAN CANDIDATE and ALL FALL DOWN#
	1978	DEATH ON THE NILE#
EVA LE GALLIENNE	1980	RESURRECTION#
CLORIS LEACHMAN	1971	THE LAST PICTURE SHOW#
HOLGER LOWENADLER	1974	LACOMBE, LUCIEN#
SHIRLEY MACLAINE	1983	TERMS OF ENDEARMENT
ANNA MAGNANI	1946	OPEN CITY
	1955	THE ROSE TATTOO
JOHN MALKOVICH	1984	PLACES IN THE HEART#
LEE MARVIN	1965	CAT BALLOU
VIRGINA MASKELL	1968	INTERLUDE#
JAMES MASON	1953	FACE TO FACE, DESERT RATS, THE MAN BETWEEN and JULIUS CAESAR
MARY STUART MASTERSON	1989	IMMEDIATE FAMILY#
FRANCES MCDORMAND	1988	MISSISSIPPI BURNING#
DOROTHY MCGUIRE	1956	FRIENDLY PERSUASION
LEO MCKERN	1968	THE SHOES OF THE FISHERMAN#
VIVIEN MERCHANT	1966	ALFIE#
BURGESS MEREDITH	1962	ADVISE AND CONSENT#
RAY MILLAND	1945	THE LOST WEEKEND
ROBERT MITCHUM	1960	HOME FROM THE HILL and THE SUNDOWNERS
PATRICIA NEAL	1963	HUD
PAUL NEWMAN	1986	THE COLOR OF MONEY
JACK NICHOLSON	1975	ONE FLEW OVER THE CUCKOO'S NEST
	1981	REDS#
	1983	TERMS OF ENDEARMENT#
PHILIPPE NOIRET	1969	TOPAZ#
LAURENCE OLIVIER	1946	HENRY V
	1978	THE BOYS FROM BRAZIL
PETER O'TOOLE	1969	GOODBYE, MR. CHIPS
	1972	THE RULING CLASS and MAN OF LA MANCHA
AL PACINO	1972	THE GODFATHER#
	1973	SERPICO
GERALDINE PAGE	1961	SUMMER AND SMOKE
	1969	TRILOGY
IRENE PAPPAS	1971	THE TROJAN WOMEN
GEORGE PEPPARD	1960	HOME FROM THE HILL#
JOE PESCI	1980	RAGING BULL#
	1990	GOODFELLAS#
VALERIE PERRINE	1974	LENNY#
MICHELLE PFEIFFER	1989	THE FABULOUS BAKER BOYS
RIVER PHOENIX	1988	RUNNING ON EMPTY#
ROBERT PRESTON	1982	VICTOR/VICTORIA#
ANTHONY QUINN	1964	ZORBA THE GREEK
MARJORIE RAMBEAU	1955	A MAN CALLED PETER and THE VIEW FROM POMPEY'S HEAD#
MICHAEL REDGRAVE	1947	MOURNING BECOMES ELECTRA

DEBBIE REYNOLDS	1956	THE CATERED AFFAIR#
MARJORIE RHODES	1967	THE FAMILY WAY#
RALPH RICHARDSON	1949	THE HEIRESS and THE FALLEN IDOL
	1952	BREAKING THE SOUND BARRIER
JASON ROBARDS, JR.	1962	LONG DAY'S JOURNEY INTO NIGHT
	1976	ALL THE PRESIDENT'S MEN#
CLIFF ROBERTSON	1968	CHARLY
GENA ROWLANDS	1974	A WOMAN UNDER THE INFLUENCE
MARGARET RUTHERFORD	1963	THE V.I.P.'S#
ROBERT RYAN	1973	THE ICEMAN COMETH
WINONA RYDER	1990	MERMAIDS#
ALBERT SALMI	1958	THE BROTHERS KARAMAZOV and THE BRAVADOS#
PAUL SCOFIELD	1966	A MAN FOR ALL SEASONS
GEORGE C. SCOTT	1970	PATTON
VICTOR SEASTROM	1959	WILD STRAWBERRIES
PETER SELLERS	1979	BEING THERE
ROBERT SHAW	1966	A MAN FOR ALL SEASONS#
TALIA SHIRE	1976	ROCKY#
SYLVIA SIDNEY	1973	SUMMER WISHES, WINTER DREAMS#
SIMONE SIGNORET	1959	ROOM AT THE TOP
JEAN SIMMONS	1953	YOUNG BESS, THE ROBE and THE ACTRESS
TOM SKERRITT	1977	THE TURNING POINT#
SISSY SPACEK	1980	COAL MINER'S DAUGHTER
KIM STANLEY	1964	SEANCE ON A WET AFTERNOON
JAN STERLING	1951	THE BIG CARNIVAL
MERYL STREEP	1979	KRAMER VS. KRAMER, MANHATTAN and THE SEDUCTION OF JOE TYNAN#
	1982	SOPHIE'S CHOICE
GLORIA SWANSON	1950	SUNSET BOULEVARD
ELIZABETH TAYLOR	1966	WHO'S AFRAID OF VIRGINIA WOOLF?
DAME SYBIL THORNDIKE	1957	THE PRINCE AND THE SHOWGIRL#
SPENCER TRACY	1958	THE OLD MAN AND THE SEA and THE LAST HURRAH
JOHN TRAVOLTA	1977	SATURDAY NIGHT FEVER
KATHLEEN TURNER	1986	PEGGY SUE GOT MARRIED
CICELY TYSON	1972	SOUNDER
LIV ULLMANN	1968	HOUR OF THE WOLF and SHAME
	1973	THE NEW LAND
	1976	FACE TO FACE
JON VOIGHT	1978	COMING HOME
KAY WALSH	1958	THE HORSE'S MOUTH#
MONA WASHBOURNE	1981	STEVIE#
DIANNE WIEST	1986	HANNAH AND HER SISTERS#
JOHN WILLIAMS	1954	SABRINA and DIAL M FOR MURDER#
ROBIN WILLIAMS	1990	AWAKENINGS
JOANNE WOODWARD	1957	THREE FACES OF EVE and NO DOWN PAYMENT

NOTES: The first awards were given in 1945; supporting awards were added in 1954 (indicated with a #). All those listed won awards. There were ties for Best Actor in 1973, 1978, 1985 and 1990, for Best Actress in 1987, and for Best Supporting Actor in 1972. There was no Best Actress award given in 1949.

THE AWARDS OF THE NATIONAL SOCIETY OF FILM CRITICS

ISABELLE ADJANI	1975	THE STORY OF ADELE H.
EDDIE ALBERT	1972	THE HEARTBREAK KID#
BIBI ANDERSSON	1967	PERSONA
	1974	SCENES FROM A MARRIAGE#
KATHY BAKER	1987	STREET SMART#
ANNETTE BENING	1990	THE GRIFTERS#
INGRID BERGMAN	1978	AUTUMN SONATA
JEANNIE BERLIN	1972	THE HEARTBREAK KID#
SANDRA BERNHARD	1983	THE KING OF COMEDY#
MARLON BRANDO	1973	LAST TANGO IN PARIS
BEAU BRIDGES	1989	THE FABULOUS BAKER BOYS#
ELLEN BURSTYN	1971	THE LAST PICTURE SHOW#
GARY BUSEY	1978	THE BUDDY HOLLY STORY
MICHAEL CAINE	1966	ALFIE
ART CARNEY	1977	THE LATE SHOW
SEYMOUR CASSEL	1968	FACES#
VALENTINA CORTESE	1973	NIGHT FOR DAY#
JUDY DAVIS	1988	HIGH TIDE
BRUCE DAVISON	1990	LONGTIME COMPANION#
DANIEL DAY-LEWIS	1989	MY LEFT FOOT
ROBERT DE NIRO	1973	MEAN STREETS#
	1976	TAXI DRIVER
GÉRARD DEPARDIEU	1983	DANTON and THE RETURN OF MARTIN GUERRE
BRUCE DERN	1971	DRIVE, HE SAID#
RICHARD FARNSWORTH	1978	COMES A HORSEMAN#
SALLY FIELD	1979	NORMA RAE
PETER FINCH	1971	SUNDAY, BLOODY SUNDAY
JANE FONDA	1971	KLUTE
FREDERIC FORREST	1979	APOCALYPSE NOW and THE ROSE#
JODIE FOSTER	1976	TAXI DRIVER#
EDWARD FOX	1977	A BRIDGE TOO FAR#
MORGAN FREEMAN	1987	STREET SMART#
CHIEF DAN GEORGE	1970	LITTLE BIG MAN#
HENRY GIBSON	1975	NASHVILLE#
JOHN GIELGUD	1985	PLENTY and THE SHOOTING PARTY#
JOEL GREY	1972	CABARET#
MELANIE GRIFFITH	1984	BODY DOUBLE#
GENE HACKMAN	1967	BONNIE AND CLYDE#
DUSTIN HOFFMAN	1979	KRAMER VS. KRAMER and AGATHA
	1982	TOOTSIE
DENNIS HOPPER	1986	BLUE VELVET#
BOB HOSKINS	1986	MONA LISA
ANJELICA HUSTON	1985	PRIZZI'S HONOR#
	1989	ENEMIES: A LOVE STORY#
	1990	THE GRIFTERS and THE WITCHES
JEREMY IRONS	1990	REVERSAL OF FORTUNE
GLENDA JACKSON	1970	WOMEN IN LOVE
DIANE KEATON	1977	ANNIE HALL
MICHAEL KEATON	1988	BEETLEJUICE and CLEAN AND SOBER
BURT LANCASTER	1981	ATLANTIC CITY
JESSICA LANGE	1982	TOOTSIE#
EMILY LLOYD	1987	WISH YOU WERE HERE
HOLGER LOWENADLER	1974	LACOMBE, LUCIEN#
JOHN MALKOVICH	1984	PLACES OF THE HEART and THE KILLING FIELDS#
STEVE MARTIN	1984	ALL OF ME
	1987	ROXANNE
ROBERT MORLEY	1978	WHO IS KILLING THE GREAT CHEFS OF EUROPE?#
JACK NICHOLSON	1969	EASY RIDER#
	1974	CHINATOWN and THE LAST DETAIL
	1975	ONE FLEW OVER THE CUCKOO'S NEST
	1983	TERMS OF ENDEARMENT#
	1985	PRIZZI'S HONOR
PER OSCARSSON	1968	HUNGER

PETER O'TOOLE	1980	THE STUNT MAN
AL PACINO	1972	THE GODFATHER
MARILIA PERA	1981	PIXOTE
JOE PESCI	1980	RAGING BULL#
MICHELLE PFEIFFER	1989	THE FABULOUS BAKER BOYS
SIAN PHILLIPS	1969	GOODBYE, MR. CHIPS#
ROBERT PRESTON	1981	S.O.B.#
VANESSA REDGRAVE	1969	ISADORA
	1984	THE BOSTONIANS
	1985	WETHERBY
MARJORIE RHODES	1967	THE FAMILY WAY#
JASON ROBARDS	1976	ALL THE PRESIDENT'S MEN#
MICKEY ROURKE	1982	DINER#
MERCEDES RUEHL	1988	MARRIED TO THE MOB#
GEORGE C. SCOTT	1970	PATTON
LOIS SMITH	1970	FIVE EASY PIECES#
SISSY SPACEK	1976	CARRIE
	1980	COAL MINER'S DAUGHTER
MAUREEN STAPLETON	1981	REDS#
MARY STEENBURGEN	1980	MELVIN AND HOWARD#
ROD STEIGER	1967	IN THE HEAT OF THE NIGHT
DEAN STOCKWELL	1988	MARRIED TO THE MOB#
MERYL STREEP	1978	THE DEER HUNTER#
	1979	MANHATTAN, KRAMER VS. KRAMER and THE SEDUCTION OF JOE TYNAN#
	1982	SOPHIE'S CHOICE
SYLVIE	1966	THE SHAMELESS OLD LADY
LILY TOMLIN	1975	NASHVILLE#
CICELY TYSON	1972	SOUNDER
LIV ULLMANN	1968	SHAME
	1973	THE NEW LAND
	1974	SCENES FROM A MARRIAGE
JON VOIGHT	1969	MIDNIGHT COWBOY
CHLOE WEBB	1986	SID AND NANCY
ANN WEDGEWORTH	1977	HANDLE WITH CARE#
BILLIE WHITELAW	1968	CHARLIE BUBBLES#
DIANNE WIEST	1986	HANNAH AND HER SISTERS#
DEBRA WINGER	1983	TERMS OF ENDEARMENT

NOTES: The first awards were given in 1966; supporting awards were added the following year (indicated with a #). All those listed won awards. There were ties for Best Supporting Actor in 1972 and 1978.

THE AWARDS OF THE NEW YORK FILM CRITICS CIRCLE

ISABELLE ADJANI	1975	THE STORY OF ADELE H.
ALAN ALDA	1989	CRIMES AND MISDEMEANORS#
NORMA ALEANDRO	1985	THE OFFICIAL STORY
ALAN ARKIN	1968	THE HEART IS A LONELY HUNTER
	1975	HEARTS OF THE WEST#
DAME PEGGY ASHCROFT	1984	A PASSAGE TO INDIA
TALLULAH BANKHEAD	1944	LIFEBOAT
INGRID BERGMAN	1945	SPELLBOUND and THE BELLS OF ST. MARY'S
	1956	ANASTASIA
	1978	AUTUMN SONATA
JEANNIE BERLIN	1972	THE HEARTBREAK KID#
SHIRLEY BOOTH	1952	COME BACK, LITTLE SHEBA
ERNEST BORGNINE	1955	MARTY
CHARLES BOYER	1974	STAVISKY#
KLAUS-MARIA BRANDAUER	1985	OUT OF AFRICA#
MARLON BRANDO	1954	ON THE WATERFRONT
	1973	LAST TANGO IN PARIS
JAMES CAGNEY	1938	ANGELS WITH DIRTY FACES
	1942	YANKEE DOODLE DANDY
CHARLES CHAPLIN	1940	THE GREAT DICTATOR
JULIE CHRISTIE	1965	DARLING
GARY COOPER	1941	SERGEANT YORK
VALENTINA CORTESE	1973	DAY FOR NIGHT#
BRODERICK CRAWFORD	1949	ALL THE KING'S MEN
BETTE DAVIS	1950	ALL ABOUT EVE
BRUCE DAVISON	1990	LONGTIME COMPANION#
DANIEL DAY-LEWIS	1986	ROOM WITH A VIEW#
	1989	MY LEFT FOOT
OLIVIA DE HAVILLAND	1948	THE SNAKE PIT
	1949	THE HEIRESS
ROBERT DE NIRO	1973	MEAN STREETS#
	1976	TAXI DRIVER
	1980	RAGING BULL
	1990	AWAKENINGS and GOODFELLAS
KIRK DOUGLAS	1956	LUST FOR LIFE
MELVYN DOUGLAS	1979	BEING THERE#
ROBERT DUVALL	1972	THE GODFATHER#
	1983	TENDER MERCIES
DAME EDITH EVANS	1967	THE WHISPERERS
SALLY FIELD	1979	NORMA RAE
ALBERT FINNEY	1963	TOM JONES
BARRY FITZGERALD	1944	GOING MY WAY
JANE FONDA	1969	THEY SHOOT HORSES, DON'T THEY?
	1971	KLUTE
JOAN FONTAINE	1941	SUSPICION
MORGAN FREEMAN	1987	STREET SMART#
GRETA GARBO	1935	ANNA KARENINA
	1937	CAMILLE
JOHN GIELGUD	1977	PROVIDENCE
	1981	ARTHUR#
ALEC GUINNESS	1957	THE BRIDGE ON THE RIVER KWAI
GENE HACKMAN	1971	THE FRENCH CONNECTION
REX HARRISON	1964	MY FAIR LADY
SUSAN HAYWARD	1958	I WANT TO LIVE!
AUDREY HEPBURN	1953	ROMAN HOLIDAY
	1959	THE NUN'S STORY
KATHARINE HEPBURN	1940	THE PHILADELPHIA STORY
DUSTIN HOFFMAN	1979	KRAMER VS. KRAMER
BOB HOSKINS	1986	MONA LISA
LINDA HUNT	1983	THE YEAR OF LIVING DANGEROUSLY#
HOLLY HUNTER	1987	BROADCAST NEWS
WALTER HUSTON	1936	DODSWORTH
ANJELICA HUSTON	1985	PRIZZI'S HONOR#
JEREMY IRONS	1988	DEAD RINGERS
GLENDA JACKSON	1970	WOMEN IN LOVE

	1981	STEVIE
CELIA JOHNSON	1946	BRIEF ENCOUNTER
DIANE KEATON	1977	ANNIE HALL
GRACE KELLY	1954	THE COUNTRY GIRL, REAR WINDOW and DIAL M FOR MURDER
ARTHUR KENNEDY	1951	BRIGHT VICTORY
DEBORAH KERR	1947	BLACK NARCISSUS and THE ADVENTURESS
	1957	HEAVEN KNOWS, MR. ALLISON
	1960	THE SUNDOWNERS
BEN KINGSLEY	1982	GANDHI
CHRISTINE LAHTI	1984	SWING SHIFT#
BURT LANCASTER	1953	FROM HERE TO ETERNITY
	1960	ELMER GANTRY
	1981	ATLANTIC CITY
JESSICA LANGE	1982	TOOTSIE#
CHARLES LAUGHTON	1935	MUTINY ON THE BOUNTY and RUGGLES OF RED GAP
JENNIFER JASON LEIGH	1990	LAST EXIT TO BROOKLYN and MIAMI BLUES#
VIVIEN LEIGH	1939	GONE WITH THE WIND
	1951	A STREETCAR NAMED DESIRE
JOHN LITHGOW	1982	THE WORLD ACCORDING TO GARP#
SOPHIA LOREN	1961	TWO WOMEN
PAUL LUKAS	1943	WATCH ON THE RHINE
IDA LUPINO	1943	THE HARD WAY
SHIRLEY MACLAINE	1983	TERMS OF ENDEARMENT
ANNA MAGNANI	1955	THE ROSE TATTOO
STEVE MARTIN	1984	ALL OF ME
RAY MILLAND	1945	THE LOST WEEKEND
AGNES MOOREHEAD	1942	THE MAGNIFICENT AMBERSONS
PAUL MUNI	1937	THE LIFE OF EMILE ZOLA
PATRICIA NEAL	1963	HUD
JACK NICHOLSON	1974	CHINATOWN
	1975	ONE FLEW OVER THE CUCKOO'S NEST
	1983	TERMS OF ENDEARMENT#
	1985	PRIZZI'S HONOR
	1987	IRONWEED, THE WITCHES OF EASTWICK and BROADCAST NEWS
DAVID NIVEN	1958	SEPARATE TABLES
LENA OLIN	1989	ENEMIES, A LOVE STORY#
LAURENCE OLIVIER	1946	HENRY V
	1948	HAMLET
	1972	SLEUTH
GREGORY PECK	1950	TWELVE O'CLOCK HIGH
VALERIE PERRINE	1974	LENNY#
JOE PESCI	1980	RAGING BULL#
MICHELLE PFEIFFER	1989	THE FABULOUS BAKER BOYS
WILLIAM POWELL	1947	LIFE WITH FATHER and THE SENATOR WAS INDISCREET
LUISE RAINER	1936	THE GREAT ZIEGFELD
LYNN REDGRAVE	1966	GEORGY GIRL
VANESSA REDGRAVE	1987	PRICK UP YOUR EARS#
RALPH RICHARDSON	1952	BREAKING THE SOUND BARRIER
	1984	GREYSTOKE: THE LEGEND OF TARZAN, LORD OF THE APES#
JASON ROBARDS	1976	ALL THE PRESIDENT'S MEN#
MAXIMILIAN SCHELL	1961	JUDGMENT AT NUREMBERG
	1977	JULIA#
PAUL SCOFIELD	1966	A MAN FOR ALL SEASONS
GEORGE C. SCOTT	1970	PATTON
TALIA SHIRE	1976	ROCKY#
SISSY SPACEK	1977	THREE WOMEN#
	1980	COAL MINER'S DAUGHTER
	1986	CRIMES OF THE HEART
KIM STANLEY	1964	SEANCE ON A WET AFTERNOON
MAUREEN STAPLETON	1978	INTERIORS#
MARY STEENBURGEN	1980	MELVIN AND HOWARD#
ROD STEIGER	1967	IN THE HEAT OF THE NIGHT
JAMES STEWART	1939	MR. SMITH GOES TO WASHINGTON
	1959	ANATOMY OF A MURDER
DEAN STOCKWELL	1988	MARRIED TO THE MOB and

		TUCKER: THE MAN AND HIS DREAM#
MERYL STREEP	1979	KRAMER VS. KRAMER and THE SEDUCTION OF JOE TYNAN
	1982	SOPHIE'S CHOICE
	1988	A CRY IN THE DARK
MARGARET SULLAVAN	1938	THREE COMRADES
ELIZABETH TAYLOR	1966	WHO'S AFRAID OF VIRGINIA WOOLF?
LILY TOMLIN	1975	NASHVILLE#
LIV ULLMANN	1972	CRIES AND WHISPERS
	1974	SCENES FROM A MARRIAGE
	1976	FACE TO FACE
DIANE VENORA	1988	BIRD#
JON VOIGHT	1969	MIDNIGHT COWBOY
	1978	COMING HOME
CHRISTOPHER WALKEN	1978	THE DEER HUNTER#
MONA WASHBOURNE	1981	STEVIE#
OSKAR WERNER	1965	SHIP OF FOOLS
DIANNE WIEST	1986	HANNAH AND HER SISTERS#
JOANNE WOODWARD	1968	RACHEL, RACHEL
	1973	SUMMER WISHES, WINTER DREAMS
	1990	MR. AND MRS. BRIDGE

NOTES: The awards were first given in 1935; supporting awards were added in 1972 (indicated with a #). All those listed won awards. There was a tie for Best Actress in 1966; no awards were given in 1962 due to the newspaper strike.

INDEX: FILMS AND PERSONALITIES

Note: The dates used here are original release dates; dates in the awards appendix may vary.